S0-BHD-114

EXEGETICAL DICTIONARY OF THE NEW TESTAMENT

EXEGETICAL DICTIONARY OF THE NEW TESTAMENT

VOLUME 1

ʼΑαρών – ʽΕνώχ

edited by
Horst Balz and
Gerhard Schneider

WILLIAM B. EERDMANS PUBLISHING COMPANY
GRAND RAPIDS, MICHIGAN

Originally published as
Exegetisches Wörterbuch zum Neuen Testament
Band I, Lieferungen 1-9

Printed in the United States of America

Library of Congress Cataloging-in-Publication Data

Exegetisches Wörterbuch zum Neuen Testament. English.
Exegetical dictionary of the New Testament / edited by Horst Balz and Gerhard Schneider.
p. cm.
Translation of: Exegetisches Wörterbuch zum Neuen Testament.
Includes bibliographical references.
ISBN 0-8028-2409-9 (v. 1)
1. Bible. N.T.—Dictionaries—Greek. 2. Bible. N.T.—Criticism, interpretation, etc. 3. Greek language, Biblical—Dictionaries—English. I. Balz, Horst Robert. II. Schneider, Gerhard, 1926- . III. Title.
BS2312.E913 1990
225.4′8′03—dc20 90-35682
CIP

CONTENTS

EDITORS' FOREWORD vi

INTRODUCTION viii

CONTRIBUTORS x

ABBREVIATIONS xii

- **1. The Bible and Other Ancient Literature** xii
  - *a. Old Testament* xii
  - *b. Apocrypha and Septuagint* xii
  - *c. New Testament* xii
  - *d. Pseudepigrapha and Early Church Writings* xii
  - *e. Qumran and Related Texts* xiii
  - *f. Rabbinic Literature* xiii
  - *g. Targums* xiv
  - *h. Other Ancient Authors and Writings* xiv
  - *i. Inscriptions, Fragments, Papyri, and Anthologies* xvi
- **2. Modern Writings** xvi
- **3. General** xxiii

TRANSLITERATION SCHEME xxiv

Ἀαρών–Ἑνώχ 1

EDITORS' FOREWORD

The *Exegetical Dictionary of the New Testament (EDNT)* is a translation of the *Exegetisches Wörterbuch zum Neuen Testament (EWNT)* and seeks to meet a broad range of needs of the student, pastor, and scholar. It is a complete English dictionary of New Testament Greek that includes definitions of every word appearing in the New Testament, a guide to the usage in different New Testament literary and theological contexts of every significant New Testament word, a systematic summation of the results of recent exegetical study of the New Testament, and a valuable source of bibliographical data for New Testament exegesis and theology.

EDNT stands in the tradition of the *Theological Dictionary of the New Testament (TDNT):* both go beyond the mere defining functions of a dictionary to discuss the historical, theological, and exegetical significance of words. *EDNT* acknowledges its debt to *TDNT,* which has long remained unique and even now is the most significant document of the exegetical work of more than a generation of scholarship. *EDNT* now brings the discussion forward, summarizing more recent treatments of numerous questions of New Testament study and giving attention to the abundance of changes and new approaches both in scholarly discussion and in study of and practical work with the New Testament in schools and churches.

EDNT meets the demands for a dictionary of the writings of the New Testament by giving for every word in the Greek text, including every proper name: transliteration, declension information for adjectives and nouns, meaning, and indication of the contexts in which the word is found. The data necessary for translation and exegesis are provided for every word.

More significant words of the New Testament are treated in longer articles in which the emphasis lies on the understanding of the words as they appear in varied contexts. A typical longer article proceeds, as much as possible, from the oldest strata of New Testament tradition in which the pertinent word carries a significant weight of meaning. The treatment of later strata follows, but it is not assumed that any idea of an evolution or of a gradual transformation should, by overschematizing, distort the presentation. Comparison with the rich material from outside the New Testament is brought in as the need arises (and not in a religio-historical discussion preliminary to the main part of the article). Words related by root and meaning are usually treated together (and cross-references from each word's normal alphabetical location are included).

The distinctiveness and goal of *EDNT* lie not only in its limitation to the vocabulary of the New Testament, but also in its presentation and working out of the implications of the exegetical and theological contexts of the different words, including the necessary historical backgrounds. Newer linguistic viewpoints are taken into consideration, but no definite system of linguistic theory is presupposed.

EDNT seeks to serve scholars, pastors, and students. It always begins with the Greek language, but the results are made available to those who have not mastered Hebrew and Greek. All Hebrew words are transliterated as they arise in the course of discussion, and Greek words are transliterated in the headings of articles. An English index in Volume III will enable those who have not studied Greek to find articles on particular words.

From the very beginning *EWNT* was planned as ecumenical. The numerous contributors are Protestant and Catholic exegetes from German-speaking countries, from other European countries, and from overseas. Thus *EWNT,* and now *EDNT,* serves as a sign of worldwide cooperation in the understanding of the New Testament. All major articles are signed. Unsigned articles are the responsibility of the editors.

The editors have many people to thank, first of all, our colleagues who have shared in the work. Often the writing of *EWNT/EDNT* articles has caused them to put aside other work. We must also thank a series of unnamed assistants for many labors in connection with the dictionary.

Our best wishes accompany *EDNT* on its way to those on the scene in classroom, study, and pulpit who participate in the interpretation and preaching of the biblical message.

Bochum, December 1979 / May 1990 *Horst Balz* *Gerhard Schneider*

Our special thanks go to the translators of this volume of the *Exegetical Dictionary of the New Testament.* Virgil P. Howard translated the material through the article on ἀσάλευτος. James W. Thompson translated the balance of the articles, beginning with Ἀσάφ.

The Publishers

INTRODUCTION

The *Exegetical Dictionary of the New Testament (EDNT)* is a guide to the forms, meaning, and usage of every word in the text of the third edition of *The Greek New Testament (UBSGNT),* which is equivalent to the text of the twenty-sixth edition of the Nestle-Aland *Novum Testament Graece (NTG)* and the text followed in the *Vollständige Konkordanz zum griechischen Neuen Testament* (*VKGNT;* see abbreviations list for full publication data on these works). Words in the most important textual variants in *UBSGNT* and *NTG* are also included, and the authors of *EDNT* articles have been granted the freedom to depart from the basic text of these two editions where they have deemed it appropriate.

The *heading* of each *EDNT* article, along with identifying the word to be discussed, supplies the following information:

The gender of common nouns is identified by inclusion of the nominative singular article.
The declension of nouns is identified by inclusion of the genitive singular ending.
Whether an adjective has one, two, or three sets of endings (corresponding to the three genders) is specified by a boldface number.[1]
The word is transliterated.
The meaning of the word is indicated by one or more English translations (sometimes divided according to verb voice or adjectival or substantival use of an adjective).[2]
An asterisk (*) appears at the end of the heading line if all New Testament occurrences of a word are at least mentioned in the body of the article.

A group of words related by form and meaning is sometimes treated in one article with multiple heading lines. In that case, a cross reference (→) is placed at each word's normal alphabetical location.

ἀλήθεια, ας, ἡ *alētheia* truth
ἀληθεύω *alētheuō* tell the truth, be truthful*
ἀληθής, 2 *alēthēs* true, honest, genuine
ἀληθινός, 3 *alēthinos* true, honest, dependable
ἀληθῶς *alēthōs* truly, actually

ἀληθεύω *alētheuō* be truthful, speak truthfully
→ ἀλήθεια.

ἀπόκρυφος, 2 *apokryphos* hidden*

ἀπολύτρωσις, εως, ἡ *apolytrōsis* redemption*

ἀπολύω *apolyō* set free, release; dismiss

1. **1:** third declension adjectives in which the three genders have the same forms; **2:** adjectives in which masculine and feminine forms are identical, including second declension adjectives in -ος, -ον and third declension adjectives in -ης, -ες and -ων, -ον; **3:** adjectives in which the three genders have different forms, including first and second declension adjectives in -ος, -η/-α, -ον and -οῦς, -ῆ/-ᾶ, -οῦν, first and third declension adjectives in -υς, -εια, -υ and those formed like πᾶς, πᾶσα, πᾶν, and a few adjectives which combine declensional patterns in ways not listed here.

2. The headings of articles are usually not a complete guide to meaning, since in some cases only a selection of documented meanings is included and since the bodies of articles discuss the meanings of words as they appear in context in different usages.

The *body* of a shorter article normally mentions all New Testament occurrences of a word, grouped, if appropriate, according to different usages and different kinds of contexts in which the word is found, and discusses the more interesting, difficult, or controversial occurrences. Shorter articles also often include some bibliography listing discussions in reference works, journal articles, monographs, and commentaries of New Testament usage of the word and of passages in which the word plays a decisive role.

More is provided for more significant words—actually many of the words in the New Testament, including both words of great frequency and words that express significant New Testament concepts. *Longer articles* are usually divided into numbered sections, sometimes with lettered subsections, and often include an outline listing the sections and subsections. An extended bibliography, which emphasizes recent works, usually precedes the body of a longer article.

ἀρχή, ῆς, ἡ *archē* beginning; power*

1. Occurrences in the NT — 2. Meaning — 3. Usage

Lit.: H. CONZELMANN, " 'Was von Anfang war' (ἀπ' ἀρχῆς)," *idem, Theologie als Schriftauslegung* (BEvT 65, 1974) 207-14. — G. DELLING, *TDNT* I, 478-84 (bibliography). — W. FOERSTER, *TDNT* II, 1 (bibliographic note), 571-73. — J. Y. LEE, "Interpreting the Demonic Powers in Pauline Thought," *NovT* 12 (1970) 54-69. — S. LEVIN, *Ἄρχω and ἀρχή* (Diss. Chicago, 1950). — G. MILLER, "Ἀρχόντων τοῦ αἰῶνος τούτου—A New Look at 1 Corinthians 2:6-8," *JBL* 91 (1972) 522-28. — I. DE LA POTTERIE, "La notion de 'commencement' dans les écrits johanniques," FS Schürmann 379-403. — H. RINGGREN, *RGG* II, 1302f. — E. SAMAIN, "La notion de APXH dans l'oeuvre lucanienne," *L'Évangile de Luc* (ed. F. Neirynck; 1973) 299-328. — H. SCHLIER, *Mächte und Gewalten im NT* (1958). — E. SJÖBERG, *TDNT* VI, 375f.

The body of a longer article generally proceeds from a statistical summary of the word's New Testament occurences, through discussion of the word's range of meanings and of the variety of usages in which it is found in the New Testament, to treatment of the exegetical and theological significance of the word in the different blocks of New Testament literature. Included where relevant is treatment of the background of New Testament usage of the word in classical Greek, the Septuagint, post-Old Testament Judaism, and Hellenistic literature. For names of persons and places, consideration is given to the historical background of the person's or place's significance in the New Testament. Where one of these longer *EDNT* articles touches on matters of significant disagreement among scholars, the author of the article summarizes and enters into the discussion.

Both shorter and longer articles include cross-references (→) to other articles where further treatment of words or exegetical problems under discussion are touched on. An English index will appear in Volume III.

CONTRIBUTORS

Franz Annen, Chur, Switzerland
Horst Balz, Bochum
Gerhard Barth, Wuppertal
Johannes B. Bauer, Graz, Austria
Günther Baumbach, Berlin
Jörg Baumgarten, Cologne
Hans Dieter Betz, Chicago
Otto Betz, Tübingen
Johannes Beutler, Frankfurt am Main
Werner Bieder, Basel, Switzerland
Peter Bläser, Paderborn
Otto Böcher, Mainz
Udo Borse, Bonn
Ingo Broer, Siegen
Jan-Adolf Bühner, Mössingen
Ulrich Busse, Duisberg
Rolf Dabelstein, Uetersen
Gerhard Dautzenberg, Giessen
Detlev Dormeyer, Münster
Jost Eckert, Trier
Winfried Elliger, Tübingen
Josef Ernst, Paderborn
Peter Fiedler, Freiburg
Hubert Frankemölle, Paderborn
†Gerhard Friedrich, Kiel
Albert Fuchs, Linz, Austria
Mark E. Glasswell, Nsukka, Nigeria
Horst Goldstein, Worpswede
Wolfgang Hackenberg, Witten
Victor Hasler, Bern, Switzerland
Günter Haufe, Greifswald
Harald Hegermann, Munich
Adolf Johann Hess, Kiel
Otfried Hofius, Tübingen
Traugott Holtz, Halle
Axel Horstmann, Hamburg
Hans Hübner, Göttingen
Ulrich Kellermann, Mülheim
Karl Kertelge, Münster
Otto Knoch, Passau
Helmut Krämer, Bethel
Reinhard Kratz, Frankfurt am Main
Jacob Kremer, Vienna, Austria
Armin Kretzer, Würzburg
Horst Kuhli, Königstein
Jan Lambrecht, Louvain, Belgium
Peter Lampe, Göttingen
Michael Lattke, Brisbane, Australia
Simon Légasse, Toulouse, France
Herbert Leroy, Augsburg
Meinrad Limbeck, Stuttgart
Gerd Lüdemann, Göttingen
Ulrich Luz, Bern, Switzerland
Bernhard Mayer, Eichstädt
Otto Merk, Erlangen
Helmut Merkel, Osnabrück
Helmut Merklein, Bonn
Hans-Jürgen van der Minde, Göttingen
Paul-Gerd Müller, Trier
Kurt Niederwimmer, Vienna, Austria
Johannes M. Nützel, Freiburg
Lorenz Oberlinner, Freiburg
Peter von der Osten-Sacken, Berlin
Hermann Patsch, Munich
Henning Paulsen, Hamburg
Rudolf Pesch, Munich
Wilhelm Pesch, Mainz
Gerd Petzke, Kelkheim
Eckhard Plümacher, Berlin
Wiard Popkes, Hamburg
Felix Porsch, Stuttgart
Karl-Heinz Pridik, Wuppertal
Walter Radl, Augsburg
†Bo Reicke, Basel, Switzerland
Hans-Joachim Ritz, Schwelm
Jürgen Roloff, Erlangen
Dieter Sänger, Bretten
Alexander Sand, Bochum
Berndt Schaller, Göttingen
Wolfgang Schenk, Epstein
Gottfried Schille, Borsdorf bei Leipzig
Walter Schmithals, Berlin
Gerhard Schneider, Bochum
Franz Schnider, Regensburg
Ulrich Schoenborn, São Leopoldo, Brazil
Luise Schottroff, Kassel
Tim Schramm, Hamburg
Gerd Schunack, Marburg
Benedikt Schwank, Beuron and Jerusalem
Ferdinand Staudinger, Sankt Pölten, Austria
Werner Stenger, Cologne
Wolfgang Trilling, Leipzig

Peter Trummer, Graz, Austria
Franz Georg Untergassmair, Paderborn
Martin Völkel, Dortmund
Nikolaus Walter, Naumburg
Joachim Wanke, Erfurt
Hans Weder, Zurich, Switzerland
Alfons Weiser, Vallendar
Hans-Friedrich Weiss, Rostock
†Konrad Weiss, Rostock
Dieter Zeller, Mainz
Josef Zmijewski, Bonn

Unsigned articles have been written by the editors, those on pp. 1-72 (ἀμοιβή), 119 (ἄπειρος)-178, 256-338, and 427-462 by Gerhard Schneider, and those on pp. 72 ('Αμπλιᾶτος)-119 (ἄπειμι [II]), 179-255, and 340-426 by Horst Balz.

ABBREVIATIONS

1. The Bible and Other Ancient Literature

a. Old Testament

Gen	Genesis
Exod	Exodus
Lev	Leviticus
Num	Numbers
Deut	Deuteronomy
Josh	Joshua
Judg	Judges
Ruth	Ruth
1–2 Sam	1–2 Samuel
1–2 Kgs	1–2 Kings
1–2 Chr	1–2 Chronicles
Ezra	Ezra
Neh	Nehemiah
Esth	Esther
Job	Job
Ps(s)	Psalm(s)
Prov	Proverbs
Eccl	Ecclesiastes
Cant	Canticles
Isa	Isaiah
Jer	Jeremiah
Lam	Lamentations
Ezek	Ezekiel
Dan	Daniel
Hos	Hosea
Joel	Joel
Amos	Amos
Obad	Obadiah
Jonah	Jonah
Mic	Micah
Nah	Nahum
Hab	Habakkuk
Zeph	Zephaniah
Hag	Haggai
Zech	Zechariah
Mal	Malachi

b. Apocrypha and Septuagint

1–4 Kgdms	1–4 Kingdoms
Add Esth	Additions to Esther
Bar	Baruch
Bel	Bel and the Dragon
1–2 Esdr	1–2 Esdras
4 Ezra	4 Ezra
Jdt	Judith
Ep Jer	Epistle of Jeremiah
1–4 Macc	1–4 Maccabees
Pr Azar	Prayer of Azariah
Pr Man	Prayer of Manasseh
Sir	Sirach (Ecclesiasticus)
Tob	Tobit
Wis	Wisdom of Solomon

c. New Testament

Matt	Matthew
Mark	Mark
Luke	Luke
John	
Acts	Acts
Rom	Romans
1–2 Cor	1–2 Corinthians
Gal	Galatians
Eph	Ephesians
Phil	Philippians
Col	Colossians
1–2 Thess	1–2 Thessalonians
1–2 Tim	1–2 Timothy
Titus	Titus
Phlm	Philemon
Heb	Hebrews
Jas	James
1–2 Pet	1–2 Peter
1–3 John	1–3 John
Jude	Jude
Rev	Revelation

d. Pseudepigrapha and Early Church Writings

Acts Thom.	*Acts of Thomas*
Adam and Eve	*Books of Adam and Eve*
Apoc. Abr.	*Apocalypse of Abraham*
Apoc. Elijah	*Apocalypse of Elijah*

Apoc. Mos.	*Apocalypse of Moses*
Apoc. Paul	*Apocalypse of Paul*
Apoc. Pet.	*Apocalypse of Peter*
Apoc. Zeph.	*Apocalypse of Zephaniah*
Asc. Isa.	*Ascension of Isaiah*
Augustine	
Civ. D.	*De Civitate Dei*
2–3 Bar.	Syriac, Greek *Apocalypse of Baruch*
Barn.	*Barnabas*
Bib. Ant.	Pseudo-Philo *Biblical Antiquities*
1–2 Clem.	*1–2 Clement*
Clement of Alexandria	
Paed.	*Paedagogus*
Prot.	*Protrepticus*
Strom.	*Stromata*
Did.	*Didache*
Diog.	*Epistle to Diognetus*
1–3 Enoch	Ethiopic, Slavonic, Hebrew *Enoch*
Ep. Arist.	*Epistle of Aristeas*
Epiphanius	
Haer.	*Haereses*
Eusebius	
HE	*Historia Ecclesiastica*
PE	*Praeparatio Evangelica*
Vit. Const.	*Vita Constantini*
Gk. Apoc. Ezra	*Greek Apocalypse of Ezra*
Gos. Eb.	*Gospel of the Ebionites*
Gos. Heb.	*Gospel of the Hebrews*
Gos. Naz.	*Gospel of the Nazarenes*
Gos. Nicod.	*Gospel of Nicodemus*
Gos. Pet.	*Gospel of Peter*
Gos. Thom.	*Gospel of Thomas*
Herm.	*Shepherd of Hermas*
Man.	*Mandates*
Sim.	*Similitudes*
Vis.	*Visions*
Hippolytus	
Haer.	*Refutatio Omnium Haeresium*
Philos.	*Philosophumena*
Ign.	Ignatius
Eph.	*Ephesians*
Magn.	*Magnesians*
Phld.	*Philadelphians*
Pol.	*Polycarp*
Rom.	*Romans*
Smyrn.	*Smyrnaeans*
Trall.	*Trallians*
Irenaeus	
Haer.	*Adversus Haereses*
Jerome	
De Vir. Ill.	*De Viris Illustribus*
Jos. As.	*Joseph and Aseneth*
Jub.	*Jubilees*
Justin	
Apol.	*Apologia*
Dial.	*Dialogue with Trypho*
Mart. Isa.	*Martyrdom of Isaiah*
Mart. Pol.	*Martyrdom of Polycarp*
Odes Sol.	*Odes of Solomon*
Origen	
Cels.	*Contra Celsum*
Par. Jer.	*Paralipomena Jeremiou*
Pol.	Polycarp
Phil.	*Epistle to the Philippians*
Prot. Jas.	*Protevangelium of James*
Ps.-Clem. Hom.	*Pseudo-Clementine Homilies*
Ps.-Clem. Rec.	*Pseudo-Clementine Recognitions*
Ps.-Ign.	Pseudo-Ignatius
Magn.	*Magnesians*
Pss. Sol.	*Psalms of Solomon*
Sib. Or.	*Sibylline Oracles*
T. Abr.	*Testament of Abraham*
T. Adam	*Testament of Adam*
T. Mos.	*Testament* ("Assumption") *of Moses*
T. 12 Patr.	*Testaments of the Twelve Patriarchs*
T. Ash.	*Testament of Asher*
T. Benj.	*Testament of Benjamin*
T. Dan	*Testament of Dan*
T. Gad	*Testament of Gad*
T. Iss.	*Testament of Issachar*
T. Jos.	*Testament of Joseph*
T. Jud.	*Testament of Judah*
T. Levi	*Testament of Levi*
T. Naph.	*Testament of Naphtali*
T. Reu.	*Testament of Reuben*
T. Sim.	*Testament of Simeon*
T. Zeb.	*Testament of Zebulun*
Tertullian	
Apol.	*Apologia*
Cult. Fem.	*De Cultu Feminarum*
Marc.	*Adversus Marcionem*
Pud.	*De Pudicitia*
Vit. Proph.	*Lives of the Prophets (Vita Prophetarum)*

e. Qumran and Related Texts

The standard abbreviations are used (see J. A. Fitzmyer, *The Dead Sea Scrolls: Major Publications and Tools for Study* [Sources for Biblical Study 8, [2]1977]).

f. Rabbinic Literature

m.	Mishnah
t.	Tosefta
b.	Babylonian Talmud
y.	Jerusalem Talmud

'Abot	*'Abot*	*Nazir*	*Nazir*
'Arak.	*'Arakin*	*Ned.*	*Nedarim*
'Abod. Zar.	*'Aboda Zara*	*Neg.*	*Nega'im*
B. Bat.	*Baba Batra*	*Nez.*	*Neziqin*
Bek.	*Bekorot*	*Nid.*	*Niddah*
Ber.	*Berakot*	*Ohol.*	*Oholot*
Beṣa	*Beṣa (= Yom Ṭob)*	*'Or.*	*'Orla*
Bik.	*Bikkurim*	*Para*	*Para*
B. Meṣ.	*Baba Meṣi'a*	*Pe'a*	*Pe'a*
B. Qam.	*Baba Qamma*	*Pesaḥ*	*Pesaḥim*
Dem.	*Demai*	*Qinnim*	*Qinnim*
'Erub.	*'Erubin*	*Qidd.*	*Qiddušin*
'Ed.	*'Eduyyot*	*Qod.*	*Qodašin*
Giṭ.	*Giṭṭin*	*Roš Haš.*	*Roš Haššana*
Ḥag.	*Ḥagiga*	*Sanh.*	*Sanhedrin*
Ḥal.	*Ḥalla*	*Šabb.*	*Šabbat*
Hor.	*Horayot*	*Šeb.*	*Šebi'it*
Ḥul.	*Ḥullin*	*Šebu.*	*Šebu'ot*
Kelim	*Kelim*	*Šeqal.*	*Šeqalim*
Ker.	*Keritot*	*Soṭa*	*Soṭa*
Ketub.	*Ketubot*	*Sukk.*	*Sukka*
Kil.	*Kil'ayim*	*Ta'an.*	*Ta'anit*
Ma'aś.	*Ma'aśerot*	*Tamid*	*Tamid*
Mak.	*Makkot*	*Tem.*	*Temura*
Makš.	*Makširin (= Mašqin)*	*Ter.*	*Terumot*
Meg.	*Megilla*	*Ṭohar.*	*Ṭoharot*
Me'il.	*Me'ila*	*Ṭ. Yom*	*Ṭebul Yom*
Menaḥ.	*Menaḥot*	*'Uq.*	*'Uqṣin*
Mid.	*Middot*	*Yad.*	*Yadayim*
Miqw.	*Miqwa'ot*	*Yebam.*	*Yebamot*
Mo'ed	*Mo'ed*	*Yoma*	*Yoma (= Kippurim)*
Mo'ed Qaṭ.	*Mo'ed Qaṭan*	*Zabim*	*Zabim*
Ma'aś. Š.	*Ma'aśer Šeni*	*Zebaḥ.*	*Zebaḥim*
Našim	*Našim*	*Zer.*	*Zera'im*

Bar.	*Baraita*	*Pesiq.*	*Pesiqta*
Mek.	*Mekilta*	*Pesiq. Rab Kah.*	*Pesiqta de Rab Kahana*
Midr. Qoh.	*Midrash Qoheleth*	*Rab.*	*Rabbah*

g. Targums

Tg. Esth I, II	*First or Second Targum of Esther*	*Tg. J.*	*Targum Jonathan on the prophets*

h. Other Ancient Authors and Writings

Aeschylus

A.	*Agamemnon*
Ch.	*Choephori*
Th.	*Septem contra Thebas*

Apollonius Dyscolus

Synt.	*De Syntaxi*

Aristophanes

Lys.	*Lysistrata*

Appianus

BC	*Bella Civilia*

Aristotle

Cael.	*De Caelo*
EN	*Ethica Nicomachea*
HA	*Historia Animalium*
Int.	*De Interpretatione*
Po.	*Poetica*
Pol.	*Politica*
Pr.	*Problemata*
Rh.	*Rhetorica*

Callimachus

Epigr.	*Epigrammata*
Hymn.	*Hymni*

Cicero

Att.	*Epistulae ad Atticum*
Nat. Deor.	*De Natura Deorum*

Corp. Herm.	*Corpus Hermeticum*

Demosthenes

Or.	*Orationes*

Epictetus
- *Diss.* — *Dissertationes*
- *Ench.* — *Enchiridion*

Euripides
- *Alc.* — *Alcestis*
- *Ba.* — *Bacchae*
- *Fr.* — *Fragmenta*
- *Hec.* — *Hecuba*
- *HF* — *Hercules Furens*
- *Ion* — *Ion*
- *Or.* — *Orestes*

Hesiod
- *Th.* — *Theogonia*

Homer
- *Il.* — *Iliad*
- *Od.* — *Odyssey*

Horace
- *Carm.* — *Carmina*
- *Sat.* — *Satirae*

Iamblichus
- *VP* — *De Vita Pythagorica*

Josephus
- *Ant.* — *Antiquitates Judaicae*
- *Ap.* — *Contra Apionem*
- *B.J.* — *De Bello Judaico*
- *Vita* — *Vita Josephi*

Juvenal
- *Sat.* — *Satirae*

Libanius
- *Or.* — *Orationes*

Lucian
- *Alex.* — *Alexander*
- *Anach.* — *Anacharsis*
- *DMort.* — *Dialogi Mortuorum*
- *Herm.* — *Hermotimus*
- *Peregr.* — *De Morte Peregrini*
- *Philops.* — *Philopseudes*
- *Pr. Im.* — *Pro Imaginibus*
- *Vit. Auct.* — *Vitarum Auctio*

Philo
- *Abr.* — *De Abrahamo*
- *Aet.* — *De Aeternitate Mundi*
- *Agr.* — *De Agricultura*
- *All.* — *Legum Allegoriae*
- *Cher.* — *De Cherubim*
- *Conf.* — *De Confusione Linguarum*
- *Congr.* — *De Congressu Eruditionis Gratia*
- *Decal.* — *De Decalogo*
- *Det.* — *Quod Deterius Potiori insidiari soleat*
- *Ebr.* — *De Ebrietate*
- *Flacc.* — *In Flaccum*
- *Fug.* — *De Fuga et Inventione*
- *Gig.* — *De Gigantibus*
- *Her.* — *Quis Rerum Divinarum Heres Sit*
- *Jos.* — *De Josepho*
- *Leg. Gai.* — *Legatio ad Gaium*
- *Migr.* — *De Migratione Abrahami*
- *Mut.* — *De Mutatione Nominum*
- *Omn. Prob. Lib.* — *Quod Omnis Probus Liber Sit*
- *Op.* — *De Opificione Mundi*
- *Plant.* — *De Plantatione*
- *Sacr.* — *De Sacrificiis Abelis et Caini*
- *Som.* — *De Somniis*
- *Spec. Leg.* — *De Specialibus Legibus*
- *Virt.* — *De Virtutibus*
- *Vit. Cont.* — *De Vita Contemplativa*
- *Vit. Mos.* — *De Vita Mosis*

Philodemus
- *Herc.* — *Herculanensia Volumina*
- *Piet.* — *De Pietate*

Philostratus
- *VA* — *Vita Apollonii*

Plato
- *Alc.* — *Alcibiades*
- *Ap.* — *Apologia*
- *Cra.* — *Cratylus*
- *Criti.* — *Critias*
- *Ep.* — *Epistulae*
- *Euth.* — *Euthydemus*
- *Grg.* — *Gorgias*
- *La.* — *Laches*
- *Lg.* — *Leges*
- *Phd.* — *Phaedo*
- *Phdr.* — *Phaedrus*
- *Phlb.* — *Philebus*
- *R.* — *Republic*
- *Smp.* — *Symposium*
- *Sph.* — *Sophista*
- *Tht.* — *Theaetetus*
- *Ti.* — *Timaeus*

Plotinus
- *Enn.* — *Enneaden*

Plutarch
- *Alex.* — *Alexander*
- *Apophth.* — *Apophthegmata Regum et Imperatorum*
- *Cic.* — *Cicero*
- *Demetr.* — *Demetrius*
- *Quaest. Conv.* — *Quaestiones Convivales*
- *Sept. Sap.* — *Septem Sapientum Convivum*
- *Sol.* — *Solon*
- *Suav. Viv. Epic.* — *Non Posse Suaviter Vivi secundum Epicurum*

Pseudo-Aeschylus
- *Th.* — *Septem contra Thebas*

Ptolemy
- *Geog.* — *Geographica*
- *Tetr.* — *Tetrabibiblos*

Quintillian
- *Inst.* — *Institutio Oratia*

Seneca
- *Ep.* — *Epistulae Morales*

Sextus Empiricus
- *P.* — *Pyrrhoneae Hypotyposes*

Sophocles
- *Aj.* — *Ajax*
- *Ant.* — *Antigone*
- *OC* — *Oedipus Coloneus*
- *Ph.* — *Philoctetes*

Suetonius
- *Caes.* — *De Vita Caesarum*

Tacitus
- *Ann.* — *Annales*
- *Hist.* — *Historiae*

Theodoret	
Hist.	*Historia*
Theophrastus	
Char.	*Characteres*
HP	*Historia Plantarum*
Virgil	
Aen.	*Aeneid*
Ecl.	*Eclogues*
Xenophon	
Ages.	*Agesilaus*
An.	*Anabasis*
Cyr.	*Institutio Cyri (Cyropaedia)*
Eq.	*De Equitandi Ratione*
HG	*Historia Graeca (Hellenica)*
Mem.	*Memorabilia*

i. Inscriptions, Fragments, Papyri, and Anthologies

ÄgU	Ägyptische Urkunden aus den Staatlichen Museen zu Berlin, Griechische Urkunden I-XI (1895-1970)
CIG	*Corpus Inscriptionum Graecarum* I-IV (ed. A. Boeckh, et al.; 1828-77)
CIJ	*Corpus Inscriptionum Judaicarum* I-II (1936, 1952)
CIL	*Corpus Inscriptionum Latinarum* I-XVI (1862-1943, ^{2}1893-)
Diels, *Fragmente*	H. Diels and W. Kranz, *Die Fragmente der Vorsokratiker* I-III (^{11}1964)
Epigr. Graec.	*Epigrammata Graeca ex lapidibus conlecta* (ed. G. Kaibel; 1878)
OGIS	*Orientis Graeci Inscriptiones Selectae* I-II (ed. W. Dittenberger; 1903, 1905, reprint 1960)
Pap. Eleph.	*Die Elephantine-Papyri* (ed. O. Rubensohn; Ägyptische Urkunden aus den Königlichen Museen zu Berlin, Griechische Urkunden, Sonderheft, 1907)
Pap. Hibeh	*The Hibeh Papyri* I (ed. B. P. Grenfell and A. S. Hunt; 1906), II (ed. E. G. Turner; 1955)
Pap. London	*Greek Papyri in the British Museum* I-II (ed. F. G. Kenyon; 1893, 1898), III (ed. F. G. Kenyon and H. I. Bell; 1907), IV-V (ed. H. I. Bell; 1910, 1917)
Pap. Oxy.	*The Oxyrynchus Papyri* I-XLI (ed. B. P. Grenfell, A. S. Hunt, et al.; 1898-1972)
Pap. Petrie	*The Flinders Petrie Papyri* I-II (ed. J. P. Mahaffy; 1891, 1893), III (ed. J. P. Mahaffy and J. G. Smyly; 1905)
Pap. Tebt.	*The Tebtunis Papyri* I-III (ed. B. P. Grenfell, A. S. Hunt, et al.; 1902-38)
PGM	*Papyri Graecae Magicae. Die griechischen Zauberpapyri* (ed. K. Preisendanz, et al.; ^{2}1973, 1974)
Preisigke, *Sammelbuch*	F. Preisigke, F. Bilabel, and E. Kiessling, *Sammelbuch griechischer Urkunden aus Ägypten* I-XI (1915-73)
SIG	*Sylloge Inscriptionum Graecarum* I-IV (ed. W. Dittenberger; ^{3}1915-24, reprinted 1960)

2. Modern Writings

AB	Anchor Bible
Abel, *Géographie*	F.-M. Abel, *Géographie de la Palestine* I-II (1933-38)
Abel, *Grammaire*	F.-M. Abel, *Grammaire du Grec biblique* (1927)
Abel, *Histoire*	F.-M. Abel, *Histoire de la Palestine depuis la conquête d'Alexandre jusqu'à l'invasion arabe* I-II (1952)
ABR	*Australian Biblical Review*
Abr-N	*Abr-Nahrain*
ADAW.PH	Abhandlungen der Deutschen (before 1944: Preußischen) Akademie der Wissenschaften zu Berlin. Philosophisch-historische Klasse
AER	*American Ecclesiastical Review*
AnBib	Analecta Biblica
Ang	*Angelicum*
AnGr	Analecta Gregoriana
ANRW	*Aufstieg und Niedergang der römischen Welt*
AsSeign	*Assemblées du Seigneur*
ASNU	Acta seminarii Neotestamentici Upsaliensis
ASTI	*Annual of the Swedish Theological Institute*
ATANT	Abhandlungen zur Theologie des Alten und Neuen Testaments
AuC	*Antike und Christentum. Kultur- und religionsgeschichtliche Studien*
AUSS	Andrews University Seminary Studies
AV	Authorized (King James) Version
BAGD	W. Bauer, W. F. Arndt, F. W. Gingrich, and F. Danker, *A Greek-English Lexicon of the NT and Other Early Christian Literature* (^{2}1979)
BBB	Bonner biblische Beiträge
BDB	F. Brown, S. R. Driver, and C. A. Briggs, *Hebrew and English Lexicon of the OT* (1907)
BDF	F. Blass, A. Debrunner, and R. W. Funk, *A Greek Grammar of the NT and Other Early Christian Literature* (1961)
BeO	*Bibbia e oriente*

Beginnings	*The Beginnings of Christianity,* Part I: *The Acts of the Apostles* (ed. F. J. Foakes-Jackson and K. Lake; 1920-33)
BETL	Bibliotheca ephemeridum theologicarum Lovaniensium
BEvT	Beiträge zur evangelischen Theologie
Beyer, *Syntax*	K. Beyer, *Semitische Syntax im NT* I/1 (1962)
BFCT	Beiträge zur Förderung christlicher Theologie
BGBE	Beiträge zur Geschichte der biblischen Exegese
BGE	Beiträge zur Geschichte der neutestamentlichen Exegese
BHH	*Biblisch-historisches Handwörterbuch* I-III (single pagination; ed. B. Reicke and L. Rost; 1962-66)
BiH	Biblische Handbibliothek
Bib	*Biblica*
BibLeb	*Bibel und Leben*
Bijdr.	*Bijdragen. Tijdschrift voor philosophie en theologie*
Billerbeck	(H. Strack and) P. Billerbeck, *Kommentar zum NT aus Talmud und Midrasch* I-IV (1922-28)
BJRL	*Bulletin of the John Rylands Library*
BKAT	Biblischer Kommentar: Altes Testament
BL	*Bibel-Lexikon,* ed. H. Haag (^{2}1968)
Black, *Approach*	M. Black, *An Aramaic Approach to the Gospels and Acts* (^{3}1967)
Bornkamm, *Aufsätze*	G. Bornkamm, *Gesammelte Aufsätze.* I: *Das Ende des Gesetzes. Paulusstudien;* II: *Studien zu Antike und Christentum;* III-IV: *Geschichte und Glauben* (1952-1971)
Bousset/Gressmann	W. Bousset, *Die Religion des Judentums im späthellenistischen Zeitalter* (ed. H. Gressmann; ^{4}1966 = ^{3}1926)
BR	*Biblical Research*
Braun, *Qumran*	H. Braun, *Qumran und das NT* I-II (1966)
BRL	*Biblisches Reallexikon* (ed. K. Galling; ^{2}1977)
BSac	*Bibliotheca Sacra*
BTB	*Biblical Theology Bulletin*
BU	Biblische Untersuchungen
Bultmann, *Glauben*	R. Bultmann, *Glauben und Verstehen. Gesammelte Aufsätze* I-IV (1933-65)
Bultmann, *History*	R. Bultmann, *History of the Synoptic Tradition* (1963)
Bultmann, *Theology*	R. Bultmann, *Theology of the NT* I-II (1951, 1955)
BVC	*Bible et vie chrétienne*
BWANT	Beiträge zur Wissenschaft vom Alten und Neuen Testament
ByZ	*Byzantinische Zeitschrift*
BZ	*Biblische Zeitschrift*
BZAW	Beihefte zur *Zeitschrift für die alttestamentliche Wissenschaft*
BZNW	Beihefte zur *Zeitschrift für die neutestamentliche Wissenschaft*
CBL	*Calwer Bibellexikon* (^{5}1959-61)
CBQ	*Catholic Biblical Quarterly*
Chantraine, *Dictionnaire*	P. Chantraine, *Dictionnaire étymologique de la langue grecque* (1968-)
Conzelmann, *Theology*	H. Conzelmann, *An Outline of the Theology of the NT* (1969)
ConNT	Coniectanea neotestamentica
CP	*Classical Philology*
CQR	*Church Quarterly Review*
Cremer/Kögel	H. Cremer and J. Kögel, *Biblisch-theologisches Wörterbuch des neutestamentlichen Griechisch* (^{11}1923)
DACL	*Dictionnaire d'archéologie chrétienne et de liturgie* I-XV (ed. Cabrol, Lelercq, et al.; 1903-53)
Dalman, *Arbeit*	G. Dalman, *Arbeit und Sitte in Palästina* I-VII (1928-42, reprinted 1964)
Dalman, *Words*	G. Dalman, *The Words of Jesus* (1902)
Dalman, *Worte*	G. Dalman, *Die Worte Jesu* (^{2}1930)
DB	*Dictionnaire de la Bible* I-V (ed. F. Vigouroux; 1895-1912)
DBSup	*Dictionnaire de la Bible, Supplément* (1928-)
DBT	*Dictionary of Biblical Theology* (ed. X. Léon-Dufour; 1967, ^{2}1972)
Deissmann, *Light*	A. Deissmann, *Light from the Ancient East* (^{4}1922)
Denniston, *Particles*	J. D. Denniston, *The Greek Particles* (^{2}1954, reprinted 1970)
Dibelius, *Botschaft*	M. Dibelius, *Botschaft und Geschichte. Gesammelte Studien* I-II (1953, 1956)
Dibelius, *Tradition*	M. Dibelius, *From Tradition to Gospel* (n.d.)
DJD	Discoveries in the Judean Desert
DNTT	*New International Dictionary of NT Theology* I-III (ed. C. Brown; 1975-78)
DR	*Downside Review*
ÉBib	Études Bibliques
ÉeT	*Église et théologie*
EHS	Europäische Hochschulschriften
Eichrodt, *Theology*	W. Eichrodt, *Theology of the OT* I-II (1961, 1967)

EKKNT	Evangelisch-katholischer Kommentar zum NT
EKKNT (V)	EKKNT Vorarbeiten
EncJud	*Encyclopaedia Judaica* I-XVI (1971-72)
EPM	*Evangelische Predigtmeditationen*
EstBib	*Estudios biblicos*
ETL	*Ephemerides theologicae Lovanienses*
ETS	Erfurter theologische Schriften
ETSt	Erfurter theologische Studien
EvDia	*Evangelische Diaspora*
EvK	*Evangelische Kommentare*
EvT	*Evangelische Theologie*
EWG	J. B. Hofmann, *Etymologisches Wörterbuch des Griechischen* (reprinted 1950)
ExpTim	*Expository Times*
FDV	Franz-Delitzsch-Vorlesungen
Frisk, *Wörterbuch*	H. Frisk, *Griechisches etymologisches Wörterbuch* I-III (1960-72)
FRLANT	Forschungen zur Religion und Literatur des Alten und Neuen Testaments
FS	Festschrift
FS Bardtke	*Bibel und Qumran* (FS H. Bardtke; 1968)
FS Black	*Neotestamentica et Semitica* (FS M. Black; 1969)
FS Braun	*Neues Testament und christliche Existenz* (FS H. Braun; 1973)
FS Bruce	*Apostolic History and the Gospel* (FS F. F. Bruce; 1970)
FS Bultmann (1954)	*Neutestamentliche Studien* (FS R. Bultmann; 1954)
FS Bultmann (1964)	*Zeit und Geschichte* (FS R. Bultmann; 1964)
FS Conzelmann	*Jesus Christus in Historie und Theologie* (FS H. Conzelmann; 1975)
FS Cullmann (1962)	*Neotestamentica et Patristica* (FS O. Cullmann; 1962)
FS Cullmann (1967)	*Oikonomia. Heilsgeschichte als Thema der Theologie* (FS O. Cullmann; 1967)
FS Cullmann (1972)	*Neues Testament und Geschichte* (FS O. Cullmann; 1972)
FS Dahl	*God's Christ and His People* (FS N. A. Dahl; 1977)
FS Friedrich	*Das Wort und die Wörter* (FS G. Friedrich; 1973)
FS Fuchs	*Festschrift für Ernst Fuchs* (1973)
FS Gingrich	*Festschrift to Honor F. W. Gingrich* (1972)
FS Goguel	*Aux sources de la tradition chrétienne* (FS M. Goguel; 1950)
FS Jeremias (1960)	*Judentum, Urchristentum, Kirche* (FS J. Jeremias; 1960)
FS Jeremias (1970)	*Der Ruf Jesu und die Antwort der Gemeinde* (FS J. Jeremias; 1970)
FS Käsemann	*Rechtfertigung* (FS E. Käsemann; 1976)
FS Kuhn	*Tradition und Glaube. Das frühe Christentum in seiner Umwelt* (FS K. G. Kuhn; 1971)
FS Kümmel	*Jesus und Paulus* (FS W. G. Kümmel; 1975)
FS Meinertz	*Vom Wort des Lebens* (FS M. Meinertz; 1951)
FS Michel	*Abraham unser Vater. Juden und Christen im Gespräch über die Bibel* (FS O. Michel; 1963)
FS Moule	*Christ and Spirit in the NT* (FS C. F. D. Moule; 1973)
FS Rigaux	*Mélanges Bibliques en hommage au B. Rigaux* (1970)
FS Schlier	*Die Zeit Jesu* (FS H. Schlier; 1970)
FS Schmid (1963)	*Neutestamentliche Aufsätze* (FS J. Schmid; 1963)
FS Schmid (1973)	*Orientierung an Jesus* (FS J. Schmid; 1973)
FS Schnackenburg	*Neues Testament und Kirche* (FS R. Schnackenburg; 1974)
FS Schürmann	*Die Kirche des Anfangs* (FS H. Schürmann; 1977)
FS Sevenster	*Studies in John Presented to J. N. Sevenster* (1970)
FS Smith	*Christianity, Judaism, and Other Greco-Roman Cults* I-IV (FS M. Smith; 1975)
FS Stählin	*Verborum Veritas* (FS G. Stählin; 1970)
FS Vögtle	*Jesus und der Menschensohn* (FS A. Vögtle; 1975)
FS Wikenhauser	*Synoptische Studien* (FS A. Wikenhauser; 1953)
FS Wikgren	*Studies in the NT and Early Christian Literature* (FS A. P. Wikgren; 1972)
FS de Zwaan	*Studia Paulinum in honorem Johannis de Zwaan* (1953)
FTS	Frankfurter theologische Studien
FzB	Forschungen zur Bibel
Gesenius/Buhl	H. F. W. Gesenius and F. Buhl, *Hebräisches und Aramäisches Handwörterbuch über das AT* (^{17}1915, reprinted 1962)
GGA	*Göttingische gelehrte Anzeigen*
Glotta	*Glotta. Zeitschrift für die griechische und lateinische Sprache*
Goppelt, *Theology*	L. Goppelt, *Theology of the NT* I, II (1981, 1982)
GuL	*Geist und Leben*
Hahn, *Titles*	F. Hahn, *The Titles of Jesus in Christology* (1969)

Harnack, *Mission*	A. von Harnack, *The Mission and Expansion of Christianity in the First Three Centuries* I-II (1904, 1905)
Hatch/Redpath	E. Hatch and H. A. Redpath, *A Concordance to the Septuagint* I-III (1897-1906)
HDB	*Dictionary of the Bible* I-V (ed. J. Hastings; 1901-04)
Helbing, *Kasussyntax*	R. Helbing, *Die Kasussyntax der Verba bei den Septuaginta* (1928)
Hengel, *Judaism*	M. Hengel, *Judaism and Hellenism* I-II (1974)
Hennecke/ Schneemelcher	E. Hennecke, *New Testament Apocrypha* I-II (ed. W. Schneemelcher and [English translation] R. McL. Wilson; 1963, 1965)
Hermeneia	Hermeneia—A Critical and Historical Commentary on the Bible
HNT	Handbuch zum NT
HNTC	Harper's NT Commentaries
HTG	*Handbuch theologischer Grundbegriffe* I-II (ed. H. Fries; 1962, 1963)
HTKNT	Herders theologischer Kommentar zum NT
HTR	*Harvard Theological Review*
HUCA	*Hebrew Union College Annual*
HUT	Hermeneutische Untersuchungen zur Theologie
HWP	*Historisches Wörterbuch der Philosophie* (1971-)
ICC	International Critical Commentary
IDB	*Interpreter's Dictionary of the Bible* I-IV (ed. G. A. Buttrick, et al.; 1962)
IDBSup	*Interpreter's Dictionary of the Bible, Supplementary Volume* (ed. K. Crim; 1976)
Int	*Interpretation*
ISBE	*International Standard Bible Encyclopedia* I-IV (revised edition ed. G. W. Bromiley, et al.; 1979-88)
JAAR	*Journal of the American Academy of Religion*
JAC	Jahrbuch für Antike und Christentum
Jastrow, *Dictionary*	M. Jastrow, *A Dictionary of the Targumim, the Talmud Babli and Yerushalmi, and the Midrashic Literature* (1903)
JB	Jerusalem Bible
JBL	*Journal of Biblical Literature*
Jeremias, *Parables*	J. Jeremias, *The Parables of Jesus* (^{2}1972)
Jeremias, *Theology*	J. Jeremias, *NT Theology* (1971)
JETS	*Journal of the Evangelical Theological Society*
JHS	*Journal of Hellenic Studies*
Johannessohn, *Präpositionen*	M. Johannessohn, *Der Gebrauch der Präpositionen in der Septuaginta* (1926)
JQR	*Jewish Quarterly Review*
JR	*Journal of Religion*
JSHRZ	*Jüdische Schriften aus hellenistisch-römischer Zeit* I-V (ed. W. G. Kümmel; 1973-)
JSJ	*Journal for the Study of Judaism*
JTS	*Journal of Theological Studies*
JTSB	*Jahrbuch der theologischen Schule Bethel*
Judaica	*Judaica. Beiträge zum Verständnis des jüdischen Schicksals in Vergangenheit und Gegenwart*
Jülicher I-II	A. Jülicher, *Die Gleichnissreden Jesu* I-II (1910)
Kairos	*Kairos. Zeitschrift für Religionswissenschaft und Theologie*
Käsemann, *Versuche*	E. Käsemann, *Exegetische Versuche und Besinnungen* I-II (^{4}1965, ^{3}1968)
KBL^{2,3}	L. Koehler and W. Baumgartner, *Lexicon in Veteris Testamenti Libros* (^{2}1958); *Hebräisches und Aramäisches Lexikon zum AT* (^{3}1974-)
KD	*Kerygma und Dogma*
KEK	Kritisch-exegetischer Kommentar über das NT
KIT	Kleine Texte
KNT	Kommentar zum NT
Kopp, *Stätten*	C. Kopp, *Die heiligen Stätten der Evangelien* (1959)
KP	*Der Kleine Pauly. Lexikon der Antike* I-V (ed. von Ziegler and Sontheimer; 1964-75)
KQT	*Konkordanz zu den Qumrantexten* (ed. K. G. Kuhn; 1960)
Kühner, *Grammatik*	R. Kühner, *Ausführliche Grammatik der griechischen Sprache* I by F. Blass, II by B. Gerth (1890-1904)
Kümmel, *Introduction*	W. G. Kümmel, *Introduction to the NT* (^{2}1975)
Kuss I-III	O. Kuss, *Auslegung und Verkündigung* I-III (1963-71)
LAW	*Lexikon der Alten Welten* (ed. C. Andresen, H. Erbse, et al.; 1965)
LCL	Loeb Classical Library
LD	Lectio Divina
LingBibl	*Linguistica Biblica*
Lipsius/Bonnet	R. A. Lipsius and M. Bonnet, *Acta Apostolorum Apocrypha* I-II (1891, 1903)
Lohse, *Texte*	*Die Texte aus Qumran. Hebräisch und Deutsch* (ed. E. Lohse; ^{2}1971)
LSJ	H. G. Liddell, R. Scott, H. S. Jones, and R. McKenzie, *A Greek-English Lexicon* (^{9}1940)

LTK	*Lexikon für Theologie und Kirche* I-XI (ed. J. Höfer and K. Rahner; ^{2}1957-67)
Maier/Schreiner	*Literatur und Religion des Frühjudentums. Eine Einführung* (ed. J. Maier and J. Schreiner; 1973)
Mayser, *Grammatik*	E. Mayser, *Grammatik der griechischen Papyri aus der Ptolemäerzeit* I-II (1906, 1934)
MGWJ	*Monatsschrift für Geschichte und Wissenschaft des Judentums*
MNTC	Moffatt NT Commentary
Morgenthaler, *Statistik*	R. Morgenthaler, *Statistik des neutestamentlichen Wortschatzes* (1958)
Moulton, *Grammar*	*A Grammar of NT Greek:* I by J. H. Moulton (^{2}1908), II by W. F. Howard (1963), III, IV by N. Turner (1963, 1976)
Moulton/Milligan	J. H. Moulton and G. Milligan, *The Vocabulary of the Greek Testament, Illustrated from the Papyri and Other Non-literary Sources* (1930)
MTS	Münchener theologische Studien
MTSt	Marburger theologische Studien
MTZ	*Münchener theologische Zeitschrift*
NAB	New American Bible
Nägeli, *Wortschatz*	T. Nägeli, *Der Wortschatz des Apostels Paulus* (1905)
NASB	New American Standard Bible
NEB	New English Bible
NedTTs	*Nederlandse theologisch tijdschrift*
Neot	*Neotestamentica*
N.F.	Neue Folge
NIGTC	New International Greek Testament Commentary
Nilsson, *Geschichte*	M. P. Nilsson, *Geschichte der griechischen Religion.* II: *Die hellenistische und römische Zeit* (^{2}1961)
NIV	New International Version
NJKA	*Neue Jahrbücher für das klassische Altertum, Geschichte, deutsche Literatur und für Pädagogik*
NorTT	*Norsk Teologisk Tidsskrift*
NovT	*Novum Testamentum*
NovTSup	Novum Testamentum Supplements
NRT	*La nouvelle revue théologique*
NSNU	*Nuntius sodalicii neotestamentici Upsaliensis*
NTAbh	Neutestamentliche Abhandlungen
NTD	Das Neue Testament Deutsch
NTF	Neutestamentliche Forschungen
NTG	*Novum Testamentum Graece* (ed. E. Nestle and K. Aland; ^{25}1963; ed. K. Aland, M. Black, C. M. Martini, B. M. Metzger, and A. Wikgren; ^{26}1979)
NTS	*New Testament Studies*
NTSR	New Testament for Spiritual Reading
OBO	Orbis Biblicus et Orientalis
OCD	*The Oxford Classical Dictionary* (ed. H. G. L. Hammond and H. H. Scullard; ^{2}1970)
ÖTK	Ökumenischer Taschenbuch-Kommentar
OTS	*Oudtestamentische Studiën*
Pape, *Wörterbuch*	W. Pape, *Griechisch-deutsches Wörterbuch* I-II (^{6}1914)
Passow I-II	F. Passow, *Handwörterbuch der griechischen Sprache* I-II (^{5}1841, 1857)
PEQ	*Palestine Exploration Quarterly*
PG	J.-P. Migne, *Patrologiae cursus completus. Series Graeca* (1857-1936)
PGL	G. W. H. Lampe, *A Patristic Greek Lexicon* (^{4}1976)
Ph.	*Philologus. Zeitschrift für das klassische Altertum*
Ph. S.	*Philologus* Supplements
PL	J.-P. Migne, *Patrologiae cursus completus. Series Latina* (1841-64)
PLSup	J.-P. Migne, *Patrologiae cursus completus. Series Latina. Supplementa* (1958-70)
PosLuth	*Positions luthériennes*
Preisigke, *Wörterbuch*	F. Preisigke, *Wörterbuch der griechischen Papyruskunden* I-III (1925-31), Supplement I (1971)
PVTG	Pseudepigrapha Veteris Testamenti graece
PW	(A.) *Paulys Real-Encyclopädie der classischen Altertumswissenschaft* (ed. G. Wissowa and W. Kroll; 1893-)
QD	Quaestiones Disputatae
RAC	*Reallexikon für Antike und Christentum* (ed. T. Klauser; 1941-)
Radermacher, *Grammatik*	L. Radermacher, *Neutestamentliche Grammatik* (^{2}1925)
RB	*Revue Biblique*
RCB	*Revista de cultura biblica*
RE	*Realencyclopädie für protestantische Theologie und Kirche* I-XXIV (^{3}1896-1913)
RechBib	Recherches bibliques

Reicke, *NT Era*	B. Reicke, *The NT Era* (1968)
RevQ	*Revue de Qumran*
RevScRel	*Revue des sciences religieuses*
RevThom	*Revue thomiste*
RGG	*Die Religion in Geschichte und Gegenwart* I-VI (ed. K. Galling, et al.; [3]1957-62)
RHPR	*Revue d'histoire et de philosophie religieuses*
Ristow/Matthiae	*Der historische Jesus und der kerygmatische Christus* (ed. H. Ristow and K. Matthiae; [3]1964)
RivB	*Rivista Biblica*
RivLi	*Rivista Liturgica*
RMP	*Rheinisches Museum für Philologie*
RNT	Regensburger Neues Testament
Robertson, *Grammar*	A. T. Robertson, *A Grammar of the Greek NT in the Light of Historical Research* ([4]1934)
Roscher, *Lexikon*	*Ausführliches Lexikon der griechischen und römischen Mythologie* (ed. H. W. Roscher; 1884-1937)
RRef	*Revue réformée*
RSPT	*Revue des sciences philosophiques et théologiques*
RSR	*Recherches de science religieuse*
RSV	Revised Standard Version
RTL	*Revue théologique de Louvain*
RTM	*Revista di Teologia Morale*
RTP	*Revue de théologie et de philosophie*
RTR	*Reformed Theological Review*
RVV	Religionsgeschichtliche Versuche und Vorarbeiten
SacVb	*Sacramentum Verbi* (= *Encyclopedia of Biblical Theology;* ed. J. B. Bauer; [3]1967)
SANT	Studien zum Alten und Neuen Testament
SBFLA	*Studii biblici franciscani liber annuus*
SBLDS	Society of Biblical Literature Dissertation Series
SBLSP	Society of Biblical Literature Seminar Papers
SBM	Stuttgarter biblische Monographien
SBS	Stuttgarter Bibelstudien
SBT	Sources in Biblical Theology
ScEc	*Sciences Ecclésiastiques*
ScEs	*Science et esprit*
Schelkle, *Theology*	K. H. Schelkle, *Theology of the NT* I-IV (1971-78)
Schlier I-III	H. Schlier, *Exegetische Aufsätze und Vorträge* I-III (1956-71)
Schmidt, *Synonymik*	J. H. H. Schmidt, *Synonymik der griechischen Sprache* I-IV (1876-86, reprinted 1967-69)
Schnackenburg I-II	R. Schnackenburg, *Christian Existence in the NT* (1968, 1969)
Schnackenburg, *Botschaft*	R. Schnackenburg, *Die sittliche Botschaft des NT* ([2]1962)
Schulz, *Q*	S. Schulz, *Q. Die Spruchquelle der Evangelisten* (1972)
Schürer, *History*	E. Schürer, *The History of the Jewish People in the Age of Jesus Christ* I-III/1-2 (revised and ed. G. Vermes, F. Millar, and M. Black; 1973-87)
Schwyzer, *Grammatik*	E. Schwyzer, *Griechische Grammatik* I-IV (1939-71)
Scr	*Scripture*
SDAW	*Sitzungsberichte der deutschen Akademie der Wissenschaft zu Berlin*
SE	*Studia Evangelica* (= TU 73, 87, 88, etc.)
SEÅ	*Svensk exegetisk årsbok*
SHVL	Skrifter utgivna av k. humanistiska vetenskapssamfundet i Lund
SJT	*Scottish Journal of Theology*
SM	*Sacramentum Mundi: An Encyclopedia of Theology* I-IV (ed. K. Rahner, et al.; 1968-70)
SNT	Studien zum NT
SNTSMS	Society for NT Studies Monograph Series
Sophocles, *Lexicon*	E. A. Sophocles, *Greek Lexicon of the Roman and Byzantine Periods* I-II ([3]1888)
SPAW	*Sitzungsberichte der preußischen Akademie der Wissenschaften*
SPB	Studia postbiblica
ST	*Studia theologica*
Staab, *Paulus-kommentare*	K. Staab, *Pauluskommentare aus der griechischen Kirche* (1933)
STDJ	Studies on the Texts of the Desert of Judah
StudNeot	Studia Neotestamentica
SUNT	Studien zur Umwelt des NT
SWJT	*Southwestern Journal of Theology*
TB	*Tyndale Bulletin*

TBT	Theologische Bibliothek Töpelmann
TBer	*Theologische Berichte*
TBl	*Theologische Blätter*
TBü	Theologische Bücherei
TCGNT	B. Metzger, *A Textual Commentary on the Greek NT* (1971)
TDNT	*Theological Dictionary of the NT* I-X (ed. G. Kittel and G. Friedrich; 1964-76)
TDOT	*Theological Dictionary of the OT* (ed. J. Botterweck and H. Ringgren; [2]1974-)
TEH	Theologische Existenz heute
TEV	Today's English Version (Good News Bible)
Textus	*Textus. Annual of the Hebrew University Bible Project*
TF	*Theologische Forschung*
TGl	*Theologie und Glaube*
THAT	*Theologisches Handwörterbuch zum AT* I-II (ed. E. Jenni and C. Westermann; 1971, 1976)
ThDiss	Theologische Dissertationen (Basel)
ThGL	*Thesaurus Graecae Linguae ab H. Stephano constructus* I-IX (ed. Hase and Dindorf; 1831-65)
ThJb(L)	*Theologisches Jahrbuch* (Leipzig)
THKNT	Theologischer Handkommentar zum NT
Thrall, *Particles*	M. Thrall, *Greek Particles in the NT* (1962)
TLZ	*Theologische Literaturzeitung*
TP	*Theologie und Philosophie*
TPQ	*Theologisch-Praktische Quartalschrift*
TQ	*Theologische Quartalschrift*
TRE	*Theologische Realenzyklopädie* (ed. G. Krause and G. Müller; 1976-)
Trench, *Synonyms*	R. C. Trench, *Synonyms of the NT* ([9]1880)
TRev	*Theologische Revue*
TRu	*Theologische Rundschau*
TS	*Theological Studies*
TSK	*Theologische Studien und Kritiken*
TTS	Trierer Theologische Studien
TTZ	*Trierer Theologische Zeitschrift*
TU	Texte und Untersuchungen zur Geschichte der altchristlichen Literatur
TViat	*Theologia Viatorum*
TWAT	*Theologisches Wörterbuch zum Alten Testament* I- (ed. G. J. Botterweck and H. Ringgren; 1970-)
TWNT	*Theologisches Wörterbuch zum NT* I-X (ed. G. Kittel and G. Friedrich; 1933-79)
TZ	*Theologische Zeitschrift*
UBSGNT	*The Greek NT* (ed. K. Aland, M. Black, C. M. Martini, B. M. Metzger, and A. Wikgren; [3]1975)
UNT	Untersuchungen zum NT
UUÅ	*Uppsala universitetsårsskrift*
VD	*Verbum Domini*
VF	*Verkündigung und Forschung*
VKGNT	*Vollständige Konkordanz zum griechischen NT* I-II (ed. K. Aland; 1978, 1983)
VT	*Vetus Testamentum*
WdF	Wege der Forschung
Wettstein, *NT*	J. J. Wettstein, *Novum Testamentum Graecum* I-II (1751-52, reprinted 1962)
WiWei	*Wissenschaft und Weisheit*
WMANT	Wissenschaftliche Monographien zum Alten und Neuen Testament
WuD	*Wort und Dienst. Jahrbuch der Kirchlichen Schule Bethel*
WUNT	Wissenschaftliche Untersuchungen zum NT
WZKM	*Wiener Zeitschrift für die Kunde des Morgenlandes*
Zahn, *Kanon*	T. Zahn, *Forschungen zur Geschichte des neutestamentlichen Kanons und der altkirchlichen Literatur* I-IX (1881-1916)
ZAW	*Zeitschrift für die Alttestamentliche Wissenschaft*
ZBK	Zürcher Bibelkommentare
ZDMG	*Zeitschrift der deutschen morgenländischen Gesellschaft*
ZDPV	*Zeitschrift des deutschen Palästina-Vereins*
ZEE	*Zeitschrift für evangelische Ethik*
Zerwick, *Biblical Greek*	M. Zerwick, *Biblical Greek* (1963)
Zetemata	Zetemata. Monographien zur klassischen Altertumswissenschaft
ZKG	*Zeitschrift für Kirchengeschichte*
ZKT	*Zeitschrift für katholische Theologie*
ZNW	*Zeitschrift für die neutestamentliche Wissenschaft*
ZPE	*Zeitschrift für Papyrologie und Epigraphik*

ZST	*Zeitschrift für systematische Theologie*
ZTK	*Zeitschrift für Theologie und Kirche*
ZVRW	*Zeitschrift für vergleichende Rechtswissenschaft*

3. General

Sigla in textual notes are from the twenty-fifth and twenty-sixth editions of *NTG*.

acc.	accusative
act.	active (voice)
adj.	adjective
adv.	adverb
aor.	aorist
Aram.	Aramaic
art.	(definite) article
AT	Altes Testament
b.	ben, bar (in names of Rabbis)
ch(s).	chapter(s)
dat.	dative
def. art.	definite article
dir. obj.	direct object
diss.	dissertation
Eng.	English
esp.	especially
fem.	feminine
fig.	figurative(ly)
fut.	future
g.	gram(s)
gen.	genitive
Germ.	German
Gk.	Greek
Heb.	Hebrew
impf.	imperfect
imv(s).	imperative(s)
ind.	indicative
inf.	infinitive
intrans.	intransitive(ly)
km.	kilometer(s)
κτλ.	etc. (Greek)
L	Material in Luke not found in Matthew or Mark
l(l).	line number(s)
Lat.	Latin
LXX	Septuagint
M	Material in Matthew not found in Mark or Luke
m.	meter(s)
masc.	masculine
mg.	margin(al)
mid.	middle
mm.	millimeter(s)
ms(s).	manuscript(s)
MT	Masoretic Text
neut.	neuter
nom.	nominative
NT	New Testament, Neues Testament, Nouveau Testament
obj.	object
opt.	optative
OT	Old Testament
partc.	participle
par.	parallel
pass.	passive
pf.	perfect
pl.	plural
pred.	predicate
prep(s).	preposition(s), prepositional
pres.	present
pron.	pronoun
Q	Hypothetical source of material common to Matthew and Luke but not found in Mark
rel.	relative
sg.	singular
subj.	subject
subjunc.	subjunctive
subst.	substantive, substantival
t.t.	technical term
TR	Textus Receptus
trans.	transitive(ly)
v(v).	verse(s)
v.l.	variant reading
vb(s).	verb(s)
Vg.	Vulgate
voc.	vocative

TRANSLITERATION SCHEME

Greek

α	*a*	η	*ē*	ρ	*r*
ᾳ	*ą*	ῃ	*ę̄*	ῥ	*rh*
β	*b*	θ	*th*	σ, ς	*s*
γ	*g*	ι	*i*	τ	*t*
γγ	*ng*	κ	*k*	υ	*y* (*u* in diphthongs)
γκ	*nk*	λ	*l*	φ	*ph*
γξ	*nx*	μ	*m*	χ	*ch*
γχ	*nch*	ν	*n*	ψ	*ps*
δ	*d*	ξ	*x*	ω	*ō*
ε	*e*	ο	*o*	ῳ	*ǭ*
ζ	*z*	π	*p*	ʽ	*h*

Hebrew and Aramaic

Consonants

א	ʾ	ח	*ḥ*	פ	*p̱*
ב	*ḇ*	ט	*ṭ*	פּ	*p*
בּ	*b*	י	*y*	צ	*ṣ*
ג	*g̱*	כ	*ḵ*	ק	*q*
גּ	*g*	כּ	*k*	ר	*r*
ד	*ḏ*	ל	*l*	שׂ	*ś*
דּ	*d*	מ, ם	*m*	שׁ	*š*
ה	*h*	נ, ן	*n*	ת	*ṯ*
ו	*w*	ס	*s*	תּ	*t*
ז	*z*	ע	ʿ		

Vowels

ַ	*a*	ֻ	*u*	ְ (vocal)	^{e}
ָ	*ā, o*	ָה	*â*	ֲ	^{a}
ֶ	*e*	ֵי	*ê*	ֱ	$^{\breve{e}}$
ֵ	*ē*	ִי	*î*	ֳ	^{o}
ִ	*i*	וֹ	*ô*		
ֹ	*ō*	וּ	*û*		

A α

Ἀαρών *Aarōn* Aaron*

Elder brother of Moses (cf. Exod 4:14; 7:7; 28:1): Luke 1:5; Acts 7:40; Heb 5:4; 7:11; 9:4. K. G. Kuhn, *TDNT* I, 3f.; H. Junker, *LTK* I, 3f.; *TRE* I, 1-7.

Ἀβαδδών *Abaddōn* Abaddon*

The name, meaning "destruction" (?), of the angel ruling over the abyss: Rev 9:11. J. Jeremias, *TDNT* I, 4. → ἄβυσσος 2, ἄγγελος 2.

ἀβαρής, 2 *abarēs* not burdensome*

2 Cor 11:9; cf. 12:16; 1 Thess 2:9.

ἀββά *abba* Father (vocative)*

1. In Aramaic — 2. Occurrences in early Christian literature — 3. Ἀββά in Paul — 4. Ἀββά in the sayings of Jesus

Lit.: CONZELMANN, *Theology,* 103f. — G. DALMAN, *Grammatik des jüdisch-palästinischen Aramäisch* ([2]1905; repr. 1960) §§14:7d, f; 36:1γ; 40:4. — DALMAN, *Worte,* 150-59, 296-304. — E. HAENCHEN, *Der Weg Jesu* (1968) 59, 492-94. — O. HOFIUS, *DNTT* I, 614f. — J. JEREMIAS, "Abba," *idem, The Prayers of Jesus* (SBT 2/6, 1967) 11-65. — JEREMIAS, *Theology,* 61-68. — G. KITTEL, *TDNT* I, 5f. — W. MARCHEL, *Abba, Père! La prière du Christ et des chrétiens* (1963); condensed edition, *Abba, Vater! Die Vaterbotschaft des NT* (1963). — S. V. MCCASLAND, "Abba, Father," *JBL* 72 (1953) 79-91. — G. SCHRENK, *TDNT* V, 974-1014, esp. 984f., 1006. — T. M. TAYLOR, " 'Abba, Father' and Baptism," *SJT* 11 (1958) 62-71.

1. *'Abbā'* in Aramaic was originally a nursery word, part of the speech of children (not the determinative form of the noun "father"), with the meaning "Daddy." In NT times it was no longer limited to the speech of small children, but was used also by grown children and was even used as a form of address for old men. Even in Hebrew texts *'abbā'* replaced "my father" and, similarly, could mean "his father" and "our father." It could also replace the determinative form.

2. In early Christian literature (as given by the list in BAGD xxix) ἀββά occurs only twice in Paul (Gal 4:6; Rom 8:15) and once in Mark (14:36) and is always addressed to God. In all three cases it is followed by the same translation: ὁ πατήρ (instead of the expected vocative πάτερ; cf. BDF §147.3). The direct address to God, "Father" (without preceding ἀββά), occurs elsewhere in the NT only in the words of Jesus in the Gospels (19 or 20 times): in the secondary form of the Gethsemane story, Matt 26:39, 42 par. Luke 22:42; in the Lord's Prayer, Luke 11:2 par. Matt 6:9; twice in Jesus' cry of rejoicing, Luke 10:21 par. Matt 11:25f.; in the expansion of the account of Jesus' death, Luke 23:46; in what might be a later addition to the ms. tradition, Luke 23:34; and in John 11:41; 12:27f.; 17:1, 5, 11, 21, 24f.; cf. 1 Pet 1:17.

'Abbā' is not found in direct address to God in ancient Judaism, although the collective address "our Father" is found in two Jewish prayers (KIT 58, pp. 6, 28f.) from around the time of the NT (through the influence of the pagan world, πάτερ as an address in prayer is also found occasionally in Diaspora Judaism, e.g., Wis 14:3), and in Palestinian Judaism, apart from a direct address in prayer, one could occasionally even speak of God as "my father" (as early as Sir 51:10). A fundamental difference from Jewish usage cannot be demonstrated (*contra* esp. Jeremias, e.g., *Theology,* 63-67).

3. In Gal 4:6 and Rom 8:15 the believers "cry" (κράζειν in the sense of the ecstatic cry in the congregational meeting) to God because they are "children of God" and have received "the spirit of his son" or "a spirit of sonship." In Galatians it is the divine spirit in the human heart that "cries" ἀββά, in Romans it is the believers who "cry" it "in" the divine spirit.

4. In the mouth of Jesus ἀββά occurs literally only in the oldest form of the prayer in Gethsemane (Mark 14:36), as an expression of a childlike trust in God and of the obligation to obedience (both aspects are characteristic of the designation of God as "father" in ancient Judaism; cf., e.g., 3 Macc 6:3, 8; 1QH 9:35f. or Wis 11:10; *Sipra Lev.* on 20:26). An Aramaic original, with corresponding *'abbā',* should probably be assumed for the Lord's Prayer and perhaps the cry of rejoicing (→ 2). The prayer in

Gethsemane and the (Wisdom-christological) cry of rejoicing are, however, early Christian formulations, so that the Lord's Prayer, a prayer for disciples, remains as the *only* text likely to be authentic (if the Lukan πάτερ—as probable—is authentic, or the Matthean πάτερ ἡμῶν goes back to a simple *'abbā'*).

H.-W. Kuhn

῞Αβελ *Habel* Abel*

Younger brother of Cain (Gen 4:1-16): Matt 23:35; Luke 11:51; Heb 11:4; 12:24. *DB* I, 28-30; K. G. Kuhn, *TDNT* I, 6-8; C. Westermann, *Genesis 1–11* (1984) 279-320 (bibliography).

᾿Αβιά *Abia* Abijah*

Personal name (cf. 2 Chr 13:1–14:1): Matt 1:7b, c; Luke 1:5.

᾿Αβιαθάρ *Abiathar* Abiathar*

Priest under David and Solomon (2 Sam 20:25; 1 Kgs 2:26f.): Mark 2:26.

᾿Αβιληνή, ῆς *Abilēnē* Abilene*

Territory controlled by the city of Abila (northwest of Damascus): Luke 3:1. Schürer, *History* I, 567-69; R. Savignac, *RB* 21 (1912) 533-40. → Λυσανίας.

᾿Αβιούδ *Abioud* Abiud*

Personal name (1 Chr 8:3): Matt 1:13a, b.

᾿Αβραάμ *Abraam* Abraham*

1. Abraham in the OT and early Judaism — 2. In the NT — a) Gospels and Acts — b) Epistles

Lit.: M. A. Beek, et al., *BHH* I, 15-17. — K. Berger, "Abraham in den paulinischen Hauptbriefen," *MTZ* 17 (1966) 47-89. — Billerbeck III, 186-201; IV, 1213 (index s.v. Abraham). — R. E. Clements, *TDOT* I, 52-58. — N. A. Dahl, "The Story of Abraham in Luke-Acts," *Studies in Luke-Acts* (ed. L. Keck and J. L. Martyn; 1968) 139-58. — *Encyclopedia Miqra'îth* I (1965) 61-67. — J. Jeremias, *TDNT* I, 8-10. — E. Käsemann, *Perspectives on Paul* (1971) 79-101. — T. Klauser, *RAC* I, 18-27. — H. E. Lona, *Abraham in Johannes 8* (1976). — R. Martin-Achard, K. Berger, et al., *TRE* I, 364-87. — G. Mayer, "Aspekte des Abrahambildes in der hellenistisch-jüdischen Literatur," *EvT* 32 (1972) 118-227. — L. Pirot, *DBSup* I, 8-28. — O. Schilling, *SacVb* I, 3-6. — O. Schmitz, "Abraham im Spätjudentum und im Urchristentum," in *Aus Schrift und Geschichte* (FS Adolf Schlatter, 1922) 99-123.

1. The name *'abrām* is probably a northern Semitic form meaning "(my) father (God?) is exalted"; from Gen 17:5 on the expanded form *'abrāhām,* which is interpreted as "father of many nations," is used. In the narratives of Gen 11:26–25:9 Abraham is presented as one who is called by God, receives the promise of numerous descendants (12:3; 13:16; 15:5; 17:4f.; 22:17f.) and possession of the land (12:7; 13:14f.; 17:8; 24:7), is found worthy of a covenant with God (15:18; 17:7-14), and preserves his election through believing obedience (12:4; 15:6; 22:3-19). He is called "friend of God" (Isa 41:8; 2 Chr 20:7), and Israel is regarded as the "offspring of Abraham" (Isa 41:8; Ps 105:6).

In early Judaism the faith of Abraham is stressed (1 Macc 2:52; Philo *Abr.* 268-276; *Her.* 90-95) and his faithfulness elaborated in haggadic style. In Sir 44:19-21 it is more precisely described as faithfulness to the law; in *Jubilees* Abraham is a determined opponent of idolatry and the one who restores the Hebrew language and tradition (*Jub.* 11–12; 20–22). He withstood ten temptations (19:8) and through prayer and laying on of hands cured Pharaoh of leprosy (1QapGen 20:16-29); he was rescued from the furnace (*Gen. Rab.* 44:13; *Bib. Ant.* 6:15-18). The results of the blessing originating in Abraham are extensive: Israel's deliverance at the Sea of Reeds is due to the faith of Abraham or his willingness to sacrifice Isaac (*Mek. Exod.* on 14:15); descent from Abraham guarantees a place in the eternal kingdom (Justin *Dial.* 140). On the basis of the binding of Isaac, Abraham appears as intercessor for Israel (*y. Ta'an.* 2:65d). On the other hand, 1QS 2:9 argues against the efficacy of the merits of "the fathers" for an Israelite under a curse.

The Hellenistic Jewish *Apoc. Abr.* (1st cent. A.D.?) describes Abraham as a monotheist and recipient of revelations of the future; the contemporary *T. Abr.* describes the announcement of his death and his ascension to heaven.

2. In the NT Abraham's significance in salvation history for Israel is acknowledged, but any automatic effect of Abrahamic descent is placed in question.

a) John the Baptist criticized the reliance on physical descent from Abraham as a guarantee of salvation and expounded the possibility of a spiritual descent from Abraham (Matt 3:9; Luke 3:8). Jesus saw in God's self-revelation as the God of Abraham, Isaac, and Jacob (Exod 3:6) the Torah pointing to the resurrection of the dead (Mark 12:26; Matt 22:32; Luke 20:37): Abraham must be alive if the living God (cf. Exod 3:14) refers to him. In the parable of Luke 16:19-31 Abraham is alive and constitutes a place of bliss for the soul of Lazarus (v. 22); he can also be addressed by the soul of the rich man and remain for him, too, "Father Abraham" (vv. 23f., 27, 30). For the rich man, however, the blessing is exhausted in the material possessions of earthly life (v. 25); the enduring efficacy of the blessing is guaranteed by obedience to the law and the prophets, of which Abraham quite naturally appears as the advocate (vv. 29, 31). According to Matt 8:11; Luke 13:28f., the blessing of Abraham had universal significance; together with Isaac and Jacob, Abraham constitutes the goal of the eschatological pilgrimage of the nations so that in his table fellowship at the heavenly banquet Gentiles are included as well. According to Luke, Israel's descent from Abraham signifies a special obligation for Jesus the Savior: A "daughter of Abraham" may not be enslaved by the devil (13:16; cf. John 8:33-40), and even a tax collector remains Abraham's son and a candidate for salvation (Luke 19:9).

In Matthew the genealogy of Jesus begins with Abraham (1:2) and proceeds from him to David in fourteen generations (1:17): as Israel's Messiah, Jesus is the Son not only of David but of Abraham as well (1:1; cf. 1:21). Luke mentions Abraham only as one member in the genealogy of Jesus, which reaches back to Adam (Luke 3:34), but he is the most prominent representative of the three patriarchs whom God acknowledges (Acts 3:13; 7:32). Israel is Abraham's family (13:26); the covenant and blessing of Abraham are fulfilled in the appearance of the Christ (3:25). Stephen's speech (7:2-8, 16f.) recalls the high points of Abraham's history as well as the announcement of Israel's enslavement made to Abraham (7:6f.; cf. Gen 15:13f.); at the beginning stands the circumcision of Abraham (Acts 7:8), at the conclusion the uncircumcised heart of Israel (v. 51).

In John 8 the difference between the physical descendants ("seed of Abraham," vv. 33, 37; cf. v. 39) and those who believe in Christ is emphasized. The latter prove they are the authentic children of the patriarch by behaving as he did; the freedom they enjoy is interpreted as freedom from the power of sin and death (vv. 33, 39f.). Abraham is regarded as the visionary witness of this freedom of the Messiah, who was before him and ranks above him (vv. 52-58).

b) Paul, with the phrase "seed of Abraham," expresses both the historical advantage of Israel and his own origins (2 Cor 11:22; Rom 9:7; 11:1). But he disputes the equation of the "seed of Abraham" with genuine, eschatological sonship. The latter is applicable only to the children of the promise (Rom 9:7-9), i.e., those who believe, as the example of Isaac over against Ishmael makes clear. For Paul, Abraham's faith in the creative word of promise is of primary importance.

In Romans 4 Paul uses Gen 15:6 to show that, as in the case of Abraham, the prototype of the believer, not only Jews but Gentiles as well can attain to the salvation that comes through justification *sola fide*. In contrast to Jewish tradition, Paul sets Abraham apart from the law, relativizes the value of the circumcision that he underwent, and makes clear the temporal and material priority of the promise and faith: even before his circumcision and before the time of the law (cf. Rom. 4:13f.) Abraham was justified by virtue of faith through the promise given by grace (vv. 13-15), and in connection with circumcision received the pledge of the divine covenant and the new name "Abraham," which honors him as "father of many nations," i.e., as the father of all believers (vv. 10-12, 17); both Jews and Gentiles are his seed (vv. 16f.). Accordingly, Paul sees in the circumcision of Abraham not the "sign of the covenant" (as in Gen 17:10f.), but rather the "seal of justification" based on the faith that Abraham had demonstrated before circumcision (Rom 4:11f.). Abraham's fatherhood also is redefined: the physical forefather of the Jews (v. 1) is a "father of the circumcised" in the sense of a circumcision of the heart, which consists in the imitation of his faith; also the promise of inheriting the earth (v. 13) is to be understood in a spiritual sense. The faith of Abraham takes on a fundamental character and an eschatological significance: contrary to all human hope, he grasped the promise of numerous descendants and thus honored the creative word of the one who brings the dead to life and calls into being the things that do not exist (vv. 17-21); so also faith in Christ honors the God who made of the crucified one the risen Lord (vv. 24f.) and, through the forgiveness thus made possible, wills to justify the ungodly (v. 5).

In Galatians 3 Paul contrasts the blessing originating in Abraham (vv. 6-9) with the curse under which the unsuccessful obedience to the law stands (vv. 10-13). The blessing of Abraham for the nations is understood as a proto-gospel of the justification of the Gentiles (vv. 8f.); only those who believe in Christ are descendants of Abraham and heirs of the promise (v. 29). Since the blessing of Abraham is eschatologically instituted as the salvation accomplished by the one who was hanged on a tree (vv. 13f.), Paul can also apply the expression "seed of Abraham" specifically to Christ (v. 16), especially since the eternal validity of the covenant (Gen 17:7) is guaranteed only by the eternally reigning Messiah (2 Sam 7:12-14; cf. Rom 1:3f.). In Gal 4:22 Abraham is mentioned as the husband of Hagar and Sarah, who symbolize respectively Sinai and the Jerusalem above. Rom 8:32 calls to mind Gen 22:16: God's giving of the Son is brought into relation to Abraham's offering of Isaac.

In Hebrews Abraham embodies the ideal of eschatologically oriented faith as defined in 11:1: he left his homeland, dwelt as a stranger in the land of Canaan, waited for the invisible city of God (11:8-10), and offered up Isaac as a sacrifice (11:17-19); patiently he held fast to the promise of God, confirmed as it was by an oath (6:13-15). Heirs of the promise to Abraham are, above all, those who believe (6:17), who are designated "seed of Abraham" (2:16). By virtue of having given to Melchizedek a tenth of everything and thus acknowledging Melchizedek's God and his priestly authority (Gen 14:17-20), Abraham became a witness to the eternal high-priesthood of Ps 110:4, which finds its eschatological realization in the priestly service of Christ (Heb 7:1-10).

In Jas 2:20-24, over against a false understanding of Paulinism, the justification of Abraham is based upon his action in response to God. Although the author is fully aware of the meaning of Gen 15:6 (Jas 2:23), he nevertheless sees the faith of Abraham as completed by the offering of Isaac and hence as justified, subsequently as it were, by God's justifying judgment (vv. 22f.). In the household code in 1 Peter 3 the fact that Sarah addressed Abraham as "lord" (Gen 18:12) is held to be evidence of an exemplary wife (v. 6).

O. Betz

ἄβυσσος, ου, ἡ *abyssos* abyss, underworld*

Lit.: H. Bietenhard, *DNTT* II, 205-10. — J. Jeremias, *TDNT* I, 9f., 146-49, 657f. — B. Reicke, *RGG* III, 404-6. — S. Schulz, *BHH* III, 2057f.

1. The NT takes over the Jewish three-level cosmology: the world consists of heaven, earth, and underworld (Phil 2:10· Rev 5:13; → οὐρανός). In the underworld (ἄβυσσος) is not only the realm of the dead (Hades, → ᾅδης) but also Gehenna, the place of punishment ("hell," → γέεννα).

Of the 9 occurrences of ἄβυσσος in the NT, 7 are found in Revelation alone; the term occurs once in Luke (8:31) and once in Paul (Rom 10:7, citing Ps 107:26). As in the LXX (e.g., Ps 70:20 LXX), ἄβυσσος in Rom 10:7 is the translation of Heb. *t^ehôm* (flood, deep, abyss).

2. In apocalyptic Judaism the abyss is regarded as the prison of punished demons (e.g., *1 Enoch* 10:4-6; 18:11-16; *Jub.* 5:6-10). The NT shares this view (→ δαιμόνιον). Thus in Luke 8:31 the exorcised demons of Gerasa implore Jesus not to banish them into the ἄβυσσος. Those held there under lock and key (Rev 9:1; 20:1) and governed by Abaddon-Apollyon, the ruler of demons (9:11), are briefly freed by a fallen star (v. 2); with the smoke of hell (→ γέεννα) they rise to the earth (vv. 2f.). The Antichrist-"Beast" (cf. 12:17 [Greek editions v. 18]–13:10) also rises out of the abyss (11:7; 17:8), which is equated in Rev 17:8 with the sea of 12:18; 13:1 (cf. Ps 42:8; Dan 7:3). During the thousand-year reign (→ χίλιοι) Satan is held prisoner in the ἄβυσσος (Rev 20:1-3). Only Paul understands ἄβυσσος less as the place of the demons than as the realm of the dead into which no one can descend (Rom 10:7; → ᾅδης).

In these statements about the ἄβυσσος as a prison for the powers opposed to God the NT demonstrates its genetic relationship to ancient Judaism. Like the OT and Judaism, however, it also holds to God's sovereignty over the demons: God decrees the opening and closing of the abyss (Rev. 9:1; 20:1, 3). With the entire post-Easter community (1 Cor 15:24-28; Phil 2:9f.; Col 2:10, 15; 1 John 3:8; etc.), Revelation praises the resurrected and exalted Christ as victor over Satan and his instruments (1:16; 2:12, 16; 17:14; 19:15, 21), which are forever consigned to the fiery place of punishment (19:20; 20:10, 14f.; → γέεννα).

O. Böcher

Ἅγαβος, ου *Hagabos* Agabus*

A prophet from Jerusalem at the time of Paul who came to Antioch and Caesarea: Acts 11:28; 21:10. H. Patsch, *TZ* 28 (1972) 228-32.

ἀγαθοεργέω *agathoergeō* do good*

Acts 14:17; 1 Tim 6:18. W. Grundmann, *TDNT* I, 17.

ἀγαθοποιέω *agathopoieō* do good*
ἀγαθοποιΐα, ας, ἡ *agathopoiïa* doing good (noun)*
ἀγαθοποιός, 2 *agathopoios* doing good, upright*

Lit.: W. Grundmann, *TDNT* I, 17f.; → ἀγαθός.

1. The vb. is attested in the NT in Luke 6:9, 33 (bis), 35; 1 Pet 2:15, 20; 3:6, 17; 3 John 11, the noun in 1 Pet 4:19, and the adj. in 1 Pet 2:14.

Ἀγαθοποιέω is used synonymously with ἀγαθὸν ποιέω (Mark 3:4; Matt 19:16; Eph 6:8), καλῶς ποιέω (Matt 12:12; Luke 6:27, cf. vv. 33, 35), and ἐργάζομαι τὸ ἀγαθόν (Gal 6:10; Rom 2:10; Eph 4:28) and designates, as an ethical summation, the behavior appropriate to faith. The contrary is usually expressed by κακοποιέω (Mark 3:4 par. Luke 6:9; 1 Pet 3:17; 3 John 11) or κακοποιός (1 Pet 2:12, 14; 4:15).

2. Only in Luke 6:9 (cf. par. Mark 3:4 v.l.) does ἀγαθοποιέω in the NT have christological and concretely ethical relevance. In the context of the critical distancing of Jesus from the Pharisees the healing miracle ("withered hand") serves as an exemplary reply of Jesus to the question: "Is it lawful on the sabbath *to do good* or to do harm?" In a double sense there is for Jesus here a matter of life and death: "Is it lawful on the sabbath . . . to save life or to destroy it?" For Luke (6:5) this miracle functions as a demonstration that "the Son of Man is lord of the sabbath." For Jesus it is a matter of life and death for the one who is healed. In Mark the direct consequence is the decision of the Pharisees and the Herodians to destroy Jesus (Mark 3:6).

Within the framework of Q's ethics of recompense ἀγαθοποιεῖν serves—alongside love of the enemy and lending—as a summary of the ethics of Jesus (Luke 6:33, 35) and opens the prospect of being sons of the Most High.

1 Pet 2:13ff. is essentially like Rom 12:2: the will of God demands the good. This means that governing authorities (Rom 13:1ff.) have the task of punishing evildoers and praising those who do good (1 Pet 2:14) and that Christians should distinguish themselves through good citizenship "for the sake of the Lord" and as "servants of God" should submit their freedom to the test through *doing good* (vv. 15f.). To suffer for *doing good* (the opposite is ἁμαρτάνοντες) is seen as the grace of God for the slaves (v. 20); in this one conforms to the call to be a disciple of the suffering Christ (vv. 21-25; cf. the application to Christians in general in 3:17). As women are called as daughters of Sarah to *doing good* and to fearlessness (3:6), so Christians prove themselves in suffering through

doing good (4:19). Thus in the ἀγαθοποιέω word group the ethics of 1 Peter is summarized.

The key question regarding "orthodoxy and heresy" (E. Käsemann, *ZTK* 48 [1951] 292-311) in 3 John brings to sharp focus the alternatives for action: τὸ κακόν or τὸ ἀγαθόν. Only the one who does good can claim to follow the truth (v. 4). According to the summary statement in 3 John 11 this alternative is the expression of one's relationship to God.

J. Baumgarten

ἀγαθοποιΐα, ας, ἡ *agathopoiïa* doing good (noun) → ἀγαθοποιέω.

ἀγαθοποιός, 2 *agathopoios* doing good, upright → ἀγαθοποιέω.

ἀγαθός, 3 *agathos* good

1. Occurrences in the NT — 2. Semantic field — 3. Usage — 4. The Pauline corpus — 5. The deutero-Pauline letters — 6. The call of the rich man, Mark 10:17-22 par. — 7. The Pastoral Epistles — 8. Hebrews — 9. Ἀγαθωσύνη

Lit.: E. Beyreuther, *DNTT* II, 98-102. — W. Grundmann, *TDNT* I, 10-18. — E. Haenchen, *Der Weg Jesu* ([2]1968) 349-60. — W. Harnisch, "Die Berufung des Reichen," *Festschrift für Ernst Fuchs* (1973) 161-76. — E. Kamlah, *Die Form der katalogischen Paränese im NT* (WUNT 7, 1964). — E. Käsemann, *Commentary on Romans* (1980). — E. Lohmeyer, *Das Evangelium des Markus* (KEK, 1967) on Mark 10:17f. — E. Lohse, *Colossians and Philemon* (Hermeneia, 1971) on Phlm 6:14. — W. Schrage, *Die konkreten Einzelgebote in der paulinischen Paränese* (1961). — L. K. Stachowiak, *SacVb* I, 321-28. — S. Wibbing, *Die Tugend- und Lasterkataloge im NT* (BZNW 25, 1959).

1. Ἀγαθός occurs 107 times in the NT and is often used synonymously with καλός and χρηστός. It is found in nearly all of the NT writings, but in the Johannine corpus it occurs strikingly seldom (John 1:46 [a proverb?]; 5:29; 7:12; 3 John 11); in Revelation it is altogether absent.

2. Ἀγαθός appears frequently as a synonymous alternative for καλός (Rom 7:16-21; 12:17, 21; Gal 6:9f.; Matt 7:17-19 [cf. 12:33]; Mark 3:4 par. Matt 12:12; Luke 8:8 par. Mark 4:8; Matt 13:8; Luke 8:15; 1 Tim 5:10) and belongs to the semantic field represented by ἅγιος (Rom 7:12), δίκαιος (Rom 7:12; Luke 23:50), τὸ εὐάρεστον (Rom 12:2; cf. Heb. 13:21), τὸ τέλειον (Rom 12:2), πιστός (Matt 25:21), ἐπιεικής (1 Pet 2:18), and χρηστός (Matt 11:30; Luke 5:39; 6:35; Eph 4:32; cf. Rom 2:4; 1 Cor 15:33; 1 Pet 2:3). The opposite is expressed frequently by κακός (1 Thess 5:15; 2 Cor 5:10 v.l.; Rom 2:9f.; 3:8; 7:19, 21; 12:21; 13:3; 16:19; Mark 3:4 par. Luke 6:9; Luke 16:25; 1 Pet 3:10f., 13, 17; 3 John 11), less often by πονηρός (Rom 12:9; Matt 5:45; 7:11 par. Luke 11:13; Matt 12:34f. par. Luke 6:45; Matt 20:15; 22:10), φαῦλος (2 Cor 5:10; Rom 9:11; John 5:29), σαπρός (Matt 7:17f.; Eph 4:29), and σκολιός (1 Pet 2:18).

3. The adj. *good* characterizes first of all the uniquely good being of God (Mark 10:17f. par. Luke 18:18f.; Matt 19:16f.; more frequently used is χρηστότης/χρηστός) or of God's will (Rom 12:2; cf. Heb 13:21) or commandment (Rom 7:12), the "eternal comfort" and the "*good* hope" which God has given the Church and by which his comfort is marked (2 Thess 2:16), and "every *good* endowment and every perfect gift" that comes from above, from the "Father of lights" (Jas 1:17).

Ἀγαθός conveys a more diluted meaning in the address, "*good* (= honored) Teacher" (Mark 10:17f. par.) or "*good* servant" (Matt 25:21 par.), but can also be said in a qualified way of any person (Matt 12:35 par. Luke 6:45; Acts 11:24). The parables of the *good* tree (Matt 7:17f.; 12:33) and of the *good, fertile* soil (Luke 8:8; cf. v. 15 where it is internalized and refers to the *good* "heart") serve to make clear how human beings are to "bear fruit." The metaphor of the fruits is used in a figurative sense to characterize the divine wisdom (Jas 3:17f.).

Statements concerning the "*good* work" of God (Phil 1:6) or the "*good* works" of human beings (Eph 2:10; Acts 9:36; 1 Tim 2:10; cf. Rom 2:7; 13:3a) and statements regarding "every *good* work" (2 Cor 9:8; 2 Thess 2:17: "every *good* work and word"; Col 1:10; 1 Tim 5:10; 2 Tim 2:21; Titus 1:16; 3:1) bear a special accent. In the later NT period the "*good* conscience" is used as a special t.t. (Acts 23:1; 1 Pet 3:16, 21; 1 Tim 1:5, 19 [cf. Heb 13:18]).

Otherwise ἀγαθός is used in a few different ways: the "*good* gifts" given to children (Matt 7:11 par. Luke 11:13), Mary's choice of the *good* portion (Luke 10:42), and the *good* memory in which Paul and his coworkers are held by the Thessalonians and which Timothy has reported to Paul (1 Thess 3:6). The Ephesians are enjoined to speak not corrupt, but *good* words for the edification of the Church and the χάρις of those who hear (4:29). Slaves are called to display "*good* [RSV "true"] fidelity" toward their masters (Titus 2:10). The question in Ps 33:13-17 LXX has become parenesis in 1 Pet 3:10-12 listing the conditions for a hopeful future. The Church is presently exposed to abuse, but the author of 1 Peter comforts it by pointing to its *good* conduct in Christ (→ ἀναστροφή).

4. Among the unquestionably genuine letters of Paul three-fourths of the occurrences of ἀγαθός are in Romans (esp. chs. 2 and 7). In Romans 7 the issue is (according to Käsemann, whom the present author essentially follows) not an "apology for the law" (W. G. Kümmel, *Römer 7 und die Bekehrung des Paulus,* reprinted in *Römer 7 und das Bild des Menschen im Neuen Testament* [TBü 53, 1974] 1-160, here 9f.) nor, in vv. 15-20, "man in contradiction" or the "divided man" who suffers under the constant

moral-ethical conflict between "good" and "evil," but rather "a Christian interpretation of pre-Christian existence" (Käsemann 210). The individual commandment (v. 12) is—true to Jewish tradition—holy, just, and *good* in view of its effects on human beings. Assuming that Paul speaks about a "supra-individual I" (Käsemann 196), about the person under the law who lives in the contradiction between willing and doing, test and failure, good and evil (vv. 18ff.), the possibility of a positive human correspondence to the will of God is nevertheless negated. The pious person's way to salvation is discredited on the basis of experience. "What a person wants is salvation. What he creates is disaster" (Käsemann 203). The doctrines of justification and judgment, in the sense of "the fundamental Jewish idea of eschatological retribution according to our works" (Käsemann 57), are closely related to each other in the thought of Paul (2 Cor 5:10; Gal 6:7ff.; cf. Eph 6:8). The justified person is always responsible. "With obedience the goal is reached, with disobedience it is missed. Obedience is accordingly the one good work, the 'good' in [Rom 2:]10 as such, the criterion of retribution in the judgment, and the standing in eschatologically anticipated blessing. In contrast, disobedience derives from a self-centered will and is a simple equivalent of evil" (Käsemann 60). A misunderstanding of the doctrine of the justification of the ungodly finds expression in the objection, which Paul regards as blasphemy, that justification leads to libertinism (Rom 3:8).

Several times in Romans (and Phil 1:6; cf. Phlm 6) τὸ ἀγαθόν is interpreted in the sense of eschatological salvation. In Rom 8:28, which is in the style of a doctrinal axiom, Paul reverts to an ancient rhetorical theme (cf. Rabbi Akiba, *b. Ber.* 60b in Billerbeck III, 256). In Rom 10:15 Paul recalls Isa 52:7. The proclamation of the "*good* news" describes the task of the apostle (cf. 2 Cor 5:18-20) in the execution of which the eschatological promise is realized. The *good* with which the Church is blessed is (Rom 14:16) the state of salvation (Käsemann 376). In Rom 15:2 the obligation of the strong toward the weak is intended to lead to the *good,* the salutary, which is interpreted by οἰκοδομή (= edification; cf. the intention of the charismata in Rom 12:6ff.; 1 Cor 12–14; Eph 4:29). In the letter of recommendation (Rom 16:19) the apostle issues the watchword to be wise concerning the *good,* i.e., concerning salvation. With that Rom 12:2 is taken up again: the goodness of God's will is the presupposition and possibility of conduct appropriate to salvation. The will of God is designated as good, acceptable, and perfect insofar as it may "in a concrete case . . . coincide with human ideals [cf. the use of the adj. in popular philosophy], but it neither merges into these nor is it to be equated with these without further ado" (Käsemann 330). The correlate to the will of God is conduct determined by the presence of salvation. Love is prepared to engage itself fully in the task of realizing the good and despising evil (vv. 9, 21); neutrality is not an option. This is not a matter of ethical idealism, but of eschatological conduct.

In connection with political authorities (Rom 13:3f.) τὸ ἀγαθόν designates for Paul "not moral qualities but . . . political good conduct" (Käsemann 353), the "ordinary uprightness" of "upright citizens" (358). In Phlm 14 τὸ ἀγαθόν σου refers to Philemon's benevolent reception of Onesimus no longer as a slave but as a "beloved brother" (v. 16). Such conduct corresponds to the exhortation of the apostle, but much more to the will of God "which commands to do what is plainly good" (Lohse 194) and which opens to faith the recognition of the good (v. 6). The summary challenge to do good (1 Thess 5:15; Gal 6:6, 10; Rom 12:21) corresponds to the way of salvation opened by God.

5. On the whole the evidence from the deutero-Pauline writings agrees essentially with that of the Pauline documents. Here, too, doing of the ethical *good* (Eph 4:28; 6:8) and "*good* works" (Eph 2:10; Col 1:10) are neither meritorious nor the prerequisite for redemption, nor are they separated from the Creator. They are rather the necessary expression of a correspondence between Creator and creature, between faith and works "which God prepared beforehand, that we should walk in them" (Eph 2:8-10). Of course, the idea of bearing fruit "in every *good* work" and of growing (Col 1:10) is a new element which reoccurs in the nature parables of the Synoptic Gospels.

6. The call of the rich man (Mark 10:17-22; Matt 19:16-22; Luke 18:18-23) gives the question of the meaning of ἀγαθός a special theological relevance. The rich man (Matthew alters it to a "young man" and Luke to a "ruler" [Haenchen 351]) kneels respectfully before Jesus and calls him "*good* (= honored) teacher." Unusual for Palestinian Judaism, such a form of address was nevertheless possible in Greek-speaking areas (in addition to Matt 25:21, 23; Luke 19:17, cf. the references in Lohmeyer 208, n. 2; the address "good teacher" is attested in *b. Ta'an.* 24b). Jesus rebukes the rich man: "No one is good but God alone."

Jesus thus resorts to OT tradition: it is essential to OT thought that Yahweh is good *(ṭôb)* and that the history of Israel testifies to him in his goodness. The emphatically personal—compared with Greek popular philosophy and the Hellenistic point of view (details in Grundmann 11-13 and Beyreuther 98f.)—and fundamental confession is: Praise Yahweh, "for he is good" (1 Chr 16:34; 2 Chr 5:13; Ezra 3:11f.; Ps 118:1ff.; cf. the Jewish personal form in Philo *All.* I, 47; *Som.* I, 149). The experience of redemption in the Exodus, the possession of the land, and Israel's preservation in the course of history all document Yahweh's "goodness" (cf. Exod 18:9; Num 10:29ff.; Hos 8:3; 14:3). In Jeremiah the "goodness" of God takes on a special eschatological accent (Jer 8:15; 14:11, 19; 17:6; etc., esp. 32:42; details in Grundmann 13f.).

Over against Mark (and Luke), Matthew has transformed the offensive form of address into a question about the *good* that is necessary to the attainment of eternal life (19:16). The answer is the call to discipleship (details in Haenchen 358f.; Harnisch 171ff.).

7. The Pastorals (in which καλός is more common) manifest two characteristics. a) "*Good* works" are made autonomous and viewed as the mark of being a good Christian as a confessional act of devotion to God (1 Tim 2:10). In the special case of women's ethics (cf. the "*good* works" which, alongside charity, serve to distinguish Tabitha in Acts 9:36) they are specified as the raising of children, showing hospitality, washing the feet of the saints, and helping the afflicted (1 Tim 5:10). "*Good* works" can also signal the discrepancy between the knowledge of God on the one hand and, on the other hand, corresponding deeds of faith (Titus 1:16) or—a radicalizing of Rom 13:3f.—helpful and benevolent conduct toward governmental authorities (Titus 3:1).

b) As a t.t. "*good* conscience" (1 Tim 1:5, 19; cf. Acts 23:1; 1 Pet 3:16, 21; Heb 13:18) belongs to the late period of the NT. Reacting against Gnosticism, the Pastorals call for conduct that corresponds to a faith that takes creation seriously and to the love commandment (1 Tim 1:14). "Thus the traditional parenesis with its household codes, lists of virtues and vices, and its emphasis on the value of marriage and family and on the indispensability for communal life of the normal virtues of good citizenship. Thus the demand for '*good* works' (1 Tim 2:10; Titus 2:14) and the good or pure conscience (1 Tim 1:5; 3:9)" (P. Vielhauer, *Geschichte der urchristlichen Literatur* [1975] 234).

8. In its concluding doxology (13:20f.) Hebrews expresses in good Pauline fashion (cf. Rom 12:2) the wish for the addressees that God will "equip [them] with everything good," i.e., enable them to live in accordance with his will. On the other hand, Hebrews is emphatic in characterizing the good things of the world to come as ἀγαθά. In 9:11 the concept is given christological and eschatological substance: Christ is the high priest of the *good things* to come (cf. 10:1). These include the eschatological entrance into the heavenly holy place and worship before the throne of God.

9. **Ἀγαθωσύνη** *kindness, goodness, uprightness** occurs 4 times in the NT: Rom 15:24; Gal 5:22; Eph 5:9; 2 Thess 1:11. The word appears in the LXX in a wide range of meanings: earthly goods (Eccl 4:8; 5:10; 6:3); prosperity (7:14); the good that one experiences (5:17; 6:6; 9:18); the goodness of God disclosed in the good things which he distributes on earth (2 Esdr 19:25, 35); or in his promises in heaven (23:31); ethical good (Judg 8:35; 9:16; 2 Chr 24:16; Ps 51:5). Of these only the ethical dimension is taken over into the NT.

In the context of an apologetically oriented final report (Rom 15:14-21) Paul acknowledges the spiritual autonomy of the Roman church. This he expresses through an abundance of compliments: "You yourselves are full of *goodness*"—i.e., uprightness, "which in contrast to malice expresses itself in mutual open-mindedness" (Käsemann 391)—"filled with all knowledge, and able to instruct one another" (v. 14).

In both Gal 5:22 and Eph 5:9 ἀγαθωσύνη is included in a catalog of virtues. Within the frame of a dualistic-eschatological understanding of salvation, toward which all else is oriented, Paul contrasts a catalog of virtues (Gal 5:22f.) to one of vices (vv. 19-21). Over against the "works of the flesh," which result in exclusion from the kingdom of God, stands walking in the Spirit or the fruit of the Spirit. The concrete realization of the "radically new possibility of life" (Grundmann 16) is the work of the Spirit: love, joy, peace, magnanimity or patience, kindness (benevolence), *goodness* (H. Schlier, *An die Galater* [KEK] ad loc.: *uprightness*), faithfulness, gentleness, and self-control (Gal 5:22f.). Parallel to this is the occurrence of ἀγαθωσύνη in the catalog of virtues in Eph 5:9, where it is connected with the pattern: once—but now. Because of their "works of darkness" (v. 11) the sons of disobedience will suffer the wrath of God (v. 6) and not obtain the inheritance in the kingdom of Christ and of God (v. 5). By contrast the children of light distinguish themselves through individual aspects of the "fruit of light": *goodness*, righteousness, and truth (v. 9).

In an eschatological petition (2 Thess 1:11) *good* resolve and the "work of faith" constitute a single request on behalf of the Thessalonians.

J. Baumgarten

ἀγαθουργέω *agathourgeō* do good*

Contract form of → ἀγαθοεργέω: Acts 14:17.

ἀγαθωσύνη, ης, ἡ *agathōsynē* kindness, goodness, uprightness
→ ἀγαθός 9.

ἀγαλλίασις, εως, ἡ *agalliasis* rejoicing, gladness
→ ἀγαλλιάω.

ἀγαλλιάω *agalliaō* rejoice, exult, be glad*
ἀγαλλίασις, εως, ἡ *agalliasis* rejoicing, gladness*

Lit.: R. E. Backherms, *Religious Joy in General in the NT and Its Sources in Particular* (Diss. Fribourg, 1963). — H. U. von Balthasar, "Die Freude und das Kreuz," *Concilium* 4 (1968) 683-88. — P. J. Bernadicou, "The Lucan Theology of Joy," *ScEc* 25 (1973) 75-98. — E. Beyreuther and G. Finkenrath, *DNTT* II, 352-61. — R. Bultmann, *TDNT* I, 19-21. — E. G. Gulin, *Die Freude im NT* (Annales Academiae Scientiarum Fennicae 26/2 [1932] and 37/3 [1936]). — W. MORRICE, *Joy in the NT* (1984), esp. 19-23 — B. REICKE, *Diakonie, Festfreude und Zelos in Verbindung mit der altchristlichen Agapenfeier* (1951). — C. W. REINES, "Laughter in Biblical and Rabbinic Literature," *Judaism* 21 (1972) 176-83. — A. B. DU TOIT, *Der Aspekt der Freude im urchristlichen Abendmahl* (1965).

1. The vb. occurs 11 times in the NT, the noun 5 times. Of these 16 occurrences 7 are in Luke-Acts, 3 in 1 Peter, 2 in John. There is one occurrence each in Matthew, Hebrews, Jude, and Revelation. In its active form the vb. appears only in Luke 1:47 and Rev 19:7, otherwise only as a deponent. The reason for the rejoicing is indicated in various ways. Both vb. and noun occur in connection with χαίρειν or χαρά: Matt 5:12; Luke 1:14; 1 Pet 1:8; 4:13; Rev 19:17; with δοξάζειν or δόξα: 1 Pet 1:8; 4:13; Jude 24; Rev 19:7; with εὐφραίνειν: Acts 2:26; and with μεγαλύνειν: Luke 1:47.

2. These words occur only in the language of the Bible and the Church, and speak of the joy which encompasses the whole person and radiates from the person. As in the LXX, so too in the NT (except for John 5:35) they have a religious sense: they designate the joy and exultation over the salvation which God has given and promised through Jesus (John 8:56 refers to Abraham's anticipatory joy). Whether the word group was used already in Q is uncertain. The only place where this is possible is Matt 5:12 (but cf. Luke 6:23). Luke 1–2 speaks of the rejoicing occasioned already by the birth of John as God's gift in the time of salvation (1:14) and of the eschatological rejoicing in which Mary (1:47) and the yet unborn John (1:44) break out in view of the time of salvation which dawns with Jesus. The introduction to Jesus' cry of rejoicing (Luke 10:21) is Lukan redaction. Acts 2:26 puts Ps 15:9 LXX in the mouth of Peter as proof that the resurrection of Jesus is in accordance with the scriptures. Moreover, Acts testifies that primitive Christian congregations had experiences which occasioned joyful gladness. The communal meal, which was connected with the celebration of the eucharist but terminologically distinguished from it, was eaten "with glad and generous hearts" (Acts 2:46). Baptism and acceptance of the faith lead to joyful gladness (16:34); here too the intimated connection with the meal is noteworthy. The rejoicing spoken of in 1 Pet 4:13; Jude 24; Rev 19:7 is clearly that of the future eschatological consummation. 1 Pet 1:8 speaks of joy in the present. Whether the rejoicing of the Christians in 1 Pet 1:6 is likewise in the present is not certain but due to its proximity to v. 8 probable. Heb 1:9 cites Ps 44:8 LXX in order to characterize the messianic anointing of the Son of God with the "oil of gladness," i.e., with the ointment used at joyous celebrations and especially at the anointing of a king.

A. Weiser

ἄγαμος, 2 *agamos* unmarried (person)
→ γαμέω.

ἀγανακτέω *aganakteō* be indignant, angry*

Matt 21:15; 26:8; Mark 10:14. The object of indignation is introduced by περί with gen.: Mark 10:41 par. Matt 20:24. Mark 14:4 refers to *mutual* indignation: ἀγανακτοῦντες πρὸς ἑαυτούς. In Luke 13:14 the reason for indignation is introduced by ὅτι.

ἀγανάκτησις, εως, ἡ *aganaktēsis* indignation*

2 Cor 7:11, in a list between ἀπολογία and φόβος.

ἀγαπάω *agapaō* love (vb.)
→ ἀγάπη.

ἀγάπη, ης, ἡ *agapē* love (noun)
ἀγαπάω *agapaō* love (vb.)
ἀγαπητός, 3 *agapētos* beloved, dear

1. Occurrences of the word group in the NT — 2. Meaning and usage — 3. 'Αγαπάω and ἀγάπη in the NT — a) Synoptics (the love commandment of Jesus) — b) Paul's letters — c) Colossians, Ephesians, 2 Thessalonians, and the Pastorals — d) John and 1–3 John — e) The remainder of the NT — 4. 'Αγάπη in Jude 12 — 5. 'Αγαπητός

Lit.: K. BERGER, *Die Gesetzesauslegung Jesu.* I. *Markus und Parallelen* (1972). — G. BORNKAMM, "Das Doppelgebot der Liebe" (1954), *idem, Aufsätze* III, 37-45. — R. BULTMANN, *Theology,* §§39.3; 50.4 — C. BURCHARD, "Das doppelte Liebesgebot in der frühen christlichen Überlieferung," FS Jeremias (1970) 39-62. — S. CIPRIANI, "Dio è amore. La dottrina della carità in S. Giovanni," *Scuola Cattolica* 94 (1966) 214-31. — J. COPPENS, "La doctrine biblique sur l'amour de Dieu et du prochain," *ETL* 40 (1964) 252-99. — *idem,* "Agapè et Agapân dans les lettres Johanniques," *ETL* 45 (1969) 125-27. — N. A. DAHL, *RGG* IV, 364-67. — J. ERNST, "Die Einheit von Gottes- und Nächstenliebe in der Verkündigung Jesu," *TGl* 60 (1970) 3-14. — G. FRIEDRICH, *Was heißt das: Liebe?* (1972). — R. H. FULLER, "The Double Commandment of Love: A Test Case for the Criteria of Authenticity," *Essays on the Love Commandment* (ed. R. Fuller; 1978) 41-56. — V. P. FURNISH, *The Love Command in the NT* (1972). — H. GREEVEN and J. FICHTNER, *TDNT* VI, 311-18. — R. JOLY, *Le vocabulaire chrétien de l'amour est-il original?* (1968). — R. KIEFFER, *Le primat de l'amour* (LD 85, 1975), on 1 Cor 13. — O. KUSS, "Die Liebe im NT," Kuss II, 196-234. — M. LATTKE, *Einheit im Wort: Die spezifische Bedeutung von ἀγάπη, ἀγαπᾶν, und φιλεῖν im Johannesevangelium* (SANT 41, 1975). — S. LÉGASSE, "L'étendue de l'amour interhumain d'après le NT," *RTL* 8 (1977) 137-59, 293-304. — J. B. LOTZ, *Die Stufen der Liebe. Eros, Philia, Agape* (1971). — D. LÜHRMANN, "Liebet eure Feinde (Lk 6, 27-36/Mt 5, 39-48)," *ZTK* 69 (1972) 412-38. —W. LÜTGERT, *Die Liebe im NT* (1905). — K. NIEDERWIMMER, "Erkennen und Lieben. Gedanken zum Verhältnis von Gnosis und Agape im Ersten Korintherbrief," *KD* 11 (1965) 75-102. — A. NISSEN, *Gott und der Nächste im antiken Judentum* (1974); review by P. Schäfer, *TLZ* 102 (1977) 432-37. — A. NYGREN,

Agape and Eros (1969). — T. OHM, *Die Liebe zu Gott in den nichtchristlichen Religionen* (1950). — A. PENNA, *Amore nella Bibbia* (Teologia biblica 1, 1972). — H. PREISKER, *Die urchristliche Botschaft von der Liebe Gottes im Lichte der vergleichenden Religionsgeschichte* (1930). — K. ROMANIUK, *L'amour du Père et du Fils dans la sotériologie de saint Paul* (AnBib 15, ²1974). — SCHELKLE, *Theology*, III, 113-36. — H. SCHLIER, "Glauben, Erkennen, Lieben nach dem Johannesevangelium," Schlier II, 279-93. — *idem*, "Die Bruderliebe nach dem Evangelium und den Briefen des Johannes," Schlier III, 124-35. — R. SCHNACKENBURG, *LTK* VI, 1043-54. — *idem*, "Die Forderung der Liebe in der Verkündigung und im Verhalten Jesu," E. Biser, A. Ganoczy, et al., *Prinzip Liebe* (1975) 76-103. — *idem*, *Die Johannesbriefe* (HTKNT, 1975) 117-21 ("Exkurs 5: Bruderliebe"); 231-39 ("Exkurs 10: Liebe als Wesen Gottes"). — G. SCHNEIDER, "Die Neuheit der christlichen Nächstenliebe," *TTZ* 82 (1973) 257-75. — L. SCHOTTROFF, "Non-Violence and the Love of One's Enemies," *Essays on the Love Commandment* (ed. R. Fuller; 1978) 9-39. — C. SPICQ, "Le verbe ἀγαπάω et ses dérivés dans le grec classique," *RB* 60 (1953) 372-97. — *idem*, *Agape in the NT* I-III (1963-66). — *idem*, *Die Nächstenliebe in der Bibel* (1961). — E. STAUFFER, *TDNT* I, 35-55. — W. C. VAN UNNIK, "Die Motivierung der Feindesliebe in Lukas VI 32-35," *NovT* 8 (1966) 284-300. — V. WARNACH, *Agape. Die Liebe als Grundmotiv der neutestamentlichen Theologie* (1951). — *idem*, *SacVb* II, 518-42 (bibliography). — O. WISCHMEYER, "Agape in der außerchristlichen Antike," *ZNW* 69 (1978) 212-38.

OT: J. BERGMAN, A. O. HALDAR, and G. WALLIS, *TDOT* I, 99-118 (bibliography). — F. BUCK, *Die Liebe Gottes beim Propheten Osee* (1953). — E. JENNI, *THAT* I, 60-73. — N. LOHFINK, *Das Hauptgebot* (AnBib 20, 1963), on Deut 5–11. — G. QUELL, *TDNT* I, 21-35. — O. SCHILLING, "Die alttestamentlichen Auffassungen von Gerechtigkeit und Liebe," FS Meinertz 9-27. — J. ZIEGLER, *Die Liebe Gottes bei den Propheten* (1930). — W. ZIMMERLI, *RGG* IV, 363f.

For further bibliography: H. RIESENFELD, "Étude bibliographique sur la notion biblique d'ΑΓΑΠΗ," *ConNT* 5 (1941). — P.-É. LANGEVIN, *Bibliographie biblique (1930-1970)* (1972) 560-66. — *SacVb* II, 541f.

1. The three words in this group occur in nearly all the writings of the NT and a total of 320 times in the NT. 'Αγαπάω occurs 143 times, most frequently in John (37) and 1–3 John (31). ἀγάπη occurs 116 times, esp. in 1–3 John (21), 1 Corinthians (14), and Ephesians (10), and ἀγαπητός a total of 61 times, esp. in 1–3 John (10), Romans (7), and 2 Peter (6). When the entire word group is viewed together, John, together with 1–3 John, has 106 occurrences (44 + 62, i.e., one-third of the total occurrences), Paul, together with the post-Pauline writings (including the Pastorals) 136 (84 + 52), the Synoptics (with Acts) altogether only 37, and the remaining NT writings 41. Again, taking *all three* words into account, the following (with corresponding number of occurrences) are dominant: 1 John (52), John (44), Romans (24), Ephesians (22), 1 Corinthians (20), Luke (16), 2 Corinthians (15), Matthew (12), and Colossians (11). The absence of ἀγαπάω and ἀγάπη from Acts and of ἀγαπητός from John, 2 John, and Revelation is striking.

2. For the NT the meaning of the three words can be almost uniformly rendered by the translations "love," "to love," and "beloved" respectively.

'Αγαπάω ordinarily corresponds in the LXX to Heb. *'āhēḇ*, and ἀγάπη or (the older) ἀγάπησις is used primarily (16 and 6 times) to render the corresponding noun *'ahᵃbâ*. By comparison the classical forms employed most frequently in Hellenistic Greek, ἐράω/ἔρως and φιλέω/φιλία, are used much less. The translators probably preferred the words of the ἀγαπάω group which convey less affective emphasis since they designate "a sober kind of love—love in the sense of placing a high value upon some person or thing, or of receiving them with favour" (Warnach, *SacVb* 518; in this connection see also Joly). Thus far it remains disputed whether ἀγάπη is attested in literature prior to the appearance of the LXX; cf. E. Peterson, *BZ* 20 (1932) 378-82; BAGD s.v. I (cf. Moulton/Milligan s.v.); Warnach, *SacVb* 518; cf. further the controversy between S. West and R. E. Witt in *JTS* 18 (1967) 142f.; 19 (1968) 209-11; 20 (1969) 228-30. The NT excludes entirely ἐράω/ἔρως (in contrast see Ign. *Rom.* 2:1; 7:2; *Pol.* 4:3) and brings the ἀγαπάω word group to fuller theological development, whereas → φιλέω is in general theologically less relevant (see M. Paeslack, *TViat* 5 [1953-54] 51-142).

The words of the ἀγαπάω group refer almost exclusively in the NT to the love of persons for persons. However, things can also be named as objects of love (cf. BAGD s.v. ἀγαπάω 2; s.v. ἀγάπη I, 1bα): Luke 11:43 (places of honor and greetings); John 3:19 ("darkness rather than light"); 12:43 ("the δόξα of men more than the δόξα of God"); 2 Tim 4:8 ("his appearing"); 4:10 (the "present world"); Heb 1:9 (Ps 44:8 LXX: righteousness); 1 Pet 3:10 (life); 2 Pet 2:15 (gain from wrongdoing); 1 John 2:15 (the world, the → κόσμος); Rev 12:11 (one's own life); 20:9 ("the beloved city," Jerusalem). A noteworthy expression is ἀγάπην ἀγαπάω in John 17:26; Eph 2:4 (cf. 2 Kgdms 13:15). An impersonal object of ἀγάπη is the "truth" in 2 Thess 2:10 (cf. *1 Clem.* 55:5, "love of fatherland"). Both the vb. (Luke 7:47ab; 1 John 3:14, 18; 4:7, 8, 19) and especially the noun (e.g., Matt 24:12; Rom 12:9; 13:10; 1 Cor 8:1; 13:1, 2, 3, 4, 8, 13; 14:1; Phil 1:9; 2:2; 1 John 4:16; for further examples, esp. of prepositional phrases and attributives, see BAGD s.v. ἀγάπη I.1) are used absolutely. 'Αγάπη stands together with → πίστις (1 Thess 3:6; 5:8; 1 Tim 1:14; 2 Tim 1:13; Phlm 5) and with πίστις and → ἐλπίς as a triad (1 Cor 13:13; 1 Thess 1:3; 5:8; Col 1:4f.; *Barn.* 1:4, 6); → 3.b.

Departures from the usual meanings are represented by ἠγάπησεν (first aor.): *he loved him* (Mark 10:21) and ἀγάπη: *love feast;* → 4 (Jude 12; Ign. *Smyrn.* 8:2).

Along with love (ἀγαπάω) of "neighbor" (→ πλησίον; above all in the Synoptics and Paul) one speaks, using either the verb or the noun, of "mutual" love (→ ἀλλήλων; John, 1–2 John, Paul), using the verb, of love for the "brother" (→ ἀδελφός 5; 1 John) and of the "enemy" (Q), and of the love of husbands for their "wives" (Ephesians). In Mark 12:30, 33 par. (also esp. in Paul, James, and 1 John) "God" is the object of loving/love, as is

Jesus/Christ above all in John (otherwise only in Eph 6:24; 1 Pet 1:8; 1 John 5:1). Besides John and 1 John, Paul in particular speaks of the *love of God* (vb. and noun); God's love for Jesus finds expression esp. in John (also in Eph 1:6; Col 1:13); cf. also ἀγαπητός (→ 5). The *love of Jesus/Christ* is spoken of (using either the vb. or the noun) esp. by John and Paul; his love for God is mentioned in John 14:31.

3. a) Apart from Mark 10:21 and Luke 7:5 the vb. ἀγαπάω and the noun (Matt 24:12; Luke 11:42) occur in the Synoptics only in words of Jesus. The command to love the enemy and the double command of love of God and neighbor occupy a special rank.

Already in Q the demand "Love your enemies" (Luke 6:27, 35 par. Matt 5:44) was connected with the notice that the disciple must break through the mutuality of loving (Luke 6:32/Matt 5:46: "if you love those who love you") with the promise of divine sonship or the reference to the goodness of God even for the evil (Luke 6:35/Matt 5:45) and, of course, with the Golden Rule (Luke 6:31/Matt 7:12). As a demand of Jesus and of the Church which stands behind Q love for the enemy means a rejection of Zealot hatred and the surpassing of love directed only to the "neighbor" (cf. Matt 5:43: "You shall . . . hate your enemy"; cf. 1 QS 1:3f., 10). The use of the pl. ("enemies," v. 44) indicates that the issue involves the Church and its conduct toward its enemies. The saying about service to two masters draws a parallel between *loving* and *serving*; indirectly it calls for love of God (and undivided service of God).

In Mark 12:28-34 Jesus answers with an apophthegm the question of a Pharisee regarding the commandment which is "first of all" (Berger, 143, 256: the "initial question of Diaspora catechesis"; cf. the question of the Gentile who is willing to convert and the answer of Hillel in *b. Šabb.* 31a) using Deut 6:4f. (undivided love for God) and adds the demand for love of neighbor (Lev 19:18) as a second primary commandment (for the working out of the love commandment in Judaism, esp. in the *Testaments of the Twelve Patriarchs,* see Burchard, Schneider, and Nissen). Both commandments of the Torah are cited in the parallel passages, Matt 22:37, 39; Luke 10:27bc, without, however, the confirmatory repetition of Mark 12:32f.

Matt 5:43 (the Lukan parallel is different) and 19:19b (the Markan parallel is different) mention the command to love the neighbor in redactional sentences. In the first text this commandment is contrasted to Jesus' new demand (love of the enemy, v. 44), in the second it is listed after the individual commandments of the second table of the Decalogue in order to characterize it as their summation (cf. 22:40 [Mark differs]: "On these two commandments depend all the law and the prophets"). In 24:12 (M) it is predicted that "most men's love will grow cold" as a result of the spread of "lawlessness" (RSV "wickedness").

The absolute use of ἀγάπη in Matt 24:12 corresponds to a later mode of expression, as do the two uses of ἀγαπάω in Luke 7:47 (L; "for she *loved* much [has shown much love]," "he . . . *loves* little"; cf. the question in v. 42). The use of ἀγαπάω in Luke 6:32b (at the beginning of the section on love of the enemy) is dependent on the Q text ("for even sinners *love* those who *love* them"). In the pronouncement of woe upon the Pharisees in 11:42 Luke has altered the Q text by the addition of τὴν ἀγάπην τοῦ θεοῦ and has created the connection with what is in v. 43. The Pharisees "neglect . . . the *love* of God" (v. 42), but "*love* the best seat in the synagogues . . ." (v. 43; Matt 23:6: φιλοῦσιν). Luke (and Acts) illustrates by means of concrete examples how love of neighbor is manifested in actions, especially in the story of the Good Samaritan, which demonstrates Jesus' interpretation of the love commandment (cf. the frame in 10:29, 36f.). It interprets love of neighbor as active mercy which has as its model the mercy of God (6:36; 10:33, 37a); cf. G. Schneider, *Lukas* (ÖTK) I, 245-51. The fact that in Luke 10:27 the "lawyer" and not Jesus cites the double commandment (as *one* commandment; Mark and Matthew differ) results from the inclusion of the story of the Samaritan which answers the question of the identity of the neighbor (v. 29) with the illustration of how love *acts.*

b) When Paul speaks about love, his starting point is the *love of God* (Rom 5:8; 8:37; 9:13; 2 Cor 9:7; 13:11, 13; 1 Thess 1:4) which he has shown in Christ (Romaniuk). God's love has been poured out into our hearts through the Holy Spirit (Rom 5:5). "God shows his love for us in that while we were yet sinners Christ died for us" (v. 8). The hymnic passage in Rom 8:31-39 (see G. Schille, *ZNW* 59 [1968] 230-44; P. Fiedler, *ZNW* 68 [1977] 23-34), which begins with the question, "If God is for us, who is against us?" concludes with the assurance that nothing "will be able to separate us from the love of God in Christ Jesus our Lord." The ἀγαπήσας (v. 37) is Christ, who has shown his love (v. 35) on the cross (2 Cor 5:14f.) and reigns as the Exalted One. He "loved me and gave himself for me" (Gal 2:20).

Although Paul frequently speaks of the love of the Christians without qualification, and thus ἀγάπη (Rom 12:9; 14:15; 1 Cor 8:1; 14:1; 16:14) could, esp. in the lists of virtues (2 Cor 6:6; Gal 5:22; Phil 2:1f.), easily be understood as one form of moral conduct among others, he emphasizes decisively the priority of ἀγάπη over other virtues (Gal 5:6; Phil 1:9; esp. in the hymn to love in 1 Cor 13, regarding which see, besides R. Kieffer, Schlier I, 186-93; Bornkamm I, 93-112 [cf. *Early Christian Experience* (1969) 180-93]; J. T. Sanders, *Int* 20 [1966] 159-87; B. Gerhardsson, *SEÅ* 39 [1974] 121-44; E. Minguens, *CBQ* 37 [1975] 76-97). Love is not ἔργον, but "fruit of the Spirit" (Gal 5:22). Paul mentions, though without reference to an instruction of Jesus, the great commandment to *love the neighbor:* "for he who loves his neighbor has fulfilled the law" (Rom 13:8). The commandments of the second table of the Decalogue are "summed up" (→ ἀνακεφαλαιόω) in the commandment to love the neighbor, so that love is "the fulfilling (→ πλήρωμα) of the law" (13:9f.; cf. Gal 5:14). 1 Thess 4:9 designates mutual love as "love of the brethren" (→ φιλαδελφία; cf. in this regard also 3:12: καὶ εἰς πάντας); see further 1 Cor 9:20f.; 10:24; 13:5; Gal 6:2. Regarding *love for God* (always the vb. ἀγαπάω) it is said that "with those who love him" (regarding this phrase see J. B. Bauer, *ZNW* 50 [1959] 106-12), "in everything God works for good" (Rom 8:28), that God "has prepared" unimaginable things for them (1 Cor 2:9), that whoever loves God "is known by him" (8:3). The triad of faith, love, and hope occurs in Paul first in 1 Thess 1:3 (additionally in 5:8; 1 Cor 13:13; see H. Lietzmann, *Korinther,* rev. W. G. Kümmel [HNT, [4]1949] 66-68; H. Conzelmann, *1 Corinthians* [Hermeneia] 229-31; W. Marxsen, FS Cullmann [1972], 223-29).

c) Col 1:4f. picks up the triad of faith, love, and hope (→ b) and speaks in that connection of the "love . . . for all the saints" (cf. Eph 1:15; 2 Thess 1:3) which is assumed to exist among the addressees. In the same connection Epaphras "our beloved fellow servant" is mentioned (v. 7), who has made known to the author τὴν ὑμῶν ἀγάπην ἐν πνεύματι (v. 8): the love of the Church being addressed is apparently understood as the work of the Spirit (E. Lohse, *Colossians* [Hermeneia] 23, n. 92). As God has "transferred us to the kingdom of his beloved Son" (v. 13), so Christians are also God's chosen and "beloved" (3:12; cf. 2 Thess 2:13, 16), and as such are exhorted to love, "which binds everything together in perfect harmony" (v. 14). The imperative ἀγαπᾶτε applies esp. to men in relation to their wives (v. 19; cf. esp. Eph 5:25-33). 2 Thess 3:5 places the "love of God," which is prayed for, alongside "the steadfastness of Christ"; on the other hand, to become or be a believer means "to love the truth" (2:10; cf. Eph 4:15: "holding fast [RSV "speaking"] the truth in love").

In Ephesians the subst. occurs 10 times (5 times in the phrase ἐν ἀγάπῃ) and the vb. 10 times, 5 of which refer to the love of a man for his wife. With love as the constant point of reference the train of thought begins with the love of God, who has pardoned us "in the Beloved (Christ)" (1:6; "in love" in v. 4 [RSV v. 5] is, as in the other texts, not to be taken as a reference to *God's* love; *contra* H. Schlier, *Der Brief an die Epheser* [1957] 52f.).

Pauline tradition is reflected in Eph 2:4f.: God has "out of the great *love* with which he *loved* us" made the sinner "alive together with Christ." The *love of Christ* surpasses all knowledge (3:19); it shows itself as love for the Church in his self-surrender as an "offering and sacrifice to God" (5:2). The parenesis begins with the exhortation to love which enables mutual "forbearing" and "upbuilds" the body of Christ (4:2, 16), and the letter closes with the petition for "love with faith" from God and Christ (6:23) and the designation of the addressees—more appeal than confirmation—as people who "love our Lord Jesus Christ with love undying" (v. 24).

In the Pastorals the subst. is dominant (10 times) whereas the vb. occurs only in 2 Tim 4:8, 10. The latter text exhibits the alternatives for love. It can be directed toward the "epiphany" (RSV "appearing") of Christ, i.e., the parousia, or toward "this present world." The "goal of instruction" (RSV "aim of our charge") is "love that issues from a pure heart and a good conscience and sincere faith" (1 Tim 1:5; "love" alongside "faith" also in 1:14; 2:15; 4:12; 6:11; 2 Tim 1:13; 2:22; 3:10; Titus 2:3). Some have wandered far away from this love (1 Tim 1:3f., 6f.). Love stands in contrast to the results of heretical agitation and can to this extent serve as a criterion for correct preaching. Timothy is admonished to hold fast to the example of the sound teaching which he received from Paul "in the faith and love" (2 Tim 1:13).

d) John and 1–3 John display both similarities and differences in the use of ἀγάπη (28 times) and ἀγαπάω (68 times). One important distinction is the fact that the fourth Gospel speaks emphatically of the love of Jesus/Christ and love for him, whereas the letters speak more frequently of God's love and love for God. But this hardly signifies a decisive material difference. Both speak of love "for one another," although only the letters speak of "brotherly love." (In addition to the contributions of Cipriani, Lattke, and Schlier, see also F. Mussner, *ΖΩΗ* [1952] 158-64; Bultmann, *Theology* §50.4 [II, 81f.]; E. Käsemann, *The Testament of Jesus* [1968] 59-65).

Of fundamental significance is John 3:16: "For God so loved the world that he gave his only Son" in order to make available "eternal life" through faith. Suggested by 14:21 is this statement: Whoever loves Jesus will also be loved by the Father and will therefore arrive at the same goal as Jesus (cf. vv. 3, 6). Whoever loves Jesus and keeps his word (cf. 15:9f.) receives the love of the Father who, like Jesus, will "come to him" in order to "make our home with him" (14:23). The disciples are there where Jesus is (v. 3), "in the sphere of God's love" (R. Schnackenburg, *The Gospel according to St. John* III [1982] 81). The world must recognize that Jesus has been sent by God and that God loves the disciples as he loved Jesus before the foundation of the world (17:23f., 26; cf. also 3:35; 10:17; 15:15f. regarding God's love for Jesus; 14:31 regarding Jesus' love for God). The love of Jesus for his own (11:5; 13:1, 34; 14:21; 15:9f., 12) was love "to the end"; it corresponds to the love of the Father and requires of the disciple that he keep the commandments of Jesus in order to remain in his love (15:9f.). Thus the disciple, for his part, brings to realization his love for Jesus (14:15, 21, 23f., 28). The demand for love of "one another" is grounded in Jesus' love for his own and has in that love its example (15:12f., 17). To this extent it is a "new commandment" (13:34f.).

The beloved disciple ("the disciple whom Jesus loved": 13:23; 19:26; 21:7, 20) is surely not merely a symbolic figure or a literary fiction; at least in the opinion of the redactor of 21:7, 20-23 he appears as an historical person (Schnackenburg, *John* III, 375-88, 484-86 [bibliography]; T. Lorenzen, *Der Lieblingsjünger im Johannesevangelium* [1971]; P. S. Minear, *NovT* 19 [1977] 105-23).

1–3 John distinguish themselves from John above all in the fact that *God's love* (1 John 3:1; 4:7-21; 2 John 3) and *love for God* (1 John 2:5, 15; 3:17; 4:10, 12, 20f.; 5:1-3) and for *Jesus* (5:1), as well as love *for one another* (3:11, 23; 4:7, 11f.; 2 John 5) and love *for the brother* (1 John 2:10; 3:10; 4:20f.; pl. 3:14; cf. 5:1f.) are placed in relationship to each other. (In addition to the works of Coppens and Schnackenburg, see R. Bultmann, *The Johannine Epistles* [Hermeneia] 65-78; P. W. van der Horst, *ZNW* 63 [1972] 280-82; H. Thyen, FS Käsemann, 527-42; on the threefold approach to the theme of the "love commandment" [1 John 2:3-11; 3:11-24; 4:7-21] see W. Thüsing, *Epistles of St. John* [NTSR, 1971].) The discussions of the divine love reach their high point in the sentence, "God is love" (4:8, 16). This is recognized on the basis of God's action. God sent his Son into the world of death in order to bestow on humankind the gift of life (v. 9). God's love is directed first at the cosmos, the world of humankind which requires salvation (vv. 9f.; cf. John 3:16). Brotherly love (→ ἀδελφός 5) is not confined to Church members, as 1 John 3:16f. and 3 John 5 indicate. The stress on brotherly love apparently pursues a double aim: the repulsion of false teachers by means of a dependable criterion (1 John 2:9-11; 4:20f.) and the strengthening of brotherly fellowship among Christians.

e) James 1:12 begins with the testing of the Christian to whom the "crown of life" is pledged; God has promised it "to those who love him." The same phrase, τοῖς ἀγαπῶσιν αὐτόν, occurs in 2:5 in connection with the promise of being "heirs of the kingdom." The command to love the neighbor (Lev 19:18) is characterized as the "royal law" (2:8; see F. Mussner, *Jakobus* [HTKNT] 124: not in the sense of "greatest commandment"). 1 Pet 1:22 demands "sincere love of the brethren," and that the readers "love one another earnestly from the heart" (cf. 2:17; 4:8). Love for Jesus Christ is spoken of in 1:7f. (cf. 2 Tim 4:8) with a view toward his ἀποκάλυψις: "Without having seen him you love him." Rev. 1:5 describes Jesus as "him who loves us and has freed us from our sins by his blood" (cf. John 13:1; Gal 2:20; Eph 5:2); similarly Christ anticipates that the Jewish opponents will come to recognize "that I have loved you [the church in Philadelphia]" (3:9).

4. In Jude 12 ἀγάπη signifies the *love feast* as an occasion of brotherly love. In this sense the subst. is further attested, e.g., in Ign. *Smyrn.* 8:2; *Acts of Paul and Thecla* 25 (Lipsius/Bonnet I, 252:11; Hennecke/Schneemelcher II, 359); *Pass. Perp. et Fel.* 17; Clement of Alexandria *Paed.* II, 1:4; *Strom.* III, 2:10 (details in *PGL* s.v. E.4). Bibliography in BAGD, s.v. II; W.-D. Hauschild, *TRE* I, 748-53.

5. The adj. ἀγαπητός is used in the NT to describe the relationship of God to his Son (the "beloved Son" in Mark 1:11 par. Matthew/Luke; 9:7 par. Matthew; 12:6 par. Luke; Matt 12:18; 2 Pet 1:17; see F. Lentzen-Deis, *Die Taufe Jesu nach den Synoptikern* [1970] 188-91), but also with proper names, joined with ἀδελφός (Eph 6:21; Col 4:7, 9; 2 Pet 3:15; cf. also Col 1:7; 4:14; 2 Tim 1:2) and in address ("beloved": 3 John 2, 5, 11; more frequently in pl.: Rom 12:19; 2 Cor 7:1; 12:19; etc.). Christians are called "God's *beloved*" in Rom 1:7, Jews in 11:28. In 1 Thess 2:8 Paul says to the readers: "You had become very dear (ἀγαπητοί) to us" (ἀγαπητοί also occurs at the end of the instructions for slaves in 1 Tim 6:1f. and refers to Christian masters as "beloved [of God])"; cf. Rom 11:28; Ign. *Phld.* 9:2); see E. A. van Leeuwen, *TS* 21 (1903) 139-51.

G. Schneider

ἀγαπητός, 3 *agapētos* beloved, dear
→ ἀγάπη.

Ἁγάρ *Hagar* Hagar*

Concubine of Abraham, mother of Ishmael (Gen 16:1-6; 21:9-21): Gal 4:24, 25. G. Kittel, *TDNT* I, 55f.; F. Mussner, *Galaterbrief* (HTKNT) 319-25; → Σάρρα.

ἀγγαρεύω *angareuō* press into (compulsory) service, compel*

Matt 5:41; 27:32 par. Mark 15:21. Ἀγγαρεύω is no doubt a Persian loanword (R. Schmitt, *Glotta* 49 [1971] 97-101), which is found also in rabbinic literature; P. Fiebig, *ZNW* 18 (1918) 64-72. Cf. Lat. *angariare.*

ἀγγεῖον, ου, τό *angeion* vessel, container*

Matt 25:4; cf. 13:48, v.l. in Koine D W.

ἀγγελία, ας, ἡ *angelia* message, commission
→ ἀγγέλλω 3.

ἀγγέλλω *angellō* inform, report
ἀναγγέλλω *anangellō* report, announce
ἀπαγγέλλω *apangellō* announce, declare

1. Occurrences in the NT — 2. Meaning — 3. Ἀγγελία

Lit.: U. Becker and D. Müller, *DNTT* III, 44-48 (bibliography, 67f.). — P. Joüon, "Le verbe ἀναγγέλλω dans Saint Jean," *RSR* 28 (1938) 234f. — J. Schniewind, *TDNT* I, 56-67 (bibliography).

1. The compounds of ἀγγέλλω are mutually interchangeable in secular Greek as well as in the LXX and NT. In accord with the preference of koine Greek for compounds, the NT offers only 2 examples of the simple form—John 4:51 (which is text-critically difficult; cf. Schniewind, 60-61) and 20:18—compared with about 14 instances of ἀναγγέλλω and 45 of ἀπαγγέλλω, which appear frequently without distinction in the manuscript tradition. The great majority of occurrences are found in the Lukan writings.

2. With all three verbs one must distinguish between cases in which the words retain their full content and those in which they are used only in a weakened sense, as well as the various stages in between. The compounds are weaker in Matt 2:8; 14:12; 28:11; Luke 8:20; 13:1; 14:21; 18:37; John 5:15, etc.: *inform, report* (cf. Acts 28:21 ἀπήγγειλεν ἢ ἐλάλησεν). The use of these words in the miracle stories belongs in this category as well (Mark 5:14; Matt 8:33; Luke 8:34, 36, cf. esp. v. 47 in which, significantly, Jesus is the indirect obj. of ἀπαγγέλλειν, to be sure "in the presence of all the people"; John 4:51 v.l.; Acts 4:23; 11:13; 12:14, 17; and perhaps 1 Thess 1:9 as well).

In the resurrection narratives of the Gospels (ἀπ-) αγγέλλω surely means more than a colorless report (Matt 28:8, 10f.; Mark 16:10, 13; Luke 24:9; John 20:18). The verb group lifts up the special significance of the event for Christian faith; in Matt 28:11 it is probably used in an extremely ironic sense. A richer tone is also present in 11:4. Barely distinguishable from εὐαγγελίζομαι is the use of ἀπαγγέλλω in 1 John 1:2, 3 (cf. also Acts 26:20; 17:30), which designates the proclamation of the eternal life "which was with the Father and was made manifest to us" and which has as its goal fellowship with the Father, the Son Jesus Christ, and other believers; thus it designates the event of salvation as the content of the gospel. The compounds of ἀγγέλλω signify, then, more than just a comprehensive announcement of God's will for salvation; they understand the announcement itself as an effective power. "The proclamation produces and confirms ever anew the faith and the state of salvation of the Christians" (R. Schnackenburg, *1–3 Johannes* [HTKNT] 64).

As Jesus himself is the herald announced by the OT (Matt 12:18; Heb 2:12), so the Paraclete, in continuity with the message of Jesus, will by means of his proclamation enable the Church to stand firm in the future (John 16:7-11). 'Απαγγέλλω is used in its fullest sense in 1 Cor 14:25 where, as in Ps 141:3 LXX and 88:2 LXX, it carries a "strong cultic note" (G. Dautzenberg, *Urchristliche Prophetie* [BWANT 104, 1975] 252) and is to be translated "confess."

3. **'Αγγελία** *message, commission** is attested only twice in the NT, 1 John 1:5; 3:11, and is in both cases textually suspect. Whereas in 1:5 ἀγγελία refers to the proclamation of Jesus, in 3:11 it designates that of the Church. The conspicuous fact that except for Rev 10:7 and 14:6 the root εὐαγγελ- is not used in the Johannine writings—which is understood by J. Schniewind as deliberate avoidance (*TDNT* I, 59)—is explained in various ways: while Schniewind, e.g., regards εὐαγγέλιον as primarily associated with the expectation of the coming messenger with good tidings and thinks that for the author "the conflict against a Gnosis which hoped for a coming messenger . . . made it advisable not to use εὐαγγελ-" *(ibid.)*, G. Friedrich points more generally to the (realized) eschatology of John's Gospel (*TDNT* II, 717f.). However, the use of ἀγγελία, at least in 1 John 1:5, may also be based on the influence of Isa 28:9. That the author of 1 John chose ἀγγελία because it is ambiguous (*TDNT* I, 59, where, however, *schwebenden Klanges* is translated "sonorous") appears questionable since both instances of the word clearly receive special stress.

The sense of ἀγγελία, which is common both in the LXX and in secular Greek, is frequently equated, in regard to 1 John 1:5, with εὐαγγέλιον, but in regard to 3:11, with παραγγελία (cf. *TDNT* I, 59; BAGD s.v.). Decisive for the understanding of ἀγγελία, however, is the question of the point at which the two expressions, which are, of course, very different, come together. The thesis "God is light (→ φῶς)" might have been common to the author of 1 John and his opponents, but the consequences which the author and his opponents derived from this sentence differed considerably (cf. K. Wengst, *Häresie und Orthodoxie im Spiegel des ersten Johannesbriefes* [1976] 38f.). For the author of 1 John, who thinks very much in terms of deeds, "the statement 'God is light' is only true in connection with a manner of living illumined and determined by this light" (*ibid.*, 74, n. 174), a manner of living which he characterizes as love for the brother. The author can, therefore, designate both the statement "God is light" and the exhortation to love the brother as ἀγγελία because the latter is a necessary implication of the former (cf. Wengst, 71; W. Thüsing, *Epistles of St. John* [NTSR, 1971] 61f.). To exist in the light of God means for the author of 1 John to exist in love for the brother. To that extent both sentences are core sentences of the proclamation.

I. Broer

ἄγγελος, ου, ὁ *angelos* messenger, angel

1. Occurrences in the NT and what they signify — 2. Specific instances — 3. Hermeneutical considerations — 4. 'Αρχάγγελος

Lit.: H. Bietenhard, *DNTT* I, 101-3. — O. Böcher, *Christus Exorcista* (1972). — G. B. Caird, *Principalities and Powers: A*

Study in Pauline Theology (1956). — G. DAVIDSON, *A Dictionary of Angels* (1967). — M. DIBELIUS, *Die Geisterwelt im Glauben des Paulus* (1909). — W. GRUNDMANN, G. VON RAD, and G. KITTEL, *TDNT* I, 74-87. — A. MANTEL, "Die Dienste der Engel nach der Apk des Johannes," *BibLeb* 2 (1961) 59-65. — J. MICHL, *Die Engelvorstellungen in der Apokalypse* I (1937). — *idem, RAC* V, 53-258. — *idem, SacVb* I, 20-28 (bibliography). — J. W. MORAN, "St. Paul's Doctrine on Angels," *AER* 132 (1955) 378-84. — F. NÖTSCHER, "Geist und Geister in den Texten von Qumran" (1955), *idem, Vom Alten zum Neuen Testament* (BBB 17, 1962) 175-87. — P. SCHÄFER, *Rivalität zwischen Engeln und Menschen. Untersuchungen zur rabbinischen Engelvorstellung* (1975). — A. SCHIMMEL and H. RINGGREN, *RGG* II, 1298-1303. — H. SCHLIER, "Die Engel nach dem NT," Schlier II, 160-75. — *idem, Principalities and Powers in the NT* (1964). — G. TAVARD, *Die Engel* (1968). — B. TSAKONAS, "Angelology According to the Later Jewish Literature," *ΘΕΟΛΟΓΙΑ* 34 (1963) 136-51. — C. WESTERMANN, *God's Angels Need No Wings* (1979). — A. WINKLHOFER, *Die Welt der Engel.*

1. The 175 occurrences of ἄγγελος are very unevenly distributed in the NT, the majority being found in the Synoptics (51; concentrated in the infancy narratives and the narratives of the women's visit to Jesus' grave and of the appearances following the resurrection), Revelation (67), and Acts (21). In the great majority of occurrences ἄγγελος is used for the (heavenly) *messenger* of God, but can also designate a human *messenger* (only 3 times in the NT: Luke 7:24; 9:52; Jas 2:25; cf. also, however, the OT quotation in Matt 11:10 par.; Mark 1:2). Both meanings are also found in secular Greek.

2. NT use of ἄγγελος is based upon that of the OT and the intertestamental literature: the *angels* are messengers sent by God; they represent the heavenly world; and their appearance is a revelation of the otherworldly in the earthly realm. But the activity and essence of the angels never become an explicit theme. Rather their existence and knowledge of their existence are simply presupposed (cf. not only the angelophanies in the Gospels, but also, e.g., Heb 13:2; 1 Tim 5:21).

In the Gospels and Acts the angels exercise the most diverse functions: The angel of the Lord appears and transmits to human beings messages and commissions from God (Matt 1:20-23; 2:13, 19-20; 28:5; Luke 1:11ff.; 2:9ff.; Acts 8:26; 10:3, 22; cf. Judg 13:3ff.; 4 Kgdms 1:3, 15; Luke 1:26ff.: Gabriel; Luke 24:23), frees and strengthens the apostles after Easter (Acts 5:19f.; 12:7ff.; 27:23f.), and punishes Herod (12:23). The life of Jesus is accompanied by angels, who are constantly at his service (Matt 26:53; Mark 1:13 par.; Luke 22:43; cf. also John 1:51). Angels will accompany the Son of Man at the execution of the final judgment and assume functions associated with it (Matt 13:39ff.; 25:31; Mark 8:38 par.; 13:37 par.; Luke 12:8; cf. also 2 Thess 1:7 [for the connection with and contradiction to Judaism present here cf. G. Kittel, *TDNT* I, 83f.]), and they bring Lazarus after his death to the bosom of Abraham (Luke 16:22; for this concept, which is taken over from Judaism, cf. Billerbeck II, 223ff.). Nevertheless, they are not omniscient (Mark 13:32 par.). The idea of the guardian angel, frequent already in the OT and in the rabbis, but less common in the apocryphal writings, occurs in Matt 18:10 (cf. also Acts 12:15).

Whereas the Evangelists clearly emphasize statements about the angels of God (the only exception is Matt 25:41), the Pauline corpus is nearly as clear in its emphasis on statements about the evil (fallen) angels and the demonic powers and authorities (regarding the latter → ἀρχή, ἐξουσία, δύναμις, κυριότης, θρόνος, στοιχεῖον and cf. texts such as Rom 8:38; 1 Cor 6:3; 11:10; Col 2:18). However, the interpretation of most such passages is disputed and difficult. For Rom 8:38 cf. v. 35 and E. Käsemann, *Commentary on Romans* (1980) 247 (bibliography). 1 Cor 6:3 most probably refers to the fallen angels rather than the angels of the nations (*contra* Dibelius 9ff.); vv. 2-3 do not emphasize the *correspondence* between "heavenly and earthly scenes" (*ibid.*, 10) and hence nothing suggests that the angels are angels *of the nations;* rather v. 3 goes beyond the thought of v. 2 (H. Conzelmann's reference, *1 Corinthians* [Hermeneia] 105, n. 22, to Jude 6; 2 Pet 2:4 is hardly conclusive). Whether or not Paul here counts the angels as belonging to "the world" is not fully clear, in contrast to 1 Cor 4:9 (for the background of this formulation cf. H. Braun, *Gesammelte Studien zum NT und seiner Umwelt* [1962] 186-91). In 13:1 Paul speaks of the language of angels as the very "epitome of the gift of tongues" (G. Dautzenberg, *Urchristliche Prophetie* [1975] 150), in order to point up the necessity of love along with exceptional gifts of the Spirit. In Gal 1:8 the reference to angels serves to emphasize the unalterable character of the gospel. The phrase regarding the mediation of the law through the angels in Heb 2:2 and Gal 3:19 has, of course, parallels in Judaism (cf. A. van Dülmen, *Die Theologie des Gesetzes bei Paulus* [1968] 44, n. 91 [bibliography]), but in contrast to these parallels is used here to demonstrate the inferiority of the law. By contrast Acts 7:53 is perfectly in line with the Jewish statements.

Hebrews gives consideration to the unequivocal superiority of Jesus over the angels (cf. 1:4ff.). These reflections reach their high point in 1:14: "Are they not all ministering spirits sent forth to serve, for the sake of those who are to obtain salvation?" In this text, as in 2:16 and 1 Pet 1:12, one can even recognize a certain priority of believers over the angels (cf. K. H. Schelkle, *Petrusbriefe, Judasbrief* [HTKNT] 43). 1 Tim 3:16 (cf. also 1 Pet 3:22) probably also includes the notion of the superiority of the Exalted One although it does refer to the "triumphal train of the One ascending to heaven" (E. Schweizer, *Erniedrigung und Erhöhung bei Jesus und seinen Nachfolgern* [[2]1962] 106).

The interpretation of 1 Cor 11:10 is problematic. Does it speak of the angels of God or of angelic attacks on the praying and prophesying woman (cf. Dibelius, 13ff.; W. Foerster, *TDNT* II, 573f. [bibliography]; Braun, *Qumran* I, 193ff. [bibliography])? The most probable interpretation remains that the reference is to evil angels (*contra TDNT* II, 573f. [Foerster]; III, 679f. [H. Schlier]), against whom the woman should protect herself by means of the veil. However, the angels are introduced here with relatively little emphasis; because of the διὰ τοῦτο, which refers back to what precedes, the entire stress rests on the indirect relationship of the woman to God, a point which then seems to be negated again in vv. 11f. by the statement that man and woman (in the same manner?) have their origin in God. Ἄγγελος is similarly unstressed in 2 Cor 12:7 (ἄγγελος Σατανᾶ), where Paul views his suffering as a work of Satan, but understands it simultaneously as a work of God (cf. v. 10). In 2 Cor 11:14 Paul uses Satan and his ability to transform himself into an angel (of light), an idea already current in Judaism (cf. *Adam and Eve* 9), as an illustration of the fact that nothing is proven by the claim of his opponents to be apostles.

To be sure, the self-evident nature of the existence of angels, so common in the time of the NT, brings with it problems for faith. This is shown—in addition to the Epistle to the Hebrews—by Col 2:18, which is not concerned with participation in the angels' worship of God, as in the angel liturgy of Qumran (cf. Schäfer, 36ff. [bibliography]), but with the worship of angels—already widespread among Jews (cf. *ibid.,* 67ff.)—by "puffed up" Christians (on this verse cf. further E. Schweizer, *Colossians* [1982], ad loc.; Rev 19:10; 22:8f.). Finally in Jude 6 and 2 Pet 2:4 the judgment on the angels is cited as a warning example (on the underlying Jewish interpretation of Gen 6 cf. K. H. Schelkle, *Petrusbriefe, Judasbrief* [HTKNT] 150f.).

With particular frequency the author of Revelation refers to angels with diverse commissions from God: they mediate the revelation and execute God's judgments. Besides the angels of the churches (2:1–3:22), which are to be understood as real angels (since ἄγγελος in Revelation always means real angels and the underlying conception is readily understandable against the background of the Jewish views on the angels of the nations and the angel of Israel), the author mentions angels of the winds (7:1) and the destructive mounted legions (9:14), an angel of the fire (14:18), one of the water (16:5), an angel of the underworld whose name Ἀβαδδών is interpreted (9:11) as Ἀπολλύων (= destroyer) and who is master of the locusts of the fifth plague, and the traditional seven archangels (8:1–9:21). Angels also surround the throne of God and fill the heavenly world with songs of praise (5:11; 7:11).

3. The central question for the exposition of the NT passages just listed is whether the NT statements about angels belong to the dispensable time-bound worldview, or whether they—at least!—contain a core which implies the existence of angelic beings. Both opinions are represented in the literature (cf. only R. Bultmann, "NT and Mythology," *Kerygma and Myth* I [ed. H. W. Bartsch; 1961] 1ff., on the one hand, and M. Seemann, *Mysterium Salutis* II [1975] 946ff., 966f. [bibliography] on the other). One may be allowed to observe that in this matter the expositor's preunderstanding is of the greatest importance.

Many of the prejudices against the existence of angels which reside in the interpreter's preunderstanding touch finally, however, the question of God, and this must be taken into account in the exposition of passages dealing with angels. If, e.g., the stories of the discovery of the empty grave and of the appearances of the Risen One are more presentations of the truths and experiences of faith than reports of historical incidents, they nevertheless speak of actions of God which must be traced mediately "through angels" or immediately to God. To that extent, the OT texts in which Yahweh and his angels alternate as acting subjects in such a way that it remains unclear which acts (Gen 16:7ff.; 21:17ff.; 22:11ff.; 31:11ff.; Exod 3:2ff.; Judg 2:1ff.) articulate an important matter. Therefore the NT statements about angels can serve to remind human beings both of the magnitude of God and of God's creation, for the world as it presents itself to human beings is not the entire world, but is subject to the lordship and will of God. The fundamental assertion, then, of the NT texts which speak of angels can to this degree also be expressed by the fundamental assertion of the Christ-event itself: God is one who is there for us, who devotes and has devoted himself to us.

4. **Ἀρχάγγελος** *archangel** is foreign to the OT and its Greek translation, but not to the early Jewish writings. It occurs only twice in the NT: Jude 9 and 1 Thess 4:16. The first occurrence mentions the archangel Michael (cf. also 4 Ezra [2 Esdr] 4:36) and says about him that not even he dares do to Satan what the blasphemers presume to do to the celestial beings. When the text speaks of the archangel Michael instead of an angel, it intends to emphasize with special force this fact: not even the *archangel* Michael, not to mention a normal angel, would have dared . . . (cf. K. H. Schelkle, *Petrusbriefe, Judasbrief* [HTKNT] 158f.). In 1 Thess 4:16 the accent is almost certainly on the sounding of the (eschatological) voice; its characterization as that of an archangel is intended to emphasize the special significance of this voice and this moment. "Such depictions introduce traditional features of the apocalyptic world which are designed, not to describe the events in detail, but to set the mood for the commencement of the end" (L. Schmid, *TDNT* III, 658).

Both passages are part of the tendency which begins in the OT and grows significantly clearer in Judaism to raise individual angels to prominence, but the concern in both cases is not the archangel as such. Rather the archangel is mentioned to emphasize the significance of the voice or the contrast in behavior. Early Jewish speculation about angels, with, e.g., its diverse statistics on the number of highest angels (cf. *1 Enoch* 20; 9:1, etc.) is completely foreign to the NT.

I. Broer

ἄγγος, ους, τό *angos* vessel*

Matt 13:48: a container for fish.

ἄγε *age* come!*

This interjection is a frozen imv. of ἄγω (cf. BDF §§144; 364.2). It is used in the NT only in ἄγε νῦν: Jas 4:13; 5:1.

ἀγέλη, ης, ἡ *agelē* herd*

Mark 5:11, 13 par. Matt 8:30, 31, 32 par. Luke 8:32, 33. R. Renehan, *Glotta* 50 (1972) 157.

ἀγενεαλόγητος, 2 *agenealogētos* without genealogy*

Heb 7:3, of Melchizedek. F. Büchsel, *TDNT* I, 665.

ἀγενής, 2 *agenēs* ignoble*

1 Cor 1:28. The meaning *inferior* is also possible; cf. BAGD s.v.

ἁγιάζω *hagiazō* make holy, consecrate
→ ἅγιος.

ἁγιασμός, οῦ, ὁ *hagiasmos* consecration
→ ἅγιος.

ἅγιος, 3 *hagios* holy, pure
ἁγιάζω *hagiazō* make holy, consecrate*
ἁγιασμός, οῦ, ὁ *hagiasmos* consecration*
ἁγιότης, ητος, ἡ *hagiotēs* holiness*
ἁγιωσύνη, ης, ἡ *hagiōsynē* holiness*

1. Occurrences in the NT — 2. Typical contexts in the NT — 3. Greek and Jewish usage (LXX) and theological consequences — 4. God, Christ, and the salvific gifts of God; πνεῦμα ἅγιον — 5. Holiness and consecration of believers

Lit.: R. Asting, *Die Heiligkeit im Urchristentum* (FRLANT 46, 1930). — J. Barr, *The Semantics of Biblical Language* (1961) 284-86. — P. Chantraine and O. Masson, "Sur quelques termes du vocabulaire religieux des Grecs: la valeur du mot ἄγος et de ses dérivés," *Sprachgeschichte und Wortbedeutung* (FS A. Debrunner; 1954) 85-107. — S. Djukanovič, *Heiligkeit und Heiligung bei Paulus* (Diss. Bern, 1939). — J. Efros, "Holiness and Glory in the Bible," *JQR* 41 (1950/51) 263-77. — J. A. Eliott, *The Elect and the Holy* (NovTSup 12, 1966). — D. Flusser, "Sanktus und Gloria," FS Michel 129-52. — E. Gaugler, *Die Heiligung im Zeugnis der Heiligen Schrift* (1948). — B. Häring, *Das Heilige und das Gute. Religion und Sittlichkeit in ihrem gegenseitigen Bezug* (1950). — J. Haspecker, *BL* 694-96. — van Imschoot and H. Haag, *BL* 686-91. — O. R. Jones, *The Concept of Holiness* (1962). — P. Jovino, *L'Église Communauté des Saints dans les Actes des Apôtres et dans les Épîtres Pauliniennes* (1975). — L. E. Keck, "The Poor Among the Saints in Jewish Christianity and Qumran," *ZNW* 57 (1966) 54-78. — K. G. Kuhn, *TDNT* I, 97-100. — G. Lanczkowski, F. Horst, H.-D. Wendland, and G. Gloege, *RGG* III, 146-55. — M. Lattke, *TRE* XIV, 703-708. — H. P. Müller, *THAT* II, 589-609. — F. Nötscher, "Heiligkeit in den Qumranschriften," *RevQ* 2 (1959/60) 163-81, 315-44. — E. Pax, *SacVb* I, 372-75. — O. Procksch, *TDNT* I, 88-91, 100-115 (A., B., E.). — S. P. J. J. van Rensburg, *Hagios in die Nieu-Testamentiese voorstelling* (Diss. Pretoria, 1958). — *idem*, "Sanctification According to the NT," *Neot* 1 (1967) 73-87. — D. W. B. Robinson, "Who Were 'the Saints?' " *RTR* 22 (1963) 45-53. — B. Schneider, "Κατὰ Πνεῦμα Ἁγιωσύνης (Romans 1, 4)," *Bib* 48 (1967) 359-87. — H. Seebass, *DNTT* II, 223-29. — J. A. Soggin and E. Esking, *BHH* II, 681-83, 694f. — G. Stählin, *RGG* III, 178-80. — G. Walther, "Übergreifende Heiligkeit und Kindertaufe im NT," *EvT* 25 (1965) 668-74. — E. Williger, *Hagios. Untersuchungen zur Terminologie des Heiligen in den hellenisch-hellenistischen Religionen* (RVV 19/1, 1922) 72-108. — R. Wolff, "La Sanctification d'après le NT," *PosLuth* 3 (1955) 138-43.

1. This word group occurs with relative frequency in the NT: Ἅγιος occurs 230 times (among others, Matt 25:31 Koine, etc.; John 7:39 𝔭[66]* L Koine W, etc.; Acts 6:3 A C* H, etc.; 8:18 𝔭[45, 74] A C Koine D, etc.; Rom 15:19 A C D G, etc.; 1 Cor 2:13 Koine, etc.; 1 Thess 5:27 88[mg]; Rev 4:11 Koine, etc.; 15:3 296 2049; 22:21 א Koine, etc.), distributed over nearly all the NT writings (except for Galatians, James, 2–3 John), with special significance attaching to Luke (20 occurrences in Luke, 53 in Acts), Romans (20 occurrences), and Hebrews (18 occurrences). Ἁγιάζω occurs 28 times, ἁγιασμός 10 times (not in the Gospels or Acts), ἁγιότης only in Heb 12:10 and 2 Cor 1:12 𝔭[46] א* A B, etc. (the v.l. ἁπλότης [א[c] D G Koine, etc.] is preferred in *UBSGNT;* πραότης 88 635 is also found), and ἁγιωσύνη only in Rom 1:4; 2 Cor 7:1; 1 Thess 3:13.

Thus ἅγιος κτλ. stands out clearly from the other NT words for "holy": → ἱερός occurs only 3 times (and once in the shorter ending of Mark), its derivatives (with the exception of ἀρχιερεύς and ἱερεύς) not more than 13 times, and only ἱερόν (almost without exception the NT t.t. for the Jewish temple) more frequently (70 times and once as a v.l.); ὅσιος only 8 times (not in the Gospels or Paul!), ὁσίως only in 1 Thess 2:10, and ὁσιότης only in Luke 1:75; Eph 4:24.

2. Ἅγιος is used in 90 of 230 cases in the combination πνεῦμα ἅγιον, which has its greatest concentration again in the Lukan writings (13 in Luke, 41 in Acts); the form πνεῦμα ἁγιωσύνης in Rom 1:4 (→ 4) is unique. In second place follows the absolute use of the subst. adj. (οἱ) ἅγιοι (the article occurs nearly without exception) for Christians in general (Rom 8:27; Eph 6:18, etc.) and by Paul for the early church in Jerusalem (e.g., Rom 15:25, 26, 31; 1 Cor 16:1, etc.), with a total of 61 occurrences.

In addition, ἅγιος is often (traditionally) associated on the one hand with things, places, and persons connected with the (Jewish) cult and the OT-Jewish tradition: with things, γραφαὶ ἅγιαι in Rom 1:2, νόμος ἅγιος in Rom 7:12, ἐντολὴ ἁγία καὶ δικαία καὶ ἀγαθή in Rom 7:12, cf. 2 Pet 2:21; with places, πόλις ἁγία in Matt 4:5; 27:53; Rev 11:2, etc., τόπος ἅγιος in Matt 24:15; Acts 6:13; 21:28, always referring to the temple, the *holy mountain* of the transfiguration, 2 Pet 1:18; and with persons, προφῆται ἅγιοι in Luke 1:70; Acts 3:21; 2 Pet 3:2 (always in gen.; in the post-Pauline period also οἱ ἅγιοι ἀπόστολοι, Eph 3:5). On the other hand, τὸ ἅγιον can designate anything at all which belongs to God (Matt 7:6; Luke 2:23; Heb 8:2), including the earthly (κοσμικόν) "sanctuary" of the first covenant in Heb 9:1, the σκηνὴ . . . ἥτις λέγεται Ἅγια (v. 2), ἡ λεγομένη Ἅγια Ἁγίων, the "Holy of Holies" (v. 3), and the temple "Holy Place" (vv. 12, 25; mss. 69 and 1912 add τῶν ἁγίων); in Heb 10:19; 13:11; 9:24 it is applied figuratively to the true heavenly sanctuary of which the earthly is only a copy (ἀντίτυπα).

Ἅγιος occurs as a designation for God in the direct address of prayer in the high-priestly prayer of Jesus in John 17:11 (πάτερ ἅγιε) and also in Luke 1:49 (Ps. 110:9 LXX: ἅγιον τὸ ὄνομα); 1 Pet. 1:15, 16 (Lev. 19:2) 1 John 2:20; Rev 4:8: ἅγιος ἅγιος ἅγιος κύριος ὁ θεός (Isa 6:3) ὁ παντοκράτωρ; 6:10 (ὁ δεσπότης ὁ ἅγιος καὶ ἀληθινός). Similarly in relation to the world of God, the angels are called "holy" in Mark 8:38 par. Luke 9:26; Acts 10:22 (sg.); Jude 14 (ἐν ἁγίαις μυριάσιν); Rev 14:10; the term is also used frequently in the christological realm: ὁ ἅγιος τοῦ θεοῦ in relation to Christ in Mark 1:24 (par. Luke 4:34); John 6:69; cf. Rev 3:7; the absolute τὸν ἅγιον καὶ δίκαιον ἠρνήσασθε in Acts 3:14 (cf. the reference to John the Baptist in Mark 6:20); τὸ γεννώμενον ἅγιον κληθήσεται υἱὸς θεοῦ in the announcement of Jesus' birth, Luke 1:35 (cf. ὁ ἅγιος παῖς, Acts 4:27, 30). Of special theological significance are statements regarding God's "holy" gifts of salvation: κλῆσις ἁγία in 2 Tim 1:9; διαθήκη ἁγία in Luke 1:72 (cf. the connection with ἀπαρχή and ῥίζα in Rom 11:16); figuratively, θυσία ζῶσα ἁγία in Rom 12:1; and ἡ ἁγιωτάτη πίστις in Jude 20. Here the salvific character of God's gifts is connected with their origin in the holy God himself.

In the same way, finally, believers themselves are regarded as holy (see above), i.e., called out of the world about them into the presence of God as a *holy* people (ἔθνος, 1 Pet 2:9), their bodies a *holy* temple of God (ὁ γὰρ ναὸς θεοῦ ἅγιός ἐστιν, 1 Cor 3:17; cf. Eph 2:21), their children *holy* in the sense of "belonging to God" (the opposite is ἀκάθαρτα: 1 Cor 7:14), which can also be said of women (v. 34; 1 Pet 3:5). This holiness manifests itself in pure and undefiled conduct (Eph 1:4; 5:27; Col 1:22 [with ἄμωμος]; cf. 1 Pet 1:15: ἅγιοι ἐν πάσῃ ἀναστροφῇ γενήθητε; similarly in 2 Pet 3:11). The holiness of the Christian life derives from the holiness of God (1 Pet 1:16, quoting Lev 19:2; cf. also Rev 22:11: ὁ ἅγιος ἁγιασθήτω ἔτι). As holy persons Christians demonstrate to each other their new solidarity by means of the *holy kiss* (φίλημα ἅγιον, Rom 16:16; 1 Cor 16:20; 2 Cor 13:12; 1 Thess 5:26). The use of ἅγιος with δίκαιος (Mark 6:20; Acts 3:14; Rom 7:12; cf. 1 Cor 6:1 [over against ἄδικοι]) makes it clear that in addition to its specific meaning the word can occasionally be used in a weakened or figurative sense.

The vb. ἁγιάζω is used 17 times pass. and 11 times act. The following are made holy or are holy (pass.): the name of God (Matt 6:9 par. Luke 11:2); those who believe (John 17:19b; Acts 20:32; 26:18; 1 Cor 1:2; 6:11; 7:14 [twice]; 2 Tim 2:21), who are all consecrated through the one Son (Heb 2:11b; cf. 10:10, 14); everything which God has created (1 Tim 4:5); and, finally, Christ himself, who is consecrated through the blood of the covenant (Heb 10:29 [referring to Exod 24:8]). In pass. constructions God is very frequently to be understood as the subject of the consecration (divine passive). Only in Rev 22:11 is the pass. ὁ ἅγιος ἁγιασθήτω ἔτι to be translated as mid.: "Let . . . the holy (person) still be holy." Similar relationships emerge in act. constructions: God sanctifies Christ (John 10:36) and believers (17:17; 1 Thess 5:23); Christ also sanctifies himself (John 17:19a), believers (Heb 2:11a), and the Church (Eph 5:26; cf. Heb 13:12). Cultic usage is reflected in Matt 23:17, 19; Heb 9:13. 1 Pet 3:15 contains the traditional formulation: κύριον δὲ τὸν Χριστὸν ἁγιάσατε (cf. Isa 8:13): "in your hearts keep Christ holy [RSV "reverence Christ"] as Lord," i.e., allow oneself to be ruled by him alone.

Ἁγιασμός has its decisive role in NT parenesis, and often appears with a prep. to characterize the comprehensive goal of the new conduct of those who believe: εἰς ἁγιασμόν in Rom 6:19 (over against εἰς τὴν ἀνομίαν), v. 22 (over against death as the fruit of the life lived under the power of sin); ἐν ἁγιασμῷ in 1 Thess 4:7 (over against ἐπὶ ἀκαθαρσίᾳ); 1 Tim 2:15; and ἐν ἁγιασμῷ πνεύματος in 2 Thess 2:13; 1 Pet 1:2: "sanctified by the Spirit"; cf. Rom 15:16 (ἡγιασμένη ἐν πνεύματι ἁγίῳ, referring to the Gentile world, presented to God as an offering). Such phrases are also used more specifically to describe the relationship of men to their wives: τὸ ἑαυτοῦ σκεῦος κτᾶσθαι ἐν ἁγιασμῷ καὶ τιμῇ in 1 Thess 4:4 ("in *holiness,*" i.e., in a manner corresponding to the will of God, "and honor," over against ἐν πάθει ἐπιθυμίας); cf. also in general the preceding verse and Heb 12:14. In 1 Cor 1:30 δικαιοσύνη and ἀπολύτρωσις are used with ἁγιασμός to refer to the final salvation accomplished through Christ.

In Heb 12:10 ἁγιότης designates the *holiness* of God in which those who belong to God participate. By contrast the same word is used to designate Christian conduct in a series of mss. at 2 Cor 1:12 (→ 1).

Paul uses ἁγιωσύνη to speak of the believers' perfect *holiness* (ἐπιτελοῦντες ἁγιωσύνην) achieved through cleansing from every defilement of flesh and spirit (2 Cor 7:1) or their holiness which proves itself in blamelessness (ἀμέμπτους ἐν ἁγιωσύνῃ) before God's judgment (1 Thess 3:13). In Rom 1:4 (→ 4) πνεῦμα ἁγιωσύνης replaces the usual πνεῦμα ἅγιον.

3. Like ἁγνός the verbal adj. ἅγιος is connected with ἅζομαι "stand in awe" and referred originally to the deity whose manifestations are accompanied by marvelous signs and call forth fear and awe. Ἅγιος is attested as early as Herodotus, who uses it in a less specific sense to refer to holy places (e.g., v.119). A similar usage appears in Aristophanes (e.g., *Lys.* 256) and Plato (e.g., *Criti.* 116c: ἱερὸν ἅγιον, a phrase which occurs frequently, esp. later, e.g., Pausanias x.32.13) among others, and has the general sense of "venerable, awe-inspiring." In the Hellenistic period ἅγιος appears as an epithet of oriental deities (e.g., Pap. Oxy. no. 1380, ll. 34, 36), and can even refer to the veneration of Epicurus by the Epicureans: ἅγιον καὶ ἁγιώτατον καὶ ἵλεων (Philodemus *Piet.* [ed T. Gomperz, 1866] 96) and—mockingly—to the Egyptian veneration of animals: ὡς ἁγιωτάτοις ἱεροῖς (Plutarch *Quaest. Conv.* iv.5.2 [670a]). On the whole ἅγιος is relatively rare; it does not occur as an expression for a human ethical or personal quality, nor does it signify holiness (of the divine) as such but rather holiness together with the proper reactions to it, i.e., respect, reverence, and awe.

In contrast to extrabiblical Hellenistic literature ἅγιος is found rather frequently in the LXX, over 700 times, preponderantly as the rendering of Heb. *qāḏôš* or *qōḏeš*); moreover, new forms appear, among others: ἁγιάζω, e.g., Gen 2:3; ἁγιασμός, e.g., Jer 6:16; ἁγιότης, only in 2 Macc 15:2; and ἁγιωσύνη, e.g., Ps 29:4 (only 5 occurrences). Ἱερός and ὅσιος, on the other hand, recede sharply. Ἅγιος appeared especially well-suited to serve as an equivalent because, like *qdš*, it made possible the articulation of the holiness of God as a claim grounded in the power and perfection of God and thus addresses human beings out of this extra- and supraworldly reality. In this way it could become an epithet of God (Lev 19:2; 1 Kgdms 2:2; Isa 31:1; Hos 11:9), of his name (Isa 60:9), of his spirit (Ps 50:13), of his places of worship (Ex 3:5; Lev 7:6; Ps 2:6), indeed of everything associated with the cult, i.e., everything in the world which directly belongs to or is oriented toward God. New is the idea that the pious, who respond appropriately to this claim of God, are also called "holy" (Exod 19:6: ἔθνος ἅγιον; Deut 7:6: λαὸς ἅγιος); this idea refers primarily to God's election of the people and thus expresses God's right of ownership over the people (Lev 11:44f.; Ps 33:9; Hos 11:12). This leads to the demand to belong entirely to God: Exod 19:22 (of the priests); Judg 13:7; 16:17 (of a Nazirite); Deut 26:19 (of the people which does God's will); 28:9. Offenses against cultic purity are defilements of the holiness of God and result in the loss of union with God (Lev 19:2ff.). The danger of cultic conformity and legalism is unmistakable. Isa 6:3-7 illustrates how the individual recoils before the holiness of God in the knowledge of one's own incommensurability, but can then be commissioned through the consolation and call of God.

From this perspective ἁγιάζω denotes the process of the dedication and surrender of objects and persons to God whereby these are removed from the claim of the ordinary (Exod 13:2), just as God himself can appropriate certain things (Gen 2:3: the sabbath; Jer 1:5: the prophets) and will finally achieve the sanctification of his name through the people (Isa 29:23) or punish their refusal (Deut 32:51).

In late texts (οἱ) ἅγιοι designates those who belong to God: Dan 7:21; Tob 8:15; 12:15; 1 Macc 1:46. The Qumran community in particular designates itself as "Community of the Holy Ones" (1QSb 1:5) or as "saints of his [God's] people" (1QM 6:6; cf. also 1QS 5:18, 20; 11:8, etc.; see also C. Brekelmans, *OTS* 14 [1965] 305-29; L. Dequeker, *OTS* 18 [1973] 108-87).

On the whole, then, it is clear that NT usage of the word group ἅγιος κτλ. presupposes the language and theology of Hellenistic Judaism. Therefore ἅγιος κτλ. is frequently shaped by traditional usage. In the NT, as in Judaism, it centers on the being and claim of God to whom persons, appearances, and objects stand in a definite relationship. On the other hand, the word group is also filled with new content and is used in new ways (→ 4, 5), just as God himself is experienced in new ways, i.e., as the merciful and redeeming one whose holiness does not create fear and distance, but who through the gift of the Spirit is immediately present to those who believe in such a way that they live primarily not from the demand but from the gift of holiness.

4. Ἅγιος κτλ. are used only 10 times in connection with God and not much more frequently in connection with Christ (→ 2). But more than one-third of all NT occurrences refer to the Holy Spirit as God's eschatological gift associated with salvation, and about one-fourth refer to those who believe as "saints" or as those who are dependent on sanctification. This points to the likelihood of a theological emphasis within the biblical use of language characterized by new beginnings—over against the OT and Judaism. The decisive center of concern is the activity

of the holy God and the new relationship of believers to God. For the most part the holiness of God itself is expressed in traditional ways; but such formulations are altogether absent from Paul's letters. The first petition of the Lord's Prayer (Matt 6:9 par. Luke 11:2), which bears a verbal resemblance to the first petition of the Jewish Kaddish prayer, has as its goal the eschatological and universal revelation of God's power and redemptive activity, both of which are included in his "name": may the Holy One secure before the entire world (ἁγιασθήτω, aor. pass.) in a final and decisive way the holiness appropriate to his name (cf. Isa 29:23; John 12:28), to which, then, human beings will respond with praise and exaltation.

As holiness traditionally belonged to the heavenly realm of God (→ 2), so now it belongs especially to the earthly envoy of God, whom the person possessed by demons recognizes as the ἅγιος τοῦ θεοῦ (Mark 1:24 par. [the LXX applies this epithet to a person only in Judg 13:7; 16:17, to the Nazirite Samson; see also Müller, *THAT* II, 606]). He is recognized as such because he represents in his person and his redemptive actions (for the demons they are destructive actions) the holiness of God. Peter's confession (John 6:69) places the revealer of eternal life in immediate proximity to God (cf. 10:36; 1 John 2:20), although even the one of whom the confession speaks cannot avoid the attack of the διάβολος (cf. John 6:70f.). The Lukan announcement of the birth of Jesus regards Christ's holiness as the result of the πνεῦμα ἅγιον (Luke 1:35).

Of decisive significance is the use of ἅγιος in connection with the divine gifts associated with salvation, especially the gift of the divine Spirit (→ πνεῦμα). Here *holy* characterizes the Spirit as the self-impartation and divestiture of God in such a way that the Spirit finally constitutes for the believer the experiential presence of God or Christ. This distinguishes the Spirit from all forms of human enthusiasm or ecstasy but allows it nonetheless to emerge as the eschatological sphere of existence for believers. A survey makes clear, however, that in only about one-third of the pertinent NT references to the πνεῦμα is the attribute ἅγιος used (5 of 13 in Matthew, 4 of 6 in Mark, 14 of 17 in Luke; 2 of 21 in John, 41 of 57 in Acts, 5 of 31 in Romans, 2 of 28 in 1 Corinthians, 2 of 14 in 2 Corinthians, 0 of 17 in Galatians, 2 of 13 in Ephesians, 5 of 7 in Hebrews, and none of 16 in Revelation).

Pauline statements containing πνεῦμα ἅγιον are largely confined to the Spirit which is given to or dwells within the believer (frequently ἐν πνεύματι ἁγίῳ), in contrast, e.g., to Eph 1:13; 4:30. Paul's uses of πνεῦμα without ἅγιον refer more to the divine Spirit as the decisive sign of the eschaton.

This sheds light on the phrase κατὰ πνεῦμα ἁγιωσύνης, which appears in the NT only in Rom 1:4 (cf. Isa 63:10f.; Ps 51:13: *rûaḥ haqqodeš*; LXX nevertheless in both cases τὸ πνεῦμα τὸ ἅγιον, in contrast to *T. Levi* 18:11: πνεῦμα ἁγιωσύνης referring to the gift of the Spirit to the saints of the end time). Without going into the question of the precise delineation of the expression which Paul has appropriated, one recognizes that the stress of the text rests on the eschatological Spirit of God as the power which has effected the enthronement of Christ. Paul has almost certainly taken over an expression (and a conception) which was foreign to him (on the whole issue see E. Käsemann, *Commentary on Romans* [1980] ad loc.); whether it was from Hellenistic Jewish Christianity (e.g., W. Kramer, *Christos, Kyrios, Gottessohn* [1963] 118f.) or was a "nostalgic" reminder of the original kerygma of Peter known in Rome through Pentecost pilgrims (Schneider, 380; cf. also O. Kuss, *Römerbrief* I [1957] ad loc.) cannot be discussed here. Paul interpreted the tradition christologically (by placing τοῦ υἱοῦ αὐτοῦ in front of it) and set κατὰ πνεῦμα ἁγιωσύνης in relation to the proclamation and acknowledgment of the Exalted One which takes place under the influence of God's Spirit.

In the post-Pauline period πνεῦμα ἅγιον is used in an increasingly formal and colorless sense, above all by Luke, especially in Acts. On the one hand, this is due to the solidification of the language of the Church. On the other hand, this change may also have taken place because of the audience of the Lukan writings, for whom the divine Spirit had to be clearly distinguished from the spirit of human ecstasy, which is all the more important since it is Luke himself who in Acts demonstrates the presence of the Spirit by means of pneumatic phenomena (1:8; 2:2-4, 15f.; see Procksch, *TDNT* I, 104f.; E. Schweizer, *TDNT* VI, 404-13). Likewise in John the phrase πνεῦμα ἅγιον (only 1:33; 14:26, referring to the παράκλητος [whereas 14:17; 15:26; 16:13 have τὸ πνεῦμα τῆς ἀληθείας]; 20:22) reveals Church language and is related to baptism and the post-Easter presence of the Exalted One in the Spirit, whereas the absolute πνεῦμα primarily signifies the power emanating from Jesus and the Father which makes possible the recognition of Jesus as the Redeemer.

5. Through God's calling and Christ's work of redemption those who believe are *saints*: κλητοὶ ἅγιοι (Rom 1:7; 1 Cor 1:2; cf. Col 3:12), ἅγιοι (2 Cor 1:1; Phil 1:1, etc.; → 2), or ἡγιασμένοι ἐν Χριστῷ Ἰησοῦ (1 Cor 1:2; cf. 6:11); Gentile Christians are an offering ἡγιασμένη ἐν πνεύματι ἁγίῳ (Rom 15:16; cf. 2 Thess 2:13; 1 Pet 1:2), grafted onto the *holy* root of the old people of God (probably the patriarchs) and therefore themselves holy (Rom 11:16f.). The Church is the *holy* people (1 Pet 1:16; 2:9); Christ gave himself up for the Church ἵνα αὐτὴν ἁγιάσῃ . . . ἵνα ᾖ ἁγία καὶ ἄμωμος (Eph 5:26f.). "Holy" does not refer here to a state or a quality of the believers, but to Christ's setting them apart for God, thus removing them from this world (Col 1:12f.). Through God Christ has become for the believers δικαιοσύνη, ἁγιασμός, and ἀπολύτρωσις (1 Cor 1:30); they have not created their own salvation.

Hebrews in particular describes the redemptive work of Christ as an atoning sacrifice for the sanctification of believers. Christ, simultaneously the one who sanctifies and the brother of those who are sanctified (2:11), overcame the provisional cult in the "Holy Place" and the "Holy of Holies" (9:1, 2, 3, 8) by entering through his bloody death "once for all" (ἐφάπαξ) into the true, heavenly sanctuary of God which he could never have entered without this offering of himself; thus he accomplished the eternal redemption (vv. 11f., 24-26; 10:10, 14). In 10:19ff. the consequences for those who believe are made clear: to fall back into sin is equivalent to destroying Christ's work of redemption and results in God's punishment (vv. 29-31). Thus the necessity: διώκετε . . . τὸν ἁγιασμόν (12:14).

Nevertheless it would be wrong to understand the holiness of believers in the NT as being determined and mediated by the cult (Procksch) or to connect it too exclusively to the work of the Holy Spirit (Seebass)—in spite of 1 Pet 1:2. The concepts borrowed from the Jewish cult serve rather to express the real and binding new position of the believers before God. In terms of content there is a great distance, at least in the earlier layers of the NT, between cultic performances and holiness. This is apparent in 1 Cor 7:14, according to which a non-Christian spouse *is sanctified* by the Christian partner since the children of members of the congregation are also regarded as ἅγια (as opposed to ἀκάθαρτα). God's gift of holiness becomes reality in the whole, new people of God, which is the *holy* temple (3:17), and in mutual διακονία (Rom 15:25, 31), κοινωνία (12:13), and ἀγάπη (Eph 1:15). It is not contact with this world and hence defilement in the classical sense, but relapse into the situation prior to the redemption and liberation achieved through Christ which would make of the very holiness in which they stand before God the occasion of the believers' failure (cf. 1 Cor 6:1f.); in that respect the Christian is not defiled by an unbelieving spouse (twice in 1 Cor 7:14). Before God the holiness of the community extends into the impurity of individual members (see Walther). There are other instances in which the component "pure" in a fig. sense plays a role (cf. 1 Cor 7:34; Eph 1:4; 5:27, and in connection with parousia and judgment cf. 1 Thess 3:13; 5:23; Col 1:22).

A consequence of the holiness of those who believe is the sanctification (ἁγιασμός) of their lives (Rom 6:19, 22), contrasted occasionally to πορνεία (1 Thess 4:3) and ἀκαθαρσία (v. 7). Rom 12:1 speaks of sanctification or surrender of the entire life to the will of God, using the cultic image of the presentation of bodies as a living (in contrast to animal sacrifice) and *holy* sacrifice to God. "Holy" here refers to the total orientation to God which includes being totally claimed by God (cf. 1 Thess 5:23). Sanctification can therefore certainly encompass the cultic-sacral realm as well, though the reverse is not the case; i.e., the cultic-sacral can no longer be the authentic realm of sanctification. Accordingly, the NT later applies phrases from the Holiness Code to the total life and conduct of believers, e.g., 1 Pet 1:15f. (ἅγιοι, over against συσχηματιζόμενοι ταῖς πρότερον . . . ἐπιθυμίαις, v. 14). Holiness or sanctification is, then, the comprehensive acceptance by believers of the holiness of God in order that they may enter into communion with God, not a gradual progression toward religious-ethical perfection.

H. Balz

ἁγιότης, ητος, ἡ *hagiotēs* holiness
→ ἅγιος.

ἁγιωσύνη, ης, ἡ *hagiōsynē* holiness
→ ἅγιος.

ἀγκάλη, ης, ἡ *ankalē* (bent) arm*

Luke 2:28: take up in his *arms.*

ἄγκιστρον, ου, τό *ankistron* fishing tackle, fishhook*

Matt 17:27: "cast a *hook.*"

ἄγκυρα, ας, ἡ *ankyra* anchor*

Acts 27:29, 30, 40: a ship's anchor; Heb 6:19, fig. for that which gives support and stability.

ἄγναφος, 2 *agnaphos* unshrunken, new*

Mark 2:21 par. Matt 9:16 of *new* cloth.

ἁγνεία, ας, ἡ *hagneia* purity, chastity
→ ἁγνός.

ἁγνίζω *hagnizō* purify, sanctify
→ ἁγνός.

ἁγνισμός, ου, ὁ *hagnismos* purification, sanctification
→ ἁγνός.

ἀγνοέω *agnoeō* not know*
ἀγνόημα, ατος, τό *agnoēma* error, transgression*
ἄγνοια, ας, ἡ *agnoia* ignorance, delusion*
ἀγνωσία, ας, ἡ *agnosia* ignorance, lack of understanding*
ἄγνωστος, 2 *agnōstos* unknown*

1. Occurrences and epistolary usage — 2. Specifically religious usage — 3. Other uses

Lit.: W. Wrede, *The Messianic Secret* (1971). — R. Bultmann, *TDNT* I, 116-21. — *idem, Der Stil der paulinischen Predigt*

und die kynisch-stoische Diatribe (1910). — E. HAENCHEN, *The Acts of the Apostles* (1971). — W. SCHMITHALS, "Die Korintherbriefe als Briefsammlung," *ZNW* 64 (1973) 263-88. — S. K. STOWERS, *The Diatribe and Paul's Letter to the Romans* (SBLDS 57, 1981).

1. 'Αγνοέω occurs 21 times in the NT, other words in this group a total of 8 times.

Paul uses ἀγνοέω 6 times in the epistolary formula "*I do not want you to be ignorant,* brethren . . ." with a ὅτι clause which follows directly or after intervening words, in order to introduce an emphatic pronouncement, particularly in the opening section of the body of a letter (Rom 1:13; 11:25; 1 Cor 10:1; 12:1; 2 Cor 1:8; 1 Thess 4:13); dissolving the litotes one translates: "I want you to know," "You should know" (cf. 1 Cor 11:3; Bultmann, *Stil* 65).

Also an element of epistolary style is the rhetorical question ἢ ἀγνοεῖτε with a following ὅτι (Rom 6:3; 7:1): "Surely you know," "Surely you have not forgotten" (cf. Bultmann, *Stil* 13, 65; Stowers 89).

2. Against the background of Greek, particularly Stoic, thought in which ignorance and error are closely related to each other, ἀγνοέω and related words attain a specifically theological meaning in the language of primitive Christianity. At this point Christian language joins Hellenistic Judaism, which saw culpable ἄγνοια (rejection) of God as a characteristic of the Gentile world (Dan 6:5, 23; 9:15; *T. Levi* 3:5; *T. Zeb.* 1:5).

According to Eph 4:18 the Gentiles are "alienated from the life of God διὰ τὴν ἄγνοιαν τὴν οὖσαν ἐν αὐτοῖς" (because *ignorance* rules them): The *rejection* of God causes a person to miss the purpose of his or her own life. Christians are exhorted as "obedient children": "Do not be conformed to the passions of your former ἄγνοια (*disobedience, disbelief*)" (1 Pet 1:14). Rather, by doing good they will "put to silence" τὴν ἀγνωσίαν, namely "the *evil intentions* [RSV "ignorance"] of foolish men" who denounce them as enemies of the state (2:15; the preferred reading is ἄγνοιαν in 𝔭[72]).

Gentiles are like false teachers who are *ignorant* of certain supernatural powers (2 Pet 2:12) or who by denying the resurrection demonstrate their ἀγνωσία of God (1 Cor 15:34), i.e., their *sinful denial* of the power of God (cf. Mark 12:24). In connection with his instructions Paul remarks bitingly about such persons: "If anyone does not wish to understand this, let him remain ignorant" (1 Cor 14:38, ἀγνοείτω: 𝔭[46] B Koine sy; if one reads ἀγνοεῖται with ℵ* A* G [Lat.] Origen [so RSV "he is not recognized"], the thought is: ". . . he will *not be recognized* by God," which does not go well with the irony in v. 37). 'Αγνοέω, etc., may have been chosen for the sake of polemical wordplay directed against Gnostic false teachers.

Jews also, it is said, participate in the culpable *ignorance* of God. They *do not recognize* that God's gracious patience is intended to lead them to repentance (Rom 2:4). But above all, they do not recognize the righteousness of God, i.e., in the explicit and precise expression of Paul, they do not *submit* to the mercy of God (10:3). The ἀγνοήματα (a NT hapax legomenon) for which the High Priest presents the sacrifice on the Day of Atonement for the benefit of the "ignorant (= offenders) and wayward" (Heb 5:2) are simply the *sins* of the (Jewish) people (9:7; cf. Sir 23:2; 1 Macc 13:39) and not "sin committed in ignorance" (so BAGD s.v.).

3. The litotes of 2 Cor 2:11, "*we are not ignorant* of his [Satan's] designs," means: *we know them exactly.* The churches of Judea had certainly heard about the conversion of Paul, nevertheless he remained "*not known* by sight" to them (Gal 1:22). In a personal (Schmithals 277f.) apology Paul defends in 2 Cor 6:9a the apostolic office: ὡς ἀγνοούμενοι καὶ ἐπιγινωσκόμενοι: the apostle is (among human beings) *unknown, i.e., not acknowledged socially, homo ignotus;* but precisely because of this he is acknowledged as a true servant of God (by God? cf. 1 Cor 13:12; by human beings? cf. 2 Cor 1:13f.; 5:11).

In the Gospels ἀγνοέω occurs only in the second Passion prediction (Mark 9:32 par.), where it serves to express the Markan theme of the disciples' incomprehension: "*they did not understand*" what Jesus meant when he spoke of the Son of Man being delivered up, killed, and raised from the dead (cf. v. 10). Luke traces this lack of understanding back to divine intent (Luke 9:45).

In Acts 3:17 and 13:27 Luke's redactional references to ἄγνοια serve to lessen the responsibility of the Jews who killed Jesus without having recognized him as the promised Messiah; the same is implied for Paul who, according to 1 Tim 1:13, "ignorantly" persecuted the Christians (this is connected with legal terminology: *per ignorantiam* = without premeditation; cf. Bultmann, *TDNT* I, 118). Such ignorance makes forgiveness possible for the penitent.

In the context of the Areopagus speech Luke's mention of the "times τῆς ἀγνοίας" (Acts 17:30) in which the Gentiles *did not know* God, has a similar exonerating function. With this statement Luke intends also to interpret v. 23b, though in v. 23b we encounter the idea that the Gentiles are not excused: the reference to the altar in Athens, though it was supposedly dedicated "*to the unknown God*" (ἄγνωστος: a NT hapax legomenon; see Haenchen 520f. on the absence of evidence for such an altar), serves Paul in his defense with the opportunity of raising the issue of the ignorant knowledge of the Gentiles: "What therefore you worship *as unknown,* this I proclaim to you" (v. 23). Most likely Luke's source went directly on to the expression of mockery and interest on the part of the hearers (v. 32).

W. Schmithals

ἀγνόημα, ατος, τό *agnoēma* error, transgression → ἀγνοέω 2.

ἄγνοια, ας, ἡ *agnoia* ignorance, delusion → ἀγνοέω.

ἁγνός, 3 *hagnos* pure, undefiled, chaste*
ἁγνεία, ας, ἡ *hagneia* purity, chastity*
ἁγνίζω *hagnizō* purify, sanctify*
ἁγνισμός, ου, ὁ *hagnismos* purification, sanctification*
ἁγνότης, ητος, ἡ *hagnotēs* purity, sincerity*
ἁγνῶς *hagnōs* purely, sincerely*

1. Occurrences in the NT — 2. Meaning — 3. Ἁγνίζω, ἁγνισμός

Lit.: H. BALTENSWEILER, *DNTT* III, 100-102. — O. BÖCHER, *Christus Exorcista. Dämonismus und Taufe im NT* (BWANT 96, 1972), esp. 58, 84, 112, 155. — W. BRANDT, *Jüdische Reinheitslehre und ihre Beschreibung in den Evangelien* (BZAW 19, 1910). — O. GAUPP, *Zur Geschichte des Wortes "rein"* (Diss. Tübingen, 1920). — F. HAUCK, *TDNT* I, 122-24 (bibliography). — P. VAN IMSCHOOT, *BL* 1467. — W. PASCHEN, *Rein und unrein. Untersuchungen zur biblischen Wortgeschichte* (SANT 24, 1970). — T. WÄCHTER, *Reinheitsvorschriften im griechischen Kult* (RVV 9/1, 1910). — E. WILLIGER, *Hagios* (RVV 19/1, 1922) 37-69.

1. Ἁγνός occurs 8 times in the NT, esp. in the Pastorals (1 Tim 5:22; Titus 2:5) and the Catholic Epistles (Jas 3:17; 1 Pet 3:2; 1 John 3:3). It does not occur in the Gospels or Acts. Ἁγνεία is found only in 1 Tim 4:12; 5:2, ἁγνότης only in 2 Cor 6:6; 11:3 (v.l.), and ἁγνῶς only in Phil 1:17. The related words ἁγνίζω and ἁγνισμός (→ 3) occur 7 times and 1 time respectively. Thus ἁγνός etc. ranks far behind → καθαρός and related words (65 occurrences) in the NT as a designation for purity. This corresponds with the usage in the LXX, where ἁγνός occurs 11 times and ἁγνότης is absent, but words more closely associated with the cult are more frequent: ἁγνίζω more than 30 times, ἁγνισμός 6 times, and ἁγνεία 5 times, compared to καθαρός and related words, which appear approximately 170 times. The relatively rare appearance of the ἁγνός word group is probably to be explained by the shift in meaning, which occurred in Hellenistic language as well as Judaism, from cultic to fig. use, which made it increasingly easy to substitute other words for this group.

2. Ἁγνός (like ἅγιος, from ἅζομαι, "to stand in [religious] awe") refers originally to the awe-inspiring holiness of the gods and their realm.

It is used in a broader sense from the time of Homer in reference to persons and things to designate the absence of any impurity such as incest or sexual intercourse which could compromise holiness (= "chaste"), thus esp. ritual purity. In the Hellenistic period it is frequently used in an ethical sense and applied to daily behavior to mean "morally blameless" (usually synonymous with δίκαιος). Ἁγνεία and ἁγνότης (the latter is found in Paul, otherwise only in the post-NT period) designate—like ἁγνός—ritual purity and, figuratively, purity of character. Ἁγνίζω and ἁγνισμός on the other hand, point in the extrabiblical context more to the cultic sphere and refer to activities which produce cultic purity: consecration and purification by means of water and fire.

In the NT ἁγνός means *pure, undefiled* in reference to the conduct of the ἀδελφοί (Phil 4:8 in a catalog of virtues alongside ἀληθῆ, σεμνά, δίκαια, προσφιλῆ, and εὔφημα; cf. Jas 3:17; in Phil 1:17 οὐχ ἁγνῶς parallels ἐξ ἐριθείας: *impure, not sincere*), esp. of (young) women (Titus 2:5, likewise in a catalog of virtues, alongside σώφρονας, οἰκουργούς, ἀγαθάς, etc.; 1 Pet 3:2 has τὴν ἐν φόβῳ ἁγνὴν ἀναστροφήν in a household code: the women should through their "reverent and *chaste* behavior" win some of their husbands "without a word" [v. 1]), but also of the disciple of the Apostle, who oversees the Christian community and who at the ordination of officeholders is not to allow himself to be drawn into the sins of others but is to keep himself *pure* in order to be able to judge others (1 Tim 5:22). The children of God *purify* their lives already in the present because they hope for the goal of salvation, i.e., for their coming to be conformed with the *pure* Christ when he appears (1 John 3:3). Paul desires to present the Corinthian congregation to Christ as a *pure, chaste* virgin (2 Cor 11:2). Like ἁγνότης (which appears in 11:3 in 𝔓[46] ℵ* B 33 and other witnesses with ἁπλότης and in 6:6 in a catalog of virtues), ἁγνός indicates in this figure of speech in 11:2 *purity,* i.e., the perfect union of the congregation with Christ. In 7:11 ἁγνός . . . τῷ πράγματι describes in legal fashion the *purity* of the Corinthians in the case being tried: they have proven themselves to be *innocent.*

In contrast to the cultic usage in the LXX, ἐν ἁγνείᾳ appears in 1 Tim 4:12 in a catalog of virtues alongside ἐν λόγῳ, ἐν ἀναστροφῇ, ἐν ἀγάπῃ, and ἐν πίστει and refers to the exemplary *pure* character of Timothy. It is used similarly in 5:2.

3. Ἁγνίζω (act.) is used in John 11:55 of the levitical purification of the Jews prior to Passover (cf. Exod 19:10f.). Acts 21:24, 26 (where ἁγνισμός is also used) and 24:18 are difficult. Luke connects the vb. (mid.) and the subst. with the Nazirite vow of four Christian men in Jerusalem which Paul, as an open demonstration, took upon himself (ἁγνίσθητι σὺν αὐτοῖς, 21:24) in order to give notice for the four (and for himself? cf. 18:18) of the termination of the vow after seven days (21:27) by means of the prescribed offering (v. 26). A new commitment by Paul to be a Nazirite would have lasted at least thirty days (*m. Nazir* 1:3f.). Either Luke has carried over the terminology and in part also the duration of the levitical prescriptions for purification (cf. Num 19:12 LXX: ἁγνισθήσεται) into his understanding of the prescriptions for Nazirites

(see also E. Haenchen, *The Acts of the Apostles* [1971] 610-12; Billerbeck II, 755-61) or we are dealing with the existence of very diverse forms of the Nazirite vow during the Pauline period (see also Böcher 112).

Otherwise ἁγνίζω is used only fig. in the NT: ἁγνίσατε καρδίας, δίψυχοι parallels καθαρίσατε χεῖρας, ἁμαρτωλοί (!) in Jas 4:8 in the sense of *purify, cleanse;* similarly 1 Pet 1:22: τὰς ψυχὰς . . . ἡγνικότες. For 1 John 3:3 → 2.

H. Balz

ἁγνότης, ητος, ἡ *hagnotēs* purity, sincerity
→ ἁγνός.

ἁγνῶς *hagnōs* purely, sincerely
→ ἁγνός.

ἀγνωσία, ας, ἡ *agnōsia* ignorance, lack of understanding
→ ἀγνοέω.

ἄγνωστος, 2 *agnōstos* unknown
→ ἀγνοέω 3.

ἀγορά, ᾶς, ἡ *agora* marketplace*

Matt 11:16 par. Luke 7:32; Matt 20:3; 23:7 par. Luke 11:43; Mark 6:56; 12:38 par. Luke 20:46. The place for legal proceedings: Acts 16:19, or for public life: 17:17. Mark 7:4, ἀπ' ἀγορᾶς (after returning) *from the marketplace* (D adds ὅταν ἔλθωσιν). R. Martin, *Recherches sur l'agora Grecque* (1951); *idem, L'agora* (1959); G. Gottlieb, *LAW* 68-70.

ἀγοράζω *agorazō* buy

Matt 13:44, 46 and often; fig.: *to purchase as one's own* (1 Cor 6:20; 7:23; 2 Pet 2:1; Rev 5:9; 14:3, 4).

ἀγοραῖος, 2 *agoraios* pertaining to a market*

Acts 17:5, referring to the rabble in the marketplace; 19:38: ἀγοραῖοι ἄγονται, "the *courts* are open" (cf. Josephus *Ant.* xiv.245).

ἄγρα, ας, ἡ *agra* catch (of fish)*

For both the action of catching fish (Luke 5:4) and the fish which are caught (v. 9, 𝔓[75] B D τῇ ἄγρᾳ τῶν ἰχθύων ὧν συνέλαβον; ℵ A C Koine read ᾗ συνέλαβον [Θ ἦν], understanding ἄγρᾳ as that which is caught).

ἀγράμματος, 2 *agrammatos* unable to write*

Acts 5:13, in a more general sense: *uneducated.*

ἀγραυλέω *agrauleō* live out of doors*

Luke 2:8, of shepherds (cf. Homer *Il.* xviii.161).

ἀγρεύω *agreuō* catch*

Mark 12:13, fig.: catch him in a (careless) word.

ἀγριέλαιος, ου, ἡ *agrielaios* wild olive tree*

Rom 11:17, 24. M. M. Bourke, *A Study of the Metaphor of the Olive Tree in Romans XI* (1947); K. H. Rengstorf, "Das Ölbaum-Gleichnis in Röm 11.16ff.," *Donum Gentilicum* (FS D. Daube, ed. E. Bammel, C. K. Barrett, and W. D. Davies; 1978) 127-64; D. Zeller, *Juden und Heiden in der Mission des Paulus* (1973) 215-18.

ἄγριος, 3 *agrios* outdoors, wild*

Mark 1:6 par. Matt 3:4: *wild* honey; Jude 13: *stormy* waves (cf. Wis 14:1; *Sib. Or.* iii.778).

Ἀγρίππας, α *Agrippas* Agrippa*

Lit.: J. Blinzler, *LTK* V, 263-66. — A. van den Born, *BL* 28-29. — J. Goldin, *IDB* I, 60f. — H. Hoehner, *ISBE* II, 696-98. — A. H. M. Jones, *The Herods of Judaea* (²1967). —S. Perowne, *The Political Background of the NT* (1965; = *The Later Herods* [1958]; see index). — Reicke, *NT Era* (see index). — A. Rosenberg, PW X/1 (1918) 146-50. — A. Schalit, *EncJud* II, 417f. — Schürer, *History* I, 471-83.

1. Two Jewish kings had the name Agrippa: Marcus Julius Agrippa I (*ca.* 9 B.C.-A.D. 44), called "Herod" in the NT (Acts 12), and his son Marcus Julius Agrippa II (*ca.* A.D. 27-93 [or 100]). Since only Agrippa II is mentioned by name in the NT, this article deals only with him. The most important sources are Josephus *Ant.* xviii-xx; *B.J.* ii-v; and *Vita.* Also informative are Dio Cassius lxvi.15.3-5; Juvenal *Sat.* vi.156-60; Suetonius *Titus* 7; Tacitus *Ann.* xiii.7; *Hist.* ii.2.

Agrippa II was born and raised in Rome. He had three sisters: Bernice, Mariamne, and Drusilla. Emporer Claudius wanted to allow him to succeed his father as king immediately following the latter's death in 44 A.D., but was advised against it because of Agrippa's youth. After Herod of Chalcis died in A.D. 48, Claudius gave Herod's nephew Agrippa the kingdom of Chalcis in the Lebanon (probably around A.D. 50). Agrippa also received from Claudius oversight of the temple in Jerusalem so that in the following years he appointed the high priests. In return for the surrender of his small kingdom he was granted in 53 A.D. the tetrarchies of Philip (Batanaea, Trachonitis, and Gaulanitis) and Lysanias (Abilene), as well as the territory of Varus. Nero expanded Agrippa's territory by adding large parts of Galilee and Perea.

Agrippa's private life gave rise to scandal because he lived together with his widowed sister Bernice. Politically, he was submissive to the Romans. Even during the Jewish War he stood completely on the Roman side. While he did value contact with Judaism, such contact was confined to externals. When Agrippa died in A.D. 93 (or 100), his kingdom was incorporated into the Roman province of Syria.

2. In the NT Agrippa is mentioned by name 11 times, all in Acts (25:13, 22, 23, 24, 26; 26:1, 2, 19, 27, 28, 32; cf. 26:7 v.l.). According to the account there, on the

occasion of the formal visit which Agrippa and Bernice made to the new procurator Porcius Festus in Caesarea, the latter aroused their interest in Paul, who was being held in protective custody. Since they wanted to hear Paul personally and since the king's opinion was important to Festus, Paul was called upon to speak before the king and his company. Paul began with the compliment that Agrippa was "especially familiar with all customs and controversies of the Jews" (26:3) and that Paul regarded himself fortunate to be allowed to defend himself before him. Paul recounted his earlier manner of life, his calling and his service as a witness for the risen Christ among Jews and Gentiles. Agrippa replied that Paul would soon persuade him to become a Christian (v. 28) and declared to Festus that Paul could have been set free had he himself not appealed to Caesar (v. 32).

Luke has composed this final great scene in the trial of Paul in such a way as to make clear that there are no justifiable objections against the Christian message, neither from the side of the Roman state (25:25) nor from the side of the Jewish religion, represented by King Agrippa. Luke thus demonstrates that Christianity is neither politically nor religiously impeachable.

A. Weiser

ἀγρός, οῦ, ὁ *agros* arable land; field; estate

1. Occurrences in the NT — 2. What is signified by the term — 3. Usage

Lit.: H. Haag, *BL* 22f. — R. Pesch, *Markusevangelium* I/II (HTKNT, 1976-77) on the relevant texts. — Schulz, *Q* 149-57, 391-403 (on Luke 12:28; 14:18 par. Matthew). — G. Theissen, *Sociology of Early Palestinian Christianity* (1978).

1. The 36 occurrences in the NT (including Mark 16:12) are limited to the Synoptic Gospels (17 in Matthew, 9 in Mark, 9 in Luke) and Acts (4:37). All Markan examples originate in the pre-Markan tradition. Four of the Lukan occurrences are from Mark, 2 from Q, and 3 from L. Two of the Matthean occurrences are from Mark, 2 from Q, 10 from M, and 2 redactional: 13:31, in conformation to the context (unlike Mark 4:31 and Luke 13:19 = Q κῆπος); and 24:40, probably under the influence of v. 18 (unlike Luke 17:34). Ἀγρός is redactional only in Matthew and is without special relevance as a Matthean redactional term.

2. In the sg. ἀγρός means either *an individual field* (e.g., Matt 13:24, 27, 31) or, in contrast to a city or village, *the open country* (e.g., Mark 13:16 par.; 15:21 par.). In the pl. it signifies *parcels of land,* property in land, fields (e.g., Mark 10:29f. par.; Luke 15:15), *rural areas* near a city (e.g., Mark 5:14 par.), or *farms* near a village (e.g., 6:36 par.; cf. v. 56).

3. Some uses of ἀγρός reflect topographical relationships and features: city vs. *country*" (e.g., Mark 16:12), inhabited settlement vs. *open field* (e.g., Matt 24:40), the juxtaposition of cities and villages with *plots of ground and farms* (e.g., Mark 5:14; 6:36, 56), or a specific plot of ground, the "potter's field" or "field of blood" (Matt 27:7, 8, 10). Some occurrences also reflect agrarian culture (esp. in the Matthean parables, in which ἀγρός also becomes an allegorical cipher for the κόσμος: Matt 13:38), problems of land ownership (Luke 14:18), and concerns about community property (Acts 4:37). Also recognizable in these uses of the word, especially in the Markan tradition, is the rural character of the Jesus movement and the early mission in Palestine.

R. Pesch

ἀγρυπνέω *agrypneō* be awake
→ ὕπνος.

ἀγρυπνία, ας, ἡ *agrypnia* wakefulness
→ ὕπνος.

ἄγω *agō* lead

Lit.: J. Baumgarten, *Paulus und die Apokalyptik* (1975) 91-98. — E. von Dobschütz, *Thessalonicherbriefe* (KEK, [8]1974) 189-92 (bibliography). — J. A. Fitzmyer, "The Use of *Agein* and *Pherein* in the Synoptic Gospels," FS Gingrich, 147-60. — P. Hoffmann, *Die Toten in Christus* ([2]1969) 207-38. — K. Kliesch, *Das heilsgeschichtliche Credo in den Reden der Apostelgeschichte* (1975) 72-74. — F. Laub, *Eschatologische Verkündigung und Lebensgestaltung nach Paulus* (1973) 123-31. — O. Michel, *An die Hebräer* (KEK, [12]1966) 142-49. — P.-G. Müller, ΧΡΙΣΤΟΣ ΑΡΧΗΓΟΣ (1973). — J. Plevnik, "The Parousia as Implication of Christ's Resurrection," *Word and Spirit* (FS D. M. Stanley, 1975) 199-277. — H. Schlier, *Der Apostel und seine Gemeinde* (1972) 75-84. — G. Schneider, *Verleugnung, Verspottung und Verhör Jesu nach Lukas 22, 54-71* (1969) 63f. — J. J. Scott, "Paul and Late Jewish Eschatology," *JETS* 15 (1972) 133-43.

1. Most of the 67 occurrences are in the Lukan writings (13 in Luke, 26 in Acts). The vb. is well attested in John (13 occurrences) but is less common in Matthew (4) and Mark (3). The Pauline epistles offer further examples (5), as do 2 Timothy (2) and Hebrews (2:10). Measured against the compounds and related substantives which together are five times as frequent as the simple form, the attestation is slight.

2. The basic meaning of ἄγω is *lead* (BAGD s.v.). It is used intransitively in exhortation: *let us go* (7 occurrences; BDF §308). Animals require leading (Matt 21:2 par. Luke 19:30; Matt 21:7 par. Luke 19:35; Acts 8:32 [quoting Isa 53:7]; fig. in John 10:16), as do the sick and injured (Luke 4:40; 10:34; Acts 20:12), and esp. the blind (Luke 18:40; cf. John 9:13). Ἄγω is frequently used of forced leading (24 occurrences, e.g., Mark 13:11; Luke 22:54; John 7:45;

Acts 5:26), sometimes under the influence of legal terminology—*lead* or *drag away*—with ἐπί with acc., bring before (the court; e.g., Acts 18:12: ἐπὶ τὸ βῆμα).

Jesus was led by spiritual powers: Luke 4:1, 9. Ἄγω is used of Jesus having already spent the third day since the crucifixion (Luke 24:21; BDF §129). God *brings* him as Savior to the people of Israel (Acts 13:23). Those who have "fallen asleep" in Jesus God will *bring* with him (1 Thess 4:14) through the resurrection (cf. v. 16), but at the time of the parousia of Jesus. Therefore Paul does not write ἐγερεῖ, but ἄξει (with F. S. Gutjahr, *Thessalonicherbriefe* [[2]1912] ad loc., *contra* Hoffmann 216). Jesus (or God, according to others, e.g., Müller 284-92) has *brought* "many sons to glory" (Heb 2:10). In their *manner of life* the brothers of the faith are to allow themselves to be *led* by God's Spirit (Gal 5:18; Rom 8:14). As heathen they were *driven* (→ ἀπάγω) by dumb idols (1 Cor 12:2). Certain women are *ruled* "by various impulses" (2 Tim 3:6).

U. Borse

ἀγωγή, ῆς, ἡ *agōgē* manner (of life)*

2 Tim 3:10 (cf. *1 Clem.* 47:6; 48:1). K. L. Schmidt, *TDNT* I, 128f.

ἀγών, ῶνος, ὁ *agōn* contest, struggle*
ἀγωνίζομαι *agōnizomai* struggle (in a contest)*

1. Occurrences in the NT — 2. Meaning — 3. Semantic field — 4. The ἀγών of Paul and his communities — 5. The ἀγών of Christians — 6. Ἀγωνία

Lit.: J. D. Ellsworth, *Agōn. Studies in the Use of a Word* (Diss. Berkeley, 1971). — V. C. Pfitzner, *Paul and the Agon Motif* (1967). — E. Stauffer, *TDNT* I, 134-40.

1. The ἀγών word group, including forms prefixed with ἀντ-, ἐπ-, κατ-, and συν-, occurs seldom in the NT and primarily in the Pauline corpus (otherwise: Luke 13:24; John 18:36; Jude 3). Ἀγών occurs 6 times, ἀγωνίζομαι 8 times, and the compounds once each.

2. In its literal sense the subst. means *contest* or *struggle,* but it is used in the NT only metaphorically and fig. (→ 3). Correspondingly the vb. means *struggle* in a contest or in general and is likewise used metaphorically or figuratively (except John 18:36, which refers to an armed struggle; cf. 2 Macc 8:16). The same is true for the compounds (except Heb 11:33, where καταγωνίζομαι means *conquer*; cf. Josephus *Ant.* iv.153; vii.53).

3. The metaphorical and fig. use of the ἀγών word group in the NT writings is related to the widespread use in the classical diatribe form of the figure of the athletic contest and the exertions and self-denials associated with it for the practice of virtue or the ethical struggle as a struggle against the passions (Plato *Grg.* 526d, e; *Phdr.* 247b; Epictetus *Diss.* i.24 superscription; ii.18.27; iii.22.51; 25.2f.; *Ench.* 29.2; Marcus Antoninus 3:4; 4:18; Seneca *Ep.* 17:1; 34:2; 109:6; cf. Pfitzner 23-35). This metaphor was taken up in Hellenistic Judaism and applied to life according to the law (Philo *Agr.* 113, 119; *Praem.* 4-6 [cf. *Som.* ii.9]; Wis 4:2; 10:12), to suffering for the sake of the law (4 Macc 9:23f.; 17:11-16), and to the life-determining struggle against Satan (*T. Ash.* 6:2; cf. *T. Job* 4; 27) or against the evil impulse (4 Ezra 7:88, 127; cf. *2 Bar.* 15:7f.; cf. Pfitzner 38-48, 54-69). A great number of other terms related to the Greek athletic contest are likewise used in a fig. sense (e.g., in the NT: ἀθλέω, → βραβεῖον, πυκτεύω, → στέφανος, → τρέχω) and belong to the semantic field of the same word group. On the other hand, philosophical concepts not employed in the NT writings, such as ἀρετή, πάθη, ἀπάθεια, ἀταραξία, and λογισμός, are found in connection with the use in popular philosophy of the ἀγών word group in the diatribe form, as well as in Hellenistic Judaism (Pfitzner 6). The connection of the ἀγών word group with events in the stadium or in the arena varies in concentration outside the NT as well as within the NT writings and is frequently absent altogether.

4. The application in 1 Cor 9:24-27 of the ἀγών terminology to the conduct of the apostle stands in the tradition of the use of the athletic metaphor (on v. 24 cf. Lucian *Anach.* 13); this is true also of the contrast in v. 25b (Philo *All.* ii.108; Seneca *Ep.* 78.16; Wis 4:2; 1 Pet 4:5). The images and comparisons are intended to illustrate the points made in vv. 3-18, which speaks of the renunciation of the apostolic right to receive a livelihood, and in vv. 19-23, which speaks of the selfless investment of oneself for the sake of the gospel. Πᾶς δὲ ὁ ἀγωνιζόμενος in v. 25 refers back to the metaphorical statement in v. 24 and forms the transition to the first application: Whoever is engaged in an athletic contest "exercises self-control in all things" (ἐγκρατεύομαι) in order to attain the wreath (→ στέφανος). As in the moral ἀγών of the Hellenistic diatribe (→ 3), so also in Paul's application of the metaphor here, the element of competition is absent (cf. the incongruity between v. 24 and v. 25). The equally traditional element of → ἐγκράτεια does not attain independent status in Paul either, although it does serve his objective, "to attain the imperishable wreath," which is that every person might be saved (v. 22b) and that he himself might share in the gospel's blessings (v. 23b, cf. v. 27b). In the case of the Corinthians the image of the apostle's ἀγών is intended as a motivation to behave in a corresponding fashion (v. 24b), to practice self-denial with a view toward the salvation of the weak brethren (8:11-13), and to imitate Paul in the exercise of their freedom (9:1; 10:29–11:1).

In the remaining texts in the Pauline letters using the

ἀγών word group the metaphorical character is considerably weaker. In 1 Thess 2:2 Paul uses ἀγών to recall the strenuous toil, labors (cf. v. 9), and conflicts (v. 16) which accompanied his proclamation of the gospel in Thessalonica. Phil 1:30 declares that because of the enmity which it experiences at the hands of its opponents (v. 28) for the sake of the gospel (v. 27; 4:3) the congregation in Philippi finds itself in the same situation of suffering and struggle (ἀγών) as Paul did when he proclaimed the gospel in Philippi and as he does in his present imprisonment (1:12ff.). Rom 15:30 asks of the congregation in Rome unceasing support in prayer (συναγωνίσασθαί μοι ἐν ταῖς προσευχαῖς) in view of the struggle which Paul must endure in Jerusalem prior to his planned arrival in Rome, a struggle occasioned by the animosity of the Jews and the reservations of the Jerusalem congregation regarding him and the collection which he brings. There is, then, no notion that prayer itself is an ἀγών, a wrestling with God (*contra* O. Michel, *Römer* [KEK, [14]1977] 467f.; E. von Severus, *RAC* VIII, 1281).

In Colossians ἀγωνίζομαι in conjunction with κοπιάω (1:29; cf. Phil 2:16) is intended to characterize the labor, effort, and sufferings (cf. 1:24) of the apostle which he takes upon himself for the sake of the proclamation of Christ and the winning of all humanity for Christ (1:28). His ἀγών (cf. also his imprisonment, 4:10) is also related to the Christians of Laodicea whom he does not know personally (2:1) but with whom he knows himself present and united in spirit (v. 5). The knowledge of this ἀγών of the apostle "for you" should encourage (v. 2) and strengthen (v. 5b) the congregations. In the same way and with the same intention (cf. 4:12b with 1:28; 2:2, 5b) Epaphras, the founder of the congregation, who is with Paul at the moment, prays earnestly from afar for the congregation of Laodicea (4:12: ἀγωνιζόμενος; cf. πόνος in v. 13).

If one begins from the assumption, for which there is evidence, that both Paul and Epaphras were already dead at the time of the writing of Colossians, then the recollection of the ἀγών of the apostle and the founder of the congregation takes on a special significance. Unlike 1 Cor 9:24ff. and Phil 1:30 it does not create a connection between the labors of the apostle and the experiences of the congregation, but is intended to call to mind the binding union of the post-apostolic congregations with their apostolic founders (4:12 calls Epaphras δοῦλος Χριστοῦ) and thus strengthen the congregations in their Christian existence.

Although the instances of ἀγών terminology in the *Pastorals* betray dependence upon the language of the Pauline letters (cf. 1 Tim 4:10 with Col 1:29; 2 Tim 4:7 with 1 Cor 9:24f.) and an appropriation of Pauline intentions, they nevertheless have also their own tradition-oriented character. Reference to the apostle's toils and struggles (1 Tim 4:10: ἀγωνιζόμεθα) based on hope in the living God are intended to make clear the necessity of strenuous training (γυμνασία) for godliness (→ εὐσέβεια), i.e., for the ideal Christian manner of life. Whereas the Paul of the Pastorals has "*fought* the good *fight* . . . , finished the race . . . , [and] kept the faith" (2 Tim 4:7) and awaits with confidence the victor's "crown (→ στέφανος) of righteousness" from the hand of the judge (v. 8), full responsibility for "sound teaching" now rests with his disciple and successor who is to fulfill his service in sobriety and in a commitment (vv. 1-5) which includes the readiness to suffer (v. 6).

Accordingly, in the "ordination parenesis" (Käsemann, *Versuche* I, 101-8) of 1 Tim 6:11-16 the exhortation to "*fight* the good *fight* of the faith" (v. 12) applies to the successor. It is possible that this exhortation and what follows derive originally from baptismal parenesis. We can say this because the material deals with general Christian responsibility: the faith is lived out in a context of conflict. The use of the definite article before ἀγών indicates the use of a traditional metaphor developed in the realm of Hellenistic Christianity. From the same realm of tradition comes the qualification of ἀγών as καλός (Philo *All.* ii.108; iii.48), which is intended not so much to distinguish it from the battles in the stadium as to identify it as the good and right struggle required of the Christian, appropriate to the gospel (W. Grundmann, *TDNT* III, 549f.; cf. also 1 Tim 1:18; καλὴ στρατεία), and demanded by "faith" (τῆς πίστεως is gen. of quality; for the expression cf. *Corp. Herm.* x.19: τὸν τῆς εὐσεβείας ἀγῶνα ἠγωνισμένη).

5. Like 1 Tim 6:12 and 2 Tim 4:7, Heb 12:1-3 shows itself to be an application—self-contained and independent of Paul—of the image of the ἀγών to the entire life of Christians, to which the author could resort for the composition of the introduction to his long concluding parenesis (12:1-29). The life-long task of Christians is seen as a contest set before them in which they are obliged to participate (προκείμενος ἀγών; for this expression cf. Herodotus ix.60; Philo *Agr.* 112; Josephus *Ant.* xix.92), which they are to run (→ τρέχω) with endurance (→ ὑπομόνη; cf. 4 Macc 17:12, 17), surrounded by the great company of witnesses to the faith from the OT who now become, like spectators in the stadium, witnesses of the Christians' bitter struggle for victory. As the righteous person looks to God in the ordering of his life (ἀφοράω: Josephus *Ant.* viii.290; *Ap.* ii.166), the martyr bears his torments by looking up to God (4 Macc 17:10; cf. v. 11: ἀγών), and as a mob directs its gaze toward its leader (Josephus *Ant.* xii.431; *B.J.* ii.410), so Christians, in their ἀγών, are to look to Jesus, the leader and perfecter of the journey of faith, who prevailed in his own ἀγών by enduring (ὑπομένω; cf. 4 Macc 17:10) the cross and who sits at

the right hand of the of the throne of God (Heb. 12:2). In the introduction to the following section, 12:4-11, the image of the great ἀγών required of all is carried over, but bears a different emphasis: Thus far the addressees have been spared that decisive battle in the great eschatological hour of testing (A. Strobel, *Hebräer* [NTD] 232), the struggle which requires the surrender of one's life (cf. 2 Macc 13:14): "In your struggle against sin you have not yet resisted (ἀντικατέστητε . . . ἀνταγωνιζόμενοι) to the point of shedding your blood" (12:4). In preparation for this struggle they are to submit themselves to the fatherly training and discipline of God (v. 7).

In the Synoptics ἀγών terminology occurs only in Luke 13:24: "Strive (ἀγωνίζεσθε) to enter by the narrow door." The opening of the corresponding logion in Matt 7:13f., simply "enter," is closer to the original form of Q. The Lukan formulation probably originated under the influence of the primitive Christian tradition, still recognizable behind Heb 12:1-3 and 1 Tim 6:11f., of the ἀγών of the Christian as that which leads to perfection and eternal life. One finds an analogy in the penetration of ἀγών terminology into originally Palestinian traditions (→ 3 on 4 Maccabees, 4 Ezra, and *Testament of Job*).

Jude 3, ". . . appealing to you to contend (ἐπαγωνίζεσθαι) for the faith which was once for all delivered to the saints," reminds one slightly of Phil 1:27, 30 (→ 4), but distinguishes itself through the restriction, growing out of the circumstances of postapostolic Christianity, of faith to *fides quae creditur* (→ πίστις), i.e., through the emphasis upon the character of faith as tradition. The struggle has less to do with the spreading of the gospel than with the preservation of doctrine in the face of the threat presented by Gnostic (?) heretics (Jude 4).

6. **᾿Αγωνία** *anxiety**. The Lukan Gethsemane pericope reports of Jesus: καὶ γενόμενος ἐν ἀγωνίᾳ ἐκτενέστερον προσηύχετο (22:44; with v. 43 missing from 𝔭[75] B א[a]). Originally ἀγωνία had the same meaning as ἀγών, but came to designate the emotional tension, frequently connected with anxiety, experienced before a decisive conflict (BAGD s.v.; Stauffer 140; Pfitzner 131-33; cf. 2 Macc 14:16f.; 15:9; Josephus *B.J.* iv.90; *Ant.* xi.326; the closest parallel to the phrasing of Luke 22:24 is Pap. Tebt. II, 423:13f.; Moulton/Milligan 8). Therefore ἀγωνία in Luke 22:44 should be translated as *anxious agitation* rather than "mortal fear" or "death agony."

G. Dautzenberg

ἀγωνία, ας, ἡ *agōnia* anxiety
→ ἀγών 6.

ἀγωνίζομαι *agōnizomai* struggle (in a contest)
→ ἀγών.

᾿Αδάμ *Adam* Adam*

1. Usage — 2. Adam in the NT — 3. Adam motifs in the NT

Lit.: O. Betz, *TRE* I, 414-24. — M. Black, "The Pauline Doctrine of the Second Adam," *SJT* 7 (1954) 170-79. — E. Brandenburger, *Adam und Christus* (WMANT 7, 1962). — B. S. Childs, *IDB* I, 43f. — J. Jeremias, *TDNT* I, 141-43. — P. Lengsfeld, *Adam und Christus* (*Koinonia* 9, 1965). — H. A. Lombard, "The Adam-Christ 'Typology' in Romans 5:12-21," *Neot* 15 (1981) 69-100. — J. Muddiman, " 'Adam, the Type of the One to Come,' " *Theology* 87 (1984) 101-10. — B. Murmelstein, "Adam, ein Beitrag zur Messiaslehre," *WZKM* 35 (1928) 242-75; 36 (1929) 51-86. — N. Oswald, *"Urmensch" und "erster Mensch"* (Diss. Berlin, 1970). — P. Schäfer, *TRE* I, 424-27. — H. M. Schenke, *Der Gott "Mensch" in der Gnosis* (1962). — R. Scroggs, *The Last Adam* (1966). — U. Wilckens, "Christus, der 'letzte Adam' und der Menschensohn," FS Vögtle 387-403.

1. As a proper name occurring in early Jewish and Christian sources Adam refers exclusively to the "first man" who is regarded as an historical figure and the progenitor of the human race. The usage is connected to the biblical primeval history in which for the first time Heb. *'ādām* assumes in addition to the usual generic and collective meaning of "man," "humanity" (as in Gen 1:26f.; 2:5, 7, etc.) the character of a proper name (MT Gen 4:25; 5:1-5; LXX Gen 2:16; 2:19–5:5).

2. In contrast to Jewish literature of the time (see the informative summary in Schäfer) Adam is seldom mentioned in the NT (only Luke 3:38; Rom 5:14 bis; 1 Cor 15:22, 45 bis; 1 Tim 2:13, 14; Jude 14).

The most important occurrences are found in the Pauline corpus. In 1 Cor 15:21-49 (v. 22, twice in v. 45) and Rom 5:12-21 (twice in v. 14) Paul compares Adam to Christ and contrasts them as type and antitype, as the two figures which determine the essence and history of the old and new humanity respectively. The starting point, nature, and intention of the typological correspondence is different in the two texts.

In 1 Cor 15:21f. Paul calls attention to the fateful action of Adam as the "founder" of humanity's bondage to death and stresses by contrast the significance of Christ, the "first fruits of those who have fallen asleep" (v. 20), for the resurrection of all humanity. In vv. 45-49 he replies to the question about the bodily nature of the resurrection (vv. 35f.) by referring to Gen 2:7 (ψυχὴ ζῶσα, ἐκ γῆς, χοϊκός) and describing the creaturely nature of Adam as the prototype (v. 49 alludes to Gen 1:26f.; 5:1-3) of human existence in this world. He follows this with a description of the heavenly nature of Christ (πνεῦμα ζῳοποιοῦν, ἐξ οὐρανοῦ, ἐπουράνιος), the "last Adam" and "second man," as the prototype of eschatological humanity.

In Rom 5:12-21 Paul picks up the motif, already employed in 1 Cor 15:21f., of the ominous power of death which has invaded the world through Adam and develops it further, adding references to the relationship of sin, law, and death and building it thematically into the framework of the doctrine of justification. Comparison and contrast of Adam and Christ serve here to illumine the superiority of the divine mercy and righteousness over human unrighteousness and to show that through Christ the fullness of salvation is made available.

The origin and development of this typological correlation of Adam and Christ have still not been sufficiently clarified. For that reason its relative importance within Pauline theology and its systematic evaluation remain contested. It is widely assumed that the background is to be seen in an "Urmensch" mythology current in Judaism (cf. Oswald) and Gnosticism (cf. Schenke), which Paul found in an already Christianized form in Corinth and which he then appropriated polemically and, by combining it with the apocalyptic notion of the two aeons, transformed into an historical scheme (foundational is Brandenburger 68-157; see further L. Schottroff, *Der Glaubende und die feindliche Welt* [WMANT 37, 1970] 115-36). The basis of this assumption is, however, uncertain in decisive matters of the history of religions. Still less secure is the assertion of a rabbinic Adam-Messiah typology (Murmelstein) or of an apocalyptic Son of Man tradition as a basis. The nearest thing to the Pauline contrast between Adam and Christ is the comparison attested in Jewish, Samaritan, and Christian sources of Adam with other figures of salvation history, esp. Noah (cf. E. Schweizer, *Neot* [1963] 280ff.; J. C. Lebram, *VT* 15 [1965] 199ff.; J. P. Lewis, *A Study of the Interpretation of Noah and the Flood in Jewish and Christian Literature* [1968] 46, 158ff.), who in this connection can be designated as "second Adam/man" (*'ādām hāššenî* in the Samaritan *Teaching of Marqah* iv.4, ed. J. Macdonald [BZAW 84, 1963] I, 91; II, 147).

In the remainder of the NT Adam is mentioned only sporadically. In Luke 3:38 he is listed in the genealogy of Jesus. A special relationship between Adam and Christ, similar to that in Pauline theology (according to Jeremias 141, among others) is hardly to be seen in that, however; the list extends past Adam to God. In 1 Tim 2:13f. the subordination of woman to man as a prescription of Christian community discipline is supported by referring to the precedence of Adam over Eve in creation and primeval history: Adam was created before Eve (cf. 1 Cor 11:8; on the form of the argument see Billerbeck III, 256, 645f.); not Adam but Eve sinned first (cf. Sir 25:24; *Apoc. Mos.* 11, 14; *Adam and Eve* 33; *2 Enoch* 31:6). Finally, in Jude 14 the name occurs in the description of Enoch as the "seventh" (in the generations of the primitive fathers) "from Adam" (cf. *1 Enoch* 60:8).

3. Motifs which recall the figure of Adam appear frequently in the NT (cf. Betz 416, 419ff.; Lengsfeld 30ff. on Mark 1:12f.; Luke 4:1-13; Rom 1:23; 3:23; 6:1-14; 7:7-12; 8:29; 1 Cor 11:7-9; 2 Cor 3:18; 4:4; Phil 2:6-9; 3:21). In most cases, however, we are dealing with the use of particular concepts and images from Genesis 1–3 and not with specific references to Adam himself. In other cases the points of contact do not go beyond similarities in motifs (cf. H.-G. Leder, *ZNW* 54 [1963] 188-216 for an interpretation of the Markan account of the testing of Jesus as a counterpart to the story of Adam's fall). Only in the case of Acts 17:26 does one clearly recognize that the author has Adam in mind: God, who gives life and breath (πνοή, cf. Gen 2:7) "made from one [human being] every nation of men."

B. Schaller

ἀδάπανος, 2 *adapanos* free of charge*

1 Cor 9:18, of proclamation of the gospel *free of charge.*

'Αδδί *Addi* Addi*

Proper name: Luke 3:28.

ἀδελφή, ῆς, ἡ *adelphē* sister
→ ἀδελφός 6.

ἀδελφός, οῦ, ὁ *adelphos* brother

1. Frequency — 2. Meaning — 3. The physical brother — 4. The "brothers of Jesus" — 5. "Brother" in wider and fig. senses — 6. Related words

Lit.: W. G. Birch, *Veritas and the Virgin: Jesus the Son of God and the Children of Joseph and Mary* (1960). — J. Blinzler, *Die Brüder und Schwestern Jesu* (SBS 21, 1967). — M. Bouttier, "La notion de frères chez saint Jean," *RHPR* 44 (1964) 179-90. — R. E. Brown, et al., *Mary in the New Testament* (1978) (see index). — F. V. Filson, *IDB* I, 470-72 (on the "brothers of Jesus"). — J. Friedrich, *Gott im Bruder? Eine methodenkritische Untersuchung von Redaktion, Überlieferung und Traditionen in Mt 25, 31-46* (1977), esp. 220-39. — D. J. Georgacas, *Glotta* 36 (1957) 106-8. — P. Marcel, "Frères et soeurs de Jésus," *RRef* 15/4 (1964) 18-30; 16/1 (1965) 12-26. — A. Meyer and W. Bauer, "The Relatives of Jesus," Hennecke/Schneemelcher I, 418-32. — W. Nauck, *BHH* I, 275. — L. Oberlinner, *Historische Überlieferung und christologische Aussage. Zur Frage der "Brüder Jesu" in der Synopse* (FzB 19, 1975). — R. Pesch, *Das Markusevangelium* I (HTKNT, 21977) 322-24. — J. Ratzinger, *Die Christliche Brüderlichkeit* (1960). — K. H. Schelkle, *RAC* II (1954) 631-40. — H. Schürmann, "Gemeinde als Bruderschaft," *idem, Ursprung und Gestalt* (1970) 61-73. — H. von Soden, *TDNT* I, 144-46. — E. Stauffer, "Petrus und Jakobus in Jerusalem," *Begegnung der Christen* (FS J. Karrer, 1959) 361-72. — A. Stöger, "Die brüderliche Ordnung unter Christen. Biblische Grundlegung," *TPQ* 117 (1969) 185-90. — T. Zahn, "Brüder und Vettern Jesu," *idem, Kanon* VI (1900) 225-364.

1. 'Αδελφός occurs 343 times in the NT (cf. Morgenthaler, *Statistik*): 97 times in the Gospels, 57 times in Acts, and 113 times in the seven authentic letters of Paul. Whereas in the Gospels it most often refers to physical brothers (approximately 68 times, with some transitions to a fig. sense), it is the fig. sense which predominates in the other writings.

2. In every case ἀδελφός can be translated with Eng.

brother. The brother in the narrower, literal sense is the *physical brother,* which can also include half-brothers (→ 3). From the perspective of the OT (cf. H. Ringgren, *TDOT* I, 188-93) it is the notion of the tribal kinship of all Israelites which permits the transition to the wider, fig. meaning. Thus in the NT ἀδελφός can mean *fellow kinsman* and *fellow countryman* (cf. Heb 8:11 [quoting Jer 38:34 LXX] where πολίτην is parallel to ἀδελφόν) as well as *neighbor* (cf. Jas 4:11f. where πλησίον is parallel to ἀδελφόν). The more specialized sense of *fellow Christian* in the NT corresponds to that of *fellow believer* which is attested in the OT. Analogous uses are found in secular and religious non-Christian literature (cf. Moulton/Milligan; Preisigke, *Wörterbuch*; LSJ s.v.; and above all Schelkle). Occasionally the word can also have the meaning of *friend, coworker,* or *fellow soldier,* as in the commission to the eleven disciples in the Easter appearance to the women or to Mary Magdalene (Matt 28:10; John 20:17) or in the singling-out of specific brothers (or sisters) in the Epistles (→ 5, 6).

3. Regarding physical brothers in the NT, see the relevant proper names. The references to the brothers of Judah (Matt 1:2) and Joseph (Acts 7:13, 23, 25) have to do, in part, with half-brothers; this is true in both cases in which the brothers of Herod Antipater (including the one erroneously called "Philip" in Mark 6:17 par. Matt 14:3; also Luke 3:1, 19). (On ἀδελφός as *half-brother* cf. also Mur 115:14 and 116a:8 in DJD II.)

4. Physical brothers of Jesus are mentioned in the NT in Mark 3:31f. par. Matt 12:46f. and Luke 8:19f.; Mark 6:3 par. Matt 13:55 with Luke 4:22 omitting reference to the brothers; John 2:12; 7:3, 5, 10; and Acts 1:14. On Mark 3:31f. cf. also v. 21: οἱ παρ' αὐτοῦ, *his kinfolk.* In Gal 1:19 Paul mentions "James, the Lord's brother" and in 1 Cor 9:5 "the brothers of the Lord."

Who were the physical brothers of Jesus, after all? The identification of the James mentioned in Gal 1:19 with the one named in Mark 6:3 is questionable, and the self-designation of Jude as the brother of James in Jude 1 is surely fictitious. Moreover, it is disputed whether the James and Joses mentioned in Mark 15:40 (par. Matt 27:56), 47; 16:1 are identical with those mentioned in Mark 6:3 par. Matt 13:55 (both Matthean texts have Joseph rather than Joses). Blinzler regards them as identical and views them, as well as Simon and Judas, as cousins of Jesus. Protestant research since Zahn disagrees and some recent Catholic scholarship as well (e.g., Pesch). According to Oberlinner also the pre-Markan tradition in Mark 6:3 presupposes physical siblings of Jesus who are not to be equated with the James and Joses of Mark 15:40, 47; 16:1. Stauffer regards James as a half-brother of Jesus from Joseph's first marriage, thus returning to an idea of the Greek Church fathers since the time of Epiphanius. Linguistically the idea is possible, but—as Mark uses the terms—unconvincing.

5. The Q saying in the Sermon on the Mount about "the speck that is in your brother's (= neighbor's) eye" (Matt 7:3-5 par. Luke 6:41-42) still sounds like the OT and Judaism (cf. Jas 4:11 → 2). Likewise in the Q saying of Matt 18:15 par. Luke 17:3 forgiveness in relation to the brother (= neighbor) is demanded (with a transition in Matthew to the brother in faith). Matthew can speak of the brother in the same sense in his special material (5:22-24) and in his redactional framing of a parable (18:21, 35); likewise Jas 1:9; 2:15; 4:11.

The transition to distinctive Christian usage is prepared for in the Markan tradition. According to Mark 3:31-35 Jesus declares those to be his brothers and sisters who sit about him and hear his word of proclamation and all who do the will of God (which he announces). The latter thought especially is taken up in the parallel passages, Matt 12:46-50 and Luke 8:19-21; according to Matthew only the disciples are the relatives of Jesus (cf. Oberlinner 243-47). Whoever leaves (ἀφίεναι) house, brothers, etc., for the sake of Jesus and the gospel, receives (λαμβάνειν) them anew already in this age: Mark 10:29f. par. Matt 19:29; Luke 18:29f.

According to Matt 25:40 Christ the judge identifies himself with any (ἑνί) of "the least of these my brethren." According to Friedrich 248f. the pre-Matthean tradition (Jesus?) probably spoke only about the "least" in the sense of the small and helpless. By the addition of ἀδελφός Matthew is supposed to have transformed the word of Jesus into an instruction for conduct toward members of the community. Here, then, as in 5:47; 23:8 the ἀδελφός becomes the brother in faith.

The Hebrew equivalent *'āḥ* undergoes the same transition in meaning from "neighbor" to "member of the community" in the Essene Qumran texts. The word appears most often in the sense of *rēa',* "neighbor" or "fellow countryman," or parallel to it (e.g., 1QS 6:10; CD 6:20; 7:1f.; 8:6; 19:18; 20:18). In the War Scroll it is used to differentiate ordinary priests from the chief priest (1QM 13:1; 15:4). Occasionally it means simply "someone else" (CD 14:5). But the word then becomes a specific designation for members of the community (cf. "registration among his brothers," 1QS 6:22; also 1QSa 1:18; 2:13? [see Lohse, *Texte*]). The rabbis distinguish between *rēa',* the "fellow countryman," and *'āḥ,* the "fellow believer"; the proselyte was also counted among the "brothers" (Billerbeck I, 276).

In Luke as well physical brotherhood is transcended in the direction of the kingdom of God (cf. 12:13f.; 14:12, 26). Following his post-Easter return Peter is to "strengthen" his "brethren," probably his fellow apostles in the first instance (22:32). In Acts (ἄνδρες) ἀδελφοί occurs as a form of direct address used by Christians speaking to Jews: 2:29 (cf. v. 37); 3:17; 7:2; 13:26, 38; 22:1 (as in 7:2 καὶ πατέρες); 23:1, 5, 6; 28:17 (cf. v. 21). The same is addressed to Christians by Christians in 1:16;

15:7, 13; ἀδελφοί without ἄνδρες is so used in 6:3. Here ἄνδρες ἀδελφοί is probably a hellenization of Jewish use of *'aḥênû* (cf. Billerbeck II, 766; Schelkle 636).

In Paul (and in the post-Pauline epistles) ἀδελφός occurs figuratively in four different senses. Ἀδελφός as *neighbor* still finds an echo in 1 Thess 4:6 and somewhat in Rom 14:10, 13, 15, 21 and 1 Cor 6:5; 8:11-13, although already there the meaning is Christianized: to offend the brother is to sin against Christ (1 Cor 8:12). In Rom 9:3 Paul speaks of the Israelites as his "brothers" in the sense of *fellow kinsmen* and *countrymen,* although this is now true only "according to the flesh" (RSV "by race"). The prevailing sense in Paul is that of *fellow Christian,* the foundational statement being Rom 8:29: the redeemed are conformed to Christ, the "first-born among many brethren." Frequently used in direct address is "brothers" or "beloved [by God] brothers" (1 Cor 15:58; Phil 4:1; Phlm 16; cf. Eph 6:21; Col 4:7, 9; Jas 1:9, 16; 2:5; 1 Thess 1:4; "brethren beloved by the Lord" in 2 Thess 2:13). In translating it should be carefully noted that ἀδελφοί (pl.) can also mean "siblings," i.e., "brothers and sisters" (cf. e.g., G. Friedrich, *An die Thessalonicher* [NTD 8] on 1 Thess 1:4). Finally, Paul knows and mentions by name individual coworkers (→ συνεργός) and a fellow soldier (συστρατιώτης, Phil 2:25), primarily in the prescripts (1–2 Corinthians, Philippians, Philemon, cf. Colossians) and conclusions of his letters. (For ἀδελφός as a self-designation and form of address among the soldiers of Bar Cochba cf. a letter published by B. Lifshitz, *Aegyptus* 42 [1962] 248-54).

In a difficult passage Hebrews (2:11) traces Christian brotherhood to the common descent of "the one who sanctifies" (Christ) and "those who are sanctified" from "one" (the one God, one principle, or one ancestor, Adam or Abraham?). On John 20:17 → 2. John 21:23, which is probably post-Johannine, speaks of "brothers" in the sense of members of the community. 1 John emphasizes the command of "love for the brother" (2:9-11; 3:12-17; 4:20f.); in the Gospel of John only love of the disciples for "one another" is spoken of (13:34f.; 15:12, 17). In 3 John 3, 5, 10 the command is given to welcome brothers, i.e., probably missionaries. In Revelation the "brothers" are those who confess the faith and are doomed to persecution and death (1:9; 6:11; 12:10) or the "prophets" and "witnesses" (19:10; 22:9).

6. **Ἀδελφή** *sister* occurs only 26 times in the NT. Its range of meaning and usage resembles that of ἀδελφός. Mark 10:29f. speaks of leaving behind and gaining *physical sisters* for Jesus' sake (cf. par. Matt 19:29; Luke 18:29 is different; Luke 14:26; cf. Matt 10:37, where the Q tradition is supplemented). Physical sisters of Jesus are mentioned in Mark 6:3 par. Matt 13:56 (πᾶσαι); Mark 3:32 (cf. Matt 12:47; Luke 8:19; → 4, 5). Martha and Mary (Luke 10:39f.) reappear in John (11:1, 3, 5, 28, 39) as sisters of Lazarus. Paul presupposes the fig. sense of *Christian woman* in 1 Cor 7:15; 9:5: "Do I not have the right to be accompanied by a sister as wife?" (RSV mg.; a different view is held by J. B. Bauer, "Uxores circumducere," *BZ* 3 [1959] 94-102). Phoebe (Rom 16:1) and Apphia (Phlm 2) are probably *coworkers* of Paul. In Jas 2:15 ἀδελφή is one's *neighbor.* In 2 John 13 the "elect sister" is a designation of the *congregation* from which the letter originates.

Ἀδελφότης* in 1 Pet 2:17; 5:9 designates all Christians collectively, the *brotherhood.* On "brotherhood" → φιλαδελφία.

J. Beutler

ἀδελφότης, ητος, ἡ *adelphotēs* brotherhood

→ ἀδελφός 6.

ἄδηλος, 2 *adēlos* unrecognizable, unclear*

Luke 11:44: graves; in 1 Cor 14:8: a bugle's sound.

ἀδηλότης, ητος, ἡ *adēlotēs* uncertainty*

1 Tim 6:17: *uncertain* wealth. BDF §165.

ἀδήλως *adēlōs* without certainty*

1 Cor 9:26: ὡς οὐκ ἀδήλως, not *aimlessly.*

ἀδημονέω *adēmoneō* be in distress*

Mark 14:33 par. Matt 26:37; Phil 2:26.

ᾅδης, ου, ὁ *hądēs* Hades, the realm of the dead*

Lit.: G. Beer, "Der biblische Hades," *Theologische Abhandlungen* (FS H. J. Holtzmann, 1902) 3-29. — G. A. Lee, *ISBE* II, 591f. — For further bibliography → ἄβυσσος.

1. According to the ancient oriental and Jewish view of the world shared by the NT, the realm of the dead is a part of the underworld (→ ἄβυσσος). In the NT ᾅδης occurs 10 times, 4 times in Revelation and twice each in Matthew, Luke, and Acts. Matt 11:23 par. Luke 10:15 cites Isa 14:11, 13, 15, and Acts 2:27, 31 cites Ps 16:10; in each case ᾅδης is, as in the LXX, the rendering of Heb. *šᵉ'ôl, the realm of the dead.* The lines of definition in relation to the more general concept ἄβυσσος (to Matt 11:23 par. Luke 10:15; cf. Rom 10:6f.) are just as fluid as is the case with γέεννα, the place of punishment and torment (to Luke 16:23f. cf. Matt 18:9 par. Mark 9:47f.).

Whereas in Matt 11:23 par. Luke 10:15 ᾅδης, as the correlate of οὐρανός, is apparently only an image of the monstrous abyss, in Acts 2:27, 31, where Ps 16:10 is understood with reference to Christ's resurrection, it simply stands for *death.* All remaining occurrences are shaped by the inherited ancient Jewish mythology, unquestionably most strongly in the 4 places in Revelation where ᾅδης is always connected with θάνατος. The exalted Christ possesses the keys of death and Hades (Rev 1:18; cf. ἄβυσσος in 9:1; 20:1); death (θάνατος), the rider of the pale horse, is accompanied by Hades, which should perhaps be imagined as sitting behind him (6:8). Death and Hades, both pictured in personal terms as demonic figures (cf. 1 Cor 15:26, 54-56), must surrender their dead at the final judgment (Rev 20:13), before they themselves are cast into the lake of fire (v. 14). The keys of Hades mentioned in Rev 1:18 belong to the gates of Hades mentioned in Matt 16:18: the realm of the dead is, like the heavenly city (Rev 21; → Ἱεροσόλυμα, Ἰερουσαλήμ), a walled fortress. In Jesus' parable of the rich man and poor Lazarus Hades is the place of torment (Luke 16:23) and thus, finally, identical with "hell" (→ γέεννα).

2. With the exception of Luke 16:23, Hades is viewed as a place where the dead remain only for a limited time (in addition to Acts 2:27, 31 cf. esp. Rev 20:13f.). The victory over death which God gives to Christ in his resurrection (Rom 6:9; 1 Cor 15:21, 26; 2 Tim 1:10, etc.; → θάνατος) is also the victory over Hades (Acts 2:27, 31; Rev 20:13f.); through baptism Jesus' followers participate in this victory (Rom 6:3-11; Col 2:12-15; 3:1-4). The gates of Hades (Matt 16:18) cannot terrify the one who is already a citizen of the heavenly city (to Rev 21:25-27; 22:14f. cf. Gal 4:26; Heb 12:22-24).

O. Böcher

ἀδιάκριτος, 2 *adiakritos* impartial*

Jas 3:17. F. Büchsel, *TDNT* III, 950f.

ἀδιάλειπτος, 2 *adialeiptos* unceasing*

Rom 9:2; 2 Tim 1:3.

ἀδιαλείπτως *adialeiptōs* unceasingly*

Rom 1:9; 1 Thess 1:2; 2:13; 5:17

ἀδιαφθορία, ας, ἡ *adiaphthoria* genuineness

Titus 2:7 Koine, etc. (in place of ἀφθορία), of genuineness of doctrine.

ἀδικέω *adikeō* do wrong, commit injustice
ἀδίκημα, ατος, τό *adikēma* wrong (done), misdeed*
ἀδικία, ας, ἡ *adikia* wrongdoing, unrighteousness, injustice
ἄδικος, 2 *adikos* unrighteous

1. Occurrences in the NT — 2. Meaning — 3. Usage — 4. Hellenistic Jewish tradition — 5. The Pauline writings — 6. The Lukan writings

Lit.: C. K. Barrett, "Ὁ ἀδικήσας (2 Cor 7:12)," FS Stählin 149-57. — F. Boll, *Aus der Offenbarung Johannis* (1914). — G. M. Camp and B. M. Ubach, "Un sentido biblico de ἄδικος, ἀδικία y la interpretación de Lc 16, 1-13," *EstBib* 25 (1966) 75-82. — G. Herold, *Zorn und Gerechtigkeit Gottes bei Paulus* (1973) 323-29. — P. Hoffmann, "Πάντες ἐργάται ἀδικίας. Redaktion und Tradition in Lc 13, 22-30," *ZNW* 58 (1967) 188-214. — E. Käsemann, *Commentary on Romans* (1980). — K. Koch, "Gibt es ein Vergeltungsdogma im AT?" *ZTK* 52 (1955) 1-42. — H. Schlier, *Römerbrief* (HTKNT, 1977). — G. Schrenk, *TDNT* I, 149-63.

1. Ἀδικέω occurs 28 times in the NT, ἀδικία 26, ἄδικος 12, ἀδίκως once, and ἀδίκημα 3 times. Although these occurrences are found in nearly all the NT documents (exceptions are Mark, Ephesians, Philippians, 1 Thessalonians, 1 Timothy, Titus, 2-3 John), the heaviest concentration is in the Pauline and Lukan writings (→5, 6).

2. In the literal sense ἀδικέω means *do wrong.* Since to do wrong usually means to damage the one wronged, ἀδικέω can take on, specifically in legal and commercial language, the sense of *doing damage.* Ἀδικία designates the *wrong,* the *unrighteousness,* whereas ἀδίκημα refers to the specific *wrong deed,* the *misdeed* (Acts 18:14; 24:20; Rev 18:5). Ἄδικος means *unrighteous* and the adv. ἀδίκως, accordingly, *unjustly* or *unrighteously.* The adj. ἄδικος can also be replaced by the more Hebraic gen. of quality (Luke 16:8, 9; 18:6; Jas 3:6; 2 Pet 2:13, 15; see BDF §165).

3. Subjects of ἀδικεῖν are either human beings (e.g., Acts 7:26; 25:10; 1 Cor 6:8), angels (Rev 7:2f.), demonic powers (Luke 10:19; Rev 6:6; 9:4, 10, 19), or "the second death" (Rev 2:11). The object (acc.) can be human beings or the earth or portions of the earth. Used intrans. ἀδικέω, like ἀδικία, ἄδικος, and ἀδίκημα, denotes a specific incongruity with divine or human law. The means by which damage is done is indicated by ἐν (Rev 9:19); the side from which the damage occurs is indicated by ἐκ (2:11; cf. Gen 16:5 LXX). Ἀδικία or ἄδικος can be used of human beings or things, but not of God (Rom 9:14; Heb 6:10), whose righteousness (→ δικαιοσύνη) is the opposite of creaturely ἀδικία (Rom 3:5).

4. Although ἀδικέω κτλ. occurs in nearly all NT documents (→ 1), there is—with the exception of Romans and the Lukan writings—no noticeable concentration. Apparently wrongdoing was for the majority of the NT authors not yet such an oppressive reality that they felt themselves challenged by it to provide a detailed, specifically Christian response. Accordingly, the majority of the NT occurrences are indebted to Hellenistic Jewish tradition both in terms of usage and thought.

Traditional usage is present wherever ἀδικέω is used to

designate some kind of (material, financial, or spiritual) harm: Matt 20:13; Luke 10:19; Gal 4:12; Phlm 18; Rev 2:11; 6:6; 7:2; 9:4, 10, 19; 11:5 (cf. LXX Gen 21:23; Lev 19:13; 1 Kgdms 12:4, Tob 6:15; *T. Sim.* 5:4). It remains worthy of note (in spite of Boll 87) that apart from Revelation no such accumulation of references to divinely ordered damages is to be found.

In correspondence with traditional OT and Jewish thought every ἀδικία is regarded as → ἁμαρτία ("sin"; 1 John 5:17). Ἀδικία and ἁμαρτία are thus interchangeable terms (Heb 8:12; 1 John 1:9). The same correspondence with traditional OT and Jewish thought is present when human beings are divided not only into δίκαιοι ("righteous") and ἁμαρτωλοί ("sinners"; Matt 9:13 par.) but also into δίκαιοι and ἄδικοι (Matt 5:45; Acts 24:15; cf. Prov 10:30-32 LXX; Philo *Spec. Leg.* iv.77; *T. Jud.* 21:6; Josephus *B.J.* ii.139), the only difference being that the criterion for this distinction in the late NT period is no longer the Torah, but the apostolic tradition as "the way of truth" (2 Pet 2:2) and "the way of righteousness" (v. 21). Whoever allows himself to be diverted from this way because he does not "love the truth" (2 Thess 2:10) belongs to the "unrighteous," whom the Lord will "keep . . . under punishment until the day of judgment" (2 Pet 2:9; cf. 2 Thess 2:12). Therefore, everyone who names the name of the Lord should avoid iniquity (2 Tim 2:19; cf. vv. 16ff.).

The influence of OT and Jewish thought is also present where the punishment for unrighteousness is thought of as corresponding to the unrighteous deed (see Koch), as is the case in the "household code" (Col 3:25): "For *the wrongdoer* will be paid back *for the wrong he has done,*" or when, according to 2 Pet 2:13a, the heretics will be destroyed, "suffering wrong" in recompense "for their wrongdoing" (as in most recent commentaries; the reading of the Koine text, κομιούμενοι, is an apparent softening of the rare construction ἀδικούμενοι μισθὸν ἀδικίας; cf. Schrenk 161).

The argument encountered in John 7:18 is also traditional: every ambassador who seeks the glory of the one who sent him is ἀληθής, "dependable, in order." Therefore, there is no ἀδικία in him. Finally, Jas 3:6 and Luke 16:9 point toward the sphere of OT and Jewish tradition insofar as ἀδικία can also serve as a translation for *šeqer,* "lie, deception" (LXX Pss 51:3; 118:29, 69, 104, 163; 143:8, 11). The tongue is therefore ὁ κόσμος τῆς ἀδικίας, *the world of lies and deception,* because with its lies and slanders (cf. Ps 51:3-6 LXX) it can set fire to everything (Jas 3:6). On the other hand, mammon is μαμωνᾶς τῆς ἀδικίας (*māmôn dišqar* or *māmôn šel šeqer*: Billerbeck II, 220), *mammon of unrighteousness,* since it can hardly be acquired without unrighteousness (Sir 26:29–27:2).

5. Paul goes a substantial step beyond the traditional Hellenistic Jewish understanding of ἀδικία. Hellenistic Judaism also connected ἀδικία and → ἀσέβεια ("godlessness") or contrasted ἀδικία and → ἀλήθεια ("truth") (cf., on the one hand, LXX Job 36:18; Ps 72:6; Hos 10:13; Philo *Spec. Leg.* i.215; *Praem.* 105, and, on the other, Tob 4:5f.; Ps 118:29f. LXX). But for Hellenistic Judaism ἀδικία was only *one* human possibility, out of which the ἀσέβεια originated (Philo *Conf.* 152: ". . . having sown injustice, they reaped impiety") and which is the result when a person resists the truth revealed in the Torah (cf. Tob 4:5f.; Philo *Congr.* 160: "It follows that if increased laxity is the parent of that greatest of ills, impiety [ἀσέβειαν], contrariwise affliction, regulated by law [ἡ μετὰ νόμου κάκωσις], breeds a perfect good, that most admirable thing, admonition").

Paul's conception of ἀδικία is different. For him it is identical with ἀσέβεια and represents the fundamental human attitude (Rom 1:18) which withholds praise and thanks from God the creator (vv. 21, 25), and thus—like a liar (3:7)—suppresses the ἀλήθεια. This ἀλήθεια is the reality of God clearly perceivable in the creation (1:18ff.), that which is nothing other than God's righteousness (3:3-7; → δικαιοσύνη), God's unwavering faithfulness to humanity which secures human life (vv. 25f.) and thus proves God to be the one who wills salvation. This fundamental refusal to honor God and "the law which was given to and which governs creation" (Schlier 50) has always been the essence of human ἀσέβεια and ἀδικία which now cause human thinking to become empty and futile and the human heart darkened (Rom 1:21f., 28). Its result is that human beings do "what is not permitted": works of uncleanness, desecration, and lovelessness (vv. 24-31). Human ἀδικία, then, consists in "not recognizing God in his reality that opens itself to us. Instead the latter is suppressed in rebellious opposition to the right established therewith" (Käsemann 38). Therefore → ἀγάπη ("love") does not rejoice over ἀδικία but over ἀλήθεια (1 Cor 13:6). Therefore, also, there is no ἀδικία when God, in order to reveal himself, has mercy on the one and hardens the heart of the other (Rom 9:14).

For Paul, however, ἀδικία is more than a characteristic of the individual person; it is at the same time a transpersonal reality which—like truth—can claim the person (Rom 2:8) and can thus be compared to sin. The person is removed from its sphere through baptism, which makes one a "slave of righteousness" (6:1-18). Therefore it is absurd for the baptized to seek to obtain their rights from the unbaptized, i.e., from the ἄδικοι, from ἄπιστοι ("unbelievers"; 1 Cor 6:1-6). Not that Paul thereby condemns every lawsuit, for it is not always better to suffer wrong than to take each other to court (thus v. 7). It can also be the case that wrong must be cleared up "not on account of the one who did the wrong, nor on account of the one who suffered the wrong" (2 Cor 7:12), but for the sake of another for whom the wrong under discussion can and should produce perplexity and grief (λύπη) and thus "repentance that leads to salvation" (vv. 9-13). But the place for this is within the congregation. Every attempt to seek justice from "outsiders" (1 Cor 5:13) obscures the eschatological existence of the baptized (6:1-5).

6. Besides the Pauline writings ἀδικέω κτλ. occur with remarkable frequency in the Lukan writings (ἀδικεῖν 6 times, ἀδικία 6 times, ἄδικος 5 times, ἀδίκημα twice). The reason for this is provided in Luke 13:27b (cf. Matt 7:23b): participation in table fellowship with the Kyrios is withheld from all who have done injustice. For the decisive judgment following the resurrection of the just and the unjust (Acts 24:15, 25; cf. 17:30f.) is still to come. Therefore it is essential in the life of every person to avoid the possibility of being accused from any quarter of any wrongdoing (24:20; 25:10f.), and for Luke that means any offense against existing law (ἀδίκημα), though not any dispute concerning "correct doctrine" (18:12-16; 24:20f.; 25:8, 11)!

That Luke is not thereby concerned about a superficial legalism is made clear not only by Luke 18:2 and Acts 7:23-27—that person acts rightly who fears God and cares for the neighbor in need—but above all by the manner in which he interprets the traditional expression μαμωνᾶς τῆς ἀδικίας, *mammon of unrighteousness* (Luke 16:9-11; → 4): mammon is ἄδικος—and thereby the opposite of ἀληθινόν (v. 11!)—insofar as it is unable to provide human life with any permanence. It can do this, however, when it is used for giving, for this is the reason it was entrusted to human beings. That means that whoever makes appropriate use of that which has been entrusted is faithful; the person is unrighteous, however, who thoughtlessly (cf. → φρόνιμος in 12:42; 16:8) acts in a manner inappropriate to the time.

M. Limbeck

ἀδίκημα, ατος, τό *adikēma* wrong (done), misdeed
→ ἀδικέω.

ἀδικία, ας, ἡ *adikia* wrongdoing, unrighteousness, injustice
→ ἀδικέω.

ἄδικος, 2 *adikos* unrighteous
→ ἀδικέω.

ἀδίκως *adikōs* unjustly*

1 Pet 2:19: suffering *unjustly*.

Ἀδμίν *Admin* Admin*

Personal name: Luke 3:33.

ἀδόκιμος, 2 *adokimos* not standing the test, useless*

Rom 1:28; 1 Cor 9:27; 2 Cor 13:5, 6, 7; 2 Tim 3:8; Titus 1:16; Heb 6:8. W. Grundmann, *TDNT* II, 255-60; H. Haarbeck, *DNNT* III, 808-11.

ἄδολος, 2 *adolos* honest, genuine*

1 Pet 2:2: *pure* milk.

Ἀδραμυττηνός *Adramyttēnos* pertaining to Adramyttium*

Adj. derived from the name of Adramyttium, a city on the northwest coast of Asia Minor: Acts 27:2. *KP* I, 73f. (s.v. Adramyttion); R. Harris, "Adramyttium," *Contemporary Review* 128 (1925) 194-202.

Ἀδρίας, ου, ὁ *Adrias* Adriatic*

The Adriatic Sea, including the portion of the Mediterranean Sea between Sicily and the Greek peninsula, now called the Ionian Sea: Acts 27:27. *KP* I, 76f.; *OCD* 10.

ἁδρότης, ητος, ἡ *hadrotēs* abundance*

2 Cor 8:20: the *abundant proceeds* of the collection.

ἀδυνατέω *adynateō* be powerless, be impossible

In the NT only impersonal; → ἀδύνατος 1.

ἀδύνατος, 2 *adynatos* unable, impossible*
ἀδυνατέω *adynateō* be powerless, be impossible*

1. The vb. occurs twice in the Gospels (impersonal: ἀδυνατήσει): for the believer "nothing will be impossible" (Matt 17:20); "for with God nothing will be impossible" (Luke 1:37; cf. Gen 18:14).

2. Ἀδύνατος occurs 10 times in the NT, once in each of the Synoptic Gospels, once in Acts, twice in Paul's letters, and 4 times in Hebrews. It is used 7 times as an adj., 3 times as a subst. (Luke 18:27; Rom 8:3; 15:1). Used actively it means *unable;* passively it means *impossible.*

The cripple in Acts 14:8 is *powerless* in his feet. In response to the question: "Who can be saved?" Jesus replies: Even with the greatest effort human beings cannot achieve it. God's creative grace makes possible the impossible: Mark 10:27; Matt 19:26; Luke 18:27 (cf. use of ἀδυνατέω in LXX Gen 18:14; Zech 8:6; Job 10:13; 42:2). In Rom 8:3 ἀδύνατος is explained by ἀσθενεῖν: the law *does not possess the power* to break sin. According to the Jewish view, by contrast, the words of the Torah are "health unto you," "life unto you" (*Mek. Exod.* on 15:26). Over against the weakness of the law stands the power of God for salvation (cf. 1:16).

What Rom 8:3 says about the law is applied specifically to the sacrificial cult in Heb 10:4: it is "impossible" for it to "take away sins." The constant repetition of cultic sacrifice shows its powerlessness (v. 11). Without faith no person can, according to the divine plan of salvation, please God (11:6). In the case of apostasy a repetition of repentance is impossible when one has already participated in the proffered salvation (6:4[-6]). The power of God is often emphasized in contrast to human impotency. There is only one thing God cannot do: lie (6:18; cf. Num 23:19; Titus 1:2).

In Romans ἀδύνατος is a designation for some Christians (Rom 15:1; cf. "weak" in faith in 14:1f.), those who ascetically avoid meat and wine as unclean (14:2, 14, 21) and observe certain days (v. 5). They are not to condemn the others (vv. 3f., 10), and the "strong" are not to despise them, nor force their convictions on them, nor cause them inner conflict and thus bring them to ruin (vv. 3f., 13, 15, 21). Rather the "strong" are to bear with them (15:1). Both groups are to be of one mind with each other (15:5), for both have the same Lord (14:8ff.).

G. Friedrich

ᾄδω *ą̄dō* sing*

Eph 5:19; Col 3:16; Rev 5:9; 14:3; 15:3. H. Schlier, *TDNT* I, 163-65.

ἀεί *aei* always (including the past), constantly*

Acts 7:51; 2 Cor 4:11; 6:10; Titus 1:12; Heb 3:10; 1 Pet 3:15; 2 Pet 1:12; cf. Mark 15:8 A C Koine D lat.

ἀετός, οῦ, ὁ *aetos* eagle*

Matt 24:28 par. Luke 17:37; Rev 4:7; 8:13; 12:14. T. Schneider and E. Stemplinger, *RAC* I, 87-94; H. van Broekhoven, *ISBE* II, 1f.

ἄζυμος, 2 *azymos* unleavened
→ ζύμη.

Ἀζώρ *Azōr* Azor*

Personal name: Matt 1:13f.

Ἄζωτος, ου, ἡ *Azōtos* Ashdod*

An old Philistine city (Josh 13:3) under the rule of Herod the Great from 30 B.C.: Acts 8:40. Schürer, *History* II, 108f. (and see index in vol. III); *DB* I, 1307-11; *BRL* 13-15; D. N. Freedman, *IDBSup* 71f.; *idem, ISBE* I, 314-16.

ἀήρ, έρος, ὁ *aēr* air*

Lit.: W. Foerster, *TDNT* I, 165f. — BAGD s.v. — H. Bietenhard, *DNTT* I, 449f.

According to the ancient worldview the air forms the intermediate sphere between earth and heaven (ether).

In Rev 9:2 the smoke-filled air darkens the sun. The bowl which the angel pours out into the air in 16:17 causes an earthquake which completes the destruction (E. Lohmeyer, *Offenbarung* [HNT, [2]1953] 137); originally an event associated with theophany (Isa 66:6; Exod 9:22ff.), it is interpreted then as a plague (hail: Exod 9:22ff.) by the author (H. Kraft, *Offenbarung* [HNT, 1974] 210f.). In 1 Thess 4:17 the air is the place where believers who have been caught up in the clouds meet the returning Lord, either to accompany him in his return to earth (E. Peterson, *ZST* 7 [1930] 682-702; Foerster; B. Rigaux, *Épîtres aux Thessaloniciens* [ÉBib] 548f.) or for reunion in heaven (E. von Dobschütz, *Thessalonicherbriefe* [KEK] 197-99).

In Eph 2:2 (on the worldview see J. Gnilka, *Epheserbrief* [HTKNT] 63-66; F. Mussner, *Christus, das All und die Kirche* [[2]1968] 9-39) the air (which belongs to the heavens: Mussner 16f.) is the sphere of influence of a ruler (ἄρχων τῆς ἐξουσίας τοῦ ἀέρος), of a personal, spiritual being (= διάβολος, πονηρός: 6:11, 16). This ruler appears as the aeon of this world, or, one might say, his atmosphere (air) allows the world to appear as Aeon, the god of eternity, whose false claim brings death to humankind (H. Schlier, *Der Brief an der Epheser* [[2]1958] 102f.). From the perspective of the history of religion this represents a combination of the Empedoclean and Pythagorean worldview, according to which the air is full of souls which cannot yet rise to the ethereal world (E. Schweizer, *The Letter to the Colossians* [1982] 128-34), and Jewish conceptions, according to which, among other things, the air is the abode of demons (Billerbeck IV, 516). New is "the idea of an *organised kingdom* under the *single* ruler" (Foerster 165, emphasis added), for which dualistic influence is decisive (possibly from Qumran? Cf. 1QS 3:20f.; Braun, *Qumran* I, 216f.). *T. Benj.* 3:4 (v.l.); *2 Enoch* 29:4f. (recension J); *Asc. Isa.* 10:29f.; 11:23; cf. 4:2 are probably secondary in terms of the history of the texts and traditions.

Ἀέρα δέρειν, *to beat the air* (1 Cor 9:26), refers to the inaccurate boxer (not "to shadow box"). Εἰς ἀέρα λαλεῖν *to speak into the air* (14:9) refers to glossolalia which is of no benefit to the community. Examples of use in other phrases are given in BAGD; Foerster; A. Robertson and A. Plummer, *1 Corinthians* (ICC) 196, 310; A. Otto, *Die Sprichwörter . . . der Römer* (1890) 6, 364.

To *throw dust into the air* (Acts 22:23) is an expression of furious agitation. The thought is hardly of preparation or substitution for stoning; rather of a (possibly apotropaic) gesture of horror (cf. Job 2:12; E. Haenchen, *The Acts of the Apostles* [1971] 633; H. J. Cadbury, *Beginnings* V, 269-77).

H. Merklein

ἀθᾶ *atha* (Aram.) he comes, has come

1 Cor 16:22 in D[2] L *al* lat. → μαρανα θα.

ἀθανασία, ας, ἡ *athanasia* immortality → θάνατος.

ἀθέμιτος, 2 *athemitos* unlawful, not permitted*

Acts 10:28; 1 Pet 4:3. A. Oepke, *TDNT* I, 166.

ἄθεος, 2 *atheos* godless*

Eph 2:12. E. Stauffer, *TDNT* III, 120f.; W. Foerster, *TDNT* VII, 186f.

ἄθεσμος, 2 *athesmos* unprincipled*

In the NT only subst.: evildoer (as in Philo *Praem.* 126; *Sib. Or.* v.177): 2 Pet 2:7; 3:17. A. Oepke, *TDNT* I, 166.

ἀθετέω *atheteō* make invalid, declare invalid*

1. Occurrences in the NT — 2. Meaning — 3. Ἀθέτησις

Lit.: C. MAURER, *TDNT* VII, 158f.; J. I. Packer, *DNTT* I, 74.

1. Ἀθετέω is not frequently used in the NT. It occurs twice in Mark (6:26; 7:9), 5 times in Luke (7:30; 4 times in 10:16), 5 times in Paul's letters (1 Cor 1:19; Gal 2:21; 3:15; twice in 1 Thess 4:8), and in John 12:48; 1 Tim 5:12; Heb 10:28; and Jude 8.

2. Ἀθετέω literally means to *make* something *an ἄθετον—something invalidated.* In other words, *something* which is θετός ("established")—a law, a covenant, an oath, a promise—is *made invalid, declared invalid, or nullified* (= destroyed); a similar result is achieved when consent to the thing in question is withheld (Pape, *Wörterbuch* s.v.; Maurer 158f.).

For this reason the LXX prefers to use ἀθετέω as a translation whenever the point under discussion is trespass against or abrogation of formal agreements (Deut 21:14; Judg 9:23; 4 Kgdms 18:7, 20; Isa 24:16, etc.), in which case the person or thing affected either stands in the acc. (Deut 21:14; Ps 32:10; 131:11; Isa 1:2; Jer 12:6) or can be introduced by ἐν (4 Kgdms 1:1; 3:5; 1 Chr 5:25; Lam 1:2); or εἰς (1 Chr 2:7; Jer 3:20; 5:11; Ezek 39:23).

Ἀθετέω occurs in this sense in Mark 7:9: the Pharisees and scribes *make* God's commandment *invalid* by means of their tradition; Gal 3:15: "*no one annuls even a man's will . . . once it has been ratified*"; 1 Tim 5:12: the widow who serves in the congregation and who wishes to remarry makes herself liable to the accusation of having "*violated* [her] *first pledge,*" i.e., the promise made to Christ; Heb 10:28: whoever *violates* the law of Moses dies without mercy. Mark 6:26 is also to be understood in this sense: "because of his oaths and his guests he [Herod] did not want to *break his word to her* [Herodias's daughter]."

Some NT texts have an even closer relationship to OT and Jewish thought, especially as it is shaped by the claim of the Torah (Luke 7:30; 10:16; John 12:48; Gal 2:21; 1 Thess 4:8; Jude 8). For Israel the Torah was not only the charter of the covenant (→ διαθήκη), but was at the same time the express means by which the divine will for salvation (→ νόμος) was made present. Thus whoever declared the Torah invalid or withheld consent from the prophetic proclamation in which Torah was actualized nullified God's will for salvation and in this opposition rejected God himself; cf. the free translation of Isa 24:16 MT in the LXX: ἐλπὶς τῷ εὐσεβεῖ . . . οὐαὶ τοῖς ἀθετοῦσιν, οἱ ἀθετοῦντες τὸν νόμον ("hope to the pious one . . . woe to the *nullifiers* who *nullify* the law"); similarly Jer 15:15f. LXX (MT is different): γνῶθι ὡς ἔλαβον περὶ σοῦ ὀνειδισμὸν ὑπὸ τῶν ἀθετούντων τοὺς λόγους σου ("consider that for your sake I endure the insults of those who *reject* your words").

It is from this perspective that Luke 7:30; 10:16; John 12:48; Gal 2:21; 1 Thess 4:8; and Jude 8 are to be understood. "The Pharisees and the lawyers *rejected* the purpose of God for themselves [i.e., the divine will for salvation]" by not allowing themselves to be baptized by John (Luke 7:30). On the other hand, Paul does not *nullify* or *destroy* the grace of God, since he seeks righteousness through faith in Jesus Christ (Gal 2:21). The double meaning—*to make invalid, nullify/withhold consent*—is also to be heard in 1 Thess 4:8: whoever among the baptized refuses to live a holy life (vv. 3-6) refuses to acknowledge not only a human being, but the divine calling (v. 7) and at the same time disregards the God who gives him his Holy Spirit (v. 8). As in Jer 15:15f. LXX, so in Luke 10:16 and John 12:48, human rejection is, in the final analysis, directed toward God, whereas in Jude 8 the heretics whom the author has in mind refuse to acknowledge the lordship of the Kyrios.

According to 1 Cor 1:19 (= Isa 29:14 LXX) God does not finally cause the wisdom of the wise to simply disappear (as in Isa 29:14: κρύψω) through the crucifixion of Jesus, but rather nullifies it (ἀθετήσω). In the word of the cross God gives reason a new foundation.

3. **Ἀθέτησις** *nullification, annulment** occurs only in Heb 7:18 in connection with the *annulment* of the former commandment due to its weakness and uselessness and in 9:26 referring to the *removal* of sin through the sacrifice of Jesus once and for all at the end of the age. In 7:18 the legal t.t. "declaration of annulment," frequently attested in inscriptions, shows through (cf. A. Strobel, *Hebräerbrief* [NTD] ad loc.).

M. Limbeck

ἀθέτησις, εως, ἡ *athetēsis* declaration of annulment → ἀθετέω.

Ἀθῆναι, ῶν, αἱ *Athēnai* Athens*

A city of Greece, the capital of Attica, in the Roman province of Achaia. Still in the 1st cent. A.D. Athens enjoyed a strong reputation in cultural affairs and was the classical university city. It is mentioned in Acts 17:15f.; 18:1; and 1 Thess 3:1. *KP* I, 686-701; *LAW* 372-81; *OCD* 140-42; H. Conzelmann, *Acts* (Hermeneia) 138.

Ἀθηναῖος, 3 *Athēnaios* Athenian (person)*

Adj. related to the place-name → Ἀθῆναι. Acts 17:21f.

ἀθλέω *athleō* compete in a contest*

2 Tim 2:5a, b. E. Stauffer, *TDNT* I, 167f.

ἄθλησις, εως, ἡ *athlēsis* contest*

In the NT only fig.: Heb 10:32, referring to the struggle with suffering. E. Stauffer, *TDNT,* I, 167f.

ἀθροίζω *athroizō* gather*

Luke 24:33: they found the eleven *gathered together.*

ἀθυμέω *athymeō* be discouraged*

Col 3:21: lest the children *become discouraged.*

ἀθῷος, 2 *athǭos* innocent*

Matt 27:4: "betraying *innocent* blood"; v. 24: "I am *innocent* of this righteous man's blood" (RSV mg.).

αἴγειος, 3 *aigeios* of a goat*

Heb 11:37: the prophets clothed in *goat*skins.

αἰγιαλός, οῦ, ὁ *aigialos* shore, beach*

Matt 13:2, 48; John 21:4; Acts 21:5; 27:39f.

Αἰγύπτιος, 3 *Aigyptios* Egyptian (person)

Adj. related to → Αἴγυπτος.

Αἴγυπτος, ου, ἡ *Aigyptos* Egypt
Αἰγύπτιος, 3 *Aigyptios* Egyptian (person)

1. Occurrences — 2. Historical Background — 3. Egypt in the NT — 4. "The Egyptian" in Acts 21:38

Lit.: BERGMAN, WILLIAMS, WEISS, and MÜLLER, *TRE* I, 465-533 (bibliography). — A. BÖHLIG, *RAC* I, 128-38. — C. I. DAVIES, "Tradition and Redaction in Matthew 1:18–2:13," *JBL* 91 (1971) 404-21. — H. BRUNNER, H. JACOBSOHN, and S. MORENZ, *RGG* I, 105-24, 404-21. — F. D. GEALY, *IDB* II, 67f. (on Acts 21:38). — W. S. LASOR, *ISBE* I, 248-55; II, 29-47 (bibliography). — E. PERETTO, "Recerce su Mt. 1-2," *Marianum* 31 (1969) 140-247. — REICKE, *NT Era* (index s.v.) — SCHÜRER, *History* III/1, 38-60 (and index s.v.) — E. SCHWEIZER, *The Good News According to Matthew* (1975) 40-45. — J. VERGOTE, "Egypte, Egyptenaren, Egyptisch," *Woordenboek der Oudheit* I (1976) 933-77 (bibliography). — J. A. WILSON, "Egypt," *IDB* II, 39-66.

1. "Egypt" and "Egyptian" (in the NT only as subst.) occur only 25 and 5 times respectively in the NT. Of these, the 4 occurrences of the noun in the Matthean infancy narrative are thematically related; the same is true of the 13 occurrences of the noun and 3 occurrences of the adj. in Stephen's speech and the 4 and 1 occurrences respectively in Hebrews; the remaining occurrences in Acts, Jude, and Revelation are independent of each other.

2. Αἴγυπτος as a name for the country appears from the time of Homer and can be traced back to an Egyptian designation for Memphis, *ḫikuptaḫ,* "house for the spirit of Ptaḫ" (Vergote 933). From the time of the Ptolemaic dynasty Egypt was the home of numerous Jewish emigrants, and the eastern section of Alexandria had a significant Hellenistic Jewish population. With Cleopatra Caesar took over Egypt, and as the richest country of the Roman world it remained the possession of the Julio-Claudian line, administered by a prefect from the equestrian class. Jews and proselytes from Egypt and Cyrene formed part of the environment of the Christian community in Jerusalem (Acts 2:10; cf. 6:9). There were also Christians who came from these countries (Acts 11:20; 13:1), esp. Apollos (Acts 18:24).

3. In the Matthean infancy narrative Joseph flees with Mary and the Christ child from Herod to Egypt and then returns to the Holy Land following the death of the king (Matt 2:13-23). Independent confirmation of the massacre in Bethlehem and the flight to Egypt is lacking; Matthew's Gospel is not interested in legends (such as the one about Moses in Josephus *Ant.* ii.201-31), but rather in explanations from Scripture. The reason for the short duration of the stay in Egypt is explained (Matt 2:15, citing Hos 11:1), as is the fact that Bethlehem and the surrounding area refused to be comforted, i.e., it did not receive the gospel (Matt 2:18, citing Jer 31:15).

Stephen emphasized that Joseph and Moses had experienced the revelation and the loving care of God in Egypt (Acts 7:9-40). Thus God is not to be thought of as bound exclusively to Zion, as Stephen's accusers believed (6:11, 13). In other passages the deliverance of Israel from Egypt forms the basis for admonition (Acts 13:17; Heb 3:16; 8:9; 11:26f., 29; Jude 5; cf. 1 Cor 10:1). Sporadically Egypt serves as an image for the sinful world like Sodom (Rev. 11:8) and Babylon (18:4; → Βαβυλών 2).

4. The "Egyptian" of Acts 21:38 was a prophet who *ca.* A.D. 55 wanted to capture Jerusalem from the Mount of Olives with thousands of sicarii (Josephus *Ant.* xx.169-72;

B.J. ii.261-63). He was driven away by Felix, but as late as 58 it was still believed that he would return.

B. Reicke

ἀΐδιος, 2 *aidios* eternal*

Rom 1:20; Jude 6. H. Sasse, *TDNT* I, 168; G. Delling, *TDNT* IX, 582 (l. 11).

αἰδώς, οῦς, ἡ *aidōs* modesty, respect*

1 Tim 2:9; Heb 12:28 M P. R. Bultmann, *TDNT* I, 169-71; C. E. von Erffa, *ΑΙΔΩΣ* (1937). → αἰσχύνομαι 5.

Αἰθίοψ, οπος, ὁ *Aithiops* Ethiopian (person)*

Acts 8:27 (bis), referring to the court official of the Candace who had traveled to Jerusalem to "worship" (→ προσκυνέω).

αἷμα, ατος, τό *haima* blood*

1. Occurrences in the NT — 2. OT and Jewish presuppositions — 3. Aversion to blood — 4. Blood rites — 5. Αἷμα in fig. language — 6. Reinterpretation of blood rites, esp. statements concerning the blood of Jesus Christ

Lit.: J. Behm, *TDNT* I, 172-77. — J. Bergman and B. Kedar-Kopfstein, *TDOT* III, 234-50. — F. Laubach, G. Beasley-Murray, and H. Bietenhard, *DNTT* I, 220-26. — E. Lohse, *Märtyrer und Gottesknecht* (²1963). — W. Nauck, *RGG* I, 1329f. — H. L. Strack, *Das Blut im Glauben und Aberglauben der Menschheit* (⁸1900). — J. H. Waszink, *RAC* II, 459-73.

1. The noun αἷμα occurs 97 times in the NT. Most of the occurrences are found in Hebrews and in the Synoptic Gospels (21 each), followed by Revelation (19) and the Pauline corpus (12). By far the greatest number of statements concern the blood of Jesus Christ, frequently in the context of the Lord's Supper. In addition to that, the speculations of Hebrews on the effect of the blood of sacrificial animals serve as a basis for christological statements. Nevertheless there are αἷμα-texts which are determined more by anthropology or which speak of blood in fig. speech. Behind the NT doctrine of the Lord's Supper and some statements regarding baptism stand elements of early Jewish blood rites and ancient blood symbolism.

2. All NT statements concerning the blood of animals and human beings, including the atoning blood of Jesus, belong in the context of the early Jewish and, ultimately, the common ancient conception of the power of blood, according to which it can be a danger as well as working apotropaically, protecting and propitiating. Blood is viewed as the carrier of life; the soul dwells in it (Heb. *nepeš,* Gk. ψυχή; cf. Gen 9:4; Lev 17:11, 14; Deut 12:23; *Jub.* 6:7; Josephus *Ant.* i.102, etc.). Spilled human blood cries for revenge (Gen 4:10; cf. Heb 12:24; Rev 6:10) and at the same time itself brings about the death of the murderer (Josh 2:19; 2 Sam 3:28f.; *m. Sanh.* 4:5; cf. also Matt 23:30, 35; 27:25; Acts 5:28). The murderer (Isa 59:3) and the land (Gen 4:11f.; Ezek 7:23) are "defiled" by the blood of the victim, but the blood of birth and menstruation also defiles (Lev 12; 15:19-33; *1 Enoch* 15:4; Josephus *Ant.* iii.261). The consumption of blood is strictly prohibited (Gen 9:4; Lev 3:17; 7:26; *Jub.* 6:12-14, etc.). A special method of slaughter, kosher butchering, guarantees the draining of the animal's blood (Deut 12:16, 23f.; Josephus *Ant.* vi.120f., etc.); salt draws out the blood from sacrificial meat (Lev 2:13; *Jub.* 21:11; cf. Mark 9:49 v.l.).

On the other hand, blood is used in the sacrificial cultus and in magic as an antidemonic means of purification and protection. Blood redemption and execution purify the land and the community of the stain of innocent blood which has been shed (Gen 9:6; Deut 19:13; *Jub.* 6:7f.; 7:33, etc.). Israel's sacrificial system (cf. Lev 1–7) is to a great extent based upon the atoning power of blood (Exod 29:20f.; Lev 3:2, 8, 13, etc.). The blood rite of circumcision (Exod 4:24-26) is directed against the life-threatening demons of the wedding night (cf. Tob 3:7f.). The blood practice of Passover also functions apotropaically (Exod 12:7, 13, 22f.). Moses instituted a blood covenant between Yahweh and Israel by sprinkling the altar and the people with the blood of the covenant (Exod 24:3-8). The blood of the martyrs was thought to have atoning power (4 Macc 6:29; 17:22; *y. Sanh.* 11.30c.28).

Of course, already in the OT there is a reinterpretation and relativizing of the sacrificial and blood rites: prophetic parenesis shifts the accent from the correct execution to the attitude (Hos 6:6; Mic 6:6-8; then 1QS 3:4-12; 8:3f.; 9:4f.; CD 11:20f.; 4QFlor 1:6f., etc.). Circumcision becomes an image for inner purification (Jer 4:4; 6:10; 9:25; Ezek 44:7, 9; *Jub.* 1:23; 1QS 5:5; 1QH 18:20; 1QpHab 11:13f., etc.). Conversely, Deutero-Isaiah uses the image of the slaughtered sheep for the vicarious suffering of God's Servant (Isa 53:4-7; cf. Acts 8:32).

3. Primitive Christianity shares with its Jewish parent religion the fear of and aversion to the consumption and shedding of blood. Of the four requirements of the so-called apostolic decree (Acts 15:20, 29; 21:25) three have to do with prohibitions related to blood: abstinence from meat offered to idols, from what is "strangled," i.e., not kosher (missing in the v.l. of the so-called Western text), and from *(consumption of) blood.* The regulations represent the minimal requirements of Jewish Christians which make fellowship with Gentile Christians possible. In the case of meat offered to idols (cf. 1 Cor 8:1-13; 10:14-31; Rev 2:14, 20) there is, in addition to the aversion to the contaminating consumption of blood, the fear of the heathen gods, which are thought of as demons (→ δαιμόνιον; cf. *Ps.-Clem. Hom.* vii.3, 8; ix.10; *Rec.* ii.71). A text such as Rev 16:4-7 shows clearly how deep-seated the Jewish Christian aversion to the consumption of blood was; the murderers of the saints and prophets are forced to drink the impure blood. The overcoming of the fear of meat sacrificed to idols was made possible by the Pauline doctrine of Christian freedom which is limited only by the conscience of the "weak" brother (1 Cor 8:4-13; 10:25-29).

Naturally, the prohibition against murder remained valid (Matt 5:21f.; Mark 10:19 par.; Rom 13:9; Jas 2:11).

The Western text of Acts apparently understands the prohibition regarding blood in the apostolic decree as forbidding the shedding of blood; it removes the warning against what is "strangled" (Acts 15:20, 29; 21:25 v.l.): the requirement of kosher preparation of meat no longer plays any role.

4. Corresponding to OT and Jewish tradition is the view of the NT authors that atonement for murder is possible only through the blood of the murderer. The innocently shed blood of the pious (cf. Matt 27:4) requires capital punishment (Matt 23:35 par. Luke 11:50f.; Rev 6:10; 16:4-7; 19:2). The apocalyptist threatens with death impenitent heretics who have defiled themselves through immorality and eating meat sacrificed to idols (Rev 2:14-16, 20-23). The blood of one unjustly executed comes with vengeance over those responsible for it (Matt 23:30; 27:25; Acts 5:28; cf. Rev 18:6; 1 Cor 11:27).

"According to the law" the sacrificial blood of animals is indispensable for purification; without *shedding of blood* (αἱματεκχυσία) there is no forgiveness of sins (Heb 9:22). The cleansing effects of sacrificial blood (9:7, 13; cf. 13:11) and the apotropaic power of the Passover blood (11:28) form the presupposition for the confession that the blood of Jesus cleanses his followers from sin (9:14; 13:12, etc.; → 6). As in Judaism, so also for the persecuted members of the Christian community the blood of the martyrs is viewed as a means of cleansing (Rev 6:11; 22:14); the death of Jesus can be interpreted as a baptism of blood (Mark 10:38f.; Luke 12:50).

The blood rite of circumcision, instituted by God (Acts 7:8, based on Gen 17:10; cf. John 7:22f.), was retained at first by Jewish Christianity influenced by Palestinian practice as an initiation rite for Gentile Christians (Acts 15:5; Gal 6:12f.; cf. Acts 16:1-3). Only Paul's struggle against circumcision (Gal 5:1-12; 6:12f.; Phil 3:2f.; cf. Gal 2:3-5) led to a gradual supplanting of the blood rite of circumcision by the water rite of baptism.

5. Jewish literature already emphasizes, by means of the double concept "flesh and blood," earthly humanity's transitoriness and subjection to death (Sir 14:18; 17:31; *1 Enoch* 15:4; *b. Sanh.* 91a, etc.). In the same way the NT characterizes the weakness of humanity, its limitation through death, sin, and error (Matt 16:17; 1 Cor 15:50; Gal 1:16; Eph 6:12; Heb 2:14; cf. John 1:13). By assuming αἷμα καὶ σάρξ, the elements by which humankind is destined to die, Christ becomes through his death the victor over the devil and humanity's Redeemer (Heb 2:14-17). In the Lord's Supper bread and wine are consumed as the flesh and blood of Christ (John 6:53-56; cf. Mark 14:22-24 par.; 1 Cor 11:23-27).

The experience of witnessing people bleed to death (cf. Luke 13:1) leads to the equation of blood and death, of the shedding of blood and murder (Matt 23:35 par. Luke 11:50; Mark 14:24 par.; Acts 22:20; Rom 3:15 [cf. Isa 59:7]; Rev 16:6; cf. *blood money* in Matt 27:6 and the *field of blood* in Matt 27:8 and Acts 1:19). Pilate wishes to be innocent of Jesus' *blood,* i.e., *of his death* (Matt 27:24). One is to struggle against sin *to the point of shedding blood,* i.e., *to the point of death* (Heb 12:4). *Innocent blood* (cf. Matt 27:4) must be avenged, i.e., *murder* requires atoning punishment (Rev 6:10; 19:2). The whore Babylon is drunk on the *blood* of the saints and witnesses of Jesus: Rome intoxicates itself on the *death* of the Christian martyrs (Rev 17:6). The juridical assumption of responsibility rests upon the ancient Jewish notion that, in a sense, innocently shed blood itself produces the death of the guilty (Matt 27:25; cf. Acts 20:26)—likewise the placement of responsibility upon another person (Matt 23:35; Acts 5:28; 18:6); of course the wide spectrum indicated by the texts shows that out of the magical blood curse has emerged a formalized expression. The statement of Pilate (Matt 27:24) corresponds precisely to the cry of the Jews (v. 25).

As a symbol of death blood appears in the visionary images of Jewish (*T. Mos.* 10:5; 4 Ezra 5:5) as well as Christian apocalyptic (Acts 2:19f. and Rev 16:12, based on Joel 3:3f.; Rev 8:7; 14:20). The robe of the victorious rider is stained with the blood of the defeated enemies (Rev 19:13; cf. Isa 63:1f.); water is transformed into blood (Rev 8:8; 11:6; 16:3f.; cf. Exod 4:9; 7:17-25; and, referring to the sweat of Jesus, Luke 22:44).

6. The Synoptic Gospels report that Jesus neither refused nor scolded the "woman who had suffered from a hemorrhage" (αἱμοῤῥοοῦσα: Matt 9:20), but acknowledged her faith and healed her (Mark 5:25-34 par.); here the Jewish aversion to blood is already partially overcome. Likewise the atoning and apotropaic blood rites of Judaism lose to a great degree their relevance in the NT, which follows the prophetic tradition in this respect. Forgiveness replaces blood vengeance (with Gen 4:15, 24 cf. Matt 18:21f. par. Luke 17:4). According to Acts 20:26 guilt for eternal death is for Paul blood guilt (cf. Acts 18:6; 1 Cor 11:27). Baptism is the carrying-out of capital punishment on the "old self" (Rom 6:4, 6, 8; Col 2:20; 3:3; cf. Gal 2:19).

Baptism replaces circumcision not only in missionary praxis (→ 4) but also in theological reflection; it is the "circumcision of Christ" which is not accomplished by human hands, the absolute removal of sin (Col 2:11f.). According to 1 Cor 7:19 the observance of the commandments of God surpasses the rite of circumcision in importance (cf. Gal 5:6; 6:15); the circumcision of the heart occurs in the Spirit, not in the letter of the law (Rom 2:29).

The NT interprets the death of Christ as a blood sacrifice. Jesus, at once Passover lamb (John 1:29, 36; 19:36; Acts 8:32; 1 Pet 1:19), ram (Rev 5:6, 12; 13:8, etc.), and "scapegoat" (John 1:29; cf. Lev 16:20-22), presented himself representatively as a sacrifice (Eph 5:2); he is simultaneously high priest and sacrificial animal (Heb 9:11–10:18). All the hopes which ancient piety placed in the power of sacrificial blood to cleanse and to eradicate sin reach their zenith in the NT statements regarding the blood of Jesus. The blood of Christ cleanses the conscience of dead works and thus surpasses the blood of goats and bulls (Heb 9:11-14, 25; 10:4); it justifies by purifying from sin (Rom 3:25; 5:9; Eph 1:7; Heb 9:13f.; 10:19, 29; 13:11f.; 1 John 1:7-9; Rev 1:5; 7:14; 12:11). Like the OT Mosaic covenant (Exod 24:6-8) with its "blood of the covenant" (v. 8), to which Matt 26:28 par. Mark 14:24 refer (cf. Luke 22:20; 1 Cor 11:25; Heb 10:29), the blood covenant of Jesus (1 Cor 10:16; Heb 9:15-22; 13:20) is established by means of "sprinkling" (ῥαντισμός in Heb 12:24; 1 Pet 1:2; ῥαντίζεσθαι in Heb 10:22; ῥάντισμα in *Barn.* 5:1); with his blood Christ purchased those who belong to him (Acts 20:28; 1 Pet 1:18f.; Rev 5:9; cf. Eph 2:13) and instituted cosmic reconciliation on the cross (Col 1:20).

Already in the thought world of the OT and Judaism blood and water on the one hand (cf. Exod 4:9; 7:17-25; 29:4, 20; Lev 14:5-7, 50-52; *b. Ker.* 81a, etc.) and blood and wine on the other (cf. Gen 49:11; Deut 32:14; Isa 63:1-6; Jer 13:12f.; 25:15-28; Sir 39:26; 50:15; 1 Macc 6:34; *b. Šabb.* 110a, etc.) are viewed as being related. Thus it is no wonder that the symbolic thought of the NT can experience and celebrate both in the water of baptism and in the drinking of the wine of the Lord's Supper an effective representation of the blood sacrifice of Jesus. Baptism and Lord's Supper belong together in the strictest sense (1 Cor 10:1-6; 12:13; 1 John 5:6-8). Consequently in John 19:34 they are traced, as "blood and water," to the corpse of Jesus, i.e., based on his sacrificial death; participation in this death which eradicates sin and makes life possible (cf. 1:29) comes through both the Lord's Supper (cf. 6:53-56) and baptism (cf. 3:5; 13:2-11). The death of Jesus is the drinking of wine and the baptism of blood (Mark 10:38f.; cf. Matt 20:22f.; Luke 12:50).

The theology of martyrdom can interpret the witness of blood as baptism (Mark 10:38f.; Luke 12:50); conversely, baptism is, according to Col 2:11f., the true circumcision. For this reason references to the atoning and redeeming blood of Christ find a secure place in baptismal parenesis at an early date (Heb 10:19, 22, 29; 1 Pet 1:18f.; cf. Rom 6:3; Heb 9:14).

But it is primarily in the Lord's Supper that the celebrating community is granted participation in the blood sacrifice of its Lord. The wine covenant of the eucharist (1 Cor 10:16), expressly related by the interpreting remark of Jesus to the blood shed in his death (Mark 14:24 par.; 1 Cor 11:25; cf. John 6:55f.), is the new blood covenant (cf. Heb 9:15-22; 10:29; 13:20) analogous to the old blood covenant of Exod 24:6-8 (Matt 26:28 par. Mark 14:24; Heb 9:18-22). Without need of additional atoning blood rites, the primitive community experiences in the sacramental drinking of wine the purifying power of a blood which is incomparably more effective than the blood of all sacrificial animals (Heb 9:13f.).

O. Böcher

αἱματεκχυσία, ας, ἡ *haimatekchysia* shedding of blood*

Heb 9:22. J. Behm, *TDNT* I, 176f.; H. Christ, *Blutvergiessen im AT* (ThDiss 12, 1977); B. Kedar-Kopfstein, *TDOT* III, 241-44. → αἷμα 4.

αἱμορροέω *haimorroeō* suffer from hemorrhage*

Matt 9:20: a woman who had *suffered from a hemorrhage* for twelve years. → αἷμα 6.

Αἰνέας, ου *Aineas* Aeneas*

The crippled Aeneas was healed by Peter in Lydda (Lod): Acts 9:33f.

αἴνεσις, εως, ἡ *ainesis* praise (noun)
→ αἰνέω.

αἰνέω *aineō* laud, praise*
αἴνεσις, εως, ἡ *ainesis* praise (noun)*
αἶνος, ου, ὁ *ainos* praise (noun)*

Lit.: R. Deichgräber, *Gotteshymnus und Christushymnus in der frühen Christenheit* (SUNT 5, 1967) 197-214. — J. C. Lambert and B. L. Martin, *ISBE* III, 929-31. — R. J. Ledogar, "Verbs of Praise in the LXX Translation of the Hebrew Canon," *Bib* 48 (1967) 29-56. — LSJ s.v. — J. H. Quincey, "Greek Expressions of Thanks," *JHS* 86 (1966) 133-58. — H. Ringgren, *TDOT* III, 404-10. — H. Schlier, *TDNT* I, 177f. — H. Schultz, *DNTT* III, 816f.

1. Αἰνέω occurs 8 times in the NT: 6 times in the Lukan writings (3 in Luke, 3 in Acts) and in Rom 15:11 (quoting Ps 117:1) and Rev 19:5 (cf. Ps 135:1, etc.). Αἶνος occurs twice (Matt 21:16, quoting Ps 8:3 LXX; Luke 18:43), and αἴνεσις occurs only in Heb 13:15 (cf. Ps 49:14, 23 LXX). The praise indicated by these words is consistently directed toward God (6 times τὸν θεόν; once τὸν κύριον; once τῷ θεῷ with the vb. [Rev 19:5; see BDF §187.4], similar to ἀναφέρωμεν θυσίαν αἰνέσεως . . . τῷ θεῷ in Heb 13:15; πᾶς ὁ λαὸς . . . ἔδωκεν αἶνον τῷ θεῷ in Luke 18:43; see also Matt 21:16). In this respect the NT follows the customary usage of the LXX, whereas, e.g., in the Hebrew OT *hillēl* can often refer to praise of humans. Those who praise are angels (Luke 2:13), shepherds (v. 20), children (Matt 21:16), the crowd (Luke 18:43), the disciples (19:37), the primitive Church (Acts 2:47), a healed cripple (3:8f.), the nations (Rom 15:11), the congregation (Heb 13:15), and the redeemed in heaven (Rev 19:5).

While sharing basic meanings with them, the αἰνέω word group also distinguishes itself clearly in the NT from the derivative forms → ἔπαινος and ἐπαινέω, which can be used of the praise of God as well as of human beings. Αἰνέω is used together with → δοξάζω (Luke 2:20; cf. 18:32; *Mart. Pol.* 14:3), ἐπαινέω (Rom 15:11), and εὐλογέω (Luke 24:53 A Koine lat; αἰνέω only in D it; cf. *Acts of John* 77).

2. The αἰνέω word group designates the *praise of God* from the mouth of a redeemed individual or the congregation, of the nations, or of the angels. Praise can be brought forth by joy (χαίροντες, Luke 19:37), sight of the newborn Christ (2:20), the experience of salvation (Matt 21:16; Acts 2:47; Rom 15:11; Heb 13:15), or an act of healing (Luke 18:43; Acts 3:8f.). Praise is also a response to God's action in Christ, a response which joins in the heavenly praise of God (Luke 2:13; Rev 19:5) and includes the one who praises in the praise and glorification of God that belong to him universally by virtue of Christ's salvific action (cf. Rom 15:7: ὁ Χριστὸς προσελάβετο ὑμᾶς εἰς δόξαν τοῦ θεοῦ). Praise of God expresses itself in fixed and, in part, traditional expressions of doxology and prayer (καὶ λέγοντες: Luke 2:13f.; 19:37f.; cf. Rev 19:5-8), as in obligatory praise "offered" or "given" to God (Matt 21:16; Luke 18:43). As the "fruit of the lips," confession of God's name and unceasing praise of him is the true *sacrifice of praise* (→ θυσία αἰνέσεως) of those who have been redeemed by the sacrifice of Christ. Such praise finally replaces the earlier sacrifices, including the praise offering (Ps 49:14, 23 LXX) because it is the praise of those who, since the Christ-event, are moving out of this world toward the future heavenly city (Heb 13:[12-]15; cf. A. Strobel, *Hebräerbrief* [NTD] ad loc.; O. Michel, *Hebräerbrief,* [KEK] ad loc.).

H. Balz

αἴνιγμα, ατος, τό *ainigma* riddle*

1 Cor 13:12, referring to a blurred outline (cf. Num 12:8). G. Kittel, *TDNT* I, 178-80.

αἶνος, ου, ὁ *ainos* praise (noun)
→ αἰνέω.

Αἰνών, ἡ *Ainōn* Aenon*

One of the places where John baptized: John 3:23. M. Avi-Yonah, *IDB* I, 52; Kopp, *Stätten* 166-72; R. Schnackenburg, *The Gospel according to St. John* I (1968) 412f.

αἱρέομαι *haireomai* choose, prefer*

Phil 1:22; 2 Thess 2:13; Heb 11:25. H. Schlier, *TDNT* I, 180; G. Nordholt, *DNTT* I, 533-35.

αἵρεσις, εως, ἡ *hairesis* doctrine, party, dissension*
αἱρετικός, 3 *hairetikos* heretical*

Lit.: M. Meinertz, "Σχίσμα und αἵρεσις im NT," *BZ* 1 (1957) 114-18. — G. Nordholt, *DNTT* I, 533-35. — H. Schlier, *TDNT* I, 180-85. — C. Thoma, "Das jüdische Volk-Gottes-Verständnis zur Zeit Jesu," *Theologische Berichte* III (1974) 93-117. — W. Wiefel, "Erwägungen zur soziologischen Hermeneutik urchristlicher Gottesdienstformen," *Kairos* 14 (1972) 36-51.

1. Of the 9 occurrences of the subst. in the NT, 6 are found in Acts and refer to Sadducees (5:17), Pharisees (15:5; 26:5), and "Nazarenes" (24:5, 14; 28:22). In agreement with the usage of Josephus (*B.J.* ii.118, 122, 137, 142, 162; *Ant.* vii.347; xiii.171, 288, 293; xv.6; xx.199; *Vita* 10, 12, 191, 197) and other ancient writers (Diodorus Siculus ii.29.6; Diogenes Laertius i.18f.; Epictetus *Diss.* ii.19.20), the meaning which emerges is *doctrine, school,* or *(religious) party*—without any negative connotation. The Jewish αἱρέσεις mentioned in Acts 5:17; 15:5; and 26:5 were voluntary alliances—αἱρέω, the vb. cognate with αἵρεσις, meaning to *choose*—in the Greek sense of private societies, for the purpose of an intensive occupation with the Torah (cf. the characterization of the Hasidim in 1 Macc 2:42 and of the Essenes of Qumran in 1QS 1:7, 11; 5:1, 6, 8, 10, etc.), within the people of God, i.e., "special teams for the accomplishment of certain concerns and tasks within the people of God" (Thoma 97).

Prior to A.D. 70, Jewish Christians who understood themselves to be obligated to the Torah and who participated in synagogue worship, but who had, in addition, their own assemblies with fellowship meals (cf. Acts 2:42, 46f.; Luke 4:16ff.), still had their place, as a "society of the Nazarenes" (cf. the designation of Jesus as → Ναζωραῖος in Matt 2:23), within the Jewish people of God, a people characterized by pluralism of opinion. For the author of Acts, however, Christianity is no longer an inner-Jewish party and therefore he places that designation only in the mouth of Jews.

2. For Paul as well the Church is no Jewish αἵρεσις; rather he uses the word twice in an emphatically derogatory manner: in 1 Cor 11:18f. parallel to σχίσματα to mean *dissensions, divisions* and in Gal 5:20 in a vice list ("works of the flesh") along with "plots" (ἐριθεῖαι, RSV "selfishness") and "divisions" (διχοστασίαι, RSV "dissension"). For Paul, then, αἱρέσεις are *dissensions* based on false teachings which threaten the Church's unity.

The meaning that αἱρέσεις had later in the Church, *heretical groups, sects* (cf. Ign. *Eph.* 6:2; *Trall.* 6:1; *Mart. Pol.,* epilogus alius; Justin *Apol.* i.26, 33, etc.), appears in 2 Pet 2:1, where the false prophets are said to lead into destruction through *false teaching.* The αἱρετικὸς ἄνθρωπος of Titus 3:10 is, therefore, the *heretic* who has turned aside from "true doctrine."

G. Baumbach

αἱρετίζω *hairetizō* choose*

Matt 12:18: "Behold, my servant whom I *have chosen*" begins a fulfillment quotation (cf. Hag 2:23 LXX). H. Schlier, *TDNT* I, 184.

αἱρετικός, 3 *hairetikos* heretical
→ αἵρεσις.

αἴρω *airō* lift, take, carry (away)

Lit.: BAGD s.v. — J. JEREMIAS, *TDNT* I, 185f.

The word occurs *ca.* 100 times in the NT, of which only 7 are outside the Gospels and Acts. Like Lat. *tollo* it has several meanings: 1. *lift,* 2. *take,* 3. *take upon oneself,* 4. *carry,* 5. *remove.*

1. Mark 11:23, e.g., speaks of *lifting up* in the literal sense. In the same category is *picking up* leftover pieces of bread (Mark 6:43, etc.), *carrying* a corpse (Acts 20:9), and *weighing* an anchor (27:13). In a fig. sense αἴρω also means to *raise* one's hand in taking an oath (Rev 10:5), to raise one's eyes (John 11:41) or voice (Luke 17:13; Acts 4:24), and to *hold* the soul *in suspense* (John 10:24).

2. Αἴρω can stand unemphasized in relation to another verb to designate an object which a person *takes up* as he or she commences some other action, as in, e.g., Mark 2:11f. par.; John 5:8f., 11f. ("*with* your bed"). The act of taking can receive more emphasis when it speaks of *taking along* a thing (Mark 6:8 par.), *taking* something *to oneself* (Luke 22:36), or even *fetching* something (e.g., Mark 13:15f. par.; 6:29 par.; John 20:15).

3. The disciple of Jesus is to *take upon himself or herself (and carry)* the yoke (Matt 11:29) or the cross (Mark 8:34 par.; cf. Matt 10:38 [λαμβάνω]; Luke 14:27 [βαστάζω]). On the origin and original meaning of the saying about cross-bearing see J. Schneider, *TDNT* VII, 577-79. In Mark it characterizes readiness for discipleship to the point of martyrdom and in Luke, ultimately, conduct of life which is continually (καθ' ἡμέραν in 9:23, differing from Mark at this point) oriented toward the example of the Lord who goes on before.

4. The meaning *carry* is found, e.g., in John 5:10, in this case immediately alongside *take* (→ 2).

5. The meaning *remove* occurs in the sense of a change of location in John 2:16; 11:39, 41; 19:31, 38; 20:1f., 13. In Mark 2:21 αἴρω is transitive: *tear off* (BAGD s.v. 4). According to John 17:15 the disciples are not *taken out of* the world. Evil is *removed* from the Church according to Eph 4:31 (cf. 1 Cor 5:2; John 15:2). According to John's Gospel, Jesus, as the lamb (cf. 19:36; Exod. 12:46), does not take sin(s) upon himself, but rather *takes* them *away* (John 1:29; 1 John 3:5); see Billerbeck II, 363-70; Jeremias 186.

Αἴρω can also indicate removal in the sense of *destruction* (cf. Germ. *beseitigen*). A judgment can be *declared invalid* or *annulled* (Acts 8:33 = Isa 53:8 LXX) or a statement of liabilities *destroyed* (so BAGD s.v. 4 on αἴρω ἐκ τοῦ μέσου, Col 2:14). As the flood *swept* people *away* (Matt 24:39; cf. ἀπώλεσεν, Luke 17:27), so the cry of the crowd, *"Away with him!"* demands the death of Jesus (Luke 23:18; John 19:15) or of Paul (Acts 21:36; 22:22).

Finally, αἴρω also means remove in the sense of *take away, steal,* and refers in this usage, e.g., to property (Mark 4:25), the word (Mark 4:15 par.; cf. ἁρπάζει, Matt 13:19), or the kingdom of God (Matt 21:43).

6. Meanings which cannot be classified with certainty are *withdraw* (from the bank, Luke 19:21f.) and *acquire* (by lot, Mark 15:24); cf., however, → 2.

W. Radl

αἰσθάνομαι *aisthanomai* perceive, understand*

Luke 9:45 (in contrast to ἀγνοέω). G. Delling, *TDNT* I, 187f.

αἴσθησις, εως, ἡ *aisthēsis* experience*

Phil 1:9. G. Delling, *TDNT* I, 187f.; E. Schütz, *DNTT* II, 391.

αἰσθητήριον, ου, τό *aisthētērion* sense*

Heb 5:14, referring to the capacity for moral decision. G. Delling, *TDNT* I, 187f.

αἰσχροκερδής, 2 *aischrokerdēs* repulsively greedy*

1 Tim 3:8; Titus 1:7; cf. 1 Tim 3:3 Koine.

αἰσχροκερδῶς *aischrokerdōs* in repulsive greed*

1 Pet 5:2: "Not *for shameful gain* but eagerly."

αἰσχρολογία, ας, ἡ *aischrologia* obscene speech*

Col 3:8: *abusive talk* (cf. Polybius viii.11.8; xxxi.6.4; ÄgU 909, 11).

αἰσχρός, 3 *aischros* repulsive, shameful*

1 Cor 11:6; 14:35; Eph 5:12; Titus 1:11. R. Bultmann, *TDNT* I, 189-91.

αἰσχρότης, ητος, ἡ *aischrotēs* repulsiveness*

Eph 5:4 in a list of vices (vv. 3-5; RSV "filthiness"). R. Bultmann, *TDNT* I, 189-91.

αἰσχύνη, ης, ἡ *aischynē* disgrace, (feeling of) shame
→ αἰσχύνομαι 5.

αἰσχύνομαι *aischynomai* be ashamed*

1. Occurrences in the NT — 2. Meaning — 3. Usage — 4. Ἐπαισχύνομαι — 5. Αἰσχύνη

Lit.: C. K. BARRETT, "I am Not Ashamed of the Gospel," *Foi et Salut selon S. Paul* (AnBib 42, 1970) 19-41, esp. 19-22. — R. BULTMANN, *TDNT* I, 169-71, 189-91. — C. E. FREIHERR VON ERFFA, *ΑΙΔΩΣ und verwandte Begriffe in ihrer Entwicklung von Homer bis Demokrit* (*Ph.* S. 30/2, 1937). — H.-G. LINK and E. TIEDTKE, *DNTT*, III, 561-64. — W. TRILLHAAS, *Ethik* (1970) 231-36.

1. The vb. is denominative of τό αἶσχος (see Frisk, *Wörterbuch* s.v.) and attested from the time of Homer *Od.* It occurs in the NT in Luke 16:3; 2 Cor 10:8; Phil 1:20 (all ind.); 1 Pet 4:16 (imv.); and 1 John 2:28 (subjunc.).

2. It means (like Heb. *bôš*) either *be ashamed* (mid.) or *be put to shame* (pass.; Bultmann 190; BAGD s.v.).

3. The subj. of αἰσχύνομαι is always a person (e.g., Paul in 2 Cor 10:8; Phil 1:20) or group of persons, though persons never appear as a dir. obj. (cf., e.g., Euripides *Ion* 934). Besides the absolute use (cf., e.g., Homer *Od.* xviii.12) in 1 Pet 4:16 (mid.); 2 Cor 10:8; and Phil 1:20 (pass.), αἰσχύνομαι is used with a complementary inf. (cf., e.g., Aeschylus *Ch.* 917) in Luke 16:3 (mid.) and with ἀπό with gen. (cf. Sophocles, *Lexicon* s.v.) in 1 John 2:28 (pass.; "before him" or "from him"). Use with the complementary partc. occurs first in (pseudo-)Aeschylus *Th.* 1035f. (on the difference from the inf. see Kühner, *Grammatik* II, 2, 73), but not in the NT or the papyri (see Mayser, *Grammatik* II, 1, 317), and not again until Justin *Dial.* 123.4. With the exception of Luke 16:3 the vb. is connected with a negative; the following stand as opposites: δοξάζω (1 Pet 4:16); καυχάομαι (2 Cor 10:8; cf. 7:14; Ps 96:7 LXX); μεγαλύνω (Phil 1:20; cf. J. Gnilka, *Philipperbrief* [HTKNT] ad loc.); and παρρησίαν ἔχω (1 John 2:28; cf. Prov 13:5; Phil 1:20).

The sense of *being put to shame* is here more pronounced than that of *being ashamed* (Luke 16:3; 1 Pet 4:16), which is more frequent in Hellenistic usage. When, in the conflict with his Corinthian opponents, Paul is forced to boast, he does so in the conviction that he will not *be put to shame* in such a way that he would have to be ashamed (2 Cor 10:8); always the point of his hope is that in striving for success in his efforts on behalf of Christ, nothing will cause him to be disgraced (Phil 1:20; cf. 1 John 2:28).

4. The compound **ἐπαισχύνομαι** (attested since Aeschylus; only 3 occurrences in the LXX) occurs 11 times in the NT (8 times ind., 3 subjunc.), of which 4 are in the Gospels (twice in Mark 8:38 par. Luke 9:26). It always has the subjective meaning of *be ashamed* (mid.; Bultmann 190; BAGD s.v.). Here also the subj. is always a person (Christ in Heb 2:11; God in 11:16; the Son of Man in Mark 8:38 par. Luke; Paul in Rom 1:16) or group of persons. A person is the dir. obj. in the second instance in Mark 8:38 par. Luke (cf. Xenophon *HG* iv.1.34), a thing in Rom 1:16 (the εὐαγγέλιον) and in 2 Tim 1:16 (cf. Plato *Sph.* 247c; Ign. *Smyrn.* 10:2), and a person and a thing conjoined (in classical usage only with the uncompounded forms, e.g., Thucydides iii.14.1) in the first instance in Mark 8:38 par. Luke and in 2 Tim 1:8. As in the case of the simple form, one finds, in addition to the absolute use (cf. Plato *R.* 573b [ix.2]) in 2 Tim 1:12, the complementary inf. (cf. Aeschylus *A.* 1373) in Heb 2:11 and (together with an acc. of the person) 11:16, but not the partc. (cf., e.g., Sophocles *Aj.* 1307). The vb. occurs with ἐπί and the dat. of the thing (Isa 1:29; in classical usage only with the uncompounded form, e.g., Aristotle *Rh.* i.9.20 [1367a]) in Rom 6:21 ("of which"). Ἐπαισχύνομαι is connected with a negative in only 6 places.

Ἐπαισχύνομαι plays a special role in the confessional language of primitive Christianity. It can designate the renunciation of Jesus Christ by a human being or the renunciation of a human being by the Son of Man (Mark 8:38 par.). As a fixed formula the negatived ἐπαισχύνομαι of Rom 1:16 replaces ὁμολογέω ("confess") by "emphatic negation" (E. Käsemann, *Commentary on Romans* [1980] 22; cf. 2 Tim 1:8). To confess the gospel means not to be put to shame before God and humankind and therefore to have no need to be ashamed of this gospel, no matter how offensive its form and consequence.

5. The subst. **αἰσχύνη*** is a back-formation from the vb. which corresponds roughly to τὸ αἰσχύνεσθαι (Thucydides v.9.9) and is first attested in Theognis 1272. It occurs in the NT in Rev 3:18 (nom. sg.); 2 Cor 4:2; Heb 12:2 (both gen. sg.); Luke 14:9 (μετά with gen. sg.; cf. Euripides *Fr.* 953.44); Phil 3:19 (ἐν with dat. sg.); Jude 13 (acc. pl.). As a rule it has the objective meaning of *disgrace* (Bultmann 190; BAGD s.v. 2), whereby the subjective reaction of *feeling of shame* can also be present (Luke 14:9).

2 Cor 4:2 allows of several translations (R. Bultmann, *The Second Letter to the Corinthians* [1985] ad loc.), including the subjective *(feeling of) shame* (cf. BAGD s.v. 1; von Erffa 112, 121; on the difference from → αἰδώς see Schmidt, *Synonymik* III, 536-43; Trench, *Synonyms* 66-68; R. Bultmann, *TDNT* I, 169-71). Probably, however, the renunciation of *hidden, disgraceful intentions* is meant.

Likewise the enemies of the cross of Christ seek their glory in that which *disgraces* them (before God; Phil 3:19). Christ, by contrast, despised the public disgrace of the cross (Heb 12:2). Rev 3:18 uses the image of the *shame of your nakedness* to speak about the spiritual poverty of the church in Laodicea; it would also be possible to translate the phrase as *your naked shame* (cf. Alcidamas in Aristotle *Rh.* iii.3.3 [1406a]; Sophocles *Lexicon* s.v. 2). The pl. (cf. Euripides *HF* 1423, with the commentary thereon by U. von Wilamowitz-Moellendorff [[2]1895] ad loc.) in Jude 13 can be translated *shameful deeds* or *shameless acts* (BAGD s.v. 3 or s.v. ἐπαφρίζω). Αἰσχύνη is always related to a person or group of persons. Opposites are δόξα (Luke 14:9f.; Phil 3:19; cf. Thucydides i.5.1) or παρρησία (2 Cor 3:12; cf. R. Bultmann, *The Second Letter to the Corinthians* [1985] on 4:2).

A. Horstmann

αἰτέω *aiteō* ask for, demand

1. Occurrences — 2. Usage — 3. Meaning — 4. Differences in usage — 5. Αἴτημα

Lit.: H. Schönweiss, *DNTT* II, 855-58. — G. Stählin, *TDNT* I, 191-95.

1. Αἰτέω occurs *ca.* 70 times in the NT. It is used frequently by the four Evangelists, only in 1 Cor 1:22 in genuine letters of Paul, and otherwise only in Ephesians, Colossians, James, and 1 Peter.

2. In nearly half of its occurrences αἰτέω is used in the mid. Apart from the absolute use (1 John 5:16) it can be connected with a double acc. (Mark 6:22f.), not, however, in the mid. The person to whom the request or demand is addressed can also be mentioned by means of παρά (John 4:9) or ἀπό (Matt 20:20) and that which is requested by means of an (acc. with) inf. (Luke 23:23) or a ἵνα clause (Col 1:9; BDF §155.2; 392.1c). Where that which is requested is expressed by a rel. clause, αἰτέω frequently appears in the subjunc. following ἄν (ἐάν; Mark 10:35; cf. BAGD s.v. ἄν 2).

3. "There is no striking distinction between the act. and the mid." (Stählin 192). On the distinction—not applicable to the NT texts, however (Jas 4:2f.)—between a commercial claim (mid.) and the request which does not include the idea of any return (act.) see Mayser, *Grammatik* II/1, 109f.; Stählin 192; BDF §316.2.

The basic meaning, *ask for* or *demand,* is used in a variety of ways in the NT: *ask (for)* (e.g., Matt 7:7, 8, 9, 10, 11 par. Luke); *wish for* (e.g., in Mark 6:22, 23, 24, 25 par. Matthew; Mark 10:35, 38 par. Matthew); *solicit* (e.g., Mark 15:8); *request* (Mark 15:43 par. Matthew/Luke; Acts 9:2); *demand* (Luke 12:20, 48; Acts 25:15); *insist upon* (Luke 23:23; Acts 13:28); *call for* (Luke 1:63; Acts 16:29); *beg* (Acts 3:2); *petition* (12:20); *desire* (13:21); *seek, wish to see* (signs; 1 Cor 1:22); *demand* (an accounting; 1 Pet 3:15); *pray* (1 John 5:16).

4. Paul avoids αἰτέω, with one significant exception (1 Cor 1:22; → 3). According to the Gospels Jesus never used it in connection with his own praying; they employ αἰτέω in relation to prayer only in Q material, in Matthean special material (Matt 6:8; 18:19), and in John 11:22; chs. 14–16. According to Luke 11:13 (cf. Matt 7:11), the desired gift is not simply the good, but the Holy Spirit. Matt 20:20 (cf. Mark 10:35) places the immodest wish of the sons of Zebedee in the mouth of their mother. Matt 21:22 offers a conceptual correction of Mark.

5. According to Matt 21:22 the noun **αἴτημα*** as well can be qualified (Luke 23:24; Phil 4:6; 1 John 5:15): it designates the individual *petition* and its content, the *request* as distinct from prayer as an event.

W. Radl

αἴτημα, ατος, τό *aitēma* petition, request (noun)
→ αἰτέω 5.

αἰτία, ας, ἡ *aitia* cause (noun)*
αἴτιος, 3 *aitios* guilty*

1. Occurrences — 2. Meaning — 3. Usage

Lit.: BAGD s.v. — H. Conzelmann, *Die Mitte der Zeit* ([5]1964) 128-35; cf. *The Theology of St. Luke* (1961) 137-44. — W. Radl, *Paulus und Jesus im lukanischen Doppelwerk* (1975) 252-65, 325-45. — F. Thiele and C. Brown, *DNTT* II, 137-39.

1. Αἰτία occurs 20 times in the NT, of which 8 are in the phrase δι' ἣν αἰτίαν or (2 of the 8) αἰτία(ν) δι' ἣν and a further 9 appear as a t.t. in connection with the legal proceedings against Jesus and Paul. The neut. of αἴτιος is also so used 4 times, and the masc. once in a different context, the only other use of the adj. (Heb 5:9).

2. a) Αἰτία means, first, *cause, reason, occasion.* 1) The issue in Matt 19:3 is the—sometimes ridiculous—*grounds* for divorce (cf. Billerbeck I, 312-20). 2) Αἰτία with διά in the phrase mentioned above usually has the meaning of *cause* in a general sense, whether in the context of a rel. clause (Acts 10:21; 2 Tim 1:6, 12; Titus 1:13; Heb 2:11: *therefore*) or in an indirect question (Luke 8:47; Acts 22:24: *why;* cf. also the use with ταύτην in Acts 28:20: *for this reason*). In Heb 5:9 αἴτιος designates a person as a cause, i.e., as the *originator.* 3) In Matt 19:10 αἰτία is the *issue,* how the matter stands, the *relationship* (between husband and wife).

b) Αἰτία is also a t.t. in legal language and in this case means: 1) *guilt* or *crime* (Mark 15:26 par. Matthew; John 18:38; 19:4, 6; Acts 13:28; 23:28; 28:18) and 2) *charge* or *accusation* (25:18, 27). To the first of these meanings belongs also the αἴτιον of Luke 23:4, 14, 22; Acts 19:40.

3. The primary function of αἰτία and αἴτιος in the NT is, therefore, in accounts of legal trials. Luke and John emphasize the innocence of Jesus by repeating the sentence: "I find (found) no crime in this man (him)" (Luke 23:4, 14, 22, αἴτιον; John 18:38; 19:4, 6, αἰτία; cf. Acts

13:28). On the other hand, it is surely intentional that in his version of the inscription over the cross Luke (23:38; Mark and Matthew present it differently) does not speak of an αἰτία. Moreover, that there is already here a political apologetic for Christianity is esp. clear in Acts, according to which in the case of Paul as well (as in the case of all Christians; cf. 19:40) there exists no αἰτία for legal proceedings (25:18, 27; 28:18). While the benevolent Romans recognize this, they cannot resist "the Jews"—just as in the case of Jesus (cf. 28:18f. with 3:13; 13:28).

W. Radl

αἴτιος, 3 *aitios* guilty
→ αἰτία.

αἰτίωμα, ατος, τό *aitiōma* charge*

Acts 25:7: the Jews brought "many serious *charges*" against Paul before Festus.

αἰφνίδιος, 2 *aiphnidios* suddenly*

Luke 21:34; 1 Thess 5:3, in each case referring to the unexpected in-breaking of eschatological events.

αἰχμαλωσία, ας, ἡ *aichmalōsia* captivity (in war)*

Rev 13:10a, b; Eph 4:8: *prisoners of war;* cf. Heb 7:1 v.l. G. Kittel, *TDNT* I, 195-97.

αἰχμαλωτεύω *aichmalōteuō* take into captivity*

Eph 4:8 (Ps 67:19 LXX); cf. 2 Tim 3:6 Koine. G. Kittel, *TDNT* I, 195-97.

αἰχμαλωτίζω *aichmalōtizō* capture in war*

Luke 21:24; fig. *take captive:* Rom 7:23; 2 Cor 10:5; meaning *deceive, ensnare:* 2 Tim 3:6. G. Kittel, *TDNT* I, 195-97.

αἰχμάλωτος, ώτου, ὁ *aichmalōtos* imprisoned, prisoner*

Luke 4:18 (Isa 61:1). G. Kittel, *TDNT* I, 195-97. H.-G. Link and R. Tuente, *DNTT* III, 590f.

αἰών, ῶνος, ὁ *aiōn* (span of) time, age, eternity, world

1. Occurrences — 2. Pre-Christian usage — 3. Αἰών as a time concept in the NT — 4. The idea of the two aeons — 5. Αἰών = *world* — 6. Aeon as a personified being

Lit.: J. Barr, *Biblical Words for Time* (²1969). — O. Cullmann, *Christ and Time* (1950). — G. Delling, *Zeit und Endzeit* (1970). — S. J. De Vries, *Yesterday, Today, and Tomorrow* (1975) — J. Guhrt, *DNTT* III, 826-33. — W. Harnisch, *Verhängnis und Verheißung der Geschichte* (1969) 90-106. — E. Jenni, *THAT* II, 228-43. — E. C. E. Owen, "αἰών and αἰώνιος," *JTS* 37 (1936) 265-83 (with 390-404). —H. D. Preuss, *TWAT* V, 1144-59. — H. Sasse, *TDNT* I, 197-209. — *idem, RAC* I, 193-204.

1. Αἰών appears over 100 times in the NT, in every group of NT writings, and in nearly every individual document. However, a few use it only in very specific constructions; in John and 1–2 John it appears only with the preps. εἰς and ἐκ, in Revelation only in the phrase εἰς τοὺς αἰῶνας τῶν αἰώνων, in Acts only in ἀπ' αἰῶνος, and in 1–2 Peter only in prep. phrases.

2. In Gentile pre-Christian Greek αἰών has the temporal sense of *life, lifetime, generation.* But already in Hesiod *Th.* 609 we read ἀπ' αἰῶνος, *from time immemorial.* Lycurgus 106 has εἰς ἅπαντα τὸν αἰῶνα, *forever.* Likewise the noun can designate a "long, indeterminate timespan," past as well as future. It is noteworthy that Plato in *Ti.* 37d sets αἰών, eternity, over against χρόνος, time (cf. Philo *Fug.* 57; *Leg. Gai.* 85), although for him also αἰών means *lifetime* (*Grg.* 448c; *Lg.* iii [701c]; see Barr 76). In the Hellenistic period αἰών is personified and becomes a name for God (cf. Sasse, *RAC*).

In the LXX αἰών primarily represents Heb. *ʿôlām.* The use of αἰών in Jewish Greek, influenced as it is by the LXX, is thus decisively shaped by *ʿôlām,* which basically refers to *remotest time,* both past and future. It does not, however, occur in the OT as an independent subj. or obj. The meaning *eternal* does not reside as such in the word, but is derived from construct-absolute phrases and prepositional phrases in which it is found (thus Deut 15:17: *forever, lifelong;* Isa 40:28: *eternal, imperishable*). After the time of Deutero-Isaiah *ʿôlām* becomes "the code word for God's world and for the activity of God which remains as the sole determining reality in the eschaton" (Jenni 239). In the Psalms it also refers to the religious activity and conduct of the pious and has its place—also in various stages of intensification—in liturgical contexts.

In the Qumran literature the use of the word remains completely within the bounds of OT usage, becoming, if anything, narrower. Especially striking is the frequent use in gen. constructions to indicate religious relevance, whereby quite often the thought concerns also an (eschatologically) eternal future. In 1QH 13:10; CD 2:7 *qeḏem ʿôlām* designates the *primeval time* of the decrees of God; much more frequently, however, it concerns the future *eternity*; in order to express its unending quality various forms of intensification are developed. Apparently there is no material difference in meaning between the sg. and the pl.

Incidentally, the pl. is rare in the Hebrew OT, as the pl. of αἰών is in the LXX other than in Tobit, where "the difference is a stylistic one" (Barr 70). Although the LXX can express temporal *infinity* by a simple αἰών (sg. and pl.; e.g., Ps 89:2 LXX: ἀπὸ τοῦ αἰῶνος ἕως τοῦ αἰῶνος σὺ εἶ; in v. 8, incidentally, αἰών means *lifetime*), the temporal limitations of the word are occasionally so acutely sensed that Heb. *leʿôlām wāʿeḏ* of Mic 4:5 is translated by εἰς τὸν αἰῶνα καὶ ἐπέκεινα. At the periphery of the LXX the meaning *world* appears (Wis 13:9: *course of the world*; Tob 3:2 S [13:15 S]; 13:18 B A). *T. 12 Patr.* and *Jos. As.* know αἰών primarily in a future-temporal, frequently eschatological, meaning. Josephus uses the word for *epochs* (thus *Ant.* xviii.287: τὸν μέλλοντα αἰῶνα, *in the future*); an eschatological note may sound in the words concerning the reign of the Davidic line: διὰ τοῦ παντὸς αἰῶνος, *for all time* (*Ant.* vii.385). Only in *B.J.* does Josephus use the pl.; in his later writings he used only the sg.

3. a) Reflecting normal Greek usage, the phrase ἐκ τοῦ αἰῶνος as a designation for the endless time of the past appears in the NT in John 9:32, where a negative is attached: *never before* (has one heard of the healing of one born blind). Ἀπ' αἰῶνος in Luke 1:70; Acts 3:21; 15:18 is similar; these texts speak of the announcement of eschatological salvation which God has made known *all along,* as long as there has been prophetic proclamation (thus also Acts 15:18, which is no longer part of the quotation, but a conclusion in OT language). These texts seem to be related to a train of Pauline thought in which the past is viewed as the time before the world existed (1 Cor 2:7; Col 1:26; Eph 3:9, 11); these Pauline texts speak of God's eternal decree of salvation before the world had come into existence. The negatived εἰς τὸν αἰῶνα in Mark 11:14 par. Matt 21:19 refers to the unlimited time of the future in connection with the cursing of the fig tree: *never (again);* very similar is Paul's decision in 1 Cor 8:13 *never* to eat meat if it might become a temptation for his brother; in John 13:8 Jesus is *never* to wash the feet of Peter. An eschatological reference may be included in the image of the slave who does not remain in the house *for ever* (John 8:35); clearer still from its context is John 10:38: My sheep will *never* be lost. In 14:16 the promise that the Paraclete will be with the community εἰς τὸν αἰῶνα probably refers to the temporal future of this community (similarly 2 John 2). The objection of the crowd in John 12:34 against the way of Jesus refers to the unlimited time of God's future: the Christ will remain *for ever.* It is the eschatological future, no longer bound to the world and its restrictions, which is finally meant by the promises to the believers in John 4:14, etc.; 1 John 2:17. In these cases it is, of course, the context which determines such an interpretation. This is true also for Mark 3:29 (cf. Matt 12:32; → 4b); Jude 13; 2 Cor 9:9 where explicit quotation of the OT already gives to each sentence an eschatological reference. This is likewise the case with 1 Pet 1:25 and the priestly promise according to Ps 109:4 LXX in Heb 5:6 (and the parts of Hebrews 6 and 7 which are dependent on 5:6).

b) The εἰς τὸν αἰῶνα τοῦ αἰῶνος of Heb 1:8 is also a portion of an OT quotation, but by the use of two forms of the word in a phrase bears the meaning *eternity.* The same is true for the pl. form of the same phrase which has its place in doxologies in Paul's letters, the deutero-Pauline writings, Hebrews, 1 Peter, and Revelation (Eph 3:21 has an expanded variation). Only in Luke 1:33 (referring to the Messianic reign of Jesus) and in Revelation is the use of this phrase expanded; in Revelation it designates God (4:9 etc.) and Christ (1:18)—as living *eternally*—their *eternal* reign (11:15) and that of the redeemed (22:5), but also the *eternal* torment (14:11; 20:10). The pl. is not intended to add up a number of discrete courses of time, nor is the gen. construction intended to raise them to a higher power; the structure as a whole raises the infinity of God's future to *eternity.* The same result is achieved by the simple pl. in liturgically formed sentences such as Rom 1:25; 11:36; Heb 13:8; and Jude 25 (πρὸ παντὸς τοῦ αἰῶνος καὶ νῦν καὶ εἰς πάντας τοὺς αἰῶνας for the *eternal* glory of God). Peculiar is the doxology of 2 Pet 3:18, which corresponds to Jude 25 but refers to Christ: καὶ νῦν καὶ εἰς ἡμέραν αἰῶνος; here, apparently, αἰῶνος is adjectival and means *eternal,* being therefore similar to *ʿôlām* in the Qumran literature; ἡμέρα refers to *salvation* (cf. 1:19); incidentally, the expression appears also in Sir 18:10, but probably in the sense of Ps 90:4. Also adjectival is τῶν αἰώνων in 1 Tim 1:17: "the *eternal* king" (RSV "the King of ages").

c) From the use of αἰών for *eternity* some have concluded that the eschatological future as well is temporal in nature (so Cullmann). This has been disputed on linguistic grounds (Barr). In fact, the use of αἰών to express *eternity* indicates that it is difficult to think of eternity in any way other than temporally. This is confirmed precisely by the attempts to avoid such a way of thinking of eternity, such as Mic 4:5 or Jude 25. The decisive point theologically is that "eternity" and "time" are understood as sequential possibilities for the world, and not as though they existed simultaneously. The history of the world comes from the infinity of God and moves in a temporally irreversible direction toward the infinity of God. On the other hand, however, "eternity" is not naively understood as an eternal continuation of time; the various expansions of the expression are intended to express the completely different character of eternity (cf. also Rev 21:23, 25; 22:5).

4. a) Talk of the two aeons encounters us as a new phenomenon in the NT. According to *'Abot* 2:7 Hillel spoke already about the "life of the age to come" (cf. also *1 Enoch* 48:7 with 71:15); the expression is with certainty attested for Johanan b. Zakkai and is widespread at the end of the 1st cent. A.D. (cf. Dalman, *Worte* 120-23).

b) In the Jesus tradition the idea of the two aeons is old, perhaps original. It occurs in Matt 12:32 in the Q tradition of the saying about blasphemy, in Luke 16:8; 20:34f. in L, and in Mark 10:30 par. Luke 18:30 in the Markan material (certainly the latest text; Luke 16:8 could be original). Luke 20:34f. speaks about the different character of life in *that world*; Mark 10:30 names eternal life as the gift of the *world to come*; Luke 16:8 clearly contrasts the *"sons of this world"* to the "sons of light," whereby "this world" appears qualified in a sharply negative way. Also συντέλεια (τοῦ) αἰῶνος (Matt 13:39, etc.; 28:20), *end of the age,* presupposes the two-aeon scheme.

c) Only in Paul is the phrase ὁ αἰὼν οὗτος or ὁ αἰὼν ὁ

ἐνεστώς attested, although other corresponding expressions are implied (cf. Rom 8:38; 1 Cor 3:22). In Gal 1:4 the *present age* is expressly characterized as "evil"—an analytical judgment! "The god of *this world*" closes off unbelievers to the gospel (2 Cor 4:4); the (demonic) "rulers of this age" oppose God's "plan of salvation" (1 Cor 2:6, 8), just as the thinkers "of *this* age" must give way before God's redeeming activity (1:20; 3:18).

The Pastorals follow Paul insofar as they speak only of the *present aeon* (ὁ νῦν αἰών). 1 Tim 6:17; Titus 2:12 thus simply characterize the place of the present time; 2 Tim 4:10 places the present in a characteristic contrast to the situation of Paul. By contrast ὁ αἰὼν μέλλων is attested in Eph 1:21: Christ is enthroned to reign "not only *in this age* but also in *that which is to come*"; cf. also 2:7: ἐν τοῖς αἰῶσιν τοῖς ἐπερχομένοις should be understood as referring to the *world of God to come* (the conspicuous pl. belongs to the literary distinctiveness of Ephesians). Finally, Heb 6:5 speaks of the "powers" of *the age to come* already experienced by the one who has once come to faith. This passage is particularly characteristic.

In Luke 16:8 and for Paul (cf. Phil 3:20 and esp. Gal 4:25f.) the *present world* is no longer the real world for believers. To this extent the original strict temporal distinction between the two aeons is overcome: the "aeon to come" is for the believers already present to the degree that they are no longer imprisoned by the "present aeon." It is surely also for this reason that discussion of the "aeon to come" is not found in Paul. For every Jew as well the "aeon to come" as the time and realm of God's reign has always existed, but it is not the reality of this world. For Christians, however, it has already become reality in the ministry of Jesus Christ, even though temporally, of course, they continue to live in "this world," at the end of this aeon (1 Cor 10:11 [cf. *T. Levi* 14:1]; Heb 9:26 [on the pl. cf. *T. Levi* 10:2; *T. Benj.* 11:3]). Furthermore, in the sphere of this way of thinking there is no place for authentically dualistic conceptions; God always remains Lord of this aeon as well as of the one to come (as is classically expressed in 4 Ezra 7:50). Only in its own time does the present aeon have the right to exist, and therein lies the temporal significance which αἰών has in this case also. At the same time, however, that sphere is also contemplated which is encompassed by the particular time of the respective aeons, so that one could perhaps translate αἰών with *history (Geschichte).*

5. It is possible that the perception of the world's time as being filled with the history of this world led to αἰών having the meaning *world* (as it did in the case of *ʿôlām*; cf. Sasse, *TDNT* I, 203f.; E. Jenni, *ZAW* 65 [1953] 29-35). In Mark 4:19 (par. Matt 13:22) αἱ μέριμναι τοῦ αἰῶνος are the *cares brought on by life in the world.* According to Hebrews God created the αἰῶνες (in 1:2 through the Son, in 11:3 by means of God's word). Formally the pl. is of Semitic origin; materially it designates the *sequence of worlds,* esp. perhaps the sequence of this world and the "world" to come. It thus retains here too a historical dimension (and does not refer to *levels in the structure of the world*).

6. Whether αἰών also occurs in the NT as a designation for personified Aeon-beings is debated. Only in Eph 2:2 could αἰών be so understood: "this world encountering us as a unified and personified god of eternity" (H. Schlier, *Der Brief an die Epheser* [1957] 102). But more probable is a meaning which remains within the sphere of NT usage (including that of Ephesians): *the historical realm of this world.* It is the following statement which then introduces the personal power, and a third statement, in the form of an antithesis, acknowledges this power as that which is presently at work in the unbeliever.

T. Holtz

αἰώνιος, 2 *aiōnios* eternal, everlasting*

1. Occurrences in the NT — 2. Meaning and usage — 3. "Eternal life" — 4. Phlm 15

Lit.: BAGD s.v. — L. Cerfaux, "L'Évangile éternel (Apoc 14, 6)," *ETL* 39 (1963) 672-81. — G. Delling, *Das Zeitverständnis des NT* (1940) 109f., 142-49. — J. Guhrt, *DNTT* III, 826-33, esp. 832f. — G. E. Jennings, A Survey of αἰών and αἰώνιος and Their Meanings in the NT (Diss. Louisville, 1948). — E. Lohse, D. Georgi, and H. Conzelmann, *RGG* II, 801-5. — F. Mussner, *ΖΩΗ. Die Anschauung vom "Leben" im vierten Evangelium* (MTS, Historische Abteilung, 5, 1952). — J. Nelis, *BL* 1026f. — E. C. E. Owen, "Αἰών and αἰώνιος," *JTS* 37 (1963) 265-83, 390-404, esp. 390f. — H. Sasse, *TDNT* I, 208f. — P. Stuhlmacher, *Das paulinische Evangelium.* I. *Vorgeschichte* (FRLANT 95, 1968) 210-18. — R. J. Wyatt, *ISBE* II, 160-62.

1. The adj. αἰώνιος occurs 70 times in 19 NT writings. Of these the Synoptics offer 13 instances, John 17, 1 John 6, the Pauline writings 11, and Hebrews 6. 1 Corinthians, Ephesians, Philippians, Colossians, 1 Thessalonians, James, and 2–3 John do not use the word. 43 of the 70 occurrences have the phrase ζωὴ αἰώνιος, including all of the texts in John and 1 John, but this phrase is absent from, e.g., 2 Corinthians, Hebrews, and Revelation. The following combinations, among others, also occur: χρόνοι αἰώνιοι 3 times (only in deutero- or post-Pauline writings: 2 Tim 1:9; Titus 1:2b; Rom 16:25); πῦρ αἰώνιον 3 times (Matthew and Jude); and δόξα αἰώνιος or αἰώνιον βάρος δόξης (2 Cor 4:17) 3 times. In addition to the occurrences already mentioned, αἰώνιος also appears in the short ending of Mark and in 1 Tim 6:19 v.l.

In addition to the fem. in -ος, αἰώνιος also occasionally appears in the NT, as in classical Greek, with 3 endings: 2 Thess 2:16; Heb 9:12 (see BDF §59.1).

2. Throughout the NT αἰώνιος can be rendered by *eternal.* In the LXX it often represents Heb. *ʿôlām* and thus

infuses a statement which referred originally to a distant time (→ αἰών 2) with the dimension of the "eternal." In the Greek sphere αἰώνιος can be a predicate of God or the gods (cf. Plato *Lg.* x (904a): "eternal" as distinct from the merely imperishable which had a beginning), and finally in the later Empire becomes a honorific title for the emperor (*OGIS* II, 580, 3); otherwise it is primarily used to refer to a time span of long duration.

In the NT αἰώνιος refers to: a) the eternity of God and the divine realm, b) the blessings of eschatological salvation, and c) everlasting conditions which have no beginning or end.

a) Philosophical reflections on the nature of the eternal in contrast to changeable time are not to be found in the NT (there are only hints in 2 Cor 4:18). Even the pl. χρόνοι (→ 1) can, in the context of a "revelation-formula," be combined with αἰώνιος as a paraphrase for the pl. αἰῶνες, yielding what is for the Platonist a harsh self-contradiction. Αἰώνιος as a divine predicate in Rom 16:26 (there only in the NT!) stresses rather—as often in Hellenistic Judaism—the temporally transcendent validity and authority of God's commission. The eternity of God consists in God's faithfulness, which is without beginning and end and remains unchanged throughout the changing of the times (cf. Gen 21:33 LXX). In the same way, everything belonging to the nature and sphere of God endures and is not subject to the circumstantiality of this world, e.g., δόξα (1 Pet 5:10), πνεῦμα (Heb 9:14), κράτος (1 Tim 6:16, in a doxology), σωτηρία (Heb 5:9; Mark 16 [short ending]), the abiding, heavenly οἰκία which replaces the perishable earthly body (2 Cor 5:1; cf. also Luke 16:9: αἰωνίους σκηνάς), but also *eternal* fire and judgment (cf. Matt 18:8; 25:41, 46a; 2 Thess 1:9; Heb 6:2; Jude 7). In this negative accentuation the meaning *unceasing, everlasting* comes through even more strongly than is true in cases where there is a positive stress. On the whole αἰώνιος assumes in such contexts in primitive Christianity an increasingly fixed character. By contrast 2 Cor 4:17–5:1 thoughtfully compares the coming eternal salvation in the fullness of God with the present, the visible, and the perishable. As little as Paul allows himself to be captivated by that which the eye can see, he nonetheless knows that those who believe are already now borne by the hope in God's salvation which endures, which alone matters, and which is, therefore, eternal.

b) Very closely related to the verbal relationships discussed under a) are statements containing αἰώνιος which deal with the eschatological gifts associated with God's salvation; as a rule they cannot be separated from statements dealing with God and the divine realm. To this group belong the phrase ζωὴ αἰώνιος (→ 3) and phrases which appear with increasing frequency, esp. in the later writings of the NT, such as παράκλησις αἰωνία, *eternal* (= originating from God) consolation (2 Thess 2:16); δόξα αἰώνιος (2 Tim 2:10); λύτρωσις αἰωνία, referring to the eschatologically effective redemption through Christ (Heb 9:12); αἰώνιος κληρονομία, referring to the eschatological and enduring blessing of salvation in contrast to the preliminary one of the old covenant (Heb 9:15; cf. διαθήκη αἰώνιος in 13:20 and see Gen 13:19 LXX; Exod 31:16 LXX); αἰώνιος βασιλεία (2 Pet 1:11); and finally εὐαγγέλιον αἰώνιον (Rev 14:6) referring to the eschatological proclamation of God's universally effective message of salvation for humankind prior to the judgment (see Stuhlmacher 210ff.).

c) In the formulaic expression χρόνοι αἰώνιοι (→ 1, 2a; 2 Tim 1:9; Titus 1:2b [with πρό]) αἰώνιος refers to time which has always continued (in the form of endless ages), prior to which God devoted himself to the believers; it refers, then, to the absolute priority of God's revelation (→ αἰών 3b). Similarly, in Mark 3:29b αἰώνιον ἁμάρτημα is connected, in terms of content, with the familiar and fixed expression for eternity, εἰς τὸν αἰῶνα (e.g., v. 29a); blasphemy against the Holy Spirit represents an offense which remains *for all time* unpardonable.

3. Like the subst. ζωή (→ ζάω), the combination ζωὴ αἰώνιος in the NT is most heavily concentrated in the Johannine writings (→ 1), whereas it occurs 8 times in the Synoptics and only 4 times in Paul (all the αἰώνιος texts of Romans—with the exception of the secondary concluding doxology—and Galatians).

The closest parallel to the Jewish hope for an eternal life (following the resurrection of the dead) in the aeon to come (Dan 12:2 LXX, picked up by Matt 25:46b; *Pss. Sol.* 3:12; 13:11; Wis 5:15, etc.), in which "eternal" life is the antithesis of the fragmentary and frail life of this world, is found in the Synoptic account of the rich man's question to Jesus concerning the inheritance of eternal life (Mark 10:17 par. Matt 19:16; Luke 18:18; cf. Mark 10:30 par. Matt 19:29; Luke 18:30; the secondary addition in Luke 10:25; cf. also John 5:39; Acts 13:46, 48). Here ζωὴ αἰώνιος is a summarizing and interchangeable expression for being in God's salvation, in which the pious already participate but the ultimate fulfillment of which they hope for in God's new creation (cf. also 1 Tim 1:16; 6:12; Titus 1:2a; 3:7; Jude 21).

Paul emphasizes esp. the christological foundation of the shift from death to ζωὴ αἰώνιος (Rom 5:21; 6:[21], 22). As sin leads to death, so eternal life is a free gift of God ἐν Χριστῷ Ἰησοῦ (6:23), which, like the liberation of believers from bondage to death, already operates in their lives. Ζωὴ αἰώνιος is the fruit of the Spirit (Gal 6:8) and thus confirms the authenticity of the life of those who believe. Integral to this is the knowledge that the royal reign of grace, which has eternal life as its goal, will finally reveal its superiority over sin's reign of death (Rom 5:21; cf. 2:7).

Johannine theology knows Jesus to be life itself (John 11:25; 14:6; 1 John 5:20) so that ζωή and ζωὴ αἰώνιος can be used synonymously as designations for the salvation mediated by Jesus (John 3:36; 5:24; 1 John 1:2; 5:11ff.). Every believer has eternal life and is thus within the sphere of salvation (John 3:15f., 36; 5:24; 6:40, 47; 1 John 5:13, always with ἔχειν; cf. John 4:36; 1 John 2:25; 3:15). At the same time, the believer is dependent upon the one who bestows life (John 4:14; 6:54; 10:28; 17:2), who through his blood (6:54), his "food" (v. 27), and his word (v. 68; 12:50) gives eternal life to his followers so that they need never again fear destruction (10:28). For the believer this means the renunciation of one's earthly life (ψυχή) in favor of ζωὴ αἰώνιος: only in this way will one keep one's life (12:25). On the other hand, eternal life exists already as the "knowledge" of the only true God and Jesus Christ whom he has sent (17:3).

The combination ζωὴ αἰώνιος is absent from Revelation, whereas ζωή alone (always gen.) occurs there 17 times.

4. Phlm 15 is the only place in the NT where αἰώνιος refers to a person. Paul offers Philemon his own understanding of the flight of Onesimus: Onesimus may either be released by his master in order to serve the apostle or may—after a brief "separation"—return to Philemon in order that the latter may now, precisely through the separation, keep him *forever.* This refers, first, to the future service of Onesimus (cf. οἰκέτης εἰς τὸν αἰῶνα, "a bondman for ever," Deut 15:17; cf. Exod 21:6; Lev 25:46; P. Stuhlmacher, *Philemon* [EKKNT] ad loc.); but more than that, the conspicuous use of αἰώνιος in vv. 13 and 16 makes it clear that the allusion is also to the newly attained status of brother which "remains in effect" before God, for otherwise Paul's suggestion ("perhaps," v. 15a) is left hanging in the air. After all, Onesimus was a slave for life prior to his escape.

H. Balz

ἀκαθαρσία, ας, ἡ *akatharsia* impurity
→ καθαρός.

ἀκαθάρτης, ητος, ἡ *akathartēs* uncleanness, filth

Rev 17:4 TR: a golden cup "full of abominations and filthiness of her fornication" (AV).

ἀκάθαρτος, 2 *akathartos* impure, filthy
→ καθαρός.

ἀκαιρέομαι *akaireomai* have no time (opportunity)*

Phil 4:10. G. Delling, *TDNT* III, 462.

ἀκαίρως *akairōs* untimely, unseasonable*

2 Tim 4:2. G. Delling, *TDNT* III, 462.

ἄκακος, 2 *akakos* guileless*

Rom 16:18: the *simpleminded;* Heb 7:26: Christ the high priest is "holy, *blameless,* unstained."

ἄκανθα, ης, ἡ *akantha* thorn plant*

Thorny weeds (in the field): Matt 7:16; 13:7 (bis), 22; Mark 4:7 (bis), 18; Luke 6:44; 8:7 (bis), 14; Heb 6:8. Jesus' crown of thorns: Matt 27:29; John 19:2.

ἀκάνθινος, 3 *akanthinos* thorny*

Jesus' crown of *thorns* (ἀκάνθινος στέφανος): Mark 15:17; John 19:5 (cf. *Gos. Pet.* 3:8).

ἄκαρπος, 2 *akarpos* fruitless
→ καρπός.

ἀκατάγνωστος, 2 *akatagnōstos* incontestable*

Titus 2:8: the sound, *incontestable* teaching (λόγος).

ἀκατακάλυπτος, 2 *akatakalyptos* uncovered*

1 Cor 11:5, 13: the woman who prays "with her head *unveiled*" or "*uncovered.*"

ἀκατάκριτος, 2 *akatakritos* uncondemned*

Acts 16:37; 22:25: *without a proper trial.*

ἀκατάλυτος, 2 *akatalytos* indestructible*

Heb 7:16. F. Büchsel, *TDNT* IV, 338f.

ἀκατάπαυστος, 2 *akatapaustos* restless*

2 Pet 2:14: eyes which restlessly look for sin (ἁμαρτίας).

ἀκαταστασία, ας, ἡ *akatastasia* confusion, disorder*

Luke 21:9 (tumults); 1 Cor 14:33; 2 Cor 6:5; 12:20; Jas 3:16. A. Oepke, *TDNT* III, 446.

ἀκατάστατος, 2 *akatastatos* unstable, unsettled*

Jas 1:8; 3:8. A. Oepke, *TDNT* III, 447.

ἀκατάσχετος, 2 *akataschetos* uncontrollable

Jas 3:8 C Koine 33 *pl* sy. *Mart. Pol.* 12:2.

Ἀκελδαμάχ *Hakeldamach* Akeldama*

Acts 1:19: a place in Jerusalem; transliteration of Aram. *hᵃqēl dᵉmā'* (field of blood); cf. Matt 27:8.

ἀκέραιος, 2 *akeraios* unspoiled, pure*

Matt 10:16; Rom 16:19; Phil 2:15. G. Kittel, *TDNT* I, 209f.

ἀκλινής, 2 *aklinēs* unchangeable*

Heb 10:23: hold fast the confession *without wavering.*

ἀκμάζω *akmazō* be ripe*

Rev 14:18, of the ripeness of grapes.

ἀκμήν *akmēn* (adverbial acc.) still, now as before*

Matt 15:16; cf. Heb 5:13 D. BDF §160.

ἀκοή, ῆς, ἡ *akoē* (act of) hearing, (faculty of) hearing, report, preaching
→ ἀκούω.

ἀκολουθέω *akoloutheō* follow

1. Occurrences in the NT — 2. Meaning — 3. Usage — 4. Ἀκολουθέω as a term for discipleship to Jesus — 5. Compounds

Lit.: T. AERTS, "Suivre Jésus. Évolution d'un thème biblique dans les Évangiles synoptiques," *ETL* 42 (1966) 476-512. — H. D. BETZ, *Nachfolge und Nachahmung Jesu Christi im NT* (1967). — C. BLENDINGER, *DNTT* I, 480-83. — W. BRACHT, "Jüngerschaft und Nachfolge. Zur Gemeindesituation im Markusevangelium," *Kirche im Werden* (ed. J. Hainz; 1976) 143-65. — H. FRANKEMÖLLE, *Jahwebund und Kirche Christi* (1974) esp. 84-158 (on Matthew). — M. H. FRANZMAN, *Follow Me. Discipleship According to Saint Matthew* (1961). — A. FUCHS, *Sprachliche Untersuchungen zu Mt und Lk* (1971) 63-83. — F. HAHN, "Pre-Easter Discipleship," F. Hahn, G. Strobel, and E. Schweizer, *The Beginnings of the Church in the NT* (1970) 9-39. — *idem,* "Die Jüngerberufung Joh 1, 35-51," FS Schnackenburg 172-90. — M. HENGEL, *The Charismatic Leader and His Followers* (1981). — G. KITTEL, *TDNT* I, 210-16. — U. LUZ, "Die Jünger im Matthäusevangelium," *ZNW* 62 (1971) 141-71. — D. K. MCKIM, *ISBE* II, 32f. — H. MERKLEIN, "Der Jüngerkreis Jesu," *Die Aktion Jesu und die Re-Aktion der Kirche* (ed. K. Müller; 1972) 65-100. — E. NEUHÄUSLER, *Anspruch und Antwort Gottes* (1962) 186-214. — K.-G. REPLOH, *Markus, Lehrer der Gemeinde* (1969). — J. SCHMID, *Lukas* (RNT, ⁴1960) 178-82. — R. SCHNACKENBURG, "The Imitation of Christ," Schnackenburg I, 99-127. — A. SCHULZ, *Nachfolgen und Nachahmen* (1962). — E. SCHWEIZER, *Erniedrigung und Erhöhung bei Jesus und seinen Nachfolgern* (²1962) 7-21. — G. THEISSEN, " 'Wir haben alles verlassen' (Mc. X 28)," *NovT* 19 (1977) 161-96. —H. ZIMMERMANN, "Christus nachfolgen. Eine Studie zu den Nachfolge-Worten der synopt. Evv.," *TGl* 53 (1963) 241-55.

1. Of 90 occurrences in the NT only 11 are found outside the Gospels (4 in Acts, 6 in Revelation, and 1 in 1 Cor 10:4). In the Gospels ἀκολουθέω stands primarily as a term for discipleship to Jesus (→ 4). Apart from the Gospels only Rev 14:4; 19:14 speak of Christ (as "the Lamb" or the victorious "King of kings"). Altogether 73 of the 90 occurrences of the vb. refer to being a disciple of Jesus (or Christ).

2. The vb. literally means *follow* (Germ. *folgen*), go behind someone, and also bears the fig. sense of *follow as a disciple* (*nachfolgen*; Kittel 210; BAGD s.v.). In the NT both meanings are used with Jesus as the obj., e.g., when it is said that the crowd *followed* Jesus and, on the other hand, that the disciples *followed* Jesus. Other objects of the vb. rarely occur (→ 3). Following in the literal secular sense is mentioned in Mark 11:9 par. Matthew; Mark 14:13 par. Luke; Matt 9:19; John 11:31; 20:6.

3. Subjects of ἀκολουθεῖν normally are persons; an exception is Rev 14:13: the "deeds" of those who have died in the Lord "follow them" (cf. Diodorus Siculus xiii.105.4: "reproach" follows behind). The obj. of ἀκολουθεῖν is always a person or group of persons. This is also the case where no object is expressed, which is esp. the case with the partc. (Matt 8:10; Mark 3:7; 10:32; 11:9 par Matt 21:9; Luke 9:49; 22:54; John 1:38; 21:20; Acts 12:9; 21:36; 1 Cor 10:4; Rev 14:8). The one who is followed stands in the dat. (cf. Xenophon *HG* v.2.26; Ign. *Phld.* 11:1; *Herm. Vis.* iii.8.4, 7). The Hebraicized ἀκολουθέω ὀπίσω with gen. can also be used (Mark 8:34; Matt 10:38 [cf. Luke 14:27]); perhaps ἔρχομαι ὀπίσω with gen. (cf. Heb. *hālaḵ 'aḥᵃrê* in 1 Kgs 19:20 [represented by ἀκολουθεῖν ὀπίσω in 3 Kgdms 19:20]; Isa 45:14; Ezek 29:16) serves here as a basis (cf. Matt 16:24; Luke 9:23; 14:27). The combination of ἀκολουθέω and μετά with gen. (Thucydides vii.57.9; Plato *La.* 187e; BDF §193.1) appears in the NT only in Rev 6:8; 14:13 (μεθ' ἡμῶν in Luke 9:49 does not indicate the object of the following).

Two groups of statements dealing with following Jesus must be distinguished. Only in the case of the *disciples* can one speak of following *(Nachfolge)* in the truest sense (cf. Diogenes Laertius ix.21); the *crowd* follows *(folgen)* Jesus on his way for a time but does not as a whole take on following as disciples (*Nachfolge*; Mark 2:15; 3:7 par. Matthew; 5:24; 11:9 par. Matthew; Matt 8:1, 10 par. Luke; Matt 12:15; 14:13 par. Luke; Matt 19:2; 20:29; Luke 23:27; John 6:2). In both cases what is meant is a physical following, that they go along behind Jesus, but the disciples' following possesses a special quality (→ 4).

In the Gospels ἀκολουθέω is always related to Jesus as the object of following in discipleship (exceptions: Mark 9:38; 14:13 par. Luke 22:10; Matt 9:19; John 11:31; 20:6). It is striking that the idea of following as a disciple never in the NT has God as the object (in contrast to the OT; see

Kittel 211-13). The more general meaning of *join, obey, be led by* (cf. LSJ s.v. II; BAGD s.v. 4) does not occur in the NT. It is first attested in the Apostolic Fathers (objects are: habits in *Diog.* 5:4; the requirements of the Lord in *1 Clem.* 40:4; the way of truth in *1 Clem.* 35:5; cf. *T. Ash.* 6:1).

The following subjects and objects of the action of following are mentioned in the NT outside the Gospels: Peter *follows* an angel out of prison (Acts 12:8f.); receptive Jews *follow (go with)* Paul and Barnabas (13:43); the crowd *follows (presses)* at the arrest of Paul (21:36); the "supernatural rock," Christ, was *followed* during the crossing of the wilderness (1 Cor 10:4); in the vision of the seer "Hades," the ruler of the kingdom of the dead, *follows* "Death" (Rev 6:8); the chaste *follow* the "Lamb" wherever it goes (14:4; cf. John 1:36f.; 12:26); the three warning angels *follow* each other, i.e., they appear one after the other (Rev 14:8f.); those who died in the Lord are *followed* by "their deeds," i.e., probably the fruit of their tribulation from which they are now allowed to rest (v. 13); the heavenly hosts *follow* Christ, the rider on the white horse (19:14). Only Rev 11:4 speaks explicitly of being a disciple of Christ (not of the "earthly" Jesus), and is probably the basis for the Johannine image of the good shepherd (John 10:4, 5, 27). To be a follower of Christ now means to hear Christ's word (10:27).

4. One group of Q sayings mentions the conditions for being a disciple of Jesus (Luke 9:57-62 par. Matt 8:19-22). In each case the words of Jesus are understood as a reply to one who is willing to become a disciple. The first man affirms that he wishes to follow Jesus wherever he goes. Jesus' answer clearly warns of the homelessness of the Son of Man. The second is prepared to follow the call of Jesus but wishes to bury his father first. Jesus forbids him this: "Leave the dead to bury their own dead." The third (only Luke 9:61f.) wishes to say farewell to his family before beginning his discipleship. Jesus criticizes this intention with the saying: "No one who puts his hand to the plow and looks back is fit for the kingdom of God." The discipleship into which Jesus summons persons thus demands a break with custom and piety, with law and family. Behind the demand of Jesus stands the unique authority of the one who announces the imminent kingdom of God (Hengel 15). The conceptual background is not the figure of the rabbinical teacher whom the student joins (*contra* Schulz), but that of the eschatological-charismatic prophet (Hengel, ch. III). Behind Luke 9:57-62 par. Matt 8:19-22 (and Mark 1:16-18) stands the call of Elisha to be a disciple of Elijah (1 Kgs 19:19-21).

Whereas the group of Q sayings just mentioned employs ἀκολουθέω as a t.t. for being a disciple of Jesus, one finds in the saying about cross-bearing (Luke 14:27) the expression "whoever . . . come[s] after me." However, the parallel in Matt 10:38 has ἀκολουθεῖ ὀπίσω μου and could therefore represent the Q version. The saying about cross-bearing is also found in the Markan tradition (Mark 8:34 par. Matt 16:24; Luke 9:23). Here Matthew and Luke have: "If any man would come after me" (ἐλθεῖν and ἔρχεσθαι); Mark 8:34, on the other hand, reads: "If any man would *follow* [RSV come] after me" (ἀκολουθεῖν, 𝔭[45] C* Koine D W Θ). The catchword ἀκολουθέω is picked up again at the end of the main clause: καὶ ἀκολουθείτω μοι. In Q the saying about cross-bearing is preceded by the saying about breaking with the family (Luke 14:26 par. Matt 10:37). That the one desiring to be a disciple should hate family members and be prepared for crucifixion is a requirement of the same eschatological situation. It is the readiness for martyrdom as a condition for discipleship which clearly distinguishes the disciples of Jesus from other "disciples/students."

In Mark that the great multitude "follows" is mentioned (intentionally) only in the period in which Jesus' ministry is beginning in Galilee (3:7; 5:24). In the paradigmatic account of the calling of the first disciples, the initiative originates entirely with Jesus' authoritative summons and his assurance: "Follow me, and I will make you become fishers of men" (1:17). The discipleship to which Jesus calls stands finally then in the service of missionary proclamation. Ἀκολουθεῖν occurs first in the notice that the summons was obeyed: "And immediately they left their nets and *followed* him" (v. 18; that discipleship involves leaving work immediately [εὐθέως] is emphasized in the Elisha episode in Josephus *Ant.* viii.354, which differs from 3 Kgdms 19:20f.).

In the calling of Levi (Mark 2:14) the special use of ἀκολουθέω for discipleship to Jesus (ἀκολούθει μου) appears. The one called "rose and and followed him." When, immediately thereafter (v. 15), the "many who followed" Jesus are mentioned, the thought is hardly that of a merely "external" following. Progressively from 2:15 through 3:7 to 5:24 the Evangelist describes the growing crowd of "followers," which becomes a "great multitude." Nevertheless he distinguishes from this crowd which presses about Jesus (3:7; 5:24) the "disciples" who go with him to Nazareth (6:1).

But the saying about the necessity for self-denial and readiness for martyrdom must be spoken to the disciples and not just to the people (Mark 8:34). Discipleship to Jesus is viewed here (following the announcement of the Passion in 8:31) as the willingness to lay down one's life in sharing the destiny of Jesus by sharing in his crucifixion. However, only Peter made an attempt at such discipleship (14:54: at least he followed "at a distance"), though he finally denies (not "himself" but) Jesus (vv. 66-72). In addition to the failure of the disciples (cf. the flight of the disciples, v. 50), their lack of comprehension comes to expression when they say that the strange exorcist does not follow *them* (9:38).

Jesus tells the rich man that as a condition for discipleship, he must sell his possessions and give the proceeds to the poor (Mark 10:21). What the latter refuses to do, the disciples have done. They have "left everything" and inquire indirectly about the reward for discipleship (v. 28). In spite of the promised reward, those who follow are "afraid" in view of the nearness of Jerusalem and of suffering (v. 32). The blind Bartimaeus, when his sight has been restored, follows Jesus "on the way" (v. 52). He is the only non-Galilean who follows Jesus (cf. 15:41). Since he is, at the time, the only healed person who becomes a disciple, he represents symbolically all people who (after Easter) come to faith and become disciples of Jesus even though they were unable to see the earthly Jesus previously.

Matthew has taken over 12 of the 18 Markan uses of ἀκολουθέω. He does not use those in Mark 2:15; 6:1; 8:34bα; 9:38; 10:32; and 14:13. Of the further 13 instances in Matthew only 3 or 4 go back to Q (Matt 8:10, 19, 22; possibly 10:38 as well); 9 or 10 are therefore probably "redactional." (It is worth noting that in two of the Markan texts missing in Matthew the vb. was not applied to being a disciple of Jesus [Mark 9:38; 14:13].) In the Matthean use of the vb. two considerations are noteworthy. The Evangelist speaks about the crowds which followed Jesus *after* the Galilean beginnings right up to the gates of Jerusalem (8:1, 10; 12:15; 14:13; 19:2; 20:29). And he connects ἀκολουθέω redactionally with miracle stories (4:22; 8:1, 10, 23; 9:27; 12:15; 14:13; 19:2; 20:29) in such a way that the experience of the miracle follows (the mention of) discipleship (Luz 155, n. 64). From this one can deduce the Evangelist's opinion that it is only in following Jesus that the experience of his miraculous power becomes possible. Matt 4:22 replaces the Markan ἀπῆλθον ὀπίσω αὐτοῦ with ἠκολούθησαν αὐτῷ in order to make clearer the idea of discipleship (so perhaps also in 10:38 over against Luke 14:27).

In contrast to Matthew the occurrences of ἀκολουθέω in *Luke* are taken almost entirely from the sources. Of a total of 17 occurrences, 3 come with certainty from Q (Luke 7:9; 9:57, 59) and 9 from Mark. But the remaining 5 are likewise occasioned in large part by sources: 5:11 depends on Mark 1:18; 9:11 reproduces Mark 6:33 (cf. Matt 14:13); 9:61 is probably from a part of Q which Matthew has ignored; 22:39 is redactional and underscores (unlike Mark 14:32) the accompaniment of the disciples at the beginning of the Passion; whether 23:27 belongs to the L tradition of the mourning women or (more probably) originates with the Evangelist, remains finally undecided.

The "following" of the crowds and the women is not, however, authentic discipleship to Jesus. Therefore, in 8 places Luke has omitted a Markan use of ἀκολουθέω or replaced it. In 4:16 (cf. Mark 6:1) no disciples who follow can yet be mentioned. Luke 5:29 (cf. Mark 2:15) omits (like Matt 9:10) the "many" who follow. Luke 6:17 (cf. Mark 3:7) likewise removes the notice of the "following" of the crowd (so also Luke 8:42; cf. Mark 5:24). In Luke 9:23 (cf. Mark 8:34bα) ἀκολουθεῖν is replaced by ἔρχεσθαι in the dependent clause. Luke 18:31 (cf. Mark 10:32) omits the statement that "those who followed"—disciples—"were afraid" (cf. also Matt 20:17). Luke 19:37 (cf. Mark 11:9) does not mention those who went ahead and those who followed at Jesus' entry into Jerusalem. Luke 23:49 (cf. Mark 15:41) calls the Galilean women αἱ συνακολουθοῦσαι αὐτῷ, while Mark 15:41 says ἠκολούθουν αὐτῷ (→ 5).

It is instructive how Luke can, even where he retains the Markan ἀκολουθέω, alter the sense of a statement: Luke 5:11 emphasizes that the disciples "left everything" before they assumed their discipleship (cf. 5:27f.; 18:22, 28). In the saying about the discipleship of the cross in 9:23 the inserted "daily" serves to transfer the idea of discipleship to the post-Easter existence of the disciple. In 9:49 Luke replaces a Markan ἡμῖν (Mark 9:38) with μεθ' ἡμῶν so that the community does not appear as the object of discipleship, but is characterized as the community of those who follow *Jesus.* In Luke 22:10 the secular "following" (behind the one who carries the water) is distinguished from the special use of ἀκολουθεῖν in connection with being a disciple of Jesus by the addition of the words εἰς τὴν οἰκίαν. Perhaps the same purpose is served by the omission of αὐτῷ, referring to Jesus, in 22:54 (cf. Mark 14:54 par. Matt. 26:58).

The Gospel of John has 19 occurrences of ἀκολουθέω. Of these 17 refer to being a follower of Jesus; 6:2 mentions the crowd following him, the remaining 16 refer to the disciples (1:37f., 40, 43; 8:12; 10:4f., 27; 12:26; 13:36a, b, 37; 18:15; 21:19f., 22). Compared to the Synoptics (5 instances in each) the occurrences of the word in sayings of Jesus increase to 10.

At the beginning the Baptist testifies before two of his disciples that Jesus is the "Lamb of God," whereupon two disciples of John follow Jesus (John 1:36f., 38, 40). Jesus himself summons Philip to discipleship, and, although it would fit the style of a call story, there is no concluding report of the call having been obeyed (1:43). In 6:2 the motive of the great multitude in "following" is explicitly mentioned ("because they saw the signs which he did on those who were diseased"). The discipleship logion in 8:12 does not state the condition for discipleship as do the corresponding Synoptic sayings, but rather gives the follower a promise: the person who follows Jesus as "the light of the world" "will not walk in darkness, but will have the light of life." In the parabolic discourse about the Good Shepherd the image of the sheep who follow only the shepherd and not a stranger (10:4f.) is applied to Jesus and his followers. They hear his voice, Jesus "knows" them and they "follow" him (v. 27). The post-Easter situation of the disciples is clearly taken into account. *Hearing* Jesus is decisive, not *seeing* him (cf. 1:36-42). Hearing Jesus means "believing" (10:26f.). A second discipleship logion articulates by means of its context the association of discipleship and the cross (12:24-26; cf. Mark 8:34 par.; Luke 14:27 par. Matt 10:38).

These sayings are further and more deeply developed in John 13:36-38. In 18:15-17 it is disclosed how Peter's "discipleship" appears at first: Peter denies being a disciple of Jesus. The theme is picked up again by the resurrected Jesus. He calls Peter to discipleship (21:19), and it is clear that faithful obedience will lead to death. The disciple whom Jesus loved (cf. already 18:15: the "other" disciple) has already entered upon post-Easter discipleship to Jesus (21:20). Peter wishes to know what is to become of him (v. 21). The implication is: Peter cannot imagine that the discipleship in which, after all, the beloved disciple also participates, is a discipleship which must involve martyrdom (cf. R. Bultmann, *The Gospel of John* [1971] 714f.). But Jesus merely repeats his command to Peter: You likewise "follow me" (21:22).

5. The five compounds of ἀκολουθέω do not have the theological significance of the simple form. **Ἐξακολουθέω***—frequently used in the papryi in reference to "deserved" punishment (see Moulton/Milligan s.v.)—appears in three places in 2 Peter (1:16; 2:2, 15). That it bears the fig. sense of *obey* is certain because the objects of the *obedience* are things (cleverly devised myths, licentiousness, the way of Balaam).

Ἐπακολουθέω *come after** occurs 4 times in late NT texts. Mark 16:20 speaks of signs "ensuing as a result" (Kittel 215). 1 Tim 5:10 requires that the widow devote herself "to doing good in every way" (literally "pursue every good work"). According to 1 Tim 5:24 sins follow some people to judgment (cf. Rev 14:13) because they are not immediately apparent. In 1 Pet 2:21 the thought of being a disciple of Jesus is transferred to the post-Easter situation by being combined with the idea of an example: to follow in the footsteps of Christ means, above all, to imitate the example of the suffering Christ (cf. vv. 18-20, 23).

Κατακολουθέω *follow** is attested in the NT only in the Lukan writings. It designates discipleship. Luke 23:55 speaks of the Galilean women who "followed" (κατακολουθήσασαι with no expressed object) and refers to female disciples who follow Jesus (cf. the second [relative] clause in the verse); nevertheless it is noteworthy that Luke did not take over the ἠκολούθουν αὐτῷ of Mark 15:41. The same compound occurs in a dat. construction in Acts 16:17, where it clearly does not bear the specialized sense of discipleship. The girl with the sprit of divination "followed Paul and us." In Philippi she followed the missionaries for days (v. 18a). The fig. meaning of κατακολουθέω is unknown to the NT (by contrast see Dan 9:10 LXX; instances in the papyri [Moulton/Milligan s.v.] Josephus *Ant.* vi.147; *Ap.* ii.281; Pol. *Phil.* 3:2).

Παρακολουθέω* occurs with the meanings *go along beside, accompany* (Mark 16:17) and *investigate* a thing (Luke 1:3; cf. Josephus *Ap.* i.53; Moulton/Milligan s.v. 2). 1 Tim 4:6 and 2 Tim 3:10 use it to refer to the preservation of received teaching on which one must *concentrate* in order to *follow* it faithfully (cf. Kittel 215).

Συνακολουθέω *accompany** in the NT has only companions of Jesus as its subjects, but it refers to them in such a way that the pregnant sense of following Jesus as a disciple is weakened (Luke 23:49; cf. Mark 15:41), or merely an external accompanying is expressed (Mark 5:37; 14:51).

G. Schneider

ἀκούω *akouō* hear, come to know
ἀκοή, ῆς, ἡ *akoē* (act of) hearing, (faculty of) hearing, report, preaching*

1. Occurrences in the NT — 2. Meaning — 3. Compounds and related words — 4. Syntactic observations — 5. Characteristic contexts of ἀκούω — 6. Ἀκοή

Lit.: R. Deichgräber, "Gehorsam und Gehorchen in der Verkündigung Jesu," *ZNW* 52 (1961) 119-22. — E. von Dobschütz, "Die fünf Sinne im NT," *JBL* 48 (1929) 378-411. — J. Gnilka, "Zur Theologie des Hörens nach den Aussagen des NT," *BibLeb* 2 (1961) 71-81. — J. Horst, *TDNT* V, 543-59. — J. Kaufmann, *Der Begriff des Hörens im Johannesevangelium* (Diss. Gregorian University, Rome, 1969-70). — G. Kittel, *TDNT* I, 216-25. — K. Lammers, *Hören, Sehen und Glauben im NT* (1966). — G. A. Lee, *ISBE* II, 649f. — H. R. Moehring, "The Verb ἀκούειν in Acts IX 7 and XXII 9," *NovT* 3 (1959) 80-99. — M. Mundle, *DNTT* II, 172-80. — S. Pancaro, "The Metamorphosis of a Legal Principle in the Fourth Gospel. A Closer Look at Jn 7, 51," *Bib* 53 (1972) 340-61, esp. 347-53. — H. Schult, *THAT* II, 974-82. → οὖς.

1. Ἀκούω occurs nearly 430 times in the NT, most frequently in the Gospels (Matthew 63 times, Mark 44, Luke 65, John 58), Acts (89), and Revelation (46). The unquestionably authentic letters of Paul exhibit 19 occurrences, 1–3 John have 16, and Hebrews 8; the remaining examples are divided among Ephesians (5), Colossians (4), 2 Thessalonians (1), the Pastorals (5), James (3), and 2 Peter (1). Ἀκοή occurs a total of 24 times, esp. in the Pauline letters (8), Matthew (4), and Mark (3). The remaining writings have the subst. only twice each (Acts, 2 Timothy, Hebrews) or once (Luke, John, 2 Peter). Both words are lacking in 3 writings (Titus, 1 Peter, Jude).

2. Ἀκούω means *hear,* but also more generally *come to know.* The vb. is seldom used as a t.t. of legal terminology (John 7:51; Acts 25:22: *listen to, interrogate*). The mean-

ing *listen* to someone, *obey* is present, e.g., in Mark 9:7 par. Matthew/Luke; Acts 3:22 (in each case referring to Deut 18:15).

The subst. ἀκοή designates the faculty of *hearing* (1 Cor 12:17 bis), the act of *hearing* (2 Pet 2:8; also in the phrase ἀκοῇ ἀκούσετε in Matt 13:14; Acts 28:26), the organ of hearing, the *ear* (Mark 7:35; Luke 7:1; Acts 17:20; 2 Tim 4:3, 4; Heb 5:11). Moreover, the meanings *account, reputation,* and *rumor* occur (Mark 1:28; 13:7; Matt 4:24; 14:1; 24:6), as well as *report, preaching* (John 12:38; Rom 10:16, 17 bis; Gal 3:2, 5; 1 Thess 2:13; Heb 4:2).

3. Of the compounds derived from ἀκούω the following are attested in the NT: διακούω (Acts 23:35); εἰσακούω (5 times); ἐπακούω (2 Cor 6:2); παρακούω (3 times), and → παρακοή (3 times); προακούω (Col 1:5); ὑπακούω (21 times), → ὑπακοή (15 times), and ὑπήκοος (3 times). To the conceptual realm of hearing belong also: ἀκροατής, *hearer* (4 times), ἐπακροάομαι, *listen* (Acts 16:25), and ἐνωτίζομαι, *listen attentively* (Acts 2:14).

4. The vb. occurs with no obj. (Matt 11:5; 13:16; Mark 7:37; cf. the phrase ἀκοῇ ἀκούσετε [Isa 6:9]: Matt 13:14; Acts 28:26; the partc. οἱ ἀκούοντες, *the listeners,* Luke 6:27; and the imv. in Mark 4:3; 12:29; Acts 7:2; 13:16) as well as with an obj. following. Impersonal objects are usually acc. (BDF §173; e.g., Matt 10:14; 11:4; 12:19; Luke 7:22; John 3:8; 5:24; 8:47; Acts 2:22; 22:9; 2 Cor 12:4; 1 John 1:1, 3, 5; Rev 9:16), less often gen. (Mark 14:64; Luke 6:47; 15:25; John 5:25, 28; 12:47; Acts 9:7; 11:7; 22:7). The person whom one hears speaking is in the gen. (Mark 7:14; Luke 2:46, etc.; Acts 24:4; 26:3), frequently with an additional partc. (Mark 14:58; Acts 2:6, 11; Rev 5:13; 16:5, 7). Phrases which follow the rule that the impersonal obj. is acc. are: ἀκούω τί τινος, *hear something from someone* (Acts 1:4); ἀκούω τὶ ἔκ τινος (2 Cor 12:6); ἀκούω τὶ παρά τινος (John 8:26, 40; Acts 10:22); and ἀκούω τὶ ἀπό τινος (1 John 1:5). The gen. of the personal obj. also occurs in the phrase ἀκούω τινὸς περί τινος (Acts 17:32; 24:24). Also occurring are phrases with ὅτι (e.g., Matt 2:22; see BAGD s.v. 3e) and with the acc. with an inf. (e.g., 1 Cor 11:18; see BAGD s.v. 3f).

5. a) In the NT subjects of ἀκούειν are primarily human beings, esp. insofar as hearing "in biblical religion . . . is . . . the essential form in which . . . divine revelation is appropriated" (Kittel 216). In the Gospels one encounters primarily those who hear the preaching of Jesus and those who hear reports about him. Acts and the Epistles speak of hearing the "word" (Acts 4:4; 10:44; 15:7; 1 John 2:7; cf. Mark 4:15f., 18, 20, 33), i.e., the "word of God" (Acts 13:7, 44 v.l.; cf. Luke 8:21; 11:28; Jas 1:22f.), the "word of the Lord" (Acts 13:44; 19:10), or the "word of truth" (Eph 1:13). Much more seldom is Jesus the one who hears (Mark 2:17 par. Matthew 9:12 [the vb. is not in the Lukan parallel]; Mark 5:36 v.l.; Luke 7:9 par. Matthew; 8:50). God's hearing and granting is spoken of in John 9:31; Acts 7:34; 1 John 5:14f. (in John 11:41f. God hears Jesus).

b) In Q the vb. appears above all in words of Jesus. Here it designates primarily listening to his message, both in the simple "acoustical" sense (Luke 6:47, 49 par. Matt 7:24, 26: hearing and then doing or not doing; Luke 7:22 par.: "the deaf hear," cf. Mark 7:37) as well as in the sense of attentive or "obedient" hearing (Luke 10:16 par.: "Anyone who *listens* to you *listens* to me" [JB]). In Luke 11:31b par. it is said of the queen of the South that "she came . . . to *hear* the wisdom of Solomon" in a saying which underscores the superiority of Jesus and his preaching. In 7:22 par. "seeing and hearing" stand beside each other, as in 10:24 par.: "many prophets and kings desired to see what you see, and did not see it, and to *hear* what you *hear,* and did not *hear* it." Whatever the disciples "have said in the dark *shall be heard* in the light" (12:3).

The injunction of Jesus to listen (Mark 4:3; 7:14; Matt 13:14; 15:10; 21:33; Luke 18:6) is frequently issued with the call: "He who has ears to *hear,* let him *hear*" (Mark 4:9, 23; 7:16 v.l.; Matt 11:15; 13:9, 43; Luke 8:8; 14:35b). The voice from heaven at the transfiguration enjoins the disciples to listen to Jesus (Mark 9:7 par.; cf. also Mark 12:29 [Deut 6:4]: "Hear, O Israel").

In Mark ἀκούω occurs in the words of Jesus (e.g., 4:3, 12, 15, 16, 18, 20, 23, 24; 7:14; 8:18; 13:7). It also, and much more frequently than in Q, occurs in narrative as well. In narrative, however, it is usually used with reference to "neutral" (2:1; 3:8, 21; 5:27; 6:14, 16, 55, etc.) or to involved, willing, or "obedient" hearers of Jesus (4:33; 6:2; 12:37).

For Matthew the formula which introduces the "antitheses" (5:21, 27, 33, 38, 43)—ἠκούσατε ὅτι ἐρρέθη—is characteristic. Matt 18:15f. (found in Matthew only) lays down rules for the case of a "brother [who] sins against you" in the hope that he will *listen to* the reprimand of the (offended) disciple.

Luke underscores (frequently redactionally) the action of listening to Jesus' word and its astounding effect (2:47; 4:28; 10:39; 19:48; 21:38). But Luke also lets it be known that the words of Moses and the prophets are to be listened to (16:29, 31; cf. 2:46).

c) In John 3:8 and 5:37 ἀκούειν τὴν φωνήν refers to hearing in a simple external sense, whereas other sayings (e.g., 18:37: "Every one who is of the truth *hears* my voice") are to be understood in the sense of an obedient listening to Jesus. Of course, this distinction is not made in every case; in fact, in some cases there is deliberate ambiguity whether simple hearing or believing acceptance is spoken of (e.g., 5:25, 28). Those who believe in Jesus, who, according to 10:3, 16, 27, *hear* the voice of the shepherd, are the positive counterpart to those Jews who, according to 8:40-47, reject the truth proclaimed by Jesus

(R. Schnackenburg, *The Gospel According to St John* III [1982] 250). The "word" which the disciples hear from Jesus is, according to 14:24, "not mine but the Father's who sent me." Everything which he heard from the Father (cf. 8:26, 28, 40) Jesus has made known to his followers (15:15). Whoever (obediently) hears the word of Jesus and believes the one who sent him "has eternal life" (5:24). In 12:47 and 14:24 the emphasis is on the keeping or the following of the words of Jesus.

1 John 1:1-3 emphasizes that the proclamation of the author is identical with "that which was from the beginning, which we have *heard,* which we have seen with our eyes . . . concerning the word of life" (v. 1). The nature of the proclamation ("the *word* of life"; cf. John 1:1, 4) causes the usual sequence, "seeing and hearing," to be reversed (cf. also Luke 2:20: what the shepherds "had heard and seen"; further examples of the sequence "hearing and seeing" are Matt 11:4; 13:16). According to 1 John 4:1-5 the false prophets are not "of God," but "of the world"; thus what they say is "of the world" and "the world *listens* to them" (v. 5).

d) In Paul ἀκούω represents first of all the process by which he himself has received information about his congregations (1 Cor 5:1; 11:18; Phil 1:27; cf. Phlm 5; so also Col 1:4, 9; Eph 1:15; 2 Thess 3:11) or by which others have received information about him (Gal 1:13, 23; Phil 1:30; cf. 2:26; so also Eph 3:2). When he exhorts his readers to action, he mentions in detail "what you have learned and received and *heard* and seen in me" (Phil 4:9; cf. 2 Cor 12:6). Statements which deal with hearing as a presupposition for → πίστις carry special weight for Paul. With reference to the gospel which must be obeyed (Rom 10:16) he asks (v. 14b, c): "And how are they to believe in him of whom they have never heard? And how are they to hear without a preacher?" "Faith comes from what is heard," i.e., from preaching (ἀκοή → 6), but "what is heard comes by the word (ῥῆμα; RSV "preaching") of Christ" (v. 17). In 1 Cor 14:2 the secondary significance of speaking in tongues is based upon the fact that no one hears, i.e., *understands,* the person who speaks in this way. In 2 Cor 12:3f. Paul says of his once having been caught up to the third heaven that he was "caught up into Paradise" and "*heard* things that cannot be told" (cf. Paul's *hearing* the voice of Jesus according to Acts 9:4; 22:7, 15; 26:14).

e) In order to safeguard the traditional preaching of the gospel the later NT writings call attention to that which Christians *have heard* (Col 1:23; Eph 4:21; 2 Tim 1:13; 2:2; 2 John 6). Hebrews cites Ps 94:7f. LXX three times as a warning against unbelief and apostasy: "Today, when you *hear* his voice, do not harden your hearts . . ." (3:7f., 15; 4:7). In Jas 1:19 a wisdom saying exhorts the reader to be "quick to *hear,* slow to speak, slow to anger. . . ." In Revelation ἤκουσα (along with εἶδον) frequently refers to the reception of revelation. In each of the letters to the seven churches this exhortation occurs: "He who has an ear, let him hear what the Spirit says to the churches" (2:7, 11, 17, 29; 3:6, 13, 22).

6. The subst. ἀκοή (→ 1, 2) attains a special theological quality wherever its pass. meaning is not merely *report* or *rumor,* but rather Christian *preaching.* Of course, to translate it in such places with *preaching* or *sermon* "does not give expression to what is decisive, namely the passing on of what has *been heard* in order that it might *be heard*" (H. Schlier, *Römerbrief* [HTKNT] 317f.). Heb 4:2b observes that "the word of *preaching*" (RSV "the message which they heard") did not benefit some "because it did not meet with faith in the hearers." John 12:38 and Rom 10:16 face the problem of unbelief by asking, with Isa 53:1 LXX: "Lord, who has believed our *report* [i.e., *preaching*]?" Paul argues on the basis of this text from Isaiah: "So faith comes from what is heard [i.e., *preaching*], and what is heard [the *preaching*] comes by the *preaching* (ῥῆμα) of Christ" (Rom 10:17). Christians have received the Spirit not "by works of the law," but ἐξ ἀκοῆς πίστεως (Gal 3:2, 5). The gen. construction does not simply indicate preaching which has faith as its consequence or content, but rather expresses the essential unity between ἀκοή and the act of hearing (F. Mussner, *Galaterbrief* [HTKNT] 207 with n. 15). Preaching is λόγος ἀκοῆς παρ' ἡμῶν τοῦ θεοῦ (1 Thess 2:13), i.e., somewhat literally, the "word of the *message* of God out of our mouth." The Thessalonians have received it and accepted it in faith as God's word.

"But they have not all obeyed (ὑπήκουσαν) the gospel" (Rom 10:16a). Faith is "obedience" (→ ὑπακοή); wherefore Paul can speak of ὑπακοὴ πίστεως (1:5; 16:26).

G. Schneider

ἀκρασία, ας, ἡ *akrasia* self-indulgence*

Matt 23:25; 1 Cor 7:5. W. Grundmann, *TDNT* II, 339-42.

ἀκρατής, 2 *akratēs* uncontrolled*

2 Tim 3:3. W. Grundmann, *TDNT* II, 339-42.

ἄκρατος, 2 *akratos* unmixed*

Rev 14:10: the wrath of God *in full strength.*

ἀκρίβεια, ας, ἡ *akribeia* precision*

Acts 22:3: "educated according to the *strict* manner of the law of our fathers."

ἀκριβής, 2 *akribēs* exact, strict*

Acts 26:5: I have lived (as a Pharisee) "according to the *strictest* party (αἵρεσις) of our religion."

ἀκριβόω *akriboō* ascertain precisely*

Matt 2:7, 16, of Herod's investigations.

ἀκριβῶς *akribōs* accurately, carefully*

Matt 2:8; Luke 1:3; Acts 18:25; Eph 5:15; 1 Thess 5:2. Comparative ἀκριβέστερον: Acts 18:26; 23:15, 20; 24:22.

ἀκρίς, ίδος, ἡ *akris* grasshopper, locust*

Matt 3:4; Mark 1:6; Rev 9:3, 7. F. I. Andersen, *AbrN* 3 (1961/62) 60-74.

ἀκροατήριον, ου, τό *akroatērion* audience room*

Acts 25:23 (possibly, as in Philo *Congr.* 64, *auditorium*).

ἀκροατής, οῦ, ὁ *akroatēs* hearer*

Rom 2:13: of the law; Jas 1:22, 23, 25: of the word.

ἀκροβυστία, ας, ἡ *akrobystia* foreskin, uncircumcised, Gentile(s)*

Lit.: K. L. Schmidt, *TDNT* I, 225f. — R. Meyer, *TDNT* VI, 72-84. — T. R. Schreiner, *Circumcision: An Entrée into "Newness" in Pauline Thought* (Diss. Fuller Seminary, Pasadena, 1983). → περιτομή.

1. In the NT ἀκροβυστία occurs 20 times, 11 in Romans 2–4 and outside the Pauline corpus only in Acts 11:3 where, in the mouth of Jewish Christians, it serves as a designation for unclean Gentiles (ἄνδρες ἀκροβυστίαν ἔχοντες). In all other places ἀκροβυστία refers either to *the status of being non-Jewish* (Rom 2:25, 26b; 4:10 [bis], 11 [bis], 12; 1 Cor 7:18, 19; Gal 5:6; 6:15; Col 2:13; 3:11) or, concretely, to (uncircumcised) *Gentiles* (Rom 2:26a, 27; 3:30; 4:9; Gal 2:7; Eph 2:11).

Ἀκροβυστία (Lat. *praeputium*), foreskin, is not to be derived from ἄκρος (pointed) and the vb. βύω (stop up), but is rather an analogue to ἀκροποσθία, foreskin (Aristotle *HA* i.13.29 [493a]), which came into being as a result of the influence of Heb. *bōšeṯ* (shame). The term, which occurs only in biblical and ecclesiastical Greek, is found in 13 places in the LXX as translation for the Heb. *'orlâ* (foreskin), usually in the injunction to cut off the foreskin. In the Qumran literature there are spiritualizing references to the "foreskin of evil inclination" (1QS 5:5), "of the heart" (1QS 5:26; 1QpHab 11:13), "of the lips" (1QH 2:18f.), "of the ear" (1QH 18:20).

2. In Rom 2:25-29 Paul criticizes the Jewish view that the *uncircumcised* are lost by connecting the benefit of circumcision to the fulfilling of the law. In view of the final judgment this results in a revaluation of the physical circumstances: Because of disobedience circumcision is calculated as ἀκροβυστία and vice versa (vv. 25f.); by nature uncircumcised, the Gentiles as potential doers of the law can show the Jews, who possess scripture and circumcision, to be transgressors (v. 27). All that counts *coram Deo* is the invisible circumcision of the heart which is the gift of the Spirit and is therefore accomplished by God himself (vv. 28f.); Paul surely has Ezek 36:26-28 in mind.

Justification is conferred upon Jews and uncircumcised without distinction (Rom 3:30; 4:9). Paul points to the example of Abraham, who was justified by his faith while still in the state of uncircumcision; ἡ ἐν ἀκροβυστίᾳ πίστις becomes at the same time a new slogan for use in theological conflict (Rom 4:11f.); the same is true for τὸ εὐαγγέλιον τῆς ἀκροβυστίας with which Paul has been entrusted by God (Gal 2:7; cf. v. 9). The antithesis of circumcision and uncircumcision, of Jew and Gentile, is abolished in the Church through the power of the Spirit (1 Cor 7:19); "in Christ" it is meaningless (Col 3:11), overcome by love working through faith (Gal 5:6). In their natural, external existence, therefore, uncircumcision and circumcision are not to be altered, but are rather to be understood as an aspect of each individual's vocation (1 Cor 7:18). Furthermore, pride in circumcision is anachronistic since the believer is a new creation (Gal 6:15).

In an apparently non-Pauline manner the fleshly ἀκροβυστία, together with trespasses, is mentioned in Col 2:13 as characteristic of the spiritually dead Gentile, and in Eph 2:11f. is taken as proof of separation from God and hopelessness. However, it is intended in these places to illustrate *e contrario* the effect of baptism which is not achieved by human hands, but is rather by means of the circumcision accomplished by God's Spirit, a "putting off (of) the body of flesh in the circumcision of Christ" (Col 2:11).

O. Betz

ἀκρογωνιαῖος, 3 *akrogōniaios* subst.: cornerstone → γωνία 1, 3.

ἀκροθίνιον, ου, τό *akrothinion* firstfruits, spoils*

Heb 7:4: Abraham gave a tithe of the (firstfruits of the) *spoils.*

ἄκρον, ου, τό *akron* tip*

Luke 16:24: fingertip; Heb 11:21: tip of a staff; Matt 24:31 (bis); Mark 13:27 (bis): the *extreme limit,* i.e., the *end.*

Ἀκύλας, acc. -αν *Akylas* Aquila*
Πρίσκα, Πρίσκιλλα, ης *Priska, Priskilla* Prisca, Priscilla*

Lit.: H. W. Bartsch, *RGG* I, 524. — A. van den Born, *BL* 92. — F. F. Bruce, *The Pauline Circle* (1985) 44-51. — F. X.

Pölzl, *Die Mitarbeiter des Weltapostels Paulus* (1911). — J. W. Kapp, *ISBE* I, 217. — R. Schumacher, *TGl* 12 (1920) 86-99. — M. J. Shroyer, *IDB* I, 176. — A. Wikenhauser, *LTK* I, 779f.

1. Ἀκύλας and Πρίσκα (with the diminutive Πρίσκιλλα) are the Greek forms of the Latin names *Aquila* and *Prisca, Priscilla.* The names are frequently attested outside the NT in inscriptions and literature; however, there are no extrabiblical sources dealing with the husband and wife mentioned in the NT. In all 6 places in the NT where one of the two names occurs, the other appears as well. Whereas in the three Pauline texts the form Πρίσκα is used, only the diminutive Πρίσκιλλα appears in the three texts of Acts. It is striking that only in Acts 18:2 and 1 Cor 16:19 is Aquila named first, but that in Acts 18:18, 26; Rom 16:3; 2 Tim 4:19 the name of the woman appears first. Perhaps this reflects her greater significance in the life of the Church (thus H. Schlier, *Römerbrief* [HTKNT] 443).

2. Aquila was a Jewish native of Pontus (Acts 18:2). He was a tentmaker and lived with his wife in Rome until they were forced to leave Rome because of the edict proclaimed by Claudius in A.D. 49 (referred to in Suetonius *Claudius* 25), by which Jews were expelled from the city (Acts 18:2f.). When Paul became acquainted with the couple in Corinth and lived and worked with them, they were already Christians. This is apparent from the fact that their conversion is nowhere mentioned but rather seems to be presupposed and that the designation Ἰουδαῖος (Acts 18:2) can mean "Jewish Christian" (cf. Gal 2:13; Acts 21:20). Following a stay of *ca.* one and one-half years in Corinth, Paul, accompanied by Aquila and Prisca, traveled by ship to Ephesus (Acts 18:18f.). Paul went on to Caesarea while the couple remained in Ephesus (vv. 19-22). When the eloquent Apollos appeared in Ephesus and "taught accurately the things concerning Jesus," though he did not know the baptism of Jesus, Aquila and Priscilla are supposed to have instructed him (v. 26). Paul met Aquila and Priscilla again during his two-and-a-half-year stay in Ephesus. A Christian house church had assembled itself about the couple. Paul passed along greetings explicitly from them to the congregation in Corinth (1 Cor 16:19).

Rom 16:3-5 presupposes that in the period between the composition of 1 Corinthians and that of Romans Aquila and Prisca had returned to Rome and that there also a house church had already formed around them. This is understandable under the assumpsion that the edict of Claudius regarding the Jews was relaxed following his death in A.D. 54. Rom 16:3-5 make two further noteworthy points: 1) Paul refers to the couple as his fellow workers. We are perhaps justified "in regarding the two as among the leading early Christian missionaries in the Diaspora, who had begun their work independently of Paul and then continued it in association with him" (E. Käsemann, *Commentary on Romans* [1980] 413). For this reason Paul also expressly mentions the gratitude of the Gentiles toward them. 2) Paul himself thanks them for having risked their own lives in order to save him. The reference may be to the dangers mentioned in 2 Corinthians 6 and 11 or to the conflicts associated directly with Ephesus and mentioned in 1 Cor 15:32 and Acts 19.

That in actual history they were associated with Paul and were of significance for the mission of primitive Christianity resulted in this couple's secure place in later Pauline tradition as well. The anonymous author of 2 Timothy opens the list of greetings at the conclusion of the letter with the names of Prisca and Aquila (4:19). Of course, no biographical information is to be deduced from this note.

A. Weiser

ἀκυρόω *akyroō* invalidate*

Mark 7:13 par. Matt 15:6. As a juridical t.t., Gal 3:17 (cf. O. Eger, *ZNW* 18 [1917/18] 88-93). J. Behm, *TDNT* III, 1098f.

ἀκωλύτως *akōlytōs* without hindrance*

Acts 28:31. G. Delling, *NovT* 15 (1973) 193-204.

ἄκων, ἄκουσα, ἄκον *akōn, akousa, akon* unwilling*

1 Cor 9:17. F. Hauck, *TDNT* II, 469f.

ἀλάβαστρος, ου, ὁ and **ἡ** *alabastros* (also **ἀλάβαστρον, ου, τό** *alabastron*) alabaster, flask for ointment*

Matt 26:7; Mark 14:3 (bis); Luke 7:37. Instead of the fem. in Mark 14:3 ℵ A D *pm* have the masc. and G W Θ *al* the neut.

ἀλαζονεία, ας, ἡ *alazoneia* arrogant boasting*

Jas 4:16; 1 John 2:16. G. Delling, *TDNT* I, 226f.; E. Güting and C. Brown, *DNTT* III, 28-32.

ἀλαζών, όνος, ὁ *alazōn* boaster*

Rom 1:30; 2 Tim 3:2. G. Delling, *TDNT* I, 226f.; E. Güting and C. Brown, *DNTT* III, 28-32.

ἀλαλάζω *alalazō* wail loudly*

Mark 5:38; 1 Cor 13:1 (referring to *clanging* cymbals). E. Peterson, *TDNT* I, 227f.

ἀλάλητος, 2 *alalētos* unspoken*

Rom 8:26: "with sighs *too deep for words.*"

ἄλαλος, 2 *alalos* mute*

Mark 7:37; πνεῦμα ἄλαλον in 9:17, 25: a spirit which robs human beings of speech.

ἅλας, ατος, τό *halas* salt (noun)*
ἁλίζω *halizō* salt (vb.)*

Lit.: F. HAUCK, *TDNT* I, 228f. — K.-G. REPLOH, *Markus, Lehrer der Gemeinde* (1969) 154-56. — R. SCHNACKENBURG, "Markus 9, 33-50," FS Wikenhauser 184-206. — *idem,* "Ihr seid das Salz der Erde, das Licht der Welt. Zu Matthäus 5, 13-16," *Mélanges E. Tisserant* I (1964) 365-87. — SCHULZ, *Q* 470-72. — J. B. SOUČEK, "Salz der Erde und Licht der Welt," *TZ* 19 (1963) 169-79. — H.-T. WREGE, *Die Überlieferungsgeschichte der Bergpredigt* (1968) 27-31. — H. ZIMMERMANN, "Mit Feuer gesalzen werden," *TQ* 139 (1959) 28-39.

1. Except for Col 4:6 the subst. occurs in the NT only in the Synoptic tradition. The 7 occurrences are found in the saying about salt in Mark 9:50 (ter); Matt 5:13 (bis); Luke 14:34 (bis). In Mark the saying is joined immediately to the warning against causing offense (9:42-48); Matthew places the saying at the beginning of the Sermon on the Mount in connection with the Beatitudes (5:3-12); Luke appends it to a series of sayings about the conditions of discipleship (14:26-33). The vb. ἁλίζω, *salt,* is found twice in the same context (Mark 9:49; Matt 5:13), and the adj. ἄναλος, *unsalted, without salt,* once (Mark 9:50).

2. While Col 4:6 uses *salt* in its basic meaning of a seasoning (cf. ἀρτύω, *to season*) in order to say that Christian speech should be strong, i.e., convincing, the metaphor is employed in the Synoptics in the context of the instruction of the disciples. Luke 14:34 offers what is most likely the original version when he states that salt is good. If it has become tasteless, it is good "neither for the land nor for the dunghill"; one throws it away. A concrete application is lacking in Luke; only in the light of the appended call to attention in v. 35c and the preceding admonition to the multitudes does it become clear that the saying about salt is intended to exhort the disciples to special effort and watchfulness.

On the other hand, Matthew 5 has, by using direct address, related the Q saying directly to the disciples (cf. vv. 11f.), in order to stress their responsibility toward the entire world. He sharpens the demand by supplementing the subst. salt with the vb., by speaking of a total worthlessness, and by calling attention to a future judgment by means of a threat (it will be "trodden under foot by men"; cf. 7:6).

Mark 9:50, which shows points of contact with the Lukan version, connects the logion by means of the catchword to the preceding: "For every one will be salted with fire" (v. 49). The metaphor thereby becomes a riddle-like saying with paradoxical sharpness. The saying about fire (as a means of purification; cf. Mal 3:2f., etc.) gives the saying about salt a new sense, expressed in the catechetical application: "Have salt in yourselves, and be at peace with one another" (v. 50c); that is to say, the community which stands under the purifying judgment is obligated to be ready for peace. V. 49b, "and every sacrifice will be salted with salt," is secondary and represents an attempt to interpret the saying about salt in accordance with ritual regulations (cf. Lev 2:13; see Billerbeck II, 21-23).

A. Sand

ἀλείφω *aleiphō* anoint*

Matt 6:17 (mid.); Luke 7:38, 46 (bis); John 11:2; 12:3. Anointing of the sick: Mark 6:13; Jas 5:14; of a corpse: Mark 16:1. H. Schlier, *TDNT* I, 229-32; W. Brunotte, *DNTT* I, 119-21.

ἀλεκτοροφωνία, ας, ἡ *alektorophōnia* cockcrow*

Mark 13:35, as an indication of time: *at cockcrow.*

ἀλέκτωρ, ορος, ὁ *alektōr* cock, rooster*

Matt 26:34, 74, 75; Mark 14:30, 68, 72 (bis); Luke 22:34, 60, 61; John 13:38; 18:27.

Ἀλεξανδρεύς, έως, ὁ *Alexandreus* (an) Alexandrian*

A person from the Egyptian city of Alexandria (on which see J. G. Milne, *OCD* 42f.; W. Schubart, *RAC* I, 271-83): Acts 6:9; 18:24.

Ἀλεξανδρῖνος, 3 *Alexandrinos* Alexandrian*

Acts 27:6; 28:11, of a ship with Alexandria as its home port.

Ἀλέξανδρος, ου *Alexandros* Alexander*

The name of a number of people: Mark 15:21; Acts 4:6; 19:33a, b; 1 Tim 1:20; 2 Tim 4:14. Only the two occurrences in the Pastorals may refer to the same person.

ἄλευρον, ου, τό *aleuron* wheat flour*

Matt 13:33 par. Luke 13:21 in the parable of the leaven.

ἀλήθεια, ας, ἡ *alētheia* truth
ἀληθεύω *alētheuō* tell the truth, be truthful*
ἀληθής, 2 *alēthēs* true, honest, genuine
ἀληθινός, 3 *alēthinos* true, honest, dependable
ἀληθῶς *alethōs* truly, actually

1. Occurrences in the NT — 2. Meaning — 3. Usage — 4. Truth in Paul and John

Lit.: J. Becker, *Das Heil Gottes* (SUNT 3, 1964) 214-37. — J. Blank, "Der johanneische Wahrheitsbegriff," *BZ* 7 (1963) 163-73. — H. Boeder, "Der frühgriechische Wortgebrauch von Logos und Aletheia," *Archiv für Begriffsgeschichte* 4 (1959) 82-112. — G. W. Bromiley, *ISBE* IV, 926-28. — R. E. Brown, *The Gospel according to John* I (AB, 1966) 499f. — R. Bultmann, "Untersuchungen zum Johannesevangelium," *Exegetica* (1967) 124-97. — P. Friedländer, *Platon* I (²1954) 233-48. — L. Goppelt, "Wahrheit als Befreiung. Das neutestamentliche Zeugnis von der Wahrheit nach dem Johannesevangelium," *Was ist Wahrheit?* (Hamburger theologische Ringvorlesung, ed. H.-R. Müller-Schwefe; 1965) 80-93. — M. Heidegger, *Being and Time* (1962) §44. — *idem,* "On the Essence of Truth," *Martin Heidegger, Basic Writings* (ed. D. F. Krell; 1976) 117-41. — *idem, Logik, Die Frage nach der Wahrheit* (Gesamtausgabe, 21, 1976). — E. Heitsch, "Die nichtphilosophische Aletheia," *Hermes* 90 (1962) 24-33. — Y. Ibuki, *Die Wahrheit im Johannesevangelium* (BBB 39, 1972). — A. Jepsen, *TDOT* I, 292-323. — E. Käsemann, *The Testament of Jesus* (1968). — K. Koch, "Der hebräische Wahrheitsbegriff im griechischer Sprachraum," *Was ist Wahrheit?* (see above under Goppelt) 47-65. — J. Lozano, *El concepto de verdad en San Juan* (1963). — O. A. Piper, *IDB* IV, 713-17. — I. de la Potterie, *La vérité dans Saint Jean* (1977) (bibliography). — G. Quell, G. Kittel, and R. Bultmann, *TDNT* I, 232-51 (bibliography to 1931). — R. Schnackenburg, *The Gospel according to St John* II (1982) 225-37 (Excursus Ten: "The Johannine Concept of Truth"). — R. Schnackenburg and P. Engelhardt, *LTK* X, 912-20. — L. Schottroff, *Der Glaubende und die feindliche Welt* (WMANT 37, 1970) 228-96. — A. C. Thiselton, *DNTT* III, 874-902 (bibliography). — T. Tugendhat, *Der Wahrheitsbegriff bei Husserl und Heidegger* (1970). — H. Wildberger, *THAT* I, 177-209.

1. The Pauline, deutero-Pauline, and Johannine writings provide 92 of the 109 instances of ἀλήθεια in the NT. A similar pattern of distribution obtains in the case of ἀληθής: 21 of 26. Ἀληθινός is found in John and 1 John (13 times), Revelation (10), Paul (1), and in various other places (4). Of 18 occurrences of ἀληθῶς, 8 are in John and 1 John, 9 in the Synoptics and Acts, and 1 in Paul. Ἀληθεύω occurs twice, once each in Galatians and Ephesians.

2. According to early Greek usage, ἀλήθεια, a privative form derived from λανθάνω/λήθω (conceal something from someone, be hidden), refers to *things as they are*—but always that which is *expressed;* to speak the ἀλήθεια was to say "how it is" (Boeder 99; similarly Frisk, *Wörterbuch* I, 71). Regarding the classical period the evidence presented primarily by Heidegger and Bultmann (*Exegetica* 144f.) remains unrefuted according to which ἀλήθεια means *truth* in the sense of the *unhiddenness* (its etymological sense! Heitsch vs. Friedländer) and *disclosedness* of the state of affairs which exhibits itself and is therefore perceived in its actuality; further, and in thorough continuity with early usage, it could indicate the *reality* and *essentiality* or *rightness of the assertion of disclosing discourse* (Aristotle *Int.* 4:17a: λόγος ἀποφαντικός; Heidegger, *Logik* 127ff.). Insofar as ἀλήθεια discloses the disposition of the speaker, it means *truthfulness.*

For the meaning of ἀλήθεια in the NT it is decisive that Heb. *'ĕmeṯ* (faithfulness, firmness) is usually translated as ἀλήθεια in the LXX. Thereby the historical dimension of *'ĕmeṯ* is largely lost, and the ontological character of ἀλήθεια is modified, insofar as it no longer refers to the disclosedness of the entity in its being. Ἀλήθεια actually becomes transcendent revelation (Koch 60). Foreign to Greek usage is not only the LXX's literal translation of *'āśâ 'ĕmeṯ* with ποιεῖν ἀλήθειαν, "do the truth," but the accompanying OT understanding of truth as accomplishment (see also 1QS 1:5, etc.). In terms of content ἀλήθεια can approach δικαιοσύνη, righteousness; Heb. *ṣeḏeq* can be translated as ἀλήθεια. Thus ἀλήθεια becomes *uprightness.* In Hellenistic usage ἀλήθεια also signifies the divine reality; in Gnostic literature this meaning is further sharpened to refer to the self-disclosing and substantially conceived divine reality as opposed to the evil material world which presents itself to us.

In the NT as well, wherever it is theologically relevant (primarily in Paul and John → 4) ἀλήθεια means the truth disclosed by God in the noetic sense as well as the ontological sense.

The adjectives ἀληθής and ἀληθινός, already in classical Greek largely coterminous in terms of content, embody in the NT all the nuances on the spectrum of meaning of ἀλήθεια: *true* in the sense of *dependable, constant, real, genuine,* and *faithful.* Ἀληθῶς, like ἐπ' ἀληθείας (7 of the 10 occurrences of ἀλήθεια in the Synoptics and Acts are in this phrase), means *matter-of-fact,* almost as if to say that doubt is impermissible. Ἀληθεύω in Gal 4:16 means *speak the truth*; in Eph 4:15 *be genuine, upright* (in love).

3. Occasionally ἀλήθεια is a subj. (John 1:17; 8:32, 44; 1 John 1:8; 2:4; 2 Cor 11:10; Gal 2:5; Eph 4:21) or a pred. nom. (John 14:6; 17:17; 18:38; 1 John 5:6; 2 Cor 7:14); very often it is the acc. obj. of verbs of saying, recognizing, and knowing (primarily in John); important also are the two occurrences of the phrase *do the truth* (John 3:21; 1 John 1:6). The construction with ἀλήθεια in the dat., *not to obey the truth* (Rom 2:8; Gal 5:7; cf. 2 Thess 2:12; 1 Pet 1:22), is characteristic.

Especially for Paul the gen. qualifiers "of God" (Rom 1:25; 3:7; 15:8), "of Christ" (2 Cor 11:10), and "of the gospel" (Gal 2:5, 14; Col 1:5) in connection with ἀλήθεια are characteristic, whereas John understands ἀλήθεια in an absolute sense. Ἀλήθεια as a gen. determiner occurs with πνεῦμα, Spirit (John 14:17; 16:13; 1 John 4:6) and λόγος, word (2 Cor 6:7; Eph 1:13; Col 1:5; 2 Tim 2:15), etc. The phrase εἰς ἐπίγνωσιν ἀληθείας, *to recognition of the truth,* is characteristic in the Pastorals, whereby ἀλήθεια already approaches the sense of "authoritative teaching" (Bultmann, *TDNT* I, 244).

Of prep. phrases including ἀλήθεια, the following should be noted: *to be of the truth* (John 18:37; 1 John

2:21; 3:19; identical with: "to be of God"; Schottroff 228, → 4) and *in* (ἐν) *the truth* (*passim*, e.g., *to walk in the truth*: 2 John 4; 3 John 3f.). Ἀλήθεια occurs in parallel constructions primarily with πνεῦμα, Spirit (John 4:23f.), χάρις, grace (1:14, 17; cf. the OT phrase *ḥesed we'ĕmet*), δικαιοσύνη, righteousness (Eph 5:9), πίστις, faith (1 Tim 2:7), and ἀγάπη, love (2 John 3).

In John God is ἀληθής and ἀληθινός in that he reveals himself in the Son (3:33; 7:28; 8:26; 17:3; on 1 John 5:20 see R. Bultmann, *Johannine Epistles* [Hermeneia] 89f.). Therefore it is significant for Johannine theology that ἀληθής also occurs with μαρτυρία, witness (5:31f.; 8:13f.; 21:24; 3 John 12; ἀληθινός appears with μαρτυρία only in John 19:35 and there only because of "ecclesiastical redaction"; see Titus 1:13). "*True*" in this same way are also Christ (John 7:18; 1 John 5:20e; in Mark 12:14 par. Matt 22:16 ἀληθινός means that Jesus is *truthful*), the bread from heaven which signifies Christ (John 6:32), the sacramental flesh and blood (v. 55), etc.

For Paul (Rom 3:4) God is ἀληθινός in the sense of *truthful*; on the other hand, the phrase "a living and *true* (ἀληθής) God" in 1 Thess 1:9 is probably a fixed expression appropriated from Jewish missionary vocabulary. In Revelation ἀληθινός is an attribute of God (6:10), Christ (3:7, 14; 19:11), and God's ways (15:3), judgments (16:7; 19:2), and words (19:9; along with πιστός, dependable: 21:5; 22:6). For the remaining NT writings "true" is not a characteristic word.

4. The concept of truth was not a theme in the proclamation of the Synoptic Jesus and surely also not of the "historical" Jesus. Since it is Pauline theology for which ἀλήθεια is important and Johannine theology for which it is constitutive, it is, then, in this theological reflection that the motivating force of the proclamation of Jesus finds conceptual expression. The "Amen" (→ ἀμήν) typical in the speech of Jesus is the linguistic exercise of the authority of the divine truth which he claims (see Jeremias, *Theology* 35f.). "Amen" (see Wildberger 193ff.) is, after all, from the same root as *'ĕmet*.

a) Paul's use of ἀλήθεια is most clearly seen by viewing his letters chronologically. Of 3 occurrences in Galatians (the one in 3:1 C Koine, etc. is secondary) ἀλήθεια is twice qualified by τοῦ εὐαγγελίου (2:5, 14); in 5:7 ἀλήθεια is absolute (τῇ ἀληθείᾳ with 𝔓[46] C D Koine and other witnesses) in the same sense. Thus the concept appears clearly in the context of the proclaimed revelation. But Paul does not yet understand the gospel, as later in Romans, as the powerful quasi-presence of the God who reveals himself in the "righteousness of God" (→ δικαιοσύνη θεοῦ)—a phrase which the Paul of Galatians does not yet know. Therefore, in a certain way, ἀλήθεια in Galatians still implies "the true content of the divine message." Of course, in 5:7 ("obeying the truth," cf. Rom 2:8) the fundamental tendency to understand the gospel as the representation of the God who discloses himself in Christ is already present.

In 1 Corinthians ἀλήθεια stands in antithesis to unrighteousness, ἀδικία (13:6), and thus signifies human conduct. By means of the coordination of ἀλήθεια and purity of motive, εἰλικρίνεια, in 5:8 a thought is touched upon which will be developed in 2 Corinthians 3–4.

In the course of his discussion of self-commendation in 2 Corinthians Paul speaks in 4:2 of the revelation, φανέρωσις, of the truth. Only when the revelation of the truth is accomplished does doubt regarding the integrity and legitimacy of the one who proclaims it disappear. Thus the power requisite for its dissemination and accomplishment resides in the proclaimed truth itself. Accordingly, ἀλήθεια is not the mere object of a statement, although Paul can say in 12:6: "I am [RSV "shall be"] speaking the truth." As proclaimed truth it becomes accomplished truth and as such the shaping power for the receptive hearer so that in hearing "he himself becomes εἰλικρινής and thus can see that the proclaimer of such ἀλήθεια is also shaped by εἰλικρίνεια" (R. Bultmann, *The Second Letter to the Corinthians* [1985] 102). In 2 Cor 6:7 "(by) truthful speech (λόγῳ)" is parallel with "[by] the power (δυνάμει) of God." So also in 13:8 ἀλήθεια is the overpowering truth which enables the recognition of God (Bultmann, *Second Corinthians* 248). The use of unmodified ἀλήθεια is striking in 2 Corinthians (only in the oath in 11:10 does the gen. Χριστοῦ appear). In 7:14 ἀλήθεια stands for the *truthfulness* of Paul.

In Phil 1:18 ἀλήθεια is again the *truthfulness* of the one who proclaims, esp. as it is contrasted with subterfuge, πρόφασις.

A noticeable reticence in the use of ἀλήθεια is striking in Romans. In the decisive section 3:20–8:29 ἀλήθεια does not occur. However, in 1:18–3:20 the sinner, Gentile as well as Jew, is subjected to the very *truth* of God which he or she suppresses (1:18, 25) or even claims for himself or herself (2:8, 20). But precisely in the saying which forms the antithesis to the cardinal statement of 1:16f. ἀλήθεια appears as the disclosed *truth of God* (v. 18; R. Bultmann, *TDNT* I, 243; E. Käsemann, *Commentary on Romans* [1980] 38; *contra* O. Michel, *Röm* [KEK, [14]1978] 99: "right conduct"). This agrees with the foundational statement of vv. 16f.: God is effectively present as the one revealing himself in the δικαιοσύνη θεοῦ. Thus ἀλήθεια almost takes on the sense of δικαιοσύνη θεοῦ. In 3:7; 15:8 ἀλήθεια signifies the covenant faithfulness of God in the sense of the OT *'ĕmet*. Rom 9:1 is, like 2 Cor 11:10, an oath. In spite of Rom 1:18 and 3:7 ἀλήθεια is not a dominating concept in Romans due to its nonthematic usage; nevertheless, 1:18 itself lies along the line of development from Galatians through 2 Corinthians: truth is the presence of God which, according to divine will, is revealed through the proclamation and which, for that very reason, has the character of power.

The idea that in Rom 2:20 Paul is using a quotation from a Jewish missionary writing—"the embodiment of knowledge and truth in the law," τὴν μόρφωσιν τῆς γνώσεως καὶ τῆς ἀληθείας ἐν τῷ νόμῳ (H. Lietzmann, *An die Römer* [HNT] 43)—is a hypothesis still deserving of consideration.

b) John also understands truth as an event. He is not thereby concerned with a balanced conceptuality. On the one hand, (grace and) truth came into being through the incarnate Logos (John 1:14, 17); on the other hand, Jesus as the revealer "is" the way, the truth, and the life (14:6). Only because he "is" the truth does he "say" or testify to the truth (8:40, 45f.; 16:7; 18:37). As "God's very reality revealing itself—occurring!—in Jesus" (Bultmann, *Theology* II, 19), he signifies for the knowing and seeing (14:9) believer the realization of eternal life conceived as present reality (5:24f.). But to know the truth means to be free from "committing sin" (8:31ff.). On the other hand, the fact that John speaks of "doing the truth," through which access to the light (= the new self-understanding which is laid hold of by faith) is made possible (3:21), shows that the Evangelist does not intend to present any consistent theory of the psychology of coming to faith. This is already prohibited by the "predestination" statements (e.g., 8:34ff.; 12:37ff.: the Johannine "messianic secret"). They are the "theological" paraphrase for the idea that the ability to believe is given as a gift. As God's truth "comes into being" in the incarnation by God's initiative, so also it is by God's initiative that a person comes to be open to God's truth in believing comprehension. Whoever is of the truth hears Jesus, i.e., God's voice (18:37); whoever is not of God cannot hear his word, but is rather "of [his] father the devil" who, when he lies, "speaks according to his own nature" (8:40ff.). The unbeliever can only ask wretchedly: "What is truth?" (18:38). To sum up: Truth discloses itself to the one who does not close himself or herself to it. The disclosed character of truth is active in nature: God "exegetes" (1:18) himself as truth in the one whom he sends as the truth. God shows himself to be true.

R. Bultmann (*The Gospel of John* [1971] 434f.) distinguishes the Johannine usage of ἀλήθεια from the Greek understanding of it as the general disclosure of all that exists—on the basis that the Johannine question regarding ἀλήθεια is oriented to the question of life as the authentic being of the one who is concerned about his own being. But it must be remembered that this interpretation is based on Heidegger's existential analysis, an analysis which itself builds upon the Greek understanding of ἀλήθεια as disclosure. Thus the Johannine conception of ἀλήθεια may be understood as a specifically theological modification of the Greek concept of truth. Of course, one may ask whether Bultmann's understanding of the Johannine view of ἀλήθεια is not closer to certain thoughts from Heidegger's essay "On the Essence of Truth" (on this essay as documentation for the "turn" see Tugendhat 377f.) than to the existential interpretation of truth in *Being and Time,* §44. From Tugendhat's criticism of Heidegger's conception of truth emerge critical questions regarding the exegesis of the Johannine concept of ἀλήθεια which cannot be treated in detail here.

The most significant rejoinder to Bultmann's understanding has come from de la Potterie. More important than his rejection of the history-of-religions derivation of the Johannine ἀλήθεια theme from (Greek and) Gnostic dualism (see below) is his attempt to dispute the idea that for John ἀλήθεια is the disclosed reality of God. "The truth . . . is not identified with God, but with Christ and the Spirit" (1009). But one must ask in return whether this view does not place insufficient stress on the Johannine idea of the incarnation: God does disclose himself in the person Jesus! Is this sufficiently taken into account when de la Potterie concludes: "Only the incarnate Word was full of truth, only he *was* the revelation (1:18) . . ." (1011)? On this basis there was no "preexistent truth"!

But if truth is an occurrence of God, in fact, God as occurrence, then the connection between Spirit (→ πνεῦμα) and truth is seen to be an organic part of this scheme: God is to be worshiped in Spirit and in truth (4:23f.). The Spirit of truth (14:17; 15:26) guides one into the whole truth (16:13; with ℵ D and other witnesses: ἐν τῇ ἀληθείᾳ πάσῃ), i.e., he will show the persecution of the disciples to be "true" in the sense that it corresponds to the glorification of the truth incarnate in Jesus in the event of the cross. Thus Jesus sends them as those who have been sanctified in the truth (17:17ff.).

In terms of the history of religions the derivation of the Johannine ἀλήθεια is disputed. Bultmann's hypothesis, according to which the Johannine dualism of truth and lie is understood as a dualism of two possibilities for human existence in contrast to a Gnostic dualism focussed on substance, remains the most convincing solution, even though considerable modifications must be made to the mythological Gnosticism which he reconstructs. The views of Käsemann and Schottroff on the Gnostic character of John's Gospel fail, in different ways, to recognize the importance of John 1:14a. The merit of Becker's work, that he once again clearly delineated the close parallels between Qumran and John, is tempered only by his failure to give adequate attention to the Johannine conception of ἀλήθεια as the self-revelation of God (on the difference between Qumran and John see Braun, *Qumran* II, 121ff.) De la Potterie seeks a derivation from the OT and Judaism. His argument is only partially successful since early mutual penetration of Jewish, Hellenistic, and Gnostic thinking must be taken into account.

When one compares the Johannine letters with the Gospel, a certain shift in emphasis in the meaning of ἀλήθεια is recognizable, from "reality of God" (thus still, e.g., in 2 John 1b) to "behavior of the believer" (e.g., 1 John 1:6, 8; cf. R. Schnackenburg, *Die Johannesbriefe* [HTKNT] 81: "The ethical element is dominant here"). Of course, it should not be overlooked that the concrete Christian ethos is rooted in the divine reality (i.e., revelation!). Typical of this is 1 John 2:4, where both lines of thought intersect. All of this is expressed in the context of a polemic against heretics.

H. Hübner

ἀληθεύω *alētheuō* tell the truth, be truthful
→ ἀλήθεια.

ἀληθής, 2 *alēthēs* true, honest, genuine
→ ἀλήθεια.

ἀληθινός, 3 *alēthinos* true, honest, dependable
→ ἀλήθεια.

ἀλήθω *alēthō* grind*

Matt 24:41 par. Luke 17:35: two (women) *grinding* (with a millstone).

ἀληθῶς *alēthōs* truly, actually
→ ἀλήθεια.

ἁλιεύς, έως, ὁ *halieus* fisherman*

Pl. also ἁλεεῖς; BDF §29.5. Matt 4:18, 19; Mark 1:16, 17; Luke 5:2. W. H. Wuellner, *The Meaning of "Fishers of Men"* (1967); R. Pesch, *ETL* 46 (1970) 413-32. → ἄνθρωπος 2b.

ἁλιεύω *halieuō* fish (vb.)*

John 21:3: "I am going *fishing*"

ἁλίζω *halizō* salt (vb.)
→ ἅλας.

ἀλίσγημα, ατος, τό *alisgēma* pollution*

Acts 15:20: *pollutions* of idols (τῶν εἰδώλων).

ἀλλά *alla* rather, but

1. Occurrences — 2. Meaning — 3. Usage in John and Paul

Lit.: BAGD s.v. — BDF §448. — Kühner, *Grammatik* §534. — LSJ s.v. — Mayser, *Grammatik* II/3, 116-19. — Moulton, *Grammar* III, 329f.

1. Ἀλλά occurs in the NT primarily in Paul and John. Thus Romans, 1 Corinthians, and 2 Corinthians each offer approximately as many examples as Matthew and Luke combined, i.e., *ca.* 70. Colossians and 2 Thessalonians, on the other hand, have only 3 and 5 examples respectively, and John with 102 occurrences has more than twice as many as Mark with 45. The combination ἀλλὰ καί is found with striking frequency in Romans (12 times; cf. 2 Corinthians and John with 6 examples each), ἀλλ' οὐ (οὐδέ) occurs 12 times in 1 Corinthians, and ἀλλ' ἵνα occurs 10 times in John and in only isolated instances otherwise.

2. The adversative particle ἀλλά is etymologically derived from ἄλλος (cf. Ger. "sondern," which is both a verb, "separate," and a conjunction, "but, rather"). Therefore it actually means *differently* and refers to that which is different, to contrasts, separations, and new beginnings. a) In most cases ἀλλά means *but* (John 16:20; cf. Luke 24:21: ἀλλά γε, *but even*) or b) following (sometimes implicit) negations: *on the contrary, rather, no* (Matt 5:17; 11:8, 9 par. Luke; Luke 14:10, 13; John 7:49; Acts 19:2; Rom 8:37; 1 Cor 10:20; following οὐχί: Luke 1:60; 12:51; 13:3, 5; 16:30; John 9:9; Rom 3:27). c) Following negations in which ἄλλος (or ἕτερος) occurs or is to be understood, ἀλλά (or ἀλλ' ἤ) has the sense of εἰ μή, *other than, except* (Mark 4:22; 2 Cor 1:13; cf. Zerwick, *Biblical Greek* §§468-71). The ἀλλ' ἤ of Luke 12:51 (BDF §448.8: "nothing but") belongs more appropriately under b) (cf. BAGD s.v. 1a). d) Following conditional clauses with εἰ καί (εἴπερ) or ἐάν, ἀλλά means *certainly* (Mark 14:29; 1 Cor 4:15; 8:6; 9:2 [with ἀλλά γε, *at least*]; 2 Cor 4:16; 5:16; 11:6; Col 2:5; cf. Rom 6:5: ἀλλὰ καί *certainly also* after conditional εἰ). e) When used for rhetorical intensification ἀλλά means *indeed* or "so indeed, and what is more" (Luke 12:7; 16:21; John 16:2; Phil 1:18; and, with terms juxtaposed for intensification, 1 Cor 6:11 [bis]; 2 Cor 2:17; 7:11 [six times], 12 v.l.; as well as Phil 3:8: ἀλλὰ μενοῦνγε, *really* [BDF §448.6]. f) With exhortations ἀλλά serves to strengthen the command in the sense of *now then, so . . . then, come* (Mark 16:7; Acts 4:17; 9:6; 10:20; 26:16.

3. In John οὐκ . . . ἀλλά (or ἀλλ' ἵνα) and ἵνα . . . μὴ . . . ἀλλά underscore the redemptive intention of God and the one he has sent (3:15, 16, 17; 5:24; 6:39; 12:47). With οὐκ . . . ἀλλά Jesus points to and appeals to the one who sent him—usually ὁ πέμψας (5:30; 6:38; 7:16, 28; 8:16, 42; 12:44, 49; 14:24).

Paul uses ἀλλά esp. to express intensification and contrast. In the intensive contrasting of entire sentences with the aid of the phrase, found only in Paul, οὐ μόνον δέ, ἀλλὰ καί, *and not only* (this), *but also,* the theme is always (except in 2 Cor 8:19) the promise (Rom 5:3, 11; 8:23; 9:10). His speech is enlivened by contrasts, esp. when he speaks of justification (Rom 3:27; 4:4, 13; 6:14, 15; 8:4, 9, 15; 9:12) or of the service and office of the apostle (1 Cor 1:27; 2:4, 5, 7, 13; 4:19, 20; 2 Cor 1:12; 3:5; 4:5; 10:4, 18; Gal 1:1, 12, 17). In the dialectical description of the human being (Rom 7) οὐκ . . . ἀλλά is used repeatedly (vv. 15, 17, 19, 20); the same is true of the imperative μὴ . . . ἀλλά in parenesis (12:2, 3, 16, 19, 21). On the christological οὐκ . . . ἀλλά of Phil 2:6f. see P. Grelot, *Bib* 54 (1973) 25-42. With the phrase ἀλλ' οὐδέ Paul describes the paradox in Christian conduct (1 Cor 10:23; cf. 6:12) and in apostolic existence (4:3, 4; 9:12; 2 Cor 4:8a, b, 9a, b; cf. 2 Tim 1:12).

W. Radl

ἀλλάσσω *allassō* change, alter*

1. The vb. designates "change" in the broadest sense. At the end of his admonition to the Galatians, in which the personal dimension is prominent throughout, Paul writes that he would like to be present with them now and would like to "*change* [his] voice" (Gal 4:20). More appropriate than the assumption of a once-for-all change of tone (sterner or milder? from human to "heavenly speech"?) is the recognition of Paul's desire here to *adapt* his voice to the *specific situation in which the discussion is actually taking place* (J. Becker, *Galaterbrief* [NTD VIII, [15]1981] 54); cf. G. Wilhelmi, *ZNW* 65 (1974) 151-54.

2. In 1 Cor 15:51f. Paul writes that Christians who are still living at the time of the parousia must be *changed,* i.e., *transformed,* since flesh and blood cannot inherit the kingdom of God; mortality must be transformed into immortality (cf. J. Becker, *Auferstehung der Toten im Urchristentum* [1976] 96-105).

3. In his indictment of Gentiles who have failed to grasp the knowledge of God Paul writes that they "*exchanged* the glory of the immortal God for images resembling mortal man or birds . . ." (Rom 1:23). The formulation builds on Ps 105:20 LXX and Jer 2:11. As an adequate punishment for this replacement of the Creator by his creation God gave the Gentiles up to shameful passions: "Their women *exchanged* natural [sexual] relations for unnatural" (Rom 1:26). Here the compound μεταλλάσσω is used as a synonym for ἀλλάσσω, as in v. 25.

4. According to Acts 6:14 the Jews accuse Stephen of having taught that Jesus would destroy the temple and "*change* the customs which Moses delivered to us." According to Luke this is false testimony (v. 13), but it could reflect the critical attitude of the "Hellenists" toward the law.

5. In Heb 1:10ff. the preeminence of the Son over the entire creation is expressed by means of a quotation from Ps 102:26f.: heaven and earth will pass away, but you remain the same; then, in Heb 1:12 (= Ps 102:27): Heaven and earth will be *changed* like a mantle.

H. Merkel

ἀλλαχόθεν *allachothen* from another place*

John 10:1: climb in *by another way.*

ἀλλαχοῦ *allachou* elsewhere, in another direction*

Mark 1:38: "Let us go elsewhere" (JB).

ἀλληγορέω *allēgoreō* speak (explain) allegorically*

1. Etymology and meaning — 2. Attestation and semantic field — 3. Historical background — 4. Gal 4:24

Lit.: M. von Albrecht and C. Andresen, *LAW* 121-25. — BAGD s.v. — H. D. Betz, *Galatians* (Hermeneia) 243 (bibliography). — C. Brown, *DNTT* II, 754-56. — F. Büchsel, *TDNT* I, 260-63. — J. Ernst (ed.), *Schriftauslegung* (1972). — J. de Fraine, *BL* 46-48. — L. Goppelt, *RGG* I, 239f. — *idem, Typos* (1982) 139f. — A. T. Hanson, *Studies in Paul's Technique and Theology* (1974). — J. C. Joosen and J. H. Waszink, *RAC* I, 283-93. — H.-J. Klauck, *Allegorie und Allegorese in den synoptischen Gleichnistexten* (1978). — H. Lausberg, *Handbuch der literarischen Rhetorik* (1960) §§895-901. — R. N. Longenecker, *Biblical Exegesis in the Apostolic Period* (1975) 126-29. — L. Mowry, *IDB* I, 82-84. — F. Mussner, *Galaterbrief* (HTKNT, 1974) 319f. — H. Schlier, *An die Galater* (KEK, [4]1965) 218f. — J. Tate, *OCD* 45f.

1. Ἀλληγορέω is derived from ἄλλο ἀγορεύω, *I say something differently* (than I intend it) or *I mean something differently than I say it,* i.e., *I explain (signify) something figuratively or allegorically.* The root word ἀγορεύω, *I proclaim aloud, say openly,* points in the direction of the logos, speech, and thus belongs to the realm of rhetorical-hermeneutical concepts (Lausberg).

2. The vb. is attested first in writings of the late Hellenistic period (e.g., Athenaeus, Plutarch), esp. in Philo and Josephus. It appears in the NT only in Gal 4:24 (and not at all in the LXX). The subject matter itself is older, as attested by the synonymous use of ὑπόνοια (Xenophon, Plato, Aristotle). In a qualified sense typology, frequently employed by Paul and understood as divine guidance for the future (cf. Rom 5:14; 1 Cor 10:6, 11), belongs in this category, as do allegorical interpretations of parables (Mark 4:13-20 par.; Matt 13:37-43).

3. As a general phenomenon in the history of religions allegorical exposition relativizes the purely literal meaning of a text and aims at its deeper (usually ethical) sense. It seeks to defend offensive passages or give ancient statements fresh significance in the present (e.g., the Stoic interpretation of Hesiod's and Homer's myths of the gods). In this way the method also finds its way into Jewish rabbinic literature (*Psalms of Solomon;* 4 Ezra) and exegesis (Haggadah), esp. of the OT (cf. interpretation of Song of Songs), and, not least important, caters to the oriental preference for mysterious images and symbols, for tantalizing comparisons and riddle-like hints (in the OT, e.g., Ezek 15; 16; Hos 1:2-9). Moreover, there is revealed here a dimension of the understanding of Scripture which is dynamic and rich in promise for the future, the motif of promise and fulfillment.

4. The only NT appearance of the word (pres. pass. partc.) is in Gal 4:24: ἅτινά ἐστιν ἀλληγορούμενα, *all of which is spoken allegorically.* According to the context (vv. 22f.) Paul, looking back to the OT (Gen 16:15; 21:2), is concerned to contrast Hagar and Sarah more than their sons Ishmael and Isaac. The allegorical manner of speaking (or, more accurately, typological allegorizing) makes the point: Both women, along with their sons, symbolize the two testaments, the old covenant of slavery to the law (issued at Sinai) and the new covenant of freedom in Christ (given for the Jerusalem above, the spiritual Jerusalem). As free sons the Galatians belong to the latter. Both realms

portray realities at different levels and in different meanings. What is common to both Paul presents in a (daring) concluding analogy which points toward the future and hints at the mysterious activity of God (in the old as well as in the new covenant). Cf. F. Pastor Ramos, *EstBib* 34 (1975) 113-19; C. K. Barrett, FS Käsemann 1-16.

A. Kretzer

ἀλληλουϊά *hallēlouia* Hallelujah ("praise Yahweh")*

Lit.: Billerbeck III, 822. — F. Cabrol, *DACL* I, 1229-31. — H. Kraft, *Die Offenbarung des Johannes* (HNT 16a, 1974) 240-45. — E. Lohse, *RGG* III, 38. — H. Schlier, *TDNT* I, 264.

The liturgical formula from the Psalter is transliterated from Heb. *hal^elû-yāh* (or some similar form), which, except in Ps 135:3, is limited to headings and conclusions (*ca.* 20 occurrences in the LXX, always as a heading; also Tob 13:18; 3 Macc 7:13). In the literature of primitive Christianity (the literature covered in BAGD) it is almost entirely limited to 4 occurrences in Revelation 19, where it appears in the description of a heavenly service of thanksgiving. In vv. 1, 3, and 6 ἀλληλουϊά stands at the beginning of a brief hymn of praise sung by a heavenly multitude; in v. 4 (in an apparent reversal of usual liturgical sequence) the praise of the multitude is acknowledged by the chief members of the hierarchy by means of the responsive ἀμὴν ἀλληλουϊά (a similar case, also responsive, is in Ps 106:48). V. 5 translates ἀλληλουϊά with "Praise our God."

H.-W. Kuhn

ἀλλήλων (-οις, -ους) *allēlōn* each other

Lit.: BDF §§247.4, 287. — M. H. Bolkestein, "Het woord 'elkaar' in het NT," *Ministerium* 3 (1969) 37-40. — Moulton, *Grammar* III, 43f. — Schwyzer, *Grammatik* I, 446.

1. The reciprocal pron. ἀλλήλων (attested from the beginnings of Greek literature) is formed by the doubling of the stem ἀλλο- (→ ἄλλος). It originally means *one to the other(s)* (cf. Acts 2:12: ἄλλος πρὸς ἄλλον); thus it corresponds to Eng. *each other* (Germ. *einander*). In the NT it is neut. in Gal 5:17; 1 Cor 12:25 (*contra* F. Blass, A. Debrunner, and F. Rehkopf, *Grammatik des neutestamentlichen Griechisch* [[14]1976] §287, n. 1) and otherwise masc.

Hebrew (and Aramaic) has no corresponding single word, but says something like *a man—his neighbor (brother), this one to that one, one (person) to one (person)* (cf. 1 Thess 5:11: εἷς τὸν ἕνα), or uses reflexive vb. forms in the hithpael or niphal (this suggested by H.-P. Stähli of Bethel).

2. The understanding of ἀλλήλων in the NT is unproblematic; the translation *each other* or *mutually* is sufficient for every instance. Rarely are two individual persons meant (Luke 23:12; 24:14, 17, 32; Acts 15:39; 1 Cor 7:5). Matt 25:32 speaks of the separation of all people *from each other* into two groups. A personalization is present in Rom 2:15 (literally: the thoughts accuse or defend *among themselves,* μεταξὺ ἀλλήλων), as in Gal 5:17 (flesh and Spirit "are opposed to *each other*"). Otherwise ἀλλήλων is used in connection with groups of persons who are in some way peers and with reference to relationships within a homogeneous group in order to express communication with or, sometimes, negative conduct toward, each other. (It never refers to the relationship of Jesus to his disciples or of Christ to his people; on the other hand, and significantly, it is used with reference to Paul and the Church in Rom 1:12.)

Of theological relevance here is the use of ἀλλήλων primarily in the description of the (obligatory) conduct of Christians in the community toward each other, with emphasis on mutuality and culminating in the love commandment: ἀγαπᾶν ἀλλήλους *(passim)* or → ἀγάπη εἰς ἀλλήλους (1 Thess 3:12; 2 Thess 1:3) or ἐν ἀλλήλοις (John 13:35). The addition of καὶ εἰς πάντας (1 Thess 3:12; cf. 5:15) shows that by his use of ἀλλήλων Paul makes the love which members of the Church are to have *among themselves* the top priority (cf. also Gal 6:10). But neither there nor in the Johannine texts (esp. John 13:34f.; 15:12, 17; 1 John 3:23; 4:7, 11f.) is the comprehensive commandment to love one's neighbor made more narrow by the qualifying ἀλλήλους.

The phrase ἐσμὲν ἀλλήλων μέλη (Rom 12:5; Eph 4:25) means: "we are members *in our mutual relationship*" (RSV "one of another").

H. Krämer

ἀλλογενής, 2 *allogenēs* foreign*

Luke 17:18 (referring to the Samaritan from the perspective of a Jew). F. Büchsel, *TDNT* I, 266f.

ἅλλομαι *hallomai* leap*

Acts 3:8; 14:10; of *bubbling* water: John 4:14.

ἄλλος, 3 *allos* another

1. Occurrences in the NT — 2. Meaning — 3. Usage

Lit.: BDF §306. — F. Büchsel, *TDNT* I, 264f. — O. Cullmann, "Samaria and the Origins of the Christian Mission," *idem, The Early Church* (1956) 185-92.

1. As was the case already in pre-NT Greek, the NT uses ἄλλος and → ἕτερος interchangeably with no difference in meaning (cf. Büchsel; H. W. Beyer, *TDNT* II, 702-4). This is conspicuous in Gal 1:6f. and enumerations such as Matt 16:14; 1 Cor 12:8-10, etc. Even an unrefined statistical analysis of the NT documents, whose volume makes them relevant in this regard, demonstrates both that

the change from one of the two terms to the other is normally without meaning and that individual authors generally prefer one of the words to the other. The use of ἄλλος and ἕτερος is as follows: Matthew has 29 and 9 respectively, Mark 22 and 1, Luke 11 and 33, Acts 7 and 17, John 43 and 1, Revelation 18 and none, Paul 31 and 30, Hebrews 2 and 5, James 1 and 1. The LXX has ἄλλος *ca.* 50 times and ἕτερος *ca.* 150 times (Morgenthaler, *Statistik* 71, 101).

2. In the neutral sense ἄλλος means *another* or (several) *others, an additional person* or *persons* besides or in addition to the speaker(s) or person(s) mentioned or implied in the context (e.g., Matt 4:21; 27:42 par.; Mark 15:41; 1 Cor 9:27; 10:29; John 14:16; esp. in enumerations such as οἱ μὲν . . . ἄλλοι δέ, Matt 16:14; πολλοί . . . ἄλλοι, John 10:21; μήτε . . . μήτε . . . μήτε ἄλλον, Jas 5:12; cf. also the lists of signs, angels, animals, etc. in Revelation). Ὁ ἄλλος—in the sense of ὁ ἕτερος—is specifically *the one* or *the other of two*, as in Matt 5:39 par.; John 19:32; Rev 17:10, etc. Frequently this expresses an "antithetical parallelism" (e.g., ἄλλος . . . ἄλλος, John 4:37; ἐγώ . . . ἄλλος, 5:31f., 43; Phil 3:4) or an exclusive distinction of one over against the other. The word can also mean *different in kind* (e.g., Matt 2:12; Mark 14:57f.; John 10:16; 1 Cor 15:39-41, etc.). On the other hand, when the existence of an ἄλλος is denied, then *another, a second,* or *additional* persons or things *of the same rank or nature* are excluded (e.g., Mark 12:29-31; Acts 4:12; 1 Cor 3:11; Gal 1:6).

3. Examples of the latter meaning make clear that the real issue is the categorical uniqueness of the biblical, in particular of the NT, message, its contents, and those who represent it. The existence or even theoretical possibility of *additional things or persons of a particular kind,* of *something identical* or *of the same nature or worth* is denied. No commandment is greater than the double love commandment. *No other* is equal to it or excels it just as *no other* god exists besides the one God (Mark 12:29-32). According to John 15:24 *no other, no second one* exists who could have accomplished the deeds performed by Jesus. According to Acts 4:12 salvation is in *no other one.* Paul makes the same claim for the gospel which he preaches. Jesus Christ is the foundation of the Church, laid in the proclamation; no one can lay *any other* (1 Cor 3:11). There is *no other* gospel than that of Jesus Christ (Gal 1:6).

K. Weiss

ἀλλοτριεπίσκοπος, ου, ὁ *allotriepiskopos* busybody*

1 Pet 4:15: perhaps *someone who meddles in things that do not concern him;* see H. W. Beyer, *TDNT* II, 620-22; BAGD s.v. For the view that it means *one who misappropriates* or *embezzles,* see J. B. Bauer, *BZ* 22 (1978) 109-15.

ἀλλότριος, 3 *allotrios* belonging to another

Subst. τὸ ἀλλότριον, *that which belongs to another* (Luke 16:12), ὁ ἀλλότριος, *the stranger* (Matt 17:25, 26; John 10:5a, b). F. Büchsel, *TDNT* I, 265; H. Bietenhard, *DNTT* I, 684f.

ἀλλόφυλος, 2 *allophylos* foreign*

Acts 10:28; cf. 13:19 D sy^{h}. F. Büchsel, *TDNT* I, 267.

ἄλλως *allōs* otherwise*

1 Tim 5:25: τὰ ἄλλως ἔχοντα, *what is otherwise the case.*

ἀλοάω *aloaō* thresh*

1 Cor 9:9f.; 1 Tim 5:18, both based on Deut 25:4.

ἄλογος, 2 *alogos* mute, irrational*

Acts 25:27; 2 Pet 2:12; Jude 10. G. Kittel, *TDNT* IV, 141.

ἀλόη, ης, ἡ *aloē* aloe*

John 19:39: Nicodemus brought "a mixture of myrrh and *aloes.*" *BL* 50.

ἁλυκός, 3 *halykos* salty*

Jas 3:12, referring to a *salty* spring (?); see BAGD s.v.

ἄλυπος, 2 *alypos* without anxiety*

Phil 2:28. R. Bultmann, *TDNT* IV, 323.

ἅλυσις, εως, ἡ *halysis* chain*

Mark 5:3, 4 (bis); Luke 8:29; Acts 12:6, 7; 21:33; 28:20 (handcuffs?); Eph 6:20; 2 Tim 1:16; Rev 20:1.

ἀλυσιτελής, 2 *alysitelēs* unprofitable*

Heb 13:17: "that would be *of no advantage* to you."

Ἄλφα, τό *Alpha* Alpha*
Ὦ[μεγα], τό *Ō(mega)* Omega*

Lit.: W. J. P. Boyd, " 'I am Alpha and Omega' (Rev. 1, 8; 21, 6; 22, 13)," *SE* II (1964) 526-31. — F. Dornseiff, *Das Alphabet in Mystik und Magie* (²1925 [= 1975]). — H. Hommel, *Schöpfer und Erhalter* (1956) 32-137. — G. Kittel, *TDNT* I, 1-3. — H. Kosmala, "Anfang, Mitte und Ende," *ASTI* 2 (1963) 108-11. — E. Lohmeyer, *RAC* I, 1-4. — W. O. Moeller, *The Mithraic*

Origin and Meaning of the Rotas-Sator Square (1973). — W. C. VAN UNNIK, *Het godspredikaat 'Het begin en het einde' bij Flavius Josephus en in de openbaring van Johannes* (1976).

The name of the letter Ἄλφα appears in the NT only in the formula ἐγώ (εἰμι) τὸ Ἄλφα καὶ τὸ Ὦ (Rev 1:8; 21:6; 22:13). In 1:8 "the Lord God" (= *yhwh 'ĕlōhîm*) reveals himself as *the Alpha and the O(mega),* the one "who is and who was and who is to come, the Almighty"; in 21:6 he reveals himself as *the Alpha and the O(mega),* "the beginning and the end"; in 22:13 Christ is revealed as *the Alpha and the O(mega),* "the first and the last, the beginning and the end." The parallel phrases interpret each other, even though each carries its own peculiar emphasis. Each gives expression in its distinctive manner to power and lordship (for "the first and the last" cf. van Unnik; for the three-member statement referring to time and for παντοκράτωρ cf. G. Delling, *Studien zum NT und zum hellenistischen Judentum* [1970] 439-48).

As a predicate of God the phrase "the Alpha and the O(mega)" is attested in neither the Greek nor the Jewish sphere. A divine name constructed from all the vowels occurs occasionally in syncretistic contexts (cf. *PGM* V, 468, 472; Eusebius *PE* xi.6.37); what is important in this name, however, is the use of all the vowels and only the vowels; the sequence from alpha to omega has no significance. Nor does the manipulation of the letters of the alphabet by the Gnostic Marcus (Irenaeus *Haer.* i.14) offer a satisfactory explanation for the origin of the "Alpha and Omega" predicate.

Though first attested in the 3rd cent. A.D., a rabbinical designation for God—"Truth" (= *'ĕmeṯ*)—is more likely to be relevant here. Resh Lakish (R. Simon b. Lakish, *ca.* A.D. 250) pointed out with regard to *'ĕmeṯ that 'ālep̱* is the first letter, *mêm* the middle letter, and *tāw* the final letter and related this explicitly to Isa 44:6 (*y. Sanh.* 1:18a, 22; *Gen. Rab.* 81 [52a]; see Billerbeck II, 362; III, 789). In the Hebrew alphabet, however, *mêm* is not the middle letter—unlike μ in the Greek alphabet. Thus one can assume that behind *'-m-ṯ* as Resh Lakish speaks of it stands a Greek designation: α-μ-ω. The absence of the μ in Revelation is explicable. The formula "the first and the last" also occurs in a three-member form with the addition or insertion of "the middle" (both forms appear alongside each other in Josephus *Ant.* viii.280 and *Ap.* ii.190; and Resh Lakish related the three-member form to a two-member form [Isa. 44:6]). The late and indirect attestation in the rabbinic texts remains problematic. (But it is possible that the letters ΑΝΩ beneath the Rotas-Sator Square in Pompeii [*CIL* IV, 8623] represent the Greek divine name assumed by this reading of the rabbinic texts and demonstrate its existence for the period prior to A.D. 79).

The designation will have found its way into Revelation through Judaism. It designates God, and, through God, Christ as well, as those who encompass the whole of reality and have power over all of reality.

T. Holtz

Ἁλφαῖος, ου *Halphaios* Alphaeus*

1. The father of the tax-collector Levi (Mark 2:14; cf. Luke 5:27 D). 2. The father of James, one of the disciples (Matt 10:3; Mark 3:18; Luke 6:15; Acts 1:13). J. Blinzler, *LTK* I, 366; A. W. Fortune, *ISBE* I, 100.

ἅλων, ωνος, ἡ *halōn* threshing floor*

Matt 3:12 par. Luke 3:17: he will clear his *threshing floor.*

ἀλώπηξ, εκος, ἡ *alōpēx* fox*

Matt 8:20 par. Luke 9:58; Luke 13:32 (referring to Herod Antipas; see BAGD s.v. 2).

ἅλωσις, εως, ἡ *halōsis* *capture**

2 Pet 2:12: animals are born *to be caught.*

ἅμα *hama* at the same time (as); together (with)

Matt 20:1: ἅμα πρωΐ, *in the early morning.* As a designation for essential solidarity: Rom 3:12.

ἀμαθής, 2 *amathēs* ignorant*

2 Pet 3:16: "The *ignorant* and unstable."

ἀμαράντινος, 3 *amarantinos* unfading*

1 Pet 5:4: "You will obtain the *unfading* crown of glory."

ἀμάραντος, 2 *amarantos* unfading*

1 Pet 1:4: the *unfading* inheritance.

ἁμαρτάνω *hamartanō* sin (vb.)
→ ἁμαρτία.

ἁμάρτημα, ατος, τό *hamartēma* transgression, sin
→ ἁμαρτία.

ἁμαρτία, ας, ἡ *hamartia* sin (noun)
ἁμαρτάνω *hamartanō* sin (vb.)
ἁμάρτημα, ατος, τό *hamartēma* transgression, sin*
ἁμαρτωλός, 2 *hamartōlos* sinful, iniquitous

1. Occurrences of the word group in the NT — 2. Meanings — 3. Usage and semantic field — 4. a) Paul — b) John — c) 1 John — d) Hebrews

Lit.: G. BAUMBACH, *Das Verständnis des Bösen in den synoptischen Evangelien* (1963). — J. BECKER, *Das Heil Gottes* (1964). — G. BORNKAMM, *Paul* (1971) 120-95. — E. BRANDENBURGER, *Adam und Christus* (WMANT 7, 1962). — *idem, Fleisch und Geist* (WMANT 29, 1968). — F.-M. BRAUN, "Le péché du monde selon St. Jean," *RevThom* 65 (1965) 181-201. — BULTMANN, *Theology,* esp. §§21-27 (I, 227-69; see also the additional comments of O. Merk in the more recent German edition: *Theologie des Neuen Testaments* [⁹1984]). — C. COLPE, "Der Spruch von der Lästerung des Geistes," FS Jeremias (1970) 63-79. — P. DELHAYE, A. DESCHAMPS, et al., *Theologie du péché* (1960). — J. R. DONAHUE, "Tax Collectors and Sinners," *CBQ* 33 (1971) 39-61. — P. FIEDLER, *Jesus und die Sünder* (1976). — E. GRÄSSER, "Rechtfertigung im Hebr.," FS Käsemann, 79-93. — W. Günther, *DNTT* III, 577-83, with bibliography on 586f. — O. HOFIUS, *Jesu Tischgemeinschaft mit den Sündern* (1967). — J. JEREMIAS, "Zöllner und Sünder," *ZNW* 30 (1931) 293-300. — K. KERTELGE, "Die Vollmacht des Menschensohnes zur Sündenvergebung," FS Schmid (1973) 205-13. — W. G. KÜMMEL, *Römer 7 und das Bild des Menschen im NT* (1974). — *idem, Theology of the NT* (1973) 172-85. — K. G. KUHN, "Peirasmos—hamartia—sarx im NT und damit zusammenhängende Vorstellungen," *ZTK* 49 (1952) 200-222. — N. LAZURE, *Les valeurs morales de la théologie johannique* (1965) 285-328. — H. LEROY, *Zur Vergebung der Sünden* (SBS 73, 1974). — L. LIGIER, *Péché d'Adam et péché du monde* II (1961). — E. LÖVESTAM, *Spiritus blasphemia* (1968). — S. LYONNET, "L'histoire du salut selon le ch. 7 de l'épître aux Romains," *Bib* 43 (1962) 117-51. — S. LYONNET and L. SABOURIN, *Sin, Redemption and Sacrifice* (AnBib 48, 1970). — I. MAISCH, *Die Heilung des Gelähmten* (SBS 52, 1971). — B. J. MALINA, "Some Observations on the Origin of Sin in Judaism and St. Paul," *CBQ* 31 (1969) 18-34. — O. MERK, *Handeln aus Glauben* (1968) 4-41. — J. MICHL, "Sündenvergebung in Christus nach dem Glauben der frühen Kirche," *MTZ* 24 (1973) 25-35. — *idem*, "Sündenbekenntnis und Sündenvergebung in der Kirche des NT," *MTZ* 24 (1973) 189-207. — R. PESCH, "Das Zöllnergastmahl," FS Rigaux, 63-87. — G. QUELL, G. BERTRAM, G. STÄHLIN, and W. GRUNDMANN, *TDNT* I, 267-316. — K. H. RENGSTORF, *TDNT* I, 317-35. — SCHELKLE, *Theology* II, §8; III, §3. — R. SCHNACKENBURG, "Christ and Sin According to John," Schnackenburg II, 115-50. — A. STROBEL, *Erkenntnis und Bekenntnis der Sünde in neutestamentlicher Zeit* (1968). — H. THYEN, *Studien zur Sündenvergebung* (FRLANT 96, 1970). — U. WILCKENS, "Vergebung für die Sünderin," FS Schmid (1973) 394-424.

1. By far the most frequently used term for sin in the NT (as in the LXX) is ἁμαρτία: there are 173 occurrences (excluding 2 Thess 2:3), of which 48 are in Romans (42 in chs. 5–8), 25 in Hebrews, 17 in 1 John, 24 in the Synoptics—of which 11 are in Luke—and 8 in Acts; ἁμάρτημα occurs only 4 times (Mark 3:28, 29; Rom 3:25; 1 Cor 6:18). The use of ἁμαρτία in the sg. is striking in Paul (59 occurrences) as well as—less markedly—in John (17 occurrences) and 1 John. Ἁμαρτάνω (43 instances including John 8:11) appears in noticeable concentration in 1 John (10 occurrences) and Romans and 1 Corinthians (7 each). Ἁμαρτωλός (47 occurrences) is found chiefly in the Synoptics (29 occurrences), again led by Luke (18, but none in Acts).

2. a) Ἁμαρτία signifies primarily a *failure* to achieve a standard (whether culpable or unintentional) in the broadest sense, both as deed and as the nature of the deed. The distinction between ἁμαρτία and ἁμάρτημα which denotes the individual deed and the result (*failure* whether culpable or through oversight) is, however, largely obliterated. The preponderant use of ἁμάρτημα in secular Greek recedes far behind the use of ἁμαρτία in the LXX, where the religious dimension is determinative of the meaning of the word: "sin" as becoming and being guilty before God and one's peers. The expansion of the concept of ἁμαρτία, and this not only in regard to *ḥaṭṭā'ṯ* and *'āwôn*, is attested by the increasing importance and uniformity of the concept. Ἁμαρτία as "atoning sacrifice" is attested in the LXX quotations in Heb 10:6, 8, though the idea is not appropriated in the letter itself (though perhaps in Rom 8:3).

b) Ἁμαρτάνω meant *miss the mark, err,* and then following the Homeric period *transgress.* Like ἁμαρτία it had a decidedly religious character in the LXX and the NT (including Acts 25:8; 1 Cor 6:18; but not 1 Pet 2:20).

c) The adj. ἁμαρτωλός (Mark 8:38; John 9:16; esp. Luke) was used in the LXX (primarily subst.) for *rāšā'* and characterizes in Jewish thought both the Jewish and, prompted by adherence to the Torah, the Gentile adversary as the (godless) *guilty one,* the *evildoer* (e.g., 1 Macc 1:34). Paul distinguishes himself along with Peter from the sinful Gentile world (Gal 2:15). Mark 14:41 (par. Matt 26:45) and Luke 24:7 (cf. also Heb 12:3) may refer to Jesus' being delivered to the Gentiles (i.e., the Romans), but on the basis of Mark 9:31 the word "sinner" is more appropriate; likewise in Luke 6:32-34 (in spite of Matt 5:46f.).

3. a) A central concern in the conception of *sin* in the NT is the elimination of sin and of the accompanying guilt. The use of → ἄφεσις for "forgiveness of sins" is almost exclusively confined to the Synoptics (Mark 1:4 par. Luke 3:3; Luke 1:77 in relation to John the Baptist; in the mouth of Jesus only in Matt 26:28 and of the Risen Christ in Luke 24:47; Acts picks up on the latter reference: 2:38; 5:31; 10:43; 13:38; 26:18; additionally Col 1:14 in connection with baptism; parenthetically, Heb 10:18; 9:22); cf. also the pre-Pauline expression in Rom 3:25f.: πάρεσις (= ἄφεσις) τῶν ἁμαρτημάτων. Forgiveness is also spoken of by means of the verb ἀφίημι (Mark 2:5b-10 par.; cf. Luke 7:47-49 as well as Luke 11:4 in the Lukan version of the Lord's Prayer [the basis of the imagery in Matt 6:12]; John 20:23; 1 John 1:9; 2:12). Mark 3:28f. (par. Matt 12:31) denies the forgiveness of sins only in the case of one who rejects the divine Spirit at work in the primitive Christian mission.

The idea of removal of sin and guilt is presented in a number of other ways (Matt 1:21; John 1:29 and 1 John 3:5; Acts 3:19; 7:60; 22:16; Heb 9:26, 28 [par. 1 Pet 2:24, both based on Isa 53:12]; 10:4, 11 (cf. the quotation of the LXX in Rom 11:27]; Rev 1:5; cultic formulas are used in Heb 1:3; 2:17; 2 Pet 1:9; 1 John 1:7; 2:2; 4:10). The quotations in Rom 4:7f. (on "cover" see also Jas 5:20; 1 Pet 4:8) and Heb 8:12; 10:17 confirm that the same thing is in mind as in statements regarding "forgiveness." Romans 6 (→ 4) is dominated by the notion of dying to sin and being freed from it (pl. "sins" in Eph 2:1; 1 Pet 2:24; 4:1). Confession also belongs in the context of the removal of sin (Mark 1:5 par. Matt 3:6; Jas 5:16; 1 John 1:9). The vicarious sacrifice of life "for" sins (→ ὑπέρ; → περί) is spoken of in 1 Cor 15:3; Gal 1:4 (cf. Rom 5:8; 8:3; 2 Cor 5:21); 1 Pet 3:18. On Hebrews → 4. Statements which sound traditional are largely shaped by Christian interests, as, e.g., when the texts speak about committing sin(s) (John 8:34; 2 Cor 11:7; Jas 2:9; 5:15; 1 John 3:4, 8f.; see also 1 Pet 2:22 [based on Isa 53:9]) or give warnings against sin(s) (John 8:21-24; 1 Tim 5:22, alongside Rev 18:4; Heb 12:1, 4) and identify the sin (or the sinner) while giving the warning (John 9:34; 1 Cor 15:17; Rom 14:23; 1 Tim 5:24; Heb 3:13; 11:25; Jas 1:15; 4:17; polemically in 1 Thess 2:16; 2 Tim 3:6; 2 Pet 2:14; Rev 18:5). On 1 John → 4. Statements regarding the sinlessness of Jesus are found in various contexts (John 8:46 [cf. 9:13-34]; 2 Cor 5:21; Heb 4:15 [for a different view cf. 9:28]; 7:26; 1 Pet 2:22; 1 John 3:5).

b) The vb. appears in Church rules (Matt 18:15, 21 par. Luke 17:3f.; 1 Tim 5:20; Titus 3:11), in particular statements in 1 Corinthians (6:18; 7:28, 36; 8:12), in confessions (Matt 27:4; Luke 15:18, 21; cf. Acts 25:8), in warnings and admonitions (John 5:14; 8:11; 1 Cor 15:34; Eph 4:26 [= Ps 4:5]), as well as in various other statements (e.g., Heb 3:17 [cf. Num 14:29]; 2 Pet 2:4 [cf. Gen 6:1-4 and early Jewish expositions such as *1 Enoch* 6f.]).

c) Ἁμαρτωλός occurs, among other places, in the summary description of Jesus' works in Mark 2:17 par., in the confessional "word" in 1 Tim 1:15, and in parenetic contexts (Luke 18:13; Jas 4:8; 5:20; cf. 1 John 5:16; Matt 18:15). In the accusation against Jesus that he was a friend of "tax collectors and sinners" (Mark 2:15f.; Q: Matt 11:19 par. Luke 7:34) the post-Easter (so Pesch 73f.) comment "sinners" reflects disputes concerning acceptance into the Church of persons generally despised as sinners, among whom tax-collectors were numbered (cf. the lists in *b. Sanh.* 25b *Bar.*); in Judea and after A.D. 44 also in Galilee the explosive power of the accusation increased even more, since tax-collectors were seen as collaborators with the Gentile occupation forces. The Evangelist understands Luke 7:36-50 (he does not say why the woman is a sinner) as an illustration of v. 34. He takes up the accusation of 7:34 in 15:1f. (cf. also 19:7) as an introduction to the collection of parables in which he is concerned to demonstrate the "joy of God" over the sinner who has been led by Jesus to repentance, rather than over the (self-)"righteous" ones (15:7, 10; cf. 5:32 along with Mark 2:17).

4. a) Of great theological importance are, first of all, the statements of Paul about sin, which do not, of course, constitute a "doctrine" of sin (the sg. is used already in the LXX [e.g., Sir 21:2; 27:10] and in the Qumran literature [e.g., 1 QH 4:29f.; cf. 1:27: "service of sin"]; on Gnostic statements see Brandenburger, *Adam* 64-67). Paul himself speaks about particular sins only in Rom 7:15; 1 Cor 15:17 (dependent on v. 3) and clearly also in the sg. in Rom 14:23; 2 Cor 11:7.

Sin as (demonic) power in contrast to the proclamation of Christ is the center of attention in Romans 5–8. In the continuation of 5:10f. in vv. 12-21 the abundance of the life-giving grace "through" Christ is delineated over against its opposite (cf. v. 14: τύπος), which is death-bringing sin "through" Adam (Gen 3; → Ἀδάμ). Because of the incomparable nature of Christ's work (cf. Rom. 5:15ff.), the comparison with Adam's deed, begun in v. 12, is broken off after it has been made clear that death, which, since Adam's sin, encompasses all humankind (cf. 4 Ezra 3:7; *2 Bar.* 23:4), is not mere fate but equally a deserved punishment "since all have sinned" (cf. *2 Bar.* 54:15, 19, which refers, of course, to premature death). To this extent, then, there is no thought here of "original" sin, which is to be kept in mind in connection with Rom 5:19 as well.

For Paul this universality of sin, already articulated in Rom 3:9 as part of the argument which begins at 1:18 and is repeated in 3:23, is a firm conviction based on his faith; therefore he can also show how God has announced it in the Scriptures (Gal 3:22). Of course, in the time prior to the law sin was not reckoned as transgression (cf. 4:15); yet even those who—unlike Adam—have not broken a specific commandment are nonetheless subject to death since sin reigned from Adam to Moses as well (5:13f.; cf. 2:12). The way is thus prepared for 5:20: the law came in (only) "to increase the trespass." This, in turn, is viewed from the perspective of the Christ-event: the abundance of sin occasioned by the law is followed by the even greater abundance of grace; grace terminates the reign of sin which manifests itself in death (v. 21).

In order to guard against any misunderstanding of sin as the motivating power behind grace, a misunderstanding made possible by Rom. 5:20f., Paul turns in 6:1 (cf. 3:5-8) to the language of baptismal catechesis: death with Christ to the detriment of sin (the once-for-all character of which is emphasized in 6:10) frees from the law (v. 7; cf. 7:1f.) and excludes the possibility of continuing in sin (6:2; cf. v. 6: the destruction of the being which is subject to sin). To be dead to sin means to be alive to God (v. 11: to the "change of reign" here cf. the idea of the "change of place" in 2 Cor 5:21; the absurdity of the question in Gal 2:17 also becomes apparent). Following the transitional parenesis in Rom 6:12-14 and the question of v. 15 (a variation of v. 1), vv. 16-23 develop the idea that liberation from the death-bringing (v. 23: death as wages) slavery to sin (already in v. 6) involves the transfer "to [the reign of] righteousness for sanctification," which has as its end eternal life (cf. 5:12, 21).

Paul's exposition of the Christian's liberation from the law (Rom 7:1-6; cf. 6:14) indicates, in respect to existence "in the flesh," that sinful passions were effective "by the law" (i.e., as Paul says in 1 Cor 15:56, "sin gains its power from the law" [NEB]) for death (Rom 7:5). To forestall an equation of the law with the power of sin, Paul assigns to the indisputably holy law the role of allowing sin, which uses the commandment as an opportunity to work its deadly consequences, to spring to life in the human being (vv. 7-12). The law did this by bringing sin, specifically covetousness, to consciousness (cf. 3:20; Jas 1:15 psychologizes). A contradiction to Rom 5:12ff. is avoided if we interpret 7:9-11 as a reference to the failure of Adam, understood here as the prototype of humanity under the law (Lyonnet, esp. 130-42). The summary in 7:13 reinforces 5:20a. From 7:14 attention shifts to the "carnal" person, i.e., the person enslaved to sin (v. 14), the one totally dominated by it (vv. 17, 20) and subject to its law (v. 23), who longs for redemption (see Kümmel, *Römer* 7). The Christian who in faith has recognized this past for what it is knows that he has been rescued from it (v. 25a; v. 25b with its antithesis of flesh and mind is a gloss).

The transition to life in the Spirit having been thus accomplished, Rom 8:2-4 summarizes what has been said in chs. 5–7: liberation from the law and thus from sin and death occurs because God has executed the (death) sentence required by the law on sin in the flesh through his Son (as an expiation?), who took upon himself human—and hence temptable—existence. In so doing God has made life possible for those in the Spirit, those whose being had been subject to sin and precisely because of sin has been done away with (8:10; cf. 6:6; 2 Cor 5:21).

b) John 1:29 speaks of the sin of the (human) world which the Lamb of God (→ ἀμνός) bears away. According to 8:24 failure to believe in the divine Revealer, Jesus, produces death in one's sins. This lack of faith, which expresses itself in hatred against Jesus and his Father and also against the Church, is declared to be the sin of the world (15:22, 24) for which there is no pardon (cf. vv. 18-25; 9:41). In addition to convincing the world of the existence of righteousness and judgment, the Paraclete (through the Church) is to convict it of the sin of unbelief (16:8f. in the context of vv. 8-11; cf. on the other hand 8:46; on this idea see also Jude 15; *1 Enoch* 1:9). The statement that by committing sin one demonstrates one's subjection to sin (John 8:34; cf. Rom 6), in contrast to the liberation which comes through the truth of the Son, also refers to failure to believe, which thus takes concrete form in sinful deeds (cf. in John 19:11 the "greater" sin of the one who hands Jesus over; also 8:21 in connection with 8:24).

c) 1 John relates the discussion of sin(s) and sinning more firmly to the situation of the Church. To begin with, the issue of sinning on the part of Christians is raised (1:7b–2:2) in order to warn not only against sinning (2:1a) but also against the self-deception which attempts to make a liar of God (1:8, 10); instead, one is encouraged to confident confession of sin (1:9; 2:1b). In accordance with the unmistakable foundation given in 1:9 (cf. 2:12), assurances of salvation which appear to be traditional shape the discussion (cf. also 4:10). 1 John 1:7b speaks of cleansing by means of the blood of Jesus and 2:2 speaks of world-encompassing expiation. In contrast 3:5 understands the "taking away" of sins (cf. John 1:29, sg. "sin") through the sinless Jesus as the destruction of the "works" of the devil who (according to 1 John 3:8) was sinful from the beginning (Gen 3; cf. John 8:44) and from whom sinners (i.e., those who do not believe or believe wrongly [heretics]) are descended. Here, to be sure, that the sin of unfaith expresses itself in deeds is stressed even more (1 John 3:5 has the pl. "sins"; v. 4 equates sin and lawlessness, 5:17 sin and wrongdoing).

For 1 John as a whole the apparent discrepancy between 3:6, 9 (and 5:18) on the one hand and 1:7b–2:2 on the other is best resolved by regarding the statements in ch. 3, like the epistle's earlier statements, as also referring to the basic sin of not seeing God. This permits even the statement that the person born of God *cannot* sin (3:9): such a person demonstrates this gracious basis of one's Christian existence by loving the brother (v. 10). In like manner, finally, unbelief or wrong belief ("mortal sin") in 5:16-18 stands alongside the nonmortal sin of the Christian for whose life the brother is to pray to God; reconciliation with John 20:23 is not sought (the issue of "mortal sin" lies outside the scope of the passage).

d) Hebrews sums up the work of Christ under the theme of purification from sins (1:3). This is described as expiation for the sins of the people (of God) and is the responsibility of the high priest (2:17). This cultic orientation for christology and soteriology is developed in detail, as follows:

Christ is the perfect high priest (→ ἀρχιερεύς) as a man appointed on behalf of mankind to offer sacrifices for sin (5:1); he is subject to "weakness" and temptation (v. 2), but without sin (4:15), and therefore, unlike every other high priest, he is not bound to offer sacrifices (on every Day of Atonement) for his own sins (v. 3; cf. 7:27, where "daily" intentionally goes beyond Lev 16:29-34; in Heb 10:11 Israel's entire sacrificial system is viewed as insufficient).

The most important soteriological section of Hebrews, 8:8–10:18, has its decisive premise in 9:22 (without the shedding of blood there is no forgiveness of sins), and is framed by quotations from Jeremiah 31. Christ is the perfect sacrifice for sin once (and for all) revealed by God at the end of the ages (Heb 9:26, 28); thereafter he goes to God, and the culmination takes place in the heavenly sanctuary (10:12). By contrast, Israel's sacrifices can "never" (v. 11) take away sins: it is also "impossible" for the blood of sacrificial animals to accomplish this (v. 4); by such means the consciousness of sin is maintained rather than purged as in the case of those who have been completely purified through Christ (vv. 2f.). Since Jer 31:33f. has thus been fulfilled for these persons, an offering for sins is superfluous (Heb 10:18).

However, for one who willfully (cf. Num 15:30) renounces Christ there is no longer any sacrifice for sins, not even that of Christ (Heb 10:26; cf. 6:4-6). At issue here, then, is not a "second repentance" of a Christian. Rather, the concern here is to deal seriously and emphatically with the danger that through the enticement of sin the faith of the people of God could grow slack (12:1; cf. Moses as a counterexample in 11:25). Instead, the faithful can and should be encouraged through Jesus, the pioneer and perfecter of their faith, to resist sin with determination to the greatest extremity (12:1-4). At his second coming, distinguished in 9:28 from the first coming which served to eliminate sin, he will meet them for the purpose of bringing redemption to its final culmination.

P. Fiedler

ἀμάρτυρος, 2 *amartyros* without witness*

Acts 14:17: God did not leave himself *without witness.*

ἁμαρτωλός, 2 *hamartōlos* sinful, iniquitous
→ ἁμαρτία.

ἄμαχος, 2 *amachos* peaceable*

1 Tim 3:3; Titus 3:2. O. Bauernfeind, *TDNT* IV, 527f.

ἀμάω *amaō* mow*

Jas 5:4: mowing of fields.

ἀμέθυστος, ου, ἡ *amethystos* amethyst*

Rev 21:20: the twelfth foundation stone is *amethyst* (cf. Exod 28:19; Ezek 28:13 LXX).

ἀμελέω *ameleō* neglect*

Matt 22:5; 1 Tim 4:14; Heb 2:3; 8:9; cf. 2 Pet 1:12 Koine *pl* sy.

ἄμεμπτος, 2 *amemptos* blameless*

Luke 1:6; Phil 2:15; 3:6; 1 Thess 3:13; Heb 8:7. W. Grundmann, *TDNT* IV, 571-74.

ἀμέμπτως *amemptōs* blamelessly

1 Thess 2:10; 5:23. W. Grundmann, *TDNT* IV, 571-74.

ἀμέριμνος, 2 *amerimnos* free from care*

Matt 28:14; 1 Cor 7:32. R. Bultmann, *TDNT* IV, 589-93.

ἀμετάθετος, 2 *ametathetos* unchangeable*

Heb 6:17, 18: "the *unchangeable* character of [God's] purpose"; "through two *unchangeable* things" we have "strong encouragement."

ἀμετακίνητος, 2 *ametakinētos* immovable*

1 Cor 15:58: "Therefore . . . be steadfast, *immovable.*"

ἀμεταμέλητος, 2 *ametamelētos* without regret*

Rom 11:29; 2 Cor 7:10. O. Michel, *TDNT* IV, 626-29; F. Laubach, *DNTT* I, 356f.

ἀμετανόητος, 2 *ametanoētos* unrepentant*

Rom 2:5, referring to the *unrepentant* heart. J. Behm, *TDNT* IV, 1009; J. Goetzmann, *DNTT* I, 357-59.

ἄμετρος, 2 *ametros* boundless, immeasurable*

2 Cor 10:13, 15: "boast *beyond limit.*" K. Deissner, TDNT IV, 632-34.

ἀμήν *amēn* certainly, truly, amen

1. In Hebrew and Aramaic — 2. NT contexts — 3. As a liturgical conclusion — 4. As an opening word in sayings of Jesus — 5. As a predicate of Jesus

Lit.: K. Berger, *Die Amen-Worte Jesu* (1970). — *idem,* "Zur Geschichte der Einleitungsformel 'Amen, ich sage euch,' " *ZNW* 63 (1972) 45-75. — H. Bietenhard, *DNTT* I, 97-99. — Billerbeck I, 242-44; III, 456-61. — V. Hasler, *Amen* (1969). — J. Hempel, *IDB* I, 105. — A. Jepsen, *TDOT* I, 320-22. — Jeremias, *Theology* 35f. — *idem,* "Zum nichtresponsorischen Amen," *ZNW* 64 (1973) 122f. — *idem, TRE* II, 386-91. — H. Schlier, *TDNT* I, 335-38. — L. H. Silberman, "Farewell to O AMHN. A Note on Rev 3:14," *JBL* 82 (1963) 213-15. — G. Stählin, "Zum Gebrauch von Beteuerungsformeln im NT," *NovT* 5 (1962) 115-43. — J. Strugnell, " 'Amen, I say unto you' in the Sayings of Jesus and in Early Christian Literature," *HTR* 67 (1974) 177-82. — S. Talmon, "Amen as an Introductory Oath Formula," *Textus* 7 (1969) 124-29.

1. The word *'āmen,* attested in Hebrew (and also in Aramaic texts), is usually translated in the LXX as γένοιτο, *so be it;* otherwise the preference is for ἀμήν.

2. In most cases in the NT ἀμήν is found in connection with a formula or formulaic phrase: roughly half (12 or 13) of the occurrences outside the Gospels follow immediately after "for ever (and ever)" (εἰς τοὺς αἰῶνας [τῶν αἰώνων]; also in 4 Macc 18:24; cf. 1 Chr 16:36 LXX);

another 2 or 3 occurrences are similar. In the Gospels ἀμήν is used exclusively to introduce the phrase "I say to you" (λέγω ὑμῖν/σοι; the one exception is in the shorter ending of Mark); a single ἀμήν is used in the Synoptics (49 or 50 times) and a double ἀμήν in John (25 times). In the Synoptics the ἀμήν in the formula is occasionally replaced by, among other things, ναί, πλήν, or ἀληθῶς.

3. Ἀμήν occurs (corresponding to the OT and Jewish tradition) as a liturgical concluding word. Responsive pronouncement of the Amen (which appears first in Neh 8:6; also, e.g., *m. Ber.* 8:8) as a custom in the Church is clearly confirmed by 1 Cor 14:16. Overtones of this usage are also present in 2 Cor 1:20; furthermore, several texts from Revelation belong here: 5:14; 19:4; the ἀμήν of 7:12 which responds to v. 10; and the ἀμήν of 22:20b which responds to v. 20a. As an expression of affirmation ἀμήν can stand as the concluding word of an entire epistle (as the final word in the best mss. only in Galatians and Jude; 2 Peter v.l.; cf. Romans 15 and 16). It also closes smaller liturgical units (it functions in both ways in 4 Maccabees): at the conclusion of doxological sections (e.g., Rom 11:33-36; Eph 3:20f.) and formulas (e.g., Gal 1:5; 1 Pet 4:11), at the conclusion of a word of assurance (fut. tense, e.g., Phil 4:19f.), at the conclusion of a prayer of petition (optative, e.g., Heb 13:20f.), and following a wish for grace or peace (e.g., Gal 6:18; Rom 15:33).

4. Ἀμήν occurs as an opening word in the Gospels only in the words of Jesus. There it has the character of an oath-formula or, possibly, an authority-formula: ἀμὴν (ἀμὴν) λέγω ὑμῖν/σοι. In Q it probably appears at least twice (Matt 23:36 [the Lukan parallel has ναί]; 24:47 [the Lukan parallel has ἀληθῶς]; cf. ναί in Matt 11:9 par. Luke 7:26). In Mark it appears 13 times (probably largely traditional). Luke has only 3 occurrences from Mark (twice substituting ἀληθῶς for a Markan ἀμήν) and an additional 3 occurrences. Matthew has 9 occurrences from Mark and an additional 21 or 22 occurrences (only 2 are added to a Markan text, 10 are in texts from Q, and 9 or 10 are in M). The frequent oath-formula in John twice (13:21, 28) has a parallel in the Synoptic passion narrative. The double "Amen," the form always used in John, occurs also in the OT and in ancient Judaism (for references see J. Jeremias, *TLZ* 83 [1958] 504), but never in the opening position.

The use of an opening nonresponsive use of "Amen" has never been attested with certainty in ancient Judaism, neither in the OT (*contra* Talmon), nor on a seventh-century B.C. Hebrew ostracon (*contra* Bietenhard, Talmon, Strugnell), nor in rabbinic literature (*contra* Hasler), nor in Greek texts (*contra* Berger; on all these see Jeremias, *ZNW* [1973] 122f.; *contra* Berger see also E. Janssen, *JSHRZ* III, 222, n. 140). However, that Jesus himself used *'āmēn* before his sayings is likewise unproven.

5. In Rev 3:14 Jesus is given the title of *the "Amen"* (cf. Isa 65:16: *bē'lōhê 'āmēn* [bis]), which is explained by the phrase "the faithful and true witness" (see Ps 88:38 LXX); cf. 2 Cor 1:20.

H.-W. Kuhn

ἀμήτωρ, 1 *amētōr* without a mother*

Heb 7:3, of Melchizedek.

ἀμίαντος, 2 *amiantos* undefiled*

Heb 7:26; 13:4; Jas 1:27; 1 Pet 1:4. F. Hauck, *TDNT* IV, 647.

Ἀμιναδάβ *Aminadab* Amminadab*

Personal name (Ruth 4:19): Matt 1:4a, b; Luke 3:33.

ἄμμος, ου, ἡ *ammos* sand*

Matt 7:26; Rom 9:27; Heb 11:12; Rev 12:18; 20:8.

ἀμνός, οῦ, ὁ *amnos* lamb*
ἀρήν, ἀρνός, ὁ *arēn* lamb*
ἀρνίον, ου, τό *arnion* ram, lamb*

1. Occurrences in the NT — 2. Ἀμνός — 3. Ἀρνιόν — 4. Ἀρήν

Lit.: O. Böcher, *Die Johannesapokalypse* (1975). — J. Gess, *DNTT* II, 410-12. — J. Jeremias, *TDNT* I, 338-41. — T. Holtz, *Die Christologie der Apokalypse des Johannes* (1962) 27-48. — J. C. Moyer, *ISBE* III, 61f. — D. W. Wead, *ISBE* III, 62f.

1. Ἀμνός occurs a total of 4 times in the NT, all in christological contexts: Jesus is compared to a lamb (Acts 8:32, as a parallel to πρόβατον; 1 Pet 1:19) or called a lamb (John 1:29, 36). Of the 30 occurrences of ἀρνίον, 29 are in Revelation; of these, 28 refer to the exalted Christ (13:11 is the exception); in John 21:15 the pl. of ἀρνίον refers to the Church (parallel to πρόβατον). Ἀρήν occurs only in Luke 10:3 in the pl. to refer to the disciples of Jesus (par. Matt 10:6: πρόβατα).

2. Ἀμνός denotes a *lamb* of about one year; in the LXX ἐνιαύσιος is frequently added (Exod 29:38; Lev 9:3, etc.). In Acts 8:32 ἀμνός occurs in a quotation from Isa 53:7. LXX: "As a sheep (πρόβατον) led to the slaughter or a *lamb* (ἀμνός) before its shearer is dumb, so he opens not his mouth." Since Luke apparently uses the text only with a view toward the event of Christ's suffering and exaltation prophesied in Scripture (cf. Luke 24:26, 46; H. Conzelmann, *Acts* [Hermeneia] 68), the christological aspects of the ἀμνός statement remain undefined. One must keep in mind, on the one hand, the difference between the LXX and the MT (*rāḥēl* = ewe) and the parallel to ἀμνός, πρόβατον, which is never employed in a christological

sense in the NT, and, on the other hand, the christological statements connected with ἀμνός in 1 Peter and John and the christological reflections of the Lukan source or of Hellenistic Jewish Christian circles in general which make use of the ἀμνός statement.

1 Pet 1:18f. introduces the simile of the lamb in order to make clear the atoning power of the sacrificial death of Jesus: "You were ransomed . . . not with perishable things . . . but with the precious blood of Christ, like that of a *lamb* (ἀμνός) without blemish (ἄμωμος) or spot (ἄσπιλος)." Ἄμωμος belongs to the realm of OT sacrificial language (Exod 29:38; Lev 12:6, referring to the burnt offering); on the basis of its usage in Greek (Moulton/Milligan 86) ἄσπιλος could assume a similar function. Both attributes are intended to call attention to the perfection of the sacrifice, i.e., to the sinlessness of Christ. The simile of the lamb does not go back to Isaiah 53 nor does it contain any reference to the Passover lamb (as do 1 Cor 5:7; John 19:36), but is oriented toward the OT sacrificial system in general and belongs to the multifaceted juridical and cultic interpretations of the death of Jesus in the primitive Christian tradition. In 1 Pet 1:18f. the imagery of the sacrificial lamb is woven together with the image of ransom (→ λύτρον) and the idea of purification from sin by means of blood (cf. v. 2) to form a complex metaphorical statement (G. Delling, *Der Kreuzestod Jesu in der urchristlichen Verkündigung* [1972] 48f.).

The Fourth Gospel introduces the testimony of the Baptist to Jesus (1:29-34) with the words: "Behold, the Lamb of God, who takes away the sin of the world!" (v. 29; cf. v. 36; see C. K. Barrett, *NTS* 1 [1954/55] 210-18; F. Gryglewicz, *NTS* 13 [1966/67] 133-46). The Baptist, then, testifies not only to the preexistence of Jesus (v. 30) but also to his atoning death. We are dealing with a metaphorical statement which intends to identify Jesus and which is analogous to the Johannine ἐγώ-εἰμι sayings. The function of the gen. "of God" in 1:29 is similar to that of the adj. "true" (ἀληθινός) in 1:9; 6:32; 15:1, namely, to designate Jesus as the one who fulfills the reality to which the metaphor points, in this case the OT sacrificial lambs (cf. 1 Pet 1:19). Derivation of the statement from the symbolism of the Passover lamb cannot even begin to account for its inclusion of the idea of the removal of the guilt of the κόσμος. The ingenious but problematic attempt (Jeremias 339) to trace the gen. construction "Lamb of God" back to an original "servant of God" from Isaiah 53 on the basis of the twofold meaning of the Aram. *ṭalyā'* (lamb as well as boy/servant) is superfluous in light of the explanation given above.

3. **Ἀρνίον** was originally a diminutive of ἀρήν (→ 4) but in line with the general tendency of colloquial Greek in the NT period to use forms ending in -ιον, the diminutive sense is lost. Ἀρνίον could thus mean *ram, sheep,* or *lamb.* In Revelation ἀρνίον is the most common designation for Christ. It occurs in the vision of the enthronement of the ἀρνίον in ch. 5, in the subsequent visions of the seals in chs. 6 and 7, and then primarily in chs. 14, 19, 21, and 22.

It is a matter of debate whether the author intends ἀρνίον to convey more the picture of a *lamb* or of a *ram.* The most significant considerations for understanding the ἀρνίον as a *lamb* are the following: the appearance of the ἀρνίον "as though it had been slain" (5:6, 9, 12; 13:8) and the reference to the salvific effect of its blood point to a connection with NT statements which speak of Jesus as a sacrificial lamb (ἀμνός; → 2); in the image of the ἀρνίον the weakness and impotence of a *lamb* point to the lowliness of the crucified one, whereas its possession of seven horns and seven eyes indicate the omnipotence and omniscience of the heavenly Christ (5:6).

Certain characteristics of the ἀρνίον, however, correspond more readily to the notion of a *ram* and so cause one to suspect that Revelation, following apocalyptic tradition, has fashioned the image of the ἀρνίον into a messianic figure: the anger of the ἀρνίον (6:16) points to its function as judge (cf. 14:10; *1 Enoch* 69:27); the ἀρνίον leads his own (Rev 7:17; 14:1, 4; cf. the functions of lead-animals and the portrayal of biblical leaders as rams in *1 Enoch* 89:45-49); it is victorious in war against the enemies (Rev 17:14; cf. *1 Enoch* 89:49; *T. Jos.* 19:8); its 7 horns are not just the ordinary symbol for power, but rather symbolize the Messiah as a mighty king and warrior (*1 Enoch* 90:37f.; 90:9, 12; Rev 13:11, referring to the Antichrist).

First of all, then, ἀρνίον is to be regarded as a messianic symbol (Böcher 47: *Messiaswidder* ["Messiah-ram"]) and not as a symbol of impotence. Through the inclusion of christological traditions (sacrificial death, ransom of the Church) the author of Revelation has reshaped and given new form to the symbol so that a complex and scarcely more concrete metaphorical statement emerges: the ἀρνίον as the one who shares God's throne (5:6; 7:17; 22:1, 3) and as the Redeemer and Master of the Church (5:9f.; 7:17; 14:4; 19:7, 9). That the ἀρνίον has been slaughtered is, of course, based on christological reflection, but it does not introduce an irresolvable tension into the picture since Heb. *keḇeś* (translated ἀρνίον in Jer 11:19 LXX) denotes a *young ram,* usually referring to a sacrificial animal (KBL s.v.).

In John 21:15 pl. ἀρνία is used as a designation for the Church in a saying of the risen Christ addressed to Peter. The saying is repeated twice; in both repetitions, however, the Church is referred to as πρόβατα. No difference in content is recognizable; it is a matter of stylistic variation (cf. the alternation of the imvs. βόσκε ["feed"] in vv. 15, 17 and ποίμανε ["tend"] in v. 16; R. Schnackenburg, *The Gospel according to John* III [1987] 363). Translation of ἀρνία as "lambs" is justified only if the imvs. are varied in accordance with the Greek text (as in RSV). Otherwise the translation "sheep" is preferable.

4. **Ἀρήν,** like ἀμνός (→ 1), means *lamb.* The word occurs in the NT only in the metaphor found in Luke 10:3: "Behold, I send you out as *lambs* in the midst of wolves." The parallel in Matt 10:16 has πρόβατα (sheep), and it is nearly impossible to say which word stood in the Q source. On the contrast of lambs vs. wolves cf. Isa. 65:25; Sir 13:17; Homer *Il.* xxii. 263; *Epigr Graec* 1038:38: ὡς ἄρνας κατέχουσι λύκοι (BAGD s.v.); on the contrast of sheep vs. wolves cf. *Tanḥuma tôl^e^dôt* (ed. S. Buber [1885]) 32b; *1 Enoch* 89:55; Billerbeck I, 574; G. Bornkamm, *TDNT* IV, 310f.). The defenseless disciples of Jesus (cf. Luke 10:4) are, in their mission, like lambs (cf. *Pss. Sol.* 8:23; 4 Ezra 5:18), exposed to the most extreme danger at the hands of their own countrymen; the time of the mission is the time of the distress prior to the end (cf. Luke 12:51-53 Q).

G. Dautzenberg

ἀμοιβή, ῆς, ἡ *amoibē* recompense, return (noun)*

1 Tim 5:4: make some *return* to the parents.

ἄμπελος, ου, ἡ *ampelos* vine
ἀμπελουργός, οῦ, ὁ *ampelourgos* vinedresser*
ἀμπελών, ῶνος, ὁ *ampelōn* vineyard

1. Occurrences in the NT — 2. The Synoptics — 3. Ἄμπελος in John 15 and Revelation

Lit.: J. Behm, *TDNT* I, 342f. — R. Borig, *Der wahre Weinstock* (1967). — C. Brown, *DNTT* III, 918-23. — R. Bultmann, *The Gospel of John* (1971) 529-47. — H. J. Klauck, "Das Gleichnis vom Mord im Weinberg," *BibLeb* 11 (1970) 118-45. — E. Schweizer, *Ego Eimi* ([2]1965). — R. Schnackenburg, *The Gospel according to John* III (1987) 96-108. — *idem,* "Aufbau und Sinn von Johannes 15," *Homenaje a Juan Prado* (1975) 405-20.

1. In addition to Jas 3:12 and Rev 14:18, 19 *vine* occurs 6 times in the Gospels, *vineyard* only in Synoptic parables (22 times) and in 1 Cor 9:7, and *vinedresser* only in Luke 13:7. Fig. use in the NT goes back to the OT where vine and vineyard are primarily metaphors for Israel (Hos 10:1; Jer 2:21; Isa 27:2).

2. Alongside literal use (Matt 20:1-16; 21:18; Luke 13:6; Mark 14:25 par. [*vine*]) *vineyard* occurs in a fig. sense in Mark 12:1-13 par. Recalling Isa 5:1-7, the strongly allegorical (esp. in Matthew) parable clearly points to the rejection of the messengers ("servants" = prophets) of God (the Lord of *the vineyard*) by Israel's leaders (the *vinedressers*), threatens these leaders with judgment, and promises the transfer of salvation from Israel (the *vineyard*) to the Gentiles ("others"). The parable is, as spoken by Jesus, a final appeal for repentance, but is transformed by the Synoptics into an admonition directed to Christian hearers to produce "fruits" (Matt 21:43).

3. Ἄμπελος, *vine,* attains profound christological (and ecclesiological) significance in the "allegory" in John 15:1-8 in which Jesus designates himself as the "true *vine.*" Attempts to prove a Mandean origin for this self-designation (Bultmann) are unconvincing. Rather, all of the evidence points to the appropriation and further development of the OT motif. While it is true that the word *vine* is never applied to an individual person in the OT, nonetheless there are points at which the process begins (Ezek 15; 17; 19; Ps 80:9-17; Sir 24:17). *2 Bar.* 36 already applies "vine" to the Messiah (on the whole issue cf. Borig 79-194).

If in John 15 it is not the Church but Jesus himself who is the vine, the reason for this is that he himself represents the new people of God. The purpose of the emphatic ἀληθινή is not to polemically distinguish Jesus from all others who claim to bring salvation; it brings to positive expression the fact that in him—in contrast to the vine Israel—all expectations are uniquely fulfilled. In John ἄμπελος is not understood primarily as "tree of life." The central message has to do with bearing fruit and thus being true disciples (v. 8). To "abide" in the vine, therefore, is the unconditional presupposition. The "fruit" is the "keep[ing of] the commandments," above all the commandment enjoining love of the brethren (v. 12), and only indirectly "fruit of missionary activity."

In Rev 14:18f. the *vine* is a metaphor for (pagan) humanity.

F. Porsch

ἀμπελουργός, οῦ, ὁ *ampelourgos* vinedresser
→ ἄμπελος.

ἀμπελών, ῶνος, ὁ *ampelōn* vineyard
→ ἄμπελος.

Ἀμπλιᾶτος, ου *Ampliatos* Ampliatus

A Christian who, in Rom 16:8, receives a greeting and is designated by Paul as ὁ ἀγαπητός μου ἐν κυρίῳ (cf. also v. 5). Koine D, etc., read Ἀμπλιᾶς. The name is most frequently a slave's name and is derived from Lat. *Ampliatus.* BDF §125.1; BAGD s.v.; A. Wikenhauser, *LTK* I, 450; O. Michel, *Römer* (KEK) ad loc.; C. E. B. Cranfield, *Romans* (ICC) ad loc.

ἀμύνομαι *amynomai* ward off, come to the aid of*

In Acts 7:24 used absolutely with reference to Moses who *comes to the aid of* one being mistreated in Egypt. In

NT mid. is synonymous with act.; cf. Isa 59:16 LXX; BDF §316.1.

ἀμφιάζω *amphiazō* clothe

Luke 12:28 B; the reading preferred in the 25th edition of *NTG* (1963). → ἀμφιέζω.

ἀμφιβάλλω *amphiballō* throw out (in a circle)*

In Mark 1:16 as a t.t. for the *casting* of the (circular) casting net; used absolutely (but D Θ, etc., have δίκτυα as obj.; Koine βάλλοντας ἀμφίβληστρον, cf. par. Matt 4:18). C. Edlund, *BHH* I, 482f.

ἀμφίβληστρον, ου, τό *amphiblēstron* casting net*

Matt 4:18 (cf. par. Mark 1:16 Koine). The fishermen stood while casting the circular casting net into the water. *BHH* I, 482f.; C. G. Rasmussen, *IDB* III, 524.

ἀμφιέζω *amphiezō* clothe*

Luke 12:28 (with 𝔭[74, 75] D, etc.); used fig. of the flowers which grow wild in the field and which God *clothes* more gloriously than Solomon in his splendor. Occurs along with → ἀμφιάζω (which is found as a doricism in Koine) and can, like the latter, replace → ἀμφιέννυμι. BAGD s.v. ἀμφιάζω; BDF §§29.2; 73.

ἀμφιέννυμι *amphiennymi* clothe*

Used fig. in Matt 6:30 (par. Luke 12:28 ℵ Koine A etc. → ἀμφιέζω). Pass. referring to John the Baptist in Matt 11:8 par. Luke 7:25 who is not *clothed* in soft (i.e., genteel) raiment. BDF §159.1.

Ἀμφίπολις, εως *Amphipolis* Amphipolis*

A Macedonian city encircled by the Strymon River (whence the name), founded in 436 B.C., a commercial center, capital of the Roman province of *Macedonia prima* (southeast Macedonia), and a military post on the Egnatian Way. In Acts 17:1 Paul comes into contact with Ἀμφίπολις on his way from Philippi to Thessalonica on the so-called second missionary journey. G. Hirschfeld, PW I/2, 1949-52; H. Aschermann, *BHH* I, 87; H. Conzelmann, *Acts* (Hermeneia) 134; R. Meye, *ISBE* I, 118.

ἄμφοδον, ου, τό *amphodon* street*

Mark 11:4; Acts 19:28 D. (Jer 17:27 LXX; 30:33 LXX in the sense of a city quarter). LSJ s.v.

ἀμφότεροι, 3 *amphoteroi* both

There are 14 NT occurrences of this pronominal adj. of duality, all in Matthew, Luke, Acts, and Ephesians and all masc. or neut., most used in place of classical ἄμφω. In Eph 2:14, 16, 18 ἀμφότεροι with the art. emphasizes the previous state of separation of those now united in Christ: *both together* (cf. Luke 5:7); cf. Eph 2:15 οἱ δύο, "each single one of the two" (RSV "the two"). In accord with later usage in the papyri (e.g., Pap. London II, 336: 13 [2nd cent. A.D.] ἀμφότεροι could mean, as in Acts 23:8 (again with the art.), *all (of more than two);* similarly in 19:16, *all of them together* (cf. E. Haenchen, *The Acts of the Apostles* [1971] 564, n. 5; BDF §§64.6; 275.1, 8).

ἀμώμητος, 2 *amōmētos* blameless*

2 Pet 3:14; cf. Phil 2:15 Koine D G *pl* (for ἄμωμος). F. Hauck, *TDNT* IV, 830f.

H. Balz

ἄμωμον, ου, τό *amōmon* amomum*

An Indian spice plant which, with other delicacies and luxury articles, is available in "Babylon" (Rev 18:13).

ἄμωμος, 2 *amōmos* unblemished, blameless*

In Heb 9:14 ἄμωμος refers to Christ who offered himself as an "unblemished," because faultless, sacrifice (cf. 1 Pet 1:19; *Mart. Pol.* 17:2; thus frequently also in LXX, e.g., Exod 29:1). It is applied to the Church, which through Christ has been freed from every fault before God (Eph 1:4, with ἅγιος; Col 1:22, with ἅγιος and ἀνέγκλητος). In Eph 5:27 it is used of the ἐκκλησία which Christ has set before himself without spot or wrinkle (cf. Col 1:22) in order that it might be *without blemish* (again with ἅγιος; cf. Jude 24; Rev 14:5). Ἄμωμος is used parenetically in Phil 2:15 (parallel with ἀκέραιος). F. Hauck, *TDNT* IV, 830f.

Ἀμών *Amōn* Amon

King of Judah, the son of Manasseh and father of Josiah (2 Kgs 21:18; 1 Chr 3:14; there in each case also v.l. → Ἀμώς): Matt 1:10 (bis) Koine L W lat sy.

Ἀμώς *Amōs* Amos*

1. King of Judah (so 2 Kgs 21:18; 1 Chr 3:14 v.l.) in the genealogy of Jesus in Matt 1:10 (bis) v.l. → Ἀμών. 2. The father of Mattathias and son of Nahum in the genealogy of Jesus in Luke 3:25.

ἄν *an* (particle)

Lit.: BAGD s.v. — BDF §§360; 367; 369; 380; 383; 385f. — KÜHNER, *Grammatik* II/1, 202-59. — MAYSER, *Grammatik* II/1, 226-96. — C. F. D. MOULE, *An Idiom-Book of NT Greek* ([2]1959), 133, 138, 148-52. — MOULTON, *Grammar* III (index s.v.).

1. Ἐάν often follows relatives instead of ἄν, and NT mss. often vacillate between the two (BDF §§107; 380.1). Ἄν is a particle peculiar to Greek, impossible to translate by itself. It designates the content of the clause in which it occurs, according to the mood and tense of the vb., as conditional. In English ἄν can only be expressed through the mood of the vb. The NT uses the particle essentially—even though with less variety—in the same way as the classical language (BAGD). A few NT writings do not use ἄν at all: 1–2 Thessalonians, Philemon, Colossians, Ephesians, the Pastorals, James, 1–2 Peter, and Jude.

2. a) Ἄν with ind. aor. or impf. 1) denotes repeated action under certain conditions, esp. following relatives (BDF §367): Mark 6:56c: *whoever touched it* (aor.); 6:56a: *wherever he came* (impf.); Acts 2:45; 4:35: καθότι ἄν τις χρείαν εἶχεν, *as any had need;* 2) appears in the apodosis following a conditional clause with εἰ (BDF §360), Luke 7:39: *if he were a prophet, he would know*; 17:6; John 5:46; 8:19; 1 Cor 11:31; Gal 1:10; Heb 8:4 (impf.); Matt 11:21: *if miracles had been performed, they would long ago have repented*; 12:7; John 14:28; 1 Cor 2:8 (aor.).

b) Ἄν with subjunc.: 1) Where this combination follows a relative (BDF §380), the relative clause becomes a substitute for the protasis (Matt 5:19; 10:11; John 5:19; 1 Cor 11:27). 2) Ἄν is used in temporal clauses with the subjunc. where an event which will occur is described, but when it will occur remains uncertain (→ ὅταν). The following combinations occur: ἡνίκα ἄν, *whenever* (2 Cor 3:15), ὡς ἄν, *as soon as* (Rom 15:24; 1 Cor 11:34; Phil 2:23), ἀφ' οὗ ἄν, *after* (Luke 13:25), ἕως ἄν, *until* (Matt 10:11; Luke 9:27), ἄχρι οὗ ἄν, *until* (Rev 2:25), πρὶν (ἤ) ἄν, *before* (Luke 2:26; BDF §383.3).

c) In purpose clauses ὅπως ἄν is rarer than in Attic and the LXX (BDF §369.5); other than Rom 3:4 (which quotes Ps 50:6 LXX), it appears only in Luke 2:35; Acts 3:20; 15:17 (quoting Amos 9:12, which in LXX does not have ἄν).

d) Opt. with ἄν in the main clause has almost wholly disappeared in the NT. Only the Lukan writings (as evidence of their literary style) contain examples (Luke 1:62; 6:11; 9:46; 15:26; Acts 5:24; 8:31; 10:17; cf. John 13:24 $\mathfrak{p}^{66}$ A D). Especially significant is Acts 17:18 (a direct rhetorical question in the mouths of the Athenians); 26:29: εὐξαίμην ἄν, *I wish* (Paul before Agrippa; see BDF §385.1).

e) Ἄν with inf., in classical Greek a very common construction, is not found in the NT at all (BDF §396). In 2 Cor 10:9 ὡς ἄν can be taken as a single term (*quasi, so to speak*): *I do not want to give the impression that I wish* to frighten you (BDF §453.3; BAGD s.v. 6). Εἰ μήτι ἄν ἐκ συμφώνου in 1 Cor. 7:5 can be translated *except by agreement* (BDF §376).

G. Schneider

ἀνά *ana* up*

Lit.: On preps. in general: BAGD 49 (bibliography). — BDF §§203-40. — M. J. Harris, *DNTT* III, 1171-1215 (bibliography). — Morgenthaler, *Statistik* 14f., 160. — C. F. D. Moule, *An Idiom-Book of NT Greek* (²1959) 48-92. — Moulton, *Grammar* III, 249-80. — See also the bibliographies in *TDNT* II, 65, 420f., V, 727f., VI, 53f., 720f., etc.

BDF §203f. — Kühner, *Grammatik* II/1, 473f. — Mayser, *Grammatik* II/2, 401-404. — Moule 66f. — Radermacher, *Grammatik* 20, 138, 143.

The prep. ανά was rare already in Attic prose. The dat. construction with ἀνά has disappeared from the NT as it did from Polybius. As an independent prep. with acc. ἀνά occurs only 13 times in the NT. As a prefix to vbs. (Morgenthaler, *Statistik* 160 shows 74 different compounds) including vbs. with double prefixes (*ibid.* 161f.), however, ἀνά appears frequently; the same is true with compound nouns.

By itself ἀνά is used in the NT only in fixed phrases or in the distributive sense: a) ἀνὰ μέσον (with gen.), *in the midst of, between* (Matt 13:25; Mark 7:31; 1 Cor 6:5; Rev 7:17; Radermacher 138); b) ἀνὰ μέρος, *in turn* (1 Cor 14:27); c) ἀνά in the distributive sense, *each* (Matt 20:9, 10, *a denarius apiece;* Radermacher 20: not a hebraism); Luke 9:3, 14; 10:1; John 2:6; Rev 4:8; cf. Mark 6:40 $\mathfrak{p}^{84}$. Ἀνά was also fixed as an adv. (Rev 21:21: ἀνὰ εἷς ἕκαστος τῶν πυλώνων, *each of the gates;* BDF §§204; 305).

G. Schneider

ἀναβαθμός, οῦ, ὁ *anabathmos* step (pl.: flight of stairs)*

Acts 21:35, 40: the flight of stairs which connected the outer court of the temple with the tower Antonia.

ἀναβαίνω *anabainō* go up

1. Occurrences in NT — 2. Meanings — 3. Usage — 4. "Ascending" to heaven and to God

Lit.: C. Brown, *DNTT* II, 184-87. — I. Fritsch, "'. . . videbitis . . . angelos Dei ascendentes et descendentes super Filium Hominis' (Io. 1, 51)," *VD* 37 (1959) 3-11. — G. Lohfink, *Die Himmelfahrt Jesu* (SANT 26, 1971). — W. Michaelis, "Joh 1, 51, Gen 28, 12 und das Menschensohn-Problem," *TLZ* 85 (1960) 561-78. — E. Ruckstuhl, "Die joh. Menschensohnforschung 1957-1969," *TBer* 1 (1972) 171-284. — H. Schlier, *Der Brief an die Epheser* (⁷1971). — R. Schnackenburg, "Der Menschensohn im Johannesevangelium," *NTS* 11 (1964/65) 123-37. — *idem, The Gospel According to St. John* I (1968) 529-42. — J. Schneider, *TDNT* I, 518-23. — S. Schulz, *Untersuchungen zur Menschensohn-Christologie im Johannesevangelium* (1957).

1. The word occurs in the NT a total of 82 times: 9 times in each of the Synoptics, 19 in Acts (*contra* Morgenthaler, *Statistik*: 18), 13 in John, 4 in Paul, 3 in Ephesians, and 13 in Revelation. The preponderance in the Gospels and Acts

is explained by the frequent occurrence of "*go up* to Jerusalem" (so also Gal 2:1) or "to the feast" and "*go up* onto the mountain" (as a place of prayer), usually referring to Jesus or the apostles.

2. Translations must take into account both the subj. and the context of ἀναβαίνω (→ 3) as well as the location of the speaker. If there is movement away from the speaker, one speaks of *going up, climbing up* (a hill or mountain), or *ascending* (into heaven); if there is movement toward the speaker, of *coming out, coming up, coming out of* (water, the underworld), *coming toward* (a boat); in absolute use, of *going up* or *rising* (smoke, thoughts) or *coming up, growing up* (plants). In Acts 21:31 ἀνέβη φάσις means that *a report was made* (to the Antonia).

3. Occasionally ἀναβαίνω can be used in an absolute construction (i.e., with no indication of direction of movement), primarily with reference to plants (Mark 4:7f., 32; Matt 13:7: they *grew up*), animals (Matt 17:27: a fish *comes up*), or inanimate things such as smoke (it *goes up*, Rev 14:11; 19:3). Indication of the direction of movement is more frequent in reference to human beings; this is expressed by εἰς (usually) or by ἐπί (on the roof: Luke 5:19; Acts 10:9; on the surface of the earth: Rev 20:9). On ἐπί in John 1:51 → 4. Ἀναβαίνω ἐπὶ καρδίαν (cf. Heb. *ʿālâ ʿal-lēḇ*) means that something enters a person's mind (Acts 7:23; 1 Cor 2:9). Adverbs of place can also be used to indicate direction (John 6:62; Eph 4:10; Rev 4:1; 11:12; → 4). Πρός with acc. indicates the person to whom one ascends or whom one joins in a boat. On the dat. with no prep. in Acts 21:31 → 2. The place from whence one "comes up" is indicated by ἀπό, *from*, and ἐκ, *out of*. The purpose of the action, e.g., prayer or worship, is indicated by the inf. (Matt 14:23; Luke 9:28; 18:10: προσεύξασθαι), the fut. partc. of purpose (Acts 24:11: προσκυνήσων), or a ἵνα clause (John 12:20: προσκυνήσωσιν).

4. In Rom 10:6 Paul picks up the thought of Deut 30:12. What applied there to the word of God now applies to the righteousness based on faith: one need not ascend into heaven in order to bring it down to earth, for that would mean to bring Christ down again (on this expression cf. Prov 24:27 = 30:4 LXX; Bar 3:29; on "descent" into the "abyss" see Pss 106[107]:26; 138[139]:8; Amos 9:2, 4; Isa 14:13, 15).

In Acts 2:34 Luke interprets the "exaltation" of Jesus (v. 33) as "ascent into heaven," thus transposing the inauguration of the messianic King into his office (Ps 110:1) into a spatial scheme. (According to Lohfink 229, Luke here concretizes the exaltation kerygma of the primitive Church by relating it in historicizing fashion to the ascension which is now distinguished from the resurrection.) OT and Jewish phraseology is still discernible when, according to Acts 10:4, the "prayers and alms" of Cornelius ascend to God, so that God "remembers them" (cf. Job 20:6 LXX; 3 Macc 5:9).

In Eph 4:8 the author uses Ps 67(68):19 christologically (and freely): an address to God has become a statement about Christ who "ascended on high" and "gave gifts to people." The ἔλαβες (δόματα) of the LXX is here, as in Exod 25:5 LXX; 1 Kgs 17:10, and is understood as "receiving in order to give" (cf. Schlier 191f. and his reference to the rabbinic interpretation of Ps 68:19 as referring to Moses and his reception of the law "on high"). This "ascension" of Jesus "above all the heavens," and thus above all intermediary beings, presupposes, of course, his prior descent to the "lower parts of the earth," a point made clear in the parenthesis of vv. 9f. (cf. *ibid.*).

An already traditional statement in John 3:13 denies that anyone has ever ascended into heaven except the "Son of Man" who comes from heaven (cf. again Prov 30:4 LXX; Bar 3:29 with reference to wisdom); therefore, only Jesus, the earthly Son of Man, can bring heavenly knowledge. His "ascending where he was before" becomes an even greater offense than his "coming from heaven" as the bread of life (John 6:62). When, according to 1:51, angels are seen "ascending and descending upon him," he is thus shown to be the place of the presence of God (Gen 28:12, cf. v. 17: "the house of God and the gate of heaven" [cf. Fritsch]). According to John 20:17 his "ascension to the Father" prepares the way for the giving of his gifts (peace, joy, the Spirit, and forgiveness, vv. 19-23; cf. above on Eph 4:8ff.).

The command "Come up hither" enables the seer of Revelation (4:1) to receive the heavenly visions. If the "two witnesses" of 11:3 are Moses and Elijah (cf. E. Lohse, *Offenbarung* [NTD] ad loc.), then their being taken up into heaven in v. 12 goes back, in the case of Elijah, to the OT (2 Kgs. 2:11; Sir 48:9) and in the case of Moses to Jewish tradition (cf. *The Assumption of Moses* [lost except for fragments preserved in quotations and not equivalent to *T. Mos.*, which is sometimes called *The Assumption of Moses*]).

J. Beutler

ἀναβάλλω *anaballō* postpone, adjourn*

Acts 24:22: mid. with personal obj. αὐτούς referring to the adjournment of the trial against Paul by Felix. Common as a legal t.t. (see BAGD s.v.: "remand someone, adjourn [his trial]"), but from the context, the sense is rather that of "delay": "he *put off* the decision in their case."

ἀναβιβάζω *anabibazō* pull up*

Matt 13:48: the fishermen *drew* the net filled with the catch *up* onto the shore.

ἀναβλέπω *anablepō* look up

1. Occurrences in the NT — 2. Meanings — 3. Ἀνάβλεψις

Lit.: BAGD s.v. — E. v. DOBSCHÜTZ, "Die fünf Sinne im NT," *JBL* 48 (1929) 378-411. — K. LAMMERS, *Hören, Sehen und Glauben im NT* (SBS 11, 1966) 84-106. — W. L. LIEFELD, *DNTT* III, 519. — W. MICHAELIS, *TDNT* V, 315-82. — F. NÖTSCHER, *"Das Angesicht Gottes schauen" nach biblischer und babylonischer Auffassung* (1924) 62ff. — R. SCHNACKENBURG, *SacVb* III, 947-52 (bibliography).

1. The vb. occurs 25 times in the NT (Matthew 3 times, Mark 6, Luke 7, John 4, Acts 5). Words connected with seeing frequently have theological and hermeneutical significance in the NT where they refer to faith's more profound perception of the Christ-event.

2. In the NT the following meanings occur: a) To *look up* as neutral optical perception of objects and persons. In Luke 19:5 Jesus passes through Jericho and *looks up* at the chief tax-collector Zacchaeus sitting in a sycamore tree; Jesus knows that a person is seeking him; he calls him down and announces to him the presence of salvation "today." In 21:1 Jesus *looks up* and sees the rich putting their gifts into the treasury.

b) To *look up* to heaven as an act of hope in God. In the account of the multiplication of the loaves Jesus *looks up* to heaven (Matt 14:19; Mark 6:41; Luke 9:16); here it is already an expression from the eucharistic cult didache. This sense also appears in connection with the healing of a deaf-mute (Mark 7:34).

c) *Recovery of sight* as a sign of the dawn of the eschatological-messianic time of salvation. This sense appears in Mark 8:24 (the healing of a blind man in Bethsaida); 10:51 ("Rabbi, let me *receive my sight* [again]"), 52; Matt 20:34; Luke 18:41, 42, 43 (the believing act of seeing is a consequence of the encounter with God's eschatological offer of salvation in Jesus; cf. K. Kertelge, *Die Wunder Jesu im Markusevangelium* [1970] 179ff.). In John 9:11, 15, 18 (the healing at the pool of Siloam of one blind from birth) the ability to see leads to faith in the Son of Man (cf. F. Mussner, *Die johanneische Sehweise* [1965] 18ff.); when Jesus, the messianic bringer of salvation, restores sight, the OT eschatological promise of the healing of the blind (Isa 61:5-7; 35:5f.; 29:15ff.; also Matt 11:5; Luke 7:22) is fulfilled in the "today" of the encounter with Jesus (cf. H. Schürmann, *Lukas* [HTKNT] 406-14).

d) In the account of Saul's Damascus experience his blinding and healing are symbols of his conversion from Jewish Torah soteriology to the christological justification by faith (Acts 9:12, 17, 18; 22:13).

e) The women *looked up* when they were at the tomb of Jesus: That the heavy stone was rolled back allowed them to enter the tomb and thus come upon what was inside (Mark 16:4).

3. **Ἀνάβλεψις** *recovery of sight** occurs in the NT only in Luke 4:18, where it refers to recovery of sight by the blind. In Jesus in the synagogue at Nazareth is fulfilled the promise of Isa 61:1f.; 58:6 LXX; cf. *Barn.* 14:9.

P.-G. Müller

ἀνάβλεψις, εως, ἡ *anablepsis* recovery of sight → ἀναβλέπω 3.

ἀναβοάω *anaboaō* cry out*

Matt 27:46 (the subj. is Jesus; B *al* read ἐβόησεν); Mark 15:8 C Koine Θ *pl* sy; Luke 9:38 TR.

ἀναβολή, ῆς, ἡ *anabolē* delay, postponement*

Acts 25:17: ἀναβολὴν μηδεμίαν ποιησάμενος, *without delay;* → ἀναβάλλω.

ἀνάγαιον, ου, τό *anagaion* upstairs room*

Mark 14:15 par. Luke 22:12. BDF §§35.2; 44.1; K. Galling, *RGG* I, 930f.; R. Knierem, *BHH* II, 1326; N. J. Opperwall-Galluch, *ISBE* IV, 948.

ἀναγγέλλω *anangellō* report, announce → ἀγγέλλω.

ἀναγεννάω *anagennaō* cause to be born again*

Lit.: F. BÜCHSEL, *TDNT* I, 673-75. — K. H. SCHELKLE, *Die Petrusbriefe. Der Judasbrief* (HTKNT, [2]1964) 26-54. — J. YSEBAERT, *Greek Baptismal Terminology* (1962) 90-107.

1. Although the idea of being born occurs frequently in the NT (esp. in John), ἀναγεννάω is used only in 1 Pet 1:3, 23; thus it is not a NT t.t. denoting this process. In order to understand it, therefore, one must draw on related concepts in this sphere (→ γεννάω, εἶναι ἐκ, ἀποκυέω, → παλιγγενεσία). The limited use of ἀναγεννάω is not to be explained as a deliberate rejection of the language of the heathen mysteries since there also ἀναγεννάω cannot be proven to be a t.t. (which is the case with μεταγεννᾶν, παλιγγενεσία; cf. Büchsel 672).

2. The event denoted in 1 Peter 1 by ἀναγεννάω, *beget anew,* is neither a natural nor a magical process. According to v. 23 the creative agent is the "living and abiding word of God," which, like an "imperishable seed" (σπορά), mediates life and, according to v. 25, is identical with the word of the gospel. Thus the author refers to the biblical idea of the creative power of God's word. Indeed, it appears that all NT statements about spiritual procreation rest on a common viewpoint, namely, that a person is inwardly transformed through a believing acceptance of the word of God. (The acceptance itself is made possible by the Spirit and sealed in baptism; cf. 1 John 2:27ff.; 3:9;

John 1:12; 3:5; 1 Cor 4:15; Jas 1:18). Furthermore, the context of 1 Pet 1:3 shows that regeneration takes place through faith grounded in the resurrection of Jesus (vv. 5, 7, 8, 21).

Along with newness, ἀναγεννάω expresses the initiative of God and the unmerited character of salvation (1 Pet 1:21). The new being is not a static state but has as its purpose the dynamic maintenance of hope, love, and faith in view of the final salvation which is still to come.

The Pauline idea of the new creation (καινὴ → κτίσις) is to be distinguished from that of regeneration.

F. Porsch

ἀναγινώσκω *anaginōskō* read, read aloud, read publicly*

Lit.: BAGD s.v. — G. Bornkamm, "The Anathema in the Early Christian Lord's Supper Liturgy," *idem, Early Christian Experience* (1969) 169-76, 178f. — J. Blunck, *DNTT* I, 245f. — R. Bultmann, *TDNT* I, 343f. — B. Reicke, *BHH* II, 1074. — P. Vielhauer, *Geschichte der urchristlichen Literatur* (1975) 62f., 65-67.

There are 32 occurrences of ἀναγινώσκω in the NT (besides Rev 5:4 2050 *pc*). In the Synoptics it refers to *reading* the Scriptures (Mark 2:25 par. Matt 12:3 and Luke 6:3; Mark 12:10 par. Matt 21:42; Mark 12:26 par. Matt 22:31; Matt 19:4; 21:16) or the law (Matt 12:5; Luke 10:26). In all but one instance each in Matthew and Mark and in Luke 6:3 it is in an accusing question directed by Jesus to his Jewish listeners: οὐκ/οὐδέποτε/οὐδέ . . . ἀνέγνωτε. The partc. appears with no dir. obj. in Mark 13:14 par. Matt 24:15 (ὁ ἀναγινώσκων νοείτω, "let *the reader* understand") and in Rev 1:3, referring to *the one who reads aloud* (see below). It is used of reading (aloud) the prophet Isaiah in Acts 8:28, 30a, b (here a play on words with γινώσκω, cf. 2 Cor 1:13), 32, and to reading (or reading aloud) of a letter in Acts 15:31; 23:34. In three instances other than Mark 13:14 par. and Rev 1:3, it refers to the reading (or reading aloud) of the text it appears in (2 Cor 1:13; Eph 3:4; Col 4:16). In John 19:20 it refers to the reading of the τίτλος on the cross.

On the basis of 1 Thess 5:27 (ἀναγνωσθῆναι τὴν ἐπιστολὴν πᾶσιν τοῖς ἀδελφοῖς) it is clear that from the beginning the letters of Paul were *read aloud* or were at least intended to be read aloud in the churches. This is probably the case also in Eph 3:4; Col 4:16 and perhaps also Mark 13:14 par. In Rev 1:3 sg. ὁ ἀναγινώσκων, *the one who reads aloud,* is paralleled by οἱ ἀκούοντες, "the hearers," in connection with the public reading of the book. Cf. further *2 Clem.* 19:1 (bis); *Herm. Vis.* i.3.3, 4.1.

Jesus "stood up *to read*" the Scripture (Luke 4:16; ἀναγνῶναι with no obj.); cf. the reading of the prophets in worship (Acts 13:27) and of "Moses" on every sabbath in the synagogues (15:21; cf. 2 Cor 3:15).

In 2 Cor 3:2 ἀναγινώσκω refers figuratively to the Corinthian church as Paul's "letter of recommendation" which *is read* by all.

H. Balz

ἀναγκάζω *anankazō* compel
→ ἀνάγκη.

ἀναγκαῖος, 3 *anankaios* necessary, needful
→ ἀνάγκη.

ἀναγκαστῶς *anankastōs* by compulsion
→ ἀνάγκη.

ἀνάγκη, ης, ἡ *anankē* compulsion*
ἀναγκάζω *anankazō* compel*
ἀναγκαῖος, 3 *anankaios* necessary, needful*
ἀναγκαστῶς *anankastōs* by compulsion*

1. Occurrences in the NT — 2. Meanings — 3. Usage — 4. Adj. and adv.

Lit.: J. Drummond, *Philo Judaeus or the Jewish-Alexandrian Philosophy in its Development and Completion* (1888; reprint 1969), esp. 93ff. — J. Eckert, *Die urchristliche Verkündigung im Streit zwischen Paulus und seinen Gegnern nach dem Galaterbrief* (BU 6, 1971). — J. Friedrich, W. Pöhlmann, and P. Stuhlmacher, "Zur historischen Situation und Intention von Röm 13, 1-7," *ZTK* 73 (1976) 131-66 (esp. 160ff.). — W. Grundmann, *TDNT* I, 344-47. — J. J. Gunther, *St. Paul's Opponents and Their Background* (NovTSup 35, 1973) (bibliography). — M. Hengel, *Christ and Power* (1977) (bibliography). — G. F. Moore, "Fate and Free Will in the Jewish Philosophies according to Josephus," *HTR* 22 (1929) 371-89. — R. Morgenthaler, *DNTT* II, 663f. — D. Nestle, *Eleutheria. Studien zum Wesen der Freiheit bei den Griechen und im NT* (1969) 15, 75. — K. Niederwimmer, *Der Begriff der Freiheit im NT* (TBT 11, 1966) 31ff. — E. Peterson, "Die Befreiung Adams aus der ἀνάγκη," *Frühkirche, Judentum und Gnosis* (1959) 107-28. — W. Schrage, "Zur Frontstellung der paulinischen Ehebewertung in 1 Kor 7," *ZNW* 67 (1976) 214-34 (bibliography). — H. Schreckenberg, *Ananke. Untersuchungen zur Geschichte des Wortgebrauchs* (Zetemata 36, 1964). — F. Schröger, "Die Verfassung der Gemeinde des 1 Petr," *Kirche im Werden* (ed. J. Hainz; 1976) 239-52. — S. Schulz, "Gottes Vorsehung bei Lk," *ZNW* 54 (1963) 104-16. — A. Strobel, "Das Aposteldekret in Galatien. Zur Situation von Gal I and II," *NTS* 20 (1973/74) 177-90.

1. The vb. ἀναγκάζω with acc. of the thing or person (usually with an attached inf., see LSJ s.v. 1) occurs 9 times in the NT (Mark 1 time, Matthew 1, Luke-Acts 3, Paul 4). These are, without exception, narrative texts (cf. K. H. Rengstorf, *A Complete Concordance to Flavius Josephus* I [1973] 85).

There are 17 occurrences of the subst. ἀνάγκη (Matthew 1 time, Luke 2, Paul 9, Hebrews 4, and Jude 1). Luke 23:17 is not original (see *UBSGNT* ad loc.). Where Greek is the dominant language there is a partiality toward the use of this term (LXX, 2–3–4 Maccabees, Aristotle, Philo, Josephus). It also appears as an Aram. loanword (see Jastrow, *Dictionary* s.v. *'ᵃnanqê*).

The adj. ἀναγκαῖος occurs 8 times in the NT (Acts 2 times, Paul 4, Titus 1, Hebrews 1). The adv. ἀναγκαστῶς is a NT hapax legomenon (1 Pet 5:2).

A majority of the uses of these words are concerned with the life of the primitive Christian Church, whose members were exposed to physical and mental "tribulations." In texts marked by more strictly theological reflection (esp. Paul and Hebrews) the fig. sense of "logical *necessity*" dominates. The idea of ἀνάγκη as *the power of fate,* characteristic of the Hellenistic environment, has strong echoes only in 1 Cor 9:16.

2. The vb. ἀναγκάζω (the etymology is disputed; see Schreckenberg 165ff.) is used in the sense of *compelling someone to something.* Various factors, internal and external, of human and divine will, can play a role. E.g., Acts 26:11 deals with severe acts of repression at the hands of the persecutor, whereas 28:19 refers to insight regarding what is appropriate under the circumstances. Gal 2:3, 14; 6:12 point to the realm of religious legal constraints.

The same holds for the subst. ἀνάγκη, which in the Greek-speaking world had the special sense of fateful, divinely ordered *necessity,* but which was in the NT combined with a conviction of the providence and purposeful action of God for salvation. Biblical faith in God, opposed as it was to every form of fatalism, left no room for the philosophical-religious idea of a "deified" ἀνάγκη and equally little place for the numerous equivalents (μοῖρα, εἱμαρμένη, χρεών, τύχη, etc.). In this matter biblical thought possessed its own vocabulary (προορᾶν, προορίζειν, βουλή, οἰκονομία, etc.), which was preferred by both Hellenistic Judaism and Christianity (see Moore). Moreover, ἀνάγκη became a special, technical concept wherever primitive Christian eschatology was dominant.

'Ανάγκη could (as in Luke 21:23) become the equivalent of θλῖψις, a term common in areas dominated by Jewish linguistic usage (corresponding to Heb. *ṣar, ṣārâ*; cf. K. G. Kuhn, *Konkordanz zu den Qumrantexten* [1960] 188 s.v.). Both in the NT (4 instances) and outside of it (see Pap. Oxy. no. 1064, l. 4) the phrase ἀνάγκην ἔχειν is a circumlocution for *must;* reasons for such a necessity can be mentioned (see Jude 3; also Luke 23:17 v.l.). With two exceptions (2 Cor 6:4; 12:10, lists of *perilous experiences*) ἀνάγκη is always used in the NT in the sg. It stands primarily as an abstract designation for *necessity* (Luke 14:18; 2 Cor 9:7), including its use (4 times) in the impersonal expression *it is necessary* (ἀνάγκη ἔστιν with inf.). The prep. combination ἐξ ἀνάγκης (twice) means *under compulsion* (2 Cor 9:7) or, when used in an argument, *necessarily* (Heb 7:12). Κατὰ ἀνάγκην means *involuntarily* (Phlm 14). The adj. ἀναγκαῖος denotes that which is *essential* and *indispensable,* either in the general area of thinking and planning (2 Cor 9:5) or in the realm of human will and insight (Phil 1:24).

On the whole, the spectrum of meaning for this word group is very wide. In terms of the history of language and ideas, it is possible to construct a distinctive background for the particular subject under investigation, e.g., the ancient belief in fate, the biblical notion of providence, ethical-moral decision-making, specific perilous experiences, and fundamental anxieties concerning the end of time.

3. Only once in the Gospels (Mark 6:45 par. Matt 14:22) is it reported that Jesus *forced* his disciples, namely, to get into a boat and leave the crowds. This may be an accurate reflection of the tradition that during the time of his Galilean ministry a critical situation occurred in which Jesus could not be unfaithful to his own nonpolitical commission. John 6:66ff. is worthy of note in connection with this scene, which Luke has not included.

Matt 18:7 (M) is formulated in typical Matthean fashion as a saying of Jesus. Eschatological vexations *must* come, since they are part of God's plan.

Only in Luke, in the context of the parable of the great banquet (Q), is there the idea that people are to be compelled into fellowship with the Lord (Luke 14:23). The command "*compel* them" is a response to the "*must*" in the excuse of those who are invited (v. 18) and in the Lukan outline sharpens the focus on the missionary task of the disciples. Instructions for the conversion of heretics (so Augustine) cannot be deduced.

The depiction of the great ἀνάγκη in Luke 21:23 is formed after Mark 13:19. The "final distress" was thus impressively set forth for Hellenistic Christians (see already Zeph 1:15 LXX). In Matt 24:21 as well (par. Luke 21:23) it is distinguished as "great" because of its uniqueness. Instructive for the Jewish milieu is, e.g., 1QM 15:1. For the Qumran sect the expression "a time of distress for Israel" is a t.t.

In Acts ἀναγκάζω represents the form of the violent compulsion (26:11) as well as—in pass.—the insight forced upon Paul that he must appeal to Caesar (28:19).

The most varied use of ἀνάγκη is found in the letters of Paul. Eschatological expectation gives 1 Thess 3:7 its character. Paul emphasizes that he is comforted in his momentary *distress* and affliction because Timothy has brought good news. The hendiadys refers to the difficulties of the second journey in connection with the work in the Corinthian mission. The context confirms the overtone of experience of the eschaton.

1 Cor 7:26 gives pointed expression to belief in the *present* (eschatological) time of distress. It determines the advice to remain unmarried if one is able (cf. also v. 37) and to devote oneself completely to the affairs of the Lord.

The idea of the pressure of time (see v. 29) has probably aided Paul's choice of terms. When he emphasizes (9:16) that the apostolic office has been laid upon him as an ἀνάγκη, it is testimony to the certainty of the unconditional commission from God which is now the sole content of his thought and action (cf. v. 1; Gal 1:1, 12ff.).

In classical literature ἀνάγκη stands for the *constraint* under which human beings exist and which makes free decision impossible (e.g., Euripides *Or.* 1330: "There is nothing more to do, we are under the yoke of ἀνάγκη"; cf., e.g., 2 Cor 12:11). In addition, that it could mean *torture* is attested since Herodotus (e.g., i.116); in general, the sense can move toward that of *tribulation* and *suffering* as such. Ἀνάγκη is also the fundamental bond with nature and the basic necessity of life (Xenophon *Mem.* iv.5.9). To the sphere of influence of the ἀνάγκη φύσεως belongs, finally, even death (Xenophon *An.* iii.1.43), i.e., the absolute inevitability. Plato's ἀνάγκη-myth (*R.* x.616ff.) teaches that ἀνάγκη is enthroned as the center of the world and is the axis of the world rotating as a world spindle. The concept of the ἀνάγκη was also significant for, among others, the Stoics and the Orphics, as well as in the whole field of theurgy and magic. Differentiated definitions are provided in the *Corp. Herm.* (iii.12.1f.; 14.1). To the realm of Jewish mysticism belongs a "prayer of Adam" which asks for liberation in the ὥρα ἀνάγκης (*PGM* I, 212f., 221).

The *afflictions* mentioned in 2 Cor 6:4; 12:10 are to be understood in the context of the various conflicts Paul experienced during his third journey. The firm confidence which makes it possible to bear all grievous constraints is based upon the experience that it is precisely in weakness that one is strong. For Paul this inner freedom is possessed only by those who know freedom from the law (Niederwimmer 168ff.). It presents itself concretely as freedom from the *necessity* of circumcision. In the midst of heated controversies Paul defends in Galatians the gospel which is free from the law, not only against (judaizing) opponents who *insist* (6:12) on circumcision, but also against the unclear, compromising attitude of someone like Peter, whom he accused in Antioch (2:14) of *coercing*—against his better judgment—Gentile Christians to become Jews. The momentous dispute, which probably overshadowed the third journey, provides the occasion for Paul to appeal in the course of the discussion to the acknowledgment of his law-free gospel by the original apostles up to this point. At a conference in Jerusalem they had not, e.g., *compelled* (a very difficult formulation!) Titus to be circumcised. How much Paul valued the free decision of the Christian in personal affairs as well is apparent in Phlm 14. The passage expresses vividly what constitutes a "free decision."

In Rom 13:5 ἀνάγκη (here without ἔστιν) stands in the context of a theological demonstration. Since the divinely decreed authority of the state guarantees order in human society, subjection is *indispensable.* An additional reason is appended: not only out of fear of the state's power to punish, but also for conscience' sake, i.e., out of a critical sense of responsibility. Behind the text stands a perception widely shared in the Jewish and Hellenistic world.

In Hebrews the argumentation frequently shows strong contacts with Philo (see G. Mayer, *Index Philoneus* [1974] 21). A tendency to use ἀνάγκη in theological reflection is, therefore, unmistakable. From the change in the priesthood *necessarily follows,* e.g., the abolition of the law (Heb 7:12). Christ, who suffered sacrificial death once for all, is not like the priests who *need* to offer sacrifices daily for themselves and the people (7:27). The christocentric, allegorical-typological thinking of the letter is supported throughout by the knowledge of a *necessity* which has been realized (9:16, 23).

In Jude 3 the writer declares that he regards it as *necessary* (epistolary aor.) to exhort the recipients to contend for the faith. In view of the existence of the heretics he is moved by concern for that which has already been achieved.

4. Ἀναγκαῖος appears as an attributive adj. in Acts 10:24 denoting the *closest* friends (Lat. *necessarius*), in 1 Cor 12:22, the *indispensable* members of the body, and in Titus 3:14, *urgent* necessities of life. It also occurs in the impersonal expression *to be necessary* and in the phrase *to think it necessary* (2 Cor 9:5; Phil 2:25; comparative in 1:24). A specifically Lukan thought appears in Acts 13:46: according to the witness of the apostles it was *necessary* that the word should be preached first to the Jews, but this priority, however, has been forfeited through their guilt. The conclusion in Heb 8:3 is typical for that epistle (impersonal use with understood ἔστιν): even Christ *needed* to have something to offer.

The adv. ἀναγκαστῶς in 1 Pet 5:2 means *under constraint.* The context has to do with service based on "free decision" and "free will."

A. Strobel

ἀναγνωρίζω *anagnōrizō* recognize*

Acts 7:13, aor. pass., referring to Joseph, who *made himself known* (causative) to his brothers; cf. Gen 45:1 LXX; *NTG*[25] reads ἐγνωρίσθη with B A p t vg.

ἀνάγνωσις, εως, ἡ *anagnōsis* reading; reading aloud*

Acts 13:15, of reading the Scriptures (the law and the prophets) in the synagogue; 2 Cor 3:14, reading (aloud) of the OT in general; 1 Tim 4:13, reading (Scripture) from the OT (and the Pauline letters?) in Christian worship; cf. W. Bauer, *Der Wortgottesdienst der ältesten Christen* (1930) 39-54; H. Riesenfeld, *RGG* II, 1761f.; J. Jeremias, *1–2 Timotheus und Titus* (NTD) ad loc. → ἀναγινώσκω.

ἀνάγω *anagō* lead or bring up, bring before, put out to sea*

There are 23 occurrences in the NT (besides Mark 11:2

A D Koine, et al.; Luke 22:66 A Koine, et al.; 1 Cor 12:2 B[3]), primarily in Acts (17 occurrences).

According to Matt 4:1 Jesus was *led up* by the Spirit (out of the Jordan Valley) into the (highland of the Judean) wilderness; according to Luke 4:5 the διάβολος *led* him *up* (Koine Θ add εἰς ὄρος ὑψηλόν; cf. Matt 4:8 [Q?]; 17:1 D); see G. Schneider, *Lukas* (ÖTK) ad loc. In both texts it would be possible to suspect an "assumption" (see W. Grundmann, *Matthäus* [THKNT[3]] ad loc.; BAGD s.v.) or a lifting up into the air (see Schneider). Cf. further Luke 2:22 (to Jerusalem); Acts 9:39 (to the upper room); 16:34 (out of the prison [in the cellar?] into the house); similarly Rom 10:7; Heb 13:20 with reference to Christ's being brought up ἐκ νεκρῶν.

Ἀνάγω is also found in the special meaning of *bring before* in Acts 12:4 and is used fig. of the *presentation* of an offering in 7:41. The remainder of the texts employ the pass. as a t.t. of marine language: *put out to sea, set sail, depart for* (Luke 8:22; Acts 13:13; 16:11; 18:21; 20:3, 13; 21:1, 2; 27:2, 4, 12, 21; 28:10, 11).

H. Balz

ἀναδείκνυμι *anadeiknymi* commission, install, exhibit*

Luke 10:1; Acts 1:24: make plain. H. Schlier, *TDNT* II, 30.

ἀνάδειξις, εως, ἡ *anadeixis* installation, commissioning*

Luke 1:80: the commissioning of John to a public ministry to Israel, in the sense of a "sending." H. Schlier, *TDNT* II, 31; BAGD s.v.

ἀναδέχομαι *anadechomai* receive, receive a guest, accept*

Acts 28:7; Heb 11:17: Abraham *had received* the promise of God.

ἀναδίδωμι *anadidōmi* hand over, deliver*

Acts 23:33: delivery of a letter.

ἀναζάω *anazaō* come to life (again)*

Lit.: E. Käsemann, *Commentary on Romans* (1980) 197. — O. Kuss, *Der Römerbrief* ([2]1963) 462-85. — H. Schlier, *Der Römerbrief* (HTKNT, 1977) 224f. — F. Schnider, *Die verlorenen Söhne, Strukturanalytische und historisch-kritische Untersuchungen zu Lukas 15* (OBO 17, 1977) 43-47.

In Rom 7:9 the vb. has the inchoative sense: Sin *comes to life, awakens.* In the context of Paul's teaching on justification 7:1-25 emphasizes that the justified person has "died" not only to sin (6:1-11), but also to that power through which sin makes its appearance, namely, the law. The commandment, which in fact "promised life" (7:10a), caused sin to come to life in selfish human covetousness (vv. 7f.) and thus caused human death (v. 10b). In 14:9 the reading ἔζησεν (with Christ as the subj.) is preferable to ἀνέζησεν (Schlier 410).

The vb. is used metaphorically in Luke 15:24. In the parable of the lost sons the father describes the younger son's absence from his father as lostness and death and his return to his father as his being found again and "coming to life again" (ἀνέζησεν; cf. v. 32 v.l.). Accordingly, the return of the lost son produces joy.

In Rev 20:5 the seer sees in a vision that those who have been beheaded for their testimony to Jesus and for the word of God and those who have died under persecution remaining true to Christ *came to life again* and reigned with Christ a thousand years. They alone came to life already and not the rest of the dead. The fact that they participate in the first resurrection reveals that they are not affected by the "second death," which is condemnation to eternal perdition (cf. 2:11; 20:14; 21:8).

F. Schnider

ἀναζητέω *anazēteō* look for, search*

Luke 2:44, 45; Acts 11:25, the obj. always a person (Jesus, Paul).

ἀναζώννυμαι *anazōnnymai* gird up*

Fig. in 1 Pet 1:13: διὸ ἀναζωσάμενοι τὰς ὀσφύας τῆς διανοίας ὑμῶν, νήφοντες . . . ἐλπίσατε. The girding up of the robe is a sign that one is ready for departure; cf. Prov 31:17 LXX; Pol. *Phil.* 2:1 (quotation of 1 Pet 1:13). L. Goppelt, *Der Erste Petrusbrief* (KEK) ad loc.

ἀναζωπυρέω *anazōpyreō* fan, rekindle*

Fig. in 2 Tim 1:6: ἀναζωπυρεῖν τὸ χάρισμα, "to *fan into a flame* the gift that God gave you" (JB).

ἀναθάλλω *anathallō* (cause to) bloom again*

Both a trans. (causative) and an intrans. translation are possible in Phil 4:10. BDF §101 s.v. θάλλειν.

ἀνάθεμα, ατος, τό *anathema* accursed (thing or person), curse*

1. Occurrences in early Christian literature — 2. In Paul — 3. In Acts

Lit.: J. Behm, *TDNT* I, 354f. — G. Bornkamm, "The Anathema in the Early Christian Lord's Supper Liturgy," *Early Christian Experience* (1969) 169-79. — N. Brox, "ΑΝΑΘΕΜΑ ΙΗΣΟΥΣ (1 Kor 12:3)," *BZ* N.F. 12 (1968) 103-11. — L. Brun, *Segen und Fluch im Urchristentum* (1932). — H. Conzelmann,

1 Corinthians (Hermeneia) 204f., esp. nn. 9f. — K. HOFMANN, *RAC* I, 427-30. — B. A. PEARSON, "Did the Gnostics Curse Jesus?" *JBL* 86 (1967) 301-5. — W. SCHMITHALS, *Gnosticism in Corinth* (1971) 124-30, 349-51. — W. C. VAN UNNIK, "Jesus: Anathema or Kyrios (1 Cor 12:3)," FS Moule 113-26.

1. In all of early Christian literature (according to the categorization of BAGD) ἀνάθεμα occurs only 5 times in the authentic letters of Paul and once in Acts, always with human beings as the obj. (though never with a human as the agency by which the curse is carried out). It is also found in the pagan table of curses from Megara (KIT 20 [²1912]; cf. Deissmann, *Light* 95), where Jewish influence is present. Its NT use corresponds to its use in the LXX.

2. Making use of liturgical formulas which mark the transition to the Lord's Supper (cf. *Did.* 10:6), Paul concludes 1 Corinthians in 16:22 with a curse on anyone who "has no love for the Lord": "let that person *be accursed*" (cf. Deut 7:26a; Josh 6:17; above all, see 1 Cor 11:27f. and the formulas for excommunication in the Eleusinian mysteries, Lucian *Alex.* 38). Paul turns over the heretics as well to the judgment of God in Gal 1:8f.

It is difficult to understand the cursing of Jesus in 1 Cor 12:3 ("Jesus *be cursed*"; cf. Gal 3:13; *Did.* 16:5) as a mere ad hoc formulation serving as a contrast for the following acclamation ("Jesus is Lord"). Rather, Paul is combatting a curse which, while almost certainly no one—including Jewish opponents—articulated it *per se,* was nonetheless real (and in Paul's mind really present) and corresponded to the gnosticizing tendency of the opponents in 1 Corinthians. Whether one can relate the underlying rejection of the merely earthly Jesus (cf. 1 John 2:22) with the entrance requirements of the Ophites mentioned by Origen (*Catena* fragment 47 in 1 Cor 12:3: εἰ μὴ ἀναθεματίσῃ τὸν Ἰησοῦν; *Cels.* 6:28; cf. Conzelmann 205, n. 10) is disputed (for: Schmithals and Brox in particular; against: Pearson in particular).

In Rom 9:3 Paul expresses the impossible wish that for the sake of the salvation of his people he might take upon himself vicarious rejection: "would that I myself were *accursed* and cut off from Christ," i.e., so that he would be banned from association with Christ. A remote parallel in a rabbinical phrase is noted in Billerbeck III, 261.

3. According to Acts 23:14 (cf. vv. 12, 21) a group of Jews pledge themselves through an oath in the form of a self-curse (*to bind oneself unconditionally with a curse* in the sense of "swear"; cf. *1 Enoch* 6:4f.) neither to eat nor to drink until Paul was killed.

H.-W. Kuhn

ἀναθεματίζω *anathematizō* curse (vb.)

Used absolutely in Mark 14:71 of Peter's laying a curse on himself with the intention of decisively reinforcing the truth of his statement, though he thereby denies Jesus (v. 72), and in Acts 23:12, 14 (ἀναθέματι ἀνεθεματίσαμεν), and 21 with the obj. ἑαυτούς referring to more than forty Jews who pronounced God's curse upon themselves if they ate or drank before they killed Paul. J. Behm, *TDNT* I, 355f.; H. Aust and D. Müller, *DNTT* I, 415; → ἀνάθεμα 3.

ἀναθεωρέω *anatheōreō* look at again and again, observe carefully*

Acts 17:23; fig. in Heb 13:7, with the obj. the outcome of the lives of earlier leaders of the congregation.

ἀνάθημα, ατος, τό *anathēma* votive offering*

Luke 21:5, of the temple in Jerusalem, which is decorated with votive offerings, e.g., the gold-plated vine above the curtain before the sanctuary (Josephus *B.J.* v.210). On the combination with κοσμέω cf. 2 Macc 9:16; Herodotus i.183. → Ἀνάθεμα is a late (Hellenistic) form used in a special meaning in the LXX and the NT. J. Behm, *TDNT* I, 354f.; H. Köster, *RGG* V, 1651f.; H. Aust and D. Müller, *DNTT* I, 413-15.

ἀναίδεια, ας, ἡ *anaideia* shamelessness*

Luke 11:8: *audacity, obtrusiveness.*

ἀναίρεσις, εως, ἡ *anairesis* destruction, murder*

Acts 8:1: the murder of Stephen; cf. 22:20 Koine; 13:28 D*.

ἀναιρέω *anaireō* take up, do away with, kill

The meaning of the compound corresponds to the basic meaning of the prep. ἀνά, *up, up to* (Schwyzer, *Grammatik* II, 440) and the classical simple form αἱρέω, *take* (in the NT only in mid.: αἱρέομαι, "choose, prefer"); thus Acts 7:21 and Heb 10:9. Otherwise the stem (vb.) and the determiner (prep.) form a new concept which is already a classical t.t.: *kill, do away with, murder, execute* (as a synonym for θανατόω and ἀποκτείνω). This is the usual meaning in the NT in connection with the death of the apostles (Acts 5:33; 9:23f., 29) and the death of Jesus (Luke 22:2; Acts 2:23). In connection with the destruction of the Antichrist the subj. is "Jesus the Lord" (2 Thess 2:8 with reference to Isa 11:4). In Acts 16:27 the vb. is used reflexively: ἑαυτὸν ἀναιρεῖν, to *commit suicide.*

Both the Haggadah on Pharaoh's plan to murder Moses and the fulfillment quotation (Jer 31:15, quoted in Matt 2:18) have influenced the form of Herod's command "to *kill* all the male children in Bethlehem and in all that region who were two years old or under" (Matt 2:16); cf. A. Vögtle, *Messias und Gottessohn* (1971) 32-41, 68-70, and W. Grundmann, *Matthäus* (THKNT) 84 ("there is no evidence for the historicity of the incident," esp. since there is no trace of it in Josephus). As in the case of Moses, the narrative interest is wholly in God's rescue of the child.

H. Frankemölle

ἀναίτιος *anaitios* innocent, guiltless*

Matt 12:5, 7 (sg.); cf. *b. Šabb.* 132b: "the temple service supplants the Sabbath"; Lev 24:8f.; John 7:22f. Acts 16:37 D.

ἀνακαθίζω *anakathizō* sit up, sit upright*

Luke 7:15: ἀνεκάθισεν ὁ νεκρός; Acts 9:40.

ἀνακαινίζω *anakainizō* renew
→ καινός.

ἀνακαινόω *anakainoō* renew
→ καινός.

ἀνακαίνωσις, εως, ἡ *anakainōsis* renewal
→ καινός.

ἀνακαλύπτω *anakalyptō* uncover, unveil, take away*

Fig. in 2 Cor 3:14: "for to this day . . . that same veil remains *unlifted*" (μὴ ἀνακαλυπτόμενον is related to κάλυμμα and is not acc. absolute); v. 18: ἀνακεκαλυμμένῳ προσώπῳ, "with *unveiled* face." A. Oepke, *TDNT* III, 560f.; W. Mundle, *DNTT* II, 212-14; R. Bultmann, *The Second Letter to the Corinthians* (1985) ad loc.

ἀνακάμπτω *anakamptō* return, turn around*

Matt 2:12; Acts 18:21; Heb 11:15; fig. in Luke 10:6. 2 Pet 2:21 ℵ A in the sense of *turn back again.*

ἀνάκειμαι *anakeimai* lie, recline at table*

There are 14 occurrences of ἀνάκειμαι in the NT (besides Mark 5:40; Luke 7:37 v.l.). It bears the general meaning of *lie* only in Mark 5:40 C Koine *pm.* Otherwise it always has the sense of *being at table, eating a meal*; the subst. partc. ὁ ἀνακείμενος is *the one invited to the meal, the guest, the one sharing table fellowship* (Matt 9:10; 22:10, 11; 26:7; Mark 6:26; 14:18 par. Matt 26:20; Mark 16:14; Luke 22:27a [over against ὁ διακονῶν, "the one who serves at table"], b; John 6:11; 12:2; 13:28; 13:23 [ἦν ἀνακείμενος εἷς . . . ἐν τῷ κόλπῳ τοῦ Ἰησοῦ, "One . . . *was lying (at table)* close to the breast of Jesus," i.e., occupying the place of honor]; cf. also Luke 16:23, ἀναπαυόμενον D Θ it). BAGD s.v.; B. Reicke, *BHH* III, 1991-93.

ἀνακεφαλαιόω *anakephalaioō* sum up; combine, unite*

1. Basic meaning — 2. Rom 13:9 — 3. Eph 1:10

Lit.: C. Brown, *DNTT* II, 163. — H. Schlier, *TDNT* III, 681f.; — W. Staerk, *RAC* I, 411-14.

On Rom 13:9: K. Berger, *Die Gesetzesauslegung Jesu* (1972). — A. Feuillet, "Loi ancienne et moral chrétienne," *NRT* 92 (1970) 785-805. — E. Käsemann, *Commentary on Romans* (1980) 360f. — A. Nissen, *Gott und der Nächste* (1974).

On Eph 1:10: M. Barth, *Ephesians* (AB) I, 89-92 (bibliography on 411). — J. Gnilka, *Der Brief an der Epheser* (HTKNT). — S. Hanson, *The Unity of the Church* (1946). — A. Lindemann, *Die Aufhebung der Zeit* (1975). — F. Mussner, *Christus, das All und die Kirche* ([2]1968). — H. Schlier, *Christus und die Kirche* (1930). — F. J. Steinmetz, *Protologische Heilszuversicht* (1969).

1. The basic meaning of the vb. is *bring something to a* κεφάλαιον (i.e., *to the main point* [*of a structure*]), *to recapitulate* or *summarize.* A secondary meaning is *break* (some train of thought or expression) *down into its major sections.* Because of constructions using πλήρωμα and πληρόω, ἀνακεφαλαιόω is used in the NT only in the first sense.

2. In Rom 13:9 the commandments of the second table of the Decalogue (Deut 5:17ff. LXX; cf. Luke 18:20 [different from Mark 10:19]) are summarized in the commandment of love for the neighbor (Lev 19:18), i.e., they are brought together in the single major and fundamental statement from which they can be deduced or to which they can be reduced. (On the genre of the "social ethical list" which contains in this instance commandments of the Decalogue and in typically Christian fashion [Jas 2:8, 11; Matt 19:18f., unlike the Markan parallel] the love commandment, see Berger 362-95.) According to Rom 13:8-10, however (on the structure see A. L. Bencze, *NTS* 20 [1973/74] 90-92), Lev 19:18 is not only a summary of the commandments of the Decalogue, but of the law (→ νόμος) as a whole (Feuillet 797); cf. Gal 5:14.

From a tradition-historical perspective we are dealing with a Hellenistic Jewish conception of the law, which has been appropriated here. This conception of the law, which concentrates on social obligations, is exemplified in *Testaments of the Twelve Patriarchs,* Wisdom, and Sirach (cf. Berger 38-55) and has been absorbed into the NT in other places as well (Matt 7:12 [cf. 22:40]; Jas 2:8; cf. Mark 10:17ff. Since the rabbinic "summations" of the Torah (Billerbeck I, 357ff., 460; III, 306) are not summaries in any strict sense (Nissen 389-415, esp. 398f.), they are only remotely related.

In the Christian context the use of Lev 19:18 as a summary of the law is, in the final analysis, the result of the acceptance of Jesus, whose demands culminate in the love of the enemy (Matt 5:44f., 48 par.) in such a way that the specifically Christian content lies in the abolition of limitations regarding the identity of the "neighbor" (cf. Luke 10:29-37; for Paul Rom 12:14-21). For Paul, however, the essential basis for love is christology; thus the mercy of God, on which Jesus based the love commandment (Luke 6:36 par.), is replaced by the sacrifice of Christ on the cross: Gal 5:13-24; 2:20f.; Phil 2:1-11; cf. Eph 4:32–5:2.

3. Eph 1:10 specifies that the content of "the mystery" is: ἀνακεφαλαιώσασθαι τὰ πάντα ἐν τῷ Χριστῷ. Christ is the "cardinal point" in which all lines of the universe come together *(recapitulatio omnium).* But the idea of the representation of the universe (Hanson 123-26) is insufficient. The aor. is to be interpreted as indicating a unique act of God, historically located in the Christ-event. Ἀνακεφαλαιόω converges with vv. 9b, 10a, according to which history reaches its goal in Christ (Gnilka 79). Therefore, "universe" does not mean a self-contained cosmos, but rather the purposeful creation (cf. v. 4). Eph 1:10b, c, then, describes the act of God which establishes in Christ the eschatological goal for the sake of which the entire creation was brought into being so that it encompasses the universe in its spatio-temporal dimensions.

Syntactic considerations lead Lindemann 69f. rightly to criticize the interpretation of the text as referring to the restoration of the universe's unity or of the old order (Mussner 66; Gnilka 80; Steinmetz 79f.). Moreover, the etymology (κεφάλαιον, not → κεφαλή: Staerk 412) prohibits a direct interpretation of it as the installation of Christ as Head of the Universe (H. Schlier, *Der Brief an die Epheser* [1957] 65), esp. where this idea is fused with the Gnostic Anthropos myth (Schlier, *Christus* 60ff.).

Such connotations arise only from the larger context of Ephesians or from pragmatic considerations of the text. If a sense of the world similar to that in Colossians is assumed (E. Schweizer, *Kolosserbrief* [EKK] 100-104), Eph 1:10 could cause the reader to think of the reconciliation of the universe. But, unlike Colossians, Ephesians explicates this idea not in relation to the universe, but in relation to the Church (2:16) and thus interprets 1:10 in a historical perspective. Precisely for this reason it does not deduce from 1:10 the unguarded statement "Christ = Head of the universe," but says rather that Christ has been given to *the Church* as head over all things (1:22; cf. 4:15f.). Accordingly, the anakephalaiosis sets in motion a process that enables the sovereignty of Christ to assert itself through the Church before the nations and powers (3:8ff.) and that thus lends a historical dimension to the fulfillment of the universe (1:23; 4:10).

H. Merklein

ἀνακλίνω *anaklinō* lay down, cause to lie down (act.); lie down (pass.)*

Act. in Luke 2:7; in causative sense in 12:37: the returning master makes himself the servant of the watchful servants and *causes them to lie down,* i.e., invites them to the table; cf. pass. in Mark 6:39 (ℵ B* Θ, et al.; cf. par. Matt 14:19); Luke 9:15 (C Koine A W, et al.). Pass. *recline at the meal:* Matt 8:11; 14:19; Luke 13:29; 7:36 Koine A W Θ *pm.*

ἀνακόπτω *anakoptō* repel, restrain (from running)

Gal 5:7 TR: ἀνέκοψεν; preferred reading: ἐνέκοψεν.

ἀνακράζω *anakrazō* cry out*

Mark 1:23 par. Luke 4:33; Mark 6:49; Luke 8:28; 23:18. W. Grundmann, *TDNT* III, 900-903.

ἀνακρίνω *anakrinō* question, examine, investigate, test

→ κρίνω.

ἀνάκρισις, εως, ἡ *anakrisis* investigation, hearing

→ κρίνω.

ἀνακυλίω *anakyliō* roll away (trans.)

Mark 16:4, of the stone that closed the tomb of Jesus (B ℵ L).

ἀνακύπτω *anakyptō* raise oneself erect*

Luke 13:11; John 8:7, 10; fig. in Luke 21:28: ἀνακύψατε καὶ ἐπάρατε τὰς κεφαλὰς ὑμῶν.

ἀναλαμβάνω *analambanō* take up, lift up*
ἀνάλημψις, εως, ἡ *analēmpsis* ascension, taking up*

1. Basic meanings — 2. "Take up" — 3. Exaltation and ascension — 4. Ἀνάλημψις

Lit.: G. Delling, *TDNT* IV, 7-9. — G. Friedrich, "Lk 9, 51 und die Entrückungschristologie des Lukas," FS Schmid (1973) 48-77. — J. Lambrecht, "De oudste Christologie: verrijzenis of verhoging," *Bijdr.* 36 (1975) 119-44. — G. Lohfink, *Die Himmelfahrt Jesu* (SANT 26, 1971).

1. The compound vb. ἀναλαμβάνω has the basic meanings *take up* and *take again.* It appears in the NT in the general sense of *take up* (→ 2) and as the term for exaltation and ascension (→ 3). The subst. ἀνάλημψις occurs in the Bible only in Luke 9:51 (→ 4).

2. In Acts 20:13, 14; 23:31 and 2 Tim 4:11 ἀναλαμβάνω means to *take along* or *take with* in reference to travel companions. In Acts 7:43 (quotation from Amos 5:26 LXX) ἀναλαμβάνω denotes the *taking up* and *carrying along* of pagan cultic objects as signs of idolatry. In Eph 6:13, 16, as in documents outside the NT (e.g., 2 Macc 10:17; Jdt 6:12; 7:5; 14:3), ἀναλάμβανω is used as a fig. expression for *putting on* armor. In Acts 10:16 it refers to

taking up, taking away (cf. v. 3) of what is seen in the vision, the container which descended from heaven (v. 11).

3. In 1 Tim 3:16 ἀναλαμβάνω occurs in a hymnic text that apparently reflects early tradition: "*taken up* in glory." As the conclusion of the traditional material and in contrast to the beginning thereof, the phrase announces the exaltation of Christ. As indicated by the parallels in Phil 2:9; Acts 2:33; 5:31; John 3:14; 12:34 and by the addition of "in glory," this has to do with an invisible event belonging to the heavenly realm. (On the question whether these and other exaltation pronouncements constitute the earliest form of the Easter proclamation or a later, secondary form, cf. Lohfink 95f.; Lambrecht). In Mark 16:19 (a later conclusion of Mark) ἀναλαμβάνω could be interpreted in just this way (esp. because of the phrase, "and sat down at the right hand of God"; Delling 8); more likely, however, is a sense similar to and dependent upon Acts 1:11. With the phrase "who was taken up from you into heaven" Acts 1:11c unmistakably denotes an event visible to the disciples ("why do you stand looking," v. 11a; "as you saw him go into heaven," v. 11d; cf. v. 9). The ascension, which only here and in Luke 24:51 (→ ἀναφέρω) is described as a being carried away, is linguistically dependent upon the OT Elijah or Enoch traditions (2 Kgs 2:9-11; Sir 48:9; 49:14; 2 Macc 2:58); thematically it is at home in the thought world of extrabiblical assumption stories. In Acts 1:2, 22 "when he was *taken up*" refers to a literally conceived ascension and designates that day as the conclusion of the earthly activity of Jesus.

4. Ἀνάλημψις (basic meaning: *taking up, restoration*) has various kinds of content outside the Bible, including *death* (e.g., *Pss. Sol.* 4:18). In Luke 9:51 ἀνάλημψις as *taking up* denotes not only the death of Jesus (Friedrich) but also his resurrection, ascension, and exaltation; for in the Lukan two-volume work these mark the conclusion of the earthly activity of Jesus (cf. Luke 24:51; Acts 1:2, 22): it is only with reference to them that the pl. "days" is appropriate (Lohfink 212-14).

J. Kremer

ἀνάλημψις, εως, ἡ *analēmpsis* ascension, taking up
→ ἀναλαμβάνω.

ἀναλίσκω, ἀναλόω *analiskō, analoō* consume, devour*

The two forms are synonymous (see BDF §101 s.v.). Ἀναλῶσαι appears in Luke 9:54 in a question of a disciple regarding fire to come down from heaven and *consume* the inhabitants of a Samaritan village (ὡς καὶ Ἠλίας ἐποίησεν is added in C Koine D Θ *pm* it; cf. 2 Kgs 1:10-14; cf. also 2 Thess 2:8 ℵ* Origen). Ἀναλωθῆτε is fig. in Gal 5:15 of the consequences of misunderstanding freedom: "take heed that you are not *consumed* by one another."

ἀναλογία, ας, ἡ *analogia* right relationship, agreement*

Rom 12:6: εἴτε προφητείαν, κατὰ τὴν ἀναλογίαν τῆς πίστεως, ". . . in agreement with the faith" (NIV mg.). The admonition applies to the charisma of prophecy which is endangered by individual and libertine enthusiasm. It is to be measured by the πίστις that has been handed down, expressed in fixed formulas, and believed by the Church. G. Kittel, *TDNT* I, 347f.; W. Pannenberg, *RGG* I, 351; E. Käsemann, *Commentary on Romans* (1980) 332-42; H. Schlier, *Römerbrief* (HTKNT) ad loc.

ἀναλογίζομαι *analogizomai* consider, ponder*

Heb 12:3: ἀναλογίσασθε with personal dir. obj.: *consider* him. . . .

ἄναλος, 2 *analos* unsalted, without salt*

Used in Mark 9:50 in reference to salt which has lost its seasoning effect as an image for the loss of the true spirit of discipleship. Natural salt could become worthless due to dampness or the influence of the sun. At issue in the image of salt which is salty and which seasons is the real "point" of discipleship, namely, for action to be in accord with what one is. Cf. Matt 5:13 and the rabbinic ridicule of this saying in *b. Bek.* 8b. Billerbeck I, 232-36; R. J. Forbes, *BHH* III, 1653f.; E. Schweizer, *The Good News According to Mark* (1970) 199f. → ἅλας.

ἀναλόω *analoō* consume, devour
→ ἀναλίσκω.

ἀνάλυσις, εως, ἡ *analysis* release, dissolution; departure*

Fig. in 2 Tim 4:6 of *departure from life*; cf. *1 Clem.* 44:5. F. Büchsel, *TDNT* IV, 337.

ἀναλύω *analyō* break apart; depart*

Luke 12:36: *departure* from a marriage feast, i.e., the *return home*; fig. in Phil 1:23: *depart* (from this life) as a euphemism for "to die." F. Büchsel, *TDNT* IV, 337; C. J. de Vogel, *NovT* 19 (1977) 262-74. → ἀνάλυσις.

ἀναμάρτητος, 2 *anamartētos* sinless*

John 8:7: ὁ ἀναμάρτητος ὑμῶν, he "who is *without sin.*" K. H. Rengstorf, *TDNT* I, 333-35; H. Clavier, *RHPR* 47 (1967) 150-64.

ἀναμένω *anamenō* expect*

1 Thess 1:10, with dir. obj. the Son of God; cf. Ign. *Phld.* 5:2. P.-É. Langevin, *Jésus Seigneur et l'eschatologie* (1967) 67-73; BDF §148.1.

ἀναμέσον *anameson* between*

Improper prep. in 1 Cor 6:5: ἀναμέσον τοῦ ἀδελφοῦ. The sense requires the addition of καὶ τοῦ ἀδελφοῦ (as in f g sy[p]): "*between* the brethren" or "*between* the brother and his opponent." BDF §§204; 215.3. → ἀνά, μέσον.

ἀναμιμνῄσκω *anamimnēskō* remind
→ ἀνάμνησις 4.

ἀνάμνησις, εως, ἡ *anamnēsis* remembrance

1. Occurrences and meaning — 2. Eucharistic tradition — 3. Hebrews — 4. (Ἐπ-)ἀναμιμνῄσκω.

Lit.: K.-H. Bartels, *Dies tut zu meinem Gedächtnis. Zur Auslegung von 1 Kor 11, 24.25* (Diss. Mainz, 1959). — P. A. H. de Boer, *Gedenken und Gedächtnis in der Welt des AT* (1962) 64-70. — N. A. Dahl, "Anamnesis," *ST* 1 (1948) 69-95. — G. Delling, *TRE* I, 47-58 (bibliography). — H. Feld, *Das Verständnis des Abendmahls* (1976). — Goppelt, *Theology* II, 147-50. — J. Jeremias, *The Eucharistic Words of Jesus* (1966) 237-55. — H. Kosmala, "Das tut zu meinem Gedächtnis," *NovT* 4 (1960) 81-94. — P. Neuenzeit, *Das Herrenmahl* (1960). — H. Patsch, *Abendmahl und historischer Jesus* (1972) 79 (bibliography). — J. Roloff, "Heil als Gemeinschaft," *Gottesdienst und Öffentlichkeit* (ed. P. Cornehl and H.-E. Bahr; 1970) 88-117. — W. Theiler, *RAC* VI, 43-54. — K. H. Schelkle, "Das Herrenmahl," FS Käsemann 385-402.

1. Ἀνάμνησις is rare in the the NT, occurring only in cultic-liturgical contexts in Luke 22:19; 1 Cor 11:24f.; Heb 10:3. In regard to its meaning one must be sensitive to the OT and Jewish content of the semantic field represented by the root *zkr* in the sense of re-presentation, making present the past which can never remain merely past but becomes effective in the present (cf. the Passover memorial in Exod 12:14; 13:3, 8, etc.).

2. The command for repetition ("Do this *in remembrance of me*") is found only in one strand of the eucharistic tradition (1 Cor 11:24f.; Luke 22:19). Luke connects the command with the word over the bread (cf. Justin *Apol.* i.66.3). Paul connects it with both the word over the bread and the word over the cup and expands the word over the cup by the addition of "as often as you drink it." As is seen by comparison with Mark and Matthew, the memorial command is literarily secondary and therefore unlikely to be authentic.

Earlier research pointed to the widespread ancient commemorative meals for the dead which were celebrated "in remembrance" of the founder as the background for these NT texts. But "memorial formulae" are so widespread in Palestine from the OT period to that of the rabbis that it is unnecessary to trace the remembrance command to the Hellenistic Church. The Passover celebration in particular, which is most comparable to the celebration of the Last Supper (and which was certainly the historical setting for the final meal of Jesus), was from the beginning a celebration of "commemoration" (Exod 12:14; 13:3, 8; Deut 16:3; *Jub.* 49:7ff.; cf. *m. Pesaḥ.* 10:5). Since in most examples God is the subj. of the remembering, Jeremias concludes that the eucharistic command is to be translated: "This do, that God may remember me (as his Messiah)." The Passover memorial makes clear that this suggestion is not compelling; it is not, on the basis of the wording, the most obvious.

Paul cites the eucharistic formula as a binding authority in the face of the abuses in the Corinthian eucharistic praxis. In his opinion there was in Corinth no real "Lord's Supper" at all because every person of means ate his own meal in order to satisfy his hunger prior to the actual eucharistic meal without waiting for the poorer brethren who came later (1 Cor 11:20-22, 33). Paul bases his judgment in ecclesiology (v. 22b) as well as in soteriology (vv. 27ff.). He develops the decisive transition in this argument in v. 26 in connection with the command to remember: "For as often as you eat this bread and drink the cup, you proclaim the Lord's death until he comes." The "as often as" forms a clear connection with the "as often as" of the second command to remember (v. 25); but the "Lord's death" was, according to the eucharistic words, "for you" (v. 24), i.e., it occurred as a vicarious sacrifice for all "brethren" (cf. 15:3: "for our sins"). Until the return of the Lord (cf. → μαρανα θα, 16:22), it is in the celebration of the Lord's Supper that the memory of the vicarious, reconciling death of the Lord "for you" is proclaimed in word and deed and thus becomes effective. This command to remember obligates them, then, not only to a repetition of the meal as a ritual event, but also to the proclamation of the saving significance of the death of Jesus which excludes, on theological grounds, a eucharistic praxis such as that of the Corinthians.

3. In Heb 10:3 the author emphasizes that the annual sacrifices on the great Day of Atonement (10:1; Lev 16:1ff.) do not produce an enduring purification from sin, but rather a constant *reminder* of sin (cf. *Jub.* 34:19), whether through the sacrifice itself or in the confession of sin connected with the sacrificial act. Precisely through this reminder the "consciousness of sin" (10:2) is maintained. Only the sanctification which comes through the offering of the body of Jesus Christ "once for all" (vv. 10, 14), which means the forgiveness of sins (v. 18), annuls this function of memory.

4. The vb. **(ἐπ-)ἀναμιμνῄσκω** *remind* (someone [*again*] of something)* occurs in the Gospels only in Mark: Peter remembered (pass.) Jesus' curse upon the fig tree (11:21) and Jesus' "word" predicting Peter's denial

(14:72). The use of remembering in parenesis (11:22ff.) is dominant in Paul as well: memory "of my ways in Christ" (1 Cor 4:17) and of "the obedience of you all" (2 Cor 7:15). The content of this remembering is binding (Rom 15:15 [the compound]; cf. Heb 10:32). Thus, in the post-Pauline period the vb. can acquire the meaning of *admonish* (2 Tim 1:6).

H. Patsch

ἀνανεόω *ananeoō* renew
→ νέος.

ἀνανήφω *ananēphō* become sober*

Fig. in 2 Tim 2:26: καὶ ἀνανήψωσιν ἐκ τῆς τοῦ διαβόλου παγίδος, that "they may *come to their senses* and escape from the devil's snare" (NEB). In Philo *All.* ii.60 ἀνανήφω = μετανοέω.

Ἁνανίας, ου *Hananias* Ananias*

1. A Christian in the early Church in Jerusalem.

Lit.: J. D. M. DERRETT, "Ananias, Sapphira, and the Right of Property," *DR* 296 (1971) 225-32. — W. DIETRICH, *Das Petrusbild der lukanischen Schriften* (1972) 232-37. — P.-H. MENOUD, "La mort d'Ananias et de Saphira (Actes 5, 1-11)," FS Goguel 146-54. — G. THEISSEN, *Urchristliche Wundergeschichten* (1974) 117-20.

According to Acts 5:1-11 Ananias (vv. 1, 3, 5) and his wife **Σάπφιρα***/Sapphira (v. 1) were punished for fraud with death by divine decree. The text is in the form of an example story: the guilty verdict is confirmed by means of a miracle which guarantees the norms of the community (Theissen 117). Only the first half of the narrative must have belonged to its earliest form.

2. A Jewish Christian in Damascus.

Lit.: C. BURCHARD, *Der dreizehnte Zeuge* (1970) 51-136. — D. GILL, "The Structure of Acts 9," *Bib* 55 (1974) 546-48. — G. KLEIN, *Die Zwölf Apostel* (1961) 144-62. — K. LÖNING, *Die Saulustradition in der Apostelgeschichte* (1973). — G. LOHFINK, *Paulus vor Damaskus* (1966) 64-67. — S. LUNDGREN, "Ananias and the Calling of Paul," *ST* 25 (1971) 117-22. — V. STOLLE, *Der Zeuge als Angeklagter* (1973) 155-212.

Acts 9:10-19 reports that Ananias was commissioned in a vision to go and find Saul (vv. 10, 12, 13). Following initial resistance he went, healed Saul, and baptized him (v. 17). In 22:12-16 the role of Ananias is considerably curtailed, and in ch. 26 it is absent altogether. It is generally acknowledged that the role of Ananias belonged to the earliest form of the tradition. It is debated whether the double vision in 9:10-16 is pre-Lukan tradition or Lukan redaction and what office Ananias held.

3. A Jewish high priest (*ca.* A.D. 47-59).

Lit.: D. COX, "Paul before the Sanhedrin: Acts 22,30–23,11," *SBFLA* 21 (1971) 54-75. — J. JEREMIAS, *Jerusalem in the Time of Jesus* (1969) 147-221. — W. RADL, *Paulus und Jesus im lukanischen Doppelwerk* (1975) 169-221. — SCHÜRER I, 486f.; II, 231, 233. — STOLLE (→ 2) 32-64, 91-140, 213-84.

Ananias, the son of Nedebaeus, was very wealthy and therefore had great influence even after he was removed from office. But he was also hated because of his greed and was murdered by rebels at the beginning of the Jewish War because of his friendship with the Romans. See Josephus *Ant.* xx; *B.J.* ii.

In Acts 23 Paul stands before the Sanhedrin. The high priest Ananias orders that Paul be struck on the mouth in the presence of the court (v. 2), whereupon Paul calls him a "whitewashed wall." In 24:1-23 the spokesman for the Sanhedrin, Tertullus, in the presence of Ananias and a few elders (v. 1), presents the case against Paul before the Roman governor Felix (A.D. 52-59). After Paul's defense Felix postpones judgment and orders a relaxation in the conditions of Paul's imprisonment—in the mind of Luke a declaration of innocence. Even if the speeches are literary constructions, the accusations against Paul by the Jews before the Romans as well as the participation of Ananias are nonetheless historically credible.

A. Weiser

ἀναντίρρητος, 2 *anantirrētos* undeniable, irrefutable*

Acts 19:36: *true beyond doubt.*

ἀναντιρρήτως *anantirrētōs* without raising any objection, without contradiction*

Acts 10:29, referring to Peter going to Cornelius.

ἀνάξιος, 2 *anaxios* unworthy, inappropriate*

1 Cor 6:2: ἀνάξιοι . . . κριτηρίων ἐλαχίστων, "*incompetent* to try trivial cases." W. Foerster, *TDNT* I, 379f.; E. Tiedtke, *DNTT* III, 348f.

ἀναξίως *anaxiōs* unworthily, inappropriately*

1 Cor 11:27 (and v. 29 Koine D G *pl* lat sy). W. Foerster, *TDNT* I, 379f.

ἀνάπαυσις, εως, ἡ *anapausis* ceasing, rest*
ἀναπαύω *anapauō* rest, relax; refresh*

Lit.: H. D. BETZ, "The Logion of the Easy Yoke and of Rest: Matt 11:28-30," *JBL* 86 (1967) 10-24. — F. CHRIST, *Jesus Sophia* (ATANT 57, 1970) 100-119. — O. HOFIUS, *Katapausis* (WUNT 11, 1970) 29-90, 248-57. — U. LUCK, "Weisheit und Christologie in Mt 11, 25-30," *WuD* 13 (1975) 35-51.

The subst. occurs 5 times, the vb. 12. Ἀνάπαυσις is used in Rev 4:8; 14:11 in the sense of *ceasing,* in Matt

12:43 par. Luke 11:24 of a *resting-place,* and in Matt 11:20 of *rest.* As in secular Greek, ἀναπαύω is used both trans. and intrans. It is trans. in Matt 11:28, in Paul (1 Cor 16:18; Phlm 20 [act.]; 2 Cor 7:13; Phlm 7 [pass.]), and in Rev 14:13 (2nd fut. pass.). The intrans. mid., *rest,* occurs in the Synoptics (Mark 6:31; 14:41 par. Matt 26:45; Luke 12:19), in 1 Pet 4:14 (cf. Isa 11:2 LXX), and in Rev 6:11 in the sense of *to wait.*

In Paul the word has to do with inner rest (through joy, comfort, etc.), in the Synoptics, except for Matt 11:28f. and 12:43 par., more with natural relaxation. In Revelation the subst. refers both to the perpetual praise of God (4:8) and to the equally perpetual torment of the idolaters (14:11). The vb. undergirds the confidence of the witnesses to the faith regarding the time (6:11; cf. Dan 12:13) and the manner of the culmination (14:13; cf., e.g., 4 Ezra 7:95f.).

In the call of Matt 11:28-30 the phrase "you will find rest for your souls" (v. 29; cf. *Gos. Thom.* 60) recalls Jer 6:16. The motifs of laboring, the yoke, and *rest* are prefigured in Sir 6:18ff. (v. 28); 51:13ff. (v. 26) and are placed in the mouth of Jesus as the personified Wisdom. In the OT and Judaism the promise of *rest* as one of the benefits of salvation continues to be oriented to divine instruction (*b. Šabb.* 152b; *2 Bar.* 73:1 [the messianic kingdom]; Philo *Fug.* 174 [the "rest" of the blessed wise man "in God"]). In Gnosticism (cf. J.-E. Ménard, "Le repos, salut du gnostique," *RevScRel* 51 [1977] 71-88) it is oriented to the heavenly revelation (e.g., *Odes Sol.* 30:1-3, 7). In Matthew, in any case (for the "anti-pharisaic" emphasis in Wisdom-christology cf. 21:5; 23:4), it has to do with the salvation which the disciple even now finds in Jesus as (the bringer of) the divine revelation (of God's will).

P. Fiedler

ἀναπαύω *anapauō* rest, relax; refresh
→ ἀνάπαυσις.

ἀναπείθω *anapeitho* persuade, entice*

Acts 18:13: παρὰ τὸν νόμον ἀναπείθει . . . σέβεσθαι τὸν θεόν (a Jewish accusation against Paul).

ἀνάπειρος, 2 *anapeiros* crippled*

In the NT only subst. in Luke 14:13, 21: cripple. A B D read ἀνάπειρος, ℵ has ἀνάπιρος, otherwise the (classical) form ἀνάπηρος. BDF §24.

ἀναπέμπω *anapempō* send; send up; send back*

Fig. of the *sending* of a person to a superior: Luke 23:7; Acts 25:21; *send back* in Luke 23:11, 15; Phlm 12.

ἀναπηδάω *anapēdaō* jump up*

Mark 10:50, of the blind man Bartimaeus.

ἀνάπηρος, 2 *anapēros* crippled
→ ἀνάπειρος.

ἀναπίπτω *anapiptō* lie down at table; lie down, lean back*

Mark 6:40, of *taking one's place* in connection with the feeding of the 5,000 (cf. John 6:10 bis) or of the 4,000 in Mark 8:6 (ἐπὶ τῆς γῆς) par. Matt 15:35 (ἐπὶ τὴν γῆν). *Recline at table* in Luke 11:37; 14:10; 17:7; 22:14; John 13:12. John 13:25: he who was "*leaning back* on Jesus' breast" (JB), i.e., who lay beside him at table; cf. 21:20.

ἀναπληρόω *anaplēroō* make complete, fulfill, fill up
→ πληρόω.

ἀναπολόγητος, 2 *anapologētos* inexcusable*

Rom 1:20, acc. with inf. (with εἰς), to be interpreted consecutively: "so they are without excuse," i.e., unable to present anything in their defense (on this construction see A. Oepke, *TDNT* II, 430); 2:1. F. Thiele, *DNTT* II, 137-39.

ἀναπτύσσω *anaptyssō* unwrap, unroll*

Unrolling the scroll of the prophet Isaiah: Luke 4:17 ℵ Koine D Θ *pl;* ἀνοίξας in A B L W, et al.

ἀνάπτω *anaptō* ignite, kindle*

Jas 3:5: A great forest is *set ablaze* by a small fire; Acts 28:2 Koine: *kindle* a fire; Luke 12:49 (pass.): πῦρ . . . ἤδη ἀνήφθη, "a fire . . . *has* already *been kindled,*" i.e., *is burning* already.

ἀναρίθμητος, 2 *anarithmētos* innumerable*

Heb 11:12, of the sand by the seashore as an image for the descendants of Abraham; cf. Gen 32:13 LXX.

ἀνασείω *anaseiō* incite, stir up*

Mark 15:11: τὸν ὄχλον; Luke 23:5: τὸν λαόν. G. Bornkamm, *TDNT* VII, 198-200.

ἀνασκευάζω *anaskeuazō* tear down; upset; confuse*

Fig. with obj. τὰς ψυχάς: Acts 15:24.

ἀνασπάω *anaspaō* draw up, draw out*

Luke 14:5: out of a well; Acts 11:10: εἰς τὸν οὐρανόν.

ἀνάστασις, εως, ἡ *anastasis* resurrection*
ἀνίστημι *anistēmi* raise; get up, rise*
ἐξανάστασις, εως, ἡ *exanastasis* resurrection*
ἐξανίστημι *exanistēmi* raise up, stand up*

1. Occurrences in the NT — 2. General (nontechnical) meanings — 3. The rising of individuals from the dead — 4. The eschatological resurrection — 5. The resurrection of Jesus

Lit.: For bibliography: G. GHIBERTI in Dhanis, ed. (see below) 645-764. — *idem,* "Resurrexit. Gli Atti di un simposio e la discussione successiva," *RivB* 23 (1975) (413-)424-40. — PERKINS (see below) 453-79. — BROWN and COENEN (see below) 305-9. For further bibliography → ἐγείρω.

Besides the commentaries see esp.: S. AMSLER, *THAT* II, 635-41. — J. BECKER, "Das Gottesbild Jesu und die älteste Auslegung von Ostern," FS Conzelmann 105-26. — *idem, Auferstehung der Toten im Urchristentum* (SBS 82, 1976). — K. BERGER, *Die Auferstehung des Propheten und die Erhöhung des Menschensohnes* (SUNT 13, 1976). — G. BERTRAM, *RAC* I, 919-30. — H. BRAUN, "Zur Terminologie der Acta von der Auferstehung Jesu," *idem, Gesammelte Studien zum NT und seiner Umwelt* ([2]1967) 173-77. — C. BROWN and L. COENEN, *DNTT* 259-309. — R. BULTMANN, "New Testament and Mythology," *Kerygma and Myth* (ed. H. W. Bartsch; 1972) 1-44. — G. DELLING, "Zur Beurteilung des Wunders durch die Antike," *idem, Studien zum NT und zum hellenistischen Judentum* (1970) 53-71. — E. DHANIS, ed., *Resurrexit. Actes du Symposion International sur la Résurrection de Jésus (Rome 1970)* (1974). — J. DUPONT, "Les discours missionaires des Actes des Apôtres d'après un ouvrage récent," *idem, Études sur les Actes des Apôtres* (LD 45, 1967) 133-55. — E. FASCHER, "Anastasis—Resurrectio—Auferstehung," *ZNW* 40 (1941) 166-229. — E. S. Fiorenza, "Die tausendjährige Herrschaft der Auferstandenen (Apk 20, 4-6)," *BibLeb* 13 (1972) 107-24. — J. A. FITZMYER, "To Know Him and the Power of His Resurrection (Phil 3, 10)," FS Rigaux 411-25. — G. FRIEDRICH, "Die Auferweckung Jesu, eine Tat Gottes oder ein Interpretament der Jünger?" *KD* 17 (1971) 153-87. — R. H. FULLER, *The Formation of the Resurrection Narratives* (1972). — H. GRASS, *Ostergeschehen und Osterbericht* ([3]1964). — H. P. HASENFRATZ, *Die Rede von der Auferstehung Jesu Christi* (1975). — M. HENGEL, "Ist der Osterglaube noch zu retten?" *TQ* 153 (1973) 252-69. — P. HOFFMANN, *Die Toten in Christus* (NTAbh N.F. 2, [2]1969). — *idem,* "Markus 8, 31. Zur Herkunft und markanischem Rezeption einer alten Überlieferung," FS Schmid (1973) 170-204. — Jeremias, *Theology* 276-311. — G. KEGEL, *Auferstehung Jesu—Auferstehung der Toten* (1970). — R. KILIAN, "Die Totenerweckungen Elias und Elisas — eine Motivwanderung?" *BZ* 10 (1966) 44-56. — J. KREMER, *Das älteste Zeugnis von der Auferstehung Christi* (SBS 17, [3]1970). — *idem,* "Entstehung und Inhalt des Osterglaubens," *TRev* 72 (1976) 1-14. — *idem, Die Osterevangelien—Geschichten um Geschichte* (1977). — K. LEHMANN, *Auferweckt am dritten Tage nach der Schrift* (QD 38, 1968). — X. LÉON-DUFOUR, *Résurrection de Jésus et message pascal* (1971). — W. MARXSEN, *The Resurrection of Jesus of Nazareth* (1970). — J. MOLITOR, *Grundbegriffe der Jesusüberlieferung im Lichte ihrer orientalischen Sprachgeschichte* (1968). — F. MUSSNER, *Die Auferstehung Jesu* (BiH 7, 1969). — A. OEPKE, *RAC* I, 930-38. — *idem, TDNT* I, 368-72; II, 333-39. — G. R. OSBORNE, *The Resurrection Narratives* (1984). — P. PERKINS, *Resurrection: NT Witness and Contemporary Reflection* (1984). — N. PERRIN, *The Resurrection according to Matthew, Mark, and Luke* (1977). — R. PESCH, "Zur Entstehung des Glaubens an die Auferstehung Jesu," *TQ* 153 (1973) 201-28. — H. M. SCHENKE, "Auferstehungsglaube und Gnosis," *ZNW* 59 (1968) 123-26. — H. SCHLIER, *Über die Auferstehung Jesu Christi* (1968). — A. SCHMITT, "Ps 16, 8-11 als Zeugnis der Auferstehung in der Apostelgeschichte," *BZ* 17 (1973) 229-48. — *idem,* "Die Totenerweckung in 1 Kön 17, 17-24," *VT* 27 (1977) 454-74. — K. SCHUBERT, "Die Entwicklung der Auferstehungslehre von der nachexilischen bis zur rabbinischen Zeit," *BZ* 6 (1962) 177-214. — P. SIBER, *Mit Christus leben. Eine Studie zur paulinischen Auferstehungshoffnung* (ATANT 61, 1971). — B. SPÖRLEIN, *Die Leugnung der Auferstehung* (BU 7, 1971). — G. STEMBERGER, *Der Leib der Auferstehung* (AnBib 56, 1972). — *idem,* "Das Problem der Auferstehung im AT," *Kairos* 14 (1972) 273-90. — *idem,* "Zur Auferstehungslehre in der rabbinischen Literatur," *Kairos* 15 (1973) 238-66. — P. DE SURGY, et al., *La résurrection du Christ et l'exégèse moderne* (LD 50, 1969). — A. VÖGTLE and R. PESCH, *Wie kam es zum Osterglauben?* (1975). — U. WILCKENS, *Resurrection* (1977). — idem, *Die Missionsreden der Apostelgeschichte* (WMANT 5, [3]1974).

1. The compound vb. ἀνίστημι (→ ἵστημι), with its general meaning of *erect, raise up* (trans.) or *get up* (intrans.), occurs frequently in secular literature (Fascher 174-87) and in the LXX (usually for *qûm*). The vb. appears in the NT 108 times, of which 72 are in Luke-Acts, and is often used synonymously with → ἐγείρω or ἐγείρομαι. In 73 NT occurrences ἀνίστημι has the general meanings of *raise up* or *appoint* or (intrans.) *stand up, rise,* or *appear* (→ 2). In 35 instances it has the technical sense of *raise up* from the dead (trans.) or *rise* from the dead (intrans.) with reference to an individual (→ 3), all the dead (→ 4), or Jesus (→ 5).

In accord with the meaning of the vb., the subst. ἀνάστασις is attested in the secular literature in both an act. and a pass. sense. In the LXX it occurs only 6 times (pass.); no corresponding form exists in the Hebrew. It appears 42 times in the NT, always, apart from Luke 2:34 (→ 2), in conformity with the technical use of the vb., i.e., in the sense of the *raising up* or the *resurrection* of the dead (→ 3, 5).

The double compound ἐξανίστημι (Mark 12:19 par. Luke 20:28; Acts 15:5) occurs in the NT only as a synonym for ἀνίστημι in the general sense (→ 2). The subst. ἐξανάστασις appears only once (Phil 3:11), as a designation for the *resurrection* from the dead (→ 4).

2. Only occasionally does the vb. ἀνίστημι (used trans.) have a general meaning, as a rule in texts which evidence a clear dependence on OT formulations. In Matt 22:24 it has the meaning of *raise up descendants* (cf. Deut. 25:5 and Gen 19:32, 34; 38:8; ἐξανίστημι in the parallels [Mark 12:19; Luke 20:28]). In the quotation of Deut 18:15 in Acts 3:22; 7:37 ἀνίστημι means to *appoint* a prophet (on the NT's new interpretation in Acts 3:26 → 5); similarly in

Heb 7:11, 15 it means to *institute* as high priest (here, however, ἀνίστημι can also mean [intrans.] *appear*). Except for Acts 9:41 (but cf. → 3), ἀνίστημι (trans.) in the NT never has the general meaning of *raise up* with reference to persons or things, the meaning frequently attested in secular literature and the LXX (cf. LSJ s.v.).

Used intrans. and in a general meaning ἀνίστημι denotes the *standing up* of a sick person who has been lying down (Luke 4:39; 5:25; Acts 9:34; 14:10; Mark 10:50 v.l.), of one who has been stoned (Acts 14:20; here, as in Mark 9:27, there is no thought of resurrection from death, even though those present regard the one lying on the ground as dead), from sleep (Luke 11:7, 8; 22:46; Acts 12:7), from prayer or kneeling in entreaty (Luke 17:19; 22:45; Acts 9:6, 18; 10:26; 22:10, 16; 26:16), of one who is seated (Mark 2:14 [par. Matt 9:9; Luke 5:28]; Luke 6:8; 24:33; John 11:31; Acts 26:30; 1 Cor 10:7). In the variant reading of Luke 17:12 ἀνίστημι (in place of ἔστησαν) means *remain standing.*

Echoes of the idea of rising are still present when ἀνίστημι means *stand up, rise,* or *appear* in order to speak in an assembly or trial (Mark 14:57, 60 [par. Matt 26:62]; Luke 4:16; Acts 1:15; 5:34; 13:16; 15:7; ἐξανέστησαν in Acts 15:5). Related to this is the use of ἀνίστημι to mean *appear* (Mark 3:26; Luke 10:25; 11:32 par. Matt 12:41; Luke 23:1; Acts 5:6, 17, 36, 37; 6:9; 7:18; 20:30; 23:9; Rom 15:12). The idea of standing up recedes completely when ἀνίστημι appears as a partc. or in conjunction with a vb. of motion to indicate the beginning of a new action (a hebraism); in such cases it can be translated *get up, get ready* (Mark 1:35; 7:24; 10:1; Luke 1:39; 4:29, 38; 15:18, 20; 24:12; Acts 8:26, 27; 9:11, 39; 10:20, 23). In Acts 10:13; 11:7 the partc. serves to emphasize the following imv.: "*Rise* . . . ; kill and eat."

In Luke 2:34 the subst. ἀνάστασις stands as a metaphorical expression (cf. Isa 8:14f.; 28:16) for *rise* or *stand,* a movement associated with salvation, in contrast to plunge or fall (→ πτῶσις). Whether Luke has in mind here also the technical meaning of resurrection from the dead (cf. Acts 26:23) is uncertain.

If we keep in mind the varied general uses of ἀνίστημι anchored in part in Hebrew usage (Amsler 638), we will not automatically hear the technical meaning of ἀνίστημι, "to rise from the dead," in the texts mentioned above. However, ἀνίστημι always indicates a new action or movement; above all, the standing up or rising of one who lies ill expresses the turn in this person's fate. For this reason ἀνίστημι is well-suited to express the seemingly impossible change in the fate of the dead. This suggested itself esp. in an age which regarded sickness and death as intimately related.

3. Like ἐγείρομαι, ἀνίστημι (used intrans.) frequently refers to the *rising of someone from the dead* (extrabiblical examples are noted in Oepke, *TDNT* I, 369; Fascher 182-91). In Mark 5:42 par. Luke 8:55 (ἐγέρθη in Matt 9:25) "and immediately the girl *got up*" describes the effect of the call ταλιθὰ κοῦμ (Mark 5:41). The similar command, "Tabitha, *rise*" (Acts 9:40), likewise calls the dead person back into life. (The trans. use in v. 41, *lifted up,* refers first to the lifting up of one who is already sitting, but in a narrative style which imbues an earlier text with later meaning, it can also refer to the raising up of the dead person.) In John 11:23, "Your brother will *rise again,*" Jesus announces the rising up of Lazarus which is described later on; Martha, however, understands ἀνίστημι as referring to the eschatological resurrection (v. 24; → 4).

While for people of that age the rising up of an individual who had died was extremely unusual, and for many unbelievable (cf. Fascher 184f.; Delling 68), it nonetheless lay entirely within the realm of conceivable reality and divine possibility (cf. Acts 26:8; Heb 11:19; on extrabiblical cases of rising from the dead and the related myths see Bertram and Oepke in *RAC*). Heb 11:35 uses the subst. ἀνάστασις of the rising from the dead attributed to the men of God Elijah (1 Kgs 17:17-24) and Elisha (2 Kgs 4:18-37). (The Quadratus fragment from the time of Hadrian [Eusebius *HE* iv.3.2] and Irenaeus *Haer.* ii.32.4 even call attention to persons raised from the dead by Jesus [Quadratus] and by miracle-workers in the Church [Irenaeus] who are still alive at the time of writing; cf. Lucian *Philops.* 26). When one remembers that in Israel every seriously ill person was already included among the dead (e.g., Pss 30:2-4; 86:13; also Mark 9:27; Acts 20:9f.; cf. Stemberger, "Problem" 285, 289), that sinners were designated as dead persons (Luke 15:24, 32), and that as a result of his resurrection Jesus was regarded as the Lord over death (→ 5), then it is clear that in the NT stories of those who were raised from the dead one must reckon with a similar development in the history of traditions as one finds in the OT (cf. Kilian, Schmitt) and extrabiblical accounts.

The statement in Luke 9:8, 19, "one of the old prophets *has risen,*" reflects popular opinion concerning Jesus (cf. Mark 6:14 par. with reference to the Baptist). According to the context the reference is to prophetic figures whose death (in contrast to Elijah) is presupposed. To what extent we have here the idea of the rising from the dead of a martyred prophet (an idea first attested in Rev 11:3-12; *Apoc. Elijah* 4:7-19) is debated (cf. Berger; Pesch, "Entstehung"; opposed: Hengel). In any case, their rising as a return to life in this world is very different from the resurrection of Christ (→ 5).

Luke 16:31 speaks in a similar way of the return of someone from the dead to the house of the glutton. The formulaic phrase "if someone should rise from the dead" shows that this sentence was formulated from the perspective of those who were looking back upon the rejection of the message of the crucified and resurrected One.

4. As terminology for the *eschatological resurrection* from the dead, which is first represented in the later strata of the OT (cf. Schubert; Stemberger, "Problem"), the vb. ἀνίστημι and the subst. ἀνάστασις are attested already in the LXX (Isa 26:19; Dan 12:2; 2 Macc 7:9, 14; 12:43f.; Hos 6:2 at least in later interpretation; cf. *Pss. Sol.* 3:10, 12). In Acts 23:8; Mark 12:18 par. "resurrection," with no further specification, denotes "the hope and the *resurrection* of the dead" (Acts 23:6; a hendiadys), which is denied by the Sadducees and defended by the Pharisees and Paul. The addition "of the dead" (Acts 23:6; 24:21) or "from the dead" (Luke 20:35; cf. Acts 4:2) guarantees for ἀνίστημι the meaning "resurrection out of the realm of the dead" (on the phrase ἐκ νεκρῶν, which presumably originates in the Easter proclamation, see Hoffmann, *Die Toten* 180-85). Acts 24:15 mentions the hope, shared by Paul and the Pharisees, of *"a resurrection* of both the just and the unjust." According to Josephus *B.J.* ii.163; *Ant.* xviii.14, however, the Pharisees expected only a "resurrection of the just" (cf. 2 Macc 7:14; Luke 14:14).

In the dispute between Jesus and the Sadducees (Mark 12:18-27 par.) the question is: "At the *resurrection,* when they *come back to life* [figura etymologica], whose wife will she be?" (Mark 12:23 NEB; cf. par. Matthew, Luke). This question presupposes a resurrection life conceived entirely according to earthly conditions (cf. Hoffmann, *Die Toten* 156-74; Stemberger, "Auferstehungslehre" 263-66 draws more of a distinction). Jesus corrects this view: "when they *rise* from the dead, they neither marry nor are given in marriage" (Mark 12:25; Matt 20:30). According to Luke 20:35 (as in 14:14) only a resurrection of the righteous is contemplated: "those who are accounted worthy to attain to that age and to the *resurrection* from the dead." For these there is no longer marriage because they, "equal to angels," are immortal (so that a guarantee of descendants is superfluous), "and are sons of God, being sons of the *resurrection*" (Luke 20:36). That is to say, by means of the resurrection they receive the ability to participate, like the angels, as "sons of God" in a mode of existence akin to that of God. Accordingly, the eschatological resurrection is not merely a resumption of earthy life, but is rather a new kind of existence made possible through God's → δύναμις (cf. Mark 12:24) and for which there is no analogy in earthly life. Ἀνάστασις thereby attains a fully new, fig. meaning. This resurrection is, according to Mark 12:26, already hinted at in the self-presentation of Yahweh as the God of Abraham, Isaac, and Jacob (Exod 3:6; Matt 22:31: "as for the *resurrection* of the dead"); i.e., it is strictly connected to faith in Yahweh. Since the dispute does full justice to the views of the Sadducees and makes no reference to the resurrection of Jesus, it can in no way be denied that it has a basis in the life of Jesus himself (cf. the commentaries).

According to Heb 6:2 "the *resurrection* of the dead" belongs to the basic elements of Christian proclamation (cf. also Acts 23:6; 24:15, 21). The future resurrection, longed for by the martyrs of the old covenant and held up to the readers of the epistle as a worthy goal, differs from the incidences of rising from the dead in the accounts of the prophets (Heb 11:35a) by being "a better *resurrection*" (11:35b NEB). The manner in which it is better and the way in which the Christian hope of resurrection distinguishes itself from popular Jewish conceptions become esp. clear from the refutation of those in Corinth who maintain that "there is no *resurrection* of the dead" (1 Cor 15:12, 13; on this heresy see Spörlein; Becker, *Auferstehung* 69-76).

In this refutation Paul first recalls the conviction shared by all Christians that at least Christ (→ 5) has been raised from the dead (1 Cor. 15:1-11). Second, he teaches that through Christ, "the first fruits of those who have fallen asleep" (v. 20) and the new Adam, "by a man . . . the *resurrection* of the dead" (v. 21) is achieved. Third, he shows that Christ as the πνεῦμα ζῳοποιοῦν creates the new mode of bodily existence (→ σῶμα, v. 45; cf. Rom 8:11; Phil 3:21), which, according to 1 Cor 15:50-55, will be granted also to those who are not yet among the dead at the time of the parousia.

According to the picturesque presentation of 1 Thess 4:16 it will be "the dead in Christ" who are first *raised up* at the parousia. How closely the eschatological resurrection is tied to Christ is here evidenced by the fact that it is given to the "dead in Christ" to participate in it. (Ἐν Χριστῷ is hardly to be directly connected with ἀνίστημι.)

In Phil 3:11 Paul expresses his desire to attain "the resurrection from the dead." The unusual double compound used here, ἐξανάστασις, in connection with ἐκ νεκρῶν can hardly point to a special resurrection (as a privilege of the martyrs [cf. Rev 20:5]; E. Lohmeyer, *Philipper, Kolosser und Philemon* [KEK] ad loc.). Rather it gives special emphasis to the reality of the resurrection as redemption from the realm of death (more likely as a defense against enthusiasts [Siber 118-20] than against early Gnostic false teachers [J. Gnilka, *Philipperbrief* (HTKNT) ad loc.]).

How strongly the preaching of the primitive Church was still dependent upon Jewish apocalyptic ideas is made clear by the phrase "the first *resurrection*" in Rev 20:5f. This does not stand in contrast to a second (unmentioned) resurrection, but does serve to designate those who share in the life and reign of Christ already prior to the end of history and who no longer need to fear the second death (otherwise referred to as "the resurrection to judgment"; cf. 1 Cor 15:23f.; Oepke, *TDNT*; Fiorenza 115, 123).

The juxtaposition of *"resurrection* to life" and *"resurrection* to judgment" in John 5:29 speaks of the eschatological resurrection of all who are in the grave and the eschatological judgment by the Son of Man. Since there is a certain tension between this and the realized eschatology asserted in vv. 24f., it is often judged to be an interpolation (by the author or a redactor). However, future eschatology is to be found also in the speech about bread in John 6 (also in interpolations?) where ἀνίστημι (used trans.) clearly denotes Jesus as the originator of eschatological resurrection: "I will *raise* him *up* at the last day" (6:40, 44, 54, cf. v. 39). In 11:24 Martha understands Jesus' promise of resurrection for Lazarus in an eschatological sense: "he will *rise again* in the *resurrection* [figura etymologica] at the last day." Jesus corrects this hope by referring to himself as "the *resurrection* and the life" (v. 25); i.e., in Johannine language, he is in his own person the cause and embodiment of what is hoped for in the form of resurrection and → ζωή. Whoever believes in him has a share in it now already and, indeed, forever.

The terminology of the eschatological resurrection occurs in Eph 5:14 in a summons from the baptismal liturgy of the early Church: "*arise* from the dead." The vb. occurs here in a fig. sense: the sinner is numbered among the sleeping and the dead, whereas the baptized person experiences already the reality of the resurrection (cf. Rom 6:13; Clement of Alexandria *Prot.* ix.84.2: ὁ τῆς ἀναστάσεως ἥλιος; on this point see H. Schlier, *Römerbrief* [HTKNT] ad loc.). The distinctly realized eschatology involved in this understanding of baptism led, under the influence of Gnostic thought, to the assertion, characterized in 2 Tim 2:18 as heretical, that "the *resurrection* is past already." In this assertion the central doctrine of the early Church is spiritualized and, as with the Gnostics, identified with the reception of the Gnosis, i.e., the rediscovery of one's divine self (cf. Schenke; N. Brox, *Pastoralbriefe* [RNT] ad loc.).

5. The vb. ἀνίστημι (used intrans.) denotes the *resurrection of Jesus* in the pre-Pauline article of faith in 1 Thess 4:14: "Jesus died and *rose again.*" Because of its relation to "die" ἀνίστημι here clearly signifies the conquering of death. Moreover, the Pauline context presupposes a personal existence of the risen one beyond the earth (→ ὑψόω, → ἀναλαμβάνω). Only as such can the crucified one be expected by and called upon by the community of faith (cf. 1 Thess 1:10; 1 Cor 16:23; → μαρανα θα). The resurrection of Jesus is thereby distinguished from a return to the life of this world, and ἀνίστημι must be seen here as a metaphorical expression for a reality which is finally unimaginable and without analogy.

The pre-Pauline (so Becker, "Gottesbild") statements about the resurrection and other such statements are interpreted differently—as mythological speech or as a means of interpreting the significance of the death or the proclamation of Jesus—by, e.g., Bultmann and Marxsen, and similarly Becker ("Gottesbild") and Hasenfratz. On this interpretation see Kremer, *Zeugnis* 95-128, 147-49; Lehmann 340-42; Friedrich.

Ἀνέστη (1 Thess 4:14) (like Heb. *qûm*) describes resurrection not as the act of the one rising (as in later documents: John 2:19, 21; 10:17f.; Ignatius *Smyrn.* 2:1; cf. Jeremias 278, n. 1), but rather as that which is made possible by God's act (cf. Mark 9:27: "Jesus . . . lifted him up, and he *arose*"). As the one freed from death Jesus can *rise* and "live" (the combination of ἀνίστημι with ἔζησεν [→ ζάω] in Rom 14:9 Koine is textually secondary but materially accurate).

In most forms of the Synoptic Passion predictions (Mark 8:31; 9:31; 10:34 [par. Luke 18:33]; Luke 24:7) ἀνίστημι is used intrans. with reference to the crucified Son of Man and is more closely defined by the phrase "after three days" or "on the third day" (→ ἡμέρα, → τρεῖς). Although this addition can refer to the great transition from death to life (cf. Lehmann), at least in the Gospels in question it points to the connection of the Easter event with history and with a point in time prior to the end of the world. In a few texts related to the Passion predictions ἀνίστημι (again intrans.) also occurs: Mark 9:9: "Until the Son of man should have *risen* from the dead" (par. Matt 17:9 v.l.); Mark 9:10: "what the *rising* from the dead meant" (referring to the resurrection of Christ in spite of the generalized formulation); further, Luke 24:46; Acts 17:3; and John 20:9. The formulaic addition "from the dead" (→ ἐγείρω 5) here expressly defines the resurrection of Jesus as liberation from the realm of the dead; this is made clear by the traditions associated with the tomb (cf. Kremer, *Osterevangelien* 98-112). Apart from Acts 10:41 (where ἀνίστημι can also be understood as trans.) intrans. ἀνίστημι appears as a designation for the resurrection of Jesus only in secondary texts (Mark 16:9; Rom 14:9 v.l.). The consistent use of intrans. ἀνίστημι in the Markan Passion predictions is more original than ἐγείρω in Matthew and Luke (cf. Hoffmann, "Herkunft"; Wilckens, *Missionsreden* 139).

In the speeches in Acts trans. ἀνίστημι, along with ἐγείρω, denotes the raising of Jesus. In Acts 2:24 ("But God *raised* him *up*") the partc. construction "having loosed the pangs of death" clearly shows that ἀνίστημι expresses salvation out of death, here viewed as birth pangs (cf. v. 32). The announcement in 13:33 of God's fulfillment of Scripture "by *raising* Jesus" is made more precise by vv. 34ff.: God "*raised* him from the dead, no more to return to corruption" (cf. Rom 6:9; on the use of Ps 16:10 LXX cf. Schmitt). According to Acts 17:31 Paul used the resurrection of Jesus as proof that Jesus had been given authority to judge the world. In 3:26 ("God, having *raised up* his servant") ἀνίστημι means, first, to *appoint* as prophet (as in Deut 18:15, quoted in Acts 3:22), but in the context of the entire speech, *to raise from the dead.* This ambiguous usage shows that when he employs ἀνίστημι trans. Luke has in mind not only the terminus a quo of the resurrection (death), but also the terminus ad quem (installation as Kyrios-Christos; cf. 2:36). Since it is only in Acts that trans. ἀνίστημι denotes the resurrection of Christ, it seems reasonable to suspect that the author has replaced the more usual and familiar (to him also) ἐγείρω with an expression which was known in the Greek and Hellenistic environment as a t.t. for the raising of the dead (cf. Dupont 141-43 *contra* Wilckens, *Missionsreden* 137-50; John uses trans. ἀνίστημι only with reference to the eschatological resurrection of all the dead [→ 4]).

Ἀνάστασις occurs in the pre-Pauline expression in Rom 1:4: "by the *resurrection* from the dead" is parallel with "of the seed of David" (AV). The resurrection is here conceived of as a type of birth and new creation through which Christ became the mighty Son of God "according to the Spirit of holiness"; he was not merely declared to be such (enthroned), but was filled with power (cf. 1 Cor 1:24; 2 Cor 13:4; Phil 3:10; on this point see Fitzmyer 418; on the history of the tradition cf. Becker, *Auferstehung* 18-31).

In Phil 3:10 Paul expresses his longing to "know him [Jesus] and the power of his *resurrection.*" Thus, for the apostle, Christ's resurrection is an event which makes Christ a source of power for all who believe in him and who bring this faith to completion by sharing in his life and suffering. This power is finally the power of God which raised Jesus from the dead (1 Cor 6:14) and which is identical with the πνεῦμα (15:45; Rom 8:11) and the δόξα (2 Cor 4:6; 3:16-18; cf. Fitzmyer 420-25).

1 Pet 1:3 employs ἀνάστασις in a formulaic expression in order to name the event by means of which God conveys salvation to the baptized: he delivers us into the new life "through the *resurrection* of Jesus Christ from the dead." This language, which is apparently from baptismal liturgy, occurs also in 3:21, where it is said of baptism that it "saves . . . through the *resurrection* of Jesus Christ." In the context of his reference to baptism (Rom 6:5; → βαπτίζω) Paul sets up in brief fashion a contrast between future participation in the *resurrection* of Christ and union with the likeness of Jesus' death.

In Acts ἀνάστασις occurs in the same way as a fixed expression. According to Acts 1:22 the apostles are "witnesses to his *resurrection*" (cf. 2:32 [→ μάρτυς]), not as eyewitnesses to the event, but as those who have experienced the Lord (cf. Luke 24:48; Acts 1:3, 8; 10:41; 13:31; on the distinctiveness of the Lukan appearance narratives see Kremer, *Osterevangelien* 153-55) and have been called by him. They bear "testimony to the *resurrection* of the Lord Jesus" (4:33) and, according to 4:2, proclaim "in Jesus the *resurrection* from the dead," i.e., the resurrection which has occurred in Christ or is based on him as the first participant (cf. 26:23). According to 17:18, Paul preached in Athens "Jesus and the *resurrection,*" i.e., the resurrection of Jesus (not "Jesus and the [goddess] Anastasis" as this hendiadys has often been interpreted since the time of Chrysostom). How incomprehensible a "resurrection of the dead," referring concretely here to the resurrection of Jesus (v. 31), sounded for Greek hearers is shown by v. 32 (cf. H. Conzelmann, *Acts* [Hermeneia] ad loc.) In the face of manifold objections those who preach make use not only of the witness of the apostles and the testimony of the → πνεῦμα (5:31) but also of the witness of Scripture (→ γραφή; cf. Kremer, *Zeugnis* 52-54); according to 2:31 David already spoke prophetically "of the *resurrection* of Christ" (cf. 13:33ff.).

J. Kremer

ἀναστατόω *anastatoō* incite, disturb, mislead*

Acts 17:6 with obj. τὴν οἰκουμένην: "turned the whole world upside down"; Gal 5:12, of the opponents of Paul who *incite* the congregation (against the Pauline message); with no obj., Acts 21:38, of an Egyptian who *stirred up a revolt.*

ἀνασταυρόω *anastauroō* crucify*

Lit.: In addition to the commentaries on Heb 6:6: BAGD s.v. — P. PROULX and L. ALONSO SCHÖKEL, "Heb 6, 4-6: εἰς μετάνοιαν ἀνασταυροῦντας," *Bib* 56 (1975) 193-209. — L. SABOURIN, " 'Crucifying Afresh for One's Repentance' (Heb 6:4-6)," *BTB* 6 (1976) 264-71. — J. SCHNEIDER, *TDNT* VII, 583f.

In Heb 6:6 both the sense of the ἀνα- in ἀνασταυροῦντας and the syntactic relations of the partc. are debatable. Since ἀνασταυρόω never occurs in Gentile or Jewish literature (in the primitive Christian period it is found primarily in Josephus and is frequent in Plutarch) in the sense of "crucify again," one can only understand the word here also as *crucify* (ἀνα- = *up*; so as a rule in the more recent commentaries; O. Michel, *Hebräer* [KEK] ad loc. differs). This is in spite of the unanimous interpretation of ἀνασταυρόω as repeated crucifixion in early Church exegesis (earliest are Tertullian *Pud.* 9:11 and Origen *In Joh.* on 8:40) and in early translations (Tert. *Pud.* 20; it., i.e., d r^3; vg., et al.). Linguistic and contextual considerations make it unlikely that εἰς μετάνοιαν is to be related to ἀνασταυροῦντας (*contra* Proulx and Alonso Schökel; Sabourin). Most likely the verse should be taken as saying: it is impossible to restore (them) again to repentance . . . since they *crucify* the Son of God on their own account (i.e., to their detriment: dat. of disadvantage) and hold him up to contempt. Cf. the similar statement in 10:29. On fig. use of ἀνασταυρόω → σταυρόω.

H.-W. Kuhn

ἀναστενάζω *anastenazō* sigh deeply*

Mark 8:12: ἀναστενάξας τῷ πνεύματι αὐτοῦ, "*he sighed deeply* in his spirit" (i.e., inwardly); cf. 2:8.

ἀναστρέφω *anastrephō* conduct oneself, live (in a certain way)
→ ἀναστροφή.

ἀναστροφή, ῆς, ἡ *anastrophē* conduct, way of life*
ἀναστρέφω *anastrephō* conduct oneself, live (in a certain way)*

Lit.: G. BERTRAM, *TDNT* VII, 715-17. — G. EBEL, *DNTT* III, 933-35.

The vb. occurs 9 times in the NT (besides Matt 17:22 v.l.; John 2:15 v.l.), the subst. 13 times. The Hebrew term behind the compound vb. is most frequently *šûb,* less often *hālak*. The subst. occurs in the LXX only in Tob 4:14; 2 Macc 6:23.

In Acts 5:22 ἀναστρέφω means *return.* In the quotation from Amos 9:11 in Acts 15:16 God promises to "rebuild the dwelling of David, which has fallen" (ἀναστρέψω καὶ ἀνοικοδομήσω together represent *'āqîm*).

The vb. (and the subst. similarly) are used in the Pauline Epistles and the post-Pauline writings in the neutral sense of *conduct oneself, live in a certain way*; however, they are usually qualified negatively or positively by the context. Paul appeals in 2 Cor 1:12 to the testimony of conscience "that we *have behaved* in the world . . . with holiness and godly sincerity, not by earthly wisdom but by the grace of God" (here the vb. is synonymous with the more common Pauline περιπατέω). Pre- or non-Christian conduct is negatively qualified in Gal 1:13 and Eph 2:3. Terminologically, however, the "former" *conduct* is not contrasted with "new conduct." Instead, the motif of putting on the new person is employed (Eph 4:22 [-24]). *Conduct* (ἀναστροφή) describes the total human person as he or she is determined by heathenism, Judaism, or Christian faith.

In 1 Timothy *conduct* is an element alongside speech, love, faith, and purity in a catalog of virtues for officeholders (4:12; more generally in 3:15). In Hebrews the leaders are presented as models whose faith is to be imitated and whose "outcome of their life" (τὴν ἔκβασιν τῆς ἀναστροφῆς) is an example (13:7). The way of life (v. 5: ὁ τρόπος; v. 9: περιπατεῖν) becomes, along with "faith," the observable expression of one's being a Christian (10:33), but is in itself ambivalent:

1) On the one hand, the conduct of one's life should be "good" (13:18; Jas 3:13; 1 Pet 2:12; 3:16f.). The parenesis of 1 Peter interprets the present as the time of testing during which Christians live as "aliens and exiles" (2:11, 12; 1:17). The admonition to conduct themselves in "holiness" and "fear" is based upon the calling of the holy God (1:15f.), his identity as father and judge (v. 17), and the sacrificial death of Jesus understood as the ransom "from the futile *ways* inherited from your fathers" (v. 18). "Good *conduct*" becomes concrete in one's turning away from fleshly passions and one's devotion to good works (v. 14; 2:11f.) in view of the judgment of God (3:16f.: ἡ ἀγαθὴ ἀναστροφή, → ἀγαθοποιέω). "Pure" behavior can even take the place of the word as testimony between married persons in order that husbands may be won for faith (3:1, 2).

2) On the other hand, behavior can be regarded as inappropriate for the Christian and can express itself in "lawless deeds" (2 Pet 2:7f.). Accordingly, false teachers are those "who *live* in error" (v. 18). The certainty of the return of Christ requires perseverance "in *lives* of holiness and godliness" (3:11) in view of the imminent judgment.

J. Baumgarten

ἀνατάσσομαι *anatassomai* compose, compile*

The only NT occurrence is in Luke 1:1 (mid.): ἐπειδήπερ πολλοὶ ἐπεχείρησαν ἀνατάξασθαι διήγησιν, "inasmuch as many have undertaken to *compile* a [clear, orderly] narrative of the things which have been accomplished among us. . . ." The vb. originally meant "arrange in a sequence" or "reproduce a narrative" (cf. Eusebius *HE* v.8.15). The author of Luke 1:1 looks back on the work of his predecessors who have arranged the oral tradition in an orderly, because written, narrative. Luke does not reject these, but wishes to replace them by his own presentation (vv. 3f.) with the aid of a new critical and dependable examination of the tradition. On the reference to the "predecessors" cf. Diodorus Siculus i.1.1-3. BAGD s.v.; G. Delling, *TDNT* VIII, 32f. (bibliography); G. Schneider, *Lukas* (ÖTK) ad loc.

H. Balz

ἀνατέλλω *anatellō* rise
→ ἀνατολή.

ἀνατίθεμαι *anatithemai* communicate, lay before (for consideration)*

In the NT only mid.: Acts 25:14; Gal 2:2; in both texts there is surely the accompanying thought of presenting something for examination or decision. J. Behm, *TDNT* I, 353f.

ἀνατολή, ῆς, ἡ *anatolē* rising*
ἀνατέλλω *anatellō* rise*

Lit.: A. CHARBEL, "Mt 2, 1.7: Os Reis Magos eram Nabateus?," *RCB* 8 (1971) 96-103. — F. J. DÖLGER, *Sol salutis* ([2]1925) 149ff. — H. SCHLIER, *TDNT* I, 351-53.

1. Ἀνατέλλω, *rise* (9 occurrences) and ἀνατολή, *rising* (10 occurrences) are used of the appearance of the sun, stars, and clouds in the heavens (Mark 16:2; Luke 12:54; Jas 1:11). East is "the *rising* of the sun" (Rev 7:2; 16:12) or simply *"rising"* (pl. in Matt 2:1; 8:11; 24:27; Luke 13:29; sg. in Rev 21:13). The daily rising of the sun is evidence of the divine benevolence (Matt 5:45); on the other hand, heat exemplifies a destructive effect (Matt 13:6 par. Mark 4:6; Jas 1:11).

2. The wise men from *the East* (Matt 2:1) observed the *rise* of a "star" which heralded for them the birth of the king of Israel (2:2, 9). As is true for Matthew generally, so here the concern is with the fulfillment of prophecy, specifically of the oracle of Balaam concerning a star which was to arise out of Jacob (Num 24:17 LXX: ἀνατελεῖ ἄστρον, "a star shall *rise*"). During the time of Jesus this prophecy occupied esp. the Essenes of Qumran, east of Jerusalem (1QM 11:6f.; CD 7:18-21; 4QTestim 9-13), where heavenly phenomena were also studied (cf. *1 Enoch* 72:1-8; 82:1-20; *2 Enoch* 11:1–16:8). The father of the Baptist (Luke 1:78) and the Evangelist Matthew (cf. the quotation of Isa 9:1 [2] in Matt 4:16) were likewise interested in the light of the redeemer which dawns in the sky. The influence of Balaam's prophecy is also evident in the emphasis upon the Lord's being *descended* from Judah (Heb 7:14). Psychological use is also made of the image by anticipating a rising of the messianic bearer of light in human hearts (2 Pet 1:19).

B. Reicke

ἀνατρέπω *anatrepō* overturn, cause to fall*

Used literally in John 2:15 of Jesus' *overturning* the money-changers' tables (ἀναστρέφω 𝔭[75] Koine *pm*; καταστρέφω ℵ f^{13} *pc*). Fig. in 2 Tim 2:18: *upset* the faith of some (τήν τινων πίστιν); Titus 1:11, οἵτινες ὅλους οἴκους ἀνατρέπουσιν, of false teachers in Crete who "are *upsetting* whole families."

ἀνατρέφω *anatrephō* bring up, rear, raise*

Only in Luke-Acts, of the rearing of a child: Luke 4:16 v.l. (B Koine *pm* τεθραμμένος); Acts 7:20f. (ἀνεθρέψατο αὐτὸν ἑαυτῇ εἰς υἱόν, she "brought him up as her own son"); 22:3. W. C. van Unnik, *Sparsa collecta* I (1973) 259-327.

ἀναφαίνω *anaphainō* cause to appear, (pass.) appear*

Pass. in Luke 19:11: "the kingdom of God was to *appear* immediately"; act. in Acts 21:3: ἀναφάναντες δὲ τὴν Κύπρον (ἀναφανέντες in A C Koine E *pm*; see BDF §159.4), "when we had *come in sight* of Cyprus" (= when we approached near enough to see Cyprus); see BDF §309.1.

ἀναφέρω *anapherō* bring up; offer up*

1. Basic meaning — 2. Mark 9:2 par.; Luke 24:51 — 3. Sacrificial terminology

Lit.: G. Lohfink, *Die Himmelfahrt Jesu* (SANT 26, 1971). — O. Michel, *Der Brief an die Hebräer* (KEK, [12]1966). — J. M. Nützel, *Die Verklärungserzählung im Markusevangelium* (FzB 6, 1973). — K. H. Schelkle, *Die Petrusbriefe. Der Judasbrief* (HTKNT, [5]1980). — K. Weiss, *TDNT* IX, 60f., 65-68.

1. The compound ἀναφέρω with its basic meaning of *carry up, bring up* (in secular Greek also *bring back*) denotes 3 times in the NT an upward movement (→ 2) and several times is a t.t. for a sacrificial act (→ 3).

2. In Mark 9:2 par. Matt 17:1 ἀναφέρει means *he leads* (them) *up* (a high mountain). This is the only instance in the NT of the historical present of ἀναφέρω, which is common elsewhere. The historical present indicates that the Evangelist ascribes special significance to ἀναφέρω and elevates it above a mere indication of a change of location.

In Luke 24:51 ἀνεφέρετο, he was *taken up,* is questionable on text-critical grounds but probably original; it is the only occurrence in Luke. A more precise definition of διέστη is achieved by describing the process (impf.) of the ascension as Jesus' experience of being carried away (cf. Acts 1:9-11: ἐπήρθη, ἀναλημφθείς). Ἀναφέρω is not attested in this sense in the LXX (→ ἀναλαμβάνω), but is found in secular assumption narratives (Lohfink 171).

3. As a t.t. for *offering up* a sacrifice (so frequently in LXX) ἀναφέρω in Jas 2:21 designates the sacrifice of Isaac as the deed which brings to perfection the faith of Abraham (cf. Heb 11:17). In Heb 7:27a it designates the sacrifice which is to be *offered* daily, and in v. 27b the sacrifice of Christ which, by contrast, is *offered* once and for all. In close dependence on phrases that appear in the OT (e.g., Hos 14:3) and are common in the Qumran literature (1QS 9:3-5; 10:8, 14; cf. Michel 558f.), the expression ἀναφέρωμεν θυσίαν αἰνέσεως, "*offer up* a sacrifice of praise," occurs in Heb 13:15 (with the vb. used figuratively); as the author himself interprets it, this "fruit of lips" consists of the doxological confession of the name of Jesus. Ἀναφέρω has the same sense in 1 Pet 2:5: "*offer* spiritual sacrifices acceptable to God through Jesus Christ" (cf. v. 9 as well as the related sacrificial terminology [not using ἀναφέρω] of Rom 12:1; 15:16; Phil 2:17; cf. Schelkle ad loc.).

In the light of the Passion tradition ἀναφέρω in the quotation of Isa 53:12 in 1 Pet 2:24 has a new meaning: "He himself *bore* our sins in his body on the tree." The death of Jesus on the cross is here understood as a kind of sacrificial act (cf. Heb 9:14; 10:10) which effects the "removal" of sins. This statement regarding the death of Jesus, more figurative suggestion than clear definition, results from the manifold meanings of the Hebrew synonyms *nś'* and *sbl* (carry, sacrifice, remove). This meaning comes to even clearer expression in Heb 9:28 where ἀναφέρω in the newly interpreted quotation from Isa 53:12, "to *remove* the sins of many," designates the goal of the once-for-all sacrifice of Christ (see the context).

J. Kremer

ἀναφωνέω *anaphōneō* cry out, exclaim*

Luke 1:42: ἀνεφώνησεν κραυγῇ μεγάλῃ, "*exclaimed* with a loud cry."

ἀνάχυσις, εως, ἡ *anachysis* outpouring, wide stream*

In NT only fig.: 1 Pet 4:4: ἀσωτίας ἀνάχυσις, "this *flood which is rushing down* to ruin" (JB).

ἀναχωρέω *anachōreō* withdraw, move away; return*

There are 14 occurrences in the NT, of which 10 are in Matthew and 4 in Matt 2:12-22: *return* εἰς τὴν χώραν αὐτῶν, "to their own country" (v. 12; cf. v. 13), εἰς τὴν Γαλιλαίαν, "to Galilee" (4:12), *go away, escape* εἰς Αἴγυπτον, "to Egypt" (2:14), εἰς τὰ μέρη τῆς Γαλιλαίας, "to the district of Galilee" (v. 22), *withdraw* ἐκεῖθεν, "from there" (12:15; 14:13; cf. 15:21); used with ἀπελθών, he *ran away* (27:5; Mark 3:7 [par. Matt 12:15]; John 6:15 [v.l. φεύγει ℵ* lat sy^c]), ἀναχωρήσας κατ' ἰδίαν, "he *went aside* (with him)" (Acts 23:19; cf. 26:31), *retire, go out* (Matt 9:24, absolute).

ἀνάψυξις, εως, ἡ *anapsyxis* rest, refreshment*

Lit.: O. BAUERNFEIND, "Tradition und Komposition in dem Apokatastasisspruch Apg 3, 20f," FS Michel 13-23. — E. KRÄNKL, *Jesu der Knecht Gottes* (1972) 193-98. — G. LOHFINK, "Christologie und Geschichtsbild in Apg 3, 19-21," *BZ* 13 (1969) 223-41, esp. 230-33. — E. SCHWEIZER, *TDNT* IX, 664f.

1. Occurring in the NT only in Acts 3:20, the subst. (cf. ἀναψύχω, cool, refresh) also refers to the *drying out* (healing) of a wound, and *cooling off, relief,* or *recovery* (Philo *Abr.* 152). In Exod 8:11 (the only instance in the LXX) ἀνάψυξις denotes the *liberation* from the plague of frogs.

2. In Acts 3:19 (or 20, depending on where the verses are divided) ἀνάψυξις occurs in a text (vv. 19-21) which strikes one as foreign and which has often been interpreted (e.g., Bauernfeind; cf. Lohfink) as a trace of an early form of christology (originally an Elijah tradition?). In its gen. relation to καιροί the subst. ἀνάψυξις characterizes the καιροί as "times of *refreshing,*" which, in contrast to previous times, bring new life. The phrase "from the presence of the Lord" characterizes these "times," along with the benefits they bring, as gifts from God. (The interpretation yielding the meaning "breathing spaces in the distress of the messianic woes" [O. Bauernfeind, *Apostelgeschichte* (THKNT) ad loc.] can be justified neither by normal usage [→ 1] nor by the context). These times are the same as the time of "restoration" (v. 21 JB; → ἀποκατάστασις), i.e., the final time of salvation.

Although the designation of the time of salvation as καιροὶ ἀναψύξεως has no direct precedent in the LXX or in apocalyptic literature (cf. Lohfink 232), there are nonetheless many parallels to the idea expressed with this phrase (e.g., 4 Ezra 7:91, 95; 11:46; *2 Bar.* 73–74; *1 Enoch* 96:3), including, in the NT, ἄνεσις in 2 Thess 1:7 (closely connected to "from the presence of the Lord"), κατάπαυσις in Heb 3:11; 4:11, and σαββατισμός in Heb 4:9 (cf. Kränkl 194). The expectation of the time of salvation as *relief* following afflictions is a common theme in the Lukan writings (e.g., Acts 9:16; 14:22; Luke 21:7-19, 28, 36). The use of ἀνάψυξις in Acts 3:20 can, therefore, go back to Luke (possibly as his own rendering of an earlier tradition).

J. Kremer

ἀναψύχω *anapsychō* refresh, revive*

2 Tim 1:16 (trans.); in place of συναναπαύομαι in Rom 15:32 D G lat (intrans.).

ἀνδραποδιστής, ου, ὁ *andrapodistēs* kidnapper, slave trader*

In a vice-catalog which lists offenders against the commandments of the Decalogue (1 Tim 1:9f.), after the ἀνδροφόνοις (fifth commandment), πόρνοις, and ἀρσενοκοίταις (sixth commandment) and before the ψεύσταις and ἐπιόρκοις (eighth commandment) stand the ἀνδραποδισταί. This is in conformity with ancient rabbinic exposition of the seventh commandment (Exod 20:15), which distinguished between theft (of things) and kidnapping and frequently related Exod 20:15 to kidnapping; cf. *Mek. Exod.* 77b on 20:15; see also Philo *Spec. Leg.* iv.13. Billerbeck I, 810-13; J. Jeremias, *1-2 Timotheus und Titus* (NTD) ad loc.

Ἀνδρέας, ου *Andreas* Andrew*

1. Occurrences — 1. Biographical information — 3. Andrew in the redaction of the Synoptics and in John.

Lit.: P. M. PETERSON, *Andrew, Brother of Simon Peter. His History and His Legends* (NovTSup 1, 1958). — R. PESCH, *Das Markusevangelium* (HTKNT, 1976, 1977).

1. In the NT only one person is mentioned who bears the good Gk. name Ἀνδρέας. He is mentioned in Mark 4 times, in Matthew twice, in Luke once, in Acts once, and in John 5 times, in traditions dealing with the call to discipleship (Mark 1:16 par.; John 1:40, 44), in lists of the twelve (Mark 3:18 par.; Acts 1:13), in a local tradition associated with Capernaum (Mark 1:29), in the pre-Markan eschatological discourse (Mark 13:3), in the Johannine version of the feeding miracle (John 6:8), and in the distinctively Johannine material (12:22).

2. Andrew, brother of Simon Peter (Mark 1:16 par. Matt 4:18; John 1:40) was from Bethsaida (John 1:44) and had perhaps moved with Simon to Capernaum (Mark 1:29),

where the brothers worked as fishermen (1:16 par.). Andrew belonged to the first disciples of Jesus (1:16 par.; John 1:40) and to the circle of the twelve (Mark 3:18 par.; Acts 1:13). In the primitive Christian mission he may have been teamed with Peter to form a missionary pair. His rank in the primitive Church is reflected in his position as fourth in the list of the twelve (Mark 3:18; Acts 1:13; in Matt 10:2 and Luke 6:14 [redactional] he is second) and in his role of recipient of revelation in the context of the eschatological discourse (Mark 13:3). As a Greek-speaking resident of Palestine Andrew appears in John 12:22 (twice) alongside Philip as one familiar with the Greek language and hence a mediator for Greek proselytes.

3. Whereas Mark includes four traditions associated with Andrew, Matthew takes over only two (conforming 10:2 to 4:18) without wishing to detract from the role of Andrew. Luke takes over only one (assimilating in the Gospel and Acts, in an alternating fashion, lists of the twelve taken from the double tradition): in his only reference to Andrew in the Gospel Luke introduces him as the brother of Simon (Luke 6:14), eliminates him from the tradition of the call to discipleship (5:10), and omits him (as does Matthew), first, by concentrating the healing miracle from Mark 1:29-31 par. on Jesus and, second, by generalizing the introduction to the eschatological discourse of Mark 13:3 par. Greater significance is attributed to Andrew in the Johannine tradition, where he is the first called to discipleship (1:40), where his role as mediator is mentioned (12:22), and in what is perhaps redactional material (6:8).

R. Pesch

ἀνδρίζομαι *andrizomai* conduct oneself in a manly way*

1 Cor 16:13 (cf. Pss 26:14; 30:25 LXX) alongside γρηγορεῖτε, στήκετε, and κραταιοῦσθε. Cf. also 1 Macc 2:64; *Herm. Vis.* i.4.3.

Ἀνδρόνικος, ου *Andronikos* Andronicus*

A Jewish Christian missionary who, together with Junia, is the recipient of greetings from Paul (Rom 16:7). Both are designated as συγγενεῖς μου καὶ συναιχμαλώτους μου as well as ἐπίσημοι ἐν τοῖς ἀποστόλοις. Andronicus thus has the rank of an apostle (E. Käsemann, *Commentary on Romans* [1980] 414). Paul stresses that both had already become believers before him. G. Klein, *BHH* I, 93; H. E. Jacobs, *ISBE* I, 123; J. Roloff, *Apostolat—Verkündigung—Kirche* (1965) 60f.

ἀνδροφόνος, ου, ὁ *androphonos* murderer*

1 Tim 1:9 in a vice catalog with reference to the fifth commandment of the Decalogue; → ἀνδραποδιστής.

ἀνέγκλητος, 2 *anenkletos* irreproachable, blameless*

1 Cor 1:8, of the Church, which will be *blameless* in the coming judgment; similarly in Col 1:22, along with ἁγίους καὶ ἀμώμους; 1 Tim 3:10, of διάκονοι, and Titus 1:6f., of ἐπίσκοποι, who are to be *blameless* men. W. Grundmann, *TDNT* I, 356f.; H. Währisch, *DNTT* III, 923-25.

ἀνεκδιήγητος, 2 *anekdiēgētos* inexpressible, indescribable*

2 Cor 9:15, of the δωρεά of God, the abundance of which *cannot be expressed in words* but which makes itself evident in the ability of the churches of Achaia to gather a generous offering. Thus v. 15 echoes the thought expressed by διὰ τὴν ὑπερβάλλουσιν χάριν in v. 14.

ἀνεκλάλητος, 2 *aneklalētos* inexpressible*

1 Pet 1:8: χαρᾷ ἀνεκλαλήτῳ (parallel with δεδοξασμένῃ); cf. Pol. *Phil.* 1:3.

ἀνέκλειπτος, 2 *anekleiptos* inexhaustible, imperishable*

Luke 12:33: the *inexhaustible* treasure in heaven acquired by selling one's earthly possessions.

ἀνεκτός (ἀνεκτότερος), 2 *anektos (anektoteros)* bearable*

Only the neut. of the comparative occurs in the NT. The phrase ἀνεκτότερον ἔσται, *it will be more tolerable,* is used—with a view toward the final judgment—of Jewish sites of Jesus' activity, comparing them with Sodom (Gen 19:24ff.) in Matt 10:15; 11:24 par. Luke 10:12 and with Tyre and Sidon (Isa 23; Ezek 26–28) in Matt 11:22 par. Luke 10:14. It appears as a secondary v.l. from Matt 10:15 in Mark 6:11 Koine *pm.* H. Schlier, *TDNT* I, 359f.

ἀνελεήμων, 2 *aneleēmōn* unmerciful*

In a vice list in Rom 1:31 along with ἀσυνθέτους and ἀστόργους; Titus 1:9 v.l. R. Bultmann, *TDNT* II, 487; H.-H. Esser, *DNTT* II, 594, 597.

ἀνέλεος, 2 *aneleos* merciless, without pity*

Jas 2:13: the *merciless* final judgment on the one who has not shown mercy: κρίσις ἀνέλεος τῷ μὴ ποιήσαντι ἔλεος. R. Bultmann, *TDNT* II, 487; H.-H. Esser, *DNTT* II, 594, 597; BDF §120.2.

ἀνεμίζομαι *anemizomai* be moved by the wind*

The NT has only the pass.: Jas 1:6 in an image of the

doubter, who is "like a wave of the sea *driven* and tossed (ῥιπιζομένῳ) *by the wind.*"

ἄνεμος, ου, ὁ *anemos* wind*

There are 31 occurrences in the NT, of which 25 are in the Gospels and Acts and 3 in Revelation.

Wind is mentioned as a destructive power in Matt 7:25, 27 (pl.). Jesus is spoken of as Lord over the powers of the wind(s) in the Synoptic narrative of the stilling of the storm (Mark 4:37, 39 [bis], 41 par. Matt 8:26f. and Luke 8:23-25); the devastating power of the wind is emphasized by the phrase λαῖλαψ μεγάλη ἀνέμου, "a great storm of *wind*" (Mark 4:37; cf. Luke 8:23). A similar tradition appears in the narrative of Jesus' walking on the water (Mark 6:48, 51 par. Matt 14:24, 32; cf. John 6:18 [not in Luke!]) and of Peter's sinking in the sea (Matt 14:30).

The occurrences in Acts are concentrated in the account of Paul's voyage to Rome (Acts 27:4, 7, 14, 15). There are always contrary winds, esp. the "tempestuous *wind,* called the northeaster" (ἄνεμος τυφωνικὸς ὁ καλούμενος εὐρακύλων, v. 14).

The phrase ἐκ τῶν τεσσάρων ἀνέμων in Mark 13:27 par. Matt 24:31 signifies the four points of the compass, from which the winds blow, i.e., every region of the earth right up to the horizon, the boundary of earth and heaven; cf. the elaboration in Mark 13:27b (Deut 13:8; 30:4 LXX; on this see E. Schweizer, *The Good News According to Mark* 275) and the Matthean redaction in 24:31b; cf. also Rev 7:1 (bis).

Otherwise ἄνεμος occurs frequently in figures of speech and similes. Matt 11:7 par. Luke 7:24 mentions the reed shaken by the wind, from which John the Baptist is distinguished. The figure of "every *wind of doctrine,*" παντὶ ἀνέμῳ τῆς διδασκαλίας, by which "children" are "tossed to and fro" is found in Eph 4:14. Other figurative uses are in Jas 3:4; Jude 12; and Rev 6:13.

H. Balz

ἀνένδεκτος, 2 *anendektos* impossible*

Luke 17:1: ἀνένδεκτόν ἐστιν τοῦ τὰ σκάνδαλα μὴ ἐλθεῖν, it is *impossible* that temptations not come = "temptations to sin are sure to come."

ἀνεξεραύνητος, 2 *anexeraunētos* inscrutable*

Rom 11:33. The precise meaning of the word derives from the vb. ἐξερευνάω, "investigate, search out." God's actions in relation to Israel are based on his "*unsearchable* . . . judgments," in the face of which Pauline—and all other—theological reflection ends in praise of God. The reasons for God's actions remain *inaccessible* to theological reflection. G. Delling, *TDNT* I, 357; M. Seitz, *DNTT* III, 532f.

ἀνεξίκακος, 2 *anexikakos* bearing evil calmly, patient*

2 Tim 2:24, referring to the Christian (δοῦλος κυρίου) as "forbearing," alongside ἤπιος and διδακτικός. The adj. is formed on the basis of the vb. → ἀνέχομαι.

ἀνεξιχνίαστος, 2 *anexichniastos* untraceable

Rom 11:33; Eph 3:8. Like the vb. ἐξιχνιάζω on which it is based, the adj. has its origin in the Greek of the LXX (cf. Job 5:9; 9:10; 13:24). In Rom 11:33 it further intensifies the preceding ἀνεξεραύνητος (cf. Suidas s.v.: ἀνεξεύρητον οὗ μηδὲ ἴχνος ἐστὶν εὑρεῖν). Thus, according to Paul, perceptible history does not lead even to the tracks of the true ways of God. On the relationship to Gnosticism see E. Peterson, *TDNT* I, 358f.

ἀνεπαίσχυντος, 2 *anepaischyntos* having no need to be ashamed*

2 Tim 2:15, of Timothy, the disciple of the apostle, who is to be an ἐργάτης ἀνεπαίσχυντος, "a workman who *has no need to be ashamed* [of his work]."

ἀνεπίλημπτος, 2 *anepilēmptos* faultless, irreproachable*

In the NT only in 1 Timothy: 3:2: the ἐπίσκοπος; 5:7: the widows; 6:14 (alongside ἄσπιλος): Timothy. Cf. *Mart. Pol.* 17:1.

ἀνέρχομαι *anerchomai* go up*

John 6:3: εἰς τὸ ὄρος (ἀπῆλθεν in ℵ* D *pc*); Gal 1:17, 18: εἰς Ἱεροσόλυμα (v. 17 ἀπῆλθον in 𝔭[51] B D G *al*).

ἄνεσις, εως, ἡ *anesis* relief, rest, relaxation*

In Acts 24:23 Paul is to receive some *relaxation* of the conditions of imprisonment: ἔχειν τε ἄνεσιν. 2 Cor 2:13 and 7:5 deal with the lack of *rest* in Paul's mind and body respectively. Ἄνεσις stands as the opposite of θλῖψις in 2 Cor 8:13; cf. 2 Thess 1:7, where God will reward (ἀνταποδοῦναι in v. 6) the θλιβόμενοι with *refreshment* for their present affliction. R. Bultmann, *TDNT* I, 367.

ἀνετάζω *anetazō* give a hearing

A juridical t.t. used in reference to the interrogation of Paul before the Roman soldiers in the tower of Antonia (Acts 22:24, 29). The phrase μάστιξιν ἀνετάζεσθαι in v. 24 refers to the examination of someone by the use of torture (in the form of scourging), a practice not permitted against Roman citizens (cf. 16:37; 22:25).

ἄνευ *aneu* without*

Prep. with gen. with much the same meaning and use as χωρίς. Matt 10:29: ἄνευ τοῦ πατρὸς ὑμῶν, "*without* your Father's will"; 1 Pet 3:1: ἄνευ λόγου, of women who by their behavior can win their unbelieving husbands for the gospel "*without* a word"; 4:9.

ἀνεύθετος, 2 *aneuthetos* unfit, unfavorably situated*

Acts 27:12, of the harbor Καλοὶ λιμένες on Crete, which was "*not suitable* to winter in."

ἀνευρίσκω *aneuriskō* discover, search out

Luke 2:16; Acts 21:4, both times referring to persons.

ἀνέχομαι *anechomai* bear, accept, endure*

There are 15 occurrences in the NT with a special concentration in the (ironical) discussion in 2 Corinthians 11 (5 occurrences: vv. 1 bis, 4, 19, 20). The verb is always mid. in form with a gen. object (see BDF §176.1).

With personal objects: Mark 9:19 par. Matt 17:17 and Luke 9:41 in the exasperated question of Jesus, "How long *am I to bear with* you?"; with ἀλλήλων as the obj., referring to mutual *forbearance* (in love): Eph 4:2; cf. Col 3:13; in the sense of *permit* (to hold a trial): Acts 18:14.

With impersonal objects: 2 Thess 1:4: ἐν . . . ταῖς θλίψεσιν αἷς ἀνέχεσθε (on attraction of the rel. pron. see BDF §294); Heb 13:22: ἀνέχεσθε τοῦ λόγου τῆς παρακλήσεως, "*bear with* my word of exhortation"; similar statement negatived in 2 Tim 4:3.

In 2 Corinthians 11 Paul plays with the vb.: First he asks the Corinthians to *bear with* a little foolishness (impersonal obj., v. 1a) from him, even as they already *bear with* him (ind., cf. R. Bultmann, *The Second Letter to the Corinthians* [1985] 199f.). Then in v. 4 he notes sarcastically that the Corinthians "*submit* . . . readily" (καλῶς ἀνέχεσθε absolute, or to be taken with the preceding clause as its obj.) when someone comes with a different message (on the construction and the textual problem see Bultmann 201f.). Paul's use of the verb continues similarly in vv. 19 (ἀνέχεσθε τῶν ἀφρόνων) and 20 (where the obj. is the clause εἴ τις ὑμᾶς καταδουλοῖ).

The vb. is also used absolutely (or with an obj. to be supplied from the context) in 1 Cor 4:12. H. Schlier, *TDNT* I, 359f.; U. Falkenroth and C. Brown, *DNTT* II, 765-67.

H. Balz

ἀνεψιός, οῦ, ὁ *anepsios* cousin*

Col 4:10: "[John] Mark the cousin of Barnabas."

ἄνηθον, ου, τό *anēthon* dill*

Matt 23:23 mentions dill *(Anethum graveolens)* with other plants used for seasoning (ἡδύοσμον, κύμινον) that were, according to rabbinic opinion, subject to the tithe on the basis of Num 18:12; Deut 14:22f. Billerbeck I, 932f.; J. Feliks, *BHH* I, 344f.; J. C. Trever, *IDB* I, 843.

ἀνήκω *anēkō* be proper, be appropriate*

In the NT this vb. is always used impersonally (Eph 5:4; Col 3:18; Phlm 8). The expression ἐπιτάσσειν σοι τὸ ἀνῆκον, "to command you *to do what is required* (of a Christian)" (Phlm 8), has its background outside the NT, namely, in Stoic ethical thought (cf. the title of Zeno's treatise Περὶ τοῦ καθήκοντος) and came into primitive Christian parenesis through Hellenistic Judaism (cf. 1 Macc 10:42; *Ep. Arist.* 245). H. Schlier, *TDNT* I, 360; E. Schweizer, *The Letter to the Colossians* (1982) on Col. 3:18.

ἀνῆλθον *anēlthon* (2nd aor.)
→ ἀνέρχομαι.

ἀνήμερος, 2 *anēmeros* wild, untamed*

In 2 Tim 3:3 with διάβολοι, ἀκρατεῖς, ἀφιλάγαθοι, and other words referring to human behavior in the "last days."

ἀνήνεγκα *anēnegka* (2nd aor.)
→ ἀναφέρω.

ἀνήρ, ἀνδρός, ὁ *anēr* man

1. Occurrences in the NT — 2. Human beings in general — 3. Ἀνήρ in combination with certain adjs. — 4. Man in contrast to woman — 5. 1 Cor 11:7 — 6. Supernatural beings

Lit.: J. Kühlewein, *THAT* I, 130-38, 398-402. — F.-W. Eltester, *Eikon im NT* (BZNW 23, 1958) 125-27, 153-56. — J. Jervell, *Imago Dei* (FRLANT 76, 1960) 292-312. — A. Oepke, *TDNT* I, 360-63. — P. Trummer, "Einehe nach den Pastoralbriefen. Zum Verständnis der Termini *mias gynaikos anēr* und *henos andros gynē*," *Bib* 51 (1970) 471-84. — H. Vorländer and C. Brown, *DNTT* II, 562-64.

1. Ἀνήρ occurs in the NT 216 times, more than half of the occurrences being found in the Lukan writings (27 in the Gospel, 100 in Acts). The remaining occurrences are distributed among 16 other NT documents, most prominently Matthew with 8, Romans with 9 (of which 7 are in 7:2f.!), and 1 Corinthians with 32 (of which 26 are in ch. 7 and 14 in 11:3-14). Philippians, 2 Timothy, Philemon, Hebrews, 2 Peter, 1–3 John, and Jude do not use the word at all.

2. Ἀνήρ can denote any *human being*. Οἱ ἄνδρες are the *people* (Matt 14:35; Luke 5:18; 11:31; in the reporting of numbers: Mark 6:44; Luke 9:14; John 6:10 [differing from Matt 14:21, where the word designates men only]; Acts 4:4 [in contrast with 8:3, 12; 17:12, where different words are used for *men* and women]). Ἀνήρ can accompany designations of the characteristics, functions, and origins of an individual: ἀνὴρ προφήτης (Mark 6:20; Luke 24:19), ἀνὴρ ἁμαρτωλός (Luke 5:8), ἀνὴρ φονεύς (Acts 3:14), ἀνὴρ λόγιος (Acts 18:24), ἄνδρες Νινευῖται (Matt 12:41 par. Luke 11:32). The same is true in the papyri: ἀνὴρ βίαιος (Preisigke, *Sammelbuch* 4284:9 [3rd cent. A.D.]), ἀνὴρ σοφός (Pap. Hibeh 27:19 [3rd cent. B.C.]).

3. An ἀνήρ is the one who is *respected* in contrast to the poor (Jas 2:2; Sir 10:23), the *mature man* in contrast to the easily deceived child (1 Cor 13:11), a state which the Christian has already overcome in principle (Gal 4:3). According to Eph 4:13 each is to become τέλειος ἀνήρ in the fig. sense by attaining to "the unity of the faith," "the knowledge of the Son of God," the "mature manhood" of Christ. Later it was thought, on this basis, that it is only as a man that one enters the kingdom of heaven (*Gos. Thom.* 114 as opposed to 1 Pet 3:7; Tertullian *Cult. Fem.* i.2.5; Augustine *Civ. D.* xxii.17). In Jas 3:2 the τέλειος ἀνήρ is the *morally perfect person* who does not sin even in speaking.

4. Ἀνήρ can also mean *husband* (Mark 10:2, 12 par. Matt 1:16, 19; Luke 2:36; 16:18; John 4:16-18; Acts 5:9f.; Rom 7:2f.; 1 Cor 7:2-4, 10f., 13f.; 14:35, etc.). In the household codes (Eph 5:22ff.; Col 3:18f.; 1 Pet 3:1ff.; cf. Titus 2:5) the wife is enjoined to be subordinate, the *husband* to be lovingly considerate of his wife. The clergyman is to be μιᾶς γυναικὸς ἀνήρ, *true to one wife* (1 Tim 3:2, 12; Titus 1:6; but remarriage is not illegitimate). An engaged man is also called ἀνήρ (Matt 1:19; Rev 21:2 [cf. Deut 22:23]). 2 Cor 11:2 speaks of Christ as the spiritual *bridegroom*. In cases where marriage is not referred to, ἀνήρ is the *male partner* apart from whether the relationship is marital (Luke 1:34 [the biblical phrase "to know a *man*" means "to have sexual intercourse," as in Gen 19:8; Judg 11:39]; John 1:13 [cf. Tob 3:14; Jdt 16:22; Sir 23:23d).

5. In 1 Cor 11:7 Paul interprets the creation story according to a rabbinic model, attributing creation in the image of God to the *man* alone. However, his proof from Scripture is not part of a systematic discussion of the image of God, but only a part of his answer to the question concerning the obligation of a woman to wear a veil. Since woman lacks the image and glory of God she must wear the symbol of her subordination to the man on her head, a symbol which at the same time functions to protect her against demons (v. 10). The man is protected against demons by virtue of his likeness to God. Apparently the Church had drawn more far-reaching conclusions from the abolition of the distinction between the sexes (Gal 3:28), a provision which applied only in the sacramental realm ("in the Lord," 1 Cor. 11:11).

6. In accordance with Gen 18:2, 16, 22; 19:3, 8, 10, 12, 16 ἀνήρ can designate a *supernatural being* or *angel* (Gen 19:1, 15, 16 LXX; Heb 13:2), as in Luke 24:4: ἄνδρες δύο (cf. John 20:12 δύο ἀγγέλους); Acts 1:10; 10:30; *Gos. Pet.* 36, 39 (9, 10); *Herm. Vis.* i.4.3; iii.2.5, etc.

J. B. Bauer

ἀνθίστημι *anthistēmi* set oneself against, oppose, resist*

The 14 occurrences in the NT are all middle in meaning (i.e., not causative) and all have a dat. obj. or no obj. (the latter includes Rom 13:2b [the obj. is to be supplied from v. 2a]; Eph 6:13). The vb. frequently refers to human opposition to God, God's messengers, God's will, etc. (Acts 13:8; Rom 9:19; 13:2 bis [in contrast to ὑποτασσέσθω in v. 1]; 2 Tim 3:8 bis; 4:15; cf. Luke 21:15; Acts 6:10), but is also used with reference to evil that one is not to *resist* (in the sense of defense, counteraction; e.g., Matt 5:39); at the same time, it is appropriate to *oppose* evil absolutely (Jas 4:7 [the counterpart of ὑποτάγητε οὖν τῷ θεῷ]; 1 Pet 5:9; cf. also Eph 6:13). Paul uses the vb. to describe his behavior toward Peter in Antioch (Gal 2:11: κατὰ πρόσωπον αὐτῷ ἀντέστην, "I *opposed* him to his face").

ἀνθομολογέομαι *anthomologeomai* praise, extol*

Luke 2:38 with dat. τῷ θεῷ; cf. Ps 78:13 LXX; Dan 4:37 LXX (with αἰνῶ).

ἄνθος, ους, τό *anthos* flower, blossom*

The NT uses the imagery in Isa. 40:6f. of the wild flower of the field to describe the mortality of those who trust in wealth (Jas 1:10f.) and uses the quotation from Isaiah (including v. 8) as a contrast to the imperishability of God's redemptive act (1 Pet 1:24; cf. vv. 18, 23).

ἀνθρακιά, ᾶς, ἡ *anthrakia* pile of charcoal; live coal, charcoal fire*

John 18:18: ἀνθρακιὰν πεποιηκότες, they "had made *a charcoal fire*"; 21:9: βλέπουσιν ἀνθρακιὰν κειμένην, "they saw *a charcoal fire*." G. Sauer, *BHH* II, 974.

ἄνθραξ, ακος, ὁ *anthrax* charcoal*

The only NT use is fig. in Rom 12:20, which makes use of a widely used proverbial phrase (quoting Prov

25:22): ἄνθρακας πυρὸς σωρεύσεις ἐπὶ τὴν κεφαλὴν αὐτοῦ, "you will heap burning *coals* upon his head." Since the implied act is fundamentally directed toward the destruction of life (cf. Ps 140:11) and would contradict the commandment to love one's enemy, it is often assumed that there is a connection with an Egyptian penitential rite in which an offender atones for his trespasses by carrying on his head a basin containing live coals as a symbol of repentance and self-punishment. With the proverb Paul could be thinking either of divine retribution (so e.g., O. Michel, *Römer* [KEK, [14]1978] ad loc.) or of the painful remorse of the adversary produced by humiliation (BAGD s.v.; E. Käsemann, *Commentary on Romans* [1980] 349). While v. 19a suggests the first interpretation, it is already sufficiently answered in v. 19b. As a result ἀλλά in v. 20 introduces a focus on the requisite Christian behavior, i.e., to treat the adversary as a brother; in just this way, it becomes possible for the unbeliever to recognize the error in his hostile behavior (toward God and toward those who believe). BAGD s.v. (bibliography); S. Morenz, "Feurige Kohlen auf dem Haupte," *TLZ* 78 (1953) 187-92; W. Klassen, "Coals of Fire: Sign of Repentance or Revenge?" *NTS* 9 (1962/63) 337-50; L. Ramaroson, " 'Carbons ardents': 'sur la tête' ou 'pour la feu'? (Pr 25, 22a—Rm 12, 20b)," *Bib* 51 (1970) 230-34.

H. Balz

ἀνθρωπάρεσκος, 2 *anthrōpareskos* seeking to please people*

In the NT only subst.: Eph 6:6; Col 3:22. In both texts the word is more fully explicated by ὀφθαλμοδουλία and stands in contrast to devotion to the κύριος. W. Foerster, *TDNT* I, 456; H. Bietenhard, *DNTT* II, 815, 817.

ἀνθρώπινος, 3 *anthrōpinos* human
→ ἄνθρωπος 6.

ἀνθρωποκτόνος, ου, ὁ *anthrōpoktonos* murderer*

This word occurs in the NT only in the Johannine literature. John 8:44 refers to the διάβολος as the "father" of the Jewish adversaries of Jesus: as ἀνθρωποκτόνος . . . ἀπ' ἀρχῆς the devil is God's opponent from the beginning and has engendered murderous thoughts against Jesus in the minds of his offspring (cf. vv. 37, 40, the similar clause in v. 44: καὶ ἐν τῇ ἀληθείᾳ οὐκ ἔστηκεν). In 1 John 3:15 ἀνθρωποκτόνος (bis) refers to everyone who hates (i.e., does not love) his brother; eternal life does not abide in such a person and thus he finds himself in the realm of God's adversary (cf. Matt 5:21f.). Billerbeck I, 139-49; R. Bultmann, *The Gospel of John* (1971) ad loc.

ἄνθρωπος, ου, ὁ *anthrōpos* human being, person; mankind; man

1. Meaning and usage — 2. *Mankind* according to the Synoptics — a) Q — b) Mark — c) Matthew — d) Luke — 3. *Mankind* in Paul — 4. Johannine statements — 5. *Mankind* in the remaining writings — 6. Ἀνθρώπινος

Lit.: P. Althaus, *Paulus und Luther über den Menschen. Ein Vergleich* (1951) 31-67 (on mankind apart from Christ). — C. J. Bjerkelund, " 'Nach menschlicher Weise rede ich.' Funktion und Sinn des paulinischen Ausdrucks," *ST* 26 (1972) 63-100. — G. Bornkamm, "Sin, Law and Death: An Exegetical Study of Romans 7," *idem, Early Christian Experience* (1969) 87-104. — H. Braun, "Römer 7, 7-25 und das Selbstverständnis der Qumran-Frommen," *ZTK* 56 (1959) 1-18. — R. Bultmann, "Romans 7 and the Anthropology of Paul," *idem, Existence and Faith* (1960) 147-57. — *idem, Theology* II, 15-32, 70-92. — W. Eichrodt, *Das Menschenverständnis des AT* (1947). — *idem, Theology* II, 118-50. — W. Gutbrod, *Die paulinische Anthropologie* (1934). — J. Jervell, *Imago Dei* (FRLANT 76, 1960). — J. Jeremias, *TDNT* I, 364-67. — E. Käsemann, "On Paul's Anthropology," *idem, Perspectives on Paul* (1971) 1-31. — K. Kertelge, "Exegetische Überlegungen zum Verständnis der paulinischen Anthropologie nach Römer 7," *ZNW* 62 (1971) 105-14. — W. G. Kümmel, *Römer 7 und das Bild das Menschen im NT* (TBü 53, 1974). — J. W. MacGorman, "Romans 7 Once More," *SWJT* 19 (1976) 31-41. — H. Mehl-Koehnlein, *L'homme selon Apôtre Paul* (1951). — R. Pesch, *SM* III, 361-65. — R. Pesch and R. Kratz, *So liest man synoptisch* (3 vols., 1975/76). — A. Sand, *SM* IV, 412-14. — O. Schilling, *Das biblische Menschenbild* (1961). — E. Schweizer, "Die Leiblichkeit des Menschen. Leben—Tod—Auferstehung," *EvT* 29 (1969) 40-55. — H. W. Wolff, *Anthropology of the Old Testament* (1974).

1. In its basic meaning ἄνθρωπος denotes the *human being* as a living creature. It conveys a diminished meaning when it refers to some one human being (frequently without an art. or with a preceding τίς); in pl. ἄνθρωπος can refer to *the people* in a general way. The sg. voc. is a frequently unstressed but often intimate or reproachful form of address. Often it is only the context which makes clear whether what is indicated by the term is a man, husband, son, or slave.

A human being is distinct from animals but also from higher beings (angels, God); transitoriness and mortality are determinative for mankind. In the forefront of the biblical statements stands the human relationship to God: mankind is sinful (Synoptics) or enslaved to the power of sin (Paul and John). Related to this is knowledge and behavior which is *human* (κατὰ ἄνθρωπον). Connected with a gen. ἄνθρωπος undergoes a definite valuation and subordination. Speaking more anthropologically (only in Paul and the post-Pauline tradition) one distinguishes between an external and an internal, an old and a new, a psychical and a spiritual human being, in the course of which the problem of an anthropological or metaphysical dualism arises. Finally, ἄνθρωπος (used absolutely) can be a messianic designation for Jesus; in this case it stands in relation to → υἱὸς τοῦ ἀνθρώπου.

2. a) In Q the human person is spoken of in general as one who stands under the power of another (Luke 7:8 par. Matt 8:9) and who brings forth good or evil out of his or her treasure chest (Luke 6:45 par. Matt 12:35). Even the Son of Man is only human according to popular opinion (Luke: λέγετε; Matthew: λέγουσιν), when he is called "glutton and drunkard, a friend of tax collectors and sinners" (Luke 7:34 par. Matt 11:19). While this accusation is rejected as false, nevertheless all human beings are πονηροί (Luke 11:13 par. Matt 7:11) and constitute an adulterous and sinful generation before God (Luke 11:29 par. Matt 12:39; cf. Mark 8:12; Matt 16:4). In the temptation pericope Jesus responds to the first demand for a miracle with a quotation from Deut 8:3b: "*Man* shall not live by bread alone, but by every word that proceeds from the mouth of God" (Luke 4:4 par. Matt 4:4; Matthew has editorially added the second part of the quotation; cf. Schulz, *Q* 179); Jesus lives in obedience in order that God's succor is guaranteed for human beings. In the saying concerning love of neighbor (the "golden rule," Luke 6:31 par. Matt 7:12) the norm of personal desire is employed to regulate social intercourse; according to Matthew "the law and the prophets" are summarized therein. In the admonition to fearless confession (Luke 12:8f. par. Matt 10:32f.) human beings constitute the forum before which the confession of faith in Jesus (Luke: υἱὸς τοῦ ἀνθρώπου; Matthew: ἐγώ) is to be made; confessing and denying before "my Father" (thus Matthew in contrast to the original of Luke: "before the angels of God") correspond to the public testimony before a human audience.

b) Mark also speaks of *people* in the general sense (8:27; 9:31; 10:7 [quoting Gen 2:24]; etc.); but ἄνθρωπος in relation to God is more precisely described by means of the context (cf. 10:27). Thus the question concerning the legitimacy of John's baptism is clothed in the alternatives: was it "from heaven or from *men*?" (11:30). A person is an enemy of God when he or she thinks what *"men"* think (8:33; cf. Matt 16:23b); and by means of the "woe" (14:21 par.) Judas is identified as "that *man* by whom the Son of man is betrayed." Keeping one's eye on "the position [literally 'face'] of *men*" (12:14) and securing one's own existence carry within them the danger that one can gain the world and still lose (the one thing that really matters) one's own life (8:36f.). As sinner every person requires forgiveness (2:17 par.; 11:25f., etc.); this is firmly promised with, however, one exception: blasphemous speech against the Holy Spirit (3:28f.; the "sons of men" are human beings in general, as the par., Matt 12:31f., shows; Matthew has added that speaking "against the Son of man") will never be forgiven. Using a quotation from Isa 29:13 Jesus accuses the Pharisees and scribes of replacing the commandment of God by human traditions (Mark 7:8); their heart is far removed from God because they are "teaching as doctrines the precepts of men" (v. 7). According to Mark discussion of the law is essentially oriented toward human beings (cf. vv. 17-23 par.: what is within a person determines purity and impurity) and reaches its climax in the saying of Jesus: "The sabbath was made for *man,* not *man* for the sabbath" (2:27).

According to Mark 1:17 par. Matt 4:19; cf. Luke 5:10, the disciples who are called to follow Jesus are promised that they will become "fishers of men." Ἁλιεύς (4 occurrences in the LXX) as a vocational designation occurs only here in the NT (Mark 1:16 par.). The call of Jesus ("follow me") shows (καί with fut. emphasizes the objective) that the disciples are being commissioned in a new vocation. The Lukan version (5:1-11; only Simon is addressed) speaks of them as those who "will be catching men" (ζωγρέω is used only here and in 2 Tim 2:26). According to Mark the promise that they will be "fishers of men" amounts to a commissioning for missionary service. Matthew has editorially sharpened the command to missionary activity ("immediately" they leave boat and father behind, Matt. 4:20); the ἀπὸ τοῦ νῦν in Luke 5:10 likewise emphasizes the urgency of the commission. The use of the vb. "catch" in Luke does not have negative connotations (as it did for the rabbis; cf. Billerbeck I, 188). The same applies also for ἁλιεύς, a word which Jesus perhaps chose as a variation on Jer 16:16.

c) Alongside the use of the general meaning of ἄνθρωπος in Matthew (9:8; 19:10, 12, etc.), the exhortation to watchfulness and readiness for decision is prominent. "Beware of *men*" (10:17) means: Be on your guard against enemies (within and without). It is the task of the disciples to be a sign for mankind, a "light" (5:16), namely, through their exemplary behavior. The disciple must guard against prostituting his own righteousness "before men" (6:1) or making a display of his own works. In the warning against allowing oneself to be admired by others (vv. 5, 16, 18) there is a clear distinction made over against the conduct of the scribes and Pharisees (23:5, 7, 28). As in Mark so also in Matthew the question is raised—but even more radically—concerning the appropriate interpretation of the law. Jesus' devotion to the lost sheep of Israel makes clear that human need suspends the obligation of the law (12:12b); for the human being is of more value than a sheep (12:12a; cf. Luke 13:15f.), of more value than the birds (Matt. 6:26), of more value than the grass (v. 30).

d) Even where ἄνθρωπος has a less emphatic sense in Luke (Luke 1:25; 2:14, 52; 18:2, 4; Acts 17:26, 29, etc.) the thought is frequently present that human beings are accepted by God (Luke 2:14: ἄνθρωπος εὐδοκίας; cf. 5:20) or that they stand in contradiction to God (12:14; Acts 5:4). To a beatitude from Q (Luke 6:22) Luke has added: ". . . when *men* hate you, and when they exclude you." The Church is exposed to human hatred and exclusion from synagogue fellowship on account of the Son of Man (Matt 5:11 has "on my account"). In the polemic against the

Pharisees (Luke 16:14f., etc.) an important Lukan theme is sounded: the warning against wealth and greed. Service of God and service of mammon (16:13) are said to be irreconcilable. The counterpart to the warning against wealth is the requirement to take up the cause of the poor, the disenfranchised, and the oppressed (15:11-32; 16:19-31). God does not acknowledge the pious (when such a person speaks of "other *men*" or of "this tax collector": 18:9-14), but the lowly (v. 11; cf. 1:52). Therefore, the disciple is likewise not permitted to avoid or despise any human being (Acts 10:28; 15:9) because he himself is also *only a human being* (Acts 10:26; 14:15).

3. Nor does Paul offer any fully explicated anthropology. Alongside unemphatic statements about human beings (2 Cor 4:2; Rom 2:9; 1 Cor 7:23: δοῦλοι ἀνθρώπων) are those which say that mankind belongs to the κόσμος (1 Cor 1:20-22; Rom 3:19, etc.), is a created being (Rom 9:20f.; cf. Isa 29:16), and stands over against God (2 Cor 5:11; Rom 1:18, etc.). Weakness and mortality are essential characteristics of human existence (1 Cor 15:53f. [quoting Isa 25:8 and Hos 13:14]; Rom 6:12). The apostle's gospel requires no human legitimation (Gal 1:11f.). Because all people stand under the power of sin (or can fall back under it again), Paul warns against "behaving like ordinary men" (1 Cor 3:3; note the correspondence with → σαρκικός). Speaking and behaving κατὰ ἄνθρωπον not only are insufficient (Gal 3:15: in his speech Paul makes use of human analogy; 1 Cor 15:32: his human battle with beasts was useless), but also stand in contradiction to the will of God (1 Cor 9:8, in the form of a question; Rom 3:5). Above all, Paul's gospel is not κατὰ ἄνθρωπον, but was given by revelation (Gal 1:11; cf. 1 Thess. 2:13); in defending himself Paul points to the nonhuman origin of his gospel (cf. Bjerkelund 100).

In 2 Cor 4:16 Paul distinguishes between the ἔσω and ἔξω ἄνθρωπος of the baptized. In Rom 7:22 he refers only to the ἔσω ἄνθρωπος, with reference to the unbaptized. While this manner of speaking is dichotomous, it does not convey anthropological dualism. The use of other anthropological terminology and the respective contexts shows that Paul, like the OT, views the human being as a unity; however, by the use of philosophical categories certain theological points are stressed. Nor does 1 Thess 5:23 (πνεῦμα—ψυχή—σῶμα) contradict this; the good wish for the brethren emphasizes the hope that they be completely and wholly preserved for the parousia (cf. E. von Dobschütz, *Thessalonicherbriefe* [KEK] 228-32).

For Paul it is unquestionable that the whole of humanity is lost apart from the saving act in Jesus Christ (Rom 1:19–3:20). Through faith (and by baptism) a person is "in Christ" and is thereby a new person (καινὸς ἄνθρωπος), totally separated from the old, adamic person (the παλαιὸς ἄνθρωπος; Rom 6:6; cf. Col 3:9; Eph 4:22, 24). Paul sharpens this contrast by the use of Hellenistic ideas when he speaks of the ψυχικὸς ἄνθρωπος and the πνευματικός (ἄνθρωπος) in 1 Cor 2:14f., which contrasts believers with unbelievers. This distinction finds its focus in the history of salvation and rests on the knowledge that Christ as the "second man" (in contrast to the "first man" Adam) has brought forth a new creation (1 Cor 15:45, 47; cf. Rom 5:15).

In Rom 7:7-25 the question arises—due to the dense description of conflict—as to the identity of the "I" who is speaking (ἐγώ occurs 8 times in vv. 7-25): Is Paul speaking of himself or does the "I" have a more general and fundamental significance? Neither the section in the past tense (vv. 7-13) nor the intense speech in the pres. tense (vv. 14-25; v. 25 is either a gloss or is to be understood as a statement in connection with ch. 8 to be placed at the beginning of that chapter) permit an autobiographical interpretation, whether it is taken as speaking of a pre-Christian period (so, e.g., C. H. Dodd, *Romans* [MNTC] 104, 107f., 116) or of a Christian period (e.g., A. Nygren, *Commentary on Romans* [1949] 287f., 293). Rather, Paul is speaking of mankind under sin. He does this from the perspective of the believer, but it is improbable that he wishes to call attention at the same time to the inner struggle of Paul the Christian (*contra* MacGorman 40). Neither a psychological nor a transpsychological (transsubjective) understanding of human existence is presented in vv. 7-15, but rather a "historical-theological" understanding (cf. Kertelge 114).

4. Ἄνθρωπος is particularly significant theologically in the Johannine literature. It occurs with no special emphasis in John 1:4, 9; 2:25; 7:22f.; 8:17; 11:50; 16:21, etc.; even Jesus is just a man when his adversaries pass judgment upon him (19:5, with connotations of contempt; cf. 11:50: εἷς ἄνθρωπος over against the whole ἔθνος).

Echoes of the Synoptic tradition are present when, in John 10:33, Jesus is accused of blasphemy against God since he is, after all, only a *man* (cf. Mark 14:64f. par Matt 26:65 and Luke 22:71). Similarity to the message of Jesus as reported in the Synoptics is also recognizable in the question regarding the sabbath, to which it is answered that the healing of a human being is more important than the keeping of the sabbath (John 7:22f.; cf. Mark 3:4 par.). The Johannine assertion that Jesus is acquainted with mankind and knows what is in mankind (John 2:24f.; the same idea is reflected in 1:47f.; 4:17-19) has an analogy in Matt 22:18; Luke 16:15.

But according to John a fundamental truth is that people live in darkness (σκοτία 14 times; σκότος twice); they are blind though they do not know it (John 9:39-41; cf. 12:40; 1 John 2:11). As a sinner (John 3:19; 9:16b, etc.), the ἄνθρωπος is God's adversary (3:27; 5:34, 41; 12:43). Mankind living in darkness is equated with the "world" (κόσμος; 1:10f.; 3:19, etc.; cf. H. Sasse, *TDNT* III, 888-95). Of course, "world" can denote creation in a wholly general sense (1:9; 17:5; 1 John 4:1), but as a rule it refers to mankind as a whole (John 1:29; 3:16; 1 John 2:2). The "world" as the world of humanity is evil; without the coming of the Son it would remain in its evil.

The apparently almost unbridgeable separation of

mankind into two groups gives the impression of an irreconcilable opposition in John's thought, almost of a metaphysical dualism of Gnostic character. For there are human beings who are from God (John 7:17; 8:42) and those who are from the devil (8:44); those who are of the truth (18:37) stand over against those who are of this world (8:23; cf. 3:31: ἐκ τῆς γῆς); those "from above" (3:3, 7) are radically separated from those who are "from below" (8:23). Nevertheless, a Gnostic-dualistic interpretation is excluded by statements that everyone who hears and learns has the chance of being "drawn" by the Father (6:44b: ἕλκω, "pull, drag"; cf. also 12:32; the vb. is used differently in 18:10; 21:6, 11). The call to decision in 12:46-48 (ὁ ἀθετῶν . . . καὶ μὴ λαμβάνων, v. 48) and the imperative invitation in 7:37f. (cf. Prov 9:5; Sir 24:19; 51:23f.) are directed to everyone because everyone stands under the judgment, i.e., is in need of the living water. A person can refuse faith (3:19) or accept it (v. 21); thus, it is more correct to speak of "antithetical terminology" (Conzelmann, *Theology* 353 [which translates "Begrifflichkeit" as "conceptuality" rather than "terminology"]) rather than of dualism in the sense of a natural determination (G. Stemberger, *La symbolique du bien et du mal selon saint Jean* [1970] 25-147, is unclear).

5. In their understanding of human existence the remaining writers of the NT (the authors of the later writings) are by and large at home within the tradition delineated thus far. They retain (along with general statements such as πᾶς ἄνθρωπος) the idea of the old and the new person (Col 3:9f.; in v. 10 νέος [without ἄνθρωπος] instead of καινός; Eph 4:22, 24: the new person [RSV "nature"] κατὰ θεόν stands over against the παλαιὸς ἄνθρωπος), but relate it more strictly to praxis than Paul does (cf. J. Gnilka, *Epheserbrief* [HTKNT] 229f.); the christological statement of Eph 2:15 that out of two contrary persons (Jew and Gentile) one new person has come into being (εἰς ἕνα καινὸν ἄνθρωπον) is thereby transformed into an anthropological statement. Likewise the statement concerning the "inner man" (3:16: ἔσω ἄνθρωπος without the complementary term ἔξω ἄνθρωπος) is taken over from the Pauline tradition and still does not point to a body-soul dualism, as a comparison with 1 Pet 3:4 (ὁ κρυπτὸς τῆς καρδίας ἄνθρωπος) shows; in the latter text, the inner person, capable of obedience, determines what counts in the sight of God, not external things such as adornment, luxury, etc.

A more negative view presents itself when a person is characterized as hollow or empty (Jas 2:20: ὦ ἄνθρωπε κενέ) or as double-minded and divided (Jas 1:8 [→ δίψυχος]; ἀνήρ, v. 8, stands in place of ἄνθρωπος, v. 7; cf. also 4:8). F. Mussner, *Galaterbrief* (HTKNT) 71, calls attention in this connection to the similarity with Qumran, but introduces OT analogies as well (Ps 11:3; 77:37 LXX; Hos 10:2). Connected with this is a stronger emphasis on the judgment under which mankind is placed (Jas 5:9; 2 Pet 2:9 [ἡμέρα κρίσεως, also in 3:7]; Heb 9:27; 10:27 [referring to Isa 26:11], etc.). The standard for judgment consists—as already in the Synoptic tradition—of the ἔργα τοῦ ἀνθρώπου (Heb 13:4; 1 Pet 1:17; Rev 20:12). The emphasis on the fact that judgment begins with the Church, with the household of God (1 Pet 4:17: οἶκος θεοῦ; cf. 1 Tim 3:15), is traditional (cf. Mark 13:9; Luke 23:31).

The later writings tend to make greater use of Hellenistic terminology and ideas. Dichotomous and trichotomous statements concerning human existence (cf. already 1 Thess 5:24) become more numerous (1 Pet 2:11; Heb 4:12, etc.), and the ψυχή attains a certain independence (1 Pet 1:9: σωτηρία ψυχῶν). Nevertheless, the unity of the human person remains intact since ψυχή and πνεῦμα can be used interchangeably (1 Pet 3:20) and ψυχή can denote the entire person (1 Pet 3:20b: ὀκτὼ ψυχαί is the antithesis of καὶ ὑμᾶς in v. 21).

Basically, the human person can be designated as ἄνθρωπος τοῦ θεοῦ. In 1 Tim 6:11 this form of address refers, of course, only to Timothy (the expression occurs already in the OT: 1 Kgs 2:27; Deut 33:1) and is, on the one hand, a statement of his belonging to God, but on the other hand, also already a title associated with his office. In 2 Tim 3:17 by contrast ἄνθρωπος τοῦ θεοῦ has a comprehensive significance: every Christian (cf. 2:21) is, through orthodox faith, useful to the Lord and equipped for every good work (cf. also 2 Pet 1:21 א [A] vg: the OT prophets were ἅγιοι [τοῦ] θεοῦ ἄνθρωποι).

6. The adj. **ἀνθρώπινος** *human** occurs 7 times in the NT, 4 of which are in the Pauline letters. In the context of the discussion of genuine erudition the contrast in 1 Cor 2:13 between "*human* wisdom" and "the Spirit (of God)" emphasizes that the apostles' speech is not learned because of human wisdom, but because it is Spirit-filled. For Paul human wisdom is wisdom according to the flesh (cf. 2 Cor. 1:12).

According to 1 Cor 4:1-5 the sole criterion against which to judge (λογίζομαι once, κρίνομαι once, ἀνακρίνομαι three times) a person is trustworthiness (πιστός). Because his critics in Corinth are human judges, he rejects their judgment in the matter of his faithfulness; of course, he is aware that he too is only human, but as an apostle he is subject only to the judgment of the Lord (vv. 4f.) and not to a "*human* court" (v. 3).

In 1 Cor 10:1-13 Paul recalls the warning given by the example of the wilderness generation. His concluding warning against false self-confidence (vv. 11-13) summarizes the example: "No temptation has overtaken you that is not common to man" (v. 13). The πειρασμός is not human in origin, but is humanly bearable as v. 13c confirms: the temptation does not demand more than is humanly possible (cf. BAGD s.v.).

When Paul discusses the new life in Christ in Rom 6:15-23, he speaks in *human* terms (cf. κατὰ ἄνθρωπον → 3) "because you are weak in your natural selves" (v. 19 NIV). Paul knows the inadequacy of his speech; this inadequacy is due not to the inability of those addressed to understand, but to their inability to give up their position outside the context of his gospel.

The reading ἀνθρώπινος ὁ λόγος in 1 Tim 3:1 (D* it, in place of πιστὸς ὁ λόγος), which is taken over from 3:1 by a few mss. in 1:15 as well, is secondary. The major reason for this text-critical decision is that πιστὸς ὁ λόγος is characteristic of the Pastoral Epistles: in light of 1 Tim 4:9; 2 Tim 2:11; Titus 3:8 it is consistent to read the same phrase in 1 Tim 1:15; 3:1 as well.

In the "Areopagus speech" of Acts 11:22-31 Paul stresses the contrast between God and the earthly-creaturely order: God does not live in temples made by human hands (v. 24b) "nor is he served by *human* hands" (v. 25a); the adj. underscores the distance between creature and creator.

The adj. carries more anthropological significance in Jas 3:7. Because of its untamed character the human tongue becomes a dangerous tool when placed uncontrolled in the service of instruction. The *human* φύσις (RSV "humankind") is capable of taming animals (v. 7) but is incapable of taming the human tongue (v. 8). V. 8 (οὐδεὶς ἀνθρώπων) understands the *human* φύσις (v. 7) to mean simply *equivalent with mankind itself.*

1 Pet 2:13 speaks of human institutions: the Christian is admonished to be subordinate to the governing authorities (2:13-17). For the sake of the Lord the Christian is to be subject to every *human* creation (πάσῃ ἀνθρωπίνῃ κτίσει; RSV "every human institution") because it represents the order willed by God in the human realm.

A. Sand

ἀνθυπατεύω *anthypateuō* be proconsul

Acts 18:12 TR in place of ἀνθυπάτου ὄντος; *Mart. Pol.* 21.

ἀνθύπατος, ου, ὁ *anthypatos* proconsul*

Acts 13:7, 8, 12 of Sergius Paulus; 18:12 of Gallio; and 19:38 unspecified. Proconsuls were the chief administrative officials of senatorial provinces which were under civil administration, such as Cyprus, Achaea, and Asia. Lat. *pro consule* corresponds to Gk. ἀνθύπατος. E. Badian, *OCD* 880f.; A. Lejeune, *LAW* 2442; H.G. Pflaum, *PW* XXIII, 1240-79; B. Reicke, *BHH* III, 1856-58; *idem, NT Era* 229f.; G. Wesenberg, *PW* XXIII, 1232-34.

ἀνίημι *aniēmi* loosen; abandon, cease*

The vb. means *loosen, unfasten* in Acts 16:26 (1st aor. pass.; object τὰ δεσμά); and 27:40 (τὰς ζευκτηρίας, "the ropes"); *abandon, desert* in Heb 13:5 (quotation from Deut 31:6); Eph 6:9 (a fig. reference to masters in relation to slaves: ἀνιέντες τὴν ἀπειλήν, "*forbear* threatening"). R. Bultmann, *TDNT* I, 367.

ἀνίλεως *anileōs* unmercifully

Jas 2:13 TR in place of ἀνέλεος. R. Bultmann, *TDNT* II, 487.

ἄνιπτος, 2 *aniptos* unwashed*

Eating with *unwashed,* i.e., ritually impure hands: Matt 15:20; Mark 7:2; 7:5 TR in place of κοιναῖς. Billerbeck I, 695-704; F. Hauck, *TDNT* IV, 947-48.

ἀνίστημι *anistēmi* raise; get up, rise
→ ἀνάστασις.

῞Αννα, ας *Hanna* Anna*

A prophetess in the temple, the daughter of Phanuel of the tribe of Asher (Luke 2:36). T. Lohmann, *BHH* II, 646; BDF §§40; 53.3; G. Schneider, *Lukas* (ÖTK) ad loc.

῞Αννας, α *Hannas* Annas*

Lit.: Billerbeck II, 568-71. — J. Blinzler, *The Trial of Jesus* (1959) 86-89. — P. Gaechter, "Der Haß des Hauses Annas," *idem, Petrus und seine Zeit* (1958) 67-104. — J. Jeremias, *Jerusalem in the Time of Jesus* (1969) 147-50 and *passim.* — *idem, RGG* III, 66. — Schürer, *History* II, 216, 230. — E. M. Smallwood, "High Priests and Politics in Roman Palestine," *JTS* 13 (1962) 14-34. — M. Stern, *EncJud* XIII, 1086-88. — A. Wikenhauser, *LTK* I, 574.

1. Annas I, Jewish high priest A.D. 6-15.

Annas's name is the short form of ῞Ανανος (Heb. *Ḥ[a]naniâ*) and occurs also in Greek as Ἄνανος (used by Josephus) and Ἀννᾶς and in Hebrew as *Ḥannîn* and *'Elḥānān.* Sources for his life and high-priesthood are Josephus *Ant.* xviii-xx; *B.J.* ii, iv, v; *t. Menaḥ.* 13:21 = *b. Pesaḥ.* 57a; *Sipre Deut.* 14:22.

Annas was the son of Seth (on the father's name, see M. Stern, "Aspects of Jewish Society: The Priesthood and Other Classes," *The Jewish People in the First Century* II [ed. S. Safrai and M. Stern; 1976] 606, n. 5) and was appointed high priest by the Roman legate of Syria Quirinius. Since he did not come from the Zadokite line, he belongs to the series of illegitimate high priests. After his deposition by the Roman procurator Valerius Gratus, he retained the title of high priest (Schürer II, 232f.; Jeremias, *Jerusalem* 157) and, most importantly, his great influence. His five sons and a son-in-law also served as high priests (Eleazar, A.D. 16-17; Joseph Caiaphas, the son-in-law, 18-36; Jonathan, 36-37; Theophilus, 37; Matthias, 42-43/44; and Annas II, 62). The family of Annas was not held in high esteem by the Jewish people, as was the case with the high-priestly families as a whole, and was accused of bribery, corruption, repression, and intrigue.

2. The statement in Luke 3:2 that the Baptist appeared

during the high-priesthood of Annas serves the author's intention of expressing "the universal significance of the Christ event" (H. Schürmann, *Lukas* [HTKNT] I, 151). Acts 4:5-22 narrates the interrogation of the apostles Peter and John before the Sanhedrin. The membership of the former high priest Annas in the Sanhedrin (v. 6) corresponds, of course, to contemporary practices, as do the procedures of this highest authority against the Christians; but the specific delineation of the scene is very difficult to understand as the report of a specific historical event. It fits very well, however, the literary and theological compositional technique of Luke.

John 18:12-24 reports that Jesus was led to the former high priest Annas (v. 13), was interrogated by him, and then brought to the officiating high priest Caiaphas (v. 24). The Evangelist has reworked traditional material to make it fit his own conception. Presumably, the source from which he was working spoke only of a hearing before Annas, so that the inclusion of Caiaphas is probably redactional (thus F. Hahn, "Der Prozess Jesu nach dem Johannesevangelium," EKKNT [V] 2 [1970] 23-96; R. Schnackenburg, *The Gospel According to St John* III [1982] 234; *contra* A. Dauer, *Die Passionsgeschichte im Johannesevangelium* [SANT 30, 1972] 68-71).

A. Weiser

ἀνόητος, 2 *anoētos* uncomprehending, unreasonable, foolish*

Of persons: Luke 24:25 (parallel with βραδεῖς τῇ καρδίᾳ); Rom 1:14: *uneducated* (contrasted with σοφοῖς, continuing the contrast between Ἕλλησίν τε καὶ βαρβάροις in the same verse); Gal 3:1, 3, of the Galatians, who do not comprehend the righteousness based on faith; similarly Titus 3:3, of the condition prior to faith (parallel with ἀπειθεῖς and other terms). Of *foolish* desires in 1 Tim 6:9 (parallel with βλαβεράς). G. Harder, *DNTT* III, 122, 124, 126, 129.

ἄνοια, ας, ἡ *anoia* absurdity; lack of understanding*

Of heretical teachers in 2 Tim 3:9, explicated by κατεφθαρμένοι τὸν νοῦν, ἀδόκιμοι περὶ τὴν πίστιν (v. 8; cf. *2 Clem.* 13:1); fig. in connection with the emotional realm in Luke 6:11: the scribes and Pharisees allow themselves to be overcome by *senseless anger* at Jesus' healing on the sabbath and his interpretation of the sabbath, thus revealing their lack of comprehension. J. Behm, *TDNT* IV, 961f.; G. Harder, *DNTT* III, 122, 124, 126, 129.

ἀνοίγω *anoigō* open (vb.)

1. Meaning — 2. Particular occurrences in Paul's letters, the Synoptics, John, Acts, and Revelation — 3. Ἄνοιξις, διανοίγω

1. There are 77 NT occurrences (11 in Matthew, 1 in Mark, 6 in Luke, 11 in John, 16 in Acts, 5 in Paul's letters, and 27 in Revelation). The vb. means *open,* both trans. and intrans.; it is also used in the pass. In the LXX it is the equivalent of Heb. *pātaḥ* (106 times), *paqaḥ* (10 times), and other words. According to the OT God opens the human womb (Gen 29:31); the mouth (Exod 4:12, 15 and numerous other texts); the eye (Gen 21:19, etc.); the ear (Isa 50:5, etc.); the hand (Ps 145:16). NT usage resembles that of the LXX; cf. C. J. Labuschagne, *THAT* II, 409 on "to open the mouth" (i.e., begin to speak). In addition to this neutral usage (in sacral speech) the vb. frequently displays theological relevance in the NT.

2. In Paul's writings ἀνοίγω is a t.t. of missionary language (1 Cor 16:9: "a wide door for effective work *has opened* to me"; 2 Cor 2:12; Col 4:3). For Paul God is always the one who opens, never Jesus Christ (see J. Jeremias, *TDNT* III, 173f.; Billerbeck III, 631). Similarly, according to Acts 14:27, God has "*opened* a door of faith to the Gentiles"; in Rev 3:7 the holy one "who has the key of David" *opens.* But the subject is different in the quotation of Pss 5:10; 13:3 in Rom 3:13, which announces the judgment of both Jews and Gentiles: "Their throat is an *open* grave." Finally, there is 2 Cor 6:11: "Our mouth is open to you," i.e., "we have spoken very frankly to you" (NEB).

For the Synoptics God is the opening power who manifests himself in the redemptive and healing activity of the earthly Jesus as in the eschatological Christ of the parousia, but who is also represented in the healing activity of the disciples and apostles. At the baptism of Jesus heaven *is opened* and Jesus sees the Spirit of God descending (Matt 3:16; Luke 3:21; cf. F. Lentzen-Deis, *Die Taufe Jesu nach den Synoptikern* [1970] 248ff.). In the Sermon on the Mount (Matt 7:7; Luke 11:9) Jesus says, "Knock, and it will be *opened* to you." In Matt 9:30; 20:33 Jesus heals blind men and *opens* their eyes, for in the redemptive activity of Jesus the promise of Isa 61:1ff. is fulfilled in the present. In the parable of the ten virgins Christ, the eschatological bridegroom, opens the door to the kingdom of God (Matt 25:11). Cosmic and apocalyptic events make clear the eschatological significance of what takes place on Golgotha when, at the death of Jesus, graves *are opened* and the dead rise (27:52). God (Luke 1:64; 3:21) and Jesus (13:25) are subjects of the vb.; an angel of the Kyrios *opens* prison doors (Acts 5:19; 16:27) in order to make possible the progress of the Christian mission: God *opens* for the Church its future.

In John's Gospel Jesus functions as God's eschatological bearer of salvation when he *opens* human eyes (John 9:10-32; cf. Isa 35:5; 42:7; Tob 10:21). In the discourse about the true shepherd the gatekeeper opens to the shepherd (John 10:3). It is asked rhetorically whether a demon can *open* the eyes of the blind (v. 21).

The word plays an important role in the language of Revelation. God *opens* heaven (Rev. 19:11), the temple (11:19), the tent of heaven (15:5), and the entrance to the underworld (9:2). Access to God's eschatological plan for history is opened by the Christ of the parousia when he *breaks open* the scroll which has been sealed with seven seals and contains the eschatological events of the end of time (5:2ff.; 6:1-12; 8:1; 10:8, 12). The word is also significant in 3:20: "If any one hears my voice and *opens* the door, I will come in to him and eat with him, and he with me."

3. **Ἄνοιξις** *opening, the act of opening** occurs only in Eph 6:19: that my mouth may be *opened* to proclaim. **Διανοίγω** *open** occurs 8 times in the NT: Luke 2:23 (Exod 13:2), of the dedication of every firstborn male; Mark 7:34: *open* the ears (i.e., to make understanding possible); Luke 24:31: *open* the eyes; Acts 16:14 (as in 2 Macc 1:4): *open* the heart (i.e., to make understanding possible); Luke 24:32, 45; Acts 17:3: *interpret* the scriptures (see G. Delling, "'. . . als er uns die Schrift aufschloß.' Zur lukanischen Terminologie der Auslegung des AT," FS Friedrich 75-84); Acts 7:56: the *opened* heavens.

P.-G. Müller

ἀνοικοδομέω *anoikodomeō* build up (again)
→ οἰκοδομή.

ἄνοιξις, εως, ἡ *anoixis* opening, (the act of) opening (the mouth)
→ ἀνοίγω 3.

ἀνομία, ας, ἡ *anomia* lawlessness, breaking of the law*
ἄνομος, 2 *anomos* lawless, unlawful*
ἀνόμως *anomōs* not possessing the law*

1. Occurrences in the NT — 2. Meaning — 3. Usage — 4. Ἀνομία in Matthew — 5. Ἀνομία and ἄνομος in 2 Thessalonians

Lit.: M. Brunec, "De 'homine peccati' in 2Thess. 2, 1-12," *VD* 35 (1957) 3-33. — J. Ernst, *Die eschatologischen Gegenspieler in den Schriften des NT* (1967) 33-63. — H. Frankemölle, *Jahwebund und Kirche Christi* (1974) 284-86 (on Matthew). — W. Gutbrod, *TDNT* IV, 1085-87. — A. Sand, "Die Polemik gegen 'Gesetzlosigkeit' im Evangelium nach Matthäus und bei Paulus," *BZ* 14 (1970) 112-25. — W. Trilling, *Untersuchungen zum zweiten Thessalonicherbrief* (1972) 75-93.

1. Ἀνομία occurs 15 times in the NT, ἄνομος 9 times (Mark 15:28 is a late secondary addition from Luke 22:37; cf. *TCGNT* 119), and ἀνόμως twice. Except for Matthew (→ 4) and 2 Thessalonians (→ 5), the NT authors do not appear to show any special interest in ἀνομία κτλ.

2. Ἀνομία refers primarily simply to the fact of *lawlessness.* The ἄνομος, then, is *one for whom there is no such thing as a—or the—law*; in the eyes of the Jews this was the Gentile (Acts 2:23; 1 Cor 9:21). For this reason the Gentile sins ἀνόμως (Rom 2:12), i.e., *independently of the* (Mosaic) *law. Ἀνομία* can also refer to *breaking of the law* and thereby come to mean *offense* and *sin* (Matt 7:23; Rom 4:7; Heb 1:9; 1 John 3:4, etc.). In this case the ἄνομος is *one who transgresses against a—or the—law* (Luke 22:37; 2 Thess 2:8; 1 Tim 1:9), and ἔργα ἄνομα are, accordingly, *unlawful* deeds (2 Pet 2:8).

3. The NT writers employ ἀνομία and ἄνομος in two contexts: a) when the subject under discussion is the redemption effected by Jesus Christ (Rom 4:7; Titus 2:14; Heb 10:17) and b) when the discrepancy between a specific person and the will—and thus also the "world"—of God is to be expounded (Matt 7:23; 23:28; 24:12; Rom 6:19; 2 Cor 6:14; 2 Thess 2:3, 7, 8; Heb 1:9; 1 John 3:4).

4. Among the Evangelists Matthew alone speaks of human ἀνομία. The explanation for this is offered in Matt 24:12: where the ἀνομία of human beings increases, their love for each other decreases (according to Matthew); for "the law (→ νόμος) and the prophets" are merely the explication of the command to love God and the neighbor (22:34-40). Therefore, the Pharisees and scribes who "tithe mint and dill and cummin," but neglect "justice and mercy and faith" (23:23) are "full of hypocrisy and *lawlessness*" inside (23:28 JB). For the same reason those also who by *ignoring* the divine will (οἱ ποιοῦντες/ἐργαζόμενοι τὴν ἀνομίαν) cause offense (→ σκάνδαλον κτλ.) have no place in the ultimate reign of God (13:41; 7:23).

5. In 2 Thess 2:3 the eschatological adversary of Christ is characterized as ὁ ἄνθρωπος τῆς ἀνομίας ("the man of *lawlessness*"). The following verse leaves no doubt that the author is resorting to traditional categories of Jewish apocalyptic literature (so Ernst 33-46; this assumption would be further strengthened if the *Apocalypse of Elijah,* in which the "Antichrist" is called "son of lawlessness," could be traced back to Jewish circles; cf. J.-M. Rosenstiehl, *L'apocalypse d'Élie* [1972]). The phrase μυστήριον τῆς ἀνομίας ("mystery of *lawlessness,*" v. 7), by which the author of 2 Thessalonians gives current relevance to the expressions ἄνθρωπος τῆς ἀνομίας (v. 3) and ἄνομος (v. 8; Trilling 81f.), also points to the realm of Jewish apocalypticism (Braun, *Qumran* I, 235f.). In other words, ἀνομία, which is to be brought to completion by the ἄνθρωπος τῆς ἀνομίας (= the ἄνομος) and which is already working in the present in the μυστήριον τῆς ἀνομίας, is not merely "the general moral dissolution which precedes the end" (Ernst 61), but is rather the destruction of that all-encompassing order of things revealed in the → νόμος.

M. Limbeck

ἄνομος, 2 *anomos* lawless, unlawful*
→ ἀνομία.

ἀνόμως *anomōs* not possessing the law*
→ ἀνομία.

ἀνορθόω *anorthoō* rebuild; straighten (trans.)*

Literal in Acts 15:16 (cf. Amos 9:11f. LXX), of rebuilding "the dwelling of David, which has fallen," i.e., the winning of the Gentiles; Luke 13:13: παραχρῆμα ἀνωρθώθη (1st aor. pass.), "immediately she *was made straight*"; Heb 12:12 (cf. Isa 35:3): Διὸ τὰς παρειμένας χεῖρας καὶ τὰ παραλελυμένα γόνατα ἀνορθώσατε, "Come, then, *stiffen* your drooping arms and shaking knees" (NEB).

ἀνόσιος, 2 *anosios* unholy, impious, godless*

1 Tim 1:9, parallel with βεβήλοις: the *unholy,* on account of whom the law is laid down; 2 Tim 3:2, with ἀχάριστοι, ἄστοργοι, etc.: *devoid of piety.* Cf. F. Hauck, *TDNT* V, 492; → ὅσιος.

ἀνοχή, ῆς, ἡ *anochē* forbearance, postponement (of punishment)*

This subst. always refers to an action or attitude of God in the NT. In Rom 2:4 it appears between χρηστότης and μακροθυμία and refers to the *forbearance* or *self-restraint* of God in the face of human error, by means of which God desires to lead human beings to repentance and at the same time expose their arrogance in the judgment. Rom 3:26 is pre-Pauline tradition and refers to the *postponement of divine punishment,* concretized in the forgiveness of former sins (those committed prior to Christ's coming) through the death of Christ, and—like this—is a sign of the δικαιοσύνη of God (cf. E. Käsemann, *Commentary on Romans* [1980] ad loc.). H. Schlier, *TDNT* I, 359f.; U. Falkenroth and C. Brown, *DNTT* II, 765-67.

ἀνταγωνίζομαι *antagōnizomai* resist, struggle*

Heb 12:4: πρὸς τὴν ἁμαρτίαν ἀνταγωνιζόμενοι, "*in your struggle* against sin" (connected with μέχρις αἵματος ἀντικατέστητε). → ἀγών 5.

ἀντάλλαγμα, ατος, τό *antallagma* medium of exchange, equivalent*

Mark 8:37 par. Matt 16:26: ἀντάλλαγμα τῆς ψυχῆς, "What can a man give *in return* for his (lost) life?" i.e., in order to trade it in again. The answer: nothing. F. Büchsel, *TDNT* I, 252; BAGD s.v.

ἀνταναπληρόω *antanaplēroō* complete vicariously
→ πληρόω 3.c.

ἀνταποδίδωμι *antapodidōmi* pay back*
ἀνταπόδομα, ατος, τό *antapodoma* repayment; gift given in return*
ἀνταπόδοσις, εως, ἡ *antapodosis* repayment, recompense*

1. Occurrences in the NT — 2. Meanings of the vb. — 3. The derived substantives.

Lit.: G. Bornkamm, "The Revelation of God's Wrath (Romans 1–3)," *idem, Early Christian Experience* (1969) 47-70. — F. Büchsel, *TDNT* II, 169. — H. G. Degenhardt, *Lukas—Evangelist der Armen* (1965) 100f., 104f. — E. Fascher, *RGG* VI, 1347-49. — W. Pesch, *LTK* X, 697-701.

1. The vb. → ἀποδίδωμι, derived from the simple form δίδωμι, takes on by means of a prefixed ἀντί the character of finality and irrevocability. The vb. with the double prefix occurs (cf. Morgenthaler, *Statistik* 161f.) twice in Luke (both in 14:14), 4 times in Paul's letters (1 Thess 3:9; 2 Thess 1:6; Rom 11:35; 12:19), and once in Hebrews (10:30). Ἀνταπόδομα is found in Luke 14:12 (in the same context as 14:14) and Rom 11:9, and ἀνταπόδοσις in Col 3:24. In Rom 12:19 and Heb 10:30 the vb. occurs in a quotation of Deut 32:35.

2. In Paul's letters the subj. of the vb. is the apostle himself only once (1 Thess 3:9): he feels obligated to thank God for the joy which the congregation occasions in him. Otherwise God is always the subj. In the hymn of praise in Rom 11:33-36 (cf. Isa 40:13; Job 41:3) God's *recompense* is spoken of in a positive sense: God is unexcelled in benevolent activity. Usually, however, the idea of recompense is connected with the announcement of judgment. 2 Thess 1:6 promises terrible *retribution* to those who "afflict" the Church. The affliction (→ θλῖψις, θλίβω, 4 times in 2 Thess 1:3-12) is intimately connected with the future judgment of wrath (v. 5), which is the prerogative of God alone (Rom 12:9 and Heb 10:30, quoting Deut 32:35; cf. CD 9:2).

Luke uses the vb. twice (14:14) in Jesus' instruction to hosts in 14:7-14 (L). The "table-rule" in v. 13 that one should invite only the poor (cf. Billerbeck II, 206f.), since they are not able to return the favor (v. 14a), takes on the character of a general principle in v. 14b in light of the eschatological allusion: "You *will be repaid* at the resurrection of the just."

3. a) **Ἀνταπόδομα** *repayment** underscores the main point of the pericope Luke 14:7-14 (→ 2) in connection with a double imv.; the word is in an emphatic position at the end of v. 12: invitation *in return.* The case is different

in Rom 11:9; the quotation from Ps 68:23 LXX (there ἀνταπόδοσις is used) occurs in the context of the idea of rejection (Rom 11:1-10). What David once wished for his enemies has, according to Paul, come true for the greater part of Israel; the emphasis is upon the "pitfall" which thus results (cf. Paul's rearrangement of the LXX text): the (prepared) table of Israel is to be for them the *occasion of retribution.*

b) In Col 3:24 **ἀνταπόδοσις*** means *repayment* in the sense of *reward,* which must, however, be seen in connection with potential punishment (v. 25). Special attention is called to reward and punishment in a "household code" for slaves (vv. 22-25) with a view toward the coming judgment (v. 22b) and responsibility toward one's master (vv. 22, 23, 24a, b).

A. Sand

ἀνταπόδομα, ατος, τό *antapodoma* repayment; gift given in return
→ ἀνταποδίδωμι 3.a.

ἀνταπόδοσις, εως, ἡ *antapodosis* repayment, recompense
→ ἀνταποδίδωμι 3.b.

ἀνταποκρίνομαι *antapokrinomai* answer back; demand one's right*

Luke 14:6: ἀνταποκριθῆναι πρὸς ταῦτα, "they could not *reply* to this"; Rom 9:20: ἀνταποκρινόμενος τῷ θεῷ, "*cross-examine* God" (JB). F. Büchsel, *TDNT* III, 944f.

ἀντεῖπον *anteipon* (2nd aor.)
→ ἀντιλέγω.

ἀντέχομαι *antechomai* hold fast to, take an interest in*

In the NT as in the LXX this vb. appears only in mid. and always with gen. Matt 6:24 par. Luke 16:13: the servant's *confident devotion* to the master (the opposite of καταφρονήσει); 1 Thess 5:14: ἀντέχεσθε τῶν ἀσθενῶν, *help* the weak; Titus 1:9: *holding firm* to the "sure word," perhaps also in the sense of *pay attention to.* H. Hanse, *TDNT* II, 827f.; BAGD s.v.

ἀντί *anti* instead of, in place of, for*

1. Occurrences in the NT — 2. Meanings — a) In compounds — b) As a prep. — c) As an indication of syntactical structure — d) As a soteriological term

Lit.: On preps. in general → ἀνά. G. Dautzenberg, *Sein Leben bewahren. Ψυχή in den Herrenworten der Evangelien* (1966) 98-107. — J. Gnilka, "Wie urteilte Jesus über seinen Tod?" *Der Tod Jesu. Deutungen im NT* (ed. K. Kertelge; 1976) 13-50. — J. Jeremias, "Das Lösegeld für viele (Mk 10, 45)," *idem, Abba* (1966) 216-29 (cf. *idem, Theology* 292-94). — K. Kertelge, "Der dienende Menschensohn (Mk. 10, 45)," FS Vögtle 225-39. — E. Lohse, *Märtyrer und Gottesknecht* (1955) 117-22. — R. Pesch, *Das Markusevangelium* II (1977) 162-64. — J. Roloff, "Anfänge der soteriologischen Deutung des Todes Jesu (Mk. X.45 und Lk. XXII.27)," *NTS* 19 (1972/73) 38-64. — A. Vögtle, "Todesankündigungen und Todesverständnis Jesu," Kertelge, *Der Tod Jesu* 51-113. — K. Wengst, *Christologische Formeln und Lieder des Urchristentums* (1972) 55-104.

1. The use of the prep. with gen. ἀντί is greatly reduced in koine literature in comparison with classical Greek. It appears 22 times in the NT (and 22 times as a prefix with vbs.), generally in standardized phrases, and has a limited range of meanings.

2. The meaning of ἀντί is determined by context as well as by semantic field, esp. its relation to other preps. that also define the soteriological aspects of Jesus' death (διά, περί, ὑπέρ). It is only within this semantic field of theologically significant preps. and in its relationship to substantives that ἀντί attains its semantic profile.

a) The original local meaning ("opposite") is no longer attested in the NT, but it remains basic to every fig. use, as in the compounds ἀντι-παρ-ῆλθεν (Luke 10:31f.): the priest and the Levite *passed him by* "eye to eye" (opposite him); ἀντι-λέγει τῷ Καίσαρι (John 19:12): he *contradicts* Caesar; ἀντι-πίπτετε τῷ πνεύματι (Acts 7:51): you *resist* the Holy Spirit; ἀντί-χριστος (1 John 2:18): the one who *opposes* Christ; ἀντί-δικος (Matt 5:25): adversary; ἀντί-τυπος (Heb. 9:24): *antitype.* The opposition can also be neutral or benevolent (Mark 14:13; Luke 8:26; 10:40; 20:26; 24:17; Matt 6:24; Rom 8:26; Acts 20:15, 35).

b) Context continues to be decisive when ἀντί is used as a prep. Here also the basic meaning of "opposite" dominates. This accounts for the meanings *instead, in place of, for, for the benefit of, for the sake of* (in a neutral, positive, or negative sense): ὀφθαλμὸν ἀντὶ ὀφθαλμοῦ: an eye *for* an eye (Matt 5:38a); κακὸν ἀντὶ κακοῦ: evil *for* evil (Rom 12:17; cf. Matt 5:38b; 1 Thess 5:15; 1 Pet 3:9); ἀντὶ ἰχθύος ὄφιν: a serpent *instead of* a fish (Luke 11:11; cf. Heb 12:16: birthright for food); ἀντὶ ἐμοῦ καὶ σοῦ: a shekel *for* me and *for* you, corresponding (taken fig.) to a modern tax obligation (Matt 17:27); ἀντὶ τοῦ πατρός, *in place of* the father (Matt 2:22); cf. ἀντ-άλλαγμα: money given *in exchange* (Mark 8:37; cf. 1 Kgs 20:2; Josephus *Ant.* xiv.484); ἀνθ-ύπατος, *pro-consul* (Acts 13:7). The idea of an exchange or a substitution might also be present in John 1:16 (χάριν ἀντὶ χάριτος: grace *upon* grace, as a constant exchange; see BDF §208); 1 Cor 11:15 (ἡ κόμη ἀντὶ περιβολαίου: hair *for* a covering); and Heb 12:2 (ἀντὶ . . . χαρᾶς . . . σταυρόν, *for the joy the cross*; J. Schneider, *TDNT* VII, 577, gives an uncritical view, according to which ἀντί, not the context, is decisive for the meaning).

c) The use of ἀντί as a classical indicator of syntactical structure continues in good Hellenistic style (cf. LXX, papyri): ἀντὶ τούτου, *therefore* (Eph 5:31), or ἀνθ' ὧν, *instead, on behalf of, so that, i.e., because* (Luke 1:20; 12:3; 19:44; Acts 12:23; 2 Thess 2:10; Jas 4:15). Here actions or thoughts stand over against each other.

d) Of theological significance is esp. the "formula of self-sacrifice" (Wengst 55ff.) in Mark 10:45 par. Matt 20:28: δοῦναι τὴν ψυχὴν αὐτοῦ λύτρον ἀντὶ πολλῶν: to give his life as ransom, substitute payment, *for* many, *in place of* the many. The context determines the semantic structure of the prep., which contrasts the persons. In this way the death of Jesus is interpreted as a vicarious sacrifice of life, as a substitutionary offering for the life of the many which has been forfeited through their own guilt. Λύτρον (the ransom money for the manumission of slaves; BAGD s.v.) already signifies ransom money, and it is to this that ἀντί corresponds as a designation for vicarious behavior. Moreover, the idea of atonement (cf. the interchangeable preps. περί [Matt 26:28], ὑπέρ [Mark 14:24, which is par. to Matt 26:28], and ἀντί [Mark 10:45 par. Matt 20:28]) may be present as well (cf. the combination in 1 Tim 2:6: ὁ δοὺς ἑαυτὸν ἀντίλυτρον ὑπὲρ πάντων, "who gave himself as a ransom for all"). From the perspective of the history of traditions, one must say that the concept did not originate among Palestinian Jews (as believed by Jeremias 226; Lohse 118-20; Roloff 51f.; Gnilka 44f., et al.), but rather among Hellenistic Jews, where, for the first time, the idea of a life for a life as constituting ransom is attested (2 Macc 7:37f.; 4 Macc 6:27-29; 17:21f. [ἀντίψυχον]; on the beginnings of Jewish theology of martyrdom see esp. Wengst 62-75; see also Kertelge 231; Pesch 162-64; more reserved are Vögtle 94-97, 101, 105, 107 and Dautzenberg 106). In Mark and Matthew the idea of the universal, vicarious atonement through Jesus is unquestionable. It takes form in its influence on the eucharistic tradition (Mark 14:24; par. Matt 26:28) and in the christological reading of Isa 53:10-12 (which has ἀνθ' ὧν in v. 12).

H. Frankemölle

ἀντιβάλλω *antiballō* throw against; object, dispute*

Luke 24:17: λόγοι . . . οὓς ἀντιβάλλετε πρὸς ἀλλήλους, matters . . . you are *discussing* (so *passionately*).

ἀντιδιατίθεμαι *antidiatithemai* oppose, resist*

A word used in elevated colloquial speech; in the NT only mid.: 2 Tim 2:25, referring to the gentle correction of those who *oppose* the leader of the Church.

ἀντίδικος, ου, ὁ *antidikos* opponent in a lawsuit, adversary*

In biblical Greek usually in the context of a lawsuit as an image for the relationship among human beings or between human beings and God (e.g., Jer 27:34 LXX; ἀντίδικος appears in rabbinic texts as a foreign term ['*anṭîḏîqôs*]). In Matt 5:25 (bis) the way to court with one's *accuser* is an image for the way which the believer goes with his brother to the eschatological judgment; cf. Luke 12:58). The word means *adversary* in general in Luke 18:3.

In 1 Pet 5:8 (unique in the NT, otherwise cf. *Adam and Eve* 33:3) the διάβολος is called ἀντίδικος. The image of the trial hardly plays a role here (*contra* G. Schrenk, *TDNT* I, 374f.); the concern is general, i.e., the threat posed for the believers by the sufferings and temptations which are caused by or taken advantage of by the "evil one" in this time prior to the end (cf. L. Goppelt, *Der erste Petrusbrief* [KEK] ad loc.; Schrenk, *TDNT* I, 373-75; H. Bietenhard, *DNTT* I, 554).

H. Balz

ἀντίθεσις, εως, ἡ *antithesis* antithesis, contradiction*

1 Tim 6:20: *controversy, polemic* (τῆς ψευδωνύμου γνώσεως).

ἀντικαθίστημι *antikathistēmi* resist, offer opposition*

Heb 12:4: μέχρις αἵματος ἀντικατέστητε, "*resisted* [sin] to the point of shedding your blood."

ἀντικαλέω *antikaleō* invite in return*

Luke 14:12: thought of an "invitation in return" (καὶ αὐτοὶ ἀντικαλέσωσιν σε) is rejected.

ἀντίκειμαι *antikeimai* be opposite, oppose, be in conflict with*

The subst. partc. is used in Luke 13:17; 21:15; 1 Cor 16:9; Phil 1:28; 2 Thess 2:4 in reference to the Antichrist and in 1 Tim 5:14 in the sense of *adversary, enemy.* In Gal 5:17 πνεῦμα and σάρξ are said to be "*opposed* to each other" (ἀλλήλοις ἀντίκειται). 1 Tim 1:10 refers to items in a vice list as "*contrary* to sound doctrine."

ἄντικρυς *antikrys* opposite (adv.)*

Used as an improper prep. with gen. in Acts 20:15: "*opposite* Chios." BDF §§21; 214.3.

ἀντιλαμβάνομαι *antilambanomai* come to the aid of, concern oneself with*

In the NT only mid.: with reference to persons (Luke 1:54; Acts 20:35) or things (εὐεργεσίας in 1 Tim 6:2: devote oneself to). G. Delling, *TDNT* I, 375f.

ἀντιλέγω *antilegō* speak against, oppose*

There are 11 occurrences in the NT, 7 of them in the Lukan writings (Luke 2:34; 20:27; 21:15; John 19:12; Acts 4:14; 13:45; 28:19, 22; Rom 10:21; Titus 1:9; 2:9). Luke 2:34: σημεῖον ἀντιλεγόμενον, "A sign that is spoken against"; 20:27, with inf.: *disagree,* saying that. . . .

ἀντίλημψις, εως, ἡ *antilēmpsis* help, assistance*

The pl. in 1 Cor 12:28 refers to the more specialized organizational work in the Church. Paul understands it (polemically) as a charism, alongside κυβερνήσεις; both are absent from the list which follows in vv. 29f. For the use of the pl. cf. 2 Macc 8:19; 3 Macc 5:50. G. Delling, *TDNT* I, 375f.

ἀντιλογία, ας, ἡ *antilogia* contradiction, resistance, rebellion*

In a more technical sense in Heb 6:16 (πάσης . . . ἀντιλογίας πέρας . . . ὁ ὅρκος, "the oath provides a confirmation to end all *dispute*" [NEB]) and 7:7 (χωρὶς δὲ πάσης ἀντιλογίας, *indisputable*). In 12:3 in the sense of resistance; similarly Jude 11: "they . . . perish in Korah's *rebellion.*"

ἀντιλοιδορέω *antiloidoreō* revile in return*

Of Christ in 1 Pet 2:23: λοιδορούμενος οὐκ ἀντελοιδόρει.

ἀντίλυτρον, ου, τό *antilytron* ransom
→ λύτρον.

ἀντιμετρέω *antimetreō* measure out in return*

In Luke 6:38 (par. Matt 7:2 TR) as the reason for not judging each other. By contrast, similar formulations in the rabbinic literature (e.g., *m. Soṭa* 1:7) aim at establishing a norm for judgment; cf. K. Deissner, *TDNT* IV, 632-34.

ἀντιμισθία, ας, ἡ *antimisthia* wage, reward*

This form is attested only in Pauline and post-Pauline Christian writings. It is used *in sensu malo* in Rom 1:27: τὴν ἀντιμισθίαν ἣν ἔδει . . . ἀπολαμβάνοντες, "receiving . . . the due *penalty,*" of homosexual intercourse among men as the punishment decreed by God for their failure to honor God. In 2 Cor 6:13 Paul asks the Church to open their hearts to him as he has done for them: τὴν δὲ αὐτὴν ἀντιμισθίαν . . . πλατύνθητε καὶ ὑμεῖς. The acc. is probably to be understood as the cognate obj. of πλατύνθητε (cf. BDF §154: the term corresponds approximately to τὸν αὐτὸν πλατυσμὸν ὡς ἀντιμισθίαν . . .). H. Preisker, *TDNT* IV, 702; R. Bultmann, *The Second Letter to the Corinthians* (1985) 177.

'Αντιόχεια, ας *Antiocheia* Antioch*

Two cities with the name Antioch are mentioned in the NT, Antioch in Syria and Pisidian Antioch.

1. Antioch on the Orontes in Syria was the residence of the Seleucids and, after 64 B.C., of the Roman legate of the province of Syria. It came to be the third most significant city of the Empire (after Rome and Alexandria). It is mentioned in Acts 11:19f. (in connection with the mission to the Gentiles), 22 (Barnabas's presence in Antioch as a delegate from Jerusalem), 26 (bis: Paul's presence in Antioch; the origin of the term Χριστιανοί), 27; 13:1; 14:26; 15:22f., 30, 35; 18:22; Gal 2:11. G. Delling, *BHH* I, 98f.; G. Downey, *A History of Antioch in Syria from Seleucus to the Arab Conquest* (1961); *idem, IDB* I, 145-48; W. Eltester, *RGG* I, 454; J. Kollwitz, *RAC* I, 461-69; E. Hammerschmidt, *LTK* I, 648-50; R. Fellmann, *LAW* 180f.; J. Lassus, *ANRW* II/8 (1977) 54-102; F. W. Norris, *TRE* III, 99-103.

2. Pisidian Antioch (Strabo xii.8.14: *ad Pisidas*) was situated in the region of Phrygia in the Roman province of Asia; under Augustus it was a Roman colony. It is mentioned in Acts 13:14 (in connection with the founding of the Church there by Paul and Barnabas); 14:19 (Jews from Antioch, cf. 13:50), 21; 2 Tim 3:11. G. Delling, *BHH* I, 99; B. Van Elderen, *ISBE* I, 142; A. Wikenhauser, *LTK* I, 650.

H. Balz

'Αντιοχεύς, εως, ὁ *Antiocheus* a man from Antioch*

Acts 6:5, referring to the proselyte Nicolaus from Antioch in Syria.

ἀντιπαρέρχομαι *antiparerchomai* pass by on the opposite side*

Luke 10:31f., referring to the priest and the Levite, who both, seeing the man who had been attacked on the road from Jerusalem to Jericho, "*passed by* [him] *on the other side*" (of the road? or possibly, each *made a detour around him and passed by*). See also ἀντί 2.a.; C. Burchard, "Fußnoten zum neutestamentlichen Griechisch II," *ZNW* 69 (1978) 149-51.

'Αντιπᾶς, ᾶ *Antipas* Antipas*

A Christian martyr in Pergamum (Rev 2:13). The name is probably a shortened form of 'Αντίπατρος.

'Αντιπατρίς, ίδος *Antipatris* Antipatris*

A military garrison on the road between Jerusalem and Caesarea on the border of Judea. According to Acts 23:31

Paul and his Roman escort (470 soldiers! v. 23) spent the night at Antipatris. B. Reicke, *BHH* I, 102; W. S. LaSor, *ISBE* I, 148.

ἀντιπέρα *antipera* opposite (adv.)*

In the NT an improper prep. with gen.: Luke 8:26 referring to the region of the Gerasenes as *opposite* Galilee, i.e., across the Sea of Galilee from Galilee.

ἀντιπίπτω *antipiptō* resist, oppose*

Acts 7:51, of the Jews, who "always *resist* the Holy Spirit."

ἀντιστρατεύομαι *antistrateuomai* go to war against*

Fig. in Rom 7:23: the law of sin is "*at war with* the law of my mind."

ἀντιτάσσομαι *antitassomai* resist, oppose, withstand*

Rom 13:2: ὁ ἀντιτασσόμενος τῇ ἐξουσίᾳ, "he who *resists* the (governing) authorities"; with persons as obj. in the sense of *oppose*: Jas 4:6; cf. 1 Pet 5:5; Jas 5:6. Used absolutely in Acts 18:6: and when they *opposed* . . . (an obj. is supplied in most translations).

ἀντίτυπος, 2 *antitypos* corresponding to; (subst.) copy
→ τύπος.

ἀντίχριστος, ου, ὁ *antichristos* Antichrist*

1. Occurrences in the NT — 2. The origin of the concept — 3. Its prehistory — a) In the NT — b) In Jewish apocalypticism — c) In mythology — 4. The overall picture in the NT

Lit.: A. Arrighini, *L'Antichristo* (1945). — W. Bousset, *The Antichrist Legend* (1896). — G. Bouwman, *BL* 75f. — M. Brunec, "De 'homine peccati' in 2Thess 2, 1-12," *VD* 35 (1957) 3-33. — D. Buzy, *DBSup* I, 297-305. — J. Ernst, *Die eschatologischen Gegenspieler in den Schriften des NT* (1967). —E. Lohmeyer, *RAC* I, 450-57. — V. Maag, "Der Antichrist als Symbol des Bösen," *Das Böse* (1961) 63-89. — J. Michl, *SacVb* I, 28-32 (bibliography). — B. Rigaux, *L'Antéchrist et l'opposition au Royaume Messianique dans l'Ancien et le Nouveau Testament* (1932). — M. Rist, *IDB* I, 140-43. — H. Schlier, "Vom Antichrist—zum 13. Kapitel der Offenbarung Johannes," Schlier I, 16-29. — J. Schmid, "Der Antichrist und die hemmende Macht," *TQ* 129 (1949) 323-43. — R. Schnackenburg, *Die Johannesbriefe* ([2]1963), esp. 145-49. — W. Stählin, "Die Gestalt des Antichristen und das Katechon," FS J. Lortz II (1958) 1-12.

1. The term ὁ ἀντίχριστος is used in the NT only in the Johannine letters (1 John 2:18 bis, 22; 4:3; 2 John 7). On the other hand, the basic idea is more widespread.

2. The origin of the concept can be explained on the basis of a) the history of language and b) the history of theology. a) Pairs of contrasting terms are common generally and particularly in ancient usage (emperor/counter-emperor; commander/counter-commander; pope/counter-pope); the pair Christ/counter-Christ belongs to this scheme. b) The specific theological background of the term lies in the idea of a power inimical to God, which existed already in myth.

3. The prehistory of the idea of the Antichrist can still be more or less clearly traced on the basis of its development in the NT, Jewish apocalypticism, and mythology.

a) The opponent in 2 Thess 2:1-11 is an individual personality possessing the typical characteristics of the adversary of God, the false prophets, and the Antichrist. Revelation has distributed this complex of ideas among several mythical figures (Rev. 13:1-9, 11-19; 11:7; ch. 12; 20:2) with no attempt at uniformity. Here the force of the idea of the Antichrist remains strangely unfocused. The contemporary references to the Roman emperor cult make the involvement of the opposing figures in the affairs of the world part of their fundamental makeup. Knowledge of the personal adversary seems to be hinted at in the "desolating sacrilege" of Mark 13:14, but as a whole the figure is schematic and colorless. For Mark's literary sources current events (Antiochus IV Epiphanes, the destruction of the temple in the Jewish War) seem to have stood in the forefront. In the Johannine epistles the eschatological figure has become a polemical cipher in the christological controversies: the Antichrist is the one who denies Christ.

b) Jewish apocalyptic and its OT antecedents are more or less clearly recognizable in the adversary figures in the NT (Dan 11:36; Ezek 28:2 [cf. 2 Thess 2:4]; *2 Bar* 36–40; 4 Ezra 5:6; *T. Mos.* 8 and the already widespread idea of an opposition against Yahweh). The Qumran literature offers more distant parallels in the "man of lies" (1QpHab 2:1f.; CD 8:13; 20:15), in the "godless priest" (1 QpHab 8:8), and in the "man of violence" (CD 1:14), but direct influence is not recognizable.

c) The reservations occasionally expressed against the mythical derivation are insufficient to call into question the results of research in the history of religions, which, in their basic core, are indisputable. The motif of primeval and eschatological struggles of the deity against powers of destruction is not only a universal feature of the mythical interpretation of the world, but is also a sustaining element of OT-Jewish and Christian apocalyptic.

4. The concept of the opponent is not uniform in the NT. In spite of the personification occasioned by the law of contrast with the figure of Christ, the overall picture remains nonetheless disparate. It is only in the post-NT period that traditional and newly discovered motifs are concentrated in a uniform picture of the Antichrist.

J. Ernst

ἀντλέω *antleō* draw (water)*

With τὸ ὕδωρ as obj. in John 2:9; 4:7; absolute in 2:8; 4:15.

ἄντλημα, ατος, τό *antlēma* bucket*

John 4:11: "You have no *bucket,* sir" (JB).

ἀντοφθαλμέω *antophthalmeō* look directly in the face*

In the NT only fig.: Acts 27:15, of a ship caught in a storm which "could not *face* the wind" (μὴ δυναμένου ἀντοφθαλμεῖν τῷ ἀνέμῳ).

ἄνυδρος, 2 *anydros* waterless, dry*

Of the wilderness, where demons seek their dwelling places (Matt 12:43 par. Luke 11:24); 2 Pet 2:17: πηγαὶ ἄνυδροι, "*waterless* springs," an image for false teachers; a similar image is νεφέλαι ἄνυδροι ὑπὸ ἀνέμων παραφερόμεναι, "*waterless* clouds carried along by winds," in Jude 12.

ἀνυπόκριτος, 2 *anypokritos* without hypocrisy, genuine
→ ὑποκριτής.

ἀνυπότακτος, 2 *anypotaktos* not made subject, insubordinate, rebellious*

There are three instances of the pl. in the Pastorals: alongside ἄνομοι at the head of a list of vices composed of categories of insubordinate persons for whose sake the law is given (1 Tim 1:9); in reference to *rebellious* children, who are not becoming for a bishop (Titus 1:6); in reference to false teachers (v. 10). In Heb 2:8 it is said that "He [God] left nothing *outside his* [mankind's] *control.*"
G. Delling, *TDNT* VIII, 47.

ἄνω *anō* above (adv.), at the top; upward*

Lit.: BAGD s.v. — BDF §§103; 215.2. — F. Büchsel, *TDNT* I, 376f. — J. Gnilka, *Der Philipperbrief* (HTKNT, 1968) (on Phil 3:14). — LSJ s.v. — D. Mollat, "Remarques sur le vocabulaire spatial du quatrième évangile," *SE* I, 321-28 (on John 8:23). — Moulton/Milligan s.v. — Schwyzer, *Grammatik* I, 550; II, 415f.; cf. 536f.

1. Ἄνω is an adv. of place, formed with final -ω in the same way as κάτω, εἴσω, and ὀπίσω (and cf. ὧ-δε; Schwyzer I, 550). It bears the sense of both *above (at the top)* and *upward.* The attributive use with the art. occurs from the 5th cent. B.C. (Schwyzer II, 415). The NT has 3 occurrences in John, 1 in Acts, 2 in Paul's letters, 2 in Colossians, and 1 in Hebrews.

2. a) In the sense of *at the top* ἄνω appears in the combination ἕως ἄνω, *to the brim* (John 2:7). In Acts 2:19 (in the expansion of a quotation from Joel 3:3 LXX) it is syonymous with ἐν οὐρανῷ, *in the heaven above.* Paul knows the use with the art.: in Gal 4:26 ἡ δὲ ἄνω Ἰερουσαλήμ is the *heavenly* Jerusalem, which is contrasted with the present Jerusalem (v. 25). In Col 3:1, 2 the Church is exhorted: τὰ ἄνω ζητεῖτε/φρονεῖτε: seek, set your minds on *things that are above.* Τὰ ἄνω appears as a geographical term in contrast to τὸ πεδίον already in Xenophon *An.* iv.3.25; cf. *Eq.* 1.2. In John τὰ ἄνω denotes the realm of God from which Jesus comes with the divine message: "I am from *above* (John 8:23; cf. Mollat).

b) Ἄνω occurs with the meaning *upward, up* in Heb 12:15, which refers to a root which (sprouts and) springs *up.* According to John 11:41 "Jesus lifted *up* his eyes" in prayer (cf. Mark 6:41 par.), with a second use of ἦρεν in the verse. Ἡ ἄνω κλῆσις in Phil 3:14 is the *upward* call, the *heavenly* call, not in reference to the origin of the call, but in reference to its goal and prize (cf. Gnilka ad loc.; the parallel to *3 Bar.* 4:15 that he cites is irrelevant since, according to the edition of J.-C. Picard, *Apocalypsis Baruchi Graece* [1967], ἡ ἀνάκλησις is the correct reading).
J. Beutler

ἀνώγεον, ου, τό *anōgeon* upstairs room

TR in Mark 14:15 par. Luke 22:12 in place of → ἀνάγαιον.

ἄνωθεν *anōthen* from above*

Lit.: BAGD s.v. — BDF §104.2. — F. Büchsel, *TDNT* I, 378. — H. Leroy, *Rätsel und Mißverständnis. Ein Beitrag zur Formgeschichte des Johannesevangeliums* (BBB 30, 1968) 124-36 (on John 3:3, 7). — LSJ s.v. — Mayser, *Grammatik* II, 240. — Moulton/Milligan s.v. — G. Rinaldi, "'Risalendo alle più lontane origini della tradizione' (*Luca* 1, 3)," *BeO* 7 (1965) 252-58. — Schwyzer, *Grammatik* I, 618; II, 439f.; 536f.

1. Ἄνωθεν, which occurs 5 times in John, once each in each of the Synoptics and in Acts and Paul's letters, and 3 times in James, is derived from the prep. ἀν(ά), the adverbial suffix -ω (→ ἄνω 1), and the ending -θε(ν; always in the NT) as an ablative gen. (Schwyzer I, 628; II, 439f.) and means *from above, above, anew* (Schwyzer II, 536) or *from the beginning, for a long time* (→ 2.b.).

2. a) In the *spatial* meaning *(from) above,* ἄνωθεν, reinforced by ἀπ(ό) or ἐξ (cf. BDF), occurs in Mark 15:38 par. Matt 27:51 (ἀπ' ἄνωθεν ἕως κάτω, from *top* to bottom) and in John 19:23 (ἐκ τῶν ἄνωθεν, here substantive: from the *top*). In the sense of *from heaven, from God* ἄνωθεν appears in John 3:3: unless one is born *from above* (cf. v. 7; 1:13); this is cryptic language and is misunderstood by Nicodemus in the sense of *anew* (3:4; cf. Leroy). According to v. 31 Jesus is the one who comes *from above.* The

authority of Pilate is given to him *from above* (19:11). Every good gift . . . comes *from above,* i.e., *from the Father* (Jas 1:17; cf. 3:15, 17: the wisdom which comes *from above*).

b) A *temporal* meaning in the sense of *for a long time* is present in Acts 26:5 (cf. *above, earlier* in the dialogue in Plato *Phlb.* 44d; *Lg.* vi.781d) and in the sense of *from the beginning* in Luke 1:3 (cf. Pap. Oxy. no. 237, ll. 8, 31; Rinaldi).

c) The meaning *again* finds expression in Gal 4:9 through the πάλιν which stands parallel to ἄνωθεν and in John 3:3 through the δεύτερον in the understanding expressed by Nicodemus in v. 4 (→ a.; on v. 3 cf. Josephus *Ant.* i.263).

J. Beutler

ἀνωτερικός, 3 *anōterikos* upper*

Acts 19:1 refers to the *upper* regions, i.e., regions located in the highland of Asia which Paul traverses following 18:23. Thereafter he comes down to Ephesus (κατελθεῖν). On the discussion whether the meaning is "interior" or "highland," see E. Haenchen, *Acts of the Apostles* (1971) 552f., n. 1.

ἀνώτερον *anōteron* higher, further up (adv.)*

This comparative of → ἄνω (in Attic usually ἀνωτέρω) is used in Luke 14:10 of the place of honor situated *higher up* the table and thus closer to the head of the house; in Heb 10:8 of a passage quoted *further up,* i.e., *earlier,* in contrast to τότε in v. 9: "when he said *above* . . . , then he added. . . ."

ἀνωφελής, 2 *anōphelēs* useless, unprofitable, unsuitable*

Titus 3:9, with μάταιοι: *unprofitable* controversies; subst. in Heb 7:18: διὰ τὸ αὐτῆς ἀσθενὲς καὶ ἀνωφελές, "a former commandment is set aside because of its weakness and *uselessness.*"

ἀξίνη, ης, ἡ *axinē* ax*

Matt 3:10 par. Luke 3:9, in John the Baptist's sermon announcing the judgment: "Even now the *ax* is laid to the root of the trees." The image stresses the imminence and inevitability of judgment.

ἄξιος, 3 *axios* worthy, appropriate

1. Etymology and meaning — 2. Occurrences, constructions, and usage in the NT — 3. Ἀξιόω

Lit.: BAGD s.v. — W. Foerster, *TDNT* I, 379f. — Moulton/Milligan 50f. — V. Pisani, "Etimologie greche e latine," *Studia classica et orientalia Antonio Pagliaro oblata* III (1969) 157-67, esp. 161f. — G. Rinaldi, "Ebraico *šōweh* e greco ἄξιος," *BeO* 6 (1963/64) 127. — E. Tiedtke, *DNTT* III, 348f. — K. Stendahl, "Ἄξιος im Lichte der Texte der Qumran-Höhle," *NSNU* 7 (1952) 53-55.

1. This adj. is related etymologically to words for weighing and denotes that which brings up the other end of the scales (Foerster 379). In the narrower sense of the word it means *equivalent, worthy, appropriate*; in a broader sense it indicates the relationship of two quantities.

2. Ἄξιος is very rare in the LXX in spite of the subject matter which it strongly attracted to itself. But it is frequent in the papyri and appears, together with the adv. ἀξίως, 47 times in the NT (Morgenthaler, *Statistik* 75).

In addition to the impersonal ἄξιός ἐστιν, *it is fitting* (e.g., 2 Thess 1:3) and the absolute use (Matt 10:11, 13), ἄξιος usually appears in the NT with a comparative gen. (e.g., "is not worthy of me," Matt 10:37f.) or an inf. (e.g., "no longer worthy to be called your son," Luke 15:19, 21).

NT usage of the word covers a broad spectrum. Rom 8:18 uses ἄξιος in the sense of a weighing of two entities and contrasts the suffering of the present time with the future glory; impersonal use of ἄξιος in 1 Cor 16:4 also presupposes a carefully considered judgment. In the logion of Matt 10:10 par. Luke 10:7 and in 1 Tim 5:18 the word describes in a positive way the appropriate wages of the laborer. In Luke 23:15 and most of the occurrences in Acts the word is used in a negative sense to denote the appropriateness of capital punishment for a particular crime. 1 Tim 6:1 employs ἄξιος in connection with the honor which slaves are obligated to show their masters. The negatived form ἀνάξιος, *unworthy,* in 1 Cor 11:27 is directed against unworthy celebration of the Lord's Supper.

Revelation uses the adj. in reference to the eschatological allocation of reward and punishment (3:4; 16:6). In tension with this is the awareness of unworthiness resulting from the encounter with God (cf. Luke 15:19, 21) and with the person of Jesus, which is, however, expressed by → ἱκανός (Matt 8:8 par.). As a result of this awareness and in accord with Pauline theology, Paul uses the adv. ἀξίως only in parenesis (Rom 16:2; Phil 1:27; 1 Thess 2:12; cf. Eph 4:1; Col 1:10)—to denote the goal and motivation of all Christian action (Foerster 380).

3. **Ἀξιόω** *consider worthy or appropriate; request* is used frequently in secular texts to express desire (Moulton/Milligan 51; cf. Acts 28:22). NT use of the vb. with an acc. obj. corresponds completely to the use of ἄξιος and the grammatical constructions the latter is found in. In addition to the 7 occurrences of ἀξιόω, the compound καταξιόω occurs 3 times, always in a pass. construction so that the judgment regarding worthiness is left to God (Luke 20:35; Acts 5:41; 2 Thess 1:5).

P. Trummer

ἀξιόω *axioō* consider worthy or appropriate; request
→ ἄξιος 3.

ἀξίως *axiōs* appropriately, worthily, suitably*

Rom 16:2; Eph 4:1; Phil 1:27; Col 1:10; 1 Thess 2:12; 3 John 6. → ἄξιος.

ἀόρατος, 2 *aoratos* invisible
→ ὁράω.

ἀπαγγέλλω *apangellō* announce, declare
→ ἀγγέλλω.

ἀπάγχω *apanchō* strangle*

Mid. in Matt 27:5, of Judas: ἀπελθὼν ἀπήγξατο, he *hanged himself.*

ἀπάγω *apagō* lead away*

Lit.: H. CONZELMANN, *1 Corinthians* (Hermeneia, 1975) 204-6. — E. KLOSTERMANN, *Das Matthäusevangelium* (HNT, [4]1971) 68f. — G. SCHNEIDER, *Die Passion Jesu nach den drei älteren Evangelien* (1973) 43-117.

Ἀπάγω occurs 15 times in the NT. Apart from 1 Cor 12:2 it appears only in the Synoptics and Acts (3 occurrences in Mark, 5 in Matthew, 4 in Luke, and 2 in Acts). With the meaning *lead away* (BAGD s.v.) it is often very close in meaning to the uncompounded form (→ ἄγω 2). Used intrans. it refers to arrival at a goal: *lead to, end* (Matt 7:13f.). It frequently occurs as a t.t. in juridical language (*ca.* 10 times): *lead* or *lead away* a prisoner. It can bear a similar meaning without an implication of compulsion: *lead away* (Luke 13:15) or *bring* (Acts 23:17).

A *violent leading* (or *carrying*) *away* awaits the disciples (Luke 21:12), is suffered by those guarding Peter (Acts 12:19), and in particular must be endured by Jesus: Judas gives the signal (Mark 14:44; for use of ἀσφαλῶς cf. Acts 16:23) and Jesus is *led* to the high priest (Mark 14:53 par. Matt 26:57), before the Sanhedrin (Luke 22:66), to Pilate (Matt 27:2), into the praetorium (Mark 15:16), and to crucifixion (Matt 27:31 par. Luke 23:26).

In the *conduct of their lives* Christians must choose between two ways, between the way that *leads* to destruction and the way that *leads* to life (Matt 7:13f.). As Gentiles they were drawn to dumb idols and thereby in a state of ecstasy (Conzelmann 205f.) and devoid of will power *carried away* (1 Cor 12:2).

U. Borse

ἀπαίδευτος, 2 *apaideutos* uneducated, silly*

2 Tim 2:23, referring to foolish and *stupid* discussions (τὰς δὲ μωρὰς καὶ ἀπαιδεύτους ζητήσεις).

ἀπαίρω *apairō* take away, snatch away*

In the NT only pass.: Mark 2:20 par. Matt 9:15 and Luke 5:35 in the logion concerning the bridegroom who *will* one day *be taken away* from the wedding guests.

ἀπαιτέω *apaiteō* demand back, demand*

Luke 6:30: goods of which one has been robbed or which have been taken away are not to be *demanded back*; 12:20: the life of the rich farmer is *demanded back* or *called in* (as a debt); cf. v. 48 D. G. Stählin, *TDNT* I, 193f.

ἀπαλγέω *apalgeō* be callous, be impervious*

Eph 4:19, referring to the Gentiles; it is clear from the context that this is to be understood in the light of v. 18d (διὰ τὴν πώρωσιν τῆς καρδίας αὐτῶν).

ἀπαλλάσσω *apallassō* set free, release*

Act. in Heb 2:15 in a christological context, of the freeing through Christ of those who live in the fear of death (cf. Luke 9:40 D); mid. of illnesses which *leave* the sick person (ἀπαλλάσσεσθαι ἀπ' αὐτῶν, Acts 19:12); pass. in Luke 12:58: "make an effort to *settle [peaceably]* with him on the way" (ἀπηλλάχθαι ἀπ' αὐτοῦ, literally: to be *released* by him). F. Büchsel, *TDNT* I, 252f.; H. Vorländer and C. Brown, *DNTT* III, 166f., 173f..

ἀπαλλοτριόω *apallotrioō* estrange, exclude, alienate*

In the NT only the pf. pass. partc. is used, always in reference to (Gentile) existence prior to salvation. In Eph 2:12 it appears with ξένοι τῶν διαθηκῶν τῆς ἐπαγγελίας as an elaboration of χωρὶς Χριστοῦ; the Gentiles are described as "*alienated* from the commonwealth of Israel" (ἀπηλλοτριωμένοι τῆς πολιτείας τοῦ Ἰσραήλ). Eph 4:18 describes them as ἀπηλλοτριωμένοι τῆς ζωῆς τοῦ θεοῦ, "alienated from the life of God," Col 1:21 as *estranged (from God),* alongside ἐχθρούς. F. Büchsel, *TDNT* I, 265f.

ἁπαλός, 3 *hapalos* tender, fresh*

Mark 13:28 par. Matt 24:32, of the young branches of the fig tree which in summer are *full of sap* and put forth leaves.

ἀπαντάω *apantaō* meet*
ἀπάντησις, εως, ἡ *apantēsis* meeting*

1. Text-critical considerations — 2. Ἀπαντάω in the NT — 3. The problem of the expression εἰς ἀπάντησιν

Lit.: W. BRUNERS, *Die Reinigung der zehn Aussätzigen* (1977). — D. DORMEYER, *Die Passion Jesu als Verhaltensmodell* (1974). — W. HARNISCH, *Eschatologische Existenz* (1973). —

E. LINNEMANN, *Jesus of the Parables* (1966) 124-28. — W. MUNDLE and W. SCHNEIDER, *DNTT* I, 319-27. — E. PETERSON, "Die Einholung des Kyrios," *ZST* 7 (1930) 682-702. — *idem, TDNT* I, 380f. — S. WEST, "A Note on P. Oxy. 1242," *ZPE* 7 (1971) 164. — H. A. WILCKE, *Das Problem eines messianischen Zwischenreichs bei Paulus* (1967) 109-147.

1. The matter of textual variants in connection with ἀπαντάω, συναντάω, and ὑπαντάω and with ἀπάντησις, συνάντησις, and ὑπάντησις is confused because of the influence of the Synoptics on each other and because ἀπαντάω and ὑπαντάω in particular and ἀπάντησις and ὑπάντησις as well are nearly always synonymous (cf. Peterson, "Einholung," *passim*).

2. In the NT **ἀπαντάω** always refers to the everyday, nonhostile *meeting*. Other nuances are missing as well as otherwise frequent prep. constructions (see Pape, *Wörterbuch* 278; Passow I, s.v.). According to the "prediction of a sign" (Dormeyer 94) in Mark 13:14 a man carrying water will meet the disciples. In Luke 17:12 where the obj. αὐτῷ was originally absent (see Bruners 53, 171), ἀπαντάω means *come toward* (BAGD 79). There is an accumulation of vbs. of motion in the context surrounding both texts (in this regard see Mundle and Schneider).

3. NT use of **ἀπάντησις** is confined to the formulaic phrase εἰς ἀπάντησιν (Matt 25:6; Acts 28:15; 1 Thess 4:17), which in the LXX is often the translation of the inf. *liqra'ṯ* and means (*come* or *go*) *toward.* Whether ἀπάντησις/ὑπάντησις is a t.t. for the civic custom of according a public welcome to rulers upon their arrival at a city and Paul "presupposes knowledge of the technical meaning" (Peterson, "Einholung" 683) is disputed. The evidence (Peterson 683-92) is not so much proof for a t.t. (unlike πομπή: *KP* IV, 1017-19) as for the existence and form of an ancient custom. Thus one does well to translate the well-honed phrase εἰς ἀπάντησιν (in Matt 27:32 D it as well) primarily as *toward* and leave more far-reaching deductions regarding the parousia of the κύριος to the miniature apocalypse of 1 Thess 4:16f. ("caught up . . . in the clouds *to meet* the Lord"; → ἁρπάζω 3) or the delayed coming of the νυμφίος of Matt 25:1-13 to the exegesis of the respective contexts.

M. Lattke

ἀπάντησις, εως, ἡ *apantēsis* meeting → ἀπαντάω.

ἅπαξ *hapax* once, uniquely, once for all*

1. Occurrences and meanings in the NT — 2. In lists — 3. As an expression of unrepeatability and finality

Lit.: K.-H. BARTELS, *DNTT* II, 716-25, esp. 716-19. — W. STÄHLIN, *TDNT* I, 381-83. — A. WINTER, *"Απαξ, ἐφάπαξ im Hebräerbrief. Eine exegetisch-bibeltheologische Studie zur Theologie der Einmaligkeit* (Diss. Rome, 1960). — D. J. C. VAN WYK, "Die betekenis van hapax en efhapax in die Hebreerbrief," *Hervormde teologiese studies* 28 (1972) 153-64.

1. "Απαξ occurs 14 times in the NT (in addition to 1 Pet 3:20 TR): 3 times in Paul's letters, once in 1 Peter, twice in Jude, and 8 times in Hebrews. It can emphasize the uniqueness of an event in the numerical sense (in contrast to two or three times, etc.); beyond this, however, it can also stress that an event is unrepeatable *(unique)* or effective for all times *(once for all).*

2. In the numerical sense ἅπαξ occurs in lists, e.g., ἅπαξ ἐλιθάσθην (2 Cor 11:25) and the phrase ἅπαξ καὶ δίς (cf. Deut 9:13 LXX), *once and again, several times* (Phil 4:16; 1 Thess 2:18). Heb 9:7 belongs in this category also; here the continuous priestly service in the outer tent (v. 6) is contrasted to its detriment with the sacrificial service of the high priest which occurs only "*once* a year," namely, on the great Day of Atonement (cf. Lev 16:11ff.: twice on the same day; *m. Yoma* 5:1ff.; 7:4: four times on the same day) in the holy place. This juxtaposition, in which the holy place seems to bar the way to the holy of holies, is for the author a sign of the provisional character, willed by God and attested by the Spirit, of the old cult which requires for its fulfillment and dissolution the one true sacrifice.

3. The proclamation of Hebrews stresses the thought of the uniqueness of Christ's work of redemption, which cannot be complemented or subsequently strengthened by anything else because it belongs itself to the conclusiveness of the eschaton. In contrast to the annual sacrifice presented by the high priest for atonement (9:25) Christ has been revealed *once* "at the end of the age to put away sin" (v. 26). Just as death is *unique* in human destiny (v. 27) and thereafter the judgment of God has its place, so also the revelation of Christ is *unique* and finally decisive, i.e., there is no additional possibility for the forgiveness of sins (cf. 6:4); rather, the second coming of Christ following the abolition of sin will be for those who wait for him as their salvation (9:28). According to 12:26 (quotation from Hag 2:6), 27 the created things will be shaken yet *once more,* i.e., one final time, at the end, in order that what cannot be shaken may remain.

According to Heb 6:4, 6 (and in accord with 9:25-28) "it is impossible to restore again to repentance those who have *once* been enlightened" (ἀδύνατον γὰρ ἅπαξ φωτισθέντας . . . πάλιν ἀνακαινίζειν εἰς μετάνοιαν). In a similar way 1 Pet 3:18 stresses the decisive effectiveness of the atoning death of Jesus; → ἐφάπαξ. (Over against this is the impossibility in Judaism of knowing oneself once for all cleansed from sin since the sacrifice must, after all, be continually repeated [Heb 10:2].) Jude 3-5 narrows and sharpens the focus of this idea to concentrate on the reception of salvation by the believers when it calls them to "contend for the faith which was *once for all* delivered to the saints" (v. 3) now that they already know everything (necessary for salvation) *once for all* (εἰδότας ἅπαξ πάντα, v. 5; on the text-critical questions cf. *TCGNT* ad loc.).

H. Balz

ἀπαράβατος, 2 *aparabatos* unchangeable, imperishable*

This late word, absent from the LXX, is used in Heb 7:24 of the priestly office of Jesus (ἀπαράβατον ἔχει τὴν ἱερωσύνην), which, unlike that of the Levites, does not expire with the death of the priest, but is *imperishable* since Jesus himself "continues for ever." The occasionally suggested act. meaning "not to be transferred (to another)" (see J. Schneider, *TDNT* V, 742f.) is possible on the basis of the context, but cannot be otherwise attested. But v. 25, in particular, speaks for the translation "imperishable."

ἀπαρασκεύαστος, 2 *aparaskeuastos* unprepared, not equipped*

A t.t. of military vocabulary used fig. in 2 Cor 9:4 of the Corinthian church in connection with the Pauline collection.

ἀπαρνέομαι *aparneomai* refuse
→ ἀρνέομαι.

ἀπάρτι *aparti* from now on
→ ἄρτι.

ἀπαρτισμός, οῦ, ὁ *apartismos* completion*

Luke 14:28, of the *completion* of a tower.

ἀπαρχή, ῆς, ἡ *aparchē* firstfruits, firstling*

1. Meaning and occurrences in the NT —2. Paul — 3. James and Revelation

Lit.: M. Albertz, "Die 'Erstlinge' in der Botschaft des NT," *EvT* 12 (1952/53) 151-55. — G. Delling, *TDNT* I, 479-89, esp. 485f. — F. Mussner, *Der Jakobusbrief* (1964) 94-97. — B. Spörlein, *Die Leugnung der Auferstehung. Eine historisch-kritische Untersuchung zu 1 Kor 15* (BU 7, 1971) 70f., 75.

1. In addition to indicating a specific time (the beginning) and being the formal term for a birth certificate, ἀπαρχή is used in secular Greek primarily as the expression for *firstfruits* and *firstlings for sacrifice* (cf. LSJ s.v.). The LXX is likewise familiar with ἀπαρχή as a concept in sacrificial vocabulary (Exod 23:19; 25:2, 3; 36:6; Lev 22:12; Deut 12:6, 11, 17; 18:4; 26:2, 10; Ezek 44:30). In this context it has to do with the flawless firstfruits of natural products, the firstfruits of human beings, animals, and plants (in Ezekiel ἀπαρχή several times denotes a piece of farm land which must be turned over to God when land is purchased), all of which are owed to Yahweh (or the sanctuary). The connection with sacrificial language of the OT is preserved in the NT as well, both with regard to numerical sequence and to qualitative definition. With two exceptions (James and Revelation → 3) the term belongs to the realm of Pauline usage.

2. The relationship to the OT is esp. clear in Rom 11:16: Paul uses Num 15:17-21 to say in a metaphor that the whole batch of dough (φύραμα = dough, batch of dough, lump of clay; cf. BAGD s.v.) will be holy if only the essential component (cf. the image of the root in v. 16b) is holy, i.e., sanctified as a sacrificial gift to God. According to 1 Cor 16:15 the household of Stephanas were *the first* Christians of Achaia; according to Rom 16:5 Epaenetus was *the first* member of the Christian community in Asia, designated for Christ (in this sense also Acts 16:14f. and *1 Clem.* 42:4). According to Rom 8:23 the Spirit of God as the *firstfruits* has been given to Paul and his colleagues as an eschatological pledge (cf. 2 Cor 5:5 and → ἀρραβών with the same meaning in 2 Cor 1:22). Christ himself is the *firstling* (1 Cor 15:20, 23): he is raised up as the first of those who have fallen asleep (cf. *1 Clem.* 24:1). At first, the temporal meaning is primary here; but the resurrection of Jesus is determinative for all those who have fallen asleep in Christ (cf. Col 1:18; Rev 1:5), if not in the sense of strict causality, then at least in the consecutive sense of a firm promise.

The statement in 2 Thess 2:13 is disputed on text-critical grounds. Along with ℵ D K L Ψ and many minuscules as well as most of the Church Fathers, many modern exegetes read ἀπ' ἀρχῆς, "from the beginning" (in the sense of "from eternity"). In agreement with *UBSGNT* *ἀπαρχήν*, the more difficult reading, is to be preferred: the young church in Thessalonica receives the honorific title of "first converts," i.e., those sanctified by the Spirit and blessed with faith in the truth.

3. The parenetic instruction in Jas 1:16-18 speaks of the *first gift* ("firstfruits" according to Mussner) of God's creation (cf. κτίσις, "everything created," "the creatures," "the creation": 1 Tim 4:4; Rev 5:13; 8:9; καινὴ κτίσις, "the new creature," "the new creation": 2 Cor 5:17; Gal 6:15). Through the word of truth the Christians are made into a new humanity; the emphasis is thereby on the new creation, which is to be interpreted soteriologically.

In Rev 14:4 the 144,000 redeemed (cf. 7:4-8 and 7:9-17) are designated as "*first fruits* for God and the Lamb" (here also one finds—though little-attested—the v.l. ἀπ' ἀρχῆς: $\mathfrak{p}^{47}$ ℵ *pc*). In the context of 14:4-5 the two datives (τῷ θεῷ, τῷ ἀρνίῳ) cause some difficulty. It is possible that they each denote the "purchaser" (see H. Kraft, *Offenbarung* [HNT] 190; cf. BDF §191). But since the context makes clear that the concern here is with a determination of quality, the sense is surely: Because of their life and conduct the 144,000 are found to be worthy, as those elected by God and the Lamb, to be preserved in the terrors of the end time and finally saved.

A. Sand

ἅπας, 3 *hapas* whole, every, all
→ πᾶς.

ἀπασπάζομαι *apaspazomai* bid farewell*

Acts 21:6 (5 in translations): ἀπησπασάμεθα ἀλλήλους, "we . . . bade one another farewell."

ἀπατάω *apataō* deceive, cheat, mislead
→ ἀπάτη.

ἀπάτη, ης, ἡ *apatē* deception, deceit, enticement*
ἀπατάω *apataō* deceive, cheat, mislead*

1. Meaning — 2. NT Usage — 3. NT statements — 4. Ἐξαπατάω

Lit.: BAGD s.v. — A. Oepke, *TDNT* I, 384f.

1. The subst. and vb. are attested in secular Greek (papyri, Homer) in reference to *deceptive behavior* of human beings, through which persons are misled and on account of which punishment is meted out (in juridical language), i.e., as a primarily ethical concept (Plutarch). They also refer to personified *deception, deceit,* and *seduction* (Hesiod). Essentially this same content is found also in the LXX (e.g., Exod 8:25; Jdt 9:10, 13) and taken over into the NT.

2. For the basically negative meaning of ἀπάτη, ἀπατάω in the NT (7 and 3 occurrences respectively) the usage is instructive; thus the connection with wealth (Mark 4:19), sin (Heb 3:13), lust (Eph 4:22), futile, empty words (Eph 5:6; cf. Col 2:8), and unrighteousness (2 Thess 2:10) and the corresponding counter-concepts: truth (Eph 4:21, 24; 2 Thess 2:10, 12) and righteousness (Eph 4:24).

3. The 10 NT occurrences are found primarily in ethical-parenetic contexts, in part with a retrospective view toward salvation history (OT) and an eschatological expansion. Accordingly, wealth can become *seduction* (Mark 4:19 par. Matt 13:22), and lust can blind persons and turn them away from Christ (Eph 4:22). Eph 5:6 expands the idea of *seduction* on the basis of futile words and joins in thought with Col 2:8 as a warning against a philosophy which propagates empty deception and leads away from Christ to the elemental spirits of the universe. Jas 1:26 calls attention to *deception* in connection with piety which displays itself in undisciplined, loveless speech.

The word undergoes an orientation toward salvation history in 1 Tim 2:14, according to which Adam is *seduced* by Eve (cf. Gen 3:13 and 2 Cor 11:3). The sense of the word takes on an eschatological coloring and focus in 2 Thess 2:10; here *seduction* is understood as a sign of the end time with all its destructive consequences; similarly in Heb 3:13 the *deception* of sin leads to hardening and falling away. 2 Pet 2:13 identifies the eschatological tempter with persons who revel in their deceits, meaning both bodily excesses (vv. 13f.) and spiritual boasting (vv. 10, 18).

4. The compound **ἐξαπατάω** *deceive**, frequent in Attic prose (Plato, Aristotle), is used without exception in the NT as a synonym for the uncompounded form (Rom 7:11; 16:18; 1 Cor 3:18; 2 Cor 11:3; 2 Thess 2:3; 1 Tim 2:14); cf. BAGD s.v.

A. Kretzer

ἀπάτωρ, 1 *apatōr* fatherless*

Heb 7:3, referring to Melchizedek. The silence of Gen 14:18ff. regarding the origin and further circumstances of his life is taken as evidence for the imperishability of his priestly office. G. Schrenk, *TDNT* V, 1019-21; O. Hofius, *DNTT* I, 615-21.

ἀπαύγασμα, ατος, τό *apaugasma* reflection*

Lit.: F. Bleek, *Der Brief an die Hebräer* (1828-40). — G. Bornkamm, "Das Bekenntnis im Hebräerbrief" (1942), *idem, Aufsätze* II, 188-203, esp. 197-200. — R. Deichgräber, *Gotteshymnus und Christushymnus in der frühen Christenheit* (1967) 137-40, 182. — F.-W. Eltester, *Eikon im NT* (1958) esp. 149-52. — E. Grässer, "Hebräer 1, 1-4," *Text und Situation* (1973) 182-228, esp. 218f. — O. Hofius, *Der Christushymnus Philipper 2, 6-11* (1976) 80-83. — J. Jervell, *Imago Dei* (1960), esp. 214-26. — E. Käsemann, *The Wandering People of God* (1984) 101-17. — G. Kittel, *TDNT* I, 508. — O. Michel, *Der Brief an die Hebräer* (KEK, [13]1975) (on Heb. 1:3). — E. Riggenbach, *Der Brief an die Hebräer* (KNT, [2, 3]1922). — C. Spicq, *L'Épître aux Hébreux* (ÉBib, 1952-53). — K. Wengst, *Christologische Formeln und Lieder des Urchristentums* (1973) 166-80. — U. Wilckens, *TDNT* IX, 418-23, esp. 421f. — R. Williamson, *Philo and the Epistle to the Hebrews* (1970) 36-41, 409-34. — H. Windisch, *Der Hebräerbrief* (HNT, [2]1931). — H. Zimmermann, *Das Bekenntnis der Hoffnung* (1977) 53-60.

1. Ἀπαύγασμα occurs in the NT only in Heb 1:3. Verses 1:3f. are based upon a Christ-hymn that came into being in the Hellenistic Jewish Church and describes the way of Christ on the basis of the scheme: preexistence–death–exaltation (cf. Phil 2:6-11). The first line of the hymn (Heb 1:3a) describes the relationship of the eternal Son of God to God: ὃς ὢν ἀπαύγασμα τῆς δόξης καὶ χαρακτὴρ τῆς ὑποστάσεως αὐτοῦ. In agreement with Heb 1:3 Christ is called the ἀπαύγασμα τῆς μεγαλωσύνης (τοῦ θεοῦ) in *1 Clem.* 36:2.

2. The meaning of ἀπαύγασμα in Heb 1:3 is disputed. Actively, the word can denote *radiance* or *effulgence* (Philo *Spec. Leg.* iv.123) or, passively, *reflection* or *the light that is reflected* (Wis 7:26; Philo *Op.* 146; *Plant.* 50). The sentence structure in Heb 1:3 favors understanding ἀπαύγασμα and → χαρακτήρ as synonyms and, therefore, interpreting ἀπαύγασμα as pass.: Christ "reflects the glory of God and bears the very stamp of his nature." Both predicates characterize the Son as the perfect image of God and thus correspond to the expression → εἰκὼν τοῦ θεοῦ (Col 1:15; 2 Cor 4:4).

In the background of the statement is the Hellenistic Jewish concept of the εἰκών. According to Wis 7:26 preexistent Wisdom is "the reflection (ἀπαύγασμα) of eternal light, a spotless mirror of the working of God, and an image (εἰκών) of his goodness." In Philo the Logos appears as the "image" and "reflection" of God (*Op.* 25; *Plant.* 18; *Conf.* 146f.; *Som.* i.239 and frequently elsewhere). The εἰκών represents and reveals the invisible God and thus mediates the saving knowledge of God.

In Heb 1:3a—unlike *1 Clem* 36:2—the accent is not on the idea of the mediation of revelation, but rather on the mystery of the person of the revealer himself. Both christological predicates underscore the divine origin, divine nature, and divine omnipotence of the preexistent One and in this they agree with the confession of Phil 2:6. The emphasis on Christ's equality with God, further underscored by Heb 1:3b, has as its point of reference the statement in v. 3c regarding the atoning death: only the Son in the unity of his being and acting with God could bring about purification from sins through his death. Thus the work of redemption is inseparable from the person of the redeemer.

O. Hofius

ἀπεῖδον *apeidon* (2nd aor.)
→ ἀφοράω.

ἀπείθεια, ας, ἡ *apeitheia* disobedience
→ ἀπειθέω 2.

ἀπειθέω *apeitheō* disobey, be disobedient

1. Meanings and usage in the NT — 2. Ἀπείθεια — 3. Ἀπειθής

Lit.: O. Becker, *DNTT* I, 593. — R. Bultmann, *TDNT* VI, 10f.

1. In the NT the vb. ἀπειθέω always has God or his will as its obj. Thus it belongs to the fundamental theological terms of the NT. As sin was understood in the OT as disobedience of God's will and one thought thereby primarily of ethical requirements, so can the idea of *being disobedient* have this ethical quality in the NT. In Rom 2:8 it is Jews and Gentiles who "do not obey (ἀπειθοῦντες) the truth, but obey (πειθόμενοι) wickedness." In Heb 11:31 it is the inhabitants of Jericho and in 1 Pet 3:20 the contemporaries of Noah who are characterized as *disobedient.* From the context it is clear that moral errors are at issue.

The prophetic word quoted in Rom 10:21 ("All day long I have held out my hands to a disobedient and contrary people," Isa 65:2) originally possessed this same ethical nuance, but in the context of Romans it takes on a completely new meaning. Here it stands under the superscription in 10:16: "they have not all obeyed the gospel," and actually serves as scriptural proof of Israel's *unbelief:* failure to heed the gospel and being "disobedient" (ἀπειθεῖν) are identical. Ἀπειθέω can be made more specific by a dat. obj. ("the word," 1 Pet 2:8; 3:1; "the gospel," 4:17), but the same thing is always intended: rejection of Christian faith. "By virtue of being proclaimed, the gospel demands acceptance in obedience" (K. H. Schelkle, *Die Petrusbriefe. Der Judasbrief* [HTKNT] 60). Unbelief is disobedience against God.

This equation of disobedience with lack of belief and the specifically Christian focus of the stance represented by this term is very clear in John 3:36: "He who believes in the Son has eternal life; he who does not obey (ἀπειθῶν) the Son shall not see life. . . ." Ἀπειθεῖν becomes a t.t. for nonacceptance of the Christian faith. In Acts 14:1 *believing* (πιστεύειν) and *being disobedient* (ἀπειθεῖν) are used absolutely and are contrasted to each other. The Jews, who do not obey, are those who do not accept the Christian faith. And when Paul, in Rom 15:31, exhorts the recipients of the letter to pray for him "that I may be delivered from *the disobedient* in Judea," he is speaking of "unbelievers" (so RSV), i.e., Jews who have not become Christians.

In a number of Greek mss. (esp. $\mathfrak{p}^{46}$) and in the Latin versions the identity of "not obeying" and "not believing" is so much taken for granted that the former is replaced by the latter (Heb 3:18; 11:31; cf. 1 Pet 2:7).

The terminological equation of disobedience and disbelief in NT usage has great theological significance. One could say pointedly: disobedience against God's will manifests itself not primarily in the transgression of individual commandments of God, but rather in resistance against the revelation of God's salvation in the gospel.

Rom 11:30-32 forms the seam as it were in which the OT and the NT use of ἀπειθέω meet in the same sentence. When it is said of Gentile Christians that they were once *disobedient* to God, this means not only that they did not know God, but rather that they did not acknowledge God in their deeds. But when it is said that the Jews "have now been *disobedient,*" nothing is being said other than that the Jews have not accepted the Christian faith.

2. **Ἀπείθεια** *disobedience* has, like the vb., a double meaning: a) disobedience as sin in the moral-religious context; b) disobedience as sin in the sense of unbelief in relation to the kerygma of God. How near these two meanings are to each other is shown by comparison of

Rom 11:32 ("God has consigned all men to *disobedience,* that he may have mercy upon all") with Gal 3:22 ("The scripture consigned all things to sin, that what was promised to faith in Jesus Christ might be given to those who believe"). In Heb 3:19 unbelief is mentioned and in 4:6 *disobedience* as the reason that the wilderness generation was unable to enter the "rest"; of course, it should be noted that 4:6 as well speaks in the first place of the gospel ("those who formerly received the good news").

The moral-religious dimension of ἀπείθεια comes to expression above all in the formulaic phrase *"sons of disobedience"* (Eph 2:2; 5:6; Col 3:6). The formula "sons of," which is used in a fig. sense to express solidarity and still today is widespread in the Semitic-speaking world, has in this particular construction ("sons of unrighteousness") not a single parallel in the whole of Hebrew usage (cf. Billerbeck I, 476-78).

3. Rom 1:30 and 2 Tim 3:2 are the only places in the NT where disobedience, here in the adjectival form **ἀπειθής** *disobedient**, is said to be directed toward persons, specifically parents. In Titus 1:16 *disobedient* is explicated by "unfit for any good deed." In 3:3 "foolish" and "disobedient" form one thought unit and are concerned with the moral life. Luke 1:17 also points in the same direction; ἀπειθεῖς and φρόνησις δικαίων (the attitude of the righteous) are opposites. Acts 26:19 forms the bridge to the meaning "disbelief": "I was not disobedient to the heavenly vision."

P. Bläser

ἀπειθής, 2 *apeithēs* disobedient
→ ἀπειθέω 3.

ἀπειλέω *apeileō* threaten, prohibit under threat*

This vb. appears with no obj. and with Christ as the subj. in 1 Pet 2:23: πάσχων οὐκ ἠπείλει, "when he suffered, he did not *threaten*"; with a complementary inf. with μή in Acts 4:17: "let us *warn* them *[under threat of punishment]* to speak no more to any one in this name" (Koine E *pm* add ἀπειλῇ).

ἀπειλή, ῆς, ἡ *apeilē* threat*

The pl. is used in Acts 4:29 of the eschatological attack of the opponents of Jesus against those who believe. In 9:1 the sg. is used of Paul: ἐμπνέων ἀπειλῆς καὶ φόνου, "breathing threats of [RSV "and"] murder." According to Eph 6:9 masters should forego *threatening* their slaves. For Acts 4:17 v.l. → ἀπειλέω.

ἄπειμι (I) *apeimi* be absent*

In the NT only Pauline or deutero-Pauline: 1 Cor 5:3 (ἀπὼν τῷ σώματι, παρὼν δὲ τῷ πνεύματι); 2 Cor 10:1 (contrasted with κατὰ πρόσωπον), 11 (contrasted with παρόντες); cf. 13:2, 10; Phil 1:27 (contrasted with ἐλθών); Col 2:5 (τῇ σαρκὶ ἄπειμι, . . . τῷ πνεύματι σὺν ὑμίν εἰμι).

ἄπειμι (II) *apeimi* go away, go to*

Acts 17:10: εἰς τὴν συναγωγὴν τῶν Ἰουδαίων ἀπῄεσαν, "they went into the Jewish synagogue."

ἀπεῖπον *apeipon* (2nd aor.)
→ ἀπολέγομαι.

ἀπείραστος, 2 *apeirastos* untried, incapable of being tempted*

This adj. is not attested before Jas 1:13, where it is predicated to God: ὁ γὰρ θεὸς ἀπείραστός ἐστιν κακῶν. Act. and pass. translations are both possible: God does not tempt to evil or "God cannot be tempted to evil" (RSV). The context requires the latter, the pass. translation (so also H. Seesemann, *TDNT* VI, 29; BAGD s.v.; BDF §§117.1; 182.3; *contra* P. H. Davids, "The Meaning of Ἀπείραστος in James 1. 13," *NTS* 24 [1977/78] 386-92; *idem, Commentary on James* [NIGTC] 81-83); the statement provides the basis for the contention that no one can make God responsible when he or she is tempted: God himself cannot be tempted to evil and hence cannot tempt anyone else to it. V. 14 then traces the temptation of the individual back to his or her own ἐπιθυμία. But lusts, sin, and death have nothing to do with the God in whom there is no change (v. 17). Thus "tempt" in v. 13 means to seduce to sin and does not have as its aim the testing of faith (as is the case, however, in vv. 2f.).

H. Balz

ἄπειρος, 2 *apeiros* inexperienced, unskilled, unpracticed*

Heb 5:13, of beginners in Christian instruction who still require "milk." Such a person is ἄπειρος λόγου δικαιοσύνης, "*unskilled* in the word of righteousness."

ἀπεκδέχομαι *apekdechomai* wait; await, expect (eagerly)
→ ἐκδέχομαι 4.

ἀπεκδύομαι *apekdyomai* remove (something); disarm
→ ἐκδύω 1, 4.

ἀπέκδυσις, εως, ἡ *apekdysis* laying aside (noun)*

Col 2:11, referring to the *"putting off* [of] the body of flesh." A. Oepke, *TDNT* II, 321. → ἐκδύω 4.

ἀπελαύνω *apelaunō* drive away*

Acts 18:16: Gallio "*drove* them from the tribunal."

ἀπελεγμός, οῦ, ὁ *apelegmos* refutation*

Acts 19:27: "come into *disrepute*," possibly a Latinism: *in redargutionem venire.*

ἀπελεύθερος, ου, ὁ *apeleutheros* freedman
→ ἐλεύθερος.

Ἀπελλῆς, οῦ *Apellēs* Apelles*

Personal name in Rom 16:10; v.l. in Acts 18:24; 19:1 (א in place of Ἀπολλῶς).

ἀπελπίζω *apelpizō* despair; hope for, expect
→ ἐλπίς.

ἀπέναντι *apenanti* opposite, in the presence of*

Improper prep. with gen. in Matt 27:24, 61 (cf. 21:2 v.l.); Acts 17:7; Rom 3:18. Ἀπέναντι πράσσω, *oppose* in Acts 3:16.

ἀπέραντος, 2 *aperantos* endless*

1 Tim 1:4: genealogies which run on *endlessly.*

ἀπερισπάστως *aperispastōs* not distracted, undisturbed (adv.)*

1 Cor 7:35: "wait upon the Lord *without distraction*" (NEB).

ἀπερίτμητος, 2 *aperitmētos* uncircumcised*

Acts 7:51: "*uncircumcised* in heart and ears" (Lev 26:41; Jer 6:10; 9:25; Ezek 44:7, 9). R. Meyer, *TDNT* VI, 73f., 81f.; → περιτομή.

ἀπέρχομαι *aperchomai* go away

This vb. is used figuratively, e.g., of illnesses (Mark 1:42 par. Luke 5:13), and literally with εἰς (e.g., Mark 1:35; 6:32, 36, 46; 7:24, 30; 8:13; 9:43 [also in Matthew, Luke, and John]; Rom 15:28; Gal 1:17) and πρός (Mark 3:13; 14:10; John 4:47; 6:68; 11:46; 20:10; Rev 10:9) to indicate a goal: *go to.* Ἀπέρχομαι ὀπίσω ισ used in the positive sense of *to follow* as a disciple (Mark 1:20; cf. John 12:19), but also in a negative sense in Jude 7. Ἀπῆλθον εἰς τὰ ὀπίσω in John 6:66: "many disciples *drew back*" from Jesus (deserted him?); 18:6, referring to the *drawing back* of those who come to arrest Jesus. J. Schneider, *TDNT* II, 675f.

ἀπέχω *apechō* receive in full; be distant*

1. Occurrences in the NT — 2. Meaning — 3. Usage

Lit.: W. Barclay, *NT Words* ([4]1976) 51-54. — H. Hanse, *TDNT* II, 816-32, esp. 828.

1. The vb. (a compound from → ἔχω found as early as Homer *Il.*) occurs 19 times in the NT (13 act., of which 9 are ind., 1 subjunc., and 3 partc.; 6 mid., of which 1 is imv., and 5 inf.).

2. In act. ἀπέχω means a) *receive in full* or *receive one's share* (6 of the NT occurrences; actually a t.t. of commercial language often found in receipts on papyri and ostraca; see BAGD s.v. 1; Preisigke, *Wörterbuch* s.v. 4) and b) *be distant* (6 times, all in the Gospels; this meaning from the time of Herodotus; BAGD s.v. 2). In mid. it means c) *abstain* (not in the Gospels; this meaning from the time of Herodotus; BAGD s.v. 3). The act. meaning *hold at a distance* (first in Homer *Il.* vi.96) does not occur in the NT.

In Mark 14:41 ἀπέχει (omitted in Matt 26:45) permits several translations (see most recently R. Pesch, *Markusevangelium* [HTKNT] II, ad loc.), primarily: a) impersonal *it is enough* (Vg. *sufficit*; = classical ἀρκεῖ; see BDF §129; only *Anacreontea* 16.33 is comparable; see the translation in J. M. Edmonds, *Elegy and Jambus with the Anacreontea* II [1931]), with reference to the sleep of the disciples or to the ironic scolding of Jesus, or b), as in a) in the paragraph above, personal (with Judas as the subj. and the obj. supplied; cf. Mayser, *Grammatik* II/1, 82), or c) impersonal: *the account is closed* (BAGD s.v. 1). The τὸ τέλος added in a few Western mss. can be explained as a gloss (probably borrowed from Luke 22:37; see *TCGNT* ad loc.).

3. Where ἀπέχω means *receive in full* or *receive one's share* the subj. is always a person or group of persons and the obj. (acc.) can be a thing (first in Aeschines 2:50) or a person (Onesimus in Phlm 15). Where it means *be distant* the subj. can be a person or thing, and the vb. is used with ἀπό with gen. of the thing (since Herodotus) or the person (without ἀπό in Demosthenes *Or.* 21.59); absolute usage (cf., e.g., Thucydides iii.20.3) is present in Luke 15:20. Where it means *abstain* the subj. is always a group of persons, and the gen. of the thing is used (with [cf. Xenophon *Cyr.* i.6.32] or without [since Homer *Il.*] ἀπό, as in the LXX; see Helbing, *Kasussyntax* 179; in Acts 15:20 the ms. evidence varies); the inf. is always dependent upon an expression of intention.

The hypocrites, who give alms, pray, and fast in public, *have* their (human) reward *already* (Matt 6:2, 5, 16); the opposite is the possession (→ ἔχω) of the heavenly reward (v. 1; cf. Plutarch *Sol.* 22.4; similarly Gen 43:23 and Callimachus *Epigr.* 55). The pronouncement of woe upon the rich who have *already received* their comfort (Luke

6:24) uses the vb. in the same way. In Phil 4:18 Paul presents what amounts to a receipt for the collection which the church at Philippi had sent him. Philemon is to *have* Onesimus *back* forever as a brother (Phlm 15).

Jesus is said to be not *far* (μακράν; cf. Diodorus Siculus xii.33.4) from the centurion's house (Luke 7:6); while returning, the lost son is still a long way from his father (15:20). In a fig. sense, the heart of the people is far from God (Matt 15:8 par. Mark 7:6, a quotation from Isa 29:13). An indication of distance in stadia (since Herodotus vi.119.2) is given in Matt 14:24 (the distance of the ship in which the disciples of Jesus are traveling from the shore of the Sea of Gennesaret) and in Luke 24:13 (the distance of the village of Emmaus from Jerusalem).

In his speech to the apostolic council in Jerusalem (Acts 15:20) James proposes for the Gentiles certain regulations governing abstinence. The apostles then send Paul with such a decree to, among other places, Antioch (v. 29). 1 Thess 4:3 (the commandment to *abstain* from [sexual] immorality) appears within a parenetic context, as does 5:22 (the admonition to *abstain* from every form of evil, based on Job 1:1, 8; cf. also *1 Clem.* 17:3) and 1 Pet 2:11 (an exhortation to *abstain* from the passions of the flesh; cf. *Did.* 1:4; similarly Plato *Phd.* 82c). Finally, 1 Tim 4:1ff. announces the appearance of certain (ascetic) heretics who prohibit the eating of certain foods which God has created (v. 3; cf. ἀπέχεσθαι σιτίων in Plutarch *Sept. Sap.* 157d [over Epimenides of Crete in Diels, *Fragmente* I, 30:35]).

A. Horstmann

ἀπιστέω *apisteō* be unfaithful; fail to believe*
ἀπιστία, ας, ἡ *apistia* unfaithfulness; lack of faith*
ἄπιστος, 2 *apistos* unbelievable; not believing*

1. Occurrences in the NT — 2. Ἀπιστέω — 3. Ἀπιστία — 4. Ἄπιστος

Lit.: R. Bultmann, *TDNT* VI, 174-228. — G. Dautzenberg, "Der Glaube im Hebr," *BZ* 17 (1973) 161-77. — G. Ebeling, "Jesus and Faith," *idem, Word and Faith* (1963) 201-46. — E. Grässer, *Der Glaube im Hebräerbrief* (1965). — D. Lührmann, "Pistis im Judentum," *ZNW* 64 (1973) 19-38. — *idem, Glaube im frühen Christentum* (1976). — O. Michel, *DNTT* I, 593-606 (bibliography). — A. Schlatter, *Der Glaube im NT* ([5]1963). → πίστις.

1. NT occurrences of ἀπιστέω (8), ἀπιστία (11), and ἄπιστος (23) are few compared to those of πιστεύω (241) and πίστις (243). The meaning of the negative words ἀπιστέω κτλ. is largely dependent upon that of the positive words → πίστις and πιστεύω. Since there are no Hebrew equivalents to the privative forms ἀπιστέω, ἀπιστία, and ἄπιστος, only Greek texts from the sphere of Judaism are available as a basis for comparison of usage.

2. As ἀπιστία means both *unfaithfulness* and *lack of faith,* so also the vb. **ἀπιστέω** means both a) *be unfaithful* and b) *fail to believe.*

a) Occurrences of the first of these meanings are numerous for the subst. but sparse for the vb.; however, they are not completely absent (Xenophon *An.* ii.6.19, of the unfaithfulness of a soldier to his commander). This meaning is required in Rom 3:3 by the context: "What if some *were unfaithful* (ἠπίστησαν)? Does their *faithlessness* nullify the faithfulness of God?" The use here of ἀπιστία and πίστις τοῦ θεοῦ together with what follows in v. 4 shows that the issue is the covenant faithfulness of God, which cannot be nullified by the faithlessness of Israel. Nevertheless, echoes, at least, of the second meaning *(be unbelieving, refuse to believe)* can also be heard in ἠπίστησαν: the qualification τινές makes clear that ἠπίστησαν is not to be thought of as the all-encompassing subjection to sin spoken of in v. 9, but as the refusal by a part of the Jewish people to believe when confronted with the gospel (cf. 9:6; 11:1-5, 17).

The same juxtaposition of terms is found in 2 Tim 2:13 in a hymn strophe which the author quotes: "if we are *faithless,* he remains [nevertheless] faithful." In what follows, "for he cannot deny himself," the meaning of πιστός as "faithful" is established, and the meaning of the contrasting εἰ ἀπιστοῦμεν is also thereby determined. Here also there are echoes of the meaning *be unbelieving,* for otherwise a distinction between being faithless (v. 13) and the denial of Christ spoken of in the previous line (v. 12b) would hardly be possible and the two lines would merely contradict each other.

b) The meaning *put no faith in, be unbelieving,* in relation to a statement or message, is attested in Herodotus i.158; Sophocles *Ph.* 1350; Josephus *Ant.* ii.270; *B.J.* ii.54; Philo *Vit. Mos.* i.236; *Virt.* 188, etc. When confronted by the proclamation of the resurrection, the disciples *"did not believe"* the women (Luke 24:11): they *put no faith* in them. In Luke 24:41 "while they still disbelieved" means while they *were not yet able to believe;* likewise Mark 16:11, "But when they heard that he was alive and had been seen by her, they *would not believe* it," i.e., they could not yet believe it. As ἀπιστέω is thus used in relation to the message of the resurrection, so it is also used generally for unbelief in relation to the message of salvation. Thus Acts 28:24, where it is said of Paul's sermon that some were convinced by what he said, it is also said that "others *disbelieved* [continued to disbelieve: ἠπίστουν]"; similarly Mark 16:16: ὁ δὲ ἀπιστήσας κατακριθήσεται, "he who *does not believe* [= remains in unbelief] will be condemned": unbelief is defined (by the preceding command to missionary activity) as unbelief in relation to the gospel.

In 1 Pet 2:7 the partc. ἀπιστοῦντες denotes *unbelievers* in the sense of non-Christians. The development of usage in the Christian sphere becomes visible here and becomes even clearer when ἄπιστος (→ 4.b.2) is used as a fixed designation for non-Christians.

3. In the case of **ἀπιστία** one likewise encounters both meanings: a) *unfaithfulness* and b) *lack of belief.*

a) Ἀπιστία undoubtedly means *unfaithfulness* in Rom 3:3, as is apparent from its juxtaposition to πίστις τοῦ θεοῦ and from what follows in v. 4: their *lack of faithfulness* cannot nullify God's faithfulness (→ 2.a). Numerous examples outside the NT confirm this use of ἀπιστία (Josephus *B.J.* i.268; iii.349; Philo *Fug.* 152; *Decal.* 172; Xenophon *An.* ii.5.21, etc.).

b) *Unbelief.* (1) Ἀπιστία denotes, first, in the technical sense, *rejection* or *nonacceptance* of the message of salvation. The Jews as branches of the olive tree were broken off "because of their *unbelief,*" because they rejected the gospel (Rom 11:20; on the dat. of cause cf. BDF §196); they can be grafted in again if they do not persist in their *unbelief,* their refusal of the gospel (11:23). According to 1 Tim 1:13 Paul had persecuted the Church ἐν ἀπιστίᾳ, while he was still *unbelieving.*

(2) Ἀπιστία has a somewhat different meaning in Mark 16:14: "and he upbraided them for their *unbelief* and hardness of heart, because they had not believed those who saw him after he had risen." Here ἀπιστία is first an *inability* or *unwillingness to believe* in the face of the improbability of the report, but at the same time it carries a negative valuation because of its equation with → σκληροκαρδία.

(3) The understanding of ἀπιστία in Rom 4:20 is determined entirely by the context in which Paul attempts to lay out the idea of justifying faith, using the example of Abraham. The faith on account of which Abraham was pronounced righteous showed itself in the fact that he "never doubted God's promise *in unbelief*" (NEB; οὐ διεκρίθη τῇ ἀπιστίᾳ), that "he did not weaken in faith when he considered his own body, which was as good as dead" (v. 19), but believed in God, who gives life to the dead (v. 17). Thus he took God at his word and held fast to God's promise. Ἀπιστία is, then, doubting, calling into question, and not taking seriously the promise of God in the face of contrary experiences.

(4) Mark 6:6 says that Jesus "marveled because of their *unbelief.*" Ἀπιστία is here the rejection which Jesus experiences when the people of Nazareth refuse to acknowledge his claim in view of his well-known origins (cf. ἐσκανδαλίζοντο ἐν αὐτῷ, v. 3). In his version Matthew (13:58) has made a characteristic alteration: Whereas Mark 6:5 reports that Jesus could do no mighty work there, Matthew eliminates this apparent limitation of the power of Jesus and underscores the connection between faith and miracle: because of *unbelief* he did only a few mighty works there. As faith receives the mighty work as the answer to prayer, so, on the other hand, is the mighty work refused to lack of faith.

(5) The connection between faith and mighty works is seen also in the cry of the father in Mark 9:24: "I believe; help my *unbelief*!" This paradoxical saying about unbelieving faith reveals the reflection on faith and doubt which is beginning: it seeks to protect faith from the misunderstanding that what matters is an especially great faith, as though faith were an achievement. Faith always exists only in the struggle with lack of faith and with doubt (cf. G. Barth, "Glaube und Zweifel in den synoptischen Evangelien," *ZTK* 72 [1975] 269-92).

(6) Ἀπιστία has a slightly different sense in Hebrews. In 3:12 the author warns the readers lest there be in any of them a καρδία πονηρὰ ἀπιστίας, "an evil, *unbelieving* heart"; that would constitute a falling away from God. Following the mention of the sin and rebellion of the wilderness generation, v. 19 states that the Israelites were unable to enter the promised rest because of their *unbelief.* Faith means holding fast the beginning of the → ὑπόστασις to the end (v. 14): it is the attitude of patience and persistence on the way to the promised rest. To grow tired and get behind on this pilgrimage (4:1) is ἀπιστία. Since → πίστις here is an attitude and a virtue, ἀπιστία can be explicitly designated as πονηρά (3:12).

4. In the case of **ἄπιστος** also one finds two meanings: a) *unbelievable* and b) *unbelieving.*

a) The first is found in Acts 26:8: τί ἄπιστον κρίνεται παρ' ὑμῖν, "why is it thought *incredible* by any of you that God raises the dead?" Ἄπιστος is found in this sense also in Philo *Ebr.* 205; Josephus *Ant.* xiv.31; xviii.76.

b) Much more frequent and characteristic is the use of ἄπιστος in the sense of *unbelieving:*

(1) John 20:27 says in relation to the Easter message: "do not be *faithless* (μὴ γίνου ἄπιστος), but believing." According to Mark 9:19 Jesus complains about the γενεὰ ἄπιστος, the "*faithless* generation"; their lack of faith consists in mistrust or insufficient trust in relation to his sending and authority. It is instructive that in Matt 17:17 and Luke 9:41 this complaint is expanded with echoes from Deut 32:5 (cf. Phil 2:15) to "*faithless* and perverse (διεστραμμένη) generation": such lack of faith is a moral fault.

(2) Most frequently οἱ ἄπιστοι occurs as a fixed designation for *non-Christians,* outsiders who do not belong to the Church. Thus 1 Cor 7:12-14 speaks of the non-Christian spouse; 10:27 speaks of an invitation given by a non-Christian; 6:6 refers to going to court before "*unbelievers,*" i.e., before Gentile courts of law; 14:22-24 refers to non-Christians who enter a Christian service of worship (here with → ἰδιώτης); likewise in 2 Cor 6:14f.; 1 Tim 5:8; Rev 21:8; *Mart. Pol.* 16:1. In 2 Cor 4:4 the ἄπιστοι are equated with the ἀπολλύμενοι; the somewhat difficult sentence is best construed as follows: for those who are lost the gospel is veiled, "for *unbelievers,* whose

thinking the god of this world has blinded" (RSV is different).

This use of ἄπιστοι as a fixed designation for non-Christians is even more striking when one observes not only that it appeared early and came to be widely used in Christian writings, but also that it has no parallels outside Christian writings. Of course, the concept of πίστις plays a central role in Philo's interpretation of the relationship to God in the OT, but nowhere are Gentiles, those who stand outside the Jewish religious community, designated as οἱ ἄπιστοι. On the other hand, that at a relatively early stage in the NT non-Christians are consistently called οἱ ἄπιστοι is evidence not only of the powerful influence early Christianity exerted on the formation of language, but also the degree to which one perceived the essence of one's own religion to be determined by πίστις.

(3) From here it is only a small step to the use of ἄπιστος to refer to false teachers. Thus clear references to Gnostic heretical teachers in Ignatius *Trall.* 10:1; *Smyrn.* 2:1; 5:3; cf. *Magn.* 5:2. In the NT the "unbelievers" of Titus 1:15 are also apparently false teachers. It is possible that 2 Cor 4:4 is similarly directed polemically at the opponents in Corinth.

(4) A further step leads to ἄπιστος assuming the secondary implication of wickedness. Thus in 2 Cor 6:14f. ἄπιστοι stands alongside terms such as σκότος, ἀνομία, and εἴδωλον. In 1 Tim 5:8 and Titus 1:15 *unbelievers* are characterized as morally degenerate. It is significant that they are mentioned in 2 Cor 6:14f. and Rev 21:8 in a vice list (cf. also ἀπιστία in *Herm. Sim.* ix.15.3). Of course, ἄπιστος and ἀπιστία occur also in Philo *Conf.* 48 and Wis 14:25 in vice lists, but there they have the sense of unfaithful(ness) or disloyal(ty). Ἄπιστος in vice lists with the meaning *unbelieving* appears for the first time in Christian texts.

(5) Finally, it is unbelievers who are to be condemned at the judgment; this is said in *2 Clem.* 17:5 and probably also in Luke 12:46 and Rev 21:8. Luke 12:46 has: "and put him with the *unbelievers*" (RSV "unfaithful"). The par. in Matt 24:51 has the (possibly older) form μετὰ τῶν ὑποκριτῶν and thereby makes clear that the issue here is those who are condemned in the judgment in a general sense and ἄπιστοι can hardly (in contrast to 12:42: πιστός, "faithful") refer to the unfaithful, but is to be understood in the sense of *unbelieving, non-Christian.* NT usage in general, according to which the ἄπιστοι are the unbelievers, the non-Christians, as well as the special reference to the final judgment speaks for translating ἄπιστοι in Rev 21:8 as *unbelievers* (not unfaithful ones).

G. Barth

ἀπιστία, ας, ἡ *apistia* unfaithfulness; lack of faith → ἀπιστέω.

ἄπιστος, 2 *apistos* unbelievable; not believing → ἀπιστέω.

ἁπλότης, ητος, ἡ *haplotēs* simplicity, sincerity, uprightness*

ἁπλοῦς, 3 *haplous* simple, sincere*

Lit.: J. AMSTUTZ, *APLOTES* (Theophaneia 19, 1968). — H. BACHT, *RAC* IV, 821-40. — O. BAUERNFEIND, *TDNT* I, 386f. — G. BAUMBACH, *Das Verständnis des Bösen in den synoptischen Evangelien* (1963) 77-79. — M. DIBELIUS and H. GREEVEN, *James* (Hermeneia, 1976) 77-79. — C. EDLUND, *Das Auge der Einfalt* (1952). — JEREMIAS, *Parables* 122. — SCHULZ, *Q* 468-70. — C. SPICQ, "La vertu de simplicité dans l'Ancien et le Nouveau Testament," *RSPT* 22 (1933) 1-26.

1. In koine Greek ἁπλότης and, correspondingly, ἁπλοῦς (and ἁπλῶς) have a relatively broad spectrum of meaning. The basic meaning is *simplicity* or *wholeness*; it can be appropriately translated by Eng. *purity* ("pure" being understood as meaning unmixed with any other matter). In more specialized usage ἁπλότης carries a negative connotation of naive *simplicity* (e.g., Philo *Vit. Mos.* i.172; Josephus *B.J.* i.111; v.529) or a positive valuation of *rectitude, uprightness* as well as "simple goodness, which gives itself without reserve" (thus BAGD 86; so also Bauernfeind; Dibelius and Greeven; *contra,* among others, Amstutz 111).

Information on the (increasingly frequent) occurrence of the word group in early Jewish and early Christian literature is provided by Edlund 51ff.; Baumbach 77ff.; Amstutz 13ff., 116ff. In the *Testaments of the Twelve Patriarchs* ἁπλότης becomes a central concept in ethical instruction: like God himself and his law, that which is good is thoroughly simple and indivisible; only plain uprightness of behavior is consonant with it. Along with the *Testaments of Asher* and *Benjamin* cf. esp. the *Testament of Issachar,* in which the speaker describes himself as a representative of ἁπλότης—and thereby "realizes" various positive nuances of meaning of the word (cf. *T. Iss.* 4:1; differently 3:8 [simplicity in giving and generosity] and 3:2ff. [uprightness]).

2. a) The subst. occurs only in the Pauline letter corpus; 6 of the 8 occurrences stand in a context clearly shaped by parenetic concerns and all of the occurrences are in topical contexts (Amstutz 96ff.). In 2 Cor 1:12 Paul characterizes his conduct toward the Church: he behaves toward it "not by earthly wisdom," i.e., with dishonest motives, but in *uprightness* (so *NTG*[26]) and purity in accordance with the norm of God. In 11:3 he fears that the Corinthians could be led astray—as Eve once was by the serpent—"from a *sincere* and pure *devotion* to Christ."

In the household codes (Col 3:22; Eph 6:5) it is required of Christian slaves that they obey their masters "not with eyeservice, as men-pleasers, but in *singleness* of heart," i.e., wholeheartedly and without reservation.

While commending the collection for the first church Paul uses ἁπλότης 3 times. In 2 Cor 9:13 it describes the disposition of the Corinthians which moved them to contribute to the aid of others—*uprightness* in fellowship, that is, solidarity. In 8:2 and 9:11 it refers to the greatness of the gift and so means *simple goodness*; the same is true in Rom 12:8: whoever is entrusted with the charisma of giving money for the aid of others is to exercise it in *simple, gracious objectivity,* not seeking gain for self or showing partiality. God also gives → ἁπλῶς (Jas 1:5; the adv. appears only here), i.e., either *generously* (Vg. *affluenter*) or, in view of the context and diverse parallels (cf. esp. *Herm. Man.* ii.4), more likely *with pure thoughts, without ulterior motives* (Codex Corbeiensis: *simpliciter*).

b) The adj. occurs in an enigmatic wisdom saying about the eye (Matt 6:22f. par. Luke 11:34). The saying is based on the image from the Hebrew-Aramaic thought world of the "good" and "evil [i.e., envious] eye." Greek can render this image not literally but appropriately with ἁπλοῦς and πονηρός; cf. *T. Iss.* 3:3f.: ἁπλοῦς here means *pure, gracious* (Amstutz 101f.: "without envy"). As an ethical imperative, as it is esp. in Matthew, the image describes a blunt either/or: God requires ἁπλότης, i.e., the human will in its entirety.

T. Schramm

ἁπλοῦς, 3 *haplous* simple, sincere
→ ἁπλότης.

ἁπλῶς *haplōs* sincerely, uprightly*

Jas 1:5, referring to giving *without ulterior motives.* M. Dibelius and H. Greeven, *James* (Hermeneia) 79: "without hesitation" (so also O. Bauernfeind, *TDNT* I, 386); H. Riesenfeld, "ΑΠΛΩΣ: Zu Jak. 1, 5," *ConNT* 11 (1944) 33-41: "unconditionally." → ἁπλότης 2.a.

ἀπό *apo* from, away from

1. Usage in the NT — 2. Local — 3. Temporal — 4. Fig. uses — 5. Fixed phrases

Lit.: On preps. in general → ἀνά. — BAGD s.v. — BDF §§209-11. — K. Dieterich, *Indogermanische Forschungen* 24 (1909) 93-158. — Kühner, *Grammatik* II/1, 456-59. — G. Kuhring, *De praepositionum Graecarum in chartis Aegyptiis usu* (1906). — LSJ s.v. — Mayser, *Grammatik* II/2, 375-82. — Radermacher, *Grammatik* 235 (index).

1. With *ca.* 645 occurrences, distributed almost uniformly among the NT writings, ἀπό (always with gen.) ranks seventh in frequency among preps. in the NT (Morgenthaler, *Statistik* 160). However, in its use as a prefix with *ca.* 97 different vbs. (Morgenthaler 160) ἀπό ranks fifth in frequency (after σύν, ἐπί, κατά, and ἐκ/ἐξ). Moreover, ἀπό occurs as a prefix together with other prepositional prefixes (Morgenthaler 161) and in numerous nouns.

Originally ἀπό expresses departure from a person, object, or place. Further meanings developed out of this basic meaning. In the NT ἀπό also substitutes for the Attic preps. ἐκ, παρά, and ὑπό. E.g., the third Evangelist has taken over a Markan ἐκ/ἐξ 17 times, but replaced it with ἀπό 8 times. Furthermore, in the NT ἀπό assumes the function of the older partitive gen. (cf. Mayser 348).

2. Local use: a) With (1) vbs. which denote movement and frequently have ἀπό as a prep. prefix; vbs. which express separation from a place; vbs. which speak of separation in a broader sense (including Matt 14:2: raised *from* the dead [Mark has ἐκ]); and (2) vbs. with meanings such as "be ashamed," "be on guard," "conceal," or "hide," in which case the person or thing *before* which one is on guard, etc., is introduced by ἀπό.

b) In precise phrases of which there are no immediate examples in the classical language (BDF §211): μετανοεῖν ἀπὸ τῆς κακίας, repent *of* the wickedness (Acts 8:22; cf. Jer 8:6 LXX); ἀνάθεμα εἶναι ἀπὸ τοῦ Χριστοῦ, to be cut off by a curse *from* Christ (Rom 9:3); φθείρεσθαι ἀπὸ τῆς ἁπλότητος, to be led astray *from* (presently existing) sincerity (2 Cor 11:3); ἀποθνῄσκειν ἀπό, through death be *free from* (Col 2:20).

c) As a substitute for the gen. of separation (already in Herodotus vi.27; *Thucydides* vii.87.6; and Pap. Petrie III, 11:20; see further Moulton/Milligan s.v.): Matt 27:21 (which *of* the two?); Luke 9:38 (a man *from* [Mark has ἐκ] the crowd; cf. Luke 19:39); Mark 12:2 (λαμβάνειν ἀπὸ τῶν καρπῶν, receive *his portion of* the fruit); Acts 2:17, 18 (ἀπὸ τοῦ πνεύματός μου, *from (of)* my Spirit [Joel 3:1, 2 LXX]); 27:44 (τὰ ἀπὸ τοῦ πλοίου, the pieces of the ship, debris); with regard to foods from which one eats (Mark 7:28 par. Matt 15:27; Luke 16:21); Luke 22:18 similarly: drink *from* the fruit of the vine (Mark 14:25 has ἐκ).

d) In reference to a point of departure, *from, out from,* or *out of:* Mark 8:11, a sign *from* heaven (Matt 16:1; Luke 11:16 are different); Mark 15:38 par. Matt 27:51, *from* top to bottom; Matt 23:34, *from* one town to another; 24:31, ἀπ' ἄκρων οὐρανῶν, *from* one end of heaven (to the other; cf. Mark 13:27); Luke 24:47, beginning *from/in* Jerusalem; 1 Thess 1:8, (the word of the Lord sounded) *forth from* you; Rev 21:13, ἀπὸ βορρᾶ . . . ἀπὸ νότου, *on* the north . . . *on* the south (cf. Josh 18:5; 19:34; 1 Kgs 14:5).

e) In designations of distance: e.g., → μακρὰν ἀπό, *far from* (Matt 8:30; Luke 7:6) and ἀπὸ → μακρόθεν, *from a great distance* (Mark 14:54; 15:40; Luke 16:23) and in John 11:18, ὡς ἀπὸ σταδίων δεκαπέντε, about 15 stadia *(away) from;* similarly 21:8, about 200 cubits *away;* Rev 14:20, *(for)* about 1600 stadia. Ἀπὸ προσώπου (corresponding to Heb. *mipnê*), *away from* someone, *in front of* someone (Acts 3:20; 5:41; 7:45; 2 Thess 1:9 [Isa 2:10, 19, 21]; Rev 12:14; cf. Gen. 16:6; Jdt 2:14; 1 Macc 5:34; Jer 4:26; Sir 21:2; BDF §217.1).

f) Of source or origin, *from, out of* (BDF §209.3f.): Matt 3:13, *from* Galilee; John 3:2, come *from* God; 1:44, *from* Bethsaida; also Matt 4:25; 21:11; John 12:21; Acts 2:5; 6:9; 10:23; 17:13; Heb 13:24. Acts 12:1, οἱ ἀπὸ τῆς ἐκκλησίας denotes *membership* in the Church; likewise 15:5. To indicate the material from which something is made: Matt 3:4, *of camel's hair* (cf. Herodotus vii.65).

3. Temporal use: *from . . . on, since:* a) With reference to the point of time in the past from which an activity or condition is dated: Matt 9:22, *from* that hour; 22:46, *from* that day *(on)*; Luke 2:36, seven years *from* the time she was a virgin (i.e., since she had married); 8:43, *for* 12 years; Acts 23:23, *from (at)* the third hour of the night; Rom 1:20, *since* the creation of the world; 2 Cor 8:10, *since* last year; see also the expressions ἀπὸ τοῦ → νῦν, ἀπὸ → τότε, and ἀπ' → ἄρτι.

b) In the abbreviated expressions ἀφ' ἧς (Luke 7:45; Acts 24:11; 2 Pet 3:4 [cf. Col 1:6, 9]) and ἀφ' οὗ (Luke 13:7, 25; 24:21; Acts 16:18)—meaning *since*—ὥρας, ἡμέρας, or χρόνου is to be supplied.

c) Indicating a temporal limit *from* (some point) to (another point): ἀπό with ἕως (Matt 11:12; 27:45; Phil 1:5) or μέχρι (Acts 10:30; Rom 5:14).

4. Fig. meanings: a) Of source and origin: (1) with vbs. of asking and desiring to introduce the person *from* whom something is asked (Matt 5:42; Luke 11:51; 12:20; 1 Thess 2:6); (2) with vbs. of perception to indicate that *on the basis of* which something has been perceived (Mark 13:28 par. Matt 24:32, *learn from the fig tree*; Matt 7:16, 20, *by* their fruits). (3) 2 Cor 3:18 refers to source (and goal): *from* glory to glory.

b) Causal, to indicate: (1) the reason for something: *because of, as a result of, for*: Matt 18:7, *on account of* the damage caused (BDF §176.1); Luke 19:3, *because of* the crowd; Acts 22:11, *because of* the brilliance of the light; Heb 5:7, *because of* his piety (BDF §210.1); (2) the means by which a result is achieved: *with the help of, with*: Rev 18:25 (cf. Luke 15:16 A Koine, *with* the husks); (3) a motive: *from, for*: Matt 13:44, *for* joy; Luke 22:45, *for* sorrow; Acts 12:14, *for* fear; (4) the originator of that of which the vb. speaks: Matt 12:38, see a sign *from* you; Luke 22:71, ἀπὸ τοῦ στόματος, *from* his own mouth (15 times in the LXX; BDF §217.3); Acts 23:21; 1 Cor 11:23; referring to a more distant cause: Gal 1:1, *from* men; 2 Cor 3:18, ἀπὸ κυρίου πνεύματος, *from* the Lord the Spirit; in formulas of greeting: peace which proceeds *from* God (Rom 1:7; 1 Cor 1:3, etc., and, correspondingly, in the unique form of Rev 1:4); (5) *of* oneself, ἀφ' ἑαυτοῦ (-ῶν): Luke 12:57; 2 Cor 3:5; often in John (5:19, 30, etc.); (6) agency: with the pass. and vbs. with a pass. meaning the customary ὑπό is sometimes replaced by ἀπό (on classical usage see Kühner II/1, 457f.): Luke 8:43b, be healed *by*; Acts 2:22, attested *by* God; 4:36; 15:4; 20:9.

c) To indicate the beginning of a series: Matt 2:16; Luke 24:27; Jude 14. Occasionally the end is indicated with ἕως: Matt 1:17; 23:35; Acts 8:10.

5. Fixed phrases or expressions such as ἀπὸ μέρους, in part (Rom 11:25; 15:15, 24; 2 Cor 1:14; 2:5), ἀπὸ μιᾶς, at once, unanimously (Luke 14:18; an Aramaism? see BAGD s.v. ἀπό VI), ἀπὸ τῶν καρδιῶν, *from* (your) hearts (Matt 18:35), ἀπ' ἄνωθεν, *from* above (Mark 15:38).

G. Schneider

ἀποβαίνω *apobainō* go away, get out, lead to*

Luke 5:2 and John 21:9: *get out* of the ship; fig. in Luke 21:13 and Phil 1:19 (Job 13:16).

ἀποβάλλω *apoballō* throw away, take off*

Mark 10:50: *removal* of a garment; Heb 10:35 as an admonition: Do not throw away your παρρησία.

ἀποβλέπω *apoblepō* look at*

Heb 11:26: Moses "*looked to* the [heavenly] reward"; cf. Josephus *B.J.* ii.311; *Ant.* xx.61.

ἀπόβλητος, 2 *apoblētos* rejected*

1 Tim 4:4, of created things: they are good (καλός, Gen 1:31), not ἀπόβλητος (*rejected* by God).

ἀποβολή, ῆς, ἡ *apobolē* loss, rejection*

Acts 27:22: ἀποβολὴ ψυχῆς, referring to *loss* of life; Rom 11:15, referring to the *rejection* of the Jews by God.

ἀπογίνομαι *apoginomai* die*

1 Pet 2:24: ταῖς ἁμαρτίαις ἀπογενόμενοι, *died to sin* (cf. Rom 6:11). F. Büchsel, *TDNT* I, 686.

ἀπογραφή, ῆς, ἡ *apographē* list, registration, census*

ἀπογράφω *apographō* list, record (vb.)*

1. Occurrences in the NT — 2. Hellenistic usage — 3. The census in Luke 2 — 4. Heb 12:23

Lit.: P. W. Barnett, "ἀπογραφή and ἀπογράφεσθαι in Luke 2, 1-5," *ExpTim* 85 (1973/74) 377-80. — BAGD s.v. — H. Braunert, "Der römische Provinzialzensus und der Schätzungsbericht des Lk-Ev.," *Historia. Zeitschrift für alte Geschichte* 6 (1957) 192-214 (cf. E. Haenchen, *The Acts of the Apostles* [1971] 252f., n. 7). — J. Ernst, *Das Evangelium nach Lukas* (RNT, 1976) 101-4. — W. Grundmann, *Das Evangelium nach Lukas* (THKNT, 1961) 76-79. — H. U. Instinsky, *Das Jahr der Geburt Christi* (1957). — E. Klostermann, *Das Lukasevangelium* (HNT, [2]1929) 32-34. — G. M. Lee, "The Census in Luke," *CQR* 167 (1966) 431-36. — LSJ s.v. — I. H. Marshall, *Commentary on Luke* (NIGTC, 1978) 97-104. — H. R. MOEHRING, "The Census in Luke as an Apologetic Device," FS Wikgren 144-60. — G. OGG, "The Quirinius Question To-day," *ExpTim* 79 (1967/68) 231-36. — PREISIGKE, *Wörterbuch* I, 170-73; Supplement I, 30. — A. SCHALIT, *König Herodes* (1969) 265-78. — W. Schmithals, "Die Weihnachtsgeschichte Lk 2, 1-10," FS Fuchs 281-97. — SCHÜRER, *History* I, 399-427 (bibliography). — H. SCHÜRMANN, *Das Lukasevangelium* (HTKNT, 1969) I, 98-101. — E. STAUFFER, "Die Dauer des Census Augusti," FS E. Klostermann (TU 77, 1961) 9-34.

1. Ἀπογραφή occurs twice in the NT (Luke 2:2; Acts 5:37), the vb. 4 times (Luke 2:1, 3, 5; Heb 12:23). In Luke 2:1ff. the word designates a fiscal action of the Roman administration, a registration (census) for the purpose of taxation.

2. Ἀπογραφή is attested since the time of Lysias and Plato, and in inscriptions and the LXX as well. It is a t.t. of Attic and then Hellenistic legal and administrative language (as seen in the papyri). The vb. occurs (since Herodotus) in corresponding meanings and with the same circulation; it is esp. frequent in mid.: *have oneself entered in a list, inform by submitting an ἀπογραφή*.

3. The census referred to in Luke 2 did not, of course, take place in the year of Jesus' birth (at that point P. Sulpicius Quirinius was not governor in Syria) but not until A.D. 6-7 when Archelaus was deposed and Judea was incorporated into the province of Syria (Josephus *Ant.* xvii.355; xviii.1-5). It was the first time such an operation had been carried out in Judea, which may account for the lasting impression it made. Similar censuses, conducted on the basis of written or oral property declarations of the inhabitants of the provinces (not of Roman citizens) and more or less regularly repeated, but always regionally limited, are known from other provinces as well (Braunert 196ff.), e.g., from Gallia, Lusitania, and Egypt, whose census methods could have influenced the narrative in Luke 2:1-5 (cf. the census edict in Pap. London III, 904 [A.D. 104]). The connection of the Syrian census with the birth of Jesus and the expansion of this provincial census to a registration of the whole Empire (Luke 2:1) go back to Luke. Only in his conception of history are the history of Jesus and that of Christianity so closely bound to the history of the world (cf. 3:1; Acts 11:28; 26:26f.).

4. By contrast, the more general meaning of the term appears in Heb 12:23, as in *1 Enoch* 98:7f.; *Apoc. Paul* 10 (Hennecke/Schneemelcher II, 763). Ἀπογράφομαι here means to be *entered in the list* which is kept in heaven or in "the book of life" (cf. also Luke 10:20; Phil 4:3; Rev 3:5, etc.). Here an idea widespread in the OT and post-OT Jewish literature stands in the background (G. Schrenk, *TDNT* I, 618-20).

E. Plümacher

ἀπογράφω *apographō* list, record (vb.) → **ἀπογραφή**.

ἀποδείκνυμι *apodeiknymi* attest; cause (someone) to be (something); prove*
ἀπόδειξις, εως, ἡ *apodeixis* proof*

1. Occurrences in the NT and meaning — 2. Ἀποδείκνυμι — 3. Ἀπόδειξις

1. The vb. occurs 4 times in the NT. It is formed from → δείκνυμι, *show, display* and the prefix ἀπό, which here denotes a conclusion or the attainment of a goal (Schwyzer, *Grammatik* II, 445). Thus different nuances in meaning arise: *attest* (Acts 2:22; 2 Thess 2:4), *appoint, cause* (someone) *to be* (something) (1 Cor 4:9), and *prove* (Acts 25:7). The subst. occurs in the NT only in 1 Cor 2:4, where it means *proof.*

2. In Peter's speech (Acts 2:22) Jesus is spoken of as "*attested* [or *certified*] to you by God with mighty works and wonders and signs which God did through him in your midst." On the use of the vb. ἀποδείκνυμι cf. Esth 3:13c. The phrase has a primitive ring to it (M. Dibelius, *Studies in the Acts of the Apostles* [1956] 165). The christology which appears in it picks up the notion of the eschatological prophet who is attested by God (Hahn, *Titles* 376f.). The miracles of Jesus are regarded as the deeds of a charismatic person whom God has endowed (Hahn 380), indeed as the acts of God (on this "subordinationist" perspective of Lukan christology cf. Acts 2:36; H. Conzelmann, *The Theology of St. Luke* [1960] 173).

Close to the meaning *attest* is that of *proclaim* (Pap. Oxy. no. 1021, ll. 5ff., in Moulton/Milligan 60). It is behind the use of ἀποδείκνυμι in 2 Thess 2:4c: The Antichrist "takes his seat in the temple of God *proclaiming [attesting]* himself to be God" (on this subject cf. Ezek 28:2; *Sib. Or.* v.33; *Mart. Isa.* 4:6; on the Antichrist as "Son of God" see *Did.* 16:4; *Gk. Apoc. Ezra* 4:27).

Ἀποδείκνυμι is frequently used with the meaning *attest, appoint,* or *make* (cause to be). Whereas this normally refers to an honorific "appointment," e.g., as king (with God as the subject: Josephus *Ant.* vii.338; xi.3; cf. also vi.35) or as overseer (Dan 2:48 LXX; Josephus *Ant.* viii.162), Paul, in 1 Cor 4:9, verifies on the basis of his own experience and that of his coworkers Silvanus and Timothy (cf. 1 Thess 1:1) an entirely different kind of divine action: "For it seems to me that God *has made* us apostles the most abject of mankind (→ ἔσχατος). We are like men condemned to death (ἐπιθανάτιος)" (NEB). The apostles experience already in their own fate the eschatological reversal of rank (Mark 10:31; Luke 13:30), participate in Jesus' fate of suffering and death, and in precisely this way testify in their activity to the power of Jesus' life (ζωή) to overcome death (1 Cor 4:10-13; 2 Cor 4:7-12; 6:4-10).

In the legal system ἀποδείκνυμι is used in the technical sense of *prove* (Pap. London 904, 84, in Moulton/Milligan 60; cf. 4 Macc 1:8); this is true for Acts 25:7 also in the context of a trial scene which is merely sketched: "And when he [Paul] had come, the Jews who had gone down from Jerusalem stood about him, bringing against him many serious charges (αἰτίωμα) which they could not *prove.*"

3. Paul uses the subst. **ἀπόδειξις** in the sense of *proof:* "My speech and my message (→ κήρυγμα) were not in plausible (πειθός) words of wisdom (→ σοφία), but in *demonstration* of the Spirit and power (→ δύναμις)" (1 Cor 2:4). It is disputed whether in looking back to his initial proclamation, which, in view of the accomplished goal, namely, the faith of the Corinthians (2:5; cf. 1:4-7), he regards as thoroughly convincing, Paul uses ἀπόδειξις merely in the general sense of *manifestation* (H. Conzelmann, *1 Corinthians* [Hermeneia] 55; C. K. Barrett, *1 Corinthians* [HNTC] 65; cf. 3 Macc 4:20; Philo *Vit. Mos.* i.95 for the juxtaposition of two uses of ἀπόδειξις: oracular saying and the clearer ἀπόδειξις through signs and wonders), or, what is far more likely, with a deliberate play on the technical use of the word in ancient rhetoric (J. Weiss, *Der erste Korintherbrief* [KEK] 50; E. B. Allo, *Premiere Épître aux Corinthiens* [ÉBib] 25; L. Hartmann, "Some Remarks on 1 Cor 2:1-5," *SEÅ* 39 [1974] 109-20, esp. 116f.).

In ancient rhetoric ἀπόδειξις, πίστωσις, and κατασκευή denote the orderly, logical, or dialectical argumentation in the body of speech (H. Hommel and K. Ziegler, "Rhetorik," PW IV, 1396-1414, esp. 1414; cf. Plato *Ti.* 40e; Aristotle *EN* i.3.4; *Rh.* i.1355a.6ff.; Quintilian *Inst.* v.10.7 [ἀπόδειξις *est evidens probatio*]; Epictetus *Diss.* i.24.8; 4 Macc 3:19). Paul concedes the deficiencies in rhetorical performance and the art of persuasion in his initial preaching, which the Corinthian critics have censured (cf. 1 Cor. 2:1). He deliberately made no use of these things as an aid to the proclamation of the crucified One (v. 2). He claims for his preaching a special, nonrhetorical form of ἀπόδειξις which leads to persuasion. In contrast to rhetoric, this is based not on human wisdom (cf. v. 5) but on the power of God's Spirit which is effective in his preaching (subjective gen.: Weiss 49; Conzelmann 55; hendiadys: Weiss 50; Allo 25; cf. 1 Thess 1:5).

A similar juxtaposition of rhetorical skills (δεινότης λόγων, "eloquence," or ἐπίδειξις, "rhetorically ordered speech") and the sermon which is to communicate the meaning of the Scriptures, is found in Philo *Vit. Cont.* 31, 75 (cf. Plato *Phdr.* 260a: πείθειν vs. ἀλήθεια; *Ap.* 17a-c: πιθανῶς vs. ἀλήθεια, well-polished vs. simple words).

G. Dautzenberg

ἀπόδειξις, εως, ἡ *apodeixis* proof
→ ἀποδείκνυμι 1, 3.

ἀποδεκατεύω *apodekateuō* give one tenth, tithe

Luke 18:12 in $\mathfrak{p}^{75}$ B ℵ*, with πάντα (everything) as obj.: give a tithe of everything.

ἀποδεκατόω *apodekatoō* give one tenth, tithe; require a tithe, take a tithe*

Matt 23:23 par. Luke 11:42; Luke 18:12. In the meaning *require* or *take the tithe* in Heb 7:5 (cf. 1 Kgs 8:15, 16, 17).

ἀπόδεκτος, 2 *apodektos* acceptable, pleasing*

1 Tim 2:3; 5:4, both times: This is . . . ἀπόδεκτον before (ἐνώπιον τοῦ) God. W. Grundmann, *TDNT* II, 58f.

ἀποδέχομαι *apodechomai* receive (favorably)*

In the NT only in Luke-Acts. In Luke 8:40; 9:11; Acts 18:27; 21:17; 28:30; Ignatius *Eph.* 1:1; *Trall.* 1:2: *to welcome.* Referring to acceptance of the "word": Acts 2:41; referring to the respectful *reception* of Paul and Barnabas in Jerusalem: 15:4 v.l.; of the laudatory *recognition* of the administration of Felix by Tertullus: 24:3. W. Grundmann, *TDNT* II, 55.

ἀποδημέω *apodēmeō* go on a journey*

Mark 12:1 par. Matt 21:33/Luke 20:9; Matt 25:14, 15; Luke 15:13. 2 Cor 5:6 D (G): ἀποδημοῦμεν ἀπὸ τοῦ κυρίου, *be away from the Lord.*

ἀπόδημος, 2 *apodēmos* away on a journey, absent*

Mark 13:34: ἄνθρωπος ἀπόδημος, *someone who is away on a journey.*

ἀποδίδωμι *apodidōmi* give away, give back, repay*

1. Occurrences and meaning — 2. Usage — 3. In ethical contexts — 4. In theological contexts

Lit.: F. Büchsel, *TDNT* II, 166-73. — H. Braun, *Gerichtsgedanke und Rechtfertigungslehre bei Paulus* (UNT 19, 1930) 2-11, 14-31. — J. D. M. Derrett, *Law in the NT* (1970) 32-47 (the unmerciful servant), 313-37 ("Render to Caesar . . ."). — C. Dietzfelbinger, "Das Gleichnis von der erlassenen Schuld. Eine theologische Untersuchung von Mt 18, 23-35," *EvT* 32 (1972) 437-51. — L. Goppelt, "Die Freiheit zur Kaisersteuer," *Ecclesia und Res Publica* (FS K. D. Schmidt; 1961) 40-50. — C. F. D. Moule, "Punishment and Retribution," *SEÅ* 30 (1965) 21-36. — W. Pesch, *Der Lohngedanke in der Lehre Jesu* (MTS I/7, 1955). — *idem, Matthäus der Seelsorger* (SBS 1, 1966) (on Matthew 18). — J. N. Sevenster, " 'Geeft den keizer wat des keizers is, en God wat Gods is,' " *NedTTs* 17 (1962) 21-31. — S. H. Travis, *Divine Retribution in the Thought of Paul* (Diss. Cambridge, 1970). — A. Weiser, *Die Knechtsgleichnisse der synoptischen Evangelien* (SANT 24, 1971) 75-104 (on Matt 18:23-35). — For further bibliography see *TWNT* X, 1047.

1. The 48 NT occurrences of the vb. are distributed among nearly all of the NT writings. It is entirely absent in John. Paul (5 occurrences) and the post-Pauline tradi-

tion (3 occurrences in the Pastorals) use it only rarely. By contrast, it is a favorite word in Matthew, which has 18 occurrences, though 2 of these are from Q (Luke 12:59 par. Matt 5:26) and Mark (12:17); it occurs, by contrast, only 10 times in L and Acts (6 in the Gospel, 4 in Acts). But of the 16 occurrences particular to Matthew, 7 are in the parable of the king's settlement of accounts (Matt 18:23-35).

The compound of δίδωμι formed with ἀπό means *give away, give out, yield,* and *give back, repay, recompense.* Fixed phrases are ἀποδίδωμι (τὸν) λόγον, *give account* (Matt 12:36; Luke 16:2; Acts 19:40; Heb 13:17; 1 Pet 4:5; Rom 14:12 v.l.), ἀποδίδωμι τοὺς ὅρκους, *keep oaths* (Matt 5:33), ἀποδίδωμι τὸ μαρτύριον, *testify* (Acts 4:33). The mid. form means *sell* (Acts 5:8; 7:9; Heb 12:16; cf. BAGD s.v. 4; LSJ s.v. III).

2. Ἀποδίδωμι is used metaphorically in Heb 12:11 (cf. Lev 26:4 LXX): discipline is unpleasant, but finally *bears* "the peaceful fruit of righteousness." According to Rev 22:2 the tree of life (ξύλον ζωῆς, cf. Gen 2:9) *bears* fruit, i.e., the fullness of life (cf. Ezek 47:12).

Other than in those two instances the subj. of ἀποδίδωμι is always a person, who, for instance, *puts away* a book (Luke 4:20, with Jesus the subj.), *hands over* the body (of Jesus; Matt 27:58), *turns over* the fruits of the harvest (21:41), *repays* additional costs (Luke 10:35), *pays back* fraudulent charges (19:8), *pays out* wages (Matt 20:8), or *fulfills* a certain obligation (12:17 par.). The subj.-obj. relationship is more personal when a child is *given back* to his father (Luke 9:42), when a man *renders* to his wife that to which she is entitled (1 Cor 7:3), when each *gives* to the other what is due (Rom 13:7: φόρος, τέλος, φόβος, τιμή), when repayment of a debt is required of someone (Matt 5:26 par. Luke 12:59; Matt 18:23-35; Luke 7:42), or when that which one has received from one's parents is to be *returned* to them (1 Tim 5:4).

God is the subj. as the one who *rewards* persons (Matt 6:4, 6, 18: in each case καὶ ὁ πατήρ σου . . . ἀποδώσει σοι) and judges persons according to their works (Rom 2:6; 2 Tim 4:14). In three texts Jesus is the subj., he who will *repay* each one according to what that person has done (Matt 16:27), *give* to everyone the proper recompense (Rev 22:12), and at his epiphany *award* (Paul) the crown of righteousness (2 Tim 4:8).

3. The vb. takes on the sense of ethical obligation when it is used in connection with proper and just conduct or the repayment of a debt, as in Mark 12:17 par. Matt 22:21; Luke 20:25. Jesus' reply to the question whether payment of taxes to Caesar is permitted (ἔξεστιν) is in the form of an imv.: "*Render* to Caesar the things that are Caesar's, and to God the things that are God's." Since the introduction is redactional (Derrett 314: a "constructed unit"), since the apophthegm is to be taken as instruction to the disciples and not as a statement about Jesus, and, finally, since the vb. is missing from the narrative which provides the context for this logion, the sense of ἀποδίδωμι (which in Matthew and Luke is strengthened by an adv. and placed at the beginning of the quoted sentence for emphasis) is to be grasped solely on the basis of Jesus' reply. The instruction of Jesus has nothing to do with the coin as such, nor does it deal with a specific emperor or tax, but rather gives expression to the comprehensive commandment: Obey the regulations of the governing authorities, obey (to a special degree) the demand of God. To the one with a legitimate claim to legal rights one must give those legal rights. The answer of Jesus extends beyond the individual case he is asked to interpret to that which is generally obligatory.

Three times in the NT ἀποδίδωμι is used in the expression of a major rule of Christian conduct: Evil is not to be *repaid* with evil, but with good (1 Thess 5:15; Rom 12:17; 1 Pet 3:9 [sharpened by the addition of λοιδορίαν ἀντὶ λοιδορίας]). There is no corresponding rule in the OT (Prov 20:22 is only a remote analogy). Of course, the OT prohibits the repayment of good with evil (Gen 44:4; Jer 18:20, etc.), but a discussion of the question of how one is to conduct oneself when confronted by evil first begins to emerge in Rabbinic Judaism (cf. Billerbeck I, 368, 370; III, 299); the Qumran community also was a long way from a positive answer (according to 1QS 1:4 the members of the community were to "love all that he [God] has chosen and hate all that he has rejected"; cf. also 9:21; *2 Enoch* 50:4). The primitive Christian rule recalls the command of Jesus to love the enemy (Matt 5:44, 46, 47; Luke 6:27f., 32f.) and has its origin in Hellenistic Christian communities which had been decisively influenced by Paul.

In Rev 18:6 the second angel admonishes: "*Render* to her as she herself *has rendered,* and repay her double for her deeds." At the judgment Babylon is to receive what she has done to others. It is a matter of dispute who the subj. of the repayment is. But surely one is not to think here of the Antichrist or of the minor kings of ch. 17 (since they are on Babylon's side), but rather of the people of God, who accomplish the judgment under God's commission.

4. The texts mentioned above (→ 3) have already moved partially beyond a purely ethical meaning. Theological relevance is esp. clear where ἀποδίδωμι is connected with the idea of forgiveness of sins and the judgment of humanity. In Matt 6:4, 6, 18 God is presented as the Father who will reward the disciples according to their works. This idea, so important for Matthew, is fully developed in the parable of the king who settles accounts with his servants, Matt 18:23-35 (M); the motif of μακροθυμία (μακροθυμέω, vv. 26, 29) brings two narratives

together into an inner unity. The question regarding the frequency of forgiveness occurs already in Q (Luke 17:4 par. Matt 18:21f.). Whereas Luke is content to emphasize that one's forgiveness must be unlimited, Matthew attempts to clarify this further with a parable. However, the parable has a somewhat different accent; in it the issue is repayment (ἀποδίδωμι in vv. 25, 26, 28, 29, 30, 34) and forgiveness is first mentioned again in the redactional summary in v. 35. Against the background of Hellenistic financial practice (cf. Derrett 38) the parable gives expression to the idea that the life of the Church must be determined by generosity and mercy rather than by unmerciful conduct based on legal rights; for on the day of God's judgment every person will be called to render account and will be *requited* according to his or her works (Matt 12:36; Rom 2:6; 2 Tim 4:14 [according to Matt 16:27; 2 Tim 4:8; Rev 22:12 it is Christ who will conduct the judgment]).

A. Sand

ἀποδιορίζω *apodiorizō* separate*

In Jude 19 the pres. partc. designates *those who cause division.* K. L. Schmidt, *TDNT* V, 455f.

ἀποδοκιμάζω *apodokimazō* reject*

Referring to the "stone" which *is rejected* (Mark 12:10 par. Matt 21:42/Luke 20:17; 1 Pet 2:4, 7). With persons as obj.: the Son of Man (Mark 8:31 par. Luke 9:22; 17:25); Esau (Heb 12:17; cf. Gen 27:30-38). W. Grundmann, *TDNT* II, 255-60.

ἀποδοχή, ῆς, ἡ *apodochē* acceptance, approval*

1 Tim 1:15; 4:9, in the formula: "The saying is sure and worthy of full *acceptance.*" W. Grundmann, *TDNT* II, 55f.; N. Brox, *Pastoralbriefe* (RNT) 112-14.

ἀπόθεσις, εως, ἡ *apothesis* removal*

1 Pet 3:21: the *removal* of dirt (in baptism); 2 Pet 1:14 euphemistically for death: "the *putting off* of my body."

ἀποθήκη, ης, ἡ *apothēkē* barn, storehouse*

Matt 3:12 par. Luke 3:17; Matt 6:26; 13:30; Luke 12:18, 24.

ἀποθησαυρίζω *apothēsaurizō* store up
→ θησαυρός.

ἀποθλίβω *apothlibō* press upon*

Luke 8:45, referring to the ὄχλοι that *press in upon* Jesus.

ἀποθνῄσκω *apothnęskō* die
→ θάνατος.

ἀποκαθίστημι, ἀποκαθιστάνω *apokathistēmi, apokathistanō* restore*

1. Occurrences in the NT — 2. The Synoptic miracle stories — 3. The eschatological restoration of Israel (Acts 1:6) — 4. Ἀποκατάστασις (Acts 3:21)

Lit.: O. Bauernfeind, "Tradition und Komposition in den Apokatastasisspruch Apg 3, 20f," FS Michel 13-23. — R. Beauvery, "La guérison d'un aveugle à Bethsaida," *NRT* 90 (1968) 1082-91. — Billerbeck IV/2, 764-98. — Bousset/Gressmann 232ff., 249. — U. Busse, *Die Wunder des Propheten Jesus* (1977) 135-41. — J. Dey, "Restoration," *SacVb* II, 750-54. — E. L. Dietrich, שׁוב שְׁבוּת. *Die endzeitliche Wiederherstellung bei den Propheten* (1925) 38-51. — G. Molin, "Der Prophet Elijahu und sein Weiterleben in den Hoffnungen des Judentums und der Christenheit," *Judaica* 4 (1952) 65-94. — F. Mussner, "Die Idee der Apokatastasis in der Apg," *idem, Praesentia Salutis* (1967) 223-34. — F. Mussner and J. Loosen, *LTK* I, 708-12. — J. M. Nützel, *Die Verklärungserzählung im Markusevangelium* (FzB 6, 1973). — A. Oepke, *TDNT* I, 387-93. — R. Pesch, *Das Markusevangelium* (HTKNT, 1976-77) II, 69-84. — M. E. Thrall, "Elijah and Moses in Mark's Account of the Transfiguration," *NTS* 16 (1969/70) 305-17. — T. L. Wilkinson, "The Role of Elijah in the NT," *Vox Reformata* 10 (1968) 1-10. — W. Wink, *John the Baptist in the Gospel Tradition* (1968) 13-18. — A. S. van der Woude, *Die messianischen Vorstellungen der Gemeinde von Qumran* (1957) 172-76.

1. The vb. occurs 8 times in the NT (Matt 12:13; 17:11; Mark 3:5; 8:25; 9:12; Luke 6:10; Acts 1:6; Heb 13:19). In the NT as in secular Greek it has the basic meaning of *restore, put back in the original condition.* Already in the LXX the vb. is used to refer to the eschatological restoration of Israel from the Diaspora (cf. the eschatological announcement of salvation in exilic prophecy: Jer 16:15; 23:8; 24:6; Hos 2:3; 6:11; 11:11; Pss 14:7; 85:2; see H. D. Preuss, *Jahweglaube und Zukunftserwartung* [1968] 61 [bibliography]).

2. In the Synoptic account of Jesus' healing of a man with a withered (paralyzed or crippled) hand on the sabbath (Mark 3:1-6 par.) ἀποκαθίστημι designates the healing of the hand as a result of the royal-eschatological command of Jesus, "Stretch out your hand." Jesus counters the Pharisaic position in the sabbath controversy by tracing the Torah back to its original redemptive purpose, namely, to mediate God's salvation to mankind. The restoration of the crippled hand demonstrates the new, superior order of salvation which is present in the coming of Jesus, the dawn of the eschatological time of salvation which restores to the sabbath commandment its profound significance: *restoration* of human beings in their integrity as part of God's creation; the same is seen in 8:25 (the healing of the blind man of Bethsaida).

The saying of Jesus in the context of the transfiguration narrative, "Elijah does come first to *restore* all things" (Mark 9:12 par. Matt 17:11), picks up the OT and Jewish idea of the eschatological function of Elijah (cf. Mal 3:23f.; Sir 48:10; 2 Kgs 2:11). Elijah redivivus, connected to John the Baptist by Matthew (17:12f.), brings about the rehabilitation of the people of God promised in Isa 11:1-12; Jer 12:14-17; Amos 9:11. The question of the disciples in Acts 1:6 refers to this idea of restoration (→ 3).

3. In the ascension narrative (Acts 1:4-12) Jesus promises the outpouring of the Spirit as a result of which the disciples expect the restoration of Israel within the framework of the events of the end time. But Jesus corrects the restoration hope which focuses on Israel and calls the attention of his disciples to the universal mission from a worldwide perspective. The Risen One is the one "who has led the way to life" (Acts 3:15 NEB) for all peoples of the world; he frees Judaism's hope of redemption from the confines of nationalism and extends it to all the peoples of the world.

4. **Ἀποκατάστασις** *restoration** occurs in the NT only in Acts 3:21: "Then the Lord may grant you a time of recovery and send you the Messiah he has already appointed, that is, Jesus. He must be received into heaven until the time of universal *restoration* comes, of which God spoke by his holy prophets" (NEB; mg. adds "from the beginning of the world"). In accord with the Jewish principle that end time = primeval time, the Messiah is expected to bring about the eschatological return of things to their original state, the universal renewal of the world which reestablishes the original integrity of creation. The Christ of the parousia will bring about the promised restoration of the cosmic universe. The apokatastasis speculation of Origen is concerned not only with the return of the universe to the harmony of a comprehensive order of being but also with the notion of a cosmic reconciliation of the universe as the anthropological destiny of mankind (so F. Schleiermacher); it has only indirect support in Acts 3:21.

P.-G. Müller

ἀποκαλύπτω *apokalyptō* reveal*
ἀποκάλυψις, εως, ἡ *apokalypsis* disclosure, revelation*

1. Occurrences and usage — 2. The Synoptic tradition — 3. Paul and the deutero-Pauline sphere — 4. 1 Peter — 5. Ἀποκάλυψις in Revelation — 6. The understanding of revelation in the NT.

Lit.: D. Aune, *Prophecy in Early Christianity* (1983). — O. Betz, *Offenbarung und Schriftforschung in der Qumransekte* (1960). — R. Bultmann, "The Concept of Revelation in the NT," *idem, Existence and Faith* (1960) 58-91. — G. Dautzenberg, *Urchristliche Prophetie. Ihre Erforschung, ihre Voraussetzungen im Judentum und ihre Struktur im ersten Korintherbrief* (1975). — P. Hoffmann, "Die Offenbarung des Sohnes," *Kairos* 12 (1970) 270-88. — K. Kertelge, "Apokalypsis Jesou Christou (Gal 1, 12)," FS Schnackenburg 266-81. — D. Lührmann, *Das Offenbarungsverständnis bei Paulus und in paulinischen Gemeinden* (1965). — *idem, Die Redaktion der Logienquelle* (1969) 60-68, 97-100. — A. Oepke, *TDNT* III, 563-92. — A. Polag, *Die Christologie der Logienquelle* (1977) 160-62. — H. Schulte, *Der Begriff der Offenbarung im NT* (1949). — P. Stuhlmacher, *Das paulinischen Evangelium* I (1968) 76-83. — A. Vögtle, "Zum Problem der Herkunft von Mt 16, 17-19," FS Schmid (1973) 372-93. — U. Wilckens, "Das Offenbarungsverständnis in der Geschichte des Urchristentums," *Offenbarung als Geschichte* (*KD* Beiheft 1 [1961], ed. W. Pannenberg) 42-90. — C. Westermann and R. Albertz, *THAT* I, 418-26. — H.-J. Zobel, *TDOT* II, 476-88.

1. Both noun and vb. occur in the NT, always with a religious meaning. The passage which comes nearest to the (rare) pagan usage, which is wholly secular ("uncover something which is hidden"), is Luke 2:35, a passage which also corresponds partially to the usage of the words in the LXX and—significantly—completely to that in Josephus. But even there it is the Messiah, set for a sign, to whom the hidden (evil) thoughts of human beings *are to be uncovered* (cf. 1 Cor 3:13; *T. Reu.* 3:15; *T. Jos.* 6:6; *Jos. As.* 12:3 [4]). The entire word group is not esp. frequent in the NT (44 occurrences: vb. 26, noun 18); it is absent from Mark, Acts, the Pastorals, James, 2 Peter, 1–3 John, and Jude; only the vb. appears in John's Gospel and it only in 12:38 in a quotation from Isa 53:1 LXX; only the noun appears in Revelation and it only in 1:1.

2. In the Q material the vb. occurs in contexts apparently related to each other (Matt 10:26 par.; 11:25-27 par.). Matt 10:26 par. uses an apocalyptic saying (see already Deut 29:28; then *1 Enoch* 51:3; *2 Bar.* 54:1ff.; cf. G. Bornkamm, *TDNT* IV, 816) as the basis for the confidence which those who preach may have; in Matt 11:25-27 par. it is the basis for the authorization of the disciples to preach. The latter is composed of two logia, the first speaking of the concealment of God's eschatological activity from the wise and its unveiling to the simple (cf. *2 Bar.* 54:4f.), the second of the necessary mediation of such *unveiling* through the Son (cf. *1 Enoch* 48:7; 62:7). Here also the apocalyptic background is clear (see esp. Hoffmann). Now, however, ἀποκαλύπτω no longer refers so much to the uncovering of something previously concealed as it does, rather, to the opening up of a reality which is by its very nature veiled. According to Luke 2:32 (which belongs to the Palestinian Jewish Christian tradition) the Messiah is the "light for revelation [of the reality of God] to the Gentiles," a hymnic statement formed on the basis of Isa 42:6f.; 49:9. The idea that what was previously hidden is discovered in the strict apocalyptic sense is present in Luke 17:30: the still concealed Son of Man will be *revealed* by God, i.e., presented publicly.

This idea, which goes back by way of Q to the earliest tradition, has experienced a characteristic alteration in Matt 16:17. It is possible that this saying has undergone elaboration by Matthew under the influence of 11:25-27, but it must have come to him in substance together with 16:18f., since—as seems likely—it reflects the first appearance of the Risen Christ to Peter. Not for the first time at the end of days, but already now God effectively *reveals* the Christ for who he is, and thereby establishes the eschatological community (cf. *Jos. As.* 16:14 [7]!).

3. In Gal 1:12, 16 Paul also uses both noun and vb. for the "revelation" of God's Son that has been given to him, i.e., for his experience of being called. It is by means of this event, according to 1 Cor 15:8, that Paul knows himself to be included in the ranks of the apostles. There he describes the event with the word ὤφθη; in 9:1 he uses ἑόρακα. In Galatians 1 he employs the word group under discussion so as to emphasize more strongly the theological significance of the event, namely, that with the *revelation* of the crucified one as Son of God the gospel itself is disclosed to him.

Thus Rom 1:17 says that the gospel, the essential character of which resides, according to 1:1-4, in the divine sonship of Jesus, *reveals* the righteousness of God through faith for faith. That this revelation, like the "revelation" of the Son, is to be understood as eschatological event, is made clear by v. 18: along with the gospel, God's actions by which he rejects people are *revealed*—as the divine eschatological judgment. Gal 3:23 speaks of the future (seen from the perspective of the period of the law) faith *to be revealed;* v. 24 shows that again it is God's act in Christ which is meant, as seen from the perspective of the human recipient (cf. Rom 3:21).

Alongside this experience of the present disclosure of salvation and judgment which corresponds with the basic structure of Paul's theological thought there nonetheless remains in his thinking the expectation of the future revelation of Christ and the reality grounded in him. According to 1 Cor 1:7 the Church anticipates "the revealing of our Lord Jesus Christ" (cf. 4 Ezra 7:28; Luke 17:30); 2 Thess 1:7 points to the same event, though, of course, in more clearly apocalyptic detail. Apocalyptic thinking is also the source of the expectation that prior to the "parousia" (2 Thess 2:1) the incarnation of evil will *appear* (vv. 3, 6, 8); the pass. indicates that this "parousia" (vv. 8f.) is also included in God's plan.

The *appearance* of Jesus (1 Cor 1:7; 2 Thess 1:7) discloses salvation and judgment. Rom 8:18f. looks forward to the final exhibition of glory, the glory of the children of God, and 2:5 to the *appearance* of God's righteous judgment (cf. *1 Enoch* 91:7, 14). In the eschatological unveiling of present reality not merely is what already exists in somewhat hidden form disclosed, but rather the new, fulfilled reality makes its appearance.

In addition, Paul is familiar with other uses of the word group, which obviously still possessed a certain terminological flexibility. In 2 Cor 12:1, 7 the noun denotes the unveiling of heavenly matters which Paul experienced in an ecstatic state (cf. *2 Bar.* 76:1 [cf. Stuhlmacher 75f. n. 3]; *3 Apoc. Bar.* 11:7). By contrast the spiritual gift called ἀποκάλυψις in 1 Corinthians 14 is distinguished in v. 6 from glossalalia and grouped together with "knowledge or prophecy or teaching"; it is thus understood as something presented in an understandable fashion. In v. 26 prophecy does not accompany ἀποκάλυψις in the list of forms of expression in the worship service; in v. 30 the reception of a prophecy is denoted by ἀποκαλύπτεσθαι. Thus it appears that the ἀποκάλυψις is connected with the prophecy (see Dautzenberg). This makes comprehensible Gal 2:2 on the one hand (where Paul himself is surely to be understood as the recipient of the *revelation*), and Phil 3:15 and 1 Cor 2:10 on the other where, in each case, the *revealing* of a more profound knowledge of God is the issue (cf. 1 Cor. 13:2; Dautzenberg 150ff.; *idem,* "Botschaft und Bedeutung der urchristlichen Prophetie nach dem ersten Korintherbrief [2:6-16; 12–14]," *Prophetic Vocation in the NT and Today* [ed. J. Panagopoulos; NovTSup 45, 1977] 131-61 [even if Dautzenberg is somewhat one-sided]); whether an ironic and polemical undertone is heard in 1 Cor 2:10 and Phil 3:15 is uncertain since examples of usage which could serve as a basis for comparison are unknown.

In the deutero-Pauline sphere the vb. and the noun are used to designate the *revelation* of the Gospel, esp. the revelation of it received by Paul (Eph 3:3, 5; Rom 16:25). The "revelation schema" (that which was previously unknown is now revealed) is thereby employed (of course, ἀποκαλύπτω is not a terminologically firm element of the scheme; cf. Eph 3:10: γνωρισθῇ; Lührmann, *Offenbarungsverständnis* 125, n. 2). Eph 1:17 apparently speaks of the charismatic prophetic spirit.

4. Whereas in the deutero-Pauline sphere the word group refers strictly to the *revelation* of the gospel and the charismatic spirit in the Church, in 1 Peter it refers to the coming *revelation* of the parousia or to a *revelation* to the (OT) prophets who announced the salvation which comes with Christ (1:12). Apparently the latter is understood in such a way that both the announcement of salvation and the fact that it will first be effective at some future time were revealed to the prophets. The idea articulated in 1QpHab 7:1f. ("God told Habakkuk to write down the things that were to come upon the latter age, but did not inform him when that moment would come to fulfillment [*gmr hqṣ*]"), is extended to all prophets of the Messiah and understood to be an element of their prophetic knowledge, of which they are made aware (by God). In 1 Pet 1:7, 13; 4:13 the noun denotes the *parousia,* and in 1:5; 5:1 the vb.

designates the *unveiling* of eschatological salvation and its glory at the parousia.

5. Finally, the noun occurs in Rev 1:1 and is used very nearly as a book title (which it soon becomes—as well as the designation for a genre): "The *revelation* of Jesus Christ." This expression is intended to summarize the contents of the entire book which follows: the *disclosure* of history up to its goal in the holy Jerusalem, which descends from heaven, through Jesus Christ who thus exposes both God's redemptive activity and the divine work of judgment. (In 22:18 the content of the book is described as προφητεία; on the combination of concepts cf. Amos 3:7.)

6. The NT understanding of "revelation" as the term is used in dogmatics cannot be fully explicated by means of an investigation of the word group and its use in the NT. Nor would this be possible by including the synonyms (cf. φανερόω in Rom 3:21; similarly Mark 4:22 par. Luke 8:17). In the NT the word group is just in the process of attaining a firm religious content. The essential preparation for this is to be found in the Jewish apocalyptic literature.

According to the NT understanding, God reveals himself as he who acts in history. Because of this it is not surprising that in the most significant NT uses of the word group the idea of the uncovering of things which had previously already existed but were merely hidden retreats, even though this is, in fact, the original meaning of the word group. And since, according to the NT, the decisive action of God occurs in the history of Jesus Christ, the word group clearly refers, insofar as it is used with reference to the actual event of revelation at all, to the *disclosure* of the reality of God as it is given with this history.

T. Holtz

ἀποκάλυψις, εως, ἡ *apokalypsis* disclosure, revelation
→ ἀποκαλύπτω.

ἀποκαραδοκία, ας, ἡ *apokaradokia* (earnest, intense) expectation*

Lit.: W. Aly, "Herodots Sprache," *Glotta* 15 (1927) 84-117, esp. 104f. — H. Balz, *Heilsvertrauen und Welterfahrung. Strukturen der paulinischen Eschatologie nach Röm 8, 18-39* (BEvT 59, 1971) 36f. — G. Bertram, "Ἀποκαραδοκία," *ZNW* 49 (1958) 264-70. — G. Delling, *TDNT* I, 393. — D. R. Denton, "Ἀποκαραδοκία," *ZNW* 73 (1982) 138-40. — Frisk, *Wörterbuch* I, s.v. καραδοκέω. — E. Hoffmann, *DNTT* II, 244-46. — E. Käsemann, *Commentary on Romans* (1980) 230-45 (bibliography). — G. Schläger, "Das ängstliche Harren der Kreatur. Zur Auslegung von Röm 8, 19ff," *NorTT* 19 (1930) 353-60. — H. Schlier, *Der Römerbrief* (HTKNT, 1977) on 8:19. — A. Viard, "Exspectatio Creaturae (Rom. 8, 19-22)," *RB* 59 (1952) 337-54, esp. 340.

1. The subst. ἀποκαραδοκία occurs only twice in the NT (Rom 8:19; Phil 1:20). It is not attested in non-Christian sources. However, the vb. ἀποκαραδοκέω, "to await," is attested (e.g., Polybius xvi.2.8; Ps 36:7 Aquila in place of ἱκετεύω LXX for Heb. *hiṯḥôlēl*, "wait"). More widely known is the simple form καραδοκέω, used, e.g., of awaiting the outcome of a war (Herodotus vii.163, 168; Ps 129:5 Aquila in place of ὑπομένω for Heb. *hôḥîl*, "wait"). Καραδοκία occurs likewise in the version of Aquila in Ps 38:8 in place of LXX ὑπόστασις and in Prov 10:28 in place of LXX ἐγχρονίζει, both times for Heb. *tôḥelet*, as an expression for the "steadfast waiting" of the faithful for God; it occurs also in Phil 1:20 G *pc* as v.l. for ἀποκαραδοκία.

It is likely that Paul himself coined the noun ἀποκαραδοκία, formed from the prep. ἀπό, the substantive κάρα, "head," and the vb. δέκομαι (= Attic δέχομαι), "accept" (of which derivatives are δοκεύω, "watch closely," and προς-δοκάω, "expect"). Already in the early Church Pauline exegesis was unable to arrive at a uniform interpretation of ἀποκαραδοκία. Thus, e.g., Theodore of Mopsuestia, commenting on Rom 8:19, explains καραδοκέω by means of ἐλπίζω, but ἀποκαραδοκέω negatively by means of ἀπελπίζω as "lose hope" (see Staab, *Pauluskommentare* 137, 9f.), whereas the majority of the Fathers understand ἀποκαραδοκία as an intensification of καραδοκία and thus as an esp. strong expression of expectation (Bertram 268f.). Etymologically (ἀπο)-καραδοκία is frequently explained as a metaphor with the basic meaning "stretching forth the head" or "looking after something" (cf. Delling; Hoffmann), but this explanation cannot be made to agree with either the formation or the uses of the word in a completely satisfying way (cf. Frisk; Balz). The occasional attempt to detect by means of a linguistic comparison with other compounds (such as ἀπελπίζω, ἀπογινώσκω, "despair") a weakened or even reversed meaning of the compound over against the simple form (e.g., Bertram 266-68; see above)—cf. the translation "anxious longing" (Luther: "ängstliches Harren") in Rom 8:19—breaks down in the face of Phil 1:20 where ἀποκαραδοκία stands with equal force alongside ἐλπίς. Aquila likewise made no distinction between the compound and the simple form (see above). Thus it remains most probable that with ἀποκαραδοκία Paul intends to give expression to the element of earnest and eager longing. The prep. ἀπό thereby strengthens the intensive character of the expression.

2. For the interpretation of both Pauline uses the context is decisive. In Phil 1:20 Paul speaks of his *eager expectation* (ἀποκαραδοκία) and "hope" (ἐλπίς) that he will not be brought to shame (before God) by anything, not even by a rival proclamation of Christ occasioned by his imprisonment and directed against him (vv. 12-17). Whereas → ἐλπίς in this context, as always in Paul, articulates the element of trust in God, the accompanying ἀποκαραδοκία emphasizes rather the vehement and unshakable expectation which constitutes the emotional dimension of hope (*contra* J. Gnilka, *Philipperbrief* [HTKNT] ad loc.).

Rom 8:19 views the "creation" (κτίσις) in a tension between, on the one hand, meaninglessness and transitoriness and, on the other, the freedom which consists in the glorification of the children of God. Here also ἀποκαραδοκία and ἐλπίς (ἐφ' ἐλπίδι, v. 20) can designate two aspects of the theological statement: ἀποκαραδοκία speaks of the unredeemed character of creation as the inherent state of eager longing for liberation, and ἐλπίς of the hope for future freedom which God guarantees the enslaved creation. This hope, built into the creation by God, is the ground of creation's ἀποκαραδοκία. For this reason "the creation waits with *eager longing* for the revealing of the sons of God."

H. Balz

ἀποκαταλλάσσω *apokatallassō* reconcile
→ καταλλάσσω.

ἀποκατάστασις, εως, ἡ *apokatastasis* restoration
→ ἀποκαθίστημι 4.

ἀπόκειμαι *apokeimai* be held in readiness*

Luke 19:20; Col 1:5; 2 Tim 4:8; Heb 9:27 impersonal: *it awaits, it is reserved.* F. Pfister, "Zur Wendung 'Απόκειταί μοι ὁ τῆς δικαιοσύνης στέφανος," *ZNW* 15 (1914) 94-96; F. Büchsel, *TDNT* III, 655.

ἀποκεφαλίζω *apokephalizō* behead*

In the NT only in connection with the beheading of John the Baptist: Mark 6:16 par. Luke 9:9; Mark 6:27 par. Matt 14:10.

ἀποκλείω *apokleiō* close*

Luke 13:25: the *closing* of the door by the householder.

ἀποκόπτω *apokoptō* cut off*

Mark 9:43, 45 in the injunction to *cut off* the hand or foot should they cause offense. In John 18:10, 26 ὠτάριον or ὠτίον is the obj. of the cutting off; Acts 27:32 speaks of the *cutting away* of the ropes. In Gal 5:12 the mid. is used in a (sarcastic) wish for the self-castration of Paul's adversaries. G. Stählin, *TDNT* III, 852-55.

ἀπόκριμα, ατος, τό *apokrima* decision; judicial sentence*

2 Cor 1:9: ἀπόκριμα τοῦ θανάτου, death *sentence.* F. Büchsel, *TDNT* III, 945f.

ἀποκρίνομαι *apokrinomai* answer, reply, begin speaking, continue speaking

1. Etymology and general usage — 2. Occurrences in the NT — 3. Usage and possible meanings — 4. Major emphases of the expression

Lit.: C. Barth, "Die Antwort Israels," *Probleme biblischer Theologie* (FS G. von Rad; 1971) 44-56. — BDF §§78; 420. — F. Büchsel, *TDNT* III, 944f.

1. The root word κρίνω in the meaning "sort, evaluate, select" is instructive in connection with "answer" as a considered reaction to a statement. The prep. ἀπό in the sense of "suitable, based upon (an evaluation)" underscores the element of circumspect selection and judgment. For this reason κρίνω/ἀποκρίνω can also be used forensically in the sense of *reject, pass judgment upon* (papyri, Plato). The mid. form ἀποκρίνομαι adds to this the dialogical character of conversation and debate: *have words, exchange words with each other.* The various aor. forms are grammatically noteworthy (aor. pass. ἀπεκρίθην is frequently attested in biblical Greek), as is the hebraicizing expression ἀποκριθεὶς εἶπεν (cf. BDF §420.2; BAGD s.v. 2) as a signal, characteristic of narrative style, for the beginning or continuation of a speech.

2. 'Αποκρίνομαι is found principally in the Gospels and Acts (altogether *ca.* 230 occurrences). John (78 occurrences) displays a slight predominance, followed by Luke (with Acts) and Matthew. Otherwise the vb. is found only in Col 4:6 (in a parenetic context) and Rev 7:13.

3. Usage is diverse and is itself suggestive of a number of possible meanings. The most frequent conversation partners are Jesus and other human beings, but angels (Luke 1:19, 35; Matt 28:5) and demons (Mark 5:9; Acts 19:15) are also included. In each case the type and manner of the answer is instructive of its content and aim.

Thus, e.g., according to Mark Jesus answers restrictively (3:33), commandingly (6:37), questioningly (10:3), emphatically (10:24), and in such a way as to extend the reply (12:29); in debates (often with a typical structure), primarily in a challenging way (11:29f.), confirming (12:34), uncovering (12:17 v.l.), or decisively (12:29-31); in the Passion narrative the Markan Jesus replies majestically (14:48; 15:2) or with silence (14:60f.; 15:5). According to Luke in particular Jesus expresses himself as disappointed (17:17), in prophetic exhortation (19:40), in aversion (22:51). It is striking that ἀποκρίνομαι is used only in connection with the pre-Easter Jesus. Even John respects this qualification, portraying his Christ with this term primarily in revelatory sayings (3:5; 4:13; 5:17, 19) and debates (6:26, 29).

When other human beings answer, it is either the disciples (Mark 8:4), Peter (v. 29), or one of the people (9:17). The response can have various forms: a request (Mark 7:28), a confession (8:29), confusion (9:5f.), embarrassment (11:33), understanding (12:34), a question (15:9), silence (14:40), criticism (Luke 23:40), or amazement (24:18). The dialogical element comes to expression in Luke 7:40, 43; 10:27, 28, and the narrative character, opening or continuing a conversation, in Mark 9:38 v.l.; Matt 15:23f., 26; in a similar sense in the Matthean parables, e.g., Matt 13:11, 37; 22:1; 25:9, 12, 26, 37, 40, 44f. (here specifically in an eschatological milieu). An answer may (Mark 8:29) or may not (9:5f.) be preceded by a question.

4. From the various examples and diverse usages one can determine the following major emphases for ἀποκρίνομαι: For one thing, the word belongs to the colloquial speech of Jesus. But it can also be an expression of his self-consciousness and his awareness of his having been sent (in debates, in the Passion, less frequently in miracle pericopes). However, it remains limited to the pre-Easter Jesus and is thus at home "theologically" in the human sphere. With regard to other human beings ἀποκρίνομαι can characterize the different nuances of human conversation, can esp. describe reactions to Jesus, or can simply be used as a term in narrative (as in the parables). The word always attains a decidedly more profound meaning whenever "critical" points are at issue which require a conscious and circumspect response, whether on the part of Jesus (in debates) or on the part of other human beings (as in messianic confession).

A. Kretzer

ἀπόκρισις, εως, ἡ *apokrisis* answer*

Referring to the amazement at the answer(s) of Jesus: Luke 2:47; 20:26. Ἀπόκρισιν διδόναι, *give an answer:* John 1:22; 19:9. F. Büchsel, *TDNT* III, 946.

ἀποκρύπτω *apokryptō* hide, keep secret*

Luke 10:21 (par. Matt 11:25 v.l.); 1 Cor 2:7 (of God's wisdom); Col 1:26 par. Eph 3:9 (of the mystery *hidden* for ages). Cf. Matt 25:18 Koine Θ *pl* (*hide* by burying). A. Oepke, *TDNT* III, 957-61, 973-78.

ἀπόκρυφος, 2 *apokryphos* hidden*

Mark 4:22 par. Luke 8:17 (a proverb dealing with what is *hidden* and will be revealed); Col 2:3 (in Christ "are *hid* all the treasures of wisdom and knowledge"). A. Oepke, *TDNT* III, 961, 973-78.

ἀποκτείνω *apokteinō* kill

1. Occurrences — 2. Meaning — 3. Johannine texts

Lit.: J. Blinzler, *The Trial of Jesus* (1959) 157-63. — *idem, Der Prozess Jesu* ([4]1969) 229-44. — G. Dautzenberg, *Sein Leben bewahren. Ψυχή in den Herrenworten der Evangelien* (1966) 154-60. — R. Schnackenburg, *The Gospel according to St. John* III (1982) 121f., 245f.

1. As a koine form ἀποκτέννω and -ννύω are attested in the NT in the same meaning (e.g., Mark 12:5; Matt 10:28; cf. the concordances). Including these variant forms ἀποκτείνω occurs 74 times in the NT, esp. in the Gospels and Revelation. The prep. ἀπό strengthens the negative meaning of the vb. (Schwyzer, *Grammatik* II, 445: "hyper-characterizing, picture-painting").

2. As a synonym for ἀναιρέω and θανατέω the vb. denotes the violent termination of life by human beings (Matt 14:5; 16:21; 21:35, 38f., and often) or by some other cause (Luke 13:4: a tower; Rev 9:18: plagues). In accordance with OT tradition (*nepeš* = person, human being, someone) ψυχή, too (Mark 3:4 par. Luke 6:9 v.l.—only here with no indication of the possessor and with no art.), can be the obj. of σῶσαι and ἀποκτεῖναι (Dautzenberg 154f., 158ff.). Already in pre-NT Hellenistic and rabbinic anthropology one finds the distinction between body and soul (E. Sjöberg, *TDNT* VI, 377-81 [bibliography]; G. Friedrich, *TDNT* X, 657) so that in the NT σῶμα and ψυχή in opposition to each other can be objects of ἀποκτείνειν (Matt 10:28). This is the presupposition for the fig. use in Paul (2 Cor 3:6: the letter *kills,* the spirit makes alive; similarly in Rom 7:11) and in Eph 2:16 (he has *killed* the hostility).

3. The illusion attributed to Jews in John 16:2 that by *killing* the Christians (ὁ ἀποκτείνας ὑμᾶς) they are offering God a cultic sacrifice (λατρεία) has its foundation in the "holy war" and in the "holy zeal" for Yahweh, principally since the Maccabbean period, and is frequently attested (Schnackenburg 121f.). Whether John 18:31b (it is not lawful for us—the Jews—to *put* anyone *to death*) accurately indicates the juridical powers of the Sanhedrin at the time of Jesus is, of course, debated (cf. Blinzler), but is generally and correctly affirmed (Blinzler; E. Lohse, *TDNT* VII, 865f.; Schnackenburg 245f.); legal death sentences were reserved for Rome; the stoning of Stephen (Acts 7) and the execution of James by the sword (Acts 12:1f.) are acts of Jews and Herod Agrippa I which exceed the bounds of legal authority.

H. Frankemölle

ἀποκυέω *apokyeō* give birth to*

Used in a fig. sense in Jas 1:15 of personified sin which *brings forth* death, and in v. 18 of God who "*brought us forth* by the word of truth." M. Dibelius and H. Greeven, *James* (Hermeneia, 1976) 93-99, 103-7; C.-M. Edsman, *ZNW* 38 (1939) 11-44 (cf. Dibelius and Greeven, 104, n. 179).

ἀποκυλίω *apokyliō* roll away*

Referring to the *rolling away* of the (disk-shaped) stone from the entrance to the tomb of Jesus: Mark 16:3, 4 par. Matt 28:2/Luke 24:2; *Gos. Pet.* 12:53.

ἀπολαμβάνω *apolambanō* receive, obtain, recover, receive in return; welcome*

1. In secular Greek — 2. In the OT (LXX) — 3. In the NT

Lit.: BAGD s.v. — G. Delling, *TDNT* IV, 5-15. — H. H. Schmid, *THAT* I, 875-79.

1. Ἀπολαμβάνω, a compound of λαμβάνω, is frequently attested in secular Greek. It was used as a t.t. of commercial

language: *obtain* that which another is obligated to give, e.g., wages (Herodotus, Xenophon); then *regain*, e.g., supremacy (Isocrates); also *take aside* (Herodotus); *separate* (Plato).

2. In the LXX ἀπολαμβάνω is attested only 7 times (representing Heb. *lqḥ*) in the sense of *obtain* (Num 34:14), *go away* (Deut 26:5), *desert* (Isa 5:17), *take aside* (2 Macc 4:46; 6:21), *occupy* (8:6), and *receive* in an eschatological sense (4 Macc 18:23).

3. In the NT the local meaning *take aside* is established only in Mark 7:33 and the general meaning *recover (regain)* only in Luke 15:27. The sense *receive as recompense* applies both to "this aeon" (Luke 6:34 [*recover* what was loaned]; 16:25 [*receive* all good things]; 23:41 [*receive* due punishment]) and to the world to come (18:30 [here both conceptions]; 2 John 8). Paul evidences the negative understanding of *receive* (Rom 1:27) and its positive orientation (Gal 4:5: *receive* the right of sonship on the basis of Christ's redemptive act). The meaning "*receive* as an inheritance" is present in Col 3:24, whereas 3 John 8 v.l. understands *receive (welcome)* in the sense of hospitality. The significant meaning of ἀπολαμβάνω as *recompense* remains with its parenetic orientation (Luke), as does the essential statement regarding the *reception* of sonship as a gift (Galatians) out of which grow Christian obligation and motivation (Gal 4:6f.).

A. Kretzer

ἀπόλαυσις, εως, ἡ *apolausis* enjoyment*

1 Tim 6:17, referring to "God who richly furnishes us with everything *to enjoy*"; Heb 11:25, referring to the fleeting *pleasures* of sin. Cf. *Did.* 10:3; *1 Clem.* 20:10; *2 Clem.* 10:3f.

ἀπολέγομαι *apolegomai* renounce*

2 Cor 4:2: ἀπειπάμεθα (for -όμεθα, 2nd aor.) τὰ κρυπτά, "we have *renounced* disgraceful, underhanded ways" (JB).

ἀπολείπω *apoleipō* leave behind*

Jude 6: "*left* their proper dwelling"; 2 Tim 4:13, 20; Titus 1:5; pass. in Heb 4:6, 9; 10:26: *be left.*

ἀπολείχω *apoleichō* lick off, lick

Luke 16:21 Koine, referring to the *licking* of Lazarus's sores by dogs.

ἀπόλλυμι *apollymi* destroy; lose; die; be lost
ἀπώλεια, ας, ἡ *apōleia* destruction, waste, annihilation

1. Scope of meaning — 2. NT examples — 3. Central focus of the expression

Lit.: G. DAUTZENBERG, *Sein Leben bewahren. Ψυχή in den Herrenworten der Evangelien* (1966) 180 (index s.v.). — H. CH. HAHN, *DNTT* I, 462-64; E. JENNI, *THAT* I, 17-20. — A. OEPKE, *TDNT* I, 394-97. — B. OTZEN, *TDOT* I, 19-23.

1. Both vb. and subst. are richly attested in secular Greek. The simple form ὄλλυμι is found in classical writings only in epic poetry, where it is used trans. and intrans., act. and mid. in the same sense as the compound. The basic negative meaning of the entire word group, frequently with a violent tendency, aims to express loss, destruction, and annihilation (e.g., of wealth) in a very general sense which can extend to the final destruction of the human being in death (Homer, Herodotus, Plato, Xenophon).

The LXX has ἀπόλλυμι as the most frequent translation of Heb. *'āḇaḏ*. With a view toward the NT, it needs to be emphasized that the existence of the individual as well as that of the people as a whole can stand in the balance and that the loss of life is accounted for by the culpable behavior of human beings (e.g., Deut 28:20; 30:18); striking, then, is the eschatological dimension of later statements which characterize a final statement of ruin (Prov 15:11; 27:20; Sir 44:9, here the subst.) and, in connection with Hades and death (Job 26:6; 28:22), can even present the "personification" of evil.

From the intertestamental period, the conception of the Qumran community should be mentioned, according to which the godless, those who do not belong to the community, are branded as "men and sons of perdition" (1QS 9:16, 22; CD 6:15—Heb. *šāḥaṯ*).

2. In the NT the vb. occurs *ca.* 90 times, the subst. 18 times. There is a slight predominance of the occurrences of the vb. in Luke. In the trans. (act.) sense those occurrences of the vb. are significant which have to do with a value or an irretrievable good, e.g., life, human existence in a comprehensive sense. The juxtaposition "to gain life or lose it" occurs in Q (Matt 10:39; Luke 17:33) as well as in Mark 8:35 par. (cf. John 12:25). Ἀπόλλυμι is used here with a double meaning: a slipping away and thus a final loss in a negative sense (Mark 8:35a: to forfeit life) and in a positive sense as the renunciation of every human security (8:35b: to *give up* life). The consequences of such an attitude of renunciation extend beyond the mode of one's earthly existence, beyond immediate thought and imagination, and are comprehensible only in the context of radical discipleship (v. 34).

The dimension of God's activity is expressed in the salvation-historical outline in the parables of the husbandmen (Mark 12:9) and the wedding feast (Matt 22:7), and that of Jesus' activity in connection with the unclean spirit (Mark 1:24). The destructive, murderous tendency of mankind finds expression in relation to Jesus (Mark 3:6; 11:18; Matt 27:20). Originating from the evil spirit and influencing human beings, it comes into play in Mark 9:22. Eschatologically more threatening and devastating is the note sounded in Luke 17:27, 29, 33.

In regard to the intrans. (mid.) meaning it is primarily those texts which speak of the "lost" in a fig. sense that should be mentioned, such as those concerned with the lost sheep of the house of Israel (Matt 10:6 and 15:24), but esp. Luke 15 (8 occurrences, used metaphorically and fig.). Luke 19:10 represents in this connection a redemptive perspective: the Son of Man seeks and saves what is *lost.* In the sense of material loss Mark 2:22 par. (cf. John 6:12, 27) should be noted; on the other hand, when human beings are concerned, texts such as Mark 4:38 (the storm at sea), Matt 26:52 (in connection with Jesus' arrest), and Luke 13:33 (the fate of prophets; cf. also vv. 3, 5) should be mentioned (in the sense here of *perish, die*). The danger of final loss is strongly underscored in the Johannine tradition according to which it is the responsibility of human beings to attain eternal life (John 10:28) through faith (3:15f.) and discipleship (10:27).

Paul uses the vb. in a similar sense, trans. to denote the punishing intervention of God (1 Cor 1:19) and thoughtless human action (Rom 14:15; cf. 1 Cor 8:11, here intrans. with the same meaning) and intrans. to denote being lost before God (Rom 2:12; 1 Cor 1:18; 2 Cor 2:15; 4:3), personal affliction (2 Cor 4:9), or an eschatological state (1 Cor 15:18). The guilty thought finds expression esp. in 2 Thess 2:10: those who allow themselves to be deceived into unrighteousness and refuse to love the truth will perish (cf. also 1 Cor 10:9f.: Israel's fate in the wilderness is its own fault).

The transitoriness of the world and of human beings is expressed by ἀπόλλυμαι in the later writings (Heb 1:11; Jas 1:11; 2 Pet 3:6). Rev 9:11 presents a special form: the → Ἀπολλύων (from Heb. *'ᵃḇaddôn*) is the angel of the abyss who brings destruction.

The subst. ἀπώλεια (intrans.) displays a significantly deeper meaning in connection with ultimate human ruin, for which mankind is to blame (Matt 7:13; here the counterpart is "life": v. 14), esp. in Paul (Rom 9:22; Phil 1:28; the counterpart here is "salvation": Phil 3:18). Persons who have fallen into this state are called "son(s) of perdition" (2 Thess 2:3; cf. John 17:12; 18:9 and the Qumran literature → 1). The entire eschatological scenery and tension in 2 Peter is characterized by this word (6 occurrences): deceivers as well as deceived are on the way to ruin, not least of all because of their false interpretation of Scripture (2 Pet 3:16).

3. The focus of these words can be specified as follows: As destructive action ἀπόλλυμι can have persons as its obj. (Jesus: Mark 3:6; 12:9) as well as things (wages: Mark 9:41; wisdom: 1 Cor 1:19). Those texts are significant which have to do with being as such, whether of the universe (Heb 1:11; 2 Pet 3:6), of purely earthly existence (Mark 4:38; Matt 26:52), or of life in a comprehensive sense (Mark 8:35). In the latter sense ἀπόλλυμι goes beyond this present aeon and can mean "definitive destruction," or "a hopeless destiny of death" (Oepke 396), esp. in Paul and John. Thus it becomes a central concept in NT parenesis and ethics: the human being is addressed and challenged as one who is free and responsible, but who also is able to and, in fact, does fail and miss the meaning of life. "Security" is given as a gift only by the one who alone is able to save what is lost, Jesus himself (Luke 19:10).

A. Kretzer

Ἀπολλύων, ονος, ὁ *Apollyōn* Apollyon, destroyer*

Rev 9:11 (as Greek translation of → Ἀβαδδών) *destroyer, exterminator.* → ἄγγελος 2. J. Jeremias, *TDNT* I, 4; A. Oepke, *TDNT* I, 397.

Ἀπολλωνία, ας *Apollōnia* Apollonia*

A city on the Via Egnatia in Macedonia through which Paul passed on his way to Thessalonica (Acts 17:1). G. Hirschfeld, PW II, 114 (s.v. 4); E. Haenchen, *The Acts of the Apostles* (1971) 506 with n. 3.

Ἀπολλῶς, ῶ *Apollōs* Apollos*

1. Occurrences — 2. In Acts — 3. In 1 Corinthians

Lit.: K. Aland, *Taufe und Kindertaufe* (1971) 15-21. — F. F. Bruce, "Apollos in NT (Acts 18, 24–19, 1)," *Ekklesiastikos Pharos* (Addis Ababa) 57 (1975) 354-66. — *idem, The Pauline Circle* (1985) 51-57. — E. Käsemann, "The Disciples of John the Baptist in Ephesus," *idem, Essays on NT Themes* (1964) 136-48. — E. Schweizer, "Die Bekehrung des Apollos," *idem, Beiträge zur Theologie des NT* (1970) 71-79.

1. In the Hellenistic period and esp. in Egypt Ἀπολλῶς was a common short form for names such as Apollonios or Apollonides. The NT mentions a Christian Ἀπολλῶς in Acts 18:24; 19:1 and in 1 Cor 1:12; 3:4, 5, 6, 22; 4:6; 16:12. It is more than likely that Titus 3:13 refers to the same Ἀπολλῶς but provides no personal information about him beyond that given in Acts 18 and 19 and 1 Corinthians.

2. According to Acts 18:24f. Apollos was a Jew from Alexandria trained in rhetoric and exegesis who had been "instructed in the way of the Lord," was "fervent in spirit," and "taught accurately the things concerning Jesus, though he knew only the baptism of John." Priscilla and Aquila are said to have remedied this deficiency in learning, and Apollos traveled on to Corinth with a letter of recommendation from the Ephesian church.

As an explanation for the curious fact that Apollos is described as a Christian though he knew only the baptism of John, Aland assumed that Apollos was (like the disciples in Acts 19:1ff.) a follower of Jesus in the pre-Easter period when John's baptism for repentance was still practiced among the followers of Jesus. Insofar, however, as John 3:22ff. has any historical value at all, this would be accurate only for the earliest period of Jesus' ministry and it is unimaginable that in the 20 years following Easter and Pentecost Apollos should not have encountered a single "perfect Christian" (E. Haenchen, *The Acts of the Apostles* [1971] 554). Käsemann solves the problem by assuming that Luke's source spoke of Apollos as an independent Christian missionary whom Luke has degraded to the status of "semi-Christian" in order to indirectly subordinate him to Pauline authority. Such redactional intervention on Luke's part is hard to imagine. Therefore, one can assume with Schweizer that Luke's source spoke of Apollos as an unbelieving Jew who held inspiring lectures on ethics in the synagogue and was converted by Priscilla and Aquila. Luke mistakenly related Apollos's knowledge of "the way of the Lord" to the Lord Jesus Christ and thus made Apollos a "near-Christian."

3. Following Paul's departure, Apollos worked effectively in Corinth; one group appealed to him as its spiritual authority (1 Cor 1:12; 3:4ff.). Whether he made such an impression by means of allegorical interpretation of Scripture as it was practiced in Alexandria or whether Paul's controversy with "wisdom" in 1 Cor 1:18ff. is directed specifically against Apollos (thus J. Weiss, *Der erste Korintherbrief* [KEK, [9]1910] xxxiii; Haenchen, *Acts* 556) cannot be ascertained with certainty. In no case can one observe a fundamental difference between Paul and Apollos, for Apollos is recognized as a "fellow worker in God's service" (1 Cor 3:9 NEB mg.) who performs the same task as Paul, though in a different situation. Behind the activity of both stands God himself.

H. Merkel

ἀπολογέομαι *apologeomai* defend oneself*
ἀπολογία, ας, ἡ *apologia* defense*

1. Occurrences in the NT — 2. As a juridical t.t. — 3. Fig. use

Lit.: BAGD s.v. — G. Bornkamm, "Gesetz und Natur," *idem, Aufsätze* II, 93-118. — J. Dupont, "Aequitas Romana," *idem, Études sur les Actes des Apôtres* (1967) 527-52, esp. 536-38. — L. Goppelt, *Der erste Petrusbrief* (KEK, 1978) 236f. — LSJ s.v.

1. The vb. occurs 10 times, the subst. 8, of which a total of 10 occurrences are in Luke-Acts.

2. Both subst. and vb. occur esp. as t.t.s in the language of the trial court. The context presupposes hostility or imprisonment for the sake of the Christian witness. In the course of interrogation and judicial process the *defense* becomes an unexpected opportunity for missionary proclamation: Phil 1:7, 16; 2 Tim 4:16 (Paul's judicial *hearing*); 1 Pet. 3:15 (the *missionary's explanation* of hope—the heart of Christian faith—in court or in private conversation).

Luke adds to a doubly-attested saying of Jesus his own picture of Christian beginnings (cf. Acts) by more sharply delineating the "speaking" as ἀπολογεῖσθαι (Luke 12:11 [Q, cf. Matt 10:19]; 21:14 [cf. Mark 13:11]). Along with the synagogal court (2 Cor 11:24) and Roman officials of the central and local government, Luke also mentions imprisonment (Luke 21:12), intimates the possibility of preparation for defense, and by placing such apology prior to the apocalyptic catastrophies describes it as the normal situation of the Church.

In Acts 22:1; 24:10; 25:8, 16; 26:1, 2, 24 the words appear in a type of apology (chs. 22–26) which makes clear to the Christians Paul's fearlessness in confessing his faith and aims at persuading the Roman officials to tolerance by *proving* the legitimacy of the Christian faith as a Jewish movement and its political goodwill. In a rhetorically brilliant defense (with *captatio benevolentiae* directed toward the judge, *vita* with special emphasis on Paul's Jewish heritage and divine call to the Gentile mission) Paul is able to expose the false Jewish accusations (offense against the temple, law, public order, and Caesar). Only injustice, delay, and errors in the trial process prevent the demonstrably necessary acquital.

In Acts 19:33 Alexander attempts to *present a self-defense* on behalf of his fellow Jews. That is, he seeks to disassociate them from the Christians.

3. These words are used fig. esp. in the controversy between Paul and the Corinthians regarding his personal apostleship. 1 Cor 9:3 describes the enumeration of the apostolic rights and the description of the personal renunciation of them (vv. 4ff.) as *self-defense, theological proof* over against the critics. According to 2 Cor 12:19 God alone is the one who sits in judgment and before whom Paul must *defend* himself. In 7:11 Paul confirms that the Corinthians have *explained* to Timothy their *apology,* which has eliminated the cause for the letter of tears (2:3-9). Rom 2:15 applies ἀπολογέομαι to thoughts as they function as *witnesses for the defense* (and for the prosecution) in relation to the examinations of conscience; such witnesses in the consciousness of the Gentile who does not have the Torah represent something analogous to the divine judgment on the basis of the Torah.

U. Kellermann

ἀπολογία, ας, ἡ *apologia* defense
→ ἀπολογέομαι.

ἀπολούομαι *apolouomai* *wash oneself**

Acts 22:16: "*wash away* your sins" (through baptism). In 1 Cor 6:11 ἀπελούσασθε (alongside ἡγιάσθητε) is, despite the form, not to be interpreted as mid. but as pass.: "you were washed" (H. Conzelmann, *1 Corinthians* [Hermeneia] 107); it also refers to the effects of baptism (cf. Titus 3:5). A. Oepke, *TDNT* IV, 303f.; G. R. Beasley-Murray, *DNTT* I, 150-52.

ἀπολύτρωσις, εως, ἡ *apolytrōsis* redemption*

1. Occurrences in the NT — 2. Basic meaning — 3. Concrete meanings in NT texts — 4. Semantic range in the NT

Lit.: C. ANDRESEN, *RAC* VI, 54-219, esp. 98-111. — F. BOURASSA, "Rédemption," *ScEs* 21 (1969) 19-33, 189-207. — F. BÜCHSEL, *TDNT* IV, 351-56. — D. HILL, *Greek Words and Hebrew Meanings* (1967), esp. 49-81. — S. LYONNET, *De peccato et redemptione. II: De vocabulario redemptionis* ([2]1972). —*idem*, "Redemptio cosmica secundum Rom 8, 19-23," *VD* 44 (1966) 225-42. — S. LYONNET and L. SABOURIN, *Sin, Redemption, and Sacrifice* (1970). — I. H. MARSHALL, "The Development of the Concept of Redemption in the NT," *Reconciliation and Hope* (FS L. L. Morris; 1974) 153-69. — L. L. MORRIS, *The Apostolic Preaching of the Cross* ([3]1965), esp. 11-64. — P. VON DER OSTEN-SACKEN, *Römer 8 als Beispiel paulinischer Soteriologie* (1975), esp. 263-87. — P. STUHLMACHER, "Recent Exegesis on Romans 3:24-26," *idem, Reconciliation, Law, and Righteousness* (1986) 94-109. — P. VIELHAUER, *RGG* II, 588-90. — K. WENNEMER, "Ἀπολύτρωσις Römer 3, 24-25a," *Studiorum Paulinorum Congressus Internationalis Catholicus 1961* I (1963) 283-88.

1. Most of the NT texts in which ἀπολύτρωσις occurs are found in the Pauline corpus. In this connection, the use of the word in the deutero-Pauline writings Ephesians (1:7, 14; 4:30) and Colossians (1:14) is esp. striking. In terms of tradition they display a certain relationship to the three texts in Romans (3:24; 8:23) and 1 Corinthians (1:30; → 3). Other occurrences are in Heb 9:15 and 11:35 as well as the single occurrence in the Gospels, Luke 21:28 (cf., however, λύτρωσις in 1:68; 2:38, λυτροῦσθαι in 24:21, and λύτρον in Mark 10:45 par. Matt 20:28). From this overview emerges a limited textual basis for the NT understanding of ἀπολύτρωσις; in the period following the composition of the texts, however, this textual basis extends into the greater part of primitive Christian tradition. The occurrence of the word deserves attention, at least in regard to NT usage, since it is not common in secular Greek and is attested only from about the 2nd cent. B.C. (BAGD s.v.; Büchsel 352).

2. The basic meanings of ἀπολύτρωσις are, on the basis of act. ἀπολυτρόω, *freed by ransom,* and, on the basis of mid. ἀπολυτρόομαι, *redemption,* i.e., of prisoners or slaves. The first occurs in Heb 11:35 (cf. 2 Macc 6:23, 30; 7:24; 4 Macc 8:4-14): martyrs refuse *release* offered in return for denying the faith. In the remainder of the NT texts the word occurs in the second sense but in a fig., theological meaning, and in this case is to be rendered simply as *redemption.* The event thereby indicated rests decisively in the saving act of God on behalf of those in need of redemption. Even more than the redeeming event, the word designates in the NT the effect of this event, the (hoped-for) human *state of being redeemed.* It must be asked whether and to what extent the element of the payment of a ransom, suggested by the basic meaning of the word, is preserved in NT usage (→ 3, 4).

3. Ἀπολύτρωσις attains its specific meaning as it is applied by Paul to the central content of the gospel. It denotes the "redemption" which God offers in the death of God's Son; its location, therefore, is "in Christ Jesus" (Rom 3:24). The meaning of "redemption" here is explicated by the following verse (v. 25). Stress is placed upon the divine initiative which is the basis of expiation and which receives its historical representation and mediation in the self-sacrifice of Jesus ("by his blood"). Thus, according to Paul, redemption has both a *theo*logical and a *christo*logical base. Redemption is God's gracious turning to humanity in its need for redemption, and this grace is experienced as remission of sins—in faith in Jesus Christ. This Jesus "God made . . . our righteousness and sanctification and *redemption*" (1 Cor 1:30); here ἀπολύτρωσις stands in an ordered and ascending formula and designates Jesus Christ as the redeemer himself *(abstractum pro concreto)* in view of the salvation of believers established by him.

Already then in two texts, Rom 3:24 and 1 Cor 1:30, the theological limit is set for any explanation of the word which wishes to retain for the NT the basic meaning of "redemption" on the basis of a *payment of ransom* by appealing, e.g., to Mark 10:45 par. Matt 20:28 or 1 Pet 1:18f. ("ransomed . . . with the precious blood of Christ"). But even in these texts the inadequacy of a ransom in the literal sense becomes clear, namely by the allusion to Isa 52:3: "You were sold for nothing, and you shall be redeemed (λυτρωθήσεσθε) without money." Jesus' giving of his own life points to the redeeming work of God and effectively mediates it.

A. Deissmann (*Light From the Ancient Near East* [[2]1927] 319-30) sought to establish the ancient legal custom of "sacred manumission" as the model for the Pauline doctrine of redemption: As through the fictitious purchase of the slave by some deity the slave becomes the property of the deity and thus free, so human beings are ransomed from sin, death, and law. Apart from the fictitious element of this legal transaction (the slave himself pays the ransom money), the idea of the payment of a purchase price or ransom money has no such significance in the NT texts. Nevertheless, the binding of the redeemed to the redeemer by means of the "ransom" deserves attention (cf. Titus 2:14; Marshall 158f.); however, this cannot simply be traced back to the concept we have described from the Hellenistic environment, but rather to the OT and Jewish prehistory of the NT concept of redemption.

This OT and Jewish prehistory cannot be described solely on the basis of use of ἀπολύτρωσις in the Greek OT (the only occurrence is in Dan 4:34 and has no recognizable significance for NT usage) and other Jewish writings (e.g., Josephus *Ant.* xii.27; Philo *Congr.* 109; *Omn. Prob. Lib.* 114; cf. *T. Levi* 2:10: λυτρόομαι), but rather, first of all, on the basis of that foundational experience so frequently attested and interpreted in the OT—Israel's liberation from slavery in Egypt. In the Exodus Yahweh showed himself as the mighty redeemer of his people (cf., e.g., Deut 7:8; 9:26; 13:6; 15:5; Pss 74:2; 77:16 [LXX λυτρόομαι]). As from "the house of bondage," Egypt, so also from the Babylonian captivity will God "redeem" his people (Isa 41:14; 43:1, 14; 44:22-24; 52:3; 54:5). In the juxtaposition of "first" and "second" redemption the eschatological perspective is born, which the NT description of the redeeming activity of God takes up.

In many cases the fundamental idea of ransom (Heb. *gā'al, pādāh*) is still recognizable in OT usage (cf. Exod 21:8; Lev 25:48). However, the payment of a ransom plays no essential role there. Redemption is rather the sovereign action of God which secures the primarily *theo*logical aspect of the event of redemption. "Redemption" establishes the covenant relationship of Israel to its God, and (what is more) redemption from the manifold distresses of the people as well as of the individual is grounded in this covenant relationship. Explicitly contained in "redemption" according to Ps 130:7f. is the forgiveness of sin which the OT praying person expects in the form of the restoration of the old covenant relationship for Israel.

The believer now attains "redemption"—God's decisive eschatological act of salvation (cf. *1 Enoch* 51:2; Luke 21:28)—through and in Christ. Eph 1:7 and Col 1:14 take up the Pauline or pre-Pauline Jewish Christian understanding of redemption and speak of the redemption which becomes effective in baptism as "forgiveness of sins." In agreement with Rom 3:24f. "redemption" here remains determined by the idea of atonement and thus by the foundational event of Jesus' death, an idea which is retained in the description of Christ's work of salvation in Heb 9:15: for those who are "called" there is grounded in his redeeming death—over and above the forgiveness of sins and in a positive continuation of this experience of salvation—the certainty of the promised future, the "the promised eternal inheritance."

Alongside the present-eschatological perspective the future-eschatological aspect of redemption is also maintained in the NT. Christians have been "sealed for the day of *redemption*" by the Holy Spirit (Eph 4:30). The redemption already attained (v. 7) will appear on that day in completed form—as "our inheritance" toward which the eschatological gift of the Holy Spirit already now points in promise.

The tension between redemption already attained and still expected refers back to more original germinal ideas in Pauline thought, as is made clear esp. by Rom 8:23. As those who have already received "the first fruits of the Spirit," we "groan inwardly as we wait for adoption as sons, the *redemption* of our bodies." Redemption is certainly not to be understood here as "redemption *from* our bodies," taking τοῦ σώματος as genitive of separation (so H. Lietzmann, *An die Römer* [HNT [4]1933] 84). But the full flowering of the "sonship" attained in baptism (8:15; Gal 4:5) still stands under the qualification of the earthly and bodily existence of the believer.

The completed form of redemption is given when this mortal body is "further clothed" with that new corporeality which God has prepared for his own (2 Cor 5:1-5; cf. 1 Cor 15:37f.). The eschatologically final form of redemption is therefore given with the resurrection of the dead which is promised in Christ, "the first-born among many brethren" (Rom 8:29), to believers. At his parousia the Kyrios Jesus Christ as the "Savior" (σωτήρ here synonymous with "Redeemer" in the eschatological sense) "will change our lowly body to be like his glorious body" (Phil 3:20f.). The ultimate redemption through the σωτήρ is concerned with the creaturely existence in its totality of those who believe. The hope for this redemption does not leave believers alone in the preliminary manner of the experience of salvation in "this present time" (Rom 8:18), esp. in regard to "suffering with Christ," the paradoxical form of "being glorified with Christ" (von der Osten-Sacken 270); rather, this "being glorified with" Christ encompasses "present and future" *(ibid.)* and rests finally in the possibilities of God's "new creation."

4. "Ἀπολύτρωσις is not one of the chief concepts in early Christian proclamation and teaching" (Büchsel 356). Nevertheless, it should also be noted already for the NT that the concept of redemption is to attain central significance in later Christian soteriology. This is above all because already in the NT the concept of redemption can easily be added to and further developed by means of other concepts in the early Christian proclamation of salvation. Such a concept is that of atonement in Rom 3:24f. which contributes to the concept of redemption the phrase "redemption from sins" (cf. also Eph 1:7; Col 1:14; Heb 9:15). Other concepts in early Christian soteriology address the idea of redemption in various concrete ways, in each case determined by the context, but their use does not in every case establish a precise linguistic and material demarcation. Thus Gal 1:4 describes the redeeming event of Jesus' death as a "deliverance" (ἐξαιρεῖσθαι) of human beings from the dominion of "the present evil age" in which sin and death reign. A saving "deliverance" (from afflictions) is spoken of in the NT otherwise only in several places in Acts (7:10, 34; 12:11; 23:27; 26:17).

The vb. ῥύομαι (16 occurrences in the NT) develops further the usage of the LXX and denotes the redemption expected from God as "deliverance" or "preservation" from the power of evil (Matt 6:13; Rom 7:24; Col 1:13 in a significant convergence with ἀπολύτρωσις in v. 14) and from the "wrath to come" (1 Thess 1:10). The parallelism between ἀπολύτρωσις and "liberation" (ἐλευθεροῦσθαι) is clear in Rom 8:21-23. The directly soteriological use of this concept leads to the idea of liberation from the power of sin (6:18, 22; 8:2). The liberating initiative of Christ is emphasized (Gal 5:1; cf. John 8:36). Gal 3:13 and 4:5 pick up the terminology of the ransom idea (ἐξαγοράζω) to speak of the redemptive work of Christ, without, however, understanding it in the sense of sacral ransoming of slaves

(→ 3), although they do refer to the law as the master of the slave.

All these concepts (including that of σῴζειν) need to be complemented by the central (esp. for Paul) concepts of "reconciliation" (καταλλαγή) and "justification" (→ δικαιοσύνη/δικαιόομαι) in order to throw light on the positive content of the NT concept of redemption: the attainment of the relationship to God as a new realm in which to live in faith is Jesus Christ.

K. Kertelge

ἀπολύω *apolyō* set free, release; dismiss

Lit. (esp. on 2): H. BALTENSWEILER, *Die Ehe im NT* (ATANT 52, 1967). — BAGD s.v. — J. BONSIRVEN, *Le divorce dans le NT* (1948). — G. BORNKAMM, "Ehescheidung und Wiederverheiratung im NT," *idem, Aufsätze* III, 56-59. — G. DELLING, *RAC* IV, 707-19. — E. LÖVESTAM, "ΑΠΟΛΥΕΙΝ," *SEÅ* 27 (1962) 132-35. — *idem,* "Die funktionale Bedeutung der synoptischen Jesusworte über Ehescheidung und Wiederheirat," *Theologie aus dem Norden* (ed. A. Fuchs; 1977) 19-28. — U. NEMBACH, "Ehescheidung nach alttestamentlichem und jüdischem Recht," *TZ* 26 (1970) 161-71. — K. NIEDERWIMMER, *Askese und Mysterium. Über Ehe, Ehescheidung und Eheverzicht in den Anfängen des christlichen Glaubens* (FRLANT 113, 1975), esp. 13-24, 44-52. — R. PESCH, *Freie Treue. Die Christen und die Ehescheidung* (1971). — G. SCHNEIDER, "Jesu Wort über die Ehescheidung in der Überlieferung des NT," *TTZ* 80 (1971) 65-87. — C. R. TABER, *IDBSup* (1976) 244f. — B. VAWTER, "Divorce and the NT," *CBQ* 39 (1977) 528-42. — A. D. VERHEY, *ISBE* I, 976-78.

1. This compound of λύω occurs, apart from Heb 13:23, only in the Gospels and Acts, 19 times in Matthew, 12 in Mark, 14 in Luke, 15 in Acts, and 5 in John. a) In the meaning *set free, release* it is used of the release of prisoners (Mark 15:6-15 par. Matthew/Luke; John 18:39; 19:10, 12; Acts 3:13; 5:40; 16:35, 36; 26:32; 28:18; Heb 13:23 [→ b]; on Luke 22:68 v.l. see J. Duplacy, "Une variante méconnue du texte reçu: '. . . ΜΟΙ Η ΑΠΟΛΥΣΗΤΕ' (Lc. 22, 68)," FS Schmid [1963] 42-52) and also more generally: *set free, release, liberate* (Matt 15:23; 18:27; Luke 6:37; 13:12). b) The meaning *let go, dismiss* (also *divorce* → 2) is present when persons are sent off (Matt 14:15, 22, 23; 15:32, 39; Mark 6:36, 45; 8:3, 9; Luke 8:38; 14:4; Acts 19:40) and is used passively to mean *take leave, depart* (Acts 4:23; 15:30, 33 [according to BAGD s.v. 2b also Heb 13:23]) or as a euphemism for *let die* (Luke 2:29). c) The mid. means *go away* in Acts 28:25.

2. In the Synoptics (13 of the occurrences there) ἀπολύω is a (common) term for the dismissal of a woman from marriage by means of a letter of divorce (→ ἀποστάσιον), so primarily in the phrase "*send away* one's wife" (1 [3] Esdr 9:36; cf. Deut 24:1-4). It occurs in Jesus' prohibition of divorce (Mark 10:2, 11 par. Matt 19:3, 8, 9; Matt 5:31, 32a par. Luke 16:18a [Q]; see further Matt 5:32b; 19:7; Mark 10:4; Luke 16:18b) and, referring to Joseph's intention regarding Mary, in Matt 1:19 (see M. M. Bourke, review of R. E. Brown, *The Birth of the Messiah* [1977], *CBQ* 40 [1978] 121f.). On the "adultery clauses" which appear only in Matt 5:32; 19:9 → πορνεία. Mark 10:12 speaks of the dismissal of the husband by the wife; this has to do with the logical extension of Jesus' prohibition of divorce to Greco-Roman legal practice, which gave women the right to initiate divorce (cf. 1 Cor 7:10f.; see R. Pesch, *Markusevangelium* [HTKNT] II ad loc.; cf. H. Conzelmann, *1 Corinthians* [Hermeneia] 120).

G. Schneider

ἀπομάσσω *apomassō* wipe off*

Luke 10:11 (mid.): "the dust . . . we *wipe off* against you (ὑμῖν)."

ἀπονέμω *aponemō* assign*

1 Pet 3:7: "*bestowing* honor"; cf. *1 Clem.* 1:3; Ign. *Magn.* 3:1; *Mart. Pol.* 10:2.

ἀπονίπτω *aponiptō* wash off*

Matt 27:24 (mid.): *wash* one's hands, done by Pilate as a claim of his innocence (cf. BAGD s.v. [ἀπονίζω]).

ἀποπίπτω *apopiptō* fall away*

Acts 9:18: When Ananias laid his hands on Paul and prayed that he might regain his sight, "something like scales *fell from* his [Paul's] eyes."

ἀποπλανάω *apoplanaō* mislead
→ πλανάω.

ἀποπλέω *apopleō* sail away*

A nautical t.t. in Acts 13:4; 14:26; 20:15; 27:1, usually with indication of the destination (εἰς); in 20:15 with indication of the point of departure (ἐκεῖθεν).

ἀποπλύνω *apoplynō* wash off

Luke 5:2 Koine A Θ, they "*were washing* their nets."

ἀποπνίγω *apopnigō* strangle, choke, drown*

Luke 8:7 (par. Matt 13:7 v.l.), 33 (cf. Mark 5:13) pass.: the herd *was drowned.* H. Bietenhard, *TDNT* VI, 455-58; E. Schwentner, *RMP* 105 (1962) 191.

ἀπορέω *aporeō* be uncertain, at a loss*

Act. in Mark 6:20; otherwise mid.: Luke 24:4; John 13:22; Acts 25:20; 2 Cor 4:8; Gal 4:20.

ἀπορία, ας, ἡ *aporia* perplexity, anxiety*

Luke 21:25 (a non-Markan phrase), referring to anxiety at the raging of the sea.

ἀπορ(ρ)ίπτω *apor(r)iptō* throw down*

Acts 27:43 intrans.: *throw oneself down.*

ἀπορφανίζω *aporphanizō* make an orphan (of someone)*

1 Thess 2:17 fig. of Paul, who is separated from his congregation.

ἀποσκευάζω *aposkeuazō* get rid of

Acts 21:15 D, *pack up, strike* the tents.

ἀποσκίασμα, ατος, τό *aposkiasma* darkening*

Jas 1:17, of the darkening caused by the changing positions of the heavenly bodies. S. Schulz, *TDNT* VII, 399; H.-C. Hahn, *DNTT* III, 553-56.

ἀποσπάω *apospaō* draw away, draw out*

Matt 26:51: *draw* a sword; otherwise fig.: Luke 22:41; Acts 21:1 pass.: *tear oneself away, withdraw;* 20:30 act.: *draw* the disciples *away* after them.

ἀποστασία, ας, ἡ *apostasia* apostasy*

Acts 21:21 as an accusation against Paul: you teach *apostasy* from Moses; 2 Thess 2:3: the Antichrist causes rebellion before the end. H. Schlier, *TDNT* I, 513f.; W. Bauder, *DNTT* I, 606-8.

ἀποστάσιον, ου, τό *apostasion* certificate of divorce*

Lit.: E. Bammel, "Mk 10, 11f und das jüdische Eherecht," *ZNW* 61 (1970) 95-101. — Billerbeck I, 303-12. — M. J. Geller, "The Elephantine Papyri and Hosea 2, 3," *JSJ* 8 (1977) 139-48. — E. Koffmahn, *Die Doppelurkunden aus der Wüste Juda* (STDJ 5, 1968). — W. Kornfeld and W. Baier, *BL* 1535. —J. Scharbert, "Ehe und Eheschließung in der Rechtssprache des Pentateuch und beim Chronisten," FS W. Kornfeld (1977) 213-25. — F. Schmidtke, *RAC* I, 551-53. — B. N. Wambacq, "De libello repudii," *VD* 33 (1955) 331-35.

1. The issuance of a *certificate of divorce* by the man is presupposed in Deut 24:1, 3; Isa 50:1; Jer 3:8; the t.t. is Heb. *sēp̱er kᵉrîṯuṯ* or Gk. βιβλίον ἀποστασίου, which appears in Mark 10:4; Matt 19:7. Ἀποστάσιον alone is used in Matt 5:31; this special meaning of the word occurs only in Jewish Greek texts. In the papyri ἀποστασίου συγγραφή is the deed of cession upon sale (Preisigke, *Wörterbuch* I, 194).

An Aramaic certificate of divorce from Wadi Murabbaʿat (A.D. 71?) reads: "On the first of Marḥešvan of the sixth year, at Maṣada, I discharge and repudiate you of my own free will—today, I, Joseph, son of N[aqsan] of [. . .], you Mariam, daughter of Jonathan of Hanablaṭa, resident of Maṣada, you who have previously been my wife, in such a manner that you are free to go and marry any Jewish man you choose. Here, then, from me is the document of separation *(sēp̱er tirûḵîn)* and the certificate of divorce *(gēṭ šiḇûqîn);* and I give you [the wedding endowmen]t and for everything which has been ruined or damaged or [. . . I shall reimburs]e you according to my obligation and shall pay fourfold; and anytime you demand it, I will renew this document if I am still alive. Joseph, son of Naqsan, for himself; Eliʿazar, son of Malka, witness; Joseph, son of Malka, witness; Eleazar, son of Ḥanana, witness" (Pap. Murabbʿat 19, DJD II (1961) 104-9; see Koffmahn 148-55).

2. The documentation of the divorce was necessary for the protection of the woman against the accusation of adultery. Reasons are not spelled out in the text. In Deut 24:1 the occasion is "some indecency in her"; in Matt 5:32; 19:9 it is πορνεία (is the Matthean redactor following Jer 3:1-8?). The man had no right to divorce a virgin he had violated (Deut 22:29) or when he had unjustly accused a chaste woman (v. 19). According to the Talmud a woman could demand a divorce on physical or moral grounds (Billerbeck II, 23f.). The issuance of a letter of divorce by the woman is unthinkable in the realm of authentic Judaism (*m. Yebam.* 14:1) but possible in areas under Hellenistic-Roman influence (Josephus *Ant.* xv.259; cf. Bammel).

J. B. Bauer

ἀποστεγάζω *apostegazō* remove a roof*

Mark 2:4 with the obj. → στέγη (roof).

ἀποστέλλω *apostellō* send forth

1. Occurrences in the NT — 2. Meaning and usage — 3. The sending forth of Jesus' disciples — 4. Jesus as the messenger of God in John's Gospel

Lit.: J. Seynaeve, "Les verbes ἀποστέλλω et πέμπω dans le vocabulaire théologique de Saint Jean," *L'Évangile de Jean* (ed. M. de Jonge; BETL 44, 1977) 385-89. Further lit. → ἀπόστολος (Barrett, Borgen, Bühner, Burgers, Cohn, von Eicken and Lindner, Giblet, Miranda, Rengstorf, and Schmahl).

1. Of 136 occurrences in the NT only 12 appear outside the Gospels (which have 97 occurrences) and Acts (27 occurrences). John (28 occurrences) occupies a special position: here ἀποστέλλω is related primarily (19 occurrences) to christology.

2. The vb. means *send forth, send out;* when it is not used to circumscribe the successful completion of a messenger's journey (for the purpose of delivering an object or a piece of information) but is sharpened to focus on the purpose and goal of the event in question and hence on the sending forth and completion of the assignment, the vb.

assumes the meaning of *commission* (Matt 2:16; 10:40 par.; 22:3f.; Mark 6:17; 9:37 par.; Luke 1:19; 4:18, 43; 9:2; John 1:6, 24; 3:34, 4:38; 5:36, 38; 6:29, 57; 7:29; 8:42; 11:42; 17:3, 8, 21, 23, 25; 20:21; Acts 9:17; Rom 10:15; 1 Cor 1:17; Heb 1:14; Rev 22:6). This sense regularly comes to the fore in the context of missionary apologetic (→ 3) and statements directed to christological legitimation (→ 4).

Human beings as well as God can be subjects of ἀποστέλλειν. With respect to the one doing the sending the vb. indicates that such a one has messengers at his disposal and either wishes to convey a piece of information or an object or to make a claim on a third party (a householder is the subject in Matt 20:1; 21:33; a king in Matt 22:2; Mark 4:29; the high priest in Acts 5:21; the synagogue rulers in Acts 13:15). Claim and power also characterize God as sender (Mark 1:2; Luke 1:19, 26; → 4) as well as the Son of Man (obj. is angels in Matt 13:41; Mark 13:27 par.) and, finally, the earthly Jesus (obj. is the disciples; → 3). Objects of ἀποστέλλω are, correspondingly, persons of whom the sender can expect obedience and the willingness to serve as messengers (workers in Matt 20:2; servants in Mark 12:2-5; helpers in Acts 19:22; disciples in Matt 22:16; Mark 11:1; 14:13; Luke 7:18, 20; the son in Mark 12:6; → 4). The meaning of ἀποστέλλω in the NT is determined by its connection, mediated by the LXX, with Heb. *šālaḥ* as well as with the understanding found there of "send" as "let oneself be represented"; → ἀπόστολος.

3. This popular-juridical meaning pervades the Synoptic reports, according to which the earthly Jesus sent forth twelve (or 72 according to Luke 10:1 [L]) disciples (Mark 3:13-19; 6:6f.; Matt 10:1ff.; Luke 6:12-16; 9:1ff.; 10:1ff.). Corresponding to the activity of Jesus, the charge given the disciples encompasses proclamation of the βασιλεία (Mark 3:13; Matt 10:7 par. Luke 9:2; Luke 10:9) and the exorcism of demons (Mark 3:15; 6:7; Matt 10:1 par. Luke 9:1; 10:9). That the disciples are sent to represent the master who sends them and to substitute for his own presence is expressed most clearly in the legal maxims which promise that reception of the disciples who are sent brings with it the reception and presence of the Lord who sends them and thus, finally, the presence of the *šᵉḵînâ* (Matt 10:40; Luke 10:16; Mark 9:37 par.; 9:41 par.; John 5:23; 12:44f.; 13:20). The disciples who are sent forth participate in the authority of the Lord (Mark 3:15 par.; 6:7), they are protected by God as the Father, who is in the final analysis the one who sends them (Matt 10:20), and they can, in pairs (Mark 6:7 par.; Luke 10:1), bear credible witness to their commission and to the one who commissions them.

4. Already in pre-Johannine tradition the ἦλθον-sayings (Mark 1:38 par.; 2:17 par.; 10:45 par.; Matt 5:17; 10:4 par.; Luke 9:46; 12:49f.; 19:10) along with ἀπεστάλην (Matt 15:24; Luke 4:18, 43) speak of Jesus as the one who in his salvific activity has been commissioned by God. Also pre-Johannine is the confessional tradition which culminates in the statement that God sends his παῖς (Acts 3:26), his Χριστός (Acts 3:20), his Son (Gal 4:4; Rom 8:3).

Under the influence of Jewish teaching about sending, John develops this tradition (1 John 4:9, 10, 14; John 3:16f.) into the basis for christological legitimation (5:36, 38; 6:29, 57; 7:29; 10:36; 11:42; 17:3, 8, 18): ἀποστέλλω denotes commissioning and authorization from God. The sending discloses the unique manner in which the Son is bound to the Father; a believing acknowledgment of the phrase "that you have sent me" therefore constitutes the goal and content of confession (11:42; 17:3, 8, 21, 23, 25). Along with ἀποστέλλω there also appears the formula ὁ πέμψας με πατήρ (→ πέμπω).

J.-A. Bühner

ἀποστερέω *apostereō* steal, rob*

Mark 10:19 lists "You shall not *steal*" under the commandments of the second table of the law; 1 Cor 6:8 accuses the addressees of *defrauding* the brethren, and 7:5 commands marriage partners not to *refuse* each other (cf. Exod 21:10). Pass. in 1 Cor 6:7 means *allow oneself to be defrauded;* 1 Tim 6:5 refers to false teachers who are "*bereft* of the truth," and Jas 5:4 to wages kept back by *fraud.*

ἀποστολή, ῆς, ἡ *apostolē* apostolic authority; apostolic office
→ ἀπόστολος 7.

ἀπόστολος, ου, ὁ *apostolos* delegate, apostle

1. Occurrences in the NT — 2. Paul — 3. Luke-Acts — 4. The rest of the NT — 5. Presuppositions and origin of the title of apostle — 6. Christological usage — 7. Ἀποστολή

Lit.: F. Agnew, "On the Origin of the Term Apostolos," *CBQ* 38 (1976) 49-53. — C. K. Barrett, *The Signs of an Apostle* (1970). — P. Bläser, "Zum Problem des urchristlichen Apostolats," *Unio Christianorum* (FS L. Jaeger; 1962) 92-107. — P. Borgen, "God's Agent in the Fourth Gospel," *Religions in Antiquity* (E. R. Goodenough memorial volume, ed. J. Neusner; 1968) 137-48. — U. Brockhaus, *Charisma und Amt* (1972) 112-23. — C. Brown, *DNTT* I, 135f. — J.-A. Bühner, *Der Gesandte und sein Weg im vierten Evangelium* (WUNT II/2, 1977). — W. Burgers, "De instelling van de twaalf in het evangelie van Marcus," *ETL* 36 (1960) 625-54. — J. Cambier, "Le critère paulinien de l'apostolat en 2 Cor. 12, 6s.," *Bib* 43 (1962) 481-518. — M. Cohn, "Die Stellvertretung im jüdischen Recht," *ZVRW* 36 (1920) 124-213, 354-460. — E. von Eicken and H. Lindner, *DNTT* I, 126-28 (bibliography on 136f.). — P. Gaechter, *Petrus und seine Zeit* (1958) 338-450. — D. Georgi, *The Opponents of Paul in Second Corinthians* (1985). — B. Gerhardsson, "Die Boten Gottes und die Apostel Christi,"

SEÅ 27 (1962) 89-131. — J. GIBLET, "Die Zwölf: Geschichte und Theologie," *Von Christus zur Kirche* (ed. J. Giblet; 1966) 61-78. — F. HAHN, "Der Apostolat im Urchristentum. Seine Eigenart und seine Voraussetzungen," *KD* 20 (1974) 54-77. — M. HENGEL, "Die Ursprünge der christlichen Mission," *NTS* 18 (1971/72) 15-38. — T. HOLTZ, "Zum Selbstverständnis des Apostels Paulus," *TLZ* 91 (1966) 324-30. — K. KERTELGE, "Das Apostelamt des Paulus, sein Ursprung und seine Bedeutung," *BZ* 14 (1970) 161-81. — J. A. KIRK, "Apostleship since Rengstorf: Towards a Synthesis," *NTS* 21 (1974/75) 249-64. — G. KLEIN, "Die Verfolgung der Apostel (Luk 11, 49)," FS Cullmann (1972) 113-24. — *idem, Die zwölf Apostel. Ursprung und Gehalt einer Idee* (1961). — E. M. KREDEL, "Der Apostelbegriff in der neueren Exegese. Historisch-kritische Darstellung," *ZKT* 78 (1956) 169-93, 257-305. — O. MICHEL, "Zeuge und Zeugnis. Zur neutestamentlichen Traditionsgeschichte," FS Cullmann (1972) 15-31. — J. P. MIRANDA, *Die Sendung Jesu im vierten Evangelium* (SBS 87, 1977). — *idem, Der Vater, der mich gesandt hat* ([2]1976). — D. MÜLLER, *DNTT* I, 128-35. — P. VON DER OSTEN-SACKEN, "Die Apologie des paulinischen Apostolats in 1 Kor 15, 1-11," *ZNW* 64 (1973) 245-62. — K. H. RENGSTORF, *TDNT* I, 407-47. — B. RIGAUX, *The Letters of St. Paul* (1968) 55-66. — J. ROLOFF, *Apostolat–Verkündigung–Kirche* (1965). — H. ROTTMANN, "Der Apostolat Pauli nach Apg 15 und Gal 1 and 2," *Igrejia Luterana* 24 (1963) 225-42. — A. SATAKE, "Apostolat und Gnade bei Paulus," *NTS* 15 (1968/69) 96-107. — G. SCHILLE, *Die urchristliche Kollegialmission* (ATANT 48, 1967). — G. SCHMAHL, "Die Berufung der Zwölf im Markusevangelium," *TTZ* 81 (1972) 203-13. — *idem, Die Zwölf im Markusevangelium* (TTS 30, 1974). — W. SCHMITHALS, *The Office of Apostle in the Early Church* (1969). — R. SCHNACKENBURG, "Apostles before and during Paul's Time," FS Bruce 287-303. — *idem,* "Apostolizität. Stand der Forschung," *Katholizität und Apostolizität* (*KD* Beiheft 2, 1971) 51-73. — W. SCHNEEMELCHER, Hennecke/Schneemelcher II, 25-31. — G. SCHNEIDER, "Die zwölf Apostel als 'Zeugen.' Wesen, Ursprung und Funktion einer lukanischen Konzeption," *Christuszeugnis der Kirche* (ed. Scheele and Schneider; 1970) 39-65. — O. H. STECK, *Israel und das gewaltsame Geschick der Propheten* (WMANT 23, 1967). — P. STUHLMACHER, "Evangelium–Apostolat–Gemeinde," *KD* 17 (1971) 28-45.

1. Of the 80 occurrences in the NT 29 are in the Pauline corpus (incl. Ephesians and Colossians), 34 in the Lukan writings, 1 in John, 5 in the Pastorals, and 8 in the remainder of the NT. The concentration in Paul and Luke indicates the two fundamental expressions of the concept in the NT.

2. Paul employs the concept ἀπόστολος in the service of an emphatically dignified and authoritative self-introduction in the opening lines of his letters (except Philippians and 1–2 Thessalonians). With this word he describes his task of proclaiming the gospel: he is authorized, as a messenger and representative of the crucified and risen Lord, to bring the gospel to the churches of the Gentile Christians (Rom 1:1; Gal 1:15; 2:8; 2 Cor 5:19; 1 Thess 2:4-9). Paul calls other persons ἀπόστολοι (→ 5); he includes himself in their understanding of apostleship and emphasizes on this basis the particularity which belongs to him (Schnackenburg, *Apostles;* Hahn 56-61).

Paul emphasizes that he is κλητός ("called," Rom 1:1; 1 Cor 1:1; Gal 1:15), indeed ἀφωρισμένος ("set apart," Rom 1:1; Gal 1:15) for the holy service of his apostleship. The calling occurred in a christophany (1 Cor 9:1; 15:9; Gal 1:12, 16), during which, simultaneously, the content of the gospel was established (Gal 1:12f.; Roloff 44f.). In 1 Cor 1:1 and 2 Cor 1:1 Paul points to the θέλημα, the communication of the divine will which comes from outside himself and determines his course: he is not an apostle of his own will and certainly not dependent on any other human will (Gal 1:1; 2 Cor 3:5); a necessity to preach the gospel is laid upon him (1 Cor 9:16). The one who sends is master, the apostle a δοῦλος ("servant": Rom 1:1; Phil 1:1; 2 Cor 4:5) who is obligated to obedience (Gal 1:10; 1 Thess 2:4, 6; cf. Bühner 123-27, 207-9). Paul assures the recipients of the gospel that he speaks only in accordance with his commission and not from motives of human deceit (1 Thess 2:3f.): he does not seek honor from human beings (v. 6) even though as an apostle he participates in the dignity of the one who sends him (v. 7). The appeal to the one who sends him (vv. 4-6; Rom 11:13; 1 Cor 9:16f.; 2 Cor 3:6ff.; cf. John 17:4f.) and the indication of his subordination to the gospel and its recipients (1 Thess 2:7-12; 1 Cor 9:19ff.) are united in his renunciation of a dignified appearance (1 Thess 2:7) and in his renunciation of apostolic rights (1 Cor 9:18; 2 Cor 11:7). In the apostolic service of the glory of God (Rom 11:13; 2 Cor 3-5) the apostle subordinates his own person (1 Cor 9:12, 18) in order to become one with the message and the one who sends him (1 Cor 9:23; 2 Cor 4:4-6). By grace God has enabled him to perform this service (1 Cor 3:10; 2 Cor 3:6; 4:1; Rom 12:3, 6; 15:15; Gal 1:15, 2:9; Eph 3:2, 7f.) and is present in his ministry (1 Cor 15:9f.; Rom 15:18; Gal 2:8). Over against the demands and obstinacy of his adversaries the apostle is free (1 Cor 9:1); only God can judge his obedience as an apostle (1 Cor 4:3f.). As an apostle of Jesus Christ, Paul is at the same time also sent by God (Rom 15:15f.; 2 Cor 5:18-20). Paul combines the terminology of heavenly glory, which unites God and Christ (2 Cor 5:19) and is given to the apostle as well (4:4-6), with the juridical model of substitution (Cohn 393ff.; Gerhardsson 118; Roloff 122f.; Bühner 250f.).

The meaning of ἀπόστολος is tied to the peculiar character the word has attained as a result of popular-juridical usage which has drawn on its Hebrew equivalent, *šālîaḥ* (see the foundational work on this by Rengstorf; cf. Cohn). Already according to pre-NT legal practice, which the rabbinic sources merely fix in written form, the *šālîaḥ* is the direct representative of the one who sends him and can in that person's place act in a way that is authoritative and legally binding (Cohn 133ff.). He is obligated to strict obedience (Cohn 144ff., 204-13) and to act in all matters in the best interests of the one who sends him (Cohn 139f., 145). The linking of the term "apostle" with legal titles which point to the perpetual bond to the one who sends and the task given by him to the Church (→ οἰκονόμος, διάκονος, δοῦλος, ὑπερέτης) corresponds to the custom of masters who appointed deputies as their representatives in charge of the household (Cohn 175ff.; Bühner, 124-27). One must add, finally, the countless observations which testify that not only Paul's calling but also his understanding of his mission as a whole is to be understood from the perspective of the OT prophets (Holtz: Deutero-Isaiah; Gerhardsson: Moses; Rengstorf 440f.: Jeremiah; Roloff 43f.: typological correspondence; Hahn 69-73: Isa 61:1; Rigaux 83ff.: Deutero-Isaiah, Ezekiel, Jeremiah): in post-biblical Judaism the prophet was also called a *šālîaḥ* of God (Bühner 271-315).

Against this background the Pauline concept of apostle becomes clear when one inquires after the particularity of the one who sends him, the message, and the recipients: Since the power of the commissioning Lord shows itself in earthly reality as the weakness of the cross, so also the power of the message lies in the foolishness of the word of the cross (1 Cor 4:9-13; 1:21); in his mission the apostle of the crucified Lord stands under the reality of the cross; his renunciation of his own rights and honor (1 Cor 9:12; 2 Cor 11:2, 23) is more than the exemplary obedience of the delegate; rather the apostle boasts about his weakness (2 Cor 11:23-33; 12:9) because the power of the Lord which provides the messenger with protection reveals itself in weakness (12:9f.; cf. Cambier). The glory in which the apostle participates in his mission is the glory reflected in the face of the crucified Lord (4:4ff.). Such glory makes the service of the gospel an undertaking filled with earthly afflictions (v. 7) and the apostle a bearer of suffering (v. 10; 1 Cor 4:9). On the way of the Lord majesty conceals itself in humiliation (Phil 2:5-11), wisdom in foolishness (1 Cor 1:21), wealth in poverty (2 Cor 8:9), in such a way that the apostolic office bears the stamp of the uniqueness of this Lord (2 Cor 4:5; cf. Roloff 119; Barrett 70). Thus, it is through the apostle that the Lord conveys the vivifying and justifying power of the cross to the Gentile Christian churches (2 Cor 4:10-12; 5:18-21; Gal 3:1).

3. Luke restricts the title ἀπόστολος to twelve disciples and, accordingly, never calls Paul apostle (except in Acts 14:4, 14, and there one suspects that a pre-Lukan source is speaking; cf. H. Conzelmann, *Acts* [Hermeneia] ad loc.). Luke uses the expression "the twelve apostles," "the twelve," and (most often) "the apostles" without differentiation.

In Acts the twelve apostles comprise the leaders of the church in Jerusalem (4:35, 37; 5:2; cf. 6:6). They are spokesmen for the Church who proclaim the gospel to those outside (2:37) and defend the Jewish Church against attacks (5:26ff.). Their major responsibility is attending to the tradition and preserving unfalsified teaching (2:42); they authorize the Gentile mission which is beginning (8:14, 18; 15:22f.; 16:4). Acts 1:15-26 names the essential criteria which an apostle must meet: he is one who has accompanied the earthly Jesus from the beginning, has been chosen by him (1:17; cf. Luke 6:13; 9:1), has been with him the entire time up to the ascension, and is thus also a witness of the resurrection (Acts 1:21f.; cf. vv. 2f.; Luke 24:36ff.). Thus a connecting line runs from the commissioning and bestowal of the title by the earthly Jesus (Luke 6:13) through the announcement of the mission by the risen Christ (Luke 24:46-48; Acts 1:8) with the promise of the Spirit (Luke 24:49; Acts 1:5, 8) to the reception of the Spirit, and with it the proclamation of the gospel, newly initiated from heaven (Acts 2ff.).

Even though the equation of the concepts of "the twelve" and "the apostles" betrays the resolute redaction of Luke, nonetheless this conception cannot be called purely Lukan (so Klein, *Zwölf Apostel*). Rather, there are signs of it in the pre-Lukan Synoptic tradition (along with the Lukan tradition cf. Rev 21:14; Roloff 112; Schille 113, n. 14; Schmithals 267f.; E. Haenchen, *The Acts of the Apostles* [1971] 163f.), which does not know the title apart from reference to the twelve: except for the text-critically uncertain passage (probably due to the influence of the Lukan parallel) in Mark 3:14, the twelve are called ἀπόστολοι in Mark 6:30: there is clearly a concentration here of the terminology which occurs in v. 7 of → ἐξουσία and → ἀποστέλλειν; the twelve disciples who are sent out participate in the power of the Lord who sends them and are in word and deed his authorized representatives who, in accordance with ordinary legal custom, return to the Lord who sent them out to report on the mission and return the *šᵉlîḥûṯ* ("apostolic commission" → 7; Bühner 123-27, 257f.). To this Markan state of the tradition corresponds also the designation of the twelve as apostles in Matt 10:2, a text independent of Luke. Also the Lukan concept of witness (Acts 1:8, 22; 2:32; 3:15; 5:32; 10:39; 13:31; cf. Luke 24:48; see Schneider), closely connected with the title of apostle, goes back to old Palestinian tradition which understands the apostle as one who is commissioned, who is obligated to the power of the resurrected One, and who stands up for it over against stubborn Israel (Michel 25, 27; cf. *t. Qidd.* 4:1, which is concerned with the task of the *šālîaḥ*, which is to be a witness for the will and claim of the one who sends him). In this connection, the mention of apostles in Luke 11:49 is debated; but even if Luke should have inserted his concept of apostle into Q at this point (so Klein, *Verfolgung; contra* Michel 22), the reference to the deuteronomic tradition of the prophets of repentance remains noteworthy: here it is not only the reference to sending and witness (= admonition) which plays a role in pre-Christian tradition, but within that reference the designation of the prophets as apostles

(Steck 214f.; 229, n. 5; cf. Michel 19ff.; Bühner 108ff.; 194, n. 9, 282).

4. The prescripts in Ephesians and the Pastorals display Pauline terminology that has been taken over unaltered. Ephesians speaks of the apostles in a titular sense (together with the prophets in 2:20; 4:11) as the foundation of the Church, to whom the mystery of Christ was revealed (3:5) and who are appointed by the Exalted One (4:11). The apostles are called "holy" (3:5) and are elevated to the status of mediators of salvation for the church (J. Gnilka, *Epheserbrief* [HTKNT] 157, 211). The Pastorals make of Paul the archetypal holder of the office, he who guarantees the preservation of the teaching of the gospel (1 Tim 2:7; 6:20; 2 Tim 1:11-14; cf. Roloff 241, 249). On the whole, the use of the word in the Pastorals corresponds more to Lukan usage than to Pauline. In the prescripts of 1–2 Peter the Pauline apostle terminology is applied to Peter; the apostles are distinguished from the prophets of the old covenant (2 Pet 3:2) and are the only and abiding mediators of the word of Christ (Jude 17).

In Revelation the letter to the Ephesian church praises the congregation for its patience by means of which it has exposed false apostles who have appeared there (Rev 2:2). Does this refer to representatives of an original apostolic order of "wandering charismatic missionaries" (assumed frequently since Harnack) or is it a polemic against known apostles or their successors (cf. W. Bousset, *Offenbarung* [KEK; [6]1906] 204; H. Kraft, *Offenbarung* [HNT] 56)? Rev 18:20 is familiar with apostles along with saints and prophets as the great martyrs of the NT (Kraft 237); finally, in 21:14 the concept of the twelve apostles is united with the tradition of the Church as the new edifice.

5. The influences of the Palestinian popular-juridical understanding of messengers and representatives, discernible in Paul and in the Synoptic tradition regarding the sending forth of disciples, should not be historically misunderstood. The so-called institution of the *šālîaḥ* does not describe a particular historical institution (unclarity is common on this point; cf. Roloff 39; Brockhaus 119; Schmithals 98-110); therefore, the NT term "apostle" cannot be traced back historically to the sending out of specific *šelûḥîm* of the Jewish community (*šelîaḥ ṣîbbûr* = "emissary of the congregation," i.e., delegation of the Jerusalem patriarchate; *šelûḥîm* as missionaries are unproven). However, in postbiblical tradition prophets are occasionally called *šelûḥîm* of God (Bühner 281-306); thus the usual far-ranging distinction between prophetic and legal sending (Schmithals 107f.; also Rengstorf 420 burdens his foundational exposition at this point with an inappropriate differentiation). Since the later papyri (cf. Agnew) also know Gk. ἀπόστολος in the personal sense (thus not in the predominantly elevated sense of "naval expedition" common up to that time) with the meaning of "emissary, authorized representative" and probably draw on oriental law and the Semitic concept of *šelîḥā'*, it is even more likely that during the NT period this popular-juridical word *šālîaḥ*, which was available for the religious sphere as well, entered into the vocabulary of the Christian mission. Schmithals's radical attempt to derive the primitive Christian title of apostle from the "emissary" of Gnostic mythology and prophecy destroys any adequate bridges to the Palestinian sphere via the history of culture and tradition (cf. also 1 Cor 15:7; Gal 1:17).

Not even Paul makes use of an historically defined, uniform concept of apostle (Georgi 35f.). He knows apostles as qualified, primitive Christian missionaries (Schnackenburg, "Apostolizität" 54; cf. *idem,* "Apostles" 301; Brockhaus 115f.), whereby missionizing preachers (1 Cor 9:5; 12:28; 2 Cor 11:13; Rom 16:7) and representatives of the congregation appointed to special tasks (2 Cor 8:23; Phil 2:25) are to be distinguished, but not basically separated (cf. Brockhaus 115f.; *contra* Hahn 56, 60f.; however, on the issue of the charismatic qualification of congregational apostles as well in Acts 13:1-3 cf. Georgi 38f.). These (partially charismatic) apostles of the congregation are distinguished according to 1 Cor 15:7 (cf. Gal 1:17, 19; 1 Cor 9:5) from a limited circle of persons who call themselves apostles of Jesus Christ and trace their apostolic office back to an encounter with the resurrected Lord (cf. 1 Cor 9:1; 15:3f.). Members of the circle of the twelve belong to the latter group (cf. Hahn 57; Brockhaus 114; Hengel 32; Barrett 31f.; *contra* Schneemelcher 28: only Peter). These Palestinian apostles of the risen Christ were surely active as such in the mission to the Jews from the beginning (cf. Hengel 32). At first Paul works together with Barnabas as an apostle of the church in Antioch (Acts 13:1-3; Gal 2:1). Obviously the separation from Antioch, the concept of mission which now for the first time becomes universally inclusive, and the peculiar nature of the Pauline concept of apostle are closely related (cf. Hengel 18). Paul was led to a concept of mission corresponding to that of the leaders in Jerusalem (Peter), i.e., the mission to Israel and the nations (cf. Gal 2:7-10) and came to see himself as an apostle of the risen Lord (Gal 1:15f.). Nowhere in the sources, however, is the title "apostle" traced back to being sent forth by the risen Christ; similarly, an initial sending forth of the apostles by the earthly Jesus using the title (first occurring in Luke 6:13) and its essential content, "witness of the risen One," cannot be identified in the Jesus tradition. It is more probable that the origins of the use of the word lie in the Jewish Christian mission of Palestine (or was it the "Hellenists" in Jerusalem who first called their missionaries ἀπόστολοι? cf. Schneemelcher 29): the testimony to the risen Christ was carried by prophets who called for repentance (cf. Acts 2:32ff.) and who, in language analogous to that of the prophetic (Isa 61:1) and levitical tradition, were called *šelûḥîm*.

6. Only in Heb 3:1 is Christ called ἀπόστολος: he is ἀπόστολος as the high priest in the heavenly sanctuary, entrusted with his task by God. In the heavenly dwelling he is the son who is responsible to the father. The cultic service in heaven, with which the ἀπόστολος/high priest/Son is entrusted, draws on and corresponds to the attribution of absolute authority (= charismatic acclamation) by the earthly Church and makes παρρησία, the assurance of free access to the heavenly sanctuary, possible for the earthly Church. The title of apostle grows out of cultic contexts and corresponds to Jewish use of *šālîaḥ* for the priest (on the whole issue cf. O. Michel, *Hebräer* [KEK, [7]1936] 171ff.).

The Gospel of John nowhere calls Jesus ἀπόστολος. The doctrine of the messenger, connected with the vbs. → ἀποστέλλω and → πέμπω, does not take its orientation from Gnostic mythology but from Jewish teaching concerning the prophet and the *šālîaḥ* (Borgen, Bühner): the Father who sends legitimizes the Son who is sent and directs him in descent and ascent into the prescribed paths of a messenger's course.

7. **Ἀποστολή*** *authorization, sending* points back, philologically and in meaning, to *š^{e}lîḥûṯ* in a manner analogous to the relationship between ἀπόστολος and *šālîaḥ* (cf. already *Tg. J.* Hag 1:13; Judg 2:1; *Tg. Esth. II* 5:8). In 1 Cor 9:2 Paul calls the Corinthian congregation the seal (i.e., confirmation) of his ἀποστολή *(apostleship)* because it makes clear that it has come into being as the ἔργον, the "apostolic work" (cf. Bühner 203), of Paul in the Lord (and in fulfillment of the Lord's commission). According to Rom 1:5 Paul received grace and *apostleship* in his calling. God has entrusted Peter with *apostleship* in relation to the circumcision (= the Jews) and Paul with that which extends to the Gentiles (Gal 2:8).

Acts 1:25 uses the word in its Lukan technical sense of *apostolic office*.

J.-A. Bühner

ἀποστοματίζω *apostomatizō* question closely (?)*

Luke 11:53: probably *question closely* (τινὰ περί τινος); cf. Plato *Euth.* 276c, 277a, referring there to the teacher: *speak from memory, recite.* LSJ s.v. stresses that in Luke 11:53 also the vb. is to be seen against the background of the activity of the teacher who questions a student.

ἀποστρέφω *apostrephō* turn away, turn away from*

Trans.: *turn away; send* someone or something *back* (Matt 26:52 [cf. 27:3 v.l.]; Luke 23:14; Rom 11:26; 2 Tim 4:4; probably also Acts 3:26). Mid.: *turn away from* (Matt 5:42; 2 Tim 1:15); *reject* someone or something (Heb 12:25; Titus 1:14). G. Bertram, *TDNT* VII, 719-22.

ἀποστυγέω *apostygeō* abhor*

Rom 12:9: *abhor* evil.

ἀποσυνάγωγος, 2 *aposynagōgos* excluded from the synagogue*

John 9:22; 12:42 with γενέσθαι: be *excommunicated from the synagogue;* 16:2 with ποιεῖν: *expel from the synagogue.* On the synagogue ban see Billerbeck IV, 293-333; K. L. Carroll, "The Fourth Gospel and the Exclusion of Christians from the Synagogues," *BJRL* 40 (1957/58) 19-32; W. Schrage, *TDNT* VII, 848-52; L. H. Schiffman, *Who Was a Jew? Rabbinic and Halakhic Perspectives on the Jewish-Christian Schism* (1985).

ἀποτάσσομαι *apotassomai* say farewell, turn away from*

Mark 6:46; Luke 9:61; 14:33; Acts 18:18, 21; 2 Cor 2:13. G. Delling, *TDNT* VIII, 33f.

ἀποτελέω *apoteleō* finish, bring to completion*

Luke 13:32: "*I perform* cures"; Jas 1:15: pass.: sin which has *achieved its goal.*

ἀποτίθεμαι *apotithemai* put off, take off, lay down*

Lit.: BAGD s.v. ἀποτίθημι. — E. KAMLAH, *Die Form der katalogischen Paränese im NT* (1964) 183-89. — MOULTON/MILLIGAN s.v. ἀποτίθημι. — E. G. SELWYN, *The First Epistle of St. Peter* ([2]1947) 393-400.

The vb., of which the act. does not occur in the NT, can be translated *put off* in nearly all NT examples (except for Matt 14:3). It is used literally of removal of clothing, e.g., Acts 7:58 (prior to stoning) and in the phrase "*throw* someone into prison" in Matt 14:3 (on this cf. Polybius xxiv.8.8; Pap. Eleph. 12; Moulton/Milligan; Lev 24:12; Num 15:34; 2 Chr 18:26 LXX).

Fig. use of ἀποτίθεμαι is predominant in the NT. Rom 13:12 speaks of throwing off "the works of darkness," Col. 3:8 of putting off vices, Eph 4:22, in the same sense, of putting off the "old man" (cf. Col. 3:9, ἀπεκδυσάμενοι). In metaphorical language (the standard catechetical terms of [baptismal] parenesis) ἀποτίθεμαι refers to "taking off" vices (as a garment): Eph 4:25 ("falsehood"); Jas 1:21 ("all filthiness and rank growth of wickedness"); 1 Pet 2:1 ("all malice and all guile"); and Heb 12:1 ("every weight, and sin"); the partc. ἀποθέμενοι in these passages is to be understood as a challenge (cf. Rom 13:12) or an imperative (as in Col 3:8); see L. Goppelt, *Der Erste Petrusbrief* (KEK) 133, n. 32.

G. Schneider

ἀποτινάσσω *apotinassō* shake off*

Luke 9:5: *shake off* the dust from your feet; Acts 28:5: Paul *shook off* the viper which had fastened itself to his hand.

ἀποτίνω *apotinō* make compensation*

Phlm 19: *I will pay the damages.*

ἀποτολμάω *apotolmaō* be bold*

Rom 10:20: Isaiah *is bold* and says (i.e., is so bold as to say). G. Fitzer, *TDNT* VIII, 183, 185.

ἀποτομία, ας, ἡ *apotomia* severity*

Rom 11:22 bis, of God's severity in contrast to his kindness (χρηστότης). H. Köster, *TDNT* VIII, 107f.

ἀποτόμως *apotomōs* severely*

2 Cor 13:10 has ἀποτόμως χρήσομαι for ἀποτομίᾳ χρήσομαι, *use severity;* Titus 1:13: Titus is to *rebuke sharply* the deceivers (v. 10). H. Köster, *TDNT* VIII, 106-9.

ἀποτρέπομαι *apotrepomai* detest*

2 Tim 3:5b: "*Avoid* such people."

ἀπουσία, ας, ἡ *apousia* absence*

Phil 2:12: in my *absence* (over against παρουσία; cf. 2 Cor 13:10).

ἀποφέρω *apopherō* take away*

In the NT always act.: Luke 16:22; Mark 15:1 (John 21:18 v.l.): *lead away* forcibly; Rev 17:3; 21:10, of being transported by the Spirit; Acts 19:12; 1 Cor 16:3, of transporting an obj.

ἀποφεύγω *apopheugō* escape*

Escape, run away from a person or thing, with acc. in 2 Pet 2:18, 20, with gen. in 1:4.

ἀποφθέγγομαι *apophthengomai* declare loudly*

Used of the speech of the wise man (Diogenes Laertius i.63, 73), the fortune-teller or prophet (Ezek 13:9, 19; Mic 5:11; Zech 10:2; Philo *Vit. Mos.* ii.33), or the inspired person in general. In the NT only in Acts 2:4, 14 as the effect of the Holy Spirit; 26:25 in connection with Paul before Festus. J. Behm, *TDNT* I, 447.

ἀποφορτίζομαι *apophortizomai* unload*

Acts 21:3: jettisoning the ship's cargo, a nautical t.t. (cf. *ThGL* II, 1785).

ἀπόχρησις, εως, ἡ *apochrēsis* consumption*

Col 2:22: foods or created things in general are meant to "perish (εἰς φθοράν) *as they are used* [dat.]."

ἀποχωρέω *apochōreō* go away, withdraw*

Matt 7:23: *depart* from me; Luke 9:39 of the evil spirit which "will hardly *leave*" the epileptic boy (cf. *Herm. Man.* v.2.6; xii.5.4); Acts 13:13: John *left* Paul and his companions.

ἀποχωρίζομαι *apochōrizomai* separate*

Acts 15:39: Paul and Barnabas (with Mark) separated from each other in discord; Rev 6:14: "the sky *vanished* like a scroll that is rolled up" (BAGD s.v.: *was split*); cf. R. H. Charles, *Revelation* (ICC) I, 181.

ἀποψύχω *apopsychō* die*

Luke 21:26 (not in the Markan parallel): human beings will *give up the ghost* from fear and foreboding of what is coming (not "faint" as in Homer *Od.* 24:348, but *die* as in 4 Macc 15:18; Philo *Aet.* 128; Josephus *Ant.* xix.114).

Ἀππίου φόρον *Appiou phoron* Forum of Appius*

Lit.: H. Nissen, *Italische Landeskunde* II (1902), 638f. — A. Weiss, PW VII, 64.

A market station on the Via Appia, established in 312 B.C. by Appius Claudius Caecus in connection with the construction of the road which, since the time of Nerva or Trajan, was paved northward from the market (*CIL* X, 6824), which was located 43 Roman miles (= 64 km.) from Rome (*CIL* X, 6825). Alongside the road flowed a canal southward from Ἀππίου φόρον through the Pontine Marshes to Tarracina 19 miles away, so that on this stretch one could choose between travel on the road and the more comfortable waterway. According to Horace, Ἀππίου φόρον was for this reason full of boatmen and evil taverns (*Sat.* i.3f.). Because of the swamps which claimed more and more of the region, the settlement ceased to exist by the 6th cent. at the latest. According to Acts 25:18 Paul was greeted here (as in Three Taverns) by the Roman Christians on his trip to Rome.

E. Plümacher

ἀπρόσιτος, 2 *aprositos* unapproachable*

1 Tim 6:16: God dwells in *unapproachable* light.

ἀπρόσκοπος, 2 *aproskopos* giving no offense, blameless*

Acts 24:16; 1 Cor 10:32; Phil 1:10; cf. *1 Clem.* 20:10;

61:1; *Herm. Man.* vi.1.4. G. Stählin, *TDNT* VI, 747f., 753-58.

ἀπροσωπολήμπτως *aprosōpolēmptōs* without regard for persons, impartially*

1 Pet 1:17 of God's *impartial* judgment; cf. *Barn.* 4:12; *1 Clem.* 1:3; E. Lohse, *TDNT* VI, 779f.; E. Tiedtke, *DNTT* I, 587.

ἄπταιστος, 2 *aptaistos* without stumbling*

Jude 24: φυλάξαι ὑμᾶς ἀπταίστους, to keep you from *falling.*

ἅπτω *haptō* kindle; (mid.) touch

Act. in Luke 8:16; 11:33; 15:8; 22:55 v.l.; Acts 28:2. Otherwise only mid., e.g., John 20:17: "stop *clinging* to me" (BAGD s.v. 2a); Col 2:21: "do not *touch*" (i.e., eat? or is the reference to sexual intercourse as in 1 Cor 7:1?). Touching to communicate blessing (healing: Mark 1:41 par. Matthew/Luke; Mark 7:33; 8:22; 10:13 par. Luke; Matt 8:15; 9:29; 17:7; 20:34; Luke 22:51), to harm (1 John 5:18), or to seek healing (Mark 3:10 par. Luke; Mark 5:27, 28, 30, 31 par. Matthew/Luke; Mark 6:56 par. Matthew). R. Grob, *DNTT* III, 859-61.

Ἀπφία, ας *Apphia* Apphia*

A Christian woman (wife of Philemon of Colossae?): Phlm 2. Moulton/Milligan s.v.

ἀπωθέομαι *apōtheomai* push back, reject*

Acts 7:27, 39; 13:46; 1 Tim 1:19. With God as subj. in Rom 11:1, 2: God has not *rejected* the people Israel (cf. Ps 93:14 LXX). K. L. Schmidt, *TDNT,* I, 448.

ἀπώλεια, ας, ἡ *apōleia* ruin (noun), destruction → ἀπόλλυμι.

ἀρά, ᾶς, ἡ *ara* curse, malediction*

Rom 3:14 (Pss 9:28; 13:3 LXX): "Their mouth is full of *curses* and bitterness." *DNTT* I, 418 for bibliography.

ἄρα *ara* so, consequently*

Lit.: J. Blomqvist, *Greek Particles in Hellenistic Prose* (Diss. Lund, 1969), esp. 128. — K. W. Clark, "The Meaning of ἄρα," FS Gingrich 70-84. — Denniston, *Particles* 32-43. — J. Grimm, H. W. Nordheider, and H. Brandt, "ἄρα," *Lexikon des frühgriechisches Epos,* founded by B. Snell and continued by H. Erbse, fascicle 7 (1973) 1126-64. — Kühner, *Grammatik* II/2, 317-26. — C. J. Ruijgh, *Autour de "τε épique"* (1971). — Thrall, *Particles,* esp. 10f., 36.

1. This particle is usually derived from ἀραρίσκω (see, e.g., Frisk, *Wörterbuch* s.v.) and recently also from ἀρ- in ἄριστος (see Ruijgh 433). It is attested since Homer *Il.* It occurs 49 times in the NT, of which 15 are in the Synoptic Gospels and none in John.

Ἄρα stands (in accordance with Wackernagel's law) as the second word in the clause: (a) in questions, as in classical usage (Denniston 39f.), 1) following τί(ς), only in the Synoptic Gospels and Acts (in direct questions: Matt 18:1; 19:25, 27; 24:45 par. Luke 12:42; Mark 4:41 par. Luke 8:25; Luke 1:66; cf. Job 23:3; in indirect questions: Luke 22:23; Acts 12:18); 2) following εἰ (only in indirect questions: Mark 11:13; Acts 8:22; 17:27; cf. Num 22:11); b) in direct questions without an interrogative particle (Acts 21:38; 2 Cor 1:17); c) following a vb. (Rom 7:21; Gal 3:7; cf., e.g., Homer *Il.* xviii.610; cf. also Rom 8:1; similarly Theognis 788); and d) following the particles 1) εἴπερ (1 Cor 15:15; cf., e.g., Aristotle *Cael.* 268a, 22) and 2) ἐπεί (1 Cor 5:10; 7:14; cf., e.g., ἐπεὶ ἄρ in Homer *Il.* xvii.658). However, it also appears as the first word in 27 NT occurrences (non-NT examples in Blomqvist 128), namely: e) 7 times in the apodoses of conditional sentences (Matt 12:28 par. Luke 11:20; 1 Cor 15:18; Gal 2:21; 3:29; 5:11; Heb 12:8; cf., e.g., Hom *Il.* vii.360; Ps 57:12 LXX; in second place in 1 Cor 15:14); f) 8 times at the beginning of a sentence (Matt 7:20; 17:26; Luke 11:48; Acts 11:18; Rom 10:17; 2 Cor 5:14; 7:12; Heb 4:9); and g) 12 times, all in the Pauline corpus, strengthened to ἄρα οὖν (Rom 5:18; 7:3, 25; 8:12; 9:16, 18; 14:12 [reading uncertain]; Eph 2:19; in exhortations in Rom 14:19; Gal 6:10; 1 Thess 5:6; 2 Thess 2:15; this combination always involves hiatus; in classical usage only οὖν ἄρα, see Denniston 43; cf. also *1 Clem.* 35:3). Of the classical combinations of particles only ἄρα γε occurs in the NT (cf. Denniston 43), in Matt 7:20; 17:26; Acts 17:27 (cf. Gen 26:9).

2. More recent research (Denniston; Ruijgh 435) assumes that the basic meaning of ἄρα conveys lively interest (frequently nearly untranslatable). This is still felt in → 1.a.1, e.g., Luke 22:23 (the question about the one who was to betray Jesus) or Acts 12:18 (the question about what had become of Peter) and is best rendered with Eng. *then;* similarly → 1.b, in the amazed question of the tribune in Acts 21:38 and in a weakened form in → 1.a.2, in which ἄρα can also mean *perhaps* (as in Paul's question in 2 Cor 1:17 which aims to evoke a negative answer).

The question can also indicate an inference *(then, thus)* as, e.g., in the reaction of the disciples to Jesus' rejection of the rich man in Matt 19:25 (καί in par. Mark 10:26/Luke 18:26). The inference is more strongly stressed in → 1.e). The inferential meaning *consequently* (cf. Dionysius of Thrace 95:2f., who counts ἄρα among the syllogistic conjunctions), which occurs more frequently following Plato, applies to → 1.c and 1.f. In → 1.g as well ἄρα designates the consequence, and οὖν strengthens this idea (e.g., in the summaries in Rom 5:18 and 7:25) or indicates a transition (e.g., 8:12). Ἄρα is used in → 1.d.1 (1 Cor 15:15) to indicate a recapitulation: *then, as they say.* Finally, → 1.d.2, the combination ἐπεὶ ἄρα is best translated *for otherwise* (BAGD s.v. 1).

In opposition to all this, Clark views the general meaning of the word in the NT and its environment as an expression of uncertainty regarding possible alternatives, which requires that each specific context be approached on its own and given a translation appropriate to it.

A. Horstmann

ἆρα *ara* (interrogative particle)

This interrogative particle (see Kühner, *Grammatik* II/2, 527f.; Denniston, *Particles* 46-51) anticipates a negative reply. It introduces only direct questions (BDF §440.2). There are only 3 occurrences in the NT: Gal 2:17 ("is Christ then an agent of sin?"); Luke 18:8 ("will [the Son of Man] find faith on earth?"); Acts 8:30 ("Do you understand what you are reading?" [ἆρά γε]). Cf. also *Herm. Man.* iv.1.4; *Diog.* 7:30.

Ἀραβία, ας, ἡ *Arabia* Arabia*

1. Geography — 2. Ἀραβία in Galatians — 3. Inhabitants of Ἀραβία

Lit.: ABEL, *Geographie* I, 288-94; II, 164-68. — J. ASSFALG, *LTK* I, 786f. — D. BALY, *Geography of the Bible* (1974). — C. K. BARRETT, "The Allegory of Abraham, Sarah, and Hagar in the Argument of Galatians," *Essays on Paul* 154-70 (= FS Käsemann 1-16). — H. BETZ, *Galatians* (Hermeneia, 1979). — G. CORNFELD and G. J. BOTTERWECK (eds.), *Die Bibel und ihre Welt* I (1969) 84-92. — E. GÜTING, "Der geographische Horizont der sogenannten Völkerliste des Lukas (Acta 2, 9-11)," *ZNW* 66 (1975) 149-69. — M. HÖFNER, *RAC* I, 575-85. — A. JEFFERY, *HDB* I, 47f. — E. LOHSE, *TDNT* VII, 285f. — F. MUSSNER, *Der Galaterbrief* (HTKNT, [2]1974). — A. NEGEV, "The Nabateans and the Provincia Arabia," *ANRW* II/8 (1977) 520-686. — M. NOTH, *Aufsätze zur biblischen Landes- und Altertumskunde* I (1971) 55-74. — H. P. RÜGER, *BHH* I, 118f. — A. SCHIMMEL-TARI, *RGG* I, 525f.

1. As a geographical term "Arabia" designates the Syrian Desert west of Mesopotamia and east of the Orontes and Jordan valleys and encompassing to the south the peninsula bounded by the Persian Gulf, the Indian Ocean, and the Red Sea. Whether it includes the Sinai peninsula is uncertain (Baly 104; Mussner 323). In Roman terminology Ἀραβία referred to the area south and southeast of Palestine which was inhabited primarily by Nabateans.

2. The only two occurrences of Ἀραβία in the NT are in Gal 1:17; 4:25 (without and with the def. art. respectively; BDF §261.6). The travels of Paul reported in 1:17 took him into the northern areas of the Nabatean kingdom. He mentions his travels in order to contrast them with an expected trip to Jerusalem: in the case of an apostle whose message was the result of human instruction, one would have to assume that, following his conversion, he would immediately have sought out the original apostles in Jerusalem in order to be taught by them. However, Paul not only remained in Damascus, far from Jerusalem, he even undertook a journey to Ἀραβία, i.e., into a completely different region.

In 4:25 Ἀραβία is intended in a general sense. Again it has to do with a contrast to Jerusalem: Together with the present, enslaved Jerusalem, Mt. Sinai stands in contrast to the free Jerusalem "above." By locating Sinai "in Arabia" Paul establishes the impossibility of a geographic union of the two places but does not see in this any hindrance to their "allegorical" correspondence. The understanding of the text is made more difficult by the uncertain textual tradition regarding → Ἁγάρ (v. 25; see Mussner; Betz ad loc.).

3. In the OT *ʿarāḇî* (pl. *ʿarᵉḇîm*) is used several times as a general designation for desert nomads. There was no collective designation for the inhabitants of the entire region of Arabia; they were named according to tribe and location. **Ἄραβες** (sg. Ἄραψ, Arabian) in Acts 2:11 is to be understood as a reference to Jewish inhabitants of the Nabatean kingdom. Presumably the author (according to E. Haenchen, *Acts* 171, a scribe who added "Cretans and Arabians" to the list of nations) knew that there were Christians among them.

U. Borse

ἄραγε *arage* then, consequently
→ ἄρα.

Ἀράμ *Aram* Aram*

Personal name in Matt 1:3, 4; Luke 3:33 v.l. (cf. 1 Chr 2:9f.; Ruth 4:19 v.l.).

ἄραφος, 2 *araphos* seamless*

John 19:23, referring to the garment (χιτών) of Jesus (cf. Josephus *Ant.* iii.161, referring to the garment of the High Priest). J. Repond, "Le costume du Christ," *Bib* 3 (1922) 3-14.

Ἄραψ, βος, ὁ *Araps* Arabian*

Acts 2:11: "Cretans and Arabians." → Ἀραβία 3.

ἀργέω *argeō* be idle*

2 Pet 2:3: the judgment *is not idle,* i.e., it is being prepared. G. Delling, *TDNT* I, 452.

ἀργός, 3 *argos* idle; careless; useless*

Matt 12:36 ("every *careless* word"); 20:3, 6, referring to men who stand *idle* in the marketplace; 1 Tim 5:13 (bis) of *idle* widows; Titus 1:12: Cretans are *lazy* bellies (i.e., gluttons?); Jas 2:20 (faith without works is *useless*); 2 Pet 1:8, referring to virtues which abound and do not allow the Christian to be lax, i.e., "*ineffective* . . . in the knowledge of our Lord Jesus Christ." G. Delling, *TDNT* I, 452.

ἀργύριον, ου, τό *argyrion* silver; silver money

1. Meaning — 2. Silver coins mentioned in the NT — 3. Judas's "thirty pieces of silver"

Lit.: A. Kindler, *Coins of the Land of Israel* (1974).

1. Ἀργύριον literally denotes *silver.* But the word is used in this sense in only one place in the NT: 1 Cor 3:12 v.l.; the image is typical of metal-stone juxtapositions common in antiquity. The word is otherwise always used of silver currency (20 NT occurrences, of which 8, all in Matthew, are pl.).

2. In the 2nd cent. B.C. silver was as valuable as gold; thus in the OT silver is mentioned first. This usage is found in the NT in 1 Pet 1:18; Acts 3:6; 20:33. The purchasing power of silver coins was very high during the NT period (cf. Matt 20:2-13: a denarius the size of an American penny is a day's wages). Matt 26:15; 27:3, 5, 6, 9 speak of silver currency given to Judas (thirty ἀργυρία) and 28:12, 15 of the "silver" for those who guard the tomb.

The following coins were struck in silver and displayed pictures of gods or emperors: denarius (the Roman coin corresponds to the Greek drachma), double drachma, and tetradrachma (= stater and corresponding to the Hebrew shekel). No Jewish administration prior to the Jewish War of A.D. 66-70, neither the Hasmoneans (contrary to earlier opinion!), Herod I, the tetrarchs, nor the procurators, struck silver coins (in Palestine only copper coins were struck). But all coins put into circulation in Palestine during the NT period bore Greek inscriptions.

3. Temple taxes had to be paid with the heavy Tyrian silver shekel or half shekel. The tradition regarding Judas's betrayal of Jesus has such coins in mind when it speaks of the "thirty pieces of silver" (Luther: "Silberlinge"). Only Matthew knows of this number and with it refers back to the "thirty shekels of silver" in Zech 11:12.

B. Schwank

ἀργυροκόπος, ου, ὁ *argyrokopos* silversmith*

Acts 19:24, referring to the silversmith Demetrius in Ephesus.

ἄργυρος, ου, ὁ *argyros* silver*

As money in Matt 10:9; as metal (mentioned with gold) in Acts 17:29; 1 Cor 3:12; Jas 5:3; Rev 18:12.

ἀργυροῦς, 3 *argyrous* silver*

Acts 19:24: the "*silver* shrines of Artemis"; 2 Tim 2:20: "In a great house there are not only vessels of gold and *silver* . . ."; Rev 9:20: "idols of gold and *silver.*"

῎Αρειος πάγος, ὁ *Areios pagos* Areopagus*
Ἀρεοπαγίτης, ου, ὁ *Areopagitēs* Areopagite*

Lit.: H. J. Cadbury, *The Book of Acts in History* (1955) 51f., 57. — H. J. Cadbury and K. Lake, *Beginnings* IV, 212f. — T. J. Cadoux, *OCD* 102f. — H. Conzelmann, *Acts* (Hermeneia, 1987) 139. — E. Curtius, "Paulus in Athen," *SPAW* (1893) 925-38. — M. Dibelius, "Paul on the Areopagus," *Studies in the Acts of the Apostles* (1956) 26-77, esp. 67-69; cf. 80f. in the same volume (!). — B. Gärtner, *The Areopagus Speech and Natural Revelation* (ASNU 21, 1955) 52-65. — E. Haenchen, *Acts* (1971) 513-31 (further lit. in *Apostelgeschichte* [KEK, [7]1977] 709f.). — I. T. Hill, *The Ancient City of Athens* (1953, 1969) (index s.v.). — B. Keil, *Beiträge zur Geschichte des Areopags* (1920). — W. G. Morrice, "Where Did Paul Speak in Athens . . .?" *ExpTim* 83 (1971/72) 377f. — Wachsmuth and Thalheim, PW II (1895) 627-33.

1. Acts 17:19, 22a mentions the *Areopagus* (῎Αρειος πάγος) and 17:34 the *Areopagite* Dionysius in the text framing Paul's speech in Athens (the "Areopagus speech" in 17:22b-31; lit. in Haenchen 513f.).

῎Αρειος πάγος means Hill of Ares and denotes both the rocky hill northwest of the Acropolis of Athens and the legal council which met there in ancient times (Herodotus viii.52; Pausanias i.28.5; Diogenes Laertius ii.101, 116; Cicero *Att.* i.14.5; *Nat. Deor.* ii.74; *SIG* index s.v. [IV, 234]). The latter was the court for criminal and capital matters and had jurisdiction in other areas at various times (cf. Thalheim 629-33; Keil). Following the Periclean period the "royal hall" came into use as a place in the market for the sessions of the ῎Αρειος πάγος. The jurisdiction of the ῎Αρειος πάγος in the Roman period (including, among other things, possibly public education? Plutarch *Cic.* 24; Thalheim 632) is unclear. Ἀρεοπαγίτης denotes a *member of the* ῎Αρειος *πάγος.*

2. Acts 17:19 reports that "they took hold of him [Paul] and brought him to [or before: ἐπί] the *Areopagus*" in order to learn more about his "new teaching." V. 22a introduces the speech of Paul: "So Paul, standing in the middle of the *Areopagus* (ἐν μέσῳ τοῦ Ἀρείου πάγου), said. . . ." Esp. in the second text one is inclined to understand the Areopagus as the council rather than the hill itself (*contra* Dibelius, Morrice; see v. 33: "So Paul went out from among them"; 1:15; 27:21). And the phrase with ἐπί in v. 19 can refer to the council before which Paul is brought (cf. 9:21; 16:19; 18:12). That the author of Acts has (primarily) the legal court in mind is suggested, moreover, by the mention of the Areopagite in v. 34. Dionysius is mentioned by name as one of the few who come to believe.

Of course, the author does not distinguish between the alternatives, between the court or the Hill of Ares, because for him the Areopagus is significant as a literary device: according to Acts Paul presented his message before the familiar Athenian "court" which was supposed to have jurisdiction in matters of religion and doctrine and which took no action against him. It was probably the mention of the Areopagite in the tradition which caused the speech to be set in a corresponding framework (cf. Dibelius 75).

G. Schneider

Ἀρεοπαγίτης, ου, ὁ *Areopagitēs* Areopagite
→ Ἄρειος πάγος.

ἀρεσκεία, ας, ἡ *areskeia* desire to please, obsequiousness*

Used in Col 1:10 in a positive sense: εἰς πᾶσαν ἀρεσκείαν, *fully pleasing* (to God) by means of a worthy life. W. Foerster, *TDNT* I, 456; H. Bietenhard, *DNTT* II, 814-17.

ἀρέσκω *areskō* desire to please, please*

Lit.: BAGD s.v. — H. Bietenhard, *DNTT* II, 814-16. — W. Foerster, *TDNT* I, 455-57. — Nägeli, *Wortschatz* 40.

1. The vb. ἀρέσκω occurs 17 times in the NT, primarily in Paul (4 times in Romans, 4 in 1 Corinthians, twice in Galatians, 3 times in 1 Thessalonians) and otherwise only in Mark 6:22 par. Matt 14:6; Acts 6:5; 2 Tim 2:4. Originally it denotes the establishment of a positive relationship between two persons or other entities ("make reparation, make peace") and has been taken over from the legal sphere into the aesthetic: *accommodate, please* (cf. Foerster 455). Derived from the pres. stem are: ἀρεσκεία, "desire to please, obsequiousness," and ἀνθρωπάρεσκος, "seeking to please people." From the root ἀρεστός, "pleasant," come: εὐάρεστος, "well-pleasing," and εὐαρεστέω, "be agreeable."

The one(s) *pleased* by the subj. of ἀρέσκειν (pass. and mid. forms are absent from the NT) or whom the subj. *desires to please* stands in the dat. and is usually sg. (e.g., θεῷ: Rom 8:8; 1 Thess 2:4, 15; 4:1), less often pl. (as in Rom 15:1: ἑαυτοῖς; 10:33: πᾶσιν; Gal 1:10 bis; 1 Thess 2:4: ἀνθρώποις). An exception is Acts 6:5 (ἐνώπιον with gen. corresponds to the LXX: 3 Kgdms 12:24f.; Jdt 7:16; cf. Ps 55:14 LXX).

2. The meaning *to please,* corresponding to LXX usage of the vb., is present above all in non-Pauline usage: Mark 6:22 par. Matt 14:6 (the daughter of Herodias "*pleased* Herod"); Acts 6:5 (the speech "*pleased* the whole multitude"); 2 Tim 2:4 (one aims to "*satisfy* the one who enlisted him" [as a soldier]); but also perhaps 1 Cor 7:32, 34 ("the Lord," one's "wife" or "husband").

Where the vb. has theological significance in the Pauline writings (cf. the frequently occurring phrases "please God," "please human beings" → 1), ἀρέσκω means primarily *desire to please, live in order to please.* Ἑαυτοῖς ἀρέσκειν (Rom 15:1) stands in opposition to the injunction: τῷ πλησίον ἀρεσκέτω (v. 2); the injunction is based upon v. 3: "For Christ did not *please* himself." 1 Thess 4:1 underscores the necessity of conduct which is pleasing to God (δεῖ ὑμᾶς περιπατεῖν καὶ ἀρέσκειν θεῷ); such conduct is not possible for οἱ ἐν σαρκὶ ὄντες (Rom 8:8).

Ἀρέσκω in Paul thus "characterizes man in [either] a false or a valid attitude to life" (Bietenhard 816). 1 Thess 2:15 pronounces over the Jews "who killed both the Lord Jesus and the prophets" the judgment that they "do not *please* [RSV *displease*] God." The apostle himself, freed following his call from all concern to please human beings (Gal 1:10), desires to live in such a way as to please God and Christ (1 Thess 2:4); he will attempt to please Jews and Greeks in his ministry in order to save everyone (1 Cor 10:33).

G. Schneider

ἀρεστός, 3 *arestos* pleasant, pleasing*

John 8:29; Acts 6:2; 1 John 3:22 (*pleasing* to God); Acts 12:3 (*pleasing* to the Jews). W. Foerster, *TDNT* I, 456.

Ἁρέτας, α *Haretas* Aretas*

Personal name of Nabatean kings. 2 Cor 11:32 refers to Aretas IV (*ca.* 9 B.C.–A.D. 40). Schürer, *History* I, 581-83; H. Windisch, *Der zweite Korintherbrief* (KEK) 364-66; H. Lietzmann and W. G. Kümmel, *An die Korinther I/II* (HNT; [4]1949) 152; J. Starcky, *DBSup* VII, 913-16.

ἀρετή, ῆς, ἡ *aretē* good conduct, virtue*

Phil 4:8; with πίστις in 2 Pet 1:5 (bis). The meaning in 1 Pet 2:9 is disputed: *praise* (cf. Isa 42:12; 43:21) or *miracle, divine power* (as in 2 Pet 1:3). O. Bauernfeind, *TDNT* I, 457-61; BAGD s.v.; further lit.: *DNTT* III, 932.

ἀρήν, ἀρνός, ὁ *arēn* lamb
→ ἀμνός 4.

ἀριθμέω *arithmeō* count*

Matt 10:30 par. Luke 12:7; Rev 7:9; cf. *1 Clem.* 10:6 (Gen 15:5). O. Rühle, *TDNT* I, 461-64.

ἀριθμός, οῦ, ὁ *arithmos* number*

Luke 22:3; John 6:10; Acts 4:4; 5:36; Rom 9:27; Rev 5:11; 7:4; 9:16 (bis); 13:17, 18 (3 times); 15:2; 20:8. Referring to a *crowd* in Acts 6:7; 11:21; 16:5. O. Rühle, *TDNT* I, 461-64; E. D. Schmitz and C. J. Hemer, *DNTT* II, 683-86 (bibliography on 703).

῾Αριμαθαία, ας *Harimathaia* Arimathea*

A town in Judea, the same as Ramathaim and home of "Joseph of Arimathea" (→ Ἰωσήφ 6; Mark 15:43 par. Matt 27:57/Luke 23:51/John 19:38). Abel, *Géographie* II, 428f.; *BL* 1446 s.v. Rama (4).

Ἀρίσταρχος, ου *Aristarchos* Aristarchus*

A man from Thessalonica who accompanied Paul (Acts 19:29; 20:4; 27:2). Phlm 24 calls Ἀρίσταρχος a "fellow worker" and Col 4:10 a "fellow prisoner" of Paul.

ἀριστάω *aristaō* eat breakfast*

Of the first meal in the morning: John 21:12, 15; of an unspecified meal: Luke 11:37.

ἀριστερός, 3 *aristeros* left (as opposed to right)*

Mark 10:37; Luke 23:33: one on the right, one on *the left* (ἐξ ἀριστερῶν); Matt 6:3: the left (hand) is not to know what the right is doing; 2 Cor 6:7: weapons which are wielded with the right or the left hand (i.e., offensive and defensive weapons).

Ἀριστόβουλος, ου *Aristoboulos* Aristobulus*

A personal name in Rom 16:10: "those who belong to the family of *Aristobulus*" (RSV) or "the people of the house of *Aristobulus,*" i.e., his slaves and household. H. Schlier, *Römerbrief* (HTKNT) 445; C. E. B. Cranfield, *Romans* (ICC) 791f.

ἄριστον, ου, τό *ariston* breakfast*

Luke 14:12 (cf. Josephus *Ant.* viii.356). Also used of the noontime meal and of an unspecified meal: Matt 22:4; Luke 11:38.

ἀρκετός, 3 *arketos* sufficient*

Matt 6:34; 10:25; 1 Pet 4:3. G. Kittel, *TDNT* I, 464-66.

ἀρκέω *arkeō* be enough, (pass.) be satisfied*

Act.: Matt 25:9; John 6:7; 14:8; 2 Cor 12:9. Pass.: Luke 3:14; 1 Tim 6:8; Heb 13:5; 3 John 10. G. Kittel, *TDNT* I, 464-66; B. Siede, *DNTT* III, 726-28.

ἄρκος, ου, ὁ, (ἡ) *arkos* bear (noun)*

Rev 13:2 (cf. Dan 7:5): "Its feet were like *a bear's.*"

ἅρμα, ατος, τό *harma* carriage; chariot*

Carriage: Acts 8:28, 29, 38; chariot: Rev 9:9; *1 Clem.* 51:5.

῾Αρμαγεδών *Harmagedōn* Armageddon*

1. Occurrences — 2. Meaning — 3. Background — 4. The physical setting of Megiddo

Lit.: C. Brütsch, *Die Offenbarung Jesu Christi* (ZBK) III ([2]1970) esp. 215ff. — G. Cornfeld and G. J. Botterweck, *Die Bibel und ihre Welt* II (1969) 1018-24. — J. Jeremias, *TDNT* I, 468. — A. Kempinski, *BRL* 213-18. — H. Kraft, *Die Offenbarung des Johannes* (HNT, 1974) 209f. — *idem,* "Zur Offenbarung des Johannes," *TRu* 38 (1973) 81-98. — A. Strobel, "Der Berg der Offenbarung," FS Stählin 133-46.

1. The place-name derived from Hebrew occurs only in Rev 16:16 and there as an indeclinable loanword, as is Maged(d)on, the LXX's Greek form of Megiddo (Judg 5:19 [A] and Josh 17:11: Μαγεδδω; 2 Chr 35:22: Μαγεδων). Westcott and Hort support the separated form ῞Αρ Μαγεδών.

2. Literally the name means *Mt. Megiddo.* The place is seen as the battlefield for the final conflict (cf. Ezek 38:1ff.; 1 QM 1:1ff. and *passim*) where the kings of the earth are to "assemble" (see Isa 14:13 LXX), led astray by demonic spirits who have their origin in the dragon, the beast, and the false prophet. The announcement of this event, very concrete when one takes the book as a whole, occurs in the context of the sixth vision in the bowl series, which is followed by the extensive description of the destruction of "Babylon," the great adversary of God's Church (16:17–18:24). The expression *Mt. Megiddo* is peculiar to Revelation, which makes it difficult to determine compositional elements with any degree of certainty.

3. The place-name would be mysterious-sounding for readers of Greek and probably presupposes a specific combination of OT texts assembled according to the rules of Jewish rabbinic exegesis. The Song of Deborah, which perhaps bears eschatological-typological significance, mentions (Judg 5:19) "the waters of Megiddo." According to rabbinic tradition, however, with which Rev 17:15 is familiar, "waters" can mean "peoples of the world." In view of the future destruction of Babylon, Isa 14:13 (LXX as well) speaks of "the mount of assembly *(har môʿēḏ).*" The testimony of Revelation is also oriented toward the destruction of Babylon. If the *ʿayin* in *môʿēḏ* were represented by a *gamma,* which would be natural since it was pronounced like *gamma* in the Hellenistic period, it would not have been difficult to read it as *Maged(d)o* (so Jeremias 468; Kraft 209f.). Moreover, Zech 12:11 MT speaks of "mourning" "on that day" "in the plain of Megiddo," a saying with which Rev 18:9-19 is thematically consistent. Finally, it may be that the idea of the "mountain of the world," the battleground of the anti-godly powers, at home in a rich apocalyptic-mythic tradition, plays a role—consciously or unconsciously—perhaps as the antitype of the "mountain of God" (or "mount of revelation"; Jeremias).

4. Megiddo (Tell el-Mutesellim) lies at the southern edge of the plain of Jezreel. The Via Maris from the Mediterranean coast to Damascus (Isa 9:1, MT 8:23) goes through the Carmel range by way of Wâdī ʿArah and enters the plain near Megiddo. The site, inhabited continuously from the Late Stone Age to the Persian period and of strategic importance, was verified and excavated by G. Schumacher of Germany in 1903-5, later by the Americans C. S. Fisher, P. L. Guy, and G. Loud, and finally in 1960 and the years following by Y. Yadin of the Hebrew University. In the history of Israel Megiddo epitomized the blood-soaked and fateful battlefield (Judg 5:19; 2 Kgs 23:29; 2 Chr 35:22; Zech 12:11). Whether in the NT period *Mt. Megiddo* still referred to the stately hill of ruins or, perhaps, to Mt. Carmel, must remain an open question. The testimony of Revelation undoubtedly seeks to make of the geographical place a broader symbol.

A. Strobel

ἁρμόζω *harmozō* fit together; betroth*

Intrans. *fit with* something (dat.) is frequent in *Hermas* but not found in the NT. Trans. *join together* (in marriage), *betroth* is used as a t.t. (Nägeli, *Wortschatz* 25) in 2 Cor 11:2: I *betrothed* you to one man (mid. in place of act.: BDF §316.1).

ἁρμός, οῦ, ὁ *harmos* seam; joint*

Heb 4:12, of the Word of God as a sword "piercing to the division . . . of *joints* and marrow"; cf. O. Michel, *Hebräer* (KEK) 197-203.

ἀρνέομαι *arneomai* refuse*
ἀπαρνέομαι *aparneomai* refuse*

1. Occurrences in the NT — 2. Meaning — 3. The saying about the Son of Man — 4. Peter's infidelity

Lit.: J. Blinzler, *BL* 1831. — G. Bornkamm, "Das Wort Jesu vom Bekennen" (1938), *idem, Aufsätze* III, 25-36. — A. Dauer, *Die Passionsgeschichte im Johannesevangelium* (1972) 72-79, 88-90, 314-16. — D. Dormeyer, *Die Passion Jesu als Verhaltensmodell* (1974) 110-17, 149-55. — R. A. Edwards, "The Eschatological Correlative as a *Gattung* in the NT," *ZNW* 60 (1969) 9-20. — A. Fridrichsen, " 'Sich selbst verleugnen,' " *ConNT* 2 (1936) 1-8. — *idem*, "Ἀρνέομαι im NT, insonderheit in den Pastoralbriefen," *ConNT* 6 (1942) 94-96. — P. Hoffmann, *Studien zur Theologie der Logienquelle* (1972) 155f. — G. Klein, "Die Verleugnung des Petrus" (1961), *idem, Rekonstruktion und Interpretation. Gesammelte Aufsätze zum NT* (1969) 49-98. — E. Linnemann, "Die Verleugnung des Petrus," *idem, Studien zur Passionsgeschichte* (1970) 70-108. — D. Lührmann, *Die Redaktion der Logienquelle* (1969) 51f. — K.-G. Reploh, *Markus, Lehrer der Gemeinde* (1969) 123-40. — H. Riesenfeld, "The Meaning of the Verb ἀρνέομαι," *ConNT* 11 (1947) 207-19. — W. Schenk, *Naherwartung und Parusieverzögerung: Theologische Versuche* IV (1972) 47-69, esp. 56-61. — *idem, Der Passionsbericht nach Markus* (1974) 215-29. — L. Schenke, *Studien zur Passionsgeschichte des Markusevangeliums* (1971) 348-460. — *idem, Der gekreuzigte Christus* (1974) 15-22. — H. Schlier, *TDNT* I, 469-71. — G. Schneider, *Verleugnung, Verspottung und Verhör Jesu nach Lukas 22, 54-71* (1969) 42-45, 73-96, 170f. — *idem, Die Passion Jesu nach den drei älteren Evangelien* (1973) 73-82. — Schulz, *Q* 66-76. — P. Vielhauer, "Jesus und der Menschensohn," *idem, Aufsätze zum NT* (1965) 92-140, esp. 101-7. — M. Wilcox, "The Denial Sequence in Mark 14, 26-31. 66-72," *NTS* 17 (1970/71) 426-36.

1. Of the 32 NT occurrences of the simple form, more than half are distributed among the Evangelists (Mark has 2, Matthew 4, Luke 4 in the Gospel and 4 in Acts, and John, in dependence upon the Synoptics, 4). Moreover, it is a favorite word in the Pastorals (7: 1 in 1 Timothy, 4 in 2 Timothy, 2 in Titus), whereas it does not occur in Paul's letters at all. The remaining occurrences are distributed among 1 John (3), Revelation (2) and Heb 11:24; Jude 4 par. 2 Pet 2:1. The 11 occurrences of the compound are confined to the Synoptics (4 in Mark, 4 in Matthew, 3 in Luke). In contrast to these 43 occurrences, the LXX has only 6 occurrences of the simple form (5 of which are not from Hebrew: 3 in Wisdom and 2 in 4 Maccabees) and 1 of the compound. The increased usage in the Greek Church reflected in the Pastorals is also seen in the 19 occurrences of the simple form, 5 of the compound, and 2 of the subst. (which is absent from the LXX and the NT) in *Hermas* (cf. Ignatius: 3 instances of the simple form and 1 of the compound; 2 Clement: 2 instances of the simple form).

2. The vb. refers to the expression of the subject's attitude of refusal (1) in relation to a claim or demand (cf. Schlier 469), therefore, *refuse* (*decline, reject:* Wis 17:10; 12:27; 16:16; Heb 11:24), or, similarly, (2) in relation to an assertion or counterquestion, therefore, *dispute* (*deny:* Gen 18:15; Luke [redactional] 8:45; Acts 4:16). In the narrower sense involving an already existing relationship to a person or commitment ἀρνέομαι with a personal (as often in the NT, but already also in Apollonius Rhodius i.867, 932) or material obj. refers to the dissolution of this bond by direct or indirect means, therefore, *renounce* (in a situation of persecution, already in 4 Macc 8:7; 10:15).

As a designation for such a change in a relationship involving fidelity, it may be used both for *repentance* (Isa 31:7; Titus 2:12) and for *apostasy;* it is thus neutral in valuation. The decisive semantic element is not that of a false position (the assertion of something which is incorrect, which would be → ψεύδομαι) but rather that of opposition (the contesting of something already in existence); only because of this it can be used reciprocally (Luke 12:9 par.) and even reflexively (Mark [redactional] 8:34 par.; 2 Tim 2:13); thus the addition of → ψεύστης in 1 John 2:22 is necessary in order to denote a further semantic dimension (Cremer/Kögel s.v.). Thus the stress is misplaced when the usual lexical entry "deny" is at once construed in the sense of a claim not to know or be associated with someone, to renounce any relationship with that person (cf. the relationship between the Germ.

compound *verleugnen* and the simple form *leugnen* in *Synonymwörterbuch,* ed. H. Görner and G. Kempcke [1973] s.v., and the semantic evidence of current syntactical forms in E. Agricola, *Wörter und Wendungen* [81977] 677).

Partial synonyms are ἀποδοκιμάζω, ἐξουθενέω, ἐπαισχύνομαι, and σκανδαλίζω. The well-established Greek antonym in the sense of a contrasting pair, already in Aristotle *Rh.* xxxvii.1444b, 10ff. (cf. Josephus *Ant.* vi.151—but absent in the LXX), is → ὁμολογέω in the sense of "accept, affirm, acknowledge."

The compound is equivalent to the simple form in meaning (Schlier 471) and carries neither the semantic element of deceitfulness (cf. Isa 31:7) nor of intensification (cf. the interchangeability of the two in the narrower contexts, *contra* Schneider, *Passion* 76f.).

3. The earliest and decisive use occurs in the antithetical double saying of Luke 12:8f. par. (Q) within a structure of conditional parallelism. This use was formed by the later elaboration of Q (*contra* Schulz), since it alone transfers the "Son of Man" title, which had been anchored in eschatological comparative sayings (Luke 17:24-30 [Q]), to a saying in parallel form which, in fact, leads one to anticipate the naming of God in the final clause (Edwards). Employing the secular Greek antonym pair with reference to Jesus in a forensic setting (so Vielhauer on the basis of ἔμπροσθεν), the saying has to do with the acceptance or *nonacceptance* of the Jesus tradition (as presented in Q) by the Christian witnesses and by their hearers (Hoffmann).

Mark 8:38 has generalized ἀρνέομαι to ἐπαισχύνομαι, "be ashamed" (*contra* Schlier 470 not merely as an indication of motive) and has transferred ἀρνέομαι to the beginning of his compilation of sayings, in v. 34. By the word's introduction there another Q saying's image of "taking up the cross" comes to be redactionally interpreted as *self-surrender* (Fridrichsen; Reploh 126; *contra* Schlier's [471] existential spiritualizing: "radical renunciation of [self]").

A Lukan use of the Q Son of Man saying is present in the statement in Peter's speech in Acts 3:13f.: Luke can apply the accusation of *renunciation* to Israel's relationship to the death of Jesus (*contra* Schlier 469) since in the Lukan philosophy of history God has not inaugurated a new history in Jesus, but rather has continued and fulfilled Israel's history. In the same way, in Stephen's speech Acts 7:35 typologically designates a similar attitude toward Moses on the part of Israel as a whole as *renunciation.*

John 1:20 also makes use of the pair of antonyms of the Q Son of Man saying in relation to commitment to Christ (W. Schenk, "Joh 1, 19-28," *EPM* 1 [1972/73] 25-30). 12:42 makes clear the danger of "renunciation," and since the Evangelist consistently views the Baptist as "witness" (1:7f., 19) there exists here a "previous relationship of obedience and fidelity" (*contra* Schlier 470; cf. 1:15!); thus what is at issue here is really a *renunciation* which leads to the danger of apostasy.

That Rev 2:13 (over against → κρατέω, "hold fast my name") and 3:8 (over against → τηρέω, "you have kept the word") belong to the later history of our Q saying is proven by 3:5 where the latter part of the verse with its positive statement has been taken over from Matt 10:32 and the conditional construction, with syntactical modification, preserved. As in John 1:20, here also perseverance, *not falling away,* in a situation of oppression is praised (just as later in *Diog.* 7:7; 10:7).

The warning aspect of the Q saying is taken up in 2 Tim 2:12 in an admonition addressed to those who bear responsibility for teaching the word; it has already been formed by tradition (as shown by the citation formula in v. 11a) and is here a third parallel conditional sentence combined with Pauline quotations. That the issue here again is the renunciation which results in the risk of apostasy in the face of oppression is made clear by the use in the context of synonyms (in v. 13a the idea is resumed by means of → ἀπιστέω, "become faithless," and it is prepared for in the wider context by ἐπαισχύνομαι, "be ashamed," in 1:8, 12) and antonyms (συναποθνῄσκω, "die with," 2:11; → ὑπομένω, "endure," v. 12). However, the author seems to criticize the idea of retribution contained in the Q saying, for when he picks up the thought in v. 13 he completely breaks and contradicts the correspondence scheme by using in the second half of the sentence not a synonym for Jesus' "denial," but rather an antonym, referring, i.e., to Jesus' unalterable fidelity. The author thereby also guarantees that the "living with" of v. 11 and the "reigning with" of v. 12 are not earned through suffering and death, but are based solely on the fidelity of Jesus. In any case, the contradictory manner in which the thought is picked up in v. 13 makes it clear that the author does not understand Jesus' denial in the quotation in v. 12 as the definitive rejection associated with a final judgment, but rather as a punctiliar, preliminary, and repeatable act. The contradictory character of the commentary contained in the continuation of the thought is further established by the additional argument of v. 13b where the catchword ἀρνέομαι is picked up from the quotation itself and used to restate v. 13a: Jesus *cannot be untrue to himself.*

A new area of application for the pair of antonyms in our Q saying becomes apparent at the beginning of the 2nd cent. in 1 John 2:22f. (parallel and contemporary is Ign. *Smyrn.* 5:1f.; *Magn.* 1:9): in place of an external separation from the Church, now a docetic christology within the Church itself is viewed as denial. Jude 4 shows this same application to false teachers and couples it, moreover, with ethical accusations; both are taken over from Jude by 2 Pet 2:1. Finally, the Pastorals complete the process by bringing against the false teachers the charge that by their actions (Titus 1:16: ἔργοις) they are for all practical purposes *rejecting* God, the substance of their religion (2 Tim 3:5: εὐσεβείας δύναμιν in connection with the vice catalog in vv. 2-4!), or the faith (1 Tim 5:8: by not providing for the members of their own families) and hence are "worse than an unbeliever." This ethical explication is presented in a contemporary writing, *2 Clem.* 3:1; 17:7, by means of an explicit quotation of the Q saying according to Matt 10:32.

4. In the material concerning Peter's infidelity only Mark 14:30 can be regarded as pre-Markan. In the last of the four predictions which introduce the Passion (14:27a, 29, 30; cf. Dormeyer; Schenk, *Passionsbericht*) ἀπαρνέομαι is a synonym for "fall away" (σκανδαλίζομαι, vv. 27, 29), which refers to a falling away from Jesus. "Deny" refers, i.e., to the overall conduct of the disciples in view of the coming Passion. But the (redactional) prediction of Peter's *threefold* failure (v. 30) apparently refers only to his conduct in Gethsemane when Jesus is arrested and to his denial under oath. The pre-Markan account of Peter's denial was surely recounted as a single act (14:54a, c, 66b, 67b, 71a, 68b, 72a; Schenk, *Passionsbericht;* cf. also Dormeyer); it might have had no occurrence of ἀρνέομαι; and its essential point was the fulfillment of the prediction.

The Markan redactor adds to the conversation in 14:31 and thus relocates the emphasis away from Jesus' prediction to Peter's denial of the truth of it. But the latter is portrayed as doomed to failure from the outset by the divine prophecy in v. 27b (redactional). At the same time Peter's failure is diluted into a temporary breakdown which no longer represents a definitive falling away by means of the redactional preview in v. 28 of the restoration brought about by Easter. Corresponding to the confinement of Peter's denial to one episode is also the new and narrower reference to what are now three scenes in Mark 14:66-72. The content of the sentence in v. 68 is now formulated in such a way that the vb. in the introductory statement speaks only of denial, not of renunciation; this then means that the vb. with the personal obj. in vv. 30f. (and 72) is to be understood, according to the Markan redactor, in the same way: "*deny* me three times." The redactor understands the account as essentially a negative example story. This parenetic character is underscored by the redactional interweaving of it into the trial scene: at the very moment that Jesus affirms his path of suffering, Peter *denies* him (cf. the similar redactional composition in 8:27-38). Perhaps it is from this perspective as well that the generalizing "be ashamed" over against the Q-saying is to be regarded in 8:38.

Matthew takes over all five instances of the vb. in this Markan complex and follows the latter's composition as well. In Peter's prediction (Matt. 26:33) he applies the christological referent of ἀπαρνέομαι (vv. 34f.) to the synonym σκανδαλίζομαι (a favorite Matthean word). He thereby unifies and strengthens the christological orientation in the negative sense of a falling away; this in turn influences the understanding of ἀπαρνέομαι. Also of semantic significance is the redactional introduction of Peter's statement in v. 35 with an asyndetic historical pres. (W. Schenk, "Das Praesens historicum," *NTS* 22 [1975/ 76] 464-75, esp. 473); the reply of Peter is to be understood primarily as a positive reaction to Jesus' statement, as a declaration of loyalty which intensifies the narrative tension and moves the story to its continuation. That the Matthean redactor has strengthened the account in the opposite direction from Mark is also made clear by v. 70: by using ἔμπροσθεν Matthew conforms the sentence to the Q logion in 10:33 and thus interprets ἀρνέομαι in the sense of *renunciation.* Corresponding to this is the transformation of the substance of the saying into a formal oath: "I have nothing to do with the matter" (RSV is different). The same direct transgression against a saying of Jesus (5:33-37) is seen in 26:72 where by means of an added phrase Matthew expressly takes ἀρνέομαι as an oath (cf. 14:7). That the *renunciation* is final is also stressed when in 26:75, as in v. 35, με is placed at the end: Matthew is the first and only one to understand the story as a final repudiation.

By contrast, the Lukan redactor's weakening of the tradition is already evidenced by his taking over of only 3 occurrences of the vb. Mark 14:27f., 31 is omitted and with it the connection with the synonym σκανδαλίζομαι. The recasting of the saying in Luke 22:34 ("that you know me") makes clear that Luke understands ἀπαρνέομαι only as *opposition* to the statement of another. V. 57 is altered in the same sense: "he *denied* it, saying, 'Woman, I do not know him.'" V. 61 is then to be translated correspondingly. It is consistent with all of this that Luke dissolves the Markan interweaving: The story of Peter is no longer attached to the trial of Jesus but is made parallel to the mocking scene (vv. 63-65). "Since the faith of Peter has not ceased, his immediate 'return' (cf. 22:32: ἐπιστρέψας) resulting from the look of Jesus (v. 61) is possible. No appearance of the resurrected One is required!" (Schneider, *Passion* 81f.). It is clear from this why Acts 3:13f. lets Peter himself say that Israel (and not Peter) has *rejected* Jesus.

John has also taken over the episode (with only three occurrences of the vb.) and has again sharpened the understanding of it, now in the sense of 1:20. The Johannine phrase "lay down your life for me" in 13:38 is the antonym. Correspondingly, 18:25 emphatically adds "his disciples" (cf. v. 19), v. 26 gives to v. 27 the content of "with him," and in 21:15ff. an explicit rehabilitation takes place through the resurrected One.

W. Schenk

Ἀρνί *Arni* Arni*

A personal name in Luke 3:33.

ἀρνίον, ου, τό *arnion* ram, lamb
→ ἀμνός 3.

ἀροτριάω *arotriaō* plow (vb.)*

Luke 17:7, of the servant *plowing;* 1 Cor 9:10 (bis): "the *plowman* should *plow* in hope."

ἄροτρον, ου, τό *arotron* plow (noun)*

Luke 9:62: one "puts his hand to the *plow*" in order to begin the work.

ἁρπαγή, ῆς, ἡ *harpagē* robbery; plunder
→ ἁρπάζω 5.

ἁρπαγμός, οῦ, ὁ *harpagmos* robbery(?)*

Lit.: J. Carmignac, "L'importance de la place d'une négation: οὐχ ἁρπαγμὸν ἡγήσατο (Phil. II.6)," *NTS* 18 (1971/72) 131-66. — A. Feuillet, "L'hymne christologique de l'épître aux Philippiens (II, 6-11)," *RB* 72 (1965) 352-80, 481-507. — D. Georgi, "Der vor-paulinische Hymnus Phil 2, 6-11," FS Bultmann (1964) 263-93. — J. Gewiess, "Die Philipperbriefstelle 2,6b," FS Schmid (1963) 69-85. — J. Gnilka, *Der Philipperbrief* (HTKNT, 1968). — L. L. Hammerich, *An Ancient Misunderstanding (Phil 2, 6 'robbery')* (1966). — O. Hofius, *Der Christushymnus Philipper 2, 6-11* (WUNT 17, 1976). — R. Hoover, "The Harpagmos Enigma: A Philological Solution," *HTR* 64 (1971) 95-119. — R. P. Martin, *Carmen Christi: Philippians 2:5-11 in Recent Interpretation and in the Setting of Early Christian Worship* ([2]1983).

1. Ἁρπαγμός occurs in Phil 2:6 and nowhere else in the NT. It is very rare in secular Greek and does not appear in the LXX or the Apostolic Fathers. The meaning which predominates in secular Greek, *robbery,* is out of the question for Phil 2:6. For this reason it is proposed that equating it with ἅρπαγμα is linguistically possible, and it is translated accordingly (Abel, *Grammaire* 110; BAGD s.v.; W. Foerster, *TDNT* I, 473f.), although there is no example of this in non-Christian sources. Ἅρπαγμα is (1) *plunder* or *booty,* or (2) *a chance occurrence, lucky break,* or *blessing.*

2. In the Christ-hymn of Phil 2:6-11 it is said of the preexistent one (who "was in the form [μορφή] of God") that he did not ἁρπαγμὸν ἡγήσατο "equality with God." The phrase under discussion must be taken as an unceremonious expression, even as a kind of slogan: take advantage of (or seek to take advantage of) something for oneself (Foerster loc. cit.; Gnilka 116f.). But in what sense does this apply to "equality with God"—as something which seductively offers itself as booty *(res rapienda)* or as something which the preexistent one already possesses *(res rapta)*? The better arguments favor the latter interpretation, esp. in view of the antithesis in v. 7. This would yield the most likely sense: The heavenly Christ did not believe that he should regard his position of honor, i.e., his "equality with God," as something *to take advantage of for himself, to grasp, to treat as booty* (Gnilka 117; Hofius 56f. et al.; *contra* Carmignac 165f., who relates the negation to ἁρπαγμός and translates οὐχ ἁρπαγμόν as "pas une usurpation").

W. Trilling

ἁρπάζω *harpazō* steal, take away forcefully*

1. Occurrences in the NT — 2. Meaning — 3. Usage — 4. Compounds — 5. Ἁρπαγή — 6. Ἅρπαξ

Lit.: G. Braumann, " 'Dem Himmelreich wird Gewalt angetan' (Mt 11, 12 par.)," *ZNW* 52 (1961) 104-9. — W. Foerster, *TDNT* I, 472-74. — P. Hoffmann, *Studien zur Theologie der Logienquelle* (NTAbh 8, 1972), esp. 50-79. — G. Lohfink, *Die Himmelfahrt Jesu* (SANT 26, 1971). — A. H. McNeile, *The Gospel According to St. Matthew* (1915). — E. Percy, *Die Botschaft Jesu* (1953) 191-202. — G. Schrenk, *TDNT* I, 609-14. — Schulz, *Q* 261-67. — W. Trilling, *Das wahre Israel* (SANT 10, [3]1964).

1. The 14 occurrences of ἁρπάζω are distributed throughout the NT. Matthew has 3 occurrences in three different texts (the only instances in the Synoptics). John has 4, 3 of which are in ch. 10. There are 2 occurrences in Acts, 2 in 2 Corinthians, and one each in 1 Thessalonians, Jude, and Revelation.

2. The vb. means: (1) *snatch, steal,* and (2) *tear* something *away* (quickly, greedily, or firmly). It is used: (1) frequently of looting, stealing, plundering (Pape, *Wörterbuch* s.v.; Moulton/Milligan s.v.; examples from Josephus in Hoffmann 77, n. 94) and (2) of abducting, arresting, and specifically of carrying away or being carried away in visions and other ecstatic phenomena (BAGD s.v.; Foerster 472).

3. The meaning *steal* (1) with acc. obj. refers to possessions (τὰ σκεύη) in the parabolic saying of Matt 12:29 (Mark 3:27 has διαρπάζω), to the tearing out of the "seed" of the word by the devil in Matt 13:19 (Mark 4:15; Luke 8:12 are different) and to the sheep who fall prey to the thieving wolf (→ 6) in John 10:12.

The vb. is applied to the reign of God in the difficult and disputed "men of violence" saying in Matt 11:12 par. Luke 16:16. It is fairly certain that this is an independent saying, that it belongs to Q, that it has been subject to redactional activity by both Evangelists, and that Matt 11:12b with ἁρπάζουσιν (over against Luke 16:16c) is the older form. The use of this vb. lends support to an interpretation which moves in one of the many directions made possible if one takes v. 12b as an elucidation or supplement (synthetic parallelism: Hoffmann 68, n. 61) which carries forward the thought of v. 12a (so esp. Schrenk 609f.) in this sense: God's reign suffers violence—and violent people *are plundering* it. Βιάζεται is thus (as trans. pass. *in malam partem*) interpreted with reference to hostile and violent resistance to God's reign, and ἁρπάζουσιν is understood as conative pres.: they *wish* or *attempt to plunder* (or some similar rendering; cf. Kühner, *Grammatik* I, 140; Mayser, *Grammatik* II/1, 134).

Also in favor of this interpretation is that in secular literature ἁρπάζειν in connection with βιάζεσθαι alway refers to hostile plundering (Plutarch *Apophth.* II, 203c.; Lucian *Herm.* 22; see also E. Moore, "*BIAZŌ, ARPAZŌ* and Cognates in Josephus," *NTS* 21 [1974/75] 519-43). According to Dalman, *Worte* 115 (followed by Black, *Approach* 84, n. 2) the use of both vbs. in Matt 11:12 is based on the same Aram. vb., *'ns,* meaning both "use force" and "rob" (thus already McNeile 155).

Some see behind the two existing versions of this saying an authentic word of Jesus (E. Käsemann, "The Problem of the Historical Jesus," *idem, Essays on NT Themes* [1964] 42f.; Hahn, *Titles* 151), while others assume that it is a post-Easter composition (Braumann 109; Schulz 263). If the logion goes back to Jesus, as seems likely, it says that the presence of God's reign is confirmed by the resistance raised against it. Who or what exercises violence cannot be said with certainty.

The meaning *take away forcefully* (2) occurs in the NT only in connection with persons. By force Jesus is to be made king (John 6:15). Paul is forcefully brought to safety (Acts 23:10). In Jude 23 (the text is uncertain) the addressees are exhorted to save endangered fellow believers "by *snatching* them out of the fire" of impending judgment. In John 10:28f. the sheep represent those who belong to Jesus, whom no one will *snatch* out of his, i.e., the Father's, hand (on this phrase cf. 2 Sam 23:21; *Herm. Vis.* ii.1.4): no one is to be torn out of the unity of the Johannine Church with its Lord and the Father and carried off into apostasy. The influence of the image of the hireling and the wolf (John 10:12) is still discernible here.

A special area in which the vb. is used is that of experiences of being carried off supernaturally (5 occurrences in the NT). Ἁρπάζω and its compounds (corresponding to Lat. *rapio, rapior*) are the Greek terms used earliest for such experiences, including such experiences within the earthly realm (Lohfink 42 provides examples). The latter is meant in Acts 8:39 when Philip is *caught up* by the Spirit of the Lord following his baptism of the eunuch. Paul speaks of an ecstatic experience of being "*caught up* to the third heaven," "into Paradise" (2 Cor 12:2, 4; RSV vv. 2, 3) in the traditional formulas of the rapture and ascension texts of ancient and Jewish literature (cf. esp. *2 Enoch* 8; further examples in H. Windisch, *Der zweite Korintherbrief* [KEK] 369-80; Lohfink 32-73). According to 1 Thess 4:17a those "who are alive, who are left, shall be *caught up* together with [those who have already died] in the clouds to meet the Lord in the air" with the goal of unending union "with (σύν) the Lord" (v. 17b; cf. *Gos. Nicod.* 25 [Hennecke/Schneemelcher I, 475]; E. von Dobschütz, *Thessalonicherbriefe* [KEK] 197-202). Rev 12:5 describes in mythical-biblical imagery the birth of the (messianic) child of the last times and his being "*caught up* to God and to his throne."

4. Compounds of ἁρπάζω occur in the NT with but slight differences of meaning. **Διαρπάζω** *plunder thoroughly** appears in the parabolic saying of Mark 3:27 (bis) par. Matt 12:29 (cf. *Gos. Thom.* 35); **ἐξαρπάζω** *take away forcibly* in Acts 23:24 v.l.; **συναρπάζω** *seize by violence, grasp** in Luke 8:29 (of a demon-possessed person); Acts 6:12; 19:29 (of persons); 27:15 (of a ship).

5. **Ἁρπαγή** *robbery; plunder** occurs 3 times in the NT. In the "woe" Q saying in Matt 23:25 par. Luke 11:39 the conflict between attention to ceremonial purity (the cleansing of "the cup and plate") and striving for ethical purity is exposed in a polemical fashion. In the secondary Lukan version the Pharisees who "inside . . . are full of extortion and wickedness" are explicitly addressed. Since the fig. meaning of purity in an ethical sense also plays a role in Matt 23:25, perhaps in Luke as well the meaning *greediness* is to be preferred over "what has been stolen, the plunder" (thus BAGD s.v.). The connection with Matt 23:23f., 26 and the contrasts there between "weightier" and "lighter" and "outside" and "inside" should be noted here (Trilling 200f.; Schulz 94-104). In Heb 10:34 ἁρπαγή denotes the *plundering* of one's property by those who confiscate it. The Christians have endured this with joy, for they received a better and abiding possession in its place.

6. **Ἅρπαξ*** as an adj. means *ravenous* and is used as a fixed expression when speaking of a wolf (LSJ s.v.; in the LXX, however, only in Gen 49:27). Matt 7:15 warns against false prophets/*ravenous* wolves in sheep's clothing. As a subst., *(the) robber*, ἅρπαξ is attested 4 times in the NT, always in vice catalogs (1 Cor 5:10, 11; 6:10; Luke 18:11; cf. *Did.* 2:6). The meaning *swindler* is worth considering in these texts in distinction to λῃστής in 2 Cor 11:26 (thus BAGD s.v. following Deissmann, *Light* 321, n. 1).

W. Trilling

ἅρπαξ, 1 *harpax* ravenous; (subst.) robber
→ ἁρπάζω 6.

ἀρραβών, ῶνος, ὁ *arrabōn* down payment, pledge*

Lit.: J. Behm, *TDNT* I, 475. — O. Becker, *DNTT* II, 39f. (bibliography on 44). — Billerbeck III, 495f. — K. Prümm, *Diakonia Pneumatos. Auslegung des Zweiten Korintherbriefes* I

(1967) 44-49. — H. Windisch, *Der zweite Korintherbrief* (KEK, [9]1924) 70-74.

1. This Semitic loanword is from the sphere of commercial and business law (BAGD s.v.) and means *pledge* (Gen 38:17, 18, 20; cf. BDB 786 s.v. *'ērāḇôn*) or *down payment* on the total debt ("security" according to one reading of Job 17:3; cf. KBL[2] s.v.). An ἀρραβών is the earnest on the basis of which one obligates oneself to the fulfillment of a promise.

2. Ἀρραβών occurs 3 times in the NT, always in connection with the Spirit of God. According to 2 Cor 1:22 the Corinthians have received the *pledge* of the Spirit, a "down payment" (Prümm 49) to guarantee the consummation of salvation, which is yet to come. In the same way, longing for the heavenly dwelling (5:1-5) results from the certitude that the Christians have been provided with an advance installment of the Spirit (v. 5; cf. → ἀπαρχὴ τοῦ πνεύματος, Rom 8:23). Eph 1:14 speaks of the Spirit "which is the *guarantee* of our inheritance" (cf. Pol. *Phil.* 8:1: Christ is "the pledge of our righteousness"); those who believe are sealed with the Spirit (v. 13; cf. 4:30; 2 Cor 1:22a), who guarantees the future inheritance in the sense of a final taking possession. With most MSS and hence in 2 Cor 1:22 and 5:5 the reading ὅ is preferable to ὅς: ὅς "is masc. only in order to agree with ἀρραβών" (M. Dibelius, *An die Kolosser, Epheser, an Philemon* [HNT, [3]1953] 62, referring to BDF §132.1, 2).

A. Sand

ἄρρητος, 2 *arrētos* inexpressible*

2 Cor 12:4: In his experience of being taken up Paul heard "*things that cannot be told,* which a man may not utter." H. Saake, "Paulus als Ekstatiker. Pneumatologische Beobachtungen zu 2 Kor. xii 1-10," *NovT* 15 (1973) 153-60.

ἄρρωστος, 2 *arrōstos* powerless, sick*

In narratives of healings of the sick: Mark 6:5, 13; 16:18; Matt 14:14. "Many . . . weak and *ill*" in the congregation: 1 Cor 11:30.

ἀρσενοκοίτης, ου, ὁ *arsenokoitēs* male homosexual*

Referring to a male who engages in sexual activity with men or boys: 1 Cor 6:9; 1 Tim 1:10; Pol. *Phil.* 5:3.

ἄρσην, 2 *arsēn* male, man, male child*

Lit.: J. Anastassiou, *Lexikon des frühgriechischen Epos* (ed. B. Schnell and H. Erbse), pt. 8 (1976) 1353f. — BAGD s.v. — R. E. Clements, *TDOT* IV, 82-87. — A. Vögtle, "Mythos und Botschaft in Apk 12," FS Kuhn 395-415.

Etymologically related to old Indic *árṣati* ("it flows"; cf. Lat. *ros*), ἄρσην (appears frequently from Homer, and in the LXX and the papyri) literally means *that which discharges sperm* and therefore *male offspring, male child.* It appears in Luke 2:23 (Exod 13:2, 12, 15; the sacrificial animal must be male: Exod 12:5; Lev 1:3); Acts 7:19 (v.l. following Exod 1:17f.); Rev 12:5, 13 (the messianic child; cf. Isa 66:7) and serves to differentiate the sexes in the human family (Gen 1:27; 5:2; Mark 10:6; Matt 19:4 with the opposite → θῆλυ), a differentiation which becomes irrelevant as far as salvation is concerned (Gal 3:28). Ἄρσην is the male sexual partner (Num 31:17f.; Judg 21:11f.; Sir 36:26), including those in homosexual relationships (3 times in Rom 1:27; cf. Lev 18:22; 20:13).

J. B. Bauer

Ἀρτεμᾶς, ᾶ *Artemas* Artemas*

A man whom "Paul" wishes to send to Titus (Titus 3:12).

Ἄρτεμις, ιδος *Artemis* Artemis*

1. Artemis in the NT — 2. The origin of Artemis — 3. The Ephesian Artemis

Lit.: W. Fauth, *KP* I, 618-25. — R. Fleischer, *Artemis von Ephesos und verwandte Kultstatuen aus Anatolien und Syrien* (1973). — E. Lichtenecker, *Das Kultbild der Artemis von Ephesus* (Diss. Tübingen, 1952). — R. Oster, "The Ephesian Artemis as an Opponent of Early Christianity," JAC 19 (1976) 24-44. — L. R. Taylor, "Artemis of Ephesus," *Beginnings* V, 251-56.

1. Artemis is mentioned in the NT only in Acts 19:24, 27, 28, 34, 35 as the goddess of the city of Ephesus who is worshipped by the entire "world" (οἰκουμένη, v. 27). The silversmith Demetrius produced "silver shrines of Artemis" (v. 24). The epithet "the great" in connection with her name (vv. 28, 34) is attested in inscriptions; see H. Conzelmann, *Acts* (Hermeneia) 165 with n. 26; Roscher, *Lexikon* Suppl. (= VII) s.v. Ἄρτεμις (48).

2. Greek mythology worshipped Artemis (Lat. *Diana*) as the virgin goddess of the hunt, daughter of Zeus, and twin sister of Apollo. But her nature and name are pre-Greek. Esp. significant among her many epithets is "ruler of the animals," a title which points toward Asia Minor as her place of origin. In 1965, during the excavations in Çatal Hüyük and Hacilar (near Iconium) several clay statues from the 8th-6th cents. B.C. were discovered which show well-nourished maternal deities with large breasts and enthroned upon wildcats.

3. The Ephesian Artemis is portrayed wearing on her head a turret crown (of the city of Ephesus). Pictured on her close-fitting garments are various wild animals and bees (the animals of the coat of arms of Ephesus). The jewelry around her neck portrays animals. Numerous larger and smaller, more or less egg-shaped formations protrude from the clothing on her upper body; while she

was referred to in antiquity as the "many-breasted" Artemis, nonetheless the formations lack nipples and are not flesh-colored as the face and arms are.

B. Schwank

ἀρτέμων, ωνος, ὁ *artemōn* foresail*

Acts 27:40: ἐπαίρειν τὸν ἀρτέμωνα, hoisting the *foresail.*

ἄρτι *arti* now*

1. Occurrences in the NT — 2. As an independent temporal adv. — 3. In prep. phrases

Lit.: BAGD s.v. — BDF §474.4. — H. C. HAHN, *DNTT* III, 834, 837. — KÜHNER, *Grammatik* I, 134f., 136; II, 82, 119. — G. H. O. MADSEN, *The Theological Significance of "NUN/ARTI" in the Fourth Gospel* (Diss. Princeton, 1972). — MAYSER, *Grammatik* II/2, 176. — SCHWYZER, *Grammatik* I, 270f., 622; II, 158, 269, 281, 558.

1. The temporal adv. ἄρτι occurs 36 times in the NT: 7 times in Matthew, 12 in John, 11 in Paul, and once each in 2 Thessalonians 1, 1 John 1, 1 Peter 2, and Revelation 2.

2. Ἄρτι frequently occurs in its classical, basic meaning of *now* (Matt 3:15; John 9:19, 25; 13:7, 33, 37; 16:12, 31; Gal 1:9, 10; 4:20; 1 Thess 3:6; 1 Pet 1:6, 8; Rev 12:10). In 1 Cor 13:12 ἄρτι-τότε, *now–then,* reflects the relationship of present and future which Paul advocates in opposition to Gnostic groups in the Church. According to his argument it is only the unmediated self-disclosure of God which brings about unobscured sight and perfect knowledge. Ἄρτι can be acutely intensified to mean *immediately* (Matt 26:53). But it can also point toward an event in the immediate past: The daughter of the synagogue ruler has *just* died (Matt 9:18). In 1 Cor 16:7 ἄρτι expresses the element of transitoriness: Paul does not wish to visit the Corinthians *just (merely)* in passing (ἐν παρόδῳ), but wants to spend some time with them.

3. Not infrequently ἄρτι occurs in prep. phrases: ἕως ἄρτι, ἄχρι ἄρτι, ἀπ' ἄρτι. With ἕως ἄρτι we get a retrospective summary of the past from the point of view of the present. There is, however, a difference in meaning depending upon whether what has been the case so far continues to be the case or has reached its end. When it refers to a continuing situation, ἕως ἄρτι means *still, up to (and including) the present moment* (Matt 11:12; John 5:17; 1 Cor 4:13; 8:7; 15:6; 2 Thess 2:7; 1 John 2:9); this meaning is conveyed in 1 Cor 4:11 by ἄχρι τῆς ἄρτι ὥρας (ἄρτι functions as an adj.). Otherwise ἕως ἄρτι means *until now* (but no longer: John 2:10; 16:24).

Ἀπ' ἄρτι, on the other hand, speaks of the present in contrast to the future: *from now on.* It is, therefore, used in sayings concerning the eschatological future (Matt 23:39; 26:29, 64) or oriented to the future (John 13:19). The blessing in Rev 14:13 praises those who *from now on* die "in the Lord" (probably martyrs). Here ἀπ' ἄρτι suggests the "shifting of the struggle to earth" (H. Kraft, *Offenbarung* [HNT] 195); the dead are spared involvement in this struggle. Ἀπ' ἄρτι is used in a characteristic way in John 14:7, to describe not some aspect of the future but that which is happening in the present: knowledge of God is authentically given already in the person of Jesus.

H.-J. Ritz

ἀρτιγέννητος, 2 *artigennētos* newborn*

1 Pet 2:2: *newborn* babes. F. Büchsel, *TDNT* I, 672. → βρέφος 2.

ἄρτιος, 3 *artios* suitable*

2 Tim 3:17, in the sense of *capable of meeting all demands.* G. Delling, *TDNT* I, 475f.

ἄρτος, ου, ὁ *artos* bread

1. Occurrences in the NT — 2. Bread in Palestine — 3. Bread at meals, at the banquet of salvation, and in the Lord's Supper — 4. "The bread of the Presence" — 5. Fig. for food, meal, or livelihood

Lit.: J. BEHM, *TDNT* I, 477f. — O. BÖCHER, "Aß Johannes der Täufer kein Brot (Lk 7, 33)?" *NTS* 18 (1971/72) 90-92. — P. BORGEN, *Bread From Heaven* (NovTSup 10, 1965). — *idem,* "Brod fra himmel og fra jord," *NorTT* 61 (1960) 218-40. — A. VAN DEN BORN, *BL* 260-62. — F. J. DÖLGER, "Unser tägliches Brot," JAC 5 (1936) 201-10. — *idem,* "Ein Brot als Tagesbedarf," *ibid.,* 284-86. — C. FERRIÈRE, "Je suis le pain," *BVC* 26 (1959) 71-77. — F. HAUCK, "ἄρτος ἐπιούσιος," *ZNW* 33 (1934) 199-202. — J. HAUSSLEITER and A. STUIBER, *RAC* II, 611-20. — A. HEISING, *Die Botschaft der Brotvermehrung* (SBS 15, 1966). — K. KOCH, *BHH* III, 1688. — F. MERKEL, *DNTT* I, 249-51. — J. ROGGE, *BHH* I, 274. — R. SCHNACKENBURG, "Das Brot des Lebens," FS Kuhn 328-42. — G. VERMES, "He is the Bread," FS Black 256-63. For further bibliography see *DNTT* I, 253; *TWNT* X (1979), 993.

1. Ἄρτος occurs 97 times in the NT, with particular concentration in the Gospels (21 occurrences in Matthew, 21 in Mark, 15 in Luke, and 24 in John) and 5 occurrences in Acts, 7 in 1 Corinthians, 2 in 2 Thessalonians, and 1 each in 2 Corinthians (9:10) and Hebrews (9:2). The majority of the occurrences refer to the bread in the feeding miracles (32, of which only 2 are in Luke) and to bread as food in general (4 occurrences). In 18 cases the reference is to the bread of the Lord's Supper or of meals connected with appearances of the risen Christ (4 of 5 occurrences in Acts and all 7 occurrences in 1 Corinthians). Sayings concerning the "bread of heaven" (11 instances) or the "bread of life" (3) are found only in John. Four texts speak of the "bread of the Presence." A total of 22 times ἄρτος

means simply "food," although the distinction from the specific meaning *bread* is not always clearly drawn.

2. In Israel and among the Jews in Palestine bread was usually baked from barley flour or (more expensively) wheat flour, normally with the addition of yeast, in flat loaves up to 1 cm. thick and 50 cm. in diameter. Unleavened bread was baked and eaten in situations of haste (Gen 19:3), e.g., prior to a sudden departure (Exod 12:8, 11) and during a journey (vv. 34, 39), and is the bread prescribed for cultic purposes (Lev 2:4; → ζύμη). Bread is the chief foodstuff. It is torn apart or broken, not cut, before it is eaten.

3. Bread in the literal sense appears as an important food which one does not deny to a son who requests it (Matt 7:9 par. Luke 11:11 [along with fish], cf. v. 5), whereas the ascetic Baptist renounces it (7:33 [along with wine]; Böcher interprets this differently). With bread and fish Jesus feeds the multitude (5,000: Mark 6:36, 37, 38, 41 [bis], 44, 52; Matt 14:17, 19 [bis]; 16:9; Luke 9:13, 16; John 6:5, 7, 9, 11, 13, 23, 26; 4,000: Mark 8:4, 5, 6, 14 [bis], 16, 17, 19; Matt 15:34, 36; 16:10) by allowing them to take part in the eschatological salvation banquet; he takes the bread as the father of the family, breaking it, saying thanks over it, and giving it to his family. One finds the customary connections with ἀγοράζω (Mark 6:36f.; John 6:5), λαμβάνω (Mark 6:41; 8:6, 14; Matt 14:19; Luke 9:16; John 6:11), εὐλογέω καὶ (κατα-)κλάω (Mark 6:41; cf. 8:6; Matt 14:19), ἐσθίω (Mark 6:44; John 6:23, 26), δίδωμι (Mark 8:6; Matt 14:19), χορτάζω (with gen., Mark 8:6) or χορτάζομαι (absolute, John 6:26).

John interprets the bread of the feedings as ἄρτος . . . ἐκ τοῦ οὐρανοῦ (6:31, 32 [bis], 33, 34, 41, 50, 51 [bis], 58 [bis]), which recalls the manna of the desert wanderings (Exod 16:4), and, in specifically Johannine terminology, as ἄρτος τῆς ζωῆς (6:35, 48) or ἄρτος ὁ ζῶν (v. 51). Jesus is the bread of life. He is sent by the Father and comes from heaven in order that those who belong to him should not die (as did the patriarchs in the wilderness [vv. 49, 58]), but instead live ("with him" [v. 57]) eternally (vv. 51, 58). Thus the bread which Jesus gives is himself, his "flesh" and his "blood" (vv. 51, 53-56). Here "bread" becomes the image for everything a person needs to live; the feeding story is interpreted christologically and—making use of the tradition of the Lord's Supper—sacramentally.

Along with wine, bread is the major component of Jesus' final meal as of the early Christian Lord's Supper, both festive meals. As the father of the house and the Kyrios of heaven Jesus dispenses to his followers the fellowship meal with and in which he gives himself to them for their salvation (Mark 14:22 par. Matt 26:26; Luke 22:19 par. 1 Cor 11:23, cf. vv. 26, 27, 28; Luke 24:30, 35; John 21:9, 13). "Breaking of bread" has become a t.t. for the fellowship meal in Acts 2:42, 46; 20:7, 11; 1 Cor 10:16. According to 1 Cor 10:16, 17 (bis) participation in the bread of the meal mediates participation in the σῶμα Χριστοῦ.

4. In Mark 2:26 par. Matt 12:4/Luke 6:4 (cf. 1 Kgs 21:7) one encounters the pl. t.t. οἱ ἄρτοι τῆς προθέσεως for the (unleavened) "bread of the Presence" (Heb. sg. *leḥem happānîm*). According to Lev 24:5-9 twelve newly baked loaves of this bread were laid out each sabbath on a table before God's presence in the sanctuary, i.e., before the holy of holies, as a pledge that the sacrificial system would be continued eternally; thus they are literally the *bread* of God's Presence. In Mark 2:23ff. par., David's cultic offense in the sanctuary at Nob (1 Sam 21:2-7) is cited as support for Jesus' new attitude regarding the sabbath. In Heb 9:2 the "outer tent" with the table and the *bread* of the Presence is a sign of the preliminary character of the sacrificial system.

5. Ἄρτος means food and livelihood in general in the fourth petition of the Lord's Prayer (Matt 6:11 par. Luke 11:3, → ἐπιούσιος) and in Mark 3:20; 6:8 par. Luke 9:3 (those who are sent out are to take no provisions with them); Mark 7:2, 5 par. Matt 15:2; Luke 14:1; 14:15 (participation in the banquet of the kingdom of God); Matt 4:3 par. Luke 4:3 (the contrast between stones and bread); Matt 4:4 par. Luke 4:4 (quoting Deut 8:3: no person lives from food alone); Luke 15:17; Mark 7:27 par. Matt 15:26; and 2 Cor 9:10 (quoting Isa 55:10). Even in view of their eschatological expectation the Christians in Thessalonica are to submit to the rules of everyday life and earn their *bread* by working for it (2 Thess 3:12), just as the apostle himself did not allow himself to be provided for "without paying" (v. 8).

H. Balz

ἀρτύω *artyō* season*

Mark 9:50 par. Luke 14:34, referring to salt which has lost its capacity to season: "how will you *season* it?" or "how is it to be *seasoned*?" Col 4:6: speech which is *seasoned* with salt. → ἅλας.

Ἀρφαξάδ *Arphaxad* Arphaxad*

A personal name in Luke 3:36 (according to Gen 10:22, 24 Arphaxad was a son of Shem).

ἀρχάγγελος, ου, ὁ *archangelos* archangel
→ ἄγγελος 4.

ἀρχαῖος, 3 *archaios* original, old*

Rev 12:9; 20:2: the *ancient* serpent. Acts 21:16: ἀρχαῖος μαθητής, one who is a Christian *of long standing*. Matt 5:21: "You have heard that it was said to *the men of old* [the people of previous generations] . . ."; likewise vv. 27 (v.l.), 33. Luke 9:8, 19: one of the *old* prophets. Acts 15:7, 21: from *early* days (times). 2 Cor 5:17: "the *old* has passed away" (from the point of view of the new creation). 2 Pet 2:5, referring to the *ancient, earlier* cosmos which existed prior to the flood. G. Delling, *TDNT* I, 486f.; L. Coenen and H. Bietenhard, *DNTT* I, 164-69.

Ἀρχέλαος, ου *Archelaos* Archelaus*

1. Sources — 2. Biographical information — 3. Archelaus in the NT

Lit.: ABEL, *Histoire* I, 407-23. — J. BLINZLER, *LTK* I, 822f. — W. FOERSTER, *RGG* III, 266-69. — A. H. M. JONES, *The Herods of Judaea* ([2]1967) 156-68. — B. NIESE, *Flavii Iosephi opera* (index [VII, [2]1955] s.v. Archelaus 2). — W. OTTO, PW Supplement II (1913) 191-200. — S. H. PEROWNE, *The Later Herods: The Political Background of the NT* (1958). — REICKE, *NT Era* 130-33. — A. SCHALIT, *EncJud* III (1971) 333-35. — SCHÜRER, *History* I, 353-57 (bibliography). — F. D. WEINERT, "The Parable of the Throne Claimant (Luke 19, 12. 14-15a. 27) Reconsidered," *CBQ* 39 (1977) 505-14. — M. ZERWICK, "Die Parabel vom Thronanwärter," *Bib* 40 (1959) 654-74.

1. As a proper name Archelaus was in circulation in the classical and Hellenistic periods. In Matt 2:22 the name refers to the son of Herod the Great and Herod's Samaritan wife Malthace. Flavius Josephus reports about him several times (Niese, index s.v.; esp. *Ant.* xvii.194-249, 317-21, 339-55; *B.J.* ii.1-38, 80-92, 111-17); also Dio Cassius 55:27. Luke 19:11-27 probably reflects Archelaus's claim to the royal title (so Zerwick). Like his brother Antipas, Archelaus bore the name Herod (Dio Cassius 55:27; coins inscribed ΗΡΩΔΟΥ ΕΘΝΑΡΧΟΥ); in Josephus, however, Archelaus is never called Herod. The designation βασιλεύς (Matt 2:22; Josephus *Ant.* xviii.93) is imprecise.

2. Following the death of Herod the Great (4 B.C.) Judea, along with Samaria and Idumea, fell to Archelaus, Herod's eldest son, who had been born *ca.* 23 B.C. and raised in Rome (cf. *Ant.* xvii.20 and *passim*). Contrary to his father's intention, however, Archelaus was not awarded the title of king (*B.J.* i.668; ii.1-3), but only that of ethnarch (*Ant.* xvii.317, 339; on this title see Schürer I, 333). Nonetheless Augustus had promised Archelaus as well as his younger brother Antipas the royal title. Archelaus was reputed to be cruel and tyrannical (*Ant.* xvii.342; *B.J.* ii.10-13, 111). In the tenth year of his reign a Jewish-Samaritan delegation used his cruelty as the basis for formal accusations against him in Rome. Augustus summoned him to Rome and following an interrogation dismissed him from office, confiscated his wealth, and banished him to Vienne in Gaul (A.D. 6, *Ant.* xvii.342-44; *B.J.* ii.111). His territory was placed under direct Roman rule. It became a procuratorial province ruled as an annex of the province of Syria (*Ant.* xviii.1f.; *B.J.* ii.117). Archelaus died in A.D. 16.

3. When Joseph brought the child Jesus and his mother back "to the land of Israel" (Matt 2:21) he learned "that Archelaus reigned (βασιλεύει) over Judea in place of his [deceased] father Herod" and was afraid to go there (v. 22a). Following directions received in a dream, he went "to the district of Galilee" (v. 22b), came to Nazareth, and made his home there (v. 23a). Since Archelaus is the only son of Herod whom Matthew mentions in this context, it is precisely he, the successor of his father, who appears to be the true reflection of the child-murderer of Bethlehem (vv. 12-18), though he himself does not persecute the child Jesus (v. 20). Herod (Antipas) the "tetrarch," brother of Archelaus, who had John the Baptist beheaded, is designated "king" in Matt 14:9 (par. Mark 6:14, 26).

Luke 19:11-27 contains motifs which occur frequently in reports concerning Herodian claimants to the throne (*Ant.* xvii.224, 299f.; xviii.241-56). However, it is only the protest of the πολῖται αὐτοῦ against the granting of the kingly power (Luke 19:14) which has a precise parallel in the history of Archelaus (*Ant.* xvii.342). Thus it is unlikely that Luke has combined a specific incident which had become a "parable of the throne claimant" with the parable of the pounds. A more likely assumption is that he has, for his own reasons, added such motifs to the parable of the pounds. These motifs serve primarily to answer the problem of the delay of the parousia (cf. v. 11).

G. Schneider

ἀρχή, ῆς, ἡ *archē* beginning; power*

1. Occurrences in the NT — 2. Meaning — 3. Usage

Lit.: H. CONZELMANN, " 'Was von Anfang war' (ἀπ' ἀρχῆς)," *idem, Theologie als Schriftauslegung* (BEvT 65, 1974) 207-14. — G. DELLING, *TDNT* I, 478-84 (bibliography). — W. FOERSTER, *TDNT* II, 1 (bibliographic note), 571-73. — J. Y. LEE, "Interpreting the Demonic Powers in Pauline Thought," *NovT* 12 (1970) 54-69. — S. LEVIN, *Ἄρχω and ἀρχή* (Diss. Chicago, 1950). — G. MILLER, "Ἀρχόντων τοῦ αἰῶνος τούτου—A New Look at 1 Corinthians 2:6-8," *JBL* 91 (1972) 522-28. — I. DE LA POTTERIE, "La notion de 'commencement' dans les écrits johanniques," FS Schürmann 379-403. — H. RINGGREN, *RGG* II, 1302f. — E. SAMAIN, "La notion de APXH dans l'oeuvre lucanienne," *L'Évangile de Luc* (ed. F. Neirynck; 1973) 299-328. — H. SCHLIER, *Mächte und Gewalten im NT* (1958). — E. SJÖBERG, *TDNT* VI, 375f.

1. Ἀρχή occurs 55 times in the NT, of which 18 occurrences are in the Johannine writings (8 in the Gospel, 8 in 1 John, and 2 in 2 John), 7 in the Lukan writings, and 6 in Hebrews.

2. "Ἀρχή always signifies 'primacy' " (Delling 479), whether a) of time: *beginning (origin),* b) of place: *point of origin* or *departure,* or c) of rank: *power, dominion, kingdom, office.*

a) Where it is used in the temporal sense of the point at which something begins, this point can be thought of as included in the temporal process or as prior, external to, and unaffected by it, i.e., as the *origin* or *principium.* In the former case, the ἀρχή corresponds to the τέλος (Heb 3:14; 7:3); in the latter case, ἀρχή carries the sense of *pre-temporality* and *eternity.* (On the alternation between the two meanings in Greek philosophical terminology see Delling 479-81).

b) In a spatial sense the ἀρχαί in the scene in Acts 10:11; 11:5 are the *corners* of the sheet.

c) The meaning which has regard to rank—*authority, sovereignty,* or *exercise of power,* whether in a neutral or in a personal sense—is made more precise on the basis of each specific context in which the word stands. A primacy of both time and rank is expressed by the adverbial phrase τὴν ἀρχήν in John 8:25: *from the beginning, totally, principially.*

3. a) In its temporal sense the word usually occurs in the prep. phrase ἀπ' or ἐξ ἀρχῆς in the most varied contexts. It can denote the moment of creation (Matt 19:4, 8; Heb 1:10 [Ps 101:26 LXX: κατ' ἀρχάς]), sometimes specified by the addition of κτίσεως (Mark 10:6; 13:19; 2 Pet 3:4) or κόσμου (Matt 24:21); the beginning of one's life (Acts 26:4); the first public appearance of Jesus (Luke 1:2; John [2:11]; 15:27; 16:4; Heb 2:3 [ἀρχὴν λαβοῦσα]); the beginning of one's Christian experience (1 John 2:7, 24; 3:11; 2 John 5, 6 [probably also John 6:64]); the beginning of the Church's history (Acts 11:15: ἐν ἀρχῇ); the beginning of a missionary work (Phil 4:15; cf. E. Lohmeyer, *An die Philipper, Kolosser und an Philemon* [KEK] 184f.) or of missionary instruction (Heb 5:12: τὰ στοιχεῖα τῆς ἀρχῆς; cf. 6:1); and, finally, the beginning of the apocalyptic woes (Matt 24:8 par. Mark 13:8). In Mark 1:1 the ἀρχή of the gospel is found in the prophetic announcement of the Baptist. According to Heb 7:3 the priest Melchizedek, who prefigures the Christ, has no ἀρχὴν ἡμερῶν (and no ζωῆς τέλος).

That leads us to a series of primarily Johannine texts in which ἀρχή is used with reference to the essence and existence of Jesus in the sense of *before all time and creation,* first of all John 1:1, 2 (ἐν ἀρχῇ); 1 John 1:1 (on the neutral formulation cf. Delling 481f.; R. Bultmann, *The Johannine Epistles* [Hermeneia] 7f.); 2:13f. The context formed by the christological hymn of Col 1:15-20 clearly shows that ὅς ἐστιν (ἡ) ἀρχή (v. 18) does not intend to incorporate Christ into the cosmos and the creation, but rather to designate him as *the principle standing outside all time,* as *the origin* of cosmos and creation. The same is true of the self-designation of Jesus as ἡ ἀρχὴ καὶ τὸ τέλος in Rev 22:13 with the parallel statement: τὸ Ἄλφα καὶ τὸ Ὦ, ὁ πρῶτος καὶ ὁ ἔσχατος (cf. 2:8). These epitaphs apply equally to God (1:8 v.l., 17; 21:6) and signify not a temporal and worldly being, but rather the One existing *before all time* and into eternity. (On this formula [ἡ ἀρχὴ καὶ τὸ τέλος], which has a prehistory in Deutero-Isaiah, the Greeks, Philo, and the rabbis, see W. Bousset, *Offenbarung* [KEK; [6]1966] 190; Delling 479). So also the designation of wisdom as ἡ ἀρχὴ τῆς κτίσεως τοῦ θεοῦ drawn from Prov 8:22 and applied to Christ in Rev 3:14 is not to be understood as in Proverbs, namely, as referring to the first of created things, but rather as referring to the *pre-temporal origin* of all created things.

Despite its embodiment in experience ἐν ἁγιασμῷ πνεύματος καὶ πίστει ἀληθείας, the phrase ἀπ' ἀρχῆς in 2 Thess 2:13 (v.l.) points to a supratemporal process of election and hence means as much as *in eternity, before all time* (cf. E. von Dobschütz, *Thessalonicherbriefe* [KEK] 298; M. Dibelius, *Thessalonicherbriefe* [HNT] 51, also on the reading ἀπαρχήν). How ἀπ' ἀρχῆς is to be understood in John 8:44 and 1 John 3:8, where it is applied to the activity of the διάβολος as a murderer and sinner, depends upon the conception of Satan which is presupposed here, of which the element of his pre-worldly and transcendent existence is always a part (cf. G. von Rad and W. Foerster, *TDNT* II, 71-81). Thus the ἀρχή envisioned here is prior to and above the time of the world. The sense of ᾔδει ἐξ ἀρχῆς ὁ Ἰησοῦς in John 6:64 remains controversial; it might refer to the moment each of the disciples was chosen (W. Bauer, *Johannesevangelium* [HNT] 103; R. Bultmann, *The Gospel of John* [1971] 447, n. 4) or the beginning of Jesus' ministry (H. Strathmann, *Das Evangelium nach Johannes* [NTD] 123), but also perhaps to a primeval knowledge on the part of Jesus.

b) → 2.b.

c) Where ἀρχή denotes a primacy of rank, there also only context can clarify whether the reference is to earthly or supraterrestrial spheres or figures of power. In both cases the word regularly appears in connection with → ἐξουσία (Jude 6 is an exception) so that the phrase ἀρχὴ (-αὶ) καὶ ἐξουσία(-αι) represents a sort of hendiadys (attested already in Plato *Alc.* i.135a) for *powers, rulers, sphere(s) of control, authorities,* and, concretely, *governing authorities, officials.* The phrase does not define these concepts with any great degree of precision. Occasionally such precise definition comes from association with other concepts. Thus ἐπὶ τὰς συναγωγὰς καὶ τὰς ἀρχὰς καὶ τὰς ἐξουσίας in Luke 12:11 refers to being brought before Jewish and Gentile *officials*; τῇ ἀρχῇ καὶ τῇ ἐξουσίᾳ τοῦ ἡγεμόνος in 20:20 refers to "the *authority* and jurisdiction of the governor"; and Titus 3:1 refers to *government authorities* in general.

A different sphere, one which extends beyond all innerworldly boundaries, is that of the powers which exercise their influence throughout the entire cosmos. It is this sphere to which the double expression refers in the Pauline and deutero-Pauline literature, as evidenced by the relationship to and connection with other cosmic powers such as ἄγγελοι, δυνάμεις (Rom 8:38), θρόνοι, κυριότητες (Col 1:16), ὀνόματα (Eph 1:21), κοσμοκράτορες (6:12), etc., or by the addition of ἐν τοῖς ἐπουρανίοις (3:10; 6:12) (cf. Schlier 11f.). Historians of culture and religion have been unable to define these powers in detail, give a precise description of their nature and functions, or fix their exact provenance, although Babylonian (astrological), Iranian, and similar elements, mediated through Gnostic systems and reshaped in Jewish apocalyptic, are recognizable.

In the Pauline letters there is no loose or even indiscriminate summarizing of ideas and concepts, but rather an attempt to comprehend the totality of powers and forces ἐπουρανίων καὶ ἐπιγείων καὶ καταχθονίων (Phil 2:10) which exist in creation, in order to include them in the message which announces their creation, subordination, and redemption (Lee 66) by Christ and in the proclamation of the liberation of the world and humanity from their domination. The presupposition is, therefore, that they have broken out of their proper creaturely status in the universe of subordination to Christ (Col 2:10), through whom the universe, and hence also the ἀρχαί, exist (cf. 1 Cor 8:6; Col 1:16). One does not find in Paul any discussion of the occasion or manner of their defection from their proper creaturely status. (An exception may be the statement about Christ in Phil 2:5, οὐκ ἁρπαγμὸν ἡγήσατο τὸ εἶναι ἴσα θεῷ, if it is explained with reference to the rebellion of the ἄρχοντες τοῦ αἰῶνος τούτου (1 Cor 2:6, 8) and their ruler, the θεὸς τοῦ αἰῶνος τούτου (2 Cor 4:4), against God and their attempt forcibly to grasp for themselves equality with God. Cf. E. Lohmeyer, *An die Philipper, Kolosser und an Philemon* [KEK] 92 and for the opposing view W. Foerster, *TDNT* I, 473f.; E. Käsemann, *Versuche* I, 70f.)

For Paul's thought otherwise, one may presuppose the entire range of Jewish views, developed on the basis of Gen 6:1ff., of the fall of the angels and its consequences (cf. *1 Enoch* 6:15f.; 69; A. Schweitzer, *The Mysticism of Paul the Apostle* [1931] 56f.) and of related matters (Ringgren, Sjöberg). In the NT cf. Luke 10:18; 2 Pet 2:4; Jude 6, where the angels are said to have left their appointed *sphere* (R. Knopf, *Die Briefe Petri und Judä* [KEK] 222); and Rev 12:7ff. On the other hand, Paul had to oppose in his churches a worship of elemental spirits of the world which, compared to Christ, were weak and pitiful (Gal 4:3; Col 2:8, 21f.).

It is in the face of all this that Paul proclaims that the resurrected One has assumed the position appropriate to him as the preexistent One, i.e., he who is above all cosmic powers. According to 1 Cor 15:24ff. he will destroy as enemies πᾶσαν ἀρχὴν καὶ πᾶσαν ἐξουσίαν καὶ δύναμιν; according to Col 2:15 he will render them powerless, but according to 1:20 he will incorporate them into his cosmic work of redemption and pacification (Lee 66). But to his own who like him are raised and already now to his Church, his body, he gives a part in his mighty victory (Rom 8:35-39; 1 Cor 15:23; Gal 5:1; Eph 1:22f.; 6:12-16). This certainty finds its fundamental expression in the provocative questions of 1 Cor 6:2f.: "Do you not know that the saints will judge the world? . . . Do you not know that we are to judge angels?"

K. Weiss

ἀρχηγός, οῦ, ὁ *archēgos* leader*

1. Occurrences in the NT and the history of the motif — 2. Christological relevance of the title

Lit.: J. R. Bartlett, "The Use of the Word נשׂיא as a Title in the OT," *VT* 19 (1969) 1-10. — F. J. Helfmeyer, *Die Nachfolge Gottes im AT* (1968). — O. Hofius, *Der Vorhang vor dem Thron Gottes* (1972). — K. Kliesch, *Das heilsgeschichtliche Credo in den Reden der Apostelgeschichte* (1975) 89f., 149f., 154. — P.-G. Müller, *ΧΡΙΣΤΟΣ ΑΡΧΗΓΟΣ. Der religionsgeschichtliche und theologische Hintergrund einer neutestamentlichen Christusprädikation* (1973). — J. Schreiner, "Führung. Thema der Heilsgeschichte im AT," *BZ* 5 (1961) 2-18. — U. Wilckens, *Die Missionsreden der Apostelgeschichte* ([3]1974) 174-76. — H. Zimmermann, *Das Bekenntnis der Hoffnung. Tradition und Redaktion im Hebräerbrief* (1977) 161f.

1. Ἀρχηγός occurs 4 times in the NT, exclusively as a christological title for the exalted Jesus. The results of semasiological and lexicographical investigation of secular Greek indicate an extremely polyvalent spectrum of meaning for the word, the basis being *he who is the first, who stands at the head of, who leads.* The expression occurs 35 times in the LXX with 9 Heb. equivalents bearing the senses of confidant, physician, family or tribal representative, head, tip, (tree-)top, supervisor, prince, and leader. Insistence upon the continuity of the OT and Jewish theme of Yahweh's leading in the course of salvation history with Christian use of the title can serve as a corrective to earlier exegesis which derived the title too one-sidedly from the Greco-Hellenistic cult of the hero or ruler (G. Delling, *TDNT* I, 484f.) or exclusively from the Gnostic idea of the leader of souls (E. Käsemann, *The Wandering People of God* [1984] 132f.). The credo theme of "led out of Egypt" (cf. the chart in Kleisch 54-58) is here transposed into christological-titular usage and denotes the exalted Jesus as the eschatological *leader* of the new people of God on its exodus into the doxa of the resurrection.

2. In Acts 3:15 the Lukan Peter accuses the Jews of having killed the messianic one "*who has led the way* to [the] life" (NEB) of the resurrection. They acted in stubbornness and ignorance, but Jesus did not remain dead, but was raised by God and thus became the one who leads the way into the resurrection life. According to Heb 6:20 Jesus is the one who goes before into the inner sanctum behind the curtain of God's holy of holies. In contrast to Heb 5:9, "originator (αἴτιος, RSV "source") of eternal salvation," Acts 3:15 should be translated not as "originator of life," but rather as "one who leads the way into life." In a further speech of Peter Acts 5:31 says of the crucified and resurrected Jesus that "God exalted him at his right hand as [eschatological] *Leader* and Savior." The predication "Leader and Savior" is plainly near to Heb 2:10, "pioneer of their salvation." The linguistic similarities between Luke and Hebrews lead one to conclude that they reflect a common liturgical tradition; this in turn leads one to suspect that they also reflect here a fixed formula originating in an ancient christology of the Hellenistic Church.

Heb 2:10 has: "make the *leader* who delivers them perfect through sufferings" (NEB). Jesus' function as *leader* results from the cross and the resurrection from the dead (13:20); he brings to completion God's promises of salvation by leading many sons into God's doxa. In Heb 12:2 the formulation "*author* and perfecter of the faith" does not mean that Jesus "as the first man . . . gave an example of faith in God" or that "by His death He 'fulfilled' this faith in God's unconditional love" (Delling, *TDNT* I, 488), but rather that the earthly Jesus, here as the exalted Lord of his Church, is presented as the leader of the faith in order to encourage believers to endure in their christological life of faith. Since αἴτιος in "originator of eternal salvation" in Heb 5:9 is not synonymous with ἀρχηγός, 12:2 is hardly to be translated as "originator and perfecter of the faith," for Jesus is the originating source neither for the *'emûnâ* of the OT witnesses nor for christological πίστις; rather, God effects faith in Jesus as the leader.

P.-G. Müller

ἀρχιερατικός, 2 *archieratikos* high-priestly*

Acts 4:6, referring to persons of the high-priestly family. On the significance of the high-priestly families see Schürer, *History* II, 227-36; C. Thoma, *Bibel und Liturgie* 45 (1972) 4-22.

ἀρχιερεύς, εως, ὁ *archiereus* high priest

1. Occurrences in the NT — 2. Meaning — 3. History — 4. Use in Hebrews

Lit. (general): G. ALLON, "On the History of the High-Priesthood at the close of the Second Temple," *Tarbiz* 13 (1941) 1-24. — E. BAMMEL, "Die Bruderfolge im Hochpriestertum der herodianisch-römischen Zeit," *ZDPV* 70 (1954) 147-53. — *idem*, "ΑΡΧΙΕΡΕΥΣ ΠΡΟΦΗΤΕΥΩΝ," *TLZ* 79 (1954) 351-56. — N. B. BARROW, *The High Priest* (1947). — J. BLINZLER, *The Trial of Jesus* (1959) 81-89. — M. HENGEL, *Die Zeloten* (1961) 215-19. — J. JEREMIAS, *Jerusalem in the Time of Jesus* (1969) 147-221. — K. KOCH, *BHH* II, 737-40. — REICKE, *NT Era* 142-49. — *idem*, *BHH* II, 737. — E. SCHRENK, *TDNT* III, 265-83. — SCHÜRER, *History* 227-36. — A. WENDEL, *RGG* III, 427f.

On Hebrews: G. BORNKAMM, "Das Bekenntnis im Hebräerbrief," *idem, Aufsätze* II, 188-203. — O. CULLMANN, *The Christology of the NT* (1959) 83-107. — M. DIBELIUS, "Der himmlische Kultus nach dem Hebräerbrief," *idem, Botschaft* II, 160-76. — E. GRÄSSER, "Der Hebräerbrief 1938-1963," *TRu* 30 (1964), esp. 214-23 (literature up to 1963). — E. KÄSEMANN, *The Wandering People of God* (1984). — S. NOMOTO, *Die Hohepriester-Typologie im Hebräerbrief* (Diss. Hamburg, 1966). — *idem*, "Herkunft und Struktur der Hohenpriester-Vorstellung im Hebräerbrief," *NovT* 10 (1968) 10-25. — G. SCHRENK, *TDNT* III, 274-82. — G. THEISSEN, *Untersuchungen zum Hebräerbrief* (1969) 13-52. — H. ZIMMERMANN, *Die Hohepriester-Christologie des Hebräerbriefes* (1964). — *idem, Das Bekenntnis der Hoffnung* (BBB 47, 1977).

1. Except for the reference to Abiathar in Mark 2:26 (1 Sam 21:7) ἀρχιερεύς occurs in the Gospels and Acts only in connection with the trial of Jesus and the persecution of the early Church (38 times sg., 62 pl.) and in Hebrews as a christological title.

2. As a rule the pl. denotes the high priest of Jerusalem, his predecessors, and the most distinguished members of the priestly aristocracy (Acts 4:6), who together were the most influential group in the Sanhedrin (which also included scribes, elders, and ἄρχοντες; e.g., Matt 26:59; Mark 14:53, 55; Acts 22:30) and who functioned as the religious judiciary and police and the administrative consistory of the temple (e.g., Matt 21:15, 23, 45; Luke 22:4, 52; Acts 4:1; 5:24, 27). The representative of this group is the officiating *high priest* in Jerusalem. Frequently the pl. denotes the entire *Sanhedrin* (Matt 26:14; 27:6; 28:11; Mark 14:10; 15:3, 10f.; John 12:10; 19:6, 15, 21; Acts 9:14, 21; 26:10, 12), who, together with the scribes (Matt 2:4; 21:15; Mark 11:18; Luke 19:47; 20:19; 23:10) or Pharisees (Matt 21:45; 27:62; John 7:32; 11:47), is portrayed as the highest tribunal in matters of doctrine and law. The Gospels do not make clear divisions of competencies among the individual groups.

In Acts 19:14 Sceva is a member of the priestly aristocracy in the Diaspora (cf. Josephus *Ap.* i.187; *Ant.* xii.108).

3. From the time of Herod (37 B.C.) until the fall of Jerusalem (A.D. 70) the office of high priest, originally conferred for life, hereditary, and reserved for Zadokites, was subject to the political tactics of Herod and the corruptibility of the Roman procurators. During this time it was held by 28 illegitimate occupants. John 11:49, 51; 18:13 does not give the impression of an annual change in the office. The Romans appear to have accepted nepotism among the candidates, who, for financial reasons, were confined to four families (Boethus with 8 representatives, Ananus 8, Phiabi 3, and Camithus 3).

Only three members of the house of Ananus (A.D. 6-41) appear in the NT: *Annas* (Ananus), son of Sethi, was high priest A.D. 6-15, was enterprising and influential following his deposition, and died in A.D. 35 (Luke 3:2; John 18:13ff.; Acts 4:6; Josephus *Ant.* xviii.26; xx.197f.; *t. Menaḥ.* 13:21; *b. Pesaḥ.* 57a; Billerbeck II, 568ff.). Annas's son-in-law *Joseph* surnamed *Caiaphas, ca.* A.D. 18-37 (Josephus *Ant.* xviii.35, 95; *t. Yebam.* 1:10; *t. Para* 3:5; Luke 3:2; Acts 4:6), was unscrupulous (John 11:49-53) and is held responsible for the trial of Jesus (Matt 26:3, 57f., 62f., 65; Mark 14:53f., 60f., 66; Luke 22:54; John 18:13, 24). *Ananias,* son of Nebedaeus, held the office *ca.* A.D. 48-66 (Josephus *Ant.* xx.103; *B.J.* ii.429, 441f.; Acts 23:2; 24:1).

The NT yields no clarity regarding politically autonomous functions of the high priest during the period of the procurators; among other things they preside over the Sanhedrin (so the Passion narratives) and represent the Jewish people before the Romans (John 18:35; 19:6, 21;

Acts 22:30; 23:2; 25:2). According to John 11:51 "God's deputy" (cf. Acts 23:4) possesses the gift of prophecy (see Jeremias 149f.). Only in Hebrews are the cultic functions of the high priest discussed: his officiating over the sacrificial cult (8:3), the daily meal offering for the high priest (7:27; cf. Lev 6:13; Sir 45:14; Philo *Spec. Leg.* iii.131), the expiatory power of his death (Num 35:25ff.), and his execution of the ritual on the Day of Atonement (Heb 9:7, 25; 13:11; cf. Exod 30:10; Lev 16; Josephus *Ant.* iii.242ff.; Philo *Spec. Leg.* i.72; *Leg. Gai.* 307; *m. Yoma* 5:1-4).

4. Hebrews takes up the baptismal confession (3:1; 4:14; 10:19ff.) or, perhaps more broadly, the tradition of early Christian worship, to interpret the Church's confession of the Son of God as *high priest;* with the aid of Psalm 110 as well as Jewish ideas about Melchizedek and about the messianic and heavenly high priest the way of Jesus is described as high-priestly service. In contrast to Jewish and early Christian tradition this hermeneutical category is applied already to the earthly and crucified Jesus. The author circumvents the issue of Levitic descent (7:13-17), employing the phrase "after the order of Melchizedek" (5:10; 6:20; 7:11, 15, 17) typologically to make clear the legitimacy of the true high priest as eternal and permanent. Jesus surpasses the imperfect OT high-priestly office and replaces it through his own once-for-all sacrifice (chs. 7–10).

The high-priestly way to redemption is presented in four phases: a) Under the conditions of human existence, on the one hand (2:17f.; 4:15), and of perfect obedience and sinlessness (4:15; 5:5-10; 7:26-28) in solidarity with human suffering (2:17; 4:15; 5:1f.) and in fidelity to God (2:17; 3:1f.); on the other, the earthly Jesus mediates between human beings and God. Thus he becomes the high priest (2:17; 5:5; 6:20; 7:16, 21f.).

b) Decisive is the offering of his life (7:27; 10:10: martyr-theology?) or his blood (9:11ff.; 10:19) on Good Friday—the Day of Atonement—in the heavenly holy of holies (6:20; 8:1-3; 10:19f.); as an expiation, this offering effects forgiveness, eternal redemption, and purification from guilty conscience (9:11-15; 10:22). Jesus' becoming the high priest is here viewed entirely against the background of the OT cult and as typologically superior to it.

c) The ascending Jesus opens for his followers the way to God (4:14-16; 5:9; 7:19; 10:19-21; 12:2; a Gnostic-like πρόδρομος motif? So Käsemann).

d) In the present situation of the persecuted Church the exalted One appears as the heavenly *high priest* (7:26; 8:1; 10:21) before God as guarantee (7:22), intercessor (7:25; 9:24), and mediator (8:6; on the heavenly high priest see also *1 Clem.* 36:1; Ign. *Phld.* 9:1; *Pol.* 12:2).

U. Kellermann

ἀρχιποίμην, ενος, ὁ *archipoimēn* chief shepherd → ποιμήν.

Ἄρχιππος, ου *Archippos* Archippus*

A Christian in Colossae (Col 4:17; Phlm 2).

ἀρχισυνάγωγος, ου, ὁ *archisynagōgos* synagogue president*

Mark 5:22, 35, 36, 38 par. Luke 8:49; Luke 13:14; Acts 13:15; 18:8, 17. Schürer, *History* II, 433-36; W. Schrage, *TDNT* VII, 844-47; J. W. Doeve, *BHH* II, 1326.

ἀρχιτέκτων, ονος, ὁ *architektōn* master builder*

1 Cor 3:10: "like a skilled *master builder*" Paul laid the Church's foundation.

ἀρχιτελώνης, ου, ὁ *architelōnēs* chief tax collector*

Luke 19:2, referring to Zacchaeus; not otherwise attested.

ἀρχιτρίκλινος, ου, ὁ *architriklinos* one responsible for managing a banquet*

John 2:8, 9 (bis): the one responsible for the banquet (according to Luther, *the one in charge of the food).*

ἄρχω *archō* rule; begin

1. Occurrences in the NT — 2. Meaning and usage — 3. Act. meaning — 4. Mid. meaning — a) Comparison of the Synoptics — b) Pleonastic and allusive usage in the Synoptic Gospels and Acts — c) Specific meaning in the Lukan writings — 5. The remaining instances in the NT

Lit.: BAGD s.v. — H. Bietenhard, *DNTT* I, 165-69, esp. 167. — Dalman, *Words* 26-28. — G. Delling, *TDNT* I, 478-89, esp. 478f. — D. C. Hesseling, "Zur Syntax von ἄρχομαι und Verwandten," *ByZ* 20 (1911) 147-64. — J. W. Hunkin, " 'Pleonastic' ἄρχομαι in the NT," *JTS* 25 (1924) 390-402. — J. A. Kleist, *The Gospel of St. Mark* (1936) 154-61, 171, n. 1. — F. Rehkopf, *Die lukanische Sonderquelle. Ihr Umfang und Sprachgebrauch* (WUNT 5, 1959) 22f. — J. Reiling and J. L. Swellengrebel, *A Translator's Handbook on the Gospel of Luke* (1971) 203, 521, 721, etc. — H. Schürmann, *Jesu Abschiedsrede Lk 22, 21-38.* III. *Teil einer quellenkritischen Untersuchung des lukanischen Abendmahlberichtes Lk 22, 7-38* (NTAbh 20/5, 1957) 8-10. — G. Strecker, *Der Weg der Gerechtigkeit. Untersuchung zur Theologie des Matthäus* (FRLANT 82, [3]1971) 20. — J. Wanke, *Die Emmauserzählung. Eine redaktionsgeschichtliche Untersuchung zu Lk 24, 13-35* (ETS 31, 1973) 87. — U. Wilckens, *Die Missionsreden der Apostelgeschichte. Form und traditionsgeschichtliche Untersuchungen* (WMANT 5, [3]1974) 63-70, 106-9.

1. Of the 85 (+ Mark 12:14 v.l.; John 8:9) occurrences in the NT act. ἄρχω appears in Mark 10:42; Rom 15:12, the mid. ἄρχομαι 26 times in Mark (+ Mark 12:14 v.l.), 13 in Matthew, 31 in Luke, once in John (other than 8:9), 10 in Acts, and in 2 Cor 3:1; 1 Pet 4:17.

2. The original meaning of the vb. is *be first.* Act. means *rule* (or *begin*; act. is rare in the Hellenistic period; cf. Delling 478f.; BDF §177); mid. *commence, begin,* always followed by pres. inf. (BDF §414.2). In mid. the beginning itself can be emphasized or it can be contrasted with continuation, completion, or interruption (see BAGD s.v. 2aα, which has examples). The stress on the new beginning of an action frequently leads to a purely pleonastic use in the Synoptic Gospels and Acts (BDF §§392, 419.3 [bibliography in both places]; → 4) and is only a limited indication of Semitic usage (Delling 478).

3. Act. *rule* in Mark 10:42 (Matt 20:25; Luke 22:25 differ): In a saying attached to the pericope dealing with the sons of Zebedee, discipleship in the post-Easter community is given a concrete definition in view of Jesus' conduct (Mark 10:32-34), namely, as not desiring to lord it over each other; this characterizes the Church's distinctive way of existing in the world (V. P. Howard, *Das Ego Jesu in den synoptischen Evangelien* [MTS 14, 1975] 97-107, esp. 97, n. 4; R. Pesch, *Markusevangelium* II [HTKNT] 153-67 [bibliography]).

In Rom 15:12 "the accent is on the infinitive" (ἄρχειν; E. Käsemann, *Commentary on Romans* [1980] 387). With the aid of a paraphrase of Isa 11:10 LXX the universal lordship of the "resurrected and exalted one," already begun and grounded in the event of justification, is emphasized; this lordship of Christ allows the Gentiles as well to share already in the praise of the divine mercy (Käsemann 387 [bibliography]; H. Schlier, *Römerbrief* [HTKNT] 425).

4. Mid. *commence, begin:* Mark has 27 occurrences; Matthew has 13, of which 6 are parallels with Mark (Mark 2:23 par. Matt 12:1; Mark 8:31 par. Matt 16:21; Mark 8:32 par. Matt 16:22; Mark 14:19 par. Matt 22:22; Mark 14:33 par. Matt 26:37; Mark 14:71 par. Matt 26:74); of 31 occurrences in Luke, 2 are parallels with Mark (Mark 11:15 par. Luke 19:45; Mark 12:1 par. Luke 20:9; Luke 9:12 is dependent upon Mark 6:34f. and Luke 11:29 on Mark 8:11f.). There are 2 occurrences in Q (Luke 7:24 par. Matt 11:7; Luke 12:45 par. Matt 24:49). The remaining occurrences in Luke and Matthew derive from their respective traditions or redactional activity.

b) The predominantly pleonastic use in the Gospels and Acts (e.g., Mark 10:28; Acts 1:1; 11:4; Hunkin; Delling 478f.; E. Haenchen, *Acts* [1971] 137) is a significant redactional term in Mark in the areas of preaching and teaching (Mark 1:45; 4:1; 5:20; 6:2, 34; 8:31; cf. also E. Schweizer, "Anmerkungen zur Theologie des Markus," *idem, Neotestamentica* [1963] 93-104, *passim*). The same thing is reflected, though without Synoptic parallels, in the other Gospels: in Matthew it refers to the fundamental nature of the beginning of Jesus' preaching (4:17); in Luke it is significant in the stress on the beginning through Jesus (3:23; 4:21; 23:5 [the idea expressed without the vb.: Jesus as the original missionary, 8:4-8]; cf. Acts 10:37) and on the spreading of the word on the basis of the beginning in Jerusalem occasioned by the Jesus event (24:47; → c; cf. H. Schürmann, *Lukas* I [HTKNT], G. Schneider, *Lukas* [ÖTK], and Reiling and Swellengrebel on the passages cited).

c) In the peculiarly Lukan formulaic expression ἀρξάμενος ἀπό (cf. BDF §§137.3, 419.3; Wilckens 106-9; Wanke 87) a specific concern of Lukan theology is elicited: it has to do with the entire history of Jesus, *beginning with* his baptism (cf. Luke 3:23), and is geographically determinable, namely, *beginning in* Galilee (Luke 23:5; Acts 10:37); participation in this history is the decisive criterion for apostleship according to the Lukan scheme (Acts 1:22); this history has its salvation-historical center in Jerusalem (Luke 24:47; cf. 24:27) and as an event of proclamation takes from there its point of departure in the form of the "missionary speech" (Acts 10:34-43) which summarizes the gospel (of Luke) and thus signals the abiding presence of Jesus in the proclamation (on various aspects of the texts cited cf. the relevant sections in E. Haenchen, *Acts* [1971]; H. Conzelmann, *Acts* [Hermeneia]; *idem, The Theology of St. Luke* [1961] 132-35; Schneider, *Lukas* 503f.; Wilckens 63-70; 106-9; K. Kliesch, *Das heilsgeschichtliche Credo in den Reden der Apostelgeschichte* [BBB 44, 1975] 93f.; 160ff.; O. Merk, "Das Reich Gottes in den lukanischen Schriften," FS Kümmel 201ff. [with bibliography in all]).

5. a) 2 Cor 3:1, ἄρχεσθαι, here in connection with a rhetorical question, is suggestive insofar as "Paul is accustomed to hearing" the repeated "reproach" of commending himself (R. Bultmann, *The Second Letter to the Corinthians* [1985] 70; cf. 4:2; 5:12; 10:12, 18; Delling 479).

b) In 1 Pet 4:17a the present and future intervention of God in the Church is delineated in terms of "judgment"; in v. 17b it makes good sense to complete the thought by adding ἄρχεται τὸ κρίμα after εἰ δὲ πρῶτον ἀφ' ἡμῶν (L. Goppelt, *Der erste Petrusbrief* [KEK] 311-14 [bibliography], esp. 314, n. 57).

c) Ἀρξάμενοι is significant in the non-Johannine pericope of the woman taken in adultery (John 8:9), which originated perhaps in the early Church (cf. Kümmel, *Introduction* [1975] 207 with nn. 44, 45; H. Freiherr von Campenhausen, "Zur Perikope von der Ehebrecherin (Joh 7:53–8:11)," *ZNW* 68 [1977] 164-75).

In John 13:5, Jesus initiates the footwashing at the meal; it is precisely in that the beginning is made by Jesus that the significance of the statement lies, namely, the humiliating service to his followers which begins in "the fellowship of the disciples with Jesus" and has as its goal the fellowship and mutual service of love among the disciples themselves (cf. R. Bultmann, *Gospel of John*

[1971] 466-79; possible traces of Semitic or Synoptic usage [Bultmann, 462, n. 4, 466, n. 4] should not be exaggerated and hardly suffice by themselves to isolate a Johannine source; R. Schnackenburg, *Gospel according to St John* III [1987] 7-15 [includes bibliography], 17f.).

O. Merk

ἄρχων, οντος, ὁ *archōn* ruler*

1. Occurrences in the NT — 2. Range of meaning — a) References to Christ — b) Worldly rulers — c) Spiritual powers

Lit.: BAGD s.v. — H. BIETENHARD, *DNTT* I, 165-69, esp. 168f. — J. BLANK, *Krisis. Untersuchungen zur johanneischen Christologie und Eschatologie* (1964) 194, 281ff., 339. — O. BÖCHER, *Das NT und die dämonischen Mächte* (SBS 58, 1972). — W. CARR, "The Rulers of this Age—I Cor II.6-8," *NTS* 23 (1976/77) 20-35. — G. DAUTZENBERG, "Botschaft und Bedeutung der urchristlichen Propheten nach dem 1 Kor (2:6-16; 12–14)," *Prophetic Vocation in the NT and Today* (ed. J. Panagopoulos; NovTSup 45, 1977) 131-61. — G. DELLING, *TDNT* I, 478-89, esp. 488f. (bibliography). — M. DIBELIUS, *Die Geisterwelt im Glauben des Paulus* (1909) 88-97, *passim.* — A. FEUILLET, "Les 'chefs de ce siècle' et la sagesse divine d'après I Cor 2, 6-8," *Studiorum Paulinorum Congressus Internationalis Catholicus 1961* (AnBib 17/18, 1963) 383-93. — J. JEREMIAS, *Jerusalem in the Time of Jesus* (1969) 197, 222-32. — E. LOHSE, *TDNT* VII, 860-71. — F. MUSSNER, *Christus, das All und die Kirche. Studien zur Theologie des Epheserbriefes* (TTS 1, 1955) 18ff., *passim.* — A. VAN ROON, *The Authenticity of Ephesians* (NovTSup 39, 1974) 223-27, *passim.* — A. SCHLATTER, *Der Evangelist Johannes* (1930) 270-72. — *idem, Der Evangelist Matthäus* (1929) 315f. — H. SCHLIER, *Mächte und Gewalten im NT* (QD 3, 1958). — J. SCHNIEWIND, "Die Archonten dieses Äons (I. Kor 2, 6-8)," *idem, Nachgelassene Reden und Aufsätze* (ed. E. Kähler; TBT 1, 1952) 104-9. — L. SCHOTTROFF, *Der Glaubende und die feindliche Welt* (WMANT 37, 1970) 217-25, 231, n. 3, 275. — SCHÜRER, *History* II, 97, 179f., 212, 427-39; III, 92-100. — H. STRATHMANN, *TDNT* VI, 516-35, esp. 529f. — J. WANKE, *Die Emmauserzählung. Eine redaktionsgeschichtliche Untersuchung zu Lk 24, 13-35* (ETS 31, 1973) 58f., 66. — M. WINTER, *Pneumatiker und Psychiker in Korinth. Zum religionsgeschichtlichen Hintergrund von 1. Kor 2, 6–3, 4* (MTSt 9, 1975) 58ff., 199, 219, *passim.*

1. The 37 occurrences in the NT (including Matt 9:34 [cf. *TCGNT* 25f.] and excluding Titus 1:9 [v.l.; cf. *TCGNT* 653]) are distributed among three areas: a) the one reference to Christ (Rev 1:5); b) references to Roman or Jewish governing officials or individuals in distinguished positions (so usually in the Synoptic Gospels and Acts, e.g., Acts 14:5; also John 3:1; 7:26, 48; Rom 13:3); c) references to supra-worldly powers which, as a rule, exercise lordship inimical to God (Mark 3:22; Matt 9:34; 12:24; Luke 11:15; John 12:31; 14:30; 16:11; 1 Cor 2:6, 8; Eph 2:2).

2. a) Rev 1:5 is the only place in the NT where ἄρχων refers to Christ. The exalted Christ as "the *ruler* of kings on earth" is to be viewed in the context of the opening doxology as well as of the christology of Revelation; historical interpretation—and that both temporal and eschatological—are woven together to characterize "the universal reign of Christ" (cf. W. Bousset, *Offenbarung* [KEK] 187ff., 239; T. Holtz, *Die Christologie der Apokalypse* [TU 85, 1962] 58ff. [bibliography]).

b) 1) In Matt 20:25 ἄρχοντες applies to earthly lordship in general (material, though not verbatim, par. in Mark 10:42; Luke 22:25), whereas in Rom 13:3 it refers to the ruling authorities in the sense of Hellenistic-Roman administrative language (cf. A. Strobel, "Zum Verständnis von Röm 13," *ZNW* 47 [1956] 67-93, esp. 79ff.) and in Acts 16:19—there only in the NT—to municipal officials (cf. J. Weiss, *RE* XII [1903] 39; Strathmann 529). In Acts 4:26, in a prayer from Ps 2:1f., "the kings of the earth" are exegetically interpreted in a pre-Lukan sense to refer to Herod Antipas and οἱ ἄρχοντες to Pilate (cf. Acts 4:27-30 and, for clarification of the scene which Luke has created, Luke 23:6-12; M. Dibelius, "Herodes und Pilatus," *idem, Botschaft* I, 278-92, esp. 289ff.; H. Conzelmann, *Acts* [Hermeneia] ad loc.).

2) In the Synoptic Gospels and Acts persons in special positions are usually designated as ἄρχων: e.g., the judge in Luke 12:58, a member of the Sanhedrin in Luke 23:13, the high priest in Acts 23:5. As the ἄρχων of the people (Acts 7:27, 35) Moses attains typological significance in Lukan theology in connection with the Christ-event (cf. Luke 2:38; 24:21; Acts 3:15; 5:31; see E. Haenchen, *Acts* [1971]; H. Conzelmann, *Acts* [Hermeneia] ad loc.; G. Stählin, *Apostelgeschichte* [NTD] 108 [evidence]).

A comparison of the Synoptics shows that ἀρχισυνάγωγος (president of the synagogue) is used interchangeably with ἄρχων (cf. e.g., Mark 5:22 par. Matt 9:18; Luke 8:41; Mark 5:38 par. Matt 9:23). This may result from the fact that in Diaspora Judaism both offices, though clearly distinguishable, could be held by the same person (cf. also Schürer II, 435f.). More likely, however, is an imprecise knowledge of the more detailed function of the ἄρχων, as is shown also by the Lukan designation as ἄρχοντες (pl.) of Jewish "rulers," who are, among other things, only members of the Sanhedrin (cf. Schürer II, 212; Lohse 864, n. 29; Wanke 58f.). Although when an individual ἄρχων is mentioned weight is surely given to the meeting of the person with Jesus (cf. Luke 18:18, where, unlike Mark 10:17/Matt 19:16, the "rich young man" is thus designated), still pl. ἄρχοντες is also used in the Lukan writings to refer to the responsibility of the Jewish leadership as a whole for the death of Jesus (cf. Luke 14:1; 23:13, 35; 24:20; Acts 3:17; 4:5, 8; 13:27; see Wanke 59, 66; Haenchen, *Acts,* on 3:17).

In John 3:1; 7:26, 48; 12:42 ἄρχων/ἄρχοντες denotes individual members or several members of the Sanhedrin who, in contrast to "the Jews" and "the Pharisees," are open in their attitude toward the message of Jesus (cf. R. Bultmann, *John* [1971] 133, n. 4; H. F. Weiss, *TDNT* IX, 44).

c) Except in 1 Cor 2:6, 8 ἄρχων is always used in the sg. in the NT when it designates supramundane powers. (On the history of interpretation of the texts discussed below cf. the commentaries mentioned and the examples in H. Conzelmann, *1 Corinthians* [Hermeneia] 61 nn. 44f.; BAGD s.v.)

The accusation in Mark 3:22, a unitary composition in its original Q form (Matt 12:24 [does 9:34 have a Markan textual basis?] par. Luke 11:15; on the Synoptic problem at this point see Bultmann, *History* 13f., 52, 329f., 383; Schulz, *Q* 203ff. [bibliography]), is split up in Mark, though it remains substantively identical: The malevolent identification of Jesus with Beelzebul or Beelzebub (= lord of the [demonic] dwellings), the *prince* of the demons and thus Satan himself (cf. vv. 23, 26), is intended to demonstrate Jesus' demonic possession in the eyes of his opponents (v. 30) and to show that his exorcisms, which are undeniable even by his opponents, are acts of demonic power (for details see R. Pesch, *Markusevangelium* I [HTKNT] 209-21 [bibliography]; G. Schneider, *Evangelium nach Lukas* II [ÖTK] 264ff.).

In 1 Cor 2:6, 8 ἄρχοντες refers not to earthly rulers (*contra,* e.g., Schniewind; Dautzenberg), but to *demonic powers.* It is said of them that, as exponents of cosmic wisdom in its opposition to divine wisdom, they perish because they have not recognized God's eschatological action in the cross and with it the divine intervention, effective in the λόγος τοῦ σταυροῦ (1:17f.), which deprives the anti-God forces of their power (2:7f.; cf. the evidence, e.g., in Dibelius 88ff.; Kümmel in H. Lietzmann and W. G. Kümmel, *An die Korinther I/II* [HNT] 170; Conzelmann, *1 Corinthians* 60ff. [bibliography]; R. Baumann, *Mitte und Norm des Christlichen* [NTAbh N.F. 5, 1968] 209-25 [bibliography]; L. Schottroff 221, n. 1 and *passim*).

In Eph 2:2 the ἄρχων as the personification of the sphere of power opposed to God (cf. H. Schlier, *An die Epheser* [[4]1963] 102-5 [with numerous examples]) is identical with Satan. The parallel placement of αἰών and ἄρχων shows at least that they "correspond to each other in their nature" (A. Lindemann, *Die Aufhebung der Zeit* [SNT 12, 1975] 110; cf. also 49ff., 58f., 108ff.), even if their identification, otherwise demonstrable in the history of religion, is not present here also (Dibelius 156f.; M. Dibelius and H. Greeven, *An die Kolosser, Epheser, an Philemon* [HNT, [3]1953] ad loc.).

Christians are now rescued from this ἄρχων (Eph 2:1-3), and John elucidates this state of affairs in John 12:31; 14:30; 16:11 by means of a christological-eschatological sharpening: in the exaltation of Jesus on the cross the ἄρχων τοῦ κόσμου τούτου, Satan, is "stripped of his power" (cf. R. Bultmann, *John* 431, n. 2, 630f., 565f.; R. Schnackenburg, *The Gospel according to St. John* II [1979], 390f., III [1982], 86f., 113f.; Blank 194, 281ff., 339).

O. Merk

ἄρωμα, ατος, τό *arōma* spice, salve*

In the NT only pl. in Mark 16:1 par. Luke 23:56–24:1: the pleasant-smelling *oils, salves* to be used in anointing (so Mark) Jesus (in the grave); according to John 19:40 the corpse was anointed with the aromatic substances and wrapped in linen cloths *prior to* burial.

ἀσάλευτος, 2 *asaleutos* unshakable, immovable*

Acts 27:41, referring to the bow of the ship which was stuck; fig. in Heb 12:28 of the βασιλεία which *cannot be shaken.*

Ἀσάφ *Asaph* Asa*

Personal name in Matt 1:7, 8 (cf. 1 Kgs 15:8).

ἄσβεστος, 2 *asbestos* unquenchable*

Mark 9:43, of the fire of hell (v. 45 v.l.); Matt 3:12 par. Luke 3:17, "but the chaff he will burn with *unquenchable* fire."

ἀσέβεια, ας, ἡ *asebeia* evil (deed), godlessness
→ ἀσεβής.

ἀσεβέω *asebeō* commit an impious deed, act godlessly
→ ἀσεβής.

ἀσεβής, 2 *asebēs* godless, evildoer*
ἀσέβεια, ας, ἡ *asebeia* evil (deed), godlessness*
ἀσεβέω *asebeō* commit an impious deed, act godlessly*

1. Occurrences of the word group in the NT — 2. Meaning — 3. Statements about false teachers — 4. Romans and the Pastorals

Lit.: W. Foerster, *TDNT* VII, 185-91. — F. Hahn, "Genesis 15, 6 im NT," *Probleme biblischer Theologie* (FS G. von Rad; 1971) 90-107, esp. 100ff. — E. Käsemann, *Perspectives on Paul* (1971) 79-101, esp. 84f. For further bibliography → ἁμαρτία.

1. The adj. occurs 8 or 9 times. Except for 2 Pet 3:7 and perhaps Jude 4, 15 (end), it is regularly used substantively. The subst. occurs 6 times, while the vb. appears only in the etymological figure of Jude 15 (citation of *1 Enoch* 1:9), unless preference in 2 Pet 2:6 is given to the verbal form over the adjectival form. These 16 instances are distributed, except for the two OT citations (Rom 11:26;

1 Pet 4:18), among 3 occurrences each in Romans, the Pastorals, and 2 Peter, and 5 in Jude.

2. In the LXX ἀσεβής is used commonly to render Heb. *rāšā'* (like ἁμαρτωλός, but twice as often), but it is not as predominant in the NT (corresponding to the general preference for the stem ἁμαρτ-). Hellenistic Judaism breaks with the usual limitation of usage to (lack of a proper) relationship with the gods (cf., e.g., Plato *Smp.* 188c with Dio Chrysostom 31:13; but also Josephus *B.J.* vii.260), based on the OT conception of God: in whatever ways one behaves impiously, one offends against (the will of) God, who is essentially concerned with human life in community. Thus ἀσεβής and ἁμαρτωλός can stand next to each other as equivalents in 1 Tim 1:9 (hendiadys), as in the citation in 1 Pet 4:18. The pleonastic ἁμαρτωλοὶ ἀσεβεῖς in the citation in Jude 15 is unique. The active understanding of the noun is indicated both in the combined citation of Rom 11:26 (pl., as in Jude 18) and in Rom 1:18 (πᾶσα, alongside ἀδικία). 2 Tim 2:16 and Titus 2:12 aim more at discontinuity. In Jude 15, 18 the semitizing gen. replaces the adj.

3. Outside Romans and Titus 2:12, ἀσεβ- expressions occur in the context of struggle against false teachers. As in the LXX (esp. Proverbs [cf. 1 Pet. 4:18] and other wisdom literature), from the perspective of apostasy from (the instructions of) God (e.g., Prov 28:4; Jer 3:13; Dan 9:5) it was easy to identify heretics with the fundamental antithesis to δίκαιος. The practical results of false teachings are continually in view: in 1 Tim 1:9(f.) ἀσεβής occurs in connection with a vice list, while the escalation in ungodliness in 2 Tim 2:16 is illustrated in 3:1-5; in Jude 4, 18(f.) the reference is primarily to praxis, as in the parallel citation of v. 15, the prophetic word of judgment of which is anticipated in v. 4. Finally, the judgment executed on "the world of the *ungodly*" at the time of Noah and on Sodom and Gomorrah at the time of Lot (both of whom were "righteous") is established as an "example" for the future ungodly, i.e., an example of judgment to the evildoers at the time of the author of 2 Peter, those who live in opposition to God and scoff at the parousia (2 Pet 2:5f.). They will also be destroyed (3:7).

4. Paul links ἀσέβεια and ἀδικία in Rom 1:18 (corresponding, e.g., to Mic 7:18; *1 Enoch* 13:2). Against the OT and Jewish background, it is unlikely that these terms refer to a partition of offenses according to the two tablets of the Decalogue. The thought has much more to do with the objects of the divine wrath, Gentiles as well as Jews: just as Paul denies to the latter righteousness based on law because of their transgressions (Rom 2), so he denies to the former → εὐσέβεια, though he does not use that (admittedly too strong) established term for the religious life (cf., however, ἐσεβάσθησαν in 1:25). For both shut themselves off from God's truth, i.e., the order of creation. This fundamental sin results in deeds that make one culpable (1:18) and in which the punishment is already at work (vv. 21f., esp. 1:24-32). The justification of the *ungodly* (characterized in 1:18-32) by the same God—through faith alone—is referred to in 4:5; to use Abraham as an example of the believing ἀσεβής is entirely un-Jewish. Rom 5:6 focuses on faith leading to acceptance of the salvation event offered in Christ's vicarious death, and on the manifestation of the incomparable love of God and of his Son to us, who were at that time still *"ungodly."*

In Titus 2:12, by contrast (cf. vv. 11-14), the focus is on the renunciation of paganism, which is considered *godless,* at conversion (baptism). By this means grace can help the Christian to the true humanity of a life that is pleasing to God. Correspondingly, distance from Paul is suggested in 1 Tim 1:9, which designates the law as only for "the *ungodly* and sinners," while the "just" build their lives on "sound doctrine" (v. 10).

P. Fiedler

ἀσέλγεια, ας, ἡ *aselgeia* licentiousness, debauchery*

Lit.: O. BAUERNFEIND, *TDNT* I, 490. — F. MUSSNER, *Galaterbrief* (HTKNT, 1974), esp. 379-83. — A. VÖGTLE, *Die Tugend- und Lasterkataloge im NT* (1936), s.v. — S. WIBBING, *Die Tugend- und Lasterkataloge im NT* (1959).

1. In the NT ἀσέλγεια normally has a sensual meaning and refers esp. to *sexual debauchery:* Rom 13:13: κοίταις (sexual intercourse) καὶ ἀσελγείαις; 2 Cor 12:21: ἀκαθαρσίᾳ (uncleanness) καὶ πορνείᾳ (fornication) καὶ ἀσελγείᾳ; Gal 5:19: works of the flesh, which include πορνεία (fornication), ἀκαθαρσία (uncleanness), and ἀσέλγεια; cf. 2 Pet 2:2, 7, 18; *Herm. Man.* xii.4.6; *Sim.* ix.15.3; *Vis.* ii.2.2; iii.7.2. In addition, the word describes behavior in which sexual debauchery is only *one* element among many. Ἀσέλγεια is thus a comprehensive expression for evil and perversion. It is one of the vices that destroy an individual from within (Mark 7:22). The perversity of Sodom and Gomorrah (2 Pet 2:7) consisted of it. It is the characteristic of godless paganism (Eph 4:19; 1 Pet 4:3; Jude 4).

2. Characteristic of the NT usage of the word is its use in vice catalogs (Rom 13:13; Gal 5:19; 1 Pet 4:3), which have their models both in Judaism (Qumran: 1QS 4:9-11; cf. Wibbing 92-94) and in the ethic of pagan antiquity. These forms agree not only in the introductory warning against an evil lifestyle, but also in the listing of vices. They are like a cascade of charges, which—although not free of stereotypes (A. Vögtle, *LTK* VI, 807)—become a single accusation against paganism. Certainly the primary function of vice catalogs is positive. Rom 13:13 is to be understood as typical baptismal parenesis. Gal 5:19 aims to contribute to ensuring the "sphere of freedom of the baptized" (Mussner 389). The author of 1 Peter appeals to

persecuted Christians, whom he comforts and consoles with the memory of the Christ-event and of baptism (3:21).

H. Goldstein

ἄσημος, 2 *asēmos* insignificant*

Acts 21:39: from Tarsus, a not *insignificant* city of Cilicia. K. H. Rengstorf, *TDNT* VII, 267.

Ἀσήρ *Asēr* Asher*

Ἀσήρ is mentioned in Luke 2:36 as an ancestor of the prophetess Hannah and in Rev 7:6 in the enumeration of the tribes of Israel (Gen 30:13; 49:20).

ἀσθένεια, ας, ἡ *astheneia* weakness, sickness
→ ἀσθενής.

ἀσθενέω *astheneō* be weak, be sick
→ ἀσθενής.

ἀσθένημα, ατος, τό *asthenēma* weakness
→ ἀσθενής.

ἀσθενής, 2 *asthenēs* weak, sick
ἀσθένεια, ας, ἡ *astheneia* weakness, sickness
ἀσθενέω *astheneō* be weak, be sick
ἀσθένημα, ατος, τό *asthenēma* weakness*

1. Occurrences in the NT — 2. Meaning and usage of the word group — 3. In the Gospels — 4. In Paul

Lit.: J. Ernst, *Das Evangelium nach Lukas* (1977) 181f., 334. — F. Fenner, *Die Krankheit im NT* (1930), esp. 27-30. — E. Güttgemanns, *Der leidende Apostel und sein Herr* (1966). — P. Hoffmann, *Studien zur Theologie der Logienquelle* (1972), 299. — E. Kamlah, "Wie beurteilt Paulus seine Leiden?" *ZNW* 54 (1963) 217-32. — O. Michel, *Römerbrief* (KEK, [13]1966) 333-61. — H. Schlier, *Römerbrief* (1977) 402-22. — J. Schmid, *Das Evangelium nach Markus* ([4]1958) 52-55. — G. Stählin, *TDNT* I, 490-93. — E. Walter, "Die Kraft wird in der Schwachheit vollendet," *GuL* 28 (1955) 248-55. — U. Wilckens, *Weisheit und Torheit* (1959) esp. 11-53.

1. The words ἀσθενής, ἀσθένεια, and ἀσθενέω appear a total of 80 times in the NT, of which 40 occurrences are in Paul alone. The subst. ἀσθένημα is found only in Rom 15:1.

2. The word group signifies *weakness* or *powerlessness* of various kinds.

a) The reference is often to a comprehensive understanding of *weakness* as *that which is derived directly from the earthly-bodily existence of mankind* and has consequences in various realms. This understanding is present esp. in the texts in which the terms σάρξ ("flesh") or σῶμα ("body") appear in connection with ἀσθεν-. As an example Mark 14:38 par. Matt 26:41 could be mentioned; here Jesus summons the sleeping disciples to watch and pray, so that they can overcome the danger of temptation that is related to the σάρξ ἀσθενής (here contrasted to πνεῦμα πρόθυμον). Another example is 1 Cor 15:43, where Paul contrasts the earthly body (σῶμα ψυχικόν, v. 44), whose characteristic features are "perishability," "dishonor," and "*weakness,*" to the future resurrection body (σῶμα πνευματικόν), which is filled with the Spirit and which he characterizes as a body in "imperishability," "glory," and "power."

b) What can be said about weakness based on humanity's earthly-bodily existence can also be said of specific persons or groups of persons. Thus in 1 Pet 3:7, because wives are described as the "*weaker* sex," husbands should treat them with respect. According to Heb 7:28 human high priests are beset with *weakness* (cf. 5:2; also 4:15). According to 11:34 the faithful of the old covenant "were strengthened out of *weakness.*" Paul speaks of his *weak* appearance (e.g., 1 Cor 2:3: "I was with you in *weakness* and in much fear and trembling"; 2 Cor 10:10: "His bodily appearance is *weak,* and his speech of no account"; 2 Cor 11:21: "We were too *weak*"; Gal 4:13, etc.) and writes that Christ "was crucified in *weakness*" (2 Cor 13:4).

c) The characteristic and fundamental weakness of mankind has various effects. *Sickness* is one of its manifestations. The word group appears in this sense almost 40 times in the NT (Matt 8:17; 10:8; 25:36, 39, 43f.; Mark 6:56; Luke 4:40; 5:15; 8:2; 9:2; 10:9; 13:11f.; John 4:46; 5:3, 5, 7; 6:2; 11:1-4, 6; Acts 4:9; 5:15f.; 9:37; 19:12; 28:9; 1 Cor 11:30; Phil 2:26f.; 1 Tim 5:23; 2 Tim 4:20; Jas 5:14), usually in an absolute construction (even in places where a particular sickness is in view). In Matt 8:17 the synonym νόσος is found alongside ἀσθένεια. In 1 Cor 11:30 the synonymous ἄρρωστος is used in the same way. Matt 10:8 mentions the healings of the ἀσθενοῦντες (here and elsewhere, the partc. stands in place of the adj.) along with raisings from the dead, purifications from leprosy, and exorcism of demons; John 5:3 names individual groups of the sick: the blind, lame, and paralytics. Numerous causes of sicknesses are mentioned. According to Luke 13:11, e.g., they are caused by spirits (πνεύματα; cf. Luke 8:2; Acts 5:16). According to 1 Cor 11:30 they appear as a result of unworthy reception of the eucharist. The healing is normally expressed with the vb. θεραπεύειν (e.g., Luke 5:15; 8:2; 9:1; 10:9; Matt 10:8; Acts 5:16) or ἰᾶσθαι (cf. Luke 9:2; Jas 5:16). The process of healing is effected in various ways: through the laying on of hands, touch, etc., and even by applying a handkerchief (Acts 19:12) or allowing the shadow of an apostle to fall on people (Acts 5:15).

d) A further form of ἀσθένεια is *weakness in the capacity to understand.* It is intended in this way in Rom 6:19: "I am speaking in human terms, because of the *weakness* of your flesh" (RSV is different). Heb 5:2 can also be considered in this way (cf. there the vbs. ἀγνοεῖν and πλανᾶσθαι).

e) Alongside these natural forms of ἀσθένεια there is in Paul an *ethical-religious weakness.* When Paul emphasizes in Rom 5:6 that Christ died for the ungodly (cf. v. 8) at the right time, "while we were yet *helpless,*" he recognizes weakness (overcome through the death of Christ) as the condition of unredeemed humanity, which is separated from God. The Christian can also experience this kind of ἀσθένεια. Paul speaks of this in 8:26 when he says that the (divine) Pneuma comes to aid human *weakness* in prayer (i.e., the inability to pray in a way that is pleasing to God). Thus he indicates that there are groups in Rome and Corinth who are *weak* in faith (Rom 14:1: ἀσθενοῦντα τῇ πίστει; cf., however, 4:19, where it is said of Abraham: μὴ ἀσθενήσας τῇ πίστει) or who have an uneasy conscience (συνείδησις ἀσθεν-, 1 Cor 8:7, 12), just as, generally speaking, the body of the Church can include members who appear to be *weaker* (12:22).

f) Only rarely is the word group used of nonhuman persons or things to describe their power or *powerlessness.* In Gal 4:9 the "*weak* and beggarly elemental spirits" are mentioned. Rom 8:3 speaks of the *inability* of the law to bring salvation (cf. also Heb 7:18).

g) Finally, in Acts 20:35 the participle ἀσθενοῦντες designates *the economically weak, the poor.*

3. In the Gospels healings of the *sick* belong to the "signs" (John 6:2 explicitly σημεῖα) of the dawning kingdom of God. This is especially evident in the Great Commission in Q, in which the instruction to the disciples to heal the sick stands in direct relation to the mission to proclaim the imminence of the kingdom of God (Luke 10:9; Matt 10:7f.). "The healings in Q are, as other texts make clear, to be understood eschatologically as part of the end-time event" (Hoffmann 299). Mark not only reports individual healings, but also outlines in his summaries a picture of comprehensive healing activity (1:32-34; 3:7-12; 6:53-56), which forms an inseparable unity with Jesus' teaching activity (cf. 1:39). Mark understands both as proof of Jesus' dignity as Messiah and Son of God. Matt 8:16f. is characteristic of Matthew, who adds what is for him a typical "fulfillment citation" to a summary taken over from Mark (1:32-34). The citation refers to Isa 53:4, from the fourth servant song: "He has borne our sickness and carried our pains" (RSV mg.). Matthew sees this prophetic promise fulfilled in the works of Jesus. For Luke healing is connected essentially with the expansion of the λόγος (e.g., 5:15: "But so much more the report went abroad concerning him; and great multitudes gathered to hear and to be healed of their *infirmities*"). Healing has meaning, therefore, for the theology of mission. Thus it is not surprising that the proclamation of the apostles in Acts is also accompanied by healings (Acts 3–5; 19:12, 20; and often).

4. Paul develops an independent "theology of *weakness.*" For him ἀσθένεια is the place of revelation for the (divine) dynamis. This meaning is expressed particularly in the paradoxical sentence, "My power is made perfect in *weakness*" (2 Cor 12:9). Here Paul formulates a general rule, the validity of which he has derived from the Christ-event. Thus he can say of Christ: "He was crucified in *weakness,* but lives by the power of God" (13:4). For Paul, the cross and resurrection stand inseparably together. Christ is, even as the crucified one, "the power of God and the wisdom of God" (1 Cor. 1:24). The cross indicates that God selects what is *weak* in the eyes of the world in order to "shame" the "strong" (v. 27). If this basic rule is true for Christ, it must be valid for the apostle also. Consequently Paul always accents—especially in the "catalogs of sufferings" (1 Cor 4:10-13; 2 Cor. 4:8-12; 6:4-10; 11:21-29; 12:10)—his *weakness* in all of its manifestations (sufferings, persecutions, dangers, etc.). Indeed, he even boasts about it because of his conviction that it distinguishes the true apostle (cf. 2 Cor 12:10: "When I am *weak,* then I am strong").

Paul speaks of ἀσθένεια, etc., in parenetic contexts in Romans 14–15 and 1 Corinthians 8–10. In Rome there were apparently two groups of believers, the "strong" and the "*weak.*" While the "strong" were Christians with a very definite consciousness of authority and freedom, the "weak" were (Jewish Christian) believers who had an uneasy conscience. Because of their pious dread (of impurity and transgression of the law) they ate no meat (Rom 14:2) and kept certain holy days (v. 5). Paul bids the "strong" (among whom he counts himself, 15:1) to accept those in the community who are *weak* in faith (14:1), and not to despise them (v. 3), just as he encourages the "*weak*" not to judge those who have different opinions (i.e., those who believe they may eat anything), inasmuch as God has already accepted them (v. 3). One should not place an offense or hindrance in one's brother's way (v. 13). This advice is particularly aimed at the "strong." They should bear with the *weaknesses* of the *weak* and "not please themselves" (15:1), for "Christ did not please himself" (v. 3). Paul thus gives a christological basis to the parenesis.

The *weak* in Corinth are Christians who have come from paganism and have problems of conscience with eating meat sold in the market that has been offered to idols (1 Cor 10:25). They have not extricated themselves totally from their pagan past; they lacked the γνῶσις of mature Christians (8:7). In his response (which probably goes back to a concrete question from the Corinthians), Paul admonishes his readers to give no offense to the "*weak* conscience," for in so doing they would sin against Christ himself (8:12). Here also Paul directs the focus to Christ in order to provide the basis for his parenesis.

J. Zmijewski

Ἀσία, ας *Asia* Asia*

1. Occurrences in the NT — 2. Historical background — 3. Missionary history

Lit.: Articles in the journals *Anatolian Studies* (1951ff.) and *Anatolica* (1967ff.). — T. R. S. BROUGHTON, "Roman Asia Minor," *An Economic Survey of Ancient Rome* IV (ed. T. Frank; 1938, reprinted 1959) 499-916. — W. M. CALDER and E. W. GRAY, *OCD* 130f. — V. CHAPOT, *La province romaine proconsulaire d'Asie* (1904, reprinted 1967). — F. DÖLGER, *LTK* VI, 327-29. — P. R. FRANKE, *Kleinasien zur Römerzeit* (1968). — W. HOBEN, *Untersuchungen zur Stellung kleinasiatischer Dynastien* (Diss., 1969). — S. E. JOHNSON, "Early Christianity in Asia Minor," *JBL* 77 (1958) 1-17. — A. H. M. JONES, *The Cities of the Eastern Roman Provinces* (1937, reprinted 1971). — J. KEIL, *RAC* I, 740-49. — D. MAGIE, *Roman Rule in Asia Minor* I/II (1950, reprinted 1966). — M. P. NILSSON and C. ANDRESEN, *RGG* III, 1650-52. — J. NUCHELMANS, *Wordenboek der Oudheit* I (1976), 330-34. — REICKE, *NT Era* (index s.v.). — SCHÜRER, *History* III, 4f., 17-36. — For further bibliography see *ISBE* I, 329.

1. Ἀσία is mentioned 20 times in the NT. References are either to the entire Roman province of Asia (Acts 6:9; 19:10, 22, 26f.; 27:2; 1 Pet. 1:1) or to its central regions of Ionia and Lydia (Acts 2:9; 16:6; 20:16, 18; 21:27; 24:19; 2 Cor 1:8; 2 Tim 1:15; Rev 1:4; 1:11 v.l.).

2. Hittite *Assuwa,* referring to the northwestern part of Asia Minor, is the basis for the name Ἀσία (Nuchelmans 333). From the 5th cent. B.C. onward, Greek authors meant by Asia the Persian Empire or the Orient in general. The Maccabean brothers called the Seleucid kingdom by this name (1 Macc. 8:6–4 Macc 3:20 *passim*). The last king of Pergamum bequeathed his domain, which encompassed western Asia Minor, to the Roman Empire in 133 B.C. Subsequently Ἀσία was used in reference to the Roman province of *Asia,* as in the NT. This province consisted of Mysia, Ionia, Lydia, Phrygia, and Caria, and was administered by a proconsul in Ephesus commissioned by the Senate. Here fruit-growing, commerce, and industry flourished. Sources of special pride were the temples of Artemis in Ephesus (Acts 19:23-40) and of Roma and the Caesar in Pergamum, Smyrna, and Ephesus.

The Asiarchs (Ἀσιάρχαι, Acts 19:31) provided for the maintenance of the emperor cult and the popular festivals at an annual provincial assembly of Ἀσία, which was held by turns in seven cities (cf. Rev. 1:4). An asiarch who administered a local temple was called a high priest, as was the case with the Jew Sceva (Acts 19:14). Jews in Ἀσία were often citizens of the cities (Reicke 284; Schürer 22).

3. According to Acts, Paul preached *ca.* A.D. 50 in Phrygia and Mysia, but the Spirit did not allow him then to work in the center of the province of Asia (Acts 16:6f.). On the return trip from Greece in A.D. 54 he visited Ephesus for only a short time (18:21). In the interim Apollos practiced there a combination of the baptism of John and the kerygma of Jesus (vv. 24-27). Paul completed this water baptism in A.D. 55 with the giving of the Spirit (19:1-7) and worked two more years in Asia with success (vv. 8-20). This success aroused the profitable silversmith guild against him (vv. 23-40; 1 Cor. 15:32; 2 Cor. 1:8). On Paul's return trip from Macedonia in A.D. 58 he avoided a new dispute in Asia and conferred with the elders from Ephesus in Miletus (Acts 20:17-38). Judaism, Gnosticism, and fanaticism were growing problems in Asia (1 Tim 1:7; 6:20; 2 Tim 1:15; 2:18). Nevertheless, from Paul's work well-developed communities (Rom 16:5; 1 Cor 16:19) spread energetically (Eph 3:18) and were supported by other authorities (1 Pet 1:1; Rev 1:4). At the seven centers of the provincial assembly (→ 1) the seven churches of Asia (Rev 1:11) came into existence, Cyzicus in Mysia, however, being replaced by Thyatira in Lydia. Despite Roman persecution (Rev 2:13; 6:9; 13:17) numerous Jews and Gentiles were converted (7:4, 9). By the turn of the century Asia and neighboring Bithynia were strongly shaped by Christianity (Ign. *Eph.* inscription; Pliny the Younger *Epist.* x.96.9f.; cf. Reicke 303).

B. Reicke

Ἀσιανός, οῦ, ὁ *Asianos* from Asia*

Acts 20:4: Tychicus and Trophimus are *from* (the province of) *Asia.*

Ἀσιάρχης, ου, ὁ *Asiarchēs* Asiarch*

In Acts 19:31 the pl. probably means "delegate of the provincial assembly of Asia (κοινὸν Ἀσίας)." *Beginnings* V, 256-62; BAGD s.v.; E. Haenchen, *The Acts of the Apostles* (1971) 574. → Ἀσία 2.

ἀσιτία, ας, ἡ *asitia* loss or lack of appetite*

Acts 27:21: During a storm at sea those on the ship suffered great loss of appetite.

ἄσιτος, 2 *asitos* without eating, (on an) empty (stomach)*

In Acts 27:33: ἄσιτος διατελέω: They had continued *without food* for fourteen days.

ἀσκέω *askeō* practice, engage in

Acts 24:16: ἐν τούτῳ ἀσκῶ (with inf. following), I *strive* (RSV *"take pains";* cf. Xenophon *Mem.* ii.1.6). H. Windisch, *TDNT* I, 494-96; *TWNT,* X, 995.

ἀσκός, οῦ, ὁ *askos* wineskin*

Mark 2:22 par. Matt 9:17/Luke 5:37f.: new wine in old or new wineskins. In each of the Synoptics the pl. of ἀσκός occurs here 4 times.

ἀσμένως *asmenōs* gladly*

Acts 21:17: receive *gladly;* cf. 2:41 v.l.

ἄσοφος, 2 *asophos* foolish

Eph 5:15, of the change in Christians: "not as *unwise men* but as wise" (cf. 1QS 4:24: "They walk in wisdom or foolishness").

ἀσπάζομαι *aspazomai* greet, welcome; bid farewell
ἀσπασμός, οῦ, ὁ *aspasmos* greeting, welcome

Lit.: FRISK, *Wörterbuch* I, 166; III, 42. — O. ROLLER, *Das Formular der paulinischen Briefe* (1933) 67f., 472ff. — M. L. STIREWALT, JR., "Paul's Evaluation of Letter-Writing," *Search the Scriptures* (FS R. T. Stamm; 1969) 179-96. — K. THRAEDE, "Ursprünge und Formen des 'heiligen Kusses' im frühen Christentum," *JAC* 11/12 (1968/69) 124-80. — W. C. VAN UNNIK, "Dominus vobiscum. The Background of a Liturgical Formula," *NT Essays* (FS T. W. Manson; 1959) 270-305. — H. WINDISCH, *TDNT* I, 496-502.

1. The etymology is uncertain. Perhaps a connection exists with σπάω, "attract" (Frisk I, 166), as an expression of affection or friendly reception. The vb. is found in the NT 59 times, primarily in the Epistles; the noun occurs 20 times, esp. in Luke (5 times).

2. In the widest sense, the greeting is the opening of communication between individuals. Without it the meeting between two people remains neutral and, in some cases, dangerous. But the greeting clarifies the ambiguous situation. It brings together the individuals who meet and defines their further conduct. The OT wish of *šālôm* referred to the entirety of "health, good fortune, blessings, peace," etc.; the greeting not only represents a wish for these blessings, but also lets them become a reality. This aspect is entirely present in the NT. For Jesus the greeting becomes a first realization of Christian conduct. His own people should not be expecting a greeting (cf. Mark 12:38 par.); instead, a greeting should first be given by them (Windisch 496). The greeting is also the first sign of the love of enemies in actual practice (Matt 5:47); nevertheless, the practice of greeting should not hamper haste in the proclamation of the message (Luke 10:4).

The greeting receives special importance as a constituent part of the Pauline letters, in which Paul not only gives the letter itself a new function (cf. Stirewalt), but also gives the greeting formula a new function in the framework of his apostolic activity. In addition to the introductory greetings (→ χάρις, "grace"), the concluding greetings are of interest, inasmuch as their frequency and proportion is surprising in comparison with the Hellenistic culture. Except for Galatians, in which the church situation is very tense, the Pauline concluding greetings are very diverse: alongside Paul's personal greetings are greetings from coworkers or fellow Christians. The addressees are requested to *greet* specific persons or each Christian. According to Rom 16:16; 1 Cor 16:20; 2 Cor 13:12; 1 Thess 5:26 (cf. 1 Pet 5:14), they are to greet each other with a "holy kiss," which is an especially intensive—not primarily or exclusively liturgical—form of greeting (cf. Thraede 142f.).

P. Trummer

ἀσπασμός, οῦ, ὁ *aspasmos* greeting, salutation*

Mark 12:38 par. Matt 23:7/Luke 20:46; Luke 1:29, 41, 44; 11:43; 1 Cor 16:21; Col 4:18; 2 Thess 3:17. H. Windisch, *TDNT* I, 496-502. → ἀσπάζομαι.

ἄσπιλος, 2 *aspilos* without blemish, flawless*

Lit., of the flawless lamb (→ ἀμνός), 1 Pet 1:19; in the ethical sense, 1 Tim 6:14; Jas 1:27; 2 Pet 3:14; *Herm. Vis.* iv.3.5; cf. *Sim.* v.6.7; *2 Clem.* 8:6. A. Oepke, *TDNT* I, 502.

ἀσπίς, ίδος, ἡ *aspis* asp, snake*

Rom 3:13: ἰὸς ἀσπίδων, *poison of asps* (Pss 13:3; 139:4 LXX).

ἄσπονδος, 2 *aspondos* irreconcilable*

2 Tim 3:3 pl. in a list of vices; also Rom 1:31 C Koine lat.

ἀσσάριον, ου, τό *assarion* as, assarion*

Loanword from Latin *(assarius)* for a small coin ("farthing"): Matt 10:29 par. Luke 12:6, of sparrows, which are sold for one (or two) *as* (cents).

ἆσσον *asson* nearer, near*

Acts 27:13: they came *near* Crete. BDF §244.2.

Ἆσσος, ου *Assos* Assos*

A coastal city in Mysia. According to Acts 20:13f. Paul went on board in Assos. E. Haenchen, *Acts of the Apostles* (1971) 587.

ἀστατέω *astateō* be unsteady, homeless*

1 Cor 4:11, of an unsettled manner of life. A. Oepke, *TDNT* I, 503.

ἀστεῖος, 3 *asteios* beautiful, well-pleasing*

Acts 7:20: Moses was *"well-pleasing* before God" (RSV *"beautiful* before God"); Heb 11:23 (Exod 2:2) of the infant Moses, who was *"beautiful"* in form.

ἀστήρ, έρος, ὁ *astēr* star*
ἄστρον, ου, τό *astron* constellation, star*

1. Occurrences in the NT — 2. The "birth star" — 3.

ʼΑστήρ in apocalyptic references — 4. 1 Cor 15:41 and Jude 13 — 5. Ἄστρον

Lit.: F. Boll, "Der Stern der Weisen," *ZNW* 18 (1917/18) 40-48. — W. Foerster, *TDNT* I, 503-5. — O. Gerhardt, *Der Stern des Messias* (1922). — M. Hengel and H. Merkel, "Die Magier aus dem Osten und die Flucht nach Ägypten (Mt 2) im Rahmen der antiken Religionsgeschichte und der Theologie des Matthäus," FS Schmid (1973) 139-69. — E. Lohmeyer, "Der Stern der Weisen," *TBl* 17 (1938) 289-99. — P. S. Minear, "The Cosmology of the Apocalypse," *Current Issues in NT Interpretation* (FS O. A. Piper, 1962) 23-37, 261f. — E. Zinner, *Sternglaube und Sternforschung* (1953).

1. ʼΑστήρ appears 24 times in the NT, 14 of which are in Revelation. The synonymous word ἄστρον occurs only 4 times, in Luke (21:25), Acts (7:43; 27:20), and Hebrews (11:12). Neither is used with extraordinary frequency in any book of the NT.

2. The NT shares the ancient understanding (Foerster 503) according to which stars are not simply material substances but living beings; however, in the NT ἀστήρ (like ἄστρον) is regularly perceived as part of the creation. The stars do not possess a numinous character in the sense of astral powers. Yet they can stand in a close relationship to earthly events. Matt 2:2 tells of an unusually bright star at the birth of Jesus (possibly a constellation of Jupiter and Saturn, dated in 7 B.C.; on the discussion, cf. E. Lohmeyer and W. Schmauch, *Matthäus* [KEK] 22, n. 1). The extraordinary event signified the royal dignity of the child. A well-known theme of ancient historiography is the belief that stars stand over the life of an important ruler (cf. Lohmeyer and Schmauch 20). In addition, an affinity exists with OT and Jewish texts (Num 24:17; *T. Lev.* 18:3; *T. Jud.* 24:1; 6QD 7:18f.), in which the messiah is described metaphorically as a star. In this connection the name of the messiah Bar Cochba, "son of the star," is to be mentioned. (He is described in this way only in Christian sources [cf. Eusebius *HE* iv.6.2].) As an indication of political competition, the birth star arouses the concerned interest of Herod (Matt 2:7). According to Matt 2:9f. the star travels before the Magi and points the way for them.

3. ʼΑστήρ has another function in Matt 24:29. The fall of the stars occurs in the context of the apocalyptic conception of the end time (cf. Mark 13:25; Rev 6:13; 8:10; 9:1; 12:4). The eschatological fate of the world is manifested in this phenomenon.

Such conceptions are esp. pronounced in Revelation, which employs ἀστήρ with changing meanings. The ἀστήρ in Rev 9:1 is personal. The star, which falls at the angel's trumpet, is given the key to the underworld (ἄβυσσος). In the course of the cosmic catastrophe, the raging dragon causes a third of the stars of heaven to fall (12:4; cf. Dan 8:10). A variation of this portrait occurs in Rev 8:12, where the blowing of the angel's trumpet calls forth a darkening of the stars (cf. Isa 13:10; Ezek 32:7; *T. Mos.* 10:5). The plague in which the water is poisoned begins with the withdrawal of the source of light, caused by the star Ἄψινθος (Rev 8:10f.). By contrast, the "morning star," which is identified with Jesus (22:16), is the subject of the promise (2:28). Participation in the glory of Christ is granted to the one who overcomes. Another symbol is the crown of the mother of Christ, which has "twelve stars" referring to the people of the twelve tribes (12:1). The "seven stars" of Christ the world ruler (1:16; 2:1; 3:1) refer, however, to the "angels of the seven churches" (1:20 twice), which are considered heavenly representatives.

4. Paul uses ἀστήρ only in 1 Cor 15:41 (3 times). In order to illustrate the difference between earthly and heavenly forms of existence, he refers to the glory of the stars. That he sees their existence as corporeal is indicated in v. 40. Jude 13 speaks in a metaphorical sense of ἀστήρ. The author regards the libertinistic heretics as "wandering stars."

5. Ἄστρον appears to some extent in different contexts from ἀστήρ. Only in Luke 21:25 is ἄστρον connected with the concept of the end time. By contrast, in Acts 7:43 Stephen recalls polemically Israel's worship of the star divinity "Rephan" (→ Ῥαιφάν). The eclipse of the stars, on the other hand, is described in 27:20 as a weather signal. In Heb 11:12 the stars are simply a symbol of a great number (cf. Gen 15:5; Isa 40:26; Jer 33:22; Ps 147:4).

H.-J. Ritz

ἀστήρικτος, 2 *astēriktos* unstable, weak*

2 Pet 2:14: "*unsteady* souls (ψυχαί)"; 3:16: subst. "the *unstable.*" G. Harder, *TDNT* VII, 654, 657.

ἄστοργος, 2 *astorgos* unloving*

Used in vice catalogs in Rom 1:31; 2 Tim 3:3.

ἀστοχέω *astocheō* deviate, depart from*

The term is used in the NT only 3 times in the Pastorals, each time in a rel. clause with τινες (οἵτινες): in 1 Tim 1:6 of certain persons who have *deviated* from love (v. 5); in 6:21, as regards the faith (περὶ τὴν πίστιν) some *have gone astray;* in 2 Tim 2:18, with respect to the truth (περὶ τὴν ἀλήθειαν) *some have wandered away.* In a similar connection, cf. *2 Clem.* 17:7.

ἀστραπή, ῆς, ἡ *astrapē* lightning*
ἀστράπτω *astraptō* flash, sparkle (vb.)*

1. Occurrences and meaning in the NT — 2. Usage — 3. The word group in apocalyptic-eschatological contexts

Lit.: R. Bauckham, "The Eschatological Earthquake in the

Apocalypse of John," *NovT* 19 (1977) 224-33. — J. Ernst, *Das Evangelium nach Lukas* (1977) 337, 652. — W. Foerster, *TDNT* I, 505. — H. Kraft, *Die Offenbarung des Johannes* (HNT, 1974) 97, 134f., 162, 211. — F. Spitta, "Der Satan als Blitz," *ZNW* 9 (1908) 160-63. — J. Zmijewski, *Die Eschatologiereden des Lukasevangelium* (1972) (on Luke 17 par.).

1. The subst. is found twice in Matthew (24:27; 28:3), 3 times in Luke (10:18; 11:36; 17:24), and 4 times in Revelation (4:5; 8:5; 11:19; 16:18). Except for Luke 11:36, where it means *rays,* it refers to *lightning.* The vb. means *flash, sparkle* (Foerster 502; BAGD s.v.), and appears only twice, always in the pres. partc. In Luke 17:24 it is used to strengthen the noun (ἡ ἀστραπὴ ἀστράπρουσα); it has a metaphorical meaning in 24:4 (ἐν ἐσθῆτι ἀστραπτούσῃ).

2. In the Gospels ἀστραπή is used consistently in a metaphorical sense; it is preceded by ὥσπερ (Matt 24:27; Luke 17:24) or ὡς (Matt 28:3; Luke 10:18; 11:36). It is used in reference to various persons or events: in Luke 10:18 it illustrates Satan's fall from heaven; in Luke 17:24 par. Matt 24:27 it is an image of the parousia; in Matt 28:3 it describes the appearance of the angel at Easter (cf. Luke 24:4). In Revelation lightning is mentioned with other manifestations that intensify the movement between passages (ἀστραπή appears in 4:5 in a series of three; in 8:5 in a series of four; in 11:19 and 16:18, 21 in series of five).

3. The logion about lightning in Matt 24:27 par. Luke 17:24 is derived from Q, where it may already have stood together with the image of the carcass and the eagles (Matt 24:28). The logion, whose original wording (up to its end) is transmitted by Matthew, is intended to provide the basis for the previously expressed warning against attempts to track down the messiah (Matt 24:25f.; Luke 17:23). Q's report that the parousia (or the day) of the Son of Man will be "as the *lightning*" which "comes from the east and shines as far as the west" accents the suddenness and the general visibility of the parousia. While Matthew understands the logion in this way, a shift of meaning occurs in Luke: Luke uses the image with reference to the Son of Man himself, to describe his glorious appearance (cf. the compound ἐξαστράπτων in 9:29). Here, according to Luke, Jesus' glorification is preceded by his humiliation (17:25). His return is thus incorporated into the dialectic between his suffering and his glory.

The logion in Luke 10:18 (Luke's special material) stands in a context depicting the disciples' exorcisms as witnesses to the overthrow of Satan. Satan's fall from heaven "like lightning" is thus an image of his sudden, inexorable loss of power due to the arrival of the kingdom of God in the works of Jesus and his disciples. When it is reported in the Easter account in Matt 28:3 (an addition to a Markan context) that the angel's appearance was "like lightning" (Luke 24:4 speaks of "*dazzling* apparel"), this not only reflects the imagery of angelophanies, but also draws the Easter event close to the parousia.

The use of ἀστραπή in Revelation is associated with OT theophanies (esp. Exod 19:16). Whereas it is used in 4:5 for the power and glory of the God who reveals himself (cf. Pss 18:14; 50:3, etc.), in other texts (in connection with the sequence of seven plagues) it describes the horror of the divine judgment.

J. Zmijewski

ἀστράπτω *astraptō* flash, sparkle (vb.)
→ ἀστραπή.

ἄστρον, ου, τό *astron* constellation, star
→ ἀστήρ.

Ἀσύγκριτος, ου *Asynkritos* Asyncritus*

Personal name (meaning "Incomparable") in Rom 16:14 of one of those who are greeted.

ἀσύμφωνος, 2 *asymphōnos* unharmonious*

Acts 28:25 in a fig. sense, of the Roman Jews: "they were not *in harmony* with each other" (RSV is different; cf. v. 24).

ἀσύνετος, 2 *asynetos* without understanding*

The term appears in Jesus' question to the disciples in Mark 7:18 par. Matt 15:16: "Are you also *without understanding*?" It occurs also in Rom 1:21 (of the heart); 1:31 together with → ἀσύνθετος in a vice catalog; and 10:19 (Deut 32:21), of "a people *without understanding*" (RSV "*foolish* nation"). H. Conzelmann, *TDNT* VII, 888f., 892-96.

ἀσύνθετος, 2 *asynthetos* faithless*

Rom 1:31, in a vice catalog after → ἀσύνετος.

ἀσφάλεια, ας, ἡ *asphaleia* certainty, reliability
→ ἀσφαλής.

ἀσφαλής, 2 *asphalēs* secure, unshakable*
ἀσφάλεια, ας, ἡ *asphaleia* certainty, reliability*
ἀσφαλίζομαι *asphalizomai* safeguard (vb.), watch over*
ἀσφαλῶς *asphalōs* securely*

1. Occurrences of the word group in the NT — 2. Meanings — 3. Fig. meaning in Paul and Luke-Acts

Lit.: K. L. Schmidt, *TDNT* I, 506 — H. Schürmann, *Das Lukasevangelium* I (1969) 14-16.

1. The word group (a total of 15 occurrences in the NT) occurs predominantly in Luke-Acts (8 occurrences). Ἀσ-

φαλής appears also in Phil 3:1; Heb 6:19; ἀσφάλεια in 1 Thess 5:3; ἀσφαλίζομαι in Matt 27:64, 65, 66; ἀσφαλῶς in Mark 14:44.

2. Ἀσφαλής signifies in the literal sense *secure, unshakable* (from σφάλλω, "throw, bring to the ground," *EWG* 345). The word group designates in the literal sense the *certainty* or *stability* of a thing (Heb 6:19: a *sure* anchor), or the *guarding* or *safekeeping* of a person or thing (Mark 14:44, of Jesus in custody; Matt 27:64-66, of the grave of Jesus; Acts 5:23, of a *securely* locked prison; 16:23 [cf. v. 20 D], of guarding prisoners; 16:24, of *fastening* feet in stocks). The fig. sense is found in both Pauline texts and in most (5) of the passages in Luke-Acts. → 3.

The fig. meaning of ἀσφάλεια is attested in extrabiblical literature in reference to a "word" (ἀσφάλεια λόγου, Xenophon *Mem.* iv.6.15) and as a juridical t.t. (Epictetus *Diss.* ii.13.7; Moulton/Milligan s.v.). In the former it refers to (objective) *truth* (cf. ἀσφαλής in Acts 21:34; 22:30; 25:26; see Schürmann 14, n. 89); in the latter it is nearer to (subjective) *certainty.*

3. 1 Thess 5:3 mentions the watchwords ("peace and *security*") of those who, instead of having a proper expectation of the parousia, hold to a (false) *security* (cf. Jer 6:14; Luke 17:26f. par.). Phil 3:1 emphasizes that Paul writes to confirm once more the *security* of the recipients. Luke-Acts emphasizes the *reliability* (ἀσφάλεια) of the (apostolic) "words" in which the addressees have been instructed (Luke 1:4); they should recognize the "truth" (so RSV), especially in consideration of the promise it contains. In Acts 2:36 Peter summons the Jewish listeners to a *sure* (ἀσφαλῶς) knowledge (cf. Wis 18:6) that God has made Jesus "both Lord and Christ." This knowledge can be *sure* on the basis of the preceding proof from Scripture (cf. G. Schneider, *ZNW* 68 [1977] 128-31).

G. Schneider

ἀσφαλίζομαι *asphalizomai* safeguard (vb.), watch over
→ ἀσφαλής.

ἀσφαλῶς *asphalōs* securely
→ ἀσφαλής.

ἀσχημονέω *aschēmoneō* behave improperly, indecently
→ ἀσχημοσύνη.

ἀσχημοσύνη, ης, ἡ *aschēmosynē* shame (noun), shameful deed*
ἀσχημονέω *aschēmoneō* behave improperly, indecently*
ἀσχήμων, 2 *aschēmōn* dishonorable, indecent*

Lit.: W. G. Kümmel, "Verlobung und Heirat bei Paulus (1. Kor 7, 36-38)," *Heilsgeschehen und Geschichte* (1965) 310-27. — K. Niederwimmer, *Askese und Mysterium* (1975) 106ff., esp. 116-20.

The noun and vb. are found twice each, the adj. only in 1 Cor 12:23. Rom 1:27 refers to *shameful* (sexual) *misdeeds;* Rev 16:15 refers to *nakedness* (RSV "exposed"; cf. Exod 20:26), which corresponds to τὰ ἀσχήμονα ἡμῶν (μέλη), the *shameful* parts, in 1 Cor 12:23. As in 1 Cor 13:5 (RSV "be rude"), the vb. in 7:36—if also here intended in a sexual sense—has the meaning that it has in secular Greek of offense against custom (not: "undergo something dishonorable, be put to shame," as in the LXX). The clause, "If any one believes that he is *behaving shamefully* toward his virgin" (7:36; RSV is different)—because he marries her instead of practicing asceticism until the imminent parousia, which Paul prefers but does not demand—is aimed at those who wish to marry (the context determines the meaning of the unusual παρθένος), not at the "spiritual marriage" of the later subintroductae or at some kind of levirate marriage (marriage to a widowed sister-in-law). The common interpretation of a father–minor daughter relationship, widely held in the early Church, is linguistically and contextually too difficult.

In the beatitude of Rev 16:15 is found, alongside an exhortation to fulfill the law (cf. 19:8), a graphic warning of the consequences of disobedience (cf. 3:18): the disobedient will be exposed in judgment and this will bring *dishonor* (see the collective threats in Jer 13:26; Nah 3:5).

P. Fiedler

ἀσχήμων, 2 *aschēmōn* dishonorable, indecent
→ ἀσχημοσύνη.

ἀσωτία, ας, ἡ *asōtia* dissipation*

Used in Eph 5:18; Titus 1:6; 1 Pet 4:4. W. Foerster, *TDNT* I, 506f.

ἀσώτως *asōtōs* dissolutely*

Luke 15:13, of the "lost son" who wasted his fortune in *dissipated* living (ζῶν ἀσώτως). W. Foerster, *TDNT* I, 506f.

ἀτακτέω *atakteō* be idle*

2 Thess 3:7, "We [Paul] *were* not *idle* when we were with you" (cf. vv. 8f.). G. Delling, *TDNT* VIII, 47f.

ἄτακτος, 2 *ataktos* disorderly*

1 Thess 5:14, "Rebuke the *disorderly*"; cf. BAGD s.v.: *disorderly, insubordinate* or *idle, lazy* (RSV "idle"). G. Delling, *TDNT* VIII, 47f.

ἀτάκτως *ataktōs* in a disorderly manner*

2 Thess 3:6, 11, of the brother whose conduct is *disorderly* (i.e., not according to the tradition), or of those living *in an irresponsible manner,* who no longer work. G. Delling, *TDNT* VIII, 47f.

ἄτεκνος, 2 *ateknos* childless*

Luke 20:28f. (30 v.l.), to be *childless* or to die *childless;* cf. *T. Jud.* 19:2.

ἀτενίζω *atenizō* look intently at*

Used with the dat. in Luke 4:20: the eyes of all *looked intently* to Jesus (ἦσαν ἀτενίζοντες αὐτῷ); also in 22:56; Acts 3:12; 10:4; 14:9; 23:1; with εἰς: Acts 1:10; 3:4; 6:15; 7:55; 11:6; 13:9; 2 Cor 3:7, 13.

ἄτερ *ater* without*

Prep. with gen. used in Luke 22:6: ἄτερ ὄχλου, of the intent to betray Jesus *without* a crowd present; also in 22:35, of sending out *without* a purse. BDF §216.2.

ἀτιμάζω *atimazō* treat shamefully, dishonor*

Act.: Mark 12:4 par. Luke 20:11, of the mistreatment of a servant; John 8:49 (Jesus to the Jews): "You *dishonor* me"; Rom 2:23; Jas 2:6; Ign. *Phld.* 11:1. Pass. in Acts 5:41; Rom 1:24; *1 Clem.* 16:3; *Diog.* 11:3. → ἀτιμία.

ἀτιμία, ας, ἡ *atimia* dishonor (noun), contempt, shame*
ἄτιμος, 2 *atimos* dishonored, without recognition*

1. Occurrences in the NT — 2. Meaning and usage — 3. Romans 1 and John 8

Lit.: E. Käsemann, *Commentary on Romans* (1980) 36-52 (on Rom 1:18-32; bibliography). — H. Schlier, *Der Römerbrief* (1977) 47ff. (on Rom 1:18-32). — For further bibliography → τιμή, δόξα.

1. 'Ατιμία occurs in the NT almost exclusively in Paul (6 of 7 references, the seventh in the Pastorals). For ἄτιμος (4 times) and ἀτιμάζω (7 times) there is no pattern of occurrence.

2. 'Ατιμία, formed from the ἀ-privative with → τιμή, means in the NT *dishonor, contempt, shame.* In the gen. construction πάθη ἀτιμίας (used with εἰς) in Rom 1:26 it appears in the place of the adj. ἄτιμος: *shameful* passions. In 2 Cor 11:21 Paul uses κατὰ ἀτιμίαν λέγω of himself: "To my *shame,* I must say, we were too weak for that!" 'Ατιμία is most often used in antithesis to → τιμή ("honor": Rom 9:21; 2 Tim 2:20) or → δόξα ("honor": 1 Cor 11:14; 15:43; 2 Cor 6:8; "glory": Rom 1:26, → 3). Ἄτιμος means *disdained, without recognition* in Mark 6:4 par. Matt 13:57. In Paul it means *despised* in 1 Cor 4:10; used fig., the comparative form means *less honorable* in 12:23. Similarly, → ἀτιμάζω in Mark 12:4 par. Luke 20:11 means *treat disgracefully;* elsewhere it means *scorn, refuse to give heed, dishonor.*

3. In Rom 1:21-27 ἀτιμία (with ἀτιμάζω) has theological relevance. The Gentiles did not honor (ἐδόξασαν) God as God. In their foolishness they exchanged the glory (→ δόξα) of God for the mere image of the created things and thus lost the powerful radiance of the Creator (Schlier 58; cf. Rom 3:23). Consequently God gave them up to impurity, "to the *dishonoring* of their bodies" in sexual perversity and in *shameful* passions (1:24, 26). Thus *dishonor* of God has its consequences: *dishonor* of mankind even in the sphere of the body. Because God is the God of glory, to refuse him what is most primordial in his nature is to defraud oneself of one's own participation in the glory of God. Anyone who does not acknowledge God's truth (→ ἀλήθεια 4.a) becomes a victim of lies (v. 25). An analogous statement is found in John 8:49. The Jews, who *dishonor* Jesus (ὑμεῖς ἀτιμάζετέ με; and thus God also), being deceived by the devil, do not believe that Jesus is the truth, but instead accuse him of being possessed (vv. 44-52). Just as the Gentiles exchange the Creator for the creature in Romans 1, the Jews in John 8 confuse God with Satan. In both instances the denial of God's honor is self-deception.

H. Hübner

ἄτιμος, 2 *atimos* dishonored, without recognition → ἀτιμία.

ἀτιμόω *atimoō* defame, disparage

Mark 12:4 A C Koine Θ; cf. *Diog.* 5:14.

ἀτμίς, ίδος, ἡ *atmis* mist, vapor*

Acts 2:19: smoky *vapor* (Joel 3:3); Jas 4:14, of the transience of mankind: "you are a *mist*" (which one sees only briefly).

ἄτομος, 2 *atomos* indivisible*

1 Cor 15:2, with reference to time: ἐν ἀτόμῳ, in an *instant* (in a brief moment).

ἄτοπος, 2 *atopos* out of place, unusual*

According to Acts 28:6 nothing *unusual* happened to Paul after he was bitten by the snake. In references to ethical judgment the term means *wrong, evil* (Luke 23:41; Acts 25:5; 2 Thess 3:2).

'Αττάλεια, ας *Attaleia* Attalia*

A seaport in Pamphylia (R. Fellmann, *LAW* s.v. 3),

today called Antalya. According to Acts 14:25, Paul and Barnabas went from Pergamum to Attalia and then by ship from there to Antioch.

αὐγάζω *augazō* see; shine forth (intrans.)*

2 Cor 4:4: *see* the light of the gospel; because αὐτοῖς is absent from the original text, it probably should not be read as intrans. "shine forth." G. Kittel, *TDNT* I, 507f.; BAGD s.v. → ἀπαύγασμα.

αὐγή, ῆς, ἡ *augē* dawn (noun)*

Acts 20:11: ἄχρι αὐγῆς, (Paul spoke in Troas) until *the break of day.*

Αὐγοῦστος, ου *Augoustos* Augustus*

From 27 B.C., the title ("the exalted one") of the first Caesar, Octavian (died A.D. 14). Luke reports that Caesar Augustus gave the command for the registration (→ ἀπογραφή) of the whole earth (οἰκουμένη) for taxation purposes, a report which cannot be historically correct in the sense of a "census of the Empire." On Augustus, see K. Fitzler and O. Seeck, PW X, 275-381; F. Muller and K. Gross, *RAC* I, 993-1004; F. Vittinghof, *Kaiser Augustus* (1959); K. Christ, *LAW* 406-9.

αὐθάδης, 2 *authadēs* self-willed, arrogant*

According to Titus 1:7, the bishop is not to be αὐθάδης. In 2 Pet 2:10 the term is used of *arrogant* people who despise (governmental) authority. O Bauernfeind, *TDNT* I, 508f.

αὐθαίρετος, 2 *authairetos* voluntary*

2 Cor 8:3, 17, of the *voluntary* contribution of the Macedonian churches and the journey that Titus makes *voluntarily.*

αὐθεντέω *authenteō* rule (vb.)*

1 Tim 2:12: women should not *rule over* men (gen.).

αὐλέω *auleō* play the flute*

Matt 11:17 par. Luke 7:32: we *played the flute* for you; 1 Cor 14:7: τὸ αὐλούμενον, *what is played on the flute.*

αὐλή, ῆς, ἡ *aulē* court, courtyard*

Used of an enclosed area in Mark 14:54, 66 par. Matt 26:58, 69/Luke 22:55/John 10:1, 16; of a *house* (RSV "palace") in Luke 11:21; of the temple *outer court* in Rev 11:2; of the *court* or *palace* of a prince in Mark 15:6; Matt 26:3.

αὐλητής, οῦ, ὁ *aulētēs* flute player*

Matt 9:23; Rev 18:22, both pl.

αὐλίζομαι *aulizomai* spend the night, stay*

Matt 21:17 and Luke 21:37: Jesus *spent the night* outside Jerusalem (in Bethany or at the Mount of Olives).

αὐλός, οῦ, ὁ *aulos* flute*

1 Cor 14:7, with κιθάρα (as in Isa 30:32).

αὐξάνω, αὔξω *auxanō, auxō* cause to increase, cause to grow; pass.: grow, increase

1. Occurrences in the NT and meaning — 2. Αὔξησις — 3. Ὑπεραυξάνω

Lit.: G. Delling, *TDNT* VIII, 517, 519. — W. Günther, *DNTT* II, 128-30.

1. Behind NT use of the vb. lies the image of growth in the realm of creation. The phenomena of planting and harvest are applied to the reality of the kingdom of God, frequently in the parables of Jesus (Mark 4:8; Matt 13:32; Luke 13:19), and also with direct reference to the kingdom of God (Matt 6:28). The growth of the logos is interpreted in Acts 6:7 by the statement that the number of the disciples increased. In 12:24 the vb. is again used in parallelism with → πληθύνω, and in 19:20 with → ἰσχύω. This usage is perhaps dependent upon the LXX, which employs such word combinations for the power of God as it provides growth (texts in Delling 519). In the same sense Paul emphasizes in 1 Cor 3:6f. the decisive act of God, who alone provides the growth of faith, in contrast to the Corinthians' false estimate of the proclamation of Paul and Apollos. In 2 Cor 10:15 this idea is present without being explicitly named. The growing faith is displayed in the efficacy of the gospel. This idea and the fundamental image of growth are taken up in the deutero-Pauline literature. In Col 1:6, 10 αὐξάνω is used with → καρποφορέω: the gospel grows like the plant out of the seed; the knowledge of God grows in the life of the believer.

In a few texts the image is based on the natural growth of the individual. The terminology in Luke 1:80; 2:40 is taken in a literal sense from the LXX. It is used fig. in 1 Pet 2:2: as the newborn babe grows physically on the basis of milk, the believer grows spiritually on the basis of the word. In addition, Col 2:19 describes the body of Christ as in constant growth determined by God and taking place through Christ. This growth corresponds to the growth of the Church into Jesus Christ, mentioned in Eph 4:15f. The image of the growth of the Church merges finally with that of an expanding building in Eph 2:21.

In John 3:30 the saying about growth signifies, in the sense of widespread Greek usage, an increase of influence and elevation of position. An astral sense is not present, despite the texts that use αὐξάνω for an increase of light.

2. The subst. **αὔξησις** *growth* appears as a cognate acc. in Col 2:19 with the vb. Here, as in Eph 4:16, it belongs to the imagery of the growth of a body.

3. The compound **ὑπεραυξάνω** *increase abundantly* occurs only in 2 Thess 1:3. Paul is thankful for abundant growth in the faith of the church.

H. Leroy

αὔξησις, εως, ἡ *auxēsis* growth
→ αὐξάνω 2.

αὔξω *auxō* increase; cause to grow or increase
→ αὐξάνω.

αὔριον *aurion* tomorrow (adv.)*

The immediately following day is referred to in Matt 6:34 (ἡ αὔριον bis; the adv. used substantively); Luke 10:35; Acts 4:3, 5; 23:20; 25:22; and in the generalized σήμερον ἢ αὔριον in Jas 4:13; cf. v. 14. Αὔριον can also mean *tomorrow* in the sense of *soon thereafter, after a short while:* Matt 6:30 par. Luke 12:28 (σήμερον . . . καὶ αὔριον); 1 Cor 15:22; in the series σήμερον καὶ αὔριον καὶ τῇ τρίτῃ, Luke 13:32 (cf. v. 33), it is used collectively for the time allowed by God for the work of Jesus.

αὐστηρός, 3 *austēros* uncharitable, strict, exacting*

Used in Luke 19:21f. of the "nobleman" (v. 12) in the parable of the pounds.

αὐτάρκεια, ας, ἡ *autarkeia* abundance, sufficiency

Used in 2 Cor 9:8 in connection with the request for the completion of the collection: ἐν παντὶ πάντοτε πᾶσαν αὐτάρκειαν ἔχοντες, "that you may always have *enough* of everything"; and in 1 Tim 6:6 in the sense of (the Stoic virtue of) *sufficiency,* which is necessarily associated with εὐσέβεια. G. Kittel, *TDNT* I, 466f.; O. Gigon, *LAW* 414; P. Wilpert, *RAC* I, 1039-50; B. Siede, *DNTT* III, 727f.

αὐτάρκης, 2 *autarkēs* contented, in need of no support*

Phil 4:11, of Paul, who is able in every situation "to be *content*" (ἔμαθον . . . αὐτάρκης εἶναι). G. Kittel, *TDNT* I, 466f.; B. Siede, *DNTT* III, 727f.

αὐτοκατάκριτος, 2 *autokatakritos* self-condemned*

Occurs sporadically in Jewish texts; elsewhere only in Christian texts. In Titus 3:11 it is used of the αἱρετικός, who has brought about his own judgment through his behavior. F. Büchsel has argued (*TDNT* III, 952), with difficulty, that it refers here to one who "sins consciously" (after being warned twice); cf., similarly, J. Jeremias, *Timotheus und Titus* (NTD) ad loc.

αὐτόματος, 3 *automatos* (that which happens) by itself, without assistance*

Mark 4:28: the earth brings forth fruit *of itself;* Acts 12:10: the door of the prison opens *of itself.* BAGD s.v. (bibliography); E. Schweizer, *The Good News According to Mark* (1970) ad loc.; R. Pesch, *Markus* (HTKNT) I, 256f.

αὐτόπτης, ου, ὁ *autoptēs* eyewitness*

Luke 1:2: in connection with ἀπ' ἀρχῆς and with ὑπηρέται . . . τοῦ λόγου. Those who were *"eyewitnesses"* from the beginning and "ministers of the word" were the apostles (cf. Acts 1:21f.); the tradition delivered by them corresponds (καθώς) to the first "narratives" (→ διήγησις) of which Luke 1:1 speaks. W. Michaelis, *TDNT* V, 373.

αὐτός, 3 *autos* self; same

1. "Self" — 2. "Same" — 3. Personal pron.

Lit.: BAGD s.v. — BDF §§277f.; 282; 284; 286; 288; 290; 297. — J. C. Hawkins, *Horae Synopticae* (²1909, reprinted 1968). — Kühner, *Grammatik* II/1, 558-65, 568-71, 651-56. — Mayser, *Grammatik* II/2, 64-66, 75-78. — W. Michaelis, "Das unbetonte καὶ αὐτός bei Lukas," *ST* 4 (1950) 86-93. — E. Schweizer, "Eine hebraisierende Sonderquelle des Lukas?" *TZ* 6 (1950) 161-85. — Zerwick, *Biblical Greek* §§195-206.

Functionally the pron. αὐτός stands between a personal pron. and a demonstrative pron.

1. With a differentiating meaning it means *self,* Lat. *ipse.* In addition to the literal usage (Rom 8:26: αὐτὸ τὸ πνεῦμα, "the Spirit *himself*"), there are also variations (see BAGD 122f.): to emphasize a subj. which has already been named (Matt 8:24: αὐτὸς δέ, "but *he*"); to distinguish between persons and groups (Mark 2:25: "*he* and those who were with him"; cf. Luke 11:52); when someone is designated individually (Luke 24:39: "It is I *myself*"; cf. v. 36) as acting by *himself* (John 16:27) or as being dependent upon himself (Rom 7:25). When αὐτός is emphatic and connected with καί it can have a reinforcing function in the sense of *even, likewise* (Heb 11:11: *"even* Sarah"). The meaning *even* or *very* (John 5:36: "these *very* works") is close to the second basic meaning of αὐτός.

2. Ὁ αὐτός means *the same,* Lat. *idem.* It appears both with and without a subst. (2 Cor 4:13: *"the same* Spirit"; Rom 2:1: "do *the same*"). Τὸ αὐτό occurs in an adverbial function. By itself it expresses manner (Matt 27:44: *"in the same way"*); ἐπὶ τὸ αὐτό means *at the same place* (Matt

22:34); κατὰ τὸ αὐτό means *together, with each other* (Acts 14:1); τοῦτο αὐτό (2 Cor 2:3) or αὐτὸ τοῦτο (2 Pet 1:5) means *for this very reason.* In Paul are found αὐτὸ τοῦτο, *for the very purpose* (Rom 9:17 and often), and ἓν καὶ τὸ αὐτό, *one and the same* (1 Cor 11:5). In Luke simple αὐτός appears more frequently with the meaning of αὐτὸς οὗτος (ἐκεῖνος), *this* (or *that*) *very* (in Luke 10:21 ἐν αὐτῇ τῇ ὥρᾳ differs from Matt 11:25, ἐν ἐκείνῳ τῷ καιρῷ).

3. Most frequently αὐτός has the function of the third person personal pron. in the oblique cases, of which the gen. represents the missing possessive pron. But the nom. appears also; it resumes with emphasis a subj. which has already been named (Matt 1:21). Luke uses καὶ αὐτός without emphasis (certainly not on the basis of a special source). Most frequently αὐτός appears in instances such as Matt 5:40: τῷ θέλοντι . . . ἄφες αὐτῷ. In a rel. clause it can be used pleonastically (Rev 7:2: οἷς ἐδόθη αὐτοῖς) or to determine the meaning (1 Cor 8:6). The *constructio ad sensum* leads frequently to formal incongruities, i.e., changes of number after indications of place or collective concepts (2 Cor 5:19) or of gender after an abstraction (2 Cor 5:19 again) or after a diminutive designating a person (Mark 6:28).

W. Radl

αὐτοῦ *autou* here, there*

In Matt 26:36, *here;* in Acts 18:19; 21:4, *there* (cf. 15:34 TR); Luke 9:27 (cf. Mark 9:1, which has ὧδε), probably likewise: *there.*

αὑτοῦ, ῆς, οῦ *hautou* (of) oneself, his, her, one another*
→ ἑαυτοῦ.

αὐτόφωρος, 2 *autophōros* caught in the act*

In the expression ἐπ' αὐτοφώρῳ, occurring in the widely circulated account of the adulteress in John 8:4.

αὐτόχειρ, 1 *autocheir* with one's own hand*

Acts 27:19: "they cast out *with their own hands. . . .*"

αὐχέω *aucheō* boast, brag*

Jas 3:5, with acc. μεγάλα: the tongue, though only a "small member," nevertheless "*boasts* of great things."

αὐχμηρός, 3 *auchmēros* dark, obscure*

2 Pet 1:19, of a prophetic word that shines like a light "in a *dark* place."

ἀφαιρέω *aphaireō* take away, put away, cut off*

Mark 14:47 par. Matt 26:51/Luke 22:50: "*cut off* an ear"; Luke 1:25: "*take away*" something; 10:42 (pass.): with the gen. of person, "from her"; 16:3 (mid.): ἀπ' ἐμοῦ, "take away from me"; Rom 11:27 (mid., citation from Isa 27:9); Heb 10:4: of the removal of sins; at the conclusion of Revelation (22:19 bis), in a formula of assurance that depends on Deut 4:2: "if any one *takes away* from the words of the book . . . , God will *take away* his share in the tree of life"; cf. *1 Enoch* 104:11; *Ep. Arist.* 310f.; H. Kraft, *Offenbarung* (HNT) ad loc.

ἀφανής, 2 *aphanēs* invisible, hidden*

Heb 4:13: "before him no creature is *hidden.*"

ἀφανίζω *aphanizō* make invisible (unrecognizable, inconspicuous); pass.: disappear, be destroyed*

In Matt 6:16 and Jas 4:14 this vb. appears in a play on words ἀφανίζω-φαίνομαι (the antithesis of visible and invisible): in Jas 4:14, of a mist that *vanishes* (after appearing a short while); in Matt 6:16 (fig.), of hypocrites who when they fast *disfigure* their faces (i.e., do not wash and apply ointment, v. 17) so that they can show others that they are fasting. In Matt 6:19f. it refers to treasures that *are destroyed;* in Acts 13:41 (citing Hab 1:5) it means *be destroyed* (pass., with θαυμάσατε).

ἀφανισμός, οῦ, ὁ *aphanismos* disappearance, destruction*

Heb 8:13: of the first covenant, which is near to *disappearance* (ἐγγὺς ἀφανισμοῦ, RSV "ready to vanish away").

ἄφαντος, 2 *aphantos* invisible*

Luke 24:31: ἄφαντος ἐγένετο ἀπ' αὐτῶν, Jesus "*vanished* out of their sight" (in Emmaus).

ἀφεδρών, ῶνος, ὁ *aphedrōn* ditch, latrine*

Mark 7:19 par. Matt 15:17, in connection with the elimination of foods, which do not make the individual impure.

ἀφειδία, ας, ἡ *apheidia* severity*

In Col 2:23 ἀφειδία σώματος, "*severity* to the body" (along with ἐθελοθρησκία and ταπεινοφροσύνη) is represented as a demand of the false teachers in Colossae. It has the appearance of wisdom (σοφία) but actually is bound to the "elemental spirits of the universe" (στοιχεῖα τοῦ κόσμου, v. 20). E. Lohse, *Colossians and Philemon* (Hermeneia) ad loc.

ἀφελότης, ητος, ἡ *aphelotēs* simplicity, sincerity*

Acts 2:46: ἐν ἀφελότητι καρδίας, "with *simplicity* of

heart," referring to the daily breaking of bread by the early Church in Jerusalem.

ἄφεσις, εως, ἡ *aphesis* release, liberation, forgiveness
→ ἀφίημι.

ἁφή, ῆς, ἡ *haphē* joint, ligament*

Alongside συνδεσμοί in Col 2:19, ἁφαί is to be rendered either physiologically as a medical t.t. for *ligaments* or *muscles* or as a general term for *joints* or *connections*. The context (cf. v. 8) and the connection with masc. ἐξ οὗ in v. 19a unambiguously presuppose Christ as "Head" of the body. Nevertheless, the image of the rule of the head over the body is self-contained, so that the first and more technical rendering is to be preferred. In Eph 4:16 the image concerns esp. the cooperation of all members in the body of the Church under Christ the head; διὰ πάσης ἁφῆς τῆς ἐπιχορηγίας nevertheless has here primarily a physiological sense: ". . . through all of the *joints* or *muscles* giving support" (RSV is different). On the physiological meaning, cf. G. Fitzer, *TDNT* VII, 856f.; M. Dibelius and H. Greeven, *An die Kolosser, Epheser, an Philemon* (HNT) on Col 2:19; E. Lohse, *Colossians and Philemon* (Hermeneia) ad loc.

ἀφθαρσία, ας, ἡ *aphtharsia* imperishability
→ φθείρω.

ἄφθαρτος, 2 *aphthartos* imperishable
→ φθείρω.

ἀφθορία, ας, ἡ *aphthoria* incorruptibility, soundness*

Titus 2:7: Titus is instructed to show himself to the young men as a model of *"soundness"* (RSV "integrity") in teaching; v.l ἀδιαφθορία (Koine *al*).

ἀφίημι *aphiēmi* let go, leave, leave alone, release, forgive
ἄφεσις, εως, ἡ *aphesis* release (noun), liberation, forgiveness*

1. Occurrences and usage in the LXX and the NT — 2. Ἀφίημι and ἄφεσις as terms for the forgiveness of sins — a) The Sayings Source — b) Mark — c) Matthew — d) Luke and Acts — e) John — f) The Epistles

Lit.: R. Bultmann, *TDNT* I, 509-12. — P. Fiedler, *Jesus und die Sünder* (1976). — J. Gnilka, "Das Elend vor dem Menschensohn," FS Vögtle (1975) 196-209. — Articles in *EvT* 36 (1976): 1 ("Schuld und Vergebund"): A. H. J. Gunneweg, "Schuld ohne Vergebung," 2-14; K. Wengst, "Versöhnung und Befreiung. Ein Aspekt des Themas 'Schuld und Vergebung' im Lichte des Kolosserbriefes," 14-26; G. Sauter, "Versöhnung und Vergebung. Die Frage der Schuld im Horizont der Christologie," 34-52; G. Krause, "Vergebung ohne Schuld? Vorüberlegungen zur christliche Rede von Schuld und Vergebung," 53-72. — K. Kertelge, "Die Vollmacht des Menschensohnes zur Sündenvergebung (Mk 2, 10)," FS Schmid (1973) 205-13. — H. Leroy, "Vergebung und Gemeinde nach Lk 7, 36-50," FS Schelke (1973) 85-94. — *idem, Zur Vergebung der Sünden. Die Botschaft der Evangelien* (1974). — I. Maisch, *Die Heilung des Gelähmten. Eine exegetisch-traditionsgeschichtliche Untersuchung zu Markus* 2, 1-12 (1971). — J. Michl, "Sündenvergebung in Christus nach dem Glauben der frühen Kirche," *MTZ* 24 (1973) 25-35. — *idem*, "Sündenbekenntnis und Sündenvergebung in der Kirche des NT," *MTZ* 24 (1973) 189-207. — H. Thyen, *Studien zur Sündenvergebung im NT und seinen alttestamentlichen und jüdischen Voraussetzungen* (1970). — H. Vorländer, *DNTT* I, 697-703. — F. Zeilinger, "Sündenvergebung nach dem NT," *TPQ* 120 (1972) 289-99. For further bibliography see *TWNT* X, 996f.; *DNTT* I, 703.

1. The vb. occurs frequently in the NT, esp. in the Gospels.

This frequency is conditioned by nonbiblical Greek usage, in which the word has numerous nuances, from *throw away* to *release, relinquish,* and *permit,* in both literal and fig. senses. Juristic usage is often attested: ἀφίημι τινα, *discharge someone from a legal relationship,* whether it be an office, marriage, custody, debt, or punishment. Never, however, does it occur in a religious sense (Bultmann 509).

Correspondingly, the word has a wide variety of meanings in the NT: a) *release, dismiss, leave,* e.g., Mark 1:20 par. (τὸν πατέρα); 10:28f. (πάντα); John 4:3 (τὴν Ἰουδαίαν); 16:28 (τὸν κόσμον); Mark 1:31 (ἀφῆκεν αὐτὴν ὁ πυρετός); 15:37 (ἀφεὶς φωνὴν μεγάλην); Matt 27:50 (ἀφῆκεν τὸ πνεῦμα); Rom 1:27 (τὴν φυσικὴν χρῆσιν); Rev 2:4 (τὴν ἀγάπην σου τὴν πρώτην); b) *leave behind,* e.g., Mark 1:18 par. (τὰ δίκτυα); Matt 5:24 (τὸ δῶρόν σου); 18:12 (τὰ ἐνενήκοντα ἐννέα [πρόβατα]); John 14:18 (ὑμᾶς ὀρφανούς); c) *leave alone,* e.g., Mark 11:6 (ἀφῆκεν αὐτούς); Matt 19:14 (ἄφετε τὰ παιδία); d) *permit, allow,* e.g., Mark 1:34 (cf. 5:19, 37) (οὐκ ἤφιε λαλεῖν τὰ δαιμόνια); e) the Hellenistic formula of request also appears in this vb., e.g., Mark 7:27 (ἄφες πρῶτον χορτασθῆναι τὰ τέκνα; cf. BDF §364).

The LXX uses the vb. for expressions of forgiveness: for Heb. *nāśā'* (e.g., Gen 4:13; Exod 32:32; Ps 24:18 [LXX] *sālaḥ* (e.g., Lev 4:20; 5:10, 13), and the pual of *kāp̱ar* (Isa 22:14). Here it refers to the forgiveness of mankind's sins (ἁμαρτία, ἀνομία, ἀσέβεια, αἰτία [Gen 4:13]), and the one who forgives is God. This usage and the concept expressed by this word occur only in biblical and biblically influenced Greek (cf. Josephus *Ant.* vi.92). The Hebrew vbs. that it translates refer to both legal and sacral-legal acts and in the latter sense are used for cultic matters. The juristic range of meaning of the Greek vb. receives here a significant modification.

The noun ἄφεσις is used in the sense of *forgiveness* in the LXX only in Lev 16:26. Elsewhere it is the translation of Heb. *yôḇēl*, "jubilee" (Lev 25:10-12, 15, 30f.; 27:18), and *šᵉmiṭṭâ*, "release" (Deut 15:1f.; 31:10; also *šāmaṭ*, Exod 23:11); in Lev 25:10 it is used for "emancipation" (Heb. d^erôr); in Trito-Isaiah it means "liberation" in an eschatological sense (cf. Isa. 58:6; 61:1).

In the NT ἄφεσις appears 17 times, including 5 times each in Luke and Acts. The subst. almost always refers to divine *forgiveness,* in most instances defined more closely with the gen. ἁμαρτιῶν (Mark 1:4 par. Luke 3:3; Matt 26:28; Luke 1:77; 24:47; Acts 2:38; 5:31; 10:43; 13:38; 26:18; Col 1:14; cf. Heb. 10:18; τῶν παραπτωμάτων in Eph 1:7); it is used absolutely in Mark 3:29 and Heb 9:22. In connection with Isa 61:1; 58:6 (LXX), Luke 4:18 (bis) uses the word in the sense of *liberation;* yet this is also conceived as *forgiveness.*

2. a) The Sayings Source (Q) knows the old saying about the unforgivable sin against the Pneuma, which appears in its oldest form in Luke 12:10. In Matt 12:31f. the saying is revised from the version in Mark 3:28-30, the tradition of which is probably older than the Q version. In both forms it is said that one's eschatological destiny is irrevocably the result of one's decision regarding the pneumatic word of the post-Easter Church. Matthew and Luke designate blasphemy of the earthly Jesus as forgivable and contrast this to the unforgivable blasphemy of the exalted Lord who works in the pneumatic word of the Church.

b) Already the tradition underlying Mark 2:1-12 has taken Jesus' authority to heal as an occasion to demonstrate his authority to *forgive* sins. Through the healing miracle Jesus shows that he is the Son of Man, who has been given authority by God and who *forgives* sins on earth (2:10). According to the faith of the OT, God provides forgiveness as healing (cf. Pss 103:3; 41:5; 25:18; 79:9). This therapeutic view of forgiveness makes possible the particular argument of the tradition; at the same time it invalidates the charge of blasphemy (Mark 2:7) raised against Jesus. The connection with Mark 3:28-30 is unmistakable: Jesus is, according to Mark, the pneumatically gifted Son of Man (1:10, 12); to blaspheme against him is to blaspheme against the Pneuma. Forgiveness is imparted by the pneumatic Christ to his Church and remains denied to one who blasphemously works against it, scorning the Church's prophetic word.

c) Matt 9:1-8 has tightened up the Markan model and has placed the accent on the Son of Man's authority to *forgive* sins on earth (9:8). The Church represents and actualizes the Son of Man's authority, which has been given to it. The gift of divine forgiveness is tied to the forgiveness of people by one another: Matt 6:12, 14f.; 18:35; cf. Mark 11:25f. (v.l.). It is secured for mankind through Jesus' salvific death on the cross, which is represented in the celebration of the Lord's Supper. Matt 26:28 speaks explicitly of the pouring out of the blood of the covenant for the *forgiveness* of sins. The formulaic usage εἰς ἄφεσιν ἁμαρτιῶν is derived from the tradition of the Baptist (cf. Mark 1:4). Matt 3:1-6, however, denies that the baptism of John effects the forgiveness of sins. Through the joining of the Lord's Supper tradition from Mark 14:24 with the formula from the tradition of the Baptist, a usage arose that is reminiscent of the ritual of sin offering (cf. Lev 4–5). Just as the priest makes atonement by carrying out the sacrifice, with the result that Yahweh grants forgiveness, in the same way Jesus makes atonement through his bloody death on the cross, which brings about *forgiveness.* Matthew recognizes in the ἄφεσις ἁμαρτιῶν simply the salvific act of Jesus. The word of the angel in 1:21 already interprets the name "Jesus" (in dependence on Ps 130:8) in terms of salvation (→ σῴζω) from sins.

d) According to Luke 24:46-48, in the era of the Church the forgiveness of sins is tied to the preaching of repentance in Jesus' name. By accepting the kerygma of the witnesses, the believer is able to encounter the Lord who works in the gospel. According to Acts 2:38 the encounter with Jesus in baptism occurs when the → ὄνομα Ἰησοῦ Χριστοῦ is invoked over the one being baptized. This is in conscious dependence on the Baptist tradition of Luke 3:3, which has been taken over from Mark and is still recognizable behind Luke 24:46-48. The Lukan view of the Isaianic → μετάνοια is noteworthy: it includes insight into the particular situation of the ἁμαρτωλός and a turning toward the one who accepts sinners and who, without insisting on works of repentance (cf. Luke 15), grants forgiveness. As in Luke 24:46-48, in Acts 3:19; 17:30; 20:21; 26:20 repentance is a turning in faith to the Lord who responds with ἄφεσις. Luke 17:1-4 indicates clearly that the Church is the place where forgiveness is granted to people on the basis of μετάνοια (cf. Acts 5:30f. against the background of Luke 1:77).

Luke 7:36-50 (Luke's special material) contrasts Jesus' forgiveness-granting encounter with sinful people with self-righteous unwillingness to repent. The concluding saying in v. 50, which elsewhere concludes only miracle stories, describes forgiveness as healing from guilt. Jesus appears as the bearer of the gift of salvation, as is made clear by the conclusion of the "chorus" (v. 49), which comes as a question that distinctly resembles the response to the stilling of the storm (cf. 8:25b). Jesus' power is effective in the area of faith and releases the individual into the salvation of God.

Luke 5:17-26 has shaped the tradition of Mark 2:1-12 in a corresponding way. The event is described in Luke 5:26 as a παράδοξον. Jesus appears as the Savior who grants forgiveness, and the people experience this as a wonderful demonstration of the divine presence, which causes them to be in awe. What was immediately accomplished at the time of Jesus is now experienced in the time of the Church in the kerygma.

e) John 20:21-23 interprets forgiveness as the Easter

gift of the Resurrected One. The Church is given the right to share in the authority to forgive when it is commissioned by Jesus, who becomes manifest to the Church in its participation in the Pneuma.

f) The vb. and subst. do not belong to the theological language of Paul. He uses the vb. only in Rom 4:7 in the citation from Ps 31:1 (LXX). In place of the subst. and in the same sense he uses → πάρεσις, which appears only in Rom 3:25. This word does not occur in the LXX; it has the same juristic sense as the vb. παριέναι.

In Col 1:14 and Eph 1:7 the subst. ἄφεσις appears with → ἀπολύτρωσις. 1 John 1:9 uses the vb. together with καθαρίζω; Heb 9:22 uses the subst. in the same connection. Jas 5:15 uses the vb. in speaking of the prayer of healing and forgiveness of sins. Thus the association of bodily healing with forgiveness of sins, which appears in the Jesus tradition, occurs also in reference to the activities of the Church.

H. Leroy

ἀφικνέομαι *aphikneomai* arrive at, reach*

Rom 16:19: (Knowledge of) your obedience has *reached* (RSV "is known to") all.

ἀφιλάγαθος, 2 *aphilagathos* not loving the good, enemy of the good*

2 Tim 3:3, in a vice catalog referring to the people of the end time. W. Grundmann, *TDNT* I, 18.

ἀφιλάργυρος, 2 *aphilargyros* free of avarice, not covetous*

1 Tim 3:3, in a list of virtues of the bishop; Heb 13:5 (ἀφιλάργυρος ὁ τρόπος), in a series of exhortations to the Church, which lives by its trust in God and not by its possession of material goods (vv. 5b, 6, citing Ps 117:6 LXX).

ἄφιξις, εως, ἡ *aphixis* departure*

Acts 20:29, in Paul's farewell speech in Miletus: "After *my departure* fierce wolves will come in among you." Outside the NT this subst. normally means "arrival," in accordance with → ἀφικνέομαι.

ἀφίστημι *aphistēmi* cause to revolt (trans.); separate, fall away (intrans.)*

There are 14 occurrences of this vb. in the NT; it is esp. prominent in Luke (4 occurrences) and Acts (6 occurrences). It is used trans. only in Acts 5:37, where it refers to Judas the Galilean, who *caused* the people *to revolt* (RSV "drew away") ὀπίσω αὐτοῦ, so that they followed him. Used intrans. (with the gen., sometimes with ἀπό) it means *depart* (Luke 2:37; 13:27, citing Ps 6:9 LXX; Acts 12:10), *go away* from (4:13; Acts 5:38; 22:29; 2 Cor 12:8; cf. ἀπὸ ἀδικίας, 2 Tim 2:19), *withdraw from* (Acts 15:38; 19:9), *fall away* (Luke 8:13 [absolute]; 1 Tim 4:1 [τῆς πίστεως]; Heb 3:12 [ἀπὸ θεοῦ ζῶντος]). In the LXX it is frequently a t.t. for apostasy (from God), e.g., Deut 32:15; Jer 3:14; cf. also 1QS 7:18, 23 (Heb. *bgd*). H. Schlier, *TDNT* I, 512f.; W. Bauder, *DNTT* I, 606-8.

ἄφνω *aphnō* suddenly, immediately*

Acts 2:2; 16:26; 28:6: *suddenly, on the spot.*

ἀφόβως *aphobōs* fearlessly, without shyness → φοβέομαι.

ἀφομοιόω *aphomoioō* make similar, copy; pass.: resemble*

This vb. is used in Heb 7:3 in a hymnic text derived from Ps 109:4 LXX concerning Melchizedek, who *resembles* the Son of God (for the meaning cf. Wis 13:14; Ep Jer 4:62, 70), i.e., in the uniqueness of Melchizedek's origin and character as primordial priest forever, he corresponds to the eschatological Son of God and thus points to him historically. On the similarity of this statement to Philonic speculation about the logos (Philo *Fug.* 108ff. and elsewhere), see A. Strobel, *Hebräerbrief* (NTD) ad loc.; Billerbeck III, 694f.; O. Michel, *TDNT* V, 198; *idem, An die Hebräer* (KEK) ad loc.; E. Beyreuther and G. Finkenrath, *DNTT* II, 505.

ἀφοράω *aphoraō* fix one's eyes on*

Phil 2:23: ὡς ἂν ἀφίδω τὰ περὶ ἐμὲ ἐξαυτῆς, "as soon as I *see* how it will go with me"; Heb 12:2: in the image of a race on a track, of trustingly *fixing one's eyes* on Jesus (εἰς τὸν τῆς πίστεως ἀρχηγὸν . . . Ἰησοῦν; cf. 4 Macc 17:10 [εἰς θεόν]).

ἀφορίζω *aphorizō* separate; appoint*

1. Call terminology — 2. Cultic terminology — 3. Ἀφορίζω in the final judgment

Lit.: G. Delling, *Jüdische Lehre und Frömmigkeit in den Paralipomena Jeremiae* (1967) 42-53. — J. Gnilka, "2 Kor 6, 14–7, 1 im Lichte der Qumranschriften," FS Schmid (1963) 86-99. — C. H. Hunzinger, *Die jüdische Bannpraxis im neutestamentlichen Zeitalter* (Diss., 1954) 73f. — K. L. Schmidt, *TDNT* V, 454-56. — G. Strecker, "Die Makarismen der Bergpredigt," *NTS* 17 (1970/71) 255-75, esp. 268f.

1. In Rom 1:1 (*set apart* for the gospel = invested with the gospel office) Paul, in dependence on the model and language of the prophetic calls of the OT (Isa 49:1; Jer 1:5) and in an apocalyptic perspective, describes his call to be

apostle to the Gentiles as a holy requisition by God (cf. Lev 20:26) before the beginning of all existence and history (cf. *As. Mos.* 1:14). The partc. ἀφωρισμένος (Heb. *pārûš;* Aram. *p^erîšā'*) is not a reference to Paul's Pharisaic past, as this would not be understandable in Rome.

In support of such predestination Gal 1:15 cites Isa 49:1 and Jer 1:5 in reference to the OT theme of the individual's creation in his mother's womb. In Acts 13:2 the call comes through early Christian prophets and teachers under the instruction of the Spirit; cf. ὁρίζω in christological statements (Acts 10:42; 17:31; Rom 1:4).

2. Out of the emphasis of Jewish piety on purity originating from the consciousness of election (cf. Jdt 12; Tob 1:10f.) ἀφορίζω became a t.t. for the dissolution of cultic community (Gal 2:12; cf. Isa 56:3; *Jub.* 22:16; *T. Job* 10:6; 38:3; *Par. Jer.* 6:13f.). Peter *separated* himself *from* table fellowship between Gentile and Jewish Christians and held the Lord's Supper for the Jewish Christians separately when the "visitors" from James arrived. In 2 Cor 6:17 (non-Pauline, approximating the Qumran view) separation from the godless environment is encouraged, in dependence on Isa 52:11 (cf., e.g., 1QS 5:1, 10, 15ff.). In Luke 6:22 (from Q) the vb. is a t.t. of synagogue practice *(to excommunicate):* anyone who confesses that Jesus is the Son of Man in the dispute between Christianity and the synagogue must be prepared to be placed under a curse in the synagogue service or to be excluded from membership in the synagogue (cf. John 9:22; 12:42; 16:2). Acts 19:9 mentions Paul's separation of the Jewish Christians from the local synagogue as the beginning of the church at Ephesus.

3. In the parable belonging to Matthew's special material in Matt 13:49, the angels *separate* the righteous at the end of the world. Matt 25:32 refers to the daily life of the shepherd, in which sheep and goats, who graze together during the day, are separated in the evening because goats must be kept warmer at night than sheep, who are less sensitive to cold. The practice of the shepherds serves as a metaphor for the separation at the final judgment by the Son of Man.

U. Kellermann

ἀφορμή, ῆς, ἡ *aphormē* starting point, point of departure; opportunity*

Other than in 1 Tim 5:14 (and Luke 11:54 D Θ it sy^c), this noun occurs only in Paul. It is used in the positive sense of an *opportunity* for boasting in 2 Cor 5:12, and in the negative sense of the *point of departure* (RSV "claim") of Paul's opponents in 11:12 (bis; similarly 1 Tim 5:14). The role of the enemy is taken by ἁμαρτία in Rom 7:8, 11 and by σάρξ in Gal 5:13. While according to Gal 5:13 a misunderstood Christian freedom can be a *welcome opportunity* for the σάρξ, in Rom 7:8, 11 sin has found *opportunity* through the commandment (διὰ τῆς ἐντολῆς; cf. v. 7) to destroy the self. The expression ἀφορμὴν λαβοῦσα is well known (e.g., Philo *Flacc.* 47; see BAGD s.v.); it is perhaps more appropriately translated "it *gained its point of attack* through the commandment. . . ." G. Bertram, *TDNT* V, 472-74; H. H. Esser, *DNTT* I, 336.

ἀφρίζω *aphrizō* foam (vb.)*

Mark 9:18, 20, of the epileptic boy whose father brings him to Jesus.

ἀφρός, οῦ, ὁ *aphros* foam (noun)*

Luke 9:39 (par. Mark 9:18, → ἀφρίζω): μετὰ ἀφροῦ, "with foam" (on the mouth).

ἀφροσύνη, ης, ἡ *aphrosynē* lack of sense, foolishness*
ἄφρων, 2 *aphrōn* senseless, foolish; subst.: fool*

1. Occurrences in the NT — 2. Synonyms and antonyms in the NT — 3. Typical contexts

Lit.: G. Bertram, *TDNT* IX, 220-35. — H. D. Betz, *Der Apostel Paulus und die sokratische Tradition* (1972) (on 2 Cor 11–13). — T. Donald, "The Semantic Field of 'Folly' in Proverbs, Job, Psalms and Ecclesiastes," *VT* 13 (1963) 285-92. — S. A. Mandry, *There is no God! A Study of the Fool in the OT* (1972). — E. W. Seng, "Der reiche Tor," *NovT* 20 (1978) 136-55 (on Luke 12:16-21). — A. Vögtle, *Die Tugend- und Lasterkataloge im NT* (1936) 199, 231f. — J. Zmijewski, *Der Stil der paulinischen "Narrenrede"* (1978) (on 2 Cor 11–12).

1. The noun occurs 4 times in the NT, while the adj. occurs 8 times. The two words appear 8 times in 2 Corinthians 11–12 in a specific usage (→ 3.d).

2. These terms stand in direct contrast to φρόνησις, φρόνιμος (2 Cor 11:19). Corresponding antitheses occur between μωρία, μωρός, and ἄσοφος and σοφία, σοφός (cf. Eph 5:17 with v. 15); between ἀσύνετος (cf. Luke 11:40 with Matt 23:17, 19; Mark 7:22 with Rom 1:31) and σύνεσις, σύνετος. Almost synonymous with ἀφροσύνη and ἄφρων are ἄγνοια, ἀγνωσία, ἄνοια, and ἀνόητος, among others (cf. 1 Pet 2:15 with 1:14; Titus 3:3; 1 Cor 15:36 with v. 34).

3. 'Αφροσύνη and ἄφρων always signify a lack of understanding. a) In discussions relating to wisdom the address "you *fool*" is used in charges of irrationality. In the parabolic narrative in Luke 12:16-21 (Luke's special material) God exposes the meaninglessness of the future plans of the rich in a well-known motif from the wisdom tradition (v. 20; cf. Job 27:16f.; Pss 39:7; 49:11-21; Eccl 2:18-23, 26; 4:8; 6:2; Sir 11:18f.; 14:4, 15; 41:4; cf. Seng).

The model of the "fool" (Luke 12:20) is already shaped in the wisdom literature of the OT. A wide variety of terms (esp. Heb. *nāḇāl, k^esîl, 'ĕwîl, ba'ar* in Proverbs, *sāḵāl* in Ecclesiastes—all rendered normally with ἄφρων in the LXX; cf. the relevant articles in *TDOT* and *THAT*) refer to a person who rejects the order of the world articulated by the wise, i.e., one who refuses to acknowledge dependence on God. This leads to unwise and presumptuous speech and behavior, by which the fool damages the community and takes himself into destruction.

Inasmuch as Matt 23:26 begins with an invective (certainly redactional), *you fools* in Luke 11:40 could belong to Q. Such a term of abuse may belong to the dispute between the rabbis and other groups (cf. *b. Menaḥ* 65a in Billerbeck I, 280, Heb. *šōṭîm*). Similarly, Paul rebukes his imaginary opponents in 1 Cor 15:36 (voc. ἄφρων) in the style of the Cynic-Stoic diatribe (cf. R. Bultmann, *Der Stil der paulinischen Predigt und die kynisch-stoische Diatribe* [1910] 14, 66).

b) The Jewish-Christian and Hellenistic catalog of fundamental evils in Mark 7:21f. names ἀφροσύνη at the conclusion of the sixfold list of items given in the sg. (v. 22; corresponding to the more general πονηρίαι at the conclusion of the list given in the pl. [v. 22]). It is indeed also one of the four cardinal vices in the Stoa, but in the OT and Jewish tradition (cf. Vögtle 232; 1QS 4:10; *Herm. Sim.* ix.15.3) it refers to the basic defect rooted in the heart of people. According to Rom 1:29-31 (ἀσύνετος, v. 31) it is referred esp. to the Gentiles.

c) The Gentiles are lacking in insight because they do not know the law. Therefore the Jews, especially in the Diaspora, see themselves as correctors of the *foolish* (Rom 2:20, alongside "teacher of children").

Because Deut 4:6 and esp. Sirach identify wisdom with the observance of the law, lawbreakers and outsiders (on the "foolishness" of idol worship, cf. Wis 12:23f.; 15:14; etc.; *Sib. Or.* iii.722) were considered "fools." Thus, e.g., the members of the Qumran community, who were sworn to the law, remained separate from them (1QS 4:24; 1QH 1:37; 13:4; 1Q27 1:7).

Gentile Christians have a similar view of the *senseless* paganism of their own past (cf. Eph 4:18; 1 Pet 1:14). The postapostolic parenesis summons them to put to silence through good deeds slanderous words arising from ἀγνωσία (1 Pet 2:15; cf. v. 12; 3:16) and to demonstrate that they themselves are not *senseless* but understand the revealed (Eph 1:9) will of God (5:17; cf. Col 1:9; 1 Pet 4:2-4; cf. Rom 2:18-24, of the Jews).

d) In 2 Corinthians 11–12 Paul is compelled, against his basic principles, to commend himself and boast like his foolish opponents (cf. 11:19; οὐ συνιᾶσιν, 10:12). Although he perceives this as foolishness (11:1, 16b, 17, 21; as in popular philosophy; cf. H. Windisch, *Der zweite Korintherbrief* [KEK] 345; Betz, 74-76; however, self-praise is also forbidden in the OT; Prov 27:2: the fool is the "man of the tongue," the braggart, *lêṣ;* cf. also *1 Clem.* 13:1; 21:5; *Herm. Sim.* ix.22.2f.), he slips into the mask of the braggart (Windisch 316) and shows in chs. 11–12 that he is inferior to the "superlative apostles" (11:15) in nothing. Excused as a "madman" (cf. the heightened παραφρονέω in 11:23), he can speak the truth (cf. the denial of ἀφροσύνη in 11:16a; 12:6; possible literary models are named in Betz 79-82) and paradoxically transform the content of his boasting (→ καυχάομαι).

D. Zeller

ἄφρων, 2 *aphrōn* senseless, foolish; subst.: fool → ἀφροσύνη.

ἀφυπνόω *aphypnoō* fall asleep*

Luke 8:23, of Jesus, who *fell asleep* during the crossing of the lake. Outside the NT the vb. occurs also with the meaning "awaken from sleep." Cf. H. Balz, *TDNT* VIII, 553f.

ἀφυστερέω *aphystereō* withhold

Jas 5:4 ℵ B* in the place of → ἀποστερέω.

ἄφωνος, 2 *aphōnos* silent; mute, without speech*

Used with the meaning *silent* or *dumb:* in Acts 8:32 of the lamb who was *silent* before his shearers (citing Isa 53:7); in 1 Cor 12:2 of idols; in 14:10 of the great number of languages (φωναί) in the world, none of which is *without a clear meaning* (οὐδὲν ἄφωνον); in 2 Pet 2:16 of Balaam's ass, a beast of burden *without language* (ὑποζύγιον ἄφωνον) that nevertheless spoke to the prophet in human language.

'Αχάζ *Achaz* Ahaz

King of Judah (742-)735-727 B.C., son of Jotham and father of Hezekiah (cf. 2 Kgs 15:38–16:20; 2 Chr 27:9–28:27; Isa 14:28): W. S. Caldecott, *ISBE* I, 76-78; S. Laudersdorfer, *LTK* I, 107; A. Jepsen, *BHH* I, 49f.; H. Haag, *BL* (1968) 19.

'Αχαΐα, ας, ἡ *Achaïa* Achaia, Greece*

1. Occurrences — 2. Historical data — 3. Paul in 'Αχαΐα

Lit.: J. FINEGAN, *IDB* I, 25. — E. GROAG, *Die römischen Reichsbeamten von Achaia* (1939). — E. KIRSTEN and B. E. THOMASSON, *KP* I, 32-38. — J. NUCHEMANS, *Woordenboek der Oudheid* I (1976), 17f. — H. H. SCULLARD, *OCD* 3 (bibliography). — J. TOEPFFER and C. G. BRANDIS, PW I, 156-98.

1. 'Αχαΐα is referred to 3 times in Acts and 7 times in Paul's letters. It designates the Roman province of Greece (→ 2), which is also referred to once as Greece (Acts 20:2).

2. The mountainous landscape of 'Αχαΐα on the northern coast of the Peloponnesus was a center of Greek political life from 280-146 B.C. because of the Achaian League. When the Romans conquered Greece and joined it to the province of Macedonia, they named it 'Αχαΐα (Pausanias vii.16.10). Because of the significance of the new Corinth, Augustus made 'Αχαΐα an independent senatorial province under a pronconsul in Corinth in 27 B.C.

Included in the province were Greece proper, along with Thessaly and the southern part of Epirus (Strabo xvii.3.25). From A.D. 15 to 44, it was, along with Macedonia, administered imperially to ease the tax burden; but later it became an independent senatorial province again and retained the freedom granted it by Nero in A.D. 67 until Vespasian's time in A.D. 73.

3. Paul entered Ἀχαΐα in A.D. 52 (→ Γαλλίων) on his second missionary journey, coming by ship from Macedonia to Athens (Acts 17:14f.). After Paul spent 18 months working successfully in Corinth (18:11), the Jews appealed to the proconsul Gallio, but Paul was acquitted (vv. 12-17). He later expressed his joy at the expansion of the gospel in Macedonia and Achaia (1 Thess. 1:7f.). Subsequently Apollos began his activity in Ἀχαΐα (Acts 18:27). Stephanas of Corinth, called one of the firstfruits of Ἀχαΐα (1 Cor 1:16; 16:15), visited Paul in Ephesus during the third missionary journey (16:17). At that time Paul planned another visit to Ἀχαΐα (Acts 19:21; 1 Cor 16:5); to the disappointment of the Corinthians, however, this was delayed because of his activity in Macedonia (2 Cor 1:15f.; 2:13). Nevertheless, Paul was confident of the solidarity of the believers in Ἀχαΐα and of their cooperation in the collection (1:1; 9:2; 11:10). His confidence was well grounded (Rom 15:26). According to the Koine text, the Roman Christians were greeted by another of the firstfruits from Corinth (Rom 16:5). Greek culture is not mentioned by Paul, but the provinces of Macedonia and Ἀχαΐα were for him classic missionary lands.

B. Reicke

Ἀχαϊκός, οῦ *Achaikos* Achaicus*

A Christian from Corinth who, along with Stephanas and Fortunatus, visited Paul in Ephesus (1 Cor 16:17).

ἀχάριστος, 2 *acharistos* unthankful*

Used in Luke 6:35 alongside πονηροί, and in 2 Tim 3:2 in a vice list; cf. Wis 16:29; 4 Macc 9:10.

ἀχειροποίητος, 2 *acheiropoiētos* not made with hands
→ χειροποίητος.

Ἀχίμ *Achim* Achim*

Son of Zadok and father of Eliud in the genealogy of Jesus (Matt 1:14 bis).

ἀχλύς, ύος, ἡ *achlys* darkness, obscurity*

Used in Acts 13:11 with σκότος, of the temporary blinding of the magician Elymas when Saul/Paul declared his punishment: "*mist* and darkness fell upon him." In view of the LXX language used in the context, it is not to be regarded as a medical t.t.; cf. E. Haenchen, *Acts of the Apostles* (1971) ad loc.

ἀχρεῖος, 2 *achreios* useless, worthless, unsuitable*

Used in connection with δοῦλος in Matt 25:30; Luke 17:10 (pl.; absence from sy^s does not argue against its originality; cf. BAGD s.v.).

ἀχρειόω *achreioō* make useless; pass.: become unfit*

Rom 3:12 (citing Pss 13:3; 52:4 LXX): all—both Jews and Greeks—have become unfit (through sin).

ἄχρηστος, 2 *achrēstos* useless, worthless*

Used in Phlm 11 of Onesimus, who was "formerly . . . *useless*" to his master, but now is "indeed *useful*" (εὔχρηστος); for the play on words cf. *Herm. Vis.* iii.6.7; similarly *Sim.* ix.26.4.

ἄχρι, ἄχρις *achri, achris* until, as far as*

1. Occurrences — 2. As a prep. — 3. As a conjunction — 4. Spatial sense

Lit.: On preps. in general → ἀνά. — BAGD s.v. — BDF §§21; 216.3; 383.1, 2; 455.3. — MAYSER, *Grammatik* II/1, 268, n. 1; II/3, 77. — MOULTON, *Grammar* III, 110f., 276. — SCHWYZER, *Grammatik* I, 405, 450, 620, 840; II, 313, 487, 533, 549f., 637, 640, 653, 657f.

1. Ἄχρι occurs in the NT a total of 45 times, esp. in the Lukan writings (19 times). Ἄχρις, on the other hand, occurs only 3 times: Gal 3:19; Heb 3:13; Rev 2:25 (see BDF §21).

2. As a prep. ἄχρι is normally used with reference to time in the NT. Thus it stands normally in connection with words for time: ἄχρι ἧς (τῆς) ἡμέρας, *until* the day (Matt 24:38; Luke 1:20; 17:27; Acts 1:2 [22 v.l.]; 2:29; 23:1; 26:22; 2 Cor 3:14) or ἄχρι ἡμέρας Ἰησοῦ Χριστοῦ, *until* the day (of the return) of Jesus Christ (Phil 1:6); cf., however: ἄχρι ἡμερῶν πέντε, *after* five days (Acts 20:6); ἄχρι καιροῦ, *until* an opportune time (Luke 4:13; Acts 13:11); ἄχρι χρόνων, *until* the time (Acts 3:21); ἄχρι προθεσμίας, *until* the established date (Gal 4:2); ἄχρι τοῦ νῦν, *until* now (Rom 8:22; Phil 1:5); ἄχρι τοῦ δεῦρο, thus far; ἄχρι αὐγῆς, *until* the break of day (Acts 20:11); ἄχρι τῆς ἄρτι ὥρας, *to* the present moment (1 Cor 4:11); ἄχρι τέλους, *until* the end (Heb 6:11; Rev 2:26). Ἄχρι θανάτου is intended as a way of establishing a temporal limit in Rev 2:10; 12:11; a fig. usage is found in Acts 22:4, where the usage designates the intent of the action: Paul persecuted the "way" (of faith) *to* the death. The expression ἄχρι . . . νόμου, *until* the establishment of the law (Rom 5:13), is not entirely clear. Paul's actual formulation concerns the

subject of the law, but his thought is directed to the fact of the revelation of the law through Moses. The expression ἄχρι τούτου τοῦ λόγου, *up to* the statement, is a reference to time (Acts 22:22).

3. As a conjunction ἄχρι is sometimes connected with the relative οὗ: *until* the time when, where (something takes place; Luke 21:24; Acts 7:18; 27:33; Rom 11:25; 1 Cor 11:26; 15:25; Gal 3:19 [ἄχρις οὗ]; Heb 3:13 [ἄχρις οὗ *so long as*]; Rev 2:25 [ἄχρις οὗ]). Ἄχρι *until* occurs without the rel. pron. in Rev 7:3; 15:8; 17:17; 20:3, 5. Ἄχρι (οὗ) usually appears with the aor. subjunc.; with the indic. in Acts 7:18; 27:33; Rev 17:17 (see BDF §383.1, 2).

4. Ἄχρι refers comparatively seldom to a spatial distance: ἄχρι μερισμοῦ ψυχῆς καὶ πνεύματος, (the word of God pierces) *to* the division of soul and spirit (Heb 4:12); ἄχρι τῶν χαλινῶν τῶν ἵππων, *up to* the horse's bridle (Rev 14:20); ἄχρι οὐρανοῦ, *as high as* heaven (Rev 18:5). Otherwise ἄχρι refers to geographic locations (Acts 13:6; 20:4 v.l.; 28:15) or persons (11:5; 2 Cor 10:13, 14).

H.-J. Ritz

ἄχυρον, ου, τό *achyron* chaff*

Matt 3:12 par. Luke 3:17 (Q), of the *chaff,* which at the winnowing of the grain is blown away by the wind and then burned. *BL* 1624.

ἀψευδής, 2 *apseudēs* without lying, not deceptive, truthful*

Titus 1:2, with reference to God, who is *without lies;* cf. *Mart. Pol.* 14:2. The pred. corresponds to Greek thought and to Hellenistic Jewish style; cf. BAGD s.v.; H. Conzelmann, *TDNT* IX, 601 with n. 73; Wis 7:17; Philo, *Ebr.* 139.

ἄψινθος, ου, ὁ, (ἡ) *apsinthos* absinthe, wormwood*

Rev 8:11 (bis): masc., as the name of a star; fem., as the name of a bitter liquid into which a third of all water is transformed at the third trumpet sound. Because of its bitterness, ἡ ἄψινθος, *mugwort,* is translated traditionally by *wormwood,* and is an image for damnation and judgment; cf. Prov 5:4; Jer 9:15; 23:15 Aquila; LXX frequently uses ἄψινθος with ὕδωρ πικρόν, etc., or χολή. C. H. Peisker *BHH* III, 2167; *BL* 1887f.; J. Wiesner, *LAW* 3270f.

ἄψυχος, 2 *apsychos* inanimate, lifeless*

1 Cor 14:7, of musical instruments.

B β

Βάαλ *Baal* Baal*

In Rom 11:4, citing 1 Kgs 19:18, as the (indeclinable) name of the Canaanite deity before whom the seven thousand "have not bowed the knee." In 4 Kgdms 21:3 and elsewhere the word appears with the article ἡ, because at the public reading of the text the name was replaced by αἰσχύνη; cf. BDF §53.4; O. Eissfeldt, *RGG* I, 805f.; K. G. Jung, *ISBE* I, 377-79; J. Gray, *IDB* I, 328f.; H. F. Weiss, *BHH* I, 173-75; G. J. Botterweck, *LTK* I, 1162f.; *BL* 157; G. Wiessner, *LAW* 425; F. Nötscher, *RAC* I, 1063-1113.

Βαβυλών, ῶνος *Babylōn* Babylon*

1. Occurrences in the NT — 2. The Babylonian exile — 3. Babylon = Rome

Lit.: R. Borger, *BHH* I, 177f. — C. Brütsch, *Offenbarung* I-III (ZBK, 1970) ad loc. — C. H. Giblin, "Structural and Thematic Correlations in the Theology of Revelation 16–22," *Bib* 55 (1974) 487-504. — K.-P. Jörns, *Das hymnische Evangelium. Untersuchungen zu Aufbau, Funktion und Herkunft der hymnischen Stücke in der Johannesoffenbarung* (1971). — H. Kraft, *Offenbarung* (HNT, 1974) 225-40. — K. G. Kuhn, *TDNT* I, 514-17. — W. Röllig, *BRL* 26-29. — E. Schüssler-Fiorenza, *The Book of Revelation: Justice and Judgment* (1985). — *idem,* "Religion und Politik in der Offenbarung des Johannes," *Biblische Randbemerkungen* (FS R. Schnackenburg, 1974) 261-72. — S. Uhlig, "Die typologische Bedeutung des Begriffes Babylons," *AUSS* 12 (1974) 112-25. — For further bibliography see *TWNT* X, 997f.

1. The name of the city of Babylon (Heb. *bāḇel*) appears 12 times in the NT: 4 times in the genealogy of Jesus (Matt 1:11, 12, 17 bis), once each in Acts (7:43) and 1 Peter (5:13), and 6 times in Revelation (14:8; 16:19; 17:5; 18:2, 10, 21). The name thus has considerable significance, referring both to the Babylonian captivity as a salvation-historical nadir and turning point in Israel (Matthew and Acts) and to Babylon as an apocalyptic cipher for the eschatological world power in opposition to God, the overthrow of which is the object of hope (1 Peter and Revelation). Because of Israel's historical experience the name was always used in a negative way (Josephus *Ant.* x.131ff.; CD 1:6). It connoted a political enemy and a religious threat (Jer 50f.; Ezek 24).

2. Matt 1:1-17 reckons with three groups of fourteen generations from Abraham until Christ. The "deportation to Babylon," which is described with the technical language, designates the decisive turning point to the last third of the epoch. God has, despite the catastrophe of Israel, brought the promise to completion. The citation from Amos 5:25-27 LXX in Acts 7:43 is altered at the end to "beyond Babylon" (instead of "beyond Damascus"). The exile here is evidence in the argument of Stephen's word of judgment. The prophetic declaration from Amos is, in reality, not exceeded.

3. In 1 Pet 5:13 Babylon is an apocalyptic code word for the locale from which the letter was written, i.e., Rome. In the midst of the godless world-city is the Church that is "likewise chosen."

Revelation also speaks of Babylon = Rome (17:1-19) as the center and the embodiment of the anti-Christian world power. Here Babylon has taken on the form that was previously foreshadowed by the historical Babylon (see v. 5, "mystery"). The stereotypical reference to Babylon "the great" incorporates a Hellenistic pantocrator attribution (cf. Dan 4:30 [MT v. 27]; knowledge of the former greatness of Babylon was present in the NT period [Strabo xvi.1.5; Josephus *Ap.* i.128ff.]). Babylon = Rome is charged with "sexual impurity" (Rev 14:8; 17:5), i.e., adoration of the beast.

The language and the repertoire of imagery used in Revelation of Babylon has been shaped within the OT and Judaism (on the woes in 18:10, cf. Isa 21:9), and its witness concerning Babylon = Rome stands within a pronounced Jewish apocalyptic tradition (*2 Bar.* 67:7; *Sib. Or.* v.143, 158ff.; *Cant. Rab.* 1:6; Billerbeck III, 816). It took on significance in early Christian thought after the emperor cult required its first victims (see 18:24).

A. Strobel

βαθμός, οῦ, ὁ *bathmos* step; rank; reputation*

In 1 Tim 3:13 βαθμός καλός, "a good standing," is gained by the deacons who serve well. The context excludes a mystical or philosophical interpretation (as in, e.g., *Corp. Herm.* xiii.9: a level in the heavenly journey of the soul; Clement of Alexandria *Strom.* ii.54.4: a level of gnosis).

βάθος, ους, τό *bathos* depth*

1. Occurrences in the NT — 2. Meaning — 3. Usage

Lit.: H. R. BALZ, *Heilsvertrauen und Welterfahrung* (1971) 116-23. — J. BLUNK, *DNTT* II, 197f. — N. A. DAHL, "Cosmic Dimensions and Religious Knowledge (Eph 3:18)," FS Kümmel 57-75. — P. FIEDLER, "Röm 8:31-39 als Brennpunkt paulinischer Frohbotschaft," *ZNW* 68 (1977) 23-34. — H. SCHLIER, *TDNT* I, 517f. — L. SCHOTTROFF, *Der Glaubende und die feindliche Welt* (1970). — H.-F. WEISS, *Untersuchungen zur Kosmologie des hellenistischen und palästinischen Judentums* (1966). — V. VAN ZUTPHEN, *Studies on the Hymn in Rom 11, 33-36* (Diss. Würzburg, 1973). — For further bibliography see *TWNT* X, 998.

1. The 8 NT uses of βάθος are distributed among the Gospels (3: Mark 4:5 par. Matt 13:5; Luke 5:4) and the Pauline letters (5, including 1 in Ephesians). The word also appears in Rev 2:24 in a variant reading (TR).

2. The instances in the Gospels occur in narrative settings. Βάθος signifies the *spatial depth* either of earth (Mark 4:5 par. Matt 13:5) or of water (Luke 5:4). The Pauline texts employ βάθος in fig. senses, on the one hand, as the overarching dimension, both of the world and of life (Rom 8:39; 2 Cor 8:2); on the other hand, of God or Christ (Rom 11:33; 1 Cor 2:10; Eph 3:18). Thus βάθος is especially useful as one in series of terms in doxological statements, where it is employed in antithesis to ὕψος (Eph 3:18) or ὕψωμα (Rom 8:39), among other terms. The totality of the dimension named is emphasized. Pl. βάθη, which is used only in 1 Cor 2:10, accents a multi-dimensional reality (which can be negative, i.e., Satanic, e.g., in the v.l. in Rev 2:24).

3. The phrase βάθος τῆς γῆς, which is formed according to the manner of a Hebrew construct relationship, means "deep soil." Matt 13:5 has adopted this phrase from Mark 4:5, but Luke (8:6) has not, but has made the parable more concise and linguistically smoother. Luke 5:4 (Luke's special material) speaks of the *depth* of the sea. The advice of Jesus signifies: "Aim at the height."

In Rom 8:39 Paul speaks of "height" and *depth* alongside other polarities. The realm of earthly and supra-earthly powers is here in view.

As an astronomical t.t. βάθος sometimes designates the space under the horizon (Preisendanz, *Papyri* 4:575). In Gnosticism God himself can be βάθος (*Acts Thom.* 143; Hippolytus *Haer.* vi.30.7).

Paul says that the love of Christ totally permeates this realm, with the result that it loses its threatening character. In the concluding doxology in Rom 11:33, "the *depth* of the riches and wisdom and knowledge of God" encompasses, above all, the thought of the inexhaustible and unsearchable "fullness." It proceeds one step deeper in 1 Cor 2:10, for the "*depths* of God," which the Spirit alone searches, refers here finally to "depth" which, as the context shows, is illustrated in the event of the cross.

According to Hippolytus *Haer.* v.6.4 there were Gnostics who affirmed that they alone understood the βάθος. On βάθος among the Valentinians, cf. *Excerpta ex Theodoto* 29; *Gos. Truth* 22:25; 35:15; 37:8; 40:26f.: the Father, "who came forth from the depth."

The witness that is peculiar to Ephesians speaks of βάθος (3:18) within a series, which names in a formulaic and plerophoric manner "breadth and length and height and *depth*" as the absolute dimensions of existence. The passage seeks to equate an abstract cubic cosmos (cf. Rev 21:16) with the "fulness of God" (cf. Eph 3:19) on the basis of "the love of Christ which surpasses knowledge." In the Christian community this "fulness" is perceptible and available as a living organism. Βάθος, which stands significantly at the end, consciously incorporates "the unfathomable" within the glorification (cf. v. 13) that is described.

A. Strobel

βαθύνω *bathynō* make deep; go down deep*

Luke 6:48, with no obj., of a person who builds a house but first digs *deep* (ἔσκαψεν καὶ ἐβάθυνεν) in the earth.

βαθύς, 3 *bathys* deep*

Lit., of a *deep* well, John 4:11; fig., of a *deep* sleep, Acts 20:9; "at *early* dawn" (ὄρθρου βαθέως), Luke 24:1; of the *depths of Satan* (pl. τὰ βαθέα; TR τὰ βάθη), Rev 2:24. The latter refers to a widespread false teaching (Nicolaitan according to H. Kraft, *Offenbarung* [HNT] ad loc; cf. 2:6), which claimed for itself the knowledge of the depths of God; through the seer's sarcastic inversion, their knowledge of God is stigmatized as the knowledge of the depths of Satan (→ βάθος 3).

βαΐον, ου, τό *baïon* palm branch*

John 12:13: βαΐα τῶν φοινίκων. A loanword from Coptic, which actually makes the attached gen. τῶν φοινίκων superfluous; cf. BDF §6.

Βαλαάμ *Balaam* Balaam*

Lit.: W. F. ALBRIGHT and Y. M. GRINTZ, *EncJud* IV, 120-24. — BILLERBECK, III, 771f., 793. — H. KRAFT, *Offenbarung* (HNT, 1974) 65. — H. KARPP, *RAC* II, 362-66. — K. G. KUHN, *TDNT* I, 524f. — L. M. PÁKOZDY, *BHH* I, 252f. — R. RENDTORFF, *RGG* I, 1290f. — K. H. SCHELKLE, *Die Petrusbriefe. Der Judasbrief* (HTKNT, [3]1970) 160, 214f. — For further bibliography see *TWNT* X, 998.

1. The deed of the soothsayer Balaam (Heb. *bil'ām*), who cursed Israel but then had to give a blessing (Josh 24:9f.; Mic 9:5),

is already in Numbers 22–24 conditioned by the history of tradition and not to be regarded as a unified tradition (cf. 22:20-22). In the priestly tradition Balaam appears in a totally negative light (25:1; 31:8, 16; Josh 13:22). This assessment is sharpened in rabbinic tradition: The seducer Balaam (*b. Sanh.* 106a) had "an envious eye, a haughty mind, and a greedy soul" (*Num. Rab.* 20 [188[d]; cf. 189[b]], in Billerbeck 793 or 771).

2. The NT references assume the rabbinic portrait. In Rev 2:14 Balaam is the seducer with whom the Nicolaitans, possibly on etymological grounds (*bālaʿ ʿam* = devourer of the people; so Kraft on the basis of *b. Sanh.* 105a, against Kuhn 524, n. 10), can be compared; for they, like Balaam, teach (διδαχὴ Βαλαάμ—διδαχὴ [τῶν] Νικολαιτῶν, vv. 14f.) fornication, which is to be understood fig. here, since φαγεῖν εἰδωλόθυτα καὶ πορνεῦσαι is to be understood as a hendiadys. That is, they fail to stay within the line of demarcation separating the worship of God from worship of idols (Kraft). Jude 11 and 2 Pet 2:15 compare false teachers with Balaam; for they "abandon themselves for the sake of gain" (cf. Jude 16; Schelkle 160).

Βαλάκ *Balak* Balak*

Rev 2:24, of the Moabite king Balak, who wanted to have Israel cursed through Balaam (Num 22:5ff.; → Βαλαάμ). K. Baltzer, *BHH* I, 192; *BL* 163.

βαλλάντιον, ου, τό *ballantion* purse*

This noun is found only in Luke. Reference is made in 10:4 to the commissioning of the seventy without a *purse* (μὴ βαστάζετε βαλλάντιον; cf. Matt 10:9; Mark 6:8). In a double logion in Luke 22:35-36, which is probably pre-Lukan, those who have (ὁ ἔχων) a *purse* are "now" (ἀλλὰ νῦν) permitted to take (ἀράτω) it in view of the imminent time of persecution; v. 38 is to be understood as a repudiation of the disciples' misunderstanding. In 12:33 (Q) Jesus challenges his disciples to renounce property by means of the image of the *purse* which does not wear out (βαλλάντια μὴ παλαιούμενα). K. H. Rengstorf, *TDNT* I, 525f.; G. Schneider, *Lukas* (ÖTK) on Luke 22:35f.

βάλλω *ballō* throw

1. Occurrences in the NT — 2. Meanings — 3. Theological significance — a) Matt 10:34; Luke 12:49 — b) Βάλλω in judgment sayings — c) Βάλλω in Revelation

Lit.: F. HAUCK, *TDNT* I, 526f. — F. STOLZ, *THAT* II, 916-19 (on the OT equivalents).

1. The vb. βάλλω appears 122 times in the NT (including the verbal adj. βλητέον in Luke 5:38 but not βάλλω in John 8:7). There are 34 occurrences in Matthew, 18 in Mark, 19 in Luke, 16 in John, 5 in Acts, 1 in James, 1 in 1 John, and 28 in Revelation.

2. As is the case in Greek generally, βάλλω has a very wide range of meaning in the NT.

a) The basic meaning is *throw* (Matt 3:10 par.; 6:30 par.; John 8:59). When the word is present, it often describes a violent event, especially when persons are named as the obj. (e.g., Mark 9:22, 42 as well as the construction εἰς φυλακὴν βάλλειν [Matt 5:25 par.; 18:30 and frequently]; → 3.b).

Particular nuances can be added to the basic meaning. Thus βάλλω occurs in such formulations as: to *throw* something *out* or *to* animals (Mark 7:27 par.; Matt 7:6), to *cast* a net or a fishhook (Matt 4:18; 13:47; 17:27; John 21:6), and to *shed* fruit (Rev 6:13). Use of the act. to mean to *place* someone "on a sick bed" (Rev 2:22) is related to the use of the perf. pass. to say that a person is *confined* to his or her bed (Matt 8:6, 14; 9:2; Luke 16:20; cf. Mark 7:30). Further variations of the basic meaning are: *scatter* seed upon the ground (Mark 4:26), *throw* dust in the air (Acts 22:23), and *spit out* water from the mouth (Rev 12:15f.). The command βάλε ἀπὸ σοῦ (Matt 5:29f.; 18:8f.) and the phrase βάλλειν ἔξω (Matt 5:13; 13:48; Luke 14:35; John 15:6 [→ ἐκβάλλω]) mean to *throw away.* In 1 John 4:18 the latter means *drive away* or *expel.*

b) Frequently βάλλω has simply the meaning *bring* (Matt 10:34 [→ 3.a]; John 5:7) or *lay* (Mark 7:33; John 20:25, 27; Jas 3:3; Rev 2:24; 4:10).

Here also a variety of individual nuances are present: to *put* money into the treasury, etc. (Mark 12:41ff. par.; Matt 27:6; John 12:6) or *invest* it with the banker (Matt 25:27), to *fill* wineskins with wine (Mark 2:22 par.), to *pour* water into a basin (John 13:5) or *pour out* ointment onto the body (Matt 26:12), to *put* the sword into its sheath (John 18:11), to *sow* grain in the garden (Luke 13:19), to *suggest* a thought (John 13:2), or to *give* an occasion for sin (Rev 2:14), among others.

c) Βάλλω is used intrans. in Acts 27:14: ἔβαλεν ἄνεμος = the wind "struck down."

3. a) Among Synoptic uses of βάλλω the two ἦλθον sayings in Matt 10:34 and Luke 12:49 are of special interest.

According to Matt 10:34 (cf. Luke 12:51) Jesus has "not come to *bring* peace, but a sword" (on βαλεῖν εἰρήνην cf. the rabbinic phrase *hēṭîl šālôm* [*Mek. Exod.* on 20:25; *Sipre Num.* 42 on 6:26]). The original meaning may be that with the coming of Jesus the messianic peace has not yet broken in, but rather that the time of eschatological affliction, which must precede the time of salvation, has arrived (cf. Jeremias, *Theology* 127ff., 241ff.). Matthew uses the saying for the division between people brought about by the work of Jesus (vv. 35f.; likewise Luke 12:51ff.).

The meaning of the logion in Luke 12:49 as well as its relation to v. 50 is much disputed (see the commentaries on this text as well as G. Delling, *Studien zum NT und zum hellenistischen Judentum* [1970] 245ff.). As spoken by Jesus, the words πῦρ ἦλθον βαλεῖν ἐπὶ τὴν γῆν could be, as in Matt 10:34, the announcement of the eschatological affliction (cf. Jeremias, *Parables* 163f.). Luke himself probably thinks of the fire of judgment which Jesus will "*cast* upon the earth" at the parousia (cf. Luke 3:17; 17:24, 29f.). The double logion, in analogy to 17:24f., thus refers to the inner connection between the future function of Jesus at the judgment (12:49) and his passion, which must precede the judgment (v. 50). It is less probable that Luke in v. 49 has in mind the division of spirits occasioned by the proclamation of Christ (vv. 51ff.) or the pouring out of the Spirit in Acts 2:1ff. in fulfillment of Luke 3:16.

b) As an expression of forcible throwing βάλλω occurs repeatedly in judgment sayings. As in John 15:6, πῦρ βάλλειν in the speech of the Baptist in Matt 3:10 par. Luke 3:9 is originally simply an image for the destruction at the judgment (cf. Jer 22:7). In Matthew → πῦρ in 3:10 = 7:19 describes, however, the actual eschatological fire of hell. This meaning is present when it is said that on the last day those who have fallen under God's condemnation *are cast* into → γέεννα (Mark 9:45, 47; Matt 5:29; 18:9; cf. Luke 12:5), "the eternal fire" (Matt 18:8), "the furnace of fire" (13:42, 50), or "the lake of fire" (Rev 20:15). According to Matthew (see 25:41) and Revelation (19:20; 20:10, 14) the same punishment is given to Satan and to all godless powers. The basic idea and the terminology come from Jewish apocalypticism (cf. *1 Enoch* 10:6; 54:5f.; 90:24ff.; 91:9; 98:3; *T. Jud.* 25:3).

c) Revelation uses βάλλω in the sense of *cast* also to describe apocalyptic phenomena: cf. 12:4; 14:19b; 18:21; 20:3 and especially the description of the occurrence of eschatological plagues (8:5, 7f.), of the fall of Satan (12:9f., 13), and of the beginning of the harvest of judgment (14:16, 19a).

O. Hofius

βαπτίζω *baptizō* baptize*
βάπτισμα, ατος, τό *baptisma* baptism*
βαπτισμός, οῦ, ὁ *baptismos* washing*
βάπτω *baptō* dip, immerse

1. Occurrences in the NT — 2. Baptism by John — 3. Baptism by Jesus and his disciples — 4. Jesus' baptism of death — 5. The baptismal command of the resurrected one (Matt 28:19) — 6. Baptism in Acts — 7. Baptism in the Pauline corpus — 8. 1 Pet 3:21 — 9. Βάπτω and βαπτισμός

Lit.: K. ALAND, *Did the Early Church Baptize Infants?* (1963). — G. BARTH, *Die Taufe in frühchristlicher Zeit* (1981). — M. BARTH, *Die Taufe ein Sakrament?* (1951). — G. BEASLEY-MURRAY, *Baptism in the NT* ([2]1972). — W. BIEDER, *Die Verheissung der Taufe im NT* (1966). — O. CULLMANN, *Baptism in the NT* (1950). — G. DELLING, *Die Zueignung des Heils in der Taufe* (1960). — W. F. FLEMINGTON, *The NT Doctrine of Baptism* (1948). — J. JEREMIAS, *Infant Baptism in the First Four Centuries* (1960). — *idem, The Origins of Infant Baptism* (1963). — E. KLAAR, *Die Taufe nach paulinischem Verständnis* (1961). — G. W. H. LAMPE, *The Seal of the Spirit: A Study in the Doctrine of Baptism and Confirmation in the NT and the Fathers* (1951). — F. J. LEENHARDT, *Le Baptême Chrétien, son origine, sa signification* (1946). — P. LUNDBERG, *La Typologie baptismale dans l'ancienne Église* (1942). — W. MICHAELIS, *Die Sakramente im Johannesevangelium* (1946). — B. REICKE, *The Disobedient Spirits and Christian Baptism* (1946). — M. RISSI, *Die Taufe für die Toten* (1962). — G. SCHILLE, "Zur urchristlichen Tauflehre," *ZNW* 49 (1958) 31-52. — R. SCHNACKENBURG, *Baptism in the Thought of St. Paul* (1964). — H. SCHWARZMANN, *Zur Tauftheologie des heiligen Paulus in Römer 6* (1950). — J. THOMAS, *Le Mouvement Baptiste en Palestine et Syrie* (1935). — G. WAGNER, *Das religionsgeschichtliche Problem von Römer 6, 1-11* (1962; cf. *idem, Pauline Baptism and the Pagan Mysteries* [1967]). — For further bibliography see *TWNT* X, 998-1008; *DNTT* I, 160f.

1. Βαπτίζω appears 7 times in Matthew (11 times in TR of Matthew), 12 times in Mark, 10 times in Luke, 13 times in John, 21 times in Acts, twice in Romans, 10 times in 1 Corinthians, and once in Galatians. Βάπτω occurs only 4 times in the NT (Luke 16:24; John 13:26a, b; Rev 19:13). Βάπτισμα appears once each in Romans (6:4), Ephesians (4:5), Colossians (2:12), and 1 Peter (3:21), 10 times in the Lukan writings (Luke 3:3; 7:29; 12:50; 20:4; Acts 1:22; 10:37; 13:24; 18:25; 19:3, 4), and 4 times each in Matthew and Mark (Matt 3:7; 20:22, 23; 21:25; Mark 1:4; 10:38, 39; 11:30). Βαπτισμός is found 5 times in the NT (Mark 7:4, 8; Col 2:12; Heb 6:2; 9:10).

2. When one surveys the reports in the Gospels concerning John's baptism (Mark 1:2-6 par.), the origin and significance of which was debated (Matt 21:25; Mark 11:30; Luke 20:4), one notices: a) John's action of baptizing with water and his association of baptism with the preaching of repentance (Mark 1:4; Luke 3:3); b) the actions of the people and of the tax collectors in going out to John (Matt 3:7) "to be baptized by him" (Luke 3:7, 12; Matt 3:5f.; Mark 1:5); and c) the Baptist's hope that God would respond to repentance with the gift of forgiveness and purification. Consequently, when the people and the tax collectors were baptized, they acknowledged thereby the critique which touched their lives (Luke 3:1-14) and "justified God" (7:29). On the opposite side stood "the Pharisees and the lawyers." Since they were not baptized by John, they "rejected the purpose of God for themselves" and brought upon themselves the salutary judgment of God, which is directed at them (Luke 7:30).

Whereas Mark contrasts John's baptism with water to the messianic baptism with the Holy Spirit without mentioning repentance (Mark 1:8), Matthew has the Baptist, on the one hand, demand repentance (Matt 3:1f.) and, on the other hand, baptize for the purpose of repentance

(v. 11). Thus he expresses two themes: a) those who are ready for repentance come to be baptized; b) those who are baptized venture a step in the expectation of repentance as the gift of God (cf. Acts 11:18; 5:31). They will thus escape the Messiah's fiery judgment (Matt 3:11; Luke 3:16).

John may have taken two ideas from the OT: the idea of ethical purification under the image of purification with water (Isa 1:16ff.) and the expectation that God himself will execute the great purification in the end time (Ezek 36:25; Zech 13:1). John connects these two ideas and puts them to use in the urgent appeal to adapt one's life toward the Messiah's work of judgment and purification in the renunciation of sin and reorientation toward God in ethical reform. In John, the Baptist's baptism is transferred to Bethany (1:26; cf. 10:40), is called into question (1:26), and serves as preparation for the appearance of the Revealer (v. 31), who, as the bearer of the Spirit, will baptize with the Holy Spirit (v. 33). It does not bring salvation, but stands already in the light of the approaching salvation (3:23: ἐγγὺς τοῦ Σαλείμ; Bieder 52).

John's baptism was like proselyte baptism in that it was not repeated. In distinction to proselyte baptism, however, it had nothing to do with any sacrificial activity. While the Qumran sect, which John might have known, concerned itself with the privileged few and demanded repeated washings, John directed himself to the entire people, in order to declare to them in a symbolic act that an act of God had set in motion the messianic end, in which those who are prepared in baptism may be involved.

3. "Jesus . . . was baptized by John in the Jordan" (Mark 1:9). The Spirit then came upon Jesus, not upon the water. The heavenly voice named Jesus as the favored Son, he who was, as the concealed king (a reference to Isa 42 and Ps 2), ready to begin his service. In Luke (3:21f.), the solidarity of Jesus with the people is emphasized (". . . when all the people and Jesus were baptized" [cf. RSV]), and his prayer is given special notice. Thus baptism is for Jesus "the armor for prayer" (A. Schlatter, *Das Evangelium des Lukas* [[2]1960] 42). For Luke the descent of the Spirit at baptism is more important than the baptism itself. In the Matthean special material (Matt 3:13-17) John wishes to receive the baptism of the Spirit from Jesus, a wish not granted to the Baptist. With the command, "Let it be so now," John is summoned to give Jesus the sign of solidarity with sinners. Thus Jesus entered upon his path of service that would lead him to the cross. The baptism of Jesus is to be understood, however, neither as a symbol of his death and resurrection nor as a prototype of Christian baptism. It was thus a unique occurrence when Jesus obediently and voluntarily undertook the beginning phase of his messianic activity in dedication to the will of the Father who reveals himself to Jesus.

From this perspective, it is not impossible to assume that Jesus, in association with the baptism of John, initially authorized his disciples to a successful (John 3:26) baptizing ministry (3:22; 4:2), which, with this symbolic act, would point back to the Master who had himself gone that route before. But as Jesus went into the cities and villages in order to preach (Mark 1:37ff.), and increasingly experienced the resistance of the multitude, he was aware of the distance from the water rites.

Evidence of this is found in Pap. Oxy. no. 840, ll. 30-44 (Hennecke/Schneemelcher I, 94): Jesus argues against Jewish cultic water rites, which are compared with pagan practice. By contrast, "I and my disciples have been immersed in living water" (βεβάμμεθα ἐν ὕδασι ζῶσι). In solidarity with his disciples Jesus bears witness to the already approaching salvation: In a prophetic perfect the reality of the Spirit, which Jesus does not claim for himself alone, is proclaimed metaphorically.

4. In Luke 12:50 Jesus uses the image of baptism for that which he must undergo (βάπτισμα δὲ ἔχω βαπτισθῆναι). He is anxious when he thinks of the approaching period of suffering, which is compared to a raging flood of sorrow. Whether he "went under with his soul" (τὴν ψυχὴν ἐβαπτίζετο, Charito Eroticus [ed. R. Hercher] ii.48) cannot be answered by a simple Yes or No. A positive answer interprets the baptism of death as a total human submersion into the most absolute God-forsakenness (Mark). If a negative answer is given, the word from the cross transmitted by Luke comes into force: "Father, into thy hands I commit my spirit!" (23:46; cf. J. Wirsching, *Lernziel Glauben* [1976] 90-103). In contrast to the saying from Pap. Oxy. 840 (noted above), the image of baptism refers exclusively to Jesus: He goes his way alone in the expectation of the judgment (πῦρ) which brings salvation, which he brings and to which he submits himself. An allusion to Christian baptism is not present.

Jesus' baptism of death has, however, significance for the suffering which is involved in discipleship. In Mark 10:38f. (cf. Matt 20:22f. C Koine *pm*) Jesus asks the sons of Zebedee if they are able to undergo the baptism with which he must be baptized. This logion is most frequently associated with the martyrdom of the disciples. The prophecy of Jesus in Mark 10:39 can, however, be understood in view of suffering discipleship: whatever they are not capable of, with their too bold expectation "we are able" (v. 39a), they will do in the new age when the Spirit is poured out. They will suffer with their Messiah, and thus experience something of the "soul immersed in grief" (ψυχὴν λύπῃ βεβαπτισμένην, Libanius *Orationes* 64, 115) and become witnesses of Jesus. The contexts in Matthew and Luke indicate that the intentions of the Jesus logion were understood: both Evangelists have in view the witness of servanthood which awaits the uncomprehending disciples (Luke 12:42, 51-53; Mark 10:43f.).

5. It is unlikely that the shorter form of the text of the

commission to the disciples, cited frequently in Eusebius (πορευθέντες μαθητεύσατε πάντα τὰ ἔθνη ἐν τῷ ὀνόματί μου "go and make disciples from all peoples in my name," e.g., *HE* iii.5.2), is original in Matthew, inasmuch as Eusebius doubtlessly knew the longer form of the text with the baptismal command. One cannot remove the final verse of Matthew from the total context. Although no other Evangelist has a command to baptize in its authentic parts, this silence does not argue against the authenticity of the baptismal command in Matthew.

According to Paul and Acts Christian baptism was administered "in the name of Jesus." This practice does not conflict with the triadic baptismal formula reflected in the Church's later practice. The distinction between the two formulas compels us to ask concerning the original wording of the baptismal command, which must be assumed to lie behind the triadic formula.

The assumption that the resurrected one did not give a command to baptize is an uncritical bias related to a particular interpretation of Jesus' resurrection. The resurrected one did not appear suddenly in the inner circle of the disciples as a reawakened visual memory, but rather he "came . . . to them" (προσελθών, Matt 28:18). Thus just as he accomplished a movement toward them with his approach, so he expected from his disciples the movement of traveling: "Go" (πορευθέντες, v. 19). They are summoned to the journey in order to carry out the baptismal command in connection with the call to discipleship. The resurrected one sees himself as the king authorized with power. He regards it as necessary to employ the element of water, which is itself ambiguous, as a sign of the acceptance of an obligation for those who become disciples in the obedient service of faith.

The triadic baptismal formula, "in the name of the Father and of the Son and of the Holy Spirit," interprets an apparently original "baptize in my name." Εἰς τὸ ὄνομα corresponds to Heb. *l^e^šēm*, which calls for a causal or final understanding (cf. W. Bietenhard, *TDNT* V, 275). In the triadic interpretation of the christological baptismal formula the interpreters see the resurrected one in association with the Father, who acknowledged his Son in baptism and who will provide for his disciples, give to them, forgive them, see them, and hear them. They also see him in association with the Holy Spirit, with whom Jesus wants to see that the disciples are equipped and who will speak in the disciples as witnesses (Matt 10:20).

6. Acts 1:5 anticipates the cessation of John's baptism, which Luke regards as the termination of the OT epoch in salvation history and as the beginning of the ministry of Jesus (Acts 1:22; 10:37; 13:24), with the baptism of the Spirit, i.e., the eschatological gift of the end time. Thus Peter's demand, directed to those who were pierced by the pain of repentance (2:37), was especially startling: Those who had already made the step toward repentance were individually summoned to be baptized in view of Jesus, who had given the commission, in order to receive the forgiveness of sins and the gift of the Holy Spirit and be incorporated in the Christian community. Baptism becomes thus a sign of the beginning of the move toward repentance, that by which the Lord who calls adds individuals to the Church and continues the story of faith which has begun (vv. 38f., 41).

"Both men and women" were baptized after believing submission to the kingdom of God and the proclamation of the evangelist Philip in Samaria (Acts 8:12). When Simon the magician also was baptized, "seeing signs and great miracles" (v. 13), it was made evident that the act of baptism as such was not capable of protecting against religious error. But it cannot be said that the Samaritan baptismal candidates who began with faith and confession were devoid of anything associated with the Holy Spirit (v. 6, ὁμοθυμαδόν; cf. 2:46; 8:8). They had, however, received "only" the baptism "in the name of the Lord Jesus" (8:16); the Holy Spirit had not fallen on any of them as they, from the enthusiastic beginning of their faith, remained blind to the unity of the Spirit that united Samaritans and Jews.

In contrast to the Samaritan episode, the story of Philip's baptism of the African eunuch does not refer to the formation of a Church. The original text (without Acts 8:37) does not refer to faith and has no explicit confession of faith. However, the eunuch's question, "See, here is water! What is to prevent my being baptized?" (v. 36) does point to the faith of the one who is baptized. Consequently Philip carries out the act of baptism (v. 38).

In the story of Cornelius, in contrast to the Samaritan scene, baptism follows the pouring out of the Holy Spirit (Acts 10:44, 48). If God allows his Spirit to fall upon those who hear and believe and thus allows the baptism of the Spirit to occur (11:16), it would be disobedient to refuse baptism and thus to attempt to hinder God (10:47) and stand in the way of the concrete historical response of faith in the acceptance of baptism for persons who have experienced the Spirit.

In Philippi when not only Lydia and the jailer, but also "her household" (Acts 16:15) and "all his family" (v. 33) were baptized, it is to be assumed that those who heard "the word of the Lord" (v. 32) and no one else submitted to baptism. The connection between hearing, belief, and baptism is also accented in the baptismal event in Corinth (18:8). From this background the post-Lukan passage in the Markan ending is understandable: the passage refers to the connection of faith and baptism, but priority is given to faith before baptism (Mark 16:16; cf. Bieder 207-10).

Apollos, the former disciple of John, who "knew only the baptism of John," spoke so "fervently in the [Holy] Spirit" (Acts 18:25; RSV "in spirit") that he needed further instruction by Priscilla and Aquila. But apparently he did not need water baptism. But the twelve disciples of John in Ephesus, who had been baptized "into John's baptism" (19:3f.) had to receive Christian baptism (v. 5). This was so because they knew nothing of the Holy Spirit or of Jesus as the coming one. Paul was baptized in Damascus (9:18). His baptism was understood as the acceptance of purification from sins at the invocation of the name of Jesus (22:16).

7. The questions which Paul directs to the church in Rome in Rom 6:1f. call the members to remember that they (cf. 5:12-21) have experienced a change of dominion. The statement concerning baptism in 6:3f. includes three factors: 1) Baptism unites those who are baptized with the death of Christ to such a degree that Christ's death is viewed as the death of the one who is baptized. 2) Baptism causes the one who is baptized to share in Christ's burial ("We were buried therefore with him by baptism into death"). 3) Baptism allows the one who is baptized to complete the decisive change to new life which began with faith, so that he might walk from now on in "newness of life" (v. 4) and present himself as a "new creation" (2 Cor 5:17).

According to Gal 3:27, those who have been "baptized into Christ have put on Christ." Thus Christ presents himself in baptism with the proclamation of the forgiveness of sins as the protecting garment that the baptismal candidates receive upon discerning their shame.

While Col 2:12 is linked to Rom 6:4, it states more unambiguously that those who are baptized are raised with Christ in baptism (ἐν ᾧ in v. 12 refers to βαπτίσματι; the variant βαπτισμῷ is meaningless when seen in light of the explanation), and indeed "through faith in the working of God," in which they came to baptism.

1 Cor 12:13 indicates that baptism occurred in the sphere of the Holy Spirit (ἐν ἑνὶ πνεύματι), which creates harmony. Those who are baptized receive at the same moment the Holy Spirit, who was promised to all, as a gift ("all were made to drink of one Spirit"), so that they might be joined to the body of Christ, into whom they are incorporated.

In 1 Cor 10:1-13 Paul warns against a sacramental misuse of baptism that leads to a false security and hinders the obedient life of the NT community of the exodus (cf. 10:13). Thus Paul indicates either that the Israelites at the Red Sea obeyed Moses and passed through the water (they underwent baptism into Moses, v. 2) or that at their passing through the Red Sea salvation was granted to them by God when they were baptized at Moses' command (they were baptized). On the contrary, Paul says, baptism shows saving power only as a renunciation of disobedience when the one who is baptized allows himself to be called to the concrete Yes of obedience.

When Paul comments that he baptized only in exceptional situations (1 Cor 1:14, 16f.), he does not place a low value on baptism, but rather coordinates it with the manner of the proclamation of the gospel. Administering baptism has been delegated to others so that no false attachment between the baptizer and the one who is baptized might come into existence (vv. 13, 15). Thus discipleship rooted in the cross of Christ maintains its only legitimate meaning.

The one baptism (Eph 4:5) is, along with the one Spirit, the one Lord, the one faith, and the one body, testimony of the one God. In this way it stimulates the believer to live in the unity which both is given (v. 3) and is the object of hope (v. 13).

The vicarious baptism "for the dead" in 1 Cor 15:29 does not require closer examination because Paul here refers to a custom in Corinth which he does not sanction: He employs an argument that permits him to catch those who deny the resurrection with the contradiction between their theory and their practice.

8. In the setting of the universal confession of Christ (1 Pet 3:19, 22) and in the face of the threatening adversary (v. 14), Christians are reminded of the foundation of a baptismal address, instruction, or liturgy (see the commentaries) which contains the only definition of baptism in the NT: Baptism is no automatically effective means of purification, but rather the operation of the saving action of God (v. 21) "through the resurrection of Jesus Christ" by which individuals commit themselves to such a directing of the will toward God and the community that, in praying to God and confessing before mankind, they begin to live as the *militia Christi* (4:1) and as witnesses over against a hostile environment. Thus they demonstrate that they "now," like the eight who were redeemed in the generation of Noah (ἀντίτυπον does not mean "contrast," but "likeness"), must proclaim the redemption in word and life (2:9-12) before the imminent end (4:7).

9. **Βαπτισμός** *dipping, washing** (Mark 7:4 [v.l. in v. 8]; here βαπτίσωνται appears in place of ῥαντίσωνται in Koine D Θ *pl*, giving βαπτίζω the meaning of βάπτω; likewise Luke 11:38) is used in Heb 9:10 for ritual washings in Judaism, while βαπτισμῶν διδαχῆς in 6:2 refers to instruction in which the baptismal candidate is taught the difference between Christian baptism and ritual washings in Judaism and paganism. In their "faith toward God" (v. 1) they have received baptism with a view to the ministries which are expected and demanded through the distribution of the Holy Spirit in the "laying on of hands" (cf. 2:4). As a result, Christians whose faith is threatened with apostasy might again learn to take their baptism seriously in the clear knowledge of the meaning of this Christian "washing" (6:1-6).

Βάπτω *dip, immerse.** In John 13:26, in contrast to Mark 14:20 and Matt 26:23, Jesus designates the traitor with the words, "It is he to whom I shall give this morsel when I have dipped it." The "robe dipped in blood" (Rev 19:13; on the variety of textual variants, cf. J. Massyngbaerde Ford, *Revelation* [AB] 320f.) is understandable against the background of Isa 63:1-6. The author attempts to depict the "war of annihilation" against the nations with the help of clearer images and by applying the idea of the high-priestly office to the blood of Christ and the martyrs (H. Kraft, *Offenbarung* [HNT] 249). In Luke 16:24 the rich man in his torment requests Abraham to send Lazarus to "dip the end of his finger in water and cool [the rich man's] tongue."

W. Bieder

βάπτισμα, ατος, τό *baptisma* baptism
→ βαπτίζω.

βαπτισμός, οῦ, ὁ *baptismos* washing
→ βαπτίζω 1, 9.

βαπτιστής, οῦ, ὁ *baptistēs* baptizer*

Lit.: J. Becker, *Johannes der Täufer und Jesus von Nazareth* (1972). — W. H. Brownlee, "John the Baptist in the New Light of Ancient Scrolls," *The Scrolls and the NT* (ed. K. Stendahl; 1957) 33-53. — R. B. Gardnee, *Jesus' Appraisal of John the Baptist* (1973). — P. H. Menoud, *BHH* 871f. — A. Oepke, *TDNT* I, 545f. — J. A. T. Robinson, "The Baptism of John and the Qumran Community," *HTR* 50 (1957) 175-91. — A. Schlatter, *Johannes der Täufer* (1956). — W. Wink, *John the Baptist and the Gospel Tradition* (1968). — For further bibliography see *TWNT* X, 998-1008.

1. Βαπτιστής is a term formed especially and exclusively to describe John (→ Ἰωάννης) the forerunner of Jesus. The word suggests the perception of the extraordinary appearance of this man. With this Jewish Greek designation the special activity of John is indicated: as the Baptist he is not merely a witness to baptism, who stands by and watches as others immerse themselves; nor is he a "preacher of virtue" (so Josephus; cf. Menoud), but is instead the authoritative proclaimer of judgment and repentance (Matt 3:1), who immerses others and gives them instructions on how to conduct themselves (Luke 3:10-14). The Baptist did not baptize himself, but baptized instead all others of Jewish origin. As an ascetic, he fasted, eating "no [normal] food [RSV "bread"] and drinking no wine" (Luke 7:33). He wore a cloak and an undergarment made from camel's hair which had a leather girdle over it (J. Jeremias, *TDNT* II, 938f.), thus resembling Elijah the prophet. He probably did not consider himself the Elijah who was to return, but as "prophet of the most high" wanted to be nothing other than the nameless "voice in the wilderness," preparing the way for the coming baptism of fire.

2. John surpassed all "those born of women" (Matt 11:11 par. Luke 7:28 v.l.), because he brought the period of the law and the prophets to a close (Luke 16:16). As the messenger who led the way for the Messiah (Matt 11:10) in what he proclaimed, he experienced with him opposition from the enemies of God's rule (v. 23; cf. G. Schrenk, *TDNT* I, 609-14). At the same time the smallest in the kingdom of heaven is greater than John (v. 11) because the Baptist stands outside the eschatological realization.

John came into conflict with Herod Antipas, whose wife Herodias caused the tetrarch to behead him (Mark 6:24 v.l., 25 par. Matt 14:8). John had disciples (Matt 11:2 par. Luke 7:18), whom he sent from prison to Jesus and who invoked the authority of their master who had sent them when they asked Jesus about "he who is to come" (Luke 7:20). They later buried their beheaded master (Mark 6:29 par. Matt 14:12). When some said that Jesus (Mark 8:28; Luke 9:19) or the Son of Man (Matt 16:14) was John the Baptist (Mark 8:28; v.l. has βαπτίζοντα), it appears that eschatological expectations had been transferred to John the Baptist. When Herod in Matt 14:2 thinks that he recognizes John the Baptist raised from the dead in the works of Jesus, the report suggests the impact of the Baptist even after his death. He continued to be honored as the Baptist by Jesus' disciples (17:13). While the people believed that Jesus was the Elijah who was to return (16:14), Jesus recognized in the Baptist the Elijah who was to return (17:12). With the acceptance of this Jesus tradition, the early Church confessed Jesus as the Messiah.

W. Bieder

βάπτω *baptō* dip, immerse
→ βαπτίζω 1, 9.

Βαραββᾶς, ᾶ *Barabbas* Barabbas

Lit.: A. Bajsić, "Pilatus, Jesus und Barabbas," *Bib* 48 (1967) 7-28. — Billerbeck I, 1031. — J. Blinzler, *Der Prozeß Jesu* (1969) 301-20. — A. van den Born, *BL* 166. — D. Dormeyer, *Die Passion Jesu als Verhaltensmodell* (1974) 179-86. — R. Dunkerley, "Was Barabbas Also Called Jesus?" *ExpTim* 74 (1962/63) 126f. — H. Frankemölle, *Jahwebund und Kirche Christi* (1974) 202-4. — M. Hengel, *Die Zeloten* (1961) 347f. — H. Z. Maccoby, "Jesus and Barabbas," *NTS* 16 (1969/70) 55-60. — M. Herranz Marco, "Un problema de critica historica en el relato de la Pasión: La liberacion de Barabbas," *EstBib* 30 (1971) 137-60. — R. C. Nevius, "A Reply," *ExpTim* 255. — R. Pesch, *Das Markusevangelium* (HTKNT) II (1977) 459-68. — W. Schenk, *Der Passionsbericht nach Markus* (1974) 246-49. — L. Schenke, *Der gekreuzigte Christus* (1974) 42-51. — G. Schneider, *Die Passion Jesu nach den drei älteren Evangelien* (1973) 94-104. — W. Trilling, *Das wahre Israel* (1964) 66-75. — R. Walker, *Die Heilsgeschichte im ersten Evangelium* (1967) 46-48. — S. Wibbing, *BHH* 196f.

1. Barabbas (Aram. *bar 'abbā'*, son of the father/teacher) was a common patronymic (Billerbeck). According to Mark 15:7, 11, 15, a Barabbas (about whom we know nothing outside the NT) was innocently placed in

prison along with "the rebels . . . who had committed murder in the insurrection" (the article assumes that the event was known) and was a candidate for amnesty (ὁ λεγόμενος being taken as "set before") from the people. Pilate, in a futile chess play, wanted to use Barabbas in order to dispose of Jesus' case. It is disputed whether the episode was an original part of the pre-Markan Passion tradition (Dormeyer, Pesch) or whether Mark synchronized an originally independent contrast story that had nothing to do with the events leading up to Jesus' death but refers, instead, to a later incident (perhaps in vv. 6-8, 11, 15a; Schenk, Schenke, Schneider).

2. Matthew (27:15-26) has revised the Markan text most strongly and has made of it a normal condemnation scene. Here the Jewish people are responsible for the essential decision. This formulation is a key text for the origin of Christian anti-Judaism. Luke abbreviates the narrative considerably and suggests the idea of a prisoner exchange. Like Matthew, he has the Jews act collectively, so that they finally appear as initiators of the crucifixion (cf. Acts 3:13-15), while Pilate cannot even decide. The brief report in John 18:39f. is similar. Barabbas first becomes a murderer in Luke and John, a view which cannot be attributed to Mark. It is disputed whether the adj. ἐπίσημος, "famous" (RSV "notorious") added to the name in Matt 27:16 is intended in a negative sense (so Walker, in contrast to Trilling). In the same verse Matthew, according to the Caesarean text, supplies the name "Jesus," which was of course familiar to the readers (→ Ἰησοῦς 3.b). Most copyists regarded this reading as offensive and left it out (Origen *In Matt.* ad loc.: "A sinner cannot be named Jesus!"; see Metzger, *TCGNT* 67f.).

W. Schenk

Βαράκ *Barak* Barak*

Indeclinable name of a hero of Israel after the time of the Conquest (Judg 4:6ff.), who, like Gideon, Samson, Jephthah, David, Samuel, and the prophets, acted "by faith": Heb 11:32. M. Rehm, *LTK* I, 1235; E. Jenni, *BHH* I, 197; *BL* 166f.

Βαραχίας, ου *Barachias* Barachiah*

Matt 23:35 (par. Luke 11:51 D sy, etc.), in a redactional addition to the woes of Jesus against the scribes and Pharisees concerning the persecution and killing of the righteous men and the prophets, mentions Barachiah as the father of a Zechariah who was killed in the temple and who is named as the final member of the series which began with the murder of Abel. Matthew may have in mind the prophet Zechariah, who was the son of Berechiah according to Zech 1:1, 7. A martyr named Zechariah, the son of the high priest Jehoiada, was killed in the temple according to 2 Chr 24:20f., a text similar to Matt 23:35. *Gos. Naz.* 17 identifies the Zechariah of Matt 23:35 as the son of Jehoiada (Hennecke/Schneemelcher I, 149). Probably Matthew has, along with Jewish tradition (Billerbeck I, 940-43), identified the Zechariah of 2 Chronicles (named in his Bible as the last blood witness [Billerbeck IV, 422] along with Abel, the first?) with the prophet. Consequently he gives the name of his father as Barachiah (Berechiah). It is possible that there is a reference here to Zechariah, the son of a Bariskaeus/Baruch, who was murdered in the temple by the Zealots in A.D. 67-68, according to Josephus *BJ* iv.334ff. (so Steck). BAGD s.v.; S. A. Blank, "The Death of Zechariah in Rabbinic Literature," *HUCA* 12 (1937/38) 327-46; K. Stendahl, *BHH* I, 217; A. E. Rüthy, *BHH* III, 1636f.; O. H. Steck, *Israel und das gewaltsame Geschick der Propheten* (WMANT 23, 1967) 33-40, index s.v. Sacharja ben Bariscaeus/ben Jojada.

H. Balz

βάρβαρος, 2 *barbaros* speaking unintelligibly (in a foreign language); foreign; uneducated; subst.: a non-Greek person, barbarian*

1. Occurrences in the NT — 2. Meaning among Greeks and Jews — 3. Meaning in the NT

Lit.: BAGD s.v. (bibliography). — N. A. Dahl, *BHH* I, 197f. — H. Dörrie, "Die Wertung der Barbaren im Urteil der Griechen. Knechtsnaturen? Oder Bewahrer und Künder heilbringender Weisheit?" FS H. E. Stier (*Fontes et commentationes* Suppl. 1, 1972) 146-75. — T. Hermann, "Barbar und Skythe. Ein Erklärungsversuch zu Kol 3, 11," *TBl* 9 (1930) 106f. — L. Huber, *LAW* 433-35 (bibliography). — J. Jüthner, *RAC* I, 1173-76. —*idem, Hellenen und Barbaren* (Erbe der Alten Welt 9, 1923). — O. Michel, *TDNT* VII, 447-50. — E. Pax, *LTK* I, 1235. — W. Speyer and I. Opelt, "Barbar," JAC 10 (1967) 251-90. — H. Windisch, *TDNT*, I, 546-53. — For further bibliography see *TWNT* X, 1008.

1. Βάρβαρος occurs 6 times in the NT, twice in Acts (28:2, 4 subst.), 3 times in Paul's letters (Rom 1:14 subst.; 1 Cor 14:11 [bis] adj. or subst.), and in Col 3:11.

2. The onomatopoeia of the word (doubling of the initial syllable) leads to the basic meaning, "speak with a stammer, make unintelligible sounds." From this origin it designates finally anyone who speaks a non-Greek language and who is recognized as a foreigner (cf. esp. Strabo xiv.2.28; Herodotus ii.158 of the Egyptians; also Ps 113:1 LXX of the Egyptians, who from the point of view of Israel speak a foreign language). The Pauline phrase Ἕλληνες καὶ βάρβαροι (Rom 1:14) is very common (e.g., Plato *Tht.* 175a), and refers, from the Greek perspective, to the totality of all peoples. Occasionally among the Greeks the natural equality of all people is emphasized (esp. the Sophist Antipho, fragment 44.2.10ff.).

After the Persian War βάρβαρος referred less to nationality and more to education and culture. This cosmopolitanism succeeded only with difficulty, however. The Romans gained for themselves a place among the Ἕλληνες first with increasing Hellenization. In 2 Macc 2:21 the "foreign" (RSV "barbarian") Syrians are considered βάρβαροι by the Jews. According to *Ep. Arist.* 122, from the Hellenistic Jewish view one can speak of τὸ . . . βάρβαρον with reference to everything that is foreign and uneducated (see further Windisch 549-51).

3. Acts 28:2, 4 uses οἱ βάρβαροι in the national-political sense of the (predominantly Punic-speaking) inhabitants of Malta, who demonstrated "unusual kindness" to those who were stranded. The reference is surely formulated by the author on the basis of early Christian cosmopolitanism in order to say: Barbarians can be distinguished from Greeks only by language.

According to Rom 1:14 Paul's apostolic commission is meant for all peoples, Ἕλλησίν τε καὶ βαρβάροις, which is immediately followed by σοφοῖς καὶ ἀνοήτοις. Βάρβαροι thus means here, in accordance with proper Greek usage, those of non-Greek linguistic origin as well as those of non-Greek education. The Romans who are addressed are apparently included among the Ἕλληνες. Βάρβαροι alludes here most specifically to the Spaniards, who are the objects of Paul's missionary plans. In connection with his universal commission for the ἔθνη Paul emphasizes—strikingly carefully—his right to preach in Rome also (v. 15). Nevertheless, v. 16 indicates, in the formulation Ἰουδαίῳ . . . καὶ Ἕλληνι, that for Paul, a good Jew, the traditional distinction between Greek and non-Greek is irrelevant. Thus Ἕλλην here can refer comprehensively to every non-Jew.

In connection with baptism, Col 3:11 lists four pairs in a formulaic series: in the third place, after Ἕλλην καὶ Ἰουδαῖος and περιτομὴ καὶ ἀκροβυστία, βάρβαρος and Σκύθης are mentioned alongside each other, followed by δοῦλος and ἐλεύθερος. The old distinctions and tensions are taken away among those who are made new according to the image of their Creator (cf. vv. 8-10). Thus the first two groups refer to the opposition between Jews and Gentile Christians. In the following groups in the series (against Windisch 550) national and finally social barriers are mentioned. These barriers have lost their meaning for the Church. Βάρβαρος refers then, as usual, to any person of non-Greek origin, while Σκύθης refers to an especially unfamiliar people (cf. Josephus *Ap.* ii.269). Some understand the third pair in the series as opposites, taking βάρβαρος as the inhabitants of Ethiopia and Somalia and Σκύθης as a northern people (Hermann 106f.; cf. Jüthner, *Hellenen* 54ff., 143f.; see also Michel 449f., n. 11).

Βάρβαρος appears with its original meaning in 1 Cor 14:11 (bis) for one who speaks a strange, unintelligible language and for one who, from the perspective of the speaker, does not understand.

H. Balz

βαρέω *bareō* burden, oppress*

All instances of this vb. in the NT are fig. and pass.: Matt 26:43 (par. Mark 14:40 C Koine Θ, etc.) in the Gethsemane narrative, of the *heaviness* of eyelids; Luke 9:32 in the transfiguration story with ὕπνῳ, to be "*heavy* with sleep"; 21:34 in the warning against *weighing down* the heart with dissipation, drunkenness, etc.: Luke apparently adopts the widespread expression "heavy with wine" in order to express the danger of dullness and encumbrance through the pleasures and cares of this world (cf., however, βαρέω, e.g., in Exod 7:14 LXX). Βαρέω is used by Paul not to evaluate, but rather to state the facts: in 2 Cor 1:8, of his scarcely bearable and life-threatening burden or affliction in Asia; in 5:4, of the sighs of those who are *weighted down* (βαρούμενοι used absolutely) because, though they will be free from the earthly body, they want to be clothed with the heavenly body (vv. 2f.): at the present they await the parousia under the burden of the present existence. The word is used in a general sense in 1 Tim 5:16: The Church should not be *burdened* by supporting widows who have women (widows?) relatives who are capable of taking care of them. G. Schrenk, *TDNT* I, 558-61; W. Mundle, *DNTT* I, 261; BDF §101 s.v.

H. Balz

βαρέως *bareōs* with difficulty*

Matt 13:15; Acts 28:27 (both citing Isa 6:10 LXX): τοῖς ὠσὶν βαρέως ἤκουσαν, "they hardly hear[d] with their ears" (NIV), i.e., "they did not want to hear."

Βαρθολομαῖος, ου *Bartholomaios* Bartholomew*

From Aram. *bar talmay* (cf. 2 Sam 3:3), the name of a disciple-apostle from the circle of the twelve. Bartholomew is referred to only in the Synoptic lists of the twelve (Mark 3:18 par. Matt 10:3/Luke 6:14) and in the list of apostles in Acts 1:13. He is mentioned by the Synoptics in sixth place, after Philip and before Matthew or Thomas; in Acts he is in seventh place, after Thomas and before Matthew. Because of his position next to Philip he has been, since the 9th cent., often identified with Nathanael (John 1:45). According to Eusebius *HE* v.10.3 he brought the Hebrew Gospel of Matthew to India. U. Holzmeister, "Nathanael fuitne idem ac S. Bartholomaeus Apostolus?" *Bib* 21 (1940) 28-39; W. Schmauch, *RGG* I, 898f.; M. Rissi, *BHH* I, 201; *BL* 169f.

Βαριησοῦ *Bariēsou* Bar-Jesus*

Name of a Jewish magician (Aram. *bar iᵉšûaʿ*) in the entourage of Sergius Paulus at Paphos on Cyprus, according to Acts 13:6. Saul and Barnabas came into conflict with

Bar-Jesus, who was also called → Elymas (v. 8). Βαριησοῦ is the reading of 𝔭[74] ℵ 181 242 vg, etc.; the Grecized form -ους appears in B C E 33, etc.; the acc. -ουν is found in A D[2] H L, etc.; -ουαν in D*; *-uam* in d; and -ουμα in sy[p]; cf. further *TCGNT* ad loc.; W. Bieder, *BHH* I, 196; *BL* 167. → Ἰησοῦς 3.e.

Βαριωνᾶ *Bariōna* Bar-Jona*

Surname (patronymic) of Simon (Aram. *bar yônâ;* cf. Jonah 1:1): Matt 16:17. According to John 1:42; *Gos. Heb.* 9, however, Simon was the son of John; cf., however, *TRE* III, 603f. See also BAGD ad loc. (bibliography); B. Alger, "Simon Barjona," *Scr* 12 (1960) 89-92.

Βαρναβᾶς, ᾶ *Barnabas* Barnabas*

Lit.: P. Benoit, "La deuxième visite de S. Paul à Jerusalem," *Bib* 40 (1959) 778-92. — H. Conzelmann, *History of Primitive Christianity* (1973) index s.v. — H. Evans, "Barnabas the Bridge-Builder," *ExpTim* 89 (1977/78) 248-50. — B. Gärtner, "Paulus und Barnabas in Lystra. Zu Apg 14, 8-15," *SEÅ* 27 (1962) 83-93. — E. Haenchen, *Acts of the Apostles* (1971) index s.v. — C. H. Talbert, "Again: Paul's Visits to Jerusalem," *NovT* 9 (1967) 26-40.

1. The name Barnabas occurs in the NT 23 times in Acts and in 1 Cor 9:6; Gal 2:1, 9, 13; and Col 4:10, 23 as the surname of Joseph, a Jewish Levite from Cyprus (Acts 4:36). Its translation as "Son of encouragement" (Acts 4:36) is problematic (cf. Haenchen 232). Neither the letters nor Acts indicates the real meaning of the name.

As a Diaspora Jew who has become resident in Jerusalem, Barnabas appears as a Christian who, though not in the Hellenistic leadership circle there, nonetheless establishes the connection with the new church in Antioch after the persecution of the Hellenists. From that point he becomes, next to Paul, one of the most important missionaries to the Gentiles (cf. Acts 11:22-26; 13:1–14:28; 1 Cor 9:6). As "the chief mediator between the two great centers" (Conzelmann 66) Barnabas brings a collection to Jerusalem (11:30), perhaps without Paul (cf. Benoit; Haenchen 64, 377-79 against Talbert). At the Apostolic Council the "pillars" conclude their agreement with Paul and Barnabas (Gal 2:1, 9), who appear as delegates of the Antiochian church (Haenchen 443f.). At the dispute about table fellowship with the Gentile Christians (vv. 11-21), Barnabas (along with Peter) probably opposes Paul, as the further silence of Galatians allows one to assume.

2. According to Acts, Barnabas is a mediator between the apostles and Paul. In contrast to Gal 1:18f., Paul is introduced to the apostles by Barnabas shortly after Paul's conversion (9:27). Barnabas comes to Antioch (11:22) as "an official investigator" on behalf of the Jerusalem Christians (Conzelmann 66). He transmits the concern for association with the mother church to Paul. In the sending of the collection to Jerusalem (11:30; 12:25), in the mission to Cyprus and Asia Minor (13:1, 2, 7, 43, 46, 50; 14:12, 14, 20), and in connection with the Apostolic Council (15:2 bis, 12, 22, 25, 35) Barnabas and Paul are always named together, a total of 17 times, normally connected by καί. After 13:7, to be sure—in 13:9 "Saul" becomes "Paul"—Paul stands first (except for 15:12, 25), appearing from that point as the chief personality and main spokesman. Barnabas withdraws, and is almost "merely an extra" (H. Conzelmann, *Acts* [Hermeneia] on 14:12). Luke has turned a dispute over principle (Gal 2:13) into a dispute over persons (Acts 15:36f., 39; cf. Haenchen 475-77), i.e., concerning John Mark, who according to Col 4:10 was a cousin of Barnabas. After the Apostolic Council, Barnabas can withdraw from the stage, for he has functioned essentially as a mediator. In this respect Acts is not only a book about Peter and Paul, but also a book about Barnabas.

W. Radl

βάρος, ους, τό *baros* burden; weight, abundance*

All 6 NT occurrences of this word are—as is frequently the case with this word in Greek literature—used fig.: Matt 20:12 τὸ βάρος τῆς ἡμέρας, of the *burden* of the whole day's work; Acts 15:28, of the *burden* of legal requirements (cf. v. 10 ἐπιθεῖναι ζυγόν; see also 1 Macc 8:31 and, e.g., *m. 'Abot* 3:5 and many other references to the "yoke of the law"), which were limited to the necessary minimum; cf. Acts 2:24.

In Gal 6:2 Paul exhorts the readers to bear one another's *burdens* (cf. *Diog.* 10:6); the concern in v. 1 is esp. help for the fallen brother, by which the true gift of the πνευματικοί is demonstrated. From a wider standpoint τὰ βάρη refers here comprehensively to the vulnerability of Christian existence, in which even the pneumatic must carry his own part (v. 5). In contrast to this usage is the secular meaning of βάρος in 1 Thess 2:7 (ἐν βάρει εἶναι; v. 6 in English versions) in the sense of *weight, reputation* which Paul could have claimed for himself as an apostle of Christ.

In 2 Cor 4:17 Paul contrasts his present light suffering with αἰώνιον βάρος δόξης, which represents the fruit of suffering. Βάρος is used in the image of weight; αἰώνιος appears in contrast to παραυτίκα. The present suffering, which weighs little, produces a heavy weight of eternal glory, i.e., an *abundance* of eternal glory (cf. Rom 8:18). G. Schrenk, *TDNT* I, 553-56; C. von Gablenz, *BHH* II, 1050; J. G. Strelan, "Burden-Bearing and the Law of Christ," *JBL* 94 (1975) 266-76; W. Mundle, *DNTT* I, 260-62.

H. Balz

Βαρσαββᾶς, ᾶ *Barsabbas* Barsabbas*

From Aram. *bar sā'ḇā',* "son of the old man" or *bar šᵉḇā',* "son of the sabbath," the patronymic of: 1) Joseph, also called Justus, who was in the lot but was not chosen as successor for Judas (Acts 1:23; he is numbered by Eusebius *HE* i.12.3 among the seventy disciples of Luke 10:1); 2) Judas, who, with Barnabas and Silas, was a companion of Paul in the delivery of the apostolic decrees from Jerusalem to Antioch (Acts 15:22, cf. v. 27; according to v. 22 he had a leading place in Jerusalem; according to v. 32 he was, like Silas, a προφήτης). E. Kamlah, *BHH* I, 200; W. C. van Unnik, *BHH* II, 903; *BL* 169.

Βαρτιμαῖος, ου *Bartimaios* Bartimaeus*

Probably from Aram. *bar ṭimay,* the surname of a blind beggar whom Jesus healed on the road as he departed from Jericho (Mark 10:46). Mark introduces the blind man Bartimaeus with the translation of his surname as ὁ υἱὸς Τιμαίου. Since J. Wellhausen (*Das Evangelium Marci* [1909] 85) it has been assumed that Aram. *ṭimay* (-τιμαῖος) is an abbreviation of "Timothy." Cf. BAGD s.v. (bibliography); E. Gross, *BHH* I, 201; on Jewish parallels, see Billerbeck II, 25.

βαρύνω *barynō* weigh down

Luke 21:34; Acts 3:14; 28:27; 2 Cor 5:4, v.l. in all instances.

βαρύς, 3 *barys* heavy; difficult; important, weighty; fierce*

This adj. occurs 6 times in the NT, literally of *heavy* burdens in Matt 23:4; fig.: of the *more important* parts of the law (v. 23); of "*serious* charges" (Acts 25:7); of Paul's letters, which are *weighty,* unlike his personal presence (2 Cor. 10:10, with ἰσχυραί); in reference to God's commandments, which are not *difficult* to carry out (1 John 5:3); in a portrayal of the Church's destroyers as *cruel, fierce* wolves (Acts 20:29). G. Schrenk, *TDNT* I, 556-58; W. Mundle, *DNTT* I, 261f.

βαρύτιμος, 2 *barytimos* very costly, precious*

Matt 26:7, of anointing oil (v.l. has πολύτιμος; cf. John 12:3); the meaning of the word is similar to that of the expressions "very dear" and "sumptuous."

βασανίζω *basanizō* torture, torment (vb.)*
βασανισμός, οῦ, ὁ *basanismos* torture, the act of being tortured*
βασανιστής, οῦ, ὁ *basanistēs* torturer*
βάσανος, ου, ἡ *basanos* torment, torture (noun)*

Lit.: W. Mundle, *DNTT* III, 855f.; J. Schneider, *TDNT* I, 561-63.

1. Of the 12 occurrences of the vb. βασανίζω in the NT, 5 are in Revelation (9:5; 11:10; 12:2; 14:10; 20:10), 3 in Matthew (8:6, 29; 14:24), 2 in Mark (5:7; 6:48), 1 in Luke (8:28), and 1 in 2 Peter (2:8). Βασανισμός occurs only 6 times (Rev 9:5 bis; 14:11; 18:7; 10:15). Βασανιστής is a NT hapax legomenon (Matt 18:34); βάσανος occurs in Matt 4:24 and Luke 16:23, 28.

2. Βασανίζω and βάσανος can refer to bodily pain or injury and can also be used in connection with illness (Matt 4:24). The servant of the centurion was severely *tormented* by an illness (8:6). That the apocalyptic woman is tormented by the *pains* of childbirth (Rev 12:2) indicates that the word is used for especially intensive bodily pain. But mental pains can also be meant: The wicked behavior of the Sodomites caused the righteous Lot to be depressed (2 Pet 2:7) and *tormented* in his soul (v. 8). The verb has a more general meaning when the boat of the disciples (Matt 14:24) or the disciples themselves at the rudder *are harassed* by the wind and the waves (Mark 6:48). If one understands Mark 6:48 as mid. rather than pass., the text can be understood to mean that the disciples *were straining* at the helm.

Because βασανίζω and its derivatives speak of a special intensity of *torment,* it came to be used where the subject is the other-worldly or eschatological eternal punishment following the judgment. Thus the rich glutton finds himself *in torment,* namely in Hades, the "place of *torment*" (Luke 16:23, 28). The worshippers of the beast (Rev 14:10), like the devil, the beast, and the false prophet (20:10), *will be tormented* forever. The torment that will strike the whore Babylon is the recompense for her guilt (18:7, 10, 15). This torment is both mental, because it is connected with fear and mourning, and bodily, inasmuch as the other-worldly or eternal torment is depicted in the passages cited with the phenomena of heat or fire (e.g., "the smoke of her burning," v. 18). Matt 8:29, at least, understands the torment with which the demons feel tormented through the presence of Jesus or his command to depart (Mark 5:7f.; Luke 8:28f.) as a premature (from the demons' viewpoint) movement toward their eternal punishment. The *torturers* to whom a master spoken of in a parable consigns his unmerciful servant (Matt 18:34) point to the eschatological punishment.

Where, by contrast, βασανίζω describes the activity of the two eschatological prophets toward earth's inhabitants (Rev 11:10), the punishment after the judgment is not in mind. With the renewal of the Egyptian plagues (v. 6), people are to be *tormented* in order that they might be brought to repentance. Similarly, the swarm of locusts precedes the day of judgment in order to *torment* with their sting those who do not wear the seal of God on their foreheads. This torment occurs for five months, i.e., a limited amount of time. According to the wider context (cf. 9:20f.) it is intended to bring them to repentance. The comparison of this *torment* with that of scorpions (v. 5) indicates once more its intensity (the sting of the scorpion is very painful).

W. Stenger

βασανισμός, οῦ, ὁ *basanismos* torture, the act of being tortured
→ βασανίζω.

βασανιστής, οῦ, ὁ *basanistēs* torturer
→ βασανίζω.

βάσανος, ου, ἡ *basanos* torment, torture (noun)
→ βασανίζω.

βασιλεία, ας, ἡ *basileia* kingdom, reign

1. Overview — 2. Secular usage — 3. "The kingdom of God" — a) According to Jesus — b) Mark — c) Matthew —d) Luke/Acts — e) John — f) The letters —4. "The kingdom of Christ"

Lit.: S. Aalen, " 'Reign' and 'House' in the Kingdom of God in the Gospels," *NTS* 8 (1961/62) 215-40. — A. Ambrozic, *The Hidden Kingdom* (1972) (on Mark). — E. Bammel, "Erwägungen zur Eschatologie Jesu," *SE* III (1964) 3-32. — W. Barclay, *The King and His Kingdom* (1969). — G. R. Beasley-Murray, *Jesus and the Kingdom of God* (1986) (bibliography). — J. Becker, *Das Heil Gottes* (SUNT 3, 1964) 197-217. — F. Beisser, *Das Reich Gottes* (1976). — H. Bietenhard, *Das tausendjährige Reich* (1955). — H. Conzelmann, *RGG* V, 912-18 (bibliography). — *idem, The Theology of St Luke* (1961) (on Luke). — O. Cullmann, "The Kingship of Christ and the Church in the NT," *idem, The Early Church* (1956) 103-37. — Dalman, *Worte* 75-119. — C. H. Dodd, *The Parables of the Kingdom* (revised edition, 1961). — H. Flender, *Die Botschaft Jesu von der Herrschaft Gottes* (1968). — H. Frankemölle, *Jahwebund und Kirche Christi* (NTAbh 10, 1974) 264-73 (on Matthew). — E. Grässer, *Die Naherwartung Jesu* (1973). — *idem,* "Zum Verständnis der Gottesherrschaft," *ZNW* 65 (1974) 3-26. — M. Hengel, *Die Zeloten* (1976) 93-114; 308-15. — J. Héring, *Le Royaume de Dieu et sa venue* ([2]1959). — R. Hiers, *The Historical Jesus and the Kingdom of God* (1974). — E. Jüngel, *Paulus und Jesus* (1972). — W. Kelber, *The Kingdom in Mark* (1974). — J. D. Kingsbury, *Matthew: Structure, Christology, Kingdom* (1976). — B. Klappert, *DNTT* II, 372-90 (bibliography). — G. Klein, " 'Reich Gottes' als biblischer Zentralbegriff," *EvT* 30 (1970) 642-70. — A. Kretzer, *Die Herrschaft der Himmel und die Söhne des Reiches* (1971) (on Matthew). — W. G. Kümmel, *Promise and Fulfillment* (SBT 23, 1961). — *idem,* "Eschatological Expectation in the Proclamation of Jesus," *The Future of our Religious Past* (FS R. Bultmann, ed. J. M. Robinson; 1971) 29-48. — G. E. Ladd, *The Presence of the Future* (1974). — E. Lohse, "Die Gottesherrschaft in den Gleichnissen Jesu," *EvT* 18 (1958) 145-57. — T. Lorenzmeier, "Zum Logion Mt 12, 28; Lk 11, 20," FS Braun 289-304. — G. Lundström, *The Kingdom of God in the Teaching of Jesus* (1963). — F. W. Maier, *Jesus—Lehrer der Gottesherrschaft* (1965). — I. Maisch, "Die Botschaft Jesu von der Gottesherrschaft," *Gottesherrschaft und kommendes Reich* (FS A. Vögtle, 1975) 27-48. — O. Merk, "Das Reich Gottes in den lukanischen Schriften," FS Kümmel 201-20. —R. Otto, *The Kingdom of God and the Son of Man* (1943). — N. Perrin, *The Kingdom of God in the Teaching of Jesus* (1963). — *idem, Rediscovering the Teaching of Jesus* (1963). — *idem, Jesus and the Language of the Kingdom* (1976). — A. Polag, *Die Christologie der Logienquelle* (1977) 48-59. — K. H. Schelkle, "Königsherrschaft Gottes," *BibLeb* 15 (1974) 120-35. — J. Schlosser, *Les dits du 'Règne de Dieu' dans les logia de Luc et de Matthieu* (Diss. Strasbourg, 1973/74). — K. L. Schmidt, *TDNT* I, 576-93. (bibliography). — W. Schmithals, "Jesus und die Weltlichkeit des Reiches Gottes," *idem, Jesus Christus in der Verkündigung der Kirche* (1972) 91-117. — R. Schnackenburg, *God's Rule and Kingdom* (1963). — W. Trilling, *Das wahre Israel* ([3]1964) 143-54. — P. Vielhauer, "Gottesreich und Menschensohn in der Verkündigung Jesu," FS G. Dehn (1957) 51-79 = Vielhauer, *Aufsätze zum NT* (1965) 55-91. — M. Völkel, "Zur Deutung des 'Reiches Gottes' bei Lukas," *ZNW* 65 (1974) 57-70. — J. Weiss, *Jesus' Proclamation of the Kingdom of God* (1971). — H. Wenz, *Theologie des Reiches Gottes. Hat Jesus sich geirrt?* (1975). — T. Wieser, *Kingdom and Church in Luke-Acts* (Diss. Union Theological Seminary, New York, 1962). — S. G. Wilson, *The Gentiles and the Gentile Mission in Luke-Acts* (1973) 59-89. — H. Windisch, "Die Sprüche vom Eingehen in das Reich Gottes," *ZNW* 27 (1928) 163-92. — P. Wolf, "Gericht und Reich Gottes bei Johannes und Jesus," *Gottesherrschaft und kommendes Reich* (FS A. Vögtle, 1975) 43-49. — For further bibliography see *TWNT* X, 1008-14.

1. Most of the 162 uses of βασιλεία in the NT employ the word in the phrase βασιλεία τοῦ θεοῦ (or βασιλεία τῶν οὐρανῶν or τοῦ πατρός) and are found in the Synoptic Gospels. "Kingdom of God" is a typical usage of the "language of Christ," i.e., the speech of Jesus and of the Church's formulations dependent on his speech. The impressive power of this "language of Christ" is suggested by the fact that in later texts βασιλεία stands alone, obviously in place of "kingdom of God" (inconceivable in Jewish literature), especially in Matthew, but also in Luke, Hebrews, and James. In later texts especially, references speak in various ways of the βασιλεία of Christ (→ 4). By contrast, the NT texts that speak of βασιλεία without a reference to God or Christ are relatively rare.

2. In secular Greek the meaning of the word alternates between a functional sense—*royal sovereignty, monarchy, royal dignity, royal office*—and the geographical sense of *kingdom* or *realm.* Heb. *malkûṯ* can also mean not only "royal sovereignty," but also "kingdom" (KBL^2 s.v.). Both meanings are also represented in the NT: sometimes the reference is to *kingdom* or *realm* (e.g., Matt 4:8; Mark 6:23; 13:8; Rev 16:10), and sometimes to *royal sovereignty* (e.g., Luke 19:12, 15; Rev 1:6; 17:12). At times which it represents cannot be determined (e.g., Matt 12:25f.). This poses difficulties for translation, since *kingdom* (Germ. *Reich*) does not include the functional meaning, and the use of *sovereignty (Herrschaft)* to represent the geographical sense is obsolete today.

3. The kingdom of God (= KG). a) According to Jesus.

In the view of most interpreters the origin and central content of Jesus' proclamation as a whole is determined by the KG, even in texts where the word βασιλεία does not appear (otherwise: Bammel). It is important that Jesus does not teach ideologically or impart theological instruction on a branch of study known as the KG. Instead, on the basis of the beginning of the KG as a radical and unlimited love of God, he calls each person to a life in love here and now. Indeed, because Jesus is concerned primarily about a *life lived here and now on the basis of the coming of the kingdom,* there are many texts that are determined by the coming of the kingdom that do not mention the KG explicitly. This is especially true for most of the parables. Only in a few of them is the KG mentioned in the presumed original version (mustard seed, Mark 4:30; Luke 13:8; leaven, Luke 13:20; the seed growing by itself, Mark 4:25; treasure in the field, Matt 13:44; pearl, v. 45; possibly the weeds among the wheat, v. 24 and the seine net, v. 47), although many are concerned with the KG, insofar as they lead to a life based on its reality or want to concretize the love of God. Jesus' *proclamation* of the KG is to be seen in the texts which speak directly of the KG, to which the discussion here will be limited; but the information derived from these texts is not exhaustive.

Jesus proclaims the KG as an *event.* This is evident from the many temporal references associated with the βασιλεία τοῦ θεοῦ. There are statements in which the coming of the KG is expected in the future (Matt 6:10; Mark 14:25; Luke 6:20b with v. 21); elsewhere a summarizing formula appears: "the KG has come near" (Luke 10:11, etc.). Apparently Jesus lived in an imminent expectation (Grässer). He would then have shared the imminent expectation of his teacher, John the Baptist (Luke 3:9a). The imminent expectation of the first churches, newly strengthened by the resurrection of Jesus, would then have stood in continuity with Jesus. But Jesus gave little weight to the immediate expectation; he also gave no further information concerning times and stages.

Alongside the future sayings stand present sayings. They are, of course, more difficult to interpret because we no longer have the Aramaic wording. Luke 11:20 is important: φθάνω (used here in aor.!) is not just a synonym of ἐγγίζω; what is meant is that the KG has broken in with the concrete event of Jesus' exorcisms. The understanding of this passage as present is supported by 10:18 and the cryptic remark of 11:21f.: Jesus apparently saw in the exorcisms signs of the final overcoming of the kingdom of Satan through his own works. Despite the absence of the copula, 17:21 may also be understood as present: the KG is in your midst (probably also: available to you). The saying wards off time speculations and the thought that one can localize the KG in a definite place. If the saying is not connected with the perceptible presence of the KG, the text becomes meaningless in its context. Finally, Matt 11:12f., the "violence passage," is also to be understood as a reference to the present (→ βιάζομαι). Its meaning is, of course, unclear. If one accepts the Matthean wording in v. 12 as the older, one understands βιάζεται as pass. and, like the enigmatic → ἁρπάζω, in a negative sense. Thus it could be understood as a reference to the war of the political powers against the KG beginning with the murder of John the Baptist (with the period after John understood as the beginning of the violence) or to the power of the Zealots (which makes ἁρπάζω easily understood).

It is clear that the references to time are not to be harmonized. The contradictions in the time references may even have their origin in the nonobjectifying speech of Jesus about the KG. In Jesus, especially in his miracles, the future, cosmic KG exists as a present event. In such a nonobjectifying manner the two parables of the mustard seed and the leaven (Luke 13:18-21) point to the hidden beginning of the worldwide (Luke 13:19b; Mark 4:32b!) KG.

The coexistence of present and future sayings is identifiable also in Judaism. The rabbis thought primarily in terms of the continuity of God's sovereignty in history all the way to the eschaton and saw God's sovereignty as effective historically in the recitation of the confession and in the keeping of the law. The kingdom will be manifest at the eschaton with the liberation of Israel (cf. the eleventh and twelfth of the Eighteen Benedictions; other prayers in Dalman 82f.). In the apocalyptic literature the distance from God is perceptible, and the eschatological-future sovereignty of God becomes more important, although statements about the present are not entirely lacking (e.g., Dan 2:37; 4:34; 1QM 12:7). Jesus employs primarily the terminology of the apocalyptists (by way of John the Baptist?), and speaks of the presence of the *new,* eschatological sovereignty of God that is becoming realized and that is in contrast to this world. He thinks in formal terms as do the Zealots, who also anticipate the immediate coming of the cosmic sovereignty of God and whose actions are determined by this expectation (Hengel). The content of the KG is entirely different for the Zealots, however.

The particular character of Jesus' terminology demonstrates that his concern is with the present coming of the eschatological, cosmic KG, which comes from beyond and is created by God himself. The βασιλεία τοῦ θεοῦ is not only the sovereignty of God in a functional sense; it is also a particular *place, in which* one can be (Matt 8:11f.; 11:11; Mark 14:25) or into which one can enter (Mark 9:47; 10:25; cf. Matt 21:31; Mark 12:34). In comparison with Jewish texts it is striking that Jesus, in many cases, speaks of the KG in the same way that the rabbis speak of the coming aeon (the eschatological meal, to be great in the KG, to be admitted to the kingdom, to inherit it, to be prepared; cf. Dalman 91f., 93, 95, 102, 105). This language also suggests the cosmic, universal, eschatological character of the KG in the teaching of Jesus.

In contrast to history, the motif of discontinuity is dominant. It is significant that Jesus rarely speaks in general of God as king (→ βασιλεύς). In addition, any notion of national and theopolitical elements are lacking in the proclamation of Jesus about the KG. The opposite of the KG is not, as in many Jewish texts, Roman rule; Jesus does not speak of the coming political sovereignty of Israel; indeed he can employ the idea of the KG critically and polemically in a word of judgment against Israel (Matt 8:11f.).

In contrast to Judaism the decisively new element in Jesus' proclamation of the KG, apart from the association of the kingdom with his own sending, is the interpretation of the content of the kingdom as the unlimited, boundless *love of God* esp. toward the despised and the disenfranchised of Israel—the poor, women, sinners, Samaritans, etc. This love of God is defined by its connection with the eschatological KG. It is unsurpassable, ultimate, and not simply derived from God's previous salvific institutions, creation and the law. Jesus grants the (future) KG unconditionally to those who are poor (materially; Luke 6:20; cf. v. 21). The parable of the great supper, which uses imagery drawn from the idea of the joyous eschatological meal in the KG, an image that was familiar to Jesus (Matt 8:11f.; Mark 14:25), is to be understood in this way. Jesus can speak of the βασιλεία as a blessing of salvation, e.g., for children who are not of age in a legal or ethical sense (Mark 10:14f.). The exorcisms and healings are also to be understood in light of the approaching KG, which comes in the form of the love of God.

The kingdom parables of the treasure and the pearl (Matt 13:44f.) point ultimately to the dimension of decision and human involvement connected with the KG. This human engagement is not involved in the realization of the KG, which, according to Mark 4:27f., is alone a matter for God. Instead the blessing of salvation in these parables (treasure, pearl) is prior to human activity, even though it is received only by human activity. Mark 9:47 mentions the absolute battle against sin in the presence of the KG, a battle which is without compromise and for which no price is too great. How one is to conduct himself is explained in other parables that do not speak directly of the KG and in the love commandment. A particular form of involvement in the KG is discipleship, which demands the renunciation of one's occupation, families ties, and possessions in the service of a special commission of proclaiming the KG (Luke 9:60c [authenticity is disputed]; cf. v. 62). This commission is not intended for everyone. Similarly, the possibility of celibacy for the sake of the KG (Matt 19:12) is even less a matter for all disciples (cf. Peter according to Mark 1:30; 1 Cor 9:5).

The post-Easter tradition of the Church includes words of Jesus about the kingdom that are stamped by the Church's situation. Thus the Church has augmented the words of Jesus and cultivated Jesus' own characteristic terminology. Presumably the following passages, among others, are to be considered Church formulations: Matt 5:19 (levels of salvation in the KG); Mark 9:1 (post-Easter imminent expectation with a fixed terminus); Matt 16:19 (the power of the keys).

b) Mark does not employ the expression KG in a redactional way. His summary of the proclamation of Jesus in 1:15 existed prior to his Gospel and may go back to the tradition. An old logion in 4:11, which may go back to the Aramaic-speaking Church, summarizes the Christian proclamation as the "mystery of the kingdom." In the present context it describes the proclamation in parables. The indication that the disciples, in contrast to the outsiders, understand the mystery is made relative in vv. 33f. by their lack of understanding. The limited number of references to the KG in Mark is inadequate to allow one to postulate a particular Markan understanding of the KG, either in the sense of a christological dialectic of present hiddenness and future glory (Ambrozic), or as a KG in the process of development in Galilee (in contrast to one suddenly erupting in Jerusalem; Kelber).

c) In Matthew βασιλεία usually appears with the rabbinic divine circumlocution τῶν οὐρανῶν and is redactional 15 times (out of a total of *ca.* 55). It is thus a central theological concept. Characteristic for Matthew is also unmodified τῆς βασιλείας (in the sense of "kingdom of heaven") as a modifier of εὐαγγέλιον (4:23; 9:35; 24:14), υἱοί (8:12; 13:38), and λόγος (13:19). Βασιλεία is the motto in the proclamation of Jesus. When Matthew stereotypically designates Jesus' message as εὐαγγέλιον τῆς βασιλείας (4:23; 9:35; 24:14; cf. 13:19), it is because the Church's proclamation consists for him in nothing other than what Jesus taught (cf. 28:20). The imminence of the kingdom is the content of the message of John the Baptist (3:2), Jesus (4:17), and the Church (10:7). This is in keeping with the explicit identification, esp. in Matthew, of many parables as parables of the kingdom of heaven (10; only 2 each in Mark and Luke), whereby this designation lay already at hand to the evangelist.

If βασιλεία τῶν οὐρανῶν is thus a key expression of Matthew, it is not surprising if some of his important theological tendencies can be seen in what he says about "the kingdom of heaven." This has several aspects, including: 1) The concept is ethicized. Matthew adds to the traditional "seek first [God's] kingdom"—presumably epexegetically—"and his righteousness," δικαιοσύνη in Matthew being a quality of activity required of people (6:33). Entry "into the βασιλεία"—a redactional expression especially favored by Matthew—is promised as a reward to those who do a better righteousness (5:20), to the one who does the will of the Father (7:21), and to the one who repents and becomes as humble as a child (18:3f.). These passages indicate also that the kingdom can come into a relationship to the idea of judgment, which is especially accented in many of the βασιλεία parables of Matthew (cf., e.g., 13:41-43, 49f.; 18:34f.; 20:16; 22:11-14; 25:1-13, 28-30). The second request of the Lord's Prayer, "thy kingdom come," is interpreted by Matthew with the added third request, "thy will be done" (6:10). With this ethicizing of the concept Matthew stands within a certain proximity to rabbinic Judaism.

2) Βασιλεία can, however, mean the blessing of salvation that is given to people (25:34), which the righteous

"inherit." This connection is also frequently attested in the NT letters. As the use of εἰσέρχεσθαι indicates, the idea of an "area" is present in the word βασιλεία, not the functional notion of sovereignty (cf. 5:5). Βασιλεία also represents salvation in the difficult (redactional) passage in 21:43: the βασιλεία is taken away from the people of Israel who reject Jesus (Matthew apparently refers to the destruction of Jerusalem, A.D. 70; cf. 22:7) and given to another people, namely the Gentile Church, insofar as they do God's will (cf. the similar passage in 8:11f.). Βασιλεία is here the salvation promised to Israel and the Church. These passages also indicate that Matthew gives emphasis to the demands of the kingdom, whereas in the teaching of Jesus life lived on the basis of the coming of the kingdom stands in the foreground. The indicative of salvation comes to realization in a different way in Matthew—through miracles, the resurrection, and the authority of the Son of God (cf. 28:18).

d) The distribution of the expression in Luke (46 occurrences) and Acts (8 occurrences) demonstrates that βασιλεία τοῦ θεοῦ is an important key word in the teaching of Jesus. However, Luke has altered both the present and the future series of sayings independently.

In the present sayings it is striking that Luke interprets the KG christologically as the sending of Jesus. As in Matthew, βασιλεία τοῦ θεοῦ becomes the central cipher for the content of Christian proclamation (Luke 4:43; 8:1; 16:16; Acts 8:12 [εὐαγγελίζομαι]; Luke 18:29 [in place of Mark's εὐαγγέλιον]; 8:1; 9:2; Acts 20:25; 28:31 [κηρύσσω]; Luke 9:11 [λαλέω], 60 [διαγγέλλω]; Acts 1:3 [λέγω]; 19:8 [πείθω]; 28:23 [διαμαρτύρομαι]). The use of the expression in the framework of Acts is noteworthy (1:3, 6; 28:23, 31). The Markan summary of Jesus' βασιλεία proclamation (Mark 1:15) is elaborated by Luke by means of Jesus' inaugural sermon (Luke 4:14-30). The main content of the sermon is the fulfillment of the Scripture in Jesus. Only after this incident can Luke speak of the βασιλεία-proclamation of Jesus (v. 43). Since John the Baptist, i.e., starting with John the Baptist (*contra* Conzelmann, *Luke* 22ff., 113f.), the KG is preached (16:16). If we also take into consideration the traditional logia about the presence of the kingdom (especially 11:20; 17:21), we can say that for Luke the KG is historically present in Jesus (not just the message concerning the kingdom, as Conzelmann believes [*Luke* 114]), and its character as far as content is concerned is determined by Jesus. For the Church the βασιλεία is present in Jesus through the Spirit (Acts 1:6-8). The ethical nuance of βασιλεία, which is important in Matthew, is not present in Luke in the same way. Jesus' parables are not βασιλεία parables because Luke ethicizes the parables almost without exception.

In the future sayings there are various tendencies: In a few instances Luke emphasizes the imminence of the KG (Luke 10:9; 22:18 [traditional]; 10:11; 21:31f. [redactional]; cf. 18:8a [redactional]). More significant is the reduction of time references: in 9:27 the reference to the coming of the kingdom is dropped (cf. 9:2, 11, 60). In 19:11 an imminent expectation connected with Jerusalem is explicitly rejected (cf. 17:20f.; in Acts 1:6f. as well Luke corrects an imminent expectation which has a nationalistic-Jewish component; cf. Luke 24:21). He thus rejects a temporally determined imminent expectation without explicitly postulating a distant expectation considered in temporal terms. The delay of the parousia is presupposed by Luke, as it was already in Q and Mark, without its becoming the determining problem for him. Alongside sayings about the future βασιλεία there are isolated sayings which assume its presence already in heaven (Luke 23:42f.; cf. 16:19-31). The concepts are not harmonized in Luke.

An important saying for Luke, which must be discussed separately, is the statement that the Church's entrance into the KG is possible only through tribulation (Acts 14:22). The KG, which had made its appearance in Jesus and for whose future the Church lives, is thus not visible in the present, e.g., within the successful mission. The mission stands rather under the sign of persecution and suffering (cf. Luke 8:13-15 after 8:10; Luke 9:23-26 before 9:27; Luke 17:25 in 17:21-37; Luke 21:12-17; the Passion of Jesus and of Paul).

e) In John the term βασιλεία is nearly absent. John 3:3, 5 are perhaps distant variants of Mark 10:15: Baptism stands in the background, although it is not important in itself. What is important is the Johannine interpretation (rebirth: cf. Titus 3:5; Spirit: cf. John 3:6-8). The conceptual equivalent of the KG in Johannine theology is most likely the more individualizing ζωή.

f) It is clear from the NT letters that βασιλεία τοῦ θεοῦ remained an expression of the proclamation of Jesus. Thus it seldom appears. Paul interprets the christological basis and the soteriological focal point of the eschatological KG by means of the expression δικαιοσύνη θεοῦ. Βασιλεία τοῦ θεοῦ is only a marginal concept for Paul. He occasionally employs it in ways that have been shaped in the tradition (future: 1 Cor 6:9f. [cf. Eph 5:5b; Jas 2:5]; 15:50; Gal 5:21 [with κληρονομέω]; with an ethical focus: Rom 14:17; 1 Cor 4:20 [in connection with δύναμις; cf. Mark 9:1 par.!]); the usage shows no signs of thorough and independent reflection. Col 4:11 is noteworthy, because only there in the NT are humans mentioned as "fellow workers" for the KG, where the proclamation of the KG is meant.

4. In the later NT writings especially, there are a number of references to "the kingdom of Christ." These do not present any clear and unified conceptions. The Jewish concepts of the messianic interim kingdom (4 Ezra 7:26ff.; *2 Bar.* 29:3–30:1 [rabbinic, from the end of the 1st cent. A.D.]), the presence of the βασιλεία in Jesus (Luke 11:20, etc.), the royal titles of Jesus (cf. Mark 15:2 →

βασιλεύς), and esp. the kerygma of the exaltation of Jesus over the powers (Phil 2:9-11) have contributed to the emergence of the variety of sayings. The terminology of the dominion of Christ is a result of the kerygma.

The oldest text to speak of Christ's βασιλεία is 1 Cor 15:24f. Paul's argument makes use of concepts which are otherwise unknown to us: Christ's dominion is, unlike that in Phil 2:9-11 or Eph 1:20-22, a time of continuing battle against the powers; it ends with their conquest, when God comes to be all in all. In contrast with that passage, Col 1:13 understands Christ's dominion as a present realm of salvation and redemption that stands in opposition to the dominion of darkness. Yet another portrayal is found in 2 Tim 4:1 (cf. v. 18), where Christ's dominion is first manifest at his epiphany as judge of the world. 2 Pet 1:11, on the other hand, speaks of the eternal, other-worldly kingdom of Christ, into which those who believe will enter. Revelation sees the eternal sovereignty of God and his Messiah together in heavenly anticipation (11:15; 12:10). In other passages Revelation knows the idea of a thousand-year messianic interim kingdom before the final victory over Satan (20:1-4). This view has analogies in Jewish conceptions. In John's Gospel Jesus says (in 18:36) that his kingdom does not have its origin in this world (Johannine dualism), although the Johannine community lives in the world. In the Synoptics Matthew particularly knows the concept of an eschatological dominion of the Son of Man (16:28; cf. 20:21). It is uncertain in the interpretation of the parable of the weeds whether the βασιλεία of the Son of Man in 13:41 is the entire world (probably; cf. 13:38) or whether it is his eschatological kingdom which is still to come (according to v. 43, however, it is the βασιλεία τοῦ πατρός). In any case, the passage does not refer to the Church. In addition, Luke knows a kingdom of Christ, which in 22:29f. is future, but is present and heavenly in 23:42f.

The NT sayings are thus anything but uniform. Frequently the regnum Christi is associated with a subordinationist christology in some form (Paul, Matthew, Luke, Revelation). It is never directly or exclusively identified with the earthly Church. A systematizing of the NT sayings, as Cullmann attempted, is impossible.

U. Luz

βασίλειος, 2 *basileios* royal*

Lit.: E. Best, "I Peter II 4-10, A Reconsideration," *NovT* 11 (1969) 270-93. — *idem, I Peter* (NCBC, 1971) 107f. — J. H. Elliott, *The Elect and the Holy* (1966). — L. Goppelt, *Der Erste Petrusbrief* (KEK, 1978) 151-53.

In Luke 7:25 βασίλεια (subst. pl.) designates the *palace* (of a king).

Various translations are possible for 1 Pet 2:9 (Exod 19:6 LXX). In βασίλειον → ἱεράτευμα, βασίλειος can be understood as an adj.: priesthood *which serves* (God as) *the king* or priesthood *endowed with royal dignity* (Goppelt). A substantival reading of βασίλειος which takes it separately from ἱεράτευμα also comes into consideration: *a royal residence* (cf. v. 5; Elliott 149-54), *kingdom* (with God as king; cf. *2 Clem.* 6:9; Exod 19:6 MT; Rev 1:6), or *group of kings* (Best; cf. the Targum; the ending -ειον would then be an expression of collectivity—but evidence for such a use of βασίλειος is lacking).

P. Lampe

βασιλεύς, έως, ὁ *basileus* sovereign, king

1. Occurrences — 2. Secular rulers — 3. References to God and Christ in Matthew — 4. References to Jesus — a) In the Synoptics — b) In John — 5. Βασιλεύω — 6. Βασιλικός — 7. Βασίλισσα

Lit.: E. Bammel, *The Trial of Jesus* (1970) 95. — K. Berger, "Die Königlichen Messiastraditionen des NT," *NTS* 20 (1973/74) 1-44. — F. F. Bruce, *NT Development of OT Themes* (1968) 100ff. (on John). — T. A. Burkill, "The Condemnation of Jesus," *NovT* 12 (1970) 321-42. — Conzelmann, *Theology* 72-75, 101. — J. Coppens, *Le Messianisme Royal* (1968) 129ff. — N. A. Dahl, "The Crucified Messiah," *idem, The Crucified Messiah and Other Essays* (1974) 10-37. — A. Descamps, "Le Messianisme Royal dans le NT," *L'attente du Messie* (RechBib 1, 1954) 57-84. — F. Dexinger, "Die Entwicklung des jüd.-christl. Messianismus," *BibLeb* 47 (1974) 5-31, 239-66, esp. 22-27. — E. Dinkler, *Signum Crucis* (1967) 305f. — D. Dormeyer, *Die Passion Jesu als Verhaltensmodell* (1974) 186ff., 254, 263, etc. — J. Friedrich, *Gott im Bruder* (1977) 174-88. — Hahn, *Titles* 159-61, 166f., 172-89, 255-58. — M. Hengel, "Die christologischen Hoheitstitel im Urchristentum," *Der Name Gottes* (ed. H. von Stietencron; 1975) 90-111, esp. 108f. — *idem, Nachfolge und Charisma* (1968) 42f. — R. Hummel, *Die Auseinandersetzung zwischen Kirche und Judentum im Matthäusevangelium* (1963) 114. — S. E. Johnson, "The Davidic-Royal Motif in the Gospels," *JBL* 87 (1968) 136-50. — M. de Jonge, "Jesus as Prophet and King," *ETL* 49 (1973) 160-77. — J. D. Kingsbury, *Matthew: Structure, Christology, Kingdom* (1976) 97-99. — B. Klappert, *DNTT* II, 372-89. — J. Kremer, "Verurteilt als 'König der Juden'—verkündigt als 'Herr und Christus,'" *BibLeb* 45 (1972) 23-32. — W. G. Kümmel, *Theology of the New Testament* (1973) 72. — H. -W. Kuhn, "Jesus als Gekreuzigter," *ZTK* 72 (1975) 1-46, esp. 5f. — E. Lohse, *The History of the Suffering and Death of Jesus Christ* (1967) 89f. — L. Marin, "Jesus vor Pilatus," *Erzählende Semiotik nach Berichten der Bibel* (ed. C. Chabrol; 1973) 87-122. — W. A. Meeks, *The Prophet King* (1967). — P. Merendino, "Gesù 'Re dei Giudei' nella riflessione cristiana primitiva," *RivLi* 59 (1972) 479-89. — E. I. Otaduy, "Die evangelische Geschichte Christi des Königs. Untersuchung eines Mißverständnisses," *Beiträge zur biblischen Theologie* (ed. G. Rosenkranz; 1967) 164-92. — K. H. Rengstorf, "Old and New Testament Traces of a Formula of the Judean Royal Ritual," *NovT* 5 (1962) 229-44, esp. 236 (on Mark 6). — K. L. Schmidt, *TDNT* I, 576-91. — G. Schneider, *Die Passion Jesu nach den drei älteren Evangelien* (1973) esp. 104ff., 117ff. — P. Winter, *On the Trial of Jesus* (1961; [2]1974) 107ff. — For further bibliography see *DNTT* II, 389f.; *TWNT* X, 1008-14.

1. The NT has 115 occurrences of βασιλεύς. a) As in the LXX, references to the *secular ruler* predominate with 72 occurrences (25 in the Synoptics, 19 in Acts, 17 in Revelation, 7 in Hebrews, and 2 Cor 11:32; 1 Tim 2:2; 1 Pet 2:13, 17). b) 38 occurrences refer to Jesus (19 in the Synoptics and 16 in John, of which 26 are in the Passion narrative; Acts 17:7; Rev 17:14; 19:16). c) God is referred to as βασιλεύς in Matt 5:35; 1 Tim 1:17 (in a hymnic text); 6:15; Rev 15:3. d) Christians are referred to as *kings* in Rev 1:6 (v.l.); 5:10 (v.l.). e) Βασιλεύς is used for the king of the → ἄβυσσος in Rev 9:11.

2. a) Mark 6:22, 25, 26, 27 par. Matt 14:9 (with ὁ βασιλεύς used absolutely) stands in a pre-Markan (originally non-Christian) legend. Mark uses βασιλεύς also in his redactional introduction (v. 14). The title of Herod Antipas was "tetrarch"; he was called βασιλεύς only in the vernacular. Mark 13:9 par. Matt 10:18/Luke 21:12 is a pre-Markan addition to an apocalypse, a vaticinium of the time of mission and persecution (cf. Acts 9:15; chs. 25f., Paul before Agrippa II).

Matt 1:6 (Matthean special material); 17:25 (where βασιλεύς is metaphorical, since the temple tax is under discussion) are pre-Matthean. In the pre-Matthean story of the Magi the βασιλεύς title appears for Herod the Great (2:3, 9) in opposition to v. 2, "the king of the Jews." Luke 14:31 (Lukan special material) is a pre-Lukan portrayal of the necessity of self-examination before the beginning of a project. Matt 11:8 (Q) characterizes kings as those who wear soft raiment and live in palaces; the prophetic Spirit departs from them. Thus they are contrasted not only with the Baptist, but also with the itinerant preachers who stand behind Q as well; cf. the similar Q passage, Luke 10:24: what the disciples now see is hidden from kings. The redactional headings in Matt 2:1 and Luke 1:5 introduce the secular βασιλεύς (Herod the Great), in order to characterize the salvation event as an "historical" fact by this indication of place and time. With the use of the βασιλεύς title Matthew also gives added emphasis to the opposition to the "king of the Jews" (v. 2). Luke introduces βασιλεύς redactionally into the Markan text at 22:25 in order to elaborate on the difference between secular kings (v. 25) and the disciples as eschatological kings (vv. 29f.): One kind rules, the other serves.

b) In all the strata of the gospel tradition under consideration in → a, earthly kings are mentioned to form a contrast to: the Baptist (Q; Mark 6), to "the king of the Jews" (Matt 2), or to the disciples (Mark 13; Luke 22:25; the preacher in Q). In metaphorical usage (Matt 17; Luke 14; → 3.a), however, instead of contrast there is correspondence.

c) The relationship to the world is reflected in the appraisal of earthly kings. In Luke 22:25 the earthly kings are given a thoroughly critical assessment; however, the Lukan redactor weakens the pejorative connotation in contrast to Mark 10:42 (κατα-κυριεύω; κατα-ἐξουσιάζω). In Acts Herod Agrippa I is the persecutor of Christians (12:1, 20, 23; cf. 4:26-29), while Agrippa II appears in a positive light (26:26-32). 1 Tim 2:2 (generic pl.); 1 Pet 2:13, 17 portray the Roman emperor as a βασιλεύς to whom the Christian is obligated to show honor.

Revelation has a different perspective from 1 Timothy and 1 Peter: "Kings" are referred to positively first in reference to the New Jerusalem, when the contrast to the world has been taken away (21:24). Revelation speaks pointedly of the βασιλεῖς τῆς γῆς (8 times; otherwise only in Matt 17:25; Acts 4:26), who live in luxury and commit fornication with their ruler, lady Babylon (i.e., Rome; 17:2, 18; 18:3, 9; cf. 17:9, where βασιλεῖς is used of the Roman emperors). The "kings" make war against Christ, but the judgment is directed toward them (6:15; 16:12, 14; 17:12-14; 19:18f.).

3. a) Βασιλεύς appears (perhaps pre-Matthean?) in the parables of the kingdom of God in Matthew 18 and 22. This corresponds to the more frequent identification in Matthew of the parables with the → βασιλεία than in Mark and Luke. The βασιλεύς is *the ruler at the judgment,* who demands an accounting: 18:23 (vv. 23ff. is a parable with an ethical focus; vv. 32ff. is a parable focusing on judgment); 22:7 (judgment against Israel); 22:11, 13 (judgment against the Gentile Church). The βασιλεύς watches to see that only those who prove to be appropriate for his kingdom through their actions live in it. This usage of βασιλεύς corresponds to the ethicizing of the kingdom (→ βασιλεία 3.c). In Matt 5:35 (pre-Matthean) God appears as the βασιλεύς again in an ethical context.

b) Christ in his function as eschatological judge is a βασιλεύς who demands brotherly love (Matt 25:34, 40). Here the pre-Matthean tradition βασιλεύς may have referred to God (cf. the tension with "Son of man" in v. 31; P. Vielhauer, "Gottesreich und Menschensohn," *idem, Aufsätze zum NT* [1965] 55ff.). The title *king* as a term for the returning Christ and as a metaphor for God means for Matthew the Lord who demands deeds and who comes in judgment.

4. Βασιλεὺς τῶν Ἰουδαίων is a title for Jesus heard only on the lips of pagan Romans and the Magi (also Mark 15:12; an exception is John 19:21). The Jews speak of the βασιλεὺς Ἰσραήλ (Mark 15:32 par.; John 1:49; 12:13). Βασιλεύς is used in an absolute sense in Luke 23:2; 19:38; Acts 17:7; Matt 25:34, 40 and more frequently in John (for the basis of this usage → 4.b).

a) The title ὁ βασιλεὺς τῶν Ἰουδαίων (Mark 15:26) is historical as a Roman formulation of the *causa poenae.* It identifies Jesus as a political insurgent who aspires to secular rule over the Jews. The Christian tradition is reserved in its use of the title, and repeats it almost exclusively in the Passion tradition—in order to give it a new interpretation.

Mark 15:2, 9f., 12, 18, 31f. (secondary expansions of the oldest stratum of the Passion tradition) presupposes a new and positive (v. 2) content: 1) Vv. 31f. (redactional?) accentuate as one feature of the title the miraculous aid given by Jesus during his earthly ministry (σῴζω; the motif of the priestly envy in v. 10 is probably related); the aspect of the wonder-working aid is also associated with the title → υἱὸς Δαυίδ. 2) The contrast of Jesus to the political insurgent is emphasized (v. 7), and Jesus' innocence is accentuated (v. 14). 3) The title is connected with → Χριστός (v. 32; cf. Mark 14:61 par.; redactional in Luke 23:2, 39).

Matthew and Luke take over the title (Matt 27:11, 29, 37, 42; Luke 23:3, 38). Matthew also replaces it with Ἰησοῦς ὁ λεγόμενος Χριστός (27:17, 22). Luke also deletes it (23:20, 35), but in other passages inserts it redactionally: Mark 15:31f. is redactionally developed in Luke 23:37 (again βασιλεύς and σῴζω; cf. also v. 39); Luke 23:2 reports the original content in order to be able to reject it as false. Luke, more clearly than his predecessor, portrays Jesus' political innocence (vv. 4, 14f., 22) and contrasts him to the insurgents (v. 25).

Inasmuch as the title "King *of the Jews*" focuses only on Jesus' earthly mission to the people Israel (cf. "Son of David") and this mission ends at the cross with his rejection by the Jews, the βασιλεύς title is surpassed by the credo of a Gentile, → υἱὸς θεοῦ in Mark 15:39 par. Matthew (cf. Mark 14:61; redactional in Matt 27:40, 43 and 26:63). While Matthew is interested in this new title, "Son of God," it is eliminated in Luke (Luke 23:47). On the Jewish background of the theme of the royal Davidic miracle-worker, the master over the elements, demons, and illnesses, see Berger 3-9; cf. Descamps 58ff. on the wonder-working king of antiquity.

In the "triumphal entry" narrative βασιλεύς appears in a Matthean interpretative citation in 21:5 (identical in content to the redactional υἱὸς Δαυίδ in v. 9; on v. 5 → πραΰς) and redactionally in Luke 19:38. The entering βασιλεύς is identified by the context in both instances as the wonder-working helper of the oppressed: in Luke 19:37, by "mighty works" (redactional); as Son of David he heals illnesses (Matt 20:29ff. par.; 21:14f.) and receives sinners into his company (Luke 19:1ff.); cf. σῴζω/σωτηρία in Luke 18:42 and 19:9f. (cf. Zech 9:9, βασιλεὺς σῴζων); further in the context: temple (Luke 19:45 par.; redactional in v. 47) and διδάσκω (v. 47; 20:1, redactional; Matt 21:23, redactional; cf. Luke 19:39). The Lukan redactor places βασιλεύς alongside διδάσκω also in 23:2-5.

In the pre-Matthean story of the Magi the representatives of the Magi submit themselves to the βασιλεὺς τῶν Ἰουδαίων (Matt 2:2). Thus the content of the title could have been assumed to be "authoritative Ruler over elements and demons/Ruler of wisdom" (Berger 22f.). The title βασιλεὺς τῶν Ἰουδαίων moved succeeding narrators to develop the story of the Magi with vv. 3-5a, 7-9a (the story of Herod). In this context, as in the Passion narrative, the predominant role is played by the political misunderstanding of the title and the intent to kill competing pretenders to the throne (a synonym again is Χριστός, v. 4). In the Bethlehem theme the Davidic sonship is mentioned; cf., however, C. Burger, *Jesus als Davidssohn* [1970] 104f.).

In the third stratum, the pre-Matthean unit of ch. 2, Jesus is portrayed as the new Moses. Just as Moses' wonder-working power was often emphasized in the Moses tradition and commonly associated with the Moses βασιλεύς title (Philo, *Vit. Mos.* i.158; see further Berger nn. 96, 89), the pre-Matthean narrator of ch. 2 could have understood the βασιλεύς title similarly.

A more definite statement can be made for the final redactor of Matthew. For him other aspects stand in the foreground: the βασιλεὺς τῶν Ἰουδαίων, as the one prophesied in the OT (vv. 5f.) and sent to the Jews, is first worshipped by Gentiles, while the Jews persecute him.

b) John 18:36 gives a new interpretation in the Passion tradition to the title. The *king,* whose kingdom has its place in the world, does not originate there: he is the witness to the truth, whose sovereignty consists in the fact that his voice is heard by those who belong to him (v. 37; cf. ποιμήν in ch. 10).

John rejects the view that Jesus was *king* on the basis of his wonder-working activity. On three occasions John reports and criticizes this view: 1) (6:15) Anyone who comprehends Jesus' kingdom only as that of a wonder-working helper for times of distress (vv. 2, 11, 26: multiplier of bread, master of the elements) has not understood that Jesus is himself the bread (v. 35). His kingdom consists in the fact that his own believe in him (cf. v. 35 with 18:37). 2) (12:13, 15f.) The disciples understand the true meaning of Jesus' entry into Jerusalem and of his βασιλεύς title first when he comes to be glorified. Jesus is not *king* on the basis of wonders like the raising of Lazarus, as "the crowd" believes (vv. 17f., 9, 11), but because of the witness to truth which his own have believed, a truth that is not of this world (cf. 12:16 with 8:28, 31f.). 3) In 1:50f. also, it is emphasized with the reference to the glorification that Nathanael's understanding of Jesus as "King of Israel" on the basis of Jesus' miraculous knowledge (1:47-49) is only preliminary.

Jesus is a king who fits within the traditional royal expectations ("King of Israel," 12:13; 1:49; new royal prophetic Moses, 6:14f.; see Meeks on the Moses typology here) so poorly because he surpasses them. (In 18:37 and elsewhere, therefore, "of the Jews/Israel" is left out.) The Synoptics allow the kingdom of Jesus to be limited to the earthly sending of Jesus to the Jews; John associates it with the relation of the exalted one to those who believe.

5. **Βασιλεύω** *be king, rule** occurs especially in Paul and in Revelation. It is used in reference to: a) God (Rev 11:17; 19:6 [ingressive aor. as in 1 Cor 4:8 bis; Luke

19:14, 27: *begin ruling*]; b) Christ (1 Cor 15:25 [→ βασιλεία 4]; Rev 11:15 [together with God; the grammatical subj. is ἡ βασιλεία]; Luke 1:33 [tradition]); c) the dominion of death, sin, or grace (Rom 5:14, 17, 21 bis; 6:12; cf. E. Käsemann, *Romans* [1980] ad loc.); d) Christians as coregents (Rev 5:10; 20:4, 6; 22:5; Rom 5:17; 1 Cor 4:8, ironically of the Corinthians, who deny the eschatological reservation); and e) secular rulers (Matt 2:22; Luke 19:14, 27; cf. M. Zerwick, *Bib* 40 [1959] 654-74; cf. 1 Tim 6:15 in a divine predicate).

6. **Βασιλικός** *royal** is used substantively in John 4:46-49 of a *royal official* of Antipas or, less probably, of *one of royal* (i.e., Herodian) *descent* (see BAGD ad loc. for evidence). In Acts 12:20f. βασιλικός is used adjectivally for the *royal* land and robe of Herod Agrippa I. Jas 2:8 speaks of the *royal* law of love for the neighbor, possibly meaning *given by God as king* (cf. βασιλεία, v. 5) or more probably the *greatest* commandment in the sense of Gal 5:14.

7. **Βασίλισσα** *queen** occurs in the NT 4 times, in Matt 12:42 par. Luke 11:31 (Q) of "the *queen* of the south" (cf. 1 Kgs 10), in Acts 8:27 of the "*queen* of the Ethiopians," and in Rev 18:7, where Babylon (= Rome) speaks presumptuously: "I am *a queen* on my throne" (NEB).

P. Lampe

βασιλεύω *basileuō* be king, rule
→ βασιλεύς 5.

βασιλικός, 3 *basilikos* royal
→ βασιλεύς 6.

βασίλισσα, ης, ἡ *basilissa* queen
→ βασιλεύς 7.

βάσις, εως, ἡ *basis* foot*

Acts 3:7: The *feet* and ankles of the man born lame become strong. Originally βάσις meant "step"; it was not a medical t.t.; the related narrative in 14:8 has πούς (vv. 8, 10).

βασκαίνω *baskainō* bewitch, cast a spell on*

Gal 3:1: The Galatians are fascinated or spellbound by Paul's opponents, i.e., through a strange proclamation, so that they have become ἀνόητοι with respect to the Pauline gospel without noticing at all that they have been delivered over to a destructive power. G. Delling, *TDNT* I, 594f.; *TWNT* X, 1014.

βαστάζω *bastazō* pick up; carry; endure*

Lit.: F. Büchsel, *TDNT* I, 596. — For further bibliography see *TWNT* X, 1014.

1. Of 27 occurrences in the NT, 3 are in Matthew (3:11; 8:17; 20:12), 1 in Mark (14:13), 5 in Luke (7:14; 10:4; 11:27; 14:27; 22:10), 4 in Acts (3:2; 9:15; 15:10; 21:35), 5 in John (10:31; 12:6; 16:12; 19:17; 20:15), 6 in Paul (Rom 11:18; 15:1; Gal 5:10; 6:2, 5, 17), and 3 in Revelation (2:2, 3; 17:7).

2. The word is used with the literal meaning *carry* with various objects. It can refer to light things (a jar of water, Mark 14:13 par. Luke 22:10; sandals, Matt 3:11 [the loosing and carrying of sandals belongs to the service of a slave, but is not demanded of a student by his teacher; Billerbeck I, 121]) as well as heavy (the bier of the dead boy from Nain, Luke 7:14; the lame man at the Beautiful Gate of the temple, Acts 3:2). Paul *is* also *carried* by the soldiers in order to escape attack by the mob (Acts 21:35). According to John 19:17 Jesus *bears* his cross himself (in contrast to the Synoptics). The apocalyptic beast, like a beast for riding (Rev 17:7), *carries* the woman who sits upon him (v. 3). During her pregnancy, the mother *bears* her child (Luke 11:27).

Whether something is *picked up* or *carried* from another place has significance for the meaning when the Jews either *take up* or *bring along* stones in order to stone Jesus (John 10:31; cf. 8:59). It also plays a role when Judas *takes* (John 12:6) the travel money and when the presumed gardener, according to Mary Magdalene, has *taken away* the body (John 20:15; cf. vv. 2, 13). The weight of the object plays no role when the disciples are commanded *to carry with them* neither purse nor bag nor sandals (Luke 10:4). In a similar way Paul *bears* the stigmata of Jesus *on himself* (Gal 6:17).

A variety of objects give the vb. a metaphorical character in which especially the moment of *bearing* is emphasized: Jesus, the servant of God, *bears* our illnesses (Matt 8:17). The workers in the vineyard *bear* the burden and heat of the day (20:12). Anyone who troubles the Church will *bear* the judgment (Gal 5:10). The "strong" should *bear* the shortcomings of the "weak" (Rom 15:1). In the hour of Jesus' departure the disciples cannot yet *bear* the full truth (John 16:12). The church at Ephesus cannot *bear* evil men (Rev 2:2). Without an obj., however, Rev 2:3 is also to be understood metaphorically: it distinguishes the Ephesians who had patience and who *endured,* i.e., maintained unshakable steadfastness, for the sake of Christ and persevered in the face of temptations brought by false apostles.

The element of "enduring" is absent when Paul, as the "chosen vessel" (or, with RSV, "instrument") must *bear* (i.e., confess; see G. Lohfink, *BZ* 10 [1966] 108-15, with reference to *Sib. Or.* viii.331) the name of Jesus before the peoples and kings and before the sons of Israel (Acts 9:15). Paul's missionary service is in view. It is, of course, accompanied by suffering "for the sake of my name" (v. 16).

Elsewhere the vb. is not determined by its obj., but rather the entire expression is defined metaphorically by the context: for the disciple to "*bear* his own cross" means that in his discipleship he does not spare himself (Luke 14:27). The yoke which no one is able to *bear* (Acts 15:10) is circumcision and the law of Moses (v. 5). The root that *bears* the Gentile Christians, who are an engrafted branch, is Israel (Rom 11:18). The burdens that the Christians should *bear* reciprocally are sins, so that the sinners in the Church may also be included within the love command (Gal 6:2). The individual burden that everyone *will have to bear* (v. 5) is similar; it is "the burden of one's own sins, which must be brought before God's judgment" (F. Mussner, *Galaterbrief* [HTKNT] 401f.).

W. Stenger

βάτος, ου, ὁ, ἡ, (I) *batos* thornbush, thorn shrub*

Lit.: BAGD s.v. — A. VAN DEN BORN, *BL* 343. — A. HERMANN, *RAC* IV, 189-97.

The noun is fem. in Luke 20:37; Acts 7:35, masc. in Mark 12:26, the LXX, and Philo *Vit. Mos.* i.67. The masc. may be Attic, and the fem. Hellenistic. Βάτος in the sense of *thornbush* is attested since Homer *Od.* xxiv.30; *Epigr. Graec.* 546.6 and 548.2.

Moses saw the revelation of God in a thornbush (Exod 3:2-4; Deut 33:16; Josephus *Ant.* ii.266; Mark 12:26 par. Luke 20:37; Acts 7:30, 35). In this connection βάτος represents Heb. *s^eneh,* which in popular etymology is taken to refer to Sinai. Thus Yahweh, according to Deut 33:16, is called he who is in the thornbush/Sinai.

In Luke 6:44 (one does not gather figs from *thorns*) the concern is with the knowledge and assessment of authentic and hypocritical piety. Cf. Job 31:40 (thorns, *ḥôaḥ,* instead of wheat).

A. Fuchs

βάτος, ου, ὁ, (II) *batos* bath*

Lit.: A. BARROIS, "La métrologie dans la bible," *RB* 40 (1931) 185-213. — E. M. COOK, *ISBE* IV, 1050f., 1055. — B. LANG, *BL* 1951-54. — *Lexikon zur Bibel* (ed. F. Rienecker; 1969) 894f. — J. T. MILIK, "Deux jarres inscrites provenant d'une grotte de Qumran," *Bib* 40 (1959) 985-91 (= DJD III, 37-41). — A. SEGRÈ, "A Documentary Analysis of Ancient Palestinian Units of Measure," *JBL* 64 (1945) 357-75. — A. STROBEL, *BHH* II, 1162-66, 1168f. (bibliography). — J. TRINQUET, "Métrologie biblique," *DBSup* V, 1212-50. — B. N. WAMBACQ, "De mensuris in Sacra Scriptura," *VD* 32 (1954) 266-74, 325-34.

Βάτος is a loanword from Hebrew (*baṯ*).

It is rendered as βάδος by Hesychius, perhaps because the common aspiration of δ made the pronunciation conform more closely to the Hebrew (cf. mss. of Luke 16:6 and Ezra 7:22). *1 Enoch* 10:19 in the Greek version has, however, βάτος. Similar large units of liquid measure were the Egyptian ἀρτάβη and the Attic μετρητής (= "measuring jar").

In the NT it appears only in Luke 16:6: ἑκατὸν βάτους ἐλαίου. The Hebrew unit of liquid capacity corresponds to the ephah for dry materials (grain and meal). 1 *baṯ* = one-tenth *kōr* = 6 *hîn*s = 72 *lōg*s. According to Josephus *Ant.* viii.57 and other bases for comparison the *baṯ* is commonly interpreted as 39.384 liters; according to Segrè (on the basis of an Egyptian papyrus of A.D. 289) and a "royal measure" found in Lachish, it is reckoned as 22.991 liters.

A. Fuchs

βάτραχος, ου, ὁ *batrachos* frog*

In Rev 16:13 three impure spirits come out of the mouths of the dragon, the beast, and the lying prophet "like *frogs.*" The ritual uncleanness of frogs (Lev 11:10) might play a role here, as may their destructive function in the second plague of Egypt (Exod 7:26ff.; Pss 78:45; 105:30).

βατταλογέω *battalogeō* babble, chatter*

Used in Matt 6:7 in the criticism directed against Gentile "prayer," which seeks to gain a hearing by its use of many words (πολυλογία; cf. Luke 11:2 D). The word is rare in non-Christian literature. On the difficulty of explaining the etymology of the word, cf. BAGD s.v.; G. Delling, *TDNT* I, 597; BDF §40. Most probably (against those named) it is connected with the onomatopoeic word βάτ(τ)αλος/βάττος, "stammerer" (Aeschines *Oratio in Timarchum* 51; Hesychius), which βατταρίζω also takes up (cf. Passow s.v.). In early Christian literature, Aram. *btl,* "nothing," might also have played a role. Cf. also LSJ s.v. βάταλος; Frisk, *Wörterbuch* I, 225, 227; *TWNT* X, 1014.

H. Balz

βδέλυγμα, ατος, τό *bdelygma* abomination*

1. Occurrences and meaning. — 2. In Revelation and Luke — 3. The "abomination of desolation" in Mark 13:14 par. Matt 24:15

Lit.: W. FOERSTER, *TDNT* I, 598-600. — X. LÉON-DUFOUR, *Wörterbuch zum NT* (1977) 409f. — J. NELIS, *BL* 642-44. — R. PESCH, *Naherwartungen* (1968) 140-43. — *idem, Das Markusevangelium* (HTKNT) II (1977), 291f. — B. RIGAUX, "Βδέλυγμα τῆς ἐρημώσεως Mc 13, 14; Mt 24, 15," *Bib* 40 (1959) 675-83. — J. ZMIJEWSKI, *Die Eschatologiereden des Lukasevangelium* (1972) 195-98. — For further bibliography see *TWNT* X, 1014.

1. The noun occurs 6 times in the NT: Mark 13:14 par. Matt 24:15; Luke 16:15; Rev 17:4, 5; 21:27. It designates generally the *object of loathing* and has (as already in the LXX) a religious-ethical connotation. Thus it means essentially what is *an abomination before God.*

2. Rev 17:4 speaks of the βδελύγματα of the whore of

Babylon, i.e., the *loathsomeness* of paganism (represented by Babylon = Rome): idol worship and immorality (cf. also the juxtaposition of "*abomination* and [RSV "or"] falsehood" in Rev 21:27). In Luke 16:15 Jesus reproaches the "piety" of the Pharisees, saying that whatever is highly esteemed by humans is an *abomination* before God (βδέλυγμα ἐνώπιον τοῦ θεοῦ) and is thus nothing but idol worship.

3. Τὸ βδέλυγμα τῆς ἐρημώσεως (Mark 13:14 par. Matt 24:15) is an apocalyptic cipher from Daniel (9:27; 11:31; 12:11), where the allusion is to Antiochus IV's erection of an altar to Zeus in the Jerusalem temple in 168-167 B.C. (see Billerbeck I, 851).

Mark takes over the phrase from a Jewish or Jewish-Christian apocalyptic source (cf. vv. 14-22). Because it cannot be determined from what period this source is derived, the actual reference in the phrase as it appears in the source remains unclear: either the events around A.D. 40, when P. Petronius received the order from Caligula (which was not, in the course of events, carried out) to erect an image of the emperor in the Jerusalem temple, in which case what follows, masc. ἑστηκότα ὅπου οὐ δεῖ, would fit well, or events at the beginning of the Jewish war (so Pesch, *Markusevangelium* II, 291f.). In any case Mark's source intends that the "*abomination* of desolation" be understood as the desecration of the temple by a godless power (ἑστηκότα κτλ.). The traditional understanding of it as the "Antichrist" can thus be rejected for a good reason, inasmuch as it rests on a premature resort to 2 Thess 2:3f. In addition, the context of the tradition speaks against it: a demand for flight (cf. v. 14b) appears useless in the face of the Antichrist's appearance; moreover, it must be regarded as questionable to what extent false prophets and false Christs could appear with this figure or after him (cf. v. 22).

In addition, for the author of Mark the phrase is focused on the temple (cf. the explanation ἐν τόπῳ ἁγίῳ in Matt 24:15). However, nothing else is said about this desecration; rather, as the Markan context suggests (v. 2), the subject is the destruction of the temple in A.D. 70. Masc. ἑστηκότα κτλ. is intended to describe the person or power who stands behind the destruction (the Roman general and his army). The author thus actualizes the adopted cipher for the sake of his readers (cf. the apparently redactional ὁ ἀναγινώσκων νοείτω in v. 14b) in an attempt to establish an apocalyptic understanding of the destruction of the temple and to separate it (as a past event that retains, nonetheless, its eschatological meaning) from the actual end.

J. Zmijewski

βδελυκτός, 3 *bdelyktos* horrid, abominable*

Titus 1:16 (with ἀπειθής), of Jewish or Jewish Christian opponents.

βδελύσσομαι *bdelyssomai* detest, abhor*

Rom 2:22 with the obj. εἴδωλα; Rev 21:8 perf. pass. partc. ἐβδελυγμένοι alongside δειλοί, ἄπιστοι, etc., apparently of those who are stained with (Gentile) abominations and are thus *polluted.* W. Foerster, *TDNT* I, 598-600.

βέβαιος, 3 *bebaios* firm, reliable*

βεβαιόω *bebaioō* establish; strengthen; prove reliable, confirm*

βεβαίωσις, εως, ἡ *bebaiōsis* establishment; strengthening*

1. Occurrences — 2. Βεβαιόω — 3.Βέβαιος

Lit.: BAGD 138. — H. CONZELMANN, *1 Corinthians* (Hermeneia, 1975) (on 1:6, 8). — H. LIETZMANN and W. G. KÜMMEL, *An die Korinther I/II* (HNT, 51969). — H. SCHLIER, *TDNT* I, 600-4. — *idem, Der Römerbrief* (HTKNT, 1977) (on Rom 4:16; 15:8).

1. The word group appears already in Thucydides as well as in the inscriptions and papyri, but less frequently in the LXX, Philo, and Josephus. The NT has relatively numerous instances: 8 of βέβαιος, 8 of βεβαιόω, and 2 of βεβαίωσις. With a total of 7 occurrences with all three forms represented, Hebrews has the most instances; Romans, 1 Corinthians, 2 Corinthians, and 2 Peter have 2 each; other instances are in Mark 16:20; Phil 1:7; and Col 2:7.

The three forms appear in connection with the ἐπαγγελίαι of the old covenant and the proclamation and the confession of faith and its confirmation in the Christian life. Holding on to the faith or remaining firm in Christ is repeatedly spoken of with these words. Preservation of the κλῆσις or the ἐκλογή already initiated in baptism and anchoring of Christian hope for the future are also emphasized. Individual texts also occasionally have a juridical meaning in the sense of confirmation or validation.

2. **Βεβαιόω.*** According to Rom 15:8 Christ became the servant of the circumcision, in order to fulfill the promises given to the fathers and thus to *confirm* the ἀλήθεια of God, his truthfulness or his faithfulness to the covenant (Schlier, *Römerbrief* 424); a similar motif appears in Rom 4:16. Βέβαιος in 2 Pet 1:19 (προφητικὸς λόγος) is used in the same way.

Among the Christians at Corinth the testimony concerning Christ, i.e., the proclamation of faith or preaching of salvation and thus the content of faith, was *confirmed* and rooted; Christ will *keep* them *firm* in this faith and confession until the day of the Lord (1 Cor 1:6, 8). The confirmation of the testimony about Christ designates thus the foundation and development of the Church (Conzelmann ad loc.), not the validity of the gospel (Schlier, *TDNT* I, 602). The apostles' proclamation, which originates with Christ and testifies to him, has taken firm roots among the

Corinthians (Kümmel 167). 2 Cor 1:21 is similar: Establishment in Christ is establishment in faith; God binds Christians to each other and to Christ and in this way makes them true disciples (BAGD 138); cf. also Col 2:7: Christians, who have accepted Christ as Lord, should "live in him" (v. 6), because they are "rooted and built up in him, and *established* through [RSV "in"] the faith," in which they have been instructed.

Just as instruction in the faith is thus said to lead to stability, in Phil 1:7 the imprisonment of Paul, about which nothing more is known, is said to be able to contribute to the defense (ἀπολογία) and *confirmation* (βεβαίωσις) of the gospel. As is the case occasionally in secular usage, both these terms have a juridical undertone. Heb 2:3 speaks of the σωτηρία that began with the proclamation by Jesus and was transmitted by those who heard to the contemporaries of the author of Hebrews, whose reception of it has its (judicial) consequences. On the other hand, strengthening of the heart through grace spoken of in Heb 13:9 is not intended in a judicial sense, for it refers to confirmation in faith. In the inauthentic ending of Mark 16:20 βεβαιόω is used in connection with the strengthening and confirmation of the message of faith (ὁ λόγος as a t.t. of early Christian missionary terminology), which is accompanied by miraculous signs.

3. **Βέβαιος***. The act of holding fast to the confidence that first determined the Christian life guards one against unbelief and apostasy (Heb 3:14; similarly 2 Pet 1:10). On the other hand hope is "a sure and *steadfast* anchor of the soul" (Heb 6:19) which extends beyond this life. Paul's unshakable hope in the Corinthians that they remain firm in suffering and in the trials that they must endure for the sake of Christ (2 Cor 1:7) is focused on the present. In Hebrews the word is used in the sense of judicial validity or confirmation in reference to the OT law (λόγος, 2:2), to a testament (9:17), or an oath (εἰς βεβαίωσιν ὁ ὅρκος, 6:16).

The frequent occurrence of the word group in the writings mentioned allows one to draw conclusions about the situation: It is used for the early Christian message where the task is to assure permanence and stability for faith. The life of the Christian should stand the test amid temptation and persecution and hold its ground amid the enticement to unbelief. The word group stands in the service of the founding and the growth of the Christian Church or of the Christian life of the individual.

A. Fuchs

βεβαιόω *bebaioō* establish; strengthen; prove reliable, confirm
→ βέβαιος 1, 2.

βεβαίωσις, εως, ἡ *bebaiōsis* establishment; strengthening*
→ βέβαιος.

βέβηλος, 2 *bebēlos* unholy, godless; common*

Βέβηλος appears 4 times in the NT, in 1 and 2 Timothy and Heb 12:6, not in the classical sense of "accessible to everyone," "secular," rather always with reference to the distance of persons or their actions from salvation: 1 Tim 1:9: *ungodly, godless* in a vice list (with ἀνόσιοι); Heb 12:16: *unholy, common* of Esau (with πόρνος); elsewhere with reference to human speech: 1 Tim 4:7, βέβηλοι καὶ γραώδεις μῦθοι: *unholy* and old wives' tales; 6:20; 2 Tim 2:16 in the phrase βεβήλοι κενοφωνίαι, *unholy, godless chatter.* F. Hauck, *TDNT* I, 604f.; *TWNT* X, 1014 (bibliography).

βεβηλόω *bebēloō* desecrate*

Matt 12:5, of *desecrating* or breaking the sabbath, which is permitted only of priests (cf. Num 28:9f.); Acts 24:6, in the charge that Paul has *desecrated* the temple. F. Hauck, *TDNT* I, 605; *BHH* I, 415.

Βεελζεβούλ *Beelzeboul* Beelzebul*

Lit.: W. Foerster, *TDNT* I, 605f. — E. Jenni, *BHH* I, 175f. — E. C. B. MacLaurin, "Beelzeboul," *NovT* 20 (1978) 156-60. — M. J. Mulder, *TDOT* II, 192-200 (esp. 194f.). — For further bibliography → δαιμόνιον; see *TWNT* X, 1014f.

1. According to 2 Kgs 1:2-6 the name of the Philistine god of Ekron was *Lord of the Flies* (Heb. *ba'al zᵉḇûḇ*), from whom Israel's King Ahaziah requested an oracle. Comparison with Ugaritic texts and the NT forms of the name Βεελζεβούλ/Βεεζεβούλ (Matt 10:25; Mark 3:22-27 par.) shows that the OT has here a polemical dysphemism of the deity's name *ba'al zᵉḇûl* (Lord of the Abode on High; so Jenni). To the worshipper of Yahweh, the pagan deities were considered demons, whose names provoke destruction (cf. Rev 9:11: Apollyon = Ἀπολλύων).

2. In the NT Βεελζεβούλ occurs (with the secondary forms Βεεζεβούλ and Βεελζεβούβ) in 7 passages: Matt 10:25; 12:24, 27; Mark 3:22; Luke 11:15, 18f., i.e., in two Synoptic pericopes (Matt 10:17-25; Mark 3:22-27 par.). The statement that a disciple is not above his teacher (Matt 10:24, 25a par. Luke 6:40) is elucidated in a clause which appears only in Matt 10:25b to the effect that the charge of demon possession made against Jesus (cf. Mark 3:22b; John 7:20; 8:48, 52; 10:20) must surely befall his disciples (cf. Acts 2:13). Apparently Matthew alludes here to the pericope Matt 12:22-30 par. Mark 3:22-27/Luke 11:14f., 17-23, in which Jesus must respond to the charge of the Pharisees (Matt 12:24) or scribes (Mark 3:22a, c) or some Jews (Luke 11:15) that he casts out demons with the help of the prince of demons Beelzeboul (cf. Matt 9:34). Jesus takes up this charge and asks his Jewish opponents by whose authority their exorcists act if he performs his miracles with Beelzeboul's aid (Matt 12:27 par. Luke 11:19).

3. Neither in the charge of Jesus' opponents nor in the Jesus' answer is Beelzeboul identified with the devil himself; Beelzeboul is the name of a ruler of demons. Mark 3:26 par. also understands Beelzeboul apparently as a potentate of the βασιλεία of Satan (Matt 12:26 par. Luke 11:18). The NT Beelzeboul texts belong to the context of the Jewish polemic against false teachers, in which heresy is traced to demonic activity. In the NT such misunderstanding of the authority of Jesus is considered "sin against the Holy Spirit" (Mark 3:28-30 par.). It is not the diabolical power of the unclean spirit Beelzeboul (Mark 3:30) but the divine power of the Holy Spirit which enables Jesus in his eschatological battle with Satan and his demons (Matt 12:28; cf. Luke 11:20); Jesus knows that he is the stronger one who conquers and plunders the devil (Mark 3:27 par.).

O. Böcher

Βελιάρ *Beliar* Beliar*

Lit.: W. Foerster, *TDNT* I, 607. — K. Galling, *RGG* I, 1025f. — H. W. Huppenbauer, *BHH* I, 214. — P. von der Osten-Sacken, *Gott und Belial* (1969). — B. Otzen, *TDOT* II, 131-36 — For further bibliography → διάβολος; see *TWNT* X, 1015.

1. Βελιάρ, the Jewish name of the devil, appears in the NT only in 2 Cor 6:15. Heb. *bᵉlîyaʿal,* which is of uncertain etymology and perhaps of mythological origin, designates the realm of the powers of chaos in the OT, and thus means: destruction, wickedness, evil (Deut 13:14; Nah 1:11; 2:1; Pss 18:5; 41:9; 101:3; Prov 6:12, etc.). In the Qumran texts *bᵉlîyaʿal,* understood as a personal reference, is the name of the highest angel of darkness, and is synonymous with the devil (→ διάβολος) and Satan (→ σατανᾶς). Belial acts as tempter and seducer (1QS 3:20f.), exercises command over demons (1QS 3:23f.; CD 12:2; 1QM 13:2, 4, 11f.; 14:10) and human beings who have been led astray (1QS 2:4f.; 5:1f.; 1QM 4:2, etc.), and is the enemy of the princes of light (CD 5:18). The devil is consistently called Βελιάρ in the *Testaments of the Twelve Patriarchs,* where he is also the tempter and enticer (*T. Jos.* 7:4) and chief of demons (*T. Jud.* 25:3; *T. Iss.* 7:7). Beliar is the absolute enemy of God (*T. Levi* 18:12f.; 19:1; *T. Iss.* 6:1; *T. Zeb.* 9:8, etc.). In addition, *Jub.* 1:20; 15:33 and *Vit. Proph.* 21 identify Beliar as the devil. On the other hand, in *Vit. Proph.* 17:9f. and *Sib Or.* ii.167; iii.63, 73, Beliar is identified with the Antichrist.

2. Paul uses the devil's name Βελιάρ in a parenetic unit (2 Cor 6:14–7:1), which he might have taken over, together with the Hebrew word, from a dualistic Jewish tradition. His demand for the Corinthians to separate themselves from the "unclean" non-Christians is elucidated conceptually with the antitheses of Jewish polemic against Gentiles. The contrast is between believers and unbelievers, righteousness and unrighteousness, light and darkness, Beliar and the Messiah, the temple of Yahweh and idols, purity and defilement. Paul of course shifts the accent from cultic to ethical purity. Just as Paul does not intend to make a christological statement, so also he places little emphasis on the role of the devil. Nonetheless the polarity in v. 15 between Christ and Beliar approaches that of the Antichrist texts in *Sib. Or.* ii.167; iii.63, 73; *Vit. Proph.* 17:10. Anyone who evades the claim of the Χριστός remains in impurity, which is represented by the devil (cf. Heb 10:22; Jas 4:7f.).

O. Böcher

βελόνη, ης, ἡ *belonē* needle
→ ῥαφίς.

βέλος, ους, τό *belos* arrow*

Eph 6:16: τὰ βέλη τοῦ πονηροῦ τὰ πεπυρωμένα, "the flaming *arrows* [RSV "darts"] of the evil one." F. Hauck, *TDNT* I, 608f.; *BL* 1369.

βελτίων, 2 *beltiōn* better, best*

Used adverbially in the phrase βέλτιον σὺ γινώσκεις, "you well know," 2 Tim 1:18; cf. BDF §244.2; similarly also Acts 10:28 D.

Βενιαμίν *Beniamin* Benjamin*

The indeclinable name of the tribe of Benjamin, from Heb. *binyāmîn* (cf. Gen 35:16, 18; 45:12, etc.): Acts 13:21, on King Saul's origin (cf. 1 Sam 8:5; 10:21, 24); Rom 11:1; Phil 3:5, of the tribal background of Paul; Rev 7:8, in the enumeration of the twelve thousand who are sealed from each of the tribes of Israel. A. Bertsch, *LTK* II, 204f.; J. A. Soggin, *BHH* I, 216; *BL* 191f.

Βερνίκη, ης *Bernikē* Bernice*

Lit.: J. Blinzler, *LTK* II, 217. — E. Haenchen, *The Acts of the Apostles* (1971) 671f., 676, 681. — Josephus, LCL IX (1965), 630 (index s.v. 2). — É. Mireaux, *La reine Bérénice* (1951). — Schürer I, 474-76, 479, 571f. — U. Wilcken, PW III, 287-89.

1. Βερνίκη is the vernacular form of Βερενίκη, the Macedonian form of Φερενίκη (cf. Veronica) = bringer of victory. The Bernice mentioned in the NT (cf. Josephus *Ant.* and *B.J.;* Tacitus *Hist.* ii.81; Suetonius *Caes. Tit.* 7; Dio Cassius lxvi.15, 18) was the daughter of Agrippa I born in A.D. 28. After a number of "marital relations" (BAGD s.v.) she lived with her brother, Agrippa II. At the outbreak of the Jewish war in A.D. 66, she stood with her brother in Jerusalem on the side of the Jewish peace party, but changed suddenly to the Roman side and became the mistress of Titus, who later sent her away at the urging of the Romans and again later on his own accord, "invitus invitam" (Suetonius).

2. According to Acts 25:13 Agrippa and Bernice visited the Roman prefect Festus in Caesarea. In the company of noble companions (v. 23), they heard Paul's last sermon in Jewish territory. Why did Luke make, of all people, this "pretty couple who lived in incest" (Wellhausen, translated in Haenchen 674) Paul's main addressees and why

did he specifically include this woman, "who was as bigoted as she was dissolute" (Schürer 475; Acts 25:23; 26:30)? Besides providing an answer from Jewish authorities to the question of Paul's guilt (25:26; 26:31f.), Luke is concerned to provide an appropriate account concerning Christianity (cf. 26:26) in the form of ancient historiography. "What is significant for world history demanded as its framework high society, the world of the high and the mighty" (Haenchen 679).

W. Radl

Βέροια, ας *Beroia* Beroea*

A city on the Astreus River in Macedonia in which Paul and Silas conducted a successful mission on the "second missionary journey" in connection with their stay in Thessalonica (Acts 17:10, 13). According to v. 10 there was a synagogue in Beroea. D. H. Madvig, *ISBE* I, 462; E. Oberhummer, PW III, 304-6; S. Schulz, *BHH* I, 222; J. Seibert, *LAW* 456; A. Wikenhauser, *LTK* II, 261; *BL* 195.

Βεροιαῖος, 3 *Beroiaios* from Berea*

In Acts 20:4 Sopater *from Berea* is named as one of the traveling companions of Paul.

Βεώρ *Beōr* Beor

Mentioned in 2 Pet 2:15 B 453 vg^{mss} sy^{ph} and other authorities as the name of the father of Balaam; → Βοσόρ.

Βηθαβαρά *Bēthabara* Bethabara

John 1:28 TR in place of → Βηθανία 2.

Βηθανία, ας *Bēthania* Bethany*

Lit.: Abel, *Géographie* II, 243, 264-67. — A. Barrois, *DBSup* I, 968-70. — K. W. Clark, *IDB* I, 387f. — S. Dockx, "Béthanie, au-delà du Jourdain. Jn 1, 28," *idem, Chronologies néotestamentaires et Vie de l'Église primitive* (1976) 12-20. — L. Heidet, *DB* I, 1654-62. — C. Kopp, *LTK* I, 305-7. — *idem, Stätten* 153-66, 319-38.

The NT refers to two different places as Bethany, both in the Gospels:

1. Bethany near Jerusalem (Mark 11:1; John 11:18) was on the eastern slope of the Mount of Olives, 15 stadia (2.8 km. = 1.7 miles) from Jerusalem. When Jesus came near "Bethphage and Bethany," he sent two of his disciples to bring the colt for his entrance into Jerusalem (Mark 11:1 par. Luke 19:29). In the evening he returned with the twelve to Bethany to spend the night (Mark 11:11 par. Matt 21:17), and then left again on the following day (Mark 11:12). The anointing of Jesus prior to the Passion occurred in Bethany "in the house of Simon the leper" (Mark 14:3 par. Matt 26:6).

John 12:1 also places an anointing (by Mary) in Bethany, but this occurs in the house of Lazarus, Mary, and Martha (12:1-8); Bethany is called "the village of Mary and her sister Martha" (11:1, at the beginning of the narrative of the raising of Lazarus [11:1-46; see also v. 18]).

Luke 24:50f. reports that Jesus (at Easter) blessed the disciples near Bethany and then "was carried up into heaven." This statement stands in some tension with Acts 1:4-12, where the Mount of Olives is the place of the ascension.

2. The exact location of "Bethany beyond the Jordan, where John was baptizing" (mentioned only in John 1:28) cannot be identified. Already in the 3rd cent. it was not traceable (Origen). The reading can scarcely be explained as a secondary variant derived from Βηθαβαρά (the latter is the reading of C^2 K Π Ψ^c sy$^{s, c}$ sa Origen Eusebius Epiphanius) or Βηθαραβά (א^b 892^{mg} sy$^{h, mg}$ Origen). The oldest and best text witnesses (𝔭$^{66, 75}$ א* A B C* L it sy^p) have Βηθανία and thus offer the original reading (R. Schnackenburg, *The Gospel according to St John* I [1968]; *TCGNT* ad loc.).

G. Schneider

Βηθζαθά (Βηζαθά) *Bethzatha*
Βηθεσδά *Bēthesda* Bethesda*

Lit.: A. van den Born and W. Baier, *BL* 203. — J. Jeremias, *The Rediscovery of Bethesda* (1966). — R. Schnackenburg, *The Gospel according to St John* II (1979). — D. J. Wieand, "John V, 2 and the Pool of Bethesda," *NTS* 12 (1965/66) 392-404.

1. Bethesda is mentioned in the NT only in John 5:2 (RSV "Bethzatha"), where it is given as the Hebrew name of a site "by the Sheep Pool" (RSV "by the Sheep Gate a pool") which had "five porticoes." The site in Jerusalem, where according to vv. 1-9b the healing of a man who had been ill thirty-eight years took place, was venerated by Christian pilgrims for centuries. Its location has been confirmed archaeologically (cf. Jeremias).

While the name is transmitted in various forms, preference is to be given to Βηθεσδά (C Koine Θ, etc.), which best corresponds to Heb. *byt 'šdtyn* (3Q15 11:12f.). The dual form probably refers to the two (excavated) water basins. The basic element of the name is etymologically unclear. The other name Βηζαθά (L it^e) and the form Βηθζαθά (א 33 Eusebius; followed in *UBSGNT*) are Greek transcriptions of a corresponding Aramaic form (cf. *TCGNT* ad loc.).

Bethesda was a giant installation hewn 7 to 8 m. into bedrock. Four of the five porticoes surrounded the double pool on all sides. The smaller pool was to the north (ca. 40 × 50 m.) and the larger one to the south (*ca.* 50 × 60 m.). The fifth portico was erected on a 6.5 m. partition between the two pools. The porticoes were probably erected by Herod the Great. In any case the existence of the installation is assured by the Copper Scroll from Qumran (3Q15, *ca.* A.D. 35-65) for the decade before the destruction of Jerusalem. The installation was fed with rainwater which ran from the side of the valley which led into the Kidron Valley. In addition, it was probably fed also by an underground spring. Since 1961 baths have been found which had been hewn in the rock east of the two large basins. These were used to provide water for a network of smaller canals. These baths were probably where the sick went to, not the 13 m.-deep pool. The complex was probably used for sacral, not merely therapeutic, bathing already in the time of Jesus (so van den Born and Baier).

2. The authenticity of John 5:3b-4 is disputed for good reason and should not be considered part of the original text of the Gospel. Early copyists probably intensified the miraculous element of the procedure, according to which the first person into the water was healed. The angel who goes into the water thus probably depicts a popular explanation of the water's intermittent rising from the spring. The early gloss is lacking in the best mss. (𝔭[66, 75] ℵ B C* D, etc.).

H. Leroy

Βηθλέεμ *Bēthleem* Bethlehem*

1. Occurrences — 2. History — 3. Location — 4. Usage in the NT — 5. The tradition of the Grotto of the Nativity

Lit.: R. E. Brown, *The Birth of the Messiah* (1977) (index s.v.). — J. D. M. Derrett, "The Manger at Bethlehem," *SE* VI (1973) 86-94. — Kopp, *Stätten* 10-85. — G. Kroll, *Auf den Spuren Jesu* (⁵1974) 41-66. — W. Schmithals, "Die Weihnachtsgeschichte Luk 2, 1-20," FS Fuchs 281-97. — W. A. Schulze, "Zur Geschichte der Auslegung von Mt 2, 1-12," *TZ* 31 (1975) 150-60. — H. Schürmann, *Lukas* (HTKNT) I, 97-115.

1. Βηθλέεμ is an indeclinable place name (according to the LXX, for Heb. *bêṯ leḥem,* also Βαιθλέεμ, see Hatch/Redpath Sup. 33a, 39c; cf., however, Josephus: Βηθλέμα, -ων, Βηθλέεμα, -ων, and Βηθλεέμη, ης; see A. Schalit, *Namenwörterbuch zu Flavius Josephus* [1968] 27, col. b). Bethlehem is called the birthplace of Christ in the NT only in the early narrative of Matthew (2:1, 5f., 8, 16) and Luke (2:4, 15), as well as in John 7:42. In Matthew it is called "Bethlehem of Judea" (cf. also Josephus *Ant.* v.318) to distinguish it from a place in Galilee of the same name in the tribal area of Zebulun (Josh 19:15). Matt 2:6 (citing Mic 5:1 LXX) speaks of "Bethlehem, in the land of Judah." Luke gives the full expression "to Judea, to the city of David, which is called Bethlehem" (2:4). John 7:42 refers to the witness of the "Scripture" generally (see 2 Sam 7:12; Ps 89:3f.; and esp. Mic 5:2).

2. Bethlehem, about 8 km. south of Jerusalem (Josephus *Ant.* vii.312 speaks imprecisely of 20 stadia), first appears in the Amarna letters (14th cent. B.C.) as *bit ilu laḥama* ("house of the goddess Lahama"). In the OT it is most important as the place of origin of the family of David (1 Sam 16:18; 20:6; 2 Sam 2:32; 21:19; 23:14, 24; Ruth 1:22; 2:4; 4:11). Elsewhere, Bethlehem is only of secondary importance (see Judg 17:7; 19:1; 1 Chr 2:50-55; 4:4, 22; 2 Chr 11:6; Ezra 2:21; Neh 7:26).

The prophecy in Mic 5:2, which associates Bethlehem with Ephrathah (i.e., the area of origin of the Ephrathites, the smallest among the clans of Judah), became especially important for the anticipation of the messiah "from the house of David." According to 1 Sam 17:12, David was "the son of an Ephrathite of Bethlehem in Judah, named Jesse" (cf. also *T. Reu.* 3:13). An older tradition had misplaced the grave of Rachel (Gen 35:19f.; 48:7) on "the way to Ephrath (that is, Bethlehem)" (thus, at any rate, according to an earlier gloss; cf., however, Jer 31:15; 1 Sam 10:2). One must assume that in NT times the expectation of a messiah from the house of David was closely connected with the place. Jewish sources of later times understand it in the same way (Billerbeck I, 83). Josephus (e.g., *Ant.* vii.312) always calls Bethlehem a "city." John (7:42) says it is a "village."

3. Bethlehem is situated on two hills connected by a saddle, east of the road from Jerusalem to Hebron, approximately 760 to 800 m. above sea level, which falls off steeper to the south than to the north. The Judean desert extends to the east. The ice-age settlement was on the east hill, as was also probably the site during Greco-Roman times. Here Emperor Constantine or his mother Helena built the Church of the Nativity (Eusebius *Vit. Const.* iii.41ff.) over a cave that eventually was widened into a system of caves.

4. Although early texts of the NT speak confessionally of Jesus as the Messiah, "descended from David according to the flesh" (Rom 1:3; also 9:5), the problem of the place of birth remains a matter of dispute. The Gospels of Matthew and Luke both name Bethlehem but deviate considerably in their descriptions of the historical circumstances of the birth. In doing so, they are not free of apologetic and christological interests. The statement in John 7:42 shows just how much pressure the Gospel writers were under to prove the connection of Jesus with Bethlehem.

Matthew calls Bethlehem the birthplace of Jesus in the framework of the story of the Magi (2:1-12). He considers Bethlehem the home of Jesus' parents. The story culminates in the prophecy in Mic 5:2. The short attached narratives about the flight to Egypt and the murder of the children in Bethlehem (Matt 2:13-15 and vv. 16-18) betray the same interest in declaring the prophecy of the OT fulfilled (see Hos 11:1 and Jer 38:15).

In contrast to Matthew, Luke both relates Jesus' birth chronologically to the imposition of a "first" census of the Empire and also makes the census the setting for the circumstances of the birth. The parents of Jesus thus have been compelled to go from Nazareth to Bethlehem to enroll themselves there as descendants of David with the census authorities. Luke, who twice speaks emphatically of the "city of David" (2:4, 11), wants to accent the fulfillment of the biblical promise.

The other tradition of the NT starts with the fact that Jesus grew up in the hometown of Nazareth (→ Ναζαρέτ) (Mark 6:1-6; Matt 2:23; Luke 4:16-30; John 1:44-46). The Galilean origin of Jesus was reason for opponents to doubt his messianic legitimacy. One instance of the debate is reflected in John 7:42f.

5. The tradition bound to the Grotto of the Nativity is proof of an early Christian interest in the place, but it cannot assure the historicity of the Matthean and Lukan testimonies. The tradition becomes visible first with Justin (*Dial.* 78.5). He probably meant the cave by which Emperor Hadrian installed a Tammuz shrine and over which Emperor Constantine later built the Church of the Nativity (according to Jerome *Epistula ad Paulinum* 58.3). According to Origen *Cels.* i.51, the cave was "shown" to visitors in the 3rd cent. A.D. *Prot. Jas.* (17:2; 18:1) suggests a different place.

A. Strobel

Βηθσαϊδά(ν) *Bēthsaïda(n)* Bethsaida*

Lit.: ABEL, *Géographie* II, 279f. — BAGD s.v. — A. VAN DEN BORN, *BL* 204f. — G. DALMAN, *Orte und Wege Jesu* (BFCT 2/1, 1967) 173-80. — M. S. ENSLIN, *BHH* I, 234. — KOPP, *Stätten* 230-43. — C. KOPP, *LTK* II, 314f.

Heb. *bêṯ ṣayᵉḏâ* ("fishing place") is on the north end of Lake Gennesaret east of the mouth of the Jordan (Josephus *B.J.* ii.167f.; iii.506-15). It was elevated to the status of a city by Herod Philip in honor of Caesar Augustus and named *Bethsaida Julia* after his daughter (Josephus *Ant.* xviii.28). Nero allocated it to King Agrippa (*Ant.* xx.158f.; *B.J.* ii.252). Bethsaida is assumed to be the city (or village) at et-Tell or Khirbet el-ʿAraj. Because of Mark 6:45, compared with v. 53, a second Bethsaida has been assumed. But πρός in v. 45 suggests only the direction (as opposed to εἰς in 8:22); besides, "cross over" does not necessarily mean a trip to the other shore; according to Josephus (*Vita* 59), one crosses over from Tiberias to Tarichea.

In the Q tradition (Matt 11:21 par. Luke 10:13) Bethsaida is cursed by Jesus because of the unbelief of its inhabitants. According to Matt 11:20 it belongs with Chorazin and Capernaum as cities in which Jesus had worked many wonders. During the trip across the lake in the night to (πρός) Bethsaida, Jesus reveals himself to the disciples (Mark 6:45). In the vicinity of the village he heals a blind man (8:22-26). Luke 9:10 names the vicinity of the city Bethsaida as the scene of the first feeding of the multitudes (as opposed to Mark and Matthew, which speak of a solitary area). This localization is probably connected with Luke's conception that Christianity gains a foothold in the cities—or, in any case, takes from them its starting point (i.e., Hellenistic urban culture). One must also deal historically and redaction-critically with the literary preparation for 10:13. Influence from Mark 6:45 and 8:22 is very questionable. Bethsaida was the hometown of Peter, Andrew, and Philip (John 1:44; 12:21).

A. Fuchs

Βηθφαγή *Bēthphagē* Bethphage*

Lit.: ABEL, *Géographie* II, 279. — BILLERBECK I, 839f. — J. FINEGAN, *The Archeology of the NT* (1969) 88-91. — KOPP, *Stätten* 323-32. — E. LOHMEYER, *Markus* (KEK) 228f. — R. PESCH, *Markus* (HTKNT) II, 176-78. — K. L. SCHMIDT, *Der Rahmen der Geschichte Jesu* (1919, repr. 1969) 295-97.

1. The name Βηθφαγή, translatable as "house of figs," refers to a place near Jerusalem situated between the old Roman road and Bethany on the Mount of Olives, probably on the east side of the Mount (Finegan 90; but cf. Lohmeyer 228), most often identified with the present Kefr eṭ-Ṭûr. In rabbinic tradition it belongs to the municipal area of Jerusalem. The texts that speak, e.g., of the proper places for eating the paschal lamb cite Bethphage as the most remote urban district allowed (Billerbeck).

2. Βηθφαγή does not appear in the LXX and is found in the NT only in Mark 11:1 par. Matt 21:1/Luke 19:29. One variant referred to by Origen does not have the name in Mark. Its weak attestation, however, and the agreement otherwise of the Synoptics favor as the original reading "Bethphage near Bethany." Logically and topographically Matthew speaks the clearest; Mark speaks from a Jerusalem perspective. The parallel in Mark 11:2, with "the village opposite you," no doubt has Bethphage in mind because of the nearness of the descent from the Mount of Olives. Also, the area of Jerusalem began here. It underscores the meaning of the entry into the Holy City when an animal for riding is placed at Jesus' disposal right on its boundary (cf. Finegan 91).

W. Radl

βῆμα, ατος, τό *bēma* step; seat; platform*

1. Occurrences in the NT — 2. Meaning — 3. Idioms

Lit.: E. REISCH, PW III, 264f. — A. M. SCHNEIDER, *RAC* II, 129f.

1. The noun βῆμα, derived from the vb. βαίνω ("step"), appears 12 times in the NT—8 times in Acts, twice in Paul, and once each in Matthew and John.

2. The original meaning *step* is retained only in Acts 7:5 in an indication of length, βῆμα ποδός, "a foot's *length*" = "length of a step," taken from Deut 2:5 LXX. In all other cases we encounter the common use in the Hellenistic official and legal language as a t.t. for public seats or stands. In Acts 12:21 βῆμα is used for a *speaker's platform* from which Herod Agrippa addresses a group of people. In Matt 27:19 and John 19:13, just as in Acts 18:12, 16f.; 25:6, 10, 17, βῆμα indicates the portable *official seat (sella curulis)* on which the higher Roman officials sat in their function as judge (cf. Josephus *B.J.* ii.301): the judgment

seat of Pilate in Jerusalem at the trial of Jesus, of Gallio in Corinth (foundations for this βῆμα have been excavated on the south side of the agora; cf. E. Kirsten and W. Kraiker, *Griechenlandkunde* [[4]1962] 321), and of Festus in Caesarea at the interrogation of Paul.

In 2 Cor 5:10 and Rom 14:10 Paul uses the word in the description of the final judgment: "For we must all appear before the *judgment seat* of Christ" (or "of God"). Βῆμα replaces θρόνος here (cf. *Sib. Or.* ii.218; viii.222, 242; also Pol. *Phil.* 6:2), which is the commonly used term for the seat of the last judgment (cf. Dan 7:9; *1 Enoch* 45:3; 47:3; Matt 19:28; 25:31f.; Acts 20:4, 11).

3. Two idiomatic expressions are relevant for the NT use of βῆμα: "sitting on the βῆμα," as an expression of the official, esp. the judicial, function (Matt 27:19; John 19:13; Acts 12:21; 25:6, 17); and "(standing) before the βῆμα," as a description of the judicial situation (Acts 18:17; 25:10; Rom 14:10; 2 Cor 5:10).

B. Schaller

βήρυλλος, ου, ὁ (ἡ) *bēryllos* beryl*

According to Rev 21:20, the eighth cornerstone of the wall of the heavenly Jerusalem is a βήρυλλος, a precious stone of sea-green color (cf. Exod 28:20; Ezek 28:13: βηρύλλιον), perhaps an aquamarine. W. Frerichs, *BHH* I, 363; *BL* 355.

βία, ας, ἡ *bia* power; violence*

In the NT only in Acts. According to 5:26 the apostles are brought "without *violence*" (οὐ μετὰ βίας) before the Sanhedrin; in 21:35 the *violence* of the crowd is pressing against Paul (cf. 24:7 v.l.); in 27:41 Paul's ship experiences the *force* (of the waves; τῶν κυμάτων added by 𝔭[74] C Koine and others).

βιάζομαι *biazomai* use force on; use power; behave violently*
βιαστής, οῦ, ὁ *biastēs* one who is violent*

1. Occurrences in the NT — 2. Meaning in Luke and Matthew — 3. Tradition history

Lit.: P. W. Barnett, "Who Were the 'Biastai' (Mt 11, 12-13)?" *RTR* 36 (1977) 65-70. — G. Braumann, " 'Dem Himmelreich wird Gewalt angetan' (Mt 11:12 par.)," *ZNW* 52 (1961) 104-9. — *idem, DNTT* III, 711f. — F. W. Danker, "Luke 16:16—An Opposition Logion," *JBL* 77 (1958) 231-43. — Goppelt, *Theology* I, 64. — Jeremias, *Theology* 46f., 111f. — P.-H. Menoud, "Le sens du verbe βιάζεται dans Lc 16, 16," FS Rigaux 207-12. — E. Moore, "ΒΙΑΖΩ, ΑΡΠΑΖΩ, and Cognates in Josephus," *NTS* 21 (1974/75) 519-43. — N. Perrin, *The Kingdom of God in the Teaching of Jesus* (1963) 171-74. — G. Schrenk, *TDNT* I, 609-14. — Schulz, *Q* 261-67. — For further bibliography see *TWNT* X, 1015.

1. The vb. βιάζομαι appears in Matt 11:12 par. Luke 16:16 (Q). The designation of the logion as the "violence passage" originates from the noun βιαστής, which is used in the parallel verse in Matthew. This has always been a crux interpretum.

2. The changes made by Luke reveal the following: Luke replaces the predicate βιάζεται, which is difficult to understand in connection with the subj. ἡ βασιλεία τοῦ θεοῦ (cf. Matthew), with εὐαγγελίζεται. In the second sentence, which is attached paratactically, he deletes the equally difficult βιασταὶ ἁρπάζουσιν and replaces it with the new subj. πᾶς and with the vb. βιάζεται from the first sentence. He assists the understanding of βιάζεται by adding the prep. εἰς, which indicates the goal of a movement. In accordance with the salvation-historical thinking of Luke, the time of the law and the prophets extends to the time of John. From then on, the announcement of the reign of God occurs. The εἰς αὐτήν indicates that βιάζεται is to be understood as an intrans. mid.: "and every one enters it [the kingdom of God] violently." At the same time, the πᾶς also includes the avaricious Pharisees (v. 14) of the context, to whom it will signify that the proclamation of the kingdom of God does not make the law void (v. 17), so that those who do not heed Moses and the prophets will also not carry out the "repentance" demanded for entrance into the kingdom of God, even "if some one should rise from the dead" (vv. 30f.).

If one interprets βιάζεται without the obj. in Matthew likewise as an intrans. mid., one must translate, "From the days of John the Baptist until now the kingdom of heaven has forced its way powerfully, with violence." But this understanding runs aground with the second clause, which is connected by καί. The rarely used word βιασταί appears here, derived from βία and part of a family of words whose common semantic element is "violent." Thus it can be translated only as the subj. of ἁρπάζουσιν in the second clause: "and men of violence take it by force." In that case an unbearable contradiction would exist between the first and second clauses, which can be avoided only if one interprets and translates βιάζεται in a pass. sense: "From the days of John the Baptist until now the kingdom of God is *assaulted* [or *afflicted* or *has suffered violence*], and *men of violence* take it by force." Thus the two clauses form a synonymous parallelism.

If one recognizes that the saying speaks in any case of the present kingdom of God, one sees that Matthew includes John the Baptist in this kingdom and understands the ἕως ἄρτι ("finally") from the situation of Jesus, the speaker. Thus the translation is to be understood on the basis of the context: "this generation" confronts both John the Baptist and Jesus, the herald of the kingdom, with defamation and resistance (vv. 16-19); thus "the kingdom of heaven is oppressed until today." That "men of violence take it by force" is a reality already for John as he sits in prison (v. 2); for Jesus the reality is imminent.

3. Unlike the forms of the logion in Matthew and Luke, the context that is determinative for the logion in Q remains uncertain (cf. Schulz 262: ὁ νόμος καὶ οἱ προφῆται ἕως Ἰωάννου, ἀπὸ τότε ἡ βασιλεία τοῦ θεοῦ βιάζεται καὶ βιασταὶ ἁρπάζουσιν αὐτήν). Nevertheless, on the basis of the wording it is to be assumed that John is regarded in Q as "the decisive break in the continuing salvation history" (Schulz 264). After the old period in salvation history, which concluded with John, the eschaton of the kingdom of God begins in Jesus. In the persecution of Jesus and the messengers who follow him, Q portrays the fate of the kingdom of God in the time before the parousia as affliction and powerlessness.

If the logion is interpreted as ipsissima verba of Jesus, he might have spoken of the affliction of the present kingdom in his word and deed (cf. Mark 4:3-8). Of course it would also be possible to understand Jesus' logion here as a metaphor: the men of violence could be understood as tax collectors and sinners who illegitimately seize the kingdom of God and afflict it with violence. In the opinion of Jesus' opponents, such sinners have no claim to it, even though it is granted to them by Jesus (cf. Matt 21:31).

W. Stenger

βίαιος, 3 *biaios* violent; forcible*

Acts 2:2: The coming of the Spirit with a loud noise is compared to a *violent* gale.

βιαστής, οῦ, ὁ *biastēs* one who is violent
→ βιάζομαι.

βιβλαρίδιον, ου, τό *biblaridion* little book*

In the NT only in Revelation: 10:2, 9, 10 (v. 8 v.l.), of a *little book* that the seer receives from the hand of the angel and must devour (cf. Ezek 2:8f.; 3:1-3). The ms. tradition is very diverse yet consistently refers to a small book, which is not identical with the one mentioned in 5:1; cf. also *TCGNT* on 10:10.

βιβλίον, ου, τό *biblion* scroll; writing; document*

1. Occurrences and meaning in the NT — 2. As a term for OT writings — 3. In Revelation

Lit.: U. Becker, *DNTT* I, 243f. — A. van den Born, *BL* 266. — H. Hunger, *LAW* 510-13. — L. Koep, *Das himmlische Buch in Antike und Christentum* (Theophaneia 8, 1952). — L. Koep, S. Morenz, and L. L. Leipoldt, *RAC* II, 664-731. — C. C. McCown, "Codex and Roll in the NT," *HTR* 34 (1941) 219-50. — J. Müller-Bardorff, *BHH* I, 276-79. — J. Nelis, *BL* 265f. — O. Roller, "Das Buch mit den sieben Siegeln," *ZNW* 36 (1937) 98-113. — G. Schrenk, *TDNT* I, 615-20, esp. 617-20. — For further bibliography → βίβλος.

1. Βιβλίον appears 34 times in the NT, 23 instances in Revelation alone; elsewhere three times in Luke, twice each in John and Hebrews, and once each in Matthew, Mark, Galatians, and 2 Timothy. As the diminutive of → βίβλος, it is synonymous with this word in the LXX and the NT and appears more frequently. Βιβλίον and βίβλος come from the old forms βύβλος and βυβλίον and refer to the writing material made from the papyrus plant, which was generally distributed in the Greek world from Byblos (whence the name) in Phoenicia from the 6th cent. B.C. But soon documents of every form, regardless of the writing material, were called βίβλος or βιβλίον, especially in the rendering of Heb. *sēper* in the LXX.

In the NT βιβλίον designates a *book*, a *scroll*, or a *document:* e.g., John 20:30 in a reference to the Gospel itself; cf. 21:25; Rev 1:11; 22:7, 9, 10, 18 (bis), 19 (bis); in 2 Tim 4:13 probably in reference to scrolls (of papyrus, for pre-Christian writings?), contrasted with parchment rolls (or papers; μεμβράναι, for OT writings?), which were more valuable and durable than papyrus; cf. the picture of the rolling up of a scroll in Rev 6:14. Βιβλίον is used 6 times for the sacred writings (of the OT; → 2). In addition, the expression βιβλίον ἀποστασίου (Mark 10:4 par. Matt 19:7), taken from Deut 24:1, 3 *(sēper kᵉrîṯuṯ)*, refers to the letter of divorce that the Jewish husband had to issue to his wife when he put her away.

2. In Luke 4:17 (bis), 20, βιβλίον (τοῦ προφήτου Ἠσαΐου, v. 17) designates the prophetic scroll of Isaiah that was read in the synagogue worship service and that, according to vv. 17 (*UBSGNT*, with א Dᶜ K and others) and 20, was unrolled and then rolled up by Jesus. Here especially with the designation of the Torah scroll as βιβλίον τοῦ νόμου (Gal 3:10; cf. Deut 27:26) or simply as τὸ βιβλίον (Heb 9:19; cf. Exod 24:7), the language of the LXX is adopted (cf. Deut 28:58, 61; Nah 1:1; also Josephus *Ant.* xi.5; *Ap.* i.38). The phrase ἐν κεφαλίδι βιβλίου (Heb 10:7, citing Ps 39:8 LXX; cf. Ezek 2:9 LXX) refers not to the Law but rather to the scrolls generally, which promise the Christ; cf. further τὰ βιβλία for the "sacred writings" (alongside οἱ ἀπόστολοι), *2 Clem.* 14:2 (→ βίβλος).

3. In Revelation βιβλίον refers 8 times to the present book of prophecy (→ 1), of which 7 occur in ch. 22 alone: the λόγοι τῆς προφητείας τοῦ βιβλίου τούτου (22:7, 10, 18; cf. v. 19) include the entire divine revelation in the last days. The blessing of v. 7 applies to those who hold firmly to it. In contrast to Jewish apocalyptic literature (Dan 8:26; 12:4, 9), the revelation of this book is not sealed for future times, for the end is near in v. 10. The formula for the protection of the revelation in vv. 18f. (cf. Deut 4:2; *1 Enoch* 104:10-12; *Ep. Arist.* 310f.) confirms the completeness and unalterability of the revelation in the book of the prophet—in comparison with

John 20:30; 21:25—a new moment in early Christianity when the revelation is codified. This is connected with the apocalyptic tradition.

For the prophet, in Rev 5:1-5, 7 (TR), 8f., God's plan for the history of the last days is put forward in connection with Ezek 2:9 in a document sealed with seven seals (cf. also Isa 29:11; Dan 8:26; 12:4, 9; *1 Enoch* 89:71) in the form of a scroll, an opisthograph (v. 1; cf. Ezek 2:10), which points to the abundance of the events contained in the book (cf. Koep 21-25). Only the exalted Christ, as the one who completes God's will, can open the seven seals (v. 7; cf. 6:1–8:1) and thereby set in motion the history of the end time that the prophet sees and experiences already. By comparison, Rev 10:8 speaks of another book already opened (many mss. have a diminutive, which is appropriate to the context in vv. 2, 9f.), which the prophet—like the prophet in Ezek 2:8–3:3—should take and eat and which will lead him to further prophecies (possibly 11:1-13).

Rev 13:8; 17:8; 20:12c; 21:27 speak of the βιβλίον τῆς ζωῆς (cf. 3:5; 20:15; 22:19 TR: βίβλος τῆς ζωῆς) that is in the hand of the "Lamb." Since the creation of the world the names of those who will be saved (20:15) and who will go into the heavenly Jerusalem (21:27; cf. also Luke 10:20; Phil 3:4; Heb 12:23) have been in it. Thus the OT idea of a list of heavenly citizens is taken up (cf. Exod 32:32f.; Isa 4:3; Ps 68:29 LXX; Dan 12:1; also *1 Enoch* 47:3; 104:1; *1 Clem.* 53:4; *Herm. Sim.* ii.9; Schrenk 619). That idea is probably unrelated to the common Oriental conception of heavenly books of fate (see above; cf. Koep 31-39). As the believers' Book of Life, the book of the Lamb confirms the appointment to salvation; but, according to Rev 3:5, the baptized are also threatened with the danger of being blotted out of the book (cf. Exod 32:32f.; Ps 68:29 LXX) if they do not remain loyal and conquer in the battle of the end time. Also in the other places the idea is not predestinarian; believers show by their own lives that they are in the Book of Life.

In Rev 20:12b, d the Book of Life is sharply distinguished from the books (pl.) of judgment (cf. Dan 7:10; Isa 65:6; *1 Enoch* 81:4; 89:62, 70f., 76; 104:7; 4 Ezra 6:20), in which, according to the tradition, people's evil works are held for the final judgment. According to 20:12, 15, the books of the deeds are generally the basis for the judgment of God; but anyone whose deeds do not conform to God is also taken out of the Book of Life and thus falls into the final death.

H. Balz

βίβλος, ου, ἡ *biblos* scroll; book*

Lit.: F. G. Kenyon, *Books and Readers in Ancient Greece and Rome* ([2]1951). — T. Kleberg, *Buchhandel und Verlagswesen in der Antike* (1969). — G. Kuhn, "Die Geschlechtsregister Jesu bei Lukas und Matthäus nach ihrer Herkunft untersucht," *ZNW* 22 (1923) 206-28. — M. Lambertz, "Die Toledoth in Mt 1, 17 und Lc 3, 23bff.," FS F. Dornseiff (1953), 210-25. — R. Smend, *BHH* I, 240-47. — For further bibliography → βιβλίον; see also *DNTT* I, 248f.; *TWNT* X, 1015f.

Βίβλος appears 10 times in the NT (also as v.l. in Rev 13:8; 22:19a [TR for βιβλίον]; and 22:19b [TR βίβλος τῆς ζωῆς for ξύλον τῆς ζωῆς]) and thus appears less frequently than the almost synonymous noun → βιβλίον.

As with → βιβλίον (2), so βίβλος is used for the sacred writings (of the OT): in Mark 12:26 βίβλος Μωϋσέως (concretely related to Exod 3:2, 6), of the Pentateuch; in Luke 3:4, βίβλος λόγων Ἠσαΐου; in 20:42 and Acts 1:20, βίβλος ψαλμῶν; in Acts 7:42, βίβλος τῶν προφητῶν. Correspondingly, βίβλος also appears in Jewish texts, e.g., Josephus *Ant.* xi.337; Philo *Migr.* 14; in the LXX, however, less often than βιβλίον, e.g., 3 Ezra 5:48; 7:6, 9 (Pentateuch); Tob 1:1. The designation of the Torah scroll as ἡ βίβλος (or τὸ βιβλίον) could form the root for the later Christian use of the term "Bible"; cf. Josephus *Ant.* iv.303 (only sg. in Josephus); 2 Macc 8:23: ἡ ἱερὰ βίβλος; Dan 9:2: αἱ βίβλοι (similar to the use of τὰ βιβλία, e.g., 1 Macc 12:9). The phrase βίβλος γενέσεως in Matt 1:1, "book of the genealogy," i.e., genealogical table (not family tree), also has its roots in the OT, in the Hebrew phrase *sēper tôl^{e}dōt* (Gen 5:1; cf. 5:1 LXX; 2:4 LXX: "history of origins" or genesis), and refers to Matt 1:2-16, where the descent of Christ is shown from the people of Abraham and the family of David.

The "Book of Life" (→ βιβλίον 3) is called βίβλος ζωῆς in Phil 4:3; Rev 3:5; 20:15; 13:8 TR; 22:19 TR (bis).

In Acts 19:19 the pl. refers to the Ephesian books of magic (cf. Diodorus Siculus i.44:4; *PGM* 13:739), worth about 50,000 drachmas, which were burned openly as a result of the work of Paul (cf. H. Conzelmann, *Acts* [Hermeneia] ad loc.).

H. Balz

βιβρώσκω *bibrōskō* consume; eat*

John 6:13: τοῖς βεβρωκόσιν, *by those who had eaten, while eating.*

Βιθυνία, ας *Bithynia* Bithynia*

A region in northwestern Asia Minor, a senatorial province from 64 B.C. (with Pontus). According to Acts 16:7, Paul and Timothy seek in vain to go from Mysia to Bithynia; 1 Pet 1:1 assumes a Christian church in Bithynia. Cf. also the correspondence of Pliny the Younger (procurator of Bithynia) with the emperor Trajan (*Ep.* x.96). A. M. Schneider, *RAC* II, 416-22; A. Wikenhauser, *LTK* II, 512f.; C. Schneider, *BHH* I, 255; *BL* 249f.; R. Fellman, *LAW* 478.

βίος, ου, ὁ *bios* life (in its outer forms and concerns)*
βιωτικός, 3 *biōtikos* concerning life*

1. Occurrences — 2. Meaning — 3. Βιωτικά

Lit.: BAGD s.v. — G. BERTRAM, *TDNT* II, 851-54. — R. BULTMANN, *ibid.* 832-43, esp. 835-37. — A. HULTKRANTZ, *RGG* IV, 248f. — G. LINK, *DNTT* II, 845f. — L. VISCHER, *Die Auslegungsgeschichte von 1 Kor 6, 1-11* (BGE 1, 1955).

1. Βίος appears 9 times in the NT. Besides occurrences in Mark and Luke, it appears in 1–2 Timothy and 1 John. Βιωτικός occurs only in Luke 21:34 and 1 Cor 6:3, 4.

2. In contrast to → ζωή, the pair βίος/βιωτικός in the NT do not describe a benefit of salvation. They refer much more to the domain of the human or worldly and concern the affairs of material existence. Sometimes βίος appears with the meaning *possessions (wealth)* or *inheritance.* In Luke 15:12 the younger son asks the father for his share of the inheritance (οὐσία). The father complies with his wish and divides the βίος, which usage shows that οὐσία and βίος are synonymous here. Likewise, in Luke 15:30 βίος is used in this sense. In 1 John 3:17 the *wealth* (or *goods*) of one person is contrasted with the needs of another. With the gen. βίος τοῦ κόσμου the author expresses the idea that material possessions really belong to the sphere of the world. Luke 8:43 v.l. reports on a woman who had a flow of blood and who had spent ὅλον τὸν βίον, "all her living," on physicians. The same wording appears in Mark 12:44 (par. Luke 21:4: πάντα τὸν βίον). There it clearly refers to the poverty of the widow. The paraphrase πάντα ὅσα εἶχεν in v. 44 makes it clear that here the woman's *livelihood* is in mind.

Βίος is found with another meaning in 1 Tim 2:2, where a civil way of life is enjoined for the sake of protection by the government. In contrast, 2 Tim 2:4 warns against losing oneself in the normal *daily affairs* (. . . ταῖς τοῦ βίου πραγματείαις), in view of one's role as a soldier of Christ. On the other hand, in 1 John 2:16 βίος is used with a clearly negative connotation. Imposing, pretentious behavior (ἀλαζονεία τοῦ βίου) based on *worldly importance* is not from the "Father." In Luke 8:14 βίος designates simply human *life,* the cares and comforts of which lead individuals away from the purpose for which God intended it. Thus βίος is recognized within the early Christian parenesis as a realm of competition to the claim that God makes on human life.

3. **Βιωτικός** appears in the NT exclusively in the pl. and designates, in a limited sense, the *things that are a part of everyday life.* It is used as an adj. in Luke 21:34. The parenetic word of Jesus not to succumb to either the pleasures or the cares of *daily life* coincides analogously with Luke 8:14. Paul uses the noun βιωτικά in 1 Cor 6:3f. The context makes clear that there had been a dispute in the church concerning legal ownership and that the dispute was taken before heathen (= Roman) jurisdiction. Thus βιωτικὰ κριτήρια (v. 4) actually means *legal action concerning matters of possessions.* Paul refers to the eschatological judgment of angels by believers and, at the same time, reproaches the Corinthians for not being able to decide such disputes themselves.

H.-J. Ritz

βιόω *bioō* live (vb.)*

1 Pet 4:2: the earthly lifetime still remaining after baptism and before the parousia.

βίωσις, εως, ἡ *biōsis* way of life; moral conduct*

Acts 26:4: Paul refers to "my *manner of life.*"

βιωτικός, 3 *biōtikos* concerning life
→ βίος 3.

βλαβερός, 3 *blaberos* harmful, hurtful*

1 Tim 6:9, of desires (with ἀνόητος).

βλάπτω *blaptō* damage, harm, hurt (vb.)*

Mark 16:18: with subj. θανάσιμόν τι; Luke 4:35: with subj. τὸ δαιμόνιον, in each case with the negative.

βλαστάνω, βλαστάω *blastanō, blastaō* sprout, germinate; allow to grow*

Intrans. in Matt 13:26 (sg.), *sprout* (ὁ χόρτος); in Mark 4:27 (sg.), *sprout, germinate* (ὁ σπόρος); in Heb 9:4, of the budding staff of Aaron (cf. Num 17:5, 8, 10). Trans. in Jas 5:18: ἡ γῆ ἐβλάστησεν τὸν καρπὸν αὐτῆς, "the earth *brought forth* its fruit" (cf. 1 Kgs 18:41-45).

Βλάστος, ου *Blastos* Blastus*

Name of the chamberlain of Herod Agrippa I in Acts 12:20, otherwise unknown.

βλασφημέω *blasphēmeō* slander, accuse wrongfully; blaspheme*
→ βλασφημία.

βλασφημία, ας, ἡ *blasphēmia* disparagement; slander; reviling*
βλασφημέω *blasphēmeō* slander, accuse wrongfully; blaspheme*
βλάσφημος, 2 *blasphēmos* abusive; slanderous*

1. Occurrences and grammatical constructions — 2. Meaning — 3. a) Blasphemy against God — b) Reviling the crucified one — c) Blasphemy against the Holy Spirit

Lit.: K. Berger, *Die Amen-Worte Jesu* (1970) 36-41. — H. W. Beyer, *TDNT* I, 621-25. — Billerbeck I, 1007-24. — S. H. Blank, "The Curse, the Blasphemy, the Spell, and the Oath," *HUCA* 23 (1950/51) 73-95. — J. Blinzler, *The Trial of Jesus* (1969) 152-62, 186-97. — *idem, LTK* IV, 1117-19. — M. E. Boring, "The Unforgivable Sin Logion," *NovT* 18 (1976) 258-79. — H. Brichto, et al., *EncJud* IV, 1073f., 1084-87. — T. A. Burkill, "Blasphemy: St. Mark's Gospel as Damnation History," FS Smith I, 51-74. — D. Catchpole, "You Have Heard His Blasphemy," *Tyndale House Bulletin* 16 (1965) 10-18. — C. Colpe, "Der Spruch von der Lästerung des Geistes," FS Jeremias (1970) 63-79. — Dalman, *Worte* 256-59, 394f., 399. — G. Jeremias, *Der Lehrer der Gerechtigkeit* (1963) 134f. — E. Lövestam, *Spiritus Blasphemia* (1968). — R. Pesch, *Markus* (HTKNT) I, 209-21; II, 427-46. — H. E. Tödt, *The Son of Man in the Synoptic Tradition* (1965) 282-88. — H. Währisch, *DNTT* III, 340-45. — G. Wallis, *TDOT* II, 416-18. — H.-T. Wrege, *Die Überlieferungsgeschichte der Bergpredigt* (1968) 156-80 (on Matt 12:32 par.). — For further bibliography see *TWNT* X, 1016; on Mark 3:28f. par. see Pesch I, 220f.; on 14:61-64 par. see *ibid.* II, 444ff.

1. The word group βλασφημία κτλ. appears 56 times in the NT: 34 of these are vbs., 18 are nouns, and 4 are adjectives (in Acts 6:11; 2 Tim 3:2; 2 Pet 2:11; and, used substantivally, 1 Tim 1:13). In the NT the obj. of βλασφημέω normally appears in the acc. (cf. 4 Kgdms 19:4, 22; Philo *Fug.* 84; Josephus *Ant.* iv.202; BDF §152.1). Mark 3:29 par. Luke 12:10, by contrast, has εἰς with the acc., a common construction in classical and Hellenistic Greek (cf. BAGD s.v.; cf. λαλεῖν ῥήματα βλάσφημα εἰς in Acts 6:11 and *Jos. As.* 13:13[9]). The noun βλασφημία is connected in Matt 12:31b with an objective gen. (as in Philo *Vit. Mos.* ii.205); in Rev 13:6 the obj. follows πρός with the acc. (as in Iamblichus *VP* xxxii.216).

2. a) When persons are named or presupposed as obj., βλασφημέω can have the simple meaning *disparage, slander, defame* (1 Cor 4:13 v.l.; Titus 3:2; cf. Philo *Spec. Leg.* iv.197), as in secular Greek (see Beyer 621). Βλασφημία likewise means *disparagement, reviling, slander, vile gossip* (so Rev 2:9 and esp. in the vice lists: Mark 7:22 par.; Col 3:8; Eph 4:31; 1 Tim 6:4; *Herm. Man.* viii.3; also βλάσφημος, *abusive,* in 2 Tim 3:2). In 1 Cor 10:30 the vb. is to be understood as meaning *denounce, reprimand* (cf. Philo *Migr.* 115).

b) In the NT the religious use of the word group is predominant. The vb. has the meaning *slander,* while the noun has the meaning *calumny* or *defamation.*

In a more general sense the vb. can be used to express the belief that Gentiles *blaspheme* and *ridicule* the name of God (Rom 2:24 [= Isa 52:5]); that non-Christians *blaspheme* and *scorn* the name of Christ (Jas 2:7); and that false teachers *blaspheme* and *ridicule* both the Church and its faith (1 Tim 1:20; 2 Pet 2:2) as well as the angelic powers (Jude 8-10; 2 Pet 2:10-12). Similarly the vb. is used in parenetic statements: Christians are warned against any behavior that gives occasion for their salvation (Rom 14:16), "the name of God and the [Christian] teaching" (1 Tim 6:1), or the "word of God" (Titus 2:5) to be *slandered* or *brought into ill repute* among non-Christians and thus to become a subject for scorn and ridicule (cf. Ign. *Trall.* 8:2; *1 Clem.* 47:7; *2 Clem.* 13).

Most references speak of blasphemy in the literal sense. The obj. can be God himself or Jesus and the Holy Spirit (→ 3). In Acts 19:37 the obj. is the goddess Artemis (cf. Josephus *Ant.* iv.207; Philo *Spec. Leg.* i.53). Blasphemy against God can be referred to explicitly (Acts 6:11; Rev 13:6; 16:9, 11, 21). But βλασφημέω used absolutely also means *blaspheme God* (Mark 2:7 par.; Matt 26:65a; John 10:36; cf. 4 Kgdms 19:6; 2 Macc 10:34; 12:14). Absolute βλασφημία correspondingly means *blasphemy against God* (Mark 3:28 par. Matt 12:31a; Mark 14:64 par. Matt 26:65b; Luke 5:21; John 10:33; Rev 13:1, 5; 17:3). The absolute use also occurs with the Hebrew and Aramaic equivalents: *giddēp* (*Sipra Lev.* on 24:10) and *gaddēp* (*y. Sanh.* 7:25b) = "to blaspheme God"; *giddûp* (*b. Giṭ.* 56b) and *giddûpā* (*b. B. Qam.* 38a) = "blasphemy against God," *m^egaddēp* (*m. Sanh.* 7:4f./*y. Sanh.* 7:25b) = "blasphemer against God."

c) Occasionally both the secular and the religious meanings of βλασφημέω are present. In Rom 3:8 Paul designates the *charge* of the opponents that his message of justification necessarily leads to libertinism as a *slander* that strikes at the gospel itself. According to 1 Pet 4:4 God is *slandered* when Christians, who are living according to his will (v. 2), are *disparaged* by the people around them. The secular and religious usages are also connected in Mark 15:29 par. Matt 27:39 and Luke 22:65; 23:39. Like the terms ἐμπαίζω (Mark 15:31; Matt 27:41; Luke 22:63; 23:36), → ὀνειδίζω (Mark 15:32; Matt 27:44), and ἐκμυκτηρίζω (Luke 23:35), which sometimes appear together, βλασφημέω is especially an expression for *ridicule* against Jesus and *mockery* of his messianic claim. At the same time, the vb. emphasizes that through this deed both the crucified one and God himself are *mocked.*

3. a) In ancient Judaism words and deeds that impugn God's honor and injure his holiness (cf. *Sipre Deut.* 221 on 21:22: the blasphemer is one who "stretches out his hand against God" *[pôšēṭ yādô ḇā-ʿiqqār]*) are counted as blasphemy against God. Thus God is *blasphemed* when people revile him, curse his name, ascribe to themselves divine powers, or lay claim to divine dignity and position. Each blasphemy against God is a crime worthy of death (see Lev 24:10-23; Num 15:30f.). According to Lev 24:16 it is punished by stoning (*m. Sanh.* 7:4; *Sipra Lev.* on 24:11-23). According to Deut 21:22f. the further punishment included hanging the body on a cross (*m. Sanh.* 6:4; *Sipre Deut.* ad loc.). The law of punishment in the Mishnah sees the carrying out of the death penalty as applying only if the blasphemer had cursed God by clearly pronouncing his name (*m. Sanh.* 7:5). This narrow definition was not valid at the time of Jesus.

The charge of blasphemy raised against Jesus by the

Jews, which is reported in the Gospels, is to be seen against the background outlined above. In Mark 2:7 par. this charge is based on the fact that Jesus claims the right to forgive sins, a right that is reserved for God alone. According to the Markan report, taken over by Matthew, of the interrogation before the Sanhedrin, the high priest described the confession of Jesus (Mark 14:61f. par.) as an overt blasphemy against God, and the council approved the death sentence (Mark 14:63f. par. Matt 26:65f. [but cf. Luke 22:71]). The historicity of this scene is widely disputed. If one assumes it, the question is raised: In what did the Sanhedrin see the crime of blasphemy? (On this question, see Catchpole; Blinzler, *Trial;* Pesch II, 439f.). The messianic claim as such was hardly an occasion for condemnation on the basis of blasphemy (cf. Blinzler for a different view). But the offense of blasphemy could easily have been established if Jesus, in his messianic self-confession, announced his "coming" as Son of Man and judge of the world; i.e., if he claimed God's eschatological authority of judgment for himself.

According to the Gospel of John, Jesus was accused of βλασφημία and threatened with stoning because he, a human being, had made himself God or "like God" (10:33, 36 [with context]; cf. 5:18; 8:48-59). This formulation reflects the post-Easter discussion between Church and synagogue over the Christian confession of Jesus as Messiah and Son of God. John 19:7 is reminiscent of Mark 14:63f.; the Jewish accusers, who demand the crucifixion of Jesus from Pilate, refer to the law in Lev 24:16, which prescribes the death penalty for a blasphemer.

A blasphemer, according to the Jewish view, is also one who speaks impudently against the Torah (*Sipre Num.* 112 on 15:30; cf. CD 5:11f.). The accusation of Acts 6:11 is to be seen in this context, i.e., that Stephen spoke "blasphemous words (ῥήματα βλάσφημα) against Moses [i.e., the Torah] and [thus against] God" (cf. v. 13). In Stephen's words in Acts 7:56 the hearers perceive blasphemy, which is punished by stoning (vv. 57-60).

For the author of Revelation, blasphemy is a characteristic of the beast, which represents the Roman Empire (13:1-10; 17:3). The cult of Caesar is primarily in view. If Caesar claims divine veneration, it is blasphemy. The divine predicates (e.g., *divus,* "the divine"; *dominus et deus,* "Lord and God"; σωτήρ, "savior") are ὀνόματα βλασφημίας, "blasphemous names" (13:1; 17:3).

b) Blasphemy against Jesus as the crucified one is the subject when the persecutor Paul is described as a blasphemer (βλάσφημος) in 1 Tim 1:13 and when it is said in Acts 26:11 that he forced the persecuted Christians to blaspheme. Likewise βλασφημεῖν in Acts 13:45; 18:6 is used to reinforce the Jews' rejection of the proclamation of Christ. For the Judaism of the pre-Christian period, death on a cross was considered in light of Deut 21:22f. as a death under the curse of God (4QNah 1:8; 11QTemple 64:6ff.; cf. Gal 3:13; Justin *Dial.* 32:1; 89:2; 90:1). Accordingly the Jewish opponents and Paul the Pharisee see in the crucified Jesus a lawbreaker under a public curse from God. The blasphemy directed against Jesus consisted perhaps in the cry → ἀνάθεμα Ἰησοῦς, "Jesus is cursed [by God]" (1 Cor 12:3).

c) The saying about blasphemy against the Holy Spirit has been the subject of much debate. On the one hand, it is transmitted in Mark 3:28f.; on the other hand, it has come down in the logia tradition (Q) in Luke 12:10, where it is independent of Mark. (Matthew has combined the Mark and Q versions; 12:31f.) The original version may appear in Mark; it essentially can be traced back to Jesus himself.

Jesus' logion accents esp. the unlimited breadth of the forgiveness of God, who does not exclude even the blasphemer. Only a rejection of the forgiveness that has been granted to Jesus is unforgivable, for then the eschatological Spirit of God, which purifies one from sin (Ezek 36:25-27; Ps 51:11-13), and which is active in the works of Jesus, is disparaged.

According to Mark (cf. 3:22, 30), and probably also according to Matthew (cf. 12:24, 28), the unforgivable sin consists in claiming that the miracles of Jesus, which are done by the power of the Holy Spirit, are diabolical in origin. The logion in Luke is to be understood differently (12:11f.): One who has rejected the earthly Jesus can receive forgiveness, but not one who resists the Holy Spirit in the period after Pentecost, as the Spirit manifests himself in the preaching of Christ by his witnesses (cf. Luke 24:45-49; Acts 1:8; 4:31; 5:32; 7:51).

O. Hofius

βλάσφημος, 2 *blasphēmos* abusive; slanderous → βλασφημία.

βλέμμα, ατος, τό *blemma* glance; look (noun)*

With ἀκοή in 2 Pet 2:8, of Lot, who daily had to witness *with eyes* and ears the crimes of the inhabitants of Sodom and Gomorrah (cf. Gen 19:1-14).

βλέπω *blepō* see

1. Occurrences and basic meaning in the NT — 2. Usage in the Synoptics — 3. Christological seeing in John — 4. Βλέπω in the rest of the NT

Lit.: M. Barth, *Der Augenzeuge* (1946). — W. von Baudissin, *"Gott schauen" in der alttestamentlichen Religion* (1915), reprinted in F. Nötscher, *"Das Angesicht Gottes schauen" nach biblischer und babylonischer Auffassung* (1924; ²1969); 195-261. — N. Brox, *Zeuge und Märtyrer. Untersuchungen zur frühchristlichen Zeugnis-Terminologie* (1961). — O. Cullmann, "Εἶδεν καὶ ἐπίστευσεν. La vie de Jésus, objet de la 'vue' et de la 'foi' d'après le Quatrième Évangile," FS Goguel 52-61. —

K. Dahn, *DNTT* III, 511-18. — E. von Dobschütz, "Die fünf Sinne im NT," *JBL* 28 (1929) 378-411. — P. Fiedler, *Die Formel "und siehe" im NT* (1969). — H. F. Fuhs, *"Sehen" und "Schauen." Die Wurzel* ḥzh *im Alten Orient und im AT. Ein Beitrag zum prophetischen Offenbarungsempfang* (1978). — F. Hahn, "Sehen und Glauben im Johannesevangelium," FS Cullmann (1972) 125-41. — A. Jepsen, *TDOT* IV, 280-90. — H. Junker, *Prophet und Seher in Israel* (1927). — K. Lammers, *Hören, Sehen und Glauben im NT* (1966). — W. Michaelis, *TDNT* V, 315-82. — C. Mugler, *Dictionnaire historique de la terminologie optique des Grecs* (1964) 77-79. — F. Mussner, *The Historical Jesus in the Gospel of John* (1967) 18-23, 68-81. — R. Schnackenburg, *LTK* IX, 598-600. — D. Vetter, *THAT* I, 533-37. — H. Wenz, "Sehen und Glauben bei Johannes," *TZ* 17 (1961) 17-25.

1. The vb. βλέπω occurs 132 times in the NT (20 times in Matthew, 15 in Mark, 15 in Luke, 17 in John, 14 in Acts, 28 in Paul, 8 in Hebrews, 13 in Revelation, and once each in James and 2 John). It is synonymous with ὁράω, θεάομαι, and θεωρέω as well as κατανοέω and καταμανθάνω. It has the basic meaning *see, look, view, notice* (optically), and *comprehend* (visually), as in secular Greek. Already before NT times the original meaning of the literal eye's seeing had been extended to the intuitive, cognitive, critical level in the sense of "look deeply into, see through, become aware of the essence." In Greek antiquity the vb. already had the meaning of a philosophical, religious view—above all, the view of God—or an insight into the cosmic order and universal world reason.

In addition to the secular, neutral usage, in the NT the vb. manifests a very specific theological meaning when it describes the process of receiving a revelation—the prophetic, apocalyptic vision of the hidden and the future or a confirmed insight into the meaning of salvation in Jesus Christ. In the NT when the function of "seeing" as a witness refers to the miraculous presence of the invisible God (Matt 6:4, 6, 18) or the soteriological relevance of the earthly Jesus and the incarnated Son of God (i.e., the expectation of the return of Christ at the parousia), the NT usage shows the direct influence of the OT idea of "seeing" as reception of divine revelation. Cf. the Heb. vb. *ḥzh* and its derivatives with the function of the Nebiim in the OT. In several places in the NT, βλέπω also serves the hermeneutical function of identifying the processes of understanding that are implied in the act of putting faith in God and in Christ.

2. "Seeing" the wonders and signs of Jesus is a deciding factor in the Synoptics in grasping the message of salvation and the claims of Jesus. Even though "seeing" plays a smaller role in the Synoptics than does "hearing," the mission and the nature of the one sent by Yahweh can be recognized in seeing the reality of Jesus (Matt 15:31). On the other hand, unbelief indeed sees, but does not see, because it remains stubborn in the face of the secrecy of Jesus; cf. the motif of hardening from Isa 6:9; 29:10 in Mark 4:12; 8:18; Matt 13:13; Luke 8:10, but also Acts 28:26; Rom 11:8, 10. The eyes that see the salvation in Jesus are blessed (Matt 13:17; Luke 10:23). Recovery of the physical ability to see is a symptom of a believing encounter with Jesus, the eschatological bringer of salvation (Matt 15:31; Mark 8:24; Luke 7:21). The imitation of Jesus demands a consistent looking forward (Luke 9:62).

3. The "seeing" described in John is understood still more fundamentally in that the spiritual act of seeing of christological faith is understood as revelation of the reality of the Son in the believer. Faith that discerns by seeing the "signs" is the response to the revelation of God in the doxa of Jesus Christ, who is the Word become flesh. Faith causes seeing (John 6:40) and allows the Father to be seen in the Son (12:45; 14:9). For John, seeing is a new experience of perception, which results from the total, existential encounter with the reality of Jesus, a new self-understanding of the love of God and the revelation of the Logos whereby the eschatological perspective of hope in the kingdom of God remains fundamental (3:3).

4. In Paul the vb. manifests a striking parenetic usage in the sense of *pay attention, be concerned about* (1 Cor 1:26; Rom 8:24f.; 2 Cor 4:18). The call for inspection in 1 Cor 10:18, "*consider* the people of Israel" (NIV), belongs to the ecclesiological perspective of Paul. In Revelation the apocalyptic, visionary function of revelation stands out sharply in the use of βλέπω in 5:3f.; 6:1-7; 1:12, "see the voice." In Hebrews a characteristic use of βλέπω is present in the formula "see Jesus" (2:9). Close to the parenetic use in 3:12, 19, the adoption of the formula "see the Day drawing near" (10:25) is typical for the eschatology of Hebrews as expressed in the antithesis of that which is seen and that which is hoped for but not seen (11:1; cf. vv. 3, 7).

P.-G. Müller

βλητέος, 3 *blēteos* something is to be added, to be poured in*

Luke 5:38: οἶνον νέον εἰς ἀσκοὺς καινοὺς βλητέον, "new wine *must be put* into fresh wineskins"; the only -τέος verbal adj. in the NT, as in classical Greek without ἐστίν; see BDF §§65.3; 127.4; cf. also Mark 2:22 C Koine Θ *pl*; Luke 5:38 ℵ* D βάλλουσιν.

Βοανηργές *Boanērges* Boanerges*

According to Mark 3:17, when Jesus called both of the sons of Zebedee to be a part of the twelve disciples, he gave them the Aramaic name Βοανηργές, which is immediately clarified with υἱοὶ βροντῆς, "sons of thunder" (or "thunderbolts"; see BDF §162.6). Behind Βοανηργές could be Aram. *b^enê regeš* (or *b^enê rigšâ*) and similar "sons of unrest, agitation," which incidentally is also associated with Luke 9:54. Possible also is Aram. *b^e^nê r^e^gēz*, "a person of courageous wrath," or (most probably) *b^e^nê r^e^gēš*, "sons of restless noise" (the Arabic equivalent to the latter can refer to "thunder").

Βοαν- could come from *b^e^nê* by progressive assimilation of the schwa onto the labial *b*. For discussion, see also BAGD. Since the naming of the first three in the list of the twelve refers not to their character but rather to their mission, one should think of it as the calling of the sons of Zebedee to a prophetic, apocalyptic proclamation (cf. also John 12:29; Rev 6:1; 10:3f.; 14:2; 19:6). C. C. Torrey, "Studies in the Aramaic of the First Century A.D.," *ZAW* 65 (1953) 228-47; O. Betz, "Donnersöhne, Menschenfischer und der Davidische Messias," *RevQ* 3 (1961/62) 41-70; K. H. Rengstorf, *BHH* I, 349f.; *BL* 254; H. P. Rüger, *TRE* III, 604.

H. Balz

βοάω *boaō* call; scream; cry out*

Of the 12 occurrences of βοάω in the NT, 4 are in Luke and 3 are in Acts. Next to the more common use of the excited cry of a group of people (Acts 17:6; 25:24) and the reference, taken from the LXX, to the eschatological call to repentance of John the Baptist (Mark 1:3 par. Matt 3:3/Luke 3:4/John 1:23; cf. Isa 40:3), βοάω is used esp. (as often in the LXX) for the cry of the helpless and powerless: Luke 9:38, of the father of the epileptic son; 18:7, of the cry of prayer to God by the elect; 18:38, of a blind man; Mark 15:34, of the cry of the crucified one to the Father; but also of the crying out of the unclean spirits as they come out in Acts 8:7 (in both of the last passages associated with φωνῇ μεγάλῃ). The vb. is used absolutely in Gal 4:27 (citing Isa 54:1): ῥῆξον καὶ βόησον, "break forth and *shout* [with joy]." E. Stauffer, *TDNT* I, 625-28; *TWNT* X, 1016.

Βόες (Βόος) *Boes (Boos)* Boaz*

Indeclinable name (Heb. *bōʿaz*) of the son of Salmon (Σαλά, Luke 3:32) and father of Obed (cf. Ruth 4:21; 1 Chr 2:11f.) in the genealogy of Jesus: Matt 1:5: Βόες (bis; Βόοζ Koine *pl*); Luke 3:32: Βόος (Βόοζ Koine Θ *pl*).

βοή, ῆς, ἡ *boē* cry; call (noun)*

James 5:4, pl.: the *cries* of oppressed harvesters.

βοήθεια, ας, ἡ *boētheia* help; means of help*

In Acts 27:17 in connection with precautionary measures taken for a ship threatened by a storm: βοηθείας ἐχρῶντο, "they took *[protective] measures,*" probably by tying the ship's hull lengthwise with hawsers in order to prevent its breaking apart. See esp. E. Haenchen, *The Acts of the Apostles* (1971) 703. Heb 4:16: εἰς εὔκαιρον βοήθειαν, "[grace from God] to *help* in time of need." F. Büchsel, *TDNT* I, 628f.

βοηθέω *boētheō* come to the aid of, help*

There are 8 occurrences in the NT, of which 5 are imv. and refer to calls for help. The Canaanite woman asks Jesus for her daughter βοήθει μοι in Matt 15:25 (in contrast to Mark); similarly the father of the epileptic boy, βοήθησον ἡμῖν, in Mark 9:22 (cf. also Acts 16:9) or βοήθει μου τῇ ἀπιστίᾳ, "help my unbelief [to belief]" (Mark 9:24), as a cry of help that risks faith in the word of Jesus and yet knows that it cannot overcome on its own out of its → ἀπιστία (3.b). God helps (= saves) on the day of salvation in 2 Cor 6:2 (citing Isa 49:8 LXX). Christ is sought after in Heb 2:18 as the one who "is able to *help.*" The earth helped the woman who was pursued by the dragon in Rev 12:16. Acts 21:28: βοηθεῖτε, "help!" F. Büchsel, *TDNT* I, 628f.

βοηθός, 2 *boēthos* helpful*

Heb 13:6 (citing Ps 117:6 LXX): "The Lord is my *helper.*"

βόθυνος, ου, ὁ *bothynos* pit; hole; ditch*

Matt 12:11: according to rabbinic parallels, the most likely reference is to a ditch or a cistern; cf. *b. Šabb.* 128b; 15:14 par. Luke 6:39. L. Delekat, *BHH* I, 612.

βολή, ῆς, ἡ *bolē* throw (noun)*

Luke 22:41: ὡσεὶ λίθου βολήν, "about a stone's *throw.*"

βολίζω *bolizō* throw out the sounding lead, take a sounding*

A t.t. of nautical language in Acts 27:28 (bis).

βολίς, ίδος, ἡ *bolis* projectile; arrow*

V.l. in Heb 12:20 (TR).

Βόοζ (Βόος) *Booz (Boos)* Boaz
→ Βόες (Βόος).

βόρβορος, ου, ὁ *borboros* dirt, filth; mud, mire*

2 Pet 2:22: the sow, just after being washed, wallows again in the *mire* (εἰς κυλισμὸν βορβόρου [ἐπιστρέψασα]), a proverbial image referring to apostates.

βορρᾶς, ᾶ, ὁ *borras* the north*

In the phrase ἀπὸ βορρᾶ, "from the north," in Luke

13:29; "on the north," in Rev 21:13, in each case, in connection with the other three directions. BDF §253.5; R. Press, *BHH* II, 1320; *BL* 1236.

βόσκω *boskō* lead to pasture; tend; watch over; (pass.) graze*

Act., *tend* a flock or herd, e.g., pigs in Luke 15:15, lambs in John 21:15, sheep in 21:17. The substantive partc. οἱ βόσκοντες indicates the herdsmen (Mark 5:14 par. Matt 8:33/Luke 8:34). Pass. *graze* or *feed*, of a flock (Mark 5:11 par. Matt 8:30/Luke 8:32).

Βοσόρ *Bosor* Bosor*

Indeclinable name of the father of Balaam in 2 Pet 2:15 (with the majority of the Greek mss.; B 453 vg^{mss} syr^{ph} cop^{sa} arm have, with the LXX [Num 22:5; 31:8; Deut 23:5], Βεώρ; ℵ* combines the two forms into Βεωορσόρ).

βοτάνη, ης, ἡ *botanē* plant; vegetable*

Heb 6:7: the earth brings forth βοτάνην εὔθετον, *vegetation* that is "useful"; of weeds in *Herm. Man.* x.1.5; fig. of evil people in Ign. *Eph.* 10:3 and of false teachers in Ign. *Trall.* 6:1.

βότρυς, υος, ὁ *botrys* grapes; cluster of grapes*

Rev 14:18: the angel with the sharp sickle is charged with gathering "*the clusters [of grapes]* of the vine of the earth" (τοὺς βότρυας τῆς ἀμπέλου τῆς γῆς) after a harvest of grain has taken place (vv. 14-16).

βουλεύομαι *bouleuomai* consider carefully; make up one's mind, decide
→ βουλή 4.

βουλευτής, οῦ, ὁ *bouleutēs* council member
→ βουλή 3.

βουλή, ῆς, ἡ *boulē* resolution, decision, decree, intention, purpose*

1. Occurrences in the NT — 2. Meaning and Usage — 3. Βουλευτής — 4. Βουλεύομαι — 5. Βούλημα

Lit.: BAGD s.v. — H. Gross, *BL* 1891. — E. Höhne, *BHH* III, 2174f. — D. Müller, *DNTT* III, 1015-18. — B. Reicke, *BHH* III, 1551-53. — G. Schrenk, *TDNT* I, 629-37. — F. Wetter, *LTK* X, 1161-63.

1. Βουλή appears predominantly in the Lukan writings: twice in Luke and 7 times in Acts. The other 3 occurrences are in 1 Corinthians, Ephesians, and Hebrews.

2. The subj. of βουλή can be God or persons. Most of the passages, however, deal with the βουλή of God and refer to the *decree* that is in accordance with his will of salvation. As the interpretative motif in the death of Jesus, it supports the understanding of the event as one ordered by God (in Acts 2:23 βουλή is parallel to πρόγνωσις; in 4:28 βουλή is connected with χείρ), whereby those who participate in the death of Jesus (ἄνδρες Ἰσραηλῖται, 2:22; Ἡρῴδης τε καὶ Πόντιος Πιλᾶτος σὺν ἔθνεσιν καὶ λαοῖς Ἰσραήλ, 4:27) actually fulfill the *decree* of God.

The idea of the divine determination of Jesus' death does not, however, eliminate the responsibility of those who participate, in the face of whose evil *intention* and action (in Luke 23:51 βουλή is connected with πρᾶξις) God's intention reaches its goal. On the other hand, in Luke 7:30 it is assumed that the βουλή of God can be hindered. The refusal of the scribes and Pharisees to be baptized by John the Baptist shows their contempt for God's *will* for sinners. Therefore, his will remains unfulfilled in them. Positively, David appears as a model because in his time he was led by the *counsel* of God (Acts 13:36).

In Heb 6:17 the immutability and permanence of the divine *purpose* are stressed. God has confirmed the "heirs of the promise" with an oath (on the topic of constancy and unchangeableness, cf. 1QS 3:15f.). The idea of predestination to salvation appears in Eph 1:11f. The election of the faithful precedes creation. At the same time, however, this salvation, which is grounded in the *decision* of God and which manifests itself in Christ, retains the element of hope, so that the "heir" (i.e., the believer) continues under the care of God.

In Acts 20:27 βουλὴ τοῦ θεοῦ indicates the sum of the Pauline proclamation. The advice of Gamaliel to leave the development of the Church to itself assumes the contrast between the divine βουλή, which gets its own way, and human βουλή, which is doomed to failure (Acts 5:38f.). This tension between God's decision and human *intention* is the dominant theme in Acts. Against all dangers and opposition that arise because of human *designs* (Acts 27:12, 42), the gospel finds its way (by Paul) to Rome.

Paul speaks in 1 Cor 4:5 of the βουλαὶ τῶν καρδιῶν. The expression is paraphrased by τὰ κρυπτὰ τοῦ σκότους. "The things now hidden in darkness" the Lord will bring into light (at his return). The idea of judgment that is connected with the parousia leads to the warning not to pass judgment on others "before the time" (πρὸ καιροῦ). In adopting the symbolism of light and darkness, "the old teaching that God knows the inner self of mankind . . . is eschatologically modified" (H. Conzelmann, *1 Corinthians* [Hermeneia] ad loc.). Not until the judgment are the *motives* of the heart (as the locus of human intentions) made known.

3. **Βουλευτής** *council member** appears in Mark 15:43 par. Luke 23:50 as the designation of the official position

of Joseph of Arimathea (in Matt 27:57 and John 19:38, however, he is introduced as μαθητής). This title generally refers to his relationship with the Sanhedrin (cf. Josephus *B.J.* ii.405). K. H. Rengstorf (*Lukas* [NTD] ad loc.), however, believes that βουλευτής here means "a member of the council of the city of Jersualem," which at that time automatically made him a member of the Sanhedrin. By attaching the parenthetical statement οὗτος οὐκ ἦν συγκατατεθειμένος τῇ βουλῇ . . . (v. 51) to the designation βουλευτής Luke makes a wordplay, apparently wanting to suggest that the other βουλευταί have discredited themselves by their βουλή (concerning Jesus).

4. **Βουλεύομαι** *consider carefully, make up one's mind, decide** appears 6 times in the NT, once each in Luke and Acts, twice in John, and twice in 2 Corinthians. In Luke 14:31 Jesus asks, in an image peculiar to Luke, what king who, with inferior forces, is meeting an enemy twice as strong, does not first *consider carefully* whether he should even begin the battle. In John 11:53; 12:10, βουλεύομαι is used for the high priest's intention to kill Lazarus and for the high priest's and Pharisees' plan to kill Jesus; they *took counsel* to kill them. Βουλεύομαι appears in an ordinary sense in Acts 27:39. The seamen *planned* to bring the ship to the shore. Paul considers carefully the rebuke of unreliability in 2 Cor 1:17 (bis) with the imaginary question of whether what he *planned* could be described as "worldly" (κατὰ σάρκα), i.e., vacillating.

5. **Βούλημα** *intention, will, aim** is found only once each in Acts, Romans, and 1 Peter. In Acts 27:43 it appears as a parallel term to βουλή (v. 42) and here refers to the evil *intention* of the soldiers to kill the prisoners on the ship. Paul speaks of the βούλημα of God in a rhetorical objection in Rom 9:19, where the forcible *will* of God is used as an argument against human responsibility. In 1 Pet 4:3 βούλημα (τῶν ἐθνῶν) appears in a straightforward sense. The catalog of vices that follows describes the content of those practices considered pagan.

H.-J. Ritz

βούλημα, ατος, τό *boulēma* intention, will, aim → βουλή 5.

βούλομαι *boulomai* want, persist in, insist on, command*

1. Occurrences in the NT — 2. Βούλομαι as human will — 3. Βούλομαι as the will of God, of the Son, of the Lord, of the Spirit

Lit.: BAGD s.v. — H. Gross, *BL* 1891. — E. Höhne, *BHH* III, 2174f. — D. Müller, *DNTT* III, 1015-18. — G. Schrenk, *TDNT* I, 629-37. — F. Wetter, *LTK* X, 1161-63. — For further bibliography see *TWNT* X, 1016.

1. Βούλομαι appears 37 times in the NT. Acts has the most occurrences (14), followed by Paul (5), the Pastorals (4), and James (3). The vb. occurs only 6 times in all the Gospels: in Matthew twice, Mark once, Luke twice, and John once. The word appears once each in Hebrews, 2 Peter, 2 John, 3 John, and Jude.

2. Βούλομαι is generally far less frequent than → (ἐ)θέλω as a term for *will.* The exception is Acts, where use of βούλομαι definitely prevails, a peculiarity that is "linked with the fact that Acts is stylistically more akin to narrative prose such as that of Polybius, Diodorus Siculus, and Josephus, who still like βούλομαι, even in the period of transition to ἐθέλω" (Schrenk 632). Thus βούλομαι in Acts refers without exception to human will (5:28, 33; 12:4; 15:37; 17:20; 18:15, 27; 19:30; 22:30; 23:28; 25:20, 22; 27:43; 28:18), exercised to a greater or lesser degree. In Acts 15:37 Barnabas *insisted on* taking John Mark along on the missionary journey. Contrary to the intention of the soldiers to kill the prisoners on the ship, the centurion *was determined* to keep Paul alive (27:43). Earlier, however, βούλομαι refers to a wish: Agrippa *wanted* to hear Paul himself (25:22; cf. Acts 17:20; 1 Tim 6:9; Phlm 13).

Βούλομαι is used of human will also in Matt 1:19; Mark 15:15; John 18:39; 2 Cor 1:15, 17; Phil 1:12; 1 Tim 2:8; 5:14; Titus 3:8; Jas 3:4; 4:4; 2 John 12; 3 John 10; Jude 5. It has an imperative ring in 1 Tim 2:8; 5:14; and Titus 3:8, where Paul, whose apostolic authority is challenged, *commands* a certain behavior of different groups in the local church or of Titus as an individual.

3. As a reference to the will of God, of the Son, of the Lord, or of the Spirit, βούλομαι appears only 7 times. It is used here consistently in its basic meaning of *want,* which is, however, determined by the subj., the one who wants (God, Son, Lord, or Spirit). Consequently βούλομαι is not to be understood only in the intentional sense but rather implies also an event associated with this will. Βούλομαι expresses here, moreover, this will's absolute nature, which overcomes human will and therefore is unquestionable.

In Matt 11:27 par. Luke 10:22, the Son decides to whom he *wills* to reveal God. This does not indicate an arbitrary choice in the relationship but rather says that God reveals himself only in his Son and that, in the encounter with the Son, the relationship to God is determined. In referring to the different gifts of the Spirit in the Church, Paul says that the Spirit apportions to each one individually as he *wills* (1 Cor 12:11). In Luke 22:42 in the Garden of Gethsemane, Jesus appeals to the power of the will of God to spare him the "cup." In Heb 6:17 and Jas 1:18 the will of God in its salvific nature is emphasized: God had sworn an oath to the "heirs of the promise" because he *wanted* to prove to them the unchangeableness of his decision (Heb 6:17). However, in Jas 1:18 βούλομαι is connected with the generating of faith "through the word of truth." On the other hand, the Lord's intent of salvation in 2 Pet 3:9 serves as explanation of the delay of the parousia: The Lord has not yet come again because he does not *will* that anyone be lost.

H.-J. Ritz

βουνός, οῦ, ὁ *bounos* hill, knoll*

Luke 3:5: in the sermon of John the Baptist, with ὄρος (citing Isa 40:4 LXX); 23:30: in the words of Jesus to the lamenting women from Jerusalem, τότε ἄρξονται λέγειν . . . τοῖς βουνοῖς· καλύψατε ἡμᾶς (citing Hos 10:8 LXX).

βοῦς, βοός, ὁ, ἡ *bous* ox, bull, cow*

In Luke 13:15; 14:5, in the teaching of Jesus about the sabbath: each one will give his *ox* a drink or pull it out of a ditch. Another common use occurs in Luke 14:19: ζεύγη βοῶν . . . πέντε, "five yoke of [draft-]oxen"; in John 2:14f. Jesus drives the sellers of the oxen with their animals from the temple (cf. Mark 11:15 par., which refers only to sellers of pigeons; cf. Billerbeck I, 850-52). Βοῦς appears in 1 Cor 9:9 (bis) and 1 Tim 5:18 in the application of the rule of animal protection in Deut 25:4 to the duty of the Church to support its apostles (and presbyters). R. Smend, *BHH* II, 1018; M.-L. Henry, *ibid.* 1328; *BL* ([2]1968) 1481.

βραβεῖον, ου, τό *brabeion* prize, reward (noun)*
βραβεύω *brabeuō* be an arbiter, judge, or referee; direct; control*

Lit.: A. EHRHARDT, "An Unknown Orphic Writing in the Demosthenes Scholia and St. Paul," *ZNW* 48 (1957) 101-10. — V. C. PFITZNER, *Paul and the Agon Motif* (1967), 82-98, 153-56. — E. STAUFFER, *TDNT* I, 637-39.

The noun βραβεῖον appears only in Paul (1 Cor 9:24; Phil 3:14), who takes it from the Hellenistic language of sports. In both cases it refers to the *prize* granted to the winner in the form of a victory wreath (1 Cor 9:25). The essential meaning of the image is similar in the two places: The wreath that is "imperishable" because it is given by God, in 1 Cor 9:24f., when stated in a negative sense, means that Paul or the ones to whom he is speaking do not fail the test (v. 27); and in a positive sense, it means that they partake in that which the gospel promises. Thus, the victory prize, according to Phil 3:14, consists in Paul's reaching the heavenly world, in which God has placed him by divine call, which went out by Christ Jesus, or that he attains the "resurrection from the dead" (v. 11). The image of the race has different meanings in the two instances. In Philippians it shows above all that the goal of the Christian race (of life) has not yet been reached. In 1 Corinthians, however, it challenges everyone to a strenuous and methodical Christian fulfillment of life. But it does not say that only *one* will win the prize.

In Col 3:15 the vb. βραβεύω is used absolutely and has the general meaning *rule, govern, control, determine.* Christians are called to the peace of Christ in one body, the Church. One's experience in the Church context thus should be consistent with one's being set apart in feelings, thoughts, and wishes by the peace of Christ. This peace consists in the fact that the earlier differences between Jews and Gentiles, etc., are invalidated (v. 11).

W. Stenger

βραβεύω *brabeuō* be an arbiter, judge, or referee; direct; control
→ βραβεῖον.

βραδύνω *bradynō* hesitate, linger, delay*

1 Tim 3:15: ἐὰν δὲ βραδύνω, "if I *am delayed*"; 2 Pet 3:9: οὐ βραδύνει κύριος τῆς ἐπαγγελίας (gen. of separation), "the Lord is not *being slow* to carry out his promises" (JB); cf. BDF §180.5.

βραδυπλοέω *bradyploeō* sail slowly*

Acts 27:7: the ship of Paul and his companions "sailed slowly" from Alexandria.

βραδύς, 3 *bradys* slow*

Parenetically in Jas 1:19 (bis): βραδὺς εἰς τὸ λαλῆσαι, "*slow* to speak" (in contrast to ταχὺς εἰς τὸ ἀκοῦσαι, "quick to hear"), with βραδὺς εἰς ὀργήν, "*slow* to anger"; fig. in Luke 24:25: βραδεῖς τῇ καρδίᾳ τοῦ πιστεύειν, "*slow* of heart to believe."

βραδύτης, ητος, ἡ *bradytēs* delay*

2 Pet 3:9: "The Lord is not slow (→ βραδύνω) about his promise as some count *slowness.*"

βραχίων, ονος, ὁ *brachiōn* arm (noun)*

In the NT only in the image of the *arm* of God, in accord with the LXX, of the power of God against his opponents (Luke 1:51; cf. Ps 89:11 LXX). In John 12:38 (citing Isa 53:1 LXX), ὁ βραχίων κυρίου, in reference to the σημεῖα of Jesus. In Acts 13:17 μετὰ βραχίονος ὑψηλοῦ (citing Exod 6:1, 6), "with uplifted *arm.*" H. Schlier, *TDNT* I, 639f.; *TWNT* X, 1016; *BL* 107.

βραχύς, 3 *brachys* short; small, little; few*

Always neut. in the NT. In 4 of the 7 occurrences, the reference is to time: Luke 22:58: μετὰ βραχύ, "a little later"; Acts 5:34: βραχύ, "for a while"; Heb 2:7, 9: βραχύ τι, the

Son of Man was made lower than the angels "for a little while" (citing Ps 8:6 LXX, where certainly the original meaning was that mankind was placed "a little" under the angels). Others references are to a small amount: John 6:7: βραχύ τι; Heb 13:22: διὰ βραχέων, "briefly," or "in a few words"; spatially in Acts 27:28: βραχὺ δὲ διαστήσαντες, "a little farther on."

βρέφος, ους, τό *brephos* young child; infant*

Lit.: F. W. Beare, *The First Epistle of Peter* ([2]1958) 88-90. — L. Goppelt, *Der Erste Petrusbrief* (KEK, 1977) 133-38. — S. Légasse, *Jésus et l'enfant* (1969) 352 (index s.v.). — A. Oepke, *TDNT* V, 636-54. — K. H. Schelkle, *Petrusbriefe. Judasbrief* (HTKNT, [2]1964) 54-57. — E. G. Selwyn, *The First Epistle of St. Peter* ([2]1947) 154-56.

1. Βρέφος appears in the NT 8 times, 6 of which are in Luke-Acts. It designates both the *child not yet born* and the *fetus* (Luke 1:41, 44; cf. Sir 19:11), as well as—in most cases—the *infant* or the *small child* (Luke 2:12, 16; 18:15; Acts 7:19; 2 Tim 3:15; 1 Pet 2:2). An idiom is ἀπὸ βρέφους, "from childhood" (2 Tim 3:15; cf. Philo *Spec. Leg.* ii.33). In most passages βρέφος has no direct theological meaning.

2. The occurrences in Luke 18:15 and 1 Pet 2:2 are of theological interest. In the former, Luke replaces παιδία (in Mark and Matthew) with τὰ βρέφη. Apart from the Evangelist's preference for βρέφος, his word choice is based on his desire to accent the symbolism of the text. After the parable in 18:9-14, which Luke understands as an instruction about "lowliness" (→ ταπεινόω; cf. vv. 9, 14b), the βρέφη by their extreme "smallness" illustrate better than anything else can the message that the Evangelist wants to convey by this episode (Luke 18:16-17 par.)—only the lowly/meek (cf. 1:51f.) will get into the kingdom of God; cf. G. Schneider, *Lukas* (ÖTK) II, 366f.

The image of *newborn babes* (ἀρτιγέννητα βρέφη) has a corresponding parenetic function in 1 Pet 2:2. The simile is explained most satisfactorily as a reference not to Christians in general but to the newly baptized. The main point of comparison is the strong desire (cf. ἐπιποθήσατε) with which the newborn babes demand the mother's breast (→ γάλα), a symbol for the "appetite" with which the newly baptized should strive for spiritual blessings. Therefore, the motif of the innocence of children (cf. v. 1 and 1 Cor 14:20; *Herm. Sim.* ix.29.1-3) does not need to be excluded. The responsibilities that follow from the rebirth in baptism are illustrated.

S. Légasse

βρέχω *brechō* dampen, sprinkle; allow to rain; rain*

Matt 5:45: the subject is God, who "*sends rain* [or *allows it to rain*] on the just and on the unjust"; Jas 5:17 (bis): impersonal "it rains"; cf. Rev 11:6, ἵνα μὴ ὑετὸς βρέχῃ τὰς ἡμέρας, "[in order] that no rain *may fall* during the days . . ."; Luke 17:29: ἔβρεξεν (following Gen 19:24 LXX) is not meant impersonally but rather refers to the action of God; according to Luke 7:38, 44, the sinful woman *dampened* the feet of Jesus with her tears.

βροντή, ῆς, ἡ *brontē* thunder (noun)*

Besides Mark 3:17 and John 12:29, only in Revelation (4:5; 6:1; 8:5; 10:3, 4 [bis]; 11:19; 14:2; 16:18; 19:6). Of the voice of God in John 12:29; cf. similarly φωνὴ βροντῆς, "the sound of *thunder,*" or *thunderclap,* in Rev 6:1; 10:3; 14:2; 19:6. Rev 4:5: ἀστραπαὶ καὶ φωναὶ καὶ βρονταί, "flashes of lightning, and voices and peals of *thunder,*" issue forth from the throne of God as accompanying phenomena of the theophany (cf. Exod 19:16; Ezek 1:13); cf. 8:5; 11:19; 16:18. Correspondingly, the seven seals, trumpets, and bowls in 10:3f. are met by seven thunders, which adopt the voice of the angels (ὥσπερ λέων μυκᾶται, v. 3a; cf. Hos 11:10; Amos 1:2; 3:8; Joel 4:16) and intervene for the seer (cf. also Ps 29:3-9). On Mark 3:17 → Βοανηργές. W. Foerster, *TDNT* I, 640f.; G. Morawe, *BHH* I, 349; *BL* 341.

βροχή, ῆς, ἡ *brochē* rain (noun)*

Matt 7:25, 27, of the (winter) *downpour,* which has such a quantity of rain that it can result in the collapse of a house that has a bad foundation. H. W. Hertzberg, *BHH* III, 1568-71; *BL* 1458.

βρόχος, ου, ὁ *brochos* noose; trap*

In the NT only fig.: 1 Cor 7:35: βρόχον ἐπιβάλλω, (literally) "throw a noose over," i.e., "lay a restraint upon."

βρυγμός, οῦ, ὁ *brygmos* grinding of teeth*
βρύχω *brychō* grind one's teeth*

Lit.: A. Kretzer, *Die Herrschaft der Himmel und die Söhne des Reiches* (1971) 111f. — K. H. Rengstorf, *TDNT* I, 641f.; III, 722-26. — B. Schwank, "Dort wird Heulen und Zähneknirschen sein," *BZ* 16 (1972) 121f. — O. H. Steck, *Israel und das gewaltsame Geschick der Propheten* (1967) 263ff. — D. Zeller, "Das Logion Mt 8, 11f/Lk 13, 28f und das Motiv der 'Völkerwallfahrt,'" *BZ* 15 (1971) 222-37; 16 (1972) 84-93.

The noun occurs 7 times in the NT (6 times in Matthew), always in βρυγμὸς τῶν ὀδόντων in the apocalyptic expression of threat: "there shall be weeping [howling] and *gnashing of teeth*" (AV). The vb. appears only in Acts 7:54.

Matt 8:12 (Q: par. Luke 13:28) is part of a saying about exclusion from the meal with the patriarchs. Thus, in the pericope of the centurion from Capernaum, Matthew confirms the rejection of Israel. Matt 13:42, 50; 22:13; 24:51; 25:30 belong to the redactional conclusions of parables of judgment. Matthew summons the members of his church to act with the justice that Jesus demands and threatens them with damnation to the eternal torment of fire and to the darkness of Hades or with ending up in hell.

The accompanying verbal expression *gnash with the teeth* (βρύχω; Heb. *ḥāraq šinnaîm'al*) designates the enraged baring of the teeth of the mortal enemy (Acts 7:54; Job 16:9; Pss 34:16; 36:12; Lam 2:16) or the despairing gnashing of teeth of the damned in hell (Ps 111:10 LXX; *1 Enoch* 108:3-7; *Midr. Qoh.* 1:15 [11a]; cf. Billerbeck IV, 1029-1118, esp. 1040ff.). There is no association in Acts 7:54 with βρυχάομαι (Heb. *nāham*), the loud roar of the lion rushing at his prey (Prov 19:12; Sir 51:3), with the chattering teeth of the one who is sick with a fever, or with thoughts of remorse and self-reproach.

V. Hasler

βρύχω *brychō* grind one's teeth
→ βρυγμός.

βρύω *bryō* allow to pour forth*

Jas 3:11: a spring does not *pour forth* fresh and brackish water at the same time, an image of one's mouth, out of which cursing and praising should not come at the same time.

βρῶμα, ατος, τό *brōma* food*

1. Occurrences in the NT — 2. Meaning — 3. Usage

Lit.: J. Behm, *TDNT* I, 642-45. — H. Leroy, *Rätsel und Mißverständnis* (BBB 30, 1968) 147-55.

1. Βρῶμα appears in the NT 17 times, often in relation to ethical controversy (e.g., Mark 7:19; Rom 14:15, 20). Those addressed are Jews or Jewish Christians (Mark 7:19), members of a church (Rom 14:15, 20; 1 Cor 8:8, 13; Heb 13:9), or false teachers (1 Tim 4:3). Other texts reflect more specific arguments. The word is also used in the report of the feeding of the multitudes and in the words of John the Baptist (Luke 3:11).

2. Βρῶμα can be translated *food, nourishment,* or *nutriments,* literal meanings that contrast with figurative, metaphoric, and typological uses.

3. Mark 7:19c contains what is clearly Jesus' statement of the purity of all *foods,* as opposed to the Jewish regulations of purity. (It is not to be understood as a reference to some purification accomplished by defecation, which would be grammatically possible.) In Rom 14:15, 20 *food,* i.e., what one chooses to eat (v. 2: one eats "everything," another eats "only vegetables") is held by Paul to be irrelevant for the believer (v. 6; cf. 1 Cor 8:8), although it is still relevant in the exercise of brotherly love. There is a similar argument in 1 Cor 8:8-13. What is at issue is meat sacrificed to idols, which the "weak," out of old habit, still consider as belonging to the idol; therefore they feel concerned about eating it. The "strong," on the other hand, feel they can eat it because of their understanding of freedom obtained through faith. The apostle's opposing position is prepared in 1 Cor 6:13 by his statement about the purpose for food.

A warning appears in 1 Tim 4:3 against false teachers who demand abstention from wine (cf. 5:23), from marriage, and even from (certain) *foods.* Likewise food is an object of contention in Heb 13:9, where it is unclear whether the subject is excesses at cultic meals or ascetic demands. In 9:10 *food* and drink (which have their proper place in OT worship) are classed with the old order, which has only temporary validity.

The pl. is used of necessary *supplies of food* in regard to the feeding of the multitude (Matt 14:15; cf. Luke 9:12 [ἐπισιτισμός]; the Lukan interpolation in v. 13c, however, also has βρώματα, which highlights the contrast between the small amount that is available and the great need). In the words of John the Baptist in Luke 3:11, those who possess βρώματα are responsible for giving it to the poor.

Βρῶμα is used as a metaphor in 1 Cor 3:2; it indicates, in contrast to "milk," the higher demands of Christian preaching and can be translated *solid food.* In John 4:34 the idea of βρῶμα is linked with the previous bidding of the disciples (v. 31) and the question in v. 33, but it also takes up → βρῶσις, which has already been used on another level. While the disciples still understand the ideas βρῶσις and βρῶμα literally, the words here also speak to a higher spiritual reality.

Πνευματικὸν βρῶμα in 1 Cor 10:3 (possibly a familiar expression, see *Did.* 10:3), in this section referring to Israel's exodus from Egypt, is, like the baptism into Moses (v. 2) or the spiritual drink (v. 4), a type; that is to say, "future events are represented in redemptive history" (L. Goppelt, *Typos: The Typological Interpretation of the Old Testament in the New* [1982] 146), that which belongs to the future being here the eucharistic meal. In this reference Paul can speak of "spiritual *food*" because the same Spirit has already begun to work in it.

H.-J. van der Minde

βρώσιμος, 2 *brōsimos* edible*

Luke 24:41: τι βρώσιμον, "something *to eat.*"

βρῶσις, εως, ἡ *brōsis* food; eating; a meal*

1. Occurrences in the NT — 2. Meaning — 3. Usage

Lit.: J. Behm, *TDNT* I, 642-45.

1. Of 11 occurrences in the NT, 4 are in John (4:32; 6:27 [bis]; 6:55), 4 in Paul's letters (Rom 14:17; 1 Cor 8:4; 2 Cor 9:10; Col 2:16), 2 in Matthew (6:19f.), and 1 in

Hebrews (12:16). Three times the word appears in connection with πόσις, "drink" (John 6:55; Rom 14:17; Col 2:16). Βρῶσις is used in aphorisms in Matt 6:19f. and 2 Cor 9:10 (the latter perhaps coined by Paul himself). Heb 12:16 is an allusion to the OT.

2. In contrast to → βρῶμα, βρῶσις refers not only to *eating* as a human activity and *consumption* by insects, but also the *food* itself, particularly in John (then in proximity to βρῶμα). Especially in John the level of literal meaning is lost, and βρῶσις is used in a fig. sense.

3. In the aphoristic saying in Matt 6:19f., βρῶσις, in connection with σής, can only mean *eating* by insects (cf. Mal 3:11), whose activity works destructively and therefore prohibits the hoarding and collecting of earthly things.

Paul uses the word in the sense of human *eating* in 1 Cor 8:4 in connection with the question about the permissibility of eating meat offered to idols. He uses it in the same way in the saying about the kingdom of God in Rom 14:17, which is surprising in view of the context. The verse refers to the argument that has also occurred in Rome between the "strong" and the "weak" (cf. 1 Cor 8) about which foods are permissible in the Christian community (Rom 14:2). It highlights two negative statements (v. 15a, b)—regarding the violation of brotherly love and the ruin in someone's life of Christ's work of salvation—by identifying the positive principle that God's future lordship is already active in the present. Βρῶσις is also found in the sense of *eating* in 2 Cor 9:10 and Col 2:16. Heb 12:16 refers to the bargain between Esau and Jacob about the right of the firstborn (Gen 25:29-34). Here βρῶσις means *meal* or *dish.*

John 4:32 (βρῶσις in the mouth of Jesus), in the dialogue with the disciples, is only outwardly connected with their urging, "Rabbi, eat" (v. 31). "The whole expression 'to have food to eat' becomes a metaphor" (R. Schnackenburg, *The Gospel according to John* I [1968] 445). A similar difference of levels of understanding is also found in 6:27 in the speech about bread. V. 26 exposes the motive of the masses, who are looking for bread (i.e., a perishable *food* [v. 27a]) only to become full. The second use of the idea (v. 27b) lifts it to the level of metaphorical understanding ("the food which endures to eternal life"). The interpretation "eternal life" (v. 27) and "to be doing the works of God" (v. 28; cf. 4:34 in the same connection), i.e., to believe in the one who was sent, as well as the parallel sections 4:13f. and vv. 32f., rule out the idea of a "eucharistic" understanding of this passage. "Enduring *food*" consequently implies the indicative of receiving life and the imperative of doing the work of God, according to which a person believes in the one who was sent. Unlike 4:32 and 6:27, John 6:55 is not metaphorical, by virtue of the twofold usage of ἀληθής ("real *food*" and "real drink" [JB]).

Ἀληθής is favored in John 6:55 because of the better evidence for it (𝔭[66] 𝔭[75] ℵ[a] B C K, and others) and because it is the more difficult reading (compared with ἀληθῶς). However, the grammatical and linguistic function of ἀληθής must be clarified before the verse can be understood accurately. It is an adj. and modifies βρῶσις and πόσις. In general in Greek it means *true, genuine, real, authentic.* In Johannine usage, it means *true, real, reliable* (Schnackenburg II, 62f.).

On the basis of the Johannine usage, the reality of flesh and blood is assumed, but the special accent lies in the quality of this *food* (true food) and this drink (true drink; on the absence of the article with the predicate noun, see BDF §273), which arises out of the preceding verses and the following verse: flesh and blood give eternal life (6:54) and communion with the giver (v. 56).

H.-J. van der Minde

βυθίζω *bythizō* sink (vb.)*

Luke 5:7: ὥστε βυθίζεσθαι αὐτά [τὰ πλοῖα], "so that they [the boats] began to *sink*"; fig. in 1 Tim 6:9 of enticements "that *plunge* men into ruin and destruction."

βυθός, οῦ, ὁ *bythos* "the deep," open sea*

2 Cor 11:25: Paul mentions, "A night and a day I have been adrift at *sea*" (νυχθήμερον ἐν τῷ βυθῷ πεποίηκα).

βυρσεύς, έως, ὁ *byrseus* tanner*

The vocation of a Christian by the name of Simon from Joppa (Acts 9:43; 10:6, 32). The rabbis considered tanning a craft to be scorned. Because of their annoying smell, tanneries generally were outside of cities (cf. Isa 7:3). According to Acts, Peter disregarded these boundaries. Billerbeck II, 695; O. Hanssen, *BHH* I, 548.

βύσσινος, 3 *byssinos* made of fine linen*

This adj. is used substantively with the meaning *fine linen garments.* In the NT it appears only in Rev 18:12, 16; 19:8 (bis), 14 in references to the wealth of the great Babylon (18:12, 16) and to the pure, shining clothing worn by the Church as the bride of Christ (19:8) and by the heavenly armies that follow Christ (v. 14). Moreover, in 19:8b τὸ βύσσινον is explained as τὰ δικαιώματα τῶν ἁγίων, "the righteous deeds of the saints."

βύσσος, ου, ἡ *byssos* fine linen*

Luke 16:19: with πορφύρα to describe the clothing of the rich man; Rev 18:12 TR (instead of → βύσσινος). F. Olck, PW III/1, 1108-14; G. Fohrer, *BHH* II, 1072; *BL* 1038f.

βωμός, οῦ, ὁ *bōmos* altar*

Acts 17:23: the *altar* with the inscription ἀγνώστῳ θεῷ, which Paul found in Athens according to Luke. As here βωμός stands throughout the LXX only for altars of foreign gods (in contrast to θυσιαστήριον); cf. esp. the contrast in 1 Macc 1:59. Luke was probably thinking about altars for "unknown gods" (cf. Pausanias i.1.4; v.14.8; vi.3.5; and Diogenes Laertius i.110, which speaks of ἀνωνύμους βωμούς, "nameless altars") even though inscriptions like that spoken of in Acts have not yet been clearly established. J. Behm, *TDNT* III, 182; E. Reisch, PW III/1, 681f.; R. Smend, *BHH* I, 63-65, 2047; *BL* 53f.; J. P. Kirsch and T. Klauser, *RAC* I, 334-54; E. Haenchen, *The Acts of the Apostles* [1971] ad loc.; → ἀγνοέω 3.

Γ γ

Γαββαθά *Gabbatha* Gabbatha
→ λιθόστρωτος.

Γαβριήλ *Gabriēl* Gabriel*

1. Gabriel in the OT and in apocalyptic literature — 2. Gabriel in the NT

Lit.: BILLERBECK II, 89-99. — BOUSSET/GRESSMANN 320-31. — S. A. HORODEZKY, "Michael und Gabriel," *MGWJ* 72 (1928) 499-506. — C. H. HUNZINGER, *RGG* II, 1185. — R. LAURENTIN, "Traces d'allusions étymologiques en Luc 1–2," *Bib* 37 (1956) 435-56. — J. MICHL, *RAC* V, 239-43. — P. SCHÄFER, *Rivalität zwischen Engeln und Menschen* (1975).

1. Gabriel ("Man of God" or "God is my strength," perhaps also "God has shown himself to be strong," according to M. Noth, *Die israelitischen Personennamen* [1928] 190) is referred to in the OT only twice by name. According to Dan 8:16, he explains Daniel's dream vision (cf. vv. 17-26), and in 9:21 he also functions as an angelic interpreter (vv. 22-27). Whether Gabriel is also referred to in 10:4-6 and 12:6f. remains unclear, but on the basis of 8:15 it is possible.

As with angels in general, the apocalypticists in the intertestamental literature also show a great interest in Gabriel. As one of the sovereign angels (*1 Enoch* 9:1; 10:9; 40:9; 54:6; 71:8f., 13; *Apoc. Mos.* 40; 4 Ezra 6:2; cf. also 1QM 9:15f.), he is considered an archangel (*2 Enoch* 21:3). He makes intercession before God for sinful human beings (*1 Enoch* 40:6; cf. 99:3; *3 Bar.* 11:4; Job 33:22-25) and rules over paradise (*1 Enoch* 20:7). Gabriel is set with other angels over the end of life (4 Ezra 6:1f.); furthermore, God appoints him angel of punishment for the children of adultery (*1 Enoch* 10:9f.; cf. Gen 6:1-4 and C. Westermann, *Genesis 1-11* [1984] 365), and he cooperates with others in the judgment of the angels who have fallen from God (*1 Enoch* 54:5f.). On Gabriel in rabbinic literature, see Billerbeck.

2. Gabriel is the one who announces to Zechariah the birth of his son (Luke 1:19) and to Mary the birth of Jesus (v. 26). As an angel of the Lord (v. 11) who stands before God (v. 19; cf. Tob 12:14f.), Gabriel introduces himself to Zechariah, and Luke 1:26 calls him by name. Gabriel's own introduction in v. 19 is clearly connected with the prophetic office of messenger in the OT, whereby the representative of God legitimates himself by naming the subject of the mission. The objection and the request for a sign by Zechariah (v. 18) and its announcement by Gabriel (v. 20; cf. vv. 63-80) conform to the OT call narratives (Exod 3:1-4, 17; Judg 6:11-22) and point to their influence. Only here in the NT is Gabriel is presented as God's messenger. In connection with OT tradition associated with Gabriel, Luke pictures John and Jesus in the light of the old covenant, emphasized even more by John's appearing as Elijah redivivus (1:17). In other places in the NT, especially in Revelation, which contains so much discussion of angels, sometimes Gabriel may be in mind, although he is not mentioned by name.

D. Sänger

γάγγραινα, ης, ἡ *gangraina* rampant growth; gangrene*

2 Tim 2:17: fig. of unruly false teachers of Gnosticism, who were widespread. B. Reicke, *BHH* II, 1001.

Γάδ *Gad* Gad*

Rev 7:5: the third of the twelve tribes of Israel from which 12,000 servants of God were sealed (cf. also Gen 30:11; 49:19, etc.). K. Baltzer, *BHH* I, 507f.; *BL* 506.

Γαδαρηνός, 3 *Gadarēnos* from Gadara
→ Γερασηνός.

Γάζα, ης *Gaza* Gaza*

Formerly a city of the Philistines in southwest Palestine near the coast, linked with Jerusalem by an important road that went on to Egypt. The Ethiopian eunuch was traveling on this road from Jerusalem (Acts 8:26). K. Elliger, *BHH* I, 516; H. Donner, *LAW* 1028; *BL* 515; G. Downey, *RAC* VII, 1123-34.

γάζα, ης, ἡ *gaza* treasure*

Acts 8:27: the treasure of Candace, over which the eunuch (as he is called here) had charge as the minister of the treasury (ὃς ἦν ἐπὶ πάσης τῆς γάζης αὐτῆς); eunuchs as γαζοφύλακες are mentioned in Plutarch *Demetr.* xxv.900; cf. H. Conzelmann, *Acts* [Hermeneia] ad loc.

γαζοφυλάκιον, ου, τό *gazophylakion* treasury*

In the LXX this word is generally used of the storeroom and treasury of the temple (cf. 2 Esdr 20:38; 22:44; 1 Macc 14:49, etc.) and is to be so understood in John 8:20; i.e., of the magnificent treasury built by Herod in the north part of the women's court (cf. Josephus *B.J.* v.200; *Ant.* xix.294). *M. Šeqal.* 6:5 mentions thirteen receptacles for money offerings, called "trumpets" because they were shaped like funnels and tapered at the top (to prevent theft). Seven of them served for raising fixed duties, five for specific appropriations, and one for general, voluntary contributions. It is fairly certain that they stood in the vestibule of the women's court to which Josephus refers. The events of Mark 12:41 (bis), 43 par. Luke 21:1 take place here.

Yet γαζοφυλάκιον does not have to indicate a certain one of the 13 poor boxes, since the phrase βάλλειν χαλκὸν εἰς τὸ γαζοφυλάκιον (Mark 12:41; cf. vv. 42f.) can describe not only the dropping of money into a poor box but, according to *m. Šeqal. 5:6,* more generally depositing (*zrq* = βάλλειν) of gifts in the treasury, concretely in the thirteenth poor box for general gifts. Since the scrutiny of all gifts at the poor boxes by the priests was necessary (according to *Lev. Rab.* 3 [107a], e.g., a woman had to endure open ridicule by the priests because of a small gift), all those present participated in the presentation of the gift, surely a welcome opportunity for wealthy contributors to commend themselves (cf. Matt 6:2). The real concern of Mark 12:41-44 par. becomes clear in light of the background of the situation in front of the treasury in the women's court. Billerbeck II, 37-45; J. W. Doeve, *BHH* I, 597; H. Ljungman, *BHH* III, 1687; *BL* 1534.

H. Balz

Γάϊος, ου *Gaios* Gaius*

The personal name of several Christians (a name esp. frequent in Latin): 1. Gaius from Macedonia (Acts 19:29), with Aristarchus, a fellow sufferer of Paul in Ephesus. 2. Gaius from Derbe in Lycaonia (Acts 20:4), one of Paul's companions on the trip from Greece to Jerusalem. 3. Gaius from Corinth, who was baptized by Paul along with Crispus (1 Cor 1:14) and who, along with the whole church, showed Paul hospitality (Rom 16:23). 4. Gaius, τῷ ἀγαπητῷ, recipient of 3 John (v. 1). J. Blinzler, *LTK* IV, 486; E. Trocmé, *BHH* I, 508; *BL* 507.

γάλα, ακτος, τό *gala* milk*

Except in 1 Cor 9:7, where γάλα indicates in a literal sense the produce of a herd of cattle, this word is used regularly in the NT in the fig. sense and esp. (with the contrast between milk, as nourishment for young children, and solid food) for the beginning stage of the preaching of the gospel, past which Paul cannot yet proceed with the Corinthians in 1 Cor 3:2 (notice the contrast πνευματικοί–σάρκινοι/νήπιοι and the corresponding βρῶμα–γάλα). Similarly, in Heb 5:12f. (στερεὰ τροφή, "solid food," v. 12; τελείων δὲ ἐστιν ἡ στερεὰ τροφή, "solid food is for the mature," v. 14); v. 13 explains: ὁ μετέχων γάλακτος ἄπειρος λόγου δικαιοσύνης, νήπιος γάρ ἐστιν, "one who lives on *milk* is unskilled in the word of righteousness, for he is a child." In both places the figure of speech criticizes backsliding into the faith of a small child. Similar differences between elementary instruction and teaching for the advanced are linked with the image of milk and solid food in Philo (e.g., *Agr.* 9; *Migr.* 29) and Epictetus (e.g., *Diss.* ii.16.39).

In a different way 1 Pet 2:2, where τὸ λογικὸν ἄδολον γάλα, "the pure spiritual *milk,*" is an image for the pure message of salvation by which the baptized live as newborn babes. This use clearly moves toward the mystery or Gnostic understandings of milk as spiritual nourishment (cf. H. Schlier, *TDNT* I, 645-47), but the idea of the new existence of believers who, like newborn babies, need milk as their special nourishment may be present (→ βρέφος 2); cf. also L. Goppelt, *Der Erste Petrusbrief* (KEK) ad loc.; A. Stenzel, *LTK* VII, 412f.; A. S. Kapelrud, *BHH* II, 1215f.; *BL* 1154; for further bibliography see *TWNT* X, 1017.

H. Balz

Γαλάτης, ου, ὁ *Galatēs* a Galatian (Celt) → Γαλατία.

Γαλατία, ας *Galatia* Galatia*
Γαλάτης, ου, ὁ *Galatēs* a Galatian (Celt)*
Γαλατικός, 3 *Galatikos* Galatian (Celtic)*

Lit.: P. Althaus, *BHH* I, 508-10. — BAGD s.v. — L. Bürchner and G. Brandis, PW VII, 519-59. — R. Fellmann, *LAW* 1015f. — E. Haenchen, *The Acts of the Apostles* (1971) 483, n. 2. — F. Mussner, *Galater* (HTKNT, 1974) 1-3. — W. M. Ramsay and C. J. Hemer, *IDB* II, 377-79. — H. Schlier, *Galater* (KEK, [4]1965) 15-24. — *idem, LTK* IV, 488f. — J. Weiss, *RE* X, 554-59.

Γαλατία (Diocles 125; Dio Cassius 53:26; inscriptions) is the name of the geographical region (cf. the v.l. Γάλλιαν in 2 Tim 4:10) in central Asia Minor formerly inhabited by Phrygian tribes but inhabited by Celtic tribes (Gauls) since 278 B.C. Since "Galatian" more often distinguishes the Celts from other population groups (*OGIS* II, 540f.), Gal 3:1 could refer to the tribal region.

Official Roman usage of the terms is different from that of popular writers and coins. After a changing history (following the domain of the Galatian king Amyntas, who died in 25 B.C.), under Roman domination the tribal region constituted the core of a province *Galatia* with western

(Phrygia, Pisidia), southern (parts of Lycaonia and Pamphylia, Isauria), eastern (Cilicia), and northern (Paphlagonia) regions, although its boundaries continued to be rather fluid. Though there was no official usage that included, e.g., Pisidia and Lycaonia, some writers use *Galatia* for the Roman province (Ptolemy *Geog.* v.14; Tacitus *Hist.* ii.9; *Ann.* xiii.35).

Luke also uses the word that way when he frames the second missionary journey of Paul in Acts 16:6 and 18:23 and takes the route "through the Galatian region" of Lycaonia (Derbe, Lystra) toward Phrygia in the southern part of the tribal area. In 1 Pet 1:1 present-day Asia Minor is outlined: since regional names are not used, *Galatia* refers to the entire province.

The "Galatian churches" mentioned in Gal 1:2; 1 Cor 16:1 might have been in "Galatia" according to the older usage, i.e., in the tribal region (North Galatian hypothesis), but the phrase can refer just as well, in accord with the later usage, to the churches whose founding is described in Acts 13f. (South Galatian hypothesis). Those who advocate the former view refer to the extended period of time during which we find the common transcriptions for the Roman province (*CIL* III, 291, 312, 318; *CIG* III, 3991; *Mitteilungen des deutschen Archäologischen Institutes, Athenische Abteilung* 12 [1887] 182: "overseer of the Eparchy of Galatia and the people [σύνεγγυς] nearby"). Those who favor the latter view refer to Paul's letter to the Galatians and to the collective instructions of Paul in Acts 13f., where we learn nothing more of the establishment of churches in the north by Paul.

Neither hypothesis (see references in BAGD) sufficiently considers the possibility that at that time both meanings were possible and common in use. Also Acts should not be understood as providing an exhaustive description. Luke wrote on the basis of limited, incomplete material. We must remember that Paul did mission work in areas that Luke does not mention due to a lack of material (cf. Rom 15:19, which mentions Paul's work in Illyricum, of which Acts is silent).

G. Schille

Γαλατικός, 3 *Galatikos* Galatian (Celtic)
→ Γαλατία.

γαλήνη, ης, ἡ *galēnē* calm on the sea*

According to Mark 4:39 par. Matt 8:26/Luke 8:24, a (great) *calm* occurred at the command of Jesus (γαλήνη μεγάλη in Mark and Matthew; Luke has only γαλήνη).

Γαλιλαία, ας *Galilaia* Galilee
Γαλιλαῖος, 3 *Galilaios* Galilean

1. Occurrences in the NT — 2. In contemporary history — 3. Γαλιλαία in the Gospels and Acts

Lit.: A. ALT, "Galiläische Probleme," *Kleine Schriften zur Geschichte des Volkes Israel* ([3]1964) II, 363-435. — H. CONZELMANN, *The Theology of St. Luke* (1961). — M. KARNETZKI, "Die galiläische Redaktion im Markusevangelium," *ZNW* 52 (1961) 238-72. — E. LOHMEYER, *Galiläa und Jerusalem in den Evangelien* (FRLANT 52, 1936). — W. MARXSEN, *Mark the Evangelist* (1969). — W. A. MEEKS, "Galilee and Judea in the Fourth Gospel," *JBL* 85 (1966) 159-69. — M. VÖLKEL, "Der Anfang Jesu in Galiläa. Bemerkungen zum Gebrauch und zur Funktion Galiläas in den lukanischen Schriften," *ZNW* 64 (1973) 222-32.

1. Γαλιλαία appears 61 times in the NT, all in the Gospels and Acts: 16 times in Matthew, 12 in Mark, 13 in Luke, 17 in John, and 3 in Acts. Γαλιλαῖος appears in the same writings 11 times.

2. At the time of the birth of Jesus, Galilee belonged to the region under the rule of Herod I (37-4 B.C.). According to his last will and testament, Galilee along with Perea was to go to Herod Antipas, and Judea and Samaria to Archelaus, which, according to Matthew, was the basis for the immigration of Jesus' parents to Galilee (2:22). The region once called "Galilee of the Gentiles" was a prospering land in the time of Jesus. After centuries of foreign occupation, it not only was regained by Jews but became the hotbed of the Jewish national movement of the Zealots (who can clearly be called Galileans) and, after the fall of Jerusalem (A.D. 70), a vital center of Judaism.

3. According to Mark, Galilee is not only the home of Jesus (1:9) but also the center of his work (1:14, 16, 28, 39; 3:7; 9:30; particularly so Lake Gennesaret, also called the Sea of Galilee: see Mark 1:16; 7:31 par. Matthew; John 6:1). He leaves the area (Mark 7:24, 31; 8:27) only sporadically before he goes to Jerusalem (beginning at 10:1). The picture is rounded out by the promise of Jesus to return to Galilee after his resurrection (14:28; 16:7)—referring to his resurrection appearances, not to his parousia. If, in spite of the redactional origin of all references to Galilee (except 14:28; 16:7; 6:21), the general geographical report is also historically correct, then Galilee is also theologically significant as the center of Jewish resistance against Jesus (3:22; 7:1; 10:33; 11:18), as opposed to Jerusalem, and as the prefiguring of the Gentile mission by the journeys Jesus takes into non-Jewish areas from Galilee. The concentration of the work of Jesus on Galilee creates the frame for traditional individual stories and makes it possible to present the gospel as history, as fixed in place and time.

From his source, Matthew throughout treats Galilee as a topographical detail (4:18; 15:29). Moreover, the fulfillment quotation in Matt 4:15 (Isa 8:23) becomes the foundation for the messianic appearance of Jesus in Galilee. The as yet unfulfilled promise in Mark (leaving aside the secondary ending of Mark) of an appearance of Jesus in Galilee sets the scene for Jesus' final commission (Matt 28:18-20).

Luke is completely different. For him Galilee is not the center of the work of Jesus but only where it began (Luke 23:5; Acts 10:37). Because of the preaching of the kingdom of God (Luke 4:43), described programmatically as the task of Jesus, the Lukan Jesus cannot let himself be limited to Galilee in space or time. The Galilean phase of the work of Jesus consequently includes only 3:1–4:44; his further works stretch out over the entire Jewish area (4:44). The resurrection appearances take place in Jerusalem, and Galilee becomes the place of prophecy (24:6). Also the origin of the Galilean disciples corresponds to this viewpoint; their function as witnesses is based on Jesus' movement from Galilee to Jerusalem, not on their presence in Galilee during the lifetime of Jesus (Luke 23:49, 55; Acts 1:11f.; 13:31).

According to the outline of John, Jesus goes from Galilee to Jerusalem three times (2:13; 5:1; 7:10). From 7:10 on, Judea/Jerusalem is presented as the residence of Jesus. But thematically, Galilee is treated in the Fourth Gospel as the home of Jesus, although 4:43-44 could suggest the conclusion that Jesus came from Judea, not Galilee, unlike the assumption in 1:46; 2:1; 7:3, 41, 52. The passage can be explained only if the acceptance of Jesus in Galilee (4:45a) is based on the temple miracle (2:23; 4:45b, 48) but does not yet signify true faith. Jesus would not then support the change of place to Galilee with the words of the prophet in his native country but would predict that he will (also) be confirmed here. It is of theological importance that the origin of Jesus from Galilee becomes fixed in people's minds, in apparent contradiction to his position as Christ (7:41) or prophet (v. 52). In the argument in the synagogue relating to this idea, the majority reject the law cited by Nicodemus (v. 51) in favor of their own reading of the law (v. 52) and show thereby—as they do already by cursing those who accept the messiahship of Jesus, whom they consider ignorant of the law (v. 49)—the misuse of the law against the claim of revelation.

M. Völkel

Γαλιλαῖος, 3 *Galilaios* Galilean
→ Γαλιλαία.

Γαλλία, ας *Gallia* Gaul

2 Tim 4:10 v.l. (א C 81 104 etc.) in place of → Γαλατία.

Γαλλίων, ωνος *Galliōn* Gallio*

1. Occurrences — 2. Biographical material — 3. Gallio and Paul

Lit.: A. VAN DEN BORN, *Woordenboek der Oudheid* (1976) I, 1172f. (bibliography). — A. DEISSMANN, *Paul* (1912) 235-60. — J. A. FITZMYER, "The Pauline Letters and the Lucan Account of Paul's Missionary Journeys," SBLSP (1988) 82-89. — E. GROAG, *Die römischen Reichsbeamten von Achaia* (1939) 32-35. — L. HENNEQUIN, *DBSup* II, 355-73. — H. Dessau, ed., *Prosopographia Imperii Romani* II (1897) no. 494. — REICKE, *NT Era* 198, 226, 234. — O. ROSSBACH, PW I, 2236f. — H.-M. SCHENKE and K. M. FISCHER, *Einleitung in die Schriften des NT* (1978) I, 49-54.

1. Gallio appears in Acts 18:12-17 as the proconsul of Achaia (→ Ἀχαΐα).

2. Gallio was the oldest son of a Roman equestrian and rhetorician in Cordoba and was named Lucius Annaeus Novatus. As the result of an adoption, he changed his name to Lucius Junius Gallio. To his original family belonged such famous people as his brother Seneca and his nephew Lucan. In the autumn of A.D. 51 he was named proconsul of Achaia by Claudius and served in Corinth during the year 52, according to an inscription given by him and found in Delphi (*SIG* II, 801, D; Deissmann, plate I; Groag 32-35; Fitzmyer 87-89). About A.D. 55 he was a consul in Rome and a supporter of Nero. In A.D. 65, as Seneca before him, he was forced to commit suicide as a result of the Pisonian conspiracy.

3. On the basis of the inscription mentioned above, the episode described in Acts 18:12-27 can be dated in A.D. 52, an important starting point for the Pauline chronology. The Corinthian Jews took Paul before Gallio and accused him of illegal propaganda. From his judgment seat (→ βῆμα, "podium," which has been discovered by excavation), Gallio commanded the proceedings to stop because they involved an internal dispute of the Jews. At that time the Roman magistrates still saw no distinction between Judaism and Christianity. Gallio did not want to show too much favor to the Jews; on the other hand, he did not want to encroach upon the autonomy of the synagogue because Claudius had just decided in favor of the Jews in some of the cases between Jews and Greeks (Josephus *B.J.* ii.254; *Acta Alexandrinorum* IV, 16ff. [ed. H. Musurillo (1961) 11f.]; Reicke 226, 234). Paul was still being influenced by this Jewish attack when he wrote from Corinth to Thessalonica about the Jewish persecutions (1 Thess 2:16).

B. Reicke

Γαμαλιήλ *Gamaliēl* Gamaliel*

1. Jewish accounts — 2. The statements in Acts

Lit.: BILLERBECK II, 636-39. — G. BORNKAMM, *RGG* V, 167f. — C. BURCHARD, *Der dreizehnte Zeuge* (1970) 31-36. — E. HAENCHEN, *The Acts of the Apostles* (1971) (index s.v.). — C.-H. HUNZINGER, *RGG* II, 1197. — J. JEREMIAS, "Paulus als Hillelit," FS Black 88-94. — *idem, Der Schlüssel zur Theologie des Apostels Paulus* (1971) 9-17. — H.-J. SCHOEPS, *Paul* (1961) 37f. — W. C. VAN UNNIK, *Tarsus or Jerusalem: The City of Paul's Youth* (1962).

1. Two well-known Jewish scholars of NT times had the name *Gamaliel* (Heb. *gamlî'ēl*, "recompense of God"). The Gamaliel mentioned in the NT was active about A.D. 25-50 and was called "the elder" to distinguish him from his grandson. Gamaliel was the son or grandson of Hillel and was the first to hold the honorary title

"Rabban" ("our teacher"). In his school "the mild tolerance and friendliness toward proselytes typical of Hillel" dominated (Schoeps). Haenchen (252, n. 2) doubts that he was really a Pharisee. In any case, he was a highly esteemed member of the Sanhedrin, even if never its president (Billerbeck II, 636f.). How near he came to the Pharisaic ideal of piety is shown in *m. Soṭa* 9:15: "With the death of Rabban Gamaliel the elder, respect for the law stopped, and purity and temperance died" (Billerbeck II, 639).

2. In Acts 5:34-39 Gamaliel objects to the decision to kill the apostles (v. 33), which, according to v. 17, the Sadducees have precipitated. The historical accuracy is questionable (see Haenchen 256-58), but Luke makes it clear to the reader: undeniably "the most highly esteemed doctor-at-law . . . [Gamaliel] warned that Christians should not be persecuted" (*ibid.* 256).

If, according to Acts 23:6-10, the proceedings of the Sanhedrin against Paul led to the tumultuous argument between the Sadducees and Pharisees because some believed in the resurrection proclaimed by him (cf. 26:4-8), but some did not, he can in 22:3 call Gamaliel himself his teacher. The three-part biographical scheme used here (γεγεννημένος, ἀνατεθραμμένος, and πεπαιδευμένος; cf. 7:20-22) assumes that Paul was already in Jerusalem as a child and was then educated by Gamaliel (van Unnik). The truth of this claim is disputed.

According to Haenchen (625), Paul's familiarity with the LXX speaks in favor of the argument that he grew up in the Diaspora. Haenchen (625, n. 1) and Bornkamm (168) refer further to strong Hellenistic influences visible in Paul. Jeremias on the other hand (*Schlüssel* 10f., 12) considers these influences very superficial and sees Paul's familiarity with the LXX as something obtained in his home and in the Hellenistic synagogue in Jerusalem (cf. Acts 6:9). Was Paul in Jerusalem perhaps only occasionally? According to Haenchen (625), Gal 1:22 does not permit a long stay there before Paul's conversion. Bornkamm (168) thinks it was probably at least long enough for Paul to be educated as a Pharisee (Phil 3:5) in the center of the Pharisaic movement. But in spite of the echo of Hillel (Jeremias, "Paulus," 92-94), Paul also lacks, according to Jeremias, "the casuistry which is so important for the rabbinic learning of a scribe."

It is important to Acts to connect Paul and therefore the Christians closely with the Pharisees as allies who are already almost Christian in their thinking; it is even more significant to connect Christianity with Gamaliel himself.

W. Radl

γαμέω *gameō* marry*
ἄγαμος, 2 *agamos* unmarried (person)
γαμίζω *gamizō* give in marriage; marry*
γαμίσκω *gamiskō* give in marriage; get married*
γάμος, ου, ὁ *gamos* wedding; marriage*

1. Occurrences in the NT — 2. Meaning and usage — 3. The Jesus tradition — 4. Paul — 5. Later texts — 6. Concluding remarks

Lit.: D. L. Balch, "Backgrounds of 1 Cor VII: Sayings of the Lord in Q; Moses as an Ascetic ΘΕΙΟΣ ΑΝΗΡ in 2 Cor III," *NTS* 18 (1971/72) 351-64. — H. Baltensweiler, "Die Ehebruchsklauseln bei Mt. Zu Mt 5, 32; 19, 9," *TZ* 15 (1959) 340-56. —*idem, Die Ehe im NT. Exegetische Untersuchungen über Ehe, Ehelosigkeit und Ehescheidung* (1967). — H. R. Balz, "Sexualität und christliche Existenz. Zum ethischen Problem der vorehelichen Geschlechtsbeziehung," *KD* 14 (1968) 263-306. — E. Bammel, "Markus 10, 11f. und das jüdische Eherecht," *ZNW* 61 (1970) 95-101. — R. A. Batey, *NT Nuptial Imagery* (1971). — K. Berger, *Die Gesetzesauslegung Jesu. Ihr historischer Hintergrund im Judentum und im AT,* I: *Markus und Parallelen* (WMANT 40, 1972). — G. Bornkamm, "Ehescheidung und Wiederverheiratung im NT" (1959), *idem, Aufsätze* III, 56-59. — G. Delling, *Paulus' Stellung zu Frau und Ehe* (1931). — *idem, RAC* IV, 707-19. — K. P. Donfried, "The Allegory of the Ten Virgins (Matth. 25:1-13) as a Summary of Matthean Theology," *JBL* 93 (1974) 415-28. — D. J. Doughty, "Heiligkeit und Freiheit. Eine exegetische Untersuchung der Anwendung des paulinischen Freiheitsgedankens in 1. Kor. 7" (Diss. Göttingen, 1965). — J. Dupont, *Mariage et divorce dans l'Évangile. Matthieu 19, 3-12 et parallèles* (1959). — J. K. Elliott, "Paul's Teaching on Marriage in I. Corinthians: Some Problems Considered," *NTS* 19 (1972/73) 219-25. — G. Gloege, "Vom Ethos der Ehescheidung," FS W. Elert (ed. F. Hübner et al.; 1955) 335-58; = Gloege, *Verkündigung und Verantwortung: Theologische Traktate* (1967) II, 152-83. — H. Greeven, "Zu den Aussagen des NT über die Ehe," *ZEE* 1 (1957) 109-25. — *idem,* "Ehe nach dem NT," *NTS* 15 (1968/69) 365-88. — P. Hoffmann, "Jesu Wort von der Ehescheidung und seine Auslegung in der neutestamentlichen Überlieferung," *Concilium* 6 (1970) 326-32. — H. Hübner, "Zölibat in Qumran?" *NTS* 17 (1970/71) 153-67. — A. Isaksson, *Marriage and Ministry in the New Temple. A Study with Special Reference to Mt. 19, 3-12 and 1 Cor. 11, 3-16* (1965). — Jeremias, *Parables* 51ff., 63ff., 171ff., 176ff., 187ff., and *passim.* — G. D. Kilpatrick, "The Aorist of γαμεῖν in the NT," *JTS* 18 (1967) 139f. — W. G. Kümmel, "Verlobung und Heirat bei Paulus (I. Cor. 7, 36-38)," FS Bultmann (1954) 275-95 = Kümmel, *Heilsgeschehen und Geschichte. Gesammelte Aufsätze, 1933-1964* (1965) 310-27. — E. Linnemann, *Gleichnisse Jesu* ([6]1975) 94ff., 131ff., 162ff., 188ff. — P.-H. Menoud, "Mariage et célibat selon Saint Paul," *RTP* 3rd series, 1 (1951) 21-34. — U. Nembach, "Ehescheidung nach alttestamentlichem und jüdischem Recht," *TZ* 26 (1970) 161-71. — K. Niederwimmer, "Zur Analyse der asketischen Motivation in 1. Kor 7," *TLZ* 99 (1974) 241-48. — *idem, Askese und Mysterium. Über Ehe, Ehescheidung, und Eheverzicht in den Anfängen des christlichen Glaubens* (1975). — A. Oepke, *RAC* IV, 650-66. — R. Pesch, *Freie Treue. Die Christen und die Ehescheidung* (1971). — H. Preisker, *Christentum und Ehe in den ersten drei Jahrhunderte. Eine Studie zur Kulturgeschichte der Alten Welt* (1927). — J. B. Schaller, "Die Sprüche über Ehescheidung und Wiederheirat in der synoptischen Überlieferung," FS Jeremias (1970) 226-46. — E. Stauffer, *TDNT* I, 648-57. — W. Trilling, "Zur Überlieferungsgeschichte des Gleichnisses vom Hochzeitsmahl Mt. 22, 1-14," *BZ* N.F. 4 (1960) 251-65. — D. O. Via, *The Parables* (1967) 98-101, 122-32. — For further bibliography see *TWNT* X, 1017-22.

1. Of the 16 occurrences of the word γάμος, 13 are found in the Gospels (none in Mark), 1 in Hebrews, and 2 in Revelation. Γαμέω occurs 28 times, with 16 in the Synoptics, 9 in Paul, and 3 in 1 Timothy; γαμίζω appears 7 times

(5 in the Synoptics, twice in Paul). Ἄγαμος occurs 4 times in Paul's letters. Γαμίσκω is only in Luke 20:34 (Mark 12:25 par.; Matt 24:38 v.l.). Manuscripts also occasionally have ἐκγαμίζω (Matt 22:30; 24:38, etc.) and ἐκγαμίσκω (Luke 20:34), which, however, are never original.

2. Ὁ γάμος, as well as the pl. οἱ γάμοι, means *wedding* (Matt 22:2-12, etc.; for the change, cf. v. 8 with vv. 2-4 and BAGD s.v.; BDF §141.3; the pl. is more frequent in classical writers). This meaning shades over into the meaning *marriage feast* (Matt 22:2-12; 25:10; cf. Rev 19:9, τὸ δεῖπνον τοῦ γάμου); ultimately a *banquet* can be referred to even without its necessarily being a marriage celebration (Luke 12:36; 14:8). In one passage the meaning is *wedding hall* (Matt 22:10; but note the reading ὁ νυμφών attested by ℵ B* L *al*). The second basic meaning of the word is *marriage*. In the NT this sense appears only in Heb 13:4 (later in Ign. *Pol.* 5:2, etc.).

Ὁ ἄγαμος is *the unmarried man* and ἡ ἄγαμος, *the unmarried woman*. All NT instances are in 1 Corinthians 7: the man in v. 32, the woman in v. 34 (on text criticism, see Niederwimmer, *Askese* 114, n. 166), and the divorced and now unmarried woman in v. 11. Οἱ ἄγαμοι in v. 8 are, no doubt, the unmarried of both sexes.

The vb. γαμέω is used above all in the act., of the man who *takes a woman in marriage* (with acc.: Matt 5:32; 19:9; Mark 6:17; 10:11; Luke 16:18 bis); cf. Luke 14:20, γυναῖκα ἔγημα, "I have married a wife"; γαμέω = γυναῖκα λαμβάνω; cf. Matt 22:25 with Mark 12:20 par. Luke 20:29. The vb. means, used absolutely, *enter into marriage, get married* (Matt 19:10; 22:25, etc.). The pass. γαμηθῆναι with a woman as subj. (1 Cor 7:39) means *get married, marry a man* (γαμηθῆναί τινι, probably dat. of advantage, BDF §188.2). Γαμέω is used with an acc. obj. for the woman who *marries a man* only in Mark 10:12 (Koine *pm* have corrected in a characteristic way); it is used absolutely in 1 Cor 7:28b, 34; 1 Tim 5:11, 14. Finally, the vb. can be used in reference to both sexes (1 Cor 7:9f.; 1 Tim 4:3).

Paternalistic traditions are evident in the characteristic combination γαμέω/γαμίζω (Matt 24:38 Q): γαμέω of the man who marries a woman, γαμίζω of the man who gives a girl in marriage; the parallel in Luke 17:27 has the contrast γαμέω of the man who marries a woman and γαμίζομαι of the woman who is given in marriage (γαμίζομαι is *[allow oneself to] be married*, BDF §314). The same combination is in Mark 12:25 par.

The only known use of γαμίζειν outside Christian literature is Apollonius Dyscolus *Synt.* iii.153: τὴν αὐτὴν ἔχει διαφορὰν καὶ τὸ γαμῶ πρὸς τὸ γαμίζω· ἔστι γὰρ τὸ μὲν πρότερον γάμου μεταλαμβάνω, τὸ δὲ γαμίζω γάμου τινὶ μεταδίδωμι. The Alexandrian grammarian thus would define γαμίζω as *give someone in marriage* (pass., *get married*). The word is used in this sense in Matt 24:38 par. Luke 17:27 and Mark 12:25 par.

The meaning of the word in 1 Cor 7:38 (ὁ γαμίζων τὴν ἑαυτοῦ παρθένον) is disputed. If ὁ γαμίζων is understood in the sense just used, then the use refers either to a father who gives his daughter in marriage or to a guardian who gives his ward in marriage. The context suggests, though, that here γαμίζω = γαμέω. The grammarian's general rule does not, of course, necessarily exclude this interpretation, for spoken language does not always follow such rules. Often, in fact, forms with -ίζω alternate with other forms of the same stem and keep the same meaning (cf. H. Lietzmann and W. G. Kümmel, *An die Korinther I/II* [HNT [5]], 35f.; Kümmel, *Verlobung* 320ff.). Ὁ γαμίζων τὴν ἑαυτοῦ παρθένον is then *the fiancé who marries his bride* (perhaps, *contra* Kümmel, *ibid.* 322ff., there is here the transformation of a "spiritual betrothal" into a normal marriage; Niederwimmer, *Askese* 116ff.).

3. In the Jesus tradition a doctrine of marriage is not developed nor is marriage renounced. That which has been handed down simply encourages exemplary character. The use of the word group in Matt 24:38 par.; Luke 12:36; 14:8 is not specific; see also John 2:1f. The specific statement in Mark 6:17, however, is important for the rigorism of John the Baptist.

a) An eschatologically motivated rigorism leads to Jesus' prohibition of divorce (on the complicated tradition history of the prohibition, cf. Niederwimmer, *Askese* 13ff.). The oldest form is probably Matt 5:32 Q (without the introduction or the condition). Luke probably expanded the Q text by adding καὶ γαμῶν ἑτέραν (16:18). Jesus' prohibition has no connection with the contemporary scribal debate about the conditions in Jewish law under which a Jewish man is allowed to put away his wife. Rather, it follows (in the basic denial of this law) certain contemporary tendencies toward the intensification of morals, which are certainly eschatologically radicalized with Jesus. Jesus' prohibition is not a statement of law in its own right but rather appeals to an ethical understanding. The prohibition serves to protect the woman from the arbitrariness of the man.

A variation of the logion is Mark 10:11. The Q tradition forbids the dismissal of the woman and the marriage of one who has been dismissed; the (pre-)Markan tradition speaks of divorce and remarriage as a crime. It cannot be known when Mark 10:12 entered the tradition. Here the woman (!) is forbidden to dismiss the man, a restriction that quite possibly assumes legal relationships outside Palestine. Jesus' prohibition is expressed in another form in the (post-Easter?) conflict story in vv. 2-9. In v. 9 Jesus restores the original state desired at the creation ("what therefore God has joined together, let not man [i.e., mankind] put asunder"). Mark probably connected vv. 2-9 with vv. 11-12.

Matt 5:32 probably comes from Q, and 19:3-9 from

Mark. Both traditions are greatly changed in Matthew. The Q tradition is adapted in 5:32 to the "antitheses." Concerning the Matthean alteration of the (pre-)Markan conflict story, cf. Niederwimmer, *Askese* 16. Most important, Matthew has inserted in the prohibition the (probably pre-Matthean) exception to the rule: παρεκτὸς λόγου πορνείας (5:32) or μὴ ἐπὶ πορνείᾳ (19:9; i.e., it is forbidden for the man to send away his wife, except in the case of "unchastity" of the woman; → πορνεία). Here we have an applied interpretation of the word of the Lord that reflects the specifically Judeo-Christian environment of the Matthean tradition. The logion (at least in part) is again adapted to the legal relationships and values of that environment. Finally, the reasoning of the disciples in Matt 19:10 probably comes from the Matthean redaction. The verse is meant to link the preceding conflict dialogue with the following logion about the eschatologically motivated renunciation of marriage (vv. 11f., material peculiar to Matthew).

b) Mark 12:25 par. stands in the apocalyptic tradition: The new world, in which those who have been raised from the dead will live, does not know γαμεῖν/γαμίζεσθαι any longer. In the parable of the great feast, Luke 14:20 names as one of the grounds for an excuse γυναῖκα ἔγημα, καὶ διὰ τοῦτο οὐ δύναμαι ἐλθεῖν. The sentence is perhaps a parenetic addition (Linnemann 95, 98f., 167).

c) One group of statements uses γάμος as a metaphor in allegory (a thoroughly post-Easter tradition). In Matt 22:1-10 (an independent variation of the parable of the great feast in Luke 14:15-24; another variation is in *Gos. Thom.* 64) the tradition is recast as allegory. The eschatological feast (Isa 25:6; Matt 8:11 par.; Mark 14:25 par.; 4 Ezra 2:38, etc.) appears especially as a *marriage feast* (γάμους in Matt 22:2-4, 9; γάμος in v. 8; cf. the later Rev 19:9). Whether γάμος in the sg., meaning *wedding hall,* is used of the dominion of God can be questioned.

In what follows (Matt 22:11-14) ἔνδυμα γάμου (the *wedding garment,* vv. 11f.) could be a metaphor for the new righteousness that will be demanded of the ones who are called. The function of this short scene is to protect the message of undeserved grace (vv. 9f.) from a misunderstanding that would lead to ethical indifference. Those who are called (by grace) are expected to wear the "garment" of the new righteousness also. Anyone who does not is an intruder who will ultimately be shut out from salvation. The entire scene must be considered in the frame of Matthean theology.

Matt 25:10 goes still further in allegorical use of γάμος. There the clause εἰσῆλθον μετ' αὐτοῦ εἰς τοὺς γάμους not only means "[they] went in with him to the *marriage feast*" (RSV)—as a metaphor for salvation at the end time—but could also mean "they were called to celebrate a marriage with him"; i.e., this passage is probably based on the idea of the γάμος between Christ and the Church (cf. 2 Cor 11:2; Eph 5:25-32, etc.).

4. In Paul all occurrences of the word group are in 1 Corinthians 7. Even this chapter is not a systematic treatise but rather answers questions the Corinthian church posed regarding how a Christian must act in questions of marriage, renunciation of marriage, and divorce. In his answer the apostle is endeavoring to protect the eschatological motivation from a false enthusiasm.

Existing marriages should be continued; contrary to hyperascetic tendencies, marriage is declared as a *remedium incontinentiae* (7:2-5). What proves to be more difficult is the question of whether a Christian who is not (either not yet or no longer) married should enter into a marriage. In one respect Paul prefers the renunciation of marriage for the unmarried (7:7f., 26, 27b, 28b, 32-34, 37, 38b, 40a) for various reasons (in light of the tribulations that are to be expected at the end time, vv. 26, 28b; out of desire to give undivided devotion to the Lord, vv. 32-35). On the other hand, what is suitable for him in this case is not advisable for everyone. Voluntary renunciation of marriage could be dangerous to those who are not called to singleness. Therefore it is granted by Paul only to those who have received the special gift of continence (v. 7). For all others marriage is the right status (vv. 9a, 36b). Entering into a marriage is not a sin (vv. 28a, 36b): this statement is formulated expressly to counter a heretical ideology. For the case that is assumed in vv. 36-38, → 2. Also the remarriage of the widow is allowed—μόνον ἐν κυρίῳ, "only in the Lord" (v. 39; but cf. v. 9a). The comparatives κρεῖσσον (v. 38) and μακαριωτέρα (v. 40), however, again teach that in such cases renunciation of marriage (only when it is based on the gift) is nevertheless preferred.

Paul therefore differentiates: (1) that which is desirable and truly fitting, i.e., the renunciation of marriage, as a voluntary renunciation only for those who are not married and to whom the special gift of continence is given; (2) that which is ordinarily necessary and unobjectionably possible, i.e., marriage; and (3) that which is in any case to be avoided, i.e., unchastity.

Paul also knows Jesus' prohibition against divorce (the wife may not separate herself from her husband, 1 Cor 7:10b; the man may not divorce his wife, v. 11b). The authoritative weight of the commandment (it comes from the Lord) is striking (v. 10). A woman who is already divorced (clearly before baptism) should not enter into a new marriage; rather, she should remain ἄγαμος or become reconciled with her husband (v. 11a). Vv. 12-16 deal with the problem of whether the Christian should or may divorce his or her non-Christian marriage partner. There is no mandate from the Lord here, but the apostle decides: The Christian should not separate himself or herself from the non-Christian marriage partner unless the non-Christian spouse initiates the separation. In such a case, the Christian member is no longer bound.

5. In later texts there are only occasional instances of the word group. Heb 13:4 enjoins (in a traditional way) that the institution of *marriage* is to be held in respect. 1 Tim 4:3 also objects to a hyperascetic false teaching that would forbid marriage; 5:11 forbids the enrollment of a young woman in the office of widows (→ χήρα). Rather, younger widows should marry (v. 14). Most important, an early Catholic mentality opposes here a doctrine that is becoming (or already is) Gnostic. Finally, both occurrences in Revelation 19 illustrate the allegorical use of the term γάμος (→ 3.c). In v. 7, we have the *marriage* of the Lamb to his bride, the Church; in v. 9, the *marriage feast.* On the history of these ideas, see Niederwimmer, *Askese* 127ff., 186ff.

6. As a whole, it is noteworthy that the most important statements of the NT on the theme of marriage, renunciation of marriage, etc. are conveyed using terms other than those of the word group of γάμος and related words. Cf. ἀνήρ, γυνή, κεφαλή, κολλάομαι, μοιχεύω, νύμφη, πορνεία, σῶμα.

K. Niederwimmer

γαμίζω *gamizō* give in marriage; marry
→ γαμέω.

γαμίσκω *gamiskō* give in marriage; get married
→ γαμέω.

γάμος, ου, ὁ *gamos* wedding; marriage
→ γαμέω.

γάρ *gar* for; namely; therefore

1. Occurrences in the NT — 2. Cause or grounds — 3. Intensification — 4. Inference

Lit.: BAGD s.v. — K. BERGER, *Die Amen-Worte Jesu* (1970) (index s.v.). — C. H. BIRD, "Some γάρ Clauses in St. Mark's Gospel," *JTS* 4 (1953) 171-87. — BDF §§443.3; 452. — DENNISTON, *Particles* (index s.v.). — P. FIEDLER, *Die Formel "und siehe" im NT* (SANT 20, 1969). — B. GÄHRKEN, *Die Partikel γάρ* (Diss. Marburg, 1950). — MORGENTHALER, *Statistik* 165ff., 181ff. — A. PELLETIER, "L'annonce à Joseph (Mt 1, 20s)," *RSR* 54 (1966) 67f. — G. B. WINER, *Grammatik des neutestamentlichen Sprachidioms* (ed. G. Lünemann; [7]1867) 415-17. — ZERWICK, *Biblical Greek* §§472-77.

1. Γάρ is the fourth most common conjunction in the NT (after καί, δέ, and ὅτι). From Homer onward, γάρ is the most common causal particle (Pape, *Wörterbuch* s.v.), and in the NT it is the second most common. It appears 1,042 times in the NT. It is particularly common in Matthew, where it is the nineteenth most common word (ὅτι is fifteenth), in the Pauline writings, where it is eleventh, in 2 Peter, where it is ninth, and in Hebrews, where it is fourth (in each of these well ahead of ὅτι; cf. Morgenthaler 165-69). A significant connection exists between the greater frequency of γάρ and the less frequent occurrence of ὅτι in these writings, a stylistic detail that could be of use for questions of authenticity. According to the calculation of Morgenthaler (181ff.), γάρ is a significantly common word in Matthew, Paul, and Hebrews.

In about 95% of its occurrences in the NT, γάρ is in the second position in its clause; in about 85% of these cases, it follows a short word. When γάρ is the third word in its clause, a prepositional phrase or μέν precedes it in about 80% of the time. Γάρ appears in fourth place only in Luke 6:23, 26; 2 Cor 1:19. The combination ἰδοὺ γάρ occurs only in Luke (5 times) and in Acts 9:11 and 2 Cor 7:11; ἀμὴν γάρ appears only in Matthew (4 times) and in Mark 11:23 v.l. The Gospel of Mark ends with γάρ (cf. P. W. van der Horst, "Can a Book End with γάρ? A Note on Mark XVI.8," *JTS* 23 [1972] 121-24).

2. Γάρ generally indicates a causal relation between two statements, whereby the second statement gives a reason for or explains the first. A γάρ clause can also be parenthetically inserted as a preliminary remark or as a digression in the statement that is being substantiated (e.g., Rom 7:1), and a sequence of several γάρ clauses can also address several points in a single preceding clause (e.g., Luke 8:28f.; John 3:19f.). More often γάρ assumes a reaction on the part of the hearer to some incident (Gährken 103ff.) and gives, in its clause, the reasons for this reaction (see examples in BAGD s.v. 1.e: Matt 2:2; 9:13, etc.). In questions γάρ generally expresses a reason: *then* who . . . ? or *namely* who . . . ? Καὶ γάρ means "for (also)"; οὐδὲ γάρ, "for also not" or "for not once" (cf. BDF §452.2 with §452.3). In ἰδοὺ γάρ, ἀμὴν γάρ, and λέγω γάρ ὑμῖν, the particle γάρ is generally understood to express grounds (so Berger 30, etc.; Fiedler 30, etc.; on the other hand, Gährken [103f., 111] sees in γάρ in these cases only an intensification or variation of ἀμήν).

3. In some questions γάρ does not express grounds but serves rather to intensify a question and so can be translated *then.* As such, in accordance with its constituent parts, γάρ expresses with the intensification (γε) an inference (ἄρα) drawn from the preceding situation (according to Winer 416 with n. 1), e.g., Matt 27:23: "*Why,* what evil has he done [that you want to crucify him]?" John 7:41: "*Surely* the Messiah is not to come from Galilee?" (NEB). In assertions as well γάρ occasionally intensifies when it follows a question, actual or assumed. For example, Rom 2:25, "Circumcision *indeed* is of value . . . ," assumes a preceding dialogue, "Is circumcision therefore useless? No!" Acts 16:37 (οὐ γάρ, "No indeed!" [NEB]) is similar. See also John 9:30; 1 Thess 2:20; 1 Cor 9:10; Jas 1:7; 1 Pet 4:15.

4. In some cases γάρ apparently neither expresses

grounds nor functions as an intensifier. It might be that γάρ in these instances is a meaningless connecting particle (so BAGD s.v. 4 and others), possibly as it appears in divided textual traditions that sometimes have δέ. If this is unacceptable, then in individual passages it may indicate not that what follows is the ground for what precedes but vice versa. Thus (as in questions → 3), it may mean "therefore, thus, so, then" (on Rom 15:27 and 1 Cor 9:19 cf. BAGD s.v. 3; on Rom 12:3, O. Michel, *Römer* [KEK] ad loc.; H. W. Schmidt, *Römer* [THKNT] ad loc.; cf. also 1 Cor 9:19; 10:1; 2 Cor 11:5; Gal 1:11; 5:13; Heb 12:3).

K.-H. Pridik

γαστήρ, τρός, ἡ *gastēr* stomach; womb*

Γαστήρ is used figuratively in Titus 1:12 in the phrase γαστέρες ἀργαί, "lazy *gluttons,*" of the Cretans and especially the Jewish-Christian false teachers who were appearing on Crete. The phrase appears in a proverbial hexameter that is attributed to the Cretan Epimenides (6th cent. B.C.; for early Church interpretation, see Clement of Alexandria *Strom.* i.59.2; Jerome *Comm. in Titus* ad loc.; see also M. Dibelius and H. Conzelmann, *The Pastoral Epistles* [Hermeneia] ad loc.). Γαστήρ appears otherwise only in the common phrases ἐν γαστρὶ ἔχειν, "to be pregnant" (Matt 1:18, 23; Mark 13:17 par. Matt 24:19/Luke 21:23; 1 Thess 5:3; Rev 12:2) and συλλαμβάνειν ἐν γαστρί, "to conceive, become pregnant" (Luke 1:31).

γέ *ge* at least; even*

Γέ is an enclitic particle that serves to emphasize the word with which it is joined. It appears 28 times in the NT and also in the compounds → μήγε (7 occurrences), → καίτοιγε (3 occurrences), → μενοῦνγε (3 occurrences), and → εὖγε (1 occurrence). For the most part, γέ is connected to other particles and conjunctions and often has no meaning of its own. It appears 8 times in the phrase εἰ δὲ μή γε, "otherwise," a fixed phrase in which a vb. is understood (cf. BDF §§439.1; 376; 480.6; Matt 6:1; 9:17; Luke 5:36, 37; 10:6; 13:9; 14:32; 2 Cor 11:16); 6 times in εἴ γε, "if indeed" (Rom 5:6; 2 Cor 5:3; Gal 3:4; Eph 3:2; 4:21; Col 1:23); 3 times in ἄρα γε, "therefore, consequently" (Matt 7:20; 17:26), in εἰ ἄρα γε, "whether" (Acts 17:27a); once in ἆρά γε in a question (Acts 8:30); 2 (or 3) times in καί γε, "at least" (Luke 19:42 v.l.), "and even" (Acts 2:18), "and though" (Acts 17:27b); twice in ἀλλά γε, "but even" (Luke 24:21), "at least" (1 Cor 9:2; cf. BDF §439.2); once in μήτι γε, "not to mention; but finally" (1 Cor 6:3; cf. BDF §427.3); and once in ὄφελόν γε, "if only" (1 Cor 4:8). In addition, γέ appears twice in the phrase διά γε, "at least because of . . ." (Luke 11:8; 18:5) and once in ὅς γε, "[even] he who" (Rom 8:32).

H. Balz

Γεδεών *Gedeōn* Gideon*

Indeclinable proper name of one of the "great judges" (Judg 6:11–8:35), who is named among the witnesses of the faith in Heb 11:32. E. Jenni, *BHH* I, 569f.; *BL* 589f.

γέεννα, ης, ἡ *geenna* Gehenna; hell*

1. In the OT and Judaism — 2. In the NT — 3. Related expressions

Lit.: BILLERBECK IV, 1016-1165. — H. W. HUPPENBAUER, *BHH* I, 533. — J. JEREMIAS, *TDNT* I, 657-58. — For further bibliography → ἄβυσσος; see *TWNT* X, 959, 1022.

1. The NT designation of the fiery place of punishment, γέεννα, was originally a topographical proper name. The "Valley of Hinnom" (Heb. *gê-hinnōm,* Josh 15:8b; 18:16b; Aram. *gê-hinnām, b. 'Erub.* 19a), "valley of the son of Hinnom" (Josh 15:8a; 18:16a), or "valley of the sons of Hinnom" (2 Kgs 23:10), was the name of a valley in the southern part of Jerusalem that today is called Wâdī er-Rabâbi. Sacrifices of children took place here under Ahaz and Manasseh (2 Kgs 16:3; 21:6). Because of these sacrifices, Josiah allowed the valley to become unclean (2 Kgs 23:10). Prophetic threats of judgment identified the Valley of Hinnom as a future "valley of slaughter" (Jer 7:32; 19:6).

Jewish apocalyptic literature developed the idea that one day God would purify the defiled world and throw evildoers into purifying fire (cf. *1 Enoch* 10:13; 18:11-16, etc.; *Jub.* 9:15; 1QH 3:29-36; *2 Bar.* 37:1; see further the words of John the Baptist: Matt 3:10, 12 par. Luke 3:9, 17). In the conclusion of Isa 31:9; 66:24 (cf. Mark 9:48), the anticipated hell of fire is located in the Valley of Hinnom (*1 Enoch* 26:4; 27:1-3; 54:1-6; 56:3f.; 90:26f.). Eventually Jewish literature named the hell of fire itself *gêhinnōm/gêhinnām,* or γέεννα in its Greek form, without reference to the topography of Jerusalem (4 Ezra 7:36; *2 Bar.* 59:10; 85:13; *Sib. Or.* i.103; ii.292; rabbinic examples in Billerbeck 1023-25, 1029ff.).

2. In 12 places the NT also designates the place of eternal punishing fire (→ πῦρ) as γέεννα; 11 occurrences are found in the Synoptic Gospels (Matt 5:22, 29f.; 10:28; 18:9; 23:15, 33; Mark 9:43, 45, 47; Luke 12:5), 1 in James (3:6). Γέεννα is also localized in → ᾅδης in the → ἄβυσσος. But ᾅδης is considered the abode of the dead for only a limited time between death and the resurrection, while γέεννα is thought of as the place of eternal torment for the godless after the final judgment.

On the basis of Jesus' Sermon on the Mount, γέεννα threatens both the person who is scornful of a brother (Matt 5:22) and the adulterer (vv. 29f.). Another passage holds out the prospect of the judgment of γέεννα to the Pharisees (23:33) and their proselytes (v. 15). A fearless confession before other people is exhorted in reference to him who can condemn to γέεννα (where soul and body perish, Matt 10:28); God himself is meant, not the devil (Matt 10:28b par. Luke 12:5). One who leads others to rebellion or is led to rebellion must be prepared to be thrown into the eternal fire (Matt 18:9 par. Mark 9:43, 45, 47). James is thinking along similar lines when he describes the tongue as transmitting the fire of γέεννα—for those who allow themselves to be led astray by words (Jas 3:6).

3. In other places in the NT where the eternal punishment of fire is considered, the idea of γέεννα is always in the background, even when the word is not actually present. This is true especially for the use of κάμινος (Matt 13:42, 50; cf. Rev 9:2) or λίμνη τοῦ πυρός (Rev 19:20; 20:10, 14f.; 21:8; cf. 14:10); not only the godless (cf. also Luke 16:24) but also Satan with his demons will be destroyed in it by eternal fire (Matt 25:41; Rev 19:20; 20:10, 14; cf. *T. Jud.* 25:3; → ἄβυσσος 2). Perhaps 1 Cor 3:10-15; 2 Pet 3:5-13 (cf. Mark 9:49; Luke 17:29f.) teach that these expressions assume the purifying power of fire. Early Christianity shares this view of eschatology with contemporary Judaism. To be sure, the NT forgoes a detailed description of the torments of hell; its reference to hell and its fire is useful for its ethical goals, not for the satisfaction of any religious curiosity (cf. on the other hand *1 Enoch* 27:3f.). Some amount of present eschatology (cf. John 3:18f.; 12:31; 1 John 2:8f.) is encountered where γέεννα already threatens or controls human beings (Matt 5:22; 23:15; Jas 3:6).

O. Böcher

Γεθσημανί *Gethsēmani* Gethsemane*

Lit.: R. S. Barbour, "Gethsemane in the Tradition of the Passion," *NTS* 16 (1969/70) 231-51. — A. van den Born, *BL* 580. — V. Corbo, *Richerche archeologiche al Monte degli Ulivi* (1965). — Dibelius, *Botschaft* I, 258-71. — D. Dormeyer, *Die Passion Jesu als Verhaltensmodell* (1974) 124-37. — F. W. Eltester, *BHH* I, 562. — A. Feuillet, "Le récit lucanien de l'agonie de Gethsémani," *NTS* 22 (1975/76) 397-417. — *idem, L'agonie de Gethsémani* (1977). — M. Galizzi, *Gesù nel Getsemani* (1972). — J. W. Holleran, *The Synoptic Gethsemane* (1973). — W. H. Kelber, "Mark 14:32-42: Gethsemane," *ZNW* 63 (1972) 166-87. — Kopp, *Stätten* 387-99. — K. G. Kuhn, "Jesus in Gethsemane," *EvT* 12 (1952) 260-85. — T. Leskow, "Jesus in Gethsemane," *EvT* 26 (1966) 141-59. — *idem,* "Jesus in Gethsemane bei Lukas und im Hebräerbrief," *ZNW* 58 (1967) 215-39. — E. Linnemann, *Studien zur Passionsgeschichte,* (1970) 11-40. — W. Mohn, "Gethsemane (Mk 14, 32-42)," *ZNW* 64 (1973) 194-208. — W. Ott, *Gebet und Heil* (1965) 82-90. — R. Pesch, *Markus* (HTKNT) II (1977), 385-96. — W. Schenk, *Der Passionsbericht nach Markus* (1974) 193-206. — L. Schenke, *Studien zur Passionsgeschichte des Markus* (1971) 461-560. — V. Taylor, *The Passion Narrative of St. Luke* (1972) 69-72. — *TCGNT* 177.

Γεθσημανί (Aram. *gaṯ šᵉmānî* = "oil press") appears only in Mark 14:32 (par. Matt 26:36), where it is sg. and in a rel. clause. It is the proper name of the plot of land in which Jesus spent the last night praying while his disciples went to sleep and where he was taken prisoner. The reference is valid as an element of the oldest tradition, in spite of the divergent thoughts about the corruption of the account that it begins (unreduced: Pesch; short background report: Linnemann, Schenke, Kelber, Mohn, Dormeyer; two sources: Kuhn, Leskow, Ott, Barbour, Holleran, Schenk). Whether Gethsemane was on the Mount of Olives is determined by the tradition-historical view of the note in Mark 14:26.

In the shortened Lukan (Luke 22:39-46) and Johannine parallels, both of which could be dependent on Mark, the name Γεθσημανί has been lost. The Johannine localization above the Kidron valley (John 18:1)—therefore on the slope of the Mount of Olives—is primarily a typological allusion to David in 2 Sam 15:23. Whether behind that allusion, as behind the designation as a "garden," is a good knowledge of the locale is uncertain; in any case, it would have been developed subsequently and then conveyed in a literary form.

The Markan description is stylized as a contrast to the transfiguration: three chosen disciples, the beginning of the fulfillment of the call to suffering, and submission to the will of God in contrast to the failure of the disciples. On the basis of such elements Matthew has intensified the admonition to pray. Luke has generalized the admonition to pray and—if vv. 43f. are original (Feuillet against *TCGNT*)—has focused the narrative completely on Jesus' struggle with death, which took place for him already there.

W. Schenk

γείτων, ονος, ὁ, ἡ *geitōn* neighbor*

Γείτων appears with φίλοι in Luke 14:12; 15:6 and with φίλαι in 15:9; it stands alone in John 9:8.

γελάω *gelaō* laugh*

In the Lukan Sermon on the Plain the antithesis κλαίειν–γελᾶν (cf. Eccl 3:4) is found first in a blessing used on those who cry now but who will *laugh* later (6:21) and then in a cry of pain over those who *laugh* now but who later will be sad and weep (6:25). To laugh here is a picture of a carefree and unencumbered life in joy (οἱ γελῶντες νῦν in v. 25b is near οἱ πλούσιοι in v. 24 and οἱ ἐμπεπλησμένοι in v. 25a) that believers possess only as an eschatological promise, not as a way of life in this world. K. H. Rengstorf, *TDNT* I, 658-62; *TWNT* X, 1022; → κλαίω.

γέλως, ωτος, ὁ *gelōs* laughter*

Jas 4:9: "Let your *laughter* be turned to mourning." This text speaks of foolish laughter, which has no place in the presence of God (v. 8; cf. Isa 32:11f.; Jer 4:8). K. H. Rengstorf, *TDNT* I, 658-62.

γεμίζω *gemizō* fill
→ γέμω 3.

γέμω *gemō* be full (of)*

1. Occurrences and Usage — 2. Meaning — 3. Γεμίζω

1. Of the 11 occurrences of γέμω in the NT, 7 are found in Revelation (4:6, 8; 5:8; 15:7; 17:3f.; 21:9), and the others in Matt 23:25, 27 par. Luke 11:39 and Rom 3:14 (citing Ps 9:28 LXX). The verb is used generally only in the pres. and impf. tenses (cf. LSJ s.v.); in the NT it is used only in the ind. and as a pres. partc.

The obj. is usually in the gen.; in Matt 23:25 it is supported by ἐκ (in English, one is full *of* or filled *with* something). The acc. ὀνόματα in Rev 17:3 is grammatically awkward. Τὰ ἀκάθαρτα in Rev 17:4 as the obj. of γέμον (the contents of the cup, as is generally accepted) is important as a "serious incongruency" (BDF §136.1; as the obj. of ἔχουσα, it is without difficulty: a woman with "the impurities of her fornication").

2. Generally γέμω refers to that which something contains, but in Rev 4:6, 8 it refers to what is on the surface: "living creatures, *covered* with eyes" (NEB). The idea in Rev 17:3 of "a beast *full of* blasphemous names" is problematic.

In the NT the obj. is concrete or abstract, and the subj. concrete, except in Luke 11:39, where "your inward part" (AV), as the preceding comparison with cup and bowl shows, is presented as the inside of a container. Most of the objects have a negative connotation; positive ones are only in Rev 4:6, 8; 5:8. Furthermore, in Matthew and Luke, the secondary meaning "be impure" is a result of its association with καθαρίζειν/καθαρός.

3. **Γεμίζω** *fill;* pass.: *be full** occurs 9 times in the NT, with only Luke and Revelation having both γεμίζω and γέμω. Especially in the pass. it comes very close to the idea *be full:* Mark 4:37, "so that the boat was already *filling*"; so also in Luke 14:23; Rev 10:10 v.l.; 15:8. In the act. John 2:7 adds explicitly, "they filled them [= the water jugs] *up to the brim.*" In the act. it appears with acc. and gen. complements (gen. sometimes with ἐκ): Mark 15:36, ". . . a sponge full of vinegar"; Luke 15:16, ". . . his belly with (ἐκ) the pods" (NEB); John 2:7; 6:13; Rev 8:5. The gen. is lacking only in John 2:7b, after its appearance in v. 7a, and in two of the passives (Mark 4:37; Luke 14:23).

K.-H. Pridik

γενεά, ᾶς, ἡ *genea* generation; lineage*

1. Occurrences and meaning in the NT — 2. In the Synoptics — 3. In the other writings

Lit.: K. BERGER, *Die Amen-Worte Jesu* (1970) 58-74. — F. CHRIST, *Jesus Sophia* (1970) 63ff., 120ff. — V. HASLER, *Amen* (1969) 30-70. — D. LÜHRMANN, *Die Redaktion der Logienquelle* (1969) 24-48. — M. MEINERTZ, " 'Dieses Geschlecht' im NT," *BZ* 1 (1957) 283-89. — SCHULZ, *Q* 336-86. — For further bibliography see *TWNT* X, 1022.

1. Of the 43 references to γενεά in the NT, 33 are in the Synoptics, where the word refers in 25 of its occurrences to the Jewish people in the time of Jesus, 17 times in the expression "this *generation.*" In the redactional comment on the genealogy of Jesus in Matt 1:17 and in the Magnificat in Luke 1:48, 50, γενεά means the *generations to follow;* in Luke 16:8, it refers to *membership in a particular class.*

2. The Synoptic form "this *generation*" comes from the later Hellenistic Q stratum, which directs its polemic toward Israel as the last generation before the end and proclaims to it the approaching judgment. Jewish apocalyptic literature employs corresponding motifs and forms of speech. Thus *1 Enoch* 93:9 refers to a rebellious generation, 1QHab 2:6f. to a last generation, and *Jub.* 23:16ff. to an evil generation. Matt 11:16 par. Luke 7:31 begins the Q simile of the children's game, the meaning of which—that the divine wisdom has no longer given authority to Israel, but rather to John and Jesus—adopts and stresses a Deuteronomic (Deut 32:5) and Wisdom (Pss 77:8; 94:10 LXX) motif. Matt 23:36 par. Luke 11:50f. appears in a Wisdom saying that takes up a complaint against wisdom that has been despised (Prov 1:24-33; Bar 3:12f.; 11QPs[a] 18:8, 15; *1 Enoch* 93:8; 94:5; 4 Ezra 5:9f.); as an early Christian prophetic saying, it accuses the last *generation* of Israel of filling the multitude of the sins of the fathers through the murder of the prophets, including the murder of Zechariah the son of Berechiah (Josephus *B.J.* iv.335).

This same condemnation increases in the complex of sayings about the sign of Jonah: Matt 12:39 par. Luke 11:29 calls this *generation* evil; Matthew adds, as also in Matt 16:4, that it is a totally adulterous *generation.* The Q form is repeated in Matt 12:42 par. Luke 11:31 and Matt 12:41 par. Luke 11:32 in the twofold threat referring to the Queen of the South and the Ninevites. In addition, Matthew intensifies the statement by connecting it with the warning against relapse and calls Israel an evil *generation.* Luke 11:30 adds to the statement with the reference to the Son of Man who comes in judgment.

Mark transforms the demand for a sign in Q into the refusal of a sign from heaven. For Mark 8:12 only the final judgment awaits the condemned Israel of the time of Jesus. Thus in 8:38 he calls it an adulterous and sinful *generation.* Consequently in an apocalyptic threatening word 13:30 affirms, along with Matt 24:34 and Luke 21:32, that this generation must experience the horrors of the end time. Luke 17:25 connects this with the fixed plan of God promised in Scripture. Mark 9:19 has Jesus sigh in exasperation over this evil (even perverse, according to Matt 17:17 and Luke 9:41) *generation.*

3. Like Matt 17:17 and Luke 9:41, Phil 2:15 and Acts 2:40b take up Deut 32:5 LXX from the synagogue preaching. Paul summons the ekklesia to consecration in the

midst of pagan depravity. In the sermon at Pentecost, Peter turns to the population of the Jerusalem of his day. Acts 8:33 understands the obscure expression from Isa 53:8 in a genealogical sense: "Who can describe his [= the servant of God's] *generation*?" Within God's plan of salvation history, David's work was limited to his *generation,* according to Acts 13:36. Within the Hellenistic missionary preaching, 14:16 places the Gentile world under the generosity of God (cf. 3:17; 13:27; 17:30). According to Acts 15:21 James appeals to the Torah, which is read everywhere and has been read *from early generations* in order to demonstrate the worldwide validity of the prohibitions of the apostolic decree derived from Leviticus 17.

Col 1:26 accents the election of the faithful from among the Gentiles within the divine economy of salvation, while Eph 3:5 understands the gospel as the election of the Gentiles, the mystery revealed to the apostles and the prophets of the Church. Eph 3:21 belongs to a liturgical hymn that concludes the didactic part of the apostolic letter. By contrast, Heb 3:10 is a statement of the Holy Spirit that employs the harsh citation from Ps 94:10 LXX in a reference to the Jewish people of the wilderness generation. According to v. 11 the people as a whole remain excluded from salvation. The passage serves as a warning to the unrepentant Church, for the same rejection threatens the Church also. Perhaps the reference to Ps 94:10 LXX gives evidence of the source of the phrase "this *generation*" in the late Q stratum.

V. Hasler

γενεαλογέω *genealogeō* trace one's descent*

In Heb 7:6 of Melchizedek, who "does not *trace his descent*" (NEB) to the sons of Levi. F. Büchsel, *TDNT* I, 665; → γενεαλογία.

γενεαλογία, ας, ἡ *genealogia* genealogy*

Lit.: N. Brox, *Pastoralbriefe* (RNT) 35f., 102f., 311f. — M. D. Johnson, *The Purpose of the Biblical Genealogies* (1969). — D. E. Nineham, "The Genealogy in St. Matthew's Gospel and Its Significance for the Study of the Gospels," *BJRL* 58 (1976) 420-44. — S. Sandmel, "Myths, Genealogies, and Jewish Myths, and the Writing of Gospels," *HUCA* 27 (1956) 201-11. — H. Schöllig, "Die Zählung der Generationen im matthäischen Stammbaum," *ZNW* 59 (1968) 261-68. — W. Speyer, *RAC* IX, 1145-1268. — H. Stegemann, " 'Die des Uria.' Die Bedeutung der Frauennamen in der Genealogie von Mt 1, 1-17," FS Kuhn, 246-76. — K. Stendahl, "Quis et Unde? An Analysis of Mt 1–2," FS Jeremias (1960) 94-105. — A. Vögtle, "Die Genealogie Mt 1, 2-16 und die matthäische Kindheitsgeschichte," *BZ* 8 (1964) 45-58, 239-62; 9 (1965) 32-49.

The word appears in the NT only in 1 Tim 1:4 and Titus 3:9. These verses hardly refer to Gnostic lists of archons and aeons, which can be documented only later, but more probably have in mind OT and Essene or rabbinic lists (even so, an anti-Jewish polemic does not become obvious). Inasmuch as Plato (*Ti.* 22a) and Polybius (ix.2.1) issued polemics against myths and lists of genealogies, the Pastorals oppose false teachers according to established patterns. For Heb 7:3, 6, Jesus stands high over the OT priesthood according to Gen 14:17-20 and Ps 110:4. Therefore, a genealogical proof is unnecessary.

Matt 1:2-16 and Luke 3:23-38 assume a knowledge of the genealogy of Jesus from David and from ancestry tables of Jesus. They do not pursue a genealogical proof but rather have a christological purpose. Therefore differences and mistakes are not important. Matt 1:1 and 1:17 form the redactional framework, and vv. 18-25 are a midrashic, redactional footnote (Stendahl 102). The list of the bearers of the promise is important, not the sequence of generations. Jesus, the messiah who has come, has fulfilled the promise of Abraham. The four women in the ancestry refer to the universal gospel. Luke traces the ancestry back to Adam and God. He is not thinking of an Adam-messiah but rather interprets the baptism of Jesus as revealing the Son of the Most High whom God appointed as the Savior of the world from the beginning of mankind (Luke 1:32f.; 2:30-32; 4:18-21).

V. Hasler

γενέσια, ίων, τά *genesia* birthday celebration*

Of the *birthday celebration* (τοῖς γενεσίοις, temporal dat.) of Herod Antipas in Mark 6:21 par. Matt 14:6 (on the Matthean wording, see BDF §200.3). W. Rordorf, *BHH* I, 529; *BL* 523f.; A. Stuiber, *RAC* IX, 217-43.

γένεσις, εως, ἡ *genesis* source, origin, beginning; birth; descent; procreation; existence*

1. Occurrences in the NT — 2. In secular Greek and the LXX — 3. NT usages

Lit.: BAGD s.v. — F. Büchsel, *TDNT* I, 682-84. — H. Frankemölle, *Jahwebund und Kirche Christi. Studien zur Form- und Traditionsgeschichte des "Evangeliums" nach Matthäus* (1974), esp. 360-65. — F. Mussner, *Jakobusbrief* (HTKNT) (on Jas 1:23; 3:6).

1. Γένεσις is found 5 times in the NT, in the sense of *birth* (Matt 1:18; Luke 1:14), *genealogy* (Matt 1:1), and *source, root* (Jas 1:23; 3:6).

2. In secular Greek, esp. in Plato, γένεσις is attested in the sense of *origin* and *beginning,* in contrast to φθορά (dissolution); and in the sense of *becoming,* in contrast to οὐσία (being) and what has come into being, or creation (κόσμος). It is also used in temporal contexts for *lineage* and *descent.* In the latter sense it is used genealogically; i.e., every god, every hero looked proudly to his *descent;* cf. esp. Hesiod (*Th.,* "Catalog of Women"). The LXX gives the genealogical meaning in most instances (cf. Gen 2:4; 5:1), with the exception of Wisdom (e.g., 6:22; 7:5, 12). Thus it prepares the way for the NT usage.

3. Matt 1:1, in dependence on the language of Gen 5:1, speaks of the "book of the *genealogy*" (or history of the origin) of Jesus Christ and proceeds from David and

Abraham. The Evangelist intends not only to set forth the theologically shaped genealogy of the coming Messiah (vv. 2-17) but also to present his entire theological work under this aegis, to assert that this new ruler determines the fate both of Israel and of the world. "According to Matt 1:1 a new epoch of universal history begins with 'Jesus Christ'" (Frankemölle 365). Matt 1:18 emphasizes this idea once again with the reference to the special birth of this person Jesus Christ. (In this sense, cf. also Luke 1:14 as a prediction of the birth of the Baptist.)

Jas 1:23 speaks of those who only hear the word of God, but do not act. Such a person is compared to one who looks at his natural, external face (πρόσωπον τῆς γενέσεως) in a mirror and forgets what he looks like. Here the author's intent is to recognize the origin—the point of departure, the root—and to lead to that place (to his archetype). Everything else is self-deception and self-destruction. An even stronger ethical statement is found in 3:6, where the evil, uncontrollable tongue is compared to a fire that sets ablaze the "cycle *of nature*," or (RSV mg.) "wheel *of birth*" (τὸν τροχὸν τῆς γενέσεως). The exact origin of the image is unclear, as both Orphic texts dealing with the transmigration of souls and rabbinic works on the wheel of fate mention it. "James apparently thinks simply of the circle of life: There is no one and nothing before which the slanderous tongue would stop; it is capable of setting everything on fire. One is powerless against its destructive power; its fire is comparable to the fire of the eternal, unquenchable fire of hell itself" (Mussner 165).

A. Kretzer

γενετή, ῆς, ἡ *genetē* birth*

John 9:1: ἐκ γενετῆς, "from his *birth*."

γένημα, ατος, τό *genēma* plant; fruit, yield*

Γένημα is a Hellenistic neologism from γίνομαι (to be distinguished from classical → γέννημα): Mark 14:25 par. Matt 26:29/Luke 22:18 in the eschatological word of Jesus at the Last Supper, γένημα τῆς ἀμπέλου, "product" or "fruit of the vine" (cf. Deut 22:9 LXX; Isa 32:12 LXX; *m. Ber.* 6:1, *p^erî hagepen,* "at the blessing over the cup"; οἴνου γένημα, ÄgU 774:3); 2 Cor 9:10: τὰ γενήματα τῆς δικαιοσύνης ὑμῶν, "the *harvest* of your righteousness" (cf. Hos 10:12 LXX), speaks of generosity; Luke 12:18 א* D it. F. Büchsel, *TDNT* I, 685; J. Jeremias, *The Eucharistic Words of Jesus* (1966) 183.

γεννάω *gennaō* beget; give birth, bring forth

1. Occurrences in the NT — 2. Γεννάω in secular Greek and in Judaism — 3. NT uses of γεννάω

Lit.: BAGD s.v. — F. BÜCHSEL and K. H. RENGSTORF, *TDNT* I, 665-75. — J. KÜHLEWEIN, *THAT* I, 732-36. — R. SCHNACKENBURG, *Die Johannesbriefe* (HTKNT) 175-83. — A. VÖGTLE, *Messias und Gottessohn. Herkunft und Sinn der mattäischen Geburts- und Kindheitsgeschichte* (1971). — For further bibliography see *TWNT* X, 1023.

1. Γεννάω appears 97 times in the NT (Morgenthaler, *Statistik* 84), of which 40 occurrences are in Matt 1:2-16; 5 additional occurrences are elsewhere in Matthew, 18 in John, 10 in 1 John, 7 in Acts, 4 in Luke, 6 in the authentic Pauline letters, and 4 in Hebrews. Additional occurrences are in Mark 14:21; 2 Tim 2:23; 2 Pet 2:12.

2. In secular Greek γεννάω is used of the father's role in *begetting* (Sophocles, Euripides) and less frequently is used of the mother's role, in the place of τίκτω (Plutarch). Here it has the general meaning of *beget, bring forth* (Plato, Polybius). In the LXX γεννάω is frequently the translation of the Hebrew root *yld,* "give birth, beget," and appears rarely for the father-son relationship of Yahweh to his people (Deut 32:18; Isa 1:2; metaphorically in Ezek 16:20; 23:37) and in two important passages for the adoption of the messiah-king by Yahweh in the accession to the throne: Pss 2:7; 109:3. In Prov 8:25 wisdom is mentioned as the firstborn of the creative works of God. In connection with the conversion of a Gentile to Judaism, the rabbis speak of a procreation in the sense of a new being: a convert is like a newborn child (Rengstorf 666f.). According to Philo the entire creative work of God is an act of procreation: He begets the logos, the animals, and the plants; excluded are the children of God. The Qumran community knows (following 2 Sam 7:14) the idea of the begetting of the messiah from the family tree of David (4QFlor 1:10-13; cf. 1QSa 2:11-12).

3. In connection with the OT and Judaism, one may notice the usage of Ps 2:7 in the NT with messianic meaning. Thus in Acts 13:33, the accented "today" refers to the immortal life in the resurrection (cf. also Heb 1:5; 5:5, where the time reference remains open). In Luke 1:35, the begetting of the Son of God by the Spirit is, on the basis of this interpretation of Ps 2:7, regarded as the beginning of the new aeon. "Generation from God in a very real sense was here perceived by the community" (Büchsel 670). Paul may be dependent on rabbinic conceptions when he speaks in 1 Cor 4:15 and Phlm 10 of a "spiritual begetting" as an expression of his pastoral engagement and the resulting deep connection with the community (or Onesimus). The passages Rom 9:11; Gal 4:23, 24, 29 have no less weight. All of these passages stand in the salvation-theological context of the interplay of the two Testaments.

The Matthean genealogy expresses the idea of fulfillment (Matt 1:2-16). It is formed according to OT models (cf. Gen 5:3-32; 1 Chr 2:10-22, 36-49) and demonstrates the divinely intended incorporation of Jesus, who was miraculously begetted by the Holy Spirit, into the succession of Abraham and David (Vögtle). The concept of begetting receives further development and a new depth in the Johannine literature, where the birth originates with God (1 John 2:29; 3:9; 4:7) and with the Spirit (John 3:5, 6, 8), or "from above" (3:3, 7). This relationship, which is mysterious and yet determines reality, gives individuals a beginning (baptism) and a goal for their life in a relationship with God, namely, as God's child (1 John 3:1). "To be a 'child of God' is a comprehensive description of the Christian person in the inseparable unity of one's supernatural nature; it is a single expression for the exaltation and ethical perfection that together produce the model of the Christian person" (Schnackenburg 178).

In summary, γεννάω encompasses both a father's begetting and a mother's giving birth. It receives special weight in view of Jesus' becoming a man (Luke), but it also is used of the new creation of mankind through the power of the Spirit of God (John).

A. Kretzer

γέννημα, ατος, τό *gennēma* that which is produced; sprout*

In the NT only in the harsh image of γεννήματα ἐχιδνῶν, "*brood* of vipers," which appears in the preaching of judgment by John the Baptist in Matt 3:7 par. Luke 3:7 (Q) and also in Jesus' word of judgment in Matt 12:34; 23:33 (parallel to ὄφεις, "snakes"). The Jewish hearers are characterized as poisonous snakes, i.e., as insincere and rejected. This negative association of γέννημα with serpents appears neither in the LXX nor in Josephus or the rabbinic literature. *Did.* 13:1 is comparable in Christian literature. F. Büchsel, *TDNT* I, 672.

Γεννησαρέτ *Gennēsaret* Gennesaret*

Indeclinable name (actually Γεννεσάρ; cf. 1 Macc 11:67; Mark 6:53 D it sy; Matt 14:34 D* 700 lat sy, probably assimilated to Nazareth or Chinnereth) of the Sea of Galilee (Luke 5:1, λίμνη Γεννησαρέτ; cf. Josephus *B.J.* iii.506). This lake is also called θάλασσα τῆς Γαλιλαίας (Mark 1:16; Matt 4:18) and θάλασσα τῆς Τιβεριάδος (John 21:1). According to Mark 6:53 par. Matt 14:34 it is the name of a fertile area extending from the west side of the sea. According to *t. Ṭohar* 6:7; *b. Meg.* 6a, and elsewhere, a locale named Ginnesar can be assumed, which in the Greek and Roman period lay near the OT Chinnereth (cf. Num 34:11; Josh 11:2; 12:3). This locale could have given its name to the district and the sea. K. H. Rengstorf, *BHH* I, 546f.; W. E. Gerber, *BHH* II, 951f.; *BL* 554f., 948.

γέννησις, εως, ἡ *gennēsis* birth

Matt 1:18 TR; Luke 1:14 TR (in each case in place of → γένεσις).

γεννητός, 3 *gennētos* begotten; born*

A term for "mankind" in the phrase ἐν γεννητοῖς γυναικῶν, "among those *born* of women," Matt 11:11 par. Luke 7:28 (cf. Job 14:1; 15:14; see also γενόμενος ἐκ γυναικός in Gal 4:4). The term, which is also common in Judaism (Billerbeck I, 597f.), accents the earthly origin of mankind. F. Büchsel, *TDNT* I, 672.

γένος, ους, τό *genos* race; stock; kind*

1. Occurrences in the NT — 2. In the Gospels — 3. In Acts — 4. In Paul and in the other writings

Lit.: K. Maly, *Mündige Gemeinde* (1967) 176-239.

1. Γένος appears twice each in Mark and Matthew (including 17:21 v.l.), 9 times in Acts, 6 times in Paul, and once each in 1 Peter and Revelation. In most instances it is used to denote *origin* (from birth).

2. The Greek woman in Mark 7:26 (Συροφοινίκισσα τῷ γένει) was from the Syrian coastal province of Phoenicia. She learned that the Son of God also liberates the Gentiles from demonic power. In the instruction to the disciples in Mark 9:29; Matt 17:21 v.l., prayer, and in some mss. also fasting, appears as a means for exorcism in cases of possession (τοῦτο τὸ γένος). In the parable of the seine net Matt 13:47 refers to every kind of fish (ἐκ παντὸς γένους) and teaches that the selection of the righteous occurs only at the final judgment.

3. In Acts 4:36; 18:2, 24, Luke mentions the familial *origin* of the Levite Joseph Barnabas from Cyprus, and of the *origin* of Aquila from Pontus and of Apollos from Alexandria. In Stephen's speech Pharaoh recognizes Joseph's Jewish *origin,* according to Acts 7:13. V. 19 reflects the style of the speech: in v. 17 Stephen appeals to his countrymen in a passage where the concept of the people no longer resonates with its religious connotation. In the speech at Antioch, the Jews are addressed in Acts 13:26 as descendants of Abraham; here, in contrast to Paul (Rom 9:6-13; 2 Cor 11:22; Gal 3:8), there is no reflection on the promise to Abraham. In the citation from the "Heavenly Appearances" of Aratus of Cilicia (3rd cent. B.C.), Acts 17:28, 29, in the style of Hellenistic missionary preaching, refers to a Stoic motif (we are God's γένος) and emphasizes the universal character of the gospel. Acts 4:6 refers to members of the Sadducean priestly nobility (ἐκ γένους ἀρχιερατικοῦ), against whose resistance the apostolic preaching was able to succeed in accordance with God's plan of salvation.

4. With γένη γλωσσῶν Paul refers in 1 Cor 12:10, 28 to the diversity of the charismatic glossolalia and compares it with the variety of languages in 14:10. Gal 1:14; 2 Cor 11:26; Phil 3:5 employ in a secular sense the term used, e.g., in Jer 38:37 LXX to render the Heb. *zeraʿ* to accent Jewish *descent* and *membership* by birth.

The claim to election in Isa 43:20 is cited in 1 Pet 2:9 in reference to the Church, God's new race. In Rev 22:16 the shoot from the root of Jesse (Isa 11:10) refers to the exalted Jesus as the descendant of David and fulfiller of messianic hopes.

V. Hasler

Γερασηνός, 3 *Gerasēnos* from Gerasa*
Γαδαρηνός, 3 *Gadarēnos* from Gadara*
Γεργεσηνός, 3 *Gergesēnos* from Gergesa (v.l.)

Lit.: F. ANNEN, *Heil für die Heiden* (1976) 201-6. — BAGD s.v. — I. BENZINGER, PW VII, 1242-45. — A. VAN DEN BORN and W. BAIER, *BL* 555. — G. DALMAN, *Orte und Wege Jesu* ([3]1924) 192f. — E. HAENCHEN, *Der Weg Jesu* (1966) 190f. — H. HEGERMANN, *BHH* I, 508, 548. — KOPP, *Stätten,* 282-87. — C. H. KRAELING and T. KLAUSER, *RAC* X, 223-33. — K. MATTHIAE, *Chronologische Übersichten und Karten zur spätjüdischen und urchristlichen Zeit* (1977, 1978).

In the mss. of Mark 5:1, Γερασηνός (cf. *Inscriptiones Graece ad res Romanas pertinentes* IV [ed. R. Cagnat et al., 1927] 374.11) competes with the two other forms (Matt 8:28; Luke 8:26, 37). It is improbable that Γεργεσηνός originated with a conjecture by Origen (cf. Haenchen), yet as the most difficult text, the Markan "from Gerasa" is the oldest form. Gerasa (modern Jerash), however, the most important city of the Decapolis (→ Δεκάπολις), was too far distant from the Sea of Tiberias for the story of the demoniac.

Mark employs the narrative as a missionary story (5:18-20), without elaborating on topography (cf. the unrelated places listed in 7:31). Matt 8:28 replaces the original city with Gadara (modern Muqeis, *ca.* 15 km. southeast of the sea). A steep cliff 6-12 m. in height rose near the city. Although coins from Gadara with ship emblems have been attested, it is unclear whether the area around the city actually led to the sea (but cf. Josephus *Vita* ix.42). Yet it is possible that Matthew shows genuine topographical interest here. He exchanges the Markan "Decapolis" to an area near the sea, because he knows no mission outside of Israel before Easter. The variant reading "from Gergesa" (e.g., ℵ[c]), which is not an original text, is the result of an attempt to identify the locality of the demoniac narrative. Origen (in John 6:41) mentioned a place called Gergesa to the east of the sea near Kursī, at the mouth of the Wādî es-Samak. Approximately 2 km. to the south a cliff 44 m. high rises at the sea. Origen associated the east shore of the sea with the Girgashites (Gen 10:16). The influence of parallel versions on the mss. has led to a classical situation of text confusion (*TCGNT* 23f., 84, 145).

G. Schille

Γεργεσηνός, 3 *Gergesēnos* from Gergesa
→ Γερασηνός.

γερουσία, ας, ἡ *gerousia* council of elders*

Acts 5:21 mentions the γερουσία along with the συνέδριον, using a phrase (πᾶσαν τὴν γερουσίαν τῶν υἱῶν Ἰσραήλ) that is dependent on Exod 12:21. According to 1 Macc 12:6, 35; 2 Macc 1:10; Josephus *Ant.* xiii.166, etc., the γερουσία of the Jewish people assumed the role of the assembly of the elders (Ezra 5:9; 6:7) or of the "great assembly" (*'Abot* 1:1) of the postexilic time in the 2nd cent. B.C. Since the time of Herod the Great it was called the Sanhedrin, and the elders of the Jewish people were represented in it. Luke, through an imprecise knowledge of the historical situation, has both governing bodies appear alongside each other as he portrays the totality of all Israel as opponents of the apostles. H.-J. Schoeps, *BHH* II, 740f.; *BL* 751-53; E. Haenchen, *The Acts of the Apostles* (1971) ad loc.

γέρων, οντος, ὁ *gerōn* elder*

John 3:4: a reference to Nicodemus.

γεύομαι *geuomai* taste; eat*

1. Occurrences in the NT — 2. Meaning — 3. Usage

Lit.: J. BEHM, *TDNT* I, 675-77.

1. In the NT γεύομαι appears 15 times, frequently in connection with the phrase "*taste* death"; in "*taste* the meal" in the aor. subjunc., which has a future meaning (BDF §§318, 363); and once in the fut. ind. (Luke 14:24). Elsewhere the gen. or acc. obj. is connected with the aor. ind. Γεύομαι appears without an obj. 4 times, once with a ὅτι clause (1 Pet 2:3).

2. The word means *taste, savor, eat.* Along with the literal meaning it is also used metaphorically.

3. Γεύομαι is used of the steward of the feast (John 2:9) with reference to the *tasting* of the water that had been turned into wine for the purpose of examining it. Luke 14:24 associates it with the *tasting* of a meal.

Heb 6:4, 5 speaks metaphorically of the *tasting* of the heavenly gift, the word of God and the powers of the future world, and refers to the experience of such gifts as forgiveness and the gospel, which become present in the worship. In an OT citation (Ps 34:8) the imv. is transformed in 1 Pet 2:3 into the ind., "You have *tasted*"; as in Heb 6:4f., personal experience subsequent to the new birth is in mind (see 1 Pet 1:3, 23; 2:2).

In several passages γεύομαι appears in close association with the gen. θανάτου: in the eschatological saying in Mark 9:1 (par. Matt 16:28/Luke 9:27), which promises some hearers (in the original wording, perhaps, all hearers) the experience of the kingdom of God; in John 8:52, in a charge of the Jews against Jesus (referring to v. 51, where θανάτου is associated with θεωρέω, which reveals their misunderstanding of "death"; in Heb 2:9, where the reference is to Jesus, who through God's grace (so most text witnesses; not "without God") is the basis of salvation for everyone. In these verses γεύομαι implies the moment of suffering. The aor. subjunc. has a future meaning and thus is in accord with the eschatological contexts.

Γεύομαι is used with no object to mean *eat,* in the reference to Peter in Acts 10:10. In 20:11 it is used of Paul; in 23:14, of the men who have taken the oath to abstain from food until Paul is murdered; in Col 2:21, of the command by the false teachers to practice asceticism.

H.-J. van der Minde

γεωργέω *geōrgeō* cultivate, till (the land)*

Heb 6:7 pass., with the earth as the subj. and those who cultivate it as the beneficiaries: δι' οὓς καὶ γεωργεῖται, "for whose sake it is *cultivated.*"

γεώργιον, ου, τό *geōrgion* arable land; field*

1 Cor 3:9: θεοῦ γεώργιον, "God's *field,*" alongside θεοῦ οἰκοδομή in a reference to the Corinthian church. A vineyard may be in mind. The emphasis lies on the work of God, as the threefold reference to θεοῦ in v. 9 indicates.

γεωργός, οῦ, ὁ *geōrgos* farmer*

1. Occurrences in the NT and Meaning — 2. Mark 12:1-12 par. — 3. In other NT writings

Lit.: E. Haenchen, *Der Weg Jesu* ([2]1968) 396-404. — Jeremias, *Parables.* — W. Trilling, *Das wahre Israel* (SANT 10, [3]1964) 55-65.

1. Of the 19 occurrences in the NT, only two appear outside the Gospels (2 Tim 2:6; Jas 5:7). In the Gospels γεωργός occurs only in the parable of the evil vineyard workers (Mark 12:1-12 par. Matt 21:33-46/Luke 20:1-19) and in John 15:1. The word γεωργός means in the literal sense *agricultural worker, farmer, vineyard worker* (BAGD s.v.), while in a fig. sense it means *tenant.*

2. The situation assumed in the parable of the evil vineyard workers may reflect the economic and legal relationships of that period (such as the leasing of property by foreign owners to tenants; cf. Billerbeck I, 869-75). In the parable in the Gospels the vineyard workers are Jews. The question the parable does not settle is whether the workers are only the leaders of the Jews (cf. Mark 12:12; Luke 20:19) or all Israel (cf. Matt 21:43). The latter meaning is more closely related to Isa 5:1-7 (cf. the intentional allusion to Isa 5:1f. LXX in Mark 12:1 par.), where the vineyard workers (the tenants), not the vineyard itself, stand for Israel as a whole.

3. In John 15:1 God is described as the vinedresser in the address about the vine. As the true vine, Jesus' existence comes only from God; and only he as the Revealer makes God accessible to his people. In 2 Tim 2:6 the image of the farmer appears with that of the soldier and of the athlete (cf. 1 Cor 9:7, 25) in a parenetic context. Jas 5:7 employs the image of the farmer who waits for the harvest in order to encourage the faithful to perseverance in view of the delay of the parousia.

W. Hackenberg

γῆ, γῆς, ἡ *gē* earth; soil; ground; land*

Lit.: BAGD s.v. — H. Sasse, *TDNT* I, 677-81. — H. H. Schmid, *THAT* I, 228-36. For further bibliography see *TWNT* X, 1023.

1. OT use of *'ereṣ,* "earth, land," is remarkable, both numerically and in terms of content. It can be used of the earth viewed cosmologically rather than as a place of habitation for human beings (Gen 6:11), of the ground on which people and animals move (Gen 1:26; Ps 147:6: Ezek 26:16), of individual countries or regions (Gen 31:3; Num 15:2; Jer 30:10), and often with political overtones (1 Sam 13:19) or religious or social characteristics (Isa 8:22f.; cf. Matt 4:15f.). It can also be used of the earth as God's creation (Gen 1:1) and as his possession (Ps 24:1) upon which he looks down (Gen 6:12) or over which he strides (Hab 3:12) and speaks judgment (Ps 82:8). In a special way the prospect of the land is set before Israel (Gen 15:18). In Deuteronomy the land is associated closely with the proclamation of the commandments (Deut 12:1; 17:14; 19:8f.). The prophets idealize the conception in terms of eschatological fulfillment (Jer 30:3; Ezek 36:28; cf. Isa 65:17). The view of Wisdom literature and the prophets (Prov 2:21f.), which forms the background for NT statements (cf. Matt 5:5), is also noteworthy.

2. In Mark the meaning is primarily that of *ground* or *soil,* which receives the seed, brings it to maturity, and gives fruit (4:5, 8, 26, 28). Matthew employs the more geographic perspective with political and social overtones (2:6, 20f.; 4:15). The eschatological (5:5; cf. Gen 12:1) and universalistic perspective (Matt 5:13) is apparent especially in the juxtaposition of "heaven and earth," which in Matthew can appear as an element derived from the OT (Gen 1:1; 2:1) that is coordinated and held in tension, through which the hand of God as both Creator and Father forms a unity in the created cosmos (Matt 6:10). This view has consequences for the Church and its decisions (16:19; 18:18; 28:18). Luke sees the earth as the place of proclamation and of controversy (12:49, 51; 18:8) but also as the place of eschatological testing (21:23, 25). John contrasts the spiritual person who comes from above with the earthly person who is from the earth (3:31). Corresponding to this view is the christological component, namely, that the earth is the point of departure for the exaltation and glorification of the Son of Man (12:32; 17:4).

The contrast "earthly" versus "born of the Spirit" is also known to Paul (cf. 1 Cor 15:47). In addition he confesses the lordship of the *one* Lord over the entire creation (1 Cor 10:26; cf. 8:5f.), a thought that is deepened in the deutero-Pauline letters (Eph 1:10; 3:15) and extended to the perfection of mankind (Col 3:2, 5). Revelation has a special interest in the new creation of "heaven and earth" (21:1), which must be preceded by great tests, upheavals, and disorders (3:10; 6:4, 13, 15; 11:18; 13:14), until the earth is ripe for the great harvest (14:16) and for the transition to the glory of the heavenly Jerusalem (21:24).

A. Kretzer

γῆρας, ως (ους), τό *gēras* old age*

Used of Elizabeth in Luke 1:36, who has conceived a son ἐν γήρει αὐτῆς, "in her *old age.*"

γηράσκω *gēraskō* grow old; become weak with age; die out*

John 21:18, in the word of the resurrected one to Simon Peter: ὅταν δὲ γηράσῃς, "but when you *are old,*" the opposite of ὅτε ἦς νεώτερος, "when you were young" (with R. Bultmann, *The Gospel of John* [1971] ad loc., probably a proverbial formulation that originally began with ὅταν); of the old covenant in Heb 8:13: τὸ δὲ παλαιούμενον καὶ γηράσκον, "what is becoming obsolete and *growing old.*"

γίνομαι *ginomai* become; originate

1. Occurrences and meaning in the NT — 2. a) In the Pauline literature — b) In the Synoptics and Acts — c) In the Johannine literature — d) Elsewhere in the NT

Lit.: BEYER, *Syntax* 29-62. — F. BÜCHSEL, *TDNT* I, 681-89. — E. DELEBECQUE, *Études grecques sur l'Évangile de Luc* (1976) 123-65 (on καὶ ἐγένετο).

1. The verb γίνομαι appears in all NT writings except Jude. With 667 occurrences, it is one of the most commonly used words. It appears in the NT only in its Ionic-Hellenistic form (γίνομαι instead of γίγνομαι; cf. BDF §34.4). It means in the literal sense *become, originate, come into existence.* In the NT the following meanings are found: (1) *happen, occur;* (2) *become, originate;* (3) *attain to* or *arrive at* (something); (4) *be made, be created.* In addition, γίνομαι can serve as a substitute for forms of εἰμί. With few exceptions, γίνομαι is used without theological interest.

2.a) In the authentic Pauline letters γίνομαι occurs a total of 118 times. The dominant meanings are *take place* (e.g., Rom 11:25; 1 Cor 9:15; 1 Thess 1:5, 7) and *become* (e.g., Rom 2:34; 4:18; 1 Cor 3:18; 9:20; 2 Cor 1:8; 5:21). The meaning *be created* or *be born* is relatively rare (Rom 1:3; Gal 4:4). Paul employs γίνομαι also frequently with the same sense as εἰμί (e.g., Rom 7:13; 1 Cor 4:13; 7:23; 9:20f.; Gal 4:12). Characteristic of Paul is the phrase μὴ γένοιτο ("by no means!" or "far be it from me") as an answer to a rhetorical question, which occurs only in Romans, 1 Corinthians, and Galatians (elsewhere in the NT only in Luke 20:16). This phrase reflects a stylistic peculiarity of Cynic-Stoic popular philosophy (cf. BDF §§3, n. 4; 384).

b) The Synoptic Gospels and Acts use γίνομαι frequently in the phrase καὶ ἐγένετο ("and it came to pass") to indicate the continuity of the narrative. This phrase is from the LXX, which is its translation of Heb. *way^{e}hî* with waw-consecutive. The typical form with καί at the beginning and with the following clause introduced by καί is found in Luke 5:17: καὶ ἐγένετο ἐν μιᾷ τῶν ἡμερῶν καὶ αὐτὸς ἦν διδάσκων (cf. Matt 9:10; Mark 2:15; Luke 5:1, 12; 8:1, 22, etc.). The καί at the beginning is sometimes omitted; the καί at the beginning of the following clause is often either left out or the clause is replaced by another construction (e.g., acc. with the inf.), which is evidence of better Greek (esp. in Luke and Acts; cf. Büchsel 682).

Γίνομαι is frequently used with the meaning *come about, arise,* e.g., of events involving phenomena in nature (e.g., Matt 8:24, 28; 27:45; Mark 4:37; 15:33). It can replace corresponding forms of εἰμί (Mark 4:10; 16:10; Luke 2:42; Acts 19:21). In general, there is no particular theological interest in the use of γίνομαι in the Synoptic Gospels and Acts.

c) In the Johannine literature γίνομαι occurs a total of 54 times, with only 3 occurrences in the Johannine letters: 1 John 2:18; 2 John 12; 3 John 8. It is generally used with the same meaning in John as in the Synoptic Gospels; e.g., for the occurrence of phenomena in nature and times of the day (John 6:16, 17; 7:43; 10:19, 22; 12:29; 13:2, etc.) or as a substitute for corresponding forms of εἰμί (John 1:6, 15; 2:1; 3:25; 7:43; 10:22, etc.). The phrase καὶ ἐγένετο is not found in John.

In a few passages the author of John uses γίνομαι with the meaning *become, attain* in order to describe the change from being lost (darkness, slavery) to salvation within the framework of his theology (cf. John 4:14; 5:6, 9; 8:33; 9:27, 39; 12:36; 16:20). The γίνομαι in the prologue has a theological meaning (1:1-18); in vv. 3 and 10 there is a description of the role of the Logos in mediating creation. V. 4 emphasizes the function of the Logos in maintaining the creation. Finally, γίνομαι has a special meaning in John 8:58, where it appears in contrast with εἰμί: πρὶν Ἀβραὰμ γενέσθαι ἐγὼ εἰμί. The Revealer of the Father is preexistent and cannot be determined in temporal categories. Abraham, on the other hand, belongs to the created existence, to that which *has come into being.*

d) In other NT writings γίνομαι appears most frequently in Hebrews (30 times) and Revelation (38 times). It appears relatively seldom in the deutero-Pauline writings. In Heb 5:5 γίνομαι refers to Christ's office of high priest; in 9:15 it refers to the death of Christ (θανάτου γενομένου). In Revelation γίνομαι is frequently used with the meaning *arise* or *come* (for natural phenomena, etc.; cf. 6:12; 8:1, 5; 11:13, 19; 12:7; 16:18, etc.).

W. Hackenberg

γινώσκω *ginōskō* know; understand*
γνῶσις, εως, ἡ *gnōsis* recognition; knowledge*
γνωστός, 3 *gnōstos* known; knowable*

1. Occurrences in the NT — 2. Secular use — a) Learn — b) Notice — c) Ascertain — d) Know — e) Of persons: know, be known, become known — f) Other uses — 3. Religious use — a) In the OT — b) In apocalyptic literature — c) In the synagogue — d) Θεῖος ἀνήρ — e) In mysticism — f) In Gnosticism — g) The messianic secret — h) The knowledge of sin — i) In John

Lit.: L. Bieler, Θεῖος Ἀνήρ I/II (1935, 1936, repr. 1967). — M. É. Boismard, "La connaissance dans l'alliance nouvelle d'après la première lettre de Saint Jean," *RB* 56 (1949) 365-91. — R. Bultmann, *TDNT* I, 689-719. — M. Dibelius, "Ἐπίγνωσις ἀληθείας," *Neutestamentliche Studien* (FS G. Heinrici; 1914) 176-89. — J. Dupont, *Gnosis. La connaissance religieuse dans les épitres de Saint Paul* (1949). — H. J. Ebeling, *Das Messiasgeheimnis und die Botschaft des Marcus-Evangelisten* (1939). — H. M. Féret, *Connaissance biblique de Dieu* (1955). — E. Güttgemanns, *Der leidende Apostel und sein Herr* (FRLANT 90, 1966). — F. Mussner, *Galaterbrief* (HTKNT; 1974). — E. Norden, *Agnostos Theos* ([4]1956). — R. Reitzenstein, *Die hellenistischen Mysterienreligionen* ([3]1927, repr. 1966). — O. Roller, *Das Formular der paulinischen Briefe* (1933). — H. Schlier, "Glauben, Erkennen, Lieben nach dem Johannesevangelium," Schlier II, 279-93. — *idem,* "Die Erkenntnis Gottes nach den Briefen des Apostels Paulus," *ibid.* 319-39. — W. Schmithals, *Gnosticism in Corinth* (1971). — *idem, Der Römerbrief als historisches Problem* (SNT 9, 1975). — R. Schnackenburg, *The Gospel according to St. John* I (1968). — H. Windisch, *Paulus und Christus* (UNT 24, 1934). — W. Wrede, *The Messianic Secret in the Gospels* (1971). — For further bibliography see *TWNT* X, 1024f.

1. Γινώσκω appears a total of 222 times in the NT, most often in John (57), 1 John (25), Luke (28), Acts (16), Matthew (20), Mark (12), and the Pauline corpus (43, including 16 in 1 Corinthians). Γνῶσις appears 29 times, with 27 of these in the Epistles alone, esp. 1 Corinthians (10 times) and 2 Corinthians (6 times). The compounds → ἐπιγινώσκω and → ἐπίγνωσις are used in basically the same way as the simple forms; cf. the v.l. to Mark 6:33; Matt 11:27; 2 Pet 2:21; the Synoptic parallels Matt 7:16/Luke 6:44; Matt 11:27/Luke 10:22; cf. the change in 1 Cor 13:12; 2 Cor 13:5f. Thus the compounds are cited in what follows without any explicit comment. Γνωστός is a favorite word of Luke (2 times in Luke, 10 times in Acts).

The boundary between secular and religious uses of this word family is fluid. In many cases, assignment of particular uses to one category or the other is somewhat arbitrary.

2.a) One *learns* or *comes to know* a fact from information; it *becomes (is) known* (Matt 6:3; 12:15; 26:10; Mark 6:33; 15:10 ["he *knew*" = "he *learned/perceived*"; → 2.b]; Luke 1:4; 7:37; 24:18; Acts 1:19; 4:16 ["*notable* sign"]; 9:24, 30, 42; 15:18 [cf. Amos 9:12]; 17:13; 19:17; 22:29; 28:1, 22; John 4:1; 11:57 [→ 2.c]; 12:9; 19:4 ["that you may *know,*" i.e., *see*]; Phil 4:5 ["let all men *know*"; cf. Matt 10:26 par. Luke 12:2; → 3.b]; Rom 6:6 ["we *know*" = "this you should *know/consider*"]; Eph 5:5). The information comes through letters (2 Cor 2:4 ["I wrote . . . to let you *know*"]; Phil 1:12 ["I want you *to know*" = "I want *to communicate* to you"; cf. Roller 67f. and → ἀγνοέω 1]; 2 Tim 3:1; Heb 13:23 [imv. "you should *understand*"; but ind. is also possible: "as you *know*"]; Jas 5:20; 2 Pet 1:20; 3:3). Paul sends a messenger (Col 4:8; Eph 6:22 ["that you may *know*"]), or the information comes by the reader being addressed ("you should *come to know/take notice of*"; *let it be said* to you: Matt 24:43 par. Luke 12:39; Acts 2:14, 36; 4:10; 13:38; 28:28; Luke 10:11, → 3.b).

b) One *notices* or *observes* a hidden intent (Mark 12:12 par. Matt 21:45/Luke 20:19; Matt 22:18; John 16:19; cf. also Mark 15:10 [→ 2.a]). One *notices* through observation (Luke 1:22; 2:43; 9:11 ["when the crowds *learned* it"]; Acts 19:34; 21:24; 23:6). One *concludes and recognizes* a fact: John 4:53; 8:27 ["they did not *understand*"], 52; Gal 2:9 [with ἰδόντες in v. 7, with reference to v. 2; cf. 1 Cor 15:10]: "they *perceived/understood,*" or less likely, "they *acknowledged*"; cf. Mussner 118; 3:7 ["you *see,*" i.e., from the Scripture]).

c) One *ascertains* or *seeks to learn* through investigation, inquiry, and discovery (Mark 6:38; 15:45; Luke 19:15; 23:7; Acts 17:19f.; 21:34; 22:30 [→ ἐπιγινώσκω]; John 7:51 ["*learning/discovering* what he does"]; 11:57 [on 5:6 → 3.d]; 1 Cor 4:19; 2 Cor 2:9 [Paul writes "that I might . . . *know/find out* whether . . ."]; Phil 2:19; 1 Thess 3:5 [Paul sends Timothy in order to *know/learn*]). One *comes to know* through observation (Matt 7:16, 20 par. Luke 6:44; Matt 12:33), through self-examination (2 Cor 13:5f., Jas 2:20 ["do you want to *be shown*?" or perhaps "must I first *prove* to you?"—with the text of Scripture following]; similarly Luke 1:18: "How shall I *know*?" [as in Gen 15:8] as an [inappropriate] demand for a sign).

d) One *knows (about)* on the basis of experience (Matt 25:24; Mark 13:28 par. Matt 24:32/Luke 21:30 [Matt 24:43 par. Luke 12:39 → 2.a]; John 7:27; 15:18 ["*know/consider* that it has hated me"]; Acts 19:35 ["who does not *know*"]; 20:34; cf. 25:10; 27:39; Phil 2:22 [Timothy's "worth you *know,*" i.e., *know about*"]; 2 Tim 1:18 ["you well *know*"]; Jas 1:3; Heb 10:34 ["you *knew*" from the experience of faith]).

e) Of persons: *know* someone; someone *is* or *becomes known:* On Matt 7:23 (cf. Luke 13:27), → 3.b; Luke 2:44 ("kinsfolk and *acquaintances*"); 23:49; John 18:15f.; Acts 19:15; 2 Cor 3:2; 5:16 (not "*know* in a fleshly way" but rather "*know* the 'fleshly' Christ" or "no longer want to *know*" [the verse is probably an un-Pauline gloss; see Schmithals, *Gnosticism* 302ff.; Güttgemanns 282-304];

γινώσκω

→ 3.f). Someone *is recognized* or *is known* (most often ἐπιγινώσκω: Mark 6:54 par. Matt 14:35; Matt 17:12; Luke 24:16, 31, 35; John 13:35; Acts 3:10; 4:13; 12:14).

f) Miscellaneous other uses include the following: Mark 5:29 ("she *felt/sensed* in her body that she was healed"); Mark 5:30 par. Luke 8:46 (Jesus *perceived* that a power had left him); Luke 16:4 (ἔγνων, "I have *decided*"); 1 Cor 14:7, 9 (unarticulated sounds cannot be *understood*); Rom 10:18f. (Israel heard and *understood* the content of the message).

In Matt 1:25; Luke 1:34, the word refers to sexual relations and is used of both the man and the woman. This figure of speech is common in the OT (e.g., Gen 4:1, 17, 25; 19:8) but also appears in Gentile Hellenism (as a Semitism?), often in Plutarch. In 1 Pet 3:7 κατὰ γνῶσιν means *considerately* or *with understanding*.

The other meaning of γινώσκω common in secular literature, *be skilled at, be able,* is rare in the NT. Matt 16:3 ("You *know how* to interpret the appearance of the sky"; Luke has οἴδατε); Acts 21:37 (Paul *knew,* or *had a command of,* the Greek language).

3.a) God *knows* human hearts (Luke 16:15) and *knows about (sifts)* their intentions (1 Cor 3:20, citing Ps 93:11 LXX). The believer can correspondingly take comfort in the fact that God "*knows* everything" (1 John 3:20; cf. John 21:17). God "*knows* those who are his" (cares for them; does not forget them: 2 Tim 2:19 [citing Num 16:5]; cf. John 10:14, 27).

OT thought also agrees that God (through his messengers) *makes* something *known* and allows it to be known (Matt 10:26; Acts 2:36; Rom 6:6; Eph 5:5; Rev 2:23; 3:9) or spreads *knowledge* of himself (= fear of God or faith; 2 Cor 2:14; 4:6). Also, God's coworkers are *acknowledged* as such (1 Cor 16:18; 2 Cor 6:9) or are *recognized* as such in their integrity (2 Cor 1:13f.). His own *know* (= acknowledge; have fear of) God or Christ and his salvation (Luke 1:77; 1 Cor 1:5; 2 Cor 6:6; 8:7, 9; 10:5; Phil 3:8; Col 2:3; Heb 8:11 [citing Jer 38:34 LXX]; 2 Pet 3:18) and *know* or *come to know* his will (Luke 12:47f.; Acts 22:14; Rom 2:18; 15:14; 1 Cor 14:37). Jerusalem *should have known/recognized* what served the cause of peace (Luke 19:42, 44).

The godless, on the other hand, do not *know* God (= they do not ask about him or acknowledge him: Rom 3:17 [citing Isa 59:8 LXX]; Heb 3:10 [citing Ps 94:10 LXX]).

b) Various modes of speech characterize apocalyptic literature and its language. In Matt 10:26 par. Luke 12:2 is a logion from Q that adopts a secular rule from Wisdom literature. In the original tradition it apparently meant that the hidden apocalyptic truths will be *revealed* at a time that has been predetermined (cf. 1 Cor 2:6-9; 4 Ezra 46f.). Matthew associates that idea with the preaching of the gospel, which is to be *made known* publicly (→ 3.a). Luke relates the saying to the hypocrisy of the Pharisees, which will *not remain unknown* (see below). In Luke 8:17 (after the doublet in Mark 4:22) the saying is connected to interpretation of the parables (→ 3.g). At the last judgment, when what is hidden *will be revealed* (Luke 12:2), God will *not know* the evildoers; i.e., he rejects them (Matt 7:23).

The archons of this age did not *understand* the secret of God's hidden plan of salvation (1 Cor 2:8; cf. Rom 11:33f.), and thus through the crucifixion they pursued their own defeat. The exact time of the change of aeons *is not known* (Matt 24:50 par. Luke 12:46; Acts 1:7; Rev 3:3). However, one should *take notice of* (Mark 13:28f. par. Matt 24:32f./Luke 21:30f.; Matt 24:39; Luke 21:20; cf. Matt 24:43 par. Luke 12:39; Matt 16:3) its imminence (Luke 10:11: "nevertheless *know/be sure of* this") or the signs of its coming. At the appearance of Antichrist, the last hour *is known* (1 John 2:18).

c) The (Hellenistic) synagogue adapts the Greek concept of knowledge (to discern theoretically, to discover through observation; cf. Bultmann 689-92) without surrendering the OT element of *recognition.* Especially in Paul and his school the thought and the usage of the synagogue are apparent in some passages. This usage is to be seen more or less in a christologized form (Dibelius 180ff.).

There is agreement in the OT and in apocalyptic literature that God's *knowledge* (= wisdom, will) is unattainable by humankind (Rom 11:33). The creature does not *know* the mind of God (Rom 11:34 [citing Isa 40:13 LXX]; cf. 1 Cor 2:8). What is *perceptible* about God (Rom 1:19; cf. Sir 21:7), namely God's divinity and his will, is certainly *known* to the world (Rom 1:21, 32), for God has not left himself without a witness (vv. 19f.). But the world does not *know* God (1 Cor 1:21; cf. 1 Thess 4:5; 2 Thess 1:8; 1 Cor 15:34; Eph 2:12); i.e., they *gave* him *no recognition* (Rom 1:28). The Jews themselves were lacking in the *correct understanding* (Rom 10:2; Paul turns the argument of the synagogue used against the Gentiles against the Jews themselves). The knowledge of God from the creation (Rom 1:19f.) does not rest on a logical conclusion involving cause and effect but instead requires a recognition in *obedience* of the Creator (Schlier 319ff.).

Anyone who *comes to know* God (Gal 4:9; = serves him, cf. 1 Thess 1:9) turns from idols and comes to the *knowledge* of the glory of God in the face of Jesus Christ (2 Cor 4:6) or to the *knowledge* of the truth (esp. → ἐπίγνωσις, in the fixed terminology of conversion), a process that is never concluded (Eph 1:17: *to know* him, apparently also in 2 Pet 1:5f.); → ἐπίγνωσις thus takes on the meaning of "believe" (Titus 1:1). This usage is also present apparently in Luke 11:52 (cf. Matt 23:13), where Luke alters the Q text into "key of *knowledge.*"

As in the synagogue, such knowledge presupposes an *understanding* of Holy Scripture (Matt 12:7; Acts 8:30; cf. 2 Tim 3:15). The respect for the Torah common in the synagogue is indicated when the pious Jews boast that they *know* God's will (Rom 2:18f.) and possess the content of this *knowledge* in the Torah (v. 20; 7:1, of those who were previously God-fearing; see Schmithals, *Römerbrief* 87f.), while at the same time they deny that "this crowd" (John 7:49) has any knowledge of the law.

d) Jesus is often portrayed in the Gospels in a way that is analogous to the Hellenistic θεῖος ἀνήρ, who *perceives* what people say (Mark 8:17 par. Matt 16:8), think (Mark 2:8 par. Luke 5:22), intend (John 6:15; perhaps Matt 12:15), and are (Luke 7:39; John 5:6); who *knows* people and *sees through* them (John 1:48; 2:24f.; 5:42; cf. Mark 11:2f.; 14:13-16); cf. Windisch and Bieler.

e) The peculiar doublet "*know* God" and "*be known* by God" (1 Cor 8:3; 13:12; Gal 4:9) most likely goes back to the language of mysticism (Dibelius 183f.; but cf. Bultmann 710, n. 78; 693f.). For Paul, however, the idea of deification is far removed. For him, "*to be known* by God" means to be elected, loved, and accepted by God (cf. Rom 8:29; 11:2; Phil 3:12; 2 Tim 2:19; Amos 3:2); "*to know* him" means to serve him. In addition, "*to know* him and/namely . . ." (Phil 3:10, connected with v. 9a, not with the parenthesis in v. 9b) belongs, because of the continuation in v. 10, to the language of the mysteries (cf. Rom 6:1-11; Dibelius 185f.) and designates the Christian faith as a permanent existential fulfillment.

Within the framework of the Johannine idea of revelation, the motif of the unity of the Father and Son (John 10:30, 38; 17:21) or of God and the Logos (John 1:1f.), consisting of reciprocal *knowing,* belongs to this same emphasis in the history of religions; cf. John 10:15; 17:25; Matt 11:27 par. Luke 10:22. The logion is to be ascribed to the post-Markan redaction of Q. One should also note the influence of the Gnostic christology of identity.

f) In 1 Tim 6:20 there is an explicit warning against the Gnostic heresy: "What is falsely called *knowledge*." Allusions to Gnostic false teachers are also found in Rev 2:24 (they *know*) and perhaps 3:9 (they should *know*). The Pastorals contain no other mention of γνῶσις, and the Johannine corpus avoids the term entirely, which reflects the anti-Gnostic tendency of these writings.

In 1 Cor 8:1-3, 7, 10f.; 13:2f., 8f., 12, Paul gives precedence to love as the highest gift of the Spirit over the γνῶσις of the Gnostic opponents in Corinth, whose practice in eating meat offered to idols he basically approves (the *knowledge* that the gods are nothing is correct; cf. Schmithals, *Gnosticism* 224ff.). Eph 3:19 follows the framework of a Gnostic pattern (H. Schlier, *Der Brief an die Epheser* [[4]1963] ad loc.). In 1 Cor 14:37 Paul confronts the Corinthian charismatics and their claim that they *know* the will of the Lord. In 2 Cor 11:6 Paul claims to have the right γνῶσις, in opposition to them. In 1 Cor 2:11, 14, 16 Paul follows the Gnostic conception very closely: only the "spiritual man" recognizes the divine.

What Paul or the Church meant by "the utterance of *knowledge*" or "the utterance of wisdom" (1 Cor 12:8; 14:6) is not easy to determine. Perhaps a Gnostic expression is used here alongside a term from the synagogue. If a gloss from the hand of Gnostic opponents is present in 2 Cor 5:16 (→ 2.e), *know* would be used in the technical sense that it has in Gnosticism.

g) The motif of the "messianic secret," which was first described by Wrede, was essentially formulated by Mark and followed by John. According to this idea, the parables are addresses composed of riddles, which are interpreted for the disciples in order that they may *understand* (Mark 4:13; Matt 13:11 par. Luke 8:10; Luke 8:17; cf. John 10:6; 13:7, 12). One is to *learn* nothing from Jesus' works (Mark 5:43; Matt 9:30) and his presence (Mark 7:24; 9:30); indeed, the disciples often do not *understand* Jesus (Mark 9:32 par. Luke 9:45; Luke 18:34; cf. Mark 4:13; John 12:16; 13:7, 28; see Wrede 231ff. on the motif of lack of understanding).

h) The Pauline statements about the knowledge of sin are difficult. Rom 3:20 is formulated in the Jewish sense: The law teaches one to *understand* sin as transgression; i.e., it provokes the sinner into sin. Presumably Paul means this, however, in the sense of Rom 7:7 (H. Schlier, *Römer* [HTKNT] 101; E. Käsemann, *Commentary on Romans* [1980] 89f.): without the law I would not *know* sin at all; the law thus gives rise to sin (of self-righteousness). However, the sinner loses control over himself; in striving to live as a sinner, he no longer *knows* what he is doing; he no longer *understands* himself (Rom 7:15). Finally, the fact that Jesus "*knew* no sin" (2 Cor 5:21) does not mean that he personally remained sinless; rather, he did not belong to sin's sphere of power (cf. Phil 2:6f.).

i) In John γινώσκω appears 56 times, while γνῶσις is entirely absent. This may be due to John's desire to wrest the concept of "gnosis" from the Gnostics. Thus John uses γινώσκω in a theological sense parallel to "believe" or "love God" or "see God," thereby giving the Gnostics' term an OT and Christian sense. Γινώσκω designates coming to faith before the Revealer, and esp. the certainty of faith or perseverance ("abiding") in faith. Finally, it is used of understanding one's own faith (cf. Bultmann 712; *idem, The Gospel of John* [1971] 435, n. 4; Schlier, *Glauben* 284ff.). The unbelieving world (in John often "the Jews") does not *know* God or Christ; i.e., it shuts itself off from him, does not *acknowledge* him (John 1:10; 3:10; 8:27, 43, 55; 14:17; 16:3; 17:25; 1 John 3:1). However, it will find life when it *acknowledges* and *recognizes* God and the one who was sent (8:28, a text that is hardly intelligible; see Schnackenburg, *The Gospel according to St. John* II [1979] 202f.); see also 10:38 (it must *know* and *recognize*); 14:7a, 31; 17:3. As the occasion arises, the harmony of the Church is a means to the same end (17:23). Thus the praxis of faith leads the world to *know* the truth of Christian teaching (7:17).

Those who are belong to Christ have *known* him (John 6:69; 14:7b; 1 John 4:16) and *recognize* him and *know about* him, that . . . (John 10:14; 14:17; 17:7f., 25; 1 John 2:13f.; 5:20; 2 John 1; cf. also John 7:26) or should have *known* him (14:9), just as he *knows* them (10:14). They will *know* him better (or again and again; 8:28, 32; 10:38; 13:7, 12; 14:20) when they abide in him.

The first two Epistles of John follow the same terminology in a form that is clearly shaped by the Church. Christians face the problem of their sins and must confirm their faith. They *know* that they *know* him, when they keep his commandments (1 John 2:3-5), e.g., brotherly love (3:19, 24; 4:13; 2:29; note the practical syllogisms) that is produced by the Spirit, and they know that he loves them. Brotherly love is thus the characteristic of the one who *knows* God or God's love (3:16; 4:7f.; cf. 4:20f.). Sin is the characteristic of the one who does not *know* (or no longer *knows*) God (3:6). Whoever *knows* God follows the orthodox teachers and *recognizes* (distinguishes) the Spirit of truth (4:2, 6) and of falsehood. The world, which does not *know* "him," does not know the Church (3:1).

W. Schmithals

γλεῦκος, ους, τό *gleukos* sweet wine; new wine*

Acts 2:13: γλεύκους μεμεστωμένοι, "full of sweet wine" (NASB), i.e., incompletely fermented "new wine." O. Betz, "Zungenreden und süßer Wein," FS Bardtke 20-36.

γλυκύς, 3 *glykys* sweet*

Jas 3:11, of water from a spring, which cannot be both *sweet* and bitter; v. 12 likewise refers to a salt spring, which cannot give *sweet* water; Rev 10:9, 10: in the phrase γλυκὺ ὡς μέλι / ὡς μέλι γλυκύ, of a little book that was "*sweet* as honey" to the seer (cf. Ezek 3:3).

γλῶσσα, ης, ἡ *glōssa* tongue; language*
ἑτερόγλωσσος, 2 *heteroglōssos* speaking a foreign language*

1. Occurrences and meaning in the NT — 2. Γλῶσσα as a part of the body — 3. Γλῶσσα as the organ of speech — 4. Γλῶσσα as an instrument or source of sin — 5. Γλῶσσα as "language" or "people" — 6. Γλῶσσα and glossolalia in 1 Corinthians 12–14 — 7. Γλῶσσα and glossolalia in Acts and Mark 16:17

Lit.: S. Aalen, *BHH* III, 2249f. — J. Behm, *TDNT* I, 719-27. — O. Betz, "Zungenreden und süßer Wein," FS Bardtke 20-36. — G. Dautzenberg, *RAC* XI, 225-46. — N. I. Engelson, "Glossolalia and Other Forms of Inspired Speech according to 1 Corinthians 12–14," *Dissertation Abstracts* 112 (1971) 526a. — J. Gewiess, *LTK* IV, 972f. — R. A. Harrisville, "Speaking in Tongues," *CBQ* 38 (1976) 35-48 (= *Speaking in Tongues: A Guide to Research on Glossolalia* [ed. W. E. Mills; 1986] 35-51). — W. Keilbach, *RGG* VI, 1941f. — J. Kremer, *Pfingstbericht und Pfingstgeschehen* (1973) 118-26, 261-64. — E. Mosiman, *Das Zungenreden geschichtlich und psychologisch untersucht* (1911). — H. Weinel, *Die Wirkungen des Geistes und der Geister im nachapostolischen Zeitalter bis auf Irenäus* (1899) 72-101. — For further bibliography see Aalen; Behm; Gewiess; Keilbach; *TWNT* X, 1025f.

1. Γλῶσσα is used a total of 50 times in the NT writings and means: (1) in the literal sense *tongue* as a bodily organ and esp. as the organ of speech (→ 2-4); (2) any particular *language* and fig. a *people* who speak their own language (→ 5); (3) on that basis, as an early Christian t.t., *the gift of glossolalia,* i.e., the use of *heavenly and earthly languages,* and *the charismatic expression of one who practices glossolalia* (→ 6, → 7). Ἑτερόγλωσσος, *speaking a foreign language,* presupposes γλῶσσα with the meaning *language* and occurs in the NT only in 1 Cor 14:21 in the citation from Isa 28:11 (→ 5, → 6). The NT usage in → 3 and → 5 is closely related to the OT usage; in → 4 and → 6 it develops from OT and Hellenistic Jewish assumptions.

2. Rarely the tongue is viewed only as a delicate bodily organ without a connection to human language. Rev 16:10 ("men gnawed their *tongues* in anguish") follows the pouring out of the fifth bowl (darkness in the domain of the beast) and probably portrays the reaction of people to the previous plagues (H. Kraft, *Offenbarung* [HNT] 207). It is hardly a text that describes "the genuine experience of the divine" (C. Schneider, *TDNT* IV, 515, who suggests that this action is in response to "exciting hallucinations" and that the visionary's sense of pain is dulled in comparison). In *Apoc. Pet.* 9:11 the gnawing of the tongue is part of the description of hell, namely, the punishment for blasphemers (those who have sinned with the tongue), doubters, and disobedient slaves. Thirst belongs to the punishment of the ungodly in ᾅδης (4 Ezra 8:59; *Sib. Or.* ii.307; *2 Enoch* 10:2 [A]; *y. Ḥag.* 2:77d, in Billerbeck II, 231f.), causing the tongue to wither (cf. Ps 22:15; Isa 41:17; Lam 4:4). Note also Luke 16:24: "Send Lazarus to dip the end of his finger in water and cool my *tongue,* for I am in anguish in this flame."

3. In 1 Cor 14:9 γλῶσσα is understood not in the sense of a technical term (→ 6) but rather, in analogy to the comparisons with flutes, zithers, and trumpets (vv. 7f.), as the organ of speech, through which one can articulate clear speech (J. Weiss, *Der Erste Korintherbrief* [KEK] 336). The comparison is intended to support Paul's argument in favor of intelligible prophecy and is not applied to glossolalia (against H. Lietzmann, *An die Korinther I/II* [HNT] 71).

In the story of the healing of the deaf-mute in Mark 7:32-35, the inability to speak appears to be traced back to a demonic shackling and binding (→ δεσμός) of the tongue (R. Pesch, *Markus* [HTKNT] I, 397; see also Deissmann, *Light* 304ff.; Moulton/Milligan 128): after the healing manipulation of the tongue (v. 33) and the healing word (v. 34), "the impediment of his *tongue* was removed, and he began speaking plainly" (v. 35 NASB). In Luke 1:64 ("immediately his mouth was opened and his *tongue* [loosed], and he spoke, blessing God"), the original omits the verb with *tongue.* Because of the after-effects of the miracle, the γλῶσσα is mentioned, although the chief interest of the text concerns Zechariah's capacity to speak and his word of praise.

In parenesis directed to the contrast between speaking and doing (Matt 7:21; Jas 1:22-25; 2:15f.), the tongue can portray this tension in human behavior, as in 1 John 3:18: "Let us not love in word (λόγος) or *speech* (γλῶσσα) but in deed (ἔργον) and in truth" (cf. Sir 29:1-3). In accordance with the synthetic tendency of OT anthropology (H. W. Wolff, *Anthropology of the OT* [1974] 77-79), the tongue commonly stands for the whole person considered from the point of view of the capacity for speech. In Acts 2:26 it appears in the citation from Ps 16:8-11 (with → καρδία) as the bearer of jubilation. In Rom 14:11 it appears in the citation from Isa 45:23b for the person who must stand before God's judgment. The same citation is used in the hymn in Phil 2:10f. for the recognition of the lordship (→ κύριος) of Jesus Christ by the cosmic powers. Γλῶσσα can be understood only as an anthropomorphism here if the reference to "on earth" (→ ἐπίγειος) does not concern humankind. In the "complaint liturgy" (O. Michel, *Römer* [KEK] 98) of Rom 3:10-18 the tongue is parallel to the throat (→ λάρυγξ, Ps 5:9), lips (→ χείλη, Ps 140:3), and mouth (Ps 10:7) as an illustration of the human disregard for God that is demonstrated primarily in words.

4. "The striking emphasis on sins of the tongue is characteristic of practical Jewish wisdom" (Behm 721). 1 Pet 3:10 refers to the OT warning against sins of the tongue (Ps 34:14) in order to support and illustrate the exhortation to seek peace, to renounce retaliation, and to bless. In Jas 1:26 ("If any one thinks he is religious, and does not bridle his *tongue* but deceives his heart, this man's religion is vain"), the need to rule over the tongue appears to be the fundamental ethical task, although in this passage the nature of the ethical danger emanating from the tongue is not made clear.

The exhortation is understandable only against the background of widespread Jewish and Hellenistic tradition, which taught that one becomes a sinner through the tongue (Rom 3:13; 1 Pet 3:10; Ps 38:2 LXX; Prov 6:17; *Herm. Vis.* ii.2.3), that one must guard against the rashness of the tongue (Prov 15:4; Sir 4:29; Philo *Det.* 23: "the untamed impudent course of the tongue"), that the tongue is the destruction of mankind (Sir 5:13; 20:18; 25:8; Philo *Det.* 174), and thus that one must exert oneself for the training (παιδεία) of the tongue (Prov 27:20a LXX; Hos 7:16 LXX; Isa 50:4 LXX), watch over it (Prov 21:23; Sir 22:27), and bridle it (Philo *Spec. Leg.* i.53; *Det.* 23, 44, 174; *Mut.* 240).

The tongue appears even more threatening in the discourse in Jas 3:2-12, which is shaped by Jewish Wisdom literature and the Greek diatribe (on the form and tradition, cf. Sir 28:13-26). The introductory verse ("If any one makes no mistakes in what he says he is a perfect man, able to bridle the whole body also") indicates the theme: the central danger of mankind proceeds from the tongue (cf. Prov 10:19; 18:21; 25:8b; Sir 19:16).

Despite its limited size, the tongue has extraordinary power (vv. 3-5a); its devastating power is not only to be compared to that of fire—it is itself a disastrous fire (vv. 5b, 6a; cf. Sir 28:22f.; *Ps. Sol.* 12:2f.; in antiquity, a hot temper was commonly compared with fire; in Hellenistic Judaism, cf. Philo *Decal.* 32), the demonic energy of which comes from hell (→ γέεννα, v. 6d; cf. Sir 28:23) and sets on fire the entire circle of earthly life (→ τροχός, γένεσις) and hopelessly destroys it (v. 6c; cf. Sir 28:14-18, 23; *Ps. Sol.* 12:3; Philo *Det.* 174). The tongue stands among the members of the human body as "an unrighteous world" (v. 6b), a singular phrase that is scarcely intelligible, despite the parallel to the concept of the "world of unrighteousness" (*1 Enoch* 48:7). Perhaps it should be rendered as "the universal scope and eschatological destruction of this disastrous scourge" (W. Schrage, *Jakobus* [NTD] 39), which, as long as it leads an untamed life of its own, draws the body, i.e., the whole person (→ σῶμα) further and further into a worldly snare as it corrupts the person (v. 6c; cf. 1:27; Sir 28:19-21).

While a person may be able to tame the whole animal world, no one can tame the tongue (vv. 7, 8a; cf. Sir 28:20), for it is "a restless evil" (*Herm. Man.* ii.3 calls slander a restless demon), full of deadly poison (v. 8b; cf. Rom 3:13; Ps 140:4; 1QH 5:26f.). It is absurd and unnatural when one praises God with the tongue, while with the same instrument one curses mankind, his likeness (vv. 9f.; cf. vv. 11f.; Ps 62:5; *T. Benj.* 6:5; 1QS 10:21-24; *2 Enoch* 52:1f., 6).

The concluding remark, "This ought not to be so" (v. 10b), indicates that the author, despite his deeply pessimistic view, is not in despair in v. 2 over the ethical task that he formulates. He introduces the pessimistic tradition about the tongue in a parenetic context in the hope that, as the danger that proceeds from the tongue is described in drastic terms (cf. Sir 28:22, 26), the reader will be better able to resist.

5. Γλῶσσα with the meaning *language* (cf. Deut 28:49; Isa 28:11; Jer 5:15; Zech 8:23; for classical usage, see, e.g., Homer *Il.* ii.2.804) appears in the NT only in the context of early Christian glossolalia: 1 Cor 13:1 (→ 6); Acts 2:11; Mark 16:27 (→ 7). In a similar sense ἑτερόγλωσσος means

speaking a foreign language or *speaking various languages* (Philo *Conf.* 8): 1 Cor 14:21 (Isa 28:11, → 6).

The transference to various *peoples* distinguished by their languages (usually in the pl. or πᾶς with the sg., Dan 3:29) occurs in the late parts of the OT alongside literal designations for social alliances in order to emphasize the universality of the statement (Isa 66:18 with ἔθνη; Dan 3:4, 7, 29; 5:19; 6:25; 7:14 Theodotion with λαοί, φυλαί [LXX with ἔθνη, φυλαί]; Dan 4:21, 37b LXX with ἔθνη, χωραί; similarly Jdt 3:8).

The Book of Revelation is dependent on the usage of the Book of Daniel. It has groups of four terms (cf. Dan 3:4 LXX; 4 Ezra 3:7) that are artistically varied; never are the individual members in the same sequence (πᾶς with the sg. in Rev 5:9; 13:7; 14:6; with the pl. in 7:9; 10:11; 11:9; 17:15). The focus is always on all of humanity or the ancient Mediterranean world as its representative: from it come the redeemed (5:9; 7:9); it stands under the lordship of the godless powers (11:9; 13:7; 17:15); and the prophecy of judgment is addressed to it (10:11; 14:6). However, it is probably significant that they are not named abstractly and also not, as in Paul, summed up in contradictory pairs of opposites (Greeks/Barbarians in Rom 1:14; Jews/Greeks in Rom 1:16 and Gal 3:28). Instead they are named according to their collective grouping and differentiation in deliberate "biblical" terms.

6. In 1 Corinthians 12–14 Paul uses the term γλῶσσα in a variety of phrases to describe a charisma (λαλεῖν γλώσσῃ, 14:2, 4, 13, 27; ἐν γλώσσῃ, 14:19; γλώσσαις, 12:30; 13:1; 14:5, 6, 18, 23, 39; προσεύχεσθαι γλώσσῃ, 14:14; γλῶσσαν ἔχειν, 14:26; γλῶσσαι, 13:8; 14:22; γένη γλωσσῶν, 12:10, 28; ἑρμηνεία γλωσσῶν, 12:28; γλῶσσαι τῶν ἀνθρώπων καὶ τῶν ἀγγέλων, 13:1; with the exception of 14:22, always without the art.). On the basis of the phrase λαλεῖν γλώσσῃ, this spiritual gift is called "glossolalia."

The oral character of this charisma (λαλεῖν), the juxtaposition of γλῶσσα and interpretation (→ ἑρμηνεία) in the list in 12:10, 30 and in the church order in 14:26-28 (cf. also 14:5, 13), the reference to human and angelic γλῶσσαι in 13:1, and further observations (see below) indicate that the technical usage of γλῶσσα here is derived from the meaning *language.* The characterization of the gift as "speaking in tongues," which is common in older translations and studies, is thus inappropriate and misleading. The best translation is *language* or the verb phrase *speak languages* or *speak in a language;* we may designate the charisma *"the gift of language."*

The gift of language is speech that is unintelligible (14:2, 16, 23) and highly ecstatic (the → νοῦς does not participate, but only the → πνεῦμα, vv. 14-19; an outsider could come to the opinion "you are mad!" v. 23). This gift has various manifestations (γένη γλωσσῶν, 12:10, 28), as it varies in content (v. 2, telling heavenly mysteries, → μυστήριον; v. 25, the particular case of the knowledge of the heart) and form (v. 2, etc., → λαλέω; v. 14, → προσεύχομαι; v. 15, → ψάλλω; v. 16, → εὐλογέω, εὐχαριστία). Utterances of glossolalia are, in principle, translatable and thus can have a definite function of edifying (14:4f., 26), informing (v. 19), or communicating content (v. 16). The ability to interpret is founded charismatically (12:10, 30; 14:13) and cannot be explained simply as the knowledge of divination techniques or of foreign languages; the one who speaks in glossolalia (14:13) or another member of the congregation (12:10; 14:27) can "interpret." The gift of language is learned and exercised in the assembly of the congregation (14:6, 16, 23, 26, 27) and privately (vv. 18f., 28).

Prophecy (→ προφήτης) and the gift of language are related to each other. Both are emphatically classified as spiritual gifts (14:1; → πνευματικός), and both are associated with divine secrets (cf. 14:2 with 13:2), the "interpretation" as well as the glossolalia. Prophecy is associated with the process of "distinguishing" (διάκρισις, 12:10; 14:29); both have a similar effect of edification (14:3-5, 26; → οἰκοδομή) and are, to a varied extent, ecstatic (cf. vv. 30, 32). Paul considered it possible to change from exercising the gift of language to exercising prophecy (vv. 1, 12), and he himself possessed both gifts (vv. 6, 18f.). In the Corinthian assembly, uninterpreted glossolalia, which was considered the highest gift, was predominant. Paul was eager, however, to establish a more balanced relationship of interpreted glossolalia and prophecy (vv. 27-33a, 39), corresponding to the tradition and intention of worship (vv. 26, 40), and to relegate uninterpreted glossolalia to the realm of private devotion (vv. 4, 18, 28).

The place of early Christian glossolalia in the history of religions is disputed. One may argue for a derivation from the syncretistic piety of the Hellenistic Mediterranean world (Weiss 339; W. Bauer, *Der Wortgottesdienst der ältesten Christen* [1930] 33-35; H. Conzelmann, *First Corinthians* [Hermeneia] 234) on the basis of a comparison with ecstatic phenomena in the ancient religions (F. Pfister, *RAC* IV, 944-87). One may also argue for a derivation from the equally present ecstatic seers and interpreters and proclaimers (or prophets) in ancient divination (Plato *Ti.* 71e-72b), or from the concept of the gods' own language, which became known in dreams and oracular sayings to ones who were possessed (Clement of Alexandria *Strom.* i.431.1). The relationship to ancient syncretistic piety may also be suggested in the fact that the appearance of glossolalia in the church at Corinth evoked Paul's accusation that an outsider who heard them would conclude, "You are mad" (14:23). Such a response appears to place glossolalia in the category of the appearance of Dionysiac or prophetic madness. These observations are valuable not so much for tracing the derivation of glossolalia in the history of religion as for explaining its roots in the Pauline churches.

The basic presuppositions are to be sought in Judaism (W. Bousset, *GGA* 163 [1906] 757f.; S. Eitrem, *Orakel und Mysterien am Ausgang der Antike* [1947] 42). Here also ecstatic phenomena, including ecstatic speech, are known, from the beginnings of Israelite prophecy to the NT era (F. Baumgärtel,

TDNT VI, 362; R. Rendtorff, *ibid.* 797; R. Meyer, *ibid.* 825). In *T. Job* 48–52 there is ecstatic speech or singing (ὕμνος, 48:3; 49:3; 51:4; cf. 1 Cor 14:15f.; also εὐχή, 50:3; cf. 1 Cor 14:15) comparable to glossolalia (48:2; 49:1; 50:2: the daughters of Job obtain a changed heart; cf. 1 Sam 10:6, 9; *Bib. Ant.* 20:2f.) in various angelic languages, even if a different terminology is used (διάλεκτος instead of γλῶσσα, 48:3; 49:2; 50:1; 52:7; σημείωσις instead of ἑρμηνεία, 51:3f.; the topics of the speech are μεγαλεῖα instead of μυστήρια, 51:3). The topics of the songs are the creative work and glory of God, the great themes and mysteries of Jewish mysticism (J. Maier, *Geschichte der jüdischen Religion* [1972] 196f., 200-205).

Finally, both early Christian glossolalia and *T. Job* were deeply involved in various doctrines of angels and related topics that were known in Palestine and in Hellenistic Judaism: the community of the ecstatic and the one who prays with the angels (Dan 7–12; *1 Enoch;* 4 Ezra 10–13; 1QH frag. 2:6; 10:6; 1QM 10:11), participation in their knowledge (1QH 3:22f.; 11:13f.; 18:23; Philo *Vit. Cont.* 26), and the language of the angels (1QH 6:13; *b. B. Bat.* 134a, b; Billerbeck III, 449; *Apoc. Zeph.* 13:2f.; *2 Enoch* 17; 19).

The NT evidence allows one to assume a dissemination of glossolalia throughout the churches, both Pauline (cf. 1 Thess 5:19) and non-Pauline (e.g., Rome; cf. Rom 8:26f.; E. Käsemann, *Commentary on Romans* [1980] 240), beginning in the original Palestinian church (Acts 2:1-13, → 7). Thus glossolalia appears to be the early Christian form of the phenomenon of ecstatic speech, which is widely disseminated in the history of religions and was known to the Judaism of the NT era. The early Church provided its own terminology and, as will be shown, its own interpretation derived from the experience of the Spirit and an eschatological consciousness.

The oldest available interpretation in early Christianity views glossolalia as speech in human and esp. angelic languages (1 Cor 13:1; Betz 26f.), as an eschatologically provided possibility to praise God with the angels and to learn and repeat the heavenly mysteries (1 Cor 14:2).

A second and probably secondary, but nevertheless very early, interpretation appears in 1 Cor 14:21 in the citation from Isa 28:11f. This citation has been shaped in the debate with Judaism (E. E. Ellis, *Paul's Use of the OT* [1957] 98-113; B. Lindars, *NT Apologetic* [1961] 164, 175) and has thus taken on an association with glossolalia (1 Cor 14:21: ἐν ἑτερογλώσσοις; MT and LXX: "with stammering lips and in a foreign *language*" [JB]; Betz 26; Harrisville 42-45). Glossolalia is understood as the fulfillment of the promise, as the wondrous final address of God (1 Cor 14:21: "I will speak"; MT: "he will speak"; LXX: "they will speak") to his people Israel, who will remain closed to this sign (14:22; note v. 21: "even then they will not listen to me"; MT and LXX: "they did not wish to hear me"). Paul employs this citation no longer with a meaning that is critical of Israel but rather as proof of the uselessness of glossolalia in the missionary situation (vv. 22f.). But for him and the Corinthian church the first interpretation of glossolalia is decisive.

Nevertheless they give differing evaluations of the gift. The Corinthians preferred glossolalia to prophecy because of the anticipation of the eschatological communion with God that came to expression in it (cf. 1 Cor 4:7-10), because of its pronounced pneumatic character (cf. 3:1), and because of its gift of cosmological and theological mysteries (cf. the high value of → σοφία in 1:18-31; 2:6 and → γνῶσις in 8:1-3; 13:8-10). Apparently they rated it as the essential gift of the Spirit (14:1).

Paul emphasized, by contrast, that it is only one among many gifts (12:4-11) and that it is useful in public worship only under very restricted conditions because worship is intended to serve the edification of the church, not that of the individual charismatic (14:5). The ecstatic character of glossolalia could make public church meetings resemble Gentile assemblies, which were dominated by μανία, "frenzy" (14:23). Finally, if the gift is the anticipation of the perfect and the eternal, it would remain, like all gifts, transitory and imperfect (1 Cor 13:8-12). Indeed, in Rom 8:26 Paul appears even more to strip away the character of eschatological anticipation when he interprets it as a provisional eschatological gift suitable for the conditions of life before the end, as identification of the Spirit with the Christians who groan amid the suffering of this age.

7. The further history of early Christian glossolalia is lost for us in obscurity (Dautzenberg [D, I]). Perhaps Col 3:16a and Eph 5:18 refer to prayer in glossolalia. Explicit references to the charism are found only in Acts and in the secondary ending of Mark.

Acts knows glossolalia only as a sign of the reception of the Spirit (2:4; 10:45f.; 19:6) in the first Christian generation and not in association with the life of the Church; it is simply a miracle of beginning. Probably the author of Acts had no personal acquaintance with glossolalia (H. Conzelmann, *Acts* [Hermeneia] 15). He works with traditional material, which he composes for literary purposes (on Acts 10:46, μεγαλύνειν, cf. μεγαλεῖα, 2:11; *T. Job* 51:4; on the juxtaposition of glossolalia and prophecy in 19:6, cf. the identification of both gifts in 2:17f. and their juxtaposition in 1 Corinthians 12–14).

Both later mentions of glossolalia in the Book of Acts are references to the Pentecost narrative, which understands glossolalia in the sense of a miracle of language: they "began to speak foreign (ἑτέραις) *languages*" (2:4, JB). The formulation is very similar to the form of the citation from Isa 28:11f. in 1 Cor 14:21 (→ 6). The understanding of glossolalia is in agreement with the tradition cited here, insofar as they both see in it a sign for Israel: the multilingual audience who heard the glossolalia in the Pentecost narrative are Jews. The Pentecost narrative thus presupposes the tradition of 1 Cor 14:21 (cf. Betz 25f.) and pictures it in Acts 2:5-13 in a legendary way with the help of a table of peoples.

But in contrast to 1 Corinthians 12–14, the Pentecost account implies that the incident concerns not the language of angels but human languages. Glossolalia is thus intelligible here and requires no charismatic interpretation. If among the further assumptions behind the Pentecost narrative one is to include the tradition of the manifestations of glossolalia in the Jerusalem church—probably in connection with the first experience of the Spirit, which is developed legendarily in Acts 2:1-4 (on the *tongues* as of fire in 2:3, cf. Isa 51:24; it is uncertain whether a conscious association between γλῶσσα in 2:3 and 2:4 is intended)—the report then becomes one that came into existence sometime after the events themselves, given its distance from the glossolalia experienced in 1 Corinthians 12–14 and its legendary character. Thus it is best explained as a Jewish Christian midrash on the traditions recorded here (for other explanations, see Behm 725-26; Betz 33-35; E. Haenchen, *The Acts of the Apostles* [1971] 168-72; Kremer 118-26, 261-64).

The secondary ending in Mark 16:9-20, which originated in the 2nd cent. (Kümmel, *Introduction* 98-101), describes the marvelous works of believers in the context of the missionary command. This description is dependent on the traditions of Acts (K. Aland, "Der Schluß des Markus," *L'Évangile selon Marc* [ed. M. Sabbe, 1974] 435-70, esp. 454), from which comes 16:17: "they will speak in new *tongues.*" Despite the difference from Acts 2:4 (γλῶσσαι καιναί instead of ἕτεραι γλῶσσαι), the passage describes speaking in foreign and—because they are unknown—new languages. Glossolalia is thus understood as a (missionary?) sign (→ σημεῖον; cf. 1 Cor 14:22), but the estimation of it has shifted to the miraculous through its reference to Israel and the association with the possession of the Spirit (cf. the further signs in 16:18). It has become a miraculous sign of the first Christian generation, without any binding interpretation of the experience itself.

G. Dautzenberg

γλωσσόκομον, ου, τό *glōssokomon* case; money box; purse*

Originally a container "for the mouthpiece of a flute" (BDF §119.5), then with the general meaning *container*; in the NT in John 12:6; 13:29, in the phrase γλωσσόκομον ἔχειν, of Judas, who "was in charge of the common purse" (NEB) or "administered the money."

γναφεύς, έως, ὁ *gnapheus* fuller*

Mark 9:3 is probably an allusion to the bleaching of material, which was one of the tasks of a fuller. R. Knippenberg, *BHH* III, 2134f.

γνήσιος, 3 *gnēsios* genuine; legitimate; approved*

Originally of the physical or legitimate child; then frequently in a fig. sense: 2 Cor 8:8: τὸ τῆς ὑμετέρας ἀγάπης γνήσιον, "the *genuineness* of your love" (JB); Phil 4:3: γνήσιε σύζυγε, "*true* yokefellow." In 1 Tim 1:2 (Τιμοθέῳ γνησίῳ τέκνῳ ἐν πίστει, "to Timothy, my *true* child in the faith") and Titus 1:4 ("my *true* child in the common faith") the original meaning comes through. F. Büchsel, *TDNT* I, 727.

γνησίως *gnēsios* purely, sincerely*

Phil 2:20, of Timothy, who will *genuinely* concern himself with the affairs of the church.

γνόφος, ου, ὁ *gnophos* darkness; thundercloud*

Heb 12:18, alluding to Deut 4:11, one of the terrifying phenomena that accompanied the giving of the old covenant at Mount Sinai.

γνώμη, ης, ἡ *gnōmē* inclination, disposition; opinion, judgment*

Lit.: BAGD s.v. — A. Biscardi, "La 'gnomē dikaiōtatē' et l'interprétation des lois dans la Grèce ancienne," *Revue Internationale des Droits de l'Antiquité* 17 (1970) 217-32. — R. Bultmann, *TDNT* I, 717f. — Chantraine, *Dictionnaire* I, s.v. — F. Gaboriau, "Enquête sur la signification biblique de connaître," *Ang* 45 (1968) 3-43. — J. S. Morrison, "Gnōmē," *Phronesis* 8 (1963) 37-41. — S. N. Mouraviev, "Gnōmē," *Glotta* 51 (1973) 69-78. — W. C. van Unnik, "Mia gnōmē, Apocalypse of John 17:13, 17," FS Sevenster 209-20. — R. B. Zuck, "Greek Words for Teach," *BSac* 122 (1965) 158-68.

1. The word appears only 9 times in the NT: once in Acts (20:3), 5 times in the Pauline letters (1 Cor 1:10; 7:25, 40; 2 Cor 8:10; Phlm 14), and 3 times in Revelation (17:13, 17a, b). There are no compound forms in the NT.

2. The word has the following meanings: *conclusion, decision* (Acts 20:3, Paul "*determined* to return through Macedonia"); *mind, opinion* (1 Cor 1:10, in connection with νοῦς—conviction, intention, will, understanding; cf. the Pauline command "be of the same mind, of one mind, in harmony," Phil 2:2; 4:2; Rom 12:16; see also Rev 17:13, 17b); *understanding, judgment, counsel* (in contrast to a commandment, a binding admonition from Jesus, relating to the marital relationship in 1 Cor 7:25, 40; as counsel for the completion of the collection for Jerusalem in 2 Cor 8:10); *agreement, consent* (Phlm 14, in the sense of συγγνώμη, which does not appear in the NT with this meaning); *resolution, intention, plan* (Rev 17:17a, "God has put it into their hearts to carry out his purpose"). No particular theological meaning is connected to the word.

O. Knoch

γνωρίζω *gnōrizō* make known, reveal; know*

Lit.: BAGD s.v. — R. Bultmann, *TDNT* I, 718. — F. Gaboriau, "Enquête sur la signification biblique de connaître," *Ang* 45 (1968) 3-43. — R. B. ZUCK, "Greek Words for Teach," *BSac* 122 (1965) 158-68.

1. The vb. appears in the NT in 25 passages, including 2 occurrences in the Lukan prehistory (2:15, 17), 3 in John (15:15; 17:26 bis), and in Acts 2:28 and 7:13 v.l. in texts that Luke received from sources. The other appearances all belong to Paul and to the Pauline sphere of influence. Ephesians and Colossians, along with John, make special use of this word in order to give prominence to the character of the Christian message as revelation (Rom 9:22, 23; 16:26; 1 Cor 12:3; 15:1; 2 Cor 8:1; Gal 1:11; Phil 1:22; 4:6; then Col 1:27; 4:7, 9; Eph 1:9; 3:3, 5, 10; 6:19, 21; 2 Pet 1:16).

2. In the NT the word is used most frequently to mean *announce, make known publicly* or *explicitly,* and at times *communicate in a solemn way* (Luke 2:15, 17; John 15:15; 17:26 bis; Rom 9:22, 23; 16:26; 2 Pet 1:16). In all of these passages the vb. refers to revelation of the salvation from God that comes through Jesus Christ. This religious connotation of γνωρίζω in the sense of "*proclaim* God's plan of salvation, the salvation event in Christ" determines the usage of the vb., especially in John and in Colossians and Ephesians (except for Col 4:9 and Eph 6:21). Within this range of meaning also belong Rom 16:26 (liturgical usage); 1 Cor 15:1 (communication of the gospel in the form of a confessional formula); Gal 1:11; and 2 Pet 1:16. Acts 2:28 speaks of a revelation of God to the dead Jesus, as Ps 16:11 LXX is cited from the perspective of the Christian faith in the resurrection. Rom 9:22f. speaks directly of the revealing acts of God.

The saying in 1 Cor 12:3 is to be understood as the introduction to important religious facts: "I *want you to understand,*" or "I *make known* to you, I *declare* to you." A connection exists here with 1 Cor 15:1. The vb. appears in 2 Cor 8:1; Col 4:9; Eph 6:21 in the neutral sense of *make known, report.* Acts 7:13 B A vg is to be translated *reveal oneself, make oneself known, disclose one's identity,* entirely in agreement with the LXX of Gen 45:1. In Phil 1:22 οὐ γνωρίζω means "I cannot *tell*" or cannot *know* or *discern.* In Phil 4:6 the word is used for Christian prayer, which should *make known, allow to be known,* the requests of the one who prays with thanksgiving. By this means, reference is made to the distinctive character of prayer in the Christian congregations.

O. Knoch

γνῶσις, εως, ἡ *gnōsis* recognition; knowledge → γινώσκω.

γνώστης, ου, ὁ *gnōstēs* one acquainted (with)*

Acts 26:3: "because you [Agrippa] are especially *familiar* with all customs and controversies of the Jews."

γνωστός, 3 *gnōstos* known; knowable*

This adj. appears in the phrase "be/become *known*" 8 times in Acts (1:19; 2:14; 4:10; 9:42; 13:38; 19:17; 28:22, 28). The pl. subst. οἱ γνωστοί, "[one's] acquaintances," appears in Luke 2:44; 23:49. John 18:15, 16 mention the disciple who was *known* to the high priest; Acts 4:16, the undeniable "*notable* sign"; 15:18, "things *known* from of old"; and Rom 1:19, τὸ γνωστὸν τοῦ θεοῦ, "what can be *known* about God." Cf. Philo *All.* i.60f. A. Fridrichsen, "Zur Auslegung von Röm 1, 19f.," *ZNW* 17 (1916) 159-68. R. Bultmann, *TDNT* I, 718f.; → γινώσκω.

γογγύζω *gongyzō* grumble*

1. Occurrences in the NT — 2. Meaning — 3. Usage — 4. In the LXX — 5. Διαγογγύζω, γογγυσμός, γογγυστής

Lit.: BAGD s.v. — LSJ s.v. — K. H. RENGSTORF, *TDNT* I, 728-37. — For further bibliography see *TWNT* X, 1027.

1. The vb. γογγύζω appears 7 times in the NT (6 times in the Gospels).

2. Γογγύζω is onomatopoeic and speaks colloquially of personal dissatisfaction (regarding its means of expression as inappropriate). In this secular meaning it occurs twice in the NT (Matt 20:11; Luke 5:30). In other passages it is used with the connotation of people speaking against God in a reprehensible way.

3. The subjects of γογγύζω are individuals: in Matt 20:11, the workers in the vineyard; Luke 5:30, Pharisees and scribes; John 6:41, 43, the Jews; 7:32, the wavering masses; 6:61, the doubting disciples; 1 Cor 10:10, the people of Israel during the wanderings in the desert. The persons against which (κατά, πρός, περί) grumbling is directed are the householder of Matt 20:11, the disciples in Luke 5:30, Jesus in John 6:41 (43) and 7:32, a statement of Jesus in John 6:61, and the Lord, against whom the people of Israel grumbled, in 1 Cor 10:10.

4. Γογγύζω is used consistently in the LXX to render Heb. *lûn.* In Exodus 15–17 and Numbers 14–17 this refers to the complaints of the people of Israel on their desert wandering. It is taken up in this sense in 1 Cor 10:10, which forms the basis for its interpretation in other NT passages.

5. The derived forms show a similar usage. **Διαγογγύζω** *grumble** appears twice (Luke 15:2; 19:7), referring to the response of Jesus' opponents to his actions. **Γογγυσμός** *grumbling** appears 4 times. John 7:12 refers to the "*muttering* about (περί) him [Jesus] among the people." Phil 2:14 ("without *grumbling* or questioning") derives its significance from the reference to the wandering people of Israel. Acts 6:1 and 1 Pet 4:9 make no allusion to the OT. **Γογγυστής** *grumbler** appears only

in Jude 16 and refers, together with μεμψίμοιροι, to those who resist both their lot in life and God.

A. J. Hess

γογγυσμός, οῦ, ὁ *gongysmos* grumbling
→ γογγύζω 5.

γογγυστής, οῦ, ὁ *gongystēs* grumbler
→ γογγύζω 5.

γόης, ητος, ὁ *goēs* magician; swindler*

In the NT only in 2 Tim 3:13 (pl.; cf. *Diog.* 8:4), probably fig., meaning *swindler.* G. Delling, *TDNT* I, 737; BAGD s.v.; W. Burkert, "ΓΟΗΣ. Zum griechischen 'Schamanismus,'" *RMP* 105 (1962) 36-55; H. D. Betz, *Der Apostel Paulus und die sokratische Tradition* (1972) 19-39.

Γολγοθᾶ, ᾶν *Golgotha* Golgotha*
κρανίον, ου, τό *kranion* skull; head*

Lit.: E. Grässer, "Der historische Jesus im Hebräerbrief," *ZNW* 56 (1965) 63-91. — J. Jeremias, *Golgotha* (1926). — Kopp, *Stätten* 422-36. — A. Parrot, *Der Tempel von Jerusalem, Golgatha und das Heilige Grab* (1956).

1. Golgotha is the place of Jesus' crucifixion, known only in the Gospels (Mark 15:22 par. Matt 27:33/John 19:17; Luke offers only the Greek rendering κράνιον in 23:33). The name goes back to Aram. *gûlgaltā',* "skull, head." The majority of exegetes assume that the name Γολγοθᾶ designates a hill in the form of a skull or a hill in general (cf. Arab. *rās,* "head," for describing a field). However, it is probably best to forgo a conclusive interpretation, as do the Gospels.

2. According to the reports in the Gospels, Golgotha lies outside Jerusalem (Matt 27:32; John 19:17, 20; cf. Heb 13:12) but not at a great distance from it. It must have been located on a busy street (Mark 15:29; John 19:20). Nearby are gardens and the tomb of Jesus (John 19:41f.). Indications in the Gospels point to a place north of Jerusalem. The oldest tradition about the location of Golgotha centers on the Church of the Holy Sepulchre, which lies within the modern old city of Jerusalem and which was first erected by Constantine I (326-35) after the removal of a Hadrianic temple. It encompasses both the tomb of Jesus and the place of execution. The history of the tradition about the location of Golgotha and the location of the present Church of the Holy Sepulchre agree with the data of the Gospels. Thus the tradition established by Constantine is to be given credence. Final certainty cannot be achieved because the course of the second northern wall, outside of which Golgotha must have been located, cannot be determined with certainty.

3. In the Gospels the place of the crucifixion of Jesus has no particular theological interest beyond the fact that it was exposed and thus emphasized Jesus' humiliation. Explicit theological interpretation is found first in Hebrews. The "location of the cross bears and supports the typological interpretation of the death of Jesus as an OT propitiatory sacrifice" (Grässer 87) and is the occasion for parenesis in Heb 13:13-16.

M. Völkel

Γόμορρα, ων, τά (ας, ἡ) *Gomorra* Gomorrah
→ Σόδομα.

γόμος, ου, ὁ *gomos* load, burden*

Acts 21:3: a ship's *cargo;* Rev 18:11, 12: the *shipments* or *stock* of merchants—in particular, gold, silver, and other precious objects.

γονεῖς, έων, οἱ *goneis* parents*

The *parents* of: Jesus in Luke 2:27, 41, 43; the daughter of Jairus in 8:56; the man born blind, John 9:2f. in 18, 20, 22f. Elsewhere γονεῖς is used of *parents* in general: Mark 13:12 par. Matt 10:21/Luke 21:16; Luke 18:29 (cf. Mark); Rom 1:30; 2 Cor 12:14 bis; Eph 6:1; Col 3:20; 2 Tim 3:2.

γόνυ, ατος, τό *gony* knee*

1. Occurrences in the NT — 2. Usage — 3. Theological significance — 4. Γονυπετέω

Lit.: G. Fohrer, *BHH* II, 973. — H. Schlier, *TDNT* I, 738-40.

1. There are 12 occurrences of γόνυ in the NT, of which 6 are in the Lukan writings (2 in Luke, 4 in Acts), 2 in Romans, and one each in Mark, Ephesians, Philippians, and Hebrews.

2. A partc. of τίθημι with τὰ γόνατα (αὐτοῦ) and a finite vb. means "place the *knee* (on the ground)" or "kneel down, fall on one's knees." See Mark 15:19, before Jesus (gesture of mockery); Acts 7:60, probably before the exalted Jesus; Luke 22:41; Acts 9:40; 20:36; 21:5, before God.

Γόνυ with a form of κάμπτω means "bend/bow *the knee.*" At times used trans. (Rom 11:4; Eph 3:14), at times intrans. (Rom 14:11; Phil 2:10; on both passages, cf. Isa 45:23). One bows (or does not bow) the knee before God (Rom 14:11; Eph 3:14), the exalted Christ (Phil 2:10), or Baal (Rom 11:4).

The other texts cannot be placed into a single category. In Luke 5:8 (προσέπεσεν τοῖς γόνασιν Ἰησοῦ, "he fell down at Jesus' *knees*") the same conceptual framework as in the passages already named is present. Heb 12:12 has a different significance (cf. Isa 35:3, the eschatological context of which is not considered): weak knees are an expression for lack of courage and for fear. The readers should view their affliction as a temporary chastening of God and not be oppressed by it; rather, they should take on new courage.

3. Falling on the knee is frequently an expression of homage and of petition toward human beings and gods. It is frequent as a posture of prayer (explicitly so in Luke 22:41; Acts 9:40; 20:36; 21:5, probably also in Acts 7:60). Rom 11:4 gives a clear statement of Israel's situation after the rejection of Jesus: As in the time of Elijah, when Yahweh has preserved a remnant of Israel from bowing down to Baal, so he has now preserved a remnant from destruction. Rom 14:11 declares that "every *knee* shall bow," i.e., all people should worship God and must submit to his judgment. Thus, unlike Isa 45:23, which Paul cites, the universality of *salvation* is not emphasized. In addition, Phil 2:10 has in view neither salvation nor judgment for all. Isaiah's formulation referring to Yahweh is transferred to Jesus and expresses the subjection of all powers under the Christ and the Lord. In Eph 3:14 bowing the knee is an expression of worship (in response to the previously mentioned great acts of God) and of intercession for the recipients of the letter. God is here seen as the Father, from whom everything "is named" (v. 15), i.e., as Creator of the world.

4. **Γονυπετέω** *fall on the knee, request on bended knee** appears with ἔμπροσθεν with gen. (Matt 27:29) or with the acc.; it occurs as a gesture of ridicule (Matt 27:29) or of sincere request to Jesus (Matt 17:14; Mark 1:40; 10:17). G. R. Stanton, "The Oriental Background of the Compound γονυπετεῖν," *Glotta* 46 (1968) 1-6.

J. M. Nützel

γονυπετέω *gonypeteō* fall on the knee, request on bended knee
→ γόνυ 4.

γράμμα, ατος, τό *gramma* letter of the alphabet; pl.: letter (epistle); Scripture(s)*

1. Occurrences and Meaning — 2. Γράμμα in Paul

Lit.: P. Bläser, *LTK* II, 750f. — R. Bultmann, *The Second Letter to the Corinthians* (1985) 61-98. — G. Ebeling, *RGG* II, 1290-96 (bibliography). — C. J. A. Hickling, "The Sequence of Thought in 2 Cor 3," *NTS* 21 (1974/75) 380-95. — U. Luz, *Das Geschichtsverständnis des Paulus* (BEvT 49, 1968) 123-34. — P. Vielhauer, "Paulus und das AT," *Studien zur Geschichte und Theologie der Reformation* (FS E. Bizer, 1969) 45-48. — For further bibliography → γραφή.

1. Γράμμα, which in classical and koine Greek encompasses a spectrum of meaning from "letter of the alphabet" to "document" to "Scripture," is found only 14 times in the NT. In the pl. it means *account book* (Luke 16:6f.), the *Scriptures* (= OT, John 5:47; 7:15), pursuit of *learning* (Acts 26:24), *correspondence* (Acts 28:21), or *letters* of the alphabet (2 Cor 3:7; Gal 6:11); τὰ ἱερὰ γράμματα are *the Holy Scriptures* (2 Tim 3:15). In the sg. only in Paul: 2 Cor 3:6; Rom 2:27, 29; 7:6. On the common translation "letter" of the alphabet, → 2.

2. In the sg. γράμμα stands always in either direct or indirect contrast to → πνεῦμα, "Spirit." Theologically important here is 2 Cor 3:6f., which appears in the context of important theological concepts such as glory (→ δόξα), righteousness (→ δικαιοσύνη), covenant or testament (→ διαθήκη), and ministry (→ διακονία). Thus one must find its meaning particularly in the contrasting pairs. According to 2 Cor 3:6 the death-bringing γράμμα (in contrast to the life-giving Spirit; for this reason the minister of the new covenant" is not a servant of the γράμμα but of the Spirit) is clearly "the law of Moses." Does the term γράμμα disqualify the law written on stone tablets (on Exod 31:18 etc., cf. 2 Cor 3:3, 7) as necessarily bringing death (G. Schrenk, *TDNT* I, 767; Bultmann 78), or is it γράμμα only in certain respects (Bläser 750; Ebeling 1291; Luz 124)?

According to the typological interpretation of Exod 34:29-35 in 2 Cor 3:12-18, the veil of Moses lies over the (mis)reading of the Torah, and thus over the hearts of the Jews. Inasmuch as the Lord is Spirit, the veil is taken away for the one who turns to Christ. Thus the idea at the basis of 2 Corinthians 3 is that γράμμα is not in an absolute sense a law that brings death (read in isolation, vv. 4-11 can be interpreted in another way), but rather only insofar as it is written only on stone or with letters and waits to be written on "tablets of human hearts" (i.e., as a "letter from Christ"; v. 3). The law is thus intended for the Spirit. It is γράμμα when the Jew encounters it in a false way (Bultmann 78), an idea analogous to Rom 3:27 (→ νόμος). Thus γράμμα proves to be a strictly existential term characterizing the manner of existence of the Jew who is not yet justified. At the same time, the contrast between γράμμα and πνεῦμα does initiate a new hermeneutic (cf. Ebeling 1291).

This interpretation of 2 Corinthians 3 is confirmed by Rom 2:27, where γράμμα is mere outward possession of the law, which is simultaneously being transgressed (cf. Luz 124). Here γράμμα, again as a concept of existence, is not the attempt to effect justification through one's own works of the law (H. Hübner, *Law in Paul's Thought* [1984] 147). In Rom 2:28f. the antithesis between γράμμα and πνεῦμα is set in parallel with the contrast between the external and the inward, for both Jews and circumcision. The additional contrasting pair in 2 Corinthians 3—old vs. new—is connected linguistically in Rom. 7:6, which has ἐν καινότητι πνεύματος vs. (ἐν) παλαιότητι γράμματος. This can be freely translated: "in the Spirit as to the fundamentally new—in the γράμμα as to the fundamentally old." This antithesis characterizes "the standing of the Christian after the change of the aeons" (E. Käsemann, *Commentary on Romans* [1980] 190). V. 5 identifies the old manner of existence as the flesh (→ σάρξ), which for Paul is the essential contrast to "Spirit."

H. Hübner

γραμματεύς, έως, ὁ *grammateus* secretary; scribe

1. Occurrences in the NT — 2. The Synoptic Gospels — 3. History, role, and significance of the scribal office — 4. Jesus and the scribes — 5. Scribes mentioned by name in the NT

Lit.: J. Jeremias, *TDNT* I, 740-42. — *idem, Jerusalem in the Time of Jesus* (1969) 233-45. — A. F. J. Klijn, "Scribes, Pharisees, High Priests and Elders in the NT," *NovT* 2 (1959) 259-67. — E. Lohse, *The NT Environment* (1976) 115-20. — R. Meyer, *TDNT* IX, 23f. — Reicke, *NT Era* 150-52. — *idem, BHH* III, 1736f. — K. H. Rengstorf, "Die ΣΤΟΛΑΙ der Schriftgelehrten," FS Michel 383-404. — H. F. Weiss, *TDNT* IX, 35f. — E. Zenger, "Die späte Weisheit und das Gesetz," Maier/ Schreiner 43-56. — For further bibliography see *TWNT* X, 1027.

1. Of the 62 occurrences in the NT, 57 are in the Synoptic Gospels, 4 in Acts, and 1 in the Epistles. With the exception of Matt 13:52 (and possibly 23:34), where Christian scribes are in view, and Acts 19:35, where γραμματεύς is used in the sense of *secretary* (= higher [Gentile] official), as well as 1 Cor 1:20, where Isa 33:18 LXX is cited, all other texts refer to Jewish *scribes* (= teachers of the law, Heb. *sōpᵉrîm/ḥᵃḵāmîm*). Thus νομικός can stand in place of γραμματεύς 9 times (of which 7 are in the Synoptic Gospels and 2, in a more general sense, in Titus 3:9, 13) and νομοδιδάσκαλος can appear 3 times (of which 2 are in the Lukan literature and a more general usage in 1 Tim 1:7).

2. In the Passion narrative of Mark 14f. the scribes are regularly associated with high priests and/or elders and understood as members of the Sanhedrin (so also Acts 4:5; 6:12), while outside the Passion narrative this combination is not predominant (cf. also Acts 23:9). Particularly noteworthy is the way in which the individual Gospels differ from each other in identifying the people Jesus spoke with and debated. In Mark the high priests are dominant (mentioned 22 times); in Luke and Matthew, however, the Pharisees are predominant (27 and 29 times), while in Mark the scribes appear more frequently than the Pharisees (21 vs. 12 times), a relationship that is reversed in Matthew (22 vs. 29 times) and in Luke (14 vs. 27 times). All these categorizations of Jesus' opponents must be viewed critically.

The phrase γραμματεῖς τῶν Φαρισαίων in Mark 2:16 appears to be relatively reliable (cf. also Acts 23:9), because here the historically correct distinction between scribes and Pharisees is maintained and the existence of non-Pharisaic scribes is assumed (on Sadducean scribes, cf. Josephus *Ant.* xviii.16; on Essene scribes, cf. 1QS 3:13; 9:12, 21; CD 12:21; on Zealot scribes, cf. Josephus *B.J.* ii.433). The text variants (Koine and others read "scribes and Pharisees") and the texts dependent on Mark 2:16 (Luke 5:30: "Pharisees and their scribes"; Matt 9:11: "Pharisees") suggest a development that began with the mention of the scribes as the primary members of Jesus' audience in Mark 2:1–3:6 (cf. 2:6); the endpoint of the development came with the replacement of "scribes" with "Pharisees."

The individual scribal teachers who debated with Jesus (cf. Mark 2:6, 16; 3:22; 9:11; 12:28, 32, 35) appear as representatives of Pharisaic-rabbinic Judaism opposing Christ (cf. 3:22 with Matt 12:24; Mark 12:28 with Matt 22:34f.; Mark 12:35 with Matt 22:41). Thus John, the latest Gospel, speaks consistently only of Φαρισαῖοι = Ἰουδαῖοι instead of γραμματεῖς (cf. esp. John 1:19 with v. 24; 8:13 with v. 22; 9:13-16 with v. 18; the exception 8:3 is found in the secondary section 7:53–8:11). On the basis of the clearly recognizable tendency of the Gospel writers to be anti-Pharisaic and anti-Jewish, it can be assumed that the scribes have been introduced into the Passion narrative by Mark in order to portray a Sanhedrin at full strength and thus to accent the guilt of Judaism for the death of Jesus.

3. In order to recognize the nature and meaning of the scribes at the time of Jesus, we must draw upon Jewish sources. The model of the scribes (Heb. *sōp̄ēr,* "writer") was Ezra (*ca.* 450 B.C.), who is characterized in Ezra 7:6 as "a scribe skilled in the law of Moses which the . . . God of Israel had given." The list of scribes, who originally took over the priestly task of interpreting and applying the law, was derived from him. In the Hellenistic age their significance as teachers of the law grew, as they were faced with a high-priesthood that was largely Hellenized. Consequently, under Salome Alexandra (76-67 B.C.) scribes of a Pharisaic orientation took their place in the gerousia, the old representative body and earlier form of the Sanhedrin. Increasingly they gained in significance.

The scribes were *exegetes,* interpreters of Scripture, who established its instructions in a binding way for the present; *teachers,* who sought to equip the greatest possible number of pupils with the methods of interpretation; and *jurists,* who, as trial judges, administered the law in practical situations (cf. Sir 38:24-30). They exerted their greatest influence through their teaching activity in the synagogues and schools for boys, which existed after the 1st cent. A.D.

With the increasing significance of synagogues in the first century after Christ, the scribes gained more power and reputation, which is suggested by the address "rabbi" ("rabbuni," "rab"). Because knowledge of the Torah distinguished the scribes, birth and descent did not form the basis for entrance into this respected position, but rather intensive study at the feet of a famous teacher, which consisted essentially of learning by memory the rabbi's teachings. Ordination by laying on of hands later accompanied the successful completion of the course of study. Most scribes were married, in observance of the command associated with the creation in Gen 1:28, and were involved in manual work in order to earn their living, since they received no remuneration for teaching.

4. Jesus was addressed as "rabbi" according to the Gospels (e.g., Mark 9:5; 10:51; 11:21; 14:45), which indicates that he was regarded as a scribal authority, but yet as one who was removed from the scribes of that period. Jesus' ἐξουσία—the independent "authority" by which he forgave sins (cf. Mark 2:6 par.), accepted sinners and tax collectors (cf. 2:16 par.), performed healings (cf. 3:22 par.), and interpreted the will of God without relying on human intermediaries and authorities (cf. 1:22 par.; 12:28, 32; also 9:11; 12:35)—was the feature that distinguished him. This authority was resisted constantly by the scribes, who charged Jesus with blasphemy (cf. 3:28f. par.) and service to the devil (3:22 par.). Significantly, the scribe who discusses the greatest commandment with Jesus in Mark 12:34 receives a positive assessment. When the same scribe in Matt 22:35/Luke 10:25 is denigrated as "testing" him and is thus reckoned explicitly among the Pharisees, the irreconcilable opposition between Church and synagogue is evident.

Jesus' critique of the scribes in Mark 12:38-40 par. Luke 20:46f. does not come in the form of a statement of woe (otherwise in Matthew 23/Luke 11). What is criticized here are the demands for public high esteem, places of honor at the synagogue worship and banquets, respect for their (Sabbath) apparel, their practice at prayer, and payment for their legal service for widows. But the Q logia in Matthew 23/Luke 11:39, 42 represent an "originally independent word of woe from early Christian prophets directed toward the synagogue, which the Pharisees led" (Schulz, *Q* 94). These condemning judgments, with their uncompromising harshness, are distinguished in Luke by the audience addressed (cf. Luke 11:39, 42-44, and 45-52), while Matthew has them directed generally to both scribes and Pharisees.

5. The following scribes are mentioned in the NT by name: *Nicodemus* was a recognized "teacher" in Israel according to John 3:10, according to 3:1 a Pharisaic member of the Sanhedrin (cf. also 7:50f.), and according to 19:39 a secret follower of Jesus (all of this historically questionable). *Gamaliel I* (*ca.* A.D. 30) was, according to Acts 5:34, a Pharisaic member of the Sanhedrin who enjoyed the greatest reputation among the people and, according to Jewish sources, was one of the most significant representatives of the school of Hillel, receiving the honorary title "rabban." *Paul,* according to Acts 22:3, was "brought up . . . at the feet of Gamaliel," although it must remain historically questionable whether Paul really received a scribal education, because such training is never mentioned in the Pauline letters. It is also disputed whether the final redactor of Matthew was a "converted Jewish rabbi" (E. von Dobschütz) and whether a Christian scribal school (K. Stendahl) stood behind this Gospel.

G. Baumbach

γραπτός, 3 *graptos* written*

Rom 2:15, about the Gentiles: "What the law requires (τὸ ἔργον τοῦ νόμου) is *written* on their hearts." H. Schlier, *Römer* (HTKNT) 78f.

γραφή, ῆς, ἡ *graphē* Scripture
γράφω *graphō* write

1. Occurrences in the NT — 2. Meaning — 3. Usage and synonyms — 4. The Authority of Scripture — a) In general — b) For Jesus — c) For Paul — d) In the Gospels, Acts, and James — 5. NT use of the OT

Lit.: S. AMSLER, *L'Ancien Testament dans l'Église* (1960). — C. K. BARRETT, "The Allegory of Abraham, Sarah, and Hagar in the Argument of Galatians," *idem, Essays on Paul* (1982) 154-70 = FS Käsemann 1-16. — O. BETZ, *Offenbarung und Schriftforschung in der Qumransekte* (WUNT 6, 1960). — M. BLACK, "The Christological Use of the OT in the NT," *NTS* 18 (1971/72) 1-14. — J. BLANK, "Erwägungen zum Schriftverständnis des Paulus," FS Käsemann 37-56. — H. BRAUN, "Das AT im NT," *ZTK* 59 (1962) 16-31. — R. BULTMANN, "Weissagung und Erfüllung," *idem, Glauben* II, 162-86. — C. H. DODD, *According to the Scriptures* (1952). — E. E. ELLIS, *Paul's Use of the OT* (1957). — *idem, Prophecy and Hermeneutic in Early Christianity* (1978). — J. A. FITZMYER, "The Use of Explicit OT Quotations in Qumran Literature and in the NT," *NTS* 7 (1960/61) 297-333. — E. D. FREED, *OT Quotations in the Gospel of John* (NovTSup 11, 1965). — H. GESE, *Vom Sinai zum Zion* (BEvT 64, 1974). — *idem, Essays on Biblical Theology* (1981). — L. GOPPELT, *Typos: The Typological Interpretation of the Old Testament in the New* (Eng. tr. 1982) 209-37. — W. GRUNDMANN, *Matthäus* (THKNT) 71-73. — R. H. GUNDRY, *The Use of the OT in St. Matthew's Gospel* (NovTSup 18, [2]1975) (bibliography). — F. HAHN, "Das Problem 'Schrift und Tradition' im Urchristentum," *EvT* 30 (1970) 449-68. — A. T. HANSON, *Studies in Paul's Technique and Theology* (1974). — M. HENGEL and H. MERKEL, "Die Magier aus dem Osten und die Flucht nach Ägypten Mt 2 . . . ," FS Schmid (1973) 139-69. — F. HESSE, *Das AT als Buch der Kirche* (1966). — T. HOLTZ, "Zur Interpretation des AT im NT," *TLZ* 99 (1974) 19-32. — H. HÜBNER, *Das Gesetz in der synoptischen Tradition* (1973). — *idem, Law in Paul's Thought* (1984). — W. G. KÜMMEL, *RGG* V, 1517-20. — H. LIETZMANN, *An die Galater* (HNT) 34-36. — B. LINDARS, *NT Apologetic* (1961). — B. LINDARS and P. BORGEN, "The Place of the OT in the Formation of NT Theology. Prolegomena and Response," *NTS* 23 (1976/77) 59-75. — U. LUZ, *Das Geschichtsverständnis des Paulus* (BEvT 49, 1968). — R. MAYER, *DNTT* III, 482-90. — O. MICHEL, *Paulus und seine Bibel* (1929; reprint 1972). — M. P. MILLER, "Targum, Midrash and the Use of the OT in the NT," *JSJ* 2 (1971) 29-82 (bibliography). — H. J. VAN DER MINDE, *Schrift und Tradition bei Paulus* (1976). — F. MUSSNER, *Galater* (HTKNT) 334-41. — M. RESE, *Alttestamentliche Motive in der Christologie des Lukas* (SNT 1, 1969). — W. ROTHFUCHS, *Die Erfüllungszitate des Matthäus-evangelium* (BWANT 88, 1969). — G. SCHRENK, *TDNT* I, 742-

73. — K. Stendahl, *The School of St. Matthew* (ASNU 20, ²1968). — A. Suhl, *Die Funktion der alttestamentlichen Zitate und Anspielungen im Markusevangelium* (1965). — H. Ulonska, "Die Funktion der alttestamentlichen Zitate und Anspielungen in den paulinischen Briefen" (Diss. Marburg, 1963); on Suhl and Ulonska, see M. Rese, *VF* 12/2 (1967) 87-97. — P. Vielhauer, "Paulus und das AT," *Studien zur Geschichte und Theologie der Reformation* (FS E. Bizer, 1969) 33-62. — For further bibliography → λέγω, νόμος, πληρόω, τύπος; see *TWNT* X, 1027f.

1. With 192 occurrences (including γραπτός in Rom 2:15), γράφω is the twentieth most common vb. in the NT. While the pass. is characteristic in the Gospels, Acts, and Pauline letters (including γραπτός, 108 occurrences in the NT), the act. appears esp. often in the Catholic Epistles (23 times) and in Revelation (15 times). The 51 occurrences of γραφή (of which 20 are in the pl.) are, with the exception of the deutero-Paulines (except for 2 occurrences in the Pastorals), Hebrews, the Johannine letters, and Revelation, distributed throughout the entire NT: 12 are in Paul's letters, 11 in the Lukan literature, 12 in John, and 4 each in Mark and Matthew.

2. The original meaning of γράφω, *scratch, engrave,* attested since Homer, occurs only at the periphery of the NT (John 8:6, κατέγραψεν; Luke 1:63; Rev 2:17). The customary meaning in classical and Hellenistic Greek, *write,* appears in the overwhelming majority of cases in the NT. Yet reference is not exclusively to the manual process of writing; Paul's dictating of a letter can fall under this term (Schrenk 743). The pf. tense forms γέγραπται (esp. in the Synoptics, Acts, and Paul) and γεγραμμένον ἐστίν (esp. John), *it is written,* in the sense of *it stands written,* are used to express the authority and present validity of what is written; they are an appeal to ἡ γραφή, *Scripture* (the "OT" in Christian terminology). Γραφή stands also for an individual *passage of Scripture* (although it is sometimes difficult to tell when the word has this meaning). Pl. γραφαί is most often synonymous with the sg. Only 1 Tim 5:18 (citing Luke 10:7 as γραφή) and 2 Pet 3:16 (referring to Paul's letters as γραφαί) understand also the NT (or perhaps, more precisely, the NT writings) as γραφή/γραφαί. The word γραφή is nowhere used in the NT for nonbiblical literature.

3. Although γράφω is a trans. vb., it does not often appear as such in the NT. Acc. objects include a letter of divorce (Mark 10:4), a commandment (Mark 10:5), a letter (Acts 23:25), and a demonstrative pron. For some trans. uses English would translate "write about": righteousness (Rom 10:5 $\mathfrak{p}^{46}$ B Koine), a personal pron. (John 1:45). Often γράφω appears with an obj. clause introduced by ὅτι. An idiom used in 1 John is γράφω ὑμῖν ὅτι . . . , "I am writing to you that. . . ." The subj. of the act. form is often the NT author (Paul, 1 John), but also Moses (e.g., Mark 10:5; 12:19; John 5:46) or Moses and the prophets (John 1:45). In Paul's letters only in Rom 10:5 is an OT author (Moses) the subj. of γράφω. Esp. in Paul, the pass. form γέγραπται often appears with the introductory καθώς (as it does in the LXX, e.g., 4 Kgdms 14:6; 2 Chr 23:18; for the rabbinic *kakāṯûḇ* [Heb.] or *kᵉḏiḵṯîḇ* [Aram.], see Michel 69f.; Schrenk 747-48; for the Qumran *kaᵃšer kāṯûḇ,* see *KQT* 105f.; Fitzmyer 300f.) or with a following γάρ: "as *it is written*" or "for *it is written.*"

In the Lukan literature and in John, additions to the pass. formula are predominant: "in the law (of the Lord)" (Luke 2:23; 10:26), "in the law of Moses and the prophets and the psalms" (24:44), "in your law" (John 8:17; 10:34), "in the book of the prophets" (Acts 7:42), "in the prophets" (24:14), "in the book of Psalms" (1:20), "in the second psalm" (13:33). With the exception of 1 Cor 9:9; 14:21 ("in the law [of Moses]") and Gal 3:10 ("in the book of the law"), Paul does not use additions of this sort (see, however, the combinations with λέγει, e.g., Rom 9:25; 10:19; → 4.c). In Revelation the imv. γράψον, addressed to the "angel" of the respective churches in chs. 2f. (→ ἄγγελος 2) or to the author of the book, is typical, as is the idiom ὄνομα γεγραμμένον (→ ὄνομα), "the name *written,*" esp. written in the "book of life" (13:8 etc.; see Luke 10:20) or on the forehead (Rev 14:1; 17:5, of the whore Babylon) or on the thigh (19:16, of the rider on the white horse).

Γραφή, γραφαί, or the pf. pass. partc. of γράφω often appear as the subjects of "is/are fulfilled" (→ πληρόω; common in the Synoptics, Acts, and John, in the idea "in order to be fulfilled" [but usually with τὸ ῥηθέν in Matthew], but not in Paul) and "say(s)" (→ λέγω). Of the 7 occurrences of sg. γραφή in Paul, 5 are the subj. of λέγω and 3 are in a question: τί (γὰρ) ἡ γραφὴ λέγει; "what does the Scripture say?" This use of the introductory formula for a citation leads to phrases such as "Moses says," "David says," etc. (Rom 10:19; 11:9). Citations from the Scripture can, however, be introduced simply by ὅτι or γάρ, "for."

Ὁ νόμος καὶ οἱ προφῆται (e.g., Matt 7:12; Acts 24:14, → νόμος) can stand as a synonym for γραφή. On one occasion the threefold "law, prophets, and psalms" appears (Luke 24:44; → 4.d on Matthew).

In part the open question of the Jewish canon is revealed here. The threefold "Torah, prophets, and writings" was not completed until Jamnia. Indeed, "there is no Old Testament that was complete prior to the existence of the New Testament" (Gese, *Theology* 11)—at least if one applies the idea of a standard text as known in the history of religions. However, the individual NT author looks back to the closed (but for him varied) canon; in any case he has no Jewish problem of the canon in mind. In the history of the Jewish religion the law constituted the determinative part of Scripture; indeed, after Jamnia, Torah is often used as a synonym for Scripture (W. Gutbrod, *TDNT* IV, 1047). Against Gese's thesis "of the *one,* the biblical tradition," Blank (41) asserts: "The *actual scriptural authority* had long been established."

4. a) The authority of Scripture is firmly established for the NT authors, indeed where, with regard to content, they differ from OT statements. But this authority can only be viewed within the framework of a sharing of authority with Jesus and the christological kerygma, and the relationship of these three authorities to each other is viewed in different ways by the NT authors. A definite circularity is present: The kerygma of the death and resurrection of Jesus for our sakes is proclaimed as attested by Scripture (1 Cor 15:3f.: κατὰ τὰς γραφάς, "according to the *Scriptures*"; cf. 2 Esdr 6:18: κατὰ τὴν γραφὴν βιβλίου Μωϋσῆ), but Scripture receives its power to confirm the kerygma from the Easter faith, from which it is read and interpreted. Behind the latter stands the conviction, shared with Qumran, that in the eschatological present the prophecies of Scripture are fulfilled (Braun, *Qumran* II, 306; on the difference between Qumran and Paul, see, e.g., Luz 102ff.).

"It is written" is typical and constitutive neither in Jesus' preaching of the kingdom of God (→ βασιλεία 3) nor in his messianic claim (which, according to E. Käsemann, "The Problem of the Historical Jesus," *idem, Essays on NT Themes* [1964] 38, "far surpasses that of any rabbi or prophet"). Nevertheless, the Synoptics and John, each in their own way, describe Jesus' life and work as the fulfillment of Scripture (e.g., Mark 9:12f.; Luke 24:26f.; John 15:25). Thus the absolute authority claimed by Jesus is relativized by its relation to scriptural authority. In addition, the authority of the Easter witnesses requires the accompanying authority of Scripture. Behind this tension in authority stands the problem of the relationship between the oral and the written. Specifically, before Easter the preaching of Jesus and Scripture was authoritative; after Easter, it was the preaching of the gospel and Scripture (see also Hahn 455ff.).

b) Although Jesus freely and self-consciously abrogates regulations of Scripture (Mark 7:15; Matt 5:31f., 38f.; → νόμος), he appeals in many instances to its commandments, particularly the Decalogue (Matt 5:21-28; Mark 7:9-13; see Hübner, *Tradition* 146ff.; R. Pesch, *Markus* [HTKNT] I, 376). He radicalizes the love commandment in Matt 5:43-48. He does not, however, appeal to Scripture as Scripture, but rather to particular commandments that express the will of God. The Spirit, which makes Scripture "that which is written" and thus an essential authoritative court of appeal, is foreign to him, the preacher. Not only does he stand as a successor to the prophets in radicalizing their ethical demands, but he also sees in his works and in his person a typological elevation above the works of the prophets (Luke 11:31f. par.; Goppelt 65-68). Where typology is present, it concerns not the written text but rather the event that is reported (Luz 53, n. 55). (If Jesus, as is doubtful, understood his mission in the light of Isaiah 53 [as proposed recently again in Goppelt, *Theology* I, 196], he would have seen in Isaiah a prophet who knew what God wanted from him. He would not, however, have seen his atoning suffering as demanded by Scripture.)

It is not surprising, therefore, when almost all the NT tradition has the subject of "Scripture" occur in particular categories: that of the dialectical relationship of *fulfillment of Scripture* and of *abrogation of Scripture*. We may assume that the Hellenists of Acts 6, who as Jews with Greek as a native language may have carried on Jesus' critical view of the Torah "more clearly than the Twelve did" (H. Conzelmann, *Acts* [Hermeneia] 45), combined the critique of the Torah with Christian exegesis of Scripture.

In Jesus' dialectical view of the Torah the impulse toward this theological reflection was already established. Jesus may have reflected on Scripture as such, despite the immediacy of his consciousness of his mission and the resulting relative critique of the Torah, as the violence passage in Matt 11:12/Luke 16:16 indicates, despite the impossibility of an exact reconstruction of the meaning of the saying (Käsemann, "Problem," 42f.). It is difficult to say how far the theological reflection of the Hellenists went or to what extent they prepared the way for the theological work of Paul (see also Vielhauer 38-40). In any case the OT remains the Scripture not only of the Jews but also of Gentile Christianity.

The development of Christian theology occurred largely in the context of the Gentile mission; its theoretical development sprang from practical interests. Wherever the relationship of the Jesus tradition, the kerygma of Christ, and Scripture came into question, the substance of the self-understanding of the NT proclamation was affected. In varied encounters, faith was elevated as reflective and was conceptually interpreted on the level of theology. Thus the question of a "theology of the NT" is applied and developed to a certain extent within the stage of the NT tradition by the theme of "Scripture." Consequently each outline of a later NT theology must decide whether to take up the line of questioning that is set out in the NT; i.e., it must know in what sense and to what degree it is an explication of the theology/theologies already present in the NT. What Hanson says of Paul is to be noted for almost all of the NT: "He only knew one sacred book, what we call the OT. The very use of this name separates us . . . from Paul himself" (*Studies* 136).

c) For Paul in particular theological reflection on the relationship between faith and Scripture becomes an indispensable task. After his conversion he lives entirely from Scripture (more precisely, the LXX). In his letters the boundaries between formal citation, allusion, and obvious usage of the LXX are fluid (specific formal citation, partially as a proof from Scripture, partially exegeted, appears only in Galatians, 1–2 Corinthians, and Romans; see surveys in Michel 74f.; Ellis, *Paul's Use* 150ff.; for allusions, see *ibid.* 153f.). Paul employs the rabbinic method of exegesis (Michel; Hanson; Blank; Ellis, *Prophecy* 147-81; on Rom 10:5-10 see Black 8f.), i.e., haggadic midrash (or typology, → τύπος), not exegesis in the interest of halakah. His own understanding of Scripture is given in 1 Cor 9:9f.; 10:11; Rom 4:23f.; 15:4 (Scripture is written "for our instruction"). Paul's exegesis of the LXX (esp. in Galatians and Romans) is dedicated esp. to solving the pressing problem of how the indisputable authority of Scripture is to be harmonized with the enslaving role of the law, the essential part of Scripture?

In Galatians, Scripture and law are kept strictly separate. Scripture is focussed on God's evangelical purpose in making promises (Gal 3:8 [= Gen 18:18]; *Scripture* says *to* Abraham what *God* says *about* him in Genesis). The law, however, is not God's but rather the law of the angels (3:19; the "whole" law for the Christian in 5:14 is not "the whole law" of Moses mentioned in 5:3; Hübner, *Law* 36ff.). Thus Scripture belongs primarily to the Christ-event and has a share in the authority of Christ. But Scripture has also a condemning function because it pronounces a curse on all in their transgressions with the words of the law (γραφή in Gal 3:22 refers to Deut 27:26 LXX, cited in Gal 3:10).

We cannot say that Paul did not consider the divine dignity of Scripture or that Scripture was of interest to him only as illustrative material (against Ulonska 214f.). Paul depended on Scripture for the proof of his arguments (Hanson). It is improbable that the first use of Scripture was occasioned by the Galatian opponents (Ulonska 222); this view cannot be argued on the basis of 1 Thessalonians, for it is inconceivable that he had not had discussions about Scripture and the law already before 1 Thessalonians (written to a church on his Gentile mission). Rather, it is to be assumed that the specific exegeses in Galatians were answers to Galatian opponents, who had argued from Scripture (on 3:6-29, see E. de Witt Burton, *Galatians* [ICC] 153-59; Hübner, *Law* 15ff.; on the "allegorical" typology in 4:21-31 see Barrett).

In contrast to Galatians, the problem shifts in Romans in that the now more positive view of the law somewhat took the edge off the question that was pressing in Galatians. It is noteworthy that the appeal to Scripture is constitutive for the argumentation in 1:16f.; 1:18–3:20; 3:21–4:25; 9:1–11:36, and chs. 12–15, but *not* in the decisive and theologically constructive section, chs. 5–8. Paul can thus set forth both freedom from death, sin, and law and the life of the Christian "in the Spirit" (→ πνεῦμα) without appealing (except for 7:7-12; 8:36) to Scripture. Pauline theology thus proceeds in a central passage without proof from Scripture. Nevertheless, all of Romans stands under the authority of Scripture as it is understood prophetically (1:2: "through his prophets [i.e., the entire OT] in the holy Scriptures"; 3:21). On Romans, → γράμμα 2.

d) The relationship of Scripture and the Christ-event is dealt with in the Gospels particularly in terms of "fulfillment of the Scripture(s)" (the earliest reference is in Mark 14:49), a formulation unknown to Paul.

In Mark 1:1-3, "the beginning of the gospel" (i.e., the appearance of the Baptist) and thus the entire gospel is placed under the rubric of *it stands written* (for a different view, see Suhl 136 against W. Marxsen). Of the other 6 occurrences of "(as) it is written" 4 (9:12f.; 14:21, 27) refer to the death of the Baptist or the suffering and death of Jesus (note Mark's theology of the cross). The Markan Jesus appeals regularly to the OT, explicitly referring to a γραφή (= a passage of Scripture, 12:10) or to γραφαί (12:24). Although 7:15 unambiguously abrogates Leviticus 11, Mark normally understands Scripture (and Moses—note 7:10) without reservation as the fundamental authority. The result is the problem that is present in Galatians. Here, though, this problem is never the subject of reflection.

The programmatic formulation of Matt 26:56, ἵνα πληρωθῶσιν αἱ γραφαὶ τῶν προφητῶν, "that the *Scriptures* of the prophets might be fulfilled," is in a certain sense the title of Matthew. The fulfillment citations (Rothfuchs) state this basic view concretely. In them definite statements—only from the prophets—are seen as fulfilled in the Christ-event. Inasmuch as this is a typological relationship (clearly Matt 2:15 = Hos 11:1: Jesus as the Son of God is representative of the new Israel [Israel, however, as the Son of God]; see also Hengel and Merkel 157; otherwise Rothfuchs 62f.), it is an exaggeration to say that Matthew is concerned not with fulfillment of Scripture in general but with the fulfillment of isolated words in single moments of the life of Jesus (P. Vielhauer, *Geschichte der urchristlichen Literatur* [1975] 362).

Because the Scripture that Matthew cites speaks of the OT events in their connection to the Christ-event, the schema "prophecy and fulfillment" is too narrow. The prophetic word, rather, points to the alignment of the old event toward the new. Matthew's use of Scripture is in principle neither allegorical nor atomistic. Although "the law and the prophets" is used to mean "Scripture," the accent in 5:17 (as in 22:40) may lie on "law" ("prophets" only interpret the law); "fulfill the law and the prophets" (5:17) means to "bring (the law) to validity through teaching" in the sense of sharpening the Torah (Braun), as well as modifying it (G. Strecker, *Der Weg der Gerechtigkeit* [[2]1966] 147). Finally, it is remarkable that the reflective citations in Matthew, in contrast to most other Matthean citations, do not represent the LXX text but stand closer to the Hebrew (most recently, Gundry 9-150; on Stendahl's view that the fulfillment citations developed from a Christian scribal school, see Gundry's critique, 155ff.; Kümmel, *Introduction* 110-12; Rothfuchs 108f.).

For the Lukan literature, Luke 24:25-27, 32, 44-47 is decisive: Jesus is himself the interpreter of the Scriptures; he "opens" (→ ἀνοίγω 3) the minds of the disciples so that they understand the Scriptures, in particular, that everything written about him must be (→ δεῖ) fulfilled. At the beginning of his ministry Jesus proclaims that the γραφή of Isa 61:1f.; 58:6 (on the giving of the Spirit) is fulfilled in him (Luke 4:21).

According to Acts 1:16 this Spirit "spoke" Scripture "beforehand," which had to be fulfilled. In the Spirit-led Pauline mission Scripture testifies that Jesus is the Messiah (Acts 17:2f.; Paul is the subject of διανοίγω as Jesus is in Luke 24:32, 45; in Acts 18:28 it is Apollos). Again undisputed authority of Scripture stands in a singular tension with the abrogation of important legal injunctions (Acts 10: food laws, cultic ideas of purity; Acts 15: circumcision). Rese's judgment (*Motive,* 147) is correct: the γραφή in Luke 4:21 is part of a normative entity to which one can appeal; yet the "today" of v. 21 leads him to the excessive interpretation that "the fulfillment qualifies the Scripture as promise," as he exegetes 4:16-21 without reference to vv. 25-27.

In John all 4 occurrences of "fulfill the Scripture" are in fulfillment citations ("so that . . .": 13:18; 17:12; 19:24, 36; on all Johannine fulfillment citations, cf. Rothfuchs 151-57). Parallel to this idea is 15:25, "it is to fulfill the word that is *written* in their law." Significant also in this connection is 18:32, "to fulfill the word which Jesus had spoken." An understanding of Scripture is possible only in faith; anyone who cannot hear (= believe) is misled by Scripture (7:42), as Scripture itself attests (12:38-40 = Isa 53:1 and 6:9f.). However, the believer understands that Scripture (including the law) witnesses to Jesus as Revealer (5:39, in connection with vv. 45f.). For John the authority of Jesus and of Scripture coincide. Γραφή in 7:42 does not mean a NT Gospel; in 17:12 it is not the word of Jesus in John 6:70f. (against Freed 51, 96ff.).

Outside the Gospels, only James has the formula "the Scripture [= a passage of Scripture] was fulfilled" (2:23). Within the perspective of a Jewish interpretation of Genesis and as a polemic against a misunderstood Paulinism, Abraham's act of obedience (→ Ἀβραάμ 2.b) in Genesis 22 is seen as the fulfillment of Gen 15:6, a "realization of the word of God through the deed of Abraham" (W. Schrage, *Jakobus* [NTD] 32; for a similar view, see F. Mussner, *Jakobus* [HTKNT] 143, in an appeal to H. Windisch). The OT is fulfilled in the NT.

Although Hebrews has many citations and examples of exegesis from Scripture, γραφή does not appear, and γράφω occurs only once in a citation. The author instead favors → λέγω.

5. In its appeal to the OT, does the NT preserve the meaning intended by the OT? The answers move between two poles: the assumption of a complete distortion of the meaning of the OT citation because of an atomistic use of Scripture in the NT (e.g., Braun) and the belief that a careful exegesis of the text occurred with conscious observance of its context (e.g., Hanson; Hanson thus defends Paul, who almost never changes an OT text [*Studies* 147f.]; this would be consistent with use of collections of testimonies [*ibid.,* 191ff.], though the unresolved question of their existence and use cannot be treated here). Common to these controversial views is the belief that the NT authors read and interpreted Scripture in light of the Easter faith.

The statements of Scripture do not foretell the historical Jesus as the Messiah of God. Yet one may ask if decisive implications of the christology are not also implications of OT statements. Indeed, e.g., Paul has correctly understood Gen 15:6, which was important to him, in a decisive way in the sense of this correspondence of implications: The reckoning of righteousness for the Elohist is no longer cultic reckoning on the basis of human achievements. "Only faith, belief that Yahweh is serious about his promise, brings one into a right relationship; Yahweh 'reckons' " (G. von Rad, *Gesammelte Studien zum AT* [[2]1961] 134; to be considered on the other side is Vielhauer 36, n. 15). Ps 142:2 LXX, cited in Rom 3:20 with the addition of the Pauline "by works of the law," is not distorted, for Paul means any works that misuse the law against its own essential intention for the purpose of self-justification (→ νόμος).

The NT authors' practice of choosing from within the OT has its inner justification from the OT, for it compelled a selection because of its statements that do lend themselves to harmonization. From the viewpoint of the NT there was also an inner necessity, since for it the contingency of the Jesus-event is decisive. The NT authors, who agree with a portion of Judaism in reading the OT as a book of prophecy about the end time, distinguish themselves from all of Judaism essentially in not regarding Scripture primarily as Torah. They distinguish themselves especially from rabbinic Judaism insofar as they do not set out their parenesis as halakah rooted in the Torah. "What is unique about the interpretation of Scripture in the NT is that it is not only eschatological, but Christological" (Miller 67).

H. Hübner

γράφω *graphō* write
→ γραφή.

γραώδης, 2 *graōdēs* characteristic of old women*

1 Tim 4:7, of myths (→ μῦθος): *old wives'* tales, which Timothy is to avoid.

γρηγορέω *grēgoreō* be awake; be vigilant*

1. Occurrences — 2. Meaning — 3. Theological significance

Lit.: E. Lövestam, *Spiritual Wakefulness in the NT* (1967). — A. Oepke, *TDNT* II, 338f. — A. Weiser, "Von der Predigt Jesu zur Erwartung der Parusie," *BibLeb* 12 (1971) 25-31.

1. The NT contains 22 occurrences of γρηγορέω: there are 6 each in Matthew and Mark, 3 in Revelation, 2 in 1 Thessalonians, and 1 each in Luke, Acts, 1 Corinthians, Colossians, and 1 Peter. Imv. forms (γρηγορεῖτε 10 times; cf. 1 Pet 5:8, γρηγορήσατε) or partcs. in connection with imvs. (γίνου γρηγορῶν, προσκαρτερεῖτε γρηγοροῦντες) are predominant. This vb. thus belongs primarily (but not exclusively) within exhortations.

2. a) Γρηγορέω means primarily *not sleep.* Thus Jesus summons his disciples on the Mount of Olives to *stay awake* with him (Matt 26:38, 40, 41; Mark 14:34, 37, 38). In Luke 12:37 γρηγορέω is to be understood within the parable in vv. 36-38 as *not sleep.*

b) The fig. sense *be vigilant* is strongly predominant in the NT, although the transition from the first meaning is fluid. In Matt 26:41 par. Mark 14:38 γρηγορέω receives an accent in the direction of the fig. meaning. Except for 1 Thess 5:10 (→ c), γρηγορέω is to be understood clearly as *be alert* in all of the passages not yet mentioned. To be distinguished are (1) passages with a direct eschatological reference: to be prepared for the coming of Jesus Christ, the Son of Man, watchfulness is necessary (Matt 24:42; 25:13; Mark 13:35, 37; 1 Thess 5:6; Rev 3:2f.; 16:15); (2) passages without a direct eschatological reference: the danger of negative developments in the Church, the snares of Satan, among other things, demand watchfulness (Acts 20:31; 1 Cor 16:13; Col 4:2; 1 Pet 5:8); (3) passages in which normal vigilance is a metaphor for being ready for the coming of the Son of Man (Matt 24:43; Mark 13:34; cf. also the metaphorical sense in Luke 12:36-38).

c) In 1 Thess 5:10 the reference to "whether we *wake* or sleep" is, as the wider context indicates, to living or dying: Christ died for us so that whether we continue to *live* in this world or have already died we might live with him.

3. Exhortation to vigilance presupposes that Christians are always in danger of reducing their full commitment to God through Christ and of allowing themselves to be seized by things of lesser value. The focus can thus rest on the threatening danger or extend to the consequence of negligence or of not being prepared for the Son of Man. Γρηγορέω signifies vigilant constancy in faith (cf. 1 Cor 16:13).

J. M. Nützel

γυμνάζω *gymnazō* exercise; accustom*

1 Tim 4:7: "*train* yourself in godliness"; pf. pass. partc. in Heb 5:14; 12:11: "those who have their faculties *trained*," i.e., those who have advanced in piety; likewise 2 Pet 2:14: the false teachers "have their hearts *trained* in greed." A. Oepke, *TDNT* I, 775.

γυμνασία, ας, ἡ *gymnasia* exercise; training*

1 Tim 4:8: ἡ σωματικὴ γυμνασία, "bodily *training*," which is useful for little, in contrast to exercise in piety (→ γυμνάζω). A. Oepke, *TDNT* I, 775f.

γυμνητεύω *gymnēteuō* be poorly clothed

Alternative form ($\mathfrak{p}^{46}$ Koine) of → γυμνιτεύω.

γυμνιτεύω *gymniteuō* be poorly clothed*

In 1 Cor 4:11 (at the beginning of a catalog of trials) Paul says, "we hunger and thirst, we are *ill-clad* (γυμνιτεύομεν) and buffeted and homeless," even to the present hour.

γυμνός, 3 *gymnos* naked, uncovered; poorly clothed*
γυμνότης, ητος, ἡ *gymnotēs* nakedness

1. Occurrences and meaning in the NT — 2. Usage in the NT — 3. 2 Cor 5:3.

Lit.: A. van den Born, *BL* 1212. — G. Fohrer, *BHH* II, 962-65. — H. Herter, *RAC* X, 1-52, esp. 29-34, 45-48. — A. Oepke, *TDNT* I, 774-76. — F. Pfister, PW XVI/2, 1541-49. — H. Riesenfeld, "Das Bildwort vom Weizenkorn bei Paulus (zu 1 Cor 15)," *Studien zum NT und zur Patristik* (FS E. Klostermann, 1961) 43-55. — H. Ringgren, *BHH* II, 1277. — C. A. Schmitz, *RGG* IV, 1294. — J. N. Sevenster, "Some Remarks on the γυμνός in II Cor. V.3," FS de Zwaan 202-14. — H. Weigelt, *DNTT* I, 312-16. — For further bibliography see *TWNT* X, 1028.

1. Γυμνός appears 15 times in the NT. The noun γυμνότης, which is rare in Greek outside the NT and the LXX, appears 3 times (Rom 8:35; 2 Cor 11:27; Rev 3:18). Both words can be used of complete nakedness or of inadequate or meager clothing. They can also be used fig. for the condition of being unprotected, in want, and helpless.

In Gen 3:7 shame in the presence of nakedness is explained as a result of sin (cf. 2:25; 3:10; 9:21; *Jub.* 3:30f.). One begins and ends one's life in nakedness (Job 1:21; Eccl 5:14). The poor are naked and dependent on the truly pious and the righteous for clothing (Isa 58:7; Ezek 18:7, 16; Tob 4:16). Nakedness is thus predominantly an expression of defenselessness (cf. Job 26:6 on the kingdom of the dead, which cannot hide before God). Cultic nakedness (Herter 32; Ringgren; Schmitz) and the concept of the nakedness of the soul (cf. Plato *Cra.* 403b; *Corpus Hermeticum* i.24-26; xiii.6) are foreign to the biblical point of view.

2. The young man in Mark 14:51f. flees fully *unclothed* when he lets his garment, his only piece of clothing, slip from his hand. Γυμνός is used of forcible stripping in Acts 19:16 and fig. in Rev 17:16 (of the πόρνη Βαβυλών; cf. v. 5). In John 21:7 it refers, however, to the normal work clothing of a fisherman *without an outer garment.* As in the OT (→ 1), γυμνός is used of the vulnerability of the poor, who are unable to dress themselves adequately (Matt 25:36, 38, 43f.; Jas 2:15; cf. γυμνότης in Rom 8:35 with λιμός; 2 Cor 11:27 with ψύχος). Fig., γυμνός means *laid bare, unveiled* (Heb 4:13; everything is γυμνὰ καὶ τετραχηλισμένα before the eyes of God); in Rev 3:17f. it is used of the spiritual poverty of the church in Laodicea, which stands before God "poor, blind, and *naked*," unaware of its need (cf. 16:15).

Γυμνὸς κόκκος (1 Cor 15:37) designates the "*bare* kernel" of wheat, which is sown in the earth, in contrast to the future plant (τὸ σῶμα τὸ γενησόμενον, v. 37a), which God causes to grow from a particular seed. The point of the image, which is common also in rabbinic literature (Billerbeck III, 475), is that the outward appearance of the seed of grain is in every way surpassed by the future plant. The intended point becomes apparent in the image of relinquishing the naked (γυμνός) grain/body into the earth/death in consideration of the future σῶμα, so that God causes an incomparable new σῶμα to arise from it (cf. John 12:24; *1 Clem.* 24).

3. Difficult to interpret is 2 Cor 5:3: εἴ γε καὶ ἐκδυσάμενοι οὐ γυμνοὶ εὑρεθησόμεθα, "so that by taking it [the earthly dwelling] off we may not be found *naked*" (different reading followed in RSV). In vv. 1-5 a comprehensive "eschatological" basis is offered for the view that a daily renewal of the inner person through the power of God (4:7-18; 5:6-8; cf. R. Bultmann, *The Second Letter to the Corinthians* [1985] 130-33 on 5:1 with n. 120 on p. 133) corresponds to the continual dying of the earthly body. The faithful groan because they, in the midst of the destruction of their earthly existence (ἐὰν . . . καταλυθῇ, 5:1), long to be further clothed with the heavenly dwelling (v. 2), which is vouchsafed to them according to the model of Christ.

Vv. 1-2 favor neither a hope for the parousia before death (cf. v. 4) nor a fear of dying before the parousia. Thus considerations of a nakedness to be feared in the interim between death and the parousia and the assumption of a polemic against Gnostic demands for liberation from the earthly body do not account for the Pauline statements. Instead, v. 3 confirms that the knowledge making itself known in the "groaning" of the faithful concerns those who are already dying, who are in reality borne by the ζωὴ τοῦ Ἰησοῦ (4:10). At the end, they will be found before God as clothed—with heavenly glory (4:17). They are not described as those whose earthly "dying" presents them as *naked* before God, i.e., as defenselessly delivered over to death.

H. Balz

γυμνότης, ητος, ἡ *gymnotēs* nakedness
→ γυμνός.

γυναικάριον, ου, τό *gynaikarion* weak woman*

Literally *little woman* (from γυνή), used with a derogatory tone in 2 Tim 3:6: "capture *weak women,* burdened with sins. . . ."

γυναικεῖος, 3 *gynaikeios* female*

1 Pet 3:7: men are exhorted to bestow honor "on the *woman* [literally *feminine* vessel, → σκεῦος] as the weaker sex." The passage is probably influenced by 1 Thess 4:4.

γυνή, αικός, ἡ *gynē* woman; wife

Lit.: M. Adinolfi, "La donna e il matrimonio nel Giudaismo ai tempi di Cristo," *RivB* 20 (1972) 369-90. — *idem,* "Il velo della donna e la rilettura Paolina di 1 Cor. 11, 2-16," *RivB* 23 (1975) 147-73. — J. B. Bauer, "Uxores circumducere (1 Kor 9, 5)," *BZ* N.F. 3 (1959) 94-102. — G. G. Blum, "Das Amt der Frau im NT," *NovT* 7 (1964) 142-61. — M. Boucher, "Some Unexplored Parallels to 1 Cor 11:11-12 and Gal 3:28: The NT on the Role of Women," *CBQ* 31 (1969) 50-58. — R. E. Brown, "Roles of Women in the Fourth Gospel," *TS* 36 (1975) 688-99. — H. von Campenhausen, "Zur Perikope von der Ehebrecherin," *ZNW* 68 (1977) 164-75. — G. B. Caird, "Paul and Women's Liberty," *BJRL* 54 (1971/72) 268-81. — G. Dautzenberg, *Urchristliche Prophetie* (BWANT 104, 1975) 258-73 (on 1 Cor 14:34f. and 1 Tim 2:11). — A. Feuillet, "L'homme 'gloire de dieu' et la femme 'gloire de l'homme' (1 Kor 11, 7b)," *RB* 81 (1974) 161-82. — *idem,* "La dignité et le rôle de la femme d'après quelques textes Pauliniens," *NTS* 21 (1974/75) 157-91. — G. Fitzer, *Das Weib schweige in der Gemeinde. Über den unpaulinischen Charakter der mulier-taceat-Verse in 1 Kor 14* (*TEH* 110, 1963). — H. Greeven, *RGG* II, 1069f. — A. Jaubert, "Le voile des femmes 1 Cor 11, 2-16," *NTS* 18 (1971/72) 419-30. — J. Jeremias, *TDNT* IV, 1099-1106. — E. Kähler, *Die Frau in den paulinischen Briefen* (1960). — J. Kühlewein, *THAT* I, 247-51. — J. Leipoldt, *Die Frau in der antiken Welt und im Urchristentum* (1962). — A. Oepke, *TDNT* I, 776-89. — R. Scroggs, "Paul and the Eschatological Woman," *JAAR* 40 (1972) 283-303. — C. Spicq, "La femme chrétienne et ses vertus," *idem, Les Épîtres Pastorales* ([4]1969) 385-425. — K. Thraede, *RAC* VIII, 197-269. — H. Vorländer and C. Brown, *DNTT,* III, 1055-68. — For further bibliography see *DNTT* III, 1075-78; *TWNT* X, 1028-34.

Γυνή designates the *woman* as sexual partner in Matt 5:28; 1 Cor 7:1; Rev 14:4, without consideration of her age or situation. Man is born of *woman,* Matt 11:11; Luke 7:28; Gal 4:4 (John 16:21). Γυνή means *wife* in Matt 5:28, 31; 14:3, and elsewhere; 1 Cor 9:5 (Bauer believes that v.l. pl. γυναῖκας is original); *stepmother,* in 1 Cor 5:1; and occasionally also the *bride,* who remains under the *patria potestas* until her wedding but is legally considered a married woman from the time of the betrothal (Gen 29:21; Deut 22:24; Matt 1:20, 24; Luke 2:5 v.l.). Because the unfaithful wife was to be strangled (according to the rabbinic interpretation of Lev 20:10; Deut 22:22), John 8:3f., 9f. may concern an unfaithful *bride,* who was to be stoned, according to Deut 22:24 (Jeremias). If, however, one follows von Campenhausen in transferring the origin of the pericope about the adulteress to the disputes over repentance among Christians in the 2nd cent. A.D., the rabbinic argument loses its force.

In Rev 19:7; 21:9 the *bride* is the image of the Church, just as the *woman* in the sun in 12:1 symbolizes the people of God (Victorin *Comm. in Apc.* 12 [PLSup I, 149]: *ecclesia antiqua patrum et prophetarum et sanctorum apostolorum*). Voc. γύναι is not irreverent in Matt 15:28; Luke 22:57; John 2:4; 4:21; 19:26; 20:13, 15 (cf. Jdt 11:1; Josephus *Ant.* i.252: *mother of the bride;* Dio Cassius li.12.5, Augustus to Cleopatra). With designations of characteristics, function, and origin, the word serves in the formation of substantives: Canaanitess, Matt 15:22; Samaritan woman, John 4:9; Jewess, Acts 16:1; Greek woman, 17:12; wife, Rom 7:2; widow, Luke 4:26; sinner, 7:37.

J. B. Bauer

Γώγ *Gōg* Gog*
Μαγώγ *Magōg* Magog*

Lit.: H. Bietenhard, *Das tausendjährige Reich* (²1955). — Billerbeck III, 831-40. — W. Bousset, "Beiträge zur Geschichte der Eschatologie," *ZKG* 20 (1900) 103-31. — C. A. Keller, *RGG* II, 1683f. — K. G. Kuhn, *TDNT* I, 789-91. — B. Otzen, *TDOT* II, 419-25. — M. Rissi, *Die Zukunft der Welt* (1966). — A. Schlatter, *Das AT in der johanneischen Apokalypse* (1912). — M. C. Tenney, "The Importance and Exegesis of Rev 20:1-8," *BSac* 111 (1954) 137-48. — W. Zimmerli, *Ezekiel* (Hermeneia) II (1983), 300-322. — For further bibliography see *TWNT* X, 1034.

1. The OT contains many and various references to Gog and Magog. While Gog in 1 Chr 5:4 and Magog in Gen 10:2 and 1 Chr 1:5 appear as personal names, Gog in Ezek 38:2f., 14, 16, 18; 39:1, 11, 15 is chief prince from the land of Magog (38:2; cf. 39:6). Thus "Magog" is an ad hoc formulation from "Gog," and the realm of Gog is to be seen in Magog (Zimmerli 299-302). According to Ezekiel 38f., Gog is to go to war against Jerusalem at Yahweh's command with an army of troops from many nations (38:12) and capture it. However, he will be annihilated by Yahweh himself (39:1-8). Historical reality and mythic themes are merged within this Gog-Magog concept.

2. Gog and Magog are found in the NT only in Rev 20:8. As in the preceding eschatological visions of the seer, the vision in Rev 19:11–22:5 largely resembles the pattern of the prophetic announcement of Ezekiel 37–48 and is obviously dependent upon it, the mention of Gog and Magog in 20:8 being derived from the conceptual framework of Ezekiel 37–48. However, unlike the MT of Ezekiel 38f., Gog and Magog are proper names for the peoples (appearing in apposition to τὰ ἔθνη) whom Satan deceives after the thousand-year kingdom of peace (20:1-6), in order to capture Jerusalem, "the beloved city" (v. 9), the center of the rule of the Messiah. On the basis of the special emphasis on Satan in vv. 2f. and 7, it is very possible that "the nations which are at the four corners of the earth, that is, Gog and Magog" (v. 8), are thought of as demonic powers or the dead, the troops of the world below (cf. 9:1-11, 13-19). On this view Gog and Magog in 20:8 are names for a mythic entity. Thus it is moot to attempt to identify possible concrete historical references.

The Jewish Apocrypha and Pseudepigrapha are silent about Gog and Magog, except for *Sib. Or.* iii.319, 512. The rabbinic literature and Christian writings after the NT era demonstrate strong interest in them (Billerbeck, Bousset).

D. Sänger

γωνία, ας, ἡ *gōnia* corner; nook*
ἀκρογωνιαῖος, 3 (sc. **λίθος**) *akrogōniaios* cornerstone*

1. Occurrences in the NT — 2. Γωνία — 3. Κεφαλὴ γωνίας and ἀκρογωνιαῖος: a) Meanings — b) Κεφαλὴ γωνίας — c) Ἀκρογωνιαῖος

Lit.: H. Balz, *TDNT* VIII, 127-39, esp. 131-35. — K. Berger, *Exegese des NT* (1977) 61f. — G. Bornkamm, *TDNT* IV, 280-81. — Jeremias, *Parables* 73f. — J. Jeremias, *TDNT* I, 791-93 (bibliography); IV, 274-79. — *idem,* "Eckstein—Schlußstein," *ZNW* 36 (1937) 154-57. — S. Lyonnet, "De Christo summo angulari lapide secundum Eph 2, 20," *VD* 27 (1949) 74-83. — R. J. McKelvey, "Christ the Cornerstone," *NTS* 8 (1961/62) 352-59. — H. Merklein, *Das kirchliche Amt nach dem Epheserbrief* (SANT 33, 1973) 144-52 (bibliography). — W. Mundle, *DNTT* III, 381-85. — F. Mussner, *Christus, das All und die Kirche* (TTS 5, 1955) 108-11. — E. Percy, *Die Probleme der Kolosser- und Epheserbriefe* (SHVL 39, 1946) 328-35, 485-88. — J. Pfammatter, *Die Kirche als Bau* (AnGr 110, 1960) 143-51 (bibliography). — M. Rese, *Alttestamentliche Motive in der Christologie des Lukas* (1969) 113-15, 171-73. — K. T. Schäfer, "Lapis summus angularis," FS H. Lützeler (1962) 9-23. — *idem,* "Zur Deutung von ἀκρογωνιαῖος Eph 2, 20," FS Schmid (1963) 218-24 (bibliography). — K. H. Schelkle, *RAC* I, 233f. — E. Schweizer, *The Good News According to Mark* (1977) 238-42. — G. Stählin, *TDNT* VI, 745-58; VII, 339-58. — A. Suhl, *Die Funktion der alttestamentlichen Zitate und Anspielungen im Markusevangelium* (1965) 138-42. — P. Vielhauer, *Oikodome* (1940) 60-62, 124-27, 145-50. — For further bibliography see Merklein; Pfammatter; Schäfer, "Deutung"; *TDNT* 791f.; *TWNT* X, 1034.

1. Γωνία occurs 9 times in the NT—5 times in the phrase κεφαλὴ γωνίας (Matt 21:42; Mark 12:10; Luke 20:17; Acts 4:11; 1 Pet 2:7) and in 4 other places (Matt 6:5; Acts 26:26; Rev 7:1; 20:8). The compound ἀκρογωνιαῖος appears in Eph 2:20 and 1 Pet 2:6.

2. A γωνία is a *corner*; depending on whether it is viewed from the outside or the inside, it may imply either openness or seclusion. In Matt 6:5 ἐν ταῖς γωνίαις τῶν πλατειῶν, "at the street *corners,*" probably refers to road junctions or intersections, where a person is visible from more than one direction (the opposite of τὸ κρυπτόν, "the concealed place," in v. 6). The pure Greek expression ἐν γωνίᾳ, "in a *corner,*" appears in Plato *Grg.* 485d; Epictetus *Diss.* i.29.36; ii.12.17; iii.22.98, and elsewhere, as well as Acts 26:26. Γωνία expresses not only concealment from public view but also lack of significance. To describe the Messiah-event as something "not done in a corner" (Acts 26:26) affirms that it has taken place before the public as something significant.

Rev 7:1; 20:8 speaks of the τέσσαρες γωνίαι τῆς γῆς, "four *corners* of the earth." This wording hardly assumes a quadratic form of the circle of earth, for γωνίαι here has the sense of πτέρυγες, "edges, boundaries" (as in Isa 11:12; Ezek 7:2), or ἄκρα τῆς γῆς, "ends of the earth" (often in LXX; note "four ἄκρα of heaven" in Jer 25:16 LXX). The connection with the four winds in Rev 7:1 suggests rather a thought of the four *points of the compass* (so, likewise in connection with the winds, four τόποι ["regions"] καὶ γωνίαι of the horizon, corresponding to the four seasons: Ptolemy *Tetr.* i.29); furthermore, "four" is occasionally used as a symbolic number to represent totality. According to Rev 20:8 Satan incites "the nations which are at the four *corners* of the earth" (i.e., in the whole world) to battle against the Holy City, which is thought to be at the midpoint of the earth.

3. a) Κεφαλὴ γωνίας is the translation formed mechanically from the Hebrew hapax legomenon *rō'š pinnâ* in Ps 118:22. The thesis, represented particularly by J. Jeremias (since 1925), that κεφαλὴ γωνίας, as well as the synonymous ἀκρογωνιαῖος, signifies the *keystone* crowning the building, and probably installed over the portal, is unacceptable, despite the wide agreement of numerous exegetes. The texts introduced to support Jeremias's thesis are later than the NT and do not have compelling force (cf. esp. Percy; Pfammatter; Merklein). In addition, one could not stumble over such a stone and be made to fall (Luke 20:18; 1 Pet 2:7f.), and the interpretation *keystone* in Luke 20:18 requires an overly artificial interpretation in the context (→ πίπτω). Moreover, in Eph 2:20 the building to which this stone already belongs (following the clear sense of the text) is not yet completed. In NT terminology, the image of the building is to be distinguished clearly from that of the body (note the use of κεφαλή, "head"), even when the same author makes use of both images or intertwines them with each other (Eph 4:12, 16).

While *pinnâ* and γωνία unambiguously denote the corner, *rō'š* and → κεφαλή refer not only to the vertical ("head") but also to the horizontal. Note the use of *rō'š* as the place where a street begins in Ezek 16:25, 31 and elsewhere (LXX translates here with ἀρχή, in Isa 51:20 with ἄκρον) and κεφαλή for the piece of land at the perimeter in Pap. Petrie II, no. 38a, l. 21 (3d cent. B.C.) and Pap. Oxy. no. 273, l. 18 (A.D. 95). Κεφαλὴ γωνία thus refers to the *most distant corner* at the horizontal level.

A similar interpretation is associated with → ἄκρος. Ἀκρογωνιαῖος is a typical compound in the Koine intended as a strengthening of γωνιαῖος, "cornered" (this simple form is already classical; note Job 38:6, *'eḇen pinnâ*/λίθος γωνιαῖος, of a "cornerstone" of the foundation of the earth); the LXX hapax legomenon λίθος ἀκρογωνιαῖος in Isa 28:16 denotes the *cornerstone* in the foundation of a building (Symmachus uses ἀκρογωνιαῖος in Ps 117:22 LXX instead of κεφαλὴ γωνίας). The terms κεφαλὴ γωνίας and ἀκρογωνιαῖος both designate the *foundation stone at its farthest (foremost) corner,* with which a building is begun—it firmly fixes its site and determines its direction. As a (hewn) squared stone, it had a special quality; in contrast to modern building techniques, it was not sunk deeply into the ground and thus was visible.

b) In Ps 118:22f. (LXX 117:22f.) the participants in a festival praise with astonishment the acts of Yahweh toward the righteous, who, now that they are saved from contempt and the danger of death, may enter through the gates of righteousness, with the proverbial saying, "The stone which the [inspecting] builders rejected has become εἰς κεφαλὴν γωνίας." The focus is not the beginning of a building but rather the marvelous (θαυμαστή) change: once disqualified by other people, they are now recognized by God and honored. A messianic understanding in Jewish exegesis (Billerbeck I, 875f.) cannot be attested for the period before the NT. The NT uses this statement from the Psalms about the righteous five times with a christological meaning.

After Mark has already cited Ps 118:25 at Jesus' entry into Jerusalem (11:9), in 12:10f. he refers to vv. 22f. of this psalm as a scriptural proof of the parable of the evil vinegrowers, giving it a meaning beyond its context in the psalm. As is clear from the reference to Mark 8:31 (the key word is ἀποδοκιμάζω; only here and in 11:27 before the beginning of the actual Passion narrative are all three groups within the Sanhedrin explicitly enumerated as opponents of Jesus), not only Jesus' rejection (= crucifixion) is spoken of; there is also a reference to his resurrection through God's wonderful deed as a victory over the rejection. Thus new essential points are added in the witness of the Church.

In Matt 21:42 the citation from Psalms is more closely tied to the narrative of the parable through vv. 41 and 43. It is expanded through the addition of the twofold reference to the expected "fruits," supported by the explicit ὅταν οὖν ἔλθῃ ὁ κύριος in v. 40, the decisive event in pointing to the parousia, and by including the disciples in the judgment.

Luke, in 20:17, emphasizes the disastrous reverse side of the extraordinary phrase for the unbeliever by including the second verse of the citation and introducing v. 18 (from the background in Dan 2:34f., 44f.), a proverbial logion (Billerbeck I, 87; J. Jeremias, *TDNT* IV, 276), whose origin is unknown, concerning the effect of the cornerstone in judgment. Thus the second half of the verse has the sole function of expressing the inescapability of judgment (note λικμάω, "crush").

In Acts 4:11 the original usage of the word about the cornerstone appears, as in Mark 12:10f., within the interpretation of the crucifixion and resurrection of Jesus (referred to explicitly in Acts 4:10). The text follows a tradition other than the LXX (note ἐξουθενέω). On 1 Pet 2:7, → c.

c) Ἀκρογωνιαῖος in Eph 2:20 suggests the idea of a building, the spiritual building of the Church. This verse, in a clear reference to Isa 28:16 (ἀκρογωνιαῖος, θεμέλια), presents Christ Jesus as the *cornerstone,* who began this building and established its orientation. The clause ὄντος ἀκρογωνιαίου αὐτοῦ Χριστοῦ Ἰησοῦ expresses grammatically the special place of Christ in relation to the apostles and NT prophets, who belong to the foundation (→ θεμέλιος). The context demands for αὐτοῦ the exclusive or contrasting meaning "self," which refers either to the subject Χριστοῦ Ἰησοῦ (vs. the apostles and prophets) or better to the pred. nom. ἀκρογωνιαίου, *the cornerstone itself,* i.e., the essential, decisive part of the foundation (cf. 1 Cor 3:11, which contrasts the true foundation with all others).

Finally, 1 Pet 2:6f. connects ἀκρογωνιαῖος (Isa 28:16) and κεφαλὴ γωνίας (Ps 118:22) in a proof from Scripture that expresses explicitly the double effect of the work of Christ, the "living stone" (v. 4). As the ἀκρογωνιαῖος, which determines the structure of the Church, Christ provides salvation for believers, who are set into the building as "living stones" (v. 5). As κεφαλὴ γωνίας, Christ assumes a hostile stance against unbelievers, as in Luke 20:17f. In v. 8, with the additional quotation from Isa 8:14 (cf. Rom 9:33), the *cornerstone* becomes the *stone of stumbling.* The chapter thus stresses the full implications of the message of salvation.

H. Krämer

Δ δ

δαιμονίζομαι *daimonizomai* be possessed by a demon
→ δαιμόνιον 7.

δαιμόνιον, ου, τό *daimonion* demon*
δαίμων, ονος, ὁ *daimōn* demon*

1. Occurrences in the NT — 2. OT and Judaism — 3. The Synoptics and Acts — 4. The Pauline corpus — 5. The Johannine literature — 6. The Catholic Epistles — 7. Δαιμονίζομαι — 8. Δαιμονιώδης — 9. Summary

Lit.: D. E. AUNE, *ISBE* I, 919-23. — H. BIETENHARD, *DNTT* I, 449-54. — BILLERBECK IV, 501-35. — O. BÖCHER, *Dämonenfurcht und Dämonenabwehr* (BWANT 90, 1970). — *idem, Christus Exorcista* (BWANT 96, 1972). — M. DIBELIUS, *Die Geisterwelt im Glauben des Paulus* (1909). — O. EVERLING, *Die paulinische Angelologie und Dämonologie* (1888). — W. FOERSTER, *TDNT* II, 1-20. — J. MAIER, *RAC* IX, 579-85, 626-40, 668-88. — B. NOACK, *Satanás und Sotería. Untersuchungen zur neutestamentlichen Dämonologie* (1948). — B. REICKE, *The Disobedient Spirits and Christian Baptism* (ASNU 13, 1946). — H. RINGGREN, *RGG* II, 1301-3. — H. SCHLIER, *Mächte und Gewalten im NT* ([3]1963). — R. SCHNACKENBURG, *LTK* III, 141f. — E. SCHWEIZER, *RAC* IX, 688-700. — For further bibliography see *TWNT* X, 1034-36.

1. In the NT δαιμόνιον occurs a total of 63 times. Most of the references (53) are found in the Gospels: Matthew (11), Mark (13), Luke (23), and John (6). The remaining 10 passages are distributed among Acts (1), 1 Corinthians (4), 1 Timothy (1), James (1), and Revelation (3). In one instance δαίμων (Matt 8:31) stands in place of δαιμόνιον, which is the neut. form of the adj. δαιμόνιος, used as a subst. One may compare also the following synonyms, among others: πνεῦμα (esp. πνεῦμα ἀκάθαρτον, πνεῦμα πονηρόν) and ἄγγελος (τοῦ διαβόλου). Also to be noted are → ἀρχή, → δύναμις, and → ἐξουσία.

2. Whereas Israel originally attributed good and evil to Yahweh (cf. Isa 45:7; Amos 3:6) and saw in God's power to do harm messengers of both chastisment and temptation (cf. 1 Sam 16:14-23; 2 Sam 24:15f.; 1 Kgs 22:22; Job 2:1-7), the encounter with Iranian-Chaldean syncretism in the Babylonian exile led to a wide-ranging acceptance of the common dualism of ancient times by biblical and postbiblical Judaism. Angels appear as helpful spiritual powers (→ ἄγγελος), while demons are diabolical destroyers. God indeed remains the Creator and Lord also of Satan and of his demons (Job 1:6; 2:1; 1QM 13:10f.; cf. 1QS 3:25), but this increasingly loses significance in popular piety, where the pure sphere of God and his angels stands in opposition to the almost equal and impure sphere of the devil and his demons.

Demons injure and destroy (*1 Enoch* 15:11f.; *Jub.* 10:5); they are described as "unclean spirits" (*Jub.* 10:1; *T. Sim.* 4:9; *T. Benj.* 5:2; rabbinic texts in Billerbeck IV/1, 503f.). They endanger and defile individuals esp. in the realm of sexuality, so that apotropaic and cathartic countermeasures are commanded (cf. the early Lev 12:5; then, e.g., Tob 3:7f.; 8:1-3; *T. Reu.* 2:8f.; 3:3; 1QM 7:5). Illnesses of the body and the spirit (cf. Ps 91:5f.; then, e.g., *Vit. Proph.* 16:38-42 and *b. Roš Haš.* 28a and the texts in Billerbeck II, 529 and IV/1, 504f., 524-26, 532f.) and death in particular is their work (*Jub.* 10:1f.; 49:2; cf. Wis 1:14 and the texts in Billerbeck I, 144-49); contact with corpses and carcasses renders one "unclean" (cf. Lev 21:1-4; Num 6:6-12; 19:11-16; *m. Para* 8:4; Billerbeck I, 491f.). Thus impurity through contact with the dead is effected by demons in the same way as "possession" for those who are mentally ill (*Pesiq. Rab. Kah.* 40a; Billerbeck IV/1, 524), and purification is considered as exorcism (cf. Num. 19).

Healing of the sick and the possessed consists in the expulsion of the demons of sickness (cf. Josephus *B.J.* vii.185 and the texts in Billerbeck IV/1, 514-17, 524, 532-35). Angels are considered teachers of the art of healing (*Jub.* 10:10-13). God is considered the one who enabled Solomon to practice exorcism (Josephus *Ant.* viii.42, 45). The Gentiles are also unclean (cf. Deut 14:21; Ezek 4:13), for their gods are demons (Bar 4:7; *1 Enoch* 19:1; 99:7; *Jub.* 1:11; 11:4; *T. Jud.* 23:1f.; *T. Naph.* 3:3, and elsewhere), an impurity that is blotted out by proselyte baptism (cf. Billerbeck I, 102-12). Because the unclean spirits were localized in the elements, exorcism and a defense against them were accomplished magically and homeopathically with fire and smoke, liquid (water, blood, wine, oil, saliva), air, and many solid substances (earth, gems, ashes, salt, etc.) as well as with the powerful word of a physician and exorcist (see texts in Böcher, *Dämonenfurcht* 161-316).

From Gen 6:1-4, the earlier postbiblical Judaism concluded that demons had come into being through sexual intercourse between heavenly angels and the daughters of men or that they were identical with the angels who had been banished to earth by God (*1 Enoch* 6–11; 15:3-12; 18:13-16; 19:1f.; 86–88; *Jub.* 5:1-10; 10:5-11; *T. Reu.* 5:5-7; *T. Naph.* 3:5; Philo *Gig.* 6-18). Rabbinic Judaism traced demons to sexual relations between Adam and feminine spirits and to intercourse between Eve and masculine spirits (*Gen. Rab.* 20 [14a] with par.; *b. 'Erub.* 18b; Billerbeck IV/1, 505-7). Early Jewish eschatology expected the defeat of the devil and his demons in the end time (1QS 3:24f.; 4:20-22; 1QH 3:18; 1QM 1:10f.; 7:6; 12:7f.).

3. The great majority of NT occurrences of δαιμόνιον are in the reports of Jesus' miraculous healings in the Synoptic Gospels (Mark 1:23-28 par. Luke 4:33-37: healing of one who was possessed in the synagogue; Matt 8:16 par. Mark 1:32-34/Luke 4:40f.: healings in the evening; Mark 1:39: travel activity in Galilee; Matt 9:32-34 and Matt 12:22-24 par. Mark 3:22/Luke 11:14f.: the healing of a mute demoniac; Matt 12:25-30 par. Mark 3:23-27/ Luke 11:17-23: in league with the devil?; Matt 8:28-34 par. Mark 5:1-20/Luke 8:26-39: healing of the demoniac from Gadara/Gerasa; Matt 15:21-28 par. Mark 7:24-30: healing of the Syrophoenician woman's daughter; Matt 17:14-21 par. Mark 9:14-29/Luke 9:37-43a: healing of a boy who is possessed). Comparison within a text (Mark 7:25, 30; Luke 10:17, 20, etc.) and among the Synoptics (Mark 1:23, 26 par. Luke 4:33, 35; Matt 8:28, 31 par. Mark 5:2/Luke 8:27; Mark 5:8f. par. Luke 8:29f.; Matt 10:1 par. Mark 6:7/Luke 9:1; Mark 9:20 par. Luke 9:42) indicates that δαιμόνιον is used for πνεῦμα and most often for πνεῦμα ἀκάθαρτον (esp. so by Luke).

It is not to be disputed that Jesus was active as a traveling physician and exorcist. Like his contemporaries, he traced illnesses of the body and of the mind to demons (cf. Matt 12:43-45 par. Luke 11:24-26; δαιμόνιον that was dumb: Luke 11:14; πνεῦμα of muteness: Mark 9:17, 25; πνεῦμα ἀσθενείας: Luke 13:11; cf. Luke 8:2). Healing consisted in expulsion (ἐκβάλλειν) of the δαιμόνιον (Matt 9:33; Mark 7:26; Luke 11:14) or of δαιμόνια (Matt 7:22; 9:34; 10:8; 12:24, 27f.; Mark 1:34, 39; 3:15, 22; 6:13; 9:38; 16:9, 17; Luke 9:49; 11:15, 18-20; 13:32).

Jesus healed bodily infirmities such as blindness (Luke 7:21; Matt 12:22-24; Mark 10:46-52 par.), dumbness (Mark 9:14-29 par.; Matt 9:32f. par. Luke 11:14), lameness (Mark 2:1-12 par.; Luke 13:10-17), leprosy (Mark 1:40-45 par. Luke 17:11-19), and fever (Mark 1:29-31 par.), and even sicknesses of the mind and brain (Mark 1:23-28 par. Luke 4:33-37; Mark 5:1-20 par.; 7:24-30 par.; 9:14-29 par.) with the methods employed by ancient exorcists (cf. Matt 12:27 par. Luke 11:19). The exorcism of demons and the healing of sickness were identical for those of Jesus' day (Mark 1:32-34 par. Luke 6:18f.). Despite offering initial resistance (Mark 1:24 par. Luke 4:34; Mark 5:7 par.; 9:20, 26 par. Luke 9:42), the demons must yield to the stronger one.

In his answer to the Baptist (Matt 11:4-6 par. Luke 7:22f.), Jesus interprets his healings as the fulfillment of prophecy (cf. Isa 29:18f.; 35:5f.; 61:1). The hopes of ancient Judaism are being realized in Jesus' victory over the demons (Mark 3:27 par.; cf. Luke 13:32). If Jesus casts out demons by the Spirit of God (Matt 12:28a) or by the finger of God (Luke 11:20a), then God's βασιλεία has arrived (Matt 12:28b par. Luke 11:20b). Thus he guards himself emphatically against the charge that he casts out demons with the help of the prince of demons Βεελζεβούλ (Mark 3:22 par.). Anyone who so misunderstands the Spirit of Jesus commits the unforgivable sin against the Holy Spirit (Mark 3:28-30 par.).

On the other hand, Jesus recognizes the legitimacy of Jewish exorcists (Matt 12:27 par. Luke 11:19). He is even tolerant when strangers cast out demons "in the name of Jesus" (Mark 9:38-40 par. Luke 9:49f.; cf., however, Matt 7:22). Early Christianity can trace its healing exorcisms to the capacity to exorcise demons that has been mediated by Jesus (Matt 10:1 par. Mark 3:15/Mark 6:7/Luke 9:1; Matt 10:8 par. Luke 9:2; Mark 6:13; Luke 10:17, 20; cf. Mark 16:17). In contrast to Jesus, his disciples must reckon with the failure of their exorcisms (Matt 17:16 par. Mark 9:18/Luke 9:40); their lack of authority is due to their little faith (Matt 17:20) and deficiency in prayer (Mark 9:29).

The demonology assumed by Jesus and the Synoptics is clearly that of ancient Judaism. The demonological summary in Matt 12:43-45 par. Luke 11:24-26 (Q) may originate with Jesus: in order to heal the sick, the exorcist expels the "unclean spirit," who seeks a new dwelling place in a desolate place—in the ruins or in the desert. At the next best opportunity the demon returns with seven other evil spirits and possesses the person who has refused apotropaic protective measures (lustrations, asceticism). One says of a man who is possessed that he "has" a δαιμόνιον (Luke 4:33; Matt 11:18 par. Luke 7:33, of the Baptist; cf., of Jesus, John 7:20; 8:48f., 52; 10:20) or δαιμόνια (Luke 8:27). The demons enter their victims (εἰσέρχεσθαι, Luke 8:30; Mark 5:12f. par. Luke 8:32f.) and again leave them (ἐξέρχεσθαι), obeying the powerful word of the exorcist (Mark 1:26 par. Luke 4:35; Luke 4:41; 8:2; Matt 8:32 par. Mark 5:13/Luke 8:33; Luke 8:35, 38; Mark 7:29f.; Matt 17:18; Luke 11:14).

Demons are thought of in thoroughly personal terms: they know secrets such as the identity of Jesus; they know their fate, give an account of themselves, and can be brought to silence (Mark 1:24, 34 par. Luke 4:34, 41; Mark 3:11; 5:7 par.; cf. Jas 2:19). The outcry of the demoniac is viewed as the outcry of the demons (cf. Mark 1:23 par. Luke 4:33; Mark 3:11; 5:5; 5:7 par.; Mark 9:26 par. Luke 9:39; Luke 4:41). The movements, convulsions, jerks, etc. of the sick are traced back to the conscious activity of the demons (Mark 1:26 par. Luke 4:35; Luke 8:29; Mark 9:18, 20 par. Luke 9:39, 42).

Demons can unite into an "evil seven" (Luke 8:2; Matt 12:45 par. Luke 11:26; Mark 16:9). In greater numbers (Mark 5:9, πολλοί; Luke 8:30, δαιμόνια πολλά) they appear as "Legion"—in military fashion (Mark 5:9 par. Luke 8:30; Mark 5:15), just as → Βεελζεβούλ is viewed as prince and commander of the army of demons (Matt 12:24 par. Mark 3:22/Luke 11:15; cf. Matt 9:34), as potentate of the βασιλεία of Satan (Matt 12:26 par. Luke 11:18). The ancient Jewish demonology of the fall of the angels and falling stars (according to Gen 6:1-4; → 2) is reflected in Luke 10:18; the popular theme of the duping of demons is found in Matt 8:30-32 par. Mark 5:11-13/Luke 8:32f.

A common motif in the Synoptic Gospels is the confession of the eschatological victory of Jesus Christ over the world of the demons. Matthew expresses this theme most clearly: the eternal fire is the destiny of the → διάβολος and his angels (Matt 25:41; cf. Rev 19:20; 20:10, 14; → γέεννα). All powers in heaven and on earth are subjected to the resurrected one (Matt 28:18). While Matthew suppresses the pericope of the strange exorcists (cf. Mark 9:38-41 par. Luke 9:49f.), he places exorcists, insofar as they have not done the will of God, among the damned (Matt 7:21-23).

Matthew tends to separate Jesus from the category of the usual exorcists. He expunges demonic pericopes (Mark 1:23-28 par.; 9:38-41 par.) and demonic statements (Matt 8:16, 29; 9:2; 17:18). He removes demons from entire healing stories (Matt 8:28-34; 15:29-31; 17:14-21) and transforms exorcism stories into general accounts of healing (Matt 4:23b; 8:16; 12:15, 22; 15:22, 25, 28, 29-31). Jesus still appears as one who banishes demons, but he exorcises no longer with the finger of God (Luke 11:20; cf. Exod 8:15) but rather by the Spirit of God (Matt 12:28). He heals no longer with oil or spittle, but λόγῳ—with the word (Matt 8:16; cf. Mark 1:34b par. Luke 4:41a). In the post-Easter christology the battle between the historical Jesus and the individual demons of sickness was seen as the victory of the exalted one over demons in general. Thus both the fear of demons and the interest in magic against demons lose their significance.

Acts uses the term δαιμόνιον only once: Paul, to his Athenian audience, appeared as a καταγγελεύς of strange δαιμόνια (17:18). Here δαιμόνιον, apparently without a negative connotation (cf., however, 1 Cor 10:20f.), refers to the (pagan) deity (cf., with respect to Socrates, Plato *Ap.* 24b; Xenophon *Mem.* i.1.1); when Paul calls the Athenians δεισιδαιμονέστεροι, he praises their religiosity (Acts 17:22; cf. Acts 25:19, δεισιδαιμονία = religion).

Unlike the Gospels, Acts calls the destructive spirits πνεύματα—either πνεύματα ἀκάθαρτα or πνεύματα πονηρά. Healing of the sick and casting out of demons belong together throughout (Acts 5:16; 8:7; 19:12). The slave girl in Philippi has a πνεῦμα πύθων (16:16), which identifies Paul and his companions (vv. 17f.; cf. Mark 1:24, 34 par. Luke 4:34, 41) with an outcry (cf. Acts 8:7) and is cast out by Paul "in the name of Jesus Christ" (16:18). Elsewhere Jesus' disciples heal and exorcise successfully in the name of Jesus (3:6, 16; 4:7, 10, 30), while such success is denied to the seven sons of Sceva (19:13-17). A demon in the service of God is the ἄγγελος κυρίου, who punishes Herod by causing him to be eaten by worms until he dies.

4. Paul himself uses the word δαιμόνιον in only one passage, and here he uses it four times: 1 Cor 10:20f. Not only Gentiles who sacrifice to the δαιμόνια (i.e., to their gods; cf. Deut 32:17; 1 Cor 10:20) but also Christians who participate in pagan cult meals transfer themselves into the sphere of the δαιμόνια (i.e., the gods of the Gentiles; 1 Cor 10:21). The Pauline churches interpret false teachers as manifesting eschatologically the power of the spirits of seduction and of demons (1 Tim 4:1).

Demons of Jewish popular piety are the ἄγγελοι, against whose lust (cf. Gen 6:2) Paul has the women veil their heads with an ἐξουσία (1 Cor 11:10). An ἄγγελος of Satan torments Paul with sickness (2 Cor 12:7); Satan himself will destroy the one who is living in incest (1 Cor 5:5; cf. 1 Tim 1:20). Although the demons continue to do their work of temptation (Eph 2:2) and must still be fought by Christians (Eph 6:12), the fear of demons gives way to trust in God's love in Christ Jesus (Rom 8:38f.). Love is the way that leads beyond healing exorcisms and speaking in tongues (1 Cor 12:30–14:1). Already God has taken away the power of demons and placed them under the Son (1 Cor 15:24-28; Phil 2:9f.; Col 2:10, 15; cf. Eph 1:20-22; 4:8-10; Heb 2:8, 14) through the death, resurrection, and exaltation of Jesus Christ. Baptism grants participation in the lordship of Jesus over the demons (Col 2:10-15; cf. Rom 6:3-11); Christians will one day sit in judgment (1 Cor 6:3) over the "angels," i.e., the demons.

5. In the Gospel of John the Jews continually charge Jesus with having a δαιμόνιον, i.e., with being possessed (John 7:20; 8:48, 52; 10:20); 10:20 explains δαιμόνιον ἔχειν with μαίνεσθαι, "to be insane." Jesus rejects the charge (8:49). Some in his audience do not allow him to be considered a δαιμονιζόμενος because a δαιμόνιον cannot open the eyes of the blind (10:21). Although the Jewish polemic sounds like hackneyed invective in 7:20, the Evangelist wants to make it clear that the Jews reject Jesus as a false teacher; the πνεῦμα of Jesus is suspected of being of diabolical origin (cf. Mark 3:22-30 par.; 1 John 4:1-3).

According to 1 John the followers of Jesus are threatened by demonic powers, whose work is false teaching, particularly in the area of christology (1 John 4:1-3). The Spirit of truth stands in opposition to the spirit of error (v. 6) and of antichrist (v. 3). Thus it is necessary to test carefully the πνεύματα (v. 1). Like the worship of idols, false teaching from demons endangers the purity of the Church (5:21; cf. 1QS 4:5).

The Book of Revelation designates pagan gods as δαιμόνια (9:20), just as Zeus is equated with Satan (2:13). From the mouths of the diabolical trinity (chs. 12f.; 16:13; 20:10)—Satan, the Antichrist, and the provincial Roman imperial cult propaganda—three unclean spirits spring forth in the form of a frog (16:13). They are πνεύματα δαιμονίων, whom the kings of the earth have enticed into the eschatological war (v. 14; cf. *1 Enoch* 56:5f.). After the defeat and annihilation of "Babylon" (= Rome), δαιμόνια and unclean spirits will inhabit sites (18:2). Jewish popular piety is connected with the hopes of anti-Roman Christian apocalyptic literature.

Countless statements of Revelation are intelligible within the framework of Jewish demonology. The fall of angels and stars (cf. Gen 6:1-4; *1 Enoch; Jubilees;* → 2) bring the demons to earth (Rev 8:10; 9:1; 12:4, 9). The dragon, according to 12:9, is identical with the serpent, the devil, and Satan; along with his angels, he is the adversary to Michael and his angels (vv. 7-9). The ἄβυσσος is the place of punishment for the imprisoned demons (9:1; 20:1), whose prince is Abaddon/Apollyon (9:11). Demonic forces are, among others, the apocalyptic riders (6:1-8)—who apparently refer to war, revolution, hunger, and pestilence—and the locusts who are equipped for war (9:1-11). Along with the devil, the demons one day will have their end in eternal fire (19:20; 20:10, 14; → γέεννα).

6. Like Revelation, the Catholic Epistles reflect the ancient Jewish mythological theme (according to Gen 6:1-4) of the fall and imprisonment of the disobedient angels (1 Pet 3:19; 2 Pet 2:4; Jude 6). The δαιμόνια always know God and tremble before him (Jas 2:19); through the resurrection and ascension of Jesus Christ, the good and the evil spiritual powers are now brought into submission (1 Pet 3:21f.; cf. Eph 1:20f.).

7. **Δαιμονίζομαι** *be possessed by a demon** occurs 13 times in the NT, exclusively in the Gospels (7 times in Matthew, 4 times in Mark, and once each in Luke and John). It designates a condition of sickness that is explained by a demon dwelling in the person ("possession"). According to John 10:21f., δαιμονίζεσθαι is identical to δαιμόνιον ἔχειν (said of Jesus). In Matt 15:22 κακῶς δαιμονίζεται is to be translated "she is being *tormented by a demon.*" Elsewhere only the pres. partc. δαιμονιζόμενος (Matt 4:24; 8:16, 28, 33; 9:32; 12:22; Mark 1:32; 5:15f.; John 10:21) or the aor. partc. δαιμονισθείς (Mark 5:18; Luke 8:36) occurs with the meaning *be possessed.* On the attribution of illnesses of body and of mind to demons → 3.

8. **Δαιμονιώδης** *demonic** is attested only in Jas 3:15. There the "wisdom" (σοφία) of those addressed, apparently a gnosticizing heresy, is attributed to a demonic origin. False teaching is considered the work of the devil (cf. 1 Tim 4:1; 1 Pet 5:8; 1 John 4:1-6, etc.).

9. With respect to their views of demons, all strata of the NT are in agreement in adopting the structures of ancient Jewish demonology. God and his angels stand in opposition to a great host of demons, who are organized militarily under the devil (→ διάβολος). Among them are numbered both the causes of sickness (Synoptics, Acts, Paul) and the pagan gods (Paul, Revelation) or the spirits who dwell in ruins (Revelation). Demons originated from the fall of heavenly beings, in accordance with Gen 6:1-4 (Luke, Paul, Revelation, Catholic Epistles). False teaching is considered the work of demonic powers and as a sign of the end time (1 Timothy, 1 John; cf. Jas 3:15).

Jesus, however, who already in his lifetime conquered the demons as successful exorcist and passed this capability on to his disciples (Synoptics, Acts), became lord over the devil and demonic powers through his own death, resurrection, and exaltation (Synoptics, esp. Matthew; also Paul, Revelation, and the Catholic Epistles). Indeed, where now the devil, death, and the other demons are allowed to rage, they have already lost their power (Paul) and are condemned to a fiery end (Matthew, Revelation). Baptism grants the Christian a participation in Jesus' victory over the demons (Paul). The impact of the demons is overcome where regulations of purity are adopted (Mark 7:1-23 par.; Acts 10:15; Rom 14:14, 20; 1 Tim 4:4; Titus 1:15; Heb 9:13f.), and sicknesses are no longer traced back to demonic activity (John 9:1-3; Gal 4:13f.). Paul (1 Cor 12:30–14:1) and Matthew (Matt 7:22f.) place love and obedience above success in exorcism.

O. Böcher

δαιμονιώδης, 2 *daimoniōdēs* demonic
→ δαιμόνιον 8.

δαίμων, ονος, ὁ *daimōn* demon
→ δαιμόνιον.

δάκνω *daknō* bite (vb.)*

Gal 5:15: "But if you *bite* and devour (κατεσθίετε) one another. . . ."

δάκρυον, ου, τό *dakryon* tear*

Of the tears of the sinful woman (Luke 7:38, 44); μετὰ δακρύων, "amid *tears*" (Acts 20:19, 31; Heb 5:7; 12:17; Mark 9:24 v.l.) cf. διὰ πολλῶν δακρύων (2 Cor 2:4); "I remember your *tears*" (2 Tim 1:4); God will "wipe away every *tear* from their eyes" (Rev 7:17; 21:4; cf. Isa 25:8).

δακρύω *dakryō* cry, weep*

John 11:35: of Jesus, who *broke out in tears* (ἐδάκρυσεν) after the death of Lazarus.

δακτύλιος, ου, ὁ *daktylios* ring; signet ring*

Luke 15:22: "put a *ring* on his hand" (of the returned prodigal). This NT hapax legomenon appears in the LXX and in *1 Clem.* 43:2.

δάκτυλος, ου, ὁ *daktylos* finger*

1. Occurrences in the NT — 2. Usage — 3. "The finger of God" in Luke 11:20

Lit.: K. Gross, *RAC* VII, 909-46. — I. Löw, "Die Finger in Litteratur und Folklore der Juden," Gedankenbuch D. Kaufmann (ed. M. Brann and F. Rosenthal; 1900) 61-85. — H. Schlier, *TDNT* II, 20f. — For further bibliography see *TWNT* X, 1036.

1. The subst. appears in the NT only in the Gospels, a total of 8 times: Matt 23:4b par. Luke 11:46c; Mark 7:33; Luke 11:20; 16:24; John 8:6 (Koine D, etc.); 20:25, 27. → Δακτύλιος, "ring," is derived from δάκτυλος (Luke 15:22).

2. As he speaks against the scribes and Pharisees (Matt 23:1-36) Jesus says, "They bind heavy burdens . . . and lay them on men's shoulders; but they themselves will not move them *with their finger* (τῷ δακτύλῳ αὐτῶν)" (v. 4). The parallel in Luke 11:46 makes the same charge in the "woe" on the teachers of the law: "You load men with burdens hard to bear, and you yourselves do not touch the burdens *with one of your fingers* (ἑνὶ τῶν δακτύλων ὑμῶν)." The Lukan form of the woe is probably original (except for the ἑνί phrase; Schulz, *Q* 106f.). For Matthew the saying was suitable for offering an example (from another context) of the statement in 23:3. Consequently v. 4 establishes to what extent Jesus demands that one observe the teaching of the experts in the law without following their deeds. The Lukan woe charges the teachers of the law with not moving the scarcely bearable (cf. Acts 15:10) legal burdens that they want to bind on others.

Mark 7:33 reports that Jesus put his *fingers* into the ears of the man who was deaf and had a speech impediment. Thus the sign accompanying his action shows what the command → εφφαθα (v. 34) effects with reference to hearing (v. 35, ἠνοίγησαν αὐτοῦ αἱ ἀκοαί). In Luke 16:24 the rich man in Hades calls in his misery to Abraham, asking that Lazarus be sent "to dip the end of his *finger* (τὸ ἄκρον τοῦ δακτύλου) in water and cool my tongue."

In John 20:25 Thomas lays down a condition: "Unless I . . . place my *finger* in the mark of the nails . . . , I will not believe." After eight days, the resurrected Jesus grants this possibility: "Put your *finger* here . . ." (v. 27). John 8:6b says that Jesus "wrote with his *finger* on the ground," a gesture that could be understood as one of embarrassment in the narrower context (8:3-5 [6a], 7a). Inasmuch as the information from v. 6b is repeated in v. 8 (after the answer of Jesus in v. 7a), another and more important meaning must be intended. Among the previous interpretations (cf. R. Schnackenburg, *The Gospel according to St. John* II [1979] 165f.), the older view, in dependence on Jer 17:13 LXX, has the greater probability: Jesus points out to the questioner "the judgment of God, before which all men are sinners. God must write them all in the dust" (*ibid.*).

3. According to Luke 11:20 Jesus says in his defense speech (vv. 17-23), "But if it is by the *finger* of God (ἐν δακτύλῳ θεοῦ) that I cast out demons, then the kingdom of God has come (→ φθάνω) upon you." The logion is derived from Q, as the parallel in Matt 12:28 indicates; there the parallel phrase is ἐν πνεύματι θεοῦ. The latter phrase is secondary and probably comes from Matthew (see Hahn, *Titles* 292; cf. also R. G. Hamerton-Kelly, "A Note on Matthew XII.28 Par. Luke XI.20," *NTS* 11 [1964/65] 167-69, who considers πνεύματι original; T. Lorenzmeier, "Zum Logion Mt 12, 28; Lk 11, 20," FS Braun, 289-304; E. Grässer, "Zum Verständnis der Gottesherrschaft," *ZNW* 65 [1974] 3-26; G. Schneider, *Lukas* [ÖTK] II, ad loc.). By itself the logion says that Jesus' expulsion of demons marks the arrival of the kingdom of God (→ βασιλεία 3). In the context of the statement it is said that there is only one explanation for Jesus' exorcisms: the power of God (cf. "finger of God" in Exod 8:15 LXX; Ps 8:4 LXX), by which Jesus acts and through which the power of the "counter kingdom" begins to collapse.

G. Schneider

Δαλμανουθά *Dalmanoutha* Dalmanutha*

Place name of a (supposed) locale by the Lake of Gennesaret (Mark 8:10). Both the derivation of the name and the location are uncertain. Dalman, *Worte* 52f.; M.-J. Lagrange, *Marc* (ÉBib) 204f.; R. Pesch, *Markus* (HTKNT) I, 406f.

Δαλματία, ας *Dalmatia* Dalmatia*

Name of a Roman province, the southern part of Illyria, which was divided after the Dalmatian-Pannonian rebellion in 9-6 B.C. Dalmatia encompassed the coastland on the east shore of the Adriatic Sea. According to 2 Tim 4:10, Titus traveled to Dalmatia. B. Saria, PWSup VIII, 21-59; *idem, LAW* 686.

δαμάζω *damazō* subdue*

Mark 5:4, of the demoniac, "No one had the strength to *subdue* him"; Jas 3:7 (bis), of *subduing* or *taming* animals; v. 8 adds, using δαμάζω fig., "But no human being can *tame* the tongue."

δάμαλις, εως, ἡ *damalis* heifer, young cow*

Heb 9:13: "the ashes of a *heifer* used for sprinkling" (cf. Num. 19; Josephus *Ant.* iv.80; *Barn.* 8:1).

Δάμαρις, ιδος *Damaris* Damaris*

A woman in Athens who, according to Acts 17:34, joined Paul. With Dionysius, she became a believer.

Δαμασκηνός, 3 (ὁ) *Damaskēnos* from Damascus, (the) Damascene*

In the NT only in 2 Cor 11:32, used as subst.: "the city of *the Damascenes.*"

Δαμασκός, οῦ *Damaskos* Damascus*

A very old (at least 4 millennia B.C.) and important city in the fertile plain southeast of the Anti-Lebanon Range on the great caravan roads. After conquest by the Romans (64 B.C.) and incorporation into the association of the Decapolis, Damascus was temporarily in the possession of the Nabataean king Aretas IV (→ Ἀρέτας). A large percentage of Damascus was Jewish (Josephus *B.J.* ii.561; vii.368). Damascus is mentioned in the NT only in connection with Paul and his call (Gal 1:17; 2 Cor 11:32; Acts 9:2f., 8, 10, 19, 22, 27; 22:5f., 10f.; 26:12, 20).

On the history of the city, cf. *BL* 304f.; K. Galling, *BRL* 54f.; *idem, RGG* II, 22-24. On Acts 9, see W. Prentice, "St. Paul's Journey to Damascus," *ZNW* 46 (1955) 250-55; G. Lohfink, *Paulus vor Damaskus* (SBS 4, 1965); D. Gill, "The Structure of Acts 9," *Bib* 55 (1974) 546-48; O. H. Steck, "Formgeschichtliche Bemerkungen zur Darstellung des Damaskusgeschehens in der Apostelgeschichte," *ZNW* 67 (1976) 20-28. S. Sabugal, *Análisis exegético sobre la conversión de San Pablo* (1976), associates the conversion of Paul with Qumran; see critical comments in C. Bernas, *CBQ* 39 (1977) 157f.; W. Wiefel, TLZ 103 (1978) 185-88.

G. Schneider

δανείζω *daneizō* act.: lend; mid.: borrow

Alternative form of → δανίζω. BDF §23.

δάνειον, ου, τό *daneion* loan (noun)
→ δανίζω.

δανειστής, οῦ, ὁ *daneistēs* moneylender, creditor
→ δανίζω.

δανίζω *danizō* act.: lend; mid.: borrow*
δάνειον, ου, τό *daneion* loan (noun)*
δανειστής, οῦ, ὁ *daneistēs* moneylender, creditor*

1. Occurrences in the NT — 2. Matt 5:42; Luke 6:34f. — 3. Matt 18:27; Luke 7:41.

Lit.: L. Mitteis, *Reichsrecht und Volksrecht in den östlichen Provinzen des römischen Kaiserreichs* (1891) 459ff. — L. Schottroff, "Gewaltverzicht und Feindesliebe in der urchristlichen Jesustradition," FS Conzelmann 197-221. — T. Thalheim, PW IV/2, 2100-2101. — W. C. van Unnik, "Die Motivierung der Feindesliebe in Lk VI 32-35," *NovT* 8 (1966) 284-300.

1. These three words are technical terms of ancient commerce having to do with lending gold or natural objects (cf. Preisigke, *Wörterbuch* s.v.). They appear only in Matthew (5:42; 18:27) and Luke (6:34, 35 [3 times]; 7:41).

2. The widespread view that δανίζω in Matt 5:42 is original and is modified by Luke in 6:30 (who then reuses it in vv. 34f. in dependence on Matt 5:42) may be disputed. The appearance of this word in the same context but in different passages suggests that δανίζω stood in the Q original in some form. Here the concern is not with the somewhat dubious business of moneylending with interest but rather with lending as a conduct that expects the same or more than an equivalent return (cf. Aristotle *EN* 1162b; on the problem of repayment and partial cancellation cf. van Unnik 293ff.; Schottroff 204ff.). As in Sir 29:1f., one should lend, but now it is radicalized. In Matthew the borrowing is one of shameless demand; in Luke lending is explicitly lending without hope of a return. Thus lending becomes giving. This "giving" form of a loan is a type of behavior that, along with love of enemies, distinguishes disciples from sinners (Luke 6:34f.).

3. In Matt 18:27 (δάνειον) and Luke 7:41 (δανειστής) direct reference is made to ancient lending practice. The parable of the unfaithful servant reflects the cruel ancient practice of using the person as security. (Since the time of Solon this practice had been officially abolished, but it was still common in Jesus' day.) The interest rates were unbearably high (cf. Mitteis, Thalheim). Against this background the cancellation of the loan was a particularly impressive means of describing divine grace and forgiveness.

G. Petzke

Δανιήλ *Daniēl* Daniel*

The name of a "prophet" to whom the Book of Daniel is attributed. In Matt 24:15 (par. Mark 13:14 Koine A Δ Θ) the phrase "of whom the prophet *Daniel* spoke" is redactionally inserted on the basis of the reference to the "abomination of desolation" (cf. Dan 9:27; 11:31; 12:11 LXX). Outside the NT Daniel is mentioned in early Christian literature in *1 Clem.* 45:6; *2 Clem.* 6:8; *Barn.* 4:5.

δάνιον, ου, τό *danion* loan (noun)

Alternative form of → δάνειον. BDF §23.

δανιστής, οῦ, ὁ *danistēs* moneylender, creditor

Alternative form of → δανειστής. BDF §23.

δαπανάω *dapanaō* spend*

This vb. takes the acc. obj. in Mark 5:26 ("all that she had") and Luke 15:14 ("everything") and has no obj. in

Acts 21:24; 2 Cor 12:15; Jas 4:3. The fig. sense "exhaust" does not appear in the NT (but see *Herm. Man.* xii.1.2; *Barn.* 14:5).

δαπάνη, ης, ἡ *dapanē* expense, cost*

Luke 14:28: "count the *cost*"; cf. *Herm. Sim.* v.3.7.

Δαυίδ *Dauid* David

1. Occurrences in the NT — 2. Historical significance of David — 3. David in Jewish theology — 4. David in the NT

Lit.: J. Daniélou, *RAC* III, 594-603. — S. Herrmann, *Geschichte Israels in alttestamentlicher Zeit* (1973) 185-217. — E. Lohse, *TDNT* VIII, 478-88. J. A. Motyer, *DNTT* I, 425-28. — For further bibliography → υἱός.

1. In the NT David is mentioned a total of 59 times, esp. in the Synoptic Gospels and in Acts, with 17 references in Matthew, 7 in Mark, 13 in Luke, and 11 in Acts. The name appears also in John (2 times), Romans (3), 2 Timothy (1), Hebrews (2), and Revelation (3).

2. David, as the youngest of eight sons born to Jesse in Bethlehem, was primarily a regular soldier in the army of Saul, then leader of an insurgent company and a Philistine vassal. After the death of Saul the Judeans anointed him king, as did the northern tribes at a later time, so that he united the two kingdoms in a personal union. He had his soldiers conquer the Jebusite city of Jerusalem, which he made the center for all of Israel. Through conquests and shrewd diplomacy he gained control from the Euphrates to the "stream of Egypt." This widespread empire was ethnically and religiously heterogeneous, leading to several rebellions even in David's own time. After Solomon's death it collapsed. The theological legitimation of the kingdom of David was given in an oracle by the prophet Nathan (2 Sam 7), by which the dynasty of David was promised an "eternal duration" (vv. 13, 16). Until the Exile, Davidites ruled over the southern kingdom.

3. If the figure of David, with both its bright and its seamy sides, is treated in 1–2 Samuel from narratives originating from contemporary traditions that are still recognizable, the Deuteronomic historical work represents David as the ideal king. All successors are to be measured by his piety and obedience toward Yahweh (1 Kgs 3:3; 9:4; 11:4, 6, 33, 38, etc.). This characterization is strengthened in the work of the Chronicler, which not only omits David's negative elements but also leaves out the major portion of his political and military activities. David appears here primarily as the essential initiator of the building of the temple (1 Chr 22–29) and of the guild of temple singers (16:1-42). Already in 1 Samuel we meet David the composer of songs (chs. 1, 3, 22f.); later, 73 psalms are attributed to him. In the apocryphal Psalms of 11QPs[a] 27:2 (DJD IV) it is claimed that David wrote 4,050 psalms; in 11QPs[a] 151 David is made to appear like the Greek singer Orpheus. During the time of Israel's humiliation, the divine promise to David is remembered, and a David redivivus (Isa 11:1-5; Mic 5:2-4; Hos 3:5; Jer 30:9; Ezek 34:23f.; 37:24f.; on the discussion of authenticity, cf. the commentaries) is proclaimed, or the rebuilding of the fallen booth of David is promised (Amos 9:11).

Apocalyptic literature is silent about David. The rabbis describe him as learned in the Torah (Lohse 479). His failings are at times criticized, at times excused. As composer of psalms he was inspired by the Spirit of God (Billerbeck II, 132; IV/1, 445). On the authority of Ps 16:9f. he is occasionally reckoned among the men of God who were not subject to decay (J. Jeremias, *Heiligengräber in Jesu Umwelt* [1958] 129); many texts speak of his return (Billerbeck II, 335-39). More widespread, however, was the expectation of a "son of David" (→ υἱός).

4. David plays no outstanding role in the NT. He is considered an exemplary pious man who found grace before God (Luke 1:69; Acts 4:25; 7:46; 13:22; Heb 11:32). Bethlehem, his place of birth, is referred to as "the city of David" (Luke 2:4, 11; cf. John 7:42). As ancestor of Jesus Christ, David appears in the genealogies (Matt 1:1, 6; Luke 3:31). Matthew alludes to the adultery of David when he identifies Bathsheba as "the wife of Uriah." For Matthew this identification may be more important in showing Bathsheba to be a Gentile, like the other three women in the genealogy. Thus Jesus is the Messiah not only of the Jews but also of the Gentiles (cf. H. Stegemann, "'Die des Uriah.' Zur Bedeutung der Frauennamen in der Genealogie von Mt 1, 1-17," FS Kuhn 246-76).

David is also identified as the author of the Psalms (Rom 4:6; 11:9; Heb 4:7; 11:32) in passages that emphasize their inspiration by the Spirit of God (Mark 12:36/Matt 22:43; Acts 1:16; 4:25). In Acts the Psalms are interpreted as prophecies of Jesus Christ. Inasmuch as David himself did not ascend to heaven, Ps 110:1 refers to Jesus (Acts 2:34); inasmuch as David died and his grave is known to the people of Jerusalem (cf. Jeremias 56-60), Ps 16:10 must be understood as declaring the resurrection of Jesus (Acts 2:27-31; cf. 13:36f.). In addition, Amos 9:11 LXX is newly interpreted in a christological sense. No longer is the national kingdom of David anticipated, but rather "the goal of the saving activity of God for Israel is the new humanity as people of God" (H. W. Wolff, *Dodekapropheton* [BKAT] II, 409).

In the conflict story of Mark 2:23-28 par. the episode of 1 Sam 21:1-10 (the priest Ahimelech from Nob gives David and his people the showbread, although only priests were allowed to eat it) is referred to in defense of the disciples' plucking ears of grain on the sabbath. While rabbinic exegesis believed it necessary to excuse this incident (Billerbeck I, 618), the early Church (not Jesus himself) assumes that David's behavior was justified. In the background stands typological thinking: if David as a type of the Messiah could abolish the cultic law, then certainly the eschatological Son of Man could also (cf. L. Goppelt, *Typos: The Typological Interpretation of the Old Testament in the New* [1982] 82-90).

H. Merkel

δέ *de* but, rather; and, in fact

1. Occurrences in the NT — 2. Adversative δέ — 3. Copulative δέ

Lit.: BAGD s.v. —BDF, esp. §§250f.; 447; also §§442; 443.1; 459.4; 462.1. — J. BURCKHARDT, *Griechische Kulturgeschichte* (1898-1902, repr. 1977) IV, 59-159, esp. 84ff. — KÜHNER, *Grammatik* index s.v. — MAYSER, *Grammatik* II/3, 125-33. — MORGENTHALER, *Statistik* 165ff., 181ff. — MOULTON, *Grammar* III, 331f. — P. TACHAU, *"Einst" und "Jetzt" im NT* (FRLANT 105, 1972) 10f., 87. — *VKGNT* I/3-4 (1977) s.v.; II (1978).

1. The particle δέ is the fourth most frequent word in the NT. As a coordinating conjunction, it is second in frequency behind καί and ahead of ὅτι and γάρ (similarly, Mayser II/3, 125, on the language of the papyri). Δέ never stands in the first position in the sentence. In relation to the statistical count in individual NT writings (cf. Morgenthaler 166-69), δέ is most strongly represented in Galatians (4.3% of all words), 2 Corinthians (3.6%), and 1 Corinthians (3.1%) and least represented in Revelation (0.1%) and in 1–3 John and Colossians (each 0.5%). Among the Gospels, it is least represented in John (1.4%).

According to the tabulation in *VKGNT* I, 199-224, adversative use of δέ without a preceding μέν is more than twice as frequent (18.5%) as that with μέν (8.1%). The μέν-δέ construction is, compared with the total number of occurrences of δέ in the individual writings, most frequent in Jude (41.7%), Hebrews (23.9%), and 1 Peter (20.7%, all based on *VKGNT* II, 66f.). It is not represented at all in Colossians, 1–2 Thessalonians, 1 Timothy, Philemon, James, 2 Peter, 1–3 John, or Revelation.

Adversative δέ without μέν is most frequent in Matthew and Luke in relation to the total number of occurrences. It is relatively most frequent in Colossians (80%—4 of 5 occurrences), 2 Peter (42.9%), Titus (37.5%), and 1–3 John (30.8%). Both types of usage are, on the average, represented more in the Epistles than in Acts and the Gospels. Adversative δέ is not used in 1–2 Thessalonians.

Ὁ δέ, ἡ δέ, οἱ δέ, and αἱ δέ appear the greatest number of times in Matthew and Luke (76 and 75 times), with Mark showing by far the highest percentage of such usage (35%). This use of δέ with a preceding article as a pronoun occurs relatively frequently (between 6.3% and 15.5% of the total occurrences of δέ in the individual writings) only in Acts and the Gospels. It appears only once in Romans, 1 Corinthians, and Galatians, 3 times in Ephesians and Hebrews, and nowhere else in the Epistles or in Revelation. Particularly frequent is δέ after a prep. in Hebrews (11.9%), after a partc. and with the gen. absolute in Acts (20.4% and 10.2%), and in the third position in Romans (6%) and 2 Corinthians (4.8%). At the fourth or fifth position δέ stands most often in the construction καί . . . δέ (Matt 10:18; John 6:51; 8:16; Acts 5:32 v.l.; 22:29; Heb 9:21; 2 Pet 1:5; 1 John 1:3; John 8:17; 11:52 v.l.; elsewhere only in Luke 22:69 v.l.; John 17:20; Acts 3:1 v.l.; 27:14; 1 Cor 4:18; 1 John 2:2). Significant correlations with the relative frequency of other particles (e.g., καί, ἀλλά, οὖν) cannot be demonstrated.

2. As an adversative particle δέ, *but* (originally adverbial: *on the other hand*), designates a contrast—sometimes strong, sometimes weak—to a preceding statement or term. It is normally weaker than ἀλλά.

With regard to content, however, the two cannot be differentiated as signifying opposition (ἀλλά) and contrast (δέ), as is suggested in BDF §447.1. Nor can they be differentiated as referring to reversal (ἀλλά) and contrast (δέ), as is suggested in Kühner II/2, 262. Mayser II/3, 127 suggests correctly that δέ and ἀλλά are interchangeable in negative expressions, with δέ being relatively weaker.

a) Δέ is used to contrast concepts and persons: Matthew 5, *"But I* say to you" (vv. 22, 28, etc., in distinction from the ancients); Matt 6:3, 6, *"But you* . . ." (in contrast to the hypocrites).

b) It also functions to contrast statements: Matt 6:14f., "If you forgive . . . *but* if you do not forgive . . ."; and, more frequently, thought patterns: ὅτε/εἰ . . . νυνὶ δέ, etc. (e.g. Rom 7:5f.; 1 Cor 15:17-20; varied in, e.g., Gal 4:8f.: τότε μέν . . . νῦν δέ; further texts in Tachau 12.)

Parallel ideas and formulations in Col 2:13 and Eph 2:5 indicate that the author in Col 1:21f. wanted to add a temporal element to the concessive with ποτε . . . νυνὶ δέ. In view of the syntactic dissimilarity of the statements with the contrasting ποτε and νυνὶ δέ phrases—first a dependent participial clause ὄντας ἀπηλλοτριωμένους καὶ ἐχθρούς, then the finite main clause ἀποκατήλλαξεν (cf. Tachau 10f.)—the sentence is structurally unbalanced. The contrast is seen in translation by disentanglement in the two clauses: "Not long ago, you were . . . *but* now he has . . ." (JB).

c) A third usage is in the μέν . . . δέ construction (e.g., Matt 3:11; 10:13), where the two particles can be translated *certainly . . . but,* or, with the correlative use of articles ὁ/ὅς μέν . . . ὁ/ὅς δέ, *the one . . . the other* (e.g., Acts 14:4; Matt 13:8; further texts in BDF §250).

d) With preceding negation (as with ἀλλά): Luke 10:20; Acts 12:9, etc., *not . . . rather, on the contrary;* strengthened to δὲ μᾶλλον (Matt 10:6, 28; Heb 12:13) or μᾶλλον δέ (Eph 4:28; 5:11).

e) The phrase μᾶλλον δέ, without preceding negation, functions as a correction: *or rather; more correctly* (e.g., Gal 4:9).

f) With the art., ὁ δέ, οἱ δέ, etc., the meaning is *but he, but she,* more often as a copula than as an adversative. It appears as an adversative, e.g., in Matt 4:4: *"but* he answered"—in contrast to the request of the tempter. It is copulative, e.g., in Matt 2:5: "[*but/and*] they told him"—answering the question of Herod.

g) Δὲ καί means *but also, even.*

3. As a copulative particle, δέ, *but, and, in fact,* contrasts a preceding thought or term with a further, expanded,

explanatory thought or term. This view of the wider thought as a contrast corresponds to a basic structure in Greek thinking and life—the "agonistic" (cf. Burckhardt). We can usually translate this sequential δέ with *and,* since we normally regard the relationship of sequential sentences and terms as purely copulative (Kühner II/2, 274). We may list seven copulative uses:

a) Δέ indicates an enumeration: e.g., Jude 1, ἀδελφὸς δέ, "*and* brother" (also Matt 1:2-16; 2 Pet 1:5-7).

b) The particle can show addition: e.g., 1 Cor 3:15, οὕτως δὲ ὡς, "*but* only as," or "*thus* namely as" (Eph 5:32; Jas 1:6).

c) It is connective also in an explanatory parentheses with a preceding predicate: John 6:10, ἦν δέ, "*now/indeed* there was"; also ἦσαν δέ (Acts 12:3), ἀνέβην δέ (Gal 2:2).

d) Δέ also signifies the resumption or continuation of the main idea: e.g., Matt 1:18; 2 Cor 2:12; often in Acts (e.g., in the continuation of the description of the travel route); after OT citations (Matt 1:24; 2:19; 3:4); also 2 Pet 1:5 (where the return to the chain of thought begun in v. 3 is indicated after the parenthetical comments in v. 4).

e) Ὁ δέ, etc.: → 2.f; examples are indicated in *VKGNT* I, 199-224.

f) Καί . . . δέ, *and also, but also, also,* with the expression that is emphasized, "which can have as many as four words" (so Mayser II/3, 131 on the language of the papyri) between the two particles.

g) Ἔτι δὲ καί means *and even.*

K.-H. Pridik

δέησις, εως, ἡ *deēsis* request; prayer, intercession → δέομαι.

δεῖ *dei* it is necessary

1. Occurrences in the NT — 2. Meaning — 3. Δεῖ in the history of religions — 4. Mark 8:31 — 5. Luke — 6. John — 7. Revelation

Lit.: W. J. Bennett, "The Son of Man Must . . . ," *NovT* 17 (1975) 113-29. — H. Conzelmann, *The Theology of St. Luke* (1961) 151-53. — J. Ernst, *Herr der Geschichte* (1978) 52-55. — E. Fascher, "Theologische Beobachtungen zu δεῖ," FS Bultmann (1954) 228-54. — *idem,* "Theologische Beobachtungen zu δεῖ im AT," *ZNW* 45 (1954) 244-52. — W. Grundmann, *TDNT* II, 21-25. — Hahn, *Titles* 40. — P. Hoffmann, "Mk 8, 31. Zur Herkunft und markinischen Rezeption einer alten Überlieferung," FS Schmid (1973) 170-204, esp. 179-84. — E. Lohmeyer, *Markus* (KEK, [8]1967) 164f. — H. Patsch, *Abendmahl und historischer Jesus* (1972) 187-97. — J. Roloff, "Anfänge der soteriologischen Deutung des Todes Jesu (Mk X.45 und Lk XXII.27)," *NTS* 19 (1972/73) 39-42. — K. H. Schelkle, *Die Passion Jesu* (1948) 109-12. — G. Schneider, *Verleugnung, Verspottung und Verhör Jesu nach Lukas 22, 54-71* (1969) 174-81. — S. Schulz, "Gottes Vorsehung bei Lukas," *ZNW* 54 (1963) 104-16, esp. 107f. — H. E. Tödt, *The Son of Man in the Synoptic Tradition* (1965) 188-93.

1. Δεῖ, a Greek word without a Semitic equivalent, appears in the NT 101 times, distributed unevenly. It occurs 40 times in Luke-Acts, 25 in Paul's letters (of which 9 are in the Pastorals), 10 in John, 8 each in Matthew and Revelation, etc. The vb. does not occur in Galatians, Philippians, Philemon, or 1–3 John. Related ideas are expressed with μέλλω, πρέπω, ἀναγκ-, or with the fut. tense. Participial forms appear only in Acts 19:36 and 1 Pet 1:6 (δέον ἐστίν both times) and in 1 Tim 5:13 (subst. τὰ μὴ δέοντα).

2. Δεῖ designates an unconditional necessity; sentences with this vb. have fundamentally an absolute, unquestioned, and often anonymous and deterministic character. The connection with the concept of a personal God is not without problems (Grundmann, Fascher). In the NT statements with δεῖ are normally understood more or less as divine decrees. Thus God's will and nature are the norms of ethics and piety (e.g., Acts 5:29; 1 Thess 4:1; Rom 8:26; 1 Cor 8:2; 1 Tim 3:2, 7, 15; Luke 13:14, 16). Along with an immanent necessity in subject matter (e.g., Acts 19:36; John 4:4), the logic of events frequently overshadows divine determination (e.g., Rom 1:27; Acts 16:30; Heb 11:6). Human activity can demand a certain reaction (e.g., 2 Cor 11:30); nevertheless God's activity (e.g., Luke 12:12; Acts 25:10; 1 Pet 1:6) has greater influence on the situation. Thus δεῖ in the NT is normally an expression for the decree and esp. of the plan of God. Various events are dependent on this plan (e.g., Acts 1:21; 19:21; 23:11; Rev 1:1). This is esp. the case with the travels, activity, and suffering of Jesus (e.g., Mark 8:31; Matt 16:21; Luke 2:49; Acts 3:21).

3. The background in the history of religions for the δεῖ of the divine plan is not easily perceptible. The word attains a certain significance in apocalyptic literature (esp. Dan 2:28f. LXX), which must not, however, be overestimated. Here δεῖ interprets the "it is written" and serves for the consolation of the suffering righteous one (Bennett). The Hellenistic impact, which appears to be associated with the interpretation of dreams and oracular speech (K. Berger, "Zur Frage des traditionsgeschichtlichen Wertes apokrypher Gleichnisse," *NovT* 17 [1975] 75), has a certain significance, which carries over also into the NT (Hahn, Patsch).

4. It is not easy to determine the source of the saying "the Son of man must suffer many things . . ." (Mark 8:31 and elsewhere). The formulation is probably rooted in the early Hellenistic-Jewish Christian Church, which used δεῖ as a form of "it is written" (Patsch). The conceptual framework behind δεῖ cannot be determined unequivocally. The tradition of the righteous sufferer or persecuted prophet would point to a specific necessity; thus δεῖ communicates more than a conclusion from experience and instead represents a constraint based on the form of God's ways (cf. R. Pesch, *Markus* [HTKNT] ad loc.). As an eschatological statement, δεῖ would point to a particular eschatological

necessity (Lohmeyer; W. Grundmann, *Markus* [THKNT] ad loc.; M. Horstmann, *Studien zur markinischen Christologie* [1969] 24, on the "Son of Man").

At least since Mark the interpretation of δεῖ as allusion from Scripture has been dominant (Mark 9:11-13; 14:31; Matt 26:54; Luke 24:25-27). Thus δεῖ attains an objective character and is best understood within the framework of promise and fulfillment. Heb 2:10 (ἔπρεπεν) changes the idea to one of conceptual necessity and theological correctness (O. Michel, *Hebräer* [KEK] ad loc.; Schelkle).

5. Luke widens δεῖ systematically to include the entire history of salvation. The divine plan, which culminates in the death, resurrection, and exaltation of Jesus (Ernst), offers certainty for faith (Schneider). Δεῖ is the most prominent indication of the conceptual framework (Conzelmann). God's plan determines both the entire life destiny (esp. of Jesus; also, e.g., that of Paul in Acts 9:6, 16, etc., or that of Judas in Acts 1:16) and individual events (e.g., Luke 12:12; Acts 10:6; 16:30). Note that Luke writes *must* in Acts 4:12, not "can," as in *Herm. Vis.* iv.2.4.

6. John uses δεῖ in parallel to ἐὰν μή (e.g., John 3:3, 5, 7). Δεῖ designates the way given by God, to which there is no alternative. There is only the one way to enter into relationship with God (e.g., 4:20, 24), to fulfill his commission (e.g., 9:4), and to allow him to determine one's destiny (e.g., 3:30).

7. In Revelation the more generalizing eschatological ἃ δεῖ γενέσθαι (corresponding to Dan 2:28f.) appears only in the framing passages 1:1; 4:1; 22:6 (1:19 with μέλλει) and functions as an apocalyptic expression for divine determination. In the remaining passages, the word appears in reference to God's planning, as well as to the *lex talionis* (11:5; 13:10), a prophet's commission (10:11), the reign of a ruler (17:10), and proceedings that perhaps are legal in nature (20:3).

W. Popkes

δεῖγμα, ατος, τό *deigma* example*

Jude 7: πρόκεινται δεῖγμα, "[they] serve as an *example.*" In *Diogn.* 4:5; 7:9 the word has the sense *proof.*

δειγματίζω *deigmatizō* expose*

According to Matt 1:19, Joseph did not want to *expose* Mary or "*put* her *to shame.*" Col 2:15 speaks of God, who disarmed the principalities and powers (→ ἀρχή, ἐξουσία) and "*made a* public *example* of them." H. Schlier, *TDNT* II, 31f.; E. Lohse, *Colossians* [Hermeneia] 112.

δείκνυμι, δεικνύω *deiknymi, deiknyō* show*

1. Occurrences in the NT — 2. "Show, allow to see" — 3. "Explain, clarify" — 4. "Reveal, unveil"

Lit.: J. Gonda, Δείκνυμι. *Semantische Studie over den Indo-Germanischen Wortel Deik-* (1929) 15-58. — H. Schlier, *TDNT* II, 25-33. — For further bibliography see *TWNT* X, 1036f.

1. Δείκνυμι (or the alternative form δεικνύω; cf. BDF §92) appears 33 times in the NT, most often in the Gospels (3 times in Matthew, 2 in Mark, 5 in Luke, and 7 in John) and in James (3 times) and Revelation (8 times). The remaining 5 references are Acts 7:3; 10:28; 1 Cor 12:31; 1 Tim 6:15; and Heb 8:5. Along with simple δείκνυμι the NT has the following compound forms: ἀναδείκνυμι (2 times, also the noun ἀνάδειξις once), ἀποδείκνυμι (4 times, also ἀπόδειξις once), ἐπιδείκνυμι (7 times), and ὑποδείκνυμι (6 times). Cf. → ἐνδείκνυμαι, ἔνδεξις.

2. The basic meaning *show, allow to see* is dominant: Matt 4:8 par. Luke 4:5 (the obj. is: "all the kingdoms" of the world); Mark 1:44 par. Matt 8:4/Luke 5:14 ("*show* yourself to the priest"; cf. Lev 13:49 LXX); Mark 14:15 par. Luke 22:12 ("he *will show* you a large upper room"). Δείκνυμι has the sense of *display* in Luke 20:24 ("*show* me a coin"); 24:40 (Jesus "*showed* them his hands and his feet"); and similarly John 20:20 ("he *showed* them his hands and his side").

God is the one who *shows* in Acts 7:3 ("the land which I *will show* you," citing Gen 12:1 LXX). In 1 Cor 12:31b (ὁδὸν ὑμῖν δείκνυμι, "I *will show* you a way"), Paul *shows* the Corinthians the "more excellent way" of love (cf. H. Conzelmann, *1 Corinthians* [Hermeneia] 217). In 1 Tim 6:15 δείκνυμι has almost the sense of *cause* ("the appearing of our Lord Jesus Christ . . . *will be made manifest* [by God] at the proper time [καιροῖς ἰδίοις]"). Heb 8:5 (citing Exod 25:40) speaks of the pattern "which was *shown* [to Moses] on the mountain."

3. The derived meaning *explain, clarify* is present in the following contexts: According to Matt 16:21, "Jesus *began to make it clear* to his disciples" (NEB) that he had to suffer (for Matthew's δεικνύειν, Mark has διδάσκειν). In Acts 10:28 God *explains* to Peter (ἔδειξεν, with complementary inf.) that he "should not call any man common or unclean." In the three uses of the word in James the meaning *establish, prove* is present: 2:18b, "*Show* me your faith apart from your works, and I by my works will *show* you my faith"; 3:13b, "By his good life let him *show* his works."

4. In the Fourth Gospel and in Revelation δείκνυμι has the meaning *reveal, unveil* (cf. Schlier 27). As the Son, Christ has received the revelation from the Father (John 5:20, "the Father . . . *shows* him all . . . and greater works than these will he *show* him"), and he transmits it further (10:32, "I have *shown* you many good works from the Father"). In John 2 the Jews demand a sign that might prove Jesus' authority for his action in the temple (v. 18, "What sign have you to *show* us for doing this?"). The

disciples ask, "*Show* us the Father" (14:8, 9c), although Jesus has already made the Father known to them in his words and work (v. 9b, "He who has seen me has seen the Father").

The revelation that Christ received from God was intended, according to Rev 1:1, "to *show* his servants what must soon take place." This *manifestation* is accomplished through instruction to the apocalyptic writer, who "saw" and who "bore witness" (v. 2). Δείκνυμι designates as an unveiling of the future a divine announcement that follows (ἃ δεῖ γενέσθαι, 1:1; 4:1; 22:6), usually given through the angels who explain (17:1; 21:9; 22:1, 6, 8). Fixed expressions in this connection are "I will *show* you" (4:1; 17:1; 21:9) and "he *showed* me" (21:10; 22:1).

G. Schneider

δειλία, ας, ἡ *deilia* cowardice*

2 Tim 1:7: "God did not give us a spirit of *timidity* (δειλίας) but a spirit of power (δυνάμεως). . . ." W. Mundle, *DNTT* I, 622.

δειλιάω *deiliaō* be fainthearted, despondent*

John 14:27: "Let not your hearts be troubled (ταρασσέσθω), neither let them *be afraid*" (δειλιάω also appears with ταράσσομαι in Isa 13:7f.). W. Mundle, *DNTT* I, 622.

δειλός, 3 *deilos* fainthearted, despondent*

Mark 4:40 par. Matt 8:26, in the question of Jesus to the disciples: "Why are you *afraid?*" (Matthew adds the epithet ὀλιγόπιστοι); Rev 21:8 includes unbelievers (ἄπιστοι) in a list with *cowards.*

δεῖνα, ὁ (ἡ, τό) *deina* someone*

Matt 26:18, in the commission from Jesus: "Go into the city to *a certain one* (πρὸς τὸν δεῖνα)." BDF §64.5; A. C. Moorhouse, *Classical Quarterly* 13 (1963) 19-25.

δεινῶς *deinōs* dreadfully*

Matt 8:6: The centurion's servant was "in *terrible* distress," or "*grievously* tormented" (AV); Luke 11:53: the scribes and Pharisees "began to assail [Jesus] *fiercely* (δεινῶς ἐνέχειν)" (NEB).

δειπνέω *deipneō* eat a meal
→ δεῖπνον.

δεῖπνον, ου, τό *deipnon* meal*
δειπνέω *deipneō* eat a meal*

1. Ordinary meals — 2. The eschatological meal — 3. The Lord's Supper

Lit.: F. Bammel, *Das heilige Mahl im Glauben der Völker* (1950). — J. Behm, *TDNT* II, 34f., 689-95. — P. Billerbeck, "Ein altjüdisches Gastmahl," Billerbeck IV, 611-39. — G. Delling, *TRE* I, 47-58. — F. Hahn, *The Worship of the Early Church* (1973). — A. Lumpe, *RAC* VI, 612-35. — K. Schneider, PW XIV, 524-27. — H. Schürmann, *LTK* V, 271. — A. V. Ström, *TRE* I, 43-47. — For further bibliography see *TWNT* X, 1037.

1. In the NT δεῖπνον most often designates the ordinary *meal,* to which guests could be invited (cf. Mark 6:21; 12:39 par. Matt 23:6/Luke 20:46; Luke 14:16f., 24; 17:8; John 12:2). In John 13:2, 4, Jesus' farewell meal is called a δεῖπνον. The phrase μετὰ τὸ δειπνῆσαι ("after the meal," Luke 22:20; 1 Cor 11:25) signals in a highly formalized style that in Jesus' last meal the main meal took place between the cup and the wine symbolism. In Palestine one normally had two meals in a day and three on the sabbath. The Jewish δεῖπνον (= *sᵉʿûḏâ*) was the main meal, which on weekdays was taken late in the afternoon after the completion of the day's work (cf. Luke 17:7-9). On the sabbath it was taken after the worship (cf. Luke 14:1). The ἄριστον ("breakfast," cf. Luke 14:12, yet generally "meal," cf. Matt 22:4; Luke 11:38) was distinguished from the δεῖπνον.

Festive meals were held in the evening and were eaten in a reclining position. At such a meal, wine was regularly offered. This practice probably distinguished it from the ordinary meal. The rabbis distinguished the obligatory meal (on the occasion of a religious celebration, e.g., a wedding or Passover) from the voluntary meal, which was held according to one's preference. On the customs and background of the Jewish meal, cf. Billerbeck.

2. Only in Revelation are δεῖπνον (19:9, 17) and δειπνέω (3:20) associated (cf. also Luke 14:24 in a statement of Jesus). The concept of the eschatological meal of God is present in the OT (cf. Isa 25:6) and early Judaism (cf. *1 Enoch* 62:14). In Rev 19:17 it is gruesomely reversed with the reference to Ezek 39:17-20 (cf. also Isa 34:6-8; Jer 46:10; Zeph 1:7). The concept of the eschatological meal is also adopted in the Synoptic tradition, but without the use of this catchword (cf. Matt 8:11; 26:29; Luke 22:16, 18, 29f.; also Luke 14:15).

3. In 1 Cor 11:20 the common meal linked with the Eucharist is called κυριακὸν δεῖπνον, or *Lord's Supper.* This term used by Paul, which was apparently known, appears to indicate that in Corinth the meal was understood as a possibility for → κοινωνία (cf. 1 Cor 10:16) or as a place of pneumatic presence of the κύριος Jesus. Hellenistic cult terminology could have influenced the formation of this expression (see texts in Behm 35f.). Yet a connection with the Jewish-apocalyptic conception of the eschatological meal is not fully to be excluded.

Paul criticizes the Corinthians' practice of separation in eating this meal: One takes "his own *meal* (τὸ ἴδιον δεῖπνον)" (beforehand? 1 Cor 11:21). The disorder at the meal hinders the church from functioning as "one body" (cf. 10:17). Paul is not concerned with discrimination against the (late arriving?) poor. Indeed, he recommends that they eat in homes ahead of time (11:22). What is demanded is reciprocal consideration that makes possible beginning the meal together. With this directive, Paul introduces the later separation of the common meal from the eucharistic celebration. The common meal continued for a short time in the early Church as the agape feast (→ ἀγάπη 4).

J. Wanke

δεισιδαιμονία, ας, ἡ *deisidaimonia* piety; superstition; religion*

1. Occurrences, etymology, and meaning — 2. Usage — 3. Δεισιδαίμων

Lit.: BAGD s.v. — H. Bietenhard, *DNTT* I, 449-53. — H. Bolkestein, *Theophrastos' Charakter der Deisidaimonia als religionsgeschichtliche Urkunde* (1929). — H. Conzelmann, *Acts* (Hermeneia, 1972) (on Acts 17:22; 25:19). — M. Detienne, *La notion de Daïmon dans le Pythagorisme ancien* (1963). — M. Dibelius, "Paul at the Areopagus," "Paul in Athens," *Studies in the Acts of the Apostles* (1956) 26-77, 78-84. — A. M. Dubarle, "Le discours à l'Aréopage (Act 17, 22-31) et son arrière-plan biblique," *RSPT* 57 (1973) 576-610. — E. Grässer, "Acta-Forschung seit 1960," *TRu* 41 (1976) 141-94, 259-90; 42 (1977) 1-68. — E. Haenchen, *The Acts of the Apostles* (1971) (on Acts 17:22; 25:19). — H. Hommel, "Neue Forschungen zur Areopagrede Acts 17," *ZNW* 46 (1955) 145-78. — P. J. Koets, *Δεισιδαιμονία. A Contribution to the Knowledge of the Religious Terminology in Greek* (1929). — H. A. Moellering, *Plutarch on Superstition. Its Place in the Changing Meaning of δεισιδαιμονία and in the Context of His Theological Writings* (1963). — W. Nauck, "Die Tradition und Komposition der Areopagrede. Eine motivgeschichtliche Untersuchung," *ZTK* 53 (1956) 11-52. — E. Norden, *Agnostos Theos. Untersuchungen zur Formengeschichte religiöser Rede* ([4]1956). — H. Nowack, *Zur Entwicklungsgeschichte des Begriffes δαίμων. Eine Untersuchung epigraphischer Zeugnisse vom 5. Jh. v. Chr. bis zum 5. Jh. n. Chr.* (Diss. Bonn, 1960). — A. Wikenhauser, *Apostelgeschichte* (RNT, [5]1963). — U. Wilckens, *Die Missionsreden der Apostelgeschichte* (WMANT 5, [3]1974).

1. Δεισιδαιμονία appears in the NT only in Acts 25:19 and is unknown in the LXX. It belongs to later Greek and is a compound from δείδω ("be afraid") and δαίμων: "awe before the gods." The derivation follows from the vb. δεισιδαιμονέω, "have superstitious fear," and the noun thus means *fear of the gods.* From this sense the three lexical meanings of the word that are found in the literature are derived.

a) In a positive sense δεισιδαιμονία means *fear of God:* Polybius vi.56.7; Philodemus *Herc.* 1251.10; Diodorus Siculus i.70.8; xi.89.8; Dio Chrysostom 44.9; *CIG* 2737 b2 (Aphrodisias); Josephus *Ant.* x.42; *B.J.* ii.174: "deeply astonished by the fervor of their *piety.*"

b) In a disapproving or negative sense δεισιδαιμονία means *superstition:* Theophrastus *Char.* 16; Polybius xii.24.5; Plutarch *Alex.* 75.1; Diodorus Siculus i.83; Marcus Antoninus vi.30; Agatharchides in Josephus *Ant.* xii.5f. and *Ap.* i.208; *Corp. Herm.* ix.9; Philo *Spec. Leg.* iv.147; Josephus *Ant.* xv.277; *Diog.* 1:4. Plutarch discusses this theme in detail in his work Περὶ Δεισιδαιμονίας (Concerning superstition). Δεισιδαιμονία is employed in the patristic literature in order to reject various heresies; see, e.g., Theodoret *Hist.* iii.14.2 (GCS 19).

c) In a very general and neutral sense δεισιδαιμονία means *religion: OGIS* 455.11; Josephus *Ant.* xiv.228; xix.290: it is reported that Claudius forbade the Jews τὰς τῶν ἄλλων ἔθνων δεισιδαιμονίας ἐξουθενίζειν. The word is used in this neutral sense in Acts 25:19 (against *Beginnings* IV, 311, etc.). It is translated in this third sense in the more recent commentaries and translations. The fathers of the first three centuries do not cite Acts 25:19 as evidence against Judaism (*Biblia Patristica* I-II [1975, 1977] ad loc.).

2. In Acts 25:13-22 Festus reports to King Agrippa concerning the trial of Paul, which began in the time of Felix. Luke succeeds in portraying a conversation that has the ring of historical authenticity. Paul, who according to Acts 25:11 made an appeal to Caesar, had not committed a punishable offense according to Roman interpretation. The subject of discussion is the resurrection of the dead, especially the resurrection of Jesus. Festus does not use the term δεισιδαιμονία in an unfavorable way in conversation with his high-ranking Jewish guests. In v. 19, Luke characterizes the Romans' lack of understanding of the resurrection faith in the same way as the Greeks were characterized in 17:32. In Acts 26:24 Festus considers Paul mad because of his belief. Thus the Lukan intention in the brief scene in 25:13-22 is clarified. The portrayal of the trial is simplified, and Festus appears as an honorable man who wants to act according to the laws of the Roman state. The apostle appears as an imprisoned proclaimer of the gospel. The Christian message of the resurrection, which has its roots totally in the "Jewish religion," is the essential concern of the biblical author.

3. The adj. **δεισιδαίμων** *pious, religious** appears in the NT only in Acts 17:22, used in the comparative as a superlative (as in Diogenes Laertius ii.132), and not at all in the LXX.

Like the noun, δεισιδαίμων can be used in a negative sense to mean *superstitious:* Theophrastus *Char.* 16; Philodemus *Piet.* 105; Diodorus Siculus i.62; Philo *Cher.* 42; Maximus Tyrius 14.6f.; Lucian *Pr. Im.* 27 (superlative). Christian authors employ δεισιδαίμων in the battle against heretics: Justin *Apol.* ii.3; Clement of Alexandria *Prot.* 2; Origen *Cels.* 3:79; 4:5; Epiphanius *Haer.* 62:7.

From contemporary texts, the context of Acts 17:22 (cf. 25:19), and other factors (see Bolkestein, Koets, Moellering, Nowack; cf. also Grässer, esp. 44f.), one may conclude that Paul in no way uses δεισιδαίμων in an ironic or disparaging sense in his introductory statement of the Areopagus speech (Acts 17:22-31). The word here means *religious, pious* (literally, "fearing the demons"). This view is supported by Xenophon *Cyr.* iii.3.58; *Ages.* 11.8; Aristotle *Pol.* 1315a.1; *Epigr. Graec.* 607.3.

Luke, following contemporary patterns, characterizes the learned people of Athens in a twofold way: as inquisitive (Acts 17:21, so also Demosthenes *Or.* 4.10; Thucydides iii.38.4; Charito 1.11) and as *pious* (v. 22). Because of their many temples and images of the gods, the Athenians were considered especially religious in antiquity: Sophocles *OC* 260 (τάς γ' Ἀθήνας φασι θεοσεβεστάτας εἶναι); Josephus *Ap.* ii.130 (τοὺς εὐσεβεστάτους τῶν Ἑλλήνων πάντες λέγουσιν); Aelius Dionysius 24.3 (Ἀθηναίοις περισσοτερόν τι ἢ τοῖς ἄλλοις ἐς τὰ θεῖά ἐστι σπουδῆς); Pausanias i.17.1. In this positive sense Clement of Alexandria twice cites the speech at the Areopagus: *Strom.* i.9.1 (Acts 17:22-28); v.12.4 (Acts 17:22f.).

It is notable (Wikenhauser 200) that Luke does not use the technical term "godfearing" (εὐσεβής; cf. Acts 10:2, 7, of Cornelius; 22:12 v.l.; elsewhere in the NT only in 2 Pet 2:9), but rather δεισιδαίμων. (The word group εὐσεβ- is unknown in the Gospels and the authentic Pauline letters.) In Acts εὐσεβ- is appropriate only for the worshipers of the one true God (the vb. is in Acts 17:23 [cf. 1 Tim 5:4] and the noun in Acts 3:12). In Acts 17:23 Paul bases his praise on the fact that he found an altar dedicated "to an unknown God." Consequently he connects his proclamation about God with his comments about mankind and ends with the message of Christ's return and resurrection.

In presenting Paul's speech at the Areopagus, Luke has a twofold intention: to show how Christian missionary preaching looks to the pagan listeners, and to show "how that unique individual named Paul fared in this incomparable encounter with representatives of Greek civilization" (Conzelmann 147). In this composition a two-part form of the early Christian creed emerges: God, the Creator—Jesus Christ, the coming Judge (cf. 1 Thess 1:9f.; 1 Cor 8:6). Luke "employs the structure of a definite school tradition of Judaism, which is especially shaped by wisdom characteristics; then he interprets it according to his own theological purposes" (Grässer 45). He shows that the Gentiles believe in *one* God as Creator and that they repent when they believe in Jesus Christ. In the light of Acts 1:8; 14:15-17, and esp. 17:32-34, Luke shows sensitivity in not commenting on Paul's failure in Athens. What he does describe is an authentic "historic" denial: the Greek world's failure to understand (cf., however, the Cornelius story in Acts 10–11). A similar result is indicated for the Roman world in 25:13-22; 26:1-23. The faith proclaimed by Paul "knows that independent of our comprehension, God has always been near at hand" (Conzelmann 148).

F. Staudinger

δεισιδαίμων, 2 *deisidaimōn* pious, religious
→ δεισιδαιμονία 3.

δέκα *deka* ten*

1. Occurrences in the NT — 2. General significance of the number 10 — 3. Δέκα in the NT — 4. Compounds with δέκα — 5. Δέκατος

Lit.: BAGD s.v. — H. Dörrie, *KP* IV, 1267f. — E. Frank, *Plato und die sogenannten Pythagoreer* (1923) 251f., 309ff. — P. Friesenhahn, *Hellenistische Wortzahlenmystik* (1935). — H. Haag, "Die biblischen Wurzeln des *Minjan,*" FS Michel 235-42. — F. Hauck, *TDNT* II, 36f. — C. J. Hemer, *DNTT* II, 692f. — LSJ s.v. — D. Najock, "Zahlenmystik," *KP* V, 1447-49.

1. Δέκα occurs 24 times in the NT; it also appears 11 times in compounds (→ 4).

2. The decimal principle appears in early Semitic times, although it was reflected only imperfectly in the systems of weights and measures in Israel and in Mesopotamia. In the OT the number 10 is the *symbol of the perfect whole* and appears, e.g., in the 10 commandments (Exod 20; Deut 5), 10 plagues (Exod 7–11), 10 patriarchs (Gen 5), and the giving of the tenth (Gen 28:22; → δεκάτη).

In Judaism we meet the number 10, e.g., in the rule that a true worship service is made possible (*m. Meg.* 4:3) by the presence of 10 adult men (the *minyan*); in Ruth 4:2, e.g., 10 who sit in judgment represent the whole. In apocalyptic literature the idea of the full extent of the times is expressed through the division of the time of the world into 10 periods; the tenth week is the messianic time (*1 Enoch* 93:1ff.; 91:12-17, etc.).

The number 10 was significant in Greek philosophy, esp. in the school of Pythagoras. Here a value was seen in every numerical analogue or harmony. Not only numerical, but also ethical values were attributed to particular numbers—e.g., in the "tetraktys," the group of four numbers 1 + 2 + 3 + 4. Because its sum is 10, the four basic values seemed to be included in the number 10. 10 was considered the ultimate real number. This position finds expression in Gnosticism (so Irenaeus *Haer.* i.10.4: 4 elements, 10 virtues; *ibid.* 11.2: the number 10); on the other hand, Philo knows 10 as the τέλειος ἀριθμός (*Vit. Mos.* i.96, etc.).

3. In the NT 10 serves as a framework for enumerations: Rom 8:38f. (10 opposing powers); 1 Cor 6:9f. (10 vices); Matthew 8–9 (10 miracles). In Matt 1:1-17 the genealogy of Jesus is associated with the framework of the fulfillment of the world in 10 weeks.

The word δέκα itself appears as the result of doubling (2 × 5 = 10) in Matt 25:28 and as the remainder (12 - 2 = 10) in Matt 20:24; Mark 10:41, without any additional meaning. As a small round number it is found in Luke 19:13 (bis), 16f., 24f. (servants, minas, cities); 15:8 (coins); 14:31 (thousands of soldiers); 17:12, 17 (lepers); Rev 2:10 (a relatively short span of time, here in dependence on Dan 1:12, 14). In Acts 25:6 "not more than eight or ten days" is a round number. On the other hand, the 10 virgins in Matt 25:1 could be based on the *minyan* as a number that (in view of the eschatological expectation) bears elements of Passover theology. In Rev 12:3 the 10 horns reflect tradition (cf. Dan 7:7) but also take their meaning from a concrete historical allusion (cf. Dan

7:24). The same idea is present in Rev 13:1 (bis); 17:3, 7, 12 (bis), 16.

4. Compounds with δέκα normally represent concrete measurements: e.g., δεκαοκτώ in Luke 13:4 for a historical event and 13:11, 16 for a time reference; δεκαπέντε in John 11:18 for a reference to distance, in Acts 27:28 for the depth of the sea, and in Gal 1:18 for a span of time, which in ancient timekeeping is the equivalent of two weeks; δεκατέσσαρες in 2 Cor 12:2 and Gal 2:1 for a number of years. In Matt 1:17 number speculation may play a role: the numerical value of the name "David" (= 4 + 6 + 4) corresponds to the 14 generations as a significant grouping (Friesenhahn 98f.; W. Grundmann, *Matthäus* [THKNT] ad loc.).

5. **Δέκατος** *tenth** appears, as it does outside the NT, not only as an ordinal number but also in uses that correspond to the special meaning of δέκα. It occurs 3 times in the NT (not counting the subst. → δεκάτη): in Rev 11:13 it renders a (round) fractional number (one-tenth); in Rev 21:20 it is part of an enumeration that has 12 items. The special meaning of the number 10 appears to play a role in John 1:39. The exact time reference (the *tenth* hour = 4:00 p.m.) in which the first words of Jesus are given in this Gospel may refer to the tenth hour as the hour of fulfillment (R. Bultmann, *The Gospel of John* [1971] ad loc.).

A. J. Hess

δεκαδύο *dekadyo* twelve

Acts 19:7; 24:11, both TR in place of δώδεκα. Cf. also *Barn.* 8:3; *Gos. Eb.* 2.

δεκαοκτώ *dekaoktō* eighteen*

Luke 13:4, 11 (in each case material unique to Luke): *eighteen* were killed when the tower fell; a woman was sick for *eighteen* years.

δεκαπέντε *dekapente* fifteen*

John 11:18: *fifteen* stadia; Acts 27:28: *fifteen* fathoms; Gal 1:18: Paul remained with Cephas in Jerusalem for *fifteen* days (a round number for a period of time; cf. BAGD s.v. δέκα).

Δεκάπολις, εως, ἡ *Dekapolis* Decapolis*

Lit.: A. Alt, *Kleine Schriften* II ([2]1959) 384-95, 452f. — I. Benzinger, PW IV, 2415-17. — H. Bietenhard, "Die syrischen Dekapolis von Pompeius bis Traian," *ANRW* II/8 (1977) 220-61. — H. Guthe, *Die griechisch-römischen Städte des Ostjordanlandes* (1918). — A. H. M. Jones, *The Cities of the Eastern Roman Provinces* ([2]1971) 255-59. — G. Kroll, *Auf den Spuren Jesu* ([6]1975) 326, 328; maps 80, 194. — K. Matthiae, *Chronologische Übersichten und Karten zur spätjüdischen und urchristlichen Zeit* (1977). — S. T. Parker, "The Decapolis Reviewed," *JBL* 94 (1975) 437-41. — Schürer, *History* II, 125-58.

The city-states east of the Jordan (only around Scythopolis did the Decapolis extend over the Jordan between Samaria and Galilee), which had developed into Hellenistic cities after the time of Alexander the Great, were conquered by Alexander Jannaeus (103-76 B.C.) and deprived of their independence before Pompey liberated them *ca.* 63 B.C. Pompey then combined them into a league of cities under the Syrian governor, giving them an autonomous administration and the right to mint coins. The designation Δεκάπολις ("ten cities") goes back to its original number and to the numerical value of 10 as a round number. It comprises a stretch of land east of Lake Gennesaret almost to the Dead Sea (east of Perea) with an area of about 30,000 square km. The cities included in the league are noted in various ways (Pliny, Ptolemy). Herod the Great conquered Antioch ad Hippum, Gadara, and Kanatha; around A.D. 200 the Decapolis fell. Its most important cities were the temporary capitals Gadara and Scythopolis; also included were Pella, Gerasa, Hippos, Philadelphia, and Damascus.

Mark 5:20 places the exorcism of Gerasa (→ Γερασηνός) in the Decapolis, although the scene occurs at the Lake of Gennesaret, because Mark wants to speak of the effect of the first Christian mission in the Decapolis (Gerasa was centrally located; similarly 7:31). Matthew does not assume this, but in Matt 4:25 (following Mark 3:7) uses the catchword Decapolis in building a framework, thus following the Markan conception. Luke does not mention the Decapolis, presumably because in Acts he presents a portrayal of the beginnings of the Christian mission that deviates sharply from Mark's portrayal.

G. Schille

δεκατέσσαρες *dekatessares* fourteen*

This number appears three times in Matt 1:17, in the phrase "*fourteen* generations"; see A. Vögtle, *BZ* 8 (1964) 240-48; 9 (1965) 32-38; H. C. Waetjen, *JBL* 95 (1976) 205-30. In 2 Cor 12:2 Paul speaks of being "caught up" *fourteen* years ago. In Gal 2:1 Paul's second visit to Jerusalem (with Barnabas and Titus) occurred "after *fourteen* years"; see H. Schlier, *Galater* (KEK) ad loc. → δέκα 4.

δεκάτη, ης, ἡ *dekatē* tenth, tithe*
δεκατόω *dekatoō* pay tithes; receive tithes*

Lit.: A. van den Born, *BL* 1921f. — H. Volkmann, *KP* I, 1438.

Both words occur in the NT only in Heb 7:2-9 (δεκάτη 4 times, δεκατόω twice).

1. Outside the NT δεκάτη is used for the tenth portion collected as a toll—in harvest and property taxes and for dedications to the gods (captured material, portions of a sacrifice). Thus in Heb 7:2 it corresponds to the Hebrew t.t. *maʿaśēr* (see BDB 798) and means (explicitly in 7:4)

the *tenth* as a portion of the booty. In the interpretation of vv. 1-3 in vv. 8-9, it refers to the *tithe* due to the Levites. The references go back to the story of Melchizedek in Gen 14:17-20 and to the establishment of the income of the Levites in Num 18:20-32.

2. **Δεκατόω** (with acc. obj.) occurs only in the LXX and in Hebrews, with two occurrences in the latter. It corresponds to the Hebrew t.t. *ʿāśar* (e.g., Neh 10:38; see BDB ad loc.). In Heb 7:6 it means (act.) *impose the payment of the tithe;* in v. 9 (pass.), *be required to pay the tithe.*

A. J. Hess

δέκατος, 3 *dekatos* tenth
→ δέκα 5.

δεκατόω *dekatoō* pay tithes; receive tithes
→ δεκάτη.

δεκτός, 3 *dektos* acceptable; welcome

From the human side, *welcome,* in Luke 4:24 (in contrast to Mark 6:4, of the prophet in his home city), elsewhere always *acceptable* to God: Luke 4:19 (the acceptable year of the Lord; Isa 61:2 LXX); Acts 10:35 (one who fears God in every nation); 2 Cor 6:2 (with καιρός; Isa 49:8 LXX); Phil 4:18 (with θυσία). W. Grundmann, *TDNT* II, 58f.

δελεάζω *deleazō* lure, entice*

Jas 1:14: of temptation, in which one "is lured and *enticed* by his own desire (ἐπιθυμία)"; 2 Pet 2:14, 18: false teachers "*entice* unsteady souls" and those who have once escaped from error.

δένδρον, ου, τό *dendron* tree*

Lit.: T. Lohmann, *BHH* III, 1771.

1. Of the 25 occurrences in the NT, 12 are in Matthew, 7 in Luke, 4 in Revelation, and one each in Mark and Jude. Frequently recurring phrases are δένδρον καλόν (or ἀγαθόν), δένδρον σαπρόν (also σαπρὸν δένδρον), and δένδρον μὴ ποιοῦν καρπὸν καλόν, which all belong to the usage described in detail under → 2.c.

2.a) Δένδρον is used first of all in a literal sense: Matt 21:8; Mark 8:24; Luke 21:29; Rev 7:1, 3; 8:7; 9:4.

b) In Matt 13:32; Luke 13:19 the final form of the tree, which grows from a small seed, serves as a metaphor for the capacity for success and the worldwide expansion of the sovereignty of God (cf. Dan 4:9, 18f., where the sovereignty of Nebuchadnezzar appears in the dream as an enormous tree; cf. also Ezek 17:22-24).

c) Most frequent in the NT is the usage of the tree as an image for the human being, illustrating the idea that a person's actions determine his or her value before God and thus determine his or her future. "Make a *tree* sound, and its fruit will be sound; make a *tree* rotten, and its fruit will be rotten" (Matt 12:33, JB; similarly Matt 7:17 bis, 18 bis; Luke 6:43 bis). One recognizes the value of a tree by its fruits (Luke 6:44; Matt 12:33c). But woe to the tree that does not bring forth good fruits: it is cut down—an image of judgment used already in Isa 6:13; 10:33f.; 32:19—and thrown into the fire (Matt 3:10 bis; 7:19; Luke 3:9 bis).

In Jude 12 false teachers in the Church are described as "fruitless *trees* in late autumn, twice dead, uprooted." A tree that bears no fruit at the time of the harvest in autumn is like a cloud that brings forth no water; one waits in vain for something from it. Perhaps trees are here considered in which not only fruit but even foliage is lacking. Because they are uprooted, they are unfruitful. The attribute "twice dead," which abandons the image and characterizes the false teachers directly, is difficult to explain. Are they "twice dead" because they, who were originally in sin, awoke to life through faith and baptism but now have again "died" through apostasy into false doctrine? Or does it refer to both physical death and "eternal death" in God's judgment (cf. Rev 2:11; 20:6, 14; 21:8)? Cf. K. H. Schelkle, *Judas* (HTKNT) ad loc.

J. M. Nützel

δεξιολάβος, ου, ὁ *dexiolabos* light-armed soldier (?)*

This noun appears only in Acts 23:23, where 200 δεξιολάβοι belong to the military contingent that transported Paul from Jerusalem to Caesarea. The exact meaning of this military t.t. is uncertain. Witnesses from the Byzantine period (7th-10th centuries) list δεξιολάβοι alongside archers and slingers, thus apparently as *light-armed soldiers;* see E. Haenchen, *The Acts of the Apostles* (1971) 647.

δεξιός, 3 *dexios* right (side)

1. Occurrences — 2. The high estimation of "right" — 3. The right hand — 4. The right side — 5. Sitting at the right hand — 6. The right hand of God and of Jesus

Lit.: A. Gornatowski, "Rechts und links im antiken Aberglauben" (Diss. Breslau, 1936). — W. Grundmann, *TDNT* II, 37-40. — Hahn, *Titles* 129-35. — B. Hartmann, *BHH* III, 1564f. — P. Vielhauer, "Ein Weg zur neutestamentlichen Christologie? Prüfung der Thesen F. Hahns," *Aufsätze zum NT* (1965) 141-98. — C. Wolff, *Die Hand des Menschen* (1973). — For further bibliography see *TWNT* X, 1037.

1. Δεξιός occurs 54 times in the NT, most frequently in Matthew (12 times), Mark (7 times), Luke (6 times), Acts (7 times), Hebrews (5 times), and Revelation (9 times). The Pauline corpus has only 3 occurrences.

2. The meaning of the adj. (derived from δέκ[χ]ομαι, "take"), including the generally high estimation of everything on the right side, is rooted ultimately in the dominating role of the right hand as the one that is normally more active and thus more adroit and more powerful (cf. Gornatowski 5).

3. The healing of the right hand is urgent because it executes the main work (Luke 6:6; cf. Mark 3:1; Matt 12:10). The right hand gives alms (Matt 6:3) and performs the laying on of hands (Rev 1:17). It is raised to heaven in an oath (Rev 10:5) and receives the saving mark (Rev 13:16). One grasps it in order to help someone to stand (Acts 3:7). One extends it in handshake in order to seal an agreement that has been made (Gal 2:9; 2 Macc 12:11f., etc.). Its work can include forbidden sexual acts (Matt 5:30). From its dominating function (in Matt 6:3 and elsewhere it is simply ἡ δεξιά, *the right*), the right member generally is also regularly given preferential treatment: the right eye as the source of sexual desire (Matt 5:29), the right cheek, to which a slap is especially outrageous (v. 39; Billerbeck I, 343).

4. Just as left-handedness has been the object of discrimination into the modern period, so apparently it was considered unnatural in antiquity (Wolff 158). Thus "left" was considered perverse (Prov 4:27a LXX) and foolish (Eccl 10:2). Consequently "right" was, by contrast, associated with conceptions of fortune, success, and salvation (on Greek thought, cf. Gornatowski 45ff.). The resurrected one lets the disciples throw out the nets "on the *right* side (εἰς τὰ δεξιὰ μέρη) of the boat," as it is the "lucky side" (BAGD s.v.). As the royal Son of Man at the judgment, he will place the blessed at the right side and the cursed on the left (Matt 25:33f.; cf. Plato *R.* 614c). Mark 16:5 and Luke 1:11 probably have a similar interpretation. Occasionally "right and left" can be named together without any apparent value judgment (Mark 10:37 par.; 15:27 par.; 2 Cor 6:7). Nevertheless even here "right" always comes before "left."

5. Sitting at a person's right hand is a special prominence. In the earthly royal household, the highest place of honor is on the king's right (1 Kgs 2:19; Ps 44:10 LXX). In the heavenly kingdom God's right hand lends a share in God's honor and power (Ps 109:1 LXX) because of its special proximity to his throne.

Ps 109:1 LXX (κάθου ἐκ δεξιῶν μου . . .) is the basis of statements concerning the enthronement of Jesus as heavenly and messianic ruler in many different passages (by no means in all of them; Vielhauer 171f.; for further aspects of the citation see Hahn 129). Along with literal citations (Mark 12:36 par.; Acts 2:34; Heb 1:13), there are frequently more or less free renderings of the certainty that Jesus sits at the right hand of God or has sat there: the connection between κάθημαι and ἐκ δεξιῶν in Ps 109:1 LXX thus appears only in the declaration of the view of the Son of Man "seated at the right hand of Power" (= God's right hand; similarly Heb 1:3) in Mark 14:62 par. Moreover, the enthronement of Jesus at the right hand of God, which was understood early (with Vielhauer 167ff., *contra* Hahn 129) as a consequence of the resurrection, is described with → καθίζω with the connecting ἐν δεξιᾷ (Eph 1:20; Heb 1:3; 8:1; 10:12; 12:2); his present existence at the side of God is described with κάθημαι (Col 3:1) or εἰμί (Rom 8:34; 1 Pet 3:22) or with the following ἐν δεξιᾷ. The conception of the standing of Jesus ἐκ δεξιῶν of God (Acts 7:55f.) may, however, be determined by statements such as 1 Kgs 22:19; Ps 44:10 LXX.

6. In Acts 2:33; 5:31 the context suggests interpreting τῇ δεξιᾷ in a local sense (*at*—not *by*—the right hand). Thus the distinct concept of the right hand of God, used in the OT as an expression of power, is attested in the NT only in Rev 5:1, 7. In Rev 1:16f.; 2:1 the concept is transferred to the resurrected Jesus (see also 1:17). The motif of protection, as in the OT, is dominant. Here the objects of protection are the churches, whose protection comes in the form of the seven stars or angels at the right hand of Jesus. This motif also determines the phrase εἶναι ἐκ δεξιῶν, "to stand at the side" of someone (Acts 2:25, citing Ps 15:8 LXX).

P. von der Osten-Sacken

δέομαι *deomai* entreat, request; pray*
δέησις, εως, ἡ *deēsis* request; prayer, intercession*

1. Occurrences and meaning in the NT — 2. Usage in the NT — 3. Προσδέομαι

Lit.: BAGD s.v. — M. Dibelius, *Studies in the Acts of the Apostles* (1956) 26-77. — H. Greeven, *TDNT* II, 40-42. — G. Holtz, *Pastoralbriefe* (THKNT, 1965) 56f. — E. Jüngel, *Unterwegs zur Sache* (1972) 179-88. — H. Schönweiss, *DNTT* II, 855-59.

1. Use of δέομαι and δέησις, with few exceptions, is concentrated in the Pauline and Lukan literature (22 occurrences of δέομαι, 18 of δέησις). From the basic meaning "be lacking, need"—included in προσδέομαι—the meaning of the words developed into *entreat, ask for, pray* and *petition, prayer,* etc.

2. Δέομαί σου in direct address (Acts 8:34; 21:39; cf. 26:3) corresponds to the formula of politeness *please* and is characteristic of the person who speaks fluently and well. Paul depends on the rhetorical power of δέομαι when his apostolic mission is at stake (2 Cor 5:20; 8:4; 10:2; Gal 4:12).

The basic meaning is obvious in statements in which the one who makes the request communicates dependence and even perplexity (Luke 5:12; 8:28, 38; 9:38, 40). In addition, childlessness (Luke 1:13) and persecution (Acts 4:31 in reference to vv. 24-30) are occasions for prayer requests. According to Heb 5:7 the full humanity of Jesus is emphasized by his "*prayers* and supplications." One who asks for forgiveness (cf. Acts 8:22) also repents. The Church *requests* workers to be sent into the harvest (Matt 9:38 par. Luke 10:2) and responds in prayer before the imminent apocalyptic distress (cf. Luke 21:36). Prayer as entreaty, lament, and cry for help makes a claim on the saving distance between the dependent one and the powerful one.

Where δέομαι involves a third party (cf. Luke 22:32; Acts 8:24), it refers to *intercession*. In the Pauline letters the motif of intercession extends beyond the mere stylistic function that it has in the ancient letter. The *intercession* of the church (Phil 1:19) seeks the deliverance of the apostle. Thus Paul thankfully recognizes in it the work of the Spirit (v. 4). In 2 Cor 1:11 the church is summoned to intercession as an expression of solidarity (cf. 2 Cor 9:14; 2 Tim 1:3). Intercession manifests a "hope against hope" (2 Cor 1:9; Rom 10:1), the social aspect of faith, and dependence on others. Beyond the context of the Church, "the priestly calling of the Church in the world" (Holtz 56) is fulfilled in prayer for non-Christian humanity (1 Tim 2:1). Intercession can thus be called generally "the *prayer* of a righteous man" (Jas 5:16; 1 Pet 3:12).

Δέησις as "special" request (BAGD s.v.) is to be distinguished from προσευχή as the "general" request. As proof of the seriousness of his missionary plans, Paul mentions his prayer (Rom 1:10; cf. 1 Thess 3:10). Eph 6:18 calls prayer a "weapon" (cf. vv. 13-17), through which the Spirit of God works. Prayer "battles" the powers and supports the gospel.

Δέομαι and δέησις are developed into elements of a specific style of piety that describes the behavior of Christians (cf. Acts 10:2: Cornelius "*prayed* constantly to God"; Luke 2:37: Anna served "with fasting and *prayer* night and day"; cf. Luke 5:33; Phil 4:6; 1 Tim 5:5). The absolute use of this word implies God as object. Where the content of the request cannot be determined (cf. Acts 1:14; 1 Tim 2:1), the meaning of the word must be determined from the context.

3. **Προσδέομαι** *require (something)* occurs only in Acts 17:24f. in the speech at the Areopagus. The essential meaning of the word is strengthened with οὐδέ (v. 25): God is not "served by human hands, as if he *needed* anything" (cf. Dibelius 43). The OT polemic against the anthropomorphic concept of God (cf. Ps 50:9f.; Isa 42:5) is assimilated here. Nevertheless, tendencies of the Hellenistic enlightenment (e.g., the self-sufficiency of God) are determinative. Dependent mankind is contrasted with the independent God. The motif of the God who needs nothing strengthens the exhortation to repentance (cf. Acts 17:30).

This aspect of the Greek teaching of God appears nowhere else in the NT. By contrast, 2 Cor 5:20 presents God as the one who, as the crucified one and as the one who makes the request, makes himself known in the apostolic proclamation.

U. Schoenborn

δέον *deon* necessary
→ δεῖ 1.

δέος, ους, τό *deos* fear; reverence*

Heb 12:28: "Offer God acceptable worship, with reverence and *fear* (μετὰ εὐλαβείας καὶ δέους)." H. Balz and G. Wanke, *TDNT* IX, 189-219.

Δερβαῖος, 3 *Derbaios* from Derbe*

According to Acts 20:4 Paul's companion Gaius came from Derbe.

Δέρβη, ης *Derbē* Derbe*

A city in Lycaonia. Acts 14:6, 20; 16:1 mention visits of Paul on his "first" and "second" missionary journeys. A. Wikenhauser, *LTK* III, 241; G. Ogg, "Derbe," *NTS* 9 (1962/63) 367-70; B. Van Elderen, "Some Archaeological Observations on Paul's First Missionary Journey," FS Bruce 156-61.

δέρμα, ατος, τό *derma* skin (noun)*

Heb 11:37, concerning prophets and (other) martyrs from the past: "They went about in *skins* of sheep and goats." O. Michel, *Hebräer* (KEK) ad loc.

δερμάτινος, 3 *dermatinos* made of leather*

Mark 1:6 par. Matt 3:4, of the *leather* girdle of John the Baptist; cf. 2 Kgs 1:8; Josephus *Ant.* ix.22; *Gos. Eb.* 2. P. Vielhauer, *Aufsätze zum NT* (1965) 47-54.

δέρω *derō* beat, strike*

1. Occurrences in the NT — 2. Meaning — 3. Theological usage

Lit.: D. R. A. Hare, *The Theme of Jewish Persecution of Christians in the Gospel according to St. Matthew* (1967). — M. Hengel, "Das Gleichnis von den Weingärtnern Mc 12, 1-12 im Lichte der Zenonpapyri und der rabbinischen Gleichnisse," *ZNW* 59 (1968) 1-39. — R. Pesch, *Naherwartungen. Tradition und Redaktion in Mk 13* (1968) 126-29. — *idem, Markus* (HTKNT) II (1977), esp. 216f. — O. H. Steck, *Israel und das gewaltsame Geschick der Propheten* (WMANT 23, 1967), esp. 269-73. — H. Windisch, *Der zweite Korintherbrief* (ed. G. Strecker; [2]1970) (on 2 Cor 11:20).

1. This vb. occurs 15 times in the NT, of which 9 are in the Synoptics. Here the usage is concentrated in the parable of the workers in the vineyard in Mark 12:1-12 par. (Mark 12:3, 5; Matt 21:35; Luke 20:10f.). In addition δέρω is found in the speech in Mark 13:9, in another parable in Luke 12:47f., and in the Passion story in Luke 22:63. John also introduces the vb. into the Passion narrative (18:23). Finally, δέρω appears also in Acts 5:40; 16:37; 22:19; 1 Cor 9:26; 2 Cor 11:20.

2. Δέρω means literally *flay, skin.* It is used in this sense only in the LXX (Lev 1:6; 2 Chr 29:34; 35:11), which uses it in a cultic-technical sense of peeling the skin off a sacrificial animal. In the NT δέρω appears only with the fig. meaning *beat.* In the act. it is connected with the acc. It is less frequently used in the pass. (Mark 13:9; Luke 12:47f.; see BAGD s.v.). With the exception of 1 Cor 9:26 it concerns acts between persons. In this verse a person is indeed the subject, but the acc. obj. is a thing (i.e., the "air," → ἀήρ). Yet the air is introduced here ironically as replacement for a person.

In the parable of the vineyard workers the beating of the rent collectors is a realistic response of the tenants. It is illegal, of course, and thus it can be punished by the owners. On the other hand, Mark 13:9 refers to the legal beating that was permitted to the Jewish and Gentile courts and to state functionaries and kings. Acts 5:40; 16:37; 22:19 cite individual instances of the imposition of the punishment by beating against Christians. In Luke 12:47f. a reference is made to the ancient beatings within the household, which was a right especially granted to the paterfamilias under Roman law. Luke 22:63; John 18:23; and 2 Cor 11:20 refer to the gray area of the law. The δέρειν of the condemned, as long as it does not concern an explicit accompanying or additional punishment, is legally not permissible. Nevertheless, the condemned was not able to get any redress. Similarly in 2 Cor 11:20 an illegal beating is calmly accepted.

3. In the allegory of the workers in the vineyard, the reaction of the tenants has an OT reference to the Deuteronomic tradition of the persecution and killing of the prophets (Steck). At the same time, this tradition is enriched by the killing of *the* prophet (Jesus). Luke 22:63 and John 18:23 refer to another OT tradition in alluding to the suffering servant of God of Isaiah 50 and the suffering righteous one of the Psalms. This line is also in effect in regard to the significance of the persecution of the disciples according to Mark 13:9. In the incidents described in Acts the disciples continue Jesus' destiny of suffering and renew his bid to raise up the unsuffering dominion of the gospel by suffering what is given to them both legally and illegally.

D. Dormeyer

δεσμεύω *desmeuō* shackle, bind
→ δεσμός 6.

δεσμέω *desmeō* shackle, bind

Luke 8:29 C Koine A D W Θ (instead of → δεσμεύω): "He was *bound* with chains."

δέσμη, ης, ἡ *desmē* bundle
→ δεσμός 7.

δέσμιος, ου, ὁ *desmios* prisoner
→ δεσμός 3, 4.

δεσμός, οῦ, ὁ *desmos* chain; imprisonment*

1. Occurrences in the NT — 2. Meaning — 3. Δέσμιος — 4. Terms of Christian discipleship — 5. Σύνδεσμος — 6. Δεσμεύω — 7. Δέσμη

Lit.: F. ANNEN, *Heil für die Heiden. Zur Bedeutung und Geschichte der Tradition vom besessenen Gerasener (Mk 5, 1-20 parr.)* (1976). — S. ARBANDT, W. MACHEINER, and C. COLPE, *RAC* IX, 318-45, esp. 341f. — BAGD s.v. — P. BENOIT and M.-É. BOISMARD, *Synopse des quatre Évangiles en français* II (1972), esp. §§142, 158, 217, 349. — H. D. BETZ, *Lukian von Samosata und das NT* (1961), esp. 170f. — BULTMANN, *History,* esp. 13, 61-62, 271ff., 283ff. — DEISSMANN, *Light,* 346. — DIBELIUS, *Tradition,* esp. 100ff. — E. HAENCHEN, *Der Weg Jesu* (1966), esp. 257-77, 517-20. — K. KERTELGE, *Die Wunder Jesu im Markusevangelium* (1970), esp. 101-10, 157-61. — G. KITTEL, *TDNT* II, 43. — H. J. KLAUCK, "Das Amt der Kirche nach Eph 4, 1-6," *WiWei* 36 (1973) 81-110. — KUSS III, 72-75, 452-57. — D. R. DE LACEY, "Paul in Jerusalem," *NTS* 20 (1973/74) 82-86. — P. LAMARCHE, "Le possédé de Gerasa (Mt 8, 28-34; Mc 5, 1-20; Lc 8, 26-39)," *NRT* 90 (1968) 581-97. — H.-G. LINK, *DNTT* III, 591-92. — LSJ 380, 1701 (σύνδεσμος). — E. PAX, "Stilistische Beobachtungen an neutralen Redewendungen im NT," *SBFLA* 17 (1967) 335-74. — R. PESCH, *Der Besessene von Gerasa* (1972), esp. 57ff. — B. RIGAUX, *Témoignage de l'Évangile de Luc* (1970). — G. SCHNEIDER, *Lukas* (ÖTK), esp. 192-95, 298-301. — J. SCHREINER, "Die apokalyptische Bewegung," Maier/Schreiner 214-53. — H. SCHÜRMANN, *Orientierung am NT. Exegetische Aufsätze* III (1978), esp. 89-143. — E. SCHWEIZER, *The Letter to the Colossians* (1982). — P. SEIDENSTICKER, *Paulus, der verfolgte Apostel Jesu Christi* (1965). — F. STAUDINGER, "Die Sabbatkonflikte bei Lukas" (Diss. Graz, 1964). — P. STUHLMACHER, *Philemon* (EKKNT, 1975). — A. SUHL, "Der Philemonbrief als Beispiel paulinischer Paränese," *Kairos* 15 (1973) 267-79. — G. THEISSEN, *Urchristliche Wundergeschichten* (1974). — A. VANHOYE, "La structure littéraire de l'Épitre aux Hébreux," (SN 1, 1962), esp. 173-82, 191-204. — N. WALTER, "Die Philipper und das Leiden. Aus den Anfängen einer heidenchristlichen Gemeinde," FS Schürmann 417-34. — F. ZEILINGER, *Die Erstgeborene der Schöpfung. Untersuchungen zur Formalstrucktur und Theologie des Kolosserbriefs* (1974), esp. 71-73, 161-64.

1. Along with the 18 occurrences in the NT, δεσμός is added in the TR of Acts 22:30, and Heb 10:34 TR has δεσμός instead of δέσμιος. Except for Mark 7:35 and Luke

13:16 (each with the art.; Luke also with a demonstrative pron.), δεσμός always appears in the pl. (Phil 1:13 in acc. pl.; cf. Euripides *Ba.* 518), usually without the art. (Acts 20:23; 23:29; 26:31; 2 Tim 2:9; Heb 11:36; Jude 6). Matthew does not use δεσμός. The words δεσμός and δέσμιος are also unknown in the Johannine literature and in the major Pauline works.

The Synoptics use δεσμός 3 times in miracle stories: Mark 7:35 (special material); Luke 8:29 (redactional, cf. Mark 5:8, which gives an interpretive revision of a tradition that has been handed on; cf. Annen 24-26, 70-72, 206-7); Luke 13:16 (special material). Δεσμός occurs in connection with Paul's imprisonments: Acts 16:26; 20:23; 23:29; 26:29, 31; Phil 1:7, 13, 14, 17; Phlm 10, 13; Col 4:18; 2 Tim 2:9. In the LXX frequent use is made of the word group δεσμ-; it often renders *'āsar,* "bind, shackle," or *mōsēr,* "chain" (e.g., Isa 49:9; Ps 2:3; Jer 2:20).

2. The root δεσμ- has the basic meaning "bind." Δεσμός means, in the first place, *chain,* and was used since Homer (*Il.* vi.507; *Od.* xiii.100; cf. Herodotus iii.145; Plato *Lg.* ix.864e), always in the literal and concrete sense of the word. The demoniac of Gerasa, like Samson (Judg 15:13f.), repeatedly broke the fetters that bound him (Luke 8:29). In his healing activity, Jesus manifests his power over the demons and his universal mercy (note the healing story in the Gentile area). Together with Silas, Paul lies in chains at Philippi (Acts 16:26). In his farewell discourse to the elders of Ephesus at Miletus the apostle speaks of "*chains* and affliction" that await him in Jerusalem (Acts 20:23). At the end of his defense before Festus and Agrippa, Paul asks God for the conversion of his listeners to be such as he was—"except for these *chains*" (Acts 26:29).

In the word of exhortation of Heb 11:36, there is a reference to the suffering heroes of the old covenant, who experienced "mocking and scourging, and even *chains* and imprisonment." Chains are understood as the adornment of the innocent suffering martyrs (e.g., Ign. *Eph.* 11:2; *Magn.* 1:2; *Phld.* 8:1; *Pol.* 1:1). As the expression of fidelity, they are meritorious (cf. Ign. *Rom.* 2:2; 4:1).

As a derivative of the basic meaning, δεσμός can also mean *imprisonment* (e.g., Diodorus Siculus xiv.103.3; Josephus *Ant.* xiii.294, 302; *Vita* 241). In Acts 21:18-36 Luke describes the arrest of Paul in detail and then emphasizes in Acts 23:29; 26:31 the illegality of his imprisonment. He sets forth the apostle, who himself emulates the suffering Christ (Phil 3:12-17), as the model of the innocent martyr. Those who do not understand and those who are his opponents want to afflict Paul in his imprisonment (Phil 1:17). In the final greeting the author of Colossians encourages the church: "Remember I am *in prison*" (Col 4:18; cf. Eph 3:1). *In prison* Paul has become a father to the runaway slave Onesimus, who is now a Christian. The apostle sends him back with a cover letter to his "fellow worker Philemon" (v. 1). The NT generally assumes (Roman) prisons, where the prisoners were kept in chains until being sentenced (e.g., Mark 6:14-29; Acts 12:3-6; 21:33f.).

All terms associated with the word group δεσμ- have a negative and disdainful connotation. In a fig. sense in certain contexts, however, it somewhat loses the element of violence and expresses a positive statement. In connection with a typical concept of antiquity, Mark 7:35 describes how Jesus heals the tongue that was bound by a demon (Deissmann 344ff.), in order to initiate the coming of the rule of God for the deaf-mute and to make possible the praise of God in the proclamation. The Lukan sabbath conflict (Luke 13:10-17), in form-critical terms a conflict story and school conversation, finds its high point in v. 16 through the salvific act of Jesus. Just as the sabbath is not desecrated by untying livestock from the manger, so it is not desecrated by releasing a "daughter of Abraham" from the fetters of Satan. Because it corresponds to the will of God, the woman "must" therefore be freed from her fetters.

In the word of judgment against false teachers in the church, Jude 5-16 makes a warning in apocalyptic-prophetic language with a reference to the angels whom the Lord has kept "in eternal *chains* (δεσμοῖς ἀϊδίοις) in the nether gloom until the judgment"; cf. *1 Enoch* 10:4-6; *Jub.* 5:10f.; *m. Yoma* 6:8 (cf. Billerbeck III, 783-85; Schreiner 234-52).

3. **Δέσμιος** *prisoner** occurs in the NT 16 times. It appears in the LXX as the translation of *'āsar* or *'asîr* (cf. Josephus *Ant.* xiii.203; xvii.145). Of the NT uses 9 are with the art. Mark 15:6 par. Matt 27:15 (and redactional Matt 27:16) belong to the Synoptic Passion story. The crowd beseeches Pilate to release "a *prisoner* named Barabbas" as part of the Passover amnesty (Mark 15:6-14 par.). Acts 16:25 reports the nocturnal prayer and praise of Paul and Silas in the prison at Philippi and observes that "*the prisoners* were listening to them." When an earthquake freed all of them, the jailer (δεσμοφύλαξ) wanted to take his life in the first moment of shock because he believed that the prisoners had escaped (v. 27).

According to Acts 23:18 Paul the prisoner has his nephew report a conspiracy against him to the centurion. The procurator Festus takes over a prisoner from the period of Felix's time in office (25:14) and, during a conversation with Agrippa, finds it ridiculous to send the prisoner to Caesar without giving "a reasonable basis" (v. 27). Acts 28:16, describing Paul's arrival in Rome, has an expansion in the TR: "The centurion delivered the *prisoner* to the captain of the guard" (AV; see *TCGNT*). In v. 17 Paul reports that he was "delivered *prisoner* from Jerusalem into the hands of the Romans." The word, which is unknown in the Catholic Epistles and Luke, refers particularly to Paul the prisoner; it belongs to his theology

(→ 4) and to the parenetic texts of the late literature (Heb 10:34; 13:3; cf. Lucian *Peregr.* 12).

4. Δεσμός and δέσμιος signify in Paul's Prison Epistles and in the deutero-Pauline letters that the apostle is a δέσμιος Χριστοῦ Ἰησοῦ (Phlm 1, 9; generally without an art.), the prisoner (Eph 3:1) of Christ Jesus for the Gentiles "in the Lord." Only in Eph 4:1 is δέσμιος constructed with the typical Pauline ἐν κυρίῳ. Otherwise the gen. of source, quality, and possession expresses the apostle's inner relationship to Christ together with its missionary effect. This call and mission are also the basis, in the Pauline anamnesis (2 Tim 1:8, with art.), of the challenge to Timothy to practice discipleship courageously in suffering. In Phil 1:7, 13, 14, 17 Paul places δεσμός in relation to Christ and his gospel. The meaning that the apostle ascribes to imprisonment "lies in the fact that it furthers the progress and spread of the gospel. On the one hand, it has got around in the prison and elsewhere that he wears his fetters for Christ's sake; on the other hand, because he is in prison, the rest of the brethren venture the more fearlessly to proclaim the gospel of Christ" (Link 592); cf. *1 Clem.* 49:2.

5. **Σύνδεσμος** bond, shackle* (known since Euripides and Thucydides; cf. LXX: 3 Kgdms 6:10; 14:24; Isa 58:6, 9; Jer 11:9; cf. Josephus *Ant.* iii.120; τὸ σύνδεσμος, *Barn.* 3:3) means literally "that which binds." There are 4 occurrences in the NT. Eph 4:3 speaks of the "*bond* of peace." In Col 2:19 σύνδεσμος designates Christ, who holds together his body, the Church; in 3:14 it refers to love as the divine bond that connects believers to each other (cf. Hos 11:14) and liberates them. Cf. Ign. *Trall.* 3:1; Origen *Hom.* 9:4 on Jer. (see numerous examples in *PGL* 1310f.). In Acts 8:23 Peter sees Simon of Samaria in the grasp of a "*bond* of iniquity" and greed; cf. *Barn.* 3:3, 5 (citation from Isa 58:6, 9 LXX); see also BAGD s.v.

6. The vb. **δεσμεύω** *shackle, bind** occurs 3 times in the NT. It is attested in Euripides, Xenophon, Epictetus; in Judg 16:11; 3 Macc 5:5, and often in the LXX; and in Josephus *Ant.* xiv.348. The demoniac from Gerasa had been repeatedly (impf.) "*bound* hand and foot like a prisoner" (Luke 8:29, redactional). In Paul's defense speech in the outer court of the temple in Jerusalem (Acts 22:3-21), he describes how he, as one who had been zealous for God before his conversion, had persecuted and "chained" Christians and delivered them into prisons (v. 4). In Matt 23:4 (redactional) Jesus condemns the scribes and Pharisees (and warns the Church at the same time against such behavior), since they "*bind* heavy burdens" for other people but do not themselves lift a finger; cf. Gen 37:7; Amos 2:8; Jdt 8:3.

7. **Δέσμη** *bundle** (Tischendorf accents δεσμή) was known since Demosthenes and Theophrastus (*HP* ix.17.1). In Matt 13:30 (special material), the only NT reference, it is used in the parable of the weeds among the wheat for the weeds that are bound together (δῆσαι) "in *bundles*" and burned.

Among words with the root δεσμ- belong also the nouns → δεσμοφύλαξ, *keeper of the prison;* → δεσμωτήριον, *prison;* and → δεσμώτης, *prisoner.*

F. Staudinger

δεσμοφύλαξ, ακος, ὁ *desmophylax* keeper of the prison*

In the NT only in Acts 16:23, 27, 36, of the Philippian *jailer.*

δεσμωτήριον, ου, τό *desmōtērion* prison*

Matt 11:2 (cf. Luke) reports, "John heard *in prison* about the deeds of the Christ." Acts 5:21, 23 appear in the narrative of the miraculous liberation of the apostles in Jerusalem. And in 16:26, during the imprisonment of Paul and Silas in Philippi, "the foundations of *the prison* were shaken," leading to the miraculous freeing of the two.

δεσμώτης, ου, ὁ *desmōtēs* prisoner*

Acts 27:1, 42, each in the pl., of the *prisoners* who made the journey on the sea toward Italy with Paul and were rescued at Malta.

δεσπότης, ου, ὁ *despotēs* lord; owner*

1. Occurrences in the NT — 2. Sociological usage — 3. Theological usage — 4. Christological usage — 5. Compounds

Lit.: K. H. Rengstorf, *TDNT* II, 44-49. — For further bibliography see *TWNT* X, 1037f.

1. The NT has 10 occurrences, all in the later writings: 2 in the Lukan writings, 4 in the Pastorals, 3 in the Catholic Epistles, and 1 in Revelation. The relatively late appearance is conditioned by the stronger inclination to employ Hellenistic terminology in the second and third generations of early Christianity.

2. As a sociological t.t. δεσπότης appears in the rules for slaves. Here it designates, in accordance with Hellenistic usage, the *master* in contrast to the slave. As Christians, slaves should submit themselves to their masters (Titus 2:9; 1 Pet 2:18) and count them worthy of all honor (1 Tim 6:1); if the masters are Christians, they should be served even more zealously (v. 2). The reason for this counsel hinges on the opinion of pagan masters (1 Tim 6:1; Titus 2:10). Those who have ill-tempered masters must remember that unjust suffering for the sake of the faith is to win God's approval (1 Pet 2:18); those whose masters are

Christians must remember that they are brothers and should behave accordingly (1 Tim 6:2).

3. Δεσπότης has a strictly theological meaning when it is used in address to God, as it is in Simeon's song of praise (Luke 2:29), in communal prayer (Acts 4:24), and in the martyrs' cry for vengeance (Rev 6:10). When the one who prays designates himself as slave (Luke 2:29), the sociological use of the word is transferred to the relationship between human being and God, as now the Creator (Acts 4:24) and Judge (Rev 6:10) is in view. This Hellenistic way of addressing God is common in the LXX and in Josephus and takes different emphases, depending on the context.

4. Δεσπότης appears as a title for Christ in the characterization of false teachers. They deny τὸν μόνον δεσπότην καὶ κύριον ἡμῶν Ἰησοῦν Χριστόν (Jude 4), "*the Master* who bought them" (2 Pet 2:1). Μόνος δεσπότης belongs to the formal language of Jewish monotheism but may be a designation of Christ in Jude 4. In both cases denial means disobedience of the commands of Christ, who is understood as the one who commands. In 2 Tim 2:21 δεσπότης is used metaphorically for the master of the house but refers actually to Christ in the wider context of the warning against false teachers (v. 22).

5. **Οἰκοδεσπότης** *master of the house* and **οἰκοδεσποτέω** *rule the house* are late word formations without attestation in the LXX and Josephus. In Mark 14:14 par. the subst. is used for the owner of the house where Jesus celebrates the Passover. Parables and metaphors describe a definite behavior of a master of the house, which actually refers to God (Luke 14:21; Matt 13:27; 20:1, 11; 21:33), to Christ (Luke 13:25; Matt 10:25), or to a person (Matt 13:52; 24:43 par.). Οἰκοδεσποτέω appears only in the rule for widows in 1 Tim 5:14 and is, along with marriage and the bearing of children, an expression in the Pastorals of expected Christian family living.

G. Haufe

δεῦρο *deuro* to this place; until now*

This adv. is used with reference to place, meaning *to this place.* It appears with an imv. vb. (Mark 10:21 par. Matt 19:21/Luke 18:22) and with an announcement or promise (Acts 7:34; Rev 17:1; 21:9) and also can be used absolutely (John 11:43; Acts 7:3). In Rom 1:13 its meaning is temporal: *until now* (ἄχρι τοῦ δεῦρο).

δεῦτε *deute* (come) here, (come) on (imv.)*

This adv. appears normally as a particle of encouragement with the imv. or aor. subjunc. following (Mark 12:7 par. Matt 21:38/Luke 20:14 v.l.; Matt 28:6, cf. Mark; John 4:29; 21:12; Rev 19:17). It also appears absolutely (Mark 1:17 par. Matt 4:19; Mark 6:31; Matt 11:28; 22:4; 25:34).

δευτεραῖος, 3 *deuteraios* on the second day*

Acts 28:13: "*On the second day* (δευτεραῖοι) we came to Puteoli." BDF §243.

δευτερόπρωτος, 2 *deuteroprōtos* second-first (?)

Luke 6:1 C Koine A D Θ *pm* lat.: ἐν σαββάτῳ δευτεροπρώτῳ. The word δευτερόπρωτος does not appear in this passage in 𝔓[4] 𝔓[75vid] ℵ B L W λ *al* it sy[p] sa bo, and the shorter reading "on a sabbath" is to be preferred. On the textual witnesses, see more precisely *UBSGNT* ad loc.; on the textual criticism, cf. *TCGNT* ad loc. Probably marginal glosses to 6:2 (as comparisons with the sabbath days mentioned in 4:31 and 6:6) have led to the variant reading δευτερόπρωτος; see G. W. Buchanan and C. Wolfe, "The 'Second-First Sabbath' (Luke 6:1)," *JBL* 97 (1978) 259-62. The conjecture ἐν σαββάτῳ βίᾳ ("on a sabbath he was required") in place of ἐν σαββᾶτῳ δευτερόπρωτος is offered by E. Delebecque, *Études grecques sur l'Évangile de Luc* (1976) 71-83, who suggests that βίᾳ (BIAI) could have been misunderstood as the numerical reference B'A'.

δεύτερος, 3 *deuteros* second

1. Occurrences in the NT — 2. As a numeral — 3. Usage in referring back and as a connective — 4. Usage as a qualifier

Lit.: H. Conzelmann, *1 Corinthians* (Hermeneia, 1975) 284-85. — O. Hofius, "Das 'erste' und das 'zweite' Zelt. Ein Beitrag zur Auslegung von Hebr 9, 1-10," *ZNW* 61 (1970) 271-77. — E. Käsemann, *Commentary on Romans* (1980) 140-58. — W. G. Kümmel, *Theology* 155, 157f. — R. Pesch, *Markus* (HTKNT) II, 236-49 (bibliography). — H. Schlier, *Der Römerbrief* (1977) 179-89. J. L. Sharpe, "The Second Adam in the Apocalypse of Moses," *CBQ* 35 (1973) 35-46. — U. Wilckens, "Christus, der 'letzte Adam' und der Menschensohn," FS Vögtle 378-403.

1. With 13 of the 43 passages that have the word, only Revelation shows a preference for δεύτερος. The other occurrences are in the Gospels (13 occurrences), Acts (5), and Epistles (12); cf. Matt 21:30 v.l.

2. Δεύτερος appears primarily as a numeral, e.g., for the designation of a "second person" in a usually well-defined series (Mark 12:21 par.; Matt 21:30 v.l.; Luke 19:18; cf. Rev 4:7; 8:8; 14:8; 16:3); no special meaning is given to the second person. The adverbial phrases ἐκ δευτέρου (Matt 26:42; Mark 14:72; John 9:24; Acts 10:15; 11:9; Heb 9:28), (τὸ) δεύτερον (John 3:4; 21:16; 1 Cor 12:28; 2 Cor 13:2; Jude 5), and ἐν τῷ δευτέρῳ (Acts 7:13) are generally used of the second occurrence of an event (of which there are often three).

3. Δεύτερος is used to refer back and as a connective when it calls attention to something that is closely related to another item. The author of 2 Peter thus employs the

reference in 3:1 to indicate that this is already "the *second* letter"; it is to be connected with 1 Peter, which is assumed to be known already. In this way apostolic continuity and the reliability of the message are underscored. In a similar sense Mark 12:31 par. Matt 22:39 designates the command to love one's neighbor as δευτέρα (ἐντολή), second to the love of God, but at the same time maintains the indissoluble unity of the two (esp. Matt 22:39: the second is "like" the first).

4. Finally, δεύτερος can be used to emphasize the specifically *new*, which surpasses and excels the "first."

a) The "second covenant" of Heb 8:7, in comparison with the first, is "new" (v. 13; vv. 8b-12 = Jer 31:31-34) and "better" (8:6f.), founded on Christ as the surety (7:22) and mediator (9:15), the new high priest (4:14–10:18) who has been installed by God. It is the guarantee of the salvation given by God and of the redemption through his blood (9:11-15; cf. the salvation-historical interpretation of πρώτη σκηνή and δευτέρα σκηνή in vv. 1-10).

b) Δεύτερος takes on the connotation of surpassing the first in the reference to Jesus Christ in 1 Cor 15:47; as the "second man," i.e., as the "last Adam" who is contrasted with the "first man Adam" (v. 45), he stands at the end of history as the one who is eschatologically suited and decisive for salvation as a result of the resurrection. Christ and Adam are two opposite poles. Death, which is the fate brought into the world through Adam, is overcome through the resurrection (vv. 20-22). Thus Christ is the eschatologically decisive form of the "second man" = the "last Adam."

c) The reference to the "second death" (Rev 2:11; 20:6, 14; 21:8) is based on the conception of bodily death as the inescapable end of human life. Through reference to the role of God (20:11) and Christ (19:11-16) in judgment, this "second death" is described in relation to natural death as radically different and as the decisive act with regard to the future hope. It is—according to the one who endures the judgment, for whom eternal life with Jesus is in view—the irrevocable ratification of the decision against God, i.e., the eternal damnation. Only "faithfulness unto death" promises preservation from the second death (2:10f.).

L. Oberlinner

δέχομαι *dechomai* take; receive

1. Occurrences in the NT — 2. Of objects — 3. Of persons — 4. Of facts

Lit.: W. Grundmann, *TDNT* II, 50-59. — For further bibliography see *TWNT* X, 1038.

1. Δέχομαι appears 56 times in the NT. Most occurrences are in the Synoptic Gospels and Acts (10 in Matthew, 6 in Mark, 16 in Luke, 8 in Acts). Except for 2 Corinthians (5 occurrences) there are only isolated occurrences in the Epistles. NT usage coincides totally with that of the ancient world (cf. Grundmann 50-52). In the NT the grammatical subj. is always a person or a term that stands for persons, e.g., "Samaria," for the inhabitants thereof (Acts 8:14), and "every place" (Mark 6:11). The grammatical objects of δέχομαι can be divided into objects, persons, and facts.

2. *Taking* and *receiving* a object: This usage is rare in the NT. The object of δέχομαι, however, can be a bill (Luke 16:6f.), a cup (Luke 22:17), letters (Acts 22:5; 28:21), a helmet and sword (Eph 6:17), as well as gifts (Phil 4:18).

3. *Acceptance* and *receiving* of a person: In Luke 2:28 Simeon *takes* the child in his arms, which is related to → 2. More frequently the conception of a *hospitable reception* is present (Luke 16:4; 2 Cor 7:15; Col 4:10; Heb 11:31), which can designate theologically *acceptance* of the message of Jesus. This transition is apparent in Luke 9:53; 10:8, 10; John 4:45 and is unambiguously present in Matt 10:40f.: whoever *receives* the disciples, *receives* Jesus and consequently also the one who sent Jesus. This chain of commissioning going back to God is apparently dependent on Semitic law concerning envoys and is intended to express the identity of the messenger with the sender and thus to legitimate the messenger. In the form in Mark 9:37 par., which is probably original, this "chain" is used in reference to children and has the meaning: whoever *receives* children, *receives* Jesus or God. *Receiving* the disciples explicitly includes hearing the message (Mark 6:11 par.).

In scattered instances δέχομαι refers to *reception* into the life to come (Luke 16:9; Acts 3:21; cf. also 7:59, → 4). In Gal 4:14 Paul was "*received* as an angel of God"; in 2 Cor 11:16 Paul asks, "*accept* [i.e., endure, bear with] me as a fool." Finally, in Acts 7:59 Stephen prays that Jesus will *receive* his spirit (i.e., his person).

4. *Acceptance* of facts: According to Matt 11:14, the hearer should *accept* the statement that John the Baptist is Elijah, the one who is to come. According to Acts 7:38, Moses *received* the living oracles. According to 1 Cor 2:14, an unspiritual person cannot *receive*, i.e., *intelligibly accept*, the things of the Spirit of God, because he considers them foolish. Other passages speak in a variety of phrases of acceptance of the message, the gospel: as the word (of God: Luke 8:13; Acts 8:14; 11:1; 17:11; 1 Thess 1:6; 2:13; Jas 1:21), as χάρις (2 Cor 6:1), as παράκλησις (2 Cor 8:17), as love of the truth (2 Thess 2:10), and as the kingdom of God (Mark 10:15 par.).

G. Petzke

δέω *deō* bind; tie*

1. Occurrences in the NT — 2. Meaning — 3. Fig. use — 4. "Binding and loosing" in Matt 16:19; 18:18

Lit.: G. Bornkamm, "Die Binde- und Lösegewalt in der Kirche des Matthäus," FS Schlier 93-107, esp. 101-106. — F. Büchsel, *TDNT* II, 60-61. — R. Bultmann, "Die Frage nach der Echtheit von Mt 16, 17-19," in *idem, Exegetica* (1967) 255-77. — H. Frankemölle, *Jahwebund und Kirche Christi* (1972), esp. 220-47. — Goppelt, *Theology* I, 207-13. — Hahn, *Titles* 82f., 155-99. — Hengel, *Judaism* I, 47-55. — P. Hoffmann, "Der Petrus-Primat im Mt," FS Schnackenburg 94-114. — R. Hummel, *Die Auseinandersetzung zwischen Kirche und Judentum im Matthäusevangelium* ([2]1966), esp. 56-64, 74f., 154-57. — J. Jeremias, *TDNT* III, 744-53. — K. Kertelge, "Jesus, seine Wundertaten und der Satan," *Concilium* 11 (1975) 168-73. — J. Kremer, "Jesus und die Kirche," *Zeit des Geistes* (ed. J. Reikerstorfer; 1977) 41-58. — W. von Meding and D. Müller, *DNTT* I, 171-72. — O. Michel, *RAC* II, 374-80. — Pape, *Wörterbuch* 555-58. — W. Pesch, "Die sogenannte Gemeindeordnung Mt 18," *BZ* 7 (1963) 220-35. — Schelkle, *Theologie* IV/2, 95-103. — E. Schweizer, "Matthew's View of the Church in His 18th Chapter," *ABR* 21 (1973) 7-14. — W. Stenger, "Die Auferweckung des Lazarus (Joh 11, 1-45)," *TTZ* 83 (1974) 17-37. — H. Thyen, *RGG* V, 1449f. — W. Trilling, *Das wahre Israel* ([3]1964), esp. 184-230. — A. Vögtle, "Zum Problem der Herkunft von Mt 16, 17-19," FS Schmid (1973) 372-93. — *idem, LTK* II, 480-82. — For further bibliography see *TWNT* X, 1038.

1. The vb. δέω appears 43 times in the NT (10 occurrences in Matthew, 8 in Mark, 2 in Luke, 4 in John, 12 in Acts; also in Rom 7:2; 1 Cor 7:27, 39; Col 4:3; 2 Tim 2:9; Rev 9:14; 20:2; also in Acts 10:11 v.l.). In Acts δέω is a favorite word in connection with the imprisonment of Paul.

2. The vb. is derived from the root δε- and has the basic meaning *bind (together);* thus Matt 13:30 (special material) of the weeds (cf. Ezek 27:24; *1 Clem.* 43:2). Both in the NT and in the LXX δέω often appears with the literal meaning *tie up,* e.g., in Mark 11:2 (par. Matt 21:2/Luke 19:30), 4, of the colt that the disciples were to untie and bring to Jesus. Δέω appears in John 11:44 (Lazarus bound at the hands and feet) with the meaning *wrap;* cf. 19:40 (Jesus' body in linen cloths).

Frequently δέω means *bind in chains,* as in Mark 5:3f. (the demoniac from Gerasa) and Matt 22:13 (special material; parable of the man without the wedding garment). "Chain" (vb.) thus often means the same as *take prisoner* or (pass.) *be captive* (cf. Plato *Lg.* ix.864e; Diogenes Laertius ii.24; Josephus *B.J.* vii.449): Mark 3:27 par. Matt 12:29 (the metaphor of the binding of the strong man with vocabulary from exorcism); Mark 6:17 par. Matt 14:3 (arrest and imprisonment of the Baptist); John 18:12 (arrest of Jesus); 18:24 (Annas sends Jesus bound to the high priest Caiaphas); Mark 15:1 par. Matt 27:2 (Jesus is bound and led to Pilate); 15:7 (Barabbas in prison).

Paul persecuted the Christians by binding them and taking them into custody: Acts 9:2, 14, 21; 22:5. Peter was bound with two chains, 12:6. Reference is made to the imprisoned Paul in 21:11 (bis), 13, 33; 22:29; 24:27. The mission of the apostle lies in the proclamation of the mysteries of Christ, for which "I am *in prison* (δέδεμαι)," Col 4:3. Although he is *bound* like a criminal, the "word of God is not *fettered,*" 2 Tim 2:9. All of the NT passages mentioned above have a context of physical shackling.

3. Δέω is used fig. for the binding of man and woman in marriage, founded on the order of creation and in the law (Rom 7:2; 1 Cor 7:27, 39; cf. Achilles Tatius i.11; Iamblichus *VP* xi.56). The sabbath conflict story in Luke 13:16 (Lukan special material) speaks of a demonic binding common to that period (cf. Diodorus Siculus i.27; *b. Šabb.* 81b, and elsewhere). Paul, in his farewell address at Miletus (Acts 20:18-35), is "*bound* by the Spirit," i.e., by the Spirit of God, in his activities and travel plans (v. 22). In Rev 9:14 an angel is commissioned to "release the four angels who are *bound* at the great river Euphrates." In 20:2 δέω appears in connection with God's opponent who is overcome by God and bound for a definite time.

"Bind" appears repeatedly both in the literal sense (Mark 11:2 par.; 11:4; John 11:44) and fig. (Luke 13:16; Rev 9:14; 20:2) in connection with λύω, "loose."

4. Behind the much-discussed "*bind* and loose" in Matt 16:19b; 18:18 is not a formula derived from the mystery cult or a magic formula associated with binding but simply rabbinic Heb. *'āsar* (cf. also 1QH 5:36; 1QM 5:3; 1Q 22:3, 11; see *KQT* s.v.) and *hitîr* (hiphil of *ntr*) and Aram. *'^{a}sar* and *š^{e}rā'* (Billerbeck I, 738-42).

"Bind" and "loose" are technical terms in Judaism both for disciplinary force (Billerbeck IV, 304-21; cf. CD 13:10) and for Halakic teaching authority. In a disciplinary sense they frequently designate the imposition and the cancellation of the synagogue ban (cf. also Josephus *B.J.* i.111); with respect to teaching the phrase is used for authoritative exposition of the law by an authorized, ordained rabbi, who has authority "*to forbid* and to permit."

That Jesus grants authority (note "*my* Church") to bind and loose for the future to Peter alone (sg. in Matt 16:19b) or to all of the disciples (pl. in 18:18) is in conscious antithesis (i.e., a Matthean redaction) to the meanings in rabbinic Judaism. An essentially related modification of 18:18 is offered by the Easter tradition of John 20:22f. (cf. the commissioning only of Peter in 21:15-19), which combines the giving of the Spirit and the authority to forgive and retain sins.

The form (parallelism, change of images), style (double circumlocution for God with "in heaven" and the pass.), and concepts of Matt 16:17-19 point unambiguously to a Syro-Palestinian origin. According to Vögtle, Bornkamm, Frankemölle, Hoffmann, and others, Matt 16:17-19 is not originally a unit of tradition (note the change of images); v. 19a does not necessarily belong to v. 19b, as the independently transmitted Amen logion in

18:18 indicates. However, 16:18f. and 18:18 have certainly developed from a single original saying. According to some scholars, 18:18 is the more ancient. It is more probable (cf. Bornkamm, Trilling, Schelkle) that the authority (16:18f.) granted to Peter was claimed by the Church.

The conscious christological and ecclesiological redaction (cf. Frankemölle) of the group of sayings in 16:17-19 is intended to connect Peter's function as rock with the teaching authority. Other features (interest in the Church, overall structure of Matthew, the name Cephas, the special position of Simon in the circle of disciples) both portray Jesus' works and the discipleship "as belonging to each other from the beginning" and underline "the attachment of the Church from all nations to the *earthly* Jesus" (Hoffmann 109). V. 19b concludes, formulated in an open way (ὃ ἐάν twice; use of fut. tense; cf. Frankemölle 241f.), with the promise of the "power of the keys" to Peter (v. 19a; cf. Jeremias 749-53). For the "scribe" Matthew (13:52), the teaching authority as a function of Peter ensures "the *continuity* of his tradition with the earthly Jesus both historically and theologically" (giving it eschatological binding force and validity with God; Hoffmann 109f.). The function of Simon as the rock is historically unique. For Matthew it makes concrete the abiding uniqueness of the Church in its relationship to Jesus. The promise of the abiding presence of the κύριος Jesus corresponds to it (28:18-20).

Despite the disciplinary context of Matt 18:15-18, the Matthean intention in 18:18 concerns the teaching authority, as the parallel with 16:19 indicates. This corresponds totally with the Jewish conceptual world, which valued teaching that was ethically and practically oriented. The redactional intention of Matthew is to be understood, with Bornkamm and others, as follows: the Church, which is founded on the teaching of Jesus as it is authenticated by Peter, understands itself to be obligated and authorized by the Lord who is present within it to exercise discipline in its midst.

The exercise of the binding and loosing authority and the structure of the office in Matt 16:18f.; 18:18; 23:8-11 in the context of the entire Gospel of Matthew are subordinated to the criterion of the exposition of the law and the critique of the law and society by Jesus Christ. This resurrected Lord is the one who authorizes the authoritative proclamation and mediation of salvation.

F. Staudinger

δή *dē* (particle)*

This particle identifies a statement as something definitely established (Matt 13:23; 2 Cor 12:1 Koine); it appears also in commands, giving them an urgency (Luke 2:15; Acts 6:3 v.l.; 13:2; 15:36; 1 Cor 6:20).

δηλαυγῶς *dēlaugōs* (completely) clearly

Mark 8:25 ℵ B C (instead of τηλαυγῶς): "very clearly"; cf. BDF §119.4.

δῆλος, 3 *dēlos* clear, plain*

Matt 26:73: make *clear* to someone, reveal. Elsewhere only δῆλον (ἐστίν understood) with ὅτι, "it is *clear* that": 1 Cor 15:27; Gal 3:11; 1 Tim 6:7 P Koine; also Ign. *Eph.* 6:1.

δηλόω *dēloō* make known*

Lit.: R. Bultmann, *TDNT* II, 61f. — D. Lührmann, *Das Offenbarungsverständnis bei Paulus und in paulinischen Gemeinden* (WMANT 16, 1965).

1. Δηλόω appears 7 times in the NT: twice each in 1 Corinthians and Hebrews and once each in Colossians, 1 Peter, and 2 Peter.

2. The broad meaning of δηλόω is *make known, inform, explain, disclose* to another or to the public what is known through revelation or in the Holy Spirit or as an experienced fact. In 1 Cor 3:13 δηλόω along with ἀποκαλύπτω and φανερὸν γίνεσθαι (φανερόω) is used in a theologically precise sense for the revelation-event that is taking place in the proclamation; it is given to the apostles and is founded on Christ (Lührmann). "Each man's work will become manifest"—Paul speaks of the work of all who build the Church on the foundation that has been laid, on Jesus Christ—"for the Day will *disclose* it, because it will be revealed [burned] with fire." The day (of the Lord) brings to light what belongs to the Lord. What the eschatological work of Jesus Christ brings to light (from what was hidden; cf. 1 Cor 4:5) will be the content of what is revealed on that day. Whereas δηλόω refers in 1 Cor 3:13 to eschatological revelation, in 1:11 and Col 1:8 it refers to matters that come to light publicly (disputes in the congregation or love in the power of the Spirit in the congregation). In Matt 26:73, Peter's speech "betrays" him (δῆλόν σε ποιεῖ).

3. In the other uses of δηλόω a new interpretation of some part of Scripture is offered (Heb 9:8; 12:27; 1 Pet 1:11; 2 Pet 1:14; Luke 20:37 v.l. ἐδήλωσεν instead of ἐμήνυσεν: Moses *showed* the resurrection of the dead in the passage about the burning bush; see Exod 3:6); cf. the interpretive δῆλον ὅτι in 1 Cor 15:27 and Gal 3:11.

This accent on the rational or on what is exegetical or explicative in the meaning of δηλόω is found also in the LXX (where it renders Heb. *yāḏaʿ* [niphal and hiphil], "make plain"), frequently in apocalyptic literature (Daniel) and in *Hermas,* in explanation of mystery or allegory), and in Josephus, Ignatius, etc.

In Heb 9:8 δηλόω designates a typological exegesis that provides the basis in the revelation-event for the "not yet." It is used for the restriction suggested in the revelation (of the way of the saints, for whom Christ is the way; see 10:20) in the time when salvation has not yet been disclosed to the conscience. The Holy Spirit [now] *discloses* this "not yet." If the Spirit is the interpreter of the old covenant, he points to the will of God *in* it, through which it becomes a parable of the present age. In accord with this 12:27 concludes with ἔτι ἅπαξ, a time reference concerning the eschatological shaking of heaven and earth, the meaning of a word of Scripture, i.e., the unstated difference in Hag 2:6 between the temporal and that which is eschatologically real and abiding. Transformation here means that the uniquely new thing can be drawn from the old.

Thus the hermeneutical original situation of the prophecy, not only its Christian interpretation, is determined by the Spirit from a typological standpoint (cf. also 1QS 8:15f.), as is indicated finally in 1 Pet 1:11. Here the subj. of δηλόω is the Spirit of Christ, who works in OT prophecy as a whole; the content is the time of salvation, which had been the subject of inquiry. Whereas ἀπεκαλύφθη in v. 12 means that the prophetic witness concerns essentially the gospel of Christ, δηλόω (according to the model of the apocalyptic and scribal investigation of what has been said) emphasizes that the prophets already had been informed by the Spirit of Christ about the things that they investigated (i.e., the time of salvation). In 2 Pet 1:14 the word choice (ἐδήλωσεν) betrays the fact that the pseudonymous author claims foreknowledge less than he interprets on the basis of a tradition derived from the Lord (e.g., John 21:18f.).

G. Schunack

Δημᾶς, ᾶ *Dēmas* Demas*

A coworker (συνεργός) of Paul mentioned in Phlm 24; Col 4:14; 2 Tim 4:10.

δημηγορέω *dēmēgoreō* speak publicly*

Acts 12:21, of the speech (a festive oration) of Herod Agrippa I to the people.

Δημήτριος, ου *Dēmētrios* Demetrius*

Two men: in Acts 19:24, 38, a silversmith in Ephesus; in 3 John 12, a Christian who received a good testimony from everyone.

δημιουργός, οῦ, ὁ *dēmiourgos* master builder; creator*

1. Heb 11:10 (the only NT occurrence) — 2. The narrower context — 3. History of the concept — 4. The idea of the master builder in Heb 11:10

Lit.: W. Foerster, *TDNT* II, 62; III, 1000-1035. — W. Theiler, *RAC* III, 694-711. — W. Ullmann, *HWP* II, 49f. — H. Volkmann, *KP* I, 1472f. — For further bibliography see *TWNT* X, 1038.

1. The vb. δημιουργέω does not appear in the NT. The noun δημιουργός is a NT hapax legomenon, occurring only in Heb 11:10. The remarkably rare and nontheological usage of the whole word group (LSJ 386) is evident in the LXX (Foerster *TDNT* II, 62; on the relationship of δημιουργός to κτίστης and the reason for relative nonuse of the former in biblical language, see *idem, TDNT* III, 1023-28).

2. In Hebrews 11, a theological and parenetic discourse (cf. Kümmel, *Introduction* 398), δημιουργός is used with τεχνίτης ("craftsman"; see BAGD s.v.) of God. Yet one may observe that both "technical terms" (O. Michel, *Hebräer* [KEK] ad loc.) have their essential meaning in the total image of the building of a city. The context in ch. 11, which is formed by a long anaphora (BDF §491), is to be limited to the first part of the example of faith in Abraham and Sarah (11:8-12), with its preliminary summary in vv. 13-16, which comes in the form of an excursus. The cloud of witnesses of faith (12:1) is given its conclusion finally in 11:39f.

Abraham, who obediently emigrated to an unknown place for his inheritance and thus—for the author of Hebrews—into a future that could not be seen, settled in a strange land and lived in tents together with the coheirs of the promise, Isaac and Jacob (11:8f.). The reference to σκηνή, the lodging customary for nomads, which is an irrelevant fact in the history of the settling in the land (but which, in theological retrospective, provides an image of a provisional and temporary existence), strengthens antithetically the expectation of the city with foundations, whose skillful craftsman and creative founder is God (11:10). This expectation is the basis of hope.

Thus the allusion is not to the earthly city of the temple but rather, as the "insertion" (O. Kuss, *Hebräer* [RNT] ad loc.) indicates clearly, to the old and apocalyptic theme of the "heavenly city," Jerusalem (12:22), which is already prepared (cf., along with the excursus by Michel on 11:10, BAGD s.v. πόλις 2; E. Lohse, *TDNT* VII, 319-38, esp. 337; H. Strathmann, *TDNT* VI, 516-35, esp. 531). The delay of the eschatological fulfillment of the promise for those "ancients" who later died (11:2) is explained by περὶ ἡμῶν and the final clause ἵνα μὴ χωρὶς ἡμῶν τελειωθῶσιν (11:40).

3. The history of the concept δημιουργός shows considerable development of meaning. At the end of this process, the "demiurge" becomes the creator of the world in the mythological redemption system of Gnosticism (K. Rudolph, *Gnosis* [1983] index s.v.). The use of the word in religious Gnosticism, colored as it was by dualism, is not found in the same sense among the metaphysical and cosmological uses of this term that appear frequently from Plato to Plotinus (H. J. Krämer, *Der Ursprung der Geistmetaphysik* [[2]1967]; Theiler 695-704). A list of other meanings may be left out of consideration; it is interesting, nevertheless, that "occupations such as that of soothsayer, physician, singer, herald" as well as "high state officials" and "craftsmen" were identified as δημιουργοί (Volkmann 1473).

4. To understand the image in Heb 11:10 one must recall the determining and fundamental aspect of activity for the

people (δῆμος), the general public. If here the idea concerns the creative vocation of the (city) master builder, the entire phrase τεχνίτης καὶ δημιουργός may refer to the theological and philosophical work of Philo (see G. Mayer, *Index Philoneus* [1974]). The language of Alexandria, used also elsewhere in Hebrews, points to a common conceptual origin.

M. Lattke

δῆμος, ου, ὁ *dēmos* (crowd of) people*

Of the people as the inhabitants of a city: Acts 12:22; 17:5; 19:30, 33. W. Grundmann, *TDNT* II, 63; *TWNT* X, 1038f. (bibliography).

δημόσιος, 3 *dēmosios* public*

Acts 5:18: of the public (= city) prison; also δημοσίᾳ as adv., *publicly,* 16:37; 18:28; 20:20.

δηνάριον, ου, τό *dēnarion* denarius

1. Name and value of the denarius — 2. The denarius in the NT — 3. "Tribute money"

Lit.: BILLERBECK I, 884f. — H. CHANTRAINE, *KP* I, 1488-90. — E. STAUFFER, *Christ and the Caesars* (1955) 112-37.

1. Δηνάριον is a loanword from Latin. The original meaning of the phrase *denarius nummus* ("a coin having ten parts") was no longer in force in the NT period, since the denarius then equaled 16 *as,* not 10 (on the buying power of an *as,* or "cent," cf. Matt 10:29). From 209 B.C. until A.D. 215, the denarius was the standard silver coin. Originally it weighed 4.55 g., but under Nero it dropped to 3.41 g., and later to 2.3 g. The diameter decreased from 22 to 18 mm. Like the *aureus* (= 25 denarii), the denarius was minted exclusively by the ruler. When the head of Caesar was depicted on the face of the coin in 44 B.C., the prototype of the imperial denarius was created. This is the form referred to in the NT. The Greek drachma (→ δραχμή) corresponds to the Latin denarius.

2. Denarii are mentioned in the NT in several contexts: A denarius was a day's wages (Matt 20:2-13); a citizen owed 100 denarii (Matt 18:28), while two others owed 500 and 50 denarii (Luke 7:41); the first installment to an innkeeper amounted to 2 denarii (Luke 10:35); bread for 200 denarii (Mark 6:37; John 6:7) and perfume for 300 denarii are mentioned (Mark 14:5; John 12:5); and in famine the price of a day's ration of wheat climbs to a denarius (Rev 6:6).

3. All of the Synoptics mention "tribute money" (Mark 12:13-17 par.). Jesus has someone hand him a denarius and asks about the image and the inscription. If it was a denarius of Tiberius, the following words appeared around the image of the Caesar: *TIBERIUS CAESAR DIVI AUGUSTI FILIUS AUGUSTUS.* A proof of the sovereignty of a ruler was his being able to circulate currency. The power of a ruler was thus called his "coin."

B. Schwank

δήποτε *dēpote* at any time

John 5:4 v.l.: a person "was healed of *whatever* disease he had."

δήπου *dēpou* surely*

Heb 2:16: "For *surely* it is not with angels that [Jesus] is concerned but with the descendants of Abraham."

διά *dia* with gen.: through, throughout; with acc.: because of, on account of

1. Usage — 2. With gen. — 3. With acc. — 4. Semitisms

Lit.: On preps. in general → ἀνά. — BAGD s.v. — BDF §222f. — KÜHNER, *Grammatik* II/1, 480-85 (§434b). — LSJ s.v. — MAYSER, *Grammatik* II/2, 419-27 (§120). — A. OEPKE, *TDNT* II, 65-70. — For further bibliography see *TWNT* X, 1039.

1. Διά originally expressed the area *throughout which* an event took place. In the NT its range of meaning is limited in the acc. to the causal; however, in the gen. it is expanded into the realm of the instrumental dat. In addition it represents Hebrew clauses (διά with the inf. or with acc. and inf.) and phrases.

2. Διά with the gen.:

a) Spatial: *through, throughout* with vbs. that indicate or imply motion: διεσώθησαν δι' ὕδατος, "they were saved *through* water" (1 Pet 3:20).

b) Temporal: extension over a period of time until the end: *throughout, during.* Examples include διὰ παντός (sc. χρόνου), "always, constant" (Matt 18:10); διὰ νυκτός, "*during* the night" (Acts 23:31). It is used also for a period of time *during which* something occurs: διὰ νυκτός, "*by* night" (Acts 5:19). Although these usages are unclassical (Mayser 420), the meaning corresponds to classical usage when it designates length of time: *after, in the course of*. . . , as in δι' ἐτῶν πλειόνων, "*after* some years" (Acts 24:17).

c) Instrumental (substituting for instrumental dat.): γράφειν διὰ χάρτου καὶ μέλανος, "to write *with* paper and ink" (2 John 12). Modal: indicating manner (with vbs. of speaking): ἀπαγγέλλειν διὰ λόγου, "tell *by* word of mouth" (Acts 15:27); accompanying circumstances: διὰ προσκόμματος ἐσθίειν, "to eat *with* offense, misgivings" (Rom 14:20); effective cause: διὰ νόμου ἐπίγνωσις ἁμαρτίας, "*through* the law comes knowledge of sin" (Rom 3:20); occasion: διὰ τῆς χάριτος, "*in virtue of* the grace" (Rom 12:3); the urgency of a request: διὰ τῶν οἰκτιρμῶν θεοῦ, "*by* the mercies of God" (Rom 12:1; a Latinism for *per*?). Human agency: δι' ἀνθρώπου, "*through* human mediation" (Gal 1:1). Causal: διὰ τῆς σαρκός, "*because of* our unspiritual nature" (Rom 8:3, JB).

3. Διά with the acc.:

a) Spatial: only in Luke 17:11 (Koine and others have gen.).

b) Grounds: *because of, for:* διὰ τὸν φόβον τῶν Ἰουδαίων, "*for* fear of the Jews" (John 7:13); to indicate the purpose for which something exists (unclassical): *for the sake of:* διὰ τὸν ἄνθρωπον, "*for [the sake of]* man" (Mark 2:27).

c) With inf. and subj. acc. indicates (more frequently than in classical) cause: διὰ τὸ εἶναι αὐτὸν ἐξ οἴκου . . . Δαυίδ, "*because* he was of the house . . . of David" (Luke 2:4).

d) In place of διά with the gen.: ζῶ διὰ τὸν πατέρα, "I live *because of* the father" (John 6:57).

4. Semitisms with διά include the following: διὰ τί (for *lāmâ*), "why?" (Matt 9:11); διὰ χειρός with the gen. (for *b^eyaḏ*), "*by* the hands of" (Acts 2:23); διὰ στόματος with the gen. (for *b^epî*), "*by* the mouth of" (Luke 1:70); and διὰ μέσου αὐτῶν (for *b^eṯôḵ*), "*through* the midst of them" (Luke 4:30).

A. J. Hess

διαβαίνω *diabainō* go through; go across*

Luke 16:26: the impossibility of *going across* from Abraham into the realm of the dead (→ ᾅδης, v. 23); Acts 16:9, of traversing a distance: Paul is commanded in a vision to *come over* (from Troas) to Macedonia and help (διαβὰς . . . βοήθησον); Heb 11:29: "by faith the people *crossed* the Red Sea."

διαβάλλω *diaballō* accuse, charge (with)*

Luke 16:1: the unjust steward is *accused* by his master (αὐτῷ, dat., as in Herodotus v.35; Plato *R.* viii.566b, and elsewhere) of squandering the master's goods (ὡς διασκορπίζων; ὡς with partc. also in Xenophon *HG* ii.3.23; Plato *Ep.* vii.334a). W. Foerster, *TDNT* II, 71; *TWNT* X, 1039 (bibliography).

διαβεβαιόομαι *diabebaioomai* give a firm assurance*

In the NT this vb. appears with περί with the gen.: *give a firm assurance* about a matter. In 1 Tim 1:7 the author mentions "things about which [false teachers] *make assertions.*" Titus 3:8 says to the recipient of the letter, "I desire you *to insist* on these things (περὶ τούτων)."

διαβλέπω *diablepō* look intently; see (clearly)*

Matt 7:5 par. Luke 6:42b: "First take the log (τὴν δοκόν) out of your own eye, and then *you will see clearly* (διαβλέψεις) to take the speck (τὸ κάρφος) out of your brother's eye"; Mark 8:25: After Jesus laid hands on the blind man's eyes, the man "*looked intently* and was restored, and saw everything clearly."

διάβολος, 2 *diabolos* slanderous*
διάβολος, ου, ὁ *diabolos* (slanderer); adversary; devil*

1. The adj. — 2. Occurrences and synonyms of the noun — 3. Functions of the devil in the NT

Lit.: H. Bietenhard, *DNTT* III, 468-72. — W. Foerster, *TDNT* II, 72-81. — For further bibliography → σατανᾶς; see *TWNT* X, 1039.

1. The adj. διάβολος appears in the NT only in the Pastorals. Slanderous speech, a vice forbidden especially for the wives of διάκονοι (1 Tim 3:11) but also for older women (Titus 2:3), is listed with unkindness and irreconcilability (2 Tim 3:3).

2. The LXX uses the noun διάβολος to render the Hebrew designation for the *adversary* (*śāṭān,* Job 1:6-8, 12; 2:1-7; Zech 3:1, 2, and elsewhere). Διάβολος appears 34 times in the NT with this meaning, of which 12 are in the Johannine literature, 6 in Matthew, 5 each in Luke and the deutero-Pauline literature, 2 in Acts, and 1 each in Hebrews, James, 1 Peter, and Jude.

By contrast, the authentic Pauline letters and Mark use → σατανᾶς exclusively (7 and 2 references), which is attested only once in John (13:27) and is totally absent in 1–3 John. Revelation has διάβολος 5 times and σατανᾶς 8 times. There is no difference in the meaning between διάβολος and σατανᾶς (Matt 4:1 par. Luke 4:2; cf. Mark 1:13; cf. John 13:2 and 13:27; Luke 22:3). In place of ὁ διάβολος (Luke 8:12), parallel passages have ὁ πονηρός (Matt 13:19) and ὁ σατανᾶς (Mark 4:15). NT synonyms for διάβολος are ἐχθρός (Matt 13:39), πονηρός (Eph 6:11, 16; 1 John 3:8, 12), δράκων, ὄφις, and σατανᾶς (Rev 12:9; 20:2). Other terms for the διάβολος are ἄρχων (τῆς ἐξουσίας τοῦ ἀέρος, Eph 2:2; τοῦ κόσμου, John 14:30; τοῦ κόσμου τούτου, John 12:31; 16:11) and Βελιάρ (2 Cor 6:15). → Βεελζεβούλ (Mark 3:22 par.) appears as ἄρχων τῶν δαιμονίων. Eng. *devil* is derived from Gk. διάβολος by way of Lat. *diabolus.*

3. In the dualistic worldview that the NT shares with ancient Judaism, the heavenly βασιλεία stands in opposition to that of the demons (→ δαιμόνιον). The devil is the highest sovereign of the demons; the demons are his "angels" (Matt 25:41; Rev 12:7, 9). In accordance with ancient Jewish demonology the NT traces the διάβολος and his ἄγγελοι as creatures of God back to the fall of the angels in Gen 6:1-4 (Rev 12:9, 12). Before this fall the διάβολος had accused mankind before God (Rev 12:10; cf. Job 1:9-11; 2:4f.). The adversary of the διάβολος is Michael, the highest of the good angels (Jude 9; Rev 12:7-9).

The διάβολος is—by God's mandate—lord of the demons of sickness (Acts 10:38; cf. 2 Cor 12:7-9) and of death

(Heb 2:14; cf. Rev 20:10, 13f.). Through temptations (cf. Job 1:6–2:7) he desires to entice mankind to apostasy and disobedience toward God (Matt 4:1, 5, 8, 11 par. Luke 4:2, 3, 6, 13; Rev 2:10; 12:9; 20:10); he sows the weeds (Matt 13:39) and steals the good seed of the word of God (Luke 8:12). He lays the snare (1 Tim 3:7; 2 Tim 2:26) and "from the beginning" (John 8:44; 1 John 3:8b) induces human sin (1 John 3:8a) as murderer, liar, and sinner. Thus he causes the betrayal by Judas (John 13:2) as well as conceit (1 Tim 3:6) and hatred of one's brother (1 John 3:8).

Anyone who succumbs to temptation is among the children of the διάβολος (John 8:44, of the Jews; Acts 13:10, of the magus, Bar-Jesus–Elymas; 1 John 3:8, 10), and even becomes a διάβολος himself (John 6:70, of Judas; cf. Matt 16:23 par. Mark 8:33). Consequently the Christian must bravely confront the διάβολος (Eph 4:27; 6:11; Jas 4:7; 1 Pet 5:8f.), who will then flee (Jas 4:7). The dreadful work of the διάβολος lasts only a limited period of time (Rev 12:12). Before the coming of the millennium the διάβολος will be bound for one thousand years (Rev 20:2). After the decisive eschatological battle (v. 10), or after the final judgment (Matt 25:41), he will be destroyed in eternal fire (cf. 1 Tim 3:6).

His sovereignty over the world has already been broken (cf. John 12:31; 14:30; 16:11), for Jesus has appeared in order to destroy the works of the devil (1 John 3:8c). The "spiritual armament" of Christians in the battle with the διάβολος and his angels consists of truth and righteousness, of faith in the redemption through Jesus, and in obedience with respect to the Spirit and the word of God (Eph 6:11-17). The martyrs have conquered the devil (Rev 12:9) "by the blood of the Lamb and by the word of their testimony" (v. 11).

O. Böcher

διαγγέλλω *diangellō* make known; give notice*

Paul *gives notice* of the fulfillment of the days of purification in Acts 21:26. Elsewhere διαγγέλλω has the sense of a proclaiming announcement: Luke 9:60: "go and *proclaim* the kingdom of God"; Rom 9:17 (citing Exod 9:16 LXX): "that my name *may be proclaimed* in all the earth." J. Schniewind, *TDNT* I, 67f.

διαγίνομαι *diaginomai* pass, elapse*

In the NT διαγίνομαι appears only in temporal gen. absolutes: "when the sabbath *was past*" (Mark 16:1); "when some days *had passed*" (Acts 25:13); "as much time *had been lost*" (27:9).

διαγινώσκω *diaginōskō* determine, decide*

A t.t. of juridical language: *decide* a case (with acc.): Acts 23:15: "as though you were going to *determine* his case (τὰ περὶ αὐτοῦ) more exactly"; 24:22: "I [Felix] will *decide* your case (τὸ καθ' ὑμᾶς)."

διαγνωρίζω *diagnōrizō* report publicly, make known

Luke 2:17 Koine A Θ Φ: the shepherds "*made known* the saying which had been told them concerning this child." Διαγνωρίζω is also attested in Philo *Det.* 97. Passow I, 632 ad loc.

διάγνωσις, εως, ἡ *diagnōsis* decision*

Acts 25:21: "Paul appealed to be kept in custody for the *decision* [Vg. *cognitio*] of the emperor."

διαγογγύζω *diagongyzō* murmur
→ γογγύζω 5.

διαγρηγορέω *diagrēgoreō* remain awake; awaken fully*

Luke 9:32 (cf. Mark), of Peter and his companions in the story of the transfiguration: διαγρηγορήσαντες, "but *when they awoke*" (NEB), or "but *they kept awake*" (JB).

διάγω *diagō* spend (one's life)*

The acc. obj. βίον is explicitly mentioned in 1 Tim 2:2 ("that *we may lead* a quiet and peaceable life") and implicitly assumed in Titus 3:3 ("*passing our days* in malice and envy"; construction with ἐν is also found in Luke 7:25 v.l. and Ign. *Trall.* 2:2). BDF §480.2.

διαδέχομαι *diadechomai* take possession of*

Acts 7:45, of "our ancestors," who, "while they were in the desert . . . , *possessed* the Tent of Testimony (→ σκηνὴ τοῦ μαρτυρίου)" (JB). This usage corresponds to customary constructions elsewhere with the meaning *receive from a former owner* (BAGD s.v.); *1 Clem.* 44:2 (τὴν λειτουργίαν).

διάδημα, ατος, τό *diadēma* fillet; diadem*

The diadem is the sign of royal status. Rev 12:3: the dragon had "seven diadems" on his seven heads; 13:1: the beast had "ten diadems" on his ten horns; 19:12: the rider of the white horse had "many diadems" on his head. H. W. Ritter, *Diadem und Königsherrschaft* (1965); H. H. Schmitt, *LAW* 723.

διαδίδωμι *diadidōmi* distribute*

Objects *distributed* are spoil (Luke 11:22), "all that you have" (18:22), bread (John 6:11), and power and authority (Rev 17:13 v.l. in place of δίδωμι). Acts 4:35 has the pass.:

money from sales of property was "*distributed* to any who stood in need" (NEB).

διάδοχος, ου, ὁ *diadochos* successor*

Acts 24:27: Felix's *successor* was Porcius Festus.

διαζώννυμι *diazōnnymi* gird*

John 13:4, 5: Jesus *girded* himself (διέζωσεν ἑαυτόν) with a linen towel for footwashing; 21:7: Simon Peter *girded himself* (mid. διεζώσατο) with his outer garment; cf. v. 18, "another *will gird* you" (→ ζώννυμι). A. Oepke, *TDNT* V, 302-8.

διαθήκη, ης, ἡ *diathēkē* covenant; testament

1. Occurrences in the NT — 2. Meaning — 3. God's irrevocable covenant of salvation for Israel — 4. The new covenant of salvation for Israel in the Christ-event — a) The saying over the cup in the tradition of the Lord's Supper — b) The new covenant of salvation in Paul — c) Διαθήκη in Hebrews

Lit.: E. BAMMEL, "Gottes ΔΙΑΘΗΚΗ (Gal III.15-17) und das jüdische Rechtsdenken," *NTS* 6 (1959/60) 313-19. — J. BEHM, *Der Begriff ΔΙΑΘΗΚΗ im NT* (1912). — *idem, TDNT* II, 124-34. — H. FELD, *Das Verständnis des Abendmahls* (1976). — J. GUHRT, *DNTT* I, 365-72. — F. HAHN, "Die alttestamentlichen Motive in der urchristlichen Herrenmahlüberlieferung," *EvT* 27 (1967) 337-74. — *idem,* "Zum Stand der Erforschung des urchristlichen Herrenmahls," *EvT* 35 (1975) 553-63. — G. D. KILPATRICK, "Διαθήκη in Hebrews," *ZNW* 68 (1977) 263-65. — E. KUTSCH, *THAT* I, 339-52. — *idem, Neues Testament—Neuer Bund? Eine Fehlübersetzung wird korrigiert* (1978). — F. LANG, "Abendmahl und Bundesgedanke im NT," *EvT* 35 (1975) 524-38. — U. LUZ, "Der alte und der Neue Bund bei Paulus und im Hebräerbrief," *EvT* 27 (1967) 318-36. — H. PATSCH, *Abendmahl und historischer Jesus* (1972) 81-87, 155-70, 180-82. — R. PESCH, *Wie Jesus das Abendmahl hielt* (1977) 47-58. — *idem, Markus* (HTKNT) II (1977), 354-77. — E. RIGGENBACH, "Der Begriff ΔΙΑΘΗΚΗ im Hebräerbrief," *Theologische Studien* (FS T. Zahn; 1908) 289-316. — E. SCHWEIZER, "Das Herrenmahl im NT. Ein Forschungsbericht," *idem, Neotestamentica* (1963) 344-70. — V. WAGNER, "Der Bedeutungswandel von *b^erît ḥ^adāšâ* bei der Ausgestaltung der Abendmahlsworte," *EvT* 35 (1975) 538-44. — M. WEINFELD, *TDOT* II, 253-79. — For further bibliography see *DNTT* I, 375f.; Kutsch (*THAT*); Pesch, *Markus*; *TDOT* II, 253f.; *TWNT* X, 1041-46.

1. Διαθήκη is used relatively seldom: 9 times in Paul, 4 times in the Synoptics, 2 times in Acts, 1 time in Revelation, but 17 times in Hebrews. Most of the references belong either to the Lord's Supper tradition or to passages influenced by it; the significant theological weight of the word in the NT is derived from this source.

2. Only in 2 passages (Gal 3:15; Heb 9:16f.) does διαθήκη have the meaning that it has almost without exception in secular Greek usage: *last will and testament.* In all other instances διαθήκη means *covenant,* in accordance with the predominant usage in the LXX.

In connection with the early, more general usage of διαθήκη as *stipulation, regulation* in general, the LXX translators selected διαθήκη for the regular rendering of the Heb. *b^erîṯ* and filled it with all of the breadth of associations of this central OT concept.

The translation of *b^erîṯ* and διαθήκη with "covenant" is problematic. These words rarely denote a two-sided, contractual agreement between partners of equal standing (see Gk. συνθήκη). Heb. *b^erîṯ* is used almost without exception for a one-sided obligation, albeit one that has a pledge attached. Accordingly it is often connected with the taking of an oath or a blood rite conditioned by a curse on one's self. Thus the free act of obligation by the power—in theological usage, the deity (i.e., in the promise of the land to Abraham in Gen 15:7-21)—is to be distinguished from the obligation laid upon the dependent one ("the obligation of the foreigner," Kutsch), as in the case of obligation laid by God upon the people in Exod 24:3-8. A covenant idea is nevertheless involved insofar as in both instances it concerns a bilateral relation of obligation. Of course the parties are not equal. Instead, they correspond to that of the vassal relationship, which is known from the world around Israel.

Here connections from linguistic history are important. Numerous verbal analogies make it probable that the *b^erîṯ* sayings of the OT are modeled after such vassal texts and thus define Israel's relation to God as a vassal relationship of a particular kind. Even the exhortation "to 'love God with all the heart, with all the soul, and with all the might,' seems to have its origin in the loyalty oaths of the vassal to his suzerain" (Weinfeld 269). The obligations appear to be modeled after the apodictic commandments in the instructions to servants in the Hittite kingdom concerning their obligations toward royal officials. The divine covenant promise to Abraham is based on the royal gift to the loyal vassal (Weinfeld 270-75). The *b^erîṯ* theology of the OT is based upon the idea of royal sovereignty. The king's own obligation to bestow to his servants kindness, faithfulness, protection, and care precedes the covenant obligation of his subjects.

In the theological *b^erîṯ* sayings of the OT a bilateral commitment is established along with the one-sided obligatory actions, as in the pattern of relationship to a sovereign. Thus the translation "covenant" should be maintained, but also made more precise with phrases that allow differentiation, such as "covenant promise" and "covenant of obligation."

In all instances the emphasis lies on irrevocable commitment. This is indeed the case for διαθήκη in the sense of *last will and testament:* what is of significance is that what is irrevocable is valid (Gal 3:15), coming to be "in force" after death (Heb 9:17). God has firmly obligated himself to his people in his holy *covenant promise* to Abraham (Luke 1:72f.). All Israelites stand under a determination to salvation as "sons of the *covenant*" that God ordained for the fathers (Acts 3:25). As the obligatory covenant laid on Israel requiring the fulfillment of the commandment, this covenant of salvation is called the "*covenant* of circumcision" (7:8).

The notion of a divine promise appears alongside διαθήκη as a synonymous concept (Heb 8:6), one made additionally irrevocable by the divine oath (6:13-17). Because Israel's relation to God in the OT is based on a large number of divine covenant promises, διαθήκη occurs in this sense also in the pl. (Rom 9:4). The people have failed in their covenant obligation and have thus abandoned Yahweh's salvific covenant for Israel (Heb 8:3; cf. Rom 3:12; Matt 12:39; Acts 7:51-53). The covenant promise to the fathers (Gal 3:15-18; 4:21-28) precedes the covenant of obligation laid on Israel at Sinai.

In the ancient tradition of the Lord's Supper the promise of a new covenant of salvation for Israel from Jer 31:31-34 is proclaimed as fulfilled in the Jesus-event. The "old" or "first" covenant is contrasted with the "new *covenant*" (1 Cor 11:25; 2 Cor 3:6, 14; Heb 8:6-13). Jesus, who establishes the new promise of salvation in his offering of himself, is called mediator or surety of the new covenant (Heb 9:15; 7:22). As the herald of the gospel, Paul is "minister of the new *covenant*" (2 Cor 3:6). "Blood of the *covenant*" became a fixed phrase (Mark 14:24; Heb 9:20; 10:29; 13:20). Further terms derived from the OT are "ark of the *covenant*" (Heb 9:4; Rev 11:19) and "tablets of the *covenant*" (Heb 9:4).

3. According to Luke 1:72-74 "the Lord God of Israel" (v. 68) has determined, with the birth and mission of John the Baptist, to liberate his people from all enemies and thus to "remember his holy *covenant*, the oath which he swore to our father Abraham" (cf. Ps 105:8-10, 42). Here διαθήκη is used synonymously with the oath and designates the covenant promise to Abraham, understood as continuing and realized in the new salvation-event. In Rom 9:4 Paul, in an emphatic statement, mentions among the gifts of salvation to Israel "the *covenants*"; that they have further validity is explicitly stated in Rom 11:29. Furthermore, in v. 27 the future event of Israel's redemption could be interpreted as the divine realization of the continuing validity of the covenant of salvation with the fathers (→ 4.b).

This use of διαθήκη is certainly present in Gal 3:16f., for salvation in Christ is the act of God's faithfulness in realizing the covenant of salvation granted to Abraham. While in Rom 9:4 the gift of the covenants stands alongside the giving of the law (νομοθεσία), Paul works out in Galatians 3–4 a critical contrast between the covenant promise to Abraham and the Sinaitic covenant of obligation. The firm validity of the Abrahamic covenant is made clear in the transition to the meaning of διαθήκη as *testament* (3:15). Because of Paul's concern for providing a critique of the Torah, he applies the concept διαθήκη to the giving of the law only in a way that is theologically relativized (→ 4.b). In Acts 7:8, however, the obligatory covenant of circumcision belongs within the realization of the Abrahamic covenant. In the same way, according to Acts 3:25, the covenant of promise and of obligation is valid for the fathers and is realized through the Christ-event. According to Rev 11:19 the anticipated events of the end are the realization of God's continuing covenant of salvation for Israel.

4. a) For the new understanding of διαθήκη in the early Church, the saying over the cup in the Lord's Supper tradition is fundamental. The oldest attainable form of the text is probably Mark 14:24 (cf. Matt 26:28). Here already two basic sayings are connected. According to one, Jesus interprets his imminent death as God's atoning act to take away the sins of everyone. And then when the cup is given Jesus gives a share in this redemptive event: "This is my blood of the covenant, which is poured out for many" (τοῦτό ἐστιν τὸ αἷμά μου τῆς διαθήκης τὸ ἐκχυννόμενον ὑπὲρ πολλῶν). This pouring out of blood is effective in bringing a divine covenant of salvation into force. With αἷμα τῆς διαθήκης the vocabulary of the pronouncement in Exod 24:8 LXX is adopted: "Behold the blood of the covenant which the Lord has made with you in accordance with all these words." The application of Exod 24:8 was anticipated since as this passage, already before the time of Jesus, was understood as describing an act of atonement.

Originally the sprinkling of the people with blood in Exod 24:8, with the accompanying pronouncement, signified the sworn obligation of the people to do the word of Yahweh recorded in the "book of the *b^e^rîṯ*" (Exod 24:3f., 7). The simultaneous sprinkling of blood on the altar (v. 6) was reminiscent of the blood ritual on the Day of Atonement. Two targums on the passage understood the sprinkling of blood *ʿal-hāʿām*, "on the people," as meaning *on behalf of* the people, a new interpretation of this central *b^e^rîṯ* saying with significant consequences. Out of the simple covenant of obligation (the "obligation of the stranger" laid by Yahweh on the people) developed a covenant of salvation based on a gracious atonement with the blood ritual as the center.

The reference to Exod 24:8 in the saying over the cup can be taken only typologically, i.e., as an indication that the atoning act in the death of Jesus is interpreted as surpassing and corresponding to the OT act of atonement. Thus a renewal of the covenant of Sinai is not intended; instead, the passage speaks of God's surpassing new pledge of salvation in "blood," i.e., in the death of Jesus. The version of Jesus' saying about the cup transmitted by Paul (1 Cor 11:25; cf. Luke 22:20) can easily be understood as the explication of the Markan version. With the wording "this cup is the new covenant in my blood," undoubtedly there is an allusion to Jer 31:31-34 (LXX 38:31-34), where Yahweh announces that he will "make a new covenant with the house of Israel" (LXX: διαθήσομαι τῷ οἴκῳ Ἰσραὴλ . . . διαθήκην καινήν), one that is totally different compared with the Sinai covenant (v. 32): now the covenant of obligation will be replaced by a covenant of promise. Yahweh promises the forgiveness of sins and will write his instruction on the heart, so that his people will do the will of God.

With the promise of the new *b^e^rîṯ*, Yahweh responds to the abandonment of the Sinai covenant by his disobedient people (Jer

31:32). Indeed, the new b^erîṯ includes once more the obligation of the people to do the will of God. However, in this instance, Yahweh himself takes over the fulfillment of this obligation: "I will fill their hearts with fear of me, and so they will not turn away from me" (Jer 32:40, NEB). This promise is proclaimed as fulfilled in the Jesus-event. The weight of this old pre-Pauline proclamation, which is not significant in Paul himself, becomes fully visible in Hebrews (→ 4.c).

b) In Rom 11:27 Paul interprets the prophecy of a covenant of salvation from Isa 59:20f., perhaps in dependence on the Lord's Supper tradition, by adding a phrase from 27:9. He argues, along the lines of Jer 31:34, that forgiveness will effect the realization of the eschatological covenant of salvation (but see → 3).

This connection is evident in 2 Cor 3:1-14. Paul sees the divine promise in Jer 31:33 come to pass in his apostolic ministry. He is a "minister of the new covenant." He develops the greatness and dignity of his function with the help of the contrast between the new covenant and the Sinai covenant in Jeremiah 31. Paul views the ministry of the new covenant as the "ministry of the Spirit," probably in connection with a corresponding Lord's Supper interpretation (1 Cor 10:3f.). He is also dependent on OT witnesses in the context of the prophecy of Jeremiah 31, including Ezek 36:26f. In content, the ministry of the new covenant mediates righteousness and thus life (2 Cor 3:6, 9), a reminder of the promise of forgiveness (Jer 31:34) and the word of atonement (the saying over the cup). In the opposite image, the Sinai διαθήκη brings condemnation and death (2 Cor 3:6d, 9a). One passes away, while the other abides (v. 11). Paul speaks, therefore, perhaps for the first time, of the "old διαθήκη." He takes up elements of a διαθήκη theology that was already formed and already critical of the Torah and sharpens it with his own teaching on righteousness.

The allegory of the two covenants in Gal 4:21-28 is derived by Paul from the same tradition. The new διαθήκη of the Christ-event is already anticipated in the covenant promise to the fathers. To the Sinai covenant belong separation from God, slavery, and existence "according to the flesh," while a heavenly, spiritual existence and freedom belong to the covenant promise, which is founded on the creative promise of God.

c) The 17 instances of διαθήκη in Hebrews are connected with a διαθήκη theology that is developed in connection with the traditions of the Lord's Supper. Although there are no direct references to these traditions, their influence is indicated when the salvific meaning of the death of Jesus is seen in the establishment of the "new covenant" and Christ is seen as the "mediator of a new *covenant*" (διαθήκης καινῆς μεσίτης, 9:15). Thus Exod 24:8 is applied typologically, and the saying over the cup (τοῦτο τὸ αἷμα τῆς διαθήκης, v. 20) is assimilated.

The phrase "blood of the *covenant*" appears twice more in Hebrews. According to 13:20, God has brought back Christ from the dead "by the blood of the eternal *covenant*"; according to 10:29, the particular disgrace of the apostate is that he "treats the blood of the *covenant* which sanctified him as if it were not holy" (JB). The salvation brought by Christ is present in the "sprinkled blood," which speaks powerfully (12:24). It is present in Jesus' "own blood," in the "blood of Christ," in the "blood of Jesus" (9:12, 14; 10:19).

The salvation brought by the new covenant is illuminated by contrast with the Sinai covenant, God's "first" covenant with Israel (Heb 8:7, 13; 9:1, 15, 18). The first covenant is powerless, not because the people of God have broken it (8:7-13), but because it is weak in itself. It belongs to the realm of the earthly copy and could only be a weak shadowy image, pointing away from itself toward a future new διαθήκη (7:16-19; 8:5f.; 9:6-10; 10:1). Thus the first διαθήκη is evaluated from the perspective of its cult (cf. ἐντολή, 7:16-18; νόμος, 7:19, 28; 10:1) and its offer of salvation. In this evaluation there is a critical rejection of Alexandrian Jewish interpretations, according to which such symbolic cult activities point to the real, "heavenly" salvation.

According to Hebrews salvation has become real in the new, "higher" *covenant* (7:22; 8:6), in the Christ-event, and consists of access to God, authentic fellowship with God, participation in the heavenly world, participation in Christ, and divine sonship (2:10f.; 3:6, 14; 6:4f.; 7:19; 9:8, 11f., 14; 12:10). By offering himself Jesus has established the new covenant. He is "mediator of a new *covenant*" (9:15; see also 7:22; 8:6). By entering for his own as the exalted high priest, he keeps this salvation available forever (7:25; 10:19f.). He is the "surety" of the new covenant of salvation (7:22), which believers should continually grasp boldly (4:15f.; 10:19-23) to be preserved from denial and sin. The participants in the new covenant are already sanctified and perfected for priestly access to God and reception of the unshakable kingdom of God (4:16; 10:10, 14; 12:22-24, 28).

Because with a testament a new state of affairs comes into being through death, in Heb 9:15-17 the meaning of διαθήκη as *testament* is applied in a supportive way in a transition that for us is difficult to follow: in the salvation offered by God through Jesus Christ, the last will and testament of Christ comes into force through the death of the one who made the will himself (vv. 16f.). For the linguistic sensibility of that time the transition was not problematic (cf. Gal 3:15-17; Philo *Mut.* 51f., and elsewhere; Kutsch, *Neues Testament* 81-83). In the power of the "blood of the eternal covenant" is contained the promise corresponding to Jer 31:31, namely, that God himself will work "in you that which is pleasing in his sight," that he will "equip you with everything good that you may do his will" (Heb 13:21).

H. Hegermann

διαίρεσις, εως, ἡ *diairesis* distribution*

Used of the *distribution* of gifts in 1 Cor 12:4-6. This sense is suggested by διαιρέω in v. 11. Not to be excluded is the meaning *difference(s);* cf. H. Schlier, *TDNT* I, 184f.; BAGD s.v. 1; H. Conzelmann, *1 Corinthians* (Hermeneia) 207f.

διαιρέω *diaireō* distribute; divide*

Luke 15:12: "*He divided* his estate between them" (NEB); 1 Cor 12:11: the Spirit "*distributing* them [the gifts] separately to each individual at will" (NEB); → διαίρεσις. H. Schlier, *TDNT* I, 184f.

διακαθαίρω *diakathairō* clean out*

Luke 3:17: "His winnowing fork is in his hand, to *clear* his threshing floor."

διακαθαρίζω *diakatharizō* clean out*

Matt 3:12 (par. Luke 3:17 C Koine A D, etc.): the *cleaning/sweeping* of the threshing floor. → διακαθαίρω.

διακατελέγχομαι *diakatelenchomai* totally refute*

Acts 18:28, with obj. in the dat.: Apollos "powerfully *confuted* the Jews in public, showing by the Scriptures that the Christ was Jesus." → ἐλέγχω 2.

διακελεύω *diakeleuō* command

John 8:5 v.l., with dat. + inf.: "in the law Moses *commanded* us to stone such [adulteresses]"; cf. Lev 20:10; Deut 22:22-24.

διακονέω *diakoneō* serve
διακονία, ας, ἡ *diakonia* service, ministry; office
διάκονος, ου, ὁ (ἡ) *diakonos* servant

1. Occurrences in the NT — 2. Meanings — 3. Development of the concepts — a) Jesus — b) Paul and the Pauline churches — c) The Gospels and Acts — d) The deutero-Pauline letters and other late writings

Lit.: H. W. Beyer, *TDNT* II, 81-93. — W. Brandt, *Dienst und Dienen im NT* (1931). — K. Hess, *DNTT* III, 544-49. — K. Rahner and H. Vorgrimler, *Diaconia in Christo* (1962). — B. Reicke, *Diakonia, Festfreude und Zelos in Verbindung mit der altchristlichen Agapenfeier* (UUÅ 5, 1951). — J. Roloff, *Apostolat–Verkündigung–Kirche* (1965). — *idem,* "Anfänge der soteriologischen Deutung des Todes Jesu," *NTS* 19 (1972/73) 38-64. — J. Schütz, "Der Diakonat im NT" (Diss. Mainz, 1952). — W. Thüsing, "Dienstfunktion und Vollmacht kirchlicher Ämter nach dem NT," *BibLeb* 14 (1973) 77-88. — A. Weiser, *Die Knechtsgleichnisse der synoptischen Evangelien* (SANT 29, 1971). — For further bibliography see *TWNT* X, 1039-41.

1. Διακονέω appears 36 times in the NT: 21 times in the Synoptics and Acts, 3 times in John, 8 times in the Pauline collection of letters, once in Hebrews, and 3 times in 1 Peter. Among the relatively frequent occurrences in the Synoptics, the greatest number of passages belong to the words and parables of Jesus. The activities designated by the vb. are expressed abstractly with the noun διακονία, *service, office,* which appears 33 times in the NT: only once in the Gospels (Luke 10:40), 8 times in Acts, 22 times in the Pauline letters, and once each in Hebrews and Revelation. Finally, διάκονος, *servant,* is the one who executes the activities designated by διακονέω, -ία. It appears 29 times in the NT: 8 times in the Gospels and 21 times in the Pauline letters.

2. The original frame of reference for the use of the entire word group of the διακ- stem in secular Greek was that of table service. The basic meaning of the vb., correspondingly, was *wait on tables.* From this meaning the wider sense has been derived: *care for one's livelihood,* and finally *serve* in general.

The word group is distinct from other terms that are related in meaning in that it "has the special quality of indicating very personally the service rendered to another" (Beyer 81). Especially noteworthy is the difference in meaning between → δουλεύω and διακονέω with the word groups belonging to each. The δουλ- words express a relationship of dependence and the subordination of the δοῦλος to the κύριος. Διακονέω and its cognates, on the other hand, express much more strongly the idea of *service* on behalf of someone. This distinction suggests why διακονέω does not appear at all in the LXX and why διακονία and διάκονος play only a very insignificant role there, while words of the δουλ- stem are common.

Διακονέω and its cognates become in certain strata of the NT a central expression for Christian conduct oriented to Jesus' word and behavior and for specifically Christian functions in the Church: charitable activity, proclamation of the word, and the task of leadership.

The word group is used in the NT with the basic meaning *serve at table:* Matt 22:13; Mark 1:31 par. Matthew/Luke; Luke 10:40; 12:37; 17:8; 22:26f.; John 2:5, 9; 12:2; Acts 6:2. The expanded meaning *help by providing care* is present in Matt 25:44; Mark 1:13 par. Matthew; Mark 15:41 par. Matthew; Luke 8:3; Phlm 13. Jesus' entire work and his death are described as a *service:* Mark 10:45 par. Matthew; Luke 22:26f. There are also references to the *service* of the disciples in a comprehensive sense: Matt 23:11; Mark 9:35; 10:43 par. Matthew; Luke 22:26f.; John 12:26. The cognates are used to designate the apostolic service of *proclamation:* of the twelve, Acts 1:17, 25; 6:4; of Paul, Acts 20:24; 21:19; Rom 11:13; 1 Cor 3:5; 2 Cor 3:3, 6, 9; 4:1; 5:18; 6:3f.; 11:8 (15, 23: false apostles); Eph 3:7; Col 1:23, 25; 1 Tim 1:12; other proclaimers and coworkers, Acts 19:22; 1 Cor 3:5; Eph 6:21; Col 1:7; 4:7; 1 Thess 3:2; 2 Tim 4:11; 1 Pet 1:12.

The word group also designates *charitable service in*

the congregation: Acts 6:1; Rom 12:7; 1 Pet 4:11. This also extends beyond one's own congregation, as in the case of the collection for Jerusalem: Acts 11:29; 12:25; Rom 15:25, 31; 2 Cor 8:4, 19f.; 9:1, 12f. All of the *ministries* of the Church are mentioned comprehensively in 1 Cor 12:5. Next, 1 Cor 16:15; 2 Tim 1:18; Heb 6:10; 1 Pet 4:10; Rev 2:19 speak of the *ministry* of the Church as a whole. The charitable service referred to in Rom 16:1 has the character of an office, as does the ministry of the apostles, prophets, evangelists, pastors, and teachers in Eph 4:12. The word group serves to designate the official tasks of leadership in the Church in Eph 4:17; Col 4:17; 1 Tim 4:6; 2 Tim 4:5, and esp. in the references to the *office of deacon* in Phil 1:1; 1 Tim 3:8, 10, 12f. The following meanings occur separately: the power of the state as servant of God in Rom 13:4; Christ, servant of his people, Rom 15:8, not of sin, Gal 2:17; the ministry of angels for the salvation of individuals in Heb 1:14.

3. a) The root of the NT content of διακονέω, -ία, -ος lies in the speech and conduct of Jesus himself. Likewise the central meaning that the complex of words receives in the life of the early Church is derived from Jesus himself and from the earliest interpretation of his total work and death as *servanthood.* The saying about the greatness of *servanthood* in Mark 10:43f. par. Matthew; Mark 9:35; Matt 23:11 is derived from Jesus in its basic form. This can be ascertained from the age and breadth of the tradition. The interpretation of his total work and his self-sacrifice in death as *service* originated probably in the eucharistic celebrations of the Palestinian churches. This can be concluded from Mark 10:45 par. Matthew and the variant in Luke 22:27. Although Mark 10:45 is formulated in dependence on Isa 53:10-12, it is noteworthy that the vb. διακονέω is used instead of δουλεύω. This fact suggests that table service is the original context of the saying, as the variant in Luke 22:27 clearly demonstrates.

b) Paul's own apostolic understanding and the variety of "ministries" of the Pauline churches have received their essential shape and terminology from the speech and conduct of Jesus and from the early Christian understanding of his work and death as service. The image that Paul's self-understanding "makes most central is that of the servant of Jesus Christ" (Roloff, *Apostolat* 121). Thus Paul sees himself in a double relation of service with respect both to Christ and to the Church (2 Cor 3–6, 11f.). In the exercise of his apostolic service Paul regards the proclamation of the gospel as the fundamental and central activity (e.g., Rom 11:13; 2 Cor 3:3; 4:1; 5:18; 6:3; 11:8).

In the life of Paul's churches, what is considered διακονία is esp. charitable care for the needy, either in the respective churches themselves (Rom 12:7; 1 Cor 16:15) or for the Jerusalem Church in the form of a collection (Rom 15:25, 31; 2 Cor 8:4, 19f.; 9:1, 12). The word can, however, be used comprehensively for *all of the ministries* in the Church (1 Cor 12:5).

These relationships in the Church, with their terminology and their tendency to elevate the offices of service, led to the origin of the *office of deacon,* which is mentioned for the first time in the NT in Phil 1:1. Its primary tasks were probably both proclamation and charity (cf. 1 Tim 3:8-13). In addition, the servant office of the feminine διάκονος, *deaconess,* is found at an initial stage in the Pauline churches (Rom 16:1).

c) In Mark the idea of service takes on an extraordinary place through the series of parenetic sayings in 10:42-45. In contrast to normal relationships involving authority in the world, among the disciples of Jesus true greatness is demonstrated only in service. The service of the Son of Man in death is the basis for this motif, one that forms an essential part of the meaning of discipleship. This view is to be seen from the redactional arrangement of the series of sayings in connection with the third Passion prediction (vv. 33f.) and the episode where the places of honor are requested (vv. 35-40). This arrangement corresponds exactly to the manner in which Mark proceeded earlier at the second Passion prediction (9:31, 35). Both here and in the former passage the Markan community and its leaders deal with the same problem of a striving for honor and power. In both instances the Evangelist seeks to solve the problem in the same manner: by focusing on Jesus' word and work of serving and by pointing to the discipleship of the cross (cf. K. G. Reploh, *Markus—Lehrer der Gemeinde* [1969] 156-72).

Matthew takes over from Mark all of the διακονέω, -ος passages with the exception of the episode of the disciples' dispute about rank (Mark 9:33-37). However, Matthew has adapted the question about greatness that is included. He revises it and includes Jesus' answer about "becoming like children" (18:1-4). In three passages Matthew proceeds beyond the Markan material. In the portrayal of world judgment derived from the special material and then thoroughly revised by Matthew, help for the needy and the imprisoned is understood as service to Jesus and as a criterion for participating in final salvation (25:44). In the speech in Matthew 23, which is composed from Q and the special material, the Evangelist in vv. 8-12 directs his instruction to the leaders in the Christian community. They should not ambitiously demand the titles "teacher," "father," and "master." In v. 11 Matthew bases the prohibition on Jesus' statement about the greatness of service. In its form it connects elements of the Markan tradition of this word (10:43) with elements of the Lukan variant (22:26f.). In the entire section the Evangelist emphasizes fraternal relationships within the Christian community. Finally, one should not assume that the διάκονοι in the redactionally formed allegory of the guest without a wedding garment in 22:1-13 have any theological significance.

In Luke and Acts, the word group with its theological connotations plays a significant role. Of the 7 occurrences in Mark, Luke has taken over only one reference (Luke 4:39); however, it is decisive that he brings in the ideas that are expressed in the omitted Markan passages in other connections, which he at times reshapes, while at times he uses a special tradition. The saying about the greatness of service and the servanthood of Jesus (Mark 9:35; 10:43) is offered as a redactionally revised variant in the tradition in 22:26f.; the mention of the women who serve Jesus in the Passion report in Mark 15:41 is redactionally reshaped by Luke in the context of the work of Jesus in Galilee in 8:3; perhaps Luke 22:43 takes into consideration the service of the angels to Jesus, omitted from Luke's account of Mark 1:13. A special tradition belongs to 10:40 (cf. John 12:2). Indeed, the parable in 17:7-10 is also derived from a special tradition, although v. 8 with διακονέω is redactionally shaped. The parable in 12:35-38 is taken over from Q, but the promise has been redactionally formed first by Luke (cf. Weiser 109f., 168-71).

The 10 occurrences of διακονέω, -ία in Acts are distributed in two areas of meaning: *the apostolic ministry*, with emphasis on the proclamation of the word (1:17, 25; 6:4; 19:22; 20:24; 21:19), and *care for the poor* (6:1f.), to which the collection for Jerusalem belongs (11:29; 12:25). Luke adopts the content and manner of expression of the churches that Paul started among the Gentiles (cf., e.g., Rom 15:25; 2 Cor 3–6). Throughout Luke avoids the word διάκονος.

Luke emphasizes certain themes in his revision of the tradition. (1) The apostolic office, like all leading offices in the church, has the character of service. This emphasis is derived from Jesus' word and service, which Luke indicates clearly by designating the apostolate explicitly as a service (Acts 1:17, 25; 6:4, etc.), placing the service of Jesus before the eyes of Christians who hold leading positions (Luke 22:26f.), and transforming parables of Jesus into exhortations to the leaders (12:35-38, 42-46, 47f.; 17:7-10). The motif of service plays the decisive role in this transformation. (2) For Luke, apostolic service consists in the proclamation of the word (Acts 6:4, etc.) and is a witness (cf. 1:22; 20:24, etc.). (3) Finally, service to the poor and the needy (6:1f.; cf. 2:42) belongs to the basic functions of the life of the Christian community.

In Acts 6:1-6, Luke introduces a new office of service because of a conflict concerning care for the poor. If he consciously avoids the official title διάκονος, he does so because this title was probably associated with functions of the service of proclamation (Phil 1; 1 Tim 3). However, Luke wanted to subordinate an already existing group of leaders to the apostles. He did this by having them installed by the apostles, by limiting their service to the care of the poor (but cf. Acts 6:8), and by avoiding the title "deacon."

In John the only relevant passage is the saying of Jesus in 12:26 (incidental references to the word group occur in 2:5, 9; 12:2). From the perspective of tradition history, it stands close to Mark 8:34 but is expanded by the term *serve* and by two typical Johannine promises. The disciple will reach the place where Jesus himself is, and the Father will honor him. What is meant is the disciple's following to the point of death. If διακονέω, -ία, ος does not appear elsewhere in John with this meaning, 12:26 is to be seen in close connection with the serving of Jesus in 13:1-11 and the service of the disciples in 13:12-20; 15:20 (cf. R. Schnackenburg, *The Gospel according to St. John* II [1979], 385).

d) In Ephesians and Colossians διακονία appears twice, and διάκονος 6 times. The words designate the service of proclamation by "Paul" (Eph 3:7; Col 1:23, 25) and his coworkers (Eph 6:21 = Col 4:7; Col 1:7) and the *ministerial office* of the apostles, prophets, evangelists, pastors, and teachers (Eph 4:12). It is used also for the official service of leadership in the Church (Col 4:17). If the meaning of διάκονος as "minister of the gospel" comes to the foreground in the letters of Paul, it is fully developed in Ephesians and Colossians, where the word is found only in connection with proclamation. The concept has thus attained its most specific meaning (cf. H. Merklein, *Das kirchliche Amt nach dem Epheserbrief* [1973] 223, 337).

The 9 occurrences in the Pastoral Epistles also belong to specifically Christian usage: 2 Tim 1:18 speaks in general terms of the *ministry* of Onesiphorus in the church at Ephesus; 1 Tim 1:12 speaks of the *apostolic ministry* of "Paul"; 1 Tim 4:6 and 2 Tim 4:5 call Timothy's activity of proclamation a *ministry;* in 2 Tim 4:11, Mark's (missionary) *service* is requested; and 1 Tim 3:8, 10, 12f. (→ 2) speak of the *office of deacon.* Pauline language is reflected in all of these passages.

In the remaining late writings of the NT the word group appears only sporadically. Heb 6:10 and Rev 2:19 speak very generally of *ministries* in the Church; 1 Pet 1:12 speaks of the *ministry* of proclamation; 4:11 speaks of charitable *ministry.* The two are mentioned together in 4:10 with the term διακονέω.

A. Weiser

διακονία, ας, ἡ *diakonia* service, ministry; office → διακονέω.

διάκονος, ου, ὁ (ἡ) *diakonos* servant → διακονέω.

διακόσιοι, 3 *diakosioi* two hundred*

Mark 6:37 par. John 6:7: two hundred denarii worth of bread; John 21:8: the boat was about two hundred yards from shore; Acts 23:23: "Get ready two hundred soldiers . . . and two hundred spearmen." Numbers compounded with διακόσιοι appear in three places. Acts 27:37: "We were in all two hundred and seventy-six persons (ψυχαὶ . . . διακόσιαι ἑβδομήκοντα ἕξ) in the ship"; Rev 11:3 and 12:6: one thousand and sixty days (ἡμέρας χιλίας διακοσίας ἑξήκοντα—in accordance with Dan 12:11 [which includes an extra month for one thousand and ninety days], the "apocalyptic" time of forty-two months = three and one-half years).

διακούω *diakouō* hear (in court)*

Acts 23:35, Felix to Paul: "I will *hear your case* [t.t. of judicial language] when your accusers arrive" (NEB).

διακρίνω *diakrinō* distinguish; decide; doubt; interpret*

1. Occurrences and Meaning in the NT — 2. Make a distinction — 3. Decide, estimate, judge, go to court with — 4. Doubt — 5. Interpret — 6. Διάκρισις

Lit.: D. E. AUNE, *Prophecy in Early Christianity* (1983). — F. BÜCHSEL, *TDNT* III, 946-50. — G. DAUTZENBERG, "Zum religionsgeschichtlichen Hintergrund der διάκρισις πνευμάτων," *BZ* 15 (1971) 93-104. — *idem, Urchristliche Prophetie* (BWANT 104, 1975) 123-29, index.

1. Διακρίνω is used a total of 19 times in the NT: 9 times in the act., 10 times in the mid. and pass. The prefix δια- strengthens the ideas of distinguishing, seeing, and separating included in the root word → κρίνω. Thus διακρίνω extends the lexical content of κρίνω considerably in the meanings *differentiate, decide, judge* (act.) and *dispute with one another, estimate, interpret, explain* (mid.). Διακρίνω also appears in the mid. with the broader meaning *doubt.* The wealth of nuance in the usage of διακρίνω makes it difficult to determine its exact meaning in several passages.

2. According to Acts 15:9 God has "*made* no *distinction* between us and them," i.e., between Jews and Gentiles, for he has given the Holy Spirit also to Gentiles. In 11:12 ℵ A B, Peter is told to go to Caesarea with the messengers of Cornelius, "*making* no *distinction* (μηδὲν διακρίναντα)" (cf. *Herm. Man.* ii.6; H L P TR has μηδὲν διακρινόμενον, "without *misgivings,*" → 4).

Jas 2:4 has an instance of paronomasia with διακρίνω and κριταί (by their *distinctions* they become *judges* with evil thoughts); on the basis of the preceding verses (vv. 1-3), a warning against partisanship (→ προσωπολημψία), the best translation for v. 4a is probably, "have you not *made distinctions* (διεκρίθητε) among yourselves?" (cf. M. Dibelius and H. Greeven, *James* [Hermeneia] 136f.; H. Windisch, *Jakobus* [HNT] 14; F. Mussner, *Jakobus* [HTKNT] 115; *contra* Büchsel 948; BAGD s.v.), although the vb. is pass. Making distinctions between persons leads to a situation where preeminence is allowed for certain ones (Appian *BC* v.54.228; Herodotus iii.39; cf. Philo *Op.* 137).

The question in 1 Cor 4:7, "Who *sees anything different* in you?" is directed against the Corinthian tendency to misuse the grace that has been received by turning it into a personal distinction and an occasion for boasting, and thus to use it to introduce distinctions in the Church (v. 6). The concise phrase in 11:29 about one who "eats and drinks without *discerning* the body" is probably to be understood similarly. It is assumed that the bread of the Lord's Supper should be distinguished from ordinary bread and a special place given to it. *Distinctions* thus imply that special considerations are given and special behavior is exhibited (cf. Büchsel 947). Note that paronomasia may be involved in the use of διακρίνω with → κρίμα in 11:29a (see also → 3).

3. Paronomasia with the numerous terms for judging and judgment in 1 Cor 11:29-34 has led to the use of διακρίνω in v. 31: "If we *judged* ourselves truly, we should not be *judged.*" The statement demands strict self-criticism of a Christian's conduct according to the criterion of divine judgment, particularly with respect to behavior at the Lord's Supper (→ δοκιμάζω in v. 28).

In 1 Cor 6:5 διακρίνω is used of the activity of a mediator or arbitrator in distinction to that of worldly courts (vv. 1, 6), which Paul rejects, and the saints' eschatological judgment of the world (v. 2). When διακρίνω has the meaning "judge," it always has a forensic sense, which makes it difficult to find this meaning in 1 Cor 14:29 (→ 4; Dautzenberg, *Prophetie* 128f.; *contra* BAGD s.v.; Büchsel 947).

In the mid. διακρίνω has the meaning *dispute with one another* in Acts 11:2 (on the occasion of Peter's table fellowship with the uncircumcised; on the vocabulary see Ezek 20:35f. LXX) and Jude 9 (on Michael's dispute with the devil over the body of Moses).

4. Διακρίνω in the mid. voice is also used with the meaning *have misgivings, doubt.* This meaning is not attested prior to the NT. This is hardly "a product of Greek-speaking Christianity" (so Büchsel 948) but is rather a reflection of the semantic development of the Greek vernacular in the NT era. The development of the meaning can be understood both from → 2 in the sense of "make distinctions by oneself" or → 3 "be in dispute with oneself; be at odds with oneself" (BAGD s.v.). The individual usages of διακρίνω with this meaning suggest not a unified semantic or tradition-historical development within the NT but rather a variegated use of the semantic repertoire that was at hand. Acts 10:20 (and 11:12 TR → 2), "accompany them without *hesitation,*" alludes to the Jewish fear of associating with Gentiles. Luke 11:38 D has the Pharisee "*doubtful* in himself" before he reproaches Jesus with the fact that Jesus has not washed before the meal.

Διακρίνω with the meaning *doubt* has theological significance in the passages where it appears in opposition to *faith* (→ πίστις) or firm trust. The emphases are also varied. Mark 11:23 par. Matt 21:21 and Jas 1:6 see in *doubt* an endangering of faith and of the granting of petitions in (→ αἰτέω, προσεύχομαι). Mark 11:23 localizes the doubt in the heart (→ καρδία). Using an image common in diatribe, Jas 1:6b compares doubters to a wave of the sea driven here and there by the wind. In Rom 4:20 διακρίνω is included in the contrasting description of the faith of Abraham: "No distrust made him *waver* concerning the promise of God, but he grew strong in his faith as he gave glory to God."

In Rom 14:23 as well διακρίνω stands in opposition to faith. Here, however, the concern is not with faith as trust but rather with the security of daily decision and conduct that is grounded in faith. Διακρίνω designates a doubting within oneself, expressing a lack of this security in having scruples, and stands in conscious paronomasia with κρίνω in v. 22 and κατακρίνομαι in v. 23: "Happy is he who has no reason to judge himself for what he approves. But he who *doubts* is condemned, if he eats, because he does not act from faith."

In Jude 22 ℵ B C[2] the Christian use of διακρίνω appears already to have become solidified, for here an entire group of endangered Christians can be designated simply *doubters,* whom the readers should "treat with mercy."

5. Along with other forms and derivatives of the stem κριν- (κρίνω, συγκρίνω, ὑποκρίνομαι) as well as other terms for interpretation, διακρίνω is a Greek t.t. for the interpretation of oracles and dreams and for divination (for texts, see Dautzenberg, "Hintergrund" 94-96). In the Greek Bible (Gen 40:8 Symmachus) and in its sphere of influence (Philo *Jos.* 90, 104, 143), διακρίνω is a translation variant for the Hebrew term used of interpretation, *pṯr/pšr,* with the same function as κρίνω and συγκρίνω. Because a judicial evaluation of prophets' revelations in the congregational assembly (cf. 1 Cor 14:6, 26, 30) could scarcely be made (Dautzenberg, *Prophetie* 128f.), the meaning of διακρίνω in 1 Cor 14:29 must be connected with the understanding of revelation in apocalyptic literature, which is attested in the Book of Daniel. We should therefore translate, "Let two or three prophets speak, and let the others *interpret*" (*contra* RSV "weigh what is said"; Aune 220).

There is thus a close connection between prophetic revelation and interpretation, different from the connection between glossolalia (→ γλῶσσα) and translation. The revelation heard or seen by the prophets and communicated to the Church has the character of a mystery (→ μυστήριον) and requires deeper disclosure. This disclosure is analogous to the interpretation of the OT Scriptures in the Judaism of the NT era (Dan 9:4; 4 Ezra 12:11f.; Josephus *B.J.* vi.312f.; 1QpHab 2:8; note the t.t. *pšr* in Qumran) and to the disclosure by interpreting angels in the literary apocalypses (Dan 7–12; *1 Enoch* 1:2; 21:5; 40:8; 43:4; 4 Ezra 10–13; Rev 5:5; 7:13f.; 17:7; *T. Abr.* recension A 4:8: καὶ Ἰσαὰκ δὲ ἀναγγελεῖ τὸ ὅραμα, σὺ [= Michael] δὲ διακρινεῖς).

The saying about the "signs of the times" is transmitted in three versions (Matt 16:2f. C Koine D W Θ; Luke 12:54-56; *Gos. Thom.* 91). Matt 16:3b is distinguished from Luke 12:56 and *Gos. Thom.* 91 by the use of διακρίνω (Luke has δοκιμάζω, *Thomas* has πειράζω) and by the characterization of that to which διακρίνω is applied: τὰ σημεῖα τῶν καιρῶν (Luke: τὸν καιρὸν δὲ τοῦτον). It is indeed possible to understand διακρίνω as a translation variant for δοκιμάζω, "test" (cf. Job 12:11; 23:10; Dautzenberg, *Prophetie* 129). However, the relationship of διακρίνω to "signs" suggests rather that one should understand the Matthean formulation in connection with the customary interpretation of eschatological signs (Josephus *B.J.* vi.291, 295, 315; Dautzenberg, *Prophetie* 101f.) that was used in the Judaism of the NT era: "You know how to *interpret* the appearance of the sky, but you cannot *interpret* [supplied] the signs of the times."

6. **Διάκρισις** *distinguishing; quarrel; explanation** occurs in three passages in the NT (not including Acts 4:32 D), each with different meanings: Heb 5:14; Rom 14:1; 1 Cor 12:10.

a) Knowledge of good and evil is ascribed to the mature person (Deut 1:39; 1QS[a] 1:10f.; Philo *Omn. Prob. Lib.* 83). Heb 5:14 transfers this view to the comparison of the immature and the perfect (→ νήπιος, τέλειος; cf. 1 Cor 2:6; 3:1f.; 13:11) and shapes it metaphorically in dependence on the language of Hellenistic popular philosophy (for texts, see H. Windisch, *Hebräer* [HNT] 48). The mature are "those who have their faculties trained by practice to *distinguish* good from evil" (cf. Sextus Empiricus *P.* iii.168).

b) In Rom 14:1, διάκρισις has the meaning *quarrel* or *dispute.* After Paul summons the church to accept (προσλαμβάνω) the weak in faith into the community without limitation, he wants to avoid διακρίσεις διαλογισμῶν. Against the assumption that διάκρισις connotes here a judicial judgment over contested opinions (E. Käsemann, *Commentary on Romans* [1980] ad loc.), one must consider the fact that Paul fears such διακρίσεις after the weak *have been* accepted. Because there is no longer a place for a judicial judgment, a forensic judgment in this context is quite unlikely. That διάκρισις otherwise always has a forensic sense argues against the metaphorical translation "evaluation" (Büchsel 950). On the basis of the context—in 14:2 differing opinions are described, while in vv. 3-13 Paul forbids reciprocal judging and disdain directed to the person—the translation that suggests itself in v. 1 is "*disputes* over opinions" (cf. O. Michel, *Römer* [KEK, [13]1966] 334-36).

Much easier to translate is Acts 4:32 D, where the context requires the translation "and there was no *quarrel* between them."

c) Διάκρισις has the sense "interpretation, explanation"

in 1 Cor 12:10: to another (is given) *interpretations* of the revelations from the Spirit. This meaning is widely attested in Greek (including the LXX and Pausanias i.34.5; Diodorus Siculus xv.10.5; Gen 40:8 Symmachus; Philo *Jos.* 93, 110, 125; *Som.* ii.7).

Usually, however, the charisma of διακρίσεις πνευμάτων, which follows prophecy in the list in 1 Cor 12:10, is understood as "the *ability to distinguish between* spirits" (RSV; so also Aune 220f. with n. 187 on 411). A number of arguments must be made against this understanding: (1) Consideration must be given to what is required by the context (14:29; → 5). (2) When διακρίνω means "distinguishing," the context normally makes clear the two entities to be distinguished. But in 1 Cor 12:10 this is not the case (Dautzenberg, *Prophetie* 127f.). (3) There is no positive teaching about spirits or demons in 1 Corinthians 12–14, and Paul recommends prophecy in these chapters. (4) There is no indication in these chapters of a danger from doubtful or demonic prophecy (on 12:1-3, cf. Dautzenberg, *Prophetie* 143-46). (5) There are no texts illustrating "distinction between spirits" in the Pauline churches (on the sometimes differing statements applied two generations later, 1 John 4:1-6; *Did.* 11:7, cf. Dautzenberg, *Prophetie* 132-35). (6) There is a Pauline description of the procedure of revelation and interpretation in 1 Cor 2:6-16 (cf. G. Dautzenberg, "Botschaft und Bedeutung der urchristlichen Prophetie nach dem Ersten Korintherbrief (2:6-16; 12–14)," *Prophetic Vocation in NT and Today* [ed. J. Panagopoulos; NovTSup 14, 1977], 131-61, esp. 143f.). (7) There is an analogy here to the two-level Jewish understanding of revelation in the NT era (→ 5).

G. Dautzenberg

διάκρισις, εως, ἡ *diakrisis* a distinguishing; quarrel; explanation
→ διακρίνω 6.

διακωλύω *diakōlyō* vigorously prevent*

Matt 3:14: John the Baptist "would have *prevented* [impf.]" Jesus from receiving baptism.

διαλαλέω *dialaleō* discuss*

Luke 6:11: The opponents of Jesus "*discussed* with one another what they might do"; 1:65: "All these things *were talked about* through all the hill country of Judea."

διαλέγομαι *dialegomai* confer; speak*

In the NT esp. in Acts (10 times), elsewhere in Mark 9:34 (the disciples "*had been arguing over* which of them was the greatest" [JB]); Heb 12:5 (the promise of the Scripture "*addresses* you as sons"); and Jude 9 (Michael *disputed* with the devil over the body of Moses). In Acts, Paul is regularly the subj. of διαλέγομαι, which is used in the sense of *speak (argumentatively):* 17:2, 17; 18:4, 19; 19:8f.; 20:7, 9; 24:25. He *speaks* primarily in the synagogues and also in the marketplace or in a lecture hall—but not in Jerusalem (24:12). G. Schrenk, *TDNT* II, 93-95; *TWNT* X, 1041 (bibliography).

διαλείπω *dialeipō* cease*

Luke 7:45, followed by a partc.: "She *has* not *ceased* to kiss my feet."

διάλεκτος, ου, ἡ *dialektos* (spoken) vernacular; dialect*

1. Occurrences in the NT — 2. In the story of Pentecost — 3. Further references

Lit.: J. Kremer, *Pfingstbericht und Pfingstgeschehen. Eine exegetische Untersuchung zu Apg 2, 1-13* (1973) esp. 232-44. — G. Schrenk, *TDNT* II, 93-95.

1. Διάλεκτος is derived from διαλέγομαι, which in secular Greek connotes not only philosophical dialogue (Plato) but also the use of a dialect or speaking in a particular language (Polybius i.80.6). In Aristotle διάλεκτος signifies the customary vernacular (*Po.* 1449a; *Rh.* 1404b). The variety of dialects (διάλεκτοι πολλαί) distinguish the human from the animal (*Pr.* 895a), which has only one voice (μία φωνή) within a species. Διάλεκτος is thus the language that is actually spoken (in linguistic terms, *"parole,"* in contrast to *"langue"*), the language of the people of a particular region. Διάλεκτος appears 6 times with this meaning in the NT, all in Acts: 1:19; 2:6, 8; 21:40; 22:2; 26:14.

2. The two references within the Pentecost narrative are theologically significant. Do they signify a miracle of glossolalia, which the term γλῶσσα in Acts 2:3f., 11 and the reaction in v. 13 could suggest, or a miracle of language? The use of γλῶσσα in the present version of the text in vv. 4, 11 in connection with the use of διάλεκτος in vv. 6, 8 allows the conclusion that the author wants to tell of a miracle of language. The Galileans actually speak in various languages and are understood by those who are present in their own dialects; the event is thus not a miracle of hearing associated with glossolalia.

3. In other references in Acts, the author uses διάλεκτος to designate the language of the Jerusalem church (1:19), the language that Paul used in a defense speech on the barracks steps (21:40; 22:2), and the language used by the voice from heaven that spoke to Paul (26:14). The commentaries indicate that one must think in 26:14 of the Aramaic language; it is noteworthy that the "Hebrew" heavenly voice refers to a known Greek maxim, which probably was familiar to the Greek author.

G. Petzke

διαλλάσσομαι *diallassomai* reconcile oneself*

Matt 5:24: "First be *reconciled* to your brother" (note absolute use in *Did.* 14:2). F. Büchsel, *TDNT* I, 253f.

διαλογίζομαι *dialogizomai* reflect on, consider*
διαλογισμός, οῦ, ὁ *dialogismos* thought, consideration*

1. Occurrences in the NT — 2. Use of the vb. — 3. Use of the noun

Lit.: G. D. KILPATRICK, "Διαλέγεσθαι and διαλογίζεσθαι in the NT," *JTS* 11 (1960) 338-40. — G. SCHRENK, *TDNT* II, 93-98.

1. In usage outside the NT διαλογίζομαι forcefully accents more than does διαλέγομαι the thought of calculating consideration. Both the vb. and the noun are t.t. for a reckoning. In the LXX this calculating motif of consideration frequently takes on the meaning "consider evil" or "plot" (cf. Schrenk). In the NT these concepts are employed almost exclusively with a negative connotation.

The vb. appears only in the Synoptic Gospels: 3 times in Matthew, 7 in Mark, and 6 in Luke. The noun appears in 14 passages, 6 of these in Luke.

2. In the majority of occurrences of the vb., it is used for the deliberations of Jesus' opponents (cf. Mark 2:6, 8 par. Luke 5:21f.; Mark 11:31 par. Matt 21:25) or of the disciples (Mark 8:16f. par. Matt 16:7f.; Mark 9:33), which involve themselves (in their hearts) or each other (cf. the connection with πρός: e.g., Mark 8:16; 11:31) and are recognized by Jesus. These deliberations are directed against either Jesus or something in the immediate environment. In a similar way the rich fool (Luke 12:17) and the vineyard tenants in the parable (20:14) *calculate.* Luke 3:15 describes the reflective reaction of the multitude to John the Baptist, while 1:29 describes Mary's reaction to the greeting of the angel. In these two passages a faint doubt may be present.

3. The use of the noun is directly connected with the use of the vb. in Luke 5:22; 6:8; 9:46f.; 24:38. Here also it is used for the thoughts of Jesus' opponents or of the disciples about either Jesus or something in the environment (e.g., the dispute about rank in Luke 9:46f.). The sayings in Luke 2:35 and Mark 7:21 par. Matt 15:19 are more basic: (only) evil thoughts (cf. the related catalog of vices in Mark 7:21f. par.) come from people's hearts. They are revealed by the coming of Jesus (Luke 2:35). Through their wrong attitude people's thinking becomes futile and their uncomprehending heart is darkened (Rom 1:21). Likewise the thoughts of the wise are considered foolish by the Lord (1 Cor 3:20; cf. Ps 94:11).

Phil 2:14 (διαλογισμός with γογγυσμός) and 1 Tim 2:8 (διαλογισμός with ὀργή) demonstrate the juxtaposition of the negative tendencies. The concern is with anxious reflection and the consideration of doubt (Schrenk), which must be avoided. Similarly the noun in Rom 14:1 is used for the doubting reflection (of the weak). The phrase κριταὶ διαλογισμῶν πονηρῶν in Jas 2:4 is probably to be translated, "judges with evil *reasonings*" (cf. NEB, ones who "judge by false *standards*"), i.e., judges who make evil *decisions.* Even when διαλογισμός has a specialized use, the essential connection with the general NT meaning of doubting or calculating consideration is retained.

G. Petzke

διαλογισμός, οῦ, ὁ *dialogismos* thought, consideration
→ διαλογίζομαι.

διαλύω *dialyō* break up; dissolve*

Acts 5:36 (pass.): Theudas's followers *were dispersed.*

διαμαρτύρομαι *diamartyromai* swear; testify
→ μαρτυρέω.

διαμάχομαι *diamachomai* dispute vigorously*

Acts 23:9: Pharisaic scribes *disputed vigorously.*

διαμένω *diamenō* remain, abide*

Luke 1:22: Zechariah "*remained* dumb"; 22:28: "You are those who *have continued* with me in my trials (πειρασμοί)"; Gal 2:5: "that the truth of the gospel *might be preserved* for you"; Heb 1:11: "They will perish, but thou *remainest*" (citing Ps 101:27 LXX); 2 Pet 3:4: "all things *have continued* as they were from the beginning."

διαμερίζω *diamerizō* divide, distribute*

In addition to the citation of Ps 22:19 by all four Evangelists (Mark 15:24 par.), διαμερίζω appears 7 times in the Lukan work. The following meanings can be distinguished:

Divide, distribute something, with the emphasis on the meaning of the common sharing. In Mark 15:24 par. the soldiers *divide* the clothes of Jesus among themselves; the Evangelists see here the fulfillment of a prophecy referring to David (explicitly noted in John 19:24). In Luke 22:17, Jesus commands the disciples to *divide* the cup among themselves. In the ideal scene of the early Church (Acts 2:45), it is said that the members of the Church *divided* their property among the needy.

Divide, with the emphasis on separation. The tongues of fire from the Spirit are *separated* and come to rest on the disciples (Acts 2:3).

Pass.: *be divided.* As with the second meaning, the idea of separation is dominant here. In connection with the Beelzebul controversy the image of a *divided* kingdom, which cannot stand, is applied to Satan (Luke 11:17f.). According to Luke 12:51-53 the coming of Jesus will not bring peace, but discord and division (v. 51, διαμερισμός); households will be *divided* within themselves (vv. 52f.). Here a well-known conception of the end time (cf. Billerbeck IV, 977-86) is in view. Διαμερίζω in these Q passages is apparently to be traced back to Luke, who, except for the Psalm citation, is the only NT writer to use this word.

G. Petzke

διαμερισμός, οῦ, ὁ *diamerismos* dissension*

According to Luke 12:51, Jesus did not come to bring peace, but *division* (par. Matt 10:34: μάχαιραν, "sword," which may be the original version; cf. Schulz, *Q* 258f.). → διαμερίζω.

διανέμω *dianemō* distribute*

Acts 4:17: news about the miraculous activity of the apostles should "*spread* no further among the people."

διανεύω *dianeuō* make signs*

Luke 1:22: Zechariah "*made signs* to them and remained dumb."

διανόημα, ατος, τό *dianoēma* thought*

Luke 11:17: Jesus knew "their *thoughts.*" Cf. 3:16 D. J. Behm, *TDNT* IV, 968.

διάνοια, ας, ἡ *dianoia* thought, understanding; disposition*

1. Occurrences and range of meaning of διάνοια in the NT — 2. With καρδία in LXX citations — 3. The Synoptic love command — 4. Alienation from God (Colossians and Ephesians) — 5. The Catholic Epistles

Lit.: J. Behm and F. Baumgärtel, *TDNT* III, 605-14. — J. Behm and E. Würthwein, *TDNT* IV, 948-1022, esp. 963-67. — G. Bertram, A. Dihle, E. Jacob, E. Lohse, E. Schweizer, and K.-W. Tröger, *TDNT* IX, 608-66. — C. von Bormann, R. Kuhlen, and L. Oeing-Hanhoff, *HWP* II, 60-102, esp. 63-70. — H. J. Krämer, *Der Ursprung der Geistmetaphysik* (²1967). — E. A. Schmidt, *HWP* II, 229f. — H. W. Wolff, *The Anthropology of the OT* (1974), esp. 40-58.

1. The anthropological-psychological concept of διάνοια, which is especially favored in Greek and in Hellenistic Jewish literature, appears in the NT only 12 times and does not form part of Pauline anthropology (see Bultmann, *Theology* §§17-20). The related vb. does not appear at all; διανόημα, designating the outcome of thinking, appears only in Luke 11:17. Indeed, the breadth of meaning for διάνοια (BAGD s.v.; Behm, *TDNT* IV, 963f.; LSJ s.v.) is limited in the NT. It is significant that διάνοια is not used as a philosophical t.t. This is also true of related terms, including νοέω and νοῦς.

2. When διάνοια appears in the LXX, it most often translates Heb. *lēḇ* or *lēḇāḇ* (which, however, are more frequently rendered by καρδία). Within the original Hebrew anthropology (see E. Jacob, *TDNT* IX, 617-31), "the rational man" (Wolff §5) is described with "heart"; the Greek translation with διάνοια has, by way of interpretation, maintained this rational component.

In the Magnificat the phrase διανοίᾳ καρδίας (Luke 1:51) is derived from the LXX (1 Chr 29:18). Since διάνοια here is a central function of conscious existence, pride is theologically relevant (and in fact leads to eschatological disqualification).

Hebrews twice (8:10; 10:16) cites Jer 31:33 (38:33 LXX). The textual uncertainty in Heb 10:16 may be connected to a free method of citation (with O. Michel, *Hebräer* [KEK], see the excursus by O. Kuss, *Hebräer* [RNT] ad loc. on the use of Scripture in Hebrews). In the parallelisms of the prophetic text, διάνοια (for *qereḇ*) and καρδία (for *lēḇ*) are practically synonymous. In the common translation "understanding," one is not to think of reason in a narrow intellectualistic sense.

3. The textual basis of the Synoptic love commandment is also a citation from the LXX (Deut 6:4f.). Although διάνοια appears in Mark 12:30 par. Matt 22:37/Luke 10:27, it is not in the LXX of the cited text. The summons to love God is given to the total person. This fact is developed in the threefold aspect of καρδία (*lēḇ*, "heart"), ψυχή (*nepeš*, "soul"), and δύναμις (*meʾōḏ*, "strength"). The Synoptics (on the text criticism and prepositional constructions, see the commentaries) reveal the following developments: Mark has (the fourfold) καρδία, ψυχή, then διάνοια and ἰσχύς; Matthew goes back to the threefold listing; Luke agrees with Mark in the fourfold character; however, he places ἰσχύς before διάνοια. Neither Matthew nor Luke wants to reject the aspect of διάνοια, *thinking*, that Mark has introduced.

4. The only pl. use of διάνοια is Eph 2:3; on the basis of the context, the meaning intended is "(evil) impulses" (RSV "mind"; cf. M. Dibelius, *Epheser* [HNT] ad loc.; BAGD s.v.). Col 1:21 and, in dependence on it, Eph 4:18 speak of the pre-Christian situation (on the indication of a continuing condition through the periphrastic partc. cf. BDF §§352f.). Darkness and hostility to God are referred to with διάνοια (on the dat. of respect, see BDF §197). The commentary on the Colossian hymn is directed against "what is basically a false orientation of one's entire life" (E. Schweizer, *The Letter to the Colossians* [1982] ad loc.; on alienation, see E. Lohse, *Colossians* ad loc.); likewise in Eph 4:18 διάνοια has more than simply a psychological, intellectual, or ethical meaning. It concerns the whole of existence from the aspect of thought, for it is brought into relief parenetically with respect to works and behavior. Since Eph 4:17f. addresses also the mind, an exact translation is difficult (H. Conzelmann, *Epheser* [NTD] ad loc.)

and thus especially rests on one's interpretation of the passage (see esp. H. Schlier, *Epheser* [1965] ad loc.).

5. The diversity among the Catholic Epistles is evident in the use of διάνοια. With somewhat "forced metaphorical language" (K. H. Schelkle, *Die Petrusbriefe. Der Judasbrief* [HTKNT] ad loc.), 1 Pet 1:13 (cf. Luke 12:35; Exod 12:11; Jer 1:17) appeals for eschatological preparation. Hope is also a matter of thinking, of understanding. In the (redactional?) epistolary conclusion 1 John 5:14-21 emphasizes anaphora (οἴδαμεν 6 times) and reaches the climax in v. 20. Perhaps διάνοια here means "knowledge" and not merely "capacity for insight" (see, however, R. Bultmann, *The Johannine Epistles* [Hermeneia] and R. Schnackenburg, *Die Johannesbriefe,* both ad loc.). For the edifying phrase "sincere *mind*" in 2 Pet 3:1 there are striking parallels in the Apostolic Fathers (see H. Kraft, *Clavis Patrum Apostolorum* [1963] 104).

M. Lattke

διανοίγω *dianoigō* open
→ ἀνοίγω.

διανυκτερεύω *dianyktereuō* spend the night*

Luke 6:12: Jesus *"spent the whole night* in prayer" (JB).

διανύω *dianyō* complete*

Acts 21:7: ἡμεῖς δὲ τὸν πλοῦν διανύσαντες, "when we *had finished* the voyage"; *1 Clem.* 20:2 (obj.: the course).

διαπαντός *diapantos* always, constantly
→ διά 2.b.

διαπαρατριβή, ῆς, ἡ *diaparatribē* perpetual quarreling*

An intensive form of παρατριβή, "squabbling, quarreling," in 1 Tim 6:5.

διαπεράω *diaperaō* cross over*

Used absolutely in Matt 9:1; 14:34 (cf. Mark 6:53); with the statement of the destination in Mark 5:21; 6:53; Luke 16:26; Acts 21:2.

διαπλέω *diapleō* sail across*

Acts 27:5: *sail across* the sea.

διαπονέομαι *diaponeomai* be very angry*

Acts 4:2: the priests, etc., *were very angry* because the apostles taught the people; 16:18: Paul was *disturbed, annoyed* by the fortune-teller in Philippi.

διαπορεύομαι *diaporeuomai* go through
→ πορεύομαι.

διαπορέω *diaporeō* be greatly perplexed*

Διαπορέω is a strengthened form of the simple ἀπορέω and appears in Luke 9:7; Acts 5:24; 20:17. It is also used absolutely, in the mid. voice, in Luke 24:4 v.l.; Acts 2:12 א A B; *Herm. Sim.* ix.2.5.

διαπραγματεύομαι *diapragmateuomai* engage in commerce*

Luke 19:15: "that he might know what they had *gained by trading,"* τί διεπραγματεύσαντο (with א B D; on the variant -σατο [A K Θ vg], see *TCGNT* ad loc.). C. Maurer, *TDNT* VI, 641-42.

διαπρίω *diapriō* cut in pieces; pass.: be irritated, be enraged*

The members of the Sanhedrin were *infuriated* (impf. pass. διεπρίοντο) at the words of the apostles in Acts 5:33 and at the speech of Stephen in 7:54 (impf. pass. διεπρίοντο).

διαρπάζω *diarpazō* plunder thoroughly*
→ ἁρπάζω 4.

δια(ρ)ρήγνυμι, διαρήσσω *dia(r)rēgnymi, diarēssō* tear (vb.)*

Of the high priest's *tearing* of his own clothes (see Billerbeck I, 1007f.; J. Blinzler, *The Trial of Jesus* [1969], 159-61) in Mark 14:63 par. Matt 26:65; of Paul and Barnabas's *tearing* of their clothes in Acts 14:14; of the *tearing* of the nets in Luke 5:6 and of the fetters by the demoniac in 8:29.

διασαφέω *diasapheō* explain, describe accurately*

Matt 13:36: *"Explain* to us the parable of the weeds of the field"; 18:31: the servants *"reported* to their lord all that had taken place"; cf. Acts 10:25 D.

διασείω *diaseiō* shake; mistreat*

Luke 3:14: John the Baptist instructed the soldiers, *"Rob* no one *by violence"* (cf. "No *bullying!"* NEB). Διασείω is a t.t. of legal terminology (Pap. Oxy. no. 240, l. 5 [A.D. 37]; no. 284, l. 5 [A.D. 50]; Pap. Tebt. I, 43:26 [118 B.C.]) and refers most often to the exercise of force in order to extort money; see Moulton/Milligan s.v.

διασκορπίζω *diaskorpizō* scatter; waste*

1. Occurrences — 2. Meaning — 3. Usage

Lit.: BAGD s.v. — C. E. CARLSTON, "Reminiscence and Redaction in Luke 15:11-32," *JBL* 94 (1975) 368-90, esp. 374. — D. JONES, "The Background and Character of the Lukan Psalms," *JTS* 19 (1968) 19-50, esp. 24 n. 3. — JÜLICHER II, 476. — J. L. MARTYN, "Glimpses into the History of the Johannine Community," *L'Évangile de Jean: Sources, rédaction, théologie* (BETL 44, 1977) 149-75, esp. 173. — O. MICHEL, *TDNT* VII, 418-22. — R. SCHNACKENBURG, "Die Messiasfrage im Johannesevangelium," FS Schmid (1963) 240-64, esp. 258. — L. J. TOPEL, "On the Injustice of the Unjust Steward: Lk 16:1-13," *CBQ* 37 (1975) 216-27, esp. 217.

1. This compound vb. appears 8 times in the Gospels, once in Acts, and not at all in the Epistles. In Mark 14:27 it is taken over from Matt 26:31. There are no further parallels between the Synoptics. Διασκορπίζω appears chiefly in parables (Matt 25:24, 26 [Q]; Luke 15:13; 16:1 [special material]) and in biblical citations (Mark 14:27 par. Matt 26:31 [= Zech 13:7]; Luke 1:51 [= Ps 89:10 and 2 Sam 22:28]).

2. In Matt 25:24, 26 and Luke 15:13 διασκορπίζω is used as the opposite of συνάγω; hence, *divide* vs. "gather." In the framework of the repeated antithesis (Matt 25:24, 26), which forms a synonymous parallelism in which the servant characterizes his master, the agrarian contrast of sowing and harvesting is dominant. Thus the meaning of *scatter* or *disperse* is obvious. Luke uses the vb. in 15:13; 16:1 in two parables. In connection with an acc. obj. that indicates a mercantile matter (cf. Pap. Tebt. I, 24:25), it means *squander, waste* (property). When the acc. obj. of the verb is a person (Luke 1:51; Acts 5:37; Mark 14:27 par. Matt 26:31; John 11:52), one may translate *scatter*.

3. It is noteworthy that Luke does not adopt the proof text Zech 13:7, which Matt 26:31 has received from Mark (14:27). Thus the Markan Jesus predicts the flight of the disciples at his end; because the shepherd is struck, the sheep *scatter* (cf. Josephus *Ant.* viii.404). Luke pursues another thought. According to him, the disciples do not flee. Instead they watch the crucifixion from a distance. He does not place them on the same level with the followers of Judas the Zealot ("all who followed him were *scattered,*" Acts 5:37).

U. Busse

διασπάω *diaspaō* tear apart*

Mark 5:4: the demoniac "wrenched apart" the chains; Acts 23:10: the tribune was afraid "that Paul *would be torn in pieces* by them."

διασπείρω *diaspeirō* scatter
→ διασπορά.

διασπορά, ᾶς, ἡ *diaspora* dispersion*
διασπείρω *diaspeirō* scatter*

1. Occurrences in the NT — 2. Meaning and Usage

Lit.: O. BÖCHER, "Jüdische und christliche Diaspora im neutestamentlichen Zeitalter," *EvDia* 38 (1967) 147-76. — H. BRAUN, "Die Diaspora und ihre Verheißung im NT," *EvDia* 35 (1964) 97-105. — H. FISCHER, "Diaspora. Erwägungen zu einem Begriff und einer Situation," *EvDia* 37 (1966) 35-52. — L. GOPPELT, *Der erste Petrusbrief* (KEK, 1978) 77-82. — F. S. ROTHENBERG, *DNTT* I, 683-92. — K. L. SCHMIDT, *TDNT* II, 98-104. — R. SCHNACKENBURG, "Gottes Volk in der Zerstreuung. Diaspora im Zeugnis der Bibel," *idem, Schriften zum NT* (1971) 321-37. — A. VON SELMS, *RGG* II, 174-76. — M. SIMON, *Verus Israel* (1986) 52-86. — A. STUIBER, *RAC* III, 972-82. — For further bibliography see *TWNT* X, 1041.

1. The verbal subst. διασπορά appears only 3 times in the NT (John 7:35; 1 Pet 1:1; Jas 1:1), as does the vb. διασπείρω (Acts 8:1, 4; 11:19). While the noun is attested only once outside the LXX, the NT, and early Christian and Jewish literature (in Plutarch *Suav. Viv. Epic.* 27), the vb. appears frequently in ancient literature (cf. LSJ s.v.).

2. The question raised in John 7:35 by the Jews, "Does he intend to go to the *Dispersion* among the Greeks and teach the Greeks?" rests on their lack of understanding of the words of Jesus. They seek him for a short time but will not find him and will not be able to go where he will be going (v. 34). Here διασπορά, in accordance with LXX usage, is used of the Jewish minority in the midst of other religions, in this case the Greek-pagan environment.

Except for Dan 12:2 and the secondary insertion of διασπορά in the title of Ps 138:1 A, this noun is used of the exile of the scattered people of God among the Gentiles (Deut 28:25; 30:4; Ps 146:2; Isa 49:6; Jer 15:7; 41:17; 2 Macc 1:27; Jdt 5:19). Here διασπορά can refer to both the *Dispersion* and *the totality of the dispersed* (cf. Isa 49:6; Ps 146:2; 2 Macc 1:27; *Pss. Sol.* 8:28). There is no fixed Hebrew equivalent for διασπορά. The words *gōlâ* and *gālûṯ*, which became technical terms for exile or banishment after the destruction of Jerusalem and the loss of the Palestinian homeland, and which correspond essentially to διασπορά, are always rendered with some other word in the LXX.

The context of 1 Peter appears to be altogether different from that of John 7:35. The Epistle is intended for "God's elect, strangers [or "God's elect strangers"] in the world, *scattered throughout* [i.e., in the *Dispersion* in] Pontus, Galatia, Cappadocia, Asia and Bithynia" (1 Pet 1:1, NIV). These "strangers" are only "guests" (2:11), who are to conduct themselves in the fear of God "throughout the time of [their] exile" (1:17) and live for the gathering at the end time (1:8-9). With the inclusion of διασπορά in this eschatological perspective, the class of Christians addressed in 1 Peter is extended beyond the geographical realm in which other religions are in the majority. Thus διασπορά transcends the concrete historical situation of those who are addressed here and becomes a statement about the nature of the Christian Church in the world in general. Διασπορά connotes the fact that the earth is not the homeland of the Christian. The homeland is rather the heavenly world. Consequently διασπορά, in accordance with the double address in 1:1, communicates both election and alienation at the same time (Goppelt ad loc.). This idea is by no means unique or unanticipated in the NT; cf. Gal 4:26; Phil 3:10f., 20; Heb 11:13; 13:14.

The author of James greets "the twelve tribes in the *Dispersion*" in his salutation. The actual twelve-tribe federation of Israel could obviously not be intended here, for it had long since ceased to exist. Inasmuch as the addressees of the letter are Christians, one must understand the reference to the tribes in a fig. sense. The Christians intended here, and thus all of Christianity, are designated in a new interpretation as the new, true Israel. However, whether one may interpret διασπορά, as in 1 Peter, in a fig. sense and assign to it a specific theological meaning (the world as the διασπορά of the Christians; thus, e.g., M. Dibelius and H. Greeven, *James* [Hermeneia] 66-68) instead of interpreting it as a reference to the concrete situation of a minority remains uncertain. The question depends essentially on the determination of the audience and the dating of James.

While the use of διασπορά in 1 Pet 1:1 and probably also Jas 1:1 is derived only partially from the LXX, the use of the vb. διασπείρω in Acts 8:1, 4; 11:19 is entirely within the tradition history laid down in the LXX. In all the passages it refers to the *scattering* of the Christians of Hellenistic Jewish origin (despite 8:1, not the Christian community as a whole, cf. only 9:26), Greek-speaking Jewish Christians from the Diaspora (cf. Acts 6:1), in areas where there is a non-Jewish majority (11:19) but also in the area around Jerusalem and toward Samaria (8:1). According to Luke, those who are scattered are an essential factor in the expansion of early Christianity (Acts 8:4f., 40; 11:19f.).

D. Sänger

διαστέλλομαι *diastellomai* order, command*

The phrase διεστείλατο αὐτοῖς, "he *charged* them," occurs in Mark 5:43; 7:36a; 9:9 and with slight variations in 7:36b; 8:15. In three instances it is followed by a ἵνα clause and the command to silence (5:43; 7:36a; 9:9). In Matt 16:20 (cf. Mark 8:30), Jesus "*strictly charged* the disciples to tell no one. . . ." The letter to the Gentiles in Acts 15:24 mentions the activities of some persons, "although we *gave* them no *instructions.*" Along with the mid. meaning (in the passages named) pass. τὸ διαστελλόμενον, "the *order,*" appears in Heb 12:20. K. H. Rengstorf, *TDNT* VII, 591f.

διάστημα, ατος, τό *diastēma* space, interval*

Acts 5:7: ὡς ὡρῶν τριῶν διάστημα, "after *an interval* of about three hours." Cf. *Barn.* 9:8 (Gen 32:17 LXX): διάστημα ποιεῖν, "leave *an interval.*"

διαστολή *diastolē* distinction*

Rom 3:22: "For there is no *distinction*" ("all have sinned," v. 23); 10:12: explicitly "no *distinction* between Jew and Greek," here with reference to the salvation from God (v. 13); 1 Cor 14:7: διαστολὴν δίδωμι, make a *distinction* (in the sounds of various musical instruments). K. H. Rengstorf, *TDNT* VII, 592f.

διαστρέφω *diastrephō* twist; confuse*

Lit.: G. Bertram, *TDNT* VII, 714-29, esp. 717f. — J. den Boeft, *Calcidius on Fate* (1970) 58-61. — M. Dibelius, "Herodes und Pilatus," *ZNW* 16 (1915) 113-26, esp. 118f. — H. J. Michel, *Die Abschiedsrede des Paulus an die Kirche Apg 20, 17-38* (1973) 82. — W. C. van Unnik, "Die Apostelgeschichte und die Häresien," *ZNW* 58 (1967) 240-46, esp. 242. — *idem*, "Die Rücksicht auf die Reaktion der Nicht-Christen als Motiv in der altchristlichen Paränese," FS Jeremias (1960) 221-34, esp. 229.

1. This compound vb. appears 7 times in the NT (Phil 2:15; Matt 17:17 par. Luke 9:41; Luke 23:2; Acts 13:8, 10; 20:30). On three occasions it appears in connection with a citation from Deut 32:5 LXX (Phil 2:15; Matt 17:17 par.). On one occasion (Acts 13:10) Luke uses it to sum up his description of the resistance of a Jewish false prophet against the Christian faith; he was "*making crooked* the straight paths of the Lord" (= Hos 14:10 LXX). Διαστρέφω demonstrates the strong influence of biblical usage, as well as Greek influence.

2. The earliest appearance of the vb. is in the Pauline parenesis in Phil 2:15. In the framework of the LXX reminiscences of Deut 32:5 and in Acts 20:30, it appears as the perf. pass. partc. Phil 2:15 distinguishes, along with Deut 32:5, between the *crooked,* i.e., godless humanity, and the children of God. A similar distinction is made in the two major Synoptic Gospels when they complete the lament of Jesus in Mark 9:19 independently of each other in the direction of Deut 32:5 with the vb. διαστρέφω (cf. Acts 2:40; Luke 9:41).

In addition to pass. use of the compound, the act. form is employed in Luke 23:2; Acts 13:8, 10 (*1 Clem.* 46:9; 47:5). In Luke 23:2 (the Lukan) Jesus is falsely (cf. 20:20-40) accused before Pilate of *misleading* the people. This redactional verse (cf. Dibelius 118f.) indicates paradigmatically what threatens all Christians when they are taken before a government tribunal (cf. Acts 24:5-23) because of their preaching. The translation of Acts 13:8 presents difficulties. Here a person stands as the acc., but the following prep. phrase ἀπὸ πίστεως limits the clause in that it obscures the literal meaning of the compound vb. The

Jewish false prophet attempts *to lead* the proconsul *astray* from the faith.

U. Busse

διασῴζω *diasōzō* save; escape from*

Lit.: U. Busse, *Die Wunder des Propheten Jesus* (1977) 148. — M. Dibelius, *Studies in the Acts of the Apostles* (1956) 8, n. 16, 205, 213. — W. Foerster and G. Fohrer, *TDNT* VII, 965-1024, esp. 989f. — L. Goppelt, *Der erste Petrusbrief* (KEK, 1978) 255f. — E. Haenchen, *The Acts of the Apostles* (1971) 711-14. — W. Radl, *Paulus und Jesus im lukanischen Doppelwerk* (1975) 238f.

1. This compound vb. (from simple σῴζω, "save") appears 8 times in the NT. Except for Matt 14:36 and 1 Pet 3:20, it is found only in the Lukan writings (Luke 7:3; Acts 23:24; 27:43, 44; 28:1, 4). Matthew, in 14:36, takes over a summary, abbreviated from Mark 6:56, which is sacrificed by Luke in the so-called great omission, and strengthens the saying when he replaces Mark's simple vb. by the compound form.

In Luke the vb. is found in the secondary expansion of the pericope of the centurion in Capernaum (7:1-10). This narrative from Q follows the Sermon on the Plain directly and is understood by him as an example worthy of imitation for translating Jesus' message into Christian behavior (cf. 7:1-10 with Acts 10). That the centurion speaks to Jesus only through intermediaries in Luke (in contrast to Matt 8:5ff.) is a redactional means of emphasizing the humble self-assessment of the Gentile centurion over against the positive judgment of the Jewish elders who have become obligated by his contributions. Indeed, the frequent use of σῴζω and its derivatives in Acts 27:10, 20, 31, 34, 43f.; 28:1, 4 (cf. 23:24, which becomes in this way a key word of the total narrative unit) indicates that the use of the vb. in 7:3 is redactional. In 1 Pet 3:20 (cf. Josephus *Ant.* xx.25; *Ap.* i.130) διασῴζω stands in the context of an argumentative reference to the salvation of Noah in the ark (Gen 6–8) as a type of Christian baptism.

2. The use of the vb. with ἐπί in Acts 27:44 (cf. Josephus *Ant.* viii.377; xiv.377; *B.J.* v.65) and with ἐκ in Acts 28:4 (cf. Josephus *B.J.* i.47; iii.27; *Ant.* vi.247, etc.) reflects typical Hellenistic style. In the latter case the vb. is to be translated "escape from." In 1 Pet 3:20 the phrase διεσώθησαν δι' ὕδατος is to be understood in a local, and not an instrumental, sense. The eight people who "*were saved* through water" in Noah's ark boarded the ship only after the water had reached their knees. In this way they were baptized (cf. 1 Cor 10:1f.). This typology emphasizes the soteriological character of Christian baptism.

U. Busse

διαταγή, ῆς, ἡ *diatagē* commandment
→ διατάσσω 1, 5.

διάταγμα, ατος, τό *diatagma* commandment*

Heb 11:23: the *commandment* of the king; Ign. *Trall.* 7:1: the *instructions* of the apostles.

διαταράσσω *diatarassō* confuse*

Luke 1:29: Mary *was perplexed* at the word (ἐπὶ τῷ λόγῳ), i.e., by the greeting from Gabriel (v. 28; cf. v. 29b).

διατάσσω *diatassō* instruct; command
διαταγή, ῆς, ἡ *diatagē* commandment*

1. Occurrences in the NT — 2. Instructions to a subordinate — 3. Paul's claim of authority — 4. "Commandments" of Jesus — 5. The authority of God

Lit.: G. Dautzenberg, "Die Verzicht auf das apostolische Unterhaltsrecht," *Bib* 50 (1969) 212-32. — G. Delling, *TDNT* VIII, 34-36. — J. Eckert, *Die urchristliche Verkündigung im Streit zwischen Paulus und seinen Gegnern nach dem Galaterbrief* (1971) 81-86. — J. Friedrich, W. Pöhlmann, and P. Stuhlmacher, "Zur historischen Situation und Intention von Röm 13, 1-7," *ZTK* 73 (1976) 131-66, esp. 136-40. — H. Hübner, *Law in Paul's Thought* (1984) 27-30, 71-73. — E. Käsemann, *Commentary on Romans* (1980) 350-56. — P. S. Minear, "A Note on Luke 17:7-10," *JBL* 93 (1974) 82-87. — F. Mussner, *Galaterbrief* (HTKNT, [3]1977) 245-50. — A. Weiser, *Die Knechtsgleichnisse der synoptischen Evangelien* (1971) 105-20.

1. Except in Luke (Luke 4 times, Acts 5 times) and 1 Corinthians (4 times), διατάσσω (or the synonymous mid. voice) appears only in Matt 11:1; Gal 3:19, and Titus 1:5. The noun διαταγή appears only in Acts 7:53 and Rom 13:2.

2. a) In Acts 18:2; 23:31; 24:23 διατάσσω refers to orders of government authorities. The reference to the διατεταγμένον (Luke 3:13) within the framework of the threefold response of the Baptist (vv. 10-14) to the inquiry brought by the tax collectors has a specific, restricted meaning: what is *ordered* is the norm for proper conduct; it signifies the renunciation of potential personal enrichment at the expense of another (within the ancient practice of tax collection, not an easy task).

b) The dependent relationship of the subordinate is presupposed also in Luke 17:7-10. The servant who serves (v. 9) his master after the day's work according to his *duty* (τὰ διαταχθέντα) does nothing unusual. The parable, which was probably directed originally against an erroneous concept of reward on the part of the Pharisees, employs the phrase in v. 10 to demand from the apostles—in the Lukan situation, those who assume responsibility in the community—the "servant's" conviction of his "obligation" (= τὰ διαταχθέντα) in relation to his "master," i.e., "modesty, humility, and consciousness of duty" (G. Schneider, *Lukas* [ÖTK] 349).

3. As a "rule" given out of the apostle's responsibility for his churches, διατάσσομαι in 1 Cor 7:17 characterizes Paul's counsel to lead the life of eschatological freedom made available in the salvific work of God in Jesus Christ (vv. 17-24). Jew and Gentile, slave and free, all stand equally under that which "the Lord has assigned" and under God's "call." Likewise the concluding comment τὰ δὲ λοιπὰ ὡς ἂν ἔλθω διατάξομαι (11:34b) in the instructions for the celebration of the Lord's Supper (vv. 17-34a) indicates the claim of the apostle with respect to his instructions in regard to questions that concern the life of the church (also 1 Cor 16:1). The same usage is present in the Epistle to Titus, in a situation where the congregational structure has already been shaped by "offices." Here the author legitimates the installation of πρεσβύτεροι as an explicit command (διεταξάμην) of the apostle (1:5).

4. a) In Luke 8:55 the "command" of Jesus to give food to the girl who has been awakened from the dead is, in its connection with the confirmation of the "raising" (cf. Mark 5:42f.), intended to corroborate the miracle (cf. the eating by the resurrected one in Luke 24:41-43; Acts 10:40f.).

b) In the redactional note at Matt 11:1a, which concludes the commissioning speech of Jesus in 10:5-42 (cf. 7:28a; 13:53; 19:1; 26:1), the summarizing of the instructions to the disciples with διατάσσων brings into relief the fact that this is to be distinguished from Jesus' διδάσκειν καὶ κηρύσσειν to the people (11:1b; cf. 9:35). It is at the same time the confirmation of the abiding obligatory instructions to the Church, the successor of the Twelve.

c) In rejecting the claim to support by the church (1 Cor 9:14; cf. Matt 10:10b par. Luke 10:7b), which is permitted by an explicit word of Jesus (ὁ κύριος διέταξεν), Paul makes clear the "selflessness of his service" for the gospel (Dautzenberg 213).

5. When Paul describes government authorities as "God's διαταγή" (Rom 13:2) in his exhortation to the Christians to be submissive to this ἐξουσία, the use of this term indicates that he is not concerned abstractly with the nature of the state. He is concerned instead with the actual basis of submission under governmental authority as an *order* willed by God even for Christians. On the other hand, in comparison to the promise, the apostle can express the secondary significance and merely relative validity of the law when he describes it as διαταγεὶς δι' ἀγγέλων (Gal 3:19; cf., however, the positive evaluation in Acts 7:53).

L. Oberlinner

διατελέω *diateleō* endure*

Acts 27:33: ἄσιτοι διατελεῖτε, "you *have continued* without food."

διατηρέω *diatēreō* preserve

Luke 2:51: "His mother *kept* πάντα τὰ ῥήματα in her heart." The reference is probably not to "all of the words" that were remembered (so BAGD s.v.) but to "all of the events"; cf. 2:19; see H. Schürmann, *Lukas* (HTKNT) I on this passage. Acts 15:29: "*keep* yourselves from these."

διατί *diati* why?
→ διά 4.

διατίθεμαι *diatithemai* ordain; stipulate; bequeath*

In the NT only in the mid. The phrase διατίθεμαι διαθήκην (literally "*issue* a decree"), which appears frequently in the LXX (cf. Exod 24:8; Jer 38:31, 33), occurs in the NT, always in reference to acts of God, with the meaning "*establish* a covenant" (→ διαθήκη 2): Acts 3:25 (πρὸς τοὺς πατέρας ὑμῶν, "to your fathers"); Heb 8:10 (τῷ οἴκῳ Ἰσραήλ, cited from Jer 38:33 LXX); 10:16 (πρὸς αὐτούς, likewise from Jer 38:33 LXX). The subst. partc. ὁ διαθέμενος in Heb 9:16, 17, "the *one who ordains,* the *testator,*" is to be understood on the basis of the general meaning "enact or issue (a testament)" (→ διαθήκη 4.c). By contrast in Luke 22:29 (bis), Jesus *bequeathed* a share in his kingdom, just as God *has bequeathed* a share to him (not as the issuing of a testament, but rather in the sense of an allotment or participation in the kingdom). This event will be realized, to be sure, only in the future. J. Behm, *TDNT* II, 104-6; *TWNT* X, 1041-46 (bibliography).

διατρίβω *diatribō* remain; linger*

Besides John 3:22 (and 11:54 v.l., of the *abode* of Jesus), διατρίβω occurs only in the travel narratives of Acts (12:19; 14:3, 28; 15:35; 16:12; 20:6; 25:6, 14).

διατροφή, ῆς, ἡ *diatrophē* livelihood; sustenance*

1 Tim 6:8: We shall be content with "*food* and clothing (διατροφὰς καὶ σκεπάσματα)."

διαυγάζω *diaugazō* shine through; light up*

2 Pet 1:19: "until the day *dawns* and the morning star rises in your hearts."

διαυγής, 2 *diaugēs* transparent*

Rev 21:21b, of the new Jerusalem: "And the street of the city was pure gold, *transparent* as glass."

διαφανής, 2 *diaphanēs* transparent

Rev 21:21b TR in place of → διαυγής. C. Mugler, *Dictionnaire historique de la terminologie optique des Grecs* (1964) 97-100.

διαφέρω *diapherō* trans.: carry through; intrans.: be different*

1. Occurrences in the NT — 2. Trans. usage — 3. Intrans. usage — 4. Διάφορος

Lit.: E. FUCHS, "Die Verkündigung Jesu. Der Spruch von den Raben," Ristow/Matthiae 385-88. — J. GNILKA, *Philipperbrief* (HTKNT, [2]1976) 51f. — E. KÄSEMANN, *Commentary on Romans* (1980) 70f. — G. KLEIN, "Gal 2, 6-9 und die Geschichte der Jerusalemer Urgemeinde," *Rekonstruktion und Interpretation* (BEvT 50, 1969) 99-128. — F. MUSSNER, *Galaterbrief* (HTKNT, [3]1977) 111-15. — SCHULZ, *Q* 149-61. — K. WEISS, *TDNT* IX, 62-64.

1. Διαφέρω is used trans. only 3 times (Mark 11:16; Acts 13:49; 27:27). It is intrans. in the other 10 occurrences, including 5 instances in Paul's letters.

2. In Mark 11:16, within the framework of Jesus' activities in the outer court of the temple, he "would not allow any one to *carry* anything *through* the temple." The success of the sermon by Paul and Barnabas in Antioch in Asia Minor (Acts 13:14-43) on the first missionary journey is indicated not only by the conversion of the Gentiles (v. 48) but by the fact that "the word of the Lord," which was even more productive among the converts, "*spread* throughout all the region" (v. 49).

3. a) Διαφέρω has the intrans. meaning *differ* in the simple comparison of the radiance of the stars (1 Cor 15:41). In the words of Jesus it is used to indicate a higher value (Matt 6:26 par. Luke 12:24; Matt 10:31 par. Luke 12:7). From God's care for comparatively insignificant birds, consequences are derived from the order of precedence in creation about trust in the goodness of God, the "Father" who "knows" what is necessary (Matt 6:32b par. Luke 12:30b). This conclusion from the lesser to the greater is also assumed in Matt 10:31 par. The word to the disciples (in Matthew, the twelve who are sent on a mission) that they "are *of more value* than many sparrows" represents an exhortation to fearless confession. If God "forgets" none of the sparrows, which are obtainable for a ridiculously low price, how much more does he care for the disciples of Jesus, especially in the dangers of earthly life. Similarly Jesus asserts that all human life is *of more value* than property, including a single sheep according to Matt 12:12 (cf. Mark 3:1-6), and thus healing on the sabbath is permissible.

Paul describes the situation of believers, who have been accepted as "sons" and "heirs" through the sending of the Son (Gal 4:4-7), prior to the fulfillment of the promise. He uses the image of the "heir who has not come of age," who "is no *better than* [JB: *different from*] a slave" (4:1). This image is derived from the legal sphere.

b) Τὰ διαφέροντα designates what is absolutely distinctive, *that which really matters.* The phrase appears once in the polemic of Paul against the claim of the Jews that they can, on the basis of the knowledge of the law, determine τὰ διαφέροντα, "what is excellent" (Rom 2:18). On the other hand, in Phil 1:10a the capacity to recognize τὰ διαφέροντα, based on the gospel (v. 5) and mediated by the love of Christ (v. 8), is emphasized by the apostle as the actual eschatological confirmation "for the day of Christ" (v. 10b).

c) In the parenthesis in Gal 2:6 Paul provides the basis for the independence of his apostolic ministry in an argument with his opponents. Here in reference to the Jerusalem "authorities" (οἱ δοκοῦντες) he only wants to make known what they decided at the apostolic council with respect to the gospel that is free from the law (vv. 3, 7-9); any further discussion of the matter which proposes to appeal to these δοκοῦντες is cut off by Paul with the observation, "What they were *makes* no *difference* to me (οὐδέν μοι διαφέρει)."

4. The adj. **διάφορος** *different** in Rom 12:6 designates the variety and the equal value of the "gifts that *differ*" (vv. 6b-10). In the connection with the βαπτισμοί in Heb 9:10, however, it has a negative connotation. The comparative, used to describe the special place of Jesus in God's plan of salvation, appears twice in Hebrews: 1:4, in the characterization of the name (i.e., "the Son") that is *more excellent* than that of the angels; and 8:6, to describe Christ's *more excellent* ministry (διαφορωτέρα λειτουργία) in the high-priestly office, where he functions as the mediator of the new covenant (vv. 1-13).

L. Oberlinner

διαφεύγω *diapheugō* escape*

Acts 27:42: The soldiers wanted to kill the prisoners when the ship was destroyed, "lest any should swim away and *escape.*"

διαφημίζω *diaphēmizō* make known, spread (news)*

Mark 1:45, of the healed leper: ἤρξατο . . . διαφημίζειν τὸν λόγον, "he began to *spread* the news"; Matt 28:15 has the corresponding pass.: διεφημίσθη ὁ λόγος. According to Matt 9:31 the two blind men, despite being forbidden by Jesus after the healing to say anything, "*spread* his fame through all that district."

διαφθείρω *diaphtheirō* destroy, demolish*
διαφθορά, ᾶς, ἡ *diaphthora* destruction

Lit.: M. DIBELIUS, *Studies in the Acts of the Apostles* (1956) 138-85. — J. W. DOEVE, *Jewish Hermeneutics in the Synoptic Gospels and Acts* (1953) 168-76. — G. HARDER, *TDNT* IX, 102-6. — T. HOLTZ, *Untersuchungen über die alttestamentlichen Zitate bei Lukas* (TU 104, 1968) 48-51. — E. KRÄNKL, *Jesus der Knecht Gottes* (BU 7, 1972) 131-43.

1. a) This compound of φθείρω, strengthened with διά, has a literal meaning in Luke 12:33: *destroy, demolish* (D has fut.; ἀφανίζω, which appears in Matt 6:19, may be original; cf. Schulz, *Q* 142). The image is of the heavenly treasure, for which the disciples must be concerned and which will not be *destroyed* by moths. This meaning is present also in Rev 8:9; after the second vision of the trumpets (vv. 8f.) one-third of the ships in the sea are *destroyed* by a cosmic event: economics and trade are harmed, causing the people to fall into great affliction. In 11:18 the announcement of judgment (including "*destroying the destroyers* of the earth," v. 18c) is contrasted with the preceding promise of reward by the adversative καί in v. 18b. The *destroyers* of the earth are opposed to the servants of God, who are characterized more precisely as prophets, saints, and those who fear the name of God. The former will themselves be *destroyed*. The literal meaning of the twofold διαφθείρω remains determinative, even though moral destruction, which the enemies of God inflict on the Church, can also be intended; cf. 19:2.

b) Διαφθείρω has a fig. meaning in 2 Cor 4:16. Paul describes the contrast between the outer and the inner nature and emphasizes that the outer nature is *destroyed* (pass.). In the context of vv. 16-18 this is interpreted to mean that the momentary suffering burdens the earthly existence (v. 17) and that this existence is temporary (v. 18). The vb. does not refer to "the continual decrease of physical vitality" (H. Windisch, *Der zweite Korintherbrief* [KEK] 153) but instead expresses the fact that the earthly and human form of existence and life is *destroyed*, i.e., vanquished.

A fig. significance is also present in 1 Tim 6:5. In a five-part vice list, bickering by the people, which has led to their mind (→ νοῦς) being *destroyed*, is mentioned last (cf. 2 Tim 2:8). Διαφθείρω is used for the wrong attitude of mind and the ethically corrupt position of the heretics mentioned in 1 Tim 6:3-10 (N. Brox, *Pastoralbriefe* [RNT] 208-11).

2. In Acts (and only there) **διαφθορά** *destruction* appears 6 times: twice in Peter's speech at Pentecost (2:27, 31), and 4 times in Paul's speech at Antioch (13:34-37). In both texts it is used in statements about the resurrection of Jesus; in both cases Ps 15:10 LXX is the basis (see A. Schmitt, "Ps 16, 8-11 als Zeugnis der Auferstehung in der Apg," *BZ* 17 [1973] 229-48) for the statement. Although *šaḥaṯ* ("pit, grave") appears in the MT, the rendering in the LXX with διαφθορά expresses the *destruction* of the person in death. The rendering of διαφθορά with "decay" (see E. Haenchen, *The Acts of the Apostles* [1971] 182, 412; Harder 104, etc.) can scarcely be justified on linguistic or technical grounds; the anthropological terms in Ps 15:8-11 LXX are not to be understood in the sense of a dichotomy.

The statement from the Psalms is used as a basis for the statement that God did not abandon Jesus to the irrevocable fate of death. The statement is even strengthened in Acts 13:34: God does not allow Jesus to return to destruction. BAGD s.v. renders the phrase ὑποστρέφειν εἰς διαφθοράν as "*return to decay* (i.e., prob. the realm of the dead)." Even if the text in Psalms does not totally exclude this meaning and one observes that in 2:24 of the D text θάνατος is replaced by ᾅδης, it is still better to understand the noun in both Acts 2:27-31 and 13:34-37 in a comprehensive sense: Jesus' resurrection was a liberation from the *destruction* that is brought about by death; this liberation is final. There is no return to the destructive power of death (cf. ὠδῖνες τοῦ θανάτου in 2:24).

A. Sand

διαφθορά, ᾶς, ἡ *diaphthora* destruction
→ διαφθείρω 2.

διάφορος, 2 *diaphoros* different
→ διαφέρω 4.

διαφυλάσσω *diaphylassō* guard, keep*

Luke 4:10: of the angels, whom God commands "*to guard* you" (Ps 90:11 LXX).

διαχειρίζομαι *diacheirizomai* kill, murder*

With acc. obj.: Acts 5:30: Jesus, "whom you *killed*"; 26:21: the Jews attempted *to kill* Paul.

διαχλευάζω *diachleuazō* mock, ridicule*

Acts 2:13: "Others *mocking* said. . . ."

διαχωρίζω *diachōrizō* separate (vb.)*

Luke 9:33 mid. or pass.: Moses and Elijah *parted* or *were separated* from Jesus.

διδακτικός, 3 *didaktikos* qualified to teach*

1 Tim 3:2; 2 Tim 2:24, in requirements for the → ἐπίσκοπος or "servant of the Lord." K. H. Rengstorf, *TDNT* II, 165.

διδακτός, 3 *didaktos* taught, instructed*

John 6:45: "And they shall all be *taught* by God" (Isa 54:13 LXX); 1 Cor 2:13 (bis): "in words not *taught* by human wisdom but *taught* by the Spirit." K. H. Rengstorf, *TDNT* II, 165.

διδασκαλία, ας, ἡ *didaskalia* teaching*

1. Occurrences in the NT — 2. Meaning — 3. Usage — 4. Ἑτεροδιδασκαλέω

Lit.: K. H. Rengstorf, *TDNT* II, 160-63.

1. The noun appears a total of 21 times in the NT. With two exceptions, it appears only in the Epistles; remarkably, 15 of these occurrences are in the Pastorals.

2. Διδασκαλία appears in the active sense of *the action of teaching* or *instruction* in Rom 12:7 and 1 Tim 4:13; 5:17; Titus 2:7, as well as Rom 15:4 and 2 Tim 3:16. In other passages διδασκαλία denotes the *content of teaching,* most often in the sg. The pl. always has a negative connotation.

3. a) In reference to *the action of teaching* or *instruction* *διδασκαλία* in Rom 12:7 and in the Pastorals designates a specific function in the Church: Rom 12:7, the activity of the διδάσκων, in 1 Tim 4:13, one of the functions of the church leader. In 1 Tim 5:17 διδασκαλία with λόγος designates the preaching and teaching activity of the presbyters. Correspondingly the phrase ἐν τῇ διδασκαλίᾳ in Titus 2:7 can be translated "as a teacher" (→ διδάσκω). In Rom 15:4 and 2 Tim 3:16 διδασκαλία is used broadly for the instruction of the Church through the OT Scripture. In 2 Tim 3:16, where διδασκαλία is parallel to ἐλεγμός, it includes an antiheretical aspect (→ c).

b) The pl. occurs—except for 1 Tim 4:1 (→ d)—only in the citation of Isa 29:13 (LXX) in Mark 7:7 par. Matt 15:9 to describe "the tradition of the elders" as "the precepts of men" in contrast to "the command of God" (Mark 7:8). Similarly, in Col 2:22 it is used to characterize the legal injunctions of the opponents (cf. Col 2:8; Titus 1:14). This polemical use of Isa 29:13 in the NT becomes a key element in the debate about the validity of the law in the Church.

c) In the Pastoral Epistles διδασκαλία in the sg. is a t.t. for *apostolic or Christian teaching as a whole* (1 Tim 1:10; 4:6, 16; 6:1, 3; 2 Tim 3:10; 4:3; Titus 1:9; 2:1, 10). Its characterization as "sound" (1 Tim 1:10; 2 Tim 4:3; Titus 1:9; 2:1), as "good" (1 Tim 4:6), and as "the *doctrine* which is in accordance with true religion" (1 Tim 6:3, JB) demonstrates that it is regarded as the opposite of false teaching.

d) Accordingly διδασκαλία in the pl. in 1 Tim 4:1 designates the *false teaching* produced by demonic powers, which is in itself a sign of the end time. The image of the storm or wind in Eph 4:14 (cf. also Jude 12f.; Heb 13:9) is intended to portray the unreliability of human teaching in contrast to the truth of faith (v. 15).

4. Corresponding to the use of διδασκαλία in the Pastorals as a t.t. for *correct teaching* (→ 3.c), the compound **ἑτεροδιδασκαλέω** (1 Tim 1:3; 6:3) means *spread a different teaching** (cf. Ign. *Pol.* 3:1). The prefix ἑτερο-, in accordance with 1 Tim 1:10, makes the word refer to the opposite of "sound teaching." Paul's reference to "another gospel" (Gal 1:6f.) is essentially comparable (Rengstorf 163).

H.-F. Weiss

διδάσκαλος, ου, ὁ *didaskalos* teacher
→ διδάσκω.

διδάσκω *didaskō* teach
διδάσκαλος, ου, ὁ *didaskalos* teacher

1. Occurrences in the NT — 2. Meaning — 3. Constructions with διδάσκω — 4. Usage in the NT — 5. Compounds

Lit.: Dalman, *Words* 331-36. — E. Fascher, "Jesus der Lehrer," *TLZ* 79 (1954) 325-42. — F. V. Filson, "The Christian Teacher in the First Century," *JBL* 60 (1941) 317-28. — H. Flender, "Lehren und Verkündigen in den synoptischen Evangelien," *EvT* 25 (1965) 701-14. — Hahn, *Titles* 73ff. — M. Hengel, *The Charismatic Leader and His Followers* (1981) 38ff. — F. Normann, *Christos Didaskalos* (1967). — K. H. Rengstorf, *TDNT* II, 138-65. — K. H. Schelkle, "Jesus—Lehrer und Prophet," FS Schmid (1973) 300-308. — H. Schürmann, ". . . und Lehrer," *idem, Dienst der Vermittlung* (1977) 107-47. — For further bibliography see *TWNT* X, 1046.

1. The vb. appears in the NT 97 times (including John 8:2), while the noun appears 59 times (including John 8:4). In the Gospels the words appear *ca.* 50 and 40 times respectively in reference to Jesus. Moreover, the vb. denotes especially the activity of the disciples of Jesus, the apostles, and Paul. The noun is used for a specific office in the Church.

2. The vb. appears consistently in the sense of *teach* or—when the audience is named in the acc.—in the sense of *instruct,* sometimes parallel to εὐαγγελίζομαι (Luke 20:1; Acts 5:42; 15:35) or κηρύσσω (Matt 4:23; 9:35; 11:1; Acts 28:31). The noun designates a *teacher,* used in the voc. as an honorific address.

3. The subject of the vb. (both act. and pass.) is normally a person or a group of persons (Matt 28:15; Gal 1:12; Eph 4:21; Col 2:7; 2 Thess 2:15). The receivers of the teaching are, with the exception of Acts 2:14 (dat.), named with the acc.: thus the people (Mark 4:2; 10:1; Luke 4:31; Acts 4:2, etc.), the disciples of Jesus (Mark 8:31; 9:31; Matt 5:2), the brethren (Acts 15:1), the presbyters (Acts 20:20), the Greeks (John 7:35), and the Jews (Acts 21:21). The content of teaching is identified with an acc. obj. (Mark 12:14 par. 7:7 par. Matt 22:16; John 14:26, etc.), with a following inf. (Matt 28:20; Luke 11:1), with a ὅτι clause (Mark 8:31; Acts 15:1; 1 Cor 11:14), or with a prep. phrase (Mark 4:2: ἐν παραβολαῖς; Acts 21:28: κατά with the gen.; 1 John 2:27: περί with the gen.). The vb. is used relatively frequently with no indication of the content (Mark 1:21; 4:1; 6:6; Matt 4:23; 9:35, etc.); the content is determined by the context.

With the use of the subst. in the Gospels, one must distinguish between the address in the voc., which corresponds to the common Jewish address *rabbi,* and the noun used with the art., which designates Jesus absolutely as "The Teacher" (Mark 14:14 par.; Matt 23:8; John 13:13f.; cf. also Matt 10:24f. par. Luke 6:40).

4. a) An established view of the Gospels is that of *Jesus the teacher*, according to Mark 10:1; Matt 4:23; 9:35; Luke 4:15. This is true both for the pre-Synoptic Jesus tradition (on Q, cf. Matt 8:19-22 par. Luke; Matt 10:24f. par. Luke) and for its redactional shaping by the Evangelists. The connection with the Jewish tradition is thus unmistakable, especially where the reference is to the teaching of Jesus in the synagogue (Mark 1:21 par.; 6:2 par. Matthew; Matt 4:23; 9:35; 21:23; Luke 4:15; 6:6; 13:10; John 6:59; 18:20) or in the temple (Mark 11:17; 12:14 par.; 12:35; 14:49 par. Matthew; Matt 21:23 par. Luke; Luke 19:47; 21:37; John 7:14; [8:2]; 8:20; 18:20). The manner of Jesus' appearance is accordingly that of a Jewish teacher or scribe.

Jesus' sermon in the synagogue in Nazareth provides an example of his teaching (note Luke 4:15, "and he *taught* in their synagogues"). The address to Jesus as διδάσκαλε corresponds to this fact (voc.: Mark 4:38; 9:17, 38; 10:17, 35, etc.; Matt 19:16; 22:16; Luke 7:40; 11:45, etc.), as this title corresponds to the term *rabbi*, which was common in Judaism (cf. Matt 23:7f.; E. Lohse, *TDNT* VI, 964f.; Hahn 75f.). In John 1:38 the address *rabbi* is translated διδάσκαλε (cf. John 20:16). The use of διδάσκαλος with the art. in Mark 5:35 par. Luke and the reference to Jesus as "your *teacher*" in the mouth of the Jews in Matt 9:11; 17:24 (cf. Nicodemus according to John 3:2: "Rabbi, we know that you are a *teacher* come from God") are in keeping with Jewish tradition. In all of these passages the terms used reflect no particular christology.

The Evangelists emphasize, however, each in his own way, the uniqueness of Jesus' teaching in contrast to that of the Jewish teachers. According to Mark 1:22 Jesus, in his first appearance in the synagogue of Capernaum, taught "as one who had authority, and not as the scribes." The corresponding differentiation is found also in Matt 7:29 at the conclusion to the Sermon on the Mount, which begins by portraying Jesus in the manner of a Jewish teacher, to whom his disciples come (Matt 5:1f.). In connection with the summary note in Luke 4:15, Luke develops the special character of the teaching of Jesus in vv. 16-30 (cf. vv. 18, 21, 32).

The unique character of the teacher-pupil relationship with Jesus points in the same direction: one does not attach himself to Jesus the teacher; rather, one is called to discipleship (→ ἀκολουθέω 4). In addition, Jesus remains the teacher of his pupils (→ μαθητής; Hengel 50-57). Thus it is to be understood that the noun with the art. in the redaction of the tradition by the Evangelists, e.g., in Matt 23:8 (cf. v. 10), approximates a christological title (Hahn 77). The same is true for the formulation "*The Teacher* says . . ." in Mark 14:14 par. (see also John 11:28: "*The Teacher* is here and is calling for you," next to v. 27) and in the juxtaposition of διδάσκαλος and κύριος in John 13:13f. (Hahn 78, 88f.). Likewise Matt 10:24f. par. Luke is to be mentioned in this connection. Here the concern is primarily with a comparison; yet the intended christological implication of the statement is unmistakable in mentioning the household that includes master and slaves (at least such an implication is clear in the context of the commissioning speech of Matthew).

Christological reflection in connection with the tradition of Jesus the teacher is particularly apparent in Mark and Matthew. Indeed, although the noun in Mark (except at Mark 14:14) has no essential christological weight, the interest of Mark in Jesus as teacher is evident. For Mark, teaching is—as distinguished from preaching (κηρύσσω) —a typical activity of Jesus. Only once is διδάσκω used with reference to the disciples (6:30), while it is used 15 times of Jesus' activity. Thus for Mark the act of teaching is decisive, although, except for Mark 4:1-34 (Jesus' teaching "in parables"), nothing is said about the content of the teaching of Jesus (cf. 2:13; 6:2, 6, 34; 10:1). In the first part of the Gospel of Mark, the deeds of power demonstrate that "he *taught* them as one who had authority" (1:22, 27; 6:2; cf. 11:18). Only in the second part (from 8:27) is the content of the teaching of Jesus defined more closely in terms of instruction to the disciples about the Passion (8:31; 9:31). Jesus is thus not merely "the teacher"; in Mark a direct connection exists between what Jesus taught and his person and destiny. In this sense Jesus is the subject and object of his teaching at the same time (Flender 703f.).

In Matthew also Jesus as teacher stands in the center from the very beginning (4:23; 9:35; 11:1). On the other hand, it appears that Matthew consistently avoids addressing Jesus as teacher, in contrast to Mark. The voc. διδάσκαλε, like the address *rabbi*, occurs only in the mouth of nondisciples (8:19; 12:38; 19:16; 22:16, 24, 36; cf. 26:25, 49: *rabbi* as address by Judas), while the disciples address Jesus as κύριε (8:25 [cf. Mark 4:38]; 17:15 [cf. Mark 9:17]; also 17:4 is different from Mark 9:5; Hahn 80f.; E. Lohse, *TDNT* VI, 964f.). Such changes from the Markan original are based not on a lack of interest in Jesus as teacher but on the fact that Jesus is no teacher in the Jewish sense, according to Matthew; consequently for Matthew's Gospel as a whole there is a fundamental contrast between the teaching of Jesus and that of Judaism. Likewise in contrast to Mark, Matthew defines the content of the teaching of Jesus in the sense of a teaching of the law or making known the will of God, as is indicated programmatically in the Sermon on the Mount (5:1f. and 7:29). The charge of the resurrected one for the instruction of the disciples is determined accordingly, indeed, in a reference to the teaching and commandment of Jesus himself (28:20).

In contrast to Mark and Matthew, Luke and John use the noun and vb. relatively unreflectively, even if the address to Jesus, διδάσκαλε, in the Markan original is sometimes replaced by the address ἐπιστάτα (Luke 8:24 [cf. Mark 4:38]; Luke 9:49 [cf. Mark 9:38]; see also Luke 9:33 [cf. Mark 9:5]; → ἐπιστάτης). From the very beginning, Luke characterizes the activity of Jesus as that of teaching (4:15, 31; 5:3, 17, etc.; cf. Acts 1:1), without distinguishing clearly between it and Jesus' κηρύσσειν (cf. Luke 4:31 with 4:44 and Acts 28:31). In John also the vb. denotes the proclamation of Jesus in a comprehensive sense (6:59; 7:14, 28, 35; 8:20; 9:34; cf. 1:38; 20:16).

Outside the Gospels the designation of Jesus as the teacher plays no role, with the exception of Acts 1:1. The use of these terms in the Apostolic Fathers and in the apologists does not retain the focus of the vb. and noun in the Gospels (Rengstorf 158, 162f.; Fascher 337-39; Normann).

b) The vb. and the noun are used to describe a distinctive activity or *function within the Church* only in Matthew (23:8; 28:20 and 5:19). However, a wider distribution of the vb. and noun is present in Acts and in the NT Epistles. In Acts the missionary proclamation of the apostles or of Paul is frequently described in terms of the vb. διδάσκω (4:2; 5:21, 25: in the temple; 11:26), sometimes with an explicit statement of the content of the teaching as a proclamation of Christ (5:42; 15:35; 18:11, 25; 28:31; cf. 4:18; 5:28: teaching "in this [i.e., Jesus'] name"). In addition, the vb. appears also in the specific sense of teaching; i.e., in 20:20 in the sense of Paul's instruction of the presbyters and in 21:21, 28 in the sense of Paul's teaching "against the law."

In the Pauline corpus the vb. appears generally for *teaching* within the Church (Eph 4:21; Col 2:7; 3:16; 2 Thess 2:15; 1 Tim 2:12; cf. Heb 5:12) and especially for *teaching* by Paul (1 Cor 4:17; Col 1:28). In 1 Tim 2:7 and 2 Tim 1:11, Paul is described accordingly as "a *teacher* of the Gentiles." The noun is used in the specific sense to designate the position of the early Christian teacher alongside other offices and functions within the Church in 1 Cor 12:28f. Here it is one of the charisms (cf. Eph 4:11 and Rom 12:7: ὁ διδάσκων; 1 Cor 14:6, 26), as it is also in Acts 13:1 and Jas 3:1. This corresponds to the use of the vb. to designate the activity of Church leaders or those who are commissioned by them in the Pastorals (1 Tim 4:11; 6:2; 2 Tim 2:2).

c) Beyond these uses, the vb. and noun occur isolated in miscellaneous other connections: Luke 11:1 mentions the teaching of the Baptist, which corresponds to the address διδάσκαλε to the Baptist in Luke 3:12 (cf. John 3:26: *rabbi*). The Lukan (12:12) and Johannine (14:26) references to the "Holy Spirit" as the one who teaches is noteworthy. According to John 14:26, the content of this teaching is what Jesus once said to his disciples. The unique formulation of 1 John 2:27 belongs in the same connection: "as his χρῖσμα [= the ointment used at baptism] *teaches* you about everything." John 8:28 refers to Jesus' speech or his teaching, which the Father taught to him.

Jewish teachers are spoken of in Luke 2:46 and John 3:10 (Nicodemus); in Rom 2:20f. they are mentioned in a critical sense. The polemical references to the teachings (vb.) of the Jews in Mark 1:22 par. Matthew; Mark 7:7 par. Matthew should be compared in this connection.

The vb. and noun are also used in a polemical sense in reference to false teachers: Titus 1:11; Rev 2:14 (vb.); 2 Tim 4:3 (of "*teachers* to suit their own likings," in contrast to "sound *teaching*"; → διδασκαλία 3.c). The use of the vb. with reference to the guards at the tomb of Jesus, who "did as they were *directed*" (Matt 28:15), is unique.

5. Compounds of the noun appear in the NT in only a few passages, especially in the later writings (Rengstorf 159f.). Νομοδιδάσκαλος, *teacher of the law,* appears in Luke 5:17 with Φαρισαῖος as a clarifying translation of γραμματεύς, *scribe* (cf. 5:21), and in Acts 5:34 as an honorific description of the Pharisee Gamaliel. Altogether different is the description of the false teachers as "teachers of the law" (1 Tim 1:7), "who do not know what they are talking about or what they so confidently affirm" (NIV).

The compounds καλοδιδάσκαλος, *teacher of the good,* and ψευδοδιδάσκαλος, *false teacher,* occur only once each: καλοδιδάσκαλος of the teaching by the older women in the Church (Titus 2:3); ψευδοδιδάσκαλος in 2 Pet 2:1 of false teachers who, like the false prophets formerly in Israel, will introduce "destructive heresies" (αἱρέσεις).

H.-F. Weiss

διδαχή, ῆς, ἡ *didachē* instruction, teaching*

Lit.: K. H. Rengstorf, *TDNT* II, 163-65.

1. Of the 30 occurrences in the NT, διδαχή occurs in the pl. only in Heb 13:9. It has the active sense of *instruction* or of *speech* and *exhortation in the form of teaching* (Mark 4:2; 12:38; 1 Cor 14:6, 26; 2 Tim 4:2). The passive meaning of *teaching passed on through instruction* is also present. The comparison in Mark 1:22 par. Matt 7:28 indicates, of course, that one cannot always distinguish sharply between act. and pass. use. Tendencies toward the technical usage of διδαχή in the sense of Christian teaching in general are present in the NT Epistles.

2. a) In the Gospels διδαχή designates "the *teaching* of the Pharisees and Sadducees" (Matt 16:12) as well as the *teaching* of Jesus (Mark 1:22 par.; 1:27; 4:2; 11:18; 12:38; Matt 22:33). The latter is mentioned in contrast to Judaism as a "new *teaching* with authority" (Mark 1:27; cf. 1:22 and the reference to the "amazement" of the people at the *teaching* of Jesus in Mark 1:22 par. Matt 7:28/Luke 4:32;

Mark 11:18; Matt 22:33). In the answer of Jesus to the objection of the Jews (v. 15) in John 7:16f., Jesus' revelatory discourse is described as *teaching,* which is identical (cf. 8:28 and 8:26) to God's own teaching. In connection with the trial of Jesus, the high priest asks about Jesus' *teaching* (18:19; i.e., Jesus' teaching in synagogue and temple [cf. v. 20]).

b) The use of διδαχή *outside of the Gospels* is not uniform: on the one hand, the preaching of the apostles or of Paul is called *teaching* by the high priest (Acts 5:28) and by those who hear Paul in Athens (17:19). In 17:19 it is called a "new *teaching*" ("new" in the sense of ξένος; 17:18, 20f.). On the other hand, διδαχή is used in Acts 2:42 ("*teaching* of the apostles") and in the Pastorals of the firmly established tradition of instruction in the Church; this is the case esp. in Titus 1:9 in the context of the exhortation to the bishop to concern himself with the correct preaching "in accordance with the *teaching*" (cf. 2 Tim 4:2: διδαχή with the meaning of *instruction in sound teaching* in contrast to false teaching). Such usage was already prepared for by Paul in Rom 6:17 where there is an encouragement to obedience to the "form of teaching" (τύπος διδαχῆς) which was once (in baptism) transmitted to the addressees. Διδαχή is used here, as in 16:17, for definite traditions of faith that one is to learn. Similarly, διδαχῇ τοῦ Χριστοῦ in 2 John 9f. denotes the (correct) "*teaching* of Christ" in contrast to false christological teaching (v. 7). In Rev 2:14f., 24, διδαχή can designate, in references to OT traditions concerning Balaam and Jezebel, the false teaching of the Nicolaitans. In Heb 13:9 it refers to "diverse and strange *teachings*" in contrast to the Church's own (correct) teaching (cf. *Herm. Sim.* viii.6.5).

c) In Acts 13:12 and Heb 6:2 διδαχή appears with a special meaning, as it does also in the reference to the miracle of punishment by Paul on Bar-Jesus/Elymas, as a διδαχή τοῦ κυριοῦ, i.e., as "a *teaching* done by the Lord" (subj. gen.); in Heb 6:2, in the context of an enumeration of the catechetical tradition, the "*teachings* of baptisms [pl.! see the commentaries] and of the laying on of hands" is mentioned.

H.-F. Weiss

δίδραχμον, ου, τό *didrachmon* double drachma → δραχμή 2, 4.

Δίδυμος, ου *Didymos* Didymus*

The Greek name → Θωμᾶς of a disciple in the circle of the Twelve (Mark 3:18 par.; Acts 1:13) is derived from the Aramaic name *tᵉ'ômā'*, "twin," and represents the rendering of the Aramaic name with a similar-sounding Greek name (BDF §§53.2; 125.2; H. Wuthnow, *Die semitischen Menschennamen in griechischen Inschriften und Papyri des vorderen Orients* [1930], 55; P. Rüger, *TRE* III, 606). In John 14:5; 20:26, 27, 28 the Grecized name is used alone, but in 11:16; 20:24; 21:2 (cf. 14:5 D) the phrase ὁ λεγόμενος Δίδυμος, "called the *twin,*" is added. Δίδυμος is the Greek translation of the Aramaic name and also occurs as an independent Greek name (*OGIS* 519.8; cf. also W. Pape and G. E. Benseler, *Wörterbuch der griechischen Eigennamen* I [[3]1911 = 1959] 298). In *Acts Thom.* 11, 31, 39, Thomas is addressed as ὁ δίδυμος ("the twin brother") τοῦ Χριστοῦ in a speculative interpretation of the Johannine epithet; the Christ is like the apostle in appearance (11) and entrusts to him special mysteries (39). Thomas also bears the name Judas (Ἰούδας Θωμᾶς ὁ καὶ Δίδυμος, *Acts Thom.* 1; Δίδυμος Ἰούδας Θωμᾶς, *Gos. Thom.* prologue).

H. Balz

δίδωμι *didōmi* give

1. Occurrences in the NT — 2. Meaning — 3. Word pairs — 4. God as giver — 5. Christ as giver — 6. Divine gifts — 7. Usage in Mark/Matthew, Luke/Acts, the Epistles, and Revelation — 8. Usage in John

Lit.: O. BECKER and H. VORLÄNDER, *DNTT* II, 39-43. — F. BÜCHSEL, *TDNT* II, 166-73, esp. 168. — C. J. LABUSCHAGNE, *THAT* II, 117-41. — C.-J. PINTO DE OLIVEIRA, "Le verb διδόναι comme expression des rapports du Père et du Fils dans le IVᵉ Évangile," *RSPT* 49 (1965) 81-104. — W. POPKES, *Christus traditus* (ATANT, 1967). — J. RIEDL, *Das Heilswerk Jesu nach Johannes* (FTS, 1973) 83-90. — A. VANHOYE, "Opera Iesu donum Patris," *VD* 36 (1958) 83-92. — For further bibliography see *TWNT* X, 1046f.

1. With approximately 416 occurrences, δίδωμι is the ninth most frequent vb. in the NT. It is used in all writings except Philippians, Philemon, and Jude: 190 are in the Synoptics and Acts, 85 are in John and 1–3 John, 72 are in the Pauline corpus, 58 are in Revelation, and 13 are in the other letters. The distribution is based on the form of speech (esp. narrative), the style (idiomatic), and the level of discourse. On the other hand, it is also associated with the theological vocabulary (John, Revelation). On the associated form διδῶ (Rev 3:9), see BDF §94.1.

2. Δίδωμι is the most common expression for the procedure whereby a subject deliberately transfers something to someone or something so that it becomes available to the recipient. The Indo-European word is largely synonymous with the Semitic equivalent (cf. Labuschagne). The differences in origin in the figures of speech formed from *give* can be significant (BAGD; LSJ; Passow ad loc.). For example, use with the objects "fruit," "tithe," "letter of divorce," "signs and wonders," "rain," and "life" is derived from Hebrew. A large number of usages are derived from Greek, e.g., with "space," "answer," "meaning," "punishment," "peace," "tax," "opportunity," and "reward." "Make an effort" (Luke 12:58) appears to be a Latinism.

Such figures of speech are formulated ad hoc, in the NT esp. in Luke. For the determination of meaning it is important to distinguish whether a fixed clause is present or not. Thus with δόξαν δίδωμι one must distinguish between "honor" (Luke 17:18 [RSV "give praise"] and elsewhere, probably from Jewish liturgy) and the rendering of δόξα (John 17:22; transitional forms in v. 24; 1 Pet 1:21). With respect to χάριν δίδωμι one must distinguish between "*accept* a favor" (Eph 4:29 perhaps; H. Schlier, *Der Brief an die Epheser* [[2]1958] ad loc.) and "*give* grace." With respect to λόγον δίδωμι one must distinguish between "*give* an account" (Rom 14:12) and, e.g., "gift of the word" (1 Cor 12:8). Normally "to *give* law(s) or commandment(s)" is a conventional formulation. However, it can emphasize the character of the laws as a gift (H. Schlier, *Galaterbrief* [KEK, [5]1971] on Gal 3:21); the same is also true for the unusual combination διαθήκην δίδωμι (Acts 7:8; J. Behm, *TDNT* II, 126). The following are not formalized in a fundamental way: κλήρους δίδωμι (Acts 1:26), σωτήριαν δίδωμι (7:25), and ἔλεος δίδωμι (2 Tim 1:16; cf. v. 18); likewise μετάνοιαν δίδωμι (Acts 11:18; 2 Tim 2:25), which is possibly a shortened form of τόπον μετανοίας δίδωμι.

3. The vbs. αἰτέω, λαμβάνω, δέχομαι, ἔχω, and αἴρω in particular belong to the semantic field represented by δίδωμι. At times fixed word combinations come into existence with a specific content. This occurs in a most remarkable way with "take/receive and *give*" in connection with Jesus' procedure at meals (Mark 6:41 par.; 8:6 par.; 14:22 par., 23 par.; John 6:11; 13:26; 21:13), esp. in connection with the word over the eucharistic bread (not present in Luke 22:20; 1 Cor 11:22-25; cf. the reference to "fish" in Mark 8:6 and the word selection in Luke 6:4; H. Schürmann, *Lukasevangelium* [HTKNT] I [1969], 303). This combination of words appears elsewhere, partially with the character of a maxim (Matt 10:8; Acts 20:35), esp. in the paradoxical statement, "To him who has will more be *given*" (Mark 4:25 par., etc.), which contradicts the normal expectation (as in Acts 3:6 or John 5:26; Rom 12:6). Δίδωμι and αἰτέω together have a fixed place in the language of prayer (Matt 7:7, 11 par.; John 11:22; 15:16; 16:23; Jas 1:5; cf. Matt 5:42 par.; in another context, Mark 6:22, the phrase is used in a blasphemous way); but the number of passages where δίδωμι is used in prayer is not high (cf. Matt 6:11 par.; Acts 4:29).

4. God is mentioned directly as the giver in 104 passages, of which 42 are in John and 1–3 John while 19 occur in Acts, in contrast to the 28 occurrences in the Pauline corpus (of which 11 are in 1–2 Corinthians) and only 7 in the Synoptics (not in Mark). God's act of giving is nevertheless indirectly stated in most of the 73 formulations which appear as absolutes (δοθήσεται, δέδοται, ἐδόθη, etc.), which are distributed in a different way: 22 in Revelation, 11 in Matthew, 8 in Luke, 5 each in Mark, 1 Corinthians, and Ephesians, and hardly any in John, Acts, and the later Epistles. This manner of discourse is derived from Judaism (divine passive); it is esp. preferred in apocalyptic, where it designates primarily the granting of authority (e.g., Rev 6:4, 8) or the symbols that accompany authority (e.g., vv. 2, 11). The one who controls the events often remains mysteriously in the background (e.g., 13:5-7). The formulation can be polished in such a way that it approaches "*it has been given* to me" or merely "I possess" (possibly even Luke 4:6b; Popkes, 59ff., 137). In other contexts the divine passive underlines the divine guarantee of the gift (thus in the wisdom-prophetic words of Matt 7:7 par.; Mark 4:25 par.; Dalman, *Words* 224f.; *idem, Worte* 383); Paul gives it a christological focus (1 Cor 1:4; Gal 3:22; similarly Eph 4:7; 2 Tim 1:9).

5. In 68 instances Jesus Christ is the giver: 26 in John, 12 in Revelation, 7 or 8 in each of the Synoptics, seldom in the Epistles, and not at all in Acts. The subject matter and formulation are largely stereotypical: in the Synoptics, it is associated with the mandate of the disciples (Mark 6:7 par.; Matt 16:19; Mark 10:37, 40 par.); it is also associated with "he took and *gave*" at the supper (→ 3), and with Jesus' self-sacrifice (Mark 10:45 par.; cf. Gal 1:4; 1 Tim 2:6; Titus 2:14); in Revelation it is associated with the language of conquering; on John → 8.

6. The *Pneuma* is ordinarily a gift (a giver only in Acts 2:4; a mediator in 1 Cor 12:8). Together with χάρις and ἐξουσία it is reckoned among the most important gifts within early Christianity. The gift of the Spirit (normally to the Church) is mentioned in Acts, the Pauline Epistles, and 1 John (elsewhere only in John 3:34 and in the blasphemy in Rev 13:15). The gift of χάρις (often for one who is esp. commissioned, e.g., Rom 12:3) is mentioned in almost all of the Epistles (elsewhere only in Acts 7:10; χάρισμα in 1 Tim 4:14). The circle of those who receive ἐξουσία is wider: Jesus (e.g., Mark 11:28 par.), the believers (Mark 6:7 par.; John 1:12; 2 Cor 10:8, etc.), but also Pilate (John 19:11) and even the powers of destruction (Rev 6:8, etc.). Beyond that, the NT knows an abundance of further gifts, among them knowledge (Mark 4:11 par., etc.), the βασιλεία (Matt 21:43; Luke 12:32), miraculous signs (Mark 8:12 par.; Acts 14:3), confidence (Acts 4:29), harmony (Rom 15:5), (words of) wisdom (1 Cor 12:8; Acts 7:10; Eph 1:17; Jas 1:5; 2 Pet 3:15), zeal (2 Cor 8:16), encouragement (2 Thess 2:16), mercy (2 Tim 1:16, 18). Normally it is "good gifts" (cf. Jas 1:17) that are allotted to people for life in salvation and for consecrated service; however, sometimes what is granted is painful (2 Cor 12:7; Rev 16:6, 19).

7. Usage in Mark and Matthew hardly exhibits any unusual theological connotation. An exception is the saying

concerning Jesus' self-sacrifice (Mark 10:45 par.) alongside "he took and he *gave*" (→ 5). The former suggests the influence of the Lord's Supper theology, the reception of Isaiah 53, conceptions of atonement, and martyr traditions; in regard to this saying the origin (Jesus, the Aramaic or Greek-speaking Church?) and the meaning (expiation, substitutionary achievement, for the benefit/in the place of many/all) are disputed (cf. R. Pesch, *Markusevangelium* [HTKNT] ad loc.). The saying lives on in 1 Tim 2:6 and Titus 2:14; related formulations appear in Luke 22:19; John 6:51f. As the setting for these sayings, the Lord's Supper has advanced and shaped them (→ παραδίδωμι); the accent alternates between "sacrifice" (the life) and "give" (Jesus himself, symbolically in the "element").

Luke exhibits a greater preference for δίδωμι than that which is found in the common Synoptic usage. Perhaps he imitates the LXX style. However, he definitely emphasizes the gift character of the act of God (e.g., Acts 4:12, 29; 5:31; 7:8), where he has a tendency to spiritualize the content (Luke 11:13 par. Matt 7:11).

The remarkable feature in most of the Epistles is the variety used in the subject of the vb. Often God is the giver, while Christ is seldom mentioned in this way. Human giving does not appear often, and then normally in idiomatic expressions (as in Rom 4:20; 14:12). James exhibits special interest in *giving*. In Jas 1:5, 17, with help derived from wisdom statements, he treats the subject of God's giving (God gives generously, and he only gives the good). Jas 2:16 discusses the conferring of goods among people.

The references in Revelation are very stereotyped, esp. with respect to God's (apocalyptic pass.) and Christ's (Rev 2:7, etc.) giving. Thus Revelation emphasizes: what follows is irrevocably established. Alongside this, Revelation employs idioms (11:13, 18; 16:6, etc.), among them *hand over* (11:2) and "*give* authority" (v. 3; semitizing: H. Kraft, *Offenbarung* [HNT] ad loc.).

8. Δίδωμι takes on a pronounced theological quality in John (Gospel and Epistles). Fully secular usage is present only in a few conventional phrases (i.e., John 1:22; 18:22). More often they are ambiguous and enigmatic (e.g., 4:7ff.). Giving is an aspect of the divine activity. It comes from God (the subject *ca.* 42 times) through Christ (the receiver in 28 of the 42 instances) to mankind. The Father *gives* "everything" to the Son (3:35, etc.); the Son brings the divine reality to the world, esp. that which belongs to "life" (chs. 4 and 6) and δόξα (ch. 17; the vb. occurs frequently in these chapters). However, he also brings κρίσις (5:22, 27). The gift is the Son himself (3:16). The individual is totally dependent on God's gift (3:27). The world has nothing real to *give* (4:7, 10; 14:27). Only Jesus' opponents demand that one give to God (9:24); even the gifts of Moses stand in the twilight (1:17; 6:32; 7:19, 22). Δίδωμι is a Johannine expression for *sola gratia*.

W. Popkes

διεγείρω *diegeirō* awaken*

Of the waking of one who is sleeping: Luke 8:24a par. Mark 4:38 TR; pass. *wake up:* Matt 1:24 v.l.; Mark 4:39 par. Luke 8:24c; of the sea, which *is stirred up* by the wind: John 6:18; metaphorical: "by way of reminder (ἐν ὑπομνήσει)," *remain awake, awaken:* 2 Pet 1:13; 3:1. → ἐγείρω 1.

διενθυμέομαι *dienthymeomai* consider*

Acts 10:19: Peter *thought about* the vision.

διέξοδος, ου, ἡ *diexodos* exit, terminus*

Matt 22:9: διέξοδοι τῶν ὁδῶν are not "street crossings" but rather the "*outlets* of the (city) streets" where they give way to the country roads. W. Michaelis, *TDNT* V, 108f.

διερμηνευτής, οῦ, ὁ *diermēneutēs* interpreter, translator
→ ἑρμηνεύω.

διερμηνεύω *diermēneuō* translate, interpret
→ ἑρμηνεύω.

διέρχομαι *dierchomai* go through, reach*

Lit.: U. BUSSE, *Die Wunder des Propheten Jesus* (FzB, 1977) 113, n. 1, 199, 319, 353f., n. 2. — H. CONZELMANN, *First Corinthians* (Hermeneia, 1975) 105. — G. DELLING, "Die Jesusgeschichte in der Verkündigung nach Acta," *NTS* 19 (1972/73) 373-89, 378, n. 12. — E. HAENCHEN, *The Acts of the Apostles* (1971) 301. — M. KRENKEL, *Josephus und Lucas* (1894) 107. — H. LJUNGVIK, *Studien zur Sprache der apokryphen Apostelgeschichten* (1926) 80-84. — F. LUCIANI, "Camminare davanti a Dio (II)," *Aevum* 47 (1973) 468-76, esp. 470f. — A. SUHL, *Paulus und seine Briefe* (SNT, 1975) 248, 343. — J. WEISS, *Der erste Korintherbrief* (KEK, 1910) 250, 382f. — H. WINDISCH, *Der Hebräerbrief* (HNT, 1931) 37.

1. The compound vb. (based on ἔρχομαι, "come, go") is found 42 times in the NT (Matt 12:43 par. Luke 11:24 [Q]; Mark 4:35 par. Luke 8:22; Mark 10:25; Luke 2:15, 35; 4:30; 5:15; 9:6; 17:11; 19:1, 4; Acts 8:4, 40; 9:32, 38; 10:38; 11:19, 22; 12:10; 13:6, 14; 14:24; 15:3, 41; 16:6; 17:23; 18:23, 27; 19:1, 21; 20:2, 25; John 4:4, 15; Rom 5:12; 1 Cor 10:1; 16:5 bis; 2 Cor 1:16; Heb 4:14). The variant readings with διέρχομαι in Matt 19:24 (B Koine D Θ, also *GNT*) and John 8:59 (Koine) have been assimilated secondarily to texts which were already present (Matt 19:24 = Mark 10:25; John 8:59 = Luke 4:30).

Because the prefix δια- expresses both "through" and completion, context determines the exact translation. With ἕως (Luke 2:15; Acts 8:40; 9:38; 11:19) the vb. can be translated with "go as far as," with διά (Mark 10:25; Luke 4:30; 11:24 par. Matt 12:43; 17:11; Acts 9:32; John 4:4; 1 Cor 10:1; 2 Cor 1:16) as "go through," with εἰς (Mark

4:35 par. Luke 8:22; Acts 18:27; Rom 5:12) as "reach," "arrive at" (cf. Josephus *Ant.* xiv.414; xvi.129, etc.), with κατά (Luke 9:6) as "go from place to place," with ἀπό (Acts 13:14) as "continue from somewhere." Where the vb. has with it a place name or a name of a region in the acc. (Luke 19:1; Acts 13:6; 15:3, 41; 16:6; 18:23; 1 Cor 16:5; Heb 4:14), it can be translated as "travel through." In Luke 2:35 it is also to be rendered in a local sense ("penetrate"; cf. Josephus *Ant.* vi.189). Where the partc. appears in connection with an acc. and the simple ἔρχομαι, it is to be translated "come to . . ." (Acts 12:10; 14:24; 19:1, 21; 20:2). In accordance with Greek usage (Thucydides vi.46.5; Xenophon *An.* i.4, 7; Sophocles *Aj.* 978; Plato *Ep.* vii.329c; Josephus *Vita* 182; cf. *Ant.* viii.171; xix.62), the vb. in connection with the absolute λόγος can be rendered with "spread."

2. The frequent use of the vb. in the Lukan literature (31 times) is noteworthy. According to Acts 10:38 it is the t.t. for the missionary activity of Jesus in the land of the Jews. It is also used of the apostles (Luke 9:6) and missionaries (Acts 20:25). Luke portrays the activity of Jesus primarily as a mission to the city (Luke 4:14, 31, 44; 5:12), which is likewise the case with the apostles and missionaries in the post-Easter situation. The vb. belongs to the Lukan "way" terminology, along with διαπορεύομαι, διοδεύω, διαβαίνω, and διαπεράω.

In Heb 4:14 the journey through the heavens is described as an essential part of the high-priestly office of Jesus (cf. *T. Levi* 2–5; *3 Bar.* 1ff.; 2 Cor 12:2), which is a journey not only to heaven, but through heaven. In 1 Cor 10:1f. Paul refers to Exod 14:21f. and interprets the ancient event typologically as a baptismal event. For the chronology of the Pauline missionary journeys it is important that in 1 Cor 16:5 an inspection tour is not intended (against Weiss), but rather a missionary journey from which Paul wants to return to Corinth. He plans to remain in Corinth for the winter because so many Church problems are present that cannot be resolved in a short period of time.

U. Busse

διερωτάω *dierōtaō* inquire*

Acts 10:17: the emissaries of Cornelius *had inquired* about the house of Simon.

διετής, 2 *dietēs* two years old*

Matt 2:16: "all of the boys in Bethlehem *two years old and under* (ἀπὸ διετοῦς καὶ κατωτέρω)."

διετία, ας, ἡ *dietia* a period of two years*

Acts 24:27: "when *two years* were over"; 28:30: "he remained *two years* (διετίαν ὅλην)."

διηγέομαι *diēgeomai* tell, explain*

1. Occurrences in the NT — 2. Meanings and word associations — 3. Διήγησις

Lit.: BAGD ad loc. — LSJ ad loc.

1. The vb. διηγέομαι appears in the NT 10 times: twice in Mark (5:16; 9:9), 7 times in Luke (8:39; 9:10; Acts 8:33; 9:27; 12:17; 16:10, 40; Acts 16 only in the secondary Western text: D), and once in Hebrews (11:32). Inasmuch as διηγέομαι in Acts 8:33 appears in a LXX citation from Isa 53:8, the genuine NT occurrences shrink to 7.

Of the 4 instances in the Apostolic Fathers (*1 Clem.* 16:8; 27:7; 35:7; *Diogn.* 11:2 [here "recount," "discuss didactically or in a revelatory manner"]), the first 3 appear likewise in citations from the LXX, which includes the vb. more than 60 times. In classical Greek literature, διηγέομαι is attested since Heracles; papyri and writers such as Polybius, Philo, and Josephus attest it for the koine (Preisigke, *Wörterbuch* I, 377; IV, 585; Supplement I, 75; A. Mauersberger, *Polybios-Lexicon* I [1966] 541f.; G. Mayer, *Index Philoneus* [1974] 78; K. H. Rengstorf, *A Complete Concordance to Flavius Josephus* I [1973] 498).

2. In the NT διηγέομαι has almost always the meaning *explain by giving a report* to someone (τινι; of Jesus' miracles, Mark 5:16; Luke 8:39; of the transfiguration, Mark 9:9; of miraculous [Luke 9:6!] deeds of the disciples, Luke 9:10; of the miracle of deliverance in Acts 12:17; 16:40 D; of the conversion of Paul, Acts 9:27; of his vision, Acts 16:10 D). The subject of the report appears, as in other Greek literature, as an acc. obj. (Acts 16:10 D) or in a connecting rel. clause or indirect interrogative sentence with ἅ, ὅσα, or πῶς. The addressee of the report is not always mentioned (Luke 8:39; Acts 16:40 D). It is noteworthy that here only events distinguished by the miraculous are the object of the report. On the other hand, διηγέομαι in Heb 11:32 means *tell of someone* (περί τινος), here of OT war heroes and prophets. Telling has here—in the form of a paradigmatic series of figures in the history of faith—the historical realm as its object, which was also commonly associated with διηγέομαι outside the NT (e.g., in Polybius and Josephus).

3. History as the subject of the narration comes into view certainly in the Lukan proemium, where the noun **διήγησις** appears (1:1 [hapax legomenon in the NT]; 12 occurrences in the LXX). A *historical explanation* "about the events that have occurred [or "have come to fulfillment"] among us" (περὶ τῶν πεπληροφορημένων ἐν ἡμῖν πραγμάτων), like those which had been offered by the predecessors, is announced by Luke as his intention.

Obviously the announcement in Luke 1:1-4 is shaped by the conceptual framework of Hellenistic historiography; Dionysius of Halicarnassus, e.g., uses the same words when he promises in the proemium to his *Antiquitates Romanae* to clarify from his perspective "concerning which events he wants to compose a historical report" (i.7.4: περὶ τίνων ποιοῦμαι πραγμάτων τὴν διήγησιν; cf. also Polybius iii.4.1; Diodorus Siculus xi.20.1; 2 Macc 2:24, 32; Josephus *B.J.* vii.42; *Ant.* xx.157; W. C. van Unnik, "Once More St. Luke's Prologue," *Neotestamentica* 7 [1973] 7-26). It is not probable that in Luke's use of διήγησις a reference to ἐκδιηγῆται in Hab 1:5 plays a role (H. Schürmann, "Evangelienschrift und kirchliche Unterweisung," in *Das Lukasevangelium* [HTKNT, 1969] 167f.), because of the semantic association of διήγησις as a t.t. of Hellenistic history-writing.

E. Plümacher

διήγησις, εως, ἡ *diēgēsis* narrative, report → διηγέομαι 3.

διηνεκής, 2 *diēnekēs* without interruption*

Heb 7:3; 10:1, 12, 14: εἰς τὸ διηνεκές, *forever.*

διθάλασσος, 2 *dithalassos* sandy bank (?)*

Acts 27:41. Τόπος διθάλλος is probably a sandy bank extending in front of the actual shore; A. Breusing, *Die Nautik der Alten* (1886) 202.

διϊκνέομαι *diikneomai* pierce*

Heb 4:12, of the effect of the word of God: "*piercing* to the division of soul and spirit . . ."; O. Michel, *Hebräerbrief* [KEK] ad loc.

διΐστημι *diistēmi* depart*

Luke 24:51: Jesus *departed* from the disciples; 22:59, of the time: "after an *interval* of about an hour"; Acts 27:28, trans.: βραχὺ διαστήσαντες, *after they had gone a little farther.*

διϊσχυρίζομαι *diischyrizomai* firmly maintain*

Luke 22:59 (different from Mark), of the *affirmation* of Peter; Acts 12:15: the maid *insists* that Peter is at the gate.

δικαιοκρισία, ας, ἡ *dikaiokrisia* righteous judgment*

Rom 2:5, of the day "when God's *righteous judgment* will be revealed"; cf. 2 Thess 1:5 v.l.; *Sib. Or.* iii.704 (God is δικαιοκρίτης). G. Schrenk, *TDNT* II, 224f.

δίκαιος, 3 *dikaios* righteous, just; subst.: the righteous one

δικαίως *dikaiōs* righteously, justly*

1. Occurrences in the NT — 2. Meaning and usage — a) Of humans — b) Of God — c) Of Jesus

Lit.: H. Dechent, "Der 'Gerechte'—eine Bezeichnung für den Messias," *TSK* 100 (1927/28) 439-43. — D. Hill, "ΔΙΚΑΙΟΙ as a Quasi-Technical Term," *NTS* 11 (1964/65) 296-302. — *idem, Greek Words and Hebrew Meanings* (SNTSMS 5, 1967) 82-162. — K. Koch, "צדק *ṣdq* gemeinschaftstreu/heilvoll sein," *THAT* II, 507-30. — R. Mach, *Der Zaddik im Talmud und Midrasch* (1957). — F. V. Reiterer, *Gerechtigkeit als Heil: צדק bei Deuterojesaja* (1976). — L. Ruppert, *Der leidende Gerechte* (FzB 5, 1972) (index). — *idem, Jesus als der leidende Gerechte?* (SBS 59, 1972). — G. Schrenk, *TDNT* II, 182-191. — G. Strecker, *Der Weg der Gerechtigkeit* (FRLANT 82, [3]1971) (index). — J. A. Ziesler, *The Meaning of Righteousness in Paul* (SNTSMS 20, 1972) esp. 22-36, 79-85, 136-41. For further bibliography → δικαιοσύνη, δικαιόω.

1. The adj. δίκαιος occurs 79 times in the NT, of which 17 are in Matthew, 11 in Luke (+ 6 in Acts), and 10 in the authentic Pauline Epistles (7 in Romans, 1 in Galatians, 2 in Philippians). More frequent usage can be observed in 1 John (6), Revelation (5), and 2 Peter (4). The adv. occurs 5 times: Luke 23:41; 1 Cor 15:34; 1 Thess 2:10; Titus 2:12; 1 Pet 2:23.

2. In the LXX δίκαιος is used extensively for Heb. *ṣaddîq* ("righteous"; cf. Hill, *Greek Words* 104-10; Ziesler 64-67); with the exception of Deut 4:8 (where the subject is God's law: δικαιώματα καὶ κρίματα), it refers to persons, either to humans or to God. In the NT what is described by the adj. is likewise predominantly humans or God; among things so described are esp. κρίσις (John 5:30; 7:24; 2 Thess 1:5; pl. Rev 16:7; 19:2) and in individual instances αἷμα (Matt 23:35; 27:4 v.l.), ἐντολή (Rom 7:12); ἔργα (1 John 3:12), ὁδοί (Rev 15:3), and ψυχή (2 Pet 2:8).

In reference to humans δίκαιος means *righteous,* predominantly in the sense of *ṣaddîq,* i.e., acting in accordance with the requirements of law and custom toward one's fellow human being and in accordance with the demands of God (cf. BAGD s.v. 1). Δίκαιος is used of God with special reference to his activity as judge. Neut. δίκαιον denotes what is *fitting* or *to be carried out* according to an established legal requirement. It is used esp. for what is required by God—δίκαιον παρὰ θεῷ (2 Thess 1:6) or ἐνώπιον τοῦ θεοῦ (Acts 4:19; further occurrences of neut. [τὸ] δίκαιον are in Matt 20:4; 20:7 v.l.; Luke 12:57; Eph 6:1; Phil 1:7; Col 4:1; 2 Pet 1:13).

a) Δίκαιος is used primarily of humans. Pl. (οἱ) δίκαιοι appears frequently: Mark 2:17 (opposite of ἁμαρτωλοί) par. Matt 9:13/Luke 5:32; Matt 5:45 (opposite of ἄδικοι); 13:17 (with προφῆται); 13:43 (of those who survive the final judgment); 13:49 (opposite of πονηροί); 23:29 (with προφῆται); 25:37, 46 (of the "righteous" at the judgment of the world); Luke 1:17 (opposite of ἀπειθεῖς); 14:14 ("at the resurrection *of the righteous*"); 15:7 (ninety-nine *righteous* in contrast to a single "sinner"); Acts 24:15 ("resurrection of the δίκαιοι and of the ἄδικοι"); Heb 12:23 (the spirits "of the *just* who have been made perfect"); 1 Pet 3:12 (citing Ps 33:16 LXX: the eyes of the Lord are "on *the righteous*"). Δίκαιοι designates the *pious* in the OT and

Jewish sense, esp. those from an earlier time (Matt 13:17; 23:29: with "prophets"). One may question whether Matthew occasionally uses the pl. "with special reference to those in the community who witness, instruct and teach" (Hill, "ΔΙΚΑΙΟΙ," 302). If Matthew transfers the adj. to Christians (10:41; 13:49), this is associated with his "leading concept" → δικαιοσύνη (5).

The adj. is attributed to the following persons (on Jesus → c): Joseph (Matt 1:19; δίκαιος ὤν is perhaps concessive: "although he was *righteous,*" → Ἰωσήφ 4), Abel (23:35; Heb 11:4), John the Baptist (Mark 6:20: ἀνὴρ δίκαιος καὶ ἅγιος), Zechariah and Elizabeth (Luke 1:6), Simeon (2:25), Joseph of Arimathea (23:50: ἀνὴρ ἀγαθὸς καὶ δίκαιος, → Ἰωσήφ 6), Cornelius (Acts 10:22: ἀνὴρ δίκαιος καὶ φοβούμενος τὸν θεόν), and Lot (2 Pet 2:7). Δίκαιος appears with ὅσιος in Titus 1:8 as a requirement for the episkopos.

The citation from Hab 2:4 LXX ὁ (δὲ) δίκαιος ἐκ πίστεώς (μου) ζήσεται occurs 3 times in the NT (cf. H. C. C. Cavallin, *ST* 32 [1978)] 33-43). Paul employs it in Rom 1:17 and Gal 3:11 in connection with the theology of justification (→ δικαιοσύνη 3, 4). *The righteous one* is here "the one who has been justified by faith, elsewhere called δικαιωθείς by Paul" (Schrenk 191; cf. Rom 3:26; 5:1, 19). In Heb 10:38 the citation stands in a context which challenges the reader to endurance in faith (vv. 32-39), and contrasts faith to "fainthearted shrinking back" (ὑποστολή, vv. 38f.).

b) That God is *just* is stated not only frequently in the OT and Judaism, but also in pagan texts (see BAGD s.v. 2). Such statements are made relatively seldom in the NT; e.g., they do not appear in the Synoptic Gospels. With respect to God's activity as judge, he is *righteous*; as judge he is δίκαιος and ὅσιος (Rev 16:5; cf. Ps 144:17; Deut 32:4 LXX). According to 1 Pet 2:23 Christ submits in judgment τῷ κρίνοντι δικαίως. Indeed, the prayer of Jesus in John 17:25 is addressed to πάτερ δίκαιε, the God who requites justly. Whether the phrase εἰς τὸ εἶναι αὐτὸν δίκαιον in Rom 3:26 is to be understood as an elaboration of ἔνδειξις or as a declaration of purpose, the passage says that God demonstrates in the expiatory death of Jesus that he is *righteous.* God is called "faithful and *just*" in 1 John 1:9, so that he forgives our sins.

c) In the NT Jesus is designated as δίκαιος, esp. with reference to his Passion. This terminology is used not only in later (redactional) statements like Matt 27:19 (27:24 v.l.); Luke 23:47, which identify Jesus in a moralistic sense as the *innocent* one who was condemned; it is used also in the earlier christological fixed formulations of Acts 3:14 ("the Holy and *Righteous One*"); 7:52 ("the coming of *the Righteous One*" was predicted); 22:14 (Paul is "to see *the Just One*").

A Jewish tradition described the expected Messiah as the "righteous one," in both apocalyptic (*1 Enoch* 38:2; 53:6) and rabbinic literature (see Billerbeck II, 289f.; Dechent; Mach; cf. *Pss. Sol.* 17:32). One may also compare the extensive tradition of the "righteous sufferer," which is present in an apocalyptically shaped form in Wis 2:12-20; 5:1-7 (Ruppert, *Der leidende Gerechte* 70-105; *Jesus* 23f.). It was in dependence on these traditions that early Christianity formed the christological title ὁ δίκαιος.

Luke takes up the (Jewish or) early Christian term "the righteous one" and with it designates Jesus as the Messiah (Ruppert, *Jesus* 47f.). 1 John 2:29 and 3:7 derive the demand for doing "righteousness" from the relationship to Jesus the *righteous one.* In 1 John 2:1 the *righteous* Jesus is described as παράκλητος. 1 Pet 3:18 uses the idea of substitution in saying that Jesus died as δίκαιος ὑπὲρ ἀδίκων. 2 Tim 4:18 stands in the tradition of the sayings about the divine judge (→ b); the *kyrios* (Jesus, cf. v. 1) is the "*righteous* judge."

G. Schneider

δικαιοσύνη, ης, ἡ *dikaiosynē* righteousness, justice*

1. Occurrences in the NT — 2. Basic meaning — 3. In Paul — 4. Δικαιοσύνη θεοῦ in Paul — 5. In Matthew — 6. Elsewhere in the NT

Lit.: K. BERGER, "Neues Material zur 'Gerechtigkeit Gottes,' " *ZNW* 68 (1977) 266-75. — M. BRAUCH, "Perspectives on 'God's Righteousness' in Recent German Discussion," in E. P. Sanders, *Paul and Palestinian Judaism* (1977) 523-42. — R. BULTMANN, "ΔΙΚΑΙΟΣΥΝΗ ΘΕΟΥ," *JBL* 83 (1964) 12-16. — A. DESCAMPS, *Les Justes et la Justice dans les évangiles et le christianisme primitif hormis la doctrine proprement paulinienne* (1950). — A. DIHLE, *RAC* X, 233-360. — M. J. FIEDLER, "Δικαιοσύνη in der diaspora-jüdischen und intertestamentarischen Literatur," *JSJ* 1 (1970) 120-43. — E. GRÄSSER, "Rechtfertigung im Hebräerbrief," FS Käsemann, 79-93. — W. GRUNDMANN, "Der Lehrer der Gerechtigkeit von Qumran und die Frage nach der Glaubensgerechtigkeit in der Theologie des Apostels Paulus," *RevQ* 2 (1960) 237-59. — *idem*, "Zur gegenwärtigen Diskussion um das Verständnis der 'Gerechtigkeit Gottes' im neutestamentliche Verständnis," *ThJb(L)* 13 (1970) 99-117. — E. GÜTTGEMANNS, " 'Gottesgerechtigkeit' und structurale Semantic," *Studia linguistica neotestamentica* (BEvT 60, 1971) 59-98. — G. HEROLD, *Zorn und Gerechtigkeit Gottes bei Paulus* (EHS 23, 14, 1973). — H. HÜBNER, "Existentiale Interpretation der paulinischen 'Gerechtigkeit Gottes,' " *NTS* 21 (1974/75) 462-88. — E. KÄSEMANN, "The Righteousness of God in Paul," *idem, NT Questions of Today* (1969) 169-82. — *idem*, "Zum Verständnis von Römer 3, 24-26," *idem, Versuche* I, 96-100. — K. KERTELGE, *'Rechtfertigung' bei Paulus* (NTAbh N.F. 3, [2]1971). — G. KLEIN, "Gottes Gerechtigkeit als Thema der neuesten Paulus-Forschung," *VF* 12/2 (1967) 1-11 = *Rekonstruktion und Interpretation* (1969) 225-36. — K. KOCH, "Die drei Gerechtigkeiten. Die Umformung einer hebräischen Idee im aram. Denken nach dem Jesajatargum," FS Käsemann, 245-67. — O. KUSS, *Der Römerbrief* I (1957) 115-21. — B. LINDARS, "Δικαιοσύνη in Jn 16:8 and 10," FS Rigaux, 275-85. — E. LOHSE, "Die Gerechtigkeit Gottes in der paulinischen Theologie," *Einheit des NT* (1973) 209-27. — C. MÜLLER, *Gottes Gerechtigkeit und Gottes Volk* (FRLANT 86, 1964). — M. OSSEGE, "Einige Aspekte zur Gliederung des ntl. Wortschatzes (am Beispeil von dikaiosýne bei Mt)," *LingBibl* 34 (1975) 37-101. — A. PLUTA, *Gottes Bundestreue* (SBS 34, 1964). — E. PLUTTA-MESSERSCHMIDT, *Gerechtigkeit Gottes bei Paulus* (HUT 14, 1973). — SCHELKLE, *Theology* III, 178-92. — H. SCHLIER, *Grundzüge einer paulinischen Theologie* (1978) 48-54. — H. H. SCHMID, *Gerechtigkeit als Weltordnung* (BHT 40, 1968). — G. SCHRENK, *TDNT* II, 192-210. — G. STRECKER, *Der Weg der Gerechtigkeit* ([3]1971). — P. STUHLMACHER, *Gerechtigkeit Gottes bei Paulus* (FRLANT 87, 1965). — *idem*, "Recent Exegesis on Romans 3:24-26," *idem, Reconciliation, Law, and Righteousness* (1986) 94-109. — U. WILCKENS, *Der Brief an die Römer* I (EKKNT, 1978) 202-33. — D. ZELLER, *Juden und Heiden in der Mission des Paulus* (FzB 1, [2]1976) 163-188. — J. A. ZIESLER, *The Meaning of Righteousness in Paul* (SNTSMS 20, 1972). — H. ZIMMERMANN, "Jesus Christus, hingestellt als Sühne—zum Erweis der Gerechtigkeit Gottes (Röm 3,24-26)," FS J. Kardinal Höffner (1971) 71-81. — For further bibliography see Kertelge, Schmid, Wilckens, *DNTT* III, 374-77.

1. The subst. δικαιοσύνη appears in the NT 91 times, of which 57 are in the Pauline literature and 33 in Romans. Δικαιοσύνη belongs to the "preferred words" of the Pauline letters. Thus the word represents one of the most important theological concepts; consequently it is important to examine to what extent the Pauline usage has influenced the occurrence of the word in the later NT literature either directly or indirectly (→ esp. 6). The usage in Matthew (7 occurrences, and 17 occurrences of the adj. δίκαιος) appears alongside Paul and is independent of him. Also having significant usage are the Pastorals (5 occurrences), Hebrews (6), James (3, and 3 occurrences of δικαιοῦν and 2 of δίκαιος), and 1 John (3, and 6 of the adj.).

2. The meaning of δικαιοσύνη corresponds to Greek usage. In the NT *righteousness* takes on its concrete meaning within the variety of usages. The OT and Jewish meaning as "gift of salvation" (Cremer/Kögel 311) competes with the Greek meaning "righteousness, legality, honesty . . . , correct condition, especially equality" (Passow I, 688), righteousness as *iustitia distributiva*, δικαιοσύνη as an ἀρετή. In several passages both strands influence the history of the meaning of the NT δικαιοσύνη.

However, in most passages in the NT the meaning is determined by the OT and Jewish history of the concept. Repeatedly the Greek OT is explicitly referred to, e.g., Gen 15:6 in Rom 4:3-22; Gal 3:6; and Jas 2:23; Ps 111:9 LXX in 2 Cor 9:9; Ps 44:8 LXX in Heb 1:9. In addition the use of OT associations of δικαιοσύνη is exhibited in Acts 17:31 (cf. Pss 9:9; 95:13; 97:9 LXX); 2 Cor 9:9 (cf. Hos 10:12); Eph 6:14 (cf. Isa 59:17; 11:5) and Rev 19:11 (cf. Ps 95:13 LXX). The OT and Jewish background can also be noticed elsewhere, thus esp. in Matt 5:20 (cf. Ps 118:19f.; Isa 26:2); Luke 1:75 and Eph 4:24 (cf. Wis 9:3; Deut 32:4; Ps 144:17 LXX); Rom 1:17 (cf. Ps 98:2; Isa 56:1); Phil 1:11 (cf. Amos 6:12). For the elevation of the basic meaning of δικαιοσύνη in the NT, it follows that the meaning of the word "righteousness" as a concept of relationship, which was shaped in a peculiar way in the OT and Jewish tradition, is to be given precedence over the Greek meaning of "righteousness" as a category within the teaching about virtue.

According to the OT and Jewish understanding, "righteousness" (Heb. *ṣeḏeq*/*ṣᵉḏāqâ*) connotes the "right" conduct of God and of humans, not within a view of an ideal norm of what is right, but rather within the perspective of the concrete life relationships of partners to each other. In this sense righteousness is characteristic of God in his conduct toward his people (cf. Rom 3:5) in conformity with his covenant. On the other hand, he demands the performance of righteousness, which allows humankind to stand before God (Jas 1:20). In the latter sense the concept is characterized more by the dominant Greek use of ethical uprightness than by the OT usage (Acts 10:35; 13:10; 24:25; 1 Tim 6:11; 2 Tim 2:22; 3:16; 4:8; 2 Pet 2:5). Of course for the entire NT usage the fundamental idea is that of "righteousness" in the original sense of God as the Judge and Redeemer of his own (these ideas are in permanent tension) and of righteous conduct of humans, which finds its "norm" in the righteous conduct of God.

Δικαιοσύνη becomes in the phrase δικαιοσύνη θεοῦ esp. in Paul (→ 4) an expression for the unity of the eschatological judging and redeeming acts of God. The righteous conduct of God in 2 Pet 1:1 is perceived differently: "the "*righteousness* of our God and Savior Jesus Christ," which represents the basis for the "equally precious faith" of Jews and Gentiles, is here apparently to be understood as an attribute of God, with which he "distributes the same to all" (K. H. Schelkle, *Die Petrusbriefe* [HTKNT] 185). This meaning, corresponding to the Greek idea of virtue, is to be distinguished from the basic meaning derived from the OT and Jewish history of the concept.

The NT concept of δικαιοσύνη receives a certain elaboration by juxtaposition with opposing and parallel terms. Opposites include (ἀσέβεια and) ἀδικία (Rom 1:17f.; 3:5; 6:13, cf. 4:5; 5:6f.; Rev 22:11), ἁμαρτία (and θάνατος; Rom 6:16, 18, 20), and (ἀκαθαρσία and) ἀνομία (Rom 6:19; 2 Cor 6:14; Heb 1:9 = Ps 44:8 LXX). Parallel to δικαιοσύνη are βασιλεία (τοῦ θεοῦ; Matt 6:33), ὁσιότης (Luke 1:75; Eph 4:24), ἐγκράτεια (Acts 24:25), εἰρήνη and χαρά (Rom 14:17), σοφία and ἁγιασμός (1 Cor 1:30), ἀγαθωσύνη and ἀλήθεια (Eph 5:9), and εὐσέβεια, πίστις, ἀγάπη, ὑπομονή, and πραϋπάθεια (1 Tim 6:11; cf. 2 Tim 2:22). A survey of the usage confirms the assumption of a twofold dimension in the NT usage of δικαιοσύνη: as a major theological-soteriological concept and as an expression of ethically correct human conduct.

3. For Paul δικαιοσύνη stands in close relationship to the central salvific event, which has its historical place in the death and resurrection of Jesus. In agreement with OT and Jewish tradition, Paul sees in the *righteousness* not only an ethical attribute of God and/or of mankind; in-

stead, with reference to humans, it is an essential characteristic of that which allows Paul to be what he should be in relation to God and mankind. Paul is now able to affirm such "rightness"—because of the knowledge granted to him (Gal 2:16)—of the one who "lives by faith in the Son of God, who loved me and gave himself for me" (2:20). The righteousness, which determines and interweaves the life of the Christian, is neither expected from nor produced by the law and the fulfillment of its demands, as in the Judaism described by Paul; rather it is a *gift* from the loving sacrifice of Jesus in his death (Gal 2:21).

It thus becomes clear that the concept of righteousness belongs more to the subject of *soteriology* for Paul than to the subject of ethics. As a major soteriological term for the gift of salvation made available in Christ, it stands in a definite correlation with the concept of faith on the one side and with that of the law on the other side. Paul contrasts the righteousness which makes demands through the law and is based on the fulfillment of the law, i.e., the δικαιοσύνη ἐν νόμῳ (Phil 3:6) or ἐκ νόμου (3:9; Rom 10:5) or the ἰδία δικαιοσύνη (Rom 10:3; cf. Phil 3:9), with the righteousness of faith, the δικαιοσύνη ἐκ πίστεως (Rom 10:6) or the synonymous "righteousness from God," τὴν ἐκ θεοῦ δικαιοσύνην (Phil 3:9). "*Righteousness* by faith" means that God creates righteousness, not in the old way of the law, but from the new possibility of faith. In view of the event which has been fulfilled in the present, faith is defined as belief in Jesus Christ. The law cannot represent the life-giving power of God (cf. Gal 3:21). To the contrary: through the victorious power of faith, which is determined by Christ, the law has come to an end. Consequently the end of the law has come with the salvific work of Christ. The righteousness mediated by faith appears as the *universal* reality of salvation for Jews and Gentiles: Rom 10:4.

Paul endeavors to demonstrate, especially to the Jews, that the correlation of faith and righteousness is in accordance with Scripture and thus to guarantee the character of δικαιοσύνη as grace. According to Gen 15:6, the faith of Abraham "our forefather according to the flesh" (Rom 4:1) is "reckoned as *righteousness*" (Gal 3:6; Rom 4:3, 5, 6, 9, 22). One is to draw from this: Abraham attained righteousness from faith, not from works of the law. Thus Abraham becomes an extraordinary example of the righteousness of faith, and his faith becomes a type of the Christian way of salvation.

It corresponds to Paul's proclamation of salvation when the concept δικαιοσύνη is used to show the *eschatological* dimension of salvation. Already the establishment of the δικαιοσύνη granted to mankind in the act of God and its mediation by faith indicates the basic eschatological determination of Paul's concept of righteousness. Beyond that he emphasizes in Gal 5:5 the abiding eschatological character of δικαιοσύνη: the faithful await the gift of δικαιοσύνη through the (Holy) Spirit. In this perspective of faithful expectation it is and remains, indeed as already mediated in faith, *an object of hope*.

The righteousness granted to the believer requires of him a total *service of righteousness*: Rom 6:12-23. The gift of δικαιοσύνη (5:17) provides the basis for a change of masters for the believer, transferring one into a new relationship of obedience toward God (6:13, 22) or toward the gift provided by God (6:18). In a metaphorical comparison Paul characterizes the service of righteousness by the justified one as a total engagement in a battle. As such, those who have died to sin and now live for God are to commit their members as "weapons [RSV "instruments"] *of righteousness*" (6:13; cf. 2 Cor 6:7). Δικαιοσύνης here is probably not only a descriptive gen.; it designates esp. the purpose and the direction of the engagement of the weapons in battle: in the service of and for the benefit of the power of righteousness, and for the victory of its power over sin. It is to be noted that the righteousness that is granted with the ethical demand addressed to believers in Romans 6 is not simply conveyed along with a humanly achieved righteousness. The eschatological-soteriological meaning of δικαιοσύνη continues to exist even where δικαιοσύνη is bound with the ethical imperative. However, there is still the expectation that Christians bring "fruit," which consists in *righteousness* (Phil 1:11; καρπὸν δικαιοσύνης; cf. Rom 14:17; Eph 5:9), indeed a fruit made possible "through Jesus Christ."

Among the various phrases with δικαιοσύνη which occur in Paul, δικαιοσύνη θεοῦ has a special theological place. Also one may mention δικαιοσύνη τῆς πίστεως (Rom 4:11, 13)—the "*righteousness* determined by faith" and thus not entirely synonymous with δικαιοσύνη ἐκ or διὰ πίστεως (9:30; 10:6)—and phrases with δικαιοσύνη in the gen. Besides καρπὸς δικαιοσύνης (see above), δωρεὰ δικαιοσύνης (Rom 5:17) is to be explained as epexegetical gen. Objective gen. appears in the following phrases: νόμος δικαιοσύνης (Rom 9:31: the law which demands and promises righteousness), ἐλπὶς δικαιοσύνης (Gal 5:5; see above), διακονία δικαιοσύνης (2 Cor 3:9: the service which is considered righteousness) and the corresponding διάκονος δικαιοσύνης (2 Cor 11:15). In 2 Cor 9:10 a subjective gen. may be present: γενήματα τῆς δικαιοσύνης; "with characteristic restriction of meaning" (BAGD ad loc. 2a) of the word, δικαιοσύνη is, in accordance with Ps 111:9 LXX, to be understood in this verse as "mercy," "charitableness." Γενήματα τῆς δικαιοσύνης are thus the "fruits" which charitableness yields to the Corinthians.

4. For Paul the word δικαιοσύνη in the phrase δικαιοσύνη θεοῦ becomes a comprehensive expression for his proclamation, a kerygmatic "brief formula." In the gospel, which he proclaims on the basis of his calling by God, *God's righteousness* is revealed (Rom 1:17; 3:21f.).

This concept was already well known in Jewish Christianity before Paul as an expression of the salvation event, as is suggested by tradition-critical analysis of 2 Cor 5:21 and Rom 3:25f. Fundamental to the understanding of the concept is OT and Jewish usage. It was mediated and stimulated by early Christian preaching and then taken up by Paul, who gave to the phrase δικαιοσύνη θεοῦ his own distinctive emphasis and shape.

In OT writings the "righteousness of Yahweh" is Yahweh's conduct with respect to the covenant. In the "covenant" Israel experiences the righteousness of Yahweh as a condition of its existence, as Yahweh's initiative in giving himself to his people, whom he continually confirms through his "demonstration of his righteousness" (in the pl.: Yahweh's *ṣidqôt*, Judg 5:11; 1 Sam 12:7; Ps 103:6; Mic 6:5; Dan 9:16; cf. Isa 45:24, etc.). The Psalms extol the righteousness of Yahweh (Pss 22:32; 50:6; 71:24); it is demonstrated in concrete assistance with the necessities of life (40:11; 51:16; 112:9), as vindication for those who are deprived of legal rights, for the oppressed and the poor (35:24: "Vindicate me according to thy righteousness"; 5:9; 7:9; 9:5). Here the unity of the judging and redeeming activity of God is indicated. In the judgment God vindicates his own and brings salvation; this act includes the punishing righteousness of God (7:9, 12), but as an aspect of his vindicating righteousness. In deutero-Isaiah the righteousness of Yahweh becomes a comprehensive expression for the anticipated coming of salvation (Isa 45:8; 46:13; 51:5, 6, 8).

A survey of the relatively numerous appearances of the word in the OT reveals that the expression "righteousness of God" has a considerable breadth of meaning: his covenant faithfulness, his vindicating deeds, the order of life given in the covenant, the dwelling-place granted by God, his saving intervention. The self-revelation of Yahweh in his "righteousness" requires the righteousness of Israel before Yahweh, right conduct in conformity with God, which excludes all "ungodliness" (Pss 1, 15, 24, 112).

Judaism after the OT partially preserves the OT usage in literal agreement; i.e, in Qumran, where "righteousness [sg. and pl.] of God" designates God's power of salvation, which he proclaims to his "elect" in the "demonstration of salvation" through the eradication of sins and the establishment of his "covenant" (1QS 1:21; 10:23, 25; 11:3, 5, 12, 14; 1QH 7:19, etc.). In apocalyptically oriented circles the righteousness of God becomes an expression of his eschatological judgment with the double effect of redemption and justification of the faithful and condemnation of and vengeance on the "unrighteous." Paul is dependent on the eschatological-soteriological interpretation of Judaism. However, he does not employ the Jewish understanding without restricting the Jewish understanding of the righteousness of God with the catchword "one's own righteousness" (Rom 10:3), which he makes the point of attack in his own interpretation. (On the development and different levels within the Jewish understanding of the concept, cf. Stuhlmacher, *Gerechtigkeit Gottes* 145-84; Kertelge 24-45; Wilckens 212-22).

The earliest Jewish Christian proclamation before Paul, which appears in 2 Cor 5:21 and Rom 3:25-26a, exhibits an orientation to the covenant idea, in agreement with the OT and Jewish tradition. God imparts to mankind the righteousness which forgives sins and renews the covenant. This gift of salvation from God, i.e., the "demonstration of his righteousness," has been made possible by the vicarious atoning death of Christ. This view of the righteousness of God, which is both theological-christological and soteriological, was the impulse for a decisively more thoroughgoing interpretation by Paul.

In agreement with OT usage, Paul underlines the initiating act of God with the term δικαιοσύνη θεοῦ in Romans. The question about God is given precedence over the question of human salvation; the theological-christological presupposition and basis is given precedence over the anthropological-soteriological aspect of the event of righteousness. The use of δικαιοσύνη θεοῦ presupposes the question, Who is God? The God that Paul proclaims is the God who has revealed himself in abiding faithfulness to himself and to his people in Jesus Christ. His righteousness has become manifest "through faith in Jesus Christ" (Rom 3:21f.). Δικαιοσύνη θεοῦ is thus to be interpreted as subjective gen. and not as objective gen. or as gen. of origin (so Bultmann, et al.) with an appeal to Phil 3:9. "*Righteousness* of God" does not mean the righteousness which the individual receives from God and which is thus valid before God; rather, it is the claim of God upon the individual, which God demonstrates in his act upon the individual when he exercises justice.

Rom 3:21-26, which is esp. representative for the Pauline message of justification, indicates the close relationship between theological assessment and soteriological intention. Δικαιοσύνη θεοῦ thus designates the salvific act of God as his saving intervention to create something new in the context of the disaster of human history which stands under the power of sin. The righteousness of God takes on historical-eschatological character in the person and history of Jesus. It is thus brought into relationship with faith in Jesus Christ, indeed to such an extent that its revealing is made available (only) through faith in Christ and is itself grasped and "appropriated" through this faith. The righteousness of God is fully realized as a salvific power only by faith in Jesus Christ; thus it takes on universal validity in the unity of Jews and Gentiles under the grace of God which destroys unrighteousness. This righteousness, which effects salvation from faith, is refused by Israel, which fails to recognize the identity of the righteousness of God for Jews and Gentiles as his faithfulness to himself and his people, which has become manifest in Jesus Christ (Rom 10:3).

The idea of the righteousness of God is not to be interpreted in an isolated way in Paul, but rather from the context of the entire Pauline proclamation. Thus it is clear that the individual has no other salvation than that which God imparts in his just judgment. Likewise Paul sees God's deed of righteousness as insolubly bound with the cross of Jesus.

5. Outside the Pauline Epistles, the concept of δικαιοσύνη is a major theological motif in Matthew. In all

the Matthean occurrences δικαιοσύνη is redactionally placed by Matthew (Strecker 153). Thus the Evangelist interprets the way of Jesus as the "way of righteousness" (21:32), which was already proclaimed by John the Baptist, who prepared the way of the Lord (3:3; 11:10), and represented in his demand for repentance. The "way of righteousness" becomes an expression for the righteous demand of God toward mankind.

From the outset, already from the time of his baptism, Jesus' mission is directed toward the "righteousness," which is to be "fulfilled" (3:15). The "righteousness" becomes the program of Jesus. It is the content of the will of God. God wants righteousness as the salvation of mankind. This begins to be realized in the word and activity of Jesus. The righteousness is thus, on the one hand, an expression of the salvation of God, for which people "hunger and thirst" (5:6). On the other hand, it remains—in good OT and Jewish perspective—God's demand to mankind, a condition for their realization of salvation (5:20). This double-sidedness characterizes Matthew's use of the concept of δικαιοσύνη in contrast to Paul's use. At the basis is, as in Paul, the OT understanding, the expectation that God will vindicate the oppressed (cf. Ps 146:7; Isa 61:11). The "poor" (Matt 5:3), who "hunger and thirst for righteousness" (5:6), may be sure that the justice due to them will not be forgotten in the midst of the injustice which they are suffering. At the appearance of Jesus God has already begun to vindicate them. Consequently they now grasp what God has made possible and, as far as they are concerned, they seek to bring it to realization in the fulfillment of the will of God. The demand of Jesus in 6:33, "seek first his [God's] kingdom and his *righteousness*," places the imperative within the larger context of his proclamation of salvation. The eschatological *basileia* of God comes to mankind as a gift, indeed in the form of *righteousness*. The demand for a "better *righteousness*" (5:20) is thus no excessive demand on the disciples, but is rather a direction determined by the concrete exposition of the will of God in the illustrative material of the antitheses in 5:21-48 and by the "abiding" presence of Jesus as teacher of his Church (28:18-20). Indeed, in the use of the δικαιοσύνη concept in the Sermon on the Mount there is an indication of the tension between the indicative of the divine promise of salvation and the imperative of the ethical demand for the disciples of Jesus.

According to Matthew, what matters is the *doing* of righteousness (6:1). This is concretely realized in proper conduct of the disciples of Jesus, which consists of a relationship of brotherhood to each other and in the acceptance of the "brother" (perhaps according to 5:22-24; 18:15, 21-35) in his creaturely determination by God. One must endure persecutions (5:10) for the sake of this righteous conduct.

Exegetically noteworthy are the very different approaches by Matthew and Paul in the use of the δικαιοσύνη concept. As a missionary proclaimer of the gospel, Paul proceeds from the persistent human need for redemption and proclaims God's judgment over all unrighteousness and self-righteousness of mankind caused by the keeping of the law. He announces that it is a just judgment on the sinner. In Matthew, the unity of the demanding and redeeming will of God remains within the law, although the conduct of humans in the form of pharisaic self-righteousness fails to fulfill the law (ὑπόκρισις: Matt 23:28; cf. 6:2, 5, 16; 7:5). In the proclamation and activity of Jesus the true "way of righteousness" is opened, permitting the "righteous" to attain "eternal life" (25:46).

6. Alongside the use of δικαιοσύνη which is particularly shaped by theological considerations in the Pauline Epistles and in Matthew, fully one-third of the relevant passages are to be found elsewhere in the NT. Here the precise connotation of δικαιοσύνη is not easy to determine; thus one has to decide from instance to instance whether OT and Jewish usage, perhaps mediated by Paul, or the Greek linguistic background, with a primarily ethical meaning, is determinative.

It is evident that the Pauline contrast of righteousness based on works and righteousness based on faith has influenced Titus 3:5, probably in a conscious reception of the theological heritage of the apostle. However, on the basis of this isolated passage, one should not overlook the ethically oriented usage in other passages of the Pastorals (see below). 1 Pet 2:24 is reminiscent of the parenetic sequence "that we might die to sin and live *to righteousness*" in similar phrases in Romans 6. To be sure, the strictly soteriological antithesis of "sin" and "righteousness" from Romans 6 has been modified into ethical terms; "live to righteousness" has the meaning of "proper conduct of life." The same understanding is to be noted in the phrase in 3:14, "suffer for *righteousness'* sake" (identical with Matt 5:10). The influence of Pauline usage may be observed also in Heb 11:7. The righteousness that was Noah's lot is determined by faith (τῆς κατὰ πίστιν δικαιοσύνης κληρονόμος). Despite these contacts, Hebrews does not stand directly in the tradition of Paul. It combines an ethical meaning from the Greek and Hellenistic history of the word with a "righteousness" based on God's judgment of the "righteous" (11:4) and belonging to Noah as something promised because of his faith. The former is esp. evident in 11:33, when the deeds of righteousness are praised as characteristic of the extraordinary faith of the OT judges and prophets. The "peaceful fruit of *righteousness*" (12:11; cf. Jas 3:18), which is derived from ethical exertion, likewise indicates the basic ethical focus here of δικαιοσύνη.

The secondary effect of the Pauline use of δικαιοσύνη

in James may best be discussed in connection with the use of the vb. → δικαιόω. One may not overlook the fact that the citation of Gen 15:6 in Jas 2:23 is concerned with the affirmation of a righteousness *before* God (in contrast to the interpretation in Romans 4 and Galatians 3)—so also in the meaning of δικαιοσύνη θεοῦ in Jas 1:20. This righteousness is not based merely on "faith," but on a faith that is demonstrated in moral conduct.

The *ethical* meaning of δικαιοσύνη, in contrast to the "righteousness which is bestowed," which is proclaimed in Paul, is in a number of passages associated with the phrase "do righteousness," etc. (ἐργάζεσθαι, διώκειν, ποιεῖν δικαιοσύνην). According to Acts 10:35, "fear God" and "*do righteousness*" are phrases which can also be used of Gentiles. For the Gentiles, such "natural" virtues do not become the basis of salvation, but indicate instead a certain "disposition" for God's acts. The content of righteousness in Acts 13:10 is defined as "appropriate piety," which consists in the acceptance of faith (cf. 13:8). In 24:25 the concept contains more the general meaning of "proper conduct" along with the explicitly mentioned virtue of "self-control."

In 1 Tim 6:11 striving for righteousness is mentioned as the behavior appropriate for the "man of God," Timothy, together with other basic aspects of conduct such as "godliness," "faith," "love," "steadfastness," and "gentleness" which are enumerated in dependence on the catalog of virtues from Hellenistic ethics (cf. also 2 Tim 2:22). In 2 Tim 3:16 "correction" and "training in *righteousness*" are expected as a result of the correct use of the Scriptures which have been inspired by God. The "crown of *righteousness*" (2 Tim 4:8) beckons the apostle as a reward for his efforts.

"Doing *righteousness*" becomes the criterion of true Christianity and of being "born of God" in 1 John 2:29; 3:7, 10. In a combination of the christological-soteriological basis and the ethical demand, the doing of righteousness remains bound to the criterion of the "righteous one," Christ, who appeared in human form and who will come at the final parousia. In opposition to the Gnostic false teachers, the confirmation of faith in Christ in deeds (of love) becomes the distinctive characteristic of righteousness. Against the background of these texts from 1 John and in view of their significance, the singular usage in John 16:8, 10 becomes understandable. The *righteousness* that the Paraclete will demonstrate to the world—in condemning it—refers to Jesus as the Christ. It consists in the "justification" granted to him in exaltation and glorification by God, by which he appears as the criterion of conduct in relation to the world.

The use of the concept of *righteousness* in connection with the demand for authenticating deeds in numerous passages is an indication of a relatively broad early Christian tradition, in which δικαιοσύνη, in contrast to its theological usage in Paul, becomes a major parenetic motif. This is true also for the final passage in the NT, Rev 22:11, where the doing of *righteousness* is understood as the practical and consistent demonstration of the already determined election of the "righteous" and the "unrighteous."

K. Kertelge

δικαιόω *dikaioō* justify, pronounce righteous*

1. Occurrences in the NT — 2. Basic meaning — 3. Δικαιόω in Paul — 4. The "doctrine of justification" in Paul — 5. Δικαιόω elsewhere in the NT

Lit.: → δικαιοσύνη. Also: O. Betz, "Rechtfertigung in Qumran," FS Käsemann, 17-36. — J. Blank, "Warum sagt Paulus: 'Aus Werken des Gesetzes wird niemand gerecht'?" EKKNT (V) I, 79-95. — J. P. Clifton, *The Pauline Notion of Justification in the Light of Recent Literature* (Diss. Rome, 1971). — H. Conzelmann, "Paul's Doctrine of Justification: Theology or Anthropology?" *Theology of the Liberating Word* (ed. F. Herzog; 1971) 108-23. — K. P. Donfried, "Justification and Last Judgment in Paul," *ZNW* 67 (1976) 90-110. — R. Gyllenberg, *Rechtfertigung und AT bei Paulus* (FDV 1966, 1973). — F. Hahn, "Taufe und Rechtfertigung: Ein Beitrag zur paulinischen Theologie in ihrer Vor- und Nachgeschichte," FS Käsemann, 95-124. — E. Käsemann, "Justification and Salvation History in the Epistle to the Romans," *idem, Perspectives on Paul* (1971) 60-78. — L. E. Keck, "Justification of the Ungodly and Ethics," FS Käsemann, 199-209. — K. Kertelge, "Zur Deutung des Rechtfertigungsbegriffs im Galaterbrief," *BZ* N.F. 12 (1968) 211-22. — E. Lohse, "Taufe und Rechtfertigung bei Paulus," *idem, Einheit des NT* (1973) 228-44. — D. Lührmann, "Christologie und Rechtfertigung," FS Käsemann, 351-63. — *idem,* "Rechtfertigung und Versöhnung: Zur Geschichte der paulinischen Tradition," *ZTK* 67 (1970) 437-52. — U. Luz, "Rechtfertigung bei den Paulusschülern," FS Käsemann, 365-83. — F. Mussner, *Der Jakobusbrief* (HTKNT, 1964) 146-50. — B. Reicke, "Paul's Understanding of Righteousness," *Soli Deo Gloria* (FS W. C. Robinson, ed. J. M. Richards; 1966) 432-52. — J. Reumann, "The Gospel of the Righteousness of God: Pauline Reinterpretation in Rom. 3:21-31," *Int* 20 (1966) 432-52. — *idem,* et al., *"Righteousness" in the NT* (1982). — H. Graf Reventlow, *Rechtfertigung im Horizont des AT* (BEvT 58, 1971). — H. H. Schmid, "Rechtfertigung als Schöpfungsgeschehen. Notizen zur atl. Vorgeschichte eines ntl. Themas," FS Käsemann, 403-14. — G. Schrenk, *TDNT* II, 211-19. — G. Strecker, "Befreiung und Rechtfertigung: Zur Stellung der Rechtfertigungslehre in der Theologie des Paulus," FS Käsemann, 479-508. — W. Thüsing, "Rechtfertigungsgedanke und Christologie in den Korintherbriefen," FS Schnackenburg, 301-24. — U. Wilckens, "Christologie und Anthropologie im Zusammenhang der paulinischen Rechtfertigungslehre," *ZNW* 67 (1976) 64-82. — *idem,* "Die Rechtfertigung Abrahams nach Röm 4," *idem, Rechtfertigung als Freiheit* (1974) 33-49. — *idem,* "Was heißt bei Paulus, 'Aus Werken des Gesetzes wird niemand gerecht'?" EKKNT (V) I, 51-77. — W. Wolter, *Rechtfertigung und zukünftiges Heil: Untersuchungen zu Röm 5, 1-11* (BZNW 43, 1978).

1. The vb. δικαιόω appears 39 times in the NT, of which 25 are in Paul (not including the Pastorals), predominantly in the pass. Also noteworthy is the appearance of δικαιόω

in Luke-Acts (7 occurrences), James (with δικαιοσύνη, 3 occurrences), and in Matthew 11:19 par. Luke 7:35 (Q).

2. Δικαιόω is a denominative vb. from δίκαιος and means *consider just or reasonable* as well as *judge, punish* (Passow I, 688). This basic meaning in Greek usage appears in the NT only in a modified form, with the meaning of *justify, represent as just, treat as just* and esp. in Paul in the pass. with the meaning *receive acquittal* and in the act. *pronounce righteous* or *acquit* (BAGD ad loc.). Paul's usage is characteristic for the NT: he uses δικαιόω and the nouns → δικαιοσύνη and δικαίωσις with a soteriological meaning and thus places them in direct antithesis to the Greek meaning of "judge, punish." Together with the related nouns, δικαιόω is basic to Paul's proclamation of salvation, that is, to his "doctrine of justification."

The more general meaning of *justify, vindicate* is present in the following passages: Matt 11:19 par. Luke 7:35; Matt 12:37; Luke 7:29; 10:29; 16:15; 18:14 (with a soteriological element); Rom 3:4; 1 Cor 4:4; 1 Tim 3:16. Paul's usage influences Acts 13:38, 39 and Titus 3:7. The influence of Pauline usage, which is to be explained from a historical perspective, is also indicated in Jas 2:21, 24, 25.

Every NT use of δικαιόω has a forensic/juridical stamp: "justification" and "vindication" result from judgment. A juridical setting is explicitly presupposed in Matt 12:37: people must "render account on the day of judgment" (v. 36) for every idle word. "For by your words you *will be justified,* and by your words you will be condemned" (καταδικασθήση)." Equally unambiguous and explicit are Rom 3:4 (referring to Ps 50:6 LXX) and Rom 3:20. Gal 2:16, alluding to Ps 142:2 LXX, refers to God's judging and vindicating activity. The usage in the Greek OT fundamentally determines the meaning of δικαιόω in Paul and in other NT writings.

Δικαιόω is used in the LXX to represent Heb. *hiṣdîq* (hiphil of *ṣdq*) and has the meanings "acquit" in Exod 23:7; Deut 25:1; 2 Kgdms 15:4; 3 Kgdms 8:32; Isa 5:23 and "do justice (for someone)" in Ps 81:3; Isa 50:8; 53:11. Less often it renders the piel *ṣideq* with the meaning "prove someone righteous" (Jer 3:11; Ezek 16:51f.; Job 33:32). In the LXX δικαιόω appears almost always with a personal obj. The one who actually is "righteous" attains the declaration of righteousness (Deut 25:1; 3 Kgdms 8:32), which has confirmatory significance and provides public recognition. Pass. δικαιοῦσθαι appears in the LXX normally as the translation of the qal form of *ṣdq* with the meaning "be righteous," "stand as righteous," and is used with this meaning with both God (Pss 18:10; 50:6; Isa 42:21) and humans (Gen 38:26; Isa 43:9, 26; 45:25; Ps 142:2) as subj. In addition, δικαιόω is used in the act. and pass. in the LXX as the equivalent of *rîḇ*, "to secure justice for someone before the judgment," in Mic 7:9; Isa 1:17; as the equivalent of *šāpaṭ*, "judge," in 1 Kgdms 12:7; Ezek 44:24; of *zākâ*, "be pure," in Mic 6:11; Ps 73:13; and of *bāḥan*, "examine," in Ezek 21:18.

Thus in the LXX the forensic meaning of the word is predominant. The judicial "exercise of justice" reveals the uprightness of a person. It is evident that the LXX has sharpened the forensic character of statements in contrast to the Hebrew in (LXX) Pss 50:6; 142:2; Isa 42:21; Job 33:32. The focus of the translator is thus often clearly directed toward the final judgment of God, as the use of the fut. indicates in Isa 45:25; Ps 142:2 LXX; Sir 10:29; 23:11; 34:5.

Early Jewish understanding of "justification" is determined by these assumptions. The righteous one waits for the final judgment when he will be vindicated by God. In Rom 2:13 Paul takes up this Jewish expectation and contrasts mere hearing with the fulfillment of the law. Often this expectation is associated with the doubt of one's own righteousness; thus the expected vindication in the final judgment of God is thought to be connected with his goodness and mercy, as in 1QH 13:17, "only through your goodness does one become righteous"; cf. 7:28; 16:11.

3. a) In addition to his characteristic use of δικαιόω in Galatians (8 occurrences) and Romans (15), Paul uses the vb. twice in 1 Corinthians. The first of these is in 1 Cor 6:11, in an interpretation of baptism as "justification," understood here as cleansing, derived from pre-Pauline tradition; cf. also Rom 6:7, "He who has died *is freed* from sin" (δεδικαίωται ἀπὸ τῆς ἁμαρτίας). The latter statement, which Paul formulates in dependence on a similar one in Judaism, refers to "dying" in baptism.

1 Cor 4:4 has a more general meaning of δικαιόω: as a " servant of Christ" he is "not aware of anything," but still he is not "yet justified" (RSV 'acquitted'). He awaits his "justification," i.e., the evaluation of his work and thus his confirmation before the Lord's judgment (cf. 3:12-15). Both the forensic character and the strict eschatological dimension of δικαιόω in the LXX find an echo in Pauline usage.

Characteristic of Paul is nevertheless the soteriological meaning of δικαιόω, which is certainly not entirely absent in 1 Cor 4:4. It is prominent where δικαιόω stands in relation to "law" and, on the other hand, to "faith."

b) In a thematic statement in Gal 2:16a Paul excludes the justification of humans "by works of the law" in favor of justification "through faith in Jesus Christ." In this antithesis of two "ways" of righteousness, the exclusion of the former appears as a "higher" principle that is the basis of Paul's interpretation. V. 16b brings the way of faith to bear on Paul and the Jewish Christians in a repeated, axiomatic statement, in dependence on the preceding thesis. This is done in such a manner that justification by faith appears as the positive intention of the "principle." Paul has come to faith, and as a believer he awaits justification by faith in Christ or, synonymously, justification "in Christ" (v. 17).

The thesis in Gal 2:16a receives its basis and its force with the "citation" from Ps 142:2 LXX: "because by works of the law *shall* no one *be justified.*" Even if this reference to the OT passage cannot properly be viewed as a citation, the intention of Paul's use of Scripture remains clear. With the supplementary and "clarifying" interpretation of Scripture he derives the reference to the "decree" *of God,* to which Gal 2:16a has referred. The supplementary phrase, "by works of the law," gives the statement from Scripture about mankind's inability to stand before God an indirect focus on Jesus Christ, in whom God's initiative comes into view in his justifying act. Thus the Pauline understanding of δικαιόω has already been described.

One proceeds from a Jewish "pre-understanding" of justification which is bound to the law. This understanding appears above all as an indisputable "truth," grounded in the tradition. Paul is able to conform to it in Rom 2:13 insofar as it seems suitable for placing the intention of God in the correct light: "For it is not the hearers of the law who are righteous before God, but the doers of the law who *will be justified.*" Paul turns this statement critically against any self-righteousness of mankind and esp. has in mind the advantage of the Jew who has the law.

Indeed, the justification of people before God does not take place by way of the law; it takes place only when the individual humbles himself before the ways of God and recognizes what Paul recognized in his encounter with Jesus Christ. God came to mankind when he offered the way of forgiving love in his Son. Humans respond with faith in Jesus Christ, i.e., with faith in the act of God in his Son. In Jesus Christ the law comes to its "end" (Rom 10:4), and demonstrates that it is vain to seek justification "[still] by the law" (Gal 5:4).

God's "establishment" of a new way of righteousness of mankind has its basis in the fulfillment which Jesus Christ realized when he "loved me and gave himself for me" (Gal 2:20). Paul knows that in his proclamation he is appointed to be the advocate for this way.

The argument from Scripture in Gal 2:16c is expanded and deepened in Galatians 3 (from verse 6 on) by the scriptural testimony about Abraham. Thus the appeal to Gen 15:6 (cf. Rom 4:3) serves not only as a confirmation of the "new" way, so that Abraham appears as one who was justified by the same faith. Rather, Paul derives from the justification of Abraham a universal perspective in which Jews and Gentiles are united in one justifying act of God. Paul thus argues from Scripture for a Gentile mission free from the law, using a combination of Gen 15:6 with the promised blessing in Gen 12:3 and 18:18 to make his case. The Scripture "foresaw that God *would justify* the Gentiles by faith" (Gal 3:8). On the basis of Scripture—Paul cites Hab 2:4 (cf. Rom 1:17) here—it is "evident" that "no one *is justified*" on the basis of the law (Gal 3:11). In relation to the "new" way of salvation of justification by faith, only a subordinate function of a → παιδαγωγός (v. 24) is attributed to the law.

c) What Paul develops in Galatians 2 and 3 responds to the specific need in a particular setting to argue against Judaizing tendencies. This is then given a further theological development in Romans, esp. in chs. 3 and 4.

The forensic character of δικαιόω is esp. clear in Rom 3:4, where one may observe the soteriological interpretation of the term. With Ps 116:11 the setting of a legal dispute between God and mankind is presupposed. God demonstrates his righteousness; and despite the unfaithfulness of his partners in covenant, he remains faithful and keeps his promises. Thus God "triumphs" over mankind; people must acknowledge God. However, God's justice becomes his faithfulness on the basis of his justification of the sinner.

The image of the legal dispute of God with mankind (on the idea of the legal dispute in the OT and Judaism, cf. Müller 57-64) does not allow one to overlook that God is not only a party to the dispute, but is also the judge. This aspect is brought to light in the description of the act of God on people who are ensnared in unrighteousness. In this sense δικαιόω is to be rendered as *acquit.* The "justification" of the person as the result of the acquittal by God consists in the fact that one is not liberated from his own entanglement in unrighteousness. That is: in contrast to the OT, God declares as righteous not the "righteous," but rather the unrighteous, the "ungodly": Rom 4:5. This acquittal takes place "as a gift," "by his grace" (3:24; cf. Gal 2:21). In his forgiving acquittal God demonstrates that he is righteous (Rom 3:26).

As in Galatians, Paul underlines the enduring significance of faith for the justification of the sinner. The sinner receives justification through faith—without works of the law (Rom 3:28). Paul develops this thesis further with attention to its universal implications: in faith it becomes evident that God is the one who justifies. He is not only the God of the Jews, but also of the Gentiles. He demonstrates his identity as the one God in the fact that he declares righteous (Rom 3:30) both the circumcised and the uncircumcised in the same way, "through faith." In this context Paul refers to Abraham, as in Galatians 3. Abraham received righteousness not on the basis of works (Rom 4:2), but on the basis of faith (4:5). Here Abraham becomes the father and "model" of the Jewish and Gentile believer in a way that is different and more explicit than the portrayal in Galatians 3.

In referring back to the basic statements in Romans 3 and 4, Paul interprets justification in Rom 5:1, 9 as a demonstration of the *love* of God. It is the love of God poured out on the hearts of believers (v. 5), and it is finally identical with the once-for-all act of love by Jesus in his death (v. 8). It effects reconciliation and peace with God and thus an everlasting hope. The righteousness which comes through faith is further active in the life of the believer as an expression of the love of God, and finds its goal in the final salvation of the one who has been reconciled (v. 9).

In Rom 8:30, 33 Paul finally comes to the soteriological main theme of Romans when he describes the justifying activity of God in a song of praise to the "God who justifies." Once more the forensic meaning of δικαιόω becomes very clear. The individual sits at the place of the accused. He is and remains the one in need, whose sins God has forgiven by his grace. Because God intervenes on his behalf with his acquittal, his need is taken away by the grace of God; and *by this means* every destructive accusation and condemnation is withdrawn, as long as he does not allow himself to be separated (8:35, 39) from the love of Christ and the love of God.

4. The concept of justification is an essential component of the Pauline proclamation. Paul uses it to explain the salvific action of God toward mankind in its eschatological-soteriological dimension, based on the Christ-event. The concept of justification, thoroughly developed, remains consistent in the proclamation of the gospel to Jews *and* Gentiles determined by the missionary situation, even when Paul includes all statements for further developments within a systematic doctrine. Because Paul was forced to formulate a position on justification because of "judaizing" tendencies (Gal 2:14), i.e., by disputes with Jewish Christians who wanted to make circumcision and the law binding for Gentile Christians, the polemical character of the concept is appropriate ("not by works of the law"). However, it is not correct to explain Paul's "doctrine of justification" as a polemical doctrine (so W. Wrede) conceived only for the purpose of debates with Jews and Jewish Christianity. "Justification by faith" undoubtedly has a fundamental theological meaning as an essential expression of the gospel. Thus it transcends the particular situation, serving in different situations to preserve the core of the proclamation of Jesus in the critical-reflective memory.

Such a situation existed in a particular way in the period of the Reformation. Over against the deplorable oblivion into which the tradition of faith had fallen, Luther brought to light the essential content of the Christian message of salvation with his renewed appeal to the Pauline doctrine of justification. His teaching on the subject of justification was a challenge to the Catholic teaching tradition. The Council of Trent took account of the doctrine in the sixth session (1547), and in the teaching decree on justification it expounded the fundamental significance of faith and the character of justification as grace. Of course, the session offered the critique that the faith principle emphasized by the Reformers could be misunderstood to mean an "empty confidence without devotion." The efforts of Protestant and Catholic exegetes to illuminate the Pauline concept of justification in recent times and the many ecumenical-theological initiatives have contributed to more careful consideration of the universal intentions of the Pauline proclamation also with the determination of the critical function of the doctrine of justification. The result is hopeful understanding between the churches and their teaching traditions.

The Pauline doctrine of justification could gain renewed power for Jewish-Christian dialogue. Perhaps H.-J. Schoeps offers a starting point by speaking of "Paul's Fundamental Misapprehension" (*Paul* [1961] 213-19), along with F. Mussner (*Der Galaterbrief* [HTKNT] 188-204): "Has Paul misunderstood the law?" (p. 204: "The daring thesis, of course scarcely intelligible to a Jew . . . : The apostle Paul brought Judaism theologically to its fulfillment"—a thesis certainly leading to greater differences!). On the exegetical and hermeneutical difficulties of the problem of the "Pauline treatment of the problem of the Jews," cf. esp. G. Klein, "Präliminarien zum Thema 'Paulus und die Juden,' " FS Käsemann, 229-43. With the necessary consideration of the particular questions from the history of religions and hermeneutics, it should at least be possible not only to defend Paul against the charge of apostasy from orthodox Judaism, but esp. to grasp the Pauline antithesis "justification not by the law, but by faith" on its christological-theological basis and thus to liberate the theological edge of this thesis from unnecessary polemic.

5. Matt 11:19 and Luke 7:35 have transmitted the saying about the justification of the wise from Q: "yet wisdom is justified (ἐδικαιώθη) by her deeds" or "by all her children" (Luke). The saying concludes the parable of the children playing and its interpretation in Matt 11:16-19; Luke 7:31-35. The Semitic sound of the saying, esp. in Luke, indicates a Jewish Christian tradition. The predicate ἐδικαιώθη has here the forensic meaning of *it was proved to be right* and is in the present context "simply the counterpart to the disparaging words which vv. 33f. express about John the Baptist and Jesus" (Jülicher II, 34).

In two passages Luke uses δικαιόω as a reflexive vb. (Luke 10:29; 16:15). In 10:29 the phrase "but he, desiring to *justify* himself," characterizes the intention of the teacher of the law in conversation with Jesus. The reference is to the opening question about what it is necessary to "do" in v. 25. However, this reference to the preceding material remains open, so that it appears possible to see in the attempt at self-justification, corresponding to 16:15, the expression of "Pharisaic conduct" (W. Grundmann, *Lukas* [THKNT, ³1966] 223). To be sure, the "self-justification" of the teacher of the law is not to be interpreted on the basis of the Pauline concept of justification. Rather, the renewed question of the teacher of the law appears as an expression of a problem which had not yet been resolved; it was, "corresponding to the issues in rabbinic theology, the question of how far the concept of neighbor extends" (G. Eichholz, *Gleichnisse der Evangelien* [1971] 162). Literarily the question in v. 29 becomes an expression of a more precise and deepening connection between the love command and the following parable. In this sense also the "self-justification" of the teacher of the law is to be explained as more than a literary means of connecting what precedes with what follows. A theologically laden interpretation of the expression is nevertheless not brought to bear.

The "self-justification" of the Pharisee in Luke 16:15, which stands here entirely in contrast to the "lowly one"

(1:48; 14:11; 18:14) chosen by God, becomes a foil to the true "justification" in the parable of the Pharisee and the tax collector (18:9-14). This justification here occurs when God grants mercy to the "poor" sinner who has requested it. For Luke, in contrast to Paul, the connection of justification to sincere repentance, realized by the tax collector, remains decisive.

In another way Acts 13:38f. can be understood as a reminiscence of the Pauline thesis of justification by faith, not by law. The "justification" of course refers directly to the liberation from "sins" (ἀπὸ πάντων . . . ; → 3 on 1 Cor 6:11), whereby the pre-Pauline rather than the Pauline message of justification appears to be taken up. The use of the Pauline tradition in Luke does not occur without a theological generalization of the apostle's thesis as an expression of the Christian gospel of the redemption of mankind.

In contrast to Acts 13:39 (and Titus 3:7; cf., however, M. Dibelius and H. Conzelmann, *Pastoral Epistles* [Hermeneia] 150), Jas 2:14-26 exhibits a certain conflict with the Pauline proclamation of justification. Of course one must ask whether this conflict is intentional, i.e., directed against the Pauline understanding of justification by faith, or is directed against a one-sided use of the Pauline thesis (Mussner, *Jakobusbrief* [HTKNT] 130: against "Pseudopaulinism"). One must also ask whether this conflict is with libertinistic tendencies in the post-Pauline era, in response to which the Jewish tradition of law is emphatically recalled (cf. 2:8-12), in which case the Pauline doctrine of justification is only "indirectly" alluded to (Schrenk 219). The contact with the Pauline theme of justification, like the appeal to Abraham's example of faith in Gen 15:6, can scarcely be coincidental. Nevertheless it cannot be assumed to be an ostensible anti-Pauline initiative by James. Rather, the interpretation of Abraham's faith as a faith demonstrated in "works" corresponds to a general Jewish tradition of interpretation, which obviously was prevalent alongside and after Paul (cf. also the understanding of righteousness in Matthew).

Jas 2:14-26 is directed against an impotent and unfruitful faith that holds to a formulated confession (2:19: "that God is *one*"), but is unable to combine this confession with the corresponding deeds. Such a "faith apart from works is barren" (2:20). Reference is made here with a critical intent to "Abraham our father" (cf. Rom 4:1), who *"was justified"* in this sense "by works," because he was ready to sacrifice his son (2:21). On the basis of this example, the relationship of faith and works is interpreted as working together: "faith" is "completed by works" (2:22); it comes to itself in the *praxis* of faith. Such a "completed" faith was reckoned to Abraham as righteousness, according to Gen 15:6 (2:23). Thus the author of James concludes directly, in a reversal of the Pauline thesis of Rom 3:28; Gal 2:16, that "a man *is justified* by works and not by faith alone" (2:24). As a further example to confirm the point, the story of Rahab the harlot (Josh 2) is introduced in 2:25.

James 2 shares with Judaism and Paul the expectation of the justification as an eschatological event. In contrast to Paul but in striking agreement with Jewish conceptions, the relationship of faith and works is defined not exclusively, but inclusively. The different evaluations of faith and works are to be explained esp. from the different theological starting points. Paul understands "faith in Jesus Christ" as the new eschatological possibility for Jews *and* Gentiles granted by God, through which the limits of the law, based on Jewish particularism, are broken through. On the other hand, the author of James seeks, with pastoral-parenetic intent, to maintain the *practical* aspect of faith. His doctrine of justification has a different theological role than in Paul. It does not trace the old law's claim of salvation, but places those who believe in Christ (Jas 2:1) under the primacy of the love command (2:8), where "works" appear as the "completion" of faith, not as an expression of human self-affirmation toward God. In view of this fact, the intention of 2:14-26 remains totally reconcilable with the Pauline postulate of "faith working through love" (Gal 5:6).

K. Kertelge

δικαίωμα, ατος, τό *dikaiōma* regulation, requirement; righteous deed*

1. Occurrences in the NT — 2. Basic meaning — 3. Discussion of the NT texts

Lit.: E. GRÄSSER, "Rechtfertigung im Hebräerbrief," FS Käsemann, 79-93. — E. KÄSEMANN, *Commentary on Romans* (1980). — G. SCHRENK, *TDNT* II, 219-23. — U. WILCKENS, *Der Brief an die Römer* (EKKNT) I (1978).

1. Δικαίωμα occurs 10 times in the NT, of which 5 are in Paul, 1 in Luke (1:6), 2 in Hebrews (9:1, 10), and 2 in Revelation (15:4; 19:8). A definite concentration of the occurrences is apparent in Romans, particularly in the sg. The relatively few occurrences of the word in the NT are to be contrasted with surprisingly frequent usage in the LXX: two columns in Hatch/Redpath, while a mere one column is taken up by the vb. δικαιόω. Between the NT and the LXX, the frequency of the two words is just the opposite.

2. In common Greek usage, δικαίωμα designates the result of δικαιόω: "what is made right," "right conduct," "right punishment," and "legal ground" (as the result of established law; cf. Passow I, 688). The LXX frequently has δικαίωμα as the equivalent for *ḥōq, ḥuqâ* ("statute," a "legislative determination of lasting significance"; so E. König, *Hebräisches und aramäisches Wörterbuch zum AT* [[7]1937] 122, with reference to Gen 26:5), often also as

the rendering of *mišpāṭ* (possibly Exod 21:1; Num 36:13 with the meaning "legal norm").

Corresponding to LXX usage, δικαίωμα is used in the NT predominantly to mean *legal statute, requirement, commandment* (BAGD ad loc.), thus in Luke 1:6; Rom 1:32; 2:26; 8:4; Heb 9:1, 10. Except for Rom 1:32 (cf. Käsemann 51), it is used in these passages clearly for the requirement(s) of the Mosaic law; in Heb 9:1, 10 δικαίωμα refers more precisely to the ritual law. In Rom 5:18; Rev 15:4 and 19:8 δικαίωμα designates the *righteous deed*; in Rom 5:18, with a special tendency it is used for the "deed which establishes righteousness" (Wilckens 326), which Paul here ascribes to Christ.

Only in Rom 5:16 does δικαίωμα stand in "rhetorical assimilation" (Käsemann 154) to other words in the same verse which have the -μα ending, bearing there the meaning of δικαίωσις, *justification,* whether active (Schrenk 226; Wilckens ad loc.) or passive (Käsemann ad loc.). In Paul, δικαίωμα is, esp. in this passage, to be interpreted from the context of the proclamation of righteousness. This means also that δικαίωμα here largely participates in the forensic usage of → δικαιόω. Thus according to Rom 1:32 the condemnation which is deserved corresponds to the nonfulfillment of the law.

3. In dependence on LXX usage, δικαίωμα in Luke 1:6 retains the legal and ethical obligation which is characteristic of the demand of God or of the divine law. As in Gen 26:5; Num 36:13; Deut 4:40, δικαίωμα in the pl. forms a unified expression with ἐντολαί (commandments), bound together under one art. The parents of John are portrayed as "blameless in all of the commandments and *ordinances* of the Lord." Thus the characterization of them as δίκαιοι is due them, according to which their "negative perfection" of blamelessness (E. Klostermann, *Lukasevangelium* [HNT, [2]1929] 6) is raised positively through their recognition by God.

In a similar way, even with a different theological intent, Paul speaks in Rom 2:26 of the observation of the "*requirements* of the law." In contrast to Eph 2:15, the reference to the great number of demands (δικαίωμα in the pl.) does not imply the conception of the burden of the obligations, but rather Paul argues for *actual* fidelity to the law on the part of Gentiles, over against the Jews' restricted orientation to the law. Only in Rom 2:26 does δικαίωμα appear in Paul in the pl.

Otherwise δικαίωμα occurs in Paul in the sg., with a "fundamental" use by which Paul evidently "goes beyond the LXX" (Schrenk 221), as is indicated in Rom 1:32: the people, here esp. also the Gentiles, know of the divine decree and its vindicative power. With their "natural" knowledge of God's requirement they are just as responsible as are the Jews on the basis of the Mosaic law (cf. 2:14f.).

The reference to the requirement of God or of the law deserves special attention, esp. in view of Paul's thesis that no person is justified by works of the law. The Mosaic law cannot be the basis for God's eschatological announcement of salvation. Nevertheless it maintains its dignity as the "holy law" (Rom 7:12), as the "law of God" (7:22). It is not the law that is unrighteous, but humans, who do not fulfill it and who remain imprisoned in their godless desires. In relation to mankind the law is and remains the expression of God's "requirement," which is fulfilled now only because of the vicarious involvement of Jesus Christ: Rom 8:3f. with 2 Cor 5:21 and Gal 3:13. Only as those who belong to Christ (Rom 7:4) and now "serve in the new life of the Spirit" (7:6; cf. 8:4) do believers fulfill the legal claim of God which comes to expression in the law.

In Rom 5:18 δικαίωμα is ascribed to Christ with the meaning *righteous deed* (as fulfillment of the requirement of God) and contrasted to the "wrong deed" (παράπτωμα) of Adam. Indeed, the deed of Christ, which consists in his "obedience" (5:19) "to death on a cross" (Phil 2:8), results in the sacrificial act of justification, which comes to all mankind only on the basis of the "righteous deed" of the "new Adam."

Heb 9:1 refers to the δικαιώματα τῆς λατρείας, ordinances valid for the "first covenant." And 9:10 speaks of the OT commandments dealing with eating and purification as "*regulations* for the body." Thus the preliminary way of salvation of the "first covenant" (8:8, 13) is described. One may (with O. Michel, *Hebräerbrief* [KEK] 297, n. 2) ask: "Does Hebrews still refer with δικαίωμα to the demand of God?" In reference to this one must rather be cautious in judgment. The use of the word indicates, in contrast to the LXX (and Paul), a refined, more generalized meaning. Heb 9:1, 10 has in view a positive meaning for the "time of the proper regulations" and the reality of the "new covenant" (cf. Grässer 86f.).

Rev 15:4 speaks of the *righteous deeds* of God, by which "both the judicial decision and the righteous deed" are in view; "for God's judgment is his deed" (E. Lohmeyer, *Offenbarung* [HNT, [2]1953] 131f.). On the other hand, "the *righteous deeds*" in 19:8 become the subject of the song of praise. However, v. 8b ("the fine linen is the *righteous deeds* of the saints") is, because of the different meaning of the white garments in 3:5 and 6:11, suspect as a secondary gloss (cf. Lohmeyer, 155).

K. Kertelge

δικαίως *dikaiōs* righteously, justly
→ δίκαιος.

δικαίωσις, εως, ἡ *dikaiōsis* justification*

In the NT only in Rom 4:25; 5:18. G. Schrenk, *TDNT* II, 223f.; → δικαιόω 2, 3.

δικαστής, οῦ, ὁ *dikastēs* judge*

Acts 7:27, 35, in the question to Moses: "Who made you a ruler and a *judge* (over us)?" In Luke 12:14 v.l. δικαστής stands in place of κριτής.

δίκη, ης, ἡ *dikē* punishment, penalty*

2 Thess 1:9: δίκην τίνειν, *undergo punishment* (so also *Herm. Man.* ii.5; *Sim.* ix.19.3); see also Jude 7: δίκην ὑπέχειν. Δίκη κατ' αὐτοῦ, of the required *condemnation, punishment* of Paul in Acts 25:15 Koine E *pm.* In Acts 28:4 δίκη is *justice* personified as a goddess (cf. Sophocles *Ant.* 538, etc.). G. Schrenk, *TDNT* II, 178-82; *TWNT* X, 1048-53 (bibliography).

δίκτυον, ου, τό *diktyon* net*

Used in the NT only of a fish net, pl. in Mark 1:18, 19 par. Matt 4:20, 21; Luke 5:2, 4, 5, 6; sg. in John 21:6, 8, 11 (bis). Dalman, *Arbeit* VI, 346-63, esp. 362f.

δίλογος, 2 *dilogos* two-faced*

1 Tim 3:8 requires of deacons that they be, among other things, not "double-tongued." Cf. Pol. *Phil.* 5:2.

διό *dio* therefore

Διό serves to coordinate what follows with what precedes (BDF §451.5) and occurs esp. in Acts (8 times), the authentic Pauline letters (22), and in the other letters of the NT (11, of which 9 are in Hebrews); elsewhere only in Matt 27:8; Luke 1:35; 7:7. It is not used in Mark, John, Colossians, 2 Thessalonians, the Pastorals, 1–3 John, or Revelation. The conjunction appears in those passages enumerated 12 times with καί, *therefore . . . also* (BDF §§442.12; 451.5), and indicates that the conclusion is self-evident.

διοδεύω *diodeuō* travel through; wander about*

Luke 8:1, of Jesus' travels through cities and villages; Acts 17:1 in the "we narrative," of the journeys through Amphipolis and Apollonia toward Thessalonica.

Διονύσιος, ου *Dionysius* Dionysius*

A common personal name. Acts 17:34: a member of the Areopagus who, along with other Athenians, joined Paul and became a believer. On the use of his name as a pseudonym (*ca.* A.D. 500), see *RAC* III, 1075-1121; H. C. Graef, *LTK* III, 402f.

διόπερ *dioper* therefore*

This conjunction (δι' ὅπερ), like διό, indicates an inference in 1 Cor 8:13; 10:14; 14:13 v.l.

διοπετής, 2 *diopetēs* fallen from heaven*

Acts 19:35, as in Greek literature, on images of the gods: the town clerk of Ephesus speaks of the image of Artemis and calls it τὸ διοπετές. E. Haenchen, *The Acts of the Apostles* (1971) 575 with n. 5.

διόρθωμα, ατος, τό *diorthōma* improvement, reform*

In Acts 24:2 Tertullus praises Felix because of the *reforms* granted to the people.

διόρθωσις, εως, ἡ *diorthōsis* proper order*

Heb 9:10, of the ritual "regulations for the body imposed until the time of *true and proper order* [RSV *reformation*]." H. Preisker, *TDNT* V, 450.

διορύσσω *dioryssō* break through; break in*

In the NT only of breaking into a house: Matt 6:19, 20; 24:43 par. Luke 12:39.

Διόσκουροι, ων *Dioskouroi* (the) Dioscuri*

Acts 28:11: the Alexandrian ship had the *Dioscuri* (RSV "Twin Brothers"), Castor and Pollux, as a figurehead (and protective deities). F. J. Dölger, "Dioskuroi," *AuC* VI (1940/50) 276-85; O. Volk, *LTK* III, 410.

διότι *dioti* because

In clauses intended to substantiate a statement, διότι means *because* (e.g., Luke 2:7; 21:28; 1 Cor 15:9; Phil 2:26; 1 Thess 2:8); at the beginning of a clause where an inference is drawn it means *therefore* (Acts 13:35; 20:26). Διότι can also stand in place of ὅτι, which is used to confirm: *for, because* (e.g., Luke 1:13; Acts 18:10; 22:18; Rom 1:19, 21; 3:20). BDF §456.1.

Διοτρέφης, ους *Diotrephēs* Diotrephes*

A Christian criticized in 3 John 9 because he does not acknowledge the authority of the "elder" (v. 10). R. Schnackenburg, "Der Streit zwischen dem Verfasser von 3Joh und Diotrephes und seine verfassungsgeschichtliche Bedeutung," *MTZ* 4 (1953) 18-26; *idem, Die Johannesbriefe* (HTKNT, [5]1975) 326-29; A. J. Malherbe, "The Inhospitality of Diotrephes," FS Dahl, 222-32.

διπλοῦς, 3 *diplous* double, twofold*

1 Tim 5:17: presbyters who rightly exercise their authority as leaders should "be considered worthy of *double* honor"; Rev 18:6 (bis): the heavenly voice says of

"Babylon": "Repay her *double* for her deeds; mix a *double* draught for her in the cup . . ."; comparative in Matt 23:15: you make him "*twice as much* a child of hell [as you are]."

διπλόω *diploō* to double

Rev 18:6 with the obj. τὰ διπλᾶ (what has been doubled): *repay double.* → διπλοῦς.

δίς *dis* twice*

Mark 14:30, 72: "before the cock crows *twice*"; Luke 18:12: "I fast *twice* a week"; Jude 12, metaphorically: "fruitless trees . . . *twice* dead, uprooted." In the phrase καὶ ἅπαξ καὶ δίς, *once and again,* Phil 4:16; 1 Thess 2:18.

δισμυριάς, άδος, ἡ *dismyrias* a double myriad*

Two myriads (= 20,000). Rev 9:16: "the number of the troops of cavalry was *twice ten thousand* times ten thousand."

διστάζω *distazō* doubt*

Matt 14:31: Jesus says as Peter was sinking, "O man of little faith, why *did* you *doubt?*"; 28:17: as the disciples saw the resurrected one, "they worshipped him (→ προσκυνέω); but some *doubted.*" C. H. Giblin, "A Note on Doubt and Reassurance in Mt 18:16-20," *CBQ* 37 (1975) 68-75.

δίστομος, 2 *distomos* two-edged*

Heb 4:12: of the word of God, which is sharper "than any *two-edged* sword." Rev 1:16 and 2:12: "one like a son of man" (1:13), from whose mouth "a sharp *two-edged* sword" (ῥομφαία δίστομος ὀξεῖα) comes forth; cf. 19:15 v.l.

δισχίλιοι, 3 *dischilioi* two thousand*

Mark 5:13, of the size of the herd of swine which drowned: ὡς δισχίλιοι, *about two thousand.*

διϋλίζω *diylizō* strain out*

Literally, of *filtered* wine, e.g., Amos 6:6 LXX. Matt 23:24, in a woe-saying: "*straining out* a gnat [i.e., out of wine] and swallowing a camel."

διχάζω *dichazō* separate*

Matt 10:35 (cf. Luke 12:53): "*separate* a man from [κατά with gen.; RSV "set . . . against"] his father. . . ." See Schulz, *Q* 259.

διχοστασία, ας, ἡ *dichostasia* discord*

Rom 16:17: warning against those who create "*dissensions* and difficulties"; Gal 5:20, in a catalog of vices: ἐριθεῖαι, διχοστασίαι, αἱρέσεις, "selfishness, *dissension,* party spirit." In 1 Cor 3:3 $\mathfrak{p}^{46}$ Koine D G, etc., add καὶ διχοστασίαι to ζῆλος καὶ ἔρις. H. Schlier, *TDNT* I, 514.

διχοτομέω *dichotomeō* cut in two*

Matt 24:51 par. Luke 12:46, of dismemberment (quartering) of a person at the judgment.

διψάω *dipsaō* thirst*

1. Occurrences in the NT — 2. Meaning — 3. Usage

Lit.: J. Behm, *TDNT* II, 226f. — G. Bertram, *TDNT* II, 227-29. — For further bibliography see *TWNT* X, 1053.

1. Διψάω appears normally in connection with related words: a) parallel with πεινάω (be hungry): Matt 5:6; 25:35, 37, 42, 44; John 6:35; Rom 12:20; 1 Cor 4:11; Rev 7:16; b) in connection with ποτίζω (give someone a drink): Matt 25:35, 37, 42; Rom 12:20 or πίνω (drink): John 4:14; 7:37; c) in contrast to natural water: John 4:13, 14, 15; d) in reference to a special kind of water: Rev 7:16; 21:6; 22:17; cf. John 6:35; 7:37.

In Matt 5:6 the acc. obj. "righteousness" follows πεινάω and διψάω. The vb. appears without any further elaboration as Jesus' cry of death at the cross (John 19:28).

2. Διψάω means *thirst* and is used literally for a bodily need and fig. for something one is lacking (i.e., righteousness).

3. In the catalog of adversities in 1 Cor 4:11-13 Paul uses διψάω (v. 11) in a series of vbs. such as "hunger, be naked, be mistreated, be homeless" in the literal sense *be thirsty* to describe the physical deprivations of missionary activity. In Rom 12:20 he uses the word in a concrete demand to the Christians to help even the hungering and *thirsting* enemy with food and drink. In the judgment scene of Matt 25:31-46 this precise act of love (object: the least) becomes the criterion of one's relationship to Jesus (vv. 35, 37, 42, 44).

John 19:28 interprets the realistic cry of thirst from the dying one by an apparent allusion to Ps 22:16, suggesting the fulfillment of Scripture, i.e., obedience to the will of God. According to the Psalm the righteous one has to bear both persecution and bodily deprivation of every kind; one recognizes in the experience of *being thirsty* the particular depth of human misery and exhaustion. J. Beutler ("Psalm 42/43 im Johannesevangelium," *NTS* 25 [1978-79] 54-56) sees in the word of Jesus, "I thirst," a citation from Psalm 42 (41:2f. LXX).

In Matt 5:6 διψάω is used with the fig. meaning for the unquenchable desire and demand for righteousness. In John 4:13-15 one can observe a change of meaning for the same word. Διψάω is first used with the literal meaning at the well; in the following passages, in the context of Jesus' promise of water (likewise metaphorical), it is used in a fig. sense. In a similar sentence structure in Rev 21:6 and 22:17, διψάω is likewise used metaphorically. On the basis of Rev 7:17, a merely realistic interpretation of its use in v. 16 is excluded.

In the place of the metaphor "water" (John 4:14; Rev 21:6; 22:17; cf. Rev 7:16f.) Jesus himself appears (John 6:35; 7:37) as the one who gives, the one who satisfies the desires of the *thirsting* person for eternal life. In the latter two passages allusions to exodus typology (manna and rock) are present. One is to assume an association with the use of water at the Feast of Tabernacles only in 7:37 (R. Schnackenburg, *The Gospel according to St. John* II [1980] 152-55, 476f.).

H.-J. van der Minde

δίψος, ους, τό *dipsos* thirst*

2 Cor 11:27, in a catalog of adversities: "hunger and *thirst.*" J. Behm, *TDNT* II, 226-27.

δίψυχος, 2 *dipsychos* of two minds, undecided*

Jas 1:8: ἀνὴρ δίψυχος, "*a double-minded man,* unstable (ἀκατάστατος) in all his ways"; 4:8: "purify your hearts, *you men of double mind.*" The adj., along with διψυχέω and διψυχία, appears frequently in *1* and *2 Clement* and *Hermas.* O. J. F. Seitz, "Relationship of the Shepherd of Hermas to the Epistle of James," *JBL* 63 (1944) 131-40; *idem,* "Antecedents and Signification of the Term ΔΙΨΥΧΟΣ," JBL 66 (1947) 211-19; E. Schweizer, *TDNT* IX, 665.

διωγμός, οῦ, ὁ *diōgmos* persecution
→ διώκω.

διώκτης, ου, ὁ *diōktēs* persecutor*

In 1 Tim 1:13 the author of the letter calls himself: "once a blasphemer and a *persecutor* and a violent man"; cf. Gal 1:13f., 23; Phil 3:6; Acts 8:3; 9:4f.

διώκω *diōkō* hasten, run; be behind something; strive for something; persecute*
διωγμός, οῦ, ὁ *diōgmos* persecution*

1. Occurrences in the NT — 2. Meaning — 3. Persecution in the religious sense — 4. Striving for a spiritual goal — 5. Following after someone

Lit.: BAGD s.v. — W. BEILNER, *SacVb* 667-69. — C. BURCHARD, *Der dreizehnte Zeuge* (1970). — R. DEVILLE, *DBT* 424-27. — G. EBEL and R. SCHIPPERS, *DNTT* II, 805-9. — D. R. A. HARE, *The Theme of Jewish Persecution of Christians in the Gospel according to St. Matthew* (SNTSMS 6, 1967). — P. HOFFMANN, *Studien zur Theologie der Logienquelle* (1972) 158-89. — G. KLEIN, "Die Verfolgung der Apostel, Luk 11,49," FS Cullmann (1972), 113-24. — M. KÜNZI, *Das Naherwartungslogion Matthäus 10, 23* (1970). — H.-W. KUHN, *Ältere Sammlungen im Markusevangelium* (1971) 99-146. — O. KUSS, *Paulus* (1971) 35-37. — G. LOHFINK, *Paulus vor Damaskus* (SBS 4, 1965). — F. MUSSNER, *LTK* X, 694f. — W. NAUCK, "Freude im Leiden: Zum Problem einer urchristlichen Verfolgungstradition," *ZNW* 46 (1955) 68-80. — A. OEPKE, *TDNT* II, 229f. — E. SCHWEIZER, *Lordship and Discipleship* (SBT 28, 1960) 22-60. — P. SEIDENSTICKER, *Paulus, der verfolgte Apostel Jesu Christi* (SBS 8, 1965). — O. H. STECK, *Israel und das gewaltsame Geschick der Propheten* (WUNT 23, 1967). — V. STOLLE, *Der Zeuge als Angeklagter* (1973). — For further bibliography see *TWNT* X, 1053.

1. The vb. appears 45 times in the NT. It is not found in Mark, but is found in Matthew (6 times), Luke (3 in Luke, 9 in Acts), John (3), Paul (5 in Romans, 3 in 1 Corinthians, 1 in 2 Corinthians, 5 in Galatians, 3 in Philippians, 1 in 1 Thessalonians). It appears in the Pastorals (3) and in Hebrews (1), 1 Peter (1), and Revelation (1). The noun διωγμός is found once in Matthew, twice in Mark, twice in Acts, 3 times in Paul (Romans, 2 Corinthians, 2 Thessalonians), and twice in the Pastorals (2 Timothy). The special Christian term → διώκτης occurs only in 1 Tim 1:13. The overwhelming majority of these passages speaks of the persecution of the followers of Jesus; this is especially the case in the Gospels and the post-Pauline literature. Here original Christian usage is present. In addition, the vb. is used in dependence on early Judaism and Hellenism in the ethical-religious sense of religious striving toward spiritual goals and objects.

2. The original Greek sense of the word is based on the meaning *drive, set in motion, push,* which then becomes *persecute, banish* and, used metaphorically, *follow, strive for* a person or a thing, *push forward* zealously, *aspire to, be zealously behind* something, *endeavor* with zeal. The NT uses the vb. and the noun in connection with Hellenistic Judaism in the sense of religious persecution of Jesus and his followers and then, under the influence also of Greek philosophy, particularly the Stoa, as an expression for striving toward ethical and religious attitudes and goals.

3. a) The earliest NT use of the vb. is in the sayings source Q in the beatitude concerning the one who is *persecuted* for the sake of Jesus (Matt 5:10, 11, 12). Here the disciples are compared to the OT prophets, who were *persecuted* because of their striving for righteousness (social and judicial). To this group of sayings about the persecution of prophets and of Jesus the Messiah and about Israel as the one who persecutes prophets belong also Acts 7:52; Luke 11:49; Matt 23:34. One may compare also the statement in John 5:16 that "the Jews *persecuted* Jesus" because of the healings on the sabbath. Matt 23:34 and Luke 11:49, which are derived from Q, equate the

disciples of Jesus explicitly with the prophets. The logia in Matt 10:23 and Luke 21:12, which exhibit developments of old traditional material, are also to be arranged within this conceptual framework. John 15:20 formulates the basic idea as a rule for disciples: " 'A servant is not greater than his master.' If they *persecuted* me, they *will persecute* you [also]." Rev 12:13 expresses this idea with the image of the dragon who persecutes the people (the woman in childbirth) and her child (the Messiah).

The commandment to pray for the persecutors (Matt 5:44; cf. Luke 6:27f.) belongs to the oldest traditional material from Q. Paul has taken up the commandment: "Bless those who *persecute* you" (Rom 12:14) and made it concrete in his own person (1 Cor 4:12). Paul has also taken the idea that the disciple of Jesus is persecuted as was his Lord (2 Cor 4:9) and has developed it further with the reference to the death of Jesus on the cross and the message of the cross which evokes conflict (Gal 5:11; 6:12: "*persecuted* for the cross of Christ"; cf. 1 Cor 1:18-29). 2 Timothy, which appears late, affirms with reference to Paul: "all who desire to live a godly life in Christ Jesus *will be persecuted*" (3:12). Paul sees this law already represented in the OT narratives of Isaac and Ishmael (Gal 4:29).

A special group of persecution sayings use the vb. in reference to Paul, the persecuted one who was formerly a persecutor of the Church. These sayings appear both in the Epistles, where the apostle looks back to his past (1 Cor 15:9; Gal 1:13, 23; Phil 3:6), and in the corresponding passages in Acts (9:4f.; 22:4, 7f.; 26:11, 14f.).

b) The noun's usage corresponds with that of the vb. In the interpretation of the parable of the sower in Mark 4:17 par. Matt 13:21 it is said of a group in the Church that they immediately fall away "when tribulation or *persecution* arises on account of the word." In Mark 10:30 the community of disciples is promised that it already receives now a great reward, but "with *persecutions.*" Acts 8:1 refers to the "great *persecution*" which came on the Church after the stoning of Stephen. The persecutions which Paul must endure, primarily from Jews, are described in Acts 13:50; Rom 8:35 (with θλῖψις and στενοχωρία); 2 Cor 12:10 (with ἀνάγκη and στενοχωρία); and 2 Tim 3:11 (bis); on the persecution of the Christians of Thessalonica, see 2 Thess 1:4 (with θλῖψις).

4. In Paul and in the writings influenced by Paul, which belong to Hellenistic Christianity, the vb. is used in a fig. sense of striving toward religious and ethical attitudes and goals. Occurring as the obj. are: τὸ ἀγαθόν, the good (1 Thess 5:15), δικαιοσύνη, righteousness (Rom 9:30f.), φιλοξενία, hospitality (Rom 12:13), that which serves the peace (εἰρήνη) and the edification (οἰκοδομή) of the Church (Rom 14:19), ἀγάπη, love (1 Cor 14:1), δικαιοσύνη and εὐσέβεια, righteousness and piety (1 Tim 6:11), righteousness (2 Tim 2:22, as the opposite of "youthful passions"), εἰρήνη and ἁγιασμός, peace and sanctification (Heb 12:14), and peace (1 Pet 3:11, citing Ps 33:15 LXX). In Phil 3:12, 14 Paul names as his goal in life the resurrection with Christ, the victorious prize of the heavenly calling. In this use of the vb. fixed elements of parenesis and personal manner of living become palpable in the Hellenistic Christian communities.

5. The meaning *follow, run after* someone appears only in Luke 17:23 in the warning not to *follow* false messiahs and thus betray one's task of following Jesus.

O. Knoch

δόγμα, ατος, τό *dogma* opinion; decree, statute*

1. Greek and Hellenistic Jewish usage — 2. Imperial decrees — 3. Religious-ethical norms — 4. Religious statutes

Lit.: G. Kittel, *TDNT* II, 230-32. — J. Ranft and E. Fascher, *RAC* III, 1257-60; IV, 1-24. — For further bibliography see *TWNT* X, 1053.

1. The noun δόγμα is derived from the vb. δοκέω: "that which appears to someone (or to a community) as correct," "that which is considered good." Already in Plato the noun has the whole range of meanings from *opinion, intention,* to *norm,* (philosophical) *doctrine, teaching axiom* (for texts see LSJ, including the Supplement, s.v.; Kittel, 230f.). Wherever the "opinion" of a government is proclaimed, δόγμα takes on the meaning of *decree, edict, ordinance* (e.g., the senatus consultum in Polybius). In religious terminology it appears in κατὰ δόγμα θεοῦ ἀμετάθετον, *according to God's unchangeable decree* (Parisian magical papyrus = so-called Mithras Liturgy, *PGM* IV, 527).

In Hellenistic Judaism the meaning *decree, edict* (of a king or emperor or of the Roman senate) occurs in the LXX and in Josephus. In Philo the predominant meaning (more than 150 occurrences) is *teaching,* with the nuances of *opinion, correct views, true teaching.* It is important that one can speak of the Mosaic law or of its individual commandments as δόγματα θεοῦ or ἅγια δόγματα, which must be kept or followed (3 Macc 1:3; Josephus *Ap.* i.42; *Ant.* xv.136; Philo *All.* i.55; ii.55; iii.194; *Gig.* 52, etc.). Here two views coalesce: the concern is with God's *binding ordinances,* and the law of Moses contains the true philosophical "teaching" (Aristobulus, Philo, etc.).

2. In the NT δόγμα designates imperial (or royal) decrees in two passages. According to Luke 2:1, Augustus ordained a census for the purpose of taxation through an *edict.* It was to be carried out under the Syrian governorship of Quirinius (→ Κυρήνιος) both in Galilee and Judea, making necessary the journey of Jesus' parents to Bethlehem.

Nothing else is known of such an edict of Augustus. Such enrollments for taxation purposes had long been a matter of course in the Roman provinces. On the historical problem of an assessment of taxes in Judea (including Galilee) at the time of Herod the Great, who ruled his land not as a Roman province but as a client state with relative independence, → ἀπογραφή.

According to Acts 17:7, Paul and his coworkers in Thessalonica are accused by the Jews there of acting contrary to the δόγματα of Caesar because they proclaim "another," namely Jesus, to be king. The δόγματα thus contain Caesar's claim to be the sole ruler.

It is difficult to say what imperial decrees are being alluded to. Does Luke's formulation (as in v. 6b) apply to the beginning of persecutions that which was the case with the later persecutions under centralized authority (under Domitian)? It is striking how he has the Jews of Thessalonica swear their loyalty before the magistrates.

In Heb 11:23 in Codex A and a few other manuscripts διάταγμα has been changed to δόγμα (probably under the influence of Luke 2:1); the reference is to the *decree* of Pharaoh, who demands the killing of the sons of the Hebrews (Exod 1:16, 22).

3. Acts 16:4 is informative, because here the way is prepared for later ecclesiastical usage, according to which the binding doctrines of synods are called "dogmas." The subject here is the "apostolic decrees" (15:28f.), which do not impose on the Gentile Christians the keeping of the entire Mosaic law, but instead the keeping of the "Noachian commandments" in the authority of the Holy Spirit. Thus the subject is not "dogmatic" teachings in the later sense, but rather *norms of behavior*.

4. Col 2:14 speaks in a peculiar image of the forgiveness of sins (2:13): God has abolished the *certificate of indebtedness* (→ χειρόγραφον) which we ourselves drew up and which stands as a witness against us, when he cancelled it on a nail of the cross. It is unclear what τοῖς δόγμασιν refers to. The words are hardly to be understood as instrumental dat. with ἐξαλείψας (as if they were δόγματα, i.e., perhaps the *tenets* of the Christian teaching, in effect the sponge with which the recorded debts are extinguished), but probably as dat. of relationship with χειρόγραφον: it is the "certificate of indebtedness (given) *in view of (definite) statutes*" (not, as is often translated [e.g., RSV], "its" statutes, i.e., those which are laid down in the certificate of indebtedness). The general expression δόγματα may have been deliberately chosen in order to include the commandments of the Mosaic law within the prescriptions of the religious "philosophy" of the Colossians (E. Schweizer, *The Letter to the Colossians* [1982] ad loc., with reference to the use of the vb. in v. 20). The Colossians look at these statutes with religious anxiety and regard themselves as lost before God if they do not hold strictly to them. The author assures them that such slavery is removed in Christ.

Eph 2:15 is clearer. The author speaks, probably in dependence on Col 2:14, of δόγματα, but means particularly the law of Moses: Christ has abolished "in his flesh" (probably = through his self-sacrifice) "the law of commandments," which consists in (a variety of) *ordinances*. Thus the dividing wall between Jews and Gentiles, which was erected with the Mosaic law, is now removed; in the Church of Jesus Christ, composed of Gentiles and Jews, Christians are bound together in unity. The (now brought to a close) δόγματα are the rites which once separated and distinguished those Jews who were faithful to the law, even in the Diaspora, from their fellow citizens.

N. Walter

δογματίζω *dogmatizō* decree (vb.), impose regulations*

In the NT only pass. in Col 2:20 within the polemic against false teachers in vv. 16-23. Here it is used in the sense of a concession: τί ὡς ζῶντες ἐν κόσμῳ δογματίζεσθε: "Why do you *impose regulations* on yourselves" (RSV "why do you submit to regulations"), "as if you still lived within the sovereign authority of [RSV "belonged to"] the world?" G. Kittel, *TDNT* II, 230-32; BDF §314.

δοκέω *dokeō* think, believe, appear*

1. Occurrences and meaning in the NT — 2. Occurrences and meaning in the OT — 3. Trans. uses — 4. Intrans. uses — 5. The formula τί σοι (ὑμῖν) δοκεῖ

Lit.: BAGD s.v. — W. Foerster, "Die δοκοῦντες in Gal. 2," *ZNW* 36 (1937) 286-92. — E. P. Hamp, "δέχομαι, δοκέω, διδάσκω, DECET, DIGNUS, DOCTUS, DOCĒRE, DISCE," *CP* 63 (1968) 285-87. — G. Kittel, *TDNT* II, 232f. — D. Müller, *DNTT* III, 821f. — For further bibliography see *TWNT* X, 1053-55.

1. Δοκέω appears in the NT a total of 62 times, primarily in the Gospels (10 times in Matthew, 2 in Mark, 10 in Luke, 8 in John) and Acts (8). In the Epistles it appears primarily in 1 Corinthians (9 times) and Galatians (5). As a term derived from the primary vb. δέκομαι, "accept," δοκέω retains in the NT—in contrast to δόξα—the common Greek meaning (trans.) *think, believe;* (intrans.) *appear, seem.* Of course an adaptation of Hellenistic usage has an effect through the LXX and rabbinic argumentation, esp. in Matthew and Paul.

2. The Greek understanding of language and reality is already indebted very early (Parmenides 28B 8.50f.; Plato) to the ontological contrast of truth and appearance and thus makes use of the antithesis between, on the one hand, "appear" (to be) or (ethically) "allege" and, on the other hand, true being and knowledge. But the comparable antithesis in the OT is that which is related to the will of Yahweh (for salvation)—disobedience, life–death, etc. Thus δοκέω has in the LXX, without a literal equivalent in the MT, a Hellenizing tendency. In a few passages it is an interpretive device (e.g., Gen 19:14; Exod 25:2; 35:21f., 26: "which your heart prompted"; Jer 34:5: "right in my eyes"). But most often it is an interpretive addition used to approximate the antithesis in the wisdom literature between appearance and truth (= wisdom; e.g., Job, often in Proverbs, Wis 3:2). It also appears frequently in 2–3 Maccabees in the sense of "think, believe, appear (good)."

3. Except for Matt 3:9, "*let it* not *occur to you*" (RSV "*do* not *presume to say to yourselves*") δοκέω is used trans.

in the Synoptics in the sense of *think, believe:* in exhortation (Matt 6:7; 24:44 par. Luke 12:40), provocatively (Matt 26:53; Luke 12:51: *do you think . . .* ? cf. Matt 10:34: μὴ νομίσητε; Luke 13:2, 4 in reference to the Pharisaic teaching on recompense), and explicatively (Mark 6:49: "they *thought* it was a ghost"; cf. Matt 14:26: λέγοντες; similarly Luke 24:37; Luke 8:18 [δοκεῖ is added by Luke for the sake of the apodosis; cf. par. Matthew/ Mark]; 19:11 [probably redactional]). Luke obviously has a preference for δοκέω, documenting thereby not only a consciousness of style but also of history and reality. Thus it is emphasized in Acts 12:9 (paradoxical) that the liberation actually occurs and is no dream; in Acts 27:13 the vb. is chosen for stylistic reasons; ἔδοξα ἐμαυτῷ in 26:9, *I was convinced,* is used for classical δοκῶ μοι (BDF §283.1).

Trans. δοκέω is used in John for the theme of misunderstanding, for *false belief* (John 5:39, 45; 11:13, 31; 13:29; 16:2; 20:15).

Paul's phrase "if anyone *claims*" (hoping to see the claim publicly recognized) has a firm place in the theological-polemical critique of enthusiastic pneumatic tendencies and more generally where Paul speaks of boasting and trusting in oneself before God (1 Cor 3:18: "if anyone thinks that he is wise" [here δοκέω almost = κρίνω in 2:2]; 8:2: "that he knows something"; 11:16: "to be dogmatic [RSV "contentious"]"; 14:37: "that he is a prophet, or spiritual"; Gal 6:3, "[that] he is something, when he is nothing" [cf. the corresponding philosophical topos in Plato *Grg.* 527b; Epictetus *Diss.* ii.24.19]; Phil 3:4: "[that] he has reason for confidence in the flesh"). This use is also found in a participial clause in a warning statement (1 Cor 10:12; cf. also Jas 1:26). In 1 Cor 4:9; 7:4 δοκέω means *I find;* 2 Cor 11:16; 12:19 have the apologetic nuance "not *think/imagine,*" while Heb 10:29 and Jas 4:5 rhetorically call upon the reader to make a judgment.

4. With regard to intrans. δοκέω one must differentiate between *seem* and *be recognized as.* Alongside the question in Luke 10:36, which seeks to elicit the judgment and uncover the attitude of the hearer, there is the rhetorical δοκεῖ, *appear,* in Luke 22:24; Acts 17:18; similarly Heb 4:1 (if it is not to be translated forensically as *be discovered*). More significant are 2 Cor 10:9, "in order that it not *appear that I . . . ,*" and Heb 12:10, where κατὰ τὸ δοκοῦν, "at their pleasure," is contrasted in chiastic arrangement with "for our good" in relation to human and divine discipline and is followed by the wisdom saying in v. 11.

Although the partc. τὰ δοκοῦντα (μέλη) in 1 Cor 12:22, as in v. 23, designates simply the more or less highly regarded members, οἱ δοκοῦντες (εἶναί τι), *those reputed, those who are prominent,* is a fixed phrase, attested in Euripides *Hec.* 294; Plato *Grg.* 472a; Epictetus *Ench.* xxxiii.12; Josephus *Ant.* xix.307, as well as in *b. Ta'an.* 14b (Billerbeck III, 537). This designation for the Jerusalemites appears to have an accent that is for Paul, who is struggling for the unity of the Church in the freedom of faith, if not negative, at least relativizing. (Resentment against those in power can be seen in the addition of δοκοῦντες ἄρχειν in Mark 10:42).

5. The language and thought of Hellenistic Judaism are influential in the formula τί σοι (ὑμῖν) δοκεῖ (cf. Josephus *Ant.* vii.72; v.120; ix.190: τί δοκεῖ τῷ θεῷ; vi.227; vii.216) which, other than John 11:56, only Matthew employs in introducing parables (18:12; cf. Luke 15:3!; Matt 21:28) and in questions which call not only for a mere opinion but for a binding judgment (17:25; 22:17, 42; 26:66; otherwise Acts 25:37). Luke makes use of the style of official decrees and decisions in Acts 15:22, 25, 28 and in his prologue in Luke 1:3.

G. Schunack

δοκιμάζω *dokimazō* test; approve of, accept as trustworthy*

δόκιμος, 2 *dokimos* trustworthy, acknowledged, authentic*

δοκιμή, ῆς, ἡ *dokimē* proof, verification; reliability*

1. Occurrences in the NT — 2. Usage in the LXX — 3. Meaning — a) Luke — b) Paul — 4. Post-Pauline and post-NT usage

Lit.: L. Asciutto, "Decisione e libertà in Cristo: δοκιμάζειν in alcuni passi di S. Paolo," *RTM* 3 (1971) 229-45. — Bultmann, *Theology* I, 219. — W. Grundmann, *TDNT* II, 255-60. — G. Klein, "Die Prüfung der Zeit (Lukas 12, 54-56)," *ZTK* 61 (1964) 373-90. — G. Therrien, *Le discernement dans les écrits pauliniens* (ÉBib, 1973). — For further bibliography see *TWNT* X, 1055.

1. Δοκιμάζω is found in the NT primarily in Paul (15 of 22 occurrences). It is found also in Luke 12:56; 14:19; Eph 5:10; 1 Tim 3:10; 1 Pet 1:7; 1 John 4:1. A similar distribution is the case for δόκιμος: except for 2 Tim 2:15; Jas 1:12, it is found only in Paul's letters (5 times). Δοκιμή is found in the NT only in Paul's letters (5 occurrences); it does not appear in the LXX, and is indeed not known before Paul.

2. Δοκιμάζω is a denominative from δόκιμος, which is derived from δοκέω, δέκομαι ("accept"). Since Herodotus the vb. circulated with the meaning *test, approve of, accept as trustworthy,* occasionally as a t.t. *examine officially* (a sacrificial animal, an officeholder, a physician).

In the LXX the vb. appears (commonly) for Heb. *bāḥan,* "test, place on trial" (understood primarily in a religious sense; perhaps a metaphor of t.t. "purify [metals]"), for *ṣārap,* "melt, refine" (frequently synonymous with or parallel with *bāḥan*), niphal of *bāḥar,* "be selected," etc. For the NT (Pauline) understanding it is instructive that *bāḥan,* used particularly in poetic texts, has Yahweh as subj. 22 of 28 times; the objects of testing are humans, the people, individuals, the heart and kidneys (e.g., LXX Pss 16:3; 25:2; 138:1, 23; Kraus, *Psalms 1–59* [1988], e.g., 247, thinks of cultic and sacral-legal procedures such as lying-in at the temple and trial by ordeal; Jer 9:7; 11:20; 12:3; 17:10; 20:12). It is significant that the testing corresponds to "intuitive" knowledge and perception rather than being mediated through activity, experiment, or demonstration. Jeremiah's task in particular is that of testing (6:27). In the wisdom sections of the LXX the vb. is esp. used to signify the value of the object of testing (in conduct, through patience, like gold in fire; Proverbs, Wisdom, Sirach frequently). *T. Ash.* 5:4 is noteworthy: "All this have I tested (ἐδοκίμασα) in my life" (distinguishing truth from lies, righteousness from unrighteousness, etc.; cf. 5:1f.!).

Δόκιμος, used in Greek literature for "tested (by battle), proved, recognized, authentic" (of persons and things), is rare in the LXX and is used there to designate metals as authentic.

3. The Pauline texts indicate that δοκιμάζω, like δόκιμος and δοκιμή, is used in a technical sense with a broad range of meaning, esp. where it involves the proof of the authority of the apostle in the midst of weakness (of love). That is, the theological significance of the word is not undisputed, but is controversial. This argues against the biblical harmonization under such categories as "judgment (examination) of God/testing." Because of the implications in the theory of knowledge and in ethics, one should also not proceed in an unreflective way with the formal-neutral meaning "examine/authenticate."

In accordance with the formation of the vb. with -αζω one may say that δοκιμάζω refers to the thought and action in which one proves that he is δόκιμος; δοκιμή is the result of this act. The act. corresponds to an existence which consists in its fundamental referent, in knowledge and understanding. It is expressed as critical discernment (examination) and in practical testing of the experience of knowing or of being known in relation to oneself and to others. (This can imply ethical reflection.) The unique feature in Paul's letters is that it involves the critical-practical understanding and response of faith in the Kyrios, the knowledge of God in Christ, and that this act is to be accomplished by the believer himself and recognized by the Church.

a) Luke 12:56 is concerned with the essential *testing* of the signs of the time and the corresponding attitude to them (on the *appraisal* of oxen cf. 14:19). If one understands himself to be focusing on (the signs of) earth and heaven, why is the focus not first on this καιρός? Is its (eschatological) character as decision intended or an attitude within the tension now shaping history *post Christum* (between faith and disbelief, v. 51)? (So Klein, who is probably correct in distinguishing between the eschatologically determined, pre-Lukan Jesus tradition [cf. Matt 16:3b] and the Lukan redaction. Is δοκιμάζω, with its inner-historical, ethical meaning redactional?) It would appear synonymous with κρίνετε τὸ δίκαιον, v. 57, in critical observation of historical facts (cf. ὑποκριταί!) to come to a decision, to maintain the power of judgment and the steadfastness of faith.

b) Unlike OT usage, where God is most often the subj., in Paul humans are explicitly named as the subj. of δοκιμάζειν. 1 Thess 2:4 and 1 Cor 3:13 are only partial exceptions. In 1 Cor 3:13, in accordance with OT traditional imagery, fire will be used to test the work of the individual, because *the day will bring it to light* (the images of the burning house, final judgment, and trial by fire are brought together). 1 Thess 2:4 speaks of the God who *tests* the heart (citing Jer 11:20); for Paul (1 Thess 2:4a) this means that the gospel has been entrusted to him and that he must respond to this "approval" by God in the preaching of the gospel (cf. 2 Cor 2:17; Gal 1:10). Thus: δοκιμάζω in Paul refers indirectly to God, insofar as it refers to practical accomplishment, to the concrete responsibility determined by the situation and resting on the knowledge granted by the gospel in Christ of what God himself wills (in Christ!)—in relation to those who rely on the word of the cross.

Knowledge of the will of God is decisive. This is apparent in Rom 1:28; 2:18; 12:2: in the accusation in 1:28 in the corresponding lines (from the wisdom literature) "since they did not *see fit* to acknowledge God" and "God gave them up to a base mind [the loss of sensible existence]"; in the citation of the Jewish claim in 2:18, where knowledge of God's will (from the law) is equated with ability to *determine what is important*; and in the summons to worship in everyday life in the world in 12:2, the ability to *give a critical answer* with the renewed mind concerning the will of God. In its concrete but undetermined content τὰ διαφέροντα (a common Hellenistic colloquial phrase) in Phil 1:10 indicates, with respect to content, what is involved in the Church's critical testing and examining: an overflowing of the love which determines thought as well as action. (In the makarism of Rom 14:22, the concern in a more general sense is with capacity to judge which has been determined in the certainty of faith; in 1 Cor 11:28 it concerns the correct use of the sacraments, which is tested in self-examination).

Because God's power (πνεῦμα, life of Christ) is manifest in weakness, δοκιμή belongs in the situation of suffering, in the experience of discord. In a Christian adaptation of a Jewish parenetic topos (cf. *T. Jos.* 10:1; Jas 1:2-4; 1 Pet 1:6f.), Rom 5:4 concludes that affliction produces perseverance, perseverance *testing,* and *testing* (the certainty) of hope. According to 2 Cor 8:2 joy is derived from the *testing* in affliction. 1 Cor 11:19 brings to light who is *approved.* 2 Cor 10:18 emphasizes that the pred. δόκιμος is not appropriate to the one who recommends himself, but to the one whom the Lord recommends—thus the public-eschatological validity as well as the disputed character of this pred. (Each one should [scrupulously] *examine* his work, and then—not in comparison with others, but with his own certainty of faith—take pride, Gal 6:4).

Apparently in Corinth it was demanded of Paul that he prove, as did the other "tested" pneumatics, that Christ speaks in him (2 Cor 13:3-7). How could Paul achieve this proof (of the Spirit and of the power of Christ) other than by demanding of the Church that it account for its own existence in faith? Paul reckons with the fact that he will not satisfy such a false demand for the legitimizing demonstration of pneumatic power. However, he knows that his apostolate, which appears to be illegitimate, is proven in the fact that the Corinthians understand their existence in faith, i.e., prove in their own lives that Christ is in them on the basis of the gospel preached by the apostle. It is doubtful whether Paul could have proven his δοκιμή as an apostle in any other way, e.g., through a court proceeding. In addition, wherever he claims verification from the Church, he does so when he expects and gives credit to the Church (in his own words!) for the authenticity of its love (2 Cor 8:8; cf. 8:22). Thus the Church indicates its δοκιμή in 2 Cor 2:9, when it is obedient to the apostle. According to Phil 2:22, this is also true for Timothy.

Rom 14:18 formulates, in aphoristic form, the new norm for being well pleasing in God's eyes and proven in the presence of mankind: service toward Christ (cf. Rom 16:10). In the saying about the collection in 1 Cor 16:3 the concern is with "accredited people of your choice."

4. In post-Pauline (and post-NT) literature δοκιμάζειν takes on a somewhat fixed meaning in the sense that the testing and accreditation can, so to speak, be delegated according to general, ecclesiastical-ethical criteria. 1 Thess 5:21 ("*test* everything; hold fast what is good"); Eph 5:10 ("what is pleasing to the Lord"); 1 Tim 3:10 (testing whether any objection against deacons can be made on the basis of the bishop's image in vv. 6, 7); 1 John 4:1 ("*test* [in the faith] the spirits, whether they are of God"); 2 Tim 2:15 (of the bishop); Jas 1:12 ("Blessed is the man who endures trial [i.e., "stands fast in temptation"], for when he has *stood the test* [or *"if he is found approved"*] he will receive the crown of life") are transitional. *Did.* 11:11; 12:1; 15:1 interprets the meaning with respect to the testing of (wandering) prophets and bishops; similarly *1 Clem.* 42:4; 44:2; 47:4; *Herm. Man.* xi.7.16. According to Ign. *Smyrn.* 8:2 God is pleased with what the bishop approves.

G. Schunack

δοκιμασία, ας, ἡ *dokimasia* testing, examination*

Heb 3:9 (cf. Ps 94:9 LXX): ἐπείρασαν . . . ἐν δοκιμασίᾳ, "they put . . . to the *test,*" of the behavior of the Israelites in relation to God during the time in the wilderness; Koine lat sy[p, h] read ἐδοκίμασαν (μέ) with the LXX. W. Grundmann, *TDNT* II, 256.

δοκιμή, ῆς, ἡ *dokimē* proof, verification; reliability*
→ δοκιμάζω 3.b.

δοκίμιον, ου, τό *dokimion* means of testing; authenticity*

Jas 1:3: τὸ δοκίμιον ὑμῶν τῆς πίστεως, "*the testing* of your faith," in reference to temptations (cf. v. 2); 1 Pet 1:7: τὸ δοκίμιον ὑμῶν τῆς πίστεως as neut. sg. of the adj. δοκίμιος, "the *genuineness* of your faith" (v.l. δόκιμον), which surpasses the authenticity of gold, which is tested by fire. W. Grundmann, *TDNT* II, 258, 260f.; BDF §263.5; L. Goppelt, *Der Erste Petrusbrief* (KEK, 1978) ad loc.

δόκιμος, 2 *dokimos* trustworthy, acknowledged, authentic
→ δοκιμάζω.

δοκός, οῦ, ἡ *dokos* beam, log*

Matt 7:3, 4, 5 par. Luke 6:41, 42 (bis): in a hyperbolic figure of speech used by Jesus: "the *log* in your own eye" in contrast to the *"splinter"* (RSV *"speck"*) in the eye of the brother. The figure of speech is probably proverbial (cf. Billerbeck I, 446f.) and emphasizes the prohibition of judging one's brother. See Schulz, *Q* 148f.

δόλιος, 3 *dolios* malicious, insidious*

2 Cor 11:13: ἐργάται δόλιοι, "*malicious* [RSV "deceitful"] workers," alongside ψευδαπόστολοι, of the opponents of Paul; cf. also *1 Clem.* 5:5; *Herm. Sim.* ix.26.7.

δολιόω *dolioō* deceive*

Rom 3:13 (citing Ps 5:10 LXX): ταῖς γλώσσαις αὐτῶν ἐδολιοῦσαν (impf.; cf. BDF §84.3), "with their tongues *they have (always) deceived*" (RSV "they use their tongues to deceive").

δόλος, ου, ὁ *dolos* deceit, cunning; perfidy*

1. Occurrences and OT usage — 2. Description of human existence and activity — 3. Vice catalogs and household codes — 4. Defense of apostolic ministry

Lit.: D. GEORGI, *The Opponents of Paul in Second Corinthians* (1986). — O. KEEL-LEU, *Feinde und Gottesleugner* (1969). — L. RUPPERT, *Der leidende Gerechte und seine Feinde* (1972). — A. SCHULZ, *Nachfolgen und Nachahmen* (1962) 289-93. — E. SCHWEIZER, "Gottesgerechtigkeit und Lasterkataloge bei Paulus (incl. Kol und Eph)," FS Käsemann, 461-77. — A. VÖGTLE, *Die Tugend- und Lasterkataloge im NT* (1936) (index s.v.). — S. WIBBING, *Die Tugend- und Lasterkataloge im NT* (1959) 78-99. — H. W. WOLFF, *Jesaja 53 im Urchristentum* ([3]1952) 99-104.

1. Of the 11 references in the NT (including as v.l. Mark

12:14; Rev 14:5) δόλος appears once each in Matthew (par. Mark), John, Acts, Romans, 2 Corinthians, and 1 Thessalonians, twice in Mark, and 3 times in 1 Peter. In addition to actual citations from the OT, dependence on the description of the godless person as "deceitful" (in contrast to the God-fearing = "righteous"), common in the OT, esp. in the wisdom tradition (e.g., Pss 10:7; 36:4; 52:4; 55:12; Prov 12:5, 20; 16:28; 26:4; Wis 1:5; 4:11; 14:25; Sir 1:30; 19:26; cf. Jer 5:27; 9:5; Zeph 1:9), is unmistakable.

2. a) The intention of the opponents of Jesus of taking him prisoner and killing him, is described in an unambiguously negative way with the suggestion that it be done ἐν δόλῳ (Mark 14:1; Matt 26:4, δόλῳ). Besides the reason given (fear of the people), the narrative shows that the future suffering of Jesus is to be understood as that of an innocently condemned righteous man. The desire of his opponents is understood as the impious deed of the godless.

b) Just as the irreligious conduct of Elymas the magician (Acts 13:8) is described as that of a man πλήρης παντὸς δόλου (v. 10), so by contrast that of Nathanael among those first called to be disciples is that of "a true Israelite," ἐν ᾧ δόλος οὐκ ἔστιν (John 1:47)—a characterization which is intelligible only from OT passages (cf. Ps 32:2; Zeph 3:13) describing one who is truly "righteous" (cf. Rev 14:5 v.l.).

3. a) In the NT vice catalogs (Vögtle 1; Wibbing 78) δόλος appears (on the use of the term see Vögtle 13ff.; Wibbing 87f.) only in Mark 7:22; Rom 1:29; 1 Pet 2:1. In characterizing those who live in "ungodliness" and "unrighteousness" (Rom 1:18ff.) with δόλος, Paul follows the OT (cf. Vögtle 229-32). In Mark 7:22 δόλος appears at the beginning of the second series of six offenses which, according to Jesus, comprise "evil," i.e., guilt for which one is personally responsible, coming "out of the heart" of the individual. In contrast to this unspecific usage stands the command in 1 Pet 2:1 to put off "all malice, all *falsehood,*" in the service of the concrete parenesis of the Church; δόλος is one of the features of conduct which esp. trouble the relationships between individuals and opposes the Church's life together as a "holy priesthood" (v. 5), as a "chosen race" (v. 9), and as the "people of God" (v. 10).

b) The innocent suffering of the servant of God (according to deutero-Isaiah) is described in 1 Pet 2:22 as that of the one who "had done no violence" and in whose mouth "there was no *deceit*" (Isa 53:9). The citation stands in a traditional hymn about Christ (1 Pet 2:21-25), which is cited in the parenetic context of the household code: slaves should prove themselves by following the "exemplary" suffering of Jesus (2:21).

With Ps 34:13-17, 1 Pet 3:10-12 makes the concluding exhortation to "all of you" (3:8) in a parenesis aimed at a life on the basis of "the experience of Christ" (L. Goppelt, *Der Erste Petrusbrief* [KEK] 226), which breaks through the vicious circle of reciprocal retaliation against evil with the response of the "blessing" (v. 9); this implies that the Christian guards his lips from λαλῆσαι δόλον (v. 10 = Ps 34:14).

4. Already in 1 Thessalonians Paul defends his missionary service: his proclamation does not take place ἐν δόλῳ (2:3). Paul must defend himself esp. in 2 Corinthians: he does not belong to those "who tamper with God's word (δολοῦντες τὸν λόγον τοῦ θεοῦ)" (2 Cor 4:2). This is the prerogative of the "false apostles," the ἐργάται δόλιοι (11:13), who preach "another Jesus" and "a different gospel" (11:4). One can note how absurd Paul considers the necessity of his defense before the Corinthians in his ironical "concession" that he has won "by guile" (12:16), although everything occurs only for *their* sake (vv. 14f.).

L. Oberlinner

δολόω *doloō* falsify*

2 Cor 4:2: μηδὲ δολοῦντες τὸν λόγον τοῦ θεοῦ . . . , "*to falsify* [RSV "tamper with"] the word of God" in the defense of Paul's apostolate; cf. also 2 Cor 12:16; 1 Thess 2:3 (→ δόλος). A related phrase is ἄδολον γάλα in 1 Pet 2:2; cf. "falsify wine" in Lucian *Herm.* 59.

δόμα, ατος, τό *doma* gift*

Matt 7:11 par. Luke 11:13: οἴδατε δόματα ἀγαθὰ διδόναι τοῖς τέκνοις ὑμῶν, in an argument *a minori ad maius* from the conduct of parents in providing. Although they are evil (πονηροὶ ὄντες/ὑπάρχοντες), they "know how to give good *gifts* to their children." From this the argument is made to God's care for those who make requests to him as their heavenly Father; Eph 4:8 (cf. Ps 67:19 LXX), of the *gifts* of the resurrected Christ to mankind (i.e., Church, v. 11); Phil 4:17: Paul aspires not to the *gifts* of the Church for his livelihood, οὐχ ὅτι ἐπιζητῶ τὸ δόμα, but rather the fruit, the yield (→ καρπός).

δόξα, ης, ἡ *doxa* reputation, honor; radiance; glory

1. Occurrences in the NT — 2. Meaning and usage — 3. In general early Christian usage — a) *Reputation, honor, fame* — b) Heavenly-divine *radiance* — c) Spiritually perceived divine *glory* — 4. In Paul's theology of the cross — 5. In John's theology of revelation

Lit.: M.-L. Appold, *The Oneness Motif in the Fourth Gospel* (WUNT II, 1, 1976). — G. Bertram, *TDNT* VIII, 602-14. — J. Blank, *Krisis: Untersuchungen zur johanneischen Christologie und Eschatologie* (1964), esp. 264-96. — A. Dauer, *Die Passionsgeschichte im Johannesevangelium* (SANT 30, 1972), esp. 231-94. — M. Didier, "La gloire de Dieu: réalité méconnue,"

La Foi et le Temps 4 (1974) 579-602. — F.-W. Eltester, *Eikon im NT* (BZNW 23, 1958) 130-66. — G. Fischer, *Die himmlischen Wohnungen: Untersuchungen zu Joh 14, 2f* (EHS XXIII, 38, 1975) 299-348. — J. T. Forestell, *The Word of the Cross: Salvation as Revelation in the Fourth Gospel* (AnBib 57, 1974), esp. 65-74. — Y. Ibuki, *Die Wahrheit im Johannesevangelium* (BBB 39, 1972) 188-201. — E. Käsemann, *The Testament of Jesus* (1968) 4-26. — G. Kittel and G. von Rad, *TDNT* II, 232-55. — H. Kittel, *Die Herrlichkeit Gottes* (BZNW 16, 1934). — E. Larsson, *Christus als Vorbild* (ASNU 23, 1962), esp. 275-93. — C. Mohrmann, "Note sur dóxa," *Sprachgeschichte und Wortbedeutung* (FS A. Debrunner; 1954) 321-28. — J. Riedl, *Das Heilswerk Jesu nach Johannes* (Freiburger theologische Studien 93, 1973), esp. 69-188. — H. Schlier, "Doxa bei Paulus als heilsgeschichtlicher Begriff," *Studiorum Paulinorum Congressus Internationalis Catholicus 1961* I (AnBib 17, 1963) 45-50. — R. Schnackenburg, "Entwicklung und Stand der johanneischen Forschung seit 1955," *L'Evangile de Jean* (ed. M. de Jonge; 1977) 19-44. — J. Schneider, *Doxa* (1932). — *idem, TDNT* VIII, 169-80. — G. Warmuth, *TDOT* III, 335-41. — C. Westermann, *THAT* I, 794-812.

1. Δόξα appears 167 times in the NT, of which 57 are in Paul and the deutero-Pauline literature (29 in 1 Cor 3:4–4:6; 15:40-44). 28 are in the Synoptics and Acts, 18 in John, 7 in Hebrews, 20 in the Catholic Epistles (of which 1 Peter has 10), and 17 in Revelation. The word does not appear in Philemon or 1–3 John.

2. In comparison with nonbiblical Greek, the usage is surprising. The most frequent meaning of δόξα outside the Bible, "view, opinion," is missing in the NT. The other basic meaning *reputation, value, honor* (Luke 14:10; 1 Thess 2:6, 20; 1 Cor 11:15; 2 Cor 6:8, etc.) goes back to a religious usage which is unknown outside of biblical Greek: "divine *radiance,* divine *glory*" (Luke 2:9; Matt 16:27; Acts 7:55, etc.), with a transition to "visible *radiance*" in general (1 Cor 15:20f.; Acts 22:11). It is disputed whether this meaning had been prepared in the common usage of the environment, probably in the language of the Hellenistic court. This appears to be the operative meaning in the NT references where δόξα means the *radiance* of kings and kingdoms (Matt 4:8; 6:29; Rev 21:24, 26) or is used in association with throne motifs (Matt 19:28; 25:31, 34; Mark 10:37; 1 Thess 2:12) and in the sense of "majesty" as the name for angelic powers (Jude 8; 2 Pet 2:10).

This remarkable new connotation of the word goes back to the selection of δόξα as the word to translate Heb. *kāḇôḏ* in the LXX. The entire breadth of meaning of Heb. *kāḇôḏ* is taken over into the Greek equivalent δόξα. *Kāḇôḏ* refers to the weight of esteem and honor which a person, esp. the king (1 Kgs 3:13), has. It can be used fundamentally of every person, probably with respect to his or her position within the creation (Ps 8:6) or within the community of mankind, where *kāḇôḏ* is manifest in a graduated way as rank, dignity, and position of power. It is used esp. in reference to the deity as an expression of the manifestation of his sovereign rule over nature and history, on the one hand in the powerful form of divine radiance in theophanies, but even more in the majesty of his historical acts of salvation and judgment, perceptible only to the eye of faith. To acknowledge and confess this *kāḇôḏ* of Yahweh is the honor due him from his people and from all creation.

The variety of usages corresponds to the different classifications of the meaning of the word. Δόξα is used synonymously with τιμή with the meaning *esteem, honor,* (e.g., Rom 2:7, 10; 1 Tim 1:17; with ἔπαινος in Phil 1:11; 1 Pet 1:7). The opposite is ἀτιμία (2 Cor 6:8). Words connoting power are used to elaborate the idea of δόξα as *radiance of power:* δύναμις (Matt 24:30; Luke 21:27), ἐξουσία (Luke 4:6; 2 Thess 1:9), and κράτος (1 Pet 4:11; Rev 1:6). Frequently such δόξα-sayings appear in hymnic songs of praise (Luke 2:14; 19:38; Eph 1:3-14; Rev 4:11, etc.), but more often in the doxology form, derived from Jewish tradition (Rom 11:36; 16:27; Gal 1:5; Eph 3:21; Phil 4:20; Heb 13:21; 1 Tim 1:17; 2 Tim 4:18; 1 Pet 4:11; 2 Pet 3:8; Rev 1:6). Since δόξα expresses the nature of the deity in its manifestation, such concepts as θειότης, "divine nature," ὑπόστασις, "steadfastness," and μεγαλοσύνη, "majesty" can appear alongside it (Rom 1:20, 23; Heb 1:3a, d) and shift the δόξα-sayings about the manner of the divine presence in the event of revelation to the heavenly-divine sphere (Luke 2:9; 1 Tim 3:16, etc.), esp. to the heavenly messengers sent from God, particularly in the final event (Luke 9:26; Matt 16:27; Rev 18:1, etc.). This is one point of departure of the christological δόξα-sayings in the NT. Jesus comes in δόξα as the expected Son of Man (Mark 8:38, etc.) and is the κύριος τῆς δόξης (1 Cor 2:9; Jas 2:1), etc.

Participation in the divine δόξα is granted to the works of the Creator (Rom 1:21, 24), esp. mankind as that which God has created (1 Cor 11:7). But as mankind has been unfaithful to its appointed place and participation in the divine δόξα has been lost (Rom 3:23), δόξα takes on a central meaning in soteriological sayings. Here δόξα appears with δικαιοσύνη (vv. 23-25), χάρις (5:2; Eph 1:6), σωτηρία (1 Pet 1:7-10; Rev 19:1), ζωὴ αἰώνιος, τιμή, and εἰρήνη (Rom 2:7, 10), and elsewhere and is the sum of the hope for salvation (Rom 5:2; 8:21; Eph 1:18; Col 1:27), with a significant incorporation of the temporal word → δοξάζω, "glorify." Because such salvation is mediated through Christ (2 Cor 4:6, etc.) we have here the second point of departure for christological δόξα-sayings.

3. a) *Esteem, honor* as an object of human striving (Luke 14:10; 1 Cor 11:15) is evaluated from a critical perspective: one who seeks *honor* from mankind fails to seek it from God (1 Thess 2:6, 19f.; John 5:41-44; 7:18; 8:50f.; 10:43; 12:43; Phil 3:19; cf. Rom 2:7, 10). The apostle proves his freedom "in *honor* and dishonor" (2 Cor 6:8). The proverbial radiance and the *array* of kings and their kingdoms can function positively (Matt 6:29; Luke 12:27); in the final event all of the δόξα of the peoples will adorn the city of God (Rev 21:24, 26). However, the

transience of all the *splendor* of this cosmos is maintained (1 Pet 1:24; cf. 1 John 2:15-17), and its demonic and seductive *radiance* must be rejected (Matt 4:8; Luke 4:6). The humiliating suffering of the apostle for his Church, if understood correctly, is an *honor* (Eph 3:13). In the same way, on the other hand, his faithful Church will mean for him in the end *honor,* boasting, and joy (1 Thess 2:19f.). Ultimately all *honor* belongs to God alone, as is indicated in hymn and doxology. Therefore, one's situation is always significant. This is so in connection with God's repudiation of ungodliness (Rom 1:23-25), submission to God's authority as judge (John 9:24; Rev 14:7; 16:9), the rejection of blasphemy (Acts 12:23), and most of all in thanksgivings for the divine salvific gift (Luke 17:18; Rom 11:36; Eph 3:21; 1 Tim 1:17; 2 Tim 4:18; Heb 13:21; 1 Pet 4:11; Jude 24f.; Rev 4:11, etc.). In a particular sense the "yes" of faith gives God the *honor* due him (2 Cor 1:20; Rom 4:20f.).

b) OT theophany traditions have a significant, but not widespread, survival (Acts 7:2, 30-32, 35, 38; Heb 9:5; cf. Exod 25:22; 1 Cor 10:1-4; John 12:41). Such traditions are always offered as witness to the new revelation which surpasses the old (cf. esp. 1 Cor 10:6, 11). Already in the exodus event God was present in Christ (1 Cor 10:4), who "pitched his tent [RSV "dwelt"] among us" so that "we have beheld his δόξα" (John 1:14). The sight of a visible, divine radiance thus sharply recedes in the NT, with the exception of texts concerned with hope for the future consummation of the revelation that has already arrived (Mark 8:38; 13:26; Matt 16:27; 24:30; Luke 17:24; 21:27; Rev 21:11, 23f.). Nevertheless δόξα designates a perceptible and yet heavenly radiance also in Luke 9:31 (the Transfiguration), in a few of the Easter traditions (Mark 16:5; Matt 28:3; Acts 9:3), and in the Lukan infancy narrative (Luke 2:9). This is seen at times through the special capacity given to the visionary (Acts 9:3; cf. v. 7), and at times is the result of the appearance which breaks in spatially and visibly (Luke 2:9). Paul thinks of the glory of light in the new body in 1 Cor 15:43; cf. Phil 3:20f. In this context he appears to attribute to heavenly bodies a radiance of δόξα in the form of a reflection (1 Cor 15:41f.), by which an element of rank and position plays a role: "Star differs from star in δόξα." Δόξα takes on what is elsewhere called "reflected spendor," analogous to εἰκών. The human person is the "image and *reflected splendor* of God" (1 Cor 11:7). Behind the visible heavenly light stands the invisible, inaccessible divine sphere of light (1 Tim 6:16).

c) According to Rom 1:23 (cf. v. 20) God's *glory,* his eternal power and deity, is mentally perceived in his created works and calls for the thankful homage of the creation. In view of his acts in history to the patriarchs and to Israel *glory* belongs to the people of God (Rom 9:5; cf. Luke 2:32). In the midst of an Adamic humanity ensnared in guilt and in separation from God, the Creator holds firmly to his holy will and, through the Christ-event, determines for mankind a share in the δόξα of God. In the resurrection of Jesus Christ from the dead God has "given new life" to the believer (RSV "we have been born anew") and has "called [us] to his eternal *glory*" (1 Pet 1:3-9; 5:10).

Thus the δόξα which is given to mankind becomes purely a gift of grace (Rom 3:23f.; 9:23) that God has extended through Christ. God has "taken [him] up in *glory*" (1 Tim 3:16; cf. Jas 2:1; 1 Pet 1:21; 2 Pet 1:17, etc.) and "crowned him with δόξα and honor." With glory that is greater than that of Moses or the angels, he is the Son, the preexistent agent of creation, who "reflects the *glory* of God and bears the very stamp" of the nature of God, who through him began to lead "many sons to δόξα" (Heb 2:7, 9; 3:5; 1:2f.; 2:10). The "spirit of the *glory* and of God" rests already on believers (1 Pet 4:14); they are guarded through God's power until the revelation of the *glory* of Christ and of the faithful at the end (1 Pet 1:5; 4:13; 5:1). Yet just as Christ went according to God's will through suffering into *glory,* so it is also determined for the faithful (1 Pet 1:6-12; 2:20f.; 4:13; 5:1, 4, 10; cf. Rom 8:17). When the Church responds to God's *glory,* it consists fundamentally in the faithfulness of God to his lost creatures in the Christ-event (Luke 2:14; 19:38; Eph 1:3-14; Heb 13:20f., etc.).

4. Paul shares in the general early Christian usage. He allows its LXX background to become prominent, besides, in citations (Rom 1:23; cf. Ps 105:20 LXX; 1 Cor 11:7; cf. Gen 1:27). Thus δόξα expresses for Paul the basic nature of God as it appears in his revelation, perceived by the illuminated reason in his creative power (Rom 1:20, 23), from the eye of faith in his judging and salvific power in historical manifestations. It becomes the object of faithful hope for the definitive shining forth at the end.

Paul's own usage becomes perceptible when he considers the manifestations of God's δόξα in soteriological terms. The state of being lost (3:23) as the forfeiture of the δόξα is expressed in universal terms: mankind involved the whole created world in such a fall (Rom 8:19-21). Paul sees God's δόξα as present in Israel also in the Torah, but as a δόξα that condemns and causes death, which passes away (2 Cor 3:7-10) in the presence of the life-giving δόξα of Christ. For the divine instruction is "weakened by the flesh" (Rom 8:3) in the fallen creation. The christological δόξα-sayings begin with the active presence of God in the Christ-event: Christ is raised "by the δόξα of the Father" (Rom 6:4; cf. Rom 1:4 on the subject). Indeed, he was already crucified as "Lord of *glory*" (1 Cor 2:8).

The meaning of this important passage (1 Cor 2:8) is disputed. The assumption of a Gnostic descent myth, according to which the powers did not recognize the Lord of glory at his descent, probably fails to grasp the point. The passage is to be interpreted against the background of 4:6: the powers of the world did not recognize the presence of God hidden in the Christ-event; they did not recognize "the *glory* of God in the face of Christ" (4:6), which God prepared in order to reveal his saving love in the sacrifice of his Son (Rom 5:8; 8:32; cf. 3:25f.; 2 Cor 5:19), an event in which "God's truthfulness abounds to his glory" (Rom 3:7). One who recognizes the δόξα of God in the face of Christ has received "a secret and hidden wisdom of God," which God has destined for us, those who believe, in order to give us a share in his δόξα (1 Cor 2:7). This wisdom opens for us "the deep things of God," so that we are grasped and controlled by the love of God and Christ (2 Cor 5:14f.; 1 Cor 8:3).

Salvation is for Paul participation in God's glorious nature, as it is manifest in his saving love in the Christ-event. Consequently the cosmic expectation remains vivid: our body will be formed like the "body of δόξα" of the exalted Christ. Our nature will be formed by his "image": Phil 3:21; 1 Cor 15:43f., 49. However, the decisive transformation to δόξα occurs now by the vision of glory of God's love in Christ (2 Cor 3:18; 4:5). Paul himself lives and experiences this transformation (2 Cor 4:7-10, 17). His gospel mediates it, producing the "light of the knowledge of the *glory* of God in the face of Christ," a shining which is comparable to the original light at the creation of the world (2 Cor 4:3f., 6). Thus his ministry is a "dispensation of the Spirit," which "takes place in δόξα," indeed, abounds in δόξα (2 Cor 3:8f.).

The whole creation is expected to share in the *glory* of the sons of God at the end, i.e., in the universal rule of the love of the Creator, which liberates everything to the truth of its created destiny (Rom 8:21). Because the final glory of God is fundamentally his power of love, faith can already boast of it (Rom 8:30, ἐδόξασεν; cf. vv. 37-39) and God can already bring the confession of his glory: that Christ has accepted us while we were sinners, that he is exalted above everything, that the apostle in his own ministry makes the grace of Christ great, that believers bring the fruit of righteousness in a life of love, will result in the *glory* of God (Rom 15:7; 2 Cor 4:15; Phil 2:11; 1:9-11). They are able with their mortal body, indeed in their death itself, to increase the glory of God and of Christ (1 Cor 6:20; Phil 1:20). Now one can in truth devote his life to the pursuit of "*glory* and honor and immortality" (Rom 2:7), for he lives with his will and his achievements from the radiance of the presence and love of God (Rom 12:1f.; Gal 2:20; Phil 2:13), and he is summoned to do all to the *honor* of God (1 Cor 10:31).

In the deutero-Pauline letters the new theological shape of Pauline usage is developed further, but has a closer approximation to general early Christian tradition. Thus the idea of power is emphasized more in δόξα, in view of the end (2 Thess 1:9; cf. Rev 15:3), of the power of the new life in those who believe (Col 1:11; Eph 3:16), and of the heavenly majesty of God (1 Tim 1:11, 17; cf. 6:14-16). However, the idea of salvation is predominant: God is praised as the Father of δόξα; "his *glorious* grace" is proclaimed (Eph 1:6). This grace has been granted to believers, full of all the salvific gifts (1:3-10, 17-23). One knows that he is destined to praise this δόξα of God (1:12, 14; 3:21). When the perspective turns to δόξα as the object of hope (1:18; cf. 2:7; Col 1:27; 3:4; 2 Thess 2:14; cf. 1:10; 2 Tim 2:10; Titus 2:13), it involves a revelation of δόξα, of which the content is determined by grace (Titus 2:13; 2 Thess 2:16).

5. The Fourth Gospel makes its own usage prominent in a threefold way; in all three the concerns of the theology of revelation are significant.

a) In contrast to Paul the consistent view of the preexistence of δόξα is distinctive. Just as God's δόξα is prior to all created existence, so also is the glory of the Son, who was always "with God" (John 17:5; cf. 1:1f.). At death he returns to the δόξα "with the Father" (17:5), but on earth he never departs from the δόξα of the Father, for the Father is always "with him" (16:32; cf. 5:17). In his revelation in the world the *glory* as of the only begotten from the Father (1:14) is characteristic of him. The Father gives him a share of his δόξα in love (1:18; 3:35; 5:20; 17:24).

b) In Jesus' deeds of power the glorious nature of God becomes manifest (John 11:4, 40). Thus Jesus has glorified the Father on earth (17:4) in his works and his work. At the same time he has revealed the δόξα (2:11) of the Son. While the Signs Source underlines the divine presence in the works of Jesus with the intensification of the miraculous, for the Evangelist the mere experience of miracle, including the satiation at the multiplication of bread, remains in the realm of the "flesh" and "is of no avail" (6:25b-27, 63); only one who in faith "sees the signs" (6:26a)—who sees the Son whom the Father gives as the "bread of life" to the world in the miracle of the bread, who sees the Lazarus miracle as "the resurrection and the life," and who sees "the light of the world" in the healing of the blind (6:32-35; 9:3-5; 11:25-27)—that person alone sees the revelation of the δόξα of the Father and of the Son. Here one may see a critique of triumphalism *(Enthusiasmus)* related to Paul's own critique and given from the perspective of a theology of the cross.

The function of the Passion narrative in the Fourth Gospel is, of course, disputed in scholarship. Against Käsemann's thesis, according to which the Evangelist included the Passion narrative because of necessity, one should regard the Passion narrative in John as extremely significant. The glory of Jesus as light of the world is decisively the crisis of the cosmos proceeding from the cross; the creative love of God for the world, which transforms the lost into sons of light (12:31f., 36; cf. 1:12f.; 3:3; 8:34-36; 9:39) is present in it. The Son is "bread of the world" and the "good shepherd" when he gives his life for the world and for his own (6:51; 10:11, 15).

Because Jesus is "exalted" into his saving power first in the death which saves the lost world, there occurs in his death the "glorification" (13:31f.; 17:4) of him and of the Father.

In this context one may explain the programmatic δόξα saying of 1:14b. The Evangelist defines the *glory* of the Logos who has become human by taking up the OT conceptual pair *ḥeseḏ we'ᵉmeṯ*, "grace and truth." This is done in dependence on Exod 33:18–35:7, where the nature of the glory of Yahweh is summarized with this conceptual pair (Exod 34:6): mercy and faithfulness are predominant over the judging power of God. Correspondingly the revelation of the glory of Jesus is done in his loving sacrifice in death (John 13:1, 24f., 31f.; 19:25-30). It is this δόξα of love which Jesus has given and continues to give his own (17:20-23).

c) Δόξα in the sense of *reputation, honor* appears in two contexts: 1) Christological-apologetic: Even if the Son claims complete divine authority, he never seeks his own honor, but rather that of the one who has sent him (John 7:18; 8:50, 54). With the help of the common ancient idea of the messenger, the confession of the divine majesty of the revealer, of his *glory,* is defended. 2) Soteriological: As with the pursuit of one's own righteousness in Paul, the pursuit of one's own honor is regarded as one of the decisive barriers against saving faith (5:44; 12:43). Only the one who allows the shame of his sin to be disclosed, allowing himself to be purified from the service of death, has a part in Jesus (3:19f.; 4:16-19, 29; 8:31-37; 13:8).

H. Hegermann

δοξάζω *doxazō* honor, praise; glorify

1. Occurrences in the NT — 2. Meaning and usage in early Christian literature — a) Honor, praise — b) Glorify — 3. Δοξάζω in the soteriology of John

Lit.: A. Dauer, *Die Passionsgeschichte im Johannesevangelium* (SANT 30, 1972) 236-94. — G. Lohfink, *Die Himmelfahrt Jesu* (SANT 26, 1971). — M. McNamara, "The Ascension and Exaltation of Christ in the Fourth Gospel," *Scripture* 19 (1967) 65-73. — R. Schnackenburg, *The Gospel according to St. John* II (1979) 398-410. — W. Thüsing, *Die Erhöhung und Verherrlichung Jesu im Johannesevangelium* ([2]1972) (bibliography). — For further bibliography → δόξα.

1. The total of 60 instances of δοξάζω in the NT include 22 in John's Gospel alone, then 12 in Paul's letters (including 2 Thessalonians), 9 in Luke, 5 in Acts, 4 each in Matthew and 1 Peter, 2 in Revelation, and 1 each in Mark and Hebrews.

2. Δοξάζω is derived from the noun → δόξα and attains its meaning from it: a) "show honor," pass. "receive honor," b) (from the special effect of δόξα-usage in the LXX) "glorify, give or [pass.] receive a share in the divine glory."

a) Δοξάζω as *honor* of people in relation to each other is used both in a positive sense (Matt 6:2; Luke 4:15; 1 Cor 12:26; cf. v. 24) and in a critical sense of honoring oneself (John 8:54; Heb 5:5; Rev 18:7).

The predominant usage of δοξάζω in the NT concerns the honoring of God, almost always in the fixed phrase δοξάζω τὸν θεόν, which is from the Jewish traditional doxology (Luke-Acts alone 11 times; also Matt 9:8; Rom 15:6, 9; 1 Pet 2:12, etc.; in John only at 21:19). The designation for God can vary (Matt 5:16; 15:31, etc.). Very often the occasion is given (Matt 9:8; Mark 2:12). Alongside or in the passage where δοξάζω appears, traditional synonyms also appear, including αἰνέω (often in Luke-Acts), εὐλογέω (Luke 1:64; 2:28; Jas 3:9, etc.), μεγαλύνω (Luke 1:46; Acts 10:46), or also "give honor," etc. (Rom 4:20; John 9:24, etc.). This confessional honoring of God (also expressed with τιμάω: Mark 7:6; John 5:23; 8:29) has a deeper manifestation in a life and death dedicated to God (1 Cor 6:20; John 21:19). The honoring of God can be directed toward his word (Acts 13:48; 2 Thess 3:1; also Rom 11:13), particularly toward Christ (Phil 1:20; Acts 19:17; esp. John 5:23).

b) Δοξάζω is rarely used in the sense of *glorify* outside John (→ 3). It occurs in Rom 8:30 as the concluding part of a soteriological chain; in 2 Cor 3:10 in a critical interpretation of the Doxa of Moses according to Exod 34:29-35; and in Acts 3:13 (cf. v. 15) as interpretation of God's deed in Jesus Christ at Easter in dependence on Isa 52:13. Here the usage and development of δοξάζω approximates that in John.

3. The connection with the tradition of Jesus' reception into divine glory (cf. 1 Tim 3:16; Luke 24:26; Acts 3:16) is indicated clearly in John 7:39; 12:16; cf. 2:22: Jesus *was glorified* only at his resurrection. This tradition saw Jesus "exalted" into the divine sphere of glory "at the right hand of God"—participating in God's glorious power (Acts 2:33; 5:31; cf. 3:13). This is manifested in the presence of the exalted one in epiphanies of the power of the Spirit; or, said in another way: in the holy power of his name (Acts 2:33; 3:16).

The Fourth Evangelist shapes his new interpretation of δόξα (→ δόξα 5) in terms of a theology of revelation in a fourfold way: a) Already in the death of Jesus, indeed in the "now" of his self-sacrifice in death, Jesus is *glorified* (John 13:31) and thus "exalted" (3:14; 8:28; 12:32, 34; RSV "lifted up") in the great "hour" which completes everything which the Father has determined for him: "The hour has come for the Son of Man to be *glorified*" (12:23; cf. 13:1, etc.). Here the older Synoptic tradition contributes its interpretation of Jesus' Passion as that which happens to the "Son of Man."

b) Just as the saving-creative power and love of the Father becomes an event in the earthly work and in the loving self-sacrifice of Jesus for the world, John sees the reciprocal glorification of the Father through the Son (13:31b; 17:1b, 4) and of the Son through the Father (7:39; 12:16, 23; 13:31a; 17:1a, 5) occur as an event. Finally, the Father glorifies himself, "his name," in the Jesus-event (12:28), an event which radiates further after Easter (12:28; 13:32). Thus the revelation of the glory of God in the sign of Lazarus is already a glorification of the Son (11:4, despite 7:39; cf. 2:11).

c) The glorification of Jesus and of the Father is manifest, indeed increased, where the divine salvific power of Jesus becomes productive under the cooperation of the Spirit (16:14) among his own people on earth. In the death of Jesus "much fruit" is borne (12:23f.); in the "greater works," which happen in the power of prayer "in the name of Jesus," and in the life of the love of God, the Father is *glorified* in the Son (14:12f.; 15:7-13).

d) Jesus' entry into the divine glory "with the Father" (17:1, 5) is distinguished from his glorification as the revealer of salvation; it is the restoration of the preexistence glory through the generous love of the Father; to see it and to participate in it is the destiny promised to the disciple (17:5, 24; cf. 14:2f.).

H. Hegermann

Δορκάς, άδος, ἡ *Dorkas* Dorcas (gazelle)*

Acts 9:36, 39: the Greek rendering of Aram. *Ṭᵉḇîṯā'*, the name of a disciple in Jaffa (→ Ταβιθά). Δορκάς also appears as a name in, e.g., Josephus *B.J.* iv.145.

δόσις, εως, ἡ *dosis* gift; giving*

Jas 1:17: πᾶσα δόσις ἀγαθή, "every good *gift,*" with πᾶν δώρημα τέλειον of the gifts of God; Phil 4:15: εἰς λόγον δόσεως καὶ λήμψεως, "by a profit-and-loss account" (the translation of J.-F. Collange, *The Epistle of Saint Paul to the Philippians* [1979] 148), a phrase derived from commercial terminology describing here the relationship between Paul and the Philippians as the settlement of accounts; cf. also Sir 42:7; E. Lohmeyer, *Philipperbrief* (KEK) ad loc.

δότης, ου, ὁ *dotēs* giver*

2 Cor 9:7: ἱλαρὸν γὰρ δότην ἀγαπᾷ ὁ θεός, "God loves a cheerful *giver*" (cf. Prov 22:8). H. Windisch, *Der zweite Korintherbrief* (KEK) ad loc.

δουλαγωγέω *doulagōgeō* bring into slavery
→ δουλεύω.

δουλεία, ας, ἡ *douleia* slavery
→ δουλεύω.

δουλεύω *douleuō* be a slave, serve
δουλαγωγέω *doulagōgeō* bring into slavery*
δουλεία, ας, ἡ *douleia* slavery*
δούλη, ης, ἡ *doulē* female slave, maidservant*
δοῦλος, 3 *doulos* subservient, subject*
δοῦλος, ου, ὁ *doulos* slave, servant
δουλόω *douloō* enslave, subjugate*
σύνδουλος, ου, ὁ *syndoulos* fellow slave*

1. Frequency of occurrences of the different words in the NT — 2. Syntactic constructions — 3. Meanings — 4. The word group in the proclamation of Jesus, in the Synoptic tradition, and in John — 5. The word group in the Epistles of Paul and the Pauline tradition — 6. Δοῦλος and σύνδουλος in Revelation

Lit.: W. BRANDT, *Dienst und Dienen im NT* (1931). — R. GAYER, *Die Stellung des Sklaven in den paulinischen Gemeinden und bei Paulus* (1976). — H. GÜLZOW, *Christentum und Sklaverei in den ersten drei Jahrhunderten* (1969). — J. JEREMIAS, *Jerusalem in the Time of Jesus* (1969). — E. KAMLAH, "Die Parabel vom ungerechten Verwalter (Luk. 16, 1ff.) im Rahmen der Knechtsgleichnisse," FS Michel, 276-94. — G. KEHNSCHERPER, *Die Stellung der Bibel und der alten christlichen Kirche zur Sklaverei* (1957). — H.-G. LINK and R. TUENTE, *DNTT* III, 589-98. — K. H. RENGSTORF, *TDNT* II, 261-80. — G. SASS, "Zur Bedeutung von δοῦλος bei Paulus," *ZNW* 40 (1941) 24-32. — G. SCHNEIDER, *Parusiegleichnisse im Lukas-Evangelium* (1975). — S. SCHULZ, "Hat Christus die Sklaven befreit?" *EvK* 5 (1972) 13-17. — E. SCHWEIZER, "Zum Sklavenproblem im NT," *EvT* 32 (1972) 502-6. — P. STUHLMACHER, *Der Brief an Philemon* (EKKNT, 1975). — J. VOGT, *Ancient Slavery and the Ideal of Man* (1975). — A. WEISER, *Die Knechtsgleichnisse der synoptischen Evangelien* (SANT 29, 1971). — H.-D. WENDLAND, *RGG* VI, 101-4. — W. L. WESTERMANN, *The Slave Systems of Greek and Roman Antiquity* (³1964). — T. WIEDEMANN, *Greek and Roman Slavery* (1981).

1. Words with the δουλ- stem appear a total of 182 times in the NT. Most of these occurrences are of δουλεύω, *be a slave, serve* (25 occurrences) and δοῦλος, *slave, servant* (124). They appear most frequently in the Pauline Epistles (47) and in the Synoptic Gospels and Acts (71). There are also the vbs. (listed here in order of frequency): δουλόω, *enslave, subjugate, reduce to servitude* (8 occurrences); καταδουλόω, *reduce to slavery;* and δουλαγωγέω, *take into slavery* (1 Cor 9:27); and the nouns σύνδουλος, *fellow slave* (10 occurrences); δουλεία, *slavery* (5); δούλη, *female slave* (3); and ὀφθαλμοδουλία, *eye service*; and the adj. δοῦλος, *subservient, submissive* (2).

2. Where the person or the thing served is named with δουλεύω, it is always designated with the dat. (21 times). Only in Rom 7:6; Gal 4:25; 1 Tim 6:2 does the vb. appear in the absolute. In Phil 2:22 it is connected with a prep. with acc. In most instances where δοῦλος appears, the relationship is expressed: 27 times with a personal pron. indicating possession; 27 times with the gen. of the person

or thing (except for Rom 6:16). In absolute usage (with or without the art.) the word appears 39 times. In addition it is connected 11 times with an adj., 14 times with a demonstrative pron., and a few other times with a prep., a partc., ἄλλος, or ἴδιος. The person who is enslaved is indicated with acc. with δουλόω, καταδουλόω, δουλαγωγέω (5 times). Where the vb. appears in the pass., the dat. of the person or thing follows (5 times). Absolute use of these vbs. appears only in 1 Cor 7:15 and a prep. construction only in Gal 4:3.

3. In contrast to the synonyms (e.g., διακονέω) the emphasis of the words with the δουλ- stem lies "on the service being that of a slave, i.e. on a repressive or at least dependent form of service under the complete control of a superior" (Tuente 593).

In the Greek world and in Hellenism the word group has, because of the high evaluation of personal freedom, almost exclusively a demeaning, scornful significance. On this basis and because God was not considered the absolute Lord, the word group plays no role in the religious realm.

A totally different understanding is expressed in the OT and in Judaism: God is the absolute Lord. The individual knows that he is dependent on God. To be chosen by God, to be able to serve him, is not demeaning; on the contrary, it is an honor. Consequently words of the δουλ- stem in the LXX are most frequently translation equivalents for the root *ʿbd* and its denominatives (cf. W. Zimmerli, *TDNT* V, 673f.). The religious usage has developed from the Near Eastern ceremonial-court manner of expression, in which even the highest officials are δοῦλοι before their king. It articulates distance and dependence.

In Gnostic dualism the word group serves to express slavery to matter and to the world powers.

In the NT the words of the δουλ- stem serve to designate the relationship of dependence and service in the following areas:

a) In the realm of the condition of slavery as a *social reality*: Δοῦλος designates the *house slave*: Matt 8:9 par. Luke; Matt 10:24, 25; 13:24-30; 24:45-51 par. Luke; Matt. 25:14-30 (cf. Luke); Mark 12:1-9 par. Matthew/Luke; Mark 13:34-37; 14:47 par. Matthew/Luke/John; Luke 7:1-10 (cf. Matthew); Luke 12:35-38, 47; 14:16-24 (cf. Matthew); Luke 15:22; 17:7-10; John 4:51; 13:16; 15:20; 18:18, 26; Eph 6:5; Col 3:22; 4:1; 1 Tim 6:1; Titus 2:9; Phlm 16; with emphasis on the distinction between slave and son: John 8:35; Gal 4:1; between slave and free: 1 Cor 7:20-24; 12:13; Gal 3:28; Eph 6:8; Col 3:11; Rev 6:15; 13:16; 19:18; between slave and friend: John 15:15; the *high officials of the king*: Matt 18:23-35 (also σύνδουλος); 22:1-10 (cf. Luke); Luke 19:12-27 (cf. Matthew).

Δουλεύω is used of relationship: *to be a slave, to be subjugated,* John 8:33; Acts 7:7; Rom 9:12; 1 Tim 6:2. As a designation of conduct it means *to do the work of a slave, serve*: Matt 6:24 par. Luke 16:13; Luke 15:29; Eph 6:7. Δουλόω in Acts 7:6 has the meaning *enslave* and in 2 Pet 2:19 (pass.) *to have become a slave.* Ὀφθαλμοδουλία designates *eye service,* service carried out only for the sake of appearance: Eph 6:6; Col 3:22.

b) In *fig.* senses: Δοῦλος designates the individual in his or her *relationship of dependence and service* toward God, the absolute Lord, whose possession he or she is: Luke 2:29; Acts 2:18; 4:29; 16:17; Titus 1:1; 1 Pet 2:16; Jas 1:1; Rev 7:3; 10:7; 11:18; 15:3; 19:2, 5; 22:3, 6; in relation to Jesus Christ: Rom 1:1; 1 Cor 7:22b; Gal 1:10; Eph 6:6; Phil 1:1; Col 4:12; 2 Tim 2:24; Jas 1:1; 2 Pet 1:1; Jude 1; Rev 1:1; 2:20 (the relationship to Christ is described as friendship in John 15:15a and as sonship in Gal 4:7—rather than servitude). The word denotes, in its wider sense, people who should encounter each other *in the basic attitude of service*: Mark 10:44 par. Matthew; or who *serve* Christ as apostles: 2 Cor 4:5. Jesus Christ himself is called a δοῦλος in Phil 2:7. Δοῦλος serves finally to designate the person who is under the ruling power of sin (according to John 8:34; Rom 6:16f., 20) and of destruction (according to 2 Pet 2:19). It can designate one who is under the sovereign power of righteousness in Rom 6:17.

Σύνδουλος designates *coworkers* or *fellow Christians* in consideration of the common relationship to Christ in service and fidelity: Col 1:7; 4:7; Rev 6:11. Even the revealing angel of Rev 19:10; 22:9 describes himself in this way. In all of its occurrences δούλη expresses the idea of being *a maidservant* before God in the form of the oriental and OT indication of lowliness: Luke 1:38, 48; Acts 2:18.

Δουλεύω expresses the *serving* which people exercise toward the following ruling powers: to God as the absolute Lord: Matt 6:24 par. Luke; 1 Thess 1:9; Jesus Christ as Lord: Acts 20:19; Rom 12:11; 14:18; 16:18; Eph 6:7; Col 3:24; 7:6; to the law of God: Rom 7:25; to the gospel: Phil 2:22; to the idols: Gal 4:8f.; to sin: Rom 6:6; 7:25; to the desires: Titus 3:3; of people to each other: a son to his father, Luke 15:29; service to each other in love, Gal 5:13. Δουλεύω appears in an allegorical sense for the condition of Israel as that which rejects the realm of the sovereignty of Christ: Gal 4:25.

Δουλεία appears only with fig. meanings for slavery to sin, law, and death, which continues wherever the redemption through Christ is not yet effective or not yet completed: Rom 8:15, 21; Gal 4:24; 5:1; Heb 2:15. The vbs. δουλόω, καταδουλόω, δουλαγωγέω express positively the subjection of the redeemed person to the righteousness of God in Rom 6:18, 22; Paul's readiness to serve in relation to his apostolic commitment in 1 Cor 9:19; and self-control of the body in 1 Cor 9:27. Negatively they are used of *subjugation* to the elementary powers of the world in Gal 4:3; *slavish dependence* on wine in Titus 2:3; *enslavement* in interpersonal relations in Gal 2:4; 2 Cor 11:20; and, in contrast to a personal partnership in marriage, it is used for an *absolute, servile obligation* in 1 Cor 7:15. The adj. δοῦλος is used twice in Rom 6:19 to express that people before their baptism have made their members and thus their deeds of impurity and lawlessness *subservient,* but now should—i.e., after their baptism—be *subservient* to righteousness.

4. Of the words of the δουλ- stem, only the following appear in the Synoptic Gospels and Acts: δουλεύω (7 times), δοῦλος (64), σύνδουλος (5), δούλη (3), and δουλόω (1). The greatest portion of these is found in words and parables of Jesus; δουλεύω appears 5 times in them. The figure of speech from Q in Matt 6:24 par. Luke: "no one can *serve* two masters. . . . You cannot *serve* God and mammon," is drawn from contemporary slave relations and speaks of the totality with which one should belong to God and *serve* him. In Luke 15:29 Jesus uses the vb. in a parable: it designates the *service* of the son to the father.

Δοῦλος appears 5 times in sayings of Jesus other than parables: The figure in Matt 10:24f. is derived essentially from Q. Whether Matthew expanded it or Luke abbreviated it because of the context is disputed; probably the latter is the case. The double saying would say in Q: the disciples and messengers of Jesus will suffer the fate of the prophets as he does in radical discipleship to their Lord. Luke has taken up from a special tradition the figure of the punishment of the slave who did not act according to his knowledge in Luke 12:47, 48a, and added it redactionally to the preceding parable as a warning to the leaders of the Church. The important word of Jesus on the greatness of serving in Mark 10:44 par. Matthew is reshaped in the parenesis of both Gospels. Thus the expressions ὑμῶν διάκονος—πάντων δοῦλος involve an intensification.

In the parables of Jesus δοῦλος appears 47 times and σύνδουλος 5 times, the latter only in Matthew. Jesus thus employs a manner of speaking which was common in Judaism. He employs δούλος in its literal meaning in Matt 13:24-30; Luke 15:11-32, where the δοῦλοι appear only as ancillary figures and are without essential significance. In the basic form of the parable of the banquet in Matt 22:1-10 par. Luke, where the δοῦλος plays an important role, he has no significance of his own; Matthew has made from the one δοῦλος several δοῦλοι and understood them as prophets, Christian missionaries, and proclaimers. While the δοῦλοι in the parable of the vineyard (Mark 12:1-9 par. Matthew/Luke) are regarded as prophets in general by Mark and Luke, Matthew concretizes them when he mentions a stoning and thus suggests the fate of Zechariah. In the parable of the unmerciful δοῦλος in Matt 18:23-35 and in the parable of the unpretentious servant in Luke 17:7-10 the metaphor δοῦλος expresses the relation of humans to God: the parables of Jesus apparently spoke to those who had experienced the mercy of God, but stood in danger of refusing mercy to others.

Matthew has referred the parables to relationships within his own congregation, so that the δοῦλος and his σύνδουλοι (alongside Matt 18:28, 29, 31, 33 and 24:49) signify the members of the Christian Church. Luke has used the parable of the unpretentious servant, which originally had been used by Jesus against the pharisaic view of the law, with reference to the members of his church, particularly those who had been entrusted with special service. The parables of the doorkeeper in Mark 13:33-37, of the waiting δοῦλοι in Luke 12:35-38, of the faithful and unfaithful in Matt 24:45-51 par. Luke, and of the talents in Matt 25:14-30 par. Luke are closely connected with the sovereignty of God: all who have responded to the message of Jesus should expect it in watchfulness and readiness. They are thus "crisis parables," as the form of the imminent consummation of the sovereignty of God proclaimed by Jesus has a critical function because of its claim summoning to a decision and its ambivalent character. As this parable came to be applied to Christ's parousia after the resurrection, the κύριος in them came to signify him. The δοῦλοι came to signify Christians, and the lengthened time came to refer to the parousia.

In the Gospels the parables are especially placed in the service of parenesis (cf. Schneider 15-42). From the perspective of source criticism, one may recognize that certainly Matt 24:45-51 par. Luke, and probably Matt 22:1-10 par. Luke; Luke 12:35-38; 17:7-10 are derived from Q, while the origin of Matt 25:14-30 par. Luke from Q is questionable.

In the narrative material of the Synoptic Gospels and Acts words with the δουλ- stem appear only in isolation: δοῦλος is used of: the *servant* of the high priest in the Passion narrative (Mark 14:47 par. Matthew/Luke/[John]); the *servant* of the centurion of Capernaum in the narrative of the healing (Luke 7:1-10), which has been redactionally retouched (par. Matthew only 8:9); and Simeon in the style of the OT self-designation of one who prays (Luke 2:29). Three passages where δούλη appears in the NT are also shaped by OT influence, all of them found in the Lukan double work. First is Mary's designation of herself as "maidservant [RSV "handmaid"] of the Lord" in Luke 1:38 in her answer to God's call; the term indicates "in the most significant way [her] passive availability and active readiness" (H. Schürmann, *Lukasevangelium* [HTKNT] I, 58). It is used also in Luke 1:48; Acts 2:18. Within his speech Stephen cites an OT passage in Acts 7:6 describing the *servitude* of Israel in Egypt with δουλόω.

John employs only δουλεύω (1 time) and δοῦλος (11 times). In the temple dispute in John 8:33 the Jews declare that they live in the freedom of Abraham's children and have never *served as slaves* to anyone. Jesus answers them with the prophetic statement: "Every one who commits sin is a *slave* to sin" (8:34). Then he continues the metaphor: the *domestic slave* does not remain—in contrast to the son—forever in the house (8:35). Jesus has in mind here those with whom he is speaking, who do not allow themselves to be free through faith in "the Son." In the parenetic interpretation of the footwashing as a model story the Synoptic logion is found: "A *slave* is not greater than his master" (13:16). Without the introductory double Amen or the added statement out of Jewish law concerning emissaries, John sharpens the statement once more as a "reminder" to his church in the farewell address of 15:20. Jesus only shortly beforehand calls the disciples φίλοι and not δοῦλοι (15:15), but no contradiction is present: the δοῦλος-κύριος relationship stands in the context of parenesis concerning discipleship, while the φίλος terminology appears in the context of the freedom and intimacy made possible by the Son (cf. ch. 8). The four other δοῦλος-passages belong to the narrative material of the healing story of 4:51 and the Passion narrative in 18:10, 18, 26. The references here are to *slaves* in the service of an official and of the high priest.

5. In the Pauline literature all but one of the words of the δουλ- stem named in → 1 appear. They are found in the following contexts and with the following meanings: a) *Christians* are snatched away through baptism from the enslaving power of sin, of the law, of death, of the cosmos, and freed for sonship (Rom 6:6-23; 7:25; 8:15; Gal 4:1–5:1; Titus 3:3).

b) However, the sonship of Christians does not mean autonomous and certainly not unbridled freedom (Titus 2:3; 3:3), but rather *service* to God (Rom 6:22; 7:25; 1 Thess 1:9), Christ (Rom 12:11; 14:18; 16:18; Col 3:24), righteousness (Rom 6:17, 18, 19), the neighbor (Gal 5:13) "in the new life of the Spirit" (Rom 7:6). In the presence of this fundamental change of sovereignty all worldly distinctions in position have become insignificant (1 Cor 12:13; Gal 3:28; 4:7; Col 3:11).

c) Regarding *slaves* as a social class, it is said that their life is just as valuable before God as the life of those who are free (1 Cor 7:21; Eph 6:8; Col 3:25). This indicates a considerable revaluation of their human dignity. Christian slaves share in the religious activities of the Church, even with their masters, if the latter are Christians (Phlm 16). Paul himself recommends also that Christian slaves use the opportunity to become free (so probably 1 Cor 7:21; cf. Stuhlmacher 45) and that Philemon set his slave free (Phlm 13f.). Paul does not press the matter because it seems more important to him that both slave and free know that they are responsible together before the same Lord (1 Cor 7:22f.). The post-Pauline parenetic household code also corresponds to this position: it encourages Christian slaves to practice faithful, honest service and challenges masters to care for their slaves and not to mistreat them (Eph 6:5-9; Col 3:22–4:1; 1 Tim 6:1f.; Titus 2:9f.; 1 Pet 2:18-25).

d) Paul calls himself and his coworkers Timothy, Epaphras, and Tychicus *slaves* or *fellow-slaves* (with each other) of Christ or of God (Rom 1:1; Gal 1:10; Phil 1:1; Col 1:7; 4:7, 12; 2 Tim 2:24; Titus 1:1). The OT self-description of the pious as δοῦλοι θεοῦ and the self-description of Christians as δοῦλοι Χριστοῦ do not sufficiently explain this self-designation of Paul and his coworkers. Instead OT honorific titles given to such specially chosen and extraordinary characters as Moses, David, and others, have had an influence. The designation expresses for Paul not only a relationship of service, but is also a title of office and an honorific description. Corresponding to this self-understanding Paul is able to describe his commission and the commission of his coworkers as *slavery* (1 Cor 9:19; 2 Cor 4:5; Phil 2:22).

e) In the pre-Pauline hymn in Phil 2:6-11 it is said of Jesus Christ that he relinquished the divine form of existence and took on the form of a *slave* (2:7). Here the obedience of Jesus is not referred to, for it is described subsequently. Also deutero-Isaiah does not form the background, for there the servant is identified with the word παῖς while here Christ is called δοῦλος and designated besides as ἄνθρωπος in relation to θεός. Thus it is human existence that is understood as slavery. Here the biblical motifs of lowliness vs. exaltation are mixed with the pagan motifs of God's majesty vs. the enslavement of mankind to the powers of the world—Jewish Christian and Gentile Christian elements respectively (cf. J. Gnilka, *Philipperbrief* [HTKNT] 119f., 147).

6. In the remaining NT writings the word group plays a significant role only in Revelation, where, of course, the only words used are δοῦλος (14 times) and σύνδουλος (3 times). With the exception of Rev 6:15; 13:16; 19:18, where δοῦλος is used with ἐλεύθερος, the words always have a religious-figurative meaning. Under the strong influence of OT descriptions, extraordinary figures (15:3)—especially the prophets (10:7; 19:2)—as well as the people of God in general (19:2, 5; 22:3) become, as *servants* of God, the receivers of the revelation (1:1; 22:6), and members of the churches addressed are called *servants of God* or *Christ*. The pronounced δοῦλος-terminology and its connection with the OT prophetic designation indicates that the churches of Revelation are penetrated and shaped by prophetic elements (2:20; 11:18). Their situation in persecution is understood as a prophetic fate (6:11). In 19:10 and 22:9 the angel of revelation describes himself as *fellow slave* and brother of the seer.

A. Weiser

δούλη, ης, ἡ *doulē* female slave, maidservant
→ δουλεύω.

δοῦλος, 3 *doulos* subservient, subject
→ δουλεύω.

δοῦλος, ου, ὁ *doulos* slave, servant
→ δουλεύω.

δουλόω *douloō* enslave, subjugate
→ δουλεύω.

δοχή, ῆς, ἡ *dochē* meal, invitation*

This word appears only in Luke, in the phrase δοχὴν (μεγάλην) ποιέομαι, "give a (great) *banquet*" (5:29; 14:13).

δράκων, οντος, ὁ *drakōn* dragon*

1. Occurrences in the NT — 2. Mythological background — 3. The *dragon* in Revelation 12 (and 20)

Lit.: BAGD s.v. — O. EISSFELDT, "Gott und das Meer in der Bibel" (1953), *Kleine Schriften* III (1966) 256-64. — W. FOERSTER, *TDNT* II, 281-83. — H. GUNKEL, *Schöpfung und Chaos in Urzeit und Endzeit* (1895). — R. HALVER, *Der Mythos im letzten Buch der Bibel* (TF 32, 1964) esp. 96-98. — O. KAISER, *Die mythische Bedeutung des Meeres in Ägypten, Ugarit und Israel* (BZAW 78, [2]1962). — A. VÖGTLE, "Mythos und Botschaft in Apokalypse 12," FS Kuhn, 395-415. — For further bibliography see *TWNT* X, 1059.

1. The word appears in the NT only in Revelation, particularly in ch. 12 (8 times) and—in connection with it—13:2, 4, 11; 16:13 and 20:2. It regularly designates a mythical figure, the *dragon,* which is equated by the seer with "that ancient serpent, who is called the Devil and Satan" (12:9; 20:2).

2. The myth of the terrible monster that opposes the powers of light or deities of life and can only be overcome with effort, is widespread throughout the ancient world (the Pythian dragon, which Apollo kills; Typhon, whom Zeus renders incapable of battle and who falls into Tartarus [Hesiod *Th.* 820-80]; additional oriental myths in Gunkel).

In the OT such conceptions are in the background, particularly in statements which contain a theology of creation: Yahweh has overcome Leviathan, *Tannîn* (the LXX commonly renders this name with δράκων), and other land or sea monsters (Ps 74:13f.; Job 7:12: 26:12f.; 40:15ff., 25ff.) and now "sports" with them (Ps 104:26; cf. Eissfeldt; Kaiser). Out of the praise of the primeval victory of God the hope for the eschatological conquest of those powers of evil, which are experienced as oppressive, develops in Jewish apocalyptic (from Isa 27:1 on).

A "historicized" variation of the dragon myth is found in non-canonical and canonical "childhood legends": The birth of a future hero and savior is announced; the current ruler, who feels himself threatened, attempts by all means to kill the child; but it miraculously escapes, so that it can later accomplish its work (Cyrus: Herodotus i.108-128; Moses: Exodus 1–2 and esp. Josephus *Ant.* ii.201-37; Jesus: Matthew 2). Thus the mythical scene in Revelation 12 with the savior-child does "refer to" Jesus, but without equating the remaining figures with other concrete individuals (such as the woman with Mary or the dragon with a specific Caesar).

3. In Revelation 12 the dragon appears in a mythical scene ("in heaven" 12:1) and has seven heads, ten horns, seven crowns, and a powerful tail. It is red, probably "fiery red" (following Isa 14:29). It watches the birth of the savior-child in order to devour the child immediately, but the child is carried off and hidden by God (Rev 12:5). The second scene (vv. 7-12) shows Michael, the guardian angel of God's people, in dispute with the dragon. (Here the equation is made with the devil/Satan, the accuser of Israel before God's throne, and with the "ancient serpent" or "serpent of the beginning," the seducer of humanity according to Genesis 3; the equation of the serpent of Paradise with the devil is made in Wis 2:24.) The dragon is conquered and falls (cf. Luke 10:18)—but not yet finally into the abyss (as later in Rev 20:10), but rather to the earth (12:9b, 12b). Thus Satan is essentially deprived of his power, but can still exercise on earth his enticing and enslaving power. Though the dragon cannot destroy the "woman," the people of God as a whole (→ γυνή), and hinder her "child," the Messiah, it directs its wrath against the "rest of her offspring," on those who keep God's commandment and confess Jesus (12:17). In order to harm them, it has a mirror-image of itself, the "beast" (→ θηρίον), rise from the "sea." As earthly representative of the dragon the "beast" causes persecution of the faithful and general apostasy from God (13:1-10), together with the "second beast," which entices others to idolatrous worship of the "first beast" (13:11-18; cf. 16:13f.). Behind both figures stands the dragon. Thus in one impressive image, the fundamental element of all human history, the "battle between faith and unbelief," between the worship of God and the deification of creaturely powers or social forces, is portrayed.

Finally, in Rev 20:1-10 the certainty is expressed that "the *dragon,* that ancient serpent, who is the Devil and Satan" (20:2), is overcome through Jesus and can no longer separate those who belong to Jesus from the love of God. Thus in the image of the dragon, Revelation portrays the adversary of God, who in all power and tyrannical and enticing cruelty, is still without power. His "last hour" has been struck with the coming of Jesus (Luke 10:18; Rev 12:12b).

N. Walter

δράσσομαι *drassomai* catch, seize*

1 Cor 3:19: ὁ δρασσόμενος τοὺς σοφοὺς ἐν τῇ πανουργίᾳ αὐτῶν, "who *catches* the wise in their craftiness" (cf. Job 5:13: ὁ καταλαμβάνων . . .).

δραχμή, ῆς, ἡ *drachmē* drachma*
δίδραχμον, ου, τό *didrachmon* double drachma*

1. Occurrences and numismatic detail — 2. Δίδραχμον — 3. Luke 15:8f. — 4. Matt 17:24 (δίδραχμον)

Lit.: J. Babelon, *La numismatique antique* (1944). — H. Chantraine, *KP* II, 155f. — K. Christ, *Antike Numismatik* (1967). — E. Höhne and B. Kanael, *BHH* 1249-56. — F. Hultsch, *PW* V/2, 1613-33. — B. Lang, *BL* 1182-85 (bibliography). — H. W. Perkin, *ISBE* III, 406ff. (bibliography). — F. Prat, "Le cours des monnaies en Palestine au temps de Jésus-Christ," *RSR* 15 (1925) 441-48. — O. Roller, *Münzen, Geld und Vermögensverhältnisse in den Evangelien* (1929). — A. Spijkermann, "Coins Mentioned in the NT," *SBFLA* 6 (1955/56) 279-98. — W. Wirgin and S. Mandel, *The History of Coins and Symbols in Ancient Israel* (1958).

1. In the NT Jewish, Greek, and Roman coin systems are mentioned alongside each other. The *drachma,* a Greek silver coin (already in the LXX of Gen 24:22; Exod 39:2; Tob 5:14, etc.), is mentioned only in Luke 15:8a, b, 9. It had the value of one-hundredth part of a μνᾶ (mina, Luke 19:13-25) and the six-thousandth part of a τάλαντον (talent, Matt 18:24-28). The Greek drachma corresponded to a Roman silver coin, the denarius (→ δηνάριον). It was a typical silver coin (Matt 22:19) and, like the Israelite fourth shekel, the normal day's wages (Matt 20:2). The latter information assists one in converting the amount into modern currencies.

2. Along with the drachma the **δίδραχμον,** *double drachma,* which appears only at Matt 17:24 (twice in the pl.), was also in circulation. In the LXX it appears more frequently (Gen 20:14, 16; 23:15; Lev 27:3-7; Neh 5:15, etc.), as do the other multiples of this coin, e.g., the tetradrachma (Job 42:11), which may be the same as the NT stater (→ στατήρ, Matt 17:27), also corresponded to the Israelite shekel (→ ἀργύριον), and was probably the equivalent of four days' wages (→ 1).

3. The parable of the lost *drachma* (Luke 15:8f.) speaks of one of ten drachmas as a parallel to one of one hundred sheep (15:4-7). The concern of the man, which springs from his love for the single animal, is compared to the concern of the woman for the one drachma. In the background, but not referred to in the text, is probably the idea of the woman's headdress, which was her dearest possession and nest egg. She did not take it off, even when she went to sleep (J. Jeremias, *Parables* 107). As ten drachma comprise a modest decoration, the woman was extremely poor. By sweeping her dark residence she finds the jingling coin on the hard rocky floor again and rejoices, inviting her friends and neighbors to share her joy. The meaning of the parable is revealed (according to 15:7, 10) in the inner relationship of the owner to the loss of something small and in her extraordinary joy in finding it once more.

4. In the legendary traditional story of Matt 17:24-27 the *double drachma* appears as a coin for the temple tax (cf. Exod 30:11-16; Neh 10:33f.); this temple tax could be paid for two persons (Jesus and Peter) with a stater (→ 2) found in a fish. The story is more ancient than Matthew, for it reflects a time before the separation from the Jewish temple community and the introduction of Roman coins and taxes. The fundamental affirmation of Jesus, that the sons are free (Matt 17:26), is connected here with the instruction: "Give it to them for me and for yourself" (17:27). The story of the double drachma, whatever its sources may be, preserves two basic points about Peter which Matthew's church wanted to trace back to Jesus: his full and basic freedom from the Jewish temple community and his basic readiness to compromise in all questions which were not essential; it is reminiscent of Acts 15:28f. and Romans 14.

W. Pesch

δρέπανον, ου, τό *drepanon* sickle, scythe*

In the NT only at Mark 4:29 and 7 times in Rev 14:14-19, of which 4 are in the phrase δρέπανον ὀξύ (vv. 14, 17, 18 bis). Mark 4:29: ἀποστέλλει τὸ δρέπανον (cf. Joel 4:13), "he puts in the *sickle*" (as an indication of harvest); Rev 14:14ff., of the "(sharp) *sickle*" of the Son of Man or an angel (v. 17), which completes the "harvest" (with Joel 4:13, an image of judgment; cf. Mark 4:29), first a harvest of grain (vv. 15f.), then of wine (vv. 18f.). A. S. Kapelrud, *BHH* 1780f.

δρόμος, ου, ὁ *dromos* race (course); course of life*

In the NT only fig. of the *course of* a person's *life* in the phrases πληρόω τὸν δρόμον, "finish his *course,*" in Acts 13:25 and τελέω τὸν δρόμον, "accomplish my *course,*" in 20:24; 2 Tim 4:7. Fig. of the "race of faith," *1 Clem.* 6:2.

Δρούσιλλα, ης *Drousilla* Drusilla*

Lit.: BAGD s.v. — E. Haenchen, *The Acts of the Apostles* (1971) 660-63. — S. H. Perowne, *The Political Background of the NT* (1965) 59, 81, 93, 101. — Schürer, *History* I, 446, 453, 461f. — A. Stein, *PW* V/2, 1741. — R. D. Sullivan, "The Dynasty of Judaea in the First Century," *ANRW* II/8 (1977) 296-354, esp. 329-31.

Drusilla (fem. diminutive form of "Drusus") appears to have been used only seldom as a name (see F. Preisigke, *Namenbuch* [1922] Supplement 100), but is found 3 times among members of the Julio-Claudian imperial house: Livia, the wife of Augustus, Julia, the sister of Emperor Gaius (Caligula), and his daughter Julia all bore the *cognomen* Drusilla (*PW* XIII, 900; X, 935ff.).

Besides the brief reference in Acts 24:24, only Josephus reports concerning Drusilla (*Ant.* xviii.132; xix.354f.; xx.139-44; *B.J.* ii.220). The reference to her in Tacitus *Hist.* v.9 may rest on the confusion of her name with another wife of Antonius Felix, the "husband of the three queens" (Suetonius *Caes.* v.28).

Drusilla was born in A.D. 38 as the youngest daughter of King Herod Agrippa I. She probably took her name from the—already deceased?—sister of Gaius and in any case as a further expression of the loyalty of the Herods toward the imperial house. At the death of her father, who as part of his dynastic plans had already betrothed her as a child to Antiochus Epiphanes, the son of King Antiochus IV Commagene, she was six years old (*Ant.* xix.354). Antiochus Epiphanes, contrary to earlier agreements, refused to convert to Judaism at the time of the marriage ceremony with Drusilla, so in A.D. 53 she was given by her brother, Agrippa II, to be the wife of the King Azizus of neighboring Emesa, who was willing to be circumcised. Soon thereafter the procurator of Judea, Antonius Felix, succeeded in enticing her from Azizus and in marrying her. In this instance he did not at all consider it necessary to convert to Judaism. Both sons of Agrippa, and perhaps Drusilla herself, died in the eruption of Vesuvius in A.D. 79 (*Ant.* xx.139-44).

In Acts 24:24 Luke mentions Drusilla not only for her own sake, but also in order to characterize Felix: he is not only corrupt (24:26), but also lives with a woman who was won through a scandalous—and well-known—affair. Thus it is understandable why, despite his basic interest, Felix reacts with alarm (v. 25) to Paul's preaching concerning "justice and self-control and future judgment"—typical themes of post-apostolic preaching (Haenchen 660f.; cf. *Acts John* 84; *Acts Pet.* 2; *Acts Paul* 5).

E. Plümacher

δύναμαι *dynamai* can, be able

1. Occurrences in the NT — 2. Absolute usage — 3. Willing and doing — 4. John

Lit.: → δύναμις.

1. The vb. is found 210 times in the NT (including Matt 16:3; Rom 16:25). There are 27 occurrences in Matthew, 33 in Mark, 26 in Luke, 37 in John, 21 in Acts, 27 in Paul (of which 15 are in 1 Corinthians), 11 in the deutero-Paulines and Pastorals, 9 in Hebrews, 6 in James, 2 in 1 John, 1 in Jude, and 10 in Revelation. In purely statistical terms there is no great difference among the individual Synoptics. When one compares the various passages by sources, a varied picture emerges. All three Synoptics have δύναμαι only 3 times in common. Mark uses the vb. 23 times alone, 6 times together with Matthew, and once with Luke. Matthew omits δύναμαι 24 times from Mark, but uses it alone 4 times and once in agreement with Luke. The word appears 6 times in Matthew as part of a special Matthean tradition. Q uses it 4 times, besides the 3 times when it is only in Matthew and the 6 times when it appears only in Luke. Luke omits it 29 times from Mark, but inserts it 3 times by himself and once together with Matthew into the Markan text. Besides he has it 8 times in a special tradition. Thus Mark especially prefers δύναμαι. This is indicated very clearly in Mark 3:20-26.

2. As in Classical Greek (Euripides *Or.* 889; Thucydides iv.105.1; Xenophon *An.* iv.5, 11) and in the LXX (Sir 43:30; 1 Macc 6:3; 4 Macc 14:17b), δύναμαι can be used absolutely in the NT (Mark 9:22; Luke 12:16; 1 Cor 3:2; 2 Cor 13:2). In most instances the missing inf. can easily be supplied from the context: Matt 16:3, διακρίνειν; Mark 6:19, ἀποκτείνειν; Mark 10:39, πίνειν; Luke 9:40, ἐκβάλλειν; Luke 16:26, διαβαίνειν; Luke 19:3, ἰδεῖν; Acts 8:31, γινώσκειν; Acts 27:39, ἐξῶσαι; Rom 8:7, ὑποτάσσειν; 1 Cor 10:13, ὑποφέρειν.

3. The dichotomy of willing and *being able* is expressed in the NT in a variety of ways. Herodias wanted to kill John, but was not able to because Herod feared him (Mark 6:19). Although the vb. "want" is not present, it is implied in Mark 2:3f. and Luke 19:3. Jesus *could* not remain hidden, although he wanted to (Mark 7:24). In the realm of the dead, even if one desires to, he *can* not pass from one place to another (Luke 16:26). There is not always an unbridgeable chasm separating willing and being able. The sailors wanted to let the ship run aground, in Acts 27:39, if it *was possible.* In order to be able to do something, one must first want it. Thus Jesus says: "Whenever you will, *you can* do good to them [the poor]" (Mark 14:7). Because the will is the source of ability, the leper turns to Jesus: "If you will, *you can* make me clean" (Mark 1:40). Because willing and being able often lie closely together, ability comes close in meaning to willing. Peter asks if one can refuse baptism to Cornelius and his house after they have received the Spirit (Acts 10:47). When the neighbor says to his friend, "*I cannot* get up and give it [bread] to you," the statement means: I do not want to (Luke 11:7). The refusal of those who are invited is very clear: "*I cannot* come" (Luke 14:20). Of course there is also the possibility that someone can do something, but does not do it (1 Thess 2:7).

4. In John, where the noun δύναμις does not appear, δύναμαι has a particular meaning. John uses it in connection with the miracles of Jesus in 3:2. In the discussion after the healing of the man born blind, the subject is what Jesus is able to do: "How *can* a man who is a sinner do such signs?" (9:16); "If this man were not from God, he *could* do nothing" (9:33; cf. 10:21). Jesus' ability is derived from his relationship with God (5:19, 30; 12:49). In focusing on mankind, John emphasizes that no one can attain to God, because no one *can* believe (5:44); "you *cannot* bear to hear my word" (8:43); "the world *cannot* receive" "the Spirit of truth" (14:17). If it is to be different, there must be a totally new existence (3:3, 5); God must himself seize the initiative (6:44, 65). Anyone who has come to Jesus is secure. "No one *can* snatch them out of my hand" (10:29). Of course one must remain in constant relationship with Jesus: "Apart from me *you can* do nothing" (15:5).

G. Friedrich

δύναμις, εως, ἡ *dynamis* power, might

1. Occurrences in the NT — 2. Meaning — 3. God's δύναμις. — 4. Christ and δύναμις. — 5. The δύναμις of

Christian missionaries — 6. Miraculous deeds — 7. Word and power — 8. Spirit and power — 9. Spiritual powers

Lit.: O. BETZ, *DNTT* II, 601-6. — P. BIARD, *La Puissance de Dieu* (Travaux de l'Institut Catholique de Paris 7, 1960). — F. M. DU BUIT, "La Puissance de Seigneur," *Évangile* 51 (1963) 5-62. — J. CAMBIER, *L'Évangile de Dieu selon l'Épître aux Romains* I: *L'Évangile de la Justice et de la Grâce* (StudNeot 3, 1967) 28-37. — E. FASCHER, *RAC* IV, 415-58. — W. GRUNDMANN, *Der Begriff der Kraft in der neutestamentlichen Gedankenwelt* (BWANT IV, 8, 1932). — *idem, TDNT* II, 284-317. —R. HAUSER, *HTG* II, 101-4. — K. KERTELGE, *Die Wunder Jesu im Markusevangelium* (1970) 120-26, 203-10. — H. KOSMALA, *Hebräer-Essener-Christen* (SPB 1, 1959) 220-24. — *idem, TDOT* II, 367-82, esp. 369-73. — J. L. MCKENZIE, "Signs and Power: The NT Presentation of Miracles," *Chicago Studies* 3 (1964) 5-18. — R. PENNA, "La δύναμις θεοῦ: Riflessioni in Margine a 1 Cor 1, 18-25," *RivB* 15 (1967) 281-94. — B. PRETE, "La formula δύναμις θεοῦ in Rom 1, 16 e sue motivazioni," *RivB* 23 (1975) 299-328. — K. PRÜMM, "Das Dynamische als Grund-Aspekt der Heilsordnung in der Sicht des Apostels Paulus," *Greg* 42 (1961) 643-700. — *idem, Diakonia Pneumatos* II/2 (1962) 243-327. — V. K. ROBBINS, "*Dynameis* und *Sēmeia* in Mark," *BR* 18 (1973) 5-20. — L. A. ROOD, "Le Christ comme δύναμις θεοῦ" *RechBib* 5 (1960) 93-107. — H. SCHLIER, *Principalities and Powers in the NT* (1961). — O. SCHMITZ, "Der Begriff δύναμις bei Paulus," *FS A. Deissmann* (1927) 139-67. — For further bibliography see *TWNT* X, 1059-61.

1. Δύναμις appears 119 times in the NT: 12 times in Matthew, 10 in Mark, 15 in Luke, 10 in Acts, 36 in Paul's letters, of which 15 are in 1 Corinthians and 10 in 2 Corinthians, 13 in the deutero-Paulines and Pastorals, 6 in Hebrews, 2 in 1 Peter, 3 in 2 Peter, and 12 in Revelation. It is noteworthy that all three Synoptics have δύναμις in common only 3 times, in the apocalyptic texts of Mark 13:25f. and 14:62. It is found only once in Q. The usage in Luke is interesting. He inserts the word 4 times in the text of Mark and has it in special material an additional 4 times. When one considers the 10 passages in Acts, one can see clearly that the word was preferred by Luke.

2. Δύναμις has a great range of meaning. This is indicated by the variety of words with which it is associated or with which it is used in parallel statements. On the one hand, there are synonymous expressions for power: ἰσχύς, κράτος, ἐξουσία, and ἐνέργεια; then the designations for miracle: σημεῖον and τέρας; δύναμις is further associated with δόξα, ἀφθαρσία, πνεῦμα, σοφία, λόγος, and χάρις. Finally, it is mentioned in connection with ἀρχή, ἐξουσία, κυριότης, and ἄγγελος. As elsewhere in Greek literature, δύναμις can mean: *meaning* (1 Cor 14:11; Plato *Cra.* 394b; *Herm Vis.* iii.4.3; Justin *Dial.* 125.1) or *ability, capability*: κατὰ δύναμιν (Matt 25:11; 2 Cor 8:3; Sir 29:20; Josephus *Ant.* iii.102); ὑπὲρ δύναμιν (2 Cor 1:8; Sir 8:13); παρὰ δύναμιν (2 Cor 8:3; Josephus *Ant.* xiv.378).

It is the peculiarity of the NT statements that δύναμις can be used almost synonymously with and then also antithetically to the words indicated, leaving a remarkably paradoxical tension. Word and power, like wisdom and power, can be opposites and yet belong together. Weakness and power cannot be joined, but in Paul weakness offers the best possibility for the deployment of power. When the subject is the acts of God and of humans, synonymous and antithetical relationships are not mutually exclusive.

3. A characteristic of God is his δύναμις: Euripides *Alc.* 219; Plato *Cra.* 404e; 406a; Josh 4:24; Deut 3:24; LXX Pss 76:15; 144:12; Jer 16:21; Jdt 9:8; 13:4. In the OT God's power and his name can be used synonymously: Ps 53:3 LXX; Jer 16:21; cf. Acts 4:7; Exod 9:16 with Rom 9:17. Among the rabbis "power" is a circumlocution for God's name. One repeatedly finds among them the phrase "from the mouth of the power" (Billerbeck I, 1007).

In Mark 14:62; Matt 26:64 δύναμις also substitutes for the name of God; cf. *Gos. Pet.* 5:19: "My power, O power, you have forsaken me!" (Mark 15:34; Ps 22:2). In Luke 22:69, because δύναμις was not understood as a predicate for God, τοῦ θεοῦ was added, causing the original meaning to be obscured. Since the creation of the world God's eternal *power* and deity are recognizable through contemplative reflection on the creation (Rom 1:20; Wis 13:5; *Ep. Arist.* 132; Philo *All.* iii.97). God's power and deity are synonymous expressions. The essential demonstration of God's power was in the resurrection of Jesus (2 Cor 13:4) and of Christians (1 Cor 6:14). The degree to which δύναμις is thought of as God's resurrection power is indicated in the answer of Jesus to the question about the resurrection: the Sadducees know neither the Scripture nor the power of God (Mark 12:24 par. Matt 22:29). God's eschatological creative power is capable of saving people from destruction through the gospel (Rom 1:16; 1 Cor 1:18; 2:4f.). On the intimate connection between δύναμις and σωτηρία cf. LXX Pss 20:2; 139:8. Because no one can produce the result from himself, the gift of grace which allows one to be a servant of the gospel results from the effectiveness of the power of God (Eph 3:7). God's power protects Christians in the temptations of life so that they receive salvation (1 Pet 1:5). Paul speaks in 1 Cor 1:18 of the δύναμις θεοῦ τοῖς σῳζομένοις, but not τοῖς ἀπολλυμένοις. But God's power to punish is referred to in Rom 9:17. Because of the parallelism with 9:22, the reference is not to the power which brings about Israel's salvation but to that omnipotence of God that causes the hardening of Pharaoh, by which God demonstrates his wrath.

4. The NT speaks not only of the δύναμις θεοῦ, but also of the power of the Kyrios Jesus Christ: 2 Pet 1:16; 1 Cor 5:4; cf. 2 Cor 12:9; 2 Thess 1:7; 2 Pet 1:3. Already in the OT the expected one is armed with power (Isa 11:2; Mic 5:5; Ps 110:2 LXX).

Luke uses the term to emphasize the special nature of

Jesus. The conception by Mary and thus the birth of Jesus are attributed to the work of the Spirit and the power of the Most High (Luke 1:35). After the temptation Jesus returns in the power of the Spirit to Galilee (4:14). The narratives that follow, which speak of how mighty works in word and wonder go forth from Jesus, who is filled with the Spirit's power, are thus spoken of in anticipation. One says in amazement: he commands the unclean spirits with authority and power (4:36). God has attested him through δυνάμεσι καὶ τέρασι καὶ σημείοις (Acts 2:22). He was crucified in weakness, but he lives from the power of God (2 Cor 13:4). Paul calls the Crucified One the θεοῦ δύναμις (1 Cor 1:24).

It is disputed to what ἐν δυνάμει in Rom 1:4 is connected syntactically. Connection with θεοῦ is impossible; this would produce: Son of the powerful God (F. Prat, *La Théologie de S. Paul* I [1961] 512). Connection with ὁρισθέντος is grammatically possible, but unsuitable to the subject matter (cf. the commentaries of J. T. Beck, A. Schlatter, K. Barth; and Prümm, *Greg* 42 [1961] 644, 648; Hahn, *Titles* 249f.): through a powerful act, i.e., through the resurrection, Jesus is installed as son. Ἐξ ἀναστάσεως νεκρῶν would then be superfluous. Also difficult is connection with κατὰ πνεῦμα ἁγιωσύνης. Δύναμις πνεύματος ἁγίου does appear in the NT; however, it is very improbable that the traditional material taken over by Paul originally read ἐν δυνάμει πνεύματος ἁγίου (E. Linnemann, "Tradition und Interpretation in Röm 1, 3f.," *EvT* 31 [1971] 274).

In the present wording one must interpret ἐν δυνάμει instrumentally and κατὰ πνεῦμα ἁγιωσύνης as an elaboration: Jesus is the Son of God through God's power, namely in accordance with the resurrection of the dead, in the power of the Spirit (U. Wilckens, *Römer* [EKKNT] I [1978] 65). Πνεῦμα can have the meaning of power as the expression for the *praesentia dei.* However, nowhere, indeed not in Rom 8:11, has the Spirit awakened Christ from the dead; God has. Ἐξ ἀναστάσεως νεκρῶν would then be superfluous. Probably Paul inserted the words ἐν δυνάμει into the formula which he received (for another view, cf. Bultmann, *Theology* 49; Hahn, *Titles* 250) and thus transformed the apparent adoptionist christology of Jewish Christianity. As Son of God in power, Christ is the Kyrios.

As the Kyrios, Christ sits at the right hand of God. Consequently all powers and authorities are subject to him (Eph 1:20f.; 1 Pet 3:22). At the parousia he appears with great power and glory (Mark 13:26 par.), accompanied by the angels of his power (2 Thess 1:7). As in Rom 9:17 where God's δύναμις effected the hardening of Pharaoh, so in 1 Cor 5:4 the power of Kyrios Jesus serves the protection of the Church in the turning over of the one who practices incest. The result is that the incestuous person's σάρξ is destroyed, but his πνεῦμα is saved at the Day of the Lord.

5. Just as Jesus is equipped with power from God, so also he gives to his disciples δύναμιν καὶ ἐξουσίαν over all demons and illnesses to exercise healing activity (Luke 9:1; cf. 4:36). He promises them ἐξ ὕψους δύναμιν, that they might be his witnesses (Luke 24:49). This theme is repeated in Acts 1:8: one must be equipped for proclamation with the power of the Holy Spirit. The apostles witness to the resurrected one δυνάμει μεγάλῃ (Acts 4:33). Δύναμις is not used here of miraculous deeds, though, of course, miraculous deeds are included with δύναμις. When the people gaze at the disciples after the healing of the lame man as if they have done the miracle ἰδίᾳ δυνάμει and the Sanhedrin asks ἐν ποίᾳ δυνάμει ἢ ἐν ποίῳ ὀνόματι it occurred, Peter indicates that the resurrected Christ is the source of the power (Acts 4:7-10; cf. 3:12-15). Indeed, Paul ventures to do nothing from himself (Rom 15:19). Everything is based on God's working, which is powerfully active in the apostle (Col 1:29).

The power of Christ is most fully developed—this is the paradox of Christian existence—in the weakness of the earthly form. Weakness is neither a hindrance nor a precondition for the work of God. Wherever weakness stands as a human characteristic, the power of Christ can be fully demonstrated (2 Cor 12:9). In the argument with the opponents who demand a powerful form of Christian existence, Paul emphasizes that God has placed the exalted treasure of the gospel in the vessel of the weak apostle, so that it is apparent to all that the power of the gospel comes from God and not humans (4:7). From the relationship with the Christ who was crucified in weakness but raised by the power of God, Paul communicates to the Corinthians in 13:4, despite his weakness, the life from the power of God which is future but already present.

6. Δύναμις belongs to the terminology of miracle. Thus both the *miraculous powers* in Mark 5:30 par. Luke 8:46; Mark 6:14 par. Matt 14:2; 1 Cor 12:10, 28f. which one does, and the *miraculous events* which take place (γίνεσθαι) in Mark 6:2; Matt 10:20, 23; Luke 10:13 par.; Acts 8:13 or are done (ποιεῖν) in Mark 6:5 par.; 9:39; Matt 7:22; Acts 4:7; 19:11 can be designated with this word. Miracles are done by Jesus in Mark 6:2 par.; Matt 11:20-23 par., etc.; Stephen in Acts 6:8; Philip in Acts 8:13; Paul in Acts 19:11; 2 Cor 12:12. However, others do them in the name of Jesus (Matt 7:22; Mark 9:33). Even the Antichrist does them (2 Thess 2:9). Mark distinguishes between σημεῖον and δύναμις. In the Synoptics the miracles of Jesus are never called σημεῖα (Mark 8:11f.; cf. Mark 4:35–5:43 and 13:22). It is said of Stephen: πλήρης χάριτος καὶ δυνάμεως ἐποίει τέρατα καὶ σημεῖα μεγάλα (Acts 6:8); similarly of Philip in 8:13 and of Paul in 2 Cor 12:12. When in 1 Cor 12:10 ἐνεργήματα δυνάμεων are added to healings, δύναμις involves the exorcism of demons, for possession was not regarded as an illness. Δύναμις can also be magical power (Acts 8:10). Some of the miraculous stories in the NT have a strong point of contact with magic: Mark 5:30 par. Luke 8:46; cf. Luke 6:19; Mark 3:10; 6:56; Acts 19:10-12; 5:15f. The NT reports on these without offering a critical point of view. On the other hand, it distances itself again from magical views. According to Acts 19:11 the wonders are done by God. In Acts 3:12

Peter defends himself against a magical misunderstanding of the healing art. The miracles of Jesus are done by God himself (Luke 5:17), in order to authenticate him (Acts 2:22). Because God is always the active one, rather than a power streaming forth from the healer's body to do the miracle, one does not praise Jesus the miracle worker but rather God (Luke 19:34). The miracles of Jesus point beyond the concrete event to the salvation event, so that they lead people to repentance (Matt 11:20-23 par. Luke 10:13). They are the battle against demonic powers (Mark 3:27), the entry of the sovereignty of God into this world (Luke 11:20; cf. Heb 6:5).

7. Paul often connects δύναμις and λόγος with each other. This occurs in such a way that he places the two in opposition at 1 Cor 2:4f.; 4:19f. In 1 Thess 1:5 the two are not in opposition, but complement each other, as Paul speaks of word and power. As the word of proclamation is not human speech but is instead the word of God, the word of proclamation is δύναμις. As the dead can be raised, so can the lost be saved (Rom 1:16; 1 Cor 1:18). When in 2 Cor 6:7 word and δύναμις stand in fixed parallelism to each other, Paul wants to say here that his message is confirmed through the δύναμις. Here miraculous deed and not salvific power is intended.

8. Spirit and power are connected with each other even more frequently than word and power (Isa 11:2; 1 Cor 2:4; 1 Thess 1:5). In parallel statements the two words are synonymous (cf. Luke 1:17, 35; Acts 6:5, 8; 10:38). Where the Spirit is, God is at work, and something occurs. In Rom 15:19 the **δύναμις** πνεύματος (cf. Josephus *Ant.* xiii.408; *Herm. Man.* xi.2.5) are distinguished from the δύναμις σημείων καὶ τεράτων; similarly πνεῦμα and δύναμις in Gal 3:5. The deeds of power are effects of the Spirit (1 Cor 12:10ff.). The NT speaks not only of the δύναμις πνεύματος (Rom 5:13, 19; cf. Luke 4:14), but also of the πνεῦμα τῆς δυνάμεως (2 Tim 1:7). Just as the δύναμις τοῦ ἁγίου πνεύματος in Acts 1:8 gives the *power* to overcome fear, so the πνεῦμα τῆς δυνάμεως in 2 Tim 1:7 dispels fear and makes one ready to take suffering upon himself for the sake of the gospel (1 Tim 1:8). Through the Spirit of God the faithful are strengthened with the power of God in the inward person (Eph 3:16).

9. According to Mark 13:25 par. the stars of heaven will fall and αἱ δυνάμεις τῶν οὐρανῶν will be shaken. Rom 8:38 mentions δυνάμεις, 1 Cor 15:24 speaks of ἐξουσίαν καὶ δύναμιν, Eph 1:21 of ἀρχή, ἐξουσία, δύναμις, and κυριότης. In the LXX "Yahweh Sabaoth" becomes κύριος τῶν δυνάμεων in 2 Kgdms 6:2, 18; cf. Ps 102:21 LXX. According to Ps 32:6 LXX heaven and πᾶσα ἡ δύναμις were created by God. Israel falls from God and turns to the pagan astral cult in 2 Kgs 17:16; 21:3, 5; 23:4f. At the judgment of God πᾶσαι αἱ δυνάμεις τῶν οὐρανῶν wither (Isa 34:4 v.l.). Δύναμεις τοῦ οὐρανοῦ and stars are thrown to the earth (Dan 8:10 LXX). Mark 13:25 is to be understood against this background. Cosmic powers are also angelic powers. In Ps 102:21 LXX πᾶσαι αἱ δυνάμεις αὐτοῦ are summoned to offer praise. These heavenly hosts are the angels in Ps 148:2 (cf. *Adam and Eve* 28; Billerbeck III, 581ff.). Through the resurrection and exaltation of Jesus the δυνάμεις have lost their power (1 Pet 3:22; cf. Eph 1:18ff.). The powers can have no power over Christians because the love of God in Jesus Christ is stronger than the powers which disturb the relationship to God (Rom 8:38f.). The public loss of power occurs at the parousia (1 Cor 15:24).

G. Friedrich

δυναμόω *dynamoō* strengthen*

In the NT only pass.: Col 1:11: ἐν πάσῃ δυνάμει δυναμούμενοι, "*strengthened* with all power"; Heb 11:34: ἐδυναμώθησαν (v.l. ἐνεδυναμώθησαν P Koine *pl*) ἀπὸ ἀσθενείας, "where they were weak, *they were strengthened*" (RSV "*won strength* out of weakness"; cf. also Eph 6:10 v.l.

δυνάστης, ου, ὁ *dynastēs* ruler, lord*

Used of God in 1 Tim 6:15: ὁ μακάριος καὶ μόνος δυνάστης, with ὁ βασιλεὺς τῶν βασιλευόντων καὶ κύριος τῶν κυριευόντων; of earthly rulers in Luke 1:52: καθεῖλεν δυνάστας ἀπὸ θρόνων, "he has put down the *mighty* from their thrones" (cf. Job 12:19); of the *powerful court official* of Candace in Acts 8:27.

δυνατέω *dynateō* be strong, be powerful*

Only in Paul, always in reference to God or Christ: 2 Cor 13:3: δυνατεῖ ἐν ὑμῖν, "[Christ] *is powerful* in you"; in the sense of *be able, be capable for something* (with complementary inf.): Rom 14:4; 2 Cor 9:8.

δυνατός, 3 *dynatos* strong, powerful, able, possible*

1. Occurrences and meanings — 2. Usage — 3. Δυνατός as a theological, christological, and apostolic term in the NT

Lit.: R. M. Grant, *Miracle and Natural Law in Graeco-Roman and Early Christian Thought* (1952) 127-34. — W. Grundmann, *TDNT* II, 284-317. — K. Prümm, *Diakonia Pneumatos* II/2 (1962) 243-340. — W. C. van Unnik, " 'Alles ist dir möglich' (Mark 14:36)," FS Stählin, 27-36.

1. The adj. δυνατός occurs 32 times in the NT, of which 12 are in the (Synoptic) Gospels and 10 are in Paul. It has the meanings *strong, powerful, able.* The neut. δυνατόν (ἐστιν) indicates that something is *possible* (e.g., the "restricting" formula εἰ δυνατόν in Mark 13:22; 14:35; Matt

24:24; 26:39; Acts 20:16; Rom 12:18; Gal 4:15). In a few passages δυνατός has a special meaning: in Acts 25:5 pl. οἱ δυνατοί designates (a political t.t.: so E. Haenchen, *The Acts of the Apostles* [1971] 665, n. 7) those who have "authority" (cf. Josephus *B.J.* ii.242f.), and in Rom 15:1 those who are "strong" in faith. In Acts 18:24 δυνατός refers concretely to one who is *well-versed* or *expert* (in the Scriptures).

2. (Logical) subjects of δυνατός are normally persons, e.g., God: Rom 11:23; Heb 11:19; Jesus: Luke 24:19; 2 Tim 1:12; Moses: Acts 7:22; Apollos: Acts 18:24; the episkopos: Titus 1:9; the "perfect man": Jas 3:2, etc. An exception is found in 2 Cor 10:4, where the adj. refers to an impersonal subj. (τὰ ὅπλα). With δυνατόν (ἐστιν) the person for whom something is possible is referred to with (παρά and) the dat. (e.g., Mark 10:27 par.: πάντα δυνατὰ παρὰ τῷ θεῷ; cf. Mark 9:23; 14:36; Acts 20:16). That for which or in which someone is *capable* or *powerful* (or that which is *possible* for someone) is expressed with an inf. construction (Acts 2:24; 11:17; Rom 11:23; 2 Tim 1:12; Heb 11:19; Titus 1:9; Jas 3:2, etc.), with ἐν with the dat. (Luke 24:19; Acts 7:22; 18:24), or with πρός with the acc. (2 Cor 10:4). Subst. τὸ δυνατόν, *the power,* is found only in Rom 9:22 (in a statement about God).

Opposites to δυνατός within the same context are: ἀσθενεῖν (2 Cor 12:10; 13:9), σαρκικός (2 Cor 10:4; cf. 1 Cor 1:26), and ἀδύνατος (Mark 10:27 par., where it refers to the antithesis mankind–God; Rom 15:1, where the groups which are strong in faith are contrasted with those who are weak in faith).

3. In the Synoptics δυνατός appears almost always (except in Luke 14:31) in theological or christological statements:

In the Lukan Magnificat (Luke 1:49) God is referred to with the predicate ὁ δυνατός *(the mighty one),* which is known from the LXX (e.g., Pss 44:4, 6; 119:4; Zeph 3:17). He manifests his "power" immediately in his "great deed" to Mary ("for he who is mighty has done great things for me"). Similarly Mark 10:27 (par. Matt 19:26 and Luke 18:27) is based on the OT conviction (e.g., Gen 18:14; Job 10:13; Zech 8:6 LXX) that with God all things (πάντα) are possible. The disciples are concerned about Jesus' paradoxical figure of speech, "it is easier for a camel to go through the eye of a needle than for a rich man to enter the kingdom of God" (Mark 10:25), and say to each other: "Then who can be saved?" (v. 26). In his answer Jesus emphasizes that "with men this is impossible" but not with God, for "all things are *possible* with God" (v. 27). But the fact that the individual gains a portion in God's omnipotence is expressed in Mark 9:23. Jesus says to the father who requests the healing of his son: "All things are *possible* to him who believes." What is meant is probably: Jesus can help only the one who brings to him unconditional trust in his miraculous power and expresses it with a request. Just as everything is possible for Jesus (and his faith), so it is with the one who turns to him in faith and shares Jesus' faith in the omnipotence of God. Jesus himself expresses this faith in the prayer in Gethsemane. According to Mark 14:35 he requests, if it is *possible,* that the hour might pass from him. The prayer rendered literally in 14:36 begins correspondingly with the confession of the omnipotence of God: "Abba, Father, all things are *possible* to thee." That is, "Jesus praises . . . God's omnipotent will, which, according to his faith, is the will of the 'loving Father' " (R. Pesch, *Markusevangelium* [HTKNT] II, 391).

Δυνατός is used of Jesus in Luke 24:19. The disciples on the Emmaus Road testify of him: he "was a prophet, *mighty* in deed and word before God and all the people." The messianic status of Jesus is here clearly seen in "a line leading from prophetic power" (Grundmann 299f.; the idea of the Messiah already present in the OT and Jewish view reflected in the almost identical statement about Moses in Acts 7:22). Of course, for Luke himself "Christ is more than a Prophet endowed with power. He is unique in His existence. His existence is particularly determined by the power of God" (*ibid.,* 300).

Paul also speaks of the power of God, as it is manifested in the fulfillment of his promises to Abraham (Rom 4:21) or relative to the final destiny of the chosen people (cf. Rom 11:23: "if they do not persist in their unbelief, [they] will be grafted in [the olive tree], for God *has the power* to graft them in again").

Paul also uses δυνατός in statements about his apostleship. According to his view, in the life of Jesus (2 Cor 13:4) and in his own life the fundamental principle that the (divine) power (δύναμις) is perfected in (human) weakness (ἀσθένεια; 2 Cor 12:9; cf. here the catchword → ἀσθενής) is brought to bear. Thus he can at the beginning of his letter against the Corinthian opponents (2 Cor 10–13) indicate that the weapons of his warfare are not fleshly, but rather *"have* divine *power"* (10:4). Thus he can conclude the essential part of this letter, the so-called "fool's speech" (11:1–12:10), in which he wants to boast only "of the things that show (his) weakness" (11:30; 12:5) with the paradoxical confession: "For when I am weak, then I am *strong*" (12:10). He makes clear in 13:9 that his "weakness" (which in reality is the "place of revelation" of the divine δύναμις) does not portray a service to the Church: "We are glad when we are weak and you are *strong.*" Being "strong" refers, as the context indicates, to strength in doing good (cf. τὸ καλὸν ποιῆτε, v. 7).

In the remaining books of the NT one finds the theological, christological, and apostolic aspects of δυνατός. In Heb 11:19, e.g., there is the confession of God's power, which is manifest in the resurrection from the dead. In 2 Tim 1:12 it is said of Christ that he is *able* to guard what has been entrusted (the παραθήκη) until that day. In Titus 1:9 (in a catalog of duties) there is a reference to the "power" of the episkopos (standing in succession to the apostle); he must "be *able* to give instruction in sound doctrine and also to confute those who contradict it." The episcopal "power" is to be understood as essentially that of a teaching and disciplinary office.

J. Zmijewski

δύνω, δύω *dynō, dyō* go down, set (of the sun)*

Intrans., of the setting of the sun: Mark 1:32: ὅτε ἔδυ ὁ ἥλιος (ἔδυσεν B D 28 *pc*); par. Luke 4:40: δύνοντος δὲ τοῦ ἡλίου (δύναντος U *al, δυσαντος* D); cf. BDF §§75; 101 s.v.

δύο *dyo* two

1. Occurrences in the NT — 2. Meaning — 3. Theological usage

Lit.: J. Blinzler, *Der Prozeß Jesu* ([4]1969) 145-48. — C. J. Hemer, *DNTT* II, 686.— J. Jeremias, "Paarweise Sendung im NT," *idem, Abba* (1966) 132-39. — W. Pesch, *Matthäus der Seelsorger* (SBS 2, 1966) (on Matt 18). — H. Weinrich, *Sprache in Texten* (1976) 199-218.

1. Δύο appears in the NT a total of 132 times, of which 40 occurrences are in Matthew, 18 in Mark, 28 in Luke, 13 in John, 13 in Acts, 12 in the Letters, and 8 in Revelation. The emphasis lies in the narrative books (Synoptics, Acts, John, Revelation), esp. the Synoptics (86 times). This distribution indicates that δύο has a greater importance for the formation of narratives than for epistolary communication.

2. In all occurrences δύο retains its numerical value. Yet it is interesting for narratives because it stands at an elementary position in the code of numbers. The opposites of *two* are "one" and "three." "One" is singular, while all of the following numbers are plural. The grammatical dual, which of course is present in koine Greek only as a residual element, expresses most clearly the mediating function of *two* between unity and multiplicity. Thus one may observe a reciprocal movement from one to two and from two to one, and correspondingly from two to three and from three to two.

The movement from "one" to *two* has the goal of doubling. The singular "one" must be preserved but at the same time be opened to increase. Thus there is the pure numerical doubling, which proceeds from the undivided basic unit, but at the same time exhibits the possibility of added enrichment: to multiply *two* fish (Mark 6:38, 41 par.), donate *two* lepta (Mark 12:42 par.), etc. Doubling through a violent splitting occurs at the tearing of the curtain of the temple (Mark 15:38 par.).

Doubling attains an intersubjective significance as a proof of witness. The saying of one qualified witness is not sufficient, for at least *two* are required (Deut 19:15; Matt 18:16; 26:60; John 8:17; 2 Cor 13:1; 1 Tim 5:19; Heb 10:28). Thus Matthew lays great weight on the fact that at least *two* men were healed, who are thus qualified to witness to the miracle (Matt 8:28; 9:27; 20:30). When Jesus or other authorities have orders to deliver, they send *two* messengers for the sake of credibility (Mark 11:1 par., etc.). The texts go beyond the significance of witnessing where the *two* witnesses represent a specific form of community. *Two* form the basic cell of a community which one alone cannot create, but which the doubling of the one suffices for. Thus Jesus sends his disciples out *two by two* in order that they may give a credible witness to his message and, in the duality, present the new community (Mark 6:7; Luke 10:1).

The call of pairs of brothers to be disciples (Matt 4:18-22) proceeds from the numerical doubling (from one family more than one is selected), then becomes a firsthand proof (two members of a family represent the mission of Jesus in the society), and finally becomes the founding act of a new basic cell (the pairs of brothers become fishers of men). The request by the sons of Zebedee turns this point of view around (Mark 10:35 v.l.; cf. Matt 20:21). Further basic cells are mentioned in Matt 18:19, 20; 26:37; Luke 9:30, etc.

The movement from two to one takes place in some instances as division, in other instances as fusion. Division reduces the doubling to simplicity: Mark 6:9 par., etc. Where the doubling has led to a dualistic contrast, separation takes place between the good and the bad (Mark 9:43ff. par., etc.). Fusion occurs in marriage (Mark 10:8 par.; 1 Cor 6:16; Eph 5:31), through coming to faith in Christ (Eph 2:15), and through service to Christ (Phil 1:23).

The movement from two to three is above all of purely numerical value (John 2:6) and then becomes a negative expression of division (Luke 12:52) and a positive expression of the openness and the growth of the power of the witness (Matt 18:16; see above) and of the basic cell (Matt 18:20).

3. The theological result can only be suggested. Jesus prefers two as the number of the call and the mission in order, on the one hand, to trace the call and the commission to each individual; on the other hand, he wishes to avoid the individualization of the processes. Discipleship to Jesus occurs first when at least *two* are gathered in his name (Matt 18:20), formulate common prayers, and avail themselves of and enter into common tasks. Otherwise, duality, as the smallest plural, guards against having to standardize and schematize calling, sending, and community with Jesus as a mass movement. Community with Jesus lives from the common actions between *two,* which are open to being isolated (one) or being enlarged (three).

D. Dormeyer

δυσβάστακτος, 2 *dysbastaktos* hard to bear*

Matt 23:4; Luke 11:46, in the construction φορτία . . . δυσβάστακτα, "burdens *hard to bear*" (omitted in Matt 23:4 ℵ *pc* it sy Irenaeus).

δυσεντέριον, ου, τό *dysenterion* diarrhea, dysentery*

Acts 28:8: πυρετοῖς καὶ δυσεντερίῳ συνεχόμενον, "sick with fever and *dysentery*" (v.l. also sg. fem. or pl. masc. or fem.).

δυσερμήνευτος, 2 *dysermēneutos* hard to explain → ἑρμηνεύω.

δύσις, εως, ἡ *dysis* setting (of the sun); (the) west.

Only in the short Markan ending: ἀπὸ ἀνατολῆς καὶ ἄχρι δύσεως, "from the rising to the *setting* of the sun," i.e., from east to *west.*

δύσκολος, 2 *dyskolos* hard, difficult*

Mark 10:24: πῶς δύσκολόν ἐστιν, "how *hard* it is" (to enter into the kingdom of God).

δυσκόλως *dyskolōs* hardly, with difficulty*

Like the adj., only in sayings about entering the kingdom of God: those with possessions *scarcely* have a part: Mark 10:23 (πῶς δυσκόλως . . . εἰσελεύσονται) par. Matt 19:23 (δυσκόλως εἰσελεύσεται) par. Luke 18:24 (πῶς δυσκόλως . . . εἰσπορεύονται).

δυσμή, ῆς, ἡ *dysmē* setting (of the sun); (the) west*

Matt 8:11 par. Luke 13:29; Matt 24:27; Rev 21:13: in the constructions ἀπὸ δυσμῶν or ἕως δυσμῶν (Matt 24:27) in distinction to ἀπὸ ἀνατολῶν or ἀπὸ ἀνατολῆς (Rev 21:13) to describe extreme geographic contrasts; Luke 12:54: ἐπὶ δυσμῶν, *in the west.*

δυσνόητος, 2 *dysnoētos* hard to understand*

2 Pet 3:16, in reference to the letters of Paul: ἐν αἷς ἐστιν δυσνόητά τινα, "there are some things in them *hard to understand.*"

δυσφημέω *dysphēmeō* slander (vb.), revile*

1 Cor 4:13: δυσφημούμενοι παρακαλοῦμεν, "when *slandered,* we try to conciliate," with λοιδορούμενοι and διωκόμενοι.

δυσφημία, ας, ἡ *dysphēmia* slander, abuse (noun)*

2 Cor 6:8: διὰ δυσφημίας καὶ εὐφημίας, "in *abuse* and commendation" (RSV "ill repute and good repute"), with διὰ δόξης καὶ ἀτιμίας.

δύω *dyō* go down, set (of the sun) → δύνω.

δώδεκα *dōdeka* twelve

1. Δώδεκα as numerical indicator — 2. The twelve tribes — 3. The number twelve in the New Jerusalem — 4. a) "The Twelve" — b) The origin of the circle of the Twelve — c) The commission of the circle of Twelve — d) Development in the early Church — 5. A dependent reference

Lit.: E. Best, "Mark's Use of the Twelve," *ZNW* 69 (1978) 11-35. — Braun, *Qumran* I, 43f.; II, 327f. — O. Cullmann, "Der zwölfte Apostel," *idem, Vorträge und Aufsätze, 1925-1962* (1966) 214-22. — S. Freyne, *The Twelve: Disciples and Apostles* (1968). — H. Gollinger, *Das "große Zeichen" von Apokalypse 12* (SBM 2, 1971), esp. 77-89. — F. Hahn, *Mission in the NT* (1965). — M. Hengel, "The Origins of the Christian Mission," *idem, Between Jesus and Paul* (1983) 48-64, 166-79. — H. Kasting, *Die Anfänge der urchristlichen Mission* (BEvT 55, 1969). — G. Klein, *Die zwölf Apostel* (FRLANT 77, 1961). — R. P. Meye, *Jesus and the Twelve* (1968). — K. H. Rengstorf, *TDNT* II, 321-28. — B. Rigaux, "Die Zwölf in Geschichte und Kerygma," Ristow/Matthiae 468-86. — M. Rissi, *The Future of the World* (1972) 71-74. — J. Roloff, *Apostolat, Verkündigung, Kirche* (1965) esp. 138-68. — G. Schmahl, *Die Zwölf im Markusevangelium* (TTS 30, 1974). — K. Stock, *Boten aus dem Mit-Ihm-Sein* (AnBib 70, 1975). — W. Trilling, "Zur Entstehung des Zwölferkreises: Eine geschichtskritische Überlegung," FS Schürmann, 201-22. — J. Wagenmann, *Die Stellung des Apostels Paulus neben den Zwölf in den ersten zwei Jahrhunderten* (BZNW 3, 1926). — For further bibliography see *TWNT* X, 1061f.

Δώδεκα appears 75 times in the NT, with remarkable frequency in the Gospels (46 occurrences) and in Revelation (23). The word appears 4 times in Acts, and once each in 1 Corinthians and James.

1. Δώδεκα occurs in the figure of speech in John 11:9 by which the work of Jesus is characterized as temporally limited. The *twelve* days of Acts 24:11 are calculated either from 21:27 and 24:1 or by counting the days of Paul in Jerusalem. The indication of the age of Jesus in Luke 2:42 is certainly intended to be precise: Jesus is not yet fully responsible before the law (cf., however, also the second narrative of *Setme Chamoïs* [ADAW.PH, 1918/17, 68]; Josephus *Ant.* v.348; Ps.-Ign. *Magn.* 3.2.4). In Mark 5:42 the indication of the age of the daughter of Jairus is probably meant to indicate a child, but one who is at the threshold of becoming an adult; Luke 8:42, which displaces the information (mis)understands it as an approximate number.

Δώδεκα in Mark 5:25 par. may be used in this way; a relationship of the last two references to a fixed stage of the tradition is not improbable. In Acts 19:7 the preceding ὡσεί (common in Acts) indicates that δώδεκα is to be understood as an approximate number; whether any historical reminiscence stands behind it cannot be determined (a dependence on the number twelve associated with Jesus' disciples is scarcely probable).

2. The number twelve takes on decisive significance in biblical usage in that the people of Israel are traced back genealogically to the twelve sons of Jacob, resulting in the division of the people into twelve tribes (Acts 26:7). The background for this is not to be discussed here. In the NT this reality has been altered by history, inasmuch as nine tribes have disappeared through the fall of the northern kingdom and the tribe of Levi has partially disappeared (*T. Jos.* 19:1f.; 4 Ezra 13:40; *2 Bar.* 78:1). According to Jewish apocalyptic expectation these tribes will be brought back in the time of salvation (Billerbeck IV, 902-9; cf. Jer 30f.).

The *twelve* sons of Jacob mentioned in the historical sketch in Acts 7:8 are called πατριάρχαι, "patriarchs." Perhaps the crown of *twelve* stars on the head of the queen of heaven (Rev 12:1) symbolizes the twelve tribes of the people of God (cf. *T. Naph.* 5:4; Gen 37:9). If this uncertain interpretation is correct, already here the transfer of the conception of the people of the twelve tribes as the people of salvation to the Christian Church would be implied (cf., however, A. Vögtle, "Mythos und Botschaft in Apokalypse 12," FS Kuhn, 395-415). It is directly attested in Jas 1:1, where the recipients are called "the *twelve* tribes in the Dispersion," i.e., the Christians who are scattered in the world, the true Israel (cf. Gal 6:16; *Herm. Sim.* ix.17.1). This identification also stands behind the naming of those who are sealed in Rev 7:4-8, the 144,000, with 12,000 from every tribe of Israel. The number twelve is made explicit here, of course, only in the reference to the 12,000, but it is there obviously derived from the number of the twelve tribes. The countless number of those who are sealed, those who are members of the Church of Christ (cf. 14:1), is the number twelve multiplied one thousandfold.

3. From this perspective, it is evident that the number twelve has taken on a special significance for the New Jerusalem of Revelation 21, so that the number has become to a certain extent independent. Mentioned first (v. 12), in dependence on Ezek 48:30-35, are the *twelve* gates, which are inscribed with the names of the *twelve* tribes of the sons of Israel, and on which *twelve* angels keep watch (cf. Isa 62:6). According to Rev 21:21 these *twelve* gates are *twelve* pearls (cf. also on vv. 19f.: Isa 54:11f.; *b. B. Bat.* 75a [Billerbeck III, 851]). The one people of God enters through the gates to the place of salvation. The wall establishes the city built on *twelve* foundations, which bear the name of the *twelve* apostles of the lamb (Rev 21:14). The conception corresponds to Eph 2:20 (cf. also Heb 11:10; 4 Ezra 10:27); it is filled with the idea of the twelve apostles as the foundational witness to Christ (→ 4). In addition the eschatological community of salvation is built on the witness of the apostles of Christ Jesus.

The length, breadth, and height of the holy Jerusalem is uniformly measured by twelve multiplied one thousandfold (Rev 21:16; cf. the measurement of the wall, v. 17: $144 = 12 \times 12$). If a mythical tradition stands behind this (see E. Lohmeyer, *Offenbarung* [HNT, [2]1953] ad loc.), Revelation has adopted it because of the number twelve, which already determined the access and the foundation of the city of God.

The mythical-apocalyptic tradition behind Rev 22:2 is more clearly apparent. Ezek 47:12 is the basis, amplified by the concept of the tree of life (Gen 2:9). From the statement by Ezekiel (cf. also the rabbinic passages in Billerbeck III, 856) that the trees at the river of the temple are to bear fruit each month, which is taken up in Rev 21:2c, δώδεκα is computed *twelvefold.* The special significance of δώδεκα here and the missing point of reference ("annually") suggests that the "calculation" of the author of Revelation is intended to bring the number twelve explicitly into the text.

4. a) Δώδεκα has its greatest significance in the NT in reference to a fixed group of disciples, whose formation the Gospels attributed to Jesus and who seem to be known in the oldest tradition simply by the designation οἱ δώδεκα. In any case, in the tradition cited by Paul (1 Cor 15:5), Acts (6:2), Mark (and Luke), and John οἱ δώδεκα is used absolutely. Matthew alone qualifies it with ἀπόστολοι (Matt 10:2; cf. Rev 21:14) and more frequently with μαθηταί (Matt 10:1; 11:1; 20:17 v.l.; 26:20 v.l.). 1 Cor 15:5, where the term is part of a traditional formulation cited by Paul, indicates not only its antiquity, but also the "ecumenical" circulation of this designation, which must have been intelligible to a wide audience. Both are to be seen in Acts 6:2, where δώδεκα probably goes back to a written tradition (H. Conzelmann, *Acts* [Hermeneia, 1987] 45; M. Hengel, *Between Jesus and Paul* [1983] 3f.). Thus for early tradition δώδεκα was apparently the fixed name of an institution, which was in fact constituted by twelve specific people but functioned together as a unit. Thus no decisive argument can be made from 1 Cor 15:5 against the pre-Easter existence of this group.

The formula refers to the group, but not primarily to the number of its members. Indeed, the tradition of the completion of the circle of twelve (Acts 1:[15], 21-26) indicates the precedence of the institution over the number in the simultaneous necessity of filling this number. This tradition is plausible, but a later repetition (on the occasion of Acts 12:2) is not reported.

b) The four lists of "the Twelve" in the NT (Mark 3:16-19; Matt 10:2-4; Luke 6:14-16; Acts 1:13 [here of course only eleven]) permit conclusions for rather than against the pre-Easter origin of the circle of "the Twelve." A pre-Easter origin may be supported by the uncertainty with regard to the pertinent names (the varying positions of Andrew, Thomas, and Simon the Cananaean, the reversal of James and John in Acts, and the change between Thaddeus [Lebbaeus] and Judas the son of James; cf. here Cullmann) and even more the complete insignificance of the majority of the names and of "the Twelve" after Easter. Indeed, 1 Cor 15:5 indicates the constitutive significance of "the Twelve" in the post-Easter period, but only Acts 6:2, written a few (?) years later, indicates their function. However, Paul seems not to have conceded any function to them in his narrative (cf. Gal 1:18). Finally, the membership of the traitor in "the Twelve" argues for a pre-Easter origin; his membership is emphasized by εἷς (ἐκ) τῶν δώδεκα (Mark 14:10 par.; [14:20]; 14:43 par.; John 6:71; cf. 12:4; transferred to Thomas in John 20:24). Like that phrase, δώδεκα was part of the tradition which came to Mark (so already Rigaux 472-75; Best); this is the case both for the calling (Mark 3:13-19) and for the mission tradition (6:7-13). Apparently the Q tradition also had δώδεκα in connection with such a tradition (cf. H. Schürmann, *Lukasevangelium* [HTKNT, 1969] I, 318f.). The traditional material in Matt 19:28 par. Luke 22:28-30 may also belong to this tradition. The core of the tradition and of the calling-mission narrative is to be traced back to Jesus. It focuses on "the Twelve," even if the Lukan version does not directly indicate it (though it is probably to be inferred from its context).

c) Both the tradition of "the Twelve" and the calling-mission narrative are entirely joined together as eschatological-prophetic signs. With the number determined by the division of the people into twelve tribes (so perhaps also 1QS 8:1; see Braun), "the Twelve" represent proleptically the renewed people of God, whose members are measured by its standard. They are sent by Jesus and proclaim with word and deed the imminent coming of the time of salvation. They prepare the land for the time of salvation by their conduct and they summon it to repentance. They are thus at the same time important witnesses for the character and content of the works of Jesus.

d) In the post-Easter Church they soon lost their significance, as did individual members of the group. Indeed, Mark no longer understands their essential function. He identifies them with the apostles (Mark 6:30) and knows no functional difference between them and the μαθηταί (Best 32-35). This development is continued—in different ways—in the other Gospels; Matthew identifies them even more with the μαθηταί, and Luke entirely with the ἀπόστολοι (see below). John preserves them only with his tradition. It is illuminating also that in the Gospels explicit reference to "the Twelve" is on the decline (only in Matt 11:1; Luke 8:1; 9:12 beyond Mark; Matt 11:1; Luke 8:1 may belong to the Q tradition of the commission; cf. Schürmann I, 447f.; on Luke 9:12 cf. Mark 6:43 par. Luke 9:17). A "historicizing" understanding oriented to the number is indicated in the reference to "the Eleven" (→ ἕνδεκα). The tradition soon had no understanding of the institution οἱ δώδεκα. However, as it preserved the knowledge of the existence of the institution, it filled it with new content, namely that of the apostolate. Thus in the functional realm a new continuity is preserved (cf. also Roloff 166-68). In Luke this conception, which is determinative in the later period, appears in a more developed form; however, it did not originate with him (see above; [Mark 6:(7), 30; Matt 10:2; Rev 21:14]).

5. The references to δώδεκα in Mark 6:43 par. (derived from Mark 8:19) and Matt 26:53 may be dependent on the number of "the Twelve." In both instances the number is insignificant, though it does suggest a correspondence to the number of the "Twelve."

T. Holtz

δωδέκατος, 3 *dōdekatos* twelfth*

Rev 21:20: the *twelfth* cornerstone of the wall of the heavenly Jerusalem, an → ἀμέθυστος.

δωδεκάφυλον, ου, τό *dōdekaphylon* people of twelve tribes*

Acts 26:7: τὸ δωδεκάφυλον ἡμῶν: Paul includes himself before Agrippa II in the hope of Israel for the fulfillment of the promises to the fathers.

δῶμα, ατος, τό *dōma* housetop, roof*

The word appears in the NT in common phrases which presuppose the oriental flat roof as a living space in the open air: Mark 13:15 par. Matt 24:17 and Luke 17:31: ὁ ἐπὶ τοῦ δώματος, the one "who is on the *housetop*" should not enter the house; Matt 10:27 par. Luke 12:3: κηρύσσω ἐπὶ τῶν δωμάτων, "proclaim upon the *housetops*" (what has been whispered in the ear); Luke 5:19; Acts 10:9: ἀναβαίνω ἐπὶ τὸ δῶμα, (climb) "up on the *roof*." R. Knierem, *BHH* I, 311; *BL* 303.

δωρεά, ᾶς, ἡ *dōrea* gift*
δωρεάν *dōrean* (acc. as adv.) without payment, as a gift; undeserved; in vain*

1. Occurrences and meanings in the NT — 2. Δωρεά — 3. Δωρεάν

Lit.: É. Benveniste, *Le vocabulaire des institutions indo-européennes* I (1969) 65-79. — F. Büchsel, *TDNT* II, 166f. — D. N. Freedman, J. R. Lundbom, and H.-J. Fabry, *TDOT* V,

22-36. — MOULTON/MILLIGAN s.v. — H. J. STOEBE, *THAT* I, 587-97. — A. STUIBER, *RAC* X, 685-703. — H. VORLÄNDER, *DNTT* II, 40-43.

1. The noun δωρεά appears 11 times in the NT, while the acc. form δωρεάν used as an adv. occurs 9 times. Acts has the greatest number of occurrences of δωρεά with 4, while Romans has 2, Ephesians 2, and John, 2 Corinthians, and Hebrews 1 each. Δωρεάν occurs twice in Revelation, twice in Matthew (both in 10:8), and once each in John, Romans, 2 Corinthians, Galatians, and 2 Thessalonians.

Δωρεά is the (graciously offered) *gift*. In contrast to → δῶρον, δωρεά appears to be "more legal" (Büchsel 167), since in nonbiblical usage it designates formal donations (honors, bequests, fees, wedding presents; cf. LSJ s.v.; Moulton/Milligan). The adv., like Germ. *umsonst*, has a twofold meaning: *undeserved/gratis; in vain*. The NT meanings correspond, for the most part, to those of the LXX, where δωρεάν renders Heb. *ḥinnām* (favorable, in vain, unfounded) in 20 of the 24 passages which have a Hebrew equivalent. In Dan 2:48 δωρεά stands for Aram. *matᵉnā'* (gift); in 11:39 for Heb. *mᵉḥîr* (reward). Dan 2:6 and 5:17 (both Theodotion) use the noun for Aram. *nᵉbizbâ* (gift).

2. Δωρεά is used in the NT (and other early Christian literature, e.g., Ign. *Smyrn.* 7:1; *Barn.* 1:2; 9:9; *Mart. Pol.* 20:2) for the *gift* of God, always in the sg. (whereas the pl. appears in *1 Clem.* 19:2; 23:2; 32:1; 35:4), explicitly (δωρεὰ τοῦ θεοῦ) in John 4:10; Acts 8:20. In other passages the context indicates clearly that the gift comes from God: Acts 11:17; Rom 5:15, 17 (with χάρις in each instance); 2 Cor 9:15; Heb 6:4. Unique to Acts is δωρεὰ τοῦ ἁγίου πνεύματος (Acts 2:38; 10:45), but here the gen. is epexegetical: the gracious gift is the Holy Spirit. In Eph 3:7 occurs the phrase κατὰ τὴν δωρεὰν τῆς χάριτος τοῦ θεοῦ, "according to the *gift* of God's grace [= the gracious gift of God]." In a similar formulation it is said in 4:7 that to each individual Christian is the grace given κατὰ τὸ μέτρον τῆς δωρεᾶς τοῦ Χριστοῦ, "according to the measure of Christ's *gift*"; here Christ is the subject of the giving. The usage of δωρεά in the NT is concentrated on the gracious gift which has already been given by God, namely, Christ (John 4:10), the Spirit (Acts 2:38; 8:20; 10:45; 11:17), or "righteousness" (Rom 5:15, 17). Heb 6:4(f.) mentions alongside the "heavenly *gift*," which Christians have received, participation in the Holy Spirit, the word of God, and the tasting of the "powers of the age to come." Thanksgiving is due to God for the *gift* (2 Cor 9:15).

3. Δωρεάν most often means *as a gift* or *free of charge*: with λαμβάνω and (or) δίδωμι (Matt 10:8 bis; Rev 21:6; 22:17); 2 Cor 11:7: δωρεάν εὐαγγελίζομαι, "I preached God's gospel *without cost* to you"; Rom 3:24: δικαιούμενοι δωρεάν, "justified by his grace *as a gift* [= apart from merit]"; 2 Thess 3:8: we did "not eat anyone's bread *without paying*, but with toil and labor we worked night and day, that we might not burden any of you"—said here in order to set forth Paul as a model (cf. vv. 9-12).

The meaning *undeserved* is present in John 15:25: "they hated me *without a cause*" (cf. Pss 34:19; 68:5 LXX); the word of Scripture "must" be fulfilled in Jesus. Δωρεὰν ἀποθνήσκω in Gal 2:21b means "die *in vain*": "for if justification were through the law, then Christ died *to no purpose*."

G. Schneider

δωρεάν *dōrean* without payment, as a gift; undeserved; in vain
→ δωρεά 3.

δωρέομαι *dōreomai* give
→ δώρημα 2.

δώρημα, ατος, τό *dōrēma* gift*
δωρέομαι *dōreomai* give*

1. Occurrences — 2. Δωρέομαι — 3. Δώρημα.

Lit.: → δωρεά.

1. The noun δώρημα, *gift*, occurs in the NT only in Rom 5:16 and Jas 1:17, both times sg. The vb. appears only in Mark 15:45 and 2 Pet 1:3f. Δώρημα is originally "found in elevated style" (Büchsel 167). In the LXX it appears only in Sir 31(34):18, referring to (sacrificial) *gifts* of the lawless (δωρήματα ἀνόμων), which do not please God. In the NT it refers in both instances to the gifts of God to humans. The mid. vb. means *give, present*. Although it is attested in the act. in Pindar, the postclassical period knows only the mid., as do the LXX (8 occurrences), Philo, and the NT. The vb. in 2 Peter speaks of the gift of God to mankind (so also Plato *Ti.* 46e); in Mark 15:45 God is not the subject.

2. Δωρέομαι has a secular meaning in Mark 15:45: Pilate "*granted* the body [of Jesus] to Joseph [of Arimathea]." Here the release of the Crucified One is characterized as a favor done without obligation (cf. v. 43: τολμήσας . . . ᾐτήσατο); this element does not appear in the other Gospels.

The beginning of 2 Peter reminds the readers of the great gifts which they have received in being called by God and to which even greater promises belong: God has "*given* to us all things that pertain to life and godliness" (2 Pet 1:3). At the beginning of the verse causal ὡς appears with the gen. absolute; πάντα is the object of δεδωρημένης. The following verse mentions those who in their calling have been *given* (δεδώρηται) "precious and very great promises," through which Christians are to "become partakers of the divine nature." For the content of the promises (the parousia, entrance into the "eternal kingdom," the end of the world), one may compare 1:11, 16; 3:7, 13.

3. Δώρημα in Rom 5:16 appears in a context which also includes → δωρεά (vv. 15, 17). The use of δώρημα is connected with the use of other substantives with -μα within 5:12-21 (παράπτωμα 6 times; χάρισμα, κατάκριμα, and δικαίωμα 2 times each; ὁμοίωμα and κρίμα once each). V. 16a is formulated in an abbreviated way: καὶ οὐχ ὡς δι' ἑνὸς ἁμαρτήσαντος τὸ δώρημα, literally "and the *gift* is not as it is through the one who sinned."

R. Bultmann ("Adam and Christ in Romans 5," *The Old and New Man* [1967] 59) adds: "And it is not the same with the gift as (the case was) with the one who sinned." E. Brandenburger, (*Adam und Christus* [1962] 224) paraphrases: "And not: As (the effect came) through the one who sinned—(so also came) the gift." E. Käsemann translates: "What is given is not like that which the one sinner (did)" (*Commentary on Romans* [1980] 140). From v. 16b onward, the meaning is clear: the gift did not come into effect in a way corresponding to the sin, but "its results greatly exceeded it" (H. Schlier, *Römerbrief* [HTKNT] 170). V. 16a, like v. 15, contrasts the two events, the transgression of Adam and the gift which is given in Jesus Christ, and emphasizes from the very beginning the incomparability of the latter (Schlier). Thus the sequence of corresponding catchwords (on the "Christ side") goes from τὸ χάρισμα (v. 15a) to ἡ δωρεὰ ἐν χάριτι Χριστοῦ (v. 15c) to τὸ δώρημα (v. 16a).

Jas 1:17a offers (perhaps as a citation) the affirmation: "Every good endowment [→ δόσις] and every perfect *gift* is from above [→ ἄνωθεν 2.a]." V. 17b elaborates: "coming down from the Father of lights. . . ." In context v. 17a establishes that "temptation, desire, and sin" ultimately bring death, and cannot be "from above" (F. Mussner, *Jakobusbrief* [HTKNT] 90). Parallels to the statement in v. 17a are found in, e.g., Philo (*Sacr.* 3; *Migr.* 73); see also Billerbeck III, 752.

G. Schneider

δῶρον, ου, τό *dōron* gift, offering*

1. Occurrences in the NT — 2. Meaning and usage — 3. Δῶρον in Matthew

Lit.: → δωρεά.

1. The noun δῶρον appears in 19 passages of the NT, most frequently in Matthew (9 times) and in Hebrews (5 times). The remaining occurrences are in Mark 7:11; Luke 21:1, 4; Eph 2:8; and Rev 11:10. Thus the word does not appear in John and Paul. Except for Mark 7:11 par. Matt 15:5, there are no Synoptic parallels for δῶρον. Pl. δῶρα appears in Matt 2:11; Luke 21:1, 4; Rev 11:10; and in all the passages in Hebrews.

2. Δῶρον, derived from δίδωμι, means *gift.* In contrast to → δωρεά and → δώρημα only in Eph 2:8 does it designate a gift of God; elsewhere it is used of gifts of people to each other (Matt 2:11; Rev 11:10, pl.) or (more often) of *sacrificial offerings* to God (Matt 5:23, 24 bis; 8:4; 15:5; 23:18, 19 bis; Mark 7:11; Heb 5:1; 8:3, 4; 9:9; 11:4). Only in Luke 21:1, 4 (cf. Mark 12:41, 44) does the word refer (in the pl.) to an offering of money at the temple.

In the LXX δῶρον is normally (65 times) the translation of Heb. *qôrbān,* "offering, gift (to the sanctuary), sacrificial offering." → Κορβᾶν in Mark 7:11 is translated in the same way; in contrast, Matt 15:5 avoids the Hebrew word. The only occurrence of δῶρον in reference to a gift from God, Eph 2:8, underlines the Pauline thought of the gracious salvation "through faith, not because of works" (vv. 8f.) in the parenthetical θεοῦ τὸ δῶρον. Rev 11:10 characterizes the joy of "those who dwell on the earth" over the death of the two witnesses as a festival of joy in which people will exchange *gifts.* The gift-giving practice of the pagan environment (cf. also Mark 6:22f.: Herod Antipas) is here criticized by the author of Revelation (Stuiber 690). In the passages in Hebrews δῶρα is commonly the object of → προσφέρω and appears alongside θυσίαι. The high priest is to "offer *gifts* and sacrifices for sins" (Heb 5:1; cf. 8:3, 4; 9:9). These statements about the human high priest stand in the background of the explanation about the once-for-all offering through Christ, the "high priest of the good things that have come" (9:11–10:18). In Heb 11:4 δῶρα refers to Abel's sacrifice.

3. Δῶρον is a preferred word of Matthew. It appears in Matt 2:11 in the pl. and refers there to the *gifts* of homage by the Magi (gold, frankincense, and myrrh) to the newborn king. Except for 15:5 (par. Mark) the occurrences of δῶρον have no Synoptic parallels. Matt 5:23, 24a, c and 23:18, 19 (bis) appear in the special Matthean tradition.

Matt 8:4 (cf. Mark 1:40) has inserted the explanatory τὸ δῶρον in the command of Jesus: ". . . show yourself to the priest, and offer *the gift* that Moses commanded. . . ." The statement of Jesus in 5:23f. (cf. J. Jeremias, *Abba* [1966] 103-7) uses δῶρον of a "private sacrifice"; more precisely, the phrase προσφέρειν τὸ δῶρον "is used primarily for an *animal sacrifice,*" just as in the only passage in which it appears elsewhere in the Gospels, Matt 8:4, where τὸ δῶρον encompasses the sin offering, the guilt offering, and the burnt offering of the lepers (Lev. 14:10ff.)" (Jeremias 103). In the speech against the scribes and Pharisees δῶρον appears 3 times in Matt 23:16-22 (the woe concerning "blind guides"): in the phrase "if any one swears by *the gift that is on the altar* (ἐν τῷ δώρῳ)" (v. 18) and in the question of Jesus, "Which is greater, *the gift* or the altar that makes *the gift* sacred?" (v. 19). The casuistic distinctions that are rejected in illustrating the practice of the opponents (vv. 16, 18) cannot be precisely identified in the rabbinic traditions, although part of Jesus' question can be identified (*m. Zebaḥ.* 9:1: "the altar sanctifies what is meant for it"); cf. Billerbeck I, 931f.

G. Schneider

Ε ε

ἔα *ea* ha! ah!*

As an involuntary exclamation of the demonic spirit in one who is possessed: ἔα, τί ἡμῖν καὶ σοί, "Ah! What have you to do with us?" (Luke 4:34; Mark 1:24 v.l.).

ἐάν *ean* if

The conjunction ἐάν appears 351 times in the NT, primarily in Matthew (64 times), John (63 times), 1 Corinthians (48 times), Mark (36 times), and Luke (31 times). It does not appear in Philippians, Titus, Philemon, 2 Peter, 2 John, or Jude.

1. Ἐάν, normally with the pres. subjunc. or more frequently the aor. subjunc., is used in conditional sentences to designate what is expected to occur under certain circumstances from a given standpoint in the present: "if, as is to be expected . . ." (BDF §§371.4; 373.1). The pres. subjunc. in the protasis refers normally to commonly accepted assumptions, e.g., Matt 6:23; John 8:16; 1 Tim 1:8; the aor. subjunc. refers normally to non-recurring or special assumptions, e.g., Matt 5:13; 8:2; John 3:3; 1 Cor 4:19. The pres. and aor. subjunc. are used close together with this significance in 1 Cor 14:23; 2 Tim 2:5. The apodosis may have the ind.; in the case of a statement of possibility (*if* = "under the assumption that . . .") it often has the fut. ind., e.g., Matt 4:9; 9:21; Luke 10:6; Acts 13:41; Rom 7:3a, and in the case of an iterative use it often has the pres. or aor. ind., e.g., Mark 3:24; John 3:2; Rom 7:3b; 1 Cor 15:36.

2. In isolated instances ἐάν occurs with the subjunc. in the sense of → εἰ with the ind., e.g., John 21:22: ἐάν . . . θέλω, *if* it is (really) my will. Ἐάν occurs also, but rarely, with the pres. ind. in the sense of εἰ, e.g., 1 Thess 3:8; 1 John 5:15 (cf. BDF §372.1a).

3. Occasionally ἐάν can stand with the subjunc. also in the place of a contrary-to-fact statement (e.g., 1 Cor 4:15; 13:2) or a statement of potential (e.g., Acts 9:2).

4. In connection with other particles: Ἐὰν μή means *if not, unless* (Matt 6:15; Mark 3:27); *except* (Mark 4:22; cf. BDF §§376; 480.6); ἐὰν καί, *even if* (Gal 6:1); ἐὰν δὲ καί, *but if* (1 Cor 7:11; 2 Tim 2:5); ἐὰν οὖν, *if therefore* (Matt 5:23); ὁσακις ἐάν, *whenever* (1 Cor 11:25f.); καὶ ἐάν → κἄν.

5. Ἐάν frequently stands after rel. expressions, probably to underline the "conditional character" of the saying (BDF §107; see also §31.1), e.g., Matt 5:19; 21:24; John 15:7; Gal 5:10. Thus it can replace (iterative) ἄν, e.g., Matt 20:26; Mark 8:35, 38; 14:9. The ms. readings vary accordingly.

H. Balz

ἐάνπερ *eanper* if only, provided that*

The conjunction ἐάνπερ appears in the NT only in Hebrews (Heb 3:6 v.l.; 3:14; 6:3) and refers (like → εἴπερ in Paul) to still another condition besides what is said in the context; cf. BDF §454.2.

ἑαυτοῦ, 3 *heautou* (of) oneself, his, her; one another

1. Position, forms, and occurrences in the NT — 2. Usage in the NT — 3. Replacement by the personal pronoun

Lit.: BAGD s.v. — BDF §§64.1; 283 — Radermacher, *Grammatik* 72f., 110, 111f. — Moulton, *Grammar 41-43.*

1. The personal pron. has special reflexive forms where it refers to the subj. of the sentence (the reflexive forms cannot be nom. or function as the subj.). Within the sentence the reflexive pron. was normally in the attributive position (e.g., τὰ ἑαυτοῦ κτήματα or τὰ κτήματα τὰ ἑαυτοῦ), but in the course of time the predicate position came to be accepted (e.g., τὰ κτήματα ἑαυτῶν παραδιδόασιν). The reflexive pron. ἑαυτοῦ, etc., appears 321 times in the NT, of which 86 are in the Pauline corpus and 78 in the double work of Luke. The common classical Greek contracted form αὑτοῦ, αὑτῶν is rare in the NT, being replaced in koine by the less ambiguous forms: ". . . the people decided for the sake of clarity for ἑαυτοῦ where the reflexive seemed to be demanded" (Radermacher 73).

2. a) The reflexive is used "as the direct complement of the verb referring to the subject" (BDF §283.1). In the pl. the third person form ἑαυτῶν, etc., is used for first, second, and third persons with no limitation: εἰ δὲ ἑαυτοὺς διεκρίνομεν οὐκ ἂν ἐκρινόμεθα, "If we judged *ourselves* truly, we should not be judged" (1 Cor 11:31); ἵνα . . . ἀγοράσωσιν ἑαυτοῖς βρώματα, "to . . . buy food *for themselves*" (Matt 14:15); cf. Rom 8:23; Phil 2:12; Matt 3:9; John 12:8, and often. But the sg. of the third person is seldom used in place of the distinctive first and second person reflexive pronouns (cf. John 18:34; Matt 23:37 and the corresponding textual variants).

b) The reflexive of the third person sg. and pl. is used in order to maintain the identity of the persons speaking or acting: τοῦ δόντος ἑαυτὸν ὑπὲρ τῶν ἁμαρτιῶν ἡμῶν, "who gave *himself* for our sins" (Gal 1:4; cf. 2:20); ἐπείρασας τοὺς λέγοντας ἑαυτοὺς ἀποστόλους, "you . . . have tested those who call *themselves* apostles" (Rev 2:2; cf. 2:9, 20); cf. Matt 18:4; 19:12; 23:12; Mark 6:36; John 19:17, and often.

c) Prep. phrases serve the unequivocalness of the reflexive relationship: e.g., ὁ ἀφ' ἑαυτοῦ λαλῶν, "he who speaks *on his own authority*" (John 7:18); εἰς ἑαυτὸν δὲ ἐλθών, "when he came *to himself*" (Luke 15:17); ὡς ἐξ ἑαυτῶν, "as *from our own* power [RSV "competent *of ourselves*"]" (2 Cor 3:5); ὡς δὲ ἐν ἑαυτῷ διηπόρει ὁ Πέτρος, "while Peter was perplexed *inwardly*" (Acts 10:17); the prep. phrase often appears with vbs. of speaking or vbs. that point to processes taking place in the consciousness; ἡ πίστις . . . νεκρά ἐστιν καθ' ἑαυτήν, "faith *by itself*. . . is dead" (Jas 2:17).

d) In place of the possessive pron. αὐτοῦ/αὐτῆς the reflexive *can* be used to strengthen the possessive nature of the gen.: e.g., 1 Cor 7:2: ἕκαστος τὴν ἑαυτοῦ γυναῖκα ἐχέτω, καὶ ἑκάστη τὸν ἴδιον ἄνδρα . . . , "each man should have *his own* wife and each woman her own husband . . ."; cf. Gal 6:4; Rom 16:18. In Phil 2:4, 21 τὰ ἑαυτῶν, one's "*own* good/interests," takes on an idiomatic character. Text variants (e.g., Luke 14:26; Jas 1:26) nevertheless indicate that in this usage no unambiguous rule can be established.

e) The reflexive pron. replaces the reciprocal pron. ἀλλήλων, etc. on stylistic grounds (cf. Luke 23:12): εἰρηνεύετε ἐν ἑαυτοῖς, "Be at peace *among yourselves*" (1 Thess 5:13); cf. Col 3:13, 16; Eph 4:32; Mark 9:50; οἱ δὲ . . . λέγοντες πρὸς ἑαυτοῦς, "and they . . . said *to one another*" (Mark 10:26).

f) The strengthening of the reflexive by αὐτός occurs in isolated instances: e.g., 2 Cor 10:12: ἀλλὰ αὐτοὶ ἐν ἑαυτοῖς ἑαυτοὺς μετροῦντες, "instead we measure ourselves *by ourselves*" (RSV and other versions take the subj. of this clause as "they"); cf. 2 Cor 1:9.

3. The reflexive was replaced in the course of time by the simple personal pron. Increasingly other elements of the sentence have entered between the antecedent and the reflexive. Thus the NT writings avoid, wherever it is possible, using the reflexive where the subj. to which it refers does not appear in the same sentence. The variability of the text tradition (cf., e.g., Matt 25:1ff.) suggests this tendency.

U. Schoenborn

ἐάω *eaō* let, permit; let go, leave alone*

Ἐάω appears 11 times in the NT, most frequently in Acts (8 times). It also appears as a v.l. in Mark 16:14 W (the Freer logion) and elsehere.

1. The first meaning, *let* or *permit,* is used with the complementary inf. of God's forbearance, which permitted Gentiles in earlier times to follow their own customs (Acts 14:16), and also of military instructions for the escort of Paul to Caesarea (23:32). In a nautical context it is used of the work done by the seamen (27:32, → ἐκπίπτω).

In Acts 28:4 a negatived ἐάω occurs concerning "justice" (δίκη) which, according to the assumption of those present, is directed toward Paul because of his evil deeds when it sends a serpent to take his life. However, that is a Greek idea without support in the context. Negatived ἐάω means *prevent,* and is also used of the concern of God, who does not permit his people to be tempted beyond their power (1 Cor 10:13), of Jesus' act of silencing the demons (Luke 4:41), of the guarding of the house by the householder in the parable of the thief in the night (Matt 24:43), and of the destructive effect of Satan in this age (Mark 16:14 W [Freer logion]). In the same sense it is used, with the complementary inf. understood, of the work of the Spirit (Acts 16:7) and of the disciples (19:30) on the missionary journey of Paul. (Cf. the negatived προσεάω in Acts 27:7: not *permit*).

2. The second meaning appears in Gamaliel's advice *to let* the apostles *go* (Acts 5:38 v.l.) and of the forbearance toward Jezebel (Rev 2:20 v.l.), both times without the inf. and in place of → ἀφίημι. Luke 22:51 uses it in the absolute sense, where it means *stop* (imv.).

3. The vb. is used as a t.t. of the language of seafaring in Acts 27:40, where it refers to the anchors which the seamen "*left* [behind] in the sea." Ἔα in the answer of the demons to Jesus in Luke 4:34 (cf. Mark 1:24 v.l.; → ἔα) might be the imv. of ἐάω with the meaning *leave* (us alone; cf. Vg. ad loc.; *1 Clem.* 39:5).

M. E. Glasswell

ἑβδομήκοντα *hebdomēkonta* seventy

Lit.: A. Dreizehnter, *Die rhetorischer Zahl. Quellenkritische Untersuchungen anhand der Zahlen 70 und 700* (Zetemata 73, 1978). — H. Lignée, "La mission des soixante-douze.

Lc 10,1-12. 17-20," *AsSeign* 45 (1974) 64-74. — B. M. METZGER, "Seventy or Seventy-Two Disciples?" *NTS* 5 (1958/59) 299-306. — K. H. RENGSTORF, *TDNT* II, 627-35. — A. SCHIMMEL, *RGG* VI, 1861-63.

1. The sacred number seventy has significance exclusively in the mission of the seventy in Q (Luke 10:1, 17; v.l. seventy-two). On text-critical grounds the number is not easy to determine. All speculation about the identity of those who were sent (cf. Eusebius *HE* i.12) are without foundation. The group of the seventy(-two) is nevertheless thought of as excluding the Twelve (Luke 10:1).

2. For the significance of the seventy(-two) there are suggestions in the OT (on the Jewish texts, cf. Rengstorf), particularly the references to the seventy (LXX: seventy-two) Gentile peoples (Gen 10) and the seventy elders of Israel (Exod 24:1; Num 11:16). One may compare also the seventy members of the family of Jacob (Exod 1:5; according to the LXX and Acts 7:14, seventy-five), the seventy sons of Jerubbaal (Judg 9:2), the seventy years of the Exile (Jer 25:11, etc.), and the seventy (seventy-one) members of the Sanhedrin (*m. Sanh.* 1:6).

Yet in these references nothing is really learned which documents the number seventy(-two) as a customary sacred number. An intentional analogy of the seventy (-two) emissaries of Jesus to the seventy elders of Israel would overload the single mention of the seventy(-two) considerably; it fails also in regard to Luke's emphasis on the apostolate composed of twelve. The title μαθητής is not once coordinated with the seventy(-two)! Furthermore, the reference to the seventy(-two) Gentile peoples scarcely has any significance. The Gentile mission is reserved for the circle of the Twelve (Luke 24:47) and is initiated by Peter (Acts 10; 11:1-18). Besides, according to the Lukan framework the task of the seventy(-two) is only the preparation for Jesus' own arrival within *Israel* (Luke 10:1).

If one takes into consideration the tension of this statement at the beginning of the section with the content of the speech of Jesus, which assumes an independent mission of the messengers and is strongly interested in the words of Jesus, then the assumption is probable that Luke has retained the Q version of the mission because he wanted to preserve Jesus' words and to demonstrate the activity of Jesus (10:9) to all Israel (10:1). He has himself inserted the number seventy(-two) as the highest customary sacred number without offering any further interpretative help.

M. Völkel

ἑβδομηκοντάκις *hebdomēkontakis* seventy times*

Matt 18:22: ἕως ἑβδομηκοντάκις ἑπτά, "[as many as] *seventy* seven times" (D* ἑβδομηκοντάκις ἑπτάκις, "seven times seventy times" [cf. RSV]); cf. Gen 4:24; *T. Benj.* 7:4. In contrast to the unrestrained vengeance of Lamech (Gen 4:24) there should be unlimited forgiveness.

ἕβδομος *hebdomos* seventh

→ ἑπτά.

Ἔβερ, ὁ *Eber* Eber*

Son of Shelah in the genealogy of Jesus in Luke 3:35 (cf. Gen 10:24f.; Josephus *Ant.* i.147).

ἑβραϊκός, 3 *hebraïkos* Hebrew

Luke 23:38 ℵ* D Koine Θ *pl* latt sy^p: γράμμασιν . . . ἑβραϊκοῖς (alongside ἑλληνικοῖς and ῥωμαϊκοῖς), of the inscription on the cross; cf. John 19:20.

Ἑβραῖος *Hebraios* Hebrew*

Lit.: G. VON RAD, K. G. KUHN, and W. GUTBROD, *TDNT* III, 356-91.

1. "Hebrew" in the NT era normally designates the Jewish people of ancient times (e.g., Philo *Vit. Mos.* i.243; Josephus *Ant.* ii.201f., etc.). The LXX speaks of Hebrews in distinguishing the Jewish people from other peoples (Gen 39:14; 43:32, etc.). Yet "Hebrew" can (esp. in the view of non-Palestinians) refer to Jews who are from Palestine or are esp. connected with Palestine. An archaizing tendency is probably resonant in the word choice in NT times: in contrast to the (in the mouth of Gentiles) derogatory-sounding Ἰουδαῖος, the name Ἑβραῖος is deliberately used as an honored name from the past. Thus the name is preferred in the literarily ambitious writings of Hellenistic Jewish propaganda (e.g., *Sibylline Oracles,* 4 Maccabees, Judith, Ezekiel the poet, Philo, Josephus; for texts see *TDNT* III, 367f.; D. Georgi, *The Opponents of Paul in Second Corinthians* [1986] 40-49; M. Hengel, *Between Jesus and Paul* [1983], esp. 9-11), and among pagan authors (e.g., Plutarch *Quaest. Conv.* iv.6). We know in Rome and Corinth synagogues of "Hebrews" (inscription in Deissmann, *Light* 16, n. 7; cf. Hengel 15), which apparently included Jews from Palestine. Such Jews from Palestine soon gave up their Aramaic mother tongue, but apparently maintained the name *Hebrew* as a reminder of their place of origin.

2. In the NT Ἑβραῖος (4 occurrences) becomes less significant than the customary Ἰουδαῖος (195 occurrences). Acts 6:1 speaks of the "Hellenists (→ Ἑλληνιστής) [murmuring] against the *Hebrews.*" The "Hellenistic" widows have been neglected at the "table service," i.e., at the "daily distribution." "Hebrew" refers here to the Aramaic-speaking part of the Jerusalem church, which, as Acts 6 indicates, was distinguished organizationally from the Greek-speaking part, the "Hellenists."

The vernacular Hebrew in that period was probably almost totally absorbed into Aramaic. Τῇ Ἑβραΐδι διαλέκτῳ (Acts 21:40; 22:2; 26:14) or Ἑβραϊστί (John 5:2, etc.) mean "in the Aramaic language" (cf. T. Zahn, *Introduction to the NT* I (1909) 26f.; Billerbeck II, 442-53; Hengel 9-11). Philo (*Conf.* 129) distinguishes between "the Hebrew language" and "our own [Greek]" and occasionally designates Aramaic words as Hebrew words (e.g., *Abr.* 28; similarly Josephus *Ant.* iii.252). "The strongly

Aramaic coloring of the Mishnaic Hebrew might have been used in the villages of the Jewish hill country, in addition to its being used as a scribal and cultic language" (Hengel 10). Knowledge of Greek is to be assumed among the educated Palestinian Jews at the time of Jesus, i.e., the "Hebrews" of Acts 6:1 (cf. J. N. Sevenster, *Do You Know Greek?* [NovTSup 19, 1968]).

In Phil 3:5 Paul calls himself "a *Hebrew* born of *Hebrews,*" and in 2 Cor 11:22 he compares himself to his opponents: "Are they *Hebrews*? So am I. Are they Israelites? So am I. Are they descendants of Abraham? So am I." The self-designation *Hebrews* must not necessarily be understood as an affirmation of the Palestinian origin of the apostle (cf., however, the report in Jerome *De vir. ill.* 5; *Comm. on Philemon* 23: Paul was from Gischala in Galilee). Philo, e.g., says of Hagar, that she was "an Egyptian by birth, but of her own free will a Hebrew in her conduct of life (προαίρεσις, *Abr.* 251). In view of the use of the ancient concept *Hebrew* in Hellenistic Jewish propaganda, it is probable that Paul here desired primarily to claim that he was a "full-blooded Jew" (H. Lietzmann, *An die Korinther I–II* [HNT, 1949] 150), who has remained faithful to the ancestral customs and traditions (cf. Gal 1:14) and thus deserves the honorific name *Hebrew* as much as his opponents.

The late superscript of the book of Hebrews (πρὸς Ἑβραίους) says nothing about the possible recipients. A Palestinian address cannot necessarily be concluded (see above on Paul). It is not certain that the addressees were Jewish Christians.

J. Wanke

Ἑβραΐς, ΐδος, ἡ *Hebraïs* Hebrew*

In the NT only in the phrase Ἑβραΐς διάλεκτος, "*Hebrew* language": of the speech of Paul on the steps between the temple and the fortress Antonia (Acts 21:40; 22:2), which must have been in Aramaic; of the voice, which Paul heard outside Damascus *in the Hebrew language* (Acts 26:14; cf. also 9:4; 22:7: Σαούλ). W. Gutbrod, *TDNT* III, 388; R. Meyer, *BHH* 668f.; R. Mayer, *DNTT* II, 309.

Ἑβραϊστί *Hebraïsti* in the Hebrew language*

In the NT only in John (John 5:2; 19:13, 17, 20; 20:16) and in Revelation (Rev 9:11; 16:16). In John 5:2; 19:13, 17; Rev 9:11; 16:16 it is used for Greek names, which go back to an Aramaic (John) or Hebrew (Revelation) original, probably to provide historical details on the one hand (John) and to intensify the strangeness of what is portrayed on the other hand (Revelation). John 19:20 refers to the inscription on the cross (cf. Luke 23:38 v.l.); in John 20:16 the adv. is used of Mary Magdalene's address to the resurrected Jesus: ῥαββουνί. W. Gutbrod, *TDNT* III, 389f.; R. Meyer, *BHH* 668f.; R. Mayer, *DNTT* II, 309.

ἐγγίζω *engizō* come near

1. Occurrences in the NT — 2. Meaning — 3. Theological usage

Lit.: K. Löning, *Die Saulustradition in der Apostelgeschichte* (NTAbh 9, 1973) 22. — L. Marin, *Semiotik der Passionsgeschichte* (BEvT 70, 1976) 19-24. — H. Preisker, *TDNT* II, 330-32. — R. Schnackenburg, *God's Rule and Kingdom* (1963) 195-214.

1. Of the 42 occurrences in the NT, the greatest portion are in the Lukan writings (Luke has 18 and Acts has 6); Mark has 3 and Matthew 7; ἐγγίζω does not appear in John; the remaining 8 occurrences are in Paul's letters (2), Hebrews (2), James (3), and 1 Peter (1).

2. In the NT ἐγγίζω is used only intransitively. In the LXX and in secular Greek there is also the trans. sense "bring near" (Preisker 329f.). Ἐγγίζω is accompanied by the dat. of the person or thing, but can also appear absolutely or in connection with prepositions. Ἐγγίζω has a spatial or temporal significance, which remains in all further aspects of its usage.

Locations take on additional historical significance with ἐγγίζω: Jerusalem is the city in which the decision for or against Jesus will be made (Mark 11:1 par.). Jericho, Bethphage, and the Mount of Olives are the stations along the way (Luke 18:35; 19:29, 37, 41). At the gate to the city it is decided whether Jesus is to raise the deceased son of the mother (7:12) and of the city. The home of the lost son becomes the place of decision for his acceptance (15:26). After the resurrection in Jerusalem, the works of Jesus continue in Emmaus (24:28), Damascus, and Joppa (Acts 9:3; 22:6; 10:9).

Decisive moments are announced in the time references: the moment of the harvest (Matt 21:34), the decisive hour (26:45), the decisive moment (Luke 21:8), the last Passover feast of Jesus (Luke 22:1), the decisive day (Rom 13:12; Heb 10:25).

Correspondingly, critical events are established in the approaches between persons: the traitor delivers Jesus over to the Passion (Mark 14:42 par.). The tax collectors and sinners can hear Jesus (Luke 15:1). Jesus can speak with the blind man (18:40) and both disappointed disciples (24:15). The Roman captain rescues Paul (Acts 21:33), while the Jewish opponents plan his murder (23:15). The Romans destroy Jerusalem (Luke 21:20).

Finally, explicit theological subjects can *draw near*: the kingdom of God (Mark 1:15 par.; Matt 3:2; 10:7; Luke 10:9, 11), the redemption (Luke 21:28), the time of the promise (Acts 7:17), God (Jas 4:8), the return of the Lord (Jas 5:8), or the end of all things (1 Pet 4:7). Or a person can approach these entities: death (Phil 2:30), God (Heb 7:19; Jas 4:8).

3. The exceptional meaning that ἐγγίζω gives to

subjects and objects is extended *theologically* not only with respect to theological entities (kingdom of God, God, etc.), but also in the encounter between persons, in the approach toward a place, and esp. the approach of a point in time. Moment, hour, and day, used absolutely, are important elements of the apocalyptic code. Explicit theological concepts (see above) also belong to this code. Yet the significance of this encounter between Jesus and the places and times which are associated with him bring together the future apocalyptic events already in the presence of Jesus. Already in the appearance of Jesus the kingdom of God *is approaching.* In his charge the disciples also announce the approach of the eschaton. This approach is expressed in signs through healing, raising persons from the dead, in the coming of sinners and tax collectors to Jesus, in repentance. The expected eschatological centering of the world around Jerusalem is taking place in the present around Jerusalem. According to Luke the way of Jesus ends in Jerusalem, then to proceed from there after the catastrophe of the cross; in Paul's case, toward Damascus. The Feast of Passover becomes through Jesus' death on the cross the new exodus out of the early Jewish overemphasis on law, cult, and nation. What was not achieved by the levitical-priestly purity regulations which were extended by the Pharisees to all of the pious, community with the Resurrected One has achieved: the approach to God, which in the OT the priests attained through the cultic ministry (Lev 10:3).

D. Dormeyer

ἐγγράφω *engraphō* inscribe, record, write down*

Luke 10:20: τὰ ὀνόματα ὑμῶν ἐγγέγραπται (TR ἐγράφη) ἐν τοῖς οὐρανοῖς, "your names *are written* in heaven" (i.e., in the heavenly books of life; cf. *Herm. Vis.* i.3.2; → βιβλίον 3). With a fig. meaning: 2 Cor 3:2, 3: ἐπιστολὴ . . . ἐγγεγραμμένη, in reference to the Corinthian church, which represents Paul's "letter of recommendation, *written* on our hearts" (v. 2) or "*written* not with ink but with the Spirit of the living God" (v. 3). Here ἐγγράφω is certainly to be regarded as an intensive form of γράφω. In using the image of letters of recommendation and in the rejection of other customary letters of recommendation, Paul is concerned to make clear to the church that it is itself the "letter of recommendation" of Christ in the time of the "new covenant." R. Bultmann, *The Second Letter to the Corinthians* (1985) ad loc.

ἔγγυος, 2 *engyos* standing as surety, guaranteeing*

Heb 7:22: subst. of Jesus as the "*surety* of a better covenant" (κρείττονος διαθήκης . . . ἔγγυος Ἰησοῦς).

ἐγγύς *engys* near*

1. Occurrences in the NT — 2. Meaning — 3. Theological usage

Lit.: G. Gnilka, *Der Epheserbrief* (HTKNT, [2]1977) (on Eph 2:13, 17). — R. Pesch, *Naherwartungen. Tradition und Redaktion in Mk 13* (1968) 175-81. — H. Preisker, *TDNT* II, 330-32.

1. The adv., like the vb. → ἐγγίζω, appears primarily in the Gospels and Acts (22 times), and only 7 times in the Epistles and 2 times in Revelation. It is noteworthy that in the Gospels it is not—as with the vb.—Luke that has the dominant use, but John (11 times), who completely lacks the vb.

2. Like the vb. → ἐγγίζω, ἐγγύς indicates the proximity of a place, a time, a person, or a theological abstraction. In connection with γίνομαι it even receives the intrans. meaning of the vb. (John 6:19). Yet in the other instances it does not indicate movement (like the vb.), but rather location. It can be intensified (Rom 13:11) and can be used metaphorically (10:8). The places do not take on important historical significance, but rather can be used in the original local sense: baptize at Aenon *near* Salim (John 3:23; so also Acts 9:38; 27:8). More important, on the other hand, is the reference to Jerusalem. Luke indicates progression (Luke 19:11; Acts 1:12), which he has marked clearly with the vb.

In John the proximity of Jesus makes specific places the realm of decision (against Preisker 331): The approach of Jesus, walking on the water, places those who sit in the boat in the decision between fear and faith (6:19); the place of the multiplication of the bread, left behind by Jesus, stimulates the search for Jesus (6:23); the raising of Lazarus occurs in Bethany, near Jerusalem, where Jesus is raised (11:18); from Bethany he moves near the wilderness in order to be near God (11:54). His cross stands near the city which makes the final decision against him (19:20); the nearby tomb, which lies outside the city, becomes the place of the new beginning (19:42).

As with the vb. → ἐγγίζω, time is given the significance of decision (Mark 13:28 par.; Matt 26:18; Rev 1:3; 22:10; John 2:13; 6:4; 7:2; 11:55). Proximity between persons is noted only in Eph 2:13, 17. On the other hand, the nearness of theological subjects is more strongly represented (Luke 21:31; Rom 13:11; Phil 4:5; Heb 6:8; 8:13). Mark 13:29 par. Matt 24:33 is not unambiguous. Luke 21:31 has inserted "kingdom of God" in the parallel passage; this supplement for Mark 13:29 is obvious, but another term out of the apocalyptic code might have been chosen, such as "moment," or "judgment."

3. The OT background for the eschatological significance of ἐγγύς and ἐγγίζω is present in Deutero-Isaiah (Isa 50:8; 51:5; 56:6), but can also be found in the other

prophets (Ezek 7:7, etc.). This prophetic eschatology is a root of the NT apocalyptic code; the other root is contemporary apocalyptic literature. A de-apocalypticizing occurs through the early Jesus. Thus as in OT prophecy the result of God's eschatological activity takes on significance. The moment of this activity in Jesus, however, does not occur in a world-encompassing or cosmological process, but rather in the inner-historical acts of the individual person of Jesus. This beginning of the eschaton is then finally and ultimately completed by God in the future (Mark 13:29 par.; Rev 1:3; 22:10). Ephesians undertakes an ecclesiological extension. Through his death, Jesus makes possible the nearness of God for the Gentiles, who were separated from him; this proximity of God was formerly available only to the Jews. In the body of Christ both become one new person and together receive the nearness of the peace of Christ (Eph 2:13, 17). The approach of the eschaton becomes perceptible in the form of the Church. Hebrews adds that in the countermove the old covenant is near to its end (Heb 6:8; 8:13).

D. Dormeyer

ἐγείρω *egeirō* waken; raise; intrans.: rise*

1. Occurrences in the NT — 2. General meaning — 3. The raising back to life of individuals — 4. The eschatological resurrection — 5. The resurrection of Christ — 6. Ἔγερσις

Lit.: In addition to the following → ἀνάστασις. — N. Baumert, *Täglich sterben und auferstehen. Der Literalsinn von 2 Kor 4, 15–5, 10* (1973). — E. Brandenburger, "Die Auferstehung der Glaubenden als historisches und theologisches Problem," *WuD* 9 (1967) 16-33. — Bultmann, *Theology* (index s.v. resurrection). — *idem, TDNT* II, 874f. — L. Cerfaux, *Le Christ dans la Théologie de S. Paul* (1954) = *Christus in der paulinischen Theologie* (1964). — H. Conzelmann, *1 Corinthians* (Hermeneia, 1974). — M. E. Dahl, *The Resurrection of the Body. A Study of 1 Corinthians 15* (SBT 36, 1962). — E. Haenchen, *Der Weg Jesu. Eine Erklärung des Markus-Evangeliums und der kanonischen Parallelen* (1968). — Hahn, *Titles* (index s.v.). — O. Hofius, "Eine altjüdische Parallele zu Röm IV 17b," *NTS* 18 (1971/72) 93f. — H. Jankum, *Die passive Bedeutung medialer Formen untersucht an der Sprache Homers* (1969). — W. Kramer, *Christos Kyrios Son of God* (1966). — J. Lambrecht, "De oudste christologie: verrijzenis of verhoging?" *Bijdragen* 36 (1975) 118-44. — F. Mussner, *Der Jakobusbrief* (HTKNT, 1975). — *idem,* "Zur stilistischen und semantischen Struktur der Formel 1 Kor 15, 3-5," FS Schürmann 405-16. — A. Oepke, *TDNT* II, 337f. — A. Prévot, *L'aoriste grec en -θην* (1935). — M. Riebl, *Auferstehung Jesu in der Stunde seines Todes? Zur Botschaft von Mt 27, 51b-53* (1978). — R. Schnackenburg, "Zur Aussage: 'Jesus ist von den Toten auferstanden,'" *BZ* 13 (1969) 1-17. — *idem, The Gospel according to St John* I-III (1968-82). — H. Schwantes, *Schöpfung der Endzeit. Ein Beitrag zum Verständnis der Auferweckung bei Paulus* (1963). — E. Schweizer, *Lordship and Discipleship* (1960). — R. J. Sider, "The Pauline Conception of the Resurrection of the Body in 1 Corinthians XV 35-54," *NTS* 21 (1974/75) 428-43. — K. Usami, "'How are the Dead Raised?' (1 Cor 15:35-58)," *Bib* 57 (1976) 468-93. — K. Wengst, *Christologische Formeln und Lieder des Urchristentums* (1972). — J. Wilkinson, "Healing in the Epistle of James," *SJT* 24 (1971) 326-45. — H. Zimmermann, "Struktur und Aussageabsicht der johanneischen Abschiedsreden (Jo 13–17)," *BibLeb* 8 (1967) 279-90. — For further bibliography see *TWNT* X, 979-85.

1. The vb. ἐγείρω, with the basic meanings (trans.) *waken, incite, excite, raise* or (intrans.) *awaken, be active, stand up, rise* (LSJ s.v.; Oepke), appears in the NT most often as a synonym for ἀνίστημι (which is the more frequent LXX translation of Heb. *qûm*). However, a difference in the use of the two vbs. may be observed when they are examined in detail. Thus ἐγείρω appears 144 times in the NT, of which only 59 occurrences are in the general sense (→ 2); of the 108 occurrences of ἀνίστημι, however, 73 are in the general sense. In 13 occurrences ἐγείρω refers to the *raising* of deceased persons (→ 3; it is rarely so used in secular literature: Oepke 333); ἀνίστημι has this sense 34 times. The eschatological resurrection is expressed by means of ἐγείρω 20 times (→ 4) and by means of ἀνίστημι 11 times. Noteworthy for frequency are the 52 uses of ἐγείρω as a designation for the resurrection of Christ (→ 5), for which ἀνίστημι is used but 24 times. The noun ἔγερσις (→ 6) appears in the NT only in Matt 27:53, whereas ἀνάστασις, on the other hand, appears 42 times. Thus while the vb. ἐγείρω often appears with a special christological reference, the subst. ἔγερσις appears only one time; and, by contrast, while ἀνάστασις often has the special meaning, ἀνίστημι more frequently has a general meaning.

The meaning of the compounds corresponds to that of the simple vb. without a special weight being attached to the preposition: Διεγείρω appears in the NT 7 times, and indeed only with the general meaning of ἐγείρω (→ 2). Ἐξεγείρω (85 occurrences in the LXX) appears in Rom 9:17 in the general sense (likewise Mark 6:45 D) and is used in 1 Cor 6:14 of the resurrection (as also Dan 12:2 LXX; → 4). Συνεγείρω, "raise together," refers in Eph 2:6 to participation in the resurrection of Christ.

2. The basic meaning of ἐγείρω is (trans.) to *wake* from sleep (Mark 4:38 par. Matt 8:25; Acts 12:7) or (intrans.) *awaken, rise* (Mark 4:27; Matt 1:24; 2:13, 14, 20, 21; 8:26 [par. Luke 8:24 διεγερθείς]; Matt 25:7).

Used intrans., ἐγείρω does not make a distinction between *awaken* and *stand up*. In Rom 13:11 and Eph 5:14 ἐγείρω, *waken/stand up,* is a metaphor for the cessation of a manner of life which belongs to the night and death (→ ἀνάστασις 4). While in Luke 11:8; 13:25; Mark 14:42 par. Matt 26:46 the context speaks of the end of sleep, ἐγείρω means *rise.* In Matt 17:7; Luke 13:25; John 11:29; 13:4; Acts 9:8 ἐγείρω means *stand up* and is used of people who are lying or sitting. Very often ἐγείρω stands (as does ἀνίστημι) for *rise, appear* (Luke 7:16; Matt 11:11; Luke 11:31 par. Matt 12:42; Mark 13:8 par. Matt 24:7/Luke

21:10; Mark 13:22 par. Matt 24:11, 24; John 7:52). In Matt 9:19 ἐγερθείς marks (like ἀνίστημι) merely a change of location. The imvs. ἐγείρεσθε in John 14:31 and ἔγειρε in Rev 11:1 have the more significant meaning *get up*. John 14:31 may also have (though probably not) a wider, fig. meaning (analogous to 2:19-22; so Zimmermann 289 against Schnackenburg, *John* ad loc.). The aor. pass. is to be regarded as mid. in the general use of ἐγείρω (in Hellenistic Greek it stands often in place of the mid.; BDF §78; Prévot 200-208).

Peculiar to trans. use of ἐγείρω is the meaning, which is attested in the NT only in Phil 1:17: "to *raise* (prepare) tribulation in my bonds," meaning either that the persons Paul is speaking of seek to cause him grief in his imprisonment (RSV "afflict me in my imprisonment") or that his imprisonment itself (→ δέσμος) takes the character of joyful sharing of suffering with Christ (→ θλῖψις). Related to this and synonymous with ἀνίστημι is "*raise up* children [i.e., descendants]" (Luke 3:8 par. Matt 3:9) and *raise*, i.e., *send*, a savior or king (Luke 1:69 [cf. Judg 2:16; 3:9, 15]; Acts 13:22, 23 [v.l. ἤγαγεν]). In accordance with common usage in the LXX, ἐγείρω means *raise*, i.e., *build*, the temple which has been torn down (on the deeper meaning → 5). In Matt 12:11 ἐγείρω has the meaning *raise*, i.e., *help to get up* (of the sheep which has fallen into the pit); in Acts 10:26 the meaning is *lift up*, used of the centurion who had prostrated himself in homage. In Mark 1:31; 9:27; Acts 3:7 ἐγείρω means *raise* one who is sick, having taken him by the hand. In Jas 5:15 ἐγείρω is parallel to σώσει (→ σῴζω) and is a fig. expression for "heal" or refers to the effect of the healing (Wilkinson 333, 335); it is not a term for "spiritual 'raising'" (Mussner, ad loc.).

Relatively often sick people are summoned to get up with the intrans. imv. ἔγειρε, *get up*, and then the healing is conveyed to them or held in prospect (Mark 2:9, 11; 3:3; 10:49; Luke 5:23, 24; 6:8; Matt 9:5; John 5:8; Acts 3:6 [v.l.]; cf. Matt 9:6). Similarly pass. ἠγέρθη in Mark 2:12; Matt 8:15 is to be regarded as mid.: he *stood up* (cf. Matt 9:7).

3. In the description of the raising of the dead girl in Mark 5:41 par. Luke 8:54, intrans. imv. ἔγειρε (which comes after the girl's hand is taken) is not distinguished from its use in healings (→ 2). As the translation of קוּם *(qûm)*, ἐγείρω means *stand up* (Matt 9:25 mentions only the taking of the hand and its result, ἠγέρθη, *she stood up*). Indeed, the meaning of *wake up* also suggests itself (cf. Mark 5:39: she "is sleeping"); this is certainly the case for Luke 8:55 (cf. "her spirit returned"). In Luke 7:14 ἐγέρθητι (the aor. is better Greek) means both *stand up* and *wake up* (intrans.); what follows is: "[he] sat up, and began to speak" (cf. Acts 9:41; 2 Kgs 4:31, 35; also Philostratus *VA* iv.45: ἀφύπνισε). In the logion in Matt 11:5 par. Luke 7:22 ἐγείρονται is mid.: the dead *stand up, awaken* (Fascher 196 disagrees because of the following εὐαγγελίζονται, without regard to the preceding act. vbs.). This is the case also for the statements concerning John the Baptist in Mark 6:14 (ἐγήγερται ἐκ νεκρῶν, he *rose* from the dead; cf. par. Matt 14:2/Luke 9:7) and Mark 6:16 (ἠγέρθη, he *stood up*). The Markan texts are related to the sayings about the resurrection of Jesus (→ 5; on the problem of this relationship → ἀνάστασις 3) by the use of ἐγείρω and the phrase "from (the) dead" more than is the formulation of the popular opinion in Luke 9:8, 19. In all of these statements about raisings of the dead (as in 2 Kgs 4:31) pass. forms of ἐγείρω are to be regarded as mid. (as in → 2 above and in agreement with ἀνίστημι) and are used as t.t. in which the basic meanings of the vb. almost entirely fall into the background.

Trans. ἐγείρω is also a t.t.: *raise the dead, give life* (Matt 10:8; the context makes it impossible to weaken this Matthean expansion of the commission to the disciples by ascribing to ἐγείρω only a fig., spiritual meaning [as does Haenchen 228]). In John 12:1, 9 ἐγείρω refers back in formulaic language to the raising of Lazarus: "whom he had *raised* from the dead" (similarly v. 17; cf. 11:43f.). The form of these statements and the phrase "from (the) dead" (→ 5) are reminiscent of the early Christian resurrection message (on the critical evaluation of all sayings about raisings from the dead cf. ἀνάστασις 3).

4. The eschatological resurrection is expressed in the NT, as already in the LXX (Isa 26:19; Dan 12:2 both LXX and A), by ἐγείρω in addition to ἀνίστημι. In the conversation with the Sadducees only ἀνάστασις and ἀνίστημι (→ ἀνάστασις 3) appear, except in Mark 12:26 par. Luke 20:37; there pass. ἐγείρονται is to be interpreted as mid. in accordance with other uses (→ 2): that they *rise* (cf. par. Matt 22:31: "as for the resurrection of the dead"; R. Pesch, *Markus* [HTKNT] ad loc., suggests that Mark 12:26 has a divine passive). That the dead rise through God's power is said in the context (esp. Mark 12:24: "the power of God").

In accordance with Jewish conceptions of the liberation of the pious of the old covenant (→ ἅγιος) from Sheol, which is often associated with the grave (cf. P. Hoffmann, *Die Toten in Christus* [[2]1969] 62-64, 184), Matt 27:52 is connected with the opening of the tombs (cf. Ezek 37:13): "the tombs also were opened and many bodies of the saints who had fallen asleep *arose* [RSV "were raised"]." As evidence for the resurrection, v. 53 says that they came out of the tombs (after the resurrection of Jesus, → 6), went into the Holy City, and appeared to many. The passage scarcely involves an ancient tradition which the mood of the first days produced (against Jeremias, *Theology* 309), but rather a midrashic perspective (cf. Ezek 37:13) on the meaning of Jesus' death and resurrection for the divine authority of the crucified one (Riebl 80-82) and for the general resurrection (cf. 1 Cor 15:20; Col 1:18).

When Paul uses ἐγείρω throughout 1 Corinthians 15 for both Christ's resurrection and the general resurrection of the dead, it becomes evident thereby how closely the resurrection of the dead is connected with the message of Easter. The conditional sentence "if the dead *are* not *raised*" in vv. 15, 16, 29, and 32 refers to what the opponents affirm (→ ἀνάστασις 4). Paul replies to them that Christ at the very least is raised (→ 5) and bases the Christian faith on that fact (v. 14). In saying this Paul does not single out for separate consideration the fate of those who, according to vv. 51f., will be changed at the parousia without the resurrection (Brandenburger 20). In this way he does not limit resurrection to deliverance from the grave, but instead has it refer esp. to participation in the life of the resurrected Christ. Without the hope for it, the baptismal practice of the Corinthians "on behalf of the dead" (v. 29; → βαπτίζω), the apostolic activity (vv. 30-32), and a life sustained by faithful maxims and the knowledge of God (vv. 33f.) would remain unintelligible.

The fundamental question, "How *are* the dead *raised*?" (or, as it can also be translated, "Can the dead rise?" cf. Sider 429), and its concrete expression, "With what kind of body do they come?" (1 Cor 15:35), indicate that resurrection implies, on the one hand, the possession of a "body" (→ σῶμα), but, on the other hand, appears to be incompatible with a "body" of "flesh and blood" (v. 50). On the basis of the comparison with a kernel of grain (vv. 36-38) and the reference to the various kinds of "flesh" (→ σάρξ), "body" (→ σῶμα), and "glory" (→ δόξα), Paul sets forth four antitheses in rhetorical language (vv. 42b-44a) as a final conclusion (v. 42a): To "what is sown" (an image for death and burial; cf. v. 36) Paul contrasts *raised* imperishable, in glory, in power, and as a spiritual body. This suggests that ἐγείρεται, which corresponds here to pass. σπείρεται and ζῳοποιεῖται (v. 36, cf. v. 22), is pass. (*"is raised"*; cf. Moulton, *Grammar* I, 163), but a mid. understanding cannot be excluded (cf. the coexistence of "die" and "made alive," vv. 22, 36), and, in view of the usage elsewhere, mid. is to be preferred. That the beginning of the new form of existence does not occur from one's own power is expressed by the context (v. 38, δίδωσιν), esp. by σῶμα πνευματικόν (→ πνεῦμα). Later (arguing against an interpretation of Gen 2:7) Paul calls Christ "a life-giving spirit" (v. 45) and thereby ascribes to him the creative function befitting Yahweh (→ ζῳοποιέω; → 5; cf. Schwantes 56-61). According to vv. 51-54 the new form of existence is received by all, even those who are still alive at the parousia: "The dead *will be raised* imperishable, and we shall be changed" (v. 52). Resurrection and transformation occur with a view to a life beyond death (vv. 53-58; cf. 1 Thess 4:17; on the manner of argumentation and the history-of-religions problem cf. Dahl; Sider; Usami). That the resurrection of the dead is effected through the divine creative power is expressed unmistakably with the use of ἐγείρω (trans.).

The question, "Why is it thought incredible by any of you that God *raises* the dead?" (Acts 26:8), alludes to the faith, rooted in the OT, that God is lord over life and death (cf. Deut 32:39; 1 Sam 2:6; 2 Kgs 4:7; Wis 16:13; Tob 3:4); it is strikingly reminiscent of the divine predicate "Lord, who gives life to the dead" (second of the Eighteen Benedictions), which Rom 4:17 cites, adding "and calls into existence the things that do not exist" (cf. E. Käsemann, *Commentary on Romans* [1980]; H. Schlier, *Römerbrief* [HTKNT] ad loc.; Schwantes; Hofius). Thus ἐγείρω in Acts 26:8 is synonymous with → ζῳοποιέω (*ḥyh*), *give life.* Paul refers again to the Jewish confession in 2 Cor 1:9, interpreting his danger of death as the test of his hope in "God who *raises* the dead."

Of course, since the resurrection of Jesus, this Jewish belief has a new aspect: "God *raised* the Lord, and he will also raise us up (ἐξεγερεῖ) by his power" (1 Cor 6:14; see below; the compound ἐξεγερεῖ is replaced in a few later mss. by ἐξήγειρεν, making it a reference to baptism; cf. Conzelmann ad loc.). The connection between the resurrection of the dead and the resurrection of Christ (→ ἀνάστασις 4) is expressed by Paul also in 2 Cor 4:14 where the future resurrection will occur "with Jesus": the fellowship with Jesus that began at baptism finds its completion in participation in his resurrection (cf. P. Siber 72ff.; Baumert 89f. interprets ἐγείρω here as an expression for daily deliverance).

According to Heb 11:19 Abraham sacrificed Isaac, his heir, because he gave thought to the fact "that God was able to *waken* [RSV "raise"] men even from the dead." The extent to which this explication of Jewish faith in the power of God is derived from a concrete Jewish tradition cannot be demonstrated (the texts brought forward in the commentaries contribute too little). One may certainly consider a Christian interpretation; the phrase "from the dead" points to the influence of the Easter preaching of the early Church (→ 5).

An unmistakable Christian development of Jewish faith in the resurrection is present in John 5:21: "As the Father *raises* the dead and gives them life, so also the Son gives life to whom he will." Here ἐγείρω is explained by → ζῳοποιέω; the "resurrection" occurs, not, as in Jewish apocalyptic texts, as a prelude to the judgment; instead it is associated with the pronouncement of life (→ ζωή). Furthermore, the reference is not only to the power of God but also to what the *Father* does; the Son also *does* the same (cf. vv. 19f; on the life-giving function of Christ, cf. 1 Cor 15:45). As the present tense forms and the context indicate, *raise* is used in John 5:21 in a fig. sense for deliverance from the power of sin when faith is accepted (→ ἀνάστασις 4; cf. Bultmann, *TDNT* II, 874f.; Schnackenburg, *John* ad loc.).

5. The resurrection of Jesus is spoken of 31 times with a pass. form of ἐγείρω. In the ancient formulaic phrases or short references to the early resurrection preaching aor. ἠγέρθη is used (Luke 24:34; Rom 4:25; 6:4; Mark 16:6 par.; Matt 27:64; John 2:22). In other uses of the vb. in the NT

(→ 2, 3, 4) the synonym ἀνέστη and the corresponding Hebrew equivalent and its Greek translation (cf. Molitor) demand that the pass. be regarded as mid.: *stood up/awoke.* The same is true for the participles ἐγερθείς in 2 Cor 5:15; Rom 6:9; 7:4; 8:34; John 21:14 and the passives in the predictions of the Passion (Matt 16:21 par. Luke 9:22; Matt 17:9, 23; 20:19; 26:32 par. Mark 14:28; Matt 27:63). A pass. nuance of these forms cannot be excluded with certainty, as the Greeks distinguished pass. and act. differently from us (Jankum 39)—yet it recedes at least behind the mid. and forbids the extended assumption of a divine pass. (as in Fascher 197; Hahn 204; Schnackenburg, "Zur Aussage," 9; Schlier, *Auferstehung* 17; with hesitation Kremer, *Zeugnis* 43f.; Friedrich 157; Jeremias, on the other hand, correctly: *Theology* 13, n. 1). The forms of ἐγείρω to be interpreted as a mid. thus do not designate the action of the crucified one at the resurrection, but rather the manifestation of his new life made possible by that action (→ ἀνάστασις 4).

The context (e.g., "died" and "was buried," 1 Cor 15:3) and the frequent absence of a more precise definition of ἐγείρω indicate that the vb. is used in a technical sense known to the readers (→ 3, 4). The formulaic addition "from (the) dead" is often connected with ἠγέρθη or the act. forms of ἐγείρω and apparently stems from the Church's resurrection message (cf. Hoffmann, *Die Toten* 182f.). Its use means that Jesus is no longer among the dead, i.e., no longer in Sheol (cf. Rom 10:7) nor in the tomb (cf. Mark 16:6 par.). Yet ἠγέρθη, etc., expresses not only the end of the condition of death, but even more what follows death against all expectation and is a sign of new life: he *stood up* (in a fig. sense).

Whereas aor. ἠγέρθη requires that the "resurrection" of Jesus be regarded as a once-for-all event, pf. ἐγήγερται, he *is raised* (1 Cor 15:4; dependent on the expression in this verse are vv. 12, 13, 14, 16, 17, 20; cf. 2 Tim 2:8; Mark 16:14), emphasizes the abiding effect that the resurrection has for the crucified one: he lives (→ ζάω, cf. BDF §342). This is also presupposed where the Christian life is characterized as one belonging to Christ (2 Cor 5:15; cf. Rom 7:4; 14:7-9) and looking forward to his parousia (1 Thess 1:10). The resurrected Christ is no longer subjected to the law of death (Rom 6:9); therefore what 1 Cor 15:35ff. says applies to his new "body" (→ 4). In the connection of "raised" with an exaltation saying his new function is expressed (Rom 8:34): "Christ Jesus, who died, yes, and *was raised,* who is at the right hand of God, who indeed intercedes for us" (on the tradition-historical problem, see below on Rom 10:9).

As the adv. ὄντως indicates, the resurrection message was from the earliest period subject to doubt: "The Lord *has risen indeed*" (Luke 24:34). In order to demonstrate its credibility, reference was made to the witness of the Holy Scriptures: "in accordance with the scriptures" (1 Cor 15:4; → γραφή; cf. Bultmann, *Theology* I, 82; Kremer, *Zeugnis* 52-54; there also on attempts to refer "in accordance with the scriptures" to "on the third day" with an appeal to Hos 6:2, and not to ἠγέρθη; cf. Lehmann 221-30). Jesus' predictions of his Passion and resurrection serve the same apologetic purpose, at least in their extant form (cf. Kremer, *Osterevangelien* 22). For attestation of the resurrection message reference is made, esp. in Luke 24:34 and 1 Cor 15:4ff., to the witnesses to whom the resurrected one appeared (→ ὁράω; cf. Mussner, *Struktur* 412-15). In the apologetically shaped story of the tomb the resurrection message is proclaimed as the revelation of God. Reference is also made to the empty tomb as a confirming sign.

According to Rom 4:25 Christ "*was raised* for our justification," in order to liberate us from the fallen condition of death and to give us a portion in the new life (6:14) as a "new creation" (2 Cor 5:17; → 4, ἀνάστασις 4). It is for this reason that, according to 1 Cor 15:14, the resurrection of Jesus is so essential for the apostolic preaching and the Christian faith: "If Christ *has* not *been raised,* then our preaching is in vain and your faith is in vain."

It is uncertain why Matthew and Paul prefer the forms ἠγέρθη, etc., over ἀνέστη. (Both forms of expression were known in Hellenistic Judaism [LXX].) Perhaps it occurred as a result of the influence of the act. forms of ἐγείρω (cf. Oepke 335).

By means of trans. ἐγείρω the resurrection event is declared to be the act of God in 20 instances (likewise the eschatological resurrection [→ 4]) in the almost stereotypical sentence: "God *raised* him" (Rom 10:9; 1 Cor 6:14; 15:15; Acts 5:30; 10:40; 13:30), in the rel. clause "whom he *raised*" (1 Thess 1:10; Acts 3:15; 4:10; 13:37; cf. 1 Cor 15:15), and in the almost identical participial constructions with ἐγείρας, etc. (Gal 1:1; 2 Cor 4:14; Rom 4:24; 8:11a, b; Col 2:12; Eph 1:20; 1 Pet 1:21). In these passages, where it is often used without a more precise designation, the vb. is a t.t. for the deliverance from death brought about by God, as it was hoped for in the end time (→ 4). The frequent addition "from the dead" (1 Thess 1:10; Gal 1:1; Rom 8:11; 10:9; Acts 3:15; 4:10; 13:30; Col 2:12; Eph 1:20) emphasizes this. The phrase added to ἐγείρω only in Acts 10:40, "on the third day," as in 1 Cor 15:4 and in the Passion predictions, is not intended as an exact indication of the time. The act of God, which was removed from the grasp of human observation, was first evident in its effect (i.e., in the "experience": Schlier, *Auferstehung* 16; → 6). The consistent use of the aor. indicates that a solitary event is considered. (This does not exclude the possibility that later theological reflection must interpret this creative act of God as enduring and taking on a new existence.)

The frequent appeal to the resurrection of Jesus in the form of a participial construction (e.g., ὁ ἐγείρας τὸν κύριον, 2 Cor 4:14) serves to confirm belief in the power of God beyond death (so, e.g., Rom 8:11; Col 2:12) or to define faith in God more precisely (Rom 4:24; 1 Pet 1:21; Acts 5:30: "God of our fathers"). One may correctly see here a "christological variation" of the Jewish predicate for God as "Lord, who raises the dead" (→ 4; cf. Schwantes 72: ὁ ἐγείρας Ἰησοῦν as a new name of God). This indicates that belief in God as the Lord over life and death that is rooted in the OT and Judaism led the early Church to interpret the *resurrection* of Jesus, which was witnessed by the apostles on the basis of their encounter with the crucified one on Easter, as the *resurrection* brought about by God. The formulation "God *raised* Jesus" and other formulations are thus secondary, in terms of tradition-history, to the phrase *he arose* (cf. Cerfaux 57 [German edition]; *contra* Kramer 25-26). Further reflection led to the ascription of the resurrection not only to God's power (cf. Eph 1:20) but also to his πνεῦμα (Rom 8:11; cf. 6:4 [→ δόξα]; Eph 1:19f. [→ ἐνέργεια, ἰσχύς]). The use of trans. ἐγείρω in older formulaic texts indicates that this theological interpretation followed very soon after the resurrection.

The use together of the confessions "Jesus is Kyrios" and "God *raised* him from the dead" (Rom 10:9) points to the close relationship of the resurrection and the proclamation as Kyrios (→ ἀνάστασις, cf. Rom 1:4; Phil 2:9). The connection of the title κύριος with the resurrection can thus be regarded as a further early interpretation of the resurrection event (on the tradition-historical problem cf. Bultmann, *Theology* I, 51f., 81; Schweizer 56-76; Kramer 65-84; Hahn 97-114; Wengst 27-48; Vögtle and Pesch 15-24; Lambrecht 133-41): As the resurrected one Jesus is the Kyrios. He has a portion in the power of God (cf. Rom 8:34), and a function as Savior is attributed to him, which in the OT and Judaism is assigned to God alone (cf. Acts 2:21). According to 1 Thess 1:10 part of Christian existence, along with serving God (v. 9), is to wait for his Son, whom he *raised* from the dead and who saves us from the coming wrath. This salvation which belongs to God occurs, according to Paul, not least in the fact that the resurrected one as → σωτήρ has a portion in the life-giving power of God (1 Cor 15:45; → 4) and can give a part in his glory (cf. Phil 3:21). The acknowledgment of God's own power of saving and giving life led to John's ascription of Jesus' resurrection to Jesus himself (the deeper meaning of ἐγείρω in the temple logion in John 2:19-22) and to his use of ἐγείρω in this sense where Lazarus's raising is recalled (12:1, 9, 17; → ἀνάστασις 5).

6. **Ἔγερσις*** can mean both *awakening* and *resurrection* (cf. Oepke 336). In accordance with the expanded intrans. use of ἐγείρω, ἔγερσις in Matt 27:53 is to be regarded primarily as a synonym of ἀνάστασις and referred to Jesus' *resurrection,* which was first proclaimed after the sabbath. As ἔγερσις is not attested elsewhere in the NT (but in early Christian literature, cf. *PGL* s.v.) and stands here in tension with the context (which assumes the resurrection of the pious at Jesus' hour of death), one may assume that it is part of a later insertion (Oepke 337; Riebl 54f.). It fits in well with the time in which Jesus' resurrection (not simply his resurrection's becoming known) came to be connected with the third day (cf. Mark 16:9).

J. Kremer

ἔγερσις, εως, ἡ *egersis* awakening; resurrection → ἐγείρω 6.

ἐγκάθετος, 2 *enkathetos* lying in ambush

Luke 20:20 subst. partc.: ἀπέστειλαν ἐγκαθέτους, they "sent *spies.*"

ἐγκαίνια, ίων, τά *enkainia* Feast of Dedication*

In the NT only in John 10:22: ἐγένετο τότε τὰ ἐγκαίνια ἐν τοῖς Ἱεροσολύμοις, "It was the *feast of Dedication* at Jerusalem." The Feast of ἐγκαίνια (literally "renewal"; Heb. *ḥ*^{a}*nûkkâ* "[feast of] consecration"; cf. Num 7:11 LXX; 1 Esdr 7:7 [ἐγκαινισμός]; Deut 3:2 LXX [ἐγκαίνια]) was observed from the time of the Maccabees as a memorial of the purification and rededication of the temple by Judas the Maccabee on the twenty-fifth of Chislev (November/December), 164 B.C., after the three-year period of temple desecration by Antiochus IV Epiphanes (cf. 1 Macc 4:42-59 [ὁ ἐγκαινισμὸς τοῦ θυσιαστηρίου, v. 59]; 2 Macc 1:7-9, 18; 2:16; 10:1-8; Josephus *Ant.* xii.316-26). According to 2 Macc 10:5 the temple rededication fell on the same day of the year as the desecration by the Gentiles three years earlier. It was, like the Feast of Tabernacles, a festival of eight days' duration and was observed in memory both of the temple dedications under Solomon and Zerubbabel (both of which occurred on Tabernacles: 1 Kgs. 8:2; Ezra 3:4; cf. also 2 Chr 7:5; Ezra 6:16) and of the last Feast of Tabernacles during the struggles before the temple's rededication under the Maccabees (2 Macc 1:9, 18; 10:6-8). Josephus (*Ant.* xii.325) calls it "feast of lights" (Φῶτα, taken by Josephus as a reference to "the light of freedom"), probably because of the rekindling of the holy fire in the temple (cf. 2 Macc 1:18ff.). It was prescribed that, during the eight days, a light was to be kindled in front of each house (*b. Šabb.* 21b). Today the eight-armed menorah is lighted and the festival celebrated as a popular festival of lights.

According to John 10:22 Jesus, who had remained in Jerusalem since the feast of booths (cf. 7:10), is challenged by the Jews at the Feast of Dedication in "the portico of Solomon" (10:23) to declare himself openly—for the first time before "the Jews" in John—as the Messiah (v. 24). R. Hanhart and B. Reicke, *BHH* III, 1951 (bibliography); *BL* 1730f. (bibliography).

H. Balz

ἐγκαινίζω *enkainizō* renew; inaugurate*

Heb 9:18: ἡ πρώτη (διαθήκη) . . . ἐγκεκαίνισται, "the first covenant *was* not *ratified* [NEB *"inaugurated"*] without blood" (cf. Exod 24:8); Heb 10:20: ἣν ἐνεκαίνισεν ἡμῖν ὁδόν, in reference to the way into the sanctuary of God which was *newly opened* through Jesus' sacrificial death.

ἐγκακέω *enkakeō* become tired, lose heart*

In the NT always with a negative particle: in exhortations and requests (Gal 6:9; Eph 3:13; 2 Thess 3:13; cf. Luke 18:1), in reference to the conduct of Paul himself (2 Cor 4:1, 16).

ἐγκαλέω *enkaleō* accuse, blame*

Used absolutely, Acts 19:38; pass. with περί, *be accused* of (23:29; 26:2, 7), and with both gen. and a περί phrase (19:40); act. with διά (23:28) and with κατά with gen. of the person accused (Rom 8:33: "Who shall *bring any charge* against God's elect?").

ἐγκαταλείπω *enkataleipō* leave, abandon, leave behind*

Leave, abandon: Mark 15:34 par. Matt 27:46 (the cry of Jesus from the cross, following Ps 21:1 LXX); 2 Cor 4:9; 2 Tim 4:10, 16; Heb 13:5 (cf. Josh 1:5 LXX); cf. also *1 Clem.* 33:1. *Leave behind:* Rom 9:29; in the sense of *leave alone:* Acts 2:27 (οὐκ ἐγκαταλείψεις τὴν ψυχήν μου εἰς ᾅδην; cf. Ps 15:10 LXX), 31. *Forsake* (τὴν ἐπισυναγωγὴν ἑαυτῶν, "the habit of meeting together" [TEV]): Heb 10:25.

ἐγκατοικέω *enkatoikeō* dwell in, among*

2 Pet 2:8: δίκαιος ἐγκατοικῶν ἐν αὐτοῖς, of Lot, who, as a righteous man, "*lived* among them" (the inhabitants of Sodom and Gomorrah).

ἐγκαυχάομαι *enkauchaomai* boast*

2 Thess 1:4: ὥστε αὐτοὺς ἡμᾶς ἐν ὑμῖν ἐγκαυχᾶσθαι (TR καυχᾶσθαι), "Therefore we ourselves *boast* of you."

ἐγκεντρίζω *enkentrizō* graft on, graft in*

In the NT only in Rom 11:17, 19, 23 (bis), 24 (bis), in Paul's metaphor of the wild olive tree (Gentile Christians) *grafted into* the cultivated olive tree (Israel; with εἰς, v. 24a, dat., v. 24b; ἐνεκεντρίσθης ἐν αὐτοῖς, "*grafted in* among them [RSV "in their place"]," v. 17). → ἀγριέλαιος.

ἔγκλημα, ατος, τό *enklēma* accusation*

Acts 23:29: μηδὲν δὲ ἄξιον θανάτου ἢ δεσμῶν ἔχοντα ἔγκλημα, "charged with nothing deserving death or imprisonment"; 25:16: ἀπολογία . . . περὶ τοῦ ἐγκλήματος, "defense concerning the *charge*."

ἐγκομβόομαι *enkomboömai* clothe oneself; fig.: make (something) one's own*

1 Pet 5:5: πάντες δὲ ἀλλήλοις τὴν ταπεινοφροσύνην ἐγκομβώσασθε, "*Clothe yourselves,* all of you, with humility toward one another."

ἐγκοπή, ῆς, ἡ *enkopē* hindrance, restraint*

1 Cor 9:12: ἵνα μή τινα ἐγκοπὴν δῶμεν τῷ εὐαγγελίῳ, "rather than put an *obstacle* in the way of the gospel." G. Stählin, *TDNT* III, 855-57.

ἐγκόπτω *enkoptō* restrain, hinder, impede*

Paul was *hindered* from completing specific travel plans (Rom 15:22; 1 Thess 2:18); the Galatians, from obeying the truth (Gal 5:7; with inf. in each case). 1 Pet 3:7: εἰς τὸ μὴ ἐγκόπτεσθαι (TR ἐκκόπτεσθαι) τὰς προσευχὰς ὑμῶν, "in order that your prayers may not be hindered." In Acts 24:4 (ἵνα δὲ μὴ ἐπὶ πλεῖόν σε ἐγκόπτω) ἐγκόπτω is rendered best by *detain, make demands on:* "*to detain* you no further" (cf. the adv. συντόμως, "shortly," v. 4b; reference to the phrase ἔγκοπον ποιέω, "wear out," Job 19:2; Isa 43:23 [BAGD s.v.; G. Stählin, *TDNT* III 855, n. 1] do not fit the rhetorical style of the text). *TDNT* III, 857-60.

ἐγκράτεια, ας, ἡ *enkrateia* self-control; chastity*
ἐγκρατεύομαι *enkrateuomai* exercise self-control; be chaste*
ἐγκρατής, 2 *enkratēs* chaste*

Lit.: W. Grundmann, *TDNT* II, 339-42. — F. Mussner, *Der Galaterbrief* (HTKNT, 1974) 384-95, esp. 389. — H. Schlier, *Der Brief an die Galater* (KEK, 1965) 247-64, esp. 262. — A. Vögtle, *Die Tugend- und Lasterkataloge im NT* (1936), index s.v. — *idem, LTK* X, 399-401.

1. In the philosophical ethic of the Greek classical period and of later Hellenism, ἐγκράτεια (from the stem κρατ-, which refers to power and dominance) plays a significant role. The word and its derivatives take on a special importance in the writings of Philo and the Essenes. Ἐγκράτεια is normally used with regard to all human desires, including desires for food and drink, sex, and conversation. Thus ἐγκρατής signifies the free, autonomous, and independent person, who does not allow himself to be tempted or diverted by any allurements.

2. In view of the frequency of ἐγκράτεια in Greek thought, its infrequent use in the Bible is surprising. In the LXX it is found only in a few passages of Hellenistically

inspired wisdom literature (cf. Sir 18:30; 4 Macc 5:34: abstinence from sexual and other excesses; Wis 8:21: a gift of God). In the NT Gospels the word does not appear at all.

3. The ἐγκρατ- word group appears only 7 times elsewhere in the NT: the noun in Acts 24:25; Gal 5:23; and 2 Pet 1:6 (bis), the verb in 1 Cor 7:9 and 9:25, and the adj. in Titus 1:8. In Galatians, Titus, and 2 Peter these words appear in catalogs of virtues and designate the opposite of → ἀσέλγεια, which is named in the vice list in Gal 5:19. In all instances ἐγκρατ- refers first of all to sexual abstinence, but then is extended to include positive, general self-control and discipline (cf. *1 Clem.* 30:3; 35:2; 62:2; 64; *Barn.* 2:2; *Herm. Man.* viii.1ff.; cf. Schlier 262).

4. With regard to the significance of ἐγκρατ- in the sphere of the NT, three characteristic statements are to be distinguished from each other: a) In 1 Cor 9:25 Paul thinks of functional self-discipline that stands in the service of a greater good. He uses the figure of athletic victory while speaking actually of the evangelizing (cf. vv. 12, 14, 16, 18, 23) apostolate (cf. vv. 1f.).

b) The Greek and Hellenistic idea of virtue is present in Acts 24:25 (περὶ δικαιοσύνης καὶ ἐγκράτειας) and in the catalogs of virtues in Gal 5:23 (ἀγάπη, χαρά, εἰρήνη, μακροθυμία, χρηστότης, ἀγαθωσύνη, πίστις, πραΰτης, ἐγκράτεια); Titus 1:8 (qualifications for bishops: φιλόξενον, φιλάγαθον, σώφρονα, δίκαιον, ὅσιον, ἐγκρατῆ); and 2 Pet 1:5-7 (ἀρετήν . . . γνῶσιν . . . ἐγκράτειαν . . . ὑπομονήν . . . εὐσέβειαν . . . φιλαδελφίαν . . . ἀγάπην; cf. *Barn.* 2:2; *Herm. Man.* viii.1ff.).

c) Of course the NT authors do not allow their ἐγκράτεια concept to be exhausted in the Hellenistic concept of virtue (cf. Schlier 262; Vögtle, *LTK* X, 400; *contra* Grundmann 340). Luke speaks first of "faith in Christ Jesus" and then of "justice and ἐγκράτεια" (Acts 24:24f.). Paul describes his own ἐγκράτεια (1 Cor 7:9) as a "χάρισμα from God" (v. 7). In Gal 5:22f. he describes ἐγκράτεια as "fruit of the Spirit." Furthermore, before the author of 2 Peter gives his demand for the practice of virtue, knowledge, ἐγκράτεια, etc., he indicates that the addressees are recipients of a gift (1:1-7). The imv. call for the realization of chastity and self-control is based on the promise of the salvation given in Jesus Christ and in his Spirit (cf. *1 Clem.* 30:3; 35:2; 64).

5. The biblical authors are so sparing with words from the ἐγκρατ- group because of their conviction that the Christian life-style is not a matter of an autonomous ethic, but is rather to be understood only as the response to the prior gift of salvation through God himself. Thus ἐγκράτεια appeared to them to have only a limited value as a suitable instrument in verbalizing this subject.

H. Goldstein

ἐγκρατεύομαι *enkrateuomai* exercise self-control; be chaste
→ ἐγκράτεια.

ἐγκρατής, 2 *enkratēs* chaste
→ ἐγκράτεια.

ἐγκρίνω *enkrinō* place in the same category (as)*

2 Cor 10:12: ἐγκρῖναι . . . ἑαυτούς τισιν τῶν ἑαυτοὺς συνιστανόντων, "*to class* . . . ourselves with some of those who commend themselves" (parallel to συγκρῖναι, "compare").

ἐγκρύπτω *enkryptō* hide; mix*

Matt 13:33 par. Luke 13:21 of leaven, which a woman *mixed* into three measures of flour (ἐνέκρυψεν).

ἔγκυος, 2 *enkyos* pregnant*

Luke 2:5 of Mary: οὔσῃ ἐγκύῳ, "who was *with child.*"

ἐγχρίω *enchriō* rub on, smear*

Rev 3:18: κολλούριον ἐγχρῖσαι τοὺς ὀφθαλμούς σου, "salve *to anoint* your eyes."

ἐγώ *egō* I

1. General — 2. The "I" in revelatory discourses — 3. "But I say to you" in the antitheses of the Sermon on the Mount — 4. The "I" in Romans 7

Lit.: R. BULTMANN, "Romans 7 and the Anthropology of Paul" (1932), *idem, Existence and Faith* (1960) 147-57. — E. KÄSEMANN, *The Testament of Jesus* (1968) 1-55. — W. G. KÜMMEL, "Römer 7 und die Bekehrung des Paulus" (1929), *idem, Römer 7 und das Bild des Menschen im NT* (1974) 1-160. — U. LUZ, "Die Erfüllung des Gesetzes bei Matthäus," *ZTK* 73 (1978) 398-435. — *idem, Das Geschichtsverständnis des Paulus* (BEvT 49, 1968) 158-68. — G. RICHTER, "Die Fleischwerdung des Logos im Johannesevangelium," *NovT* 13 (1971) 81-126; 14 (1972) 257-76. — L. SCHOTTROFF, *Der Glaubende und die feindliche Welt* (1970) 228-96. — E. SCHWEIZER, *Ego eimi* (FRLANT 56, [2]1965). — E. STAUFFER, *TDNT* II, 343-62. — G. STRECKER, "Die Antithesen der Bergpredigt," *ZNW* 69 (1978) 36-72. — For further bibliography see *TWNT* X, 1064f.

1. The nom. of the personal pron. is most often used in the NT, as in classical Greek, to express a contrast or a point of emphasis. In addition, Hebraisms occur with the use of ἐγώ (e.g., Mark 12:26; see BDF §277). The personal pron. is used 1,802 times in the different cases; 347 of these are nom. The frequency of usage is significantly above average in John (494 occurrences; cf. Matthew: 221; Mark: 107). In the following material citations refer particularly to those cases where "I" has a special theological significance.

2. In almost all religions there are instances where the one who reveals himself introduces himself in revelatory discourse with an "I" saying, e.g., Gen 17:1, "I am God Almighty," or in an altogether different religious realm the self-introduction of the Syrian prophets with "I am God" or "God's son" or "the divine spirit" (Origen *Cels.* vii.8, 9). The "I" revelation is so widespread that no historical or theological conclusions can be drawn on the basis of parallels in the history of religions to the "I" revelatory discourse (see the comprehensive collection of material in Schweizer; see also R. Bultmann, *The Gospel of John* [1971] 225f., n. 3). To understand the "I" revelation it is important to describe the conceptions of revelation then present. These conceptions, even in almost identical "I" revelations, can be totally different. Bultmann's classification of instances of the ἐγώ-εἰμι formula by Bultmann is problematic, since it brings together different conceptions of revelation in one category (presentation formulas, qualification formulas, identification formulas, recognition formulas; on the recognition formula in John see below).

The "I" of revelatory discourse is found in the NT above all in John, Revelation, and in manifestation narratives in the Gospels and Acts. The "I" in NT revelatory discourses is almost always spoken by Christ. Self-revelation by God occurs only seldom in the NT; see esp. Rev 21:6.

In John Jesus reveals in discourses what he is (ἐγώ εἰμι, e.g., 6:35; 11:25), where he comes from (e.g., 8:42; 7:29), what he gives (e.g., 4:14; 17:14), what he speaks and to what he bears witness (e.g., 6:63; 5:36), and that he judges the κόσμος (e.g., 8:16; 7:7; 16:30). The content of his revelation is, on the one hand, his relationship to the Father and, on the other hand, the gift of salvation to mankind. In view of the revelation, human responses determine salvation or non-salvation. The gift of salvation that becomes effective in the revelation is expressed in John in numerous soteriological concepts and in graphic metaphors: The revealer is "the true vine" (15:1, 5), "the bread of life" (6:35; cf. vv. 41, 48, 51), "the light of the world" (8:12; cf. 12:46), "the door" (10:9, 7), "the good shepherd" (vv. 11, 14), "the resurrection and the life" (11:25), and "the way, the truth, and the life" (14:6).

All of these concepts and metaphors express the same content: that in revelatory discourse the Son reveals himself and that salvation and destruction are determined in this revelation. Those who believe have life. The true vine, the life, and the living water that Jesus gives, can be confused with earthly life and with water in the well (e.g., John 4:10-16); the revelation is misunderstood because it is understood in worldly terms. But the true vine is "true" because it brings life and not death. The implicit contrast to the true vine is not a so-called vine, but rather a vine which brings death. In these images and metaphors for salvation John does not refer critically to non-Christian myths (e.g., to a myth of the tree of life; so Bultmann, *John*, on 15:1) or to dreams of life which are dreamed by men. Bultmann argues on the basis of this mistaken idea that the Johannine "I am" speeches are to be understood as "recognition formulas" in which Jesus reveals himself as "the one expected and asked for" (*ibid.*, 225 with n. 3 on 225f.). *Actual* life, however, thirst, water from the well, and edible bread are for John the plane of critical confrontation: All of them can be confused with the truth. Jesus' miracles can be confused with the earthly multiplication of bread. Descriptions of misunderstandings, in which bread is confused with bread (ch. 6), water with water (4:10-16), seeing with seeing (ch. 9), and faith with faith (20:24-29), flow through John. True salvation is for John beyond reality. Faith helps one to see through the reality and to keep oneself separated from it.

The history-of-religions and literary problems of John are closely related to each other. The Gnostic structure of the revelatory discourses of John is disputed. The extent to which and manner in which Gnostic conceptions have been Christianized are disputed. For Bultmann pre-Johannine Gnostic speeches have been interpreted in a Christian way by John: The glory of the (originally Gnostic) revealer for John is to be seen only through the σάρξ of Jesus, only in the paradox, in the scandal of the incarnation. For Käsemann (see esp. 9f.) the incarnation spoken of in John 1:14 is not an abasement, and thus the understanding of the revealer comes close to that of Gnosticism ("naive docetism"). Richter distinguishes between a basic Johannine text and an antidocetic post-Johannine editing, the latter to be found in, e.g., John 1:14-18.

In manifestation narratives (e.g., call visions) in the NT, as in other religions, the ἐγώ-revelation has a firm place. The divine being who reveals himself introduces himself to the recipient of the revelation (e.g., "I am Jesus," Acts 9:5; cf. 22:8; 26:15) and commissions the recipient (e.g., "you will be a witness for him to all men," 22:15) or conveys a message (e.g., Luke 1:19; Mark 6:50 par.). According to Mark 13:6 par. a sign of the eschatological disturbances is that false prophets and false messiahs also appear with the revelatory claim ἐγώ εἰμι.

The ἐγώ of the revealer has a central meaning in the book of Revelation. The exalted Christ commissions John in a call manifestation (Rev 1:9-20) and reveals himself: "I am the first and the last, and the living one" (vv. 17f.). In the letters to the seven churches the revelation of Christ is expressed at first in the third person (τάδε λέγει, e.g., 3:14), then followed by Christ's direct speech (e.g., 3:21). The heavenly Christ who reveals himself in Revelation is like God (2:8; 22:13; cf. 21:6; 1:8). The ceremonious revelation of God and of Christ has a central significance. God reveals himself as the ruler of all history, while Christ is revealed as the judge who comes soon (22:12; cf. 1:7, etc.). From this revelation comes the threat to those who love lies and worship the beast—and the consolation for the persecuted Christians: God is the ruler also in the time of persecution by the state which claims a divine dignity for itself. The seer sees already in the revelation the coming victory of God and of Christ and the new world.

3. It is disputed whether the antitheses of Matt 5:21-48 can be traced back to the historical Jesus.

If the antitheses can be traced back to Jesus, there is a major problem in determining how Jesus understood himself in relationship to the Torah of Moses. (E.g., "the words ἐγὼ δὲ λέγω embody a claim to an authority which rivals and challenge that of Moses"—so E. Käsemann, *Essays on NT Themes* [1964] 37. The other view is that of H. Braun, *Spätjüdisch-häretischer und frühchristlicher Radikalismus* II [1957] 9f.: "Wherever ἐγὼ δὲ λέγω ὑμῖν is literarily primary, it does not introduce a sharpening of the Torah." That is, Jesus radicalizes the Torah, but not in a fundamental proclamation, but in a way that is "case by case.") The first, second, and fourth antitheses, the special material of Matthew, are attributed to Jesus by the proponents of authenticity. It is clear from the Lukan parallels to the third, fifth, and sixth antitheses that the antithetical form has been added secondarily (for further information on the debate regarding authenticity, see Strecker).

In the literary context of Matthew the antitheses can be interpreted unambiguously—independently of how one determines the question of authenticity and how one conceives the growth in the process of tradition which resulted finally in the present form of the text. Matthew believes that the entire Torah must be kept, that no commandment may be abolished (Matt 5:17-19). This does not mean for him that in a conflict where one Torah commandment falls into conflict with another commandment of the Torah may not be broken. The love commandment takes precedence, e.g., over the sabbath commandment (12:1-8).

The antitheses of the Sermon on the Mount can in this context involve no abrogation of the law. The commandment of Jesus does not annul the commandment of Moses that precedes it; otherwise the λύειν against which Matt 5:17-19 speaks unambiguously would be done by Jesus! Thus a positive relationship must exist between the thesis and the antithesis. In this way the law's "fulfillment" (5:17) is accomplished. For Matthew Jesus' *life* is the fulfillment of OT prophecy (e.g., 1:22), Jesus' *actions* (and those of the disciples) are the fulfillment of the will of God (e.g., 7:21), i.e., the Torah, and the *teaching* of Jesus (e.g., 7:29) is interpretation, i.e., fulfillment of the Torah. His interpretation of the Torah is the legitimate interpretation over against the Pharisaic interpretation of the Torah based on individual case law, which is to be rejected (e.g., 12:7). His practice (and that of the disciples), in contrast to Pharisaic practice, is the better righteousness (5:20). The better quality of the righteousness and of the interpretation of the law by Jesus depends on the meaning of the Torah's love commandment. On this basis Jesus is "Lord of the sabbath" (12:8) and he stands over the Torah: because he interprets the Torah with the help of the love commandment (as a Torah commandment).

This is precisely the case in the antitheses. The prohibition of murder is interpreted as a demand for reconciliation. The prohibition of adultery includes for Matthew also the prohibition of the lustful look and is considered by Matthew an offense against ἀγάπη. The command to write out a certificate of divorce is to be followed now, as it was formerly, but with the consequence that divorce and remarriage should be practiced only in limited, well-defined instances. The prohibition of perjury is interpreted by Jesus as saying that one should not use formulas of oath in daily speech. Here the command to love God is the guiding principle for interpretation of the Torah. The limitation of blood vengeance in the law of revenge ("an eye for an eye . . .") is to be taken further: one should not strike back at all but should totally renounce revenge. True interpretation of the command to love one's neighbor means that love is to be directed to one's enemies. Because Matthew proceeds in the sixth antithesis from the command to love one's neighbor, he thinks concretely of deeds in the sense of 25:31-46, thus of works of love that should be extended to enemies of the Church, the persecutors.

Ἐγὼ δὲ λέγω ὑμῖν thus means: Jesus is here the teacher of the Torah, teacher of the will of God. He interprets the Torah here. The legitimacy of his interpretation is based on the meaning of the love command. One can use Matt 22:36-40 as the hermeneutical key for 5:21-48.

4. As a result of the recent history of interpretation (see esp. Kümmel and Bultmann), in the interpretation of Romans 7 one can proceed with a few negative results.

The "I" is not *individual-biographical* (Paul before his conversion), but also not an embodiment of how the Jews understand themselves before the νόμος. The self-understanding of a Jew or of Paul in his past is expressed rather in Phil 3:6. The occasion for such an incorrect interpretation is given esp. in Rom 7:7-12.

Furthermore, the conflict in vv. 14-25 is not an *ethical* conflict of the "I." In the difference between θέλειν and πράσσειν the concern is not—at least primarily not—with ethical actions, for the result of πράσσειν is death and the goal of θέλειν is life. Πράσσειν is equivalent to κατεργάζεσθαι, "accomplish" (see esp. v. 17). Also, the conflict is not to be understood in *psychological* terms, for the *subjective* experience of conflict remains in the foreground. In decisive statements Paul will even leave the level of subjectivity: "It is not longer I that do it, but sin which dwells within me" (vv. 17, 20). The designation of the conflict as "trans-subjective" (Bultmann 151, 157; cf. esp. E. Käsemann, *Commentary on Romans* [1981] 193) is suitable to the character of sin as power. In addition, the conflict should not be understood in terms of the conceptions of a *dualistic anthropology.* Paul's concern is not to describe a double determination—on the one side through the body and the bodily world, and on the other side through the essential person who is separated from the world and the body. Even phrases such as ἔσω ἄνθρωπος (v. 22), σαρκινός (v. 14) or what is said in v. 23 give occasion for this interpretation. Paul sees the conflict in more radical terms. The σαρκινός is the *whole* person. "I" and σάρξ are identical (v. 18). Alongside existence as sin's puppet, there is not another true identity to which one can retreat, as in dualistic-Gnostic concepts of revelation. The radicality of the concept of sin in Paul is, on the contrary, more intelligible when one sees it in critical contrast to Gnosticism.

Along with the negative limitations which are important for the interpretation of Romans 7, one must also consider that Paul was a man in a concrete historical situation and that his letters were understood by concrete persons; thus one should consider the connection of Rom 7:7-25 with the experiences of persons in the Imperium Romanum (see especially Luz, *Geschichtsverständnis* 162, n. 101).

The "I" of Rom 7:7-25 is the "I" of the unredeemed person, the slave of sin, who desires life and produces death. Sin employs the desire for salvation in the same way that it employs the law. The law's intention is life, but the power of sin actually perverts the law. Vv. 7-13 speak of the Torah as sin's special instrument, while vv. 14-25 extend the same subject to refer not only to the existence of the Jew who has the Torah, but also more generally to the situation of mankind in a comprehensive sense as condemned. The radicality of enslavement to sin is visible as a result of the freedom that Christ points to. In the same way the imprisonment of the "I" in Gnosticism becomes visible in the presence of the revelation. Adam sat in the prison of the body, he heard the call to awake from sleep, "and he wept and shed bitter tears" and asked, "'From where has this hope come to me, while I am in the chains of the prison?'" (*Apocryphon of John* [*Nag Hammadi codex II*, 31:6, 8-10]). The "I" of Rom 7:7ff. (which also bears elements of Adam, esp. in vv. 7-12) calls for freedom, and this call is not understood just by those who are liberated. Paul at the same time describes the experiences of powerlessness and the situation of those who are enslaved and points them to their hope.

L. Schottroff

ἐδαφίζω *edaphizō* raze to the ground, strike to the ground*

Luke 19:44, of the destruction of Jerusalem by its enemies: ἐδαφιοῦσίν σε καὶ τὰ τέκνα σου ἐν σοί, they will "*dash you to the ground,* you and your children within you."

ἔδαφος, ους, τό *edaphos* ground*

Acts 22:7: ἔπεσά τε εἰς τὸ ἔδαφος, "I fell to the *ground.*"

ἑδραῖος, 3 (2) *hedraios* firm, steadfast*

1 Cor 7:37: ἐν τῇ καρδίᾳ ... ἑδραῖος, *firm* ... in heart; 15:58: ἑδραῖοι γίνεσθε, "be *steadfast,*" with ἀμετακίνητοι, "immovable"; Col 1:23: εἴ γε ἐπιμένετε τῇ πίστει τεθεμελιωμένοι καὶ ἑδραῖοι καὶ μὴ μετακινούμενοι ..., "provided that you continue in the faith, stable and *steadfast,* not shifting...." E. Stauffer, *TDNT* II, 362-64; *TWNT* X, 1065 (bibliography).

ἑδραίωμα, ατος, τό *hedraiōma* foundation

1 Tim 3:15, fig.: ἑδραίωμα τῆς ἀληθείας, *foundation* of the truth.

Ἑζεκίας, ου *Hezekias* Hezekiah*

A king of Judah (2 Kgs 18:1) mentioned in Matt 1:9f. as the son of Ahaz and father of Manasseh.

ἐθελοθρησκία, ας, ἡ *ethelothrēskia* self-chosen worship, superfluous worship*

This noun appears in the NT only in Col 2:23 in connection with the rejection of worldly elements (στοιχεῖα τοῦ κόσμου, v. 20; cf. vv. 21f.), of which it is said: λόγον μὲν ἔχοντα σοφίας ἐν ἐθελοθρησκίᾳ καὶ ταπεινοφροσύνῃ καὶ ἀφειδίᾳ σώματος, "It may be argued that true wisdom is to be found in these, with their *self-imposed devotions,* their self-abasement, and their severe treatment of the body ..." (JB). Constructions with ἐθελο- can be used to express an intent in a positive or critical manner (cf. BAGD 218). The rendering "arbitrary worship" inserts a critical component that does not correspond to the two parallel substantives (ἐθελοθρησκία and ταπεινοφροσύνη). The reference is to religious achievements taken on voluntarily, which are generally considered wise, but in reality have no value and only satisfy the carnal attitude. Christians have died with Christ to such worldly ordinances. Cf. E. Schweizer, *Kolosserbrief* (EKKNT) ad loc., n. 437; K. L. Schmidt, *TDNT* III, 159.

H. Balz

ἐθέλω *ethelō* will, be willing; want, desire
→ θέλω.

ἐθίζω *ethizō* accustom*

Luke 2:27, pf. pass. partc. used substantively: κατὰ τὸ εἰθισμένον τοῦ νόμου, "according to the *custom* of the law."

ἐθνάρχης, ου, ὁ *ethnarchēs* ethnarch, ruler*

2 Cor 11:32: ὁ ἐθνάρχης Ἁρέτα τοῦ βασιλέως, of the ethnarch (literally "ruler of the people") installed by the Nabatean King Aretas in the region of Damascus; best translated *governor.* → Ἁρέτας. G. Lindeskog, *BHH* I, 446; *BL* 443.

ἐθνικός, 3 *ethnikos* Gentile, pagan*

In the NT only as a subst.: Matt 5:47: οἱ ἐθνικοί (TR τελῶναι), the *Gentiles* (in contrast to the Jews, but at the same time placed here alongside the Jews; cf. 6:7); 18:17, of those who do not want to hear the Church's admonition: ἔστω σοι ὥσπερ ὁ ἐθνικὸς καὶ ὁ τελώνης, he will be to you as the *Gentile* or the tax collector (here in contrast to the Church!); 3 John 7: ἀπὸ τῶν ἐθνικῶν (TR ἐθνῶν), "from the *heathen.*"

ἐθνικῶς *ethnikōs* like the Gentiles*

Gal 2:14: εἰ ... ἐθνικῶς καὶ οὐχὶ Ἰουδαϊκῶς ζῇς, "if you ... live *like a Gentile* and not like a Jew."

ἔθνος, ους, τό *ethnos* people, nation; pl.: peoples, nations; Gentiles

1. Occurrences in the NT — 2. Ἔθνος = *people* (general)

— 3. Τὰ ἔθνη = *Gentiles* in contrast to Jews — a) Assumptions of the usage — b) Words of Jesus — c) Paul — d) The Synoptics — 4. Τὰ ἔθνη = *Gentiles* in contrast to Christians

Lit.: G. BERTRAM and K. L. SCHMIDT, *TDNT* II, 364-73. — P. CHRISTIAN, *Jesus und seine geringsten Brüder* (ETS 12, 1975). — J. FRIEDRICH, *Gott im Bruder?* (Calwer theologische Monographien 7, 1977). — F. HAHN, *Mission in the NT* (1965). — M. HENGEL, *Between Jesus and Paul* (1983), 1-29, 48-64. — J. LANGE, *Das Erscheinen des Auferstandenen im Ev. nach Matthäus* (1973) 295-301, 377-79. — U. WILCKENS, "Gottes geringste Brüder—zu Mt 25, 31-46," FS Kümmel 363-83. — For further bibliography see *TWNT* X, 1065f.

1. The word appears in the NT 162 times, of which only 32 are sg. (13 times general, 18 times with reference to a specific people, once in reference to Christianity). Of the 130 pl. uses 35 are anarthrous ἔθνη, but even of these anarthrous uses most pl. uses have the meaning *Gentiles* (→ 3), which presupposes a qualifying distinction between (ὁ) → λαός and (τὰ) ἔθνη.

2. Sg. ἔθνος occurs in the neutral meaning *people,* without a special theological valuation of the concept, particularly when Paul describes himself in the speeches of Acts as a member of his *"people"* (Acts 26:4; 28:19; RSV "nation") or when the Jewish people are in other contexts called an ἔθνος (Luke 7:5; 23:2; Acts 10:22; 24:2, 10). The 5 references in John also belong here (11:48, 50, 51, 52; 18:35), as does Mark 13:8 par.

It is significant that in fundamental statements Luke regards all peoples of the earth as created in the same manner by God, particularly in the Areopagus speech (Acts 17:26), which stands in the Hellenistic Jewish tradition, and in such passages as Acts 10:35 and 2:5. As "all *peoples*" (17:26; RSV "every nation"; the verse does not say πᾶν τὸ ἔθνος, "humanity as *one* people") are derived from one, Christian preaching is meant for all of them (presented in an ideal way in the Pentecost sermon, cf. 2:14 with 2:5), and persons from all peoples should be equally entitled to come to God (10:34, as the focal point of ch. 10). (In other passages Luke uses the terminology that has been shaped in Judaism, which distinguishes Jews and *Gentiles.*)

Revelation often places ἔθνος in a series with λαός, φυλή, and γλῶσσα, especially in hymnic sayings (5:9; 7:9; 14:6, etc.); thus it is said that all peoples are affected without distinction by the judgment and grace of the one God. Thus in passages in Revelation where τὰ ἔθνη stands alone, it should not be translated "Gentiles" (except possibly in 11:2); a separation of humanity into Jews and Gentiles has apparently already become unnecessary for Revelation.

3. a) The use of ἔθνος or (τὰ) ἔθνη in the NT is primarily determined by Jewish usage, which is prepared for in the OT (in the postexilic period; cf. A. R. Hulst, *THAT* II, 290-325, esp. 321ff.). In the NT period the terminological distinction is firmly fixed, so that *ʿam* designates the "people" of God and *gôyim* normally designates the "peoples," i.e., mankind outside Israel, the "Gentiles." Later rabbinic usage even uses sg. *gôy* (lit. "people") for individual non-Jews. A value judgment is consistently associated with these terms: the "peoples" are regarded as those who are far from God, even enemies of God, or at least not elect by God. According to a strict Pharisaic view, contact with them defiles (cf. the protest of those sent from James, Gal 2:12).

This Jewish usage appears unmodified in the Synoptic tradition (Matt 6:32 par. Luke 12:30 [cf. ἐθνικοί, Matt 5:47 and 6:7]; probably also Mark 10:42 par.).

The LXX translates *ʿam* primarily with λαός and *gôy* with ἔθνος; occasionally the terminological differentiation between λαός (for the elect people) and ἔθνη (for "Gentiles") is more consistently carried out than in the Hebrew text. This word choice approaches Greek usage in which, since Aristotle, there was the tendency to use ἔθνη (or ἔθνος) for the "other" peoples in contrast to the Ἕλληνες (cf. LSJ s.v.). Thus ἔθνος received a slightly unfavorable connotation and moved in the direction of βάρβαροι. In the LXX the usage is naturally determined by the self-understanding of Judaism.

Thus for the (former) Jew Paul, Ἕλληνες and βάρβαροι belong together under the generic term τὰ ἔθνη, *Gentiles* (Rom 1:14, after 1:13!); in other passages Paul can use τὰ ἔθνη and Ἕλληνες almost synonymously.

b) In the logia of Jesus (τὰ) ἔθνη has not yet taken on the new accent. Yet he holds up individual Gentiles or Gentile cities or peoples as examples which provide a warning to his own people (Matt 8:10 par.; 11:20-24 par.; 12:41f. par.); when Israel refuses the invitation into the rule of God proclaimed by Jesus, God will allot the places at his table next to Abraham, Isaac, and Jacob to others, i.e., Gentiles (8:11 par.; cf. already John the Baptist's threat, 3:9 par.).

The Synoptics portray explicitly as exceptions those instances where Jesus turns to individual Gentiles (Mark 7:25-30 par.; Matt 8:5-13 par.). Yet there is only a small step from this occasional opening to Gentiles by Jesus to his basic view, according to which he promises the kingdom of God to the "poor" (→ πτωχός), the "tax collectors and sinners," i.e., those who are considered by the Pharisees as equal to Gentiles from a religious point of view. The Samaritans, whom Jesus does not regard as excluded from the kingdom of God, are considered in the same way (Luke 10:30-37; 17:12-19).

c) Paul does use τὰ ἔθνη to mean simply "the *Gentiles*" in the same sense as in Jewish terminology: they "do not know God" (1 Thess 4:5), and one who belongs (or belonged) to them is (or was) a "sinner" (Gal 2:15; cf. 1 Cor 5:1; 12:2). But Paul regards God as the God not only of the Jews, but also of the Gentiles (Rom 3:29), and regards himself as called by God to proclaim the gospel of Christ directly to Gentiles (Gal 1:16; 2:2; Rom 1:5;

15:16-18, etc.). He derives this commission immediately from God's revelation to him that Jesus, the one he formerly persecuted, is the Lord (Gal 1:15f.).

Paul has thus entered into that direction of early Christianity which became the most significant decision of the beginning period: to call even "Gentiles" into the community of discipleship to Christ without demanding that they come by way of Judaism (through circumcision, etc.). Because of this revolutionary principle Paul had severely persecuted Christian churches in Syria. Now he himself represents this position and reflects on it anew from the basic knowledge that God justifies sinners, indeed "enemies," without works of the law. He works exegetically in Gal 3:8 with the promise to Abraham (Gen 18:18) that Abraham should be a blessing for "all *nations*" (πάντα τὰ ἔθνη). Thus Abraham is for Paul no longer the father of the Jewish people, but rather of all believers from Jews and Gentiles (Rom 4:9-18), a view he derives from Gen 17:5. The major portion of Romans (chs. 1–11) is dedicated to proving that no distinction exists between Jews and Gentiles in the presence of the God who justifies the ungodly. Thus for Paul, among others, arises the difficult problem of the place of the Mosaic law (Rom 7 throughout; → νόμος), the origin of which from God is not in doubt.

However, despite the special promises for Israel attested in the law, Paul affirms in the previously formulated thesis in Gal 3:28: In Christ the distinction between Jew and "Greek" (here = "Gentile") no longer holds (cf. Rom 11:30-32 as a resumption of Rom 3:19f., 23 and as the conclusion of the whole discussion which began at 1:18). Thus Paul has transformed the inherited theologically based distinction between Jews and Gentiles—on the basis of the proclamation of Christ (thus not on the basis of the cosmopolitan view of many Hellenistic Jews like Philo)—into a new relationship alongside and with one another. Already the introductory thesis of Romans (1:16) combines Jews and "Greeks" (= "Gentiles") additively (cf. 9:24, etc.; 1 Cor 1:23f.). This idea of an "aggregate humanity" based on the cross must have appeared to true Jews as a blasphemous surrender of Israel's election by God. This continued to bring Paul hindrances to his work and persecutions from the Jews (1 Thess 2:16; cf. Acts 17:5ff.; 18:12ff.; 20:3; 21:19-22, 27f., etc.).

The letters of the Pauline school are linked to the portrayal of Paul as the "apostle for the *Gentiles*" (Col 1:27; Eph 3:1-10; 1 Tim 2:7; 2 Tim 4:17; Rom 16:26 [secondary]). Ephesians in particular (2:11-18) places values on the equal membership of former Jews and Gentiles (who are addressed here: v. 11) in the Church of Jesus Christ.

d) In the Synoptic Gospels, all of which assume that the gospel is open for the Gentiles, the problem is considered in a variety of ways. For Mark it is self-evident that "the gospel must first be preached to all [Gentile] *nations*" before the end of the world arrives (13:10). The affirmation that the execution of the death sentence of the Jewish authorities against Jesus was carried out through "the *Gentiles*" (10:33) is given some significance.

Matthew, on the other hand, emphasizes already at the beginning of the ministry of Jesus that he lives in "Galilee of the *Gentiles*" (4:15, after vv. 12f.), in order to bring the light to "people" (λαός) who are in darkness and the shadow of death (vv. 15f., citing Isa 8:23f.). Nevertheless Matthew also emphasizes that the mission of Jesus himself and his emissaries was directed only to Israel, not to Gentiles and Samaritans (10:5f.). Yet Matthew is thereby describing an epoch which lies in the past. Israel has forfeited salvation through the rejection and killing of Jesus (23:37f.; 27:25, etc.). Thus the way is free for the resurrected one to direct his disciples to all (Gentile) *peoples* in order to make disciples of them (28:19); the context makes it improbable that Matthew includes the Jews (as one ἔθνος among others) in πάντα τὰ ἔθνη.

The same is true for Matt 25:31-46. Here in a speech from Jesus, which only begins as a parable (vv. 32f.), Matthew describes the Son of Man's judgment of "all ἔθνη." According to Matthew's usage and the context and content of the pericope, "all ἔθνη" must refer to those peoples (outside of Israel!) to whom the message of Christ has not reached or who have rejected it (so Lange, Friedrich; yet it is widely interpreted in reference to the totality of mankind; cf. Christian, Wilckens). Also among these *Gentiles* there are the δίκαιοι to whom the last judgment opens the way to salvation (vv. 1-30 speaks of the judgment of Christianity). Thus a new "ecclesiastical" usage of the word which speaks of *"Gentiles"* as distinguished from Christians is prepared for.

4. This new "ecclesiastical" terminology is prepared for also by Paul in 1 Cor 1:23f., when he contrasts Jews and Gentiles (v. 23 [on the v.l. "Greeks," cf. *TCGNT* 545]; similarly vv. 22, 24: Jews and Greeks) to "us," meaning those called from among Jews and Greeks; the contrast (in another context) in 1 Cor 5:1; 12:2, etc. is similar. 1 Peter esp. emphasizes the contrast between Christians and non-Christians when the author addresses the readers—appropriating Yahweh's address to Israel about election in Exod 19:6—as the "royal priesthood and holy *nation*" (sg. ἔθνος ἅγιον, 2:9); immediately thereafter he speaks disparagingly of non-Christians as "the *Gentiles*" (τὰ ἔθνη, 2:12; 4:3; cf. also Eph 4:17). The author of 3 John also considers such a line of demarcation as self-evident (3 John 7: ἐθνικῶν; v.l. ἐθνῶν, Koine and others).

N. Walter

ἔθος, ους, τό *ethos* habit, custom; tradition, cultic regulation, law*

1. Occurrences in the NT and usage in Hellenistic Judaism — 2. General meaning — 3. Usage in Luke-Acts

Lit.: H. H. ESSER, *DNTT* II, 436-56, esp. 436-38. — H. PREISKER, *TDNT* II, 372f.

1. Ἔθος is found in the NT most frequently in Luke-Acts (10 occurrences, 7 of which are in Acts), with one each in John and Hebrews. Although the first meaning given above occurs in classical Greek and the LXX (e.g., 1 Macc 10:89), the second meaning appears first in reference to the Jewish law in the LXX, Philo, and Josephus. The expression πάτριον ἔθος ("ancestral customs") is found in this connection in, e.g., 4 Macc 18:5 and more frequently in Philo, e.g., *Spec. Leg.* ii.149.

2. Among NT occurrences of the word the first meaning is perhaps clearest in Heb 10:25, which refers to the "*habit* of some" of absence from Christian worship (ἐπισυναγωγή). The reason for this absence is not mentioned. It need not be habitual negligence, but can include intentional defection that has become the unambiguous tendency of a group which follows a *custom* different from that of Christian practice. The noteworthy emphasis on the personal practice of Jesus of going to the Mount of Olives (Luke 22:39) indicates a distinct personal rule of conduct in which there was a fixed place and a fixed time for prayer—as the context makes clear—not a place to spend the night. Thus a religious dimension is contained in the word. In Acts 25:16, however, the word has a juridical dimension: the Romans "do not do such a thing." John 19:40, where a reference to Jewish burial customs is present, comes near to the second meaning, which concerns Jewish cultic laws.

3. In the NT the Lukan writings tend to identify ἔθος specifically with the Mosaic law (e.g., Acts 6:14; 15:1). The expression "ancestral *customs*" (τοῖς ἔθεσι τοῖς πατρῴοις) is found in Acts 28:17 (RSV "the customs of our fathers"). In 21:21 the word is associated with circumcision; its association with Judaism is emphasized in 26:3; and the strangeness of Jewish "customs" to the Romans is mentioned in 16:21. Already in the Gospel of Luke the same association of the word can be found. In Luke 1:9 it is used of the priestly tradition, which Zechariah follows. In 2:42 it is used for the presence of Jesus and his parents at the Feast of Passover. The latter example may nevertheless not involve an obligation in the law itself. It may rather suggest a parallel to 4:16 (κατὰ τὸ εἰωθός; cf. Paul in Acts 17:2) and may refer to Jesus' rootedness in the religious traditions of Israel, esp. in his birth and training, just as Luke 1:9 mentions the OT background for the birth of Jesus in the person of John, his forerunner. In Acts the word is used in accusations of Stephen (6:14) and Paul (21:21; 28:17; cf. 24:14) that they taught the Jews to reject the law of Moses. As a corrective to this accusation, Paul is portrayed as one who remains loyal to the faith of his fathers and merely liberates Gentiles from an obligation (15:1f.). In the same way Paul claims a Roman right (25:16).

For Luke, Christianity was both the continuation of the revelation to Israel and its extension to the Gentiles, and indeed within the Gentiles' own law and without any preconditions. The Jewish ἔθος is thus both vigorously affirmed for the Jews and modified for the Gentiles, who, as those who are heirs of the Roman world know, have their own ethical and juristic tradition.

M. E. Glasswell

εἰ *ei* if; whether

Lit.: BAGD s.v. — BDF (index s.v.) — C. BURCHARD, "Εἰ nach einem Ausdruck des Wissens oder Nichtwissens Joh 9, 25; Act 19, 2; I Cor 1, 16; 7, 16," *ZNW* 52 (1961) 73-82. — *idem,* "Fußnoten zum neutestamentlichen Griechisch," *ZNW* 61 (1970) 157-71. — E. D. BURTON, *Syntax of the Moods and Tenses in NT Greek* ([3]1900) (index s.v.) — J. JEREMIAS, "Die missionarische Aufgabe in der Mischehe (1 Cor 7, 16)," *idem, Abba* (1966) 292-98. — C. F. D. MOULE, *An Idiom-Book of NT Greek* ([2]1959) 151, 154, 158. — ROBERTSON, *Grammar* 1004-27. — C. A. WAHL, *Clavis Novi Testamenti Philologica* (1843) s.v. — *idem, Clavis Librorum Veteris Testamenti Apocryphorum Philologica. Indicem verborum in libris pseudepigraphis usurpatorum adiecit J. B. Bauer* (1972) s.v. — ZERWICK, *Biblical Greek* §§400-405.

Εἰ appears 507 times in the NT and is thus among the most frequently occurring words. Paul uses it most frequently (181), while the particle does not appear at all in Jude or 3 John.

1. Conditional εἰ *(if;* → ἐάν):

a) Εἰ appears in real (simple) conditions with the ind. of all tenses. Occasionally (esp. frequently in Paul) the verb of the conditional clause is not present and is to be supplied from the context (e.g., Rom 8:10, 17; 11:6).

b) Εἰ appears in the protasis of unreal (contrary-to-fact) conditional sentences with the ind. of an augmented (aor., impf., or plupf.) tense; ἄν appears in the apodosis (cf., however, an instance such as Luke 19:42, where the apodosis is missing). Because this rule is not strictly held in the NT (John 15:24; Rom 7:7b; Gal 4:15, etc.), "real" conditions concerning the past can no longer be formally distinguished from "unreal" conditions (1 Cor 15:32; Heb 7:11).

c) Εἰ followed by the optative is rarely used in the NT to express possibility (*potentialis*): Acts 20:16; 24:19; 1 Pet 3:14, 17 (BDF §385).

d) Εἰ in the indicative of reality (a above) often approaches a causal sense (cf. Germ. *wenn wirklich = da;* Eng. *if (then) = since;* see Matt 6:30 and the examples given in BDF §372.1). In 1 Thess 4:14 Paul deduces from the salvific fact of Jesus' death and resurrection that deceased Christians will be joined with Jesus at his parousia (→ παρουσία); in v. 14a (εἰ πιστεύομεν) Paul does not refer to a condition yet to be fulfilled, but rather to a fact: from the salvific content of Jesus' death and resurrection expressed in the credo follows the assurance of v. 14b in the sense of a causal relationship.

e) Εἰ can be used in oaths and asseverations in order to make an emphatic denial (*by no means:* Mark 8:12; Heb 3:11; 4:3, 5). This usage is a Hebraism corresponding to Heb. conditional *'im.* The formula of malediction ("God do this and that to me") in the main clause is left out in the NT references above and in some OT occurrences (Ps 94:11 LXX; Gen 14:23, etc.) and is sometimes retained in the OT (1 Sam 3:17; Cant 2:7, etc.).

f) Εἰ can occasionally appear after → θαυμάζω in the NT and in classical Greek where → ὅτι would have been expected. This is the case where a condition appears to be already fulfilled, as in 1 John 3:13: "Do not wonder, brethren, *that* the world hates you" (cf. Mark 15:44a, where the conditional meaning is still apparent).

2. Interrogative use:

a) Εἰ can introduce a direct question (cf. Germ. "*ob* er wohl kommt?"), as in Luke 13:23: "some one said to him, 'Lord, will those who are saved be few (κύριε, εἰ ὀλίγοι οἱ σῳζόμενοι)?' " (cf. 22:49, [67]; Acts 1:6).

b) In indirect questions introduced by εἰ the mood, negation, and tense of the direct question are normally retained (BDF §368).

c) The meaning of εἰ after expressions of knowing or not knowing is disputed and is esp. important for the understanding of 1 Cor 7:16. Here in connection with the question of mixed marriages between Christians and non-Christians it is asked "how do you know *whether* you will [not—?] save your husband/wife?" There are two possible interpretations: 1) The phrase τί γὰρ οἶδας εἰ might have a negating sense. If so, Paul gives an answer of resignation to the question whether it is possible to save the non-Christian marriage partner (i.e., he does not think it likely; H. Conzelmann, *1 Corinthians* [Hermeneia] ad loc., referring to the context). 2) On the other hand, εἰ can be understood as εἰ μή. In this case Paul encourages the maintenance of the mixed marriage because the the Christian partner has a missionary task to fulfill (Jeremias; G. D. Fee, *First Corinthians* [NICNT] ad loc.). The parenthetical "not" would then be brought into the translation. This proposal can appeal to the fact that the phrase τίς οἶδεν εἰ or similar ones have a predominantly affirming sense in Greek (Burchard, "Fußnoten" 171). In John 9:25; Acts 19:2; and 1 Cor 1:16 as well as 1 Cor 7:16 εἰ is to be translated in the sense of ὅτι (see Burchard, "Εἰ"; → 1.f).

Sometimes it can be disputed whether εἰ is to be understood in an interrogative or conditional sense: cf. Acts 13:15 (see Burchard, "Fußnoten" 166).

3. On the question of the various meanings of εἰ in connection with other particles, see BAGD s.v. VI.

G. Lüdemann

εἰ μήν *ei mēn* truly, certainly*

Heb 6:14: εἰ μὴν (TR ἦ μὴν) . . . εὐλογήσω σε (citing Gen 22:17 LXX), in an oath of God: "*Surely* I will bless you"; cf. BDF §441.1.

εἴγε *eige* if otherwise, if indeed
→ γέ.

εἰδέα, ας, ἡ *eidea* appearance*

Matt 28:3: ἦν δὲ ἡ εἰδέα αὐτοῦ ὡς ἀστραπή, "his *appearance* was like lightning." On the spelling cf. BDF §23.

εἶδον *eidon* see, perceive.

2nd aor. of → ὁράω.

εἶδος, ους, τό *eidos* (outer) appearance, form*

1. The general passive meaning — 2. The (pass.) meaning *kind, variety* — 3. The problem of 2 Cor 5:7

Lit.: G. Braumann, *DNTT* I, 703f. — J. Dupont, *Gnosis* ([2]1960) 109-11. — N. Hugedé, *La métaphore du miroir dans les Epîtres de saint Paul aux Corinthiens* (1957) (index s.v.) — G. Kittel, *TDNT* II, 373-75. — LSJ s.v. — D. Mannsperger, *Physis bei Platon* (1969) 175-91. — C. Ritter, "Εἶδος, ἰδέα und verwandte Wörter in den Schriften Platons," *idem, Neue Untersuchungen über Platon* (1910) 228-326. — H. Windisch, *Der zweite Korintherbrief* (KEK, 1924) 167.

1. Εἶδος appears only 5 times in the NT. Three of these are in the pass. meaning of that which is seen or presents itself to view, thus *appearance, form* (LSJ: *that which is seen: form, shape*; Luke 3:22 [cf. Mark 1:10]; 9:29 [cf. Mark 9:2]; John 5:37). In Luke 3:22; 9:29 the use of εἶδος goes back to the Evangelist. In 3:22 the Holy Spirit descends on Jesus "*in bodily form* (σωματικῷ εἴδει), as a dove." In 9:29 Luke avoids the Markan μετεμορφώθη ἔμπροσθεν αὐτῶν in the story of the transfiguration and reports: "as he was praying, the *appearance* (τὸ εἶδος; D and Origen read ἡ ἰδέα) of his countenance was altered (ἕτερον) . . ."; according to v. 32 this refers to Jesus' δόξα. In John 5:37 Jesus says: "And the Father who sent me has himself borne witness to me. His voice you have never heard, his *form* you have never seen." This is probably to be interpreted in the sense of 14:8f.: there is no direct access to God the Father.

2. A pass. meaning is present also in 1 Thess 5:22, although here εἶδος is to be rendered with *kind*: "abstain from every *kind* [RSV "form"] of evil." The Vg. translates εἶδος in all 5 NT passages with *species*. On the meaning *kind, variety* cf. LSJ s.v. III; BAGD s.v. 2; also Moulton/Milligan s.v., which refers to the phrase παντὸς εἴδους, "of every kind," which is found in the papyri. Josephus *Ant.* x.37 has πᾶν εἶδος πονηρίας.

3. It is disputed whether a pass. meaning is also present in 2 Cor 5:7, as Windisch, Kittel (374), and Dupont (109) affirm. BAGD s.v. 3 and H. Lietzmann and W. G. Kümmel, *An die Korinther* (HNT, [4]1949) 120f., 203, argue for the act. translation "sight." R. Bultmann, *The Second Letter to the Corinthians* (1985) ad loc. pleads (erroneously?) for both meanings. Passow I, 783 and LSJ do not know an active meaning of εἶδος.

Paul speaks in 2 Cor 5:7 in a maxim, which he applies to the Christian's life in the present (v. 6, "in the body we are away from the Lord"): "for we walk διὰ πίστεως not διὰ εἴδους." Διά with the gen. is used here modally (see A. Oepke, *TDNT* II, 66) of the manner or accompanying circumstances of the "walking." It speaks positively of the walk "in faith," but it is not certain that a negative contrast is intended (taking "by sight" in the act. sense). The sentence is correctly interpreted by Kittel as a reference to walking in the sphere "in which we are referred to faith and in which there is no visible form" (374). Of course it does not involve "the form of the Christian," as Kittel assumes (374f., with a reference to 1 John 3:2: "it does not yet appear what we shall be"). Kümmel (p. 203) observes correctly of this view that "then the subject of the believing and of the seeing are not the same, and a connection is totally lacking." The identity of the subjects is preserved when εἶδος is understood as the *appearance* vouchsafed by God of the eschatological reality (in the comprehensive sense; or of Christ, cf. vv. 6, 8) to be seen by us, or as the (reciprocal) sight "face to face" (1 Cor 13:12; cf. Num 12:8 LXX; cf. also Rom 8:24f.).

Insofar as the "eschatological" interpretation of εἶδος is maintained, the interpretation of C. K. Barrett, *2 Corinthians* (HNTC) 158f. can be followed: "we do not trust to *the appearance of things*." "We live by believing in the absent and invisible Christ, not by looking at visible forms." The maxim in 2 Cor 5:7 "expresses a contrast to the mystic-ecstatic piety" (Windisch). According to H. Jonas, *Gnosis und spätantiker Geist* II/1 (1954) 48 we have in this text "a basic Christian anti-Gnostic statement in which περιπατεῖν on the one side is as essential as πίστις: in the 'εἶδος', i.e., in the final γνῶσις, there is no longer περιπατεῖν, i.e., temporality." The identity of εἶδος and γνῶσις (so also W. Schmithals, *Gnosticism in Corinth* [1971] 270), however, as indicated above, is not admissible. Yet Paul in his polemic is perhaps not free in his selection of terminology (so Schmithals 269f.).

G. Schneider

εἰδωλεῖον, ου, τό *eidōleion* idol's temple*

1 Cor 8:10: ἐν εἰδωλείῳ κατακείμενον, "at table in an *idol's temple*"; → εἴδωλον 2, 4.b.

εἰδωλόθυτον, ου, τό *eidōlothyton* meat offered to an idol
→ εἴδωλον 4.b.

εἰδωλολάτρης, ου, ὁ *eidōlolatrēs* idolater
→ εἴδωλον 3.

εἰδωλολατρία, ας, ἡ *eidōlolatria* idolatry
→ εἴδωλον 3.

εἴδωλον, ου, τό *eidōlon* image of a deity, (pagan) deity, idol*
εἰδωλόθυτον, ου, τό *eidōlothyton* meat offered to an idol*
εἰδωλολάτρης, ου, ὁ *eidōlolatrēs* idolater*
εἰδωλολατρία, ας, ἡ *eidōlolatria* idolatry*
ἱερόθυτον, ου, τό *hierothyton* meat offered in sacrifice*

1. Occurrences in the NT — 2. Meaning — 3. Usage — 4. The word group in Paul

Lit.: F. Büchsel, *TDNT* II, 375-80. — H. Conzelmann, *1 Corinthians* (Hermeneia, 1975) 136-50, 175-80. — J. W. Drane, *Paul, Libertine or Legalist?* (1975). — G. Fohrer, B. Reicke, and K. Stendahl, *BHH* I, 602-5. — W. G. Kümmel, "Die älteste Form des Aposteldekrets," *idem, Heilsgeschehen und Geschichte* (1965) 278-88. — W. Mundle, *DNTT* II, 284-86. — H. D. Preuss, *TDOT* I, 285-87. — W. Schmithals, *Gnosticism in Corinth* (1969) 224-29. — S. Schwertner, *THAT* I, 167-69. — H. F. von Soden, "Sakrament und Ethik bei Paulus," *idem, Das Paulusbild in der neueren deutschen Forschung* (WdF 24, 1964) 338-79. — G. Theissen, *The Social Setting of Pauline Christianity* (1982) 121-43. — J. Weiss, *Der Erste Korintherbrief* (KEK, [2]1925) 210-13. — For further bibliography see *TWNT* X, 1066.

1. Εἴδωλον and the compounds εἰδωλόθυτον (from εἴδωλον and → θύω), εἰδωλολάτρης, and εἰδωλολατρία (from εἴδωλον and → λατρεία) are typical for Paul, esp. in 1 Corinthians. Of the 11 NT occurrences of εἴδωλον, 7 are in Paul's letters and 4 in 1 Corinthians; of the 9 occurrences of εἰδωλόθυτον 5 are in Paul's letters, all in 1 Corinthians; of the 7 uses of εἰδωλολάτρης 4 are Paul's, all in 1 Corinthians; of the 4 occurrences of εἰδωλολατρία 2 are in Paul's letters, 1 of those in 1 Corinthians. Furthermore, the hapax legomenon ἱερόθυτον (from → ἱερός and θύω), which is in a certain respect synonymous with εἰδωλόθυτον, appears in 1 Cor 10:28. Elsewhere, εἴδωλον appears twice in Acts and once each in 1 John and Revelation, εἰδωλόθυτον twice each in Acts and Revelation, εἰδωλολάτρης once in Ephesians and twice in Revelation, and εἰδωλολατρία once each in Colossians and 1 Peter.

2. Εἴδωλον, derived from ἰδεῖν, "see" (→ ὁράω; → εἶδος, "form"), means *form, image,* but also already in Homer *phantom, vision* (the "souls" in the underworld are εἴδωλα; → ψυχή); for Plato the individual things in their lower form of existence are, in contrast to the ideas, mere εἴδωλα. Because in OT faith pagan deities are powerless or even unreal, in the LXX εἴδωλον, which in the Greek linguistic tradition indicated loss of existence, could be best used to translate Hebrew terms both for images of Gentiles' deities and for the deities themselves. Indeed, in the OT the two meanings overflow to each other (e.g., Ps 113:12 LXX: the silver and golden εἴδωλα [Heb. *ʿaṣab̲îm*] of the Gentiles are human works; 1 Chr 16:26 LXX contrasts the human-made εἴδωλα [Heb. *ʾĕlîlîm*] of the Gentiles to God, who made heaven).

Significantly the LXX never translates Hebrew words for images of the gods with the usual Greek term τὸ ἄγαλμα (on the other hand, εἴδωλον is unknown in classical Greek with the meaning "image of a deity"). Furthermore, according to the prohibition of images in the Decalogue (Exod 20:4; Deut 5:8) God may not be depicted as an εἴδωλον (Heb. *pesel*). "Israel knew that Yahweh was never so ready to hand as the deity in the ritual forms of the ancient Near East, in which the image of the god was waited on . . ." (W. Zimmerli, *OT Theology in Outline* [1978] 121).

In the NT also εἴδωλον twice means *image of a deity* (Acts 7:41: the golden calf, which in Exod 32 is not called εἴδωλον; Rev 9:20), but elsewhere always *false deity* (Acts 15:20; Rom 2:22; 1 Cor 8:4, 7; 10:19; 12:2; 2 Cor 6:16; 1 Thess 1:9; 1 John 5:21). The Jewish polemical term **εἰδωλόθυτον** for Gentile ἱερόθυτον (in the NT only in 1 Cor 10:28) means *meat offered to idols* (Acts 15:19; 21:25; 1 Cor 8:1, 4, 7, 10; 10:19; Rev 2:14, 20). The **εἰδωλολάτρης** is an *idolater* (1 Cor 5:10f.; 6:9; 10:7; Eph 5:5; Rev 21:8; 22:15), while **εἰδωλολατρία** is *idolatry* (1 Cor 10:14; Gal 5:20; Col 3:5 [here to characterize covetousness, → πλεονεξία]; 1 Pet 4:3); both words are found only in the NT and literature dependent on it.

3. Εἴδωλον and its derivatives occur regularly with "fornication" (→ πορνεία), "fornicate" (πορνεῦσαι), or "fornicator" (πόρνος), often in parenetic contexts (sometimes in vice catalogs: cf. S. Wibbing, *Die Tugend- und Lasterkataloge im NT* [1959] 77ff.; Acts 15:20; Rev 9:20f.; εἰδωλόθυτον, Acts 15:29; 21:25—the "apostolic decree" (→ 4.b); Rev 2:14, 20; εἰδωλολάτρης, 1 Cor 5:11; 6:9; Eph 5:5; Rev 21:8; 22:15; εἰδωλολατρία, 1 Cor 10:14 with v. 8; Gal 5:19f.; Col 3:5). It is noteworthy that neither εἰδωλολάτρης nor εἰδωλολατρία appears in the first position in the vice catalogs. Yet Rom 1:18ff., where these words do not appear even though the subject does, indicates that for Paul other vices are based on the exchange of God for idols.

4. a) In 1 Thess 1:9 Paul uses εἴδωλον in a phrase derived from Jewish missionary preaching, which he gives a Christian interpretation in v. 10. The mockery which often accompanied the polemic against the idols in the OT (cf. Preuss) does not occur here. (On the other hand, in Gal 4:8f., where the concern is not with conversion to God, but rather with the charge of apostasy into paganism, the tone *is* scornful: the pagan deities, which here are not called εἴδωλα, are "weak and beggarly (world-)elements [RSV "elemental spirits"]"; → στοιχεῖον.)

b) With regard to the behavior of Christians, i.e., whether they may eat *meat offered to idols,* in 1 Cor 8:4 Paul takes up the thesis represented by Gnosticizing Corinthians as an argument against the "weak" (→ ἀσθενής 4): "an idol (εἴδωλον) has no real existence" (and thus no meat is really offered to idols). They base this thesis on "the basic statement of the confession of faith" (Conzelmann, ad loc.) that there is only one God (→ εἷς). But Paul does not understand this as an ontological statement, as if no supernatural powers existed besides the one God. Instead, in v. 5 (similarly Gal 4:3, 8f.) he reckons—as did everyone in antiquity—with the existence (εἰσίν, despite RSV "there may be") of "so-called gods in heaven and [RSV "or"] on earth," indeed with "many 'gods' and many 'lords.'" "They may very well be existent in the sense of being 'there' in the world and having a certain power—and Paul is himself convinced that they do exist. But they are not gods" (Conzelmann 143; similarly von Soden 340). In v. 6 Paul turns from the ontological to the existential : *"for us"* only one God exists; for the existence of the believer only he is the certain power. Thus "for us" no εἴδωλα exist!

For one who believes that demons can no longer trouble him, the result would follow that, wherever the occasion offers itself, he would eat as a mockery of meat offered to them (Weiss 212: "as an act of intentional bravado"). But for Paul it is not a matter of a question of dogmatics which is subject to debate but of the concrete Church: because of the weak conscience (→ συνείδησις) of the ones who eat meat offered to idols, the "strong" (this term appears in an analogous context in Rom 15:1; → δυνατός) may not allow their freedom to cause offense to the weak (1 Cor 8:7ff.; 10:28f.; see also Rom 14f.). Paul decides here on a more pastoral course than he did earlier in Galatians, where he takes no account of the weak conscience of the addressees (Drane 67ff.).

This demand for consideration of the weak may not, however, be interpreted with Mundle (285f.) to indicate that Paul does not approve this eating. Where such a consideration is not required, the strong may eat meat offered to idols just as it is.

In the course of a warning against idolatry (1 Cor 10:14ff.) Paul explains (vv. 19f.) that, for those who participate in sacrifice (→ θύω), the idols or the meat offered to the idols "is something" (RSV "anything"; τί ἐστιν = "has power"). At this point, of course, he no longer has in mind the question of the admissibility of eating or buying this meat. Instead he has in mind an invitation to a pagan cultic meal. In this case he gives a strict No, as the issue is now an invitation to a fellowship meal given specifically in the name of a pagan deity (examples are given in H. Lietzmann and W. G. Kümmel, *An die Korinther I/II* [HNT] 49ff.). Such a *communicatio in sacris* amounts to exposure to the power of demons—regardless of whether participation is understood as recognition of the efficacy of the pagan cult.

Because another situation is envisioned here than in 1 Cor 8:1-13; 10:23-33, it is not necessary, with Weiss, Schmithals, and others, to attribute 10:1-22 to an earlier letter than 8:1-13; 10:23-33 (von Soden, esp. 358ff., speaks convincingly against Weiss). It must be conceded that the partition hypothesis is plausible. Furthermore, ἐν εἰδωλείῳ, "in an idol's temple," 8:10, is a difficulty if 10:20-22 is to be read in the same epistle. On partition hypotheses for 1 Corinthians see also W. Schenk, "Der Erste Korintherbrief als Briefsammlung," *ZNW* 60 (1969) 219-43; W. Schmithals, "Die Korintherbriefe als Briefsammlung," *ZNW* 64 (1973) 263-88; Kümmel, *Introduction* 276-78.

The significance of the question whether Christians may eat meat offered to idols may not be overestimated. For most Corinthian church members (on the sociological structure see 1 Cor 1:26ff.) meat was by no means a part of the daily diet (Theissen 125ff.). For Christians of lower social position enjoyment of meat came into consideration at most with regard to occasional public distributions to all citizens (texts and literature in Theissen, loc. cit.). In addition, Conzelmann (176) disputes that everything offered at the market was derived from sacrificial animals. As correct as the objection is in some respects (otherwise "without raising any question," 10:25, 27, would be meaningless), nevertheless it was common for sacrificial meat from the pagan ritual to be at the market. (In Pompeii, where the entire installation has been preserved, the butcher's stall lies next to the chapel of the divine Caesar; see the sketch in Lietzmann and Kümmel 52. For Corinth, where a Latin inscription reading "macellum" has been found, see H. J. Cadbury, "The Macellum of Corinth," *JBL* 53 [1934] 134-41.) At the very least, beef came almost exclusively from the sacrifices connected with public feasts (H. W. Gross, *KP* III, 263). Thus Paul does not say that the Corinthians, out of consideration for the "weaker" brother, should buy meat at the market which did not originate in pagan ritual.

The question arises whether the "strong" are not to be found largely among the ranks of the wealthy in the church, who, because of their social position, tended to a more liberal position (so Theissen). Is 1 Cor 11:20 to be seen in this connection? One can at least well imagine the rich eating meat not only not slaughtered according to Jewish ritual (Deut 12:16), but also derived from pagan offerings (Exod 34:16), in the presence of the "weak" poor people—who were possibly Jewish Christians who felt themselves bound to the Torah.

The conditioned permission to eat meat offered to idols in 1 Corinthians indicates (and this is confirmed by Gal 2:6: οὐδέν!) that the "apostolic decree" (see esp. Kümmel; H. Conzelmann, *Acts* [Hermeneia] 118f.), which totally forbids this food (Acts 15:29), can in no way be regarded as the decision of a synod of the Gentile mission (the "Apostolic Council"). Mundle inappropriately harmonizes 1 Cor 10:32 with Acts 15:21 in order to allow the decree to be decided by the synod (286: "This prohibition adopted at the apostolic council . . . presupposes that in this matter Jews and Christians were agreed with regard to fundamentals" [the translation of Mundle has "basically in agreement"; Germ. *"grundsätzlich einig"*]. Thus Paul would be "agreed with regard to fundamentals" with the Jews!). The decree was also hardly accepted by Paul at a later date (Rom 14:20ff.! *contra* A. Strobel, "Das Aposteldekret in Galatien," *NTS* 20 [1973/74] 177-90).

H. Hübner

εἰκῇ *eikę̄* for nothing, in vain, to no purpose*

Rom 13:4: not *in vain,* not *without purpose;* Gal 4:11; 1 Cor 15:2: *in vain;* Gal 3:4 (bis): *in vain, useless;* Col 2:18; Matt 5:22 TR: *without cause.*

εἴκοσι *eikosi* twenty

1. Εἴκοσι appears alone only in Acts 27:28 (20 fathoms, t.t. of nautical language; 1 fathom = *ca.* 1.85 m.).

2. It also appears in combinations: εἴκοσι χιλιάδων (Luke 14:31: 20,000), εἴκοσι πέντε (John 6:19: 25 stadia = *ca.* 5 km.), ἑκατὸν εἴκοσι (Acts 1:15: 120), εἴκοσι τρεῖς χιλιάδες (1 Cor 10:8: 23,000 fell in one day, an allusion to Num 25:1ff.; 5:1ff., which reads, however, 24,000; see Num 25:9 and cf. the v.l. in 1 Cor 10:8 in 69, 81, etc.).

In Revelation εἴκοσι τέσσαρες appears frequently (4:4 [bis], 10; 5:8, 14 v.l.; 11:16; 19:4). All these passages speak of the 24 "elders" (→ πρεσβύτερος) who sit on 24 thrones and whose task is to praise God. The number is probably derived from the doubling of the number of the 12 tribes. Perhaps 1 Chr 24:5ff.; 25:1ff. plays a role (the division of the priests and Levites into 24 groups). According to *T. Adam* 1–2; 4:8 angelic powers offer veneration and honor at the (24) hours of day and night. Babylonian astrology knows 24 star deities, who are described as δικασταὶ τῶν ὅλων (Diodorus Siculus ii.31.4). Noteworthy also are the 24 Yazatas who form the divine state of Ahura Mazda (G. Bornkamm, *TDNT* VI, 668f.). One may also note that 24 was the number of the cosmos for the Pythagoreans. Probably the number symbolizes totality in Revelation.

H. Weder

εἴκω *eikō* yield, submit*

Gal 2:5: οἷς οὐδὲ πρὸς ὥραν εἴξαμεν τῇ ὑποταγῇ, "to them we did not *yield* submission even for a moment."

εἰκών, όνος, ἡ *eikōn* image, likeness, archetype*

1. Occurrences in the NT — 2. Meaning and usage — 3. Literal usage — 4. Metaphorical usage — 5. "Image of

God" as an anthropological attribute — 6. Christ as "image of God" — 7. Believers and the image of Christ

Lit.: P. ALTHAUS, "Das Bild Gottes bei Paulus," *TBl* 20 (1941) 81-92. — A. ALTMANN, "Homo Imago Dei in Jewish and Christian Theology," *JR* 48 (1968) 235-59. — J. L. AURRECOECHA, "Los titulos cristologicos de Colosenses 1, 15-16, su origen y su significado," *Estudios Trinitarios* 8 (1974) 307-28. — G. C. BERKOUWER, *Man: The Image of God* (1962). — J. M. BOVER, "Imaginis notio apud B. Paulum," *Bib* 4 (1923) 174-79. — D. M. CRESSAN, *Imago Dei. A Study in Philo and St. Paul* (Diss. St. Patrick's College, Maynooth, Ireland, 1959). — F.-W. ELTESTER, *Eikon im NT* (BZNW 23, 1958). — O. FLENDER, *DNTT* II, 286-88. — H. HEGERMANN, *Die Vorstellungen vom Schöpfungsmittler im hellenistischen Judentum und Urchristentum* (TU 82, 1961). — M. D. HOOKER, "Adam in Romans 1," *NTS* 6 (1959/60) 297-306. — N. HYLDAHL, "A Reminiscence of the OT at Romans i.23," *NTS* 2 (1955/56) 285-88. — J. JERVELL, *Imago Dei. Gen 1, 26f im Spätjudentum, in der Gnosis und in den paulinischen Briefen* (FRLANT 76, 1960). — I. D. KARIVIDOPOULOS, " 'Εἰκὼν Θεοῦ' καὶ 'κατ' εἰκόνα Θεοῦ' παρὰ τῷ 'Απ. Παύλῳ. Αἱ χριστολογικαὶ βάσεις τῆς Παυλείου ἀνθρωπολογίας (1964). — K. KERÉNYI, "Ἄγαλμα, εἰκών, εἴδωλον," *Demitizzazione e imagine, Scritti di E. Castelli* (Archivio de Filosofia 1962, I/II, 1962) 161-71. — G. KITTEL, *TDNT* II, 383-88, 392-97. — H. KLEINKNECHT, *TDNT* II, 388-90. — J. KÜRZINGER, "Συμμόρφους τῆς εἰκόνος τοῦ υἱοῦ αὐτοῦ (Röm 8, 29)," *BZ* 2 (1958) 294-99. — E. LARSSON, *Christus als Vorbild. Eine Untersuchung zu den paulinischen Tauf- und Eikontexten* (ASNU 23, 1962). — A. R. C. LEANEY, " 'Conformed to the Image of His Son' (Rom VIII.29)," *NTS* 10 (1963/64) 470-79. — E. LOHSE, "Imago Dei bei Paulus," *Libertas Christiana* (FS F. Delekat ed. W. Matthias, BEvT 26, 1957) 122-35. — B. L. MACK, *Logos und Sophia* (SUNT 10, 1973) 166-71. — S. V. MCCASLAND, " 'The Image of God' according to Paul," *JBL* 69 (1950) 85-100. — K. PRÜMM, "Reflexiones theologicae et historicae ad usum Paulinum termini 'eikon,' " *VD* 40 (1962) 233-57. — K. L. SCHMIDT, "Homo Imago Dei im Alten und NT," *Eranos-Jahrbuch* 15 (1947) 149-95. — P. SCHWANZ, *Imago Dei als christologisch-anthropologisches Problem in der Geschichte der Alten Kirche von Paulus bis Clemens Alexandrinus* (Arbeiten zur Kirchengeschichte und Religionswissenschaft 2, 1970). — F. SEN, "Se recupera la verdadera lectura de un texto muy citado," *Cultura Biblica* 24 (1967) 165-68. —A. STRUKER, *Die Gottesebenbildlichkeit des Menschen in der christlichen Literatur der ersten zwei Jahrhunderte* (1913). —H. WILLMS, *Eikon. Eine begriffsgeschichtliche Untersuchung zum Platonismus* (1935). — For further bibliography see *DNTT* II, 292; D. J. A. CLINES, "The Image of God in Man," *TB* 19 (1968) 53-103.

1. Εἰκών appears 23 times in the NT and is thus among words of moderate frequency in the NT. In the Synoptics it appears only once, in a threefold parallel reading (Mark 12:16 par. Matt 22:20/Luke 20:24), while Paul and Colossians have a greater frequency: Romans 2 times, 1 Corinthians 3 times, 2 Corinthians 2 times, Colossians 2 times; Hebrews only once (10:1). Revelation, with ten occurrences, has both the largest absolute and the largest relative frequency.

2. The relatively small number of occurrences should not obscure the broad spectrum of meaning and usage. Along with material *image* in the literal sense (image on a coin: Mark 12:16 par.; cultic statue: Revelation; probably also Rom 1:23), there is a widely dispersed metaphorical usage, which extends from the characterization of mankind as *image* of God (1 Cor 11:7) to the characterization of believers as "conformed" to Christ's *image* (Rom 8:29).

Three conceptual motifs can be distinguished in Paul's metaphorical usage (Schmidt 164; McCasland 85-88; Eltester 130-66; Schwanz 17) according to the respective bearers of the relationship prototype-copy and the manner of their relationship to each other: a) mankind as God's *image,* b) Christ as God's *image,* c) believers in their relationship to Christ's *image.* This state of affairs should provide—esp. in view of the striking independence of these conceptions from each other—a warning against attempts both to harmonize and to derive all from one cause.

3. In Mark 12:16 par. Matt 22:20/Luke 20:24 εἰκών is used for Caesar's *image on the coin* (cf. Artemidorus Onirocriticus iv.31) which, as a pictographic element together with its verbal counterpart, the title of the inscription, characterized the identity of the master on the coin. In all 10 passages in Revelation, εἰκών is used of a cultic image prepared as an "*image* of [RSV "for"] the beast" (13:14). Worship of this image is demanded (13:15; 14:9, 11; 16:2), is offered by apostates (19:20), and is refused by those who stand firmly (15:2; 20:4).

The oldest uses of εἰκών refer to statues (Herodotus ii.130, 143), and this usage always remained predominant. Use of the word for statues of the gods is only ascertainable at a late date (Plato *Lg.* 931a; cf. Kerényi 169ff.), but was quickly adopted generally (cf. Preisigke, *Wörterbuch* s.v.). In the LXX εἰκών becomes almost a t.t. for sculptures that are cultically worshipped (Dan 3:1, 2, 3, 5, 7, 10, 12, 14, 15, 18, etc.), and is there used like the above-mentioned references in Revelation (ποιέω, πίπτω, προσκυνέω κτλ.). Thus the author of Revelation has probably drawn his material directly from Daniel 3. Despite the objections of E. Lohmeyer (*Offenbarung* [HNT] 116), it cannot be doubted that the descriptions in Revelation allude to procedures in the emperor cult.

In Rom 1:23 Paul cites Ps 105:20 LXX, replacing, however, the reference to the golden calf with a reference to mankind and a series of three types of animals. Ὁμοίωμα is from the LXX and thus requires no explanation, but its (probably pleonastic) combination with εἰκών, which is normally synonymous, does. The assumption that Paul wanted to recall by this means that mankind is made in God's image in Gen 1:26 (Jervell 325ff.) fails because of the dependence also of the series of animals on εἰκών as a nomen regens (E. Käsemann, *Commentary on Romans* [1980] 45). The series of animals, like sg. ἄνθρωπος, does not refer to Genesis 1 (against Hyldahl 287; Hooker 300), but corresponds rather to anti-Gentile polemic contemporary with Paul. The combination ἐν ὁμοιώματι εἰκόνος can be resolved as a distinction between "form" (εἰκών) and "copy" (ὁμοίωμα; H. Lietzmann, *An die Römer* [HNT, [5]1971] 32; H. Schlier, *Römerbrief* [HTKNT] 58) or as the "copy" from the "original," εἰκών being "the original copied," so that both are "the thing itself and its form" (Kittel 395). Also possible is the explanation represented by C. K. Barrett (*Romans* [HNTC] ad loc.) and Käsemann that it is to be understood as an intensive form: "inferior, shadowy character" (Barrett) or "the likeness of the image of mortal humanity" (Käsemann 36). Most probable is the view of εἰκών as an epexegetical genitive: "images, which represented" (H. W. Schmidt, *An die Römer* [[2]1963] 36), and perhaps also an intentional limitation by means of εἰκών, which had become a t.t. in the LXX: "images—in the form of idols—which portrayed. . . ."

4. The contrast of σκιά and εἰκών in Heb 10:1 is noteworthy because normally both terms are used synonymously or εἰκών serves as a broader term for that which includes σκιά (e.g., Plato *R.* 509e). In order to maintain this synonymity in Heb 10:1, Sen (168) follows the reading of 𝔭[46], replacing οὐκ αὐτήν with καί. However, it is to be noted that the correlation of σκιά and εἰκών here corresponds to the correlation of σκιά and σῶμα in Col 2:17; like the latter pair of terms, σκιά and εἰκών probably distinguish the outer appearance from the essence of the thing itself. This interpretation is supported by the change of meaning in εἰκών in Hellenistic Greek such that the concept is increasingly detached from the characterization of the "true form" (RSV) and could represent a large range of nuances from "copy" (Plotinus *Enn.* iv.7) to "characteristic feature" and "visible manifestation" (ibid. v.8) to "prototype" and "original image" (Lucian *Vit. Auct.* 18).

5. a) 1 Cor 11:7 is connected to Gen 1:26f., but is singular, as Paul here limits the εἰκών to man and thus indirectly denies it to woman. Paul arrives at this view by understanding Gen 1:26f. on the basis of Gen 2:4bff. (McCasland 86; Jervell 110ff.), where *'āḏām* does not denote a classification, but is contrasted instead to the feminine proper name Eve. Paul derives woman's subordination to man from the temporal sequence of the creation of man and woman and the description of the woman's function as man's helper as described in Gen 2:4bff. The indirect assumption that woman is not made in God's image corresponds to her lack of immediacy to Christ in 1 Cor 11:3. Both are based on the strong feminine susceptibility to demons, a deficiency which does not affect man, who is the εἰκών of God and who lives in a direct association to his "head" (→ κεφαλή). The deficiency in woman can only be compensated for by the wearing of an apotropaic veil. The remarks in 1 Cor 11:2-6 are related to a typical midrash, so that the proof from Scripture in v. 7 "is not intended and cannot say anything beyond the present situation" (Schwanz 19).

b) Col 3:10 also refers to Gen 1:26f. with the phrase "after the *image* of its creator," but does not use the concept of the God's image as an anthropological category. It speaks rather in the terminology of God's creative work at the beginning to describe the continual renewal of "the new man" (RSV "new nature"), a renewal directed to the ethical insight of "the new man."

6. a) In 2 Cor 4:3f. the reference to Christ as "the *likeness* of God" has its function in opposing Corinthian attacks against the "veiled" character of the Pauline proclamation. For Paul, however, the "veiled" character of the gospel is an indication of the lost condition of the hearers, for their receptivity to the glory of Christ has failed because their minds are blinded by "the god of this world." Because Paul addresses the addressees' deficient perception and begins on the basis of a defect in the organ of their cognitive perception (→ νόημα), the anchoring of his argumentation is to be seen in the characterization of Christ as "the *likeness* of God" within the perspective of revelation.

The association of the concept of εἰκών with the idea of revelation has its analogy in Philo, for whom the logos, as the εἰκών of God, represents "the hypostatized knowability of God" (H. Jonas, *Gnosis und spätantiker Geist* II/1 [1954] 75), inasmuch as God reveals himself in the logos as his εἰκών (*Conf.* 96f.). In a way different from Philo, for whom God's revelation in the εἰκών is only a poor expedient (*Conf.* 148; *All.* iii.100), Paul indicates that the full representation of God is in his "image," which depicts his manner of existence as knowability and in relation to the believer.

b) In Col 1:15 it is not revelatory function (though it is present here) but Christ's cosmological significance that stands in the foreground, for he is not only "the *image* of the invisible God," but also "the first-born of all creation." What εἰκών means in the Colossians hymn must therefore be asked as a question concerning the relationship of Christ to cosmos (Eltester 137). Christ's designation as "the first-born of all creation" refers to his place as the mediator of creation in contrast to the things created, as is definitely indicated in the prepositional phrases in v. 16. This conceptual complex, like the idea of revelation in 2 Cor 4:4, can scarcely be derived directly from OT statements about mankind made in the image of God. Rather, both sayings about Christ as "God's *image*" are intelligible only against the background of Jewish teaching concerning Sophia as the mediator of creation and of the Gnostic myth of the *Urmensch* (primal person/man).

As the mediator in creation, Wisdom shares in the creation and preservation of the world (Wis 7:21, 27) and is understood to be the image of God's goodness (v. 26). Philo calls Wisdom ἀρχὴν καὶ εἰκόνα καὶ ὅρασιν θεοῦ (*All.* i.43). Every statement in the first strophe of the Colossians hymn can be understood against the background of this Jewish teaching about Wisdom, except for the predication of Christ as κεφαλὴ τοῦ σώματος in v. 18a (Eltester 140). The latter must be traced to the background of the prevalent conception of the *Urmensch,* which had already been closely connected in Hellenistic Judaism with Sophia speculation. Consequently the bridge between the two mythologoumena came into existence in the use of εἰκών in both spheres (E. Käsemann, *Essays on NT Themes* [1964] 155f.). Not only is Wisdom εἰκὼν θεοῦ, but also the *Urmensch* bears the εἰκών of the Father (*Corp. Herm.* i.12) and is created according to God's image (Philo *All.* i.31ff.).

7. a) In 1 Cor 15:45-49 Paul refers to the antithesis of the "first man" and "last man" within the framework of his proof for the resurrection of the dead and uses it as the basis for the contrast of σῶμα ψυχικόν and σῶμα πνευματικόν (v. 44), which corresponds to the contrast of the "earthly" and the "heavenly" (v. 47). This midrash on Gen 2:7 stands in the tradition of speculation about the *Urmensch.* In its specific form it is in the tradition of the contrast of two men, the earthly and psychic vs. the heavenly and pneumatic (E. Brandenburger, *Adam und Christus* [1962] 62ff.). This antithesis appears also in Philo, where the heavenly man, unlike the earthly man, is created in God's image (*All.* i.31f.). As the ideal man, he is distinguished from the earthly man (*Op.* 134).

With the introduction of the antithesis of the two "men," Paul proceeds from their characteristics as representatives (v. 48; Rom 5:12ff.) of those bound to them, for the earthly man (Adam) and the heavenly man (Christ) are related respectively to the members of their own groups, for they bear the εἰκών of their representatives. The figure of speech, i.e., the connection of φορέω, connoting the conception of the wearing of a garment, to εἰκών, is derived from the Gnostic mixture of the conceptions of the "garment" and the "image" (e.g., in the Hymn of the Pearl in *Acts Thom.* 108ff.). Paul accordingly uses a Gnostic schema, but modifies it in a characteristic way when he gives the fundamentally timeless prototype-copy schema an eschatological dimension through the use of fut. φορέσομεν.

b) Rom 8:29 defines the purpose of the eternal election of the faithful by God as that of being "conformed to the *image* of his Son." To limit this event to participation in the bodily resurrection would be just as wrong as to understand a purely present understanding of the process. "This event is to be understood as commencing in the present, but belongs decisively to the future" (Schwanz). The use of εἰκών with → πρωτότοκος is noteworthy, for it has common roots with the predication of Christ as God's image in the Colossians hymn (cf. Col 1:15, 18). But in Rom 8:29 the saying is not meant cosmologically, but soteriologically, as the description of the salvific event in the believer as conformation with the εἰκών of Christ (*contra* Kürzinger). In contrast to 2 Cor 4:4 and Col 1:15, εἰκών in Rom 8:29 does not mean "copy," but rather "original": The concern is with the relationship of Christ to believers, not with his relationship to God. The extrapolation from Christ being in God's image and the conformity of believers with Christ's image to the idea of Christians being in the image of God is, at any rate, misguided.

c) The statement in 2 Cor 3:18 stands in close proximity to Rom 8:29. Paul says that believers will be transformed "into the same *image*" (i.e., the Lord's image; RSV "into his likeness"). As in Rom 8:29, εἰκών means here not "copy," but is rather a way of describing the original itself, i.e., the Lord's nature. Paul means that believers will be conformed to the nature of their Lord because they also will be in glory (→ δόξα) which they "see in a mirror with unveiled face" (cf. RSV mg.). This transformation—whether conceived of as in stages or as continual—is thought of as a process ἀπὸ δόξης εἰς δόξαν, but not as a *mutatio magica,* "but as the divine power's coming into effect in the historical life of the believer" (R. Bultmann, *The Second Letter to the Corinthians* [1985] 95).

H. Kuhli

εἰλικρίνεια, ας, ἡ *eilikrineia* purity; integrity*
εἰλικρινής, 2 *eilikrinēs* uncorrupted, pure; honest*

Lit.: F. BÜCHSEL, *TDNT* II, 397f.

1. The adj. is a compound from εἵλη (poetic: sunlight, warmth [of the sun]; cf. ἥλιος) and κρίνω (test, judge); it thus means *tested in the sun* (seen in the light of day); *absolutely pure, unmixed, honest.* Along with the customary written form εἰλικρίνεια the proper aspirated forms εἱλικρίνεια and εἱλικρινής are also found.

2. These words appear rarely in the Bible and the NT. The noun is in 1 Cor 5:8; 2 Cor 1:12; 2:17. The adj. is in Wis 7:25; Phil 1:10; 2 Pet 3:1 (cf. *1 Clem.* 2:5; 32:1; *2 Clem.* 9:8).

3. With regard to meaning: a) One of the characteristic features of these words is that Paul (like the author of 2 Peter) uses it almost without exception of his apostolate. On the one hand, he wishes to express his honest pride (καύχησις) to the Corinthians that he acted "with holiness and godly *sincerity*" (2 Cor 1:12), and that he proclaims God's word with *sincerity* (2:17). With εἰλικριν- he articulates also his goal for the behavior of his addressees (Phil 1:10; 1 Cor 5:8 [he includes himself]; cf. 2 Pet 3:1). b) In 2 Cor 2:17 εἰλικρίνεια is clarified theologically by a threefold qualification: ἐκ θεοῦ (the originator), κατέναντι θεοῦ (the judge), and ἐν Χριστῷ (the means). c) 1 Cor 5:6-8 illuminates the last of these three. Leaven was used as a figure for impurity in Jewish tradition. Paul goes further and uses it as a symbol for what has become antiquated ("old"). Unleavened dough—i.e., unleavened Passover bread—is then a symbol of the new, *pure* (cf. ἐκκαθάρατε, v. 7), and authentic life. The basis of this life is the sacrifice of Christ as our Passover lamb.

H. Goldstein

εἰλικρινής, 2 *eilikrinēs* uncorrupted, pure; honest → εἰλικρίνεια.

εἰμί *eimi* be

1. Occurrences and usage in the NT — 2. As a copula — 3. As a pred. — 4. With preps. — 5. With gen. or dat.

Lit.: J. BARR, *The Semantics of Biblical Language* (1961) 58-72. — T. BOMANN, *Hebrew Thought Compared with Greek* (1960) 37-51. — F. BÜCHSEL, *TDNT* II, 398-400. — BDF §§98; 127f.; 352f.; 189f. — C. H. KAHN, "The Greek Verb 'To Be' and the Concept of Being," *Foundations of Language* 2 (1966) 245-65. — H. KRAFT, *Offenbarung* (HNT, 1974) 31. — C. H. RATSCHOW, *Werden und Wirken* (BZAW 70, 1941). — B. REICKE, *BHH* III, 1759f. — H. ZIMMERMANN, *Das absolute "Ich bin" als biblische Offenbarungsformel* (Diss. Bonn, 1951).

1. Εἰμί appears in more than 30 different grammatical forms in *ca.* 2450 passages of the NT distributed throughout all the NT writings. Most are in John (*ca.* 440), Luke (*ca.* 360), Matthew (*ca.* 290), and Acts (*ca.* 280). Εἰμί is relatively frequent in 1 John (*ca.* 100 occurrences), but relatively infrequent in 1 Peter (3), 2 Peter (13), 2 Thessalonians (7), and Philemon (3). Among the different forms of εἰμί the most frequent is ἐστίν or ἔστιν (*ca.* 900), εἰσίν (157), εἰμί (140), ἦν (*ca.* 315). In the fut. most frequent is ἔσται (118), in the pres. partc., ὤν (44). A close relationship between the style of a NT document and its use of εἰμί can be observed in the lapidary statements of 1 John (with striking dominance of ἐσμέν) and in the "revelatory sayings" of John (→ ἐγώ 2), where the inf. (only 3 occurrences) withdraws in favor of the third person pres. ind. (116 occurrences, often with ὅτι of discourse). Luke and Paul (esp. in Romans), on the other hand, use the inf. and the pres. partc. frequently.

In most passages εἰμί is used as a copula between subj. and pred. (→ 2). In such instances the subj. can be named explicitly or included in the copula; likewise the pred. nom. can be explicit or implicit in the context. The copula can be omitted in impersonal expressions, shouts, questions, and particularly in maxims and aphorisms (see BDF §§127f.). The copula originated, in any case, in the nominal clause, which was common in Hebrew and not unusual in Greek.

In connection with the pres. or perf. partc. εἰμί is used in periphrasis for corresponding vb. forms (esp. in Luke-Acts; see BDF §§352f.). Here Hebrew and Aramaic influence is to be assumed. Periphrasis involves no alteration of meaning in most instances, but sometimes indicates an intensification of the statement (→ 2.d).

Εἰμί can also be used alone as a full pred. and in such cases normally means *be present, exist, live, stay,* or impersonally *there is, it happens, it is* (→ 3). In connection with preps. εἰμί designates the origin, the affiliation, the alignment, or generally the place of things or persons (→ 4). With gen. or dat. εἰμί can express a relationship of possession (see BDF §§189f.) (→ 5).

2. a) As a copula εἰμί places subj. and pred. in relation to each other, e.g., εἰ υἱὸς εἶ τοῦ θεοῦ (Matt 4:3); καὶ γὰρ Γαλιλαῖος εἶ (Mark 14:70); εἷς ἐστιν ὁ ἀγαθός (Matt 19:17); to identify subj. with pred. ὁ λύχνος τοῦ σώματός ἐστιν ὁ ὀφθαλμός σου (11:34; cf. 1 Cor 9:2), esp. in the interpretation of a parable, e.g., ὁ δὲ ἀγρός ἐστιν ὁ κόσμος (Matt 13:38; cf. v. 37, 29 bis), and in introductory formulas for parables, e.g., ὁμοία ἐστὶν ἡ βασιλεία τῶν οὐρανῶν . . . , "the kingdom of heaven is like . . ." (vv. 33, 44).

b) In the Gospels the formula → ἐγώ εἰμι sometimes appears without explicit determination of the pred., which must be determined from the context: θαρσεῖτε, ἐγώ εἰμι (Mark 6:50 par. Matt 14:27; Mark 14:62; John 4:26; 8:28; 18:5; cf. also Matt 26:22, 25). The pred. is to be determined from the context in 1 John 3:1 as well.

c) The formula τοῦτ' ἔστιν (among others) has an explanatory function, *that is, that means, namely,* often in the translation of Aram. expressions (e.g., Matt 27:46; Mark 7:11, 34; 9:10; Luke 15:26). Τίνα θέλει ταῦτα εἶναι is translated "what these things *mean*" (Acts 17:20); as in explanations of parables (→ 2.a) the literal meaning of something already indicated or said is emphasized, but an identification is not made; similarly also in the sacrificial formula τοῦτό ἐστιν τὸ σῶμά (αἷμά) μου (Mark 14:22 (24) par.; cf. 1 Cor 11:24, 25); with the bread and cup in their literal meaning the body of Christ and the new covenant are present. The most suitable translation remains the simple "this is . . ." in the sense of "in it *is present.*"

d) Periphrastic εἰμί serves the grammatically necessary function of connecting the perf. partc. with the fut. (e.g., Matt 16:19; 18:18). It is used in other situations with no noticeable shift of meaning from the nonperiphrastic tenses. Beyond this it is used to give special emphasis to a statement or to the nominal meaning of the partc. (e.g., Matt 19:22; Mark 5:14; 6:52; Luke 23:53; John 6:50; Acts 22:20; 25:10; 1 Cor 7:29; 15:19; Gal 1:22f.). It also serves to emphasize the duration or the regular recurrence of an action or a situation (e.g., Mark 1:22 par. Matt 7:29; Mark 15:43; Matt 10:22; Luke 14:1; 19:47; Acts 1:13, 17; 2:42; 3:10; Eph 4:18). In John 1:28 ἦν has its own weight: "where John *was staying* and baptizing" (RSV is different). Cf. also the impersonal phrases πρέπον ἐστίν (1 Cor 11:13) and δέον ἐστίν (Acts 19:36).

e) Εἰμί appears in connection with adverbs, e.g., εἰμὶ ἐγγύς, *be near* (Matt 24:33; Mark 13:28), εἰμὶ μακράν, *be far away* (Mark 12:34), εἰμὶ πόρρω, *be far away* (Luke 14:32), εἰμὶ ἐντος, *be in the midst* (17:21), εἰμὶ οὕτως, *be thus* (Matt 1:18; Rom 4:18; 1 Pet 2:15), ἔστω σοι ὥσπερ τελώνης, "*let him be* to you as . . . a tax collector" (Matt 18:17), and τὸ εἶναι ἴσα (adverbial neut. pl.) θεῷ, "*be* like God" (Phil. 2:6; RSV "equality with God").

3. a) Εἰμί can be an independent pred. (normally impf.) and means in narrative connections *live, exist, be,* e.g., οὗ ἦν τὸ παιδίον, "where the child *was*" (Matt 2:9), ἦν ἐκεῖ, "and [he] *remained* there" (2:15; cf. Mark 5:21), in the introduction of narratives and parables: ἄνθρωπος ἦν, "*there was* (once) a man" (Matt 21:33; Luke 16:1, etc.; cf. also Matt 22:25; 23:30); also with the meaning *take place*: σχίσμα ἦν, "*there was* a division" (John 9:16), δεῖ γὰρ καὶ αἱρέσεις ἐν ὑμῖν εἶναι, "for there must *be* factions among you" (1 Cor 11:19; cf. also Matt 24:37), καὶ ἔσται (with a fut. vb.), "and *it shall be* that . . ." (Acts 2:17, 21; 3:23). Εἰμί is sometimes used to give information about time: ἦν . . . ὥρα ἕκτη (Luke 23:44), ἦν παρασκευή (Mark 15:42), ἦν ἑορτὴ τῶν Ἰουδαίων (John 5:1), ἦν δὲ σάββατον (9:14). It sometimes means *be there, be present:* οὔπω γὰρ ἦν πνεῦμα (John 7:39), πάλιν πολλοῦ ὄχλου ὄντος, "when again a great crowd *had gathered*" (Mark 8:1); cf. μὴ ὄντος νόμου, "where *there is* no law" (Rom 5:13). With complementary inf. οὐκ ἔστιν means "*it is impossible*" (1 Cor 11:20, NEB).

b) That which *is real,* which has been called into being by God, is τὰ ὄντα, in contrast to that which does not *exist,* τὰ μὴ ὄντα (Rom 4:17; for the creation of the world from nothing, cf. 2 Macc 7:28; *Herm. Vis.* i.1.6; fig. for conversion as a new creation, *Jos. As.* 8:15). In 1 Cor 1:28 τὰ μὴ ὄντα is a metaphor for the "despised" ones chosen by God, in contrast to τὰ ὄντα, i.e., those who could build on their own glory without relating to God.

c) In dependence on God's self-designation Ἐγώ εἰμι ὁ ὤν or Ὁ ὤν in Exod 3:14 LXX, ὁ ὤν came to be a customary name for God for Hellenistic Jews (Philo *Abr.* 12; Josephus *Ant.* viii.350). In accordance with this, ὁ ὤν appears as a name for God in Revelation. Three times it appears in the "three-tense formula," ὁ ὢν καὶ ὁ ἦν καὶ ὁ ἐρχόμενος, attested in Greek since Homer, as well as in Jewish tradition (Büchsel 397; Kraft), in a blessing (1:4), in a self-predication of God, connected with ἐγώ εἰμι (v. 8), and in a prayer (4:8). Twice it appears in the formula ὁ ὢν καὶ ὁ ἦν (11:17; 16:5; here, too, in a prayer and in a word of praise). The "three-tense formula" shows that ὁ ἦν is pressed into service as a participle; the undeclined ἀπό phrase in 1:4 is also intentional. For the seer what is involved is the praise of the name of the God who "comes" from his eternal existence, of whom it can neither be said that he has come into being (ὁ γεγονώς, as in the Greek formulas) nor that he is simply timeless "being" (ὁ ἐσόμενος). Christ's ἐγὼ εἰμί in John 8:58 is similar in its intention: "Before Abraham was [born], *I am [present].*"

In Heb 11:6 the concern is with faith "that [God] *exists*" (ὅτι ἔστιν) and can be found. 1 Cor 8:5 has the formula εἴπερ εἰσὶν λεγόμενοι θεοί . . . , but εἰμί is elided in vv. 4 and 6, where the subject is the one God. The omnipotent God is the subject of the eulogy in Rom 9:5f.: ὁ ὢν ἐπὶ πάντων θεός, "God who *has power* over everything" (RSV "God who *is* over all").

4. Εἰμί with a prep. is found in the following combinations: εἰμὶ εἰς, "*become* something" (e.g., εἰς σάρκα μίαν, Matt 19:5 [v. 6f.: εἰσὶν . . . σὰρξ μία!]; 1 Cor 6:16; εἰς σημεῖόν εἰσιν, they *serve as* a sign, 14:22; ἐμοὶ δὲ εἰς ἐλάχιστόν ἐστιν, it *does not matter* in the least to me, 4:3; in place of a pred. nom., εἰς τὸ ἕν εἰσιν, they *become* one, 1 John 5:8; cf. 2 Cor 6:18; Heb 1:5 [see BDF §145.1]), εἰμὶ ἐκ, expressing ownership or origin (e.g., ἐκ τοῦ πονηροῦ ἐστιν, "*comes from* the evil one," Matt 5:37 [RSV mg.]; cf. 26:73; John 17:16; 18:25; 1 Cor 12:15; ἐκ τοῦ διαβόλου ἐστίν, *belongs* to the devil, 1 John 3:8), εἰμὶ ἐν, "*live at* a place" or "*be in* a specific place" (Matt 18:20; Mark 2:1; Rom 8:34; fig., ἦμεν ἐν τῇ σαρκί, Rom 7:5; ἐν οἷς εἰμι, "in whatever state I am," Phil 4:11), εἰμὶ ἐπὶ τὸ αὐτό, "be together at the same place" (Acts 1:15; 1 Cor 7:5).

5. Εἰμί with gen. expresses the relationship of possession or affiliation (e.g., τίνος ἔσται γυνή, Mark 12:23; cf. Matt 19:14; Rom 8:9; ἐγὼ μέν εἰμι Παύλου, 1 Cor 1:12; πάντα ὑμῶν ἐστιν, 3:21; cf. 6:19; in reference to origin: ᾖ τοῦ θεοῦ καὶ μὴ ἐξ ἡμῶν, 2 Cor 4:7; to age: Acts 4:22). Εἰμί with dat. can also designate a relationship of possession (e.g., John 18:39), but also has the meaning *happen to* (Matt 16:22; cf. 18:8; 1 Cor 9:16).

H. Balz

εἵνεκεν *heineken* because of, for the sake of
→ ἕνεκα.

εἴπερ *eiper* if indeed, if however*

With the exception of 2 Thess 1:6, the conjunction εἴπερ appears only in the letters of Paul (Rom 3:30; 8:9, 17; 1 Cor 8:5; 15:15; 2 Cor 5:3 v.l.) and in 1 Pet 2:3 (v.l.). Like → ἐάνπερ it introduces a conditional clause which presents a new but decisive ground for the apodosis. Thus it has a secondary causal meaning (cf. BDF §454.2): *if indeed* (Rom 3:30 [v.l. ἐπείπερ, "since indeed"]; 8:9, 17; 2 Thess 1:6; καὶ γὰρ εἴπερ, "for *although,*" 1 Cor 8:5; εἴπερ ἄρα, "*if* it is true that" [cf. classical ἄρα, "as they say"], 15:15).

εἶπον *eipon* speak, command, call

1. 2nd aor. of λέγω — 2. With acc. obj. — 3. With persons spoken to — 4. With no obj. — 5. Meaning "command" — 6. Meaning "think" — 7. Meaning "name" — 8. Meaning "predict" — 9. No difference in nuance from λέγω

Lit.: BAGD s.v. — MOULTON, *Grammar* III, 64, 237. — ROBERTSON, *Grammar* (index s.v.) — SCHMIDT, *Synonymik* I (index s.v.) — G. STRECKER, *Der Weg der Gerechtigkeit* (FRLANT 82, [3]1971) (index s.v. εἰπεῖν)

1. Εἶπον (*ca.* 925 occurrences in the NT) is used as the 2nd aor. of λέγω. 1st aor. εἶπα is also used; on the additional

verb forms see BAGD s.v. Specifically, εἶπον is used in the NT in the following constructions and meanings:

2. With an acc. object: a) With the acc. of what is spoken: (τὴν) ἀλήθειαν (Mark 5:33 [2 Cor 12:6]; cf. John 4:18); λόγον (Matt 26:44; John 2:22; 7:36; 18:9, 32). The latter phrase is to be understood negatively in the sense of "defame" when it appears with → εἰς (Luke 12:10) or with → κατά with the gen. (Matt 12:32). Ὡς ἔπος εἰπεῖν, in order to *use* the right word, which is widely distributed in classical Greek, appears once in the NT (Heb 7:9; cf. Wettstein, *NT* II, 409). The question τί ἐροῦμεν, "What *should we say?*" is a transitional formula used by Paul in Romans (3:5; 6:1; 7:7; 8:31; 9:14, 30).

The OT is often introduced by the passive construction τὸ ῥηθὲν (ὑπὸ κυρίου) διὰ τοῦ προφήτου λέγοντος, etc. This is found in the introductions to the "reflexive citations" shaped by the Matthean redactor (Matt 1:22; 2:15, 17, 23; 4:14; 8:17; 12:17; 13:35; 21:4; 27:9; cf. Strecker 49-85). The antitheses of the Sermon on the Mount have ἐρρέθη (τοῖς ἀρχαίοις; Matt 5:21, 27, 31, 33, 38, 43; cf. also the expression τὸ εἰρημένον [διὰ τοῦ προφήτου], Luke 2:24; Acts 13:40; Rom 4:18 [Acts 2:16]).

b) Εἶπον appears with the acc. of a person spoken of (e.g., John 1:15; Matt 3:3 [passive]). This construction appears with the adverbs καλῶς and κακῶς: "*speak* well (ill) of someone" (Luke 6:26; Acts 23:5 [citing Exod 22:27]).

c) Εἶπον is used in elliptic constructions, where αὐτό is to be supplied from the context (Luke 22:67; John 9:27; 16:4, etc.). Σὺ εἶπας, "yes," also belongs here (Matt 26:25, 64; cf. BAGD s.v. 1); there are parallels in rabbinic and Hellenistic literature (cf. Wettstein, *NT* I, 518a; Billerbeck I, 990f.); cf. similarly σὺ λέγεις (Mark 15:2 par.; John 18:37).

3. The person(s) to whom something is said, is (are) identified a) with the dat.: εἶπον τί τινι (τισι; Matt 28:7; Luke 4:23; 7:40, and often) or b) with the prep. πρός. (Πρός is found with εἶπον only in Luke-Acts and in Mark 12:7, 12 and Rom 8:31; where its obj. is personal it indicates the person[s] spoken to [Luke 1:13, 18, 28, 34; 4:23; 5:4; 12:16, and many times in Luke-Acts] or is to be translated "in reference to" [Mark 12:12; Luke 18:9; 20:19].)

4. Εἶπον without an object. a) Εἶπον appears with adverbs or other qualifiers: with ὁμοίως (Matt 26:35), ὡσαύτως (21:30), καθώς (28:6; Luke 24:24; John 1:23; 7:38), ἐν παραβολαῖς/διὰ παραβολῆς, "*speak* in parables/a parable" (Matt 22:1), λόγῳ, "*speak* a word," in healings (λόγῳ is instrumental dat.; Matt 8:8 par. Luke 7:7).

b) Εἶπον used rhetorically in letters introduces considered objections (ἐρεῖ τις, etc.; Rom 9:19; 11:19; 1 Cor 15:35; Jas 2:18).

c) Εἶπον is used to introduce a speech in which a partc. of one of a number of vbs. provides a more precise determination (Matt 2:8; 3:7; 8:19; 9:12; 12:24; 15:10; 17:7; Mark 6:24; 8:7). Esp. important is ἀποκριθεὶς εἶπεν, which is esp. frequent in Matthew (in contrast to the Markan or Q original: Matt 3:15; 4:4; 11:4, 25; 12:48, etc.), but also appears in Mark (where it does not in Matthew and Luke: Mark 6:37; 10:51; 14:48) and Luke (against the Markan original: Luke 5:22, 31; 6:3, and often). On the other hand, John prefers to coordinate the two vbs.: ἀπεκρίθη καὶ εἶπεν (John 1:48; 2:19; 3:10, etc.; the only use of this construction in the Synoptics is Luke 17:20).

d) Ὅτι follows εἶπον in Matt 28:7, 13; Mark 16:7; John 6:36; 7:42, and often.

5. Frequently εἶπον includes the sense of a command, appearing normally thus with an inf. (Mark 5:43: he "*told* [εἶπεν] them to give her something to eat"; 8:7; Luke 12:13; 19:15, etc.) or with ἵνα with the subjunc. (Matt 4:3 par.; 20:21).

6. The phrase εἶπον ἐν ἑαυτῷ/ἐν τῇ καρδίᾳ αὐτοῦ, "think" (Matt 9:3; Luke 7:39; 12:34; 16:3; 18:4. Rom 10:6; perhaps also Mark 12:7, → 3.b) is a Hebraism corresponding to *'āmar b^elibô* (Deut 8:17; Pss 10:6; 13:1; Esth 6:6).

7. Εἶπον with the double acc. means *call by the name* (John 10:35; 15:15).

8. In Matt 28:6; Mark 14:16; Luke 23:13; John 14:28; 16:4 εἶπον has the meaning *predict*.

9. A difference between the meaning of λέγω and that of εἶπον cannot be established. Both vbs. appear in the NT as variant readings for each other, and both are also used indiscriminately in the same sentence (Matt 10:27; 26:25; John 15:15). The NT does not make a distinction between the impf. of λέγω (ἔλεγον) and εἶπον (cf. BDF §329).

G. Lüdemann

εἰρηνεύω *eirēneuō* keep peace, live in peace*

Mark 9:50: εἰρηνεύετε ἐν ἀλλήλοις, ". . . with one another"; similarly 1 Thess 5:13: εἰρηνεύετε ἐν ἑαυτοῖς, ". . . among yourselves"; Rom 12:18: εἰ δυνατόν, τὸ ἐξ ὑμῶν, μετὰ πάντων ἀνθρώπων εἰρηνεύοντες, "if possible, so far as it depends upon you, *live peaceably* with all" (cf. *T. Benj.* 5:1); used absolutely: 2 Cor 13:11; → εἰρήνη.

εἰρήνη, ης, ἡ *eirēnē* peace*

1. Occurrences in the NT — 2. Jesus' message of peace in the pre-Synoptic tradition — 3. The understanding of the Evangelists — 4. Form and content of the Pauline statements — 5. Developments in the deutero-Pauline letters — 6. The conceptions in the other writings

Lit.: G. BAUMBACH, "Das Verständnis von εἰρήνη im NT," *Theologische Versuche* V (1975) 33-44. — E. BRANDENBURGER, *Frieden im NT* (1973). — E. DINKLER, *RAC* VIII, 434-505. — W. EISENBEIS, *Die Wurzel* slm *im AT* (1969). — J. GNILKA, " 'Christus unser Friede'—ein Friedens-Erlöserlied in Eph 2, 14-17," FS Schlier 190-207. — H. HEGERMANN, "Die Bedeutung des eschatologischen Friedens . . . ," *Der Friedensdienst der Christen* (ed. W. Danielsmeyer, 1970) 17-39. — O. HOFIUS, *Katapausis* (1970). — S. MEURER, *Das Recht im Dienst der Versöhnung und des Friedens* (1972). — H. H. SCHMID, *Schālôm. Frieden im Alten Orient und im AT* (1972). — J. J. STAMM and H. BIETENHARD, *Der Weltfriede im Lichte der Bibel* (1959). — O. H. STECK, *Friedensvorstellungen im alten Jerusalem* (1972). — P. STUHLMACHER, "Der Begriff des Friedens im NT und seine Konsequenzen," *Studien zur Friedensforschung* IV (ed. G. Picht and H. E. Tödt, 1970) 21-69. — H. THYEN, "Zur Problematic einer neutestamentlichen Ekklesiologie," *Studien zur Friedensforschung* IX (ed. G. Picht, et al., 1972) 96-173. — C. WESTERMANN, "Alttestamentliche Elemente in Lk 2,1-20," FS Kuhn 317-27. — For further bibliography see *TWNT* X, 1069f.; *DNTT* II, 783.

1. Εἰρήνη appears a total of 92 times in the NT. With the exception of 1 John it appears in every NT writing, most frequently in the Gospels (25 occurrences, of which 4 are in Matthew, 1 in Mark, 14 in Luke [+ 7 in Acts], and 6 in John), and in Paul's letters (26 occurrences, with the highest frequency in Romans [10]); elsewhere most frequently in Ephesians (8).

2. In the pre-Markan tradition represented in Mark 5:34, the OT and Jewish dismissal formula "go in peace" appears (cf. Luke 8:48; Judg 18:6; 1 Sam 1:17; 20:42; 29:7; Jdt 8:35). In connection with Jesus' miracles, the blessing, as a realization of the kingdom of God, means the authoritative promise of eschatological salvation. It corresponds to the word of the "ancient one" in *1 Enoch* 71:15: "He proclaims peace to you in the name of the future world; for from there peace proceeds since the creation of the world." Against the levitical purity laws Jesus authorizes the faith of the socially despised woman and brings her back into the community.

The cryptic remark attached to the saying about salt in Mark 9:50 leads to the demand to keep peace with one another (εἰρηνεύειν, Rom 12:18; 2 Cor 13:11; 1 Thess 5:13). In the Synoptic tradition the saying about salt has a variety of forms (Mark 9:49; Matt 5:13; Luke 14:34; cf. Col 4:6). Its original place in the instruction of the disciples and the positive evaluation of salt indicate the effective power of the message. As bearers of salvation, the disciples already form a community of peace. The Essenes (CD 6:21f.; 1QM 3:5; *T. Dan* 5:2) and Pharisees (cf. Billerbeck I, 215-18) know a command for peace in reference to the final peace. Their phrase "to pursue peace," borrowed from the OT (Ps 34:15; *m. 'Abot* 1:12; *b. Sanh.* 6b; cf. Rom 14:19; 1 Pet 3:11; Heb 12:14), demands more than agreement; it demands the realization of the expected salvation in one's own social realm. The beatitude of the peacemaker in Matt 5:9, with its mention of the sons of God and of the reward in the coming kingdom (Ps 37:11; 1QS 4:7f.; 1QH 13:17; 15:16), is derived from the same milieu.

The saying in Matt 10:12f. par. Luke 10:5f.; Matt 10:34 par. Luke 12:51 is from the mission instructions in the later Q material. In it Israel's last generation is placed before a final choice. No city and no house may be entered without the accompanying word of salvation in the form of a greeting of peace or angelic greeting (Dan 10:19; Tob 12:17). Anyone who accepts the greeting becomes a "son of peace," while anyone who rejects it remains forever excluded from salvation. In the ἦλθον saying (Matt 10:34; on *hiṭîl šālôm* cf. Billerbeck I, 585f.) with the motif of the division of members of the same household (Mark 13:12; Mic 7:6; *1 Enoch* 100:1-2; *Jub.* 23:19f.) Jesus does not call the disciples to take the sword (cf. Matt 26:52), but promises a bloody persecution and the loss of domestic peace, tranquility, and order among one's own people.

3. a) Matthew understood the blessing (Matt 5:9) to refer to instruction in the wisdom tradition (cf. Pss 34; 37). Happy is the one who makes peace (Matt 5:9) before the end comes! Anyone who has not been reconciled with his brother and has not forgiven his brother's wrong will not survive the final judgment (5:23ff.; 6:12ff.; 18:21ff.). The concern is to take upon oneself the mild yoke of the Messiah king and to learn mercy from Christ (11:28ff.; 9:13; 12:7). Anyone who does not exercise the gentleness of the Prince of Peace (Zech 9:9, cited in Matt 21:1ff.) does not belong in his future kingdom (Matt 13:41; 16:19).

b) With the proclamation of peace Mark 5:34 emphasizes faith in the saving miraculous power of the hidden Son of God and indicates how the messianic secret of Jesus is made accessible in the salvific experience of faith.

c) The dismissals in Luke 7:50; 8:48 (cf. 17:19); Acts 16:36 (cf. 15:33) belong particularly to Luke's style. In Luke 24:36 (cf. RSV mg.) a secondary interpolation has been made from John 20:19, 26. We find technical usage in Luke 14:32 and Acts 12:20, where the phrase "ask for peace" (ἐρωτᾶν/αἰτεῖσθαι εἰρήνην) with *T. Jud.* 9:7 refers to prudent submission to the one who has power. The image of Luke 11:21 involves satisfactory equipment for the defense of one's possession. In the introduction to the speech by Tertullus in Acts 24:2 the use of εἰρήνη is reminiscent of the imperial idea of peace.

d) In the Lukan double work the OT and Jewish concept of *šālôm* is connected, on the one hand, with the concept of σωτηρία associated with the Hellenistic idea of epiphany and, on the other hand, with the imperial *pax* ideology (cf. the inscriptions from Priene and Halicarnassus referred to by W. Foerster, *TDNT* VII, 1012; Virgil *Ecl.* 4; *Aen.* vi.791-807; Horace *Carm.* iv.5.17-40). The Lukan birth legends are to be understood in accordance with this. Most likely motifs of ancient oriental kingship ideology dispersed in the prophetic and apocalyptic literature (Isa 52:7; Nah 2:1; *Pss. Sol.* 17:35; *T. Levi* 18:4, 12, etc.) also make an appearance, but Luke strictly limits the evidence in salvation history of the Davidic Messiah king to the past time of Jesus. Thus a combination from Isa 9:2; 42:7; Ps 107:10 (Luke 1:79) indicates the way to peace initiated by John the Baptist that leads into the time of salvation brought about by the coming king of peace through the preaching of repentance, conversion, and forgiveness.

Luke, a Hellenist, thinks historically, not apocalyptically. Thus the song of praise by the host of angels before God's throne in Luke 2:14 proclaims the epiphany of the Most High in the child in the manger as the gracious demonstration of the divine goodwill (cf. 1QH 4:32f.; 11:9). Simeon has seen the divine appearance in the child and, according to Luke 2:29, is ready to die, as he says in formulaic dying words (cf. Tob 3:6; Billerbeck II, 138f.). What the angels cry (Luke 2:14) is proclaimed in the cry of jubilation by the disciples at the public entry into Jerusalem (19:38). Luke moves from the Davidic elements and declares that the one who enters is the God-king, through whom the true peace of the kingdom of God, in contrast to the peace of Augustus, will spread from Jerusalem to the Gentiles. The appended lament over Jerusalem indicates that the city did not recognize the moment of God's gracious visitation (19:42; cf. 1:68, 78; 7:16; Acts 15:14) and must pay with siege and destruction for the rejection of the king of salvation who had been sent (Luke 13:34f.; 21:6, 20ff.; 23:27ff.). Already in 2:34 and in the instructions to the disciples in 10:5f. and 12:51 Luke mentions the conflict and the division of Israel. Indeed, Moses tried in vain to bring peaceful reconciliation to his countrymen (Acts 7:26). Despite all rejection and persecution, the universal Kyrios, according to Acts 10:36, has created a place of peace which can be built up (9:31) and expanded (15:33).

e) Behind the farewell words in John 14:27; 16:33 stands the authority of the revealer who was sent to his own chosen ones who are in the world opposed to God. He leaves to them his own supra-worldly peace, which consists in the unity of the Son with the Father. The repeated greeting of the resurrected one in John 20:19, 21, 26 indicates that the disciples remain bound together in the midst of the anxiety of the world in the indestructible security of this divine relationship. The dualistic thought structure of John separates the ontic concept of peace from the concept of shalom in apocalyptic and prevents us from assuming that he refers to the anticipation of the eschatological peace.

4. In connection with his doctrine of salvation Paul mentions peace in Rom 5:1 in a way that makes it parallel to reconciliation, spoken of in vv. 10f. (cf. 2 Cor 5:18-21). Paul goes beyond the faith formula of Rom 4:25 and takes up the justification text of 3:21ff., thinking ahead toward the completion of peace described in ch. 8. By faith in the reconciliation in the cross a person no longer stands, like the Jews and the Gentiles, under wrath, but under the gracious power of God's righteousness. Over against the breaking of the covenant and disobedience to the law (Rom 3:17) God has accomplished his claim in Christ's resurrection. In it mankind's earlier enmity, guilt, and ignominy are taken away.

The new relationship of peace with God brings the Church toward its full development. Peace effects the sanctification on the day of the parousia (1 Thess 5:23). When liberated from legal prescriptions, the righteousness and joy of God's kingdom are viewed as the result (Rom 8:6) and the fruit of the Holy Spirit (Gal 5:22; Rom 2:10; 14:17). The Spirit's structure of peace gives form to life in the Church. Thus Paul's exhortations aim in this direction: One is to pursue peace (Rom 14:19), keep peace with one another (1 Thess 5:13; 2 Cor 13:11; Rom 12:18), and make peace the watchman over heart and mind (Phil 4:7). Ethical (1 Cor 5), legal (6:1ff.), and marital relationships (7:12ff.) are to fall under the sway of peace. Peace is to be determinative in communal worship (14:33) and in communication between the apostle and his coworkers (16:11).

"Peace" is a frequent term in epistolary formulas. In the prescripts of Rom 1:7; 1 Cor 1:3; 2 Cor 1:2; Gal 1:3; Phil 1:2; 1 Thess 1:1; and Phlm 3 Paul alters a Jewish blessing formula, "mercy and peace," which is contained in *2 Bar.* 78:2 and echoed in Gal 6:16, by the use of χάρις. Except in 1 Thess 1:1 he conforms to liturgical usage by connecting it with "God our Father and the Lord Jesus Christ." With this blessing he grants to his addressees the Lord's gift of salvation, as he describes more precisely in the proemium in 1 Cor 1:4-9 and expands in Gal 1:4. (In the latter χάρις is explained in a formula of sacrifice, εἰρήνη as a process of liberation by removal from the present evil aeon.)

In the epistolary final blessing Paul repeats the doxological declaration of peace contained in the prescript. In 1 Thess 5:23; Phil 4:9; Rom 15:33; 16:20 (cf. Heb 13:20) he uses the fixed formula "the God of peace" (present also in Rom 15:13; 1 Cor 14:33; 2 Cor 13:11; 2 Thess 3:16). This is perhaps derived from *yhwh šālôm* (Judg 6:24) and is found in *T. Dan* 5:2.

Thus Paul brackets his letters with the "bond of peace" and emphasizes the unifying power of God's peaceful order. In Rom 16:20 he uses the apocalyptic image of the battle with the dragon from the ancient royal ideology (cf. *T. Levi* 18:12; Rev 12:7, 12; 20:1ff.) and makes the Church a participant in the final cosmic victory over Satan. In 1 Thess 5:3 Paul contrasts the image of the sudden onset of birth pangs to a report of peace that is opposed to expectation of the imminent end (cf. Ezek 13:10; Isa 66:8).

5. Two significant post-Pauline passages are Col 1:20 and Eph 2:14ff. The former belongs to the song of praise in Col 1:15-20. The motif of a defeat of the cosmic powers by the revealer, which is derived from Gnosticism, now describes the victory achieved by the enthroned Son of God after his resurrection. Thus those who are baptized no longer find themselves under the dominance of these powers. The record of their sins was nailed to the cross and blotted out through the blood of the Son (Col 2:13f.). Now they belong to the uppper world which has been pacified under his sovereignty (1:13, 20ff.).

Eph 2:14ff. betrays the language of the baptismal liturgy. The proclamation in v. 14 (cf. Isa 9:6; Mic 5:4f.) takes up the ideas seen in Colossians, but applies them to the universal Church made up of Jews and Gentiles. The wall of separation between the two groups consisting of the regulations of the Torah has been destroyed by Christ's death on the cross (cf. Rom 7:4; 10:4). Since then the promises, the hopes, and indeed the God of the covenant people belong also to the Gentiles (cf. Isa 57:19). Jewish and Gentile Christians have been included together in the body which spans the entire cosmos. In the two ideas of the dividing wall and the body we see a combination of the mythic conceptions of the firmament between an upper and a lower world and of the anthropos coming from heaven who fills the lower cosmos and incorporates believing humanity into its body. Christians, who have been placed under the sovereignty of *Christus Pantocrator,* now must keep the peace. Peace rules them (Col 3:15) and clasps them as a bond which encompasses the All where peace has been restored (Eph 4:3). Having been well-armed they must now spread the gospel of the rule of peace in the world (Eph 6:15; cf. Isa 52:7; Nah 2:1; Rom 2:1; Rom 10:15; Acts 10:36).

The epistolary forms in Col 1:2; Eph 1:2; 6:23 now reflect this Hellenistic understanding of the peace, and no longer the Pauline eschatological shalom. (The other salutations are assimilated to the usual Pauline salutations [2 Thess 1:2; 1 Tim 1:2; 2 Tim 1:2; Titus 1:4].) The new interpretation also appears in the final blessing in 2 Thess 3:16: "the Lord of peace" is the universal Benefactor and Savior to whom Christians, as subjects before the emperor, offer their thanks for peace and good fortune. In 2 Tim 2:22 peace (→ 2) appears in a list of virtues which oblige the Church's leaders to be concerned in an exemplary way for the pious conduct of the faithful.

6. In Hebrews the salvific significance of peace is evident only in 7:2. The concept of rest (chs. 3–4) appears in place of the concept of peace. Already 5:6 connects the name of Melchizedek typologically to an eternal and royal office of priest of the exalted Christ. In a way similar to Philo and the rabbinic literature, Ps 110:4 and motifs like those in *T. Levi* 8:14; 18:6ff. are taken up. The priestly theme is connected with the old motif of the king of peace who creates salvation and peace after the subjugation of the enemy. Thus at the cross the exalted Son of God destroyed death, the ultimate enemy, and liberated mankind from servitude to it (Heb 2:14f.). Heb 11:31; 12:11, 14 are parenetic: Rahab, in providing the spies secure refuge, is a model for the hospitality demanded in 13:2. "The peaceful fruit of righteousness" (→ εἰρηνικός) acquired in suffering (12:11) is not an inner peace of the heart, but rather a higher level of holiness. Accompanying it is a general readiness for peace. The doxology in 13:20f. in the style of a liturgical dismissal associates "the God of peace" with the royal shepherd and emphasizes once more the eternal service of peace by the priest-king in heaven.

Jas 2:16 calls for active assistance for the poverty-stricken member of the Church and contrasts such help with the pious wish which has become only an empty formula. However, good works grow only in a Church where the peace which comes from above rules. Thus 3:17f. speaks (with formulations derived from dualistic wisdom) of the fruit of righteousness (cf. Phil 1:11; Prov 11:30). The same concern for harmony shapes the exhortations in 1 Pet 3:11 (citing Ps 34) and 2 Pet 3:14, the latter speaking in view of the parousia. It accompanies also the traditional wish of peace in 1 Pet 1:2; 5:14; 2 Pet 1:2; 2 John 3; 3 John 15; Jude 2, and Rev 1:4.

The second seal, opened by the lamb in Rev 6:4, releases the rider on the red horse with the commission to take away peace from the earth. Only after the destruction of the *pax Romana* and after the bloody subjection of the imperial Antichrist will the apocalyptic Messiah-King establish an otherworldly kingdom of peace.

V. Hasler

εἰρηνικός, 3 *eirēnikos* peaceable, peaceful, ready for peace*

Heb 12:11: καρπὸν εἰρηνικὸν . . . ἀποδίδωσιν δικαιοσύνης, discipline "yields the *peaceful* fruit of righteousness" (i.e., the fruit of righteousness, which—after much suffering—brings peace with it; perhaps also fig., "the *healing* fruit"); Jas 3:17, of the ἄνωθεν σοφία . . . εἰρηνική, which is *peaceful.*

εἰρηνοποιέω *eirēnopoieō* make peace*

Col 1:20: εἰρηνοποιήσας διὰ τοῦ αἵματος τοῦ σταυροῦ αὐτοῦ, "*making peace* by the blood of his cross."

εἰρηνοποιός, 2 *eirēnopoios* bringing about peace (adj.)*

Matt 5:9: μακάριοι οἱ εἰρηνοποιοί, blessed are *those who make peace;* perhaps also subst.: "the *peacemakers.*"

εἰς *eis* with acc.: in; into; toward; to

1. Basic meaning and occurrences in the NT — 2. Spatial — 3. Temporal — 4. Of persons and things — 5. Grammatical details

Lit.: On preps. in general → ἀνά. — BAGD s.v. — BDF §§205-7. — M. J. Harris, *DNTT* III, 1184-88. — Kühner, *Grammatik* II/1, 468-71. — LSJ s.v. — Mayser, *Grammatik* II/2, 404-19. — C. F. D. Moule, *An Idiom-Book of NT Greek* (²1959) 67-71. — Moulton, *Grammar,* III, 249-57, 266f. — A. Oepke, *TDNT* I, 420-34. — P. F. Regard, *Contribution à l'étude des prépositions dans la langue du NT* (1919) 136-227. — For further bibliography see *TWNT* X, 1070.

1. Originally εἰς denoted the same spatial dimensions as → ἐν, but as an indicator of direction toward a goal, not as an indicator of location without direction. Its use in the NT corresponds largely to classical usage, from which the specifically NT phrasing is commonly derived (the influence of Hebrew is limited).

The basic meaning of εἰς as well as the many possibilities for usage can be seen in the frequent occurrences in the NT: *ca.* 1750 (fewer than ἐν). It is found in all the NT documents with no special emphasis in any of them.

2. Spatial. a) As an indication of goal, esp. with vbs. of movement: *into* the house, *into* the city, *into* the synagogue, *into* the vineyard; also with names of cities and countries: *to* Jerusalem, *to* Spain. Characteristic for the conceptual world of the NT are expanded spatial dimensions: εἰς τὸν οὐρανόν, of the ascension of Christ (Mark 16:19, etc.), of the angels (Luke 2:15; εἰς τὸν κόσμον, esp. in John in soteriological contexts: the light came *into* the world (John 3:19; cf. 1:9; 12:46; 16:28; 18:37; 1 Tim 1:15), God sent his Son *into* the world (John 10:36; cf. 3:17; 17:18; 1 John 4:9).

b) General indication of goal: εἰς τὰ ὄρη, "*to* the mountains" (Mark 13:14; sg. in 3:13); εἰς ἀγρόν, "*into* the country" (16:12); εἰς τὰς ὁδούς, "*to* the highways" (Luke 14:23); εἰς ὁδόν, "*for* their journey" (Mark 6:8; cf. 10:17; Matt 10:5); εἰς τὸ μέσον, "*in* the midst" (Mark 3:3; 14:60, etc.).

c) Approach to a goal: Matt 17:27: *at* (not in) the sea; John 4:5: *near* a city (but vv. 8, 28, *into* the city); 20:1, 3: *to the* tomb (but v. 6, *into* the tomb); hence ἐγγίζω εἰς: "come near" a place.

d) To indicate the object of a vb. of seeing: looking up *to* heaven (Mark 6:41); looking *to* him, seeing him (Acts 3:4 and often).

e) With persons and (less frequently) things: Luke 10:36: fall *among* the robbers; Mark 4:7: fall *among* the thistles; Matt 15:24: be sent *to* the sheep. Formulaic of the entry of Satan *into* a person: εἰσῆλθεν εἰς (Luke 22:3; John 13:27). To designate the center of spiritual existence: εἰς τὴν καρδίαν, "*into* the heart" (John 13:2; cf. Gal 4:6; Rev 17:17).

f) To designate the addressees with vbs. of saying (here spatial and personal concepts often merge): Mark 5:14: tell *in* the city and the country; Acts 23:11: bear witness *to* Jerusalem, *to* Rome; Mark 14:9: proclaim the gospel *to* the whole world (*before* all peoples, 13:10; cf. Luke 24:47; Rom 16:26). Similarly εἰς ὑμᾶς, *before* you (1 Thess 2:9 and often).

g) In metaphors: for heaven and hell, esp. in eschatological scenes in the NT: enter "*[into]* life" (εἰς τὴν ζωήν, Matt 18:8f., etc.), "*into* his glory" (εἰς τὴν δόξαν, Luke 24:26, etc.); enter (here closer to literal) *into* God's kingdom (Mark 9:47, etc.); go *into* destruction (Rev 17:8, 11), *into* eternal punishment (Matt 25:46), *to* death (Luke 22:33); be thrown (here again closer to literal) *into* the fire, *into* Gehenna (Mark 9:43, 45, 47, etc.). Metaphorical use also in Rom 11:32: consign *to* disobedience; 2 Cor 10:5: take prisoner *to* obedience.

The local meaning is frequently diminished: Matt 6:13: lead *into* temptation (cf. Mark 14:38 par.); Rom 2:4: lead *to* repentance; Rev 2:22: bring *into* tribulation (cf. Matt 24:9); 1 Tim 3:6: fall into judgment (cf. Luke 24:20).

Used adverbially: εἰς κενόν, *to* emptiness, i.e., "in vain" (with "run," Gal 2:2; Phil 2:16; with "labor," 1 Thess 3:5); εἰς τὰ ἄμετρα, without measure (2 Cor 10:13, 15).

3. Temporal. a) To indicate duration of time: Luke 12:19: *for* many years; 13:9: *in* the future. Esp. frequent in the formulaic designation for eternity: εἰς τὸν αἰῶνα, forever (Mark 3:29; 1 Cor 8:13, and often; similarly Luke 1:50); cf. εἰς τὸ διηνεκές, forever, only in Hebrews (7:3 and often).

b) To indicate a point in time: Acts 13:42: *on* the following sabbath; Luke 1:20: *in* their time; 2 Tim 1:12: εἰς ἐκείνην τὴν ἡμέραν, *until* that day (also to indicate purpose: *for* that day), normally in eschatological contexts.

c) To indicate a temporal goal: Matt 6:34: *for* tomorrow; 1 Tim 6:19: *for* the future. Εἰς τέλος indicates a temporal goal: *until* the end (Mark 13:13 and often), but in 1 Thess 2:16 means *finally, ultimately;* in John 13:1 *until* the end/completion. Acts 25:21: εἰς τὴν . . . διάγνωσιν, *until/for* the decision; similarly τηρέω εἰς, place in custody *until/for* the judgment (2 Pet 2:4; 3:7; Jude 6).

4. To designate the person or thing with regard to which or for which something occurs (an emphatic way of stating purpose/goal):

a) With persons in both friendly and hostile senses: ἁμαρτάνω εἴς τινα, "sin *against* someone"; ποιέω εἴς τινα, "do *to* someone"; βλασφημέω εἴς τι, "blaspheme *against* someone." The Pauline εἰς ἀλλήλους, *one another,* is used primarily of the brotherly relationship in the churches; likewise εἰς ὑμᾶς (ἡμᾶς), "*for* you (us)," of the love or grace which God has shown *to* people (similarly περισσεύω εἴς τινα, "give *to* someone in abundance"). By contrast εἰς αὐτόν, *to* him, denotes God as the final goal (Rom 11:36; 1 Cor 8:6; Col 1:16, 20); thus also πιστεύω εἰς, "believe *in*" (God or Christ; rare in the Synoptics, more than 30 occurrences in John); in this way predicate and subject (God and his people) are exchanged. Εἰς τὸ ὄνομα, "*in* the name," in the baptismal formula (Matt 28:19 and often) is derived from the language of Hellenistic accounting.

b) With abstract nouns, *to/for* to indicate purpose: εἰς μαρτύριον, "*as a* witness" (esp. common in the Synoptics); *as* a memorial (Mark 14:9 par.); *as* a demonstration (Rom 3:25); *for* the glory of God (15:7); *for* the forgiveness of sins (Acts 2:38). Εἰς ἀπ(ὑπ-)άντησιν, "*for* a meeting" = (go) toward, is formulaic. In fixed association with pronouns: εἰς τί, "why?"; εἰς τοῦτο, εἰς αὐτό, "for this reason." With substantival infinitives: "to scourge" (Matt 20:19 and often); to strengthen (Rom 1:11); *for* expiation (Heb 2:17).

c) Consecutive (nonclassical)—intended effect: Matt 3:11: βαπτίζω, "baptize *for* repentance"; repentance is the goal, but also the consequence of baptism. In Rom 6:16 εἰς θάνατον designates death the consequence of sin, and εἰς δικαιοσύνην designates righteousness the consequence of obedience (a spatial metaphor: leads *to*; so also 5:16, 18, 21; 6:12; 2 Cor 7:9). In many cases, especially with the substantival inf., a final *or* consecutive understanding is possible: You have died to the law, *so that* you belong to another (Rom 7:4; v. 5 is, however, consecutive).

5. Grammatical details (Hebraisms):

a) Εἰς in place of ἐν (point of rest [where?] as the end of a movement): Matt 2:23: settle *in* Nazareth (cf. 4:13; Mark 13:3); similarly 1:9: baptized *in* the Jordan (actually be submerged *in;* cf. John 9:7, Xenophon *Cyr.* i.3.5). Most instances of this use are in Luke/Acts: Luke 4:23: γενόμενα εἰς τὴν Καφαρναούμ, what occurred *in* Capernaum; Acts 19:22: ἐπέχω εἰς τὴν Ἀσίαν, remain *in* Asia; also Luke 11:7; Acts 7:12; 8:40; 21:13; John 1:18: εἰς τὸν κόλπον, "*in* the bosom." Hebrew influence is seen in the citation in Acts 2:27, 31.

b) Εἰς in place of the pred. nom., usually Hebraisms in OT citations: Mark 10:8 par.; Matt 21:42; Luke 3:5; Acts 13:47; 2 Cor 6:18 = Heb 1:5; 8:10. Elsewhere almost exclusively with γίνομαι, "become": Luke 13:19: εἰς δένδρον, of a grain of mustard seed which becomes a tree; also Acts 5:36; Rev 8:11; 16:19; 1 John 5:8 (cf. already Theognis 162).

c) Rarely in place of gen. or dat. (of advantage): 1 Pet 1:11: τὰ εἰς Χριστὸν παθήματα, "the sufferings *of* Christ" (those which he had to endure); Luke 9:13: εἰς πάντα τὸν λαόν, "food *for* all these people."

W. Elliger

εἷς, μία, ἕν *heis, mia, hen* one

1. Occurrences in the NT — 2. Meaning — 3. Use in NT formulaic language — 4. Use in ethics and exhortation

Lit.: BAGD s.v. — H. D. BETZ (ed.), *Plutarch's Theological Writings and Early Christian Literature* (1975) 359 and index s.v. — *idem, Galatians* (Hermeneia, 1979) 171-73. — BULTMANN, *Theology* 69-74. — BDF §247. — S. S. COHON, "The Unity of God: A Study in Hellenistic and Rabbinic Theology," *HUCA* 26 (1955) 425-79. — H. CONZELMANN, *1 Corinthians* (Hermeneia, 1975) 142-45. — A. FEUILLET, *Le Christ sagesse de dieu d'après les épîtres pauliniennes* (1966) 71ff. — C. H. GIBLIN, "Three Monotheistic Texts in Paul," *CBQ* 37 (1975) 527-47. — W. K. C. GUTHRIE, *The Sophists* (1971) 247-49. — M. HENGEL, *Judaism and Hellenism* (1974) I, 262ff. — W. HOLSTEN et al., *RGG* V, 1109-16. — E. HORNUNG, *Der Eine und die Vielen. Ägyptische Gottesvorstellungen* (1971). — T. KLAUSER, *RAC* I, 216-33, esp. 230. — N. LOHFINK and J. BERGMANN, *TDOT* I, 193-201. — R. MACUCH, "Zur Vorgeschichte der Bekenntnisformel *la ilāha illā llāhu,*" *ZDMG* 128 (1978) 20-38. — NILSSON, *Geschichte* II, 569ff. — E. PETERSON, *ΕΙΣ ΘΕΟΣ* (1926). — *idem,* "Der Monotheismus als politisches Problem," *Theologische Traktate* (1951) 46-147. — *PGL* s.v. εἷς θεός. — PREISIGKE, *Wörterbuch* IV/4, s.v. — E. STAUFFER, *TDNT* II, 434-42; III, 94-109. — K. WENGST, *Christologische Formeln und Lieder des Urchristentums* (1972) 136ff. — For further bibliography see *TWNT* X, 1071.

1. Εἷς appears a total of 337 times in the NT, and does not have special frequency in any particular text.

2. A relatively great significance is given in the NT and later Christian literature to the numeral εἷς for two reasons:

a) In koine Greek the use of εἷς is extended so that it increasingly takes the place, e.g., of the indefinite pron. τίς ("anyone, someone"). Also significant is the influence of Semitic usage (see BDF §247; BAGD s.v. 3, 4).

b) Theologically significant for ancient religion, philosophy, and politics is the influence of the distinction between the one and the many. Early Christianity shares fully in the common ancient preference of oneness and the negative evaluation of multiplicity in its various manifestations.

3. This theological manner of thinking is reflected especially in NT formulaic language.

a) Early Christianity consciously adopts from Judaism (Deut 6:4; cf. *TDOT* I, 193-201; Billerbeck II, 28-30) the monotheistic formula εἷς ὁ θεός, "God is *one*." This formula is also widely distributed in Hellenistic literature (see *Lit.*). According to Mark 12:29, 32 Jesus explicitly approves the Jewish monotheistic formula (cf., however, the parallels Matt 22:37; Luke 10:26). In Jewish Christianity also the formula is cited (Jas 2:19; *Pseudo-Clementine Epistle of Peter* 2:1 [= ch. 1]; *Pseudo-Clementine Homilies* 13:15). Among the Evangelists (Mark 2:7; 10:18 par.; 12:29, 32; Matt 23:9; John 8:41), in Paul's letters (Rom 3:30; 1 Cor 8:4, 6; Gal 3:20; cf. also 1 Thess 1:9; 1 Cor 12:2; Gal 4:8), and in the deutero-Pauline letters (Eph 4:6; 1 Tim 2:5) the formula is likewise recognized. The characteristic Christian development is also apparent in these texts in the expansion of the formula and the incorporation of christology and soteriology.

b) The expansion of the formula includes esp. incorporation of christology. "*One* Lord Jesus Christ" is placed alongside "*one* God" (1 Cor 8:6 and the v.l.; 1 Tim 2:5; Matt 23:8-10). The monotheistic formula is treated variously so that the unique place of Jesus Christ analogous to the uniqueness of God can be affirmed (Jas 4:12; Matt 23:8-10). Reference can be made to the unique sacrifice of Christ (2 Cor 5:14; John 11:50; 1 Tim 2:5f.; Heb 2:11; 10:12, 14; cf. Mark 12:6) in order to give the basis for the exalted place of Christ. Furthermore, the Adam-Christ typology can be included (Rom 5:12-19; 1 Tim 2:5; cf. Acts 17:26, 31). With the aid of the monotheistic formula the Gospel of John develops the idea of the unity of God and Christ (John 10:30; 17:11, 21, 22, 23).

c) Soteriology follows as a consequence of christology (1 Cor 8:6). Thus the redemption itself in its varied form is understood as originating in unity. In Paul's theology the redeemed are incorporated into the "*one* body of Christ" (ἓν σῶμα), the Church (Rom 12:4f.; 1 Cor 6:16f.; 10:17; 12:12, 13, 14; Gal 3:16, 28). The deutero-Pauline letters develop this teaching about the Church, giving new expansions to the formula (Col 3:14f.; Eph 2:14-22; 4:3-6). The "*one* Spirit" corresponds to the "*one* body" (Eph 4:3f.; cf. 2:18; 1 Cor 6:17; 12:9, 11; Phil 1:27). Special formulas like "*one* Lord, *one* faith, *one* baptism" (Eph 4:4) and already in Paul "*one* bread, *one* body" (1 Cor 10:17) indicate the functions of such formulas: they tell how the unity of the Church originated and is to be preserved in the midst of struggle with heresy and division. This tendency is already present in Paul: one God (Gal 3:20), one Christ (v. 16), one apostle (1:1; cf. 1 Tim 2:5-7), one gospel (Gal 1:6f.), one Church (3:26-28; 5:6; 6:15), and one fruit of the Spirit (5:22f.). The idea of unity is decisive for the entire missionary task and its relation to the churches, just as the final redemption can be equated with the unity of all things in God (1 Cor 15:20ff.). Similar theological interests are present in the Gospel of John (10:16; 11:50-52; 17:21, etc.; cf. 1 John 5:8).

4. In connection with the doctrine of redemption, ethics and parenesis are also shaped by the idea of unity (e.g., Rom 15:6; Phil 1:27; 2:2). Sexual ethics is determined by the ancient doctrine of the creation of the μία σάρξ ("*one* flesh"). The doctrine of mankind's creation as "male and female" (ἄρσεν καὶ θῆλυ) assumes that this duality is transformed to unity in the sexual union. Thus in the union there is a soteriological motif (Mark 10:1-12 par., citing and interpreting Gen 1:27; 2:24). Consequently divorce is forbidden because it is a retreat into duality (Mark 10:9). Paul uses the same teaching against the Corinthian practice of sexual relations with prostitutes: the μία σάρξ with prostitutes is incompatible with participation in the one body and "*one* Spirit" of Christ the redeemer (1 Cor 6:16f.). The teaching of the μία σάρξ is used positively in Eph 5:31-33 as a basis for monogamy (cf. also 1 Tim 3:2; 5:9; Titus 1:6). In general, unity formulas can be used parenetically in various ways: for the reduction of the Torah to the love commandment (Gal 5:14; cf. 6:2), in the prohibition of judging one's neighbor (Jas 4:12), and in the prohibition of the use of honorific titles by the disciples (Matt 23:8-10).

H. D. Betz

εἰσάγω *eisagō* bring in, lead in*

11 occurrences in the NT, of which 3 are in Luke and 6 in Acts: *lead in* (Luke 14:21; 22:54; John 18:16; Acts 9:8, with χειραγωγοῦντες, leading "by the hand"; 21:28, 29, 37; 22:24; Heb 1:6), *bring in* (Luke 2:27: τὸ παιδίον Ἰησοῦν; Acts 7:45).

εἰσακούω *eisakouō* listen to, obey, give a favorable hearing to*

In reference to the hearing of prayers, usually pass.: Matt 6:7; Luke 1:13 (cf. Dan 10:12 LXX); Acts 10:31; Heb 5:7: εἰσακουσθεὶς ἀπὸ τῆς εὐλαβείας, he was *heard* (and liberated) from his fear (RSV interprets differently); *listen to, obey:* 1 Cor 14:21 (cf. Isa 28:12 LXX).

εἰσδέχομαι *eisdechomai* accept, receive*

2 Cor 6:17: κἀγὼ εἰσδέξομαι ὑμᾶς (citing Ezek 20:34 LXX), "then I will *welcome* you [to myself]."

εἴσειμι *eiseimi* enter*

Acts 3:3; 21:26: εἰς τὸ ἱερόν; Heb 9:6: εἰς τὴν πρώτην σκηνήν; with πρός, Acts 21:18: εἰσῄει ὁ Παῦλος σὺν ἡμῖν πρὸς Ἰάκωβον, "Paul *went in* with us to James."

εἰσέρχομαι *eiserchomai* come in, go in, enter

1. Local use — 2. Entrance into the kingdom of God; related ideas — 3. Paul — 4. Hebrews — 5. Other NT documents

Lit.: J. Schneider, *TDNT* II, 676-78.

1. a) Εἰσέρχομαι with an indication of place appears primarily in the Gospels and Acts. Local use is rare in Q, frequent in Luke-Acts. Εἰσέρχομαι can be used absolutely (e.g., Luke 11:37).

b) Phrases in which εἰσέρχομαι is associated with εἰς τὸν οἶκον τοῦ θεοῦ, etc. (Mark 2:26; cf. 1:21; 3:1; 11:11, 15; Luke 1:9; 4:16) recall OT usage (e.g., Ps 5:8 LXX). Matthew never uses the word except in dependence on a source; moreover, he omits it in 12:9 par. Mark 3:1; Luke, on the other hand, has it where he does not follow Mark.

c) Εἰσέρχομαι with human beings as the location appears where evil spirits are (or an evil spirit is) the subject (*take possession*: Mark 9:25; Matt 12:45 par. Luke 11:26 [Q]). In Mark 5:12f. par. Luke 8:32f. (not in par. Matt 8:31f.) the spirits enter a herd of swine.

Similarly it is said of Judas in Luke 22:3; John 13:27 that Satan has taken hold of him. Both Gospels indicate that in the betrayal darkness itself (Luke 22:53) enters the arena. Luke 22:3 (redactional) refers to 4:13 ("until an opportune time," also redactional). Luke 22:4 connects the intervention of Satan with the execution of the betrayal. However, in John 13:26 the revealer gives the sign for the intervention of Satan, who stands under Christ's command.

Remarkably the NT has no reference to the idea of the entry of God (of the Spirit) into people (Rev 11:11 is the only exception, but there ἐν is used, and the statement is a citation applied to the resurrection); cf., however, Wis 1:4; Josephus *Ant.* iv.121. This is in response to the fact that God does not become manifest in the manner of taking possession.

2. Theologically interesting is the language of "*entering* into the kingdom of God," which has its origin in Jesus' proclamation and his understanding of the → βασιλεία. According to Mark 10:15 (cf. Luke 18:17; Matt 18:3 has a different form) entry into the kingdom is associated with access to Jesus. In the realm opened up by Jesus the individual enters and receives already a share in the future kingdom. The condition for entry is made precise in the sense that there *is no* condition. To receive the kingdom as a child is to allow it to be given. The connection between access to Jesus and entry into the kingdom is clearer in Mark 10:23-25 (discipleship, cf. 10:22).

Luke seems to take a critical view of this manner of speech. He adopts it only in 18:25, 17 from Mark, but in 11:52 changes the Q saying in Matt 23:13 (understanding . . . εἰς τὴν γνῶσιν). Matthew uses εἰσέρχομαι εἰς often with βασιλεία τῶν οὐρανῶν. The accent lies on the conditions: Matt 18:3 (cf. Mark 10:15) mentions repentance (on the pre-Matthean level στραφῆτε might render an Aramaic expression meaning "again"). Apparent conditions are given in Matt 5:20 (redactional); 7:21 (redactional). John 3:5 is related to Matt 18:3; Mark 10:15: To be "born of water and the Spirit" (i.e., to be baptized) grants entry into the kingdom. This pre-Johannine saying is interpreted in John 3:3, "be born from above," with ἰδεῖν taking the place of εἰσέρχομαι. Acts 14:22 assumes that the kingdom is *entered* at the time of the death of the individual. Matt 23:13 is difficult (cf. Luke 11:52!): Is the Pharisaic power of the keys the right interpretation of Torah and do they exclude the "laypeople" from the (present) kingdom by their exclusivity? Or is interpretation of the Law as such already the decisive hindrance? Probably the latter.

Mark 9:43-47 speaks of *entry* into ζωή (understood eschatologically; cf. Matt 18:8f.; not in Luke). Later (Matt 19:17) Matthew interprets the Markan "inherit eternal life" (Mark 10:17; par. Matt 19:16 differs) with "*enter* into life" and gives the condition: keep the commandments. "*Enter* into the joy of your master" (Matt 25:21, 23; Luke 19:17, 19 [Q] is different) is to be understood in a totally eschatological way (cf. esp. Matt 25:30). Similarly Rev 21:27; 22:14 speaks of *entry* into the heavenly Jerusalem (cf. Matt 27:53: into the Holy City).

3. Paul uses εἰσέρχομαι of the entry of outsiders into the church's assembly (1 Cor 14:23f.; cf. Jas 2:2: εἰς συναγωγήν). Rom 5:12 is significant: "sin *came* into the world through one man." This speaks of possession (→ 1.c), i.e., the invasion of sin's power. The anacolouthon in 5:12ff. indicates that Paul cannot speak of the invasion of grace, because this is not the manner in which it comes into the world. Εἰσέρχομαι is used absolutely in Rom 11:25 of the Gentiles and signifies for Paul the coming to salvation of the peoples of the world (referring to mission and dialectical eschatology).

4. Εἰσέρχομαι εἰς τὴν κατάπαυσιν appears exclusively in Hebrews (3:11, 18f.; 4:1, 3, 5, 6, 10f.; cf. Ps 94:11 LXX). The condition for entry into the rest is faith (= obedience, see 3:18f.; 4:6, 11). In exceeding the OT's manner of speech (about the high priest who *enters* into the most holy place, cf. 9:12), 6:19f.; 9:12, 24 speak of Christ, who *has entered* into the most holy place or into heaven itself. He is the basis of our hope, which "anchors" (6:19) us in the most holy place, where as the pioneer he *has entered* (v. 20). Unique to the NT is the use in 10:15 of εἰσέρχομαι εἰς τὸν κόσμον for the incarnation of the pre-existent Christ (on the idea, cf. John 1:9; 3:19, etc., but there never with εἰσέρχομαι).

5. In Luke 24:26 the way of Jesus' suffering is the path into the heavenly glory (analogous also to that of the disciple in Acts 14:22), which is completed with the resurrection. Jas 5:4 recalls OT usage (cf. Ps 87:3 LXX). According to Rev 3:20 Christ stands (cf. v. 14; 1:4-6) at the door; whoever opens it has (table) fellowship with him (the image is that of the eschatological festival of joy; cf. 3:21). The *coming* of Christ to mankind is conditioned by zeal and repentance (v. 19). Its result is victory (v. 21). Cf. the *coming* of Jesus to men in Matt 8:8 par. (Q); Luke 7:36; 11:37; 19:7; here εἰσέρχομαι has probably more than a local meaning. On the other hand Christ himself is, according to John 10:9, the door through which the believer *enters* into his salvation (cf. the reference to *entry* through the narrow gate in Matt 7:13 par. Luke 13:24 [Q]).

H. Weder

εἰσκαλέομαι *eiskaleomai* invite in*

Acts 10:23: εἰσκαλεσάμενος οὖν αὐτοὺς ἐξένισεν, "he *called* them *in* to be his guests."

εἴσοδος, ου, ἡ *eisodos* entrance, entry, access*

Εἴσοδος . . . πρὸς ὑμᾶς, "*welcome* . . . among you," "visit to you" (1 Thess 1:9; 2:1); of the *entrance* into the sanctuary: εἰς τὴν εἴσοδον τῶν ἁγίων (Heb 10:19); in the construction πρὸ προσώπου τῆς εἰσόδου αὐτοῦ, "before his [Jesus'] *coming,*" of the preparatory preaching of repentance by John (Acts 13:24); ἡ εἴσοδος εἰς τὴν αἰώνιον βασιλείαν, "*entrance* into the eternal kingdom" (2 Pet 1:11).

εἰσπηδάω *eispēdaō* rush in, run in*

Acts 16:29: αἰτήσας δὲ φῶτα εἰσεπήδησεν, he demanded lights and *rushed in* (into the prison; 14:14 v.l.).

εἰσπορεύομαι *eisporeuomai* go in, enter; appear*

Of the 18 occurrences in the NT, 8 are in Mark, 5 are in Luke, 4 are in Acts, and 1 is in Matthew. In connection with εἰς: Mark 1:21: "into Capernaum"; 6:56: "in villages, cities, or country"; 11:2: "into the village"; Luke 22:10: "into the house"; cf. Acts 3:2; 9:28 (εἰσπορευόμενος καὶ ἐκπορευόμενος); fig., Matt 15:17: "into the mouth" (par. Mark 7:19; cf. vv. 15, 18); of *entry* into the kingdom of God (v.l. εἰσελεύσονται): Luke 18:24. With κατά: Acts 8:3: κατὰ τοὺς οἴκους, "house after house." Indication of place: with the clause ὅπου ἦν τὸ παιδίον, "where the child was" (Mark 5:40); with πρός, "those who came to him" (Acts 28:30); with the attraction of the rel. pron.: κώμην, ἐν ᾗ εἰσπορευόμενοι εὑρήσετε, the village "where on entering you will find . . ." (Luke 19:30). Absolute, with the meaning *appear:* Mark 4:19; of *entry* (into a house): Luke 8:16; 11:33.

H. Balz

εἰστρέχω *eistrechō* run in*

Acts 12:14: εἰσδραμοῦσα, Rhoda *"ran in."*

εἰσφέρω *eispherō* carry in, bring in*

Luke 5:18f., of the lame man, who had to be *carried* into the house; 12:11: ὅταν εἰσφέρωσιν ὑμᾶς ἐπὶ τὰς συναγωγάς, "when they *bring* you [with force] before the synagogues"; 1 Tim 6:7: "we *brought* nothing into the world"; fig., in the construction μὴ εἰσενέγκῃς ἡμᾶς εἰς πειρασμόν, "*lead* us not into temptation" (Matt 6:13 par. Luke 11:4); ξενίζοντα . . . εἰσφέρεις εἰς τὰς ἀκοὰς ἡμῶν, "you *bring* some strange things to our ears" (Acts 17:20).

εἶτα, εἶτεν *eita, eiten* then, next, furthermore*

There are 15 occurrences in the NT (εἶτεν only as v.l. in Mark 4:28). (a) Temporal: *then, next* (Mark 4:17; 8:25; Luke 8:12; John 13:5; 19:27; 20:27; Jas 1:15); (b) In enumeration: πρῶτον . . . εἶτα (. . . εἶτα), "first . . . *then* (. . . *then)* (Mark 4:28 bis [v.l. εἶτεν]; 1 Tim 2:13; 3:10; cf. 1 Cor 15:5); ἔπειτα . . . εἶτα, "then . . . *then*" (vv. 7, 24). (c) In Heb 12:9 εἶτα introduces a new thought: *furthermore, then.*

εἴτε *eite* whether . . . or; if . . . if

There are 65 occurrences in the NT, of which 27 are in 1 Corinthians, 14 in 2 Corinthians, and none in the Gospels or Acts. As a disjunctive conjunction εἴτε . . . εἴτε separates statements from each other in order to hold them together at the same time (= *sive . . . sive*; cf. BDF §446), e.g., 1 Cor 12:13 (4 occurrences); 2 Cor 1:6 (bis); 5:9 (bis); Phil 1:27 (bis). Paul uses εἴτε . . . εἴτε frequently as a conjunction introducing hypothetical conditions (cf. BDF §454.3), primarily in series—with or without the verb—e.g., Rom 12:6-8; 1 Cor 3:22 (8 occurrences); 10:31 (3 occurrences); cf. Col 1:16 (4 occurrences); 1 Pet 2:13, 14. A single εἴτε occurs only in 1 Cor 14:27 (cf. the δέ which provides continuity in v. 29).

εἶτεν *eiten* then, afterwards
→ εἶτα.

εἴωθα *eiōtha* be accustomed (pf.)*

Plupf.: Matt 27:15: εἰώθει ὁ ἡγεμών, "the governor *was accustomed* . . ."; Mark 10:1: ὡς εἰώθει, "as *his custom was.*" Partc.: Luke 4:16: κατὰ τὸ εἰωθὸς αὐτῷ, "as his *custom* was"; Acts 17:2.

ἐκ (ἐξ) *ek (ex)* out of; since, from the time of; because of, by means of

1. Basic meaning and occurrences in the NT — 2. Local usage — 3. Temporal usage — 4. Fig. usage — 5. Other uses

Lit.: On preps. in general → ἀνά. — BAGD s.v. — BDF index s.v. — JOHANNESSOHN, *Präpositionen* 284. — MAYSER, *Grammatik* II/2, 382-90. — MORGENTHALER, *Statistik* 14f., 160. — C. F. D. MOULE, *An Idiom Book of NT Greek* (²1959) 71-74. — MOULTON/MILLIGAN s.v. — MOULTON, *Grammar* III, 208-10, 258-61. — RADERMACHER, *Grammatik* 125f., 139. — ROBERTSON, *Grammar* 596-600. — N. TURNER, *Grammatical Insights into the NT* (1965) 6, 29, 58, 107f. — C. A. WAHL, *Clavis Novi Testamenti Philologica* (1843) s.v. — *idem, Clavis Librorum Veteris Testamenti Apocryphorum Philologica. Indicem verborum in libris pseudepigraphis usurpatorum adiecit J. B. Bauer* (1972) s.v.

1. Ἐκ (ἐξ before vowels) is a prep. governing the gen. It has a fundamental spatial meaning and denotes either the way out from the inside of an object or place or from a point in general. As in classical Greek so also in the NT, much that is nonspatial is associated with ἐκ, i.e., the temporal and the fig. meaning in various aspects. Ἐκ often

overlaps with ἀπό, which, with 645 occurrences, is not yet dislodged by ἐκ. Ἐκ appears 915 times in the NT, of which 336 are in the Johannine literature alone (John, 1–3 John, Revelation). It is used in the NT as described below.

2. Ἐκ with a local meaning is often connected with verbs of movement (βαίνω, ἔρχομαι, ἥκω, φεύγω, χωρίζω), calling (καλέω), or liberation (σῴζω, ῥύομαι). In a way that is different from our own sense of language, it can also answer the question: Where? Thus ἐκ δεξιῶν (Mark 10:37, 40 par., etc.; → δεξιός) simply names a location. Here one must distinguish those instances in which ἐκ through attraction has the usage associated with ἐν: in Col 4:16 the recipients of the letter are called on to read the letter which is *in* Laodicea, which the author of Colossians has sent there and which is intended to be sent *from* Laodicea just as Colossians was sent to them (cf. similarly Matt 24:17; Luke 11:13).

3. Ἐκ with a temporal meaning *(since, from the time of)* appears in expressions such as ἐκ νεότητος (Mark 10:20 par.; Acts 26:4), ἐξ ἀρχῆς (John 6:64; 16:4), and others. At times a distinction between temporal and causal (→ 4.a) ἐκ is scarcely possible; cf. ἐκ τούτου in John 6:66 (this phrase has an unambiguous causal meaning in 19:12) or the ancient (adoptionist) christological formula in Rom 1:3f., which speaks of Jesus as Son of God *from the time of/as a consequence of* the resurrection of the dead (ἐξ ἀναστάσεως νεκρῶν).

4. Fig. usage of ἐκ is derived from its basic local meaning. It is formed in various directions, which frequently overlap:

a) Causal: see the examples given above (→ 3) and also Rev 16:10. Furthermore, with a few vbs. (in pass.) ἐκ introduces the grounds (ἀδικέω, γεμίζω, λυπέω, πληρόω, πλουτέω, μεθύω, πυρόω, ζημιόω). In all of these cases the meaning of ἐκ overlaps with that of διά and ὑπό. A causal nuance is present also, along with an instrumental sense, in the phrase ἐκ πίστεως (→ πίστις) in the Pauline literature (cf. BDF §195.1[e]), since faith is for Paul the means of justification. As with Paul ἐκ πίστεως describes formally the basic existence of the Christian in the world, ἐκ in this connection also includes a modal aspect (→ b).

b) Modal: here ἐκ πίστεως is to be translated *"by means of* faith." The change of prepositions in Rom 1:18 (cf. 2 Cor 2:16; Ps 83:8 LXX), ἐκ πίστεως εἰς πίστιν, has a rhetorical function like that of ἐκ πίστεως–διὰ πίστεως in Rom 3:30 (cf. also the alternation of ἐκ and διά in 3:22, 25; 4:13, 16; 10:17; Gal 2:16; 3:24, 26, etc.). In both cases *"by means of* faith" should be emphasized. However, a "theology of prepositions" is not to be recommended (*contra* Turner 107f.). When the apostle says in the discussion of justification: "The law is not ἐκ πίστεως" (Gal 3:12) or "Those who are *from* the works of the law (ἐξ ἔργων νόμου) are under the curse" (v. 10; cf. 2:16), he thus approaches the use of ἐκ in the Johannine literature, where this prep. expresses origin.

Modal ἐκ appears outside the Pauline literature in Matt 12:37 (in connection with the subject of righteousness!); Luke 19:22; Rev 20:12 and is to be translated in these passages as *according to.* A modal dat. (BDF §198) or a construction with διά or κατά can appear in its place.

c) Of origin: John expresses origin with the phrases εἶναι ἐκ, for the believer also γεγεννῆσθαι ἐκ (→ γεννάω) or for the revealer ἔρχεσθαι ἐκ. Thus he makes a statement about the nature of the persons involved, about that which consistently determines their speech and activity. Ἐκ (and ἀπό) serves within the background of John's cosmic dualism to qualify the various figures through the statement of their origin. The passages under → d are closely related with this particular nuance.

d) Derivation, descent: ἐκ denotes (with no difference in meaning from ἀπό) a person's (physical) origin: ἐκ Ναζαρέθ (John 1:46); ἐκ γένους Ἰσραήλ (Phil 3:5), etc. Here also belong substantival phrases like οἱ ἐξ Ἰσραήλ (Rom 9:6); οἱ ἐκ (τῆς) περιτομῆς (Rom 4:12; Gal 2:12; Acts 11:12; [Titus 1:10]); οἱ ἐκ νόμου (Rom 4:14, [16]); οἱ ἐκ πίστεως (Gal 3:7, 9 [Rom 4:16]). If these texts use ἐκ to express membership according to derivation, this occurs also and esp. where the construction with ἐκ appears for the partitive gen. (→ e; cf. BAGD s.v. 4.a).

e) The partitive gen. is strongly repressed in the NT by the use of ἐκ (and ἀπό). This is to be observed frequently in the Johannine literature, even where (the phrase in place of) the partitive gen. stands in place of the subject (John 7:40; 16:17; Rev 11:9; cf., however, Acts 19:33) or object (2 John 4; cf., however, Matt 23:34; Luke 11:49). Use of ἐκ (and ἀπό) for the partitive gen. is unusual in classical literature, but common in the Semitic languages (Heb., Aram. *min*), in LXX Greek (Johannessohn 287f.), and in koine Greek (cf. Radermacher in Robertson 1379 on koine).

5. Other uses: Phrases with ἐκ replace the subjective gen. in the NT (John 3:25; 2 Cor 8:7) and the gen. of price/value (Matt 20:2; Acts 1:18). Ἐκ is also used to indicate the material from which something is made (Matt 27:29; John 19:2; 1 Cor 15:47; perhaps also 1 Cor 11:12) and also appears in other various other adverbial connections (BAGD s.v. 6.c).

G. Lüdemann

ἕκαστος, 3 *hekastos* each (one)

1. Occurrences in the NT — 2. Basic meaning and usage — 3. A special Pauline usage

Lit.: BAGD s.v. — BDF §§64.6; 305; 164.1; 275. — R. Lazzeroni, "Ἕκαστος. Ipotesi sull' etimologia del greco ἕκαστος," *Annali della scuola normale superiore di Pisa* 25 (1956) 136-41.

1. This pron. appears *ca.* 80 times in the NT. It is used adjectivally (e.g., Luke 6:44; John 19:23; Heb 3:13; Rev 22:2) in the majority of cases, but is also used as a subst. As a subst. it appears frequently with a following partitive gen. (Luke 13:15; Acts 2:3, 38, etc.; Rom 14:12, etc.; 1 Cor 1:12; 1 Thess 2:11, etc.) A few writings prefer the strengthened form εἷς ἕκαστος, *each one* (Luke 4:40; 16:5; Acts 2:3, 6; 17:27; 20:31; 21:19, 26; Eph 4:7, 16; 5:33; also in Matt 26:22; 1 Cor 12:18; Col 4:6; 1 Thess 2:11; 2 Thess 1:3; Rev 21:21). Colloquialisms such as ἀνὰ εἷς ἕκαστος, *every single one* (Rev 21:21) and καθ' ἓν ἕκαστον, *one after another, individually* (Acts 21:19) appear sporadically.

2. Ἕκαστος refers to individual parts of a whole, as comparison with πᾶς shows. Before an anarthrous subst. πᾶς means "every" (cf. Matt 3:10: πᾶν δένδρον); therefore, used substantively it refers to "any and every person" (BDF §275.3). Substantival ἕκαστος, on the other hand, is to be distinguished from this generality and universality; it expresses the involvement (by call or offer) of *each individual* and makes the statement more direct and personal.

That this immediate concern with the individual is basic to the meaning of ἕκαστος is indicated in its use in the Pauline literature. Paul employs *each (individual)* when he gives instructions (Rom 12:3; 14:5; 15:2; 1 Cor 3:5, 10; 7:2, 17, 20, 24; 16:2; 2 Cor 9:7; Gal 6:4, 5; Phil 2:4; 1 Thess 4:4). In admonitions as well (1 Cor 1:12; 11:21; 1 Thess 2:11) *each* is directly addressed. *Each* has a gift from God (1 Cor 7:7; cf. Rom 12:3; 1 Cor 3:5; 7:20; 12:7, 11; 15:38). It is necessary that *each* be "fully convinced in his own mind" (Rom 14:5), that "*each* of us please his neighbor" (15:2), that *each* take care how he builds (1 Cor 3:10); for "*each man's* work will become manifest" (v. 13). God will recompense *each* according to his or her works (Rom 2:6) after "*each one* of us [has given] an account of himself to God" (14:12). Paul addresses everyone in his churches, and with the aid of ἕκαστος each is addressed individually.

This type of usage is also common in the Synoptics (Mark 13:34; Matt 16:27; 18:35; 25:15; Luke 2:3; 6:44; 13:15; cf. Acts 2:38; 3:26; 11:29; 17:27), in John (16:32; cf. 7:53), and in the other writings in which the pron. appears (Eph 4:7, 16, 25; 5:33; 6:8; Col 4:6; Heb 6:11 [cf. 3:13: καθ' ἑκάστην ἡμέραν, *every* day]; 8:11; 11:21; Jas 1:14; 1 Pet 1:17; 4:10; Rev 2:23, etc.).

3. Ἕκαστος, which is widely distributed in the NT, takes on a special meaning within the framework of the Pauline idea of the → σῶμα (1 Cor 12:18). On the basis of its basic meaning it was well-suited to express in this special way the idea of the call and responsibility of each one with a view to the whole, the Church.

F. G. Untergassmair

ἑκάστοτε *hekastote* always, at any time*

2 Pet 1:15: ἑκάστοτε ἔχειν ὑμᾶς, "that . . . you may be able *at any time*. . . ."

ἑκατόν *hekaton* (one) hundred*

1. Ἑκατόν appears as a simple and literal numeral only in John 19:39 ("about a *hundred* pounds' weight") and Luke 16:6f. (a sum of debts). Otherwise it has a symbolic significance or appears in compound numerals (which sometimes have symbolic significance).

2. It symbolizes a great number in Mark 4:8, 20 par. Matt 13:8, 23, inasmuch as it gives here the highest sum. The same use is present for the form ἑκατονταπλασίων, *hundredfold*, i.e., "in abundance," in Mark 10:30 par. Matt 19:29 v.l.; Luke 8:8 par. Mark 4:8.

In Matt 18:12 par. Luke 15:4 (Q) the idea of totality is in the foreground. Where one sheep is lost from the entire herd, the shepherd leaves the remaining ninety-nine behind in the wilderness (or on the mountains) in order to seek the one. The relationship of the numbers symbolizes also (in an ancillary way) the insignificance of the one sheep. Thus in ἑκατόν the aspect of a great number probably plays a role also. Totality appears in the foreground also in Mark 6:40 (both Matthew and Luke differ). This text reminds us that ἑκατόν designates finally a totality or "unity" in military language (→ ἑκατοντάρχης).

In contrast to μυρίος (Matt 18:24) ἑκατὸν δηνάρια (v. 28) suggests a relatively small number—without losing that of a totality: both numbers point to the indebtedness of the men (before God or other people). Incomprehensibly, the pardon of an extraordinary debt is not followed by the pardon of a small debt. With regard to the idea of totality, the forgiveness of debt among humans is not quantifiable (see v. 22).

3. Compound numerals: The reference in Acts 1:15 to 120 persons probably has no metaphorical meaning. The symbolism in John 21:11 (153 fish) is mysterious.

Noteworthy are 144,000 (Rev 7:4; 14:1, 3) and 144 cubits (21:17). The first refers to God's people of the end time. The number is composed as follows: 12 (symbolizing completeness, cf. the 12 tribes of Israel) × 12,000 (symbolizing determination by God's will). It signifies further extraordinary size (χιλιάδες) and perfect unity (summarizing the motifs compounded in 144,000). The number 144 is an expression of vastness and perfection (a round and complete number); → δώδεκα 2.

H. Weder

ἑκατονταετής, 2 *hekatontaetēs* one hundred years old*

Rom 4:19: ἑκατονταετής που ὑπάρχων, "because [Abraham] was about *one hundred years old.*"

ἑκατονταπλασίων, 2 *hekatontaplasiōn* (one) hundredfold*

Neut. pl. is used adverbially in Matt 19:29 par. Mark 10:30: ἑκατονταπλασίονα λαμβάνω, "receive [in return] *a hundredfold*"; Luke 8:8: ἐποίησεν καρπὸν ἑκατονταπλασίονα, "yielded [grain] *a hundredfold*"; → ἑκατόν 1.

ἑκατοντάρχης (ἑκατόνταρχος), ου, ὁ *hekatontarchēs (hekatontarchos)* centurion*

1. The centurion — 2. Terms used in the NT — 3. Centurions in the NT

Lit.: A. von Domaszewski, *Die Rangordnung des römischen Heeres* (Beihefte der Bonner Jahrbücher 14, 1908), second edition by B. Dobson (1967). — S. H. Hooke, "Jesus and the Centurion: Matthew VIII.5-10," *ExpTim* 69 (1957) 79f. — J. R. Michaels, "The Centurion's Confession and the Spear Thrust," *CBQ* 29 (1967) 102-9. — H. M. D. Parker and G. R. Watson, *OCD* 222. — C. Schneider, "Der Hauptmann am Kreuz," *ZNW* 33 (1934) 1-17.

1. In the Roman military the centurion presided over a *curia*, a division of one hundred men (one-sixtieth of a legion). A distinction was made between several ranks and different assignments of *centuriones*. Their military rank appears to have been popular. The conception of a brave, aggressive solder was associated with the centurion, comparable to the noncommissioned officer of today (Schneider 2).

2. The NT knows three different terms for the centurion. Mark uses exclusively the Latinism ὁ κεντυρίων (15:39, 44, 45). In Matthew the most frequent term is the Attic Greek translation ὁ ἑκατόνταρχος (8:5, 8; 27:54; cf. also Acts 22:25; 28:16 Koine). The Lukan double work prefers the Hellenistic Greek translation ὁ ἑκατοντάρχης (Luke 7:2, 6; 23:47; Acts 10:1, 22; 21:32; 22:26; 23:17, 23; 24:23; 27:1, 6, 11, 31, 43; cf. also Matt 8:13). The variants can be explained from the similarity of ἑκατόνταρχος and ἑκατοντάρχης.

3. Under the apparently older term ἑκατόνταρχος (Matt 8:5, 8; cf. Luke 7:2, 6), Q has preserved the memory of "the centurion of Capernaum" because of his unconditioned faith. The Lukan version emphasizes the significance of the good deeds and the popularity of this Gentile in the Jewish community (7:5).

Parallel elements are seen in the characterization of Cornelius in Acts (cf. Acts 10:1b, 2, 22 with Luke 7:3-5). Both centurions were probably active in administration, which would explain their contact with the Jewish environment.

In the Passion narratives and in the other passages in Acts the centurion has other tasks. It was their responsibility to supervise the execution of a sentence (Mark 15:39 par.: *centurio supplicio praepositus*). The confession of the centurion under the cross is used for christological purposes by the Synoptists. According to Acts 21:32 the centurion is subordinate to the military tribune (χιλίαρχος) and has duties within the cohort. In the leadership of smaller units he was, e.g., responsible for punishment (22:25f.) or for keeping persons in secure protection (watching over Paul in Jerusalem and Caesarea: 23:17, 23; 24:23, on the journey to Rome: 27:1, 6, 11, 31, 43, and in Rome itself: 28:16).

F. G. Untergassmair

ἐκβαίνω *ekbainō* go out from, come from*

Heb 11:15: ἀφ' ἧς ἐξέβησαν (v.l. ἐξῆλθον), their native land, "from which they *had gone out*."

ἐκβάλλω *ekballō* throw out, drive out

1. Occurrences in the NT — 2. Meaning and usage — 3. The Synoptics: cast out demons — 4. Matthew: cast out into darkness

Lit.: H. Bietenhard, *DNTT* I, 453f. — O. Böcher, *Dämonfurcht und Dämonenabwehr. Ein Beitrag zur Vorgeschichte der christlichen Taufe* (1970). — *idem, Christus Exorcista. Dämonismus und Taufe im NT* (1972). — F. Hauck, *TDNT* I, 527f. — O. Hofius, "Erwählung und Bewahrung. Zur Auslegung von Joh 6, 37," *Theologische Beiträge* 8 (1977) 24-49. — K. Thraede, *RAC* VII, 44-117.

1. Ἐκβάλλω, a compound of → βάλλω, appears in the NT 81 times. The majority of the occurrences are in the Synoptic Gospels (66, of which 28 are in Matt, 18 in Mark, and 20 in Luke). John uses the word 6 times, Acts 5 times. In the Pauline letters it appears only in the OT citation in Gal 4:30; elsewhere in Jas 2:25; 3 John 10, and Rev 11:2.

2. *Cast out* suggests the meaning of ἐκβάλλω in the most comprehensive sense. Location is indicated by ἐκ, ἔξω, ἀπό, or εἰς. As in Greek generally (cf. LSJ s.v.; BAGD s.v.), ἐκβάλλω also has many shades of meaning in the NT. The subject is always a person or a group of persons. Things (a), persons or groups of persons (b), and evil spirits (→ 3) appear as objects.

a) Where a thing is the object, ἐκβάλλω appears to have violent tone only in Mark 9:47 (*pluck out* the eye). Normally ἐκβάλλω is less colorful in the sense of *cast off/out* (Matt 15:17; Acts 27:38), *remove* (splinters or logs from the eye: Matt 7:4-5 par. Luke 6:42), or *take out* (two denarii: Luke 10:35; metaphorically: good or evil, old and new from the treasure: Matt 12:35; 13:52). In Rev 11:2 ἐκβάλλω has the meaning *leave out, pass over*, which is attested outside the NT (cf. BAGD s.v.). Noteworthy is the use of ἐκβάλλω in Matt 12:20, a free rendering of Isa 42:3: *lead* justice to victory (LXX ἐξοίσει). Some authors (H. Schürmann, *Lukas* [HTKNT] I, 333; J. Ernst, *Lukas* [RNT] 219) assume that technical language of banning from the synagogue is in use in Luke 6:22 (literally "*cast out* your name as evil").

b) A person or group of persons is more frequently the object of ἐκβάλλω in the NT. In the majority of cases it denotes a more or less forcible casting out, e.g., *drive out* from the temple (Mark 11:15 par. Matt 21:12; Luke 19:45; John 2:15), from the city (Luke 4:29; Acts 7:58), from the vineyard (Mark 12:8 par. Matt 21:39; Luke 20:12, 15), from the area (Acts 13:50). In addition ἐκβάλλω has the weaker meaning *send away* (Mark 1:43; 5:40 par. Matt 9:25; Acts 9:40; 16:37; Jas 2:25). In some passages it signifies discontinuance of association (*expel*: John 6:37; probably also 9:34f., though ἐκβάλλω is not attested as an expression of the formal synagogue ban; cf. R. Schnackenburg, *The Gospel according to John* II, 252; for exclusion from the Church: 3 John 10). As a t.t. of the LXX for *expulsion* of a wife, ἐκβάλλω appears in the citation of Gen 21:10 in Gal 4:30. However, it has a positive meaning in John 10:4 *(lead out)*. In Matt 9:38 par. Luke 10:2 ἐκβάλλω receives the sense *send* (workers into the vineyard) from the context. Mark 1:12 is a special case: The Spirit *drives* Jesus into the wilderness, i.e., Jesus stands entirely under the powerful impetus of the Spirit.

3. Ἐκβάλλω is theologically relevant esp. in the Synoptic Gospels as a t.t. for *expulsion* of demons (obj. normally δαιμόνιον/δαιμόνια) through exorcism from those who are possessed (34 occurrences, i.e., more than half of all Synoptic occurrences). Behind this use is the assumption that the demons live in possessed persons and are driven out by exorcists. The subject of the vb. most frequently is Jesus. Expulsion of demons belongs to his work alongside preaching and healing (cf. the summaries in Matt 8:16; Mark 1:34, 39 and the saying in Luke 13:32). He gives the same commission and the same authority to his disciples (Matt 10:1, 8; Mark 3:15; not in Luke!). According to Mark 16:17 expulsions of demons belong to the signs which accompany those who believe (cf. also Matt 17:19-20). However, the Synoptic Gospels presuppose that there are exorcists other than Jesus and his followers (Jews in Matt 12:27 par. Luke 11:19; anyone in Mark 9:38 par. Luke 9:49).

Complicated incantations, formulas, and manipulations have an important place in the environment of the NT (cf. Böcher; Thraede), but scarcely play a role in the NT itself. Jesus drives out demons through his word (λόγῳ) according to Matt 8:16. According to Mark 9:29 there are demons which can be driven out only through prayer.

More important than correct practice is the question of the authority by which exorcisms are executed (normally expressed with ἐν). The origin of Jesus' power is discussed in detail in the dialogue concerning Beelzebul (Mark 3:22-30 par. Matt 12:24-32/Luke 11:15-23): Jesus does not drive out demons in the power of Beelzebul, the prince of demons, as his opponents charge, but by God's power (Luke 11:20: "by the finger of God"; Matt 12:28: "by the Spirit of God"). The exorcisms are signs that God's kingdom is present. Jesus' followers (Mark 7:22; 16:17) and others (Mark 9:38 par. Luke 9:49) do exorcisms "in the name of Jesus." Here early Christian practice is probably reflected.

4. Ἐκβάλλω has theological weight in Matthew's formula "cast out into outer darkness, [where] there shall be weeping and gnashing of teeth" (Matt 8:12; 22:13; 25:30; in a different form, Luke 13:28). The subject here is the conclusion of the eschatological judgment and the exclusion from God's kingdom (explicitly in Matt 8:11). Darkness is an image for the place of separation from God and of punishment. John 12:31 is also to be understood as referring to punishment.

F. Annen

ἔκβασις, εως, ἡ *ekbasis* way out; conclusion*

1 Cor 10:13: τὴν ἔκβασιν τοῦ δύνασθαι ὑπενεγκεῖν, "the *way of escape* [from temptation], that you may be able to endure it"; Heb 13:7: τὴν ἔκβασιν τῆς ἀναστροφῆς, "the *conclusion* of their way of life" (RSV "the *outcome* of their life"), hardly in the sense of "fruit, yield," but looking, rather, to the steadfastness of the Church leaders in suffering to the point of death. Cf. also A. Strobel, *Hebräer* (NTD) ad loc.

ἐκβλαστάνω *ekblastanō* sprout up

Mark 4:5 $f^{1,\ 13}$ *pc* (in place of ἐξανατέλλω): The seed immediately "*sprang up.*"

ἐκβολή, ῆς, ἡ *ekbolē* discharge (noun)*

Acts 27:18: ἐκβολὴν ἐποιοῦντο, "they threw the cargo overboard" in order to save the ship in the storm.

ἐκγαμίζω *ekgamizō* marry

Only as a v.l. in TR (Matt 22:30; 24:38; Luke 17:27; 1 Cor 7:38 bis, always in place of γαμίζω).

ἐκγαμίσκω *ekgamiskō* marry

Pass. as v.l. in TR, Luke 20:34f., in place of γαμίσκω (v. 34) and γαμίζω (v. 35).

ἔκγονος, 2 *ekgonos* descendant; grandchild*

1 Tim 5:4: τέκνα ἢ ἔκγονα, "children or *grandchildren.*"

ἐκδαπανάω *ekdapanaō* spend, exhaust*

2 Cor 12:15, pass.: ἥδιστα δαπανήσω καὶ ἐκδαπανηθήσομαι, "I will most gladly spend and *be spent.*"

ἐκδέχομαι *ekdechomai* wait; await, expect*
ἀπεκδέχομαι *apekdechomai* wait; await, expect (eagerly)*

1. Occurrences in the NT — 2. Meaning — 3. Ἐκδέχομαι — 4. Ἀπεκδέχομαι

Lit.: W. Grundmann, *TDNT* II, 50-59, esp. 55f. — E. Hoffmann, *DNTT* II, 238-46, esp. 244-46. — J. Swetnam, "On Romans 8, 23 and the 'Expectation of Sonship,'" *Bib* 48 (1967) 102-8.

1. The compounds ἐκδέχομαι and ἀπεκδέχομαι (→ δέχομαι) appear in the NT 6 and 8 times respectively. They appear esp. in the letters (ἀπεκδέχομαι alone appears 6 times in the Pauline corpus).

2. In the NT ἐκδέχομαι is found only with the less frequent meaning *expect* or *await,* not with the meaning "accept" or "receive." However, the intensive ἀπεκδέχομαι, which appears rarely in classical literature and in the LXX and Josephus, is characteristic for Pauline theology with the meaning *wait with perseverance.* The common classical meaning, "draw a (usually false) conclusion" does not appear in the NT.

3. **Ἐκδέχομαι** has the simple meaning *wait for* in Acts 17:16; 1 Cor 11:33; 16:11; and John 5:3 (v.l. for ἀπεκδέχομαι). The vb. is involved in the eschatology of Heb 11:10, where Abraham's future expectation is described within the enumeration of OT examples of faith and is drawn into connection with the apocalyptic conception of the heavenly city. In the parable of the farmer who awaits the harvest in Jas 5:7, the vb. is used of eschatological waiting—a traditional eschatological motif—and is employed in connection with the counsel to have patience in view of the apparent delay in the Lord's coming. In Heb 10:13 the context is likewise eschatological, and the expression *wait until* (ἕως) follows Ps 110:1, the citation of which began in v. 12. 1 Cor 15:25 also alludes to Ps 110:1 in a context that again concerns the time between Jesus' exaltation and the end and where—in contrast to Hebrews—statements about enemies (ἐχθροί) are made. In Hebrews the surprising idea that Christ must *wait* is prepared for already in 2:8, and indeed, as in 1 Cor 15:27, with a reference to Ps 8:5-7. The subjection of all things under Christ has not yet been completed although it has begun. The time after the exaltation of Christ is a time of waiting and also of fulfillment. The Psalm citation provides the christological background and the explanation for the conflict situation in which the Church finds itself in its own time of waiting. (Cf. O. Michel, *Hebräer* [KEK] 341.)

4. a) **Ἀπεκδέχομαι** is used in Heb 9:28 of the Church's *waiting* for Christ and the future redemption which he already promises. Here in the theology of Hebrews the apocalyptic conceptual framework is dominant, in accord with which the use of ἀπεκδέχομαι in this passage might be influenced by Pauline usage. In language from the conceptual world of the Day of Atonement the *waiting* is parallel to the waiting for the return of the high priest from the most holy place by those in attendance at the worship.

But it is Paul who uses ἀπεκδέχομαι most resolutely for the situation of eschatological waiting. Rom 8:19, 23 have essentially the same object as Heb 9:28, the future full manifestation of our → υἱοθεσία (sonship) at the last and total liberation from the present existence in slavery and suffering. This liberation will take place at the resurrection. The context describes the present situation in suffering. However, in Rom 8:25 the context includes—with the same object—the certainty of the Christian hope. The Spirit comes as an aid with its longings for the benefit of those who wait. With the similar reference to the whole creation, this is seen in a universal perspective.

The positive aspect of the *waiting,* connected with the present possession of the gifts of the Spirit, is also apparent in 1 Cor 1:7, as is the end to the waiting at the return of Christ. This emerges also from Phil 3:20, where—in connection with v. 21—a combination of all aspects of the Pauline passages already mentioned is present (cf. also Heb 10:13). With the help of ἀπεκδέχομαι Gal 5:5 indicated earlier the same understanding of the relationship between present acceptance of salvation (→ δέχομαι) and future fulfillment; indeed, the reference is not only to the Spirit and hope, but these are brought into combination with faith and righteousness. Thus the eschatological nature of these concepts for Paul is exhibited.

b) 1 Pet 3:20, where the subj. of ἀπεκδέχομαι (v.l. ἐκδέχομαι) is God's patience (→ μακροθυμία), might indicate that the word lost its firmly fixed content after Paul while maintaining an eschatological meaning. The use of the vb. with no obj. *(wait for the right time)* is uncommon in the NT. Here God is seen as the one who defers his act of judgment in order to give people time for repentance. The idea is not used here for the present situation, as the ark is referred to Christian baptism (v. 21). (In Rom 2:4 and 2 Pet 3:9 it does have a reference to the present situation of the Church.) It is worthy of note that in 1 Pet 3:22—differently from the passages mentioned from Paul and Hebrews—the subjection of the powers is seen as already attained. However, realized eschatology is not otherwise a characteristic of the letter, especially not in view of 4:7ff.

M. E. Glasswell

ἔκδηλος, 2 *ekdēlos* quite apparent, fully evident*

2 Tim 3:9: ἔκδηλος ἔσται πᾶσιν, "will be *plain* to all."

ἐκδημέω *ekdēmeō* leave one's country, stay in a strange land*

In the NT only fig.: 2 Cor 5:6: ἐκδημοῦμεν ἀπὸ τοῦ κυρίου, "we *are away* from the Lord" (opposed to ἐνδημοῦντες ἐν τῷ σώματι); v. 8: ἐκδημῆσαι ἐκ τοῦ σώματος, to "*be away* from the body" (opposed to ἐνδημῆσαι πρὸς τὸν κύριον); v. 9, absolute: εἴτε ἐνδημοῦντες εἴτε ἐκδημοῦντες, "whether . . . at home or *away*."

ἐκδίδομαι *ekdidomai* lease*

In the NT only mid.: Mark 12:1 par. Matt 21:33/Luke 20:9: ἐξέδετο αὐτὸν γεωργοῖς, he "*let* it [the vineyard] *out* to tenants"; Matt 21:41: ἐκδώσεται, he *will let* it *out*.

ἐκδιηγέομαι *ekdiēgeomai* tell fully, explain*

Acts 13:41: ἐάν τις ἐκδιηγῆται ὑμῖν (citing Hab 1:5 LXX), "if one *declares* it to you"; 15:3: ἐκδιηγούμενοι τὴν ἐπιστροφὴν τῶν ἐθνῶν, "*reporting [in detail]* the conversion of the Gentiles."

ἐκδικέω *ekdikeō* avenge, punish
→ ἐκδίκησις.

ἐκδίκησις, εως, ἡ *ekdikēsis* punishment, retribution, vengeance*
ἐκδικέω *ekdikeō* avenge, punish*
ἔκδικος, 2 *ekdikos* avenging; subst.: avenger, one who requites*

Lit.: G. Schrenk, *TDNT* II, 442-46. — U. Falkenroth, *DNTT* III, 92f., 96f.

1. 'Εκδίκησις appears 9 times in the NT (Luke 18:7f.; 21:22; Acts 7:24; Rom 12:19; 2 Cor 7:11; 2 Thess 1:8; Heb 10:30; 1 Pet 2:14). 'Εκδικέω appears 6 times (Luke 18:3, 5; Rom 12:19; 2 Cor 10:6; Rev 6:10; 19:2). Ἔκδικος appears twice (Rom 13:4; 1 Thess 4:6).

2. Although ἐκδικέω in the parable of the unjust judge and the widow (Luke 18:3, 5) is best translated *procure justice for* someone (in the sense of giving legal help or advice), ποιέω τὴν ἐκδίκησιν in vv. 7f. probably means instead *avenge, execute judgment for*.

3. The word group can also designate a component of Christian conduct. Thus ἐκδίκησις in 2 Cor 7:11 is most appropriately rendered *determination* (or action) *to punish the guilty,* ἐκδικῆσαι πᾶσαν παρακοήν in 10:6 "*to requite* [RSV "punish"] every disobedience."

4. In 1 Pet 2:14 the task of the official sent by the king is described: εἰς ἐκδίκησιν κακοποιῶν, ἔπαινον δὲ ἀγαθοποιῶν. The contrast of those who do good deeds, who should be praised, with evildoers leaves no doubt that the latter are *to be punished.* But in Rom 13:4, in accordance with tradition, the power of the state has been seen as that of God's servant who executes God's judgment on one who does evil: ἔκδικος εἰς ὀργήν; in recent scholarship the ἔκδικος here has been regarded, not as the *avenger* or the *one who brings recompense,* but as the *defense attorney* who mediates between the royal official and given political communities (cf. A. Strobel, "Zum Verständnis von Röm 13," *ZNW* 47 [1956] 67-93, esp. 89f.). In this case ὀργή would be taken as a reference to an earthly law court.

5. Although the OT language of Stephen's speech in Acts 7:24 (ποιέω ἐκδίκησιν) suggests the meaning *avenge* (cf. Gen 4:24 LXX), vengeance is forbidden in the NT, in Rom 12:19a. God himself executes *vengeance* (Rom 12:19b; Heb 10:30; cf. Deut 32:35), for his will is peace among mankind (Rom 12:18). Furthermore, the claim of God that *vengeance* is his alone is also an expression of his holiness (cf. Heb 10:19).

6. The word group is suited finally to a (futurist) eschatological dimension. Luke 21:22 speaks in the language of Deut 32:35 LXX of the last judgment. Whether one translates ἔκδικος κύριος περὶ πάντων τούτων in 1 Thess 4:6 as "the Lord himself *will avenge* everything" (cf. RSV), as "*will punish . . . ,*" or as "*requite . . . ,*" depends on what is understood by "vengeance" (cf. the argument for "avenge" in the relationship of v. 7 [ἐν ἁγιασμῷ] to Heb 10:19, 30). Possibly the author of 2 Thess 1:8 also thinks of *vengeance;* the apocalyptic coloring at least speaks for as well as against such a rendering (other suggestions are *punishment, requital*). Similar considerations should be given in the translation of Rev 6:10; 19:2.

H. Goldstein

ἔκδικος, 2 *ekdikos* avenging; subst.: avenger, one who requites
→ ἐκδίκησις.

ἐκδιώκω *ekdiōkō* persecute vigorously*

1 Thess 2:15, of the Jews: τῶν καὶ τὸν κύριον ἀποκτεινάντων . . . καὶ ὑμᾶς ἐκδιωξάντων, "who killed the Lord . . . and *persecuted* us *vigorously*" (RSV is different); Luke 11:49 v.l. in place of → διώκω.

ἔκδοτος, 2 *ekdotos* handed over, surrendered*

Acts 2:23: (Ἰησοῦν) τοῦτον τῇ ὡρισμένῃ βουλῇ καὶ προγνώσει τοῦ θεοῦ ἔκδοτον, "this Jesus, *delivered up* according to the definite plan and foreknowledge of God."

ἐκδοχή, ῆς, ἡ *ekdochē* expectation*

In biblical and early Christian literature only in Heb 10:27: φοβερὰ δέ τις ἐκδοχὴ κρίσεως, "but a fearful *prospect* of judgment."

ἐκδύω *ekdyō* strip, remove*

ἀπεκδύομαι *apekdyomai* remove (something); disarm*

1. Occurrences in the NT — 2. The mid. of ἐκδύω in 2 Cor 5:3f. — 3. Ἐκδύω used literally — 4. The double compound ἀπεκδύομαι

Lit.: R. Bultmann, *The Second Letter to the Corinthians* (1985) (on 5:3). — F. G. Lang, *2. Korinther 5, 1-10 in der neueren Forschung* (1973). — A. Oepke, *TDNT* II, 318-21. — E. Schweizer, *The Letter to the Colossians* (1982). — H. Weigelt, *DNTT* I, 314-16.

1. Although the rare double compound ἀπεκδύομαι is used only twice in the NT (Col 2:15; 3:9), ἐκδύω, another compound of δύω ("sink down") appears 4 times in act. (in the Synoptic Gospels) and 2 times in mid. (in Paul), usually in direct connection with the contrasting vb. → ἐνδύω. The fundamental meaning is thus transformed by the respective lines of argumentation or narration.

2. The mid. of ἐκδύω in 2 Cor 5:4 is a fig. reference to removal in death "of the body as a garment" (BAGD s.v.). Whether the same vb. (with the same meaning) is read also in v. 3 against the stronger external attestation of ἐνδυσάμενοι is under dispute (cf., besides the form-critical conclusions in Lang 187, also Bultmann 135-38 with additional references in the German original [KEK], 263f.). In this difficult section (vv. 1ff.) Paul appears to be taking up the anthropological terminology and eschatological conceptions of his (Gnostic?) opponents.

3. In the (perhaps secondary) mocking scene of the NT Passion narratives (Mark 15:16-20 par. Matt 27:27-31; John 19:1-5 is different not only in terminology) ἐκδύω appears—as it does consistently in the LXX—in the literal sense of the word (in Mark 15:20 par. Matt 27:31 with double acc.: cf. BDF §155.5; in v. 28 only with the acc. of the person, but v.l. ἐνδύσαντες [B ℵ[1] D *pc* it] is to be followed, since it makes good sense with περιέθηκαν without the insertion ἱμάτιον πορφυροῦν [D *pc* it]). Whether or not ἐκδύω in these passages suggests some violence on the basis of the context, the vb. (again with the acc. of the person) means *strip thoroughly, plunder* in the parable of the Good Samaritan in Luke 10:29-37, which belongs to the Lukan special material (v. 30; cf. *Barn.* 10:4!).

4. **Ἀπεκδύομαι** has its own nuances in Col 2:15; 3:9. The NT hapax ἀπέκδυσις in 2:11, with the image of "*putting off* the body of the flesh," refers to "circumcision as the eschatological fulfillment" (Schweizer 142). The mid. ἀπεκδύομαι, used in place of the act. (BDF §316.1), speaks figuratively, indeed mythologically, in 2:15 of the "disarming" of "the principalities and powers." For the exhortation in 3:9 to *put off* the old person (cf. → ἀποτίθημι in v. 8; cf. E. Lohse, *Colossians* [Hermeneia] ad loc.), one may refer not only to Philo *All.* i.55; *Mut.* 233; *Som.* i.43 etc. (always with ἐκδύω, never ἀπεκδύομαι), but also to Hippolytus *Philos.* i.24.5, where report is made of the god of the Indian Brahmans who takes off the body (ἀπεκδυσάμενον δὲ τὸ σῶμα).

M. Lattke

ἐκεῖ *ekei* there; to that place

There are 95 NT occurrences of this word, which is esp. frequent in Matthew (28 occurrences), John (22), Luke (16), Mark (11), and Acts (6). It usually has the meaning *there, at that place,* e.g., Matt 2:13; 13:42; Mark 11:5; John 6:22, etc.; Matt 26:71: λέγει τοῖς ἐκεῖ, "she said to the *bystanders*"; often after rel. pronouns: οὗ, ὅπου . . . ἐκεῖ, "where . . . *there*" (Matt 18:20; 24:28; Luke 9:4; Rom 9:26; Jas 3:16); pleonastically connected directly to ὅπου: *where* (Rev 12:6a, 14). It also has the meaning *to that place:* ἐφοβήθη ἐκεῖ ἀπελθεῖν, "he was afraid to go *there*" (Matt 2:22; cf. John 11:8; 18:3; Rom 15:24); μετάβα ἔνθεν ἐκεῖ, "move from here *to there*" (Matt 17:20).

ἐκεῖθεν *ekeithen* from there

27 occurrences in the NT, esp. frequent in Matthew (12 occurrences); corresponding to ἔνθεν, "from here . . . *from there*" (Luke 16:26; v.l. οἱ ἐκεῖθεν).

ἐκεῖνος, 3 *ekeinos* that (demonstrative pron.)

1. The demonstrative pron. ἐκεῖνος occurs 243 times in the NT (and thus less frequently than οὗτος with 1388 occurrences), most frequently in the Gospels, esp. John (70 occurrences) and Matthew (56).

2. In connection with a subst. ἐκεῖνος refers to distant persons or things or to persons or things which have already been mentioned in the context (cf. BDF §291). It appears in temporal references: frequently in the phrase ἡ ἡμέρα ἐκείνη (or pl.), "*that* day," in reference to the past (Matt 3:1; 12:1; 14:1; 22:46); κατὰ τὸν καιρὸν ἐκεῖνον, "to *that* time" (Acts 19:23); in reference to the future (Matt 10:19; Mark 13:17; Rev 11:13), particularly of the "last day" (Luke 6:23; 10:12; 2 Tim 1:12, 18); cf. also ὁ αἰὼν ἐκεῖνος, "*that* age," i.e., the future aeon (Luke 20:35). It is used of things and persons: e.g., ἡ οἰκία ἐκείνη, "*that* house," i.e., the house already mentioned (Matt 7:25, 27); referring to persons (Luke 14:24); preceding a specific designation: ὁ μαθητὴς ἐκεῖνος ὃν ἠγάπα ὁ Ἰησοῦς, "*that* disciple whom Jesus loved" (John 21:7).

3. Ἐκείνης (ὁδοῦ understood) appears as a gen. of place in Luke 19:4 with the meaning *at that place, there* (cf. BDF §186.1).

4. Ἐκεῖνος is frequently used substantively. In contrast with other words: οὗτος . . . ἐκεῖνος (in the NT only in Luke 18:14; Jas 4:15); personal pronouns: ὑμῖν . . . ἐκείνοις (Matt 13:11; cf. 2 Cor 8:9), ἐκεῖνος . . . ἡμεῖς (John 9:28; 1 John 4:17); ὁ . . . ἐκεῖνος (John 10:1; cf. 21:7; Rom 14:15); αὐτός (Mark 14:21; 1 John 2:6). Referring to something spoken of directly beforehand (John 5:37; 12:48); in anticipation of a rel. clause (Rom 14:15); to emphasize something spoken of previously: ἐκεῖνον λαβών, "take *that*" (Matt 17:27; cf. John 14:21; 2 Cor 10:18). Referring to Jesus as a well-known person: with a disparaging connotation (John 7:11; 9:12); in a positive sense (1 John 2:6; 3:3). The meaning of καὶ ὁ ἑωρακὼς μεμαρτύρηκεν . . . καὶ ἐκεῖνος οἶδεν (John 19:35) is disputed; ἐκεῖνος probably does not refer to the Kyrios (as it has been frequently taken since Erasmus; however, the grammar of the reference would be very unusual), but to the witness himself, whose reliability is esp. emphasized by the redactor of John (cf. also 18:15; 21:7, 23; on the discussion cf. BDF §291.6; R. Bultmann, *The Gospel of John* [1971] ad loc.; R. Schnackenburg, *The Gospel according to St John* III [1982] ad loc.).

H. Balz

ἐκεῖσε *ekeise* to that place; there*

Acts 21:3: *to that place;* 22:5: τοὺς ἐκεῖσε ὄντας, "who were *there*" (with the meaning of → ἐκεῖ).

ἐκζητέω *ekzēteō* seek out, search, require*

With acc. obj.: Heb 12:17: ἐκζητήσας αὐτήν (μετάνοιαν), "though he *sought* it"; with God as obj.: Acts 15:17: τὸν κύριον; Rom 3:11: οὐκ ἔστιν ἐκζητῶν τὸν θεόν (citing Ps 13:2 LXX), "no one *seeks for* God"; Heb 11:6: τοῖς ἐκζητοῦσιν αὐτόν; pass. with ἀπό: Luke 11:50, 51: "*be required* of"; with περί: 1 Pet 1:10: *seek* after (with ἐξερευνάω).

ἐκζήτησις, εως, ἡ *ekzētēsis* pondering, speculation*

1 Tim 1:4: ἐκζητήσεις (v.l. ζητήσεις) παρέχουσιν μᾶλλον, "which promote *speculations.*"

ἐκθαμβέω *ekthambeō* be alarmed, be astonished*

In the NT only in Mark and only pass.: 9:15: "they *were amazed*"; 14:33: ἤρξατο ἐκθαμβεῖσθαι καὶ ἀδημονεῖν, he "began to be *greatly distressed* [perhaps "trembling"] and troubled"; 16:5f.: ἐξεθαμβήθησαν . . . μὴ ἐκθαμβεῖσθε, "they *were amazed* . . . do not *be amazed.*"

ἔκθαμβος, 2 *ekthambos* alarmed, full of astonishment*

Acts 3:11: συνέδραμεν πᾶς ὁ λαὸς . . . ἔκθαμβοι, "all the people ran together . . . *astounded*"

ἐκθαυμάζω *ekthaumazō* wonder greatly*

Mark 12:17: καὶ ἐξεθαύμαζον ἐπ' αὐτῷ, "and they *were amazed* at him" (cf. Sir 27:23).

ἔκθετος, 2 *ekthetos* exposed*

Acts 7:19: ποιεῖν τὰ βρέφη ἔκθετα, "expose their infants."

ἐκκαθαίρω *ekkathairō* purify*

1 Cor 5:7: ἐκκαθάρατε τὴν παλαιὰν ζύμην, "*purify [yourselves]* of the old leaven"; here, as in classical Greek, the thing to be eliminated is in the acc.; thus perhaps "*cleanse out* the old leaven" (so RSV). Fig. in 2 Tim 2:21: ἐὰν οὖν τις ἐκκαθάρῃ ἑαυτὸν ἀπὸ τούτων, "if anyone *has purified* [RSV "purifies"] himself from . . ."; again like classical, the one purified is acc.

ἐκκαίω *ekkaiō* kindle, pass.: be inflamed*

Rom 1:27: οἱ ἄρσενες . . . ἐξεκαύθησαν ἐν τῇ ὀρέξει αὐτῶν, "the men . . . *were consumed* with passion for one another."

ἐκκακέω *ekkakeō* be tired, be despairing

V.l. of TR in Gal 6:9; 2 Thess 3:13, both times in place of → ἐγκακέω.

ἐκκεντέω *ekkenteō* pierce through*

John 19:37: ὃν ἐξεκέντησαν, "whom they *have pierced*"; Rev 1:7: οἵτινες αὐτὸν ἐξεκέντησαν.

ἐκκλάω *ekklaō* break off*

In the NT only in the form ἐξεκλάσθησαν, of the branches *broken off* the good olive tree (Rom 11:17, 19, 20).

ἐκκλείω *ekkleiō* exclude*

Lit. in Gal 4:17: ἐκκλεῖσαι ὑμᾶς θέλουσιν, "they want to *shut* you *out* [from the community of salvation]"; fig. in Rom 3:27: ἐξεκλείσθη, boasting *"is excluded,"* i.e., *made impossible.*

ἐκκλησία, ας, ἡ *ekklesia* national assembly; congregation, congregational assembly, church; (the) Church

1. Occurrences in the NT — 2. Meanings — 3. Usage — 4. Ἐκκλησία as a Christian term — a) Paul — b) Acts — c) Deutero-Paulines — d) Matthew — e) Hebrews — f) Elsewhere in the NT

Lit.: C. K. Barrett, "Paul's Address to the Ephesian Elders,"

ἐκκλησία

FS Dahl 107-21. — K. Berger, "Volksversammlung und Gemeinde Gottes," *ZTK* 73 (1976) 167-207. — W. Bieder, *Ekklesia und Polis im NT und in der alten Kirche* (1941). — C. G. Brandis, PW V (1905) 2163-99. — L. Cerfaux, *The Church in the Theology of St. Paul* (1959). — N. A. Dahl, *Das Volk Gottes* (1941; reprint 1963). — G. Delling, "Merkmale der Kirche nach dem NT," *NTS* 13 (1966/67) 297-316. — J. Ernst, "Von der Ortsgemeinde zur Großkirche—dargestellt an den Kirchenmodellen des Philipper- und Epheserbriefes," *Kirche im Werden* (ed. J. Hainz; 1976) 109-42. — H. Frankemölle, *Jahwebund und Kirche Christi* (1974). — J. Gnilka, *Der Epheserbrief* (HTKNT, 1971) 99-111. — J. Hainz, *Ekklesia* (1972), esp. 229-55. — P. Hoffmann, "Der Petrus-Primat im Mt," FS Schnackenburg 172-90. — W. G. Kümmel, *Kirchenbegriff und Geschichtsbewußtsein in der Urgemeinde und bei Jesus* (1943). — O. Linton, *RAC* IV (1959) 906-21. — O. Michel, *Das Zeugnis des NT von der Gemeinde* (1941). — P. S. Minear, *Images of the Church in the NT* (^{2}1975). — H. P. Müller, *THAT* II, 609-19. — A. Oepke, "Leib Christi oder Volk Gottes bei Paulus?" *TLZ* 79 (1954) 363-68. — H. Schlier, "Die Kirche nach dem Brief an die Epheser," Schlier I, 159-86. — K. L. Schmidt, *TDNT* III, 501-36. — R. Schnackenburg, *The Church in the NT* (1965), esp. 55-117. — W. Schrage, "Ekklesia und Synagoge," *ZTK* 60 (1963) 178-202. — E. Schweizer, *Church Order in the NT* (1961). — *idem, Matthäus und seine Gemeinde* (1974). — K. Stendahl, *RGG* III, 1297-1304. — P. Stuhlmacher, *Gerechtigkeit Gottes bei Paulus* (1965) 210-17. — A. Vögtle, "Messiasbekenntnis und Petrusverheißung," *idem, Das Evangelium und die Evangelien* (1971) 137-70. — For further bibliography see *TWNT* X, 1127-31; *DNTT* I, 305-7.

1. The 114 occurrences of ἐκκλησία in the NT are unevenly distributed. There are only 3 occurrences in the Gospels, all in Matthew (16:18; 18:17 bis). The word appears most frequently in Paul's letters (46 occurrences, 22 of which are in 1 Corinthians), in the deutero-Pauline letters (16 occurrences), and in Acts (23 occurrences). It appears twice in Hebrews. Among the Catholic Epistles, it is found only in 3 John (3 occurrences) and James (once). Of the 20 occurrences in Revelation, 19 are in formalized phrases in the letters to the seven churches (chs. 1–3).

2. The noun ἐκκλησία is derived etymologically from ἐκ and καλέω; accordingly it was used to designate "(the totality of) those who are called out." However, this original meaning nowhere plays a recognizable role in our material. It is always displaced by terminological shifts which the concept has undergone during a long history. In classical Greek as well as in Hellenistic literature, it became a technical expression for the assembly of the people, consisting of free men entitled to vote (*CIG* I, 739, no. 1567). This political usage is present also in Acts 19:39, which refers to "the regular *assembly*" of the inhabitants of Ephesus. In a wider sense the word can be used for any public assembly; thus in Acts 19:32 it is used of an *"assembly"* "in confusion," which had come together in the theater at the urging of the silversmiths of Ephesus (cf. also v. 40).

In the overwhelming majority of the NT passages, ἐκκλησία is used as a fixed Christian term and is to be translated with *congregation* or *congregational assembly* or *c(C)hurch.* Distinguishing among passages that use ἐκκλησία with these different meanings is possible only within limits. The distinction between *congregation/church* (the body of Christians at a specific place; Germ. *Gemeinde*) and *Church* (the supra-congregational association of God's people or the totality of all Christians; Germ. *Kirche*) is foreign to the NT. Closely related is the fact that early Christianity did not conceive of ἐκκλησία primarily as an organizational, but rather as a theological entity. The *ecclesia universalis* is neither a secondary union made up of individual autonomous churches, nor is the local congregation only an organizational sub-unit of the total Church. Rather, both the local assembly of Christians and the trans-local community of believers are equally legitimate forms of the ἐκκλησία created by God.

Because there is no German word which expresses at the same time the universal and the local-particular aspect (indeed, *Versammlung,* proposed by Schmidt, *TWNT* III, 505, is unsuitable because it is too imprecise), one does best to be content with *Gemeinde* for all occurrences which refer to the concrete local ἐκκλησία or speak generically of the local ἐκκλησία. *Kirche* is best suited for all occurrences which speak abstractly from the concrete local situation of the ἐκκλησία in an all-embracing sense or make theological statements referring to its general nature. (Eng. "church" does embrace both the universal and the local-particular, but capitalization or lack thereof usually, as in the present work, eliminates this useful ambiguity. RSV's consistent use of lower-case "church" will be modified as necessary in quotations that follow.)

3. In a series of passages which reflect the earliest Christian usage, we see the phrase ἐκκλησία τοῦ θεοῦ, "*church* of God" (1 Cor 1:2; 10:32; 11:22; 15:9; 2 Cor 1:1; Gal 1:13; pl. in 1 Cor 11:16, 22; 1 Thess 2:14; 2 Thess 1:4). Here gen. "of God" is not merely an addendum defining more precisely the preceding term *church,* but is instead an integral part of a fixed terminological formulation. Indeed, this formulation might have come into existence as the translation of *q^{e}hal 'ēl,* which is attested in apocalyptic Judaism as a term for the eschatological company of God (1QM 4:10; 1QS^a 2:4; Stendahl 1299; Stuhlmacher 210f.).

This insight revises the traditional view (L. Rost, *TDNT* III, 529, n. 90), according to which the Christian term ἐκκλησία is derived from the LXX, which introduced it as the translation of the OT's *qāhāl,* "assembly, company of the people of God." Such a direct adoption from the OT is improbable for several reasons: 1) *Qāhāl* is translated in the LXX not only with ἐκκλησία, but also with συναγωγή. Indeed, the latter is the more clearly defined and theologically weighty term designating the community of salvation. 2) The LXX renders *q^{e}hal yhwh* with ἐκκλησία (συναγωγή) κυρίου, while the NT prefers ἐκκλησία τοῦ θεοῦ. 3) In the NT there is no proof from Scripture associated with ἐκκλησία (perhaps with the exception of Acts 7:38, → 4.b), although such important terms are normally connected with a direct reference to an OT term.

On the other hand, considerations must also be offered against Schrage's thesis, according to which ἐκκλησία was first taken up as a self-designation in the Hellenistic Jewish circle around Stephen (Acts 6) and then developed further by Paul in a polemical antithesis against the term συναγωγή, which was burdened by Jewish nomism. This view runs aground when it is observed that ἐκκλησία never occurs in Paul's letters where a tone critical of the law can be detected. Indeed, the term is inserted, with no inconsistency created, in Matt 16:18 within the framework of the Matthean community's Jewish Christian understanding of the law (→ 4.d). Moreover, Paul in 1 Thess 2:14 includes the early Jewish churches in the designation ἐκκλησίαι τοῦ θεοῦ.

Consequently one may proceed with the assumption that ἐκκλησία τοῦ θεοῦ *(qᵉhal 'ēl)* was first a self-designation of the early community coming into existence after Easter. The term was used because it corresponded with the eschatological self-understanding of the Church, which understood itself to be the company elect by God and determined by him to be the center and crystallization-point of the eschatological Israel now being called into existence by him. The Hellenistic Jewish Christians around Stephen, the Gentile Christians at Antioch (Acts 11:26; 13:1), and Paul were able to appropriate the name without difficulty despite the fact that they differed from the people of Jerusalem in their understanding of the law. Indeed, the common consciousness of Jewish and Gentile Christians of being the eschatological community of God proves to be the unifying thread, without which the basic recognition at the Apostolic Council of Gentiles free from the law by Jewish Christianity faithful to the law (Gal 2:6-10) was hardly conceivable.

'Εκκλησία, wherever it appears by itself as an ecclesiological term, is to be understood as an abbreviation of the original term ἐκκλησία τοῦ θεοῦ. That is, the more precise designation with the *genitivus auctoris* "of God" is to be assumed. (In this sense G vg in 1 Cor 14:4; Phil 3:6 have appropriately added "of God.")

Occasionally Paul mentions Christ also in connection with ἐκκλησία; thus in Rom 16:16, "the *churches* of Christ greet you." The fact that God is in no way replaced by Christ as the founder and initiator of the Church is indicated by 1 Thess 2:14: "For you . . . became imitators of the *churches* of God in Christ Jesus which are in Judea" ("in Christ Jesus" refers to "churches of God," not to "imitators"). The act of God in founding the Church is mediated by Christ. The church in Thessalonica was indebted for its existence, no less than the churches in Judea, to the work of Jesus Christ in the word of the gospel. The same is said in the shorter phrase in Gal 1:22: "the *churches* in [RSV "of"] Christ in Judea"; "in Christ" is not only a formulaic phrase replacing the adjective "Christian" (so F. Mussner, *Galaterbrief* [HTKNT] 98, n. 110); such a characterization would be meaningless because Paul knows no ἐκκλησία other than the Christian ἐκκλησία. What is spoken of is, rather, the origin of the Church of God in the Christ-event.

4. a) In Paul's statements about his activity as persecutor, we apparently come, in tradition-historical perspective, to the earliest usage. He calls himself "a persecutor of the *church*" (Phil 3:6) and says: "I am the least of the apostles, unfit to be called an apostle, because I persecuted the *church* of God" (1 Cor 15:9). Here he takes up the self-designation of the early Jerusalem church as "the church of God," in which, as with the designation "the saints" (2 Cor 9:1, 12), there is a manifestation of that community's self-understanding as the eschatological community of salvation. The fact that Paul in no way speaks in general of the total Church, but rather thinks in terms of a geographical area, is made probable by Gal 1:22f. and confirmed by the context of 1 Cor 15:9: Paul contrasts himself, as the last apostle called, with the other apostles of Jerusalem. That he as persecutor is "unfit to be called an apostle" is determined by this antithesis: While Peter and the other apostles constituted the church of God in Jerusalem by their witness, he, Paul, sought to destroy this church!

The transference of the name ἐκκλησία τοῦ θεοῦ to local groups of the disciples of Jesus outside of Jerusalem was certainly accomplished before Paul (→ 3).

Nevertheless Paul gives a further development to this usage. When he speaks of ἐκκλησία, he normally thinks first of the concrete assembly of those who have been baptized at a specific place. One can scarcely see here a conscious polemic against a centralized understanding of the Church held by the early Jerusalem church (*contra* Hainz 232-36). On the contrary, what is significant is, in the first place, Paul's missionary conception: The eschatological people of God came into existence, in his view, not only through the fact that individuals from all peoples in and around Jerusalem, the place of salvation, could assemble, but also through the fact that the resurrected one made him an apostle and commissioned him to bring about "the obedience of faith for the sake of his name among all the nations" through the power of the gospel entrusted to him (Rom 1:5) and to gather the community of salvation from place to place worldwide. The close connection between "apostle" and *"Church"* is expressed clearly in the coordination of both concepts in the prescripts to some of his letters (1 Cor 1:1f.; 2 Cor 1:1; Gal 1:1f.). The Church is indebted for its existence not to the apostle's work; it remains bound together in the salvation event which prevails worldwide through the gospel. Despite the local limitation in its concrete existence, by means of the obedience of faith it is fully the Church of God. It is not as an isolated entity that it is "of God"; it is "of God" in such a way that in it God's worldwide act of judgment, which leads to the Church's founding, takes on visible form.

This understanding of the Church finds programmatic expression in 1 Cor 1:1f. There (v. 2) Paul addresses the Corinthian Christians as "the *church* of God which is at Corinth" (so also in 2 Cor 1:1), i.e., as the church in whose existence the characteristic features of the coming worldwide Church of God appear and which is thereby able to represent this Church in its totality. The "ecumenical perspective" that follows in 1 Cor 2:2 (and is often attributed to a later redactor without sufficient reason) includes "all those who in every place call on the name of our Lord Jesus Christ, both their Lord and ours," i.e., the whole Church as it comes into existence through the work of the apostle.

For the Pauline understanding a great role is played by the local assembly (for worship). It is "church" whenever individuals "assemble as a *church* (ἐν ἐκκλησίᾳ)" (1 Cor 11:18). This usage has only an apparent relationship with the secular-political usage in Hellenistic literature (→ 2). For Paul the ἐκκλησία is constituted not only by the act of assembling together in order to disperse after the conclusion of assembly; it maintains this name also outside of the concrete assembly. Thus 14:23: "If, therefore, the whole *church* assembles. . . ." Assembly for worship is the center and at the same time the criterion for life in the church. Here it is determined whether it really is the church "of God." Thus the unbrotherly behavior of the rich toward the poor in the Corinthian common meal is nothing less than "despis[ing] the *church* of God" (11:22). What is despised here is, first, the power of the Lord's Supper to unite the church, but also what coming together should be for the Church of God.

The instructions in 1 Corinthians 14 are directed to the church's assembly for worship. Over against the inclination to a pneumatic individualism in Corinth Paul emphasizes the significance of the worship event for the community. While a person who speaks in tongues only "edifies" himself, because what he says is unintelligible, the prophet edifies "the [assembled] *church,*" because it understands him (vv. 4f.). Glossolalia should be permitted in principle only when care is exercised that it is intelligible for everyone present (vv. 23, 27f.). The most important principle is: Everything should be done for the edification of the church (vv. 5, 26), i.e., it should stand in the service of the act of the Spirit, which the church ruled by Christ wants to have as its living space. Here an important aspect of Paul's understanding of the church is indicated; this he elaborates, not with the word ἐκκλησία, but with the figure of the body of Christ (12:4-27; Rom 12:4ff.).

In principle, every local assembly of Christians, in whose center is the service of worship, is considered a church. Thus Paul often mentions house churches, including that of the couple Aquila and Prisca—first in Corinth (1 Cor 16:19), then in Rome (? Rom 16:3f.)—and that of Philemon (Phlm 2).

Ecclesiological statements that lead beyond the level of the local assembly are rare in Paul's letters. But they are not totally absent. Thus, according to Paul, the individual church represents God's community of salvation, that which by God's actions is coming into being throughout the world, in that definite ethical norms and patterns of conduct are valid in all individual churches equally. Paul teaches the same "ways in Christ," i.e., the same elementary moral instructions, "in every *church*" (1 Cor 4:17). He expects the Corinthians to adopt the rule accepted in the "*churches* of God," according to which women come veiled to the service of worship (11:16), and that they, "as in all the *churches* of the saints," not be allowed to give public speeches in the assembly of the church (14:33f.). In 1 Cor 10:32 Paul gives the demand for inoffensive behavior in the presence of Jews, Greeks, and "the *Church* of God." Because of the collocation here, it is clear that he is speaking not of the local congregation, but of a third comprehensive human group, one which is significant in salvation history. It is the eschatological people of God, the Church, which stands alongside Jews and Greeks. Of special importance is 12:28: "And God has appointed in the *church* first apostles, second prophets, third teachers. . . ." Paul speaks here of the fundamental structure of the Church's ministries, as it appears in all places in the past and present with individually varying significance (thus prophets and teachers were probably of little lasting significance for the Corinthian Christians). By all this Paul comes close to a fundamental statement about the nature of "the Church": whatever its historical place may be, certain norms of behavior are valid and certain offices and a holy law are established by God. In all of this the Church's inner structure as "the body of Christ" (12:27) is realized.

b) In Acts also ἐκκλησία usually designates the concrete local congregation, whether in Jerusalem (5:11; 8:1, 3; 11:22; 12:1, 5; 14:27; 15:4, 22; 18:22), in Antioch (11:26; 13:1; 15:3, 41), or in locations within the Pauline missionary areas (16:5 [Derbe and Lystra]; 20:17 [Ephesus]). In a few of these passages the earliest usage is evident: ἡ ἐκκλησία without a reference to the place as a name for the original Jerusalem church (in which Luke of course avoids the more precise genitival determination τοῦ θεοῦ). Thus in 18:22: (Paul) "went up [to Jerusalem] and greeted the *church*" (also in 12:1, 5). Repeatedly ἐκκλησία stands as a term for the local congregational assembly: In what is apparently an old Jerusalem local tradition the divine act of judgment on Ananias and Sapphira is described: "And great fear came upon the whole *church,* and upon all who heard of these things" (5:11). The church appears here to be constituted by sacral law; through the practice of this law it defends its eschatological purity. After returning from their missionary journey, Paul and Barnabas call a congregational assembly in Antioch in order to give an account to the church which sent them (14:27). What we have in 15:3 ("So, being sent on their way by the *church* . . .") is perhaps a concrete act of commissioning by the Antiochian congregational assembly. According to v. 4 ("When they came to Jerusalem, they were welcomed by the *church* and the apostles and the elders") the full congregational assembly in Jerusalem comprises its own governing body, to be distinguished from the apostles and the elders as a governing body leading the Church. The apostolic decree concluded by them (cf. v. 23) is determined by the entire congregational assembly. This could be the sense of the unsettled formulation retained in v. 22: "Then it seemed good to the apostles and the elders, with the whole *church*. . . ."

Luke conceives of the individual local churches as constituted and organized according to an arrangement which was derived from Paul. This view is assumed in the comment in Acts 14:23: Paul and Barnabas "appointed elders for them in every church." The phrase presupposes the pl. use of the word.

But the sg. usage is present in Acts 9:31. Ἐκκλησία designates here the totality of Christians in a specific geographic area and is thus to be translated with *Church*: "So the *Church* in all Judea and Galilee and Samaria had peace and was built up; and walking in the fear of the Lord. . . ." (The pl. v.l. in the Byzantine Imperial text and the majority of later manuscripts is undoubtedly secondary.)

A special position is held by Acts 20:28: "Take heed to yourselves and to all the flock, in which the Holy Spirit has made you overseers, to care for the *Church* of God which he has obtained with his own blood" (RSV mg.). It is the only theological statement by Luke about the nature of the Church. Its essential difficulty is reflected in the uncertain textual tradition: a series of important witnesses (among others 𝔭[74] A C* D) read "*Church* of the Lord," which may involve a secondary attempt to make a clear reference for the rel. clause and to avert a misunderstanding, as if it were speaking of God's blood rather than Christ's blood. It is improbable that ἰδίου is understood as a noun ("which he obtained with the blood of his own Son"), since such usage is seen nowhere else in Luke-Acts. Instead, it is likely that the apparently patripassian phrase came into existence when Luke introduced a traditional formula, whose christological reference was not in doubt for him and his readers (H. Conzelmann, *Acts* [Hermeneia] 175; Barrett 114). In favor of this argument is the fact that this is the only passage in Acts which speaks of the vicarious atoning death of Jesus. The statement's content is in harmony with Col 1:18, 24: in both passages ecclesiology is based on christology. The Church is the historical realm of salvation created by the death of Jesus. Behind Acts 20:28 is probably a deutero-Pauline ecclesiology.

Acts 7:38 is not easy to explain. In a Moses-Christ typology the function of Moses as mediator at the giving of the law is described: "This is he who was in the *congregation* in the wilderness with the angel who spoke to him at Mount Sinai, and with our fathers. . . ." It is possible that LXX use of ἐκκλησία = "assembly of the people" (Deut 4:10; 9:10; 18:16) is present here. It is not to be ruled out, however, that the typology here should be extended to the Church, indeed, in the sense that Christ as lawgiver for the Church definitively surpasses the function of Moses for the OT community of salvation.

c) In the deutero-Pauline literature ἐκκλησία is again used as a term for the individual congregation, as in Col 4:15f. (the *whole church* of Laodicea and the *house church* of Nympha there); 1 Tim 5:16 ("the *church*" in the generic sense). Characteristic of these writings is, however, a series of fundamental statements about the nature of the Church. Indeed, Colossians and Ephesians associate christology and ecclesiology most closely, so that every statement about the Church becomes a statement about Christ. The basis for this in tradition history is the Pauline concept of the Church as the body of Christ (1 Cor 12:27; Rom 12:5), which is extended into ontology and salvation history.

The relationship between Christ and the Church is determined in *a twofold way.* On the one hand Christ is *directly united* with the body, i.e., the Church. "Paul," in his own body, fulfills the remaining afflictions of Christ "for the sake of his body, that is, the *Church*" (Col 1:24). Thus it should be said that the Church is founded on the salvific deed of Christ at the cross and that its form of life—normatively represented through the apostle—is shaped by Christ's suffering. On the other hand Christ is the *head* of the Church: "He is before all things, and in him all things hold together. He is the head of the body, [that is,] the *Church*" (vv. 17f.). Today it is almost undisputed that the phrase "[that is,] the *Church*" is a gloss by which the author of Colossians interprets the hymn in 1:15-20, which originally concerned the lordship of Christ over the cosmos (E. Schweizer, *The Letter to the Colossians* [1982] 55-57). The author wants to show, as does the author of Ephesians, that the lordship of Christ over the world is presently realized visibly only in the Church insofar as it is oriented in faith to the one who is the "head."

The Church is thus not only founded on Christ; at the same time it has Christ as the one to whom it stands in relation and as the goal of its growth. The Church is a realm of salvation permeating the cosmos, tangibly initiated by the death of Christ, but nevertheless not static, but growing in a historical development toward the norm established in Christ, its head (Eph 2:20; 3:12ff.; 4:15).

The lordship of Christ over the world and his lordship over the Church are both viewed together and differentiated in Eph 1:22f. God "has put all things under his feet and has made him the head over all things for the *Church,* which is his body, the fulness of him who fills all in all." Christ is head and lord of the cosmos (Col 2:10) as of the Church, but only the Church is his body; it is permeated by his "fulness" in a special way. Consequently it alone has the capability and the mission to call the world back to Christ's lordship and thus to obedience to the world's creator. It realizes this mission through its proclamation. Thus it is "through the *Church*" that "the manifold wisdom of God" is declared "to the principalities and powers in the heavenly places" (Eph 3:10).

In an entirely characteristic way, the parenesis concerning the marital relationship of husband and wife, which is part of the traditional scheme of the household code (Col 3:18ff.), becomes in Eph 5:22-33 the occasion for instruction about the relationship between Christ and the Church. Undoubtedly the ecclesiological exposition is not only an exposition serving the marriage parenesis, but is instead the essential purpose of the section. Indeed, here again both aspects—Christ as head *and* as body of the Church—are closely intertwined. The subordination of wife to husband, which was self-evident in ancient society, serves to illustrate the former: "The husband is the head of the wife as Christ is the head of the *Church*" (v. 23). As the wife obeys her husband, so the Church maintains constant obedience to Christ (5:24). The second aspect is inferred from Gen 2:24 (Eph 5:30): The couple become "one flesh" according to the will of the creator. Consequently the husband, who gives loving care to his wife, is caring for his own body (v. 28). In the same way Christ acts on behalf of his own body, the Church (v. 29). He "loved the *Church* and gave himself up for it [RSV "her"]" (v. 25). His loving care for it is realized in the renewal which it has experienced through baptism (v. 26). The meaning of v. 32 ("This mystery is a profound one, and I am saying that it refers to Christ and the Church") is disputed, but is probably a hermeneutical comment made to justify the interpretation of Gen 2:24 with respect to Christ and the Church. "Mystery" means "the true, hidden meaning of the quotation" (H. Conzelmann, *Epheserbrief* [NTD 8] ad loc.).

The statement about the nature of the Church in 1 Tim 3:15 is unique in its static view of the Church. Here where it is called "the house [RSV "household"] of God" and "the pillar and bulwark of the truth," in the background is the image (perhaps dependent on 1 Cor 3:16; 2 Cor 6:16) of a firm house which offers protection and in which one can move and still be preserved from shock and destruction. The image of the house easily flows into that of the household: The Church is the *familia dei.* Thus an analogy can be drawn between the function of the father of the house and of those who hold office in the congregation: "For if a man does not know how to manage his own household, how can he care for God's *Church*?" (1 Tim 3:5).

d) The saying about the rock in Matt 16:18 raises a multitude of problems. It is formally the explanation of a name, in which is used a play on words, only inadequately reproduced in Greek, with the Aramaic sobriquet of Simon, *Kēpā'* (in Greek transliterated as Κηφᾶς and translated as Πέτρος). "And I tell you, you are Peter (*Kēpā'*), and on this rock (*kēpā'*; Gk. πέτρα) I will build my Church." The explanation of the name discloses the significance of Simon for the Church: just as the holy rock is the foundation of the Jerusalem temple, so Peter is the foundation of the holy building of the Church, the eschatological temple that Jesus himself will erect (cf. Mark 14:58 par. Matt 26:61; Rev 21:14).

In accord with contemporary scholarship one may regard it as impossible that this is a saying Jesus uttered before Easter with the intention of founding a special community (so even Schmidt 525f.). Matt 16:17-19 turns out to be a passage with a diverse history of tradition that Matthew has inserted radactionally into the Caesarea-Philippi scene of Mark 8:27-30. Furthermore, attempts to localize Matt 16:18 at another place within the pre-Easter history of Jesus (so O. Cullmann, *TDNT* VI, 106f.) or to place the logion at the first appearance of the resurrected one before Peter (so Vögtle 170) are ultimately not convincing.

Linguistic indications place the logion unambiguously in the second generation: 1) The statement about the ἐκκλησία as a holy building is a statement about the nature of the Church which corresponds both structurally and in its metaphorical content (cf. Eph 2:20: the apostles and prophets as the foundation of the Church as building; Rev 21:14; 1 Tim 3:15) to deutero-Pauline statements about the nature of the Church (→ 4.c). 2) The designation of the Church as the ἐκκλησία *of Jesus* hardly corresponds to earlier usage (→ 4.a on Rom 16:16; Gal 1:22), but fits well with Matthew's conception of the Church: It is the Church of Jesus because it is composed of the disciples of Jesus, constituted and held together by the authority of Jesus the teacher (Matt 28:18-20). The special meaning of Peter as the foundation of the Church probably rests for Matthew on the idea of Peter as the guarantor and interpreter of the teaching of Jesus, that which was fundamental to the Church.

Matt 18:17, unlike 16:18, uses ἐκκλησία for the assembled local church.

e) Heb 2:12 takes up Ps 21:23 LXX and gives it a christological interpretation: "in the midst of the *congregation* I will praise you." 'Εκκλησία is obviously understood as the heavenly assembly, in the midst of which Christ proclaims God's praise. This heavenly congregation is thus fundamentally an assembly for worship. Heb 12:23, on the other hand, speaks of the earthly congregation, but of course in such a way that unmistakable reference is made to the heavenly assembly for worship. The heavenly congregation is "the city of the living God, the heavenly Jerusalem," and a "festal gathering." Its counterpart stands at the distance separating heaven and earth. It is "the *assembly* of the first-born who are enrolled in heaven." It is indeed still on earth, but it is more than a mere transitory likeness of the heavenly congregation, for its members have their destiny there on the basis of their relationship to Christ.

f) The occurrences in the other NT writings are of relatively limited significance. Jas 5:14 speaks in the generic sense of "the elders of the *church.*" 3 John 6, 9, and 10 reveal a picture of a concrete local congregation with relatively well-developed legal-institutional structures. In the phrase "puts them out of the *church*" (v. 10) there is probably a reference to an official legal act. Altogether Revelation has 20 references to the local congregation.

J. Roloff

ἐκκλίνω *ekklinō* turn away, avoid*

With ἀπό, meaning *turn away:* Rom 16:17: ἐκκλίνετε ἀπ' αὐτῶν, "*avoid* them"; 1 Pet 3:11: ἐκκλινάτω δὲ ἀπὸ κακοῦ (cf. Ps 33:15 LXX), "*turn away* from evil." Used absolutely: Rom 3:12: πάντες ἐξέκλιναν (citing Ps 13:3 LXX), "all *have turned aside* [from the way]."

ἐκκολυμβάω *ekkolymbaō* swim away*

Acts 27:42: μή τις ἐκκολυμβήσας διαφύγῃ, "lest any should *swim away* and escape."

ἐκκομίζω *ekkomizō* carry out*

Luke 7:12: ἰδοὺ ἐξεκομίζετο τεθνηκώς, "behold, a man who had died *was being carried out.*"

ἐκκοπή, ῆς, ἡ *ekkopē* hindrance

1 Cor 9:12 ℵ D* L (in place of → ἐγκοπή): ἐκκοπὴν δίδωμι τινί, *hinder* something.

ἐκκόπτω *ekkoptō* cut off, fell*

Of *cutting down* a tree (which bears no good fruit; Matt 3:10 par. Luke 3:9; Matt 7:19; Luke 13:7, 9); to *chop off* a hand or a foot (Matt 5:30; 18:8); in a figure of speech, of *cutting off* a branch from the wild olive tree, in reference to Gentile Christians (Rom 11:22, 24 pass.); again fig. in 2 Cor 11:12: ἵνα ἐκκόψω τὴν ἀφορμήν, "in order to *remove* [RSV "undermine"] the claim."

ἐκκρεμάννυμι *ekkremannymi* act.: hang (something) out; mid.: hang on (to something)*

In the NT only mid.: Luke 19:48: ὁ λαὸς γὰρ ἅπας ἐξεκρέματο αὐτοῦ ἀκούων, "for all the people *hung upon* his words [and listened to him]."

ἐκλαλέω *eklaleō* let out, give away*

Acts 23:22: μηδενὶ ἐκλαλῆσαι, "*tell* no one."

ἐκλάμπω *eklampō* shine, blaze up*

Matt 13:43: οἱ δίκαιοι ἐκλάμψουσιν ὡς ἥλιος, "the righteous will *shine* like the sun" (cf. Dan 12:3 Θ; Mart. Pol. 15:1; the reference is to the transformation of the righteous at the parousia).

ἐκλανθάνομαι *eklanthanomai* forget*

With gen.: Heb 12:5: ἐκλέλησθε τῆς παρακλήσεως, "you *have forgotten* the exhortation" (or "have you forgotten. . . ? So RSV).

ἐκλέγομαι *eklegomai* choose, elect*

1. Occurrences in the NT — 2. Meaning and usage — 3. As used by the individual NT writers

Lit.: R. BULTMANN, *The Gospel of John* (1971) (index s.v.) — H. CONZELMANN, *First Corinthians* (Hermeneia, 1975) 50. — J. GNILKA, *Der Epheserbrief* (HTKNT, 1971) 69ff. — O. HOFIUS, "Erwählt vor Grundlegung der Welt (Eph 1, 4)," *ZNW* 62 (1971) 123-28. — R. SCHNACKENBURG, *The Gospel according to St. John* II (1979), 265-70. — G. SCHRENK and G. QUELL, *TDNT* IV, 144-68. — For further bibliography → ἐκλεκτός; see *TWNT* X, 1160f.

1. The verb appears 11 times in the Lukan literature and 5 times in John; it appears also in 1 Cor 1:27 (bis), 28; Eph 1:4; Jas 2:5, and as a pleonastic addition to ἐκλεκτός in Mark 13:20.

2. Ἐκλέγομαι occurs with the general meaning *choose (something)* only in Luke 10:42 and 14:7; elsewhere it denotes the election by God of the fathers (Acts 13:17), of Jesus as Son of God (Luke 9:35), and of those who believe (1 Cor 1:27 and often) and the election of the disciples by Jesus (John 6:70, etc.) and appointment to ministries and offices by the Church (Acts 6:5; 15:22, 25).

3. Just as the experience of salvation was the basis for the belief in election within Israel (cf. Deut 14:2), so the Church composed of Jews and Gentiles also viewed itself as elect on the basis of the Christ-event (Mark 13:20; → ἐκλεκτός). Paul describes the sovereign act of divine election in 1 Cor 1:26-31 in the light of the Church's composition: "God *chose* what is foolish in the world to shame the wise . . . [and the] strong" (v. 27; cf. Matt 11:25f. par.; Bar 2:22f.; Sir 10:14). This election occurred "in Christ Jesus," who is the "wisdom," "righteousness," "sanctification," and "redemption" given by God (1 Cor 1:30; cf. Greek of *1 Enoch* 51:3). In response to preference for the rich Jas 2:5 gives parenetic emphasis to the election of the poor.

In the Lukan literature fundamental theological statements are connected with ἐκλέγομαι. Israel's significance in salvation history is indicated by the election of the fathers (Acts 13:17). However, Jesus Christ is God's *chosen* Son, in whom the OT promises about the messianic Son of God (Ps 2:7), the elect suffering servant of God (Isa 42:1), and the prophet like Moses (Deut 18:15) are fulfilled (Luke 9:35, cf. par.; cf. 23:35, cf. par. ὁ ἐκλεκτός). From among the disciples Jesus *chose* the twelve (6:13), who, as the apostles chosen by him "through the Holy Spirit" (Acts 1:2; cf. v. 24), are the Jesus' primary witnesses in the time of the Church. In the opening of the Gentile mission by Peter God's *choosing* (ἐξελέξατο) is likewise evident (Acts 15:7).

The election of the twelve (the disciples) by Jesus is also emphasized by John (6:70; 13:18; 15:16, 19). However, this election did not exclude the betrayal by Judas, which Jesus saw in advance (6:70f.) and which was in accord with God's will (13:18). From the election for friendship with Jesus came the obligation to bring fruit (15:16). Because the elect are not of the world, the enmity of the world falls on them (15:19; → κόσμος).

The hymn of praise in Eph 1:3-14 shows the differentness of Christian belief in election in comparison with the consciousness of election in Jewish apocalyptic literature: it relates the idea that those who believe were chosen "before the foundation of the world" (v. 4; cf. 1QH 13:10; CD 2:7) to Christian belief in the accomplished fact of redemption by means of the added phrase "in him [Christ]" and the broader context it gives to the idea. The election is to be effective in a "holy" life in accord with the election (Eph 1:4b).

J. Eckert

ἐκλείπω *ekleipō* cease, give out, come to an end*

Luke 16:9: ὅταν ἐκλίπῃ, "when *it* ["mammon"] *runs out* [RSV "fails"]"; 22:32: ἵνα μὴ ἐκλίπῃ ἡ πίστις σου, "that your faith may not *fail*"; 23:45: τοῦ ἡλίου ἐκλιπόντος, "the sun *was darkened*" (AV); Heb 1:12: τὰ ἔτη σου οὐκ ἐκλείψουσιν (citing Ps 101:28 LXX): "thy years *will* never *end*."

ἐκλεκτός, 3 *eklektos* chosen, elect*

1. Occurrences and meaning in the NT — 2. The Synoptics — 3. Paul and the deutero-Pauline tradition — 4. 1 Peter — 5. Other NT writings — 6. Ἐκλογή

Lit.: H. Balz and W. Schrage, *Die Katholischen Briefe* (1973) 64. — H. Braun, *Spätjüdischer-häretischer und frühchristlicher Radikalismus* II (1969) 40f. — L. Coenen, *DNTT* I, 536-42. — J. H. Elliott, *The Elect and the Holy* (1966). — J. G. Fraine, *Berufung und Auserwählung* (1966). — L. Goppelt, *Der Erste Petrusbrief* (KEK, 1978) (index s.v. "Erwählung"). — E. Lohmeyer, *Die Briefe an die Philipper, Kolosser und an Philemon* (KEK, 1964). — B. Mayer, *Unter Gottes Heilsratschluß* (1974). — P. von der Osten-Sacken, *Römer 8 als Beispiel paulinischer Soteriologie* (1975). — G. Richter, *Deutsches Wörterbuch zum NT* (1962) 69-72. — G. Schneider, *Parusiegleichnisse im Lukasevangelium* (1975) 71-78. — G. Schrenk, *TDNT* IV, 179-92. — H. Zimmermann, "Das Gleichnis vom Richter und der Witwe (Lk 18, 1-8)," FS Schürmann 79-95. — For further bibliography see *TWNT* X, 1160f.

1. Ἐκλεκτός is used in the NT only in the religious sense. The adj. is used to speak of the election of Jesus Christ (Luke 23:35; 1 Pet 2:4, 6), of the angels (1 Tim 5:21), and of those who believe in Christ (15 times). In regard to the last of these ἐκλεκτός appears almost exclusively in the context of apocalyptic or eschatological sayings (Mark 13:20, 22, 27, etc.) and is christologically oriented (Rom 8:33; Col 3:12; 1 Pet 2:4-10, etc.). In the same semantic field with ἐκλεκτός are esp. → καλέω (Matt 22:14; Rom 8:30; cf. 11:29; 1 Pet 2:9; Rev 17:14) and → προορίζω (Rom 8:29f.; cf. Eph 1:5, 11).

2. Ἐκλεκτός appears in the oldest Gospels only in the eschatological discourse of Mark 13 (vv. 20, 22, 27 par. Matt 24:22, 24, 31; these texts are not in Luke). Just as the tradition history of this apocalypse, which originated in the Christian community, must be evaluated, it is evident that ἐκλεκτός as a designation for the disciples (see below on Luke 18:7), which never occurs elsewhere in the words of Jesus, appears here only in connection with apocalyptic sayings. The consoling word about the shortening of the days "for the sake of the *elect*" (Mark 13:20), which appears within the description of the great affliction (vv. 14-20), revises the apocalyptic idea of the shortening of a period of time (cf. *Apoc. Abr.* 29:13; *2 Bar.* 20:1; 4 Ezra 4:26; *1 Enoch* 80:2 [Greek]) in a positive way in order to strengthen the believers. The associated warning against false Messiahs and prophets, who do "signs and wonders" in order—if possible—"to lead astray the *elect*" (Mark 13:22), accentuates an aspect of the apocalyptic affliction that is never directly attested and indicates that, despite God's promise of support, the elect remain endangered. Again in direct dependence on the apocalyptic tradition of the coming of the Son of Man (Dan 7) and the gathering of the elect by the Son of Man (*1 Enoch* 62:2), but without articulating the idea of judgment (*contra 1 Enoch* 62:2; *T. Mos.* 10:10), the Christian apocalypse reaches its high point in the comforting promise of the parousia of the Son of Man, whose angels gather the elect "from the four winds" (Mark 13:24-27; cf. Zech 2:10 LXX; *1 Enoch* 57 [Greek]; 1 Thess 4:13-18).

Matthew alludes to the trial of the faithful when at the conclusion of the parable of the wedding feast (22:1-14; cf. Luke 14:15-24) he gives the eschatological warning against coming before the king without a wedding garment (Matt 22:11-13) and adds: "For many are called, but few are *chosen*" (v. 14). A predestinarian misunderstanding of the belief in election is thus rejected, just as is a particularistic-sectarian misunderstanding of it. The elect are those who have followed the invitation into the kingdom of God through Jesus Christ and have realized their call in a life of faith (cf. Rev 17:14).

In Luke ἐκλεκτός appears as an eschatological designation of the believers in the application of the parable of the judge and the widow (18:1-8): "And will not God vindicate his *elect,* who cry to him day and night?" (v. 7a). The tradition history of vv. 6-8 is very disputed (cf. Schneider; Zimmermann). The promise of an immediate vindication, i.e., of God's intervention on behalf of the elect to bring salvation (vv. 7a-8a), probably corresponds to the original intention of the parable. For the Lukan overcoming of the problem of the delay of the parousia (cf. v. 7b) it is decisive that in v. 8b the view of the promise of salvation in relation to the elect is linked to the required testing before the coming of the Son of Man. Jesus is himself repeatedly described in Luke as the "elect" Son (9:35) or Messiah of God (23:35; → ἐκλέγομαι).

3. Although Paul emphasizes the gracious character of the call to faith (cf. Gal 1:6; 4:9; Rom 1:6) and can also speak of predestination (Rom 8:29f.; 1 Cor 2:7), he calls believers "God's *elect*" only in Rom 8:33—in the context of the eschatological situation of judgment mentioned there. The elect need to fear neither a charge brought against them nor condemnation. Indeed, they have nothing to fear, for God's love has become manifest in Jesus Christ, who is the advocate at God's right hand (8:31-39). The trial situation for the believers is not in view in this song of praise about the salvation history experienced in Jesus Christ. The christological foundation of Paul's belief in election is to be seen also in the formulaic "*elect* [RSV "eminent"] in the Lord," with which the faith of a certain Rufus is distinguished (Rom 16:13).

The new eschatological situation of those who have died and been raised with Christ (Col 3:1-4; cf. Rom 6:1-11), and are released from God's wrath in the realization of the new life (Col 3:6), is assumed in the exhortation: "Put on, then, as (ὡς) God's *chosen ones,* [as] holy and beloved, compassion. . . ." The command is not issued to those "like the elect of God in heaven" (so Lohmeyer ad loc.), but those who, *as* God's elect, holy, and beloved people, have a new life to lead (cf. Eph 1:4; 1 Pet 2:9).

The Pastorals reveal no particular accentuation of the idea of election. In 1 Timothy there is only the reference to "the *elect* angels," who with God and Christ form the heavenly tribunal (5:21; cf. Mark 8:38), before which the church officeholder is responsible for his work. 'Εκλεκτός appears in 2 Tim 2:10 within the perspective of apocalyptic expectation, as it says of the significance of the apostle as a model of suffering: "Therefore I endure everything for the sake of the *elect,* that they also may obtain salvation in Christ Jesus with its eternal glory." It is uncertain here whether an allusion is made to the apocalyptic conception of a fixed amount of suffering (cf. Rev 6:11; Col 1:24); 2 Tim 2:11-13 emphasize the conditions for the attainment of the eschatological salvation. 'Εκλεκτός is also found in the prescript of Titus (1:1) as a formulaic designation for Christians.

4. 1 Peter intends to strengthen the Christians in the midst of an environment which is at least partially hostile. Consequently the idea of election manifests itself in a way that goes beyond any other NT book. At the very beginning the particular situation of the believers within the tension of the two worlds is addressed with the phrase "*chosen* sojourners of the dispersion" (1:1, NAB). Being foreigners is the reverse side of election. This is based on the predetermination of God the Father, consists in sanctification by the Spirit, and has as its goal the realization in obedience of the salvation effected by the death of Christ (v. 2).

The extent to which the election statements are christologically anchored and stand in the service of parenesis is indicated in 1 Pet 2:4-10. The exhortation to come to Christ (v. 4), "that living stone, rejected by men but in God's sight *chosen* and precious," and to be built up "like living stones" "into a spiritual house" (cf. *1 Enoch* 53:6), into "a holy priesthood" (v. 5), is authorized by the scriptural proof about Jesus, the *elect* stone placed in Zion (Isa 28:16)—the stone of salvation for believers and the stone of stumbling for unbelievers (vv. 6-8; Ps 118:22; Isa 8:14f.). The original terms of election, which had been given to Israel, are transferred to the Church in 2:9: "But you are a *chosen* race [Isa 43:20 LXX], a royal priesthood, a holy nation [Exod 19:6 LXX], a people for his [God's] possession [RSV mg.], that you may declare the wonderful deeds of him who called you out of darkness into his marvelous light [cf. Isa 43:21]. Once you were no people [i.e., not the people of God]; once you had not received mercy but now you have received mercy [cf. Hos 1:9f.; 2:23; Rom 9:25f.]."

5. The addressee of 2 John, called the *elect* lady, is to be understood as a (or the) Christian community (v. 1; cf. Titus 1:1; *1 Clem.* 1:1). "The children of your *elect* sister," whom the author greets at the end of his letter (v. 13), are, similarly, the believers in the church in which he is found (cf. 1 Pet 5:13).

Belief in election, which is taken over by the Church only with great caution, mostly in eschatological contexts and entirely with reference to Christ, appears once in Rev 17:14, where it is used of the followers of the lamb who has conquered, i.e., the King of kings: "and those with him are called and *chosen* and faithful." This passage indicates, in accordance with the NT understanding, that election is not automatically associated with calling and that fidelity is an essential motif of the election event (cf. Matt 22:14).

6. The idea of election is expressed in the NT in 7 passages with the noun **ἐκλογή,** *election**, which is not attested in the LXX. It appears 5 times in Paul's letters and once each in Acts and in 2 Peter.

At the beginning of 1 Thessalonians it is evident that Christian belief in election has a universal perspective and is related to history. Here, because of the faith of the Thessalonians, who had come from the Gentile world, Paul is thankful for the election of these "brethren beloved by God" (1:4). This election is manifested in the apostolic preaching accompanied by the work of the Spirit (v. 5; cf. Gal 2:8; 3:2-5; 1 Cor 2:4, etc.) and in the joyful acceptance of God's word by the Thessalonians (vv. 6-10; vv. 2f.).

In discussing the problem of Israel's election in view of the elect people's unbelief toward Christ, Paul strongly emphasizes God's sovereignty (Rom 9–11). He answers the suspicion that God's promises remain unfulfilled with the statement that not all of Abraham's descendants are his children (9:6f.). Scripture gives the proof: Just as Isaac, and not Ishmael, was the bearer of the promise (vv. 7-9; cf. Gen 21), so also God's free act of election is revealed in the preference of Jacob over firstborn Isaac (Rom 9:10-13; cf. Gen 25:23; Mal 1:2f.). "God's will in electing" (ἡ κατ' ἐκλογὴν πρόθεσις τοῦ θεοῦ, Rom 9:11; RSV translates differently), instituted already before the birth of the sons of Isaac and independently of their "works," establishes their function in salvation history. The text does not reflect on their personal salvation. God's freedom to be merciful and to harden (→ σκληρύνω) is indicated also in the call of the new community of salvation composed of Jews and Gentiles (9:14-29).

Despite Israel's guilt in unbelief (Rom 9:30–10:21), God has not rejected "his people whom he foreknew," i.e., the elect people (11:2). As it was earlier in the time of Elijah (1 Kgs 19:10, 14, 18), "so too at the present time there is a remnant, *chosen by grace*" (λεῖμμα κατ' ἐκλογὴν χάριτος, Rom 11:5). In the Jews who believe in Christ Paul sees the *election* (v. 7), which makes God's fidelity to Israel manifest. However, even the hardening of part of Israel has its significance for salvation history: "Through their trespass salvation has come to the Gentiles, so as to make them [RSV "Israel"] jealous" (v. 11). Israel's election has not been terminated, for Gentile Christianity is rooted in Israel, the olive tree (vv. 17-24), and one day "all Israel will be saved" (v. 26). Thus for the present it can be said of Israel: "As regards the gospel they are enemies [RSV adds "of God"], for your sake; but as regards *election* they are beloved for the sake of their forefathers. For the gifts and the call of God are irrevocable" (vv. 28f.).

In Ananias's vision, Paul is described as the instrument of *election* (σκεῦος ἐκλογῆς), the one appointed to confess the Lord's name "before Gentiles and kings and the sons of Israel" (Acts 9:15).

As the latest writing of the NT, 2 Peter can describe salvation in the language of Hellenistic metaphysics as participation in "the divine nature" (1:4). On the one hand 2 Peter emphasizes the ethical effort of those who are to make sure their "calling and *election*" (v. 10), while on the other hand the eschatological perspective is maintained in connection with the term ἐκλογή where 2 Peter sees in the trial of the elect the requisite for entrance into the eternal kingdom of Christ (vv. 10b, 11).

J. Eckert

ἐκλογή, ῆς, ἡ *eklogē* election, choice
→ ἐκλεκτός 6.

ἐκλύομαι *eklyomai* tire, become weak, lose courage*

Mark 8:3 (ἐκλυθήσονται ἐν τῇ ὁδῷ) par. Matt 15:32 (μήποτε ἐκλυθῶσιν), of *exhaustion* (from hunger) while traveling; Gal 6:9: θερίσομεν μὴ ἐκλυόμενοι, "we shall reap, if we do not *lose heart*"; Heb 12:3: ἐκλυόμενοι, *becoming weary* (with κάμνω, "become exhausted"); 12:5: μηδὲ ἐκλύου, do not *"lose courage";* Matt 9:36 v.l.

ἐκμάσσω *ekmassō* wipe off, dry*

In the construction ταῖς θριξὶν . . . ἐκμάσσω (. . . τοὺς πόδας), "*wipe* (the feet) with the hair" (Luke 7:38, 44; John 11:2, 3); ἐκμάσσειν τῷ λεντίῳ, *dry* (the disciples' feet) "with the towel" (John 13:5).

ἐκμυκτηρίζω *ekmyktērizō* mock, deride*

Luke 16:14: ἐξεμυκτήριζον αὐτόν, "they *scoffed at* him"; with no expressed obj.: 23:35: ἐξεμυκτήριζον . . . λέγοντες, they *were full of scorn* and said. . . .

ἐκνεύω *ekneuō* turn aside, escape*

John 5:13 (absolute): Ἰησοῦς ἐξένευσεν, "Jesus *had withdrawn.*"

ἐκνήφω *eknēphō* become sober*

1 Cor 15:34: ἐκνήψατε δικαίως, *"Come to your right mind,* and sin no more."

ἑκούσιος, 3 *hekousios* voluntarily*

Phlm 14: κατὰ ἑκούσιον, "of your own *free will*" (opposed to κατὰ ἀνάγκην).

ἑκουσίως *hekousiōs* deliberately, willingly, recklessly*

Heb 10:26: ἑκουσίως γὰρ ἁμαρτανόντων ἡμῶν, "for if we sin *deliberately*"; 1 Pet 5:2: μὴ ἀναγκαστῶς ἀλλὰ ἑκουσίως, "not by constraint but *willingly.*"

ἔκπαλαι *ekpalai* long ago, for a long time*

2 Pet 2:3: *"from of old";* 3:5: ὅτι οὐρανοὶ ἦσαν ἔκπαλαι, "that . . . heavens existed *long ago.*"

ἐκπειράζω *ekpeirazō* tempt
→ πειράζω.

ἐκπέμπω *ekpempō* send out*

Pass. in Acts 13:4: ἐκπεμφθέντες ὑπὸ τοῦ ἁγίου πνεύματος, "*being sent out* by the Holy Spirit"; act. in 17:10.

ἐκπερισσῶς *ekperissōs* extremely; with fervor*

Mark 14:31: ὁ δὲ ἐκπερισσῶς ἐλάλει, "But he said *vehemently.*"

ἐκπετάννυμι *ekpetannymi* extend, stretch out*

Rom 10:21: ἐξεπέτασα τὰς χεῖράς μου (citing Isa 65:2 LXX), "I *have held out* my hands."

ἐκπηδάω *ekpēdaō* burst loose, rush out*

Acts 14:14: ἐξεπήδησαν εἰς τὸν λαόν, they *"rushed out* among the multitude"; 10:25 D.

ἐκπίπτω *ekpiptō* fall; run aground; drift; fail, lose validity, cease*

Lit.: W. BAUDER, *DNTT* I, 608-11. — E. HAENCHEN, *The Acts of the Apostles* (1971) 705f. — W. MICHAELIS, *TDNT* VI, 161-73, esp. 167f.

1. Half of the 10 NT occurrences of ἐκπίπτω appear in Acts (3 times as a nautical t.t.), while the other half are in the Epistles (once each in Romans, Galatians, James, 1 Peter, and 2 Peter). The word is broader in meaning in the NT than in the LXX.

2. a) The meaning *fall* in 1 Pet 1:24 (citing Isa 40:6f.) and Jas 1:11 (no direct citation) is derived from the LXX. In Jas 1:11 an independent clause is taken up and explained in the next clause in order to interpret v. 10. The flower is the beauty of the grass, which passes away like the rich man. The language of Scripture is used to make a moral point. In 1 Pet 1:24 the word characterizes earthly transitoriness in contrast to the abiding word of God. In Acts 12:7 the vb. describes the supernatural deliverance of Peter from his bonds; cf. Mark 13:25 (v.l. for → πίπτω). In Acts 27:31 it probably has another meaning (→ b).

b) In Acts 27:17, 26, 29 ἐκπίπτω means *run aground,* while in v. 32 it means *drift.* The first danger the ship faced was that it might *run on* the Great Syrtis (v. 17), but later Paul prophesied that they would *run aground* on an island (v. 26), where—because of the danger of *running aground* on the rocks (v. 29)—the seamen attempted to escape in a boat which the soldiers then allowed to *drift away.* This understanding of v. 32 gives a better meaning for → ἐάω.

c) In 2 Pet 3:17 and Gal 5:4 *fall away* has two different senses. The first passage refers to a fall from an earlier position through the seduction of false teachers; the second passage to a fall from grace in which one follows the law of works, in place of grace, in order to be justified by the law (cf. Rom 6:19; 11:5f.; Gal 2:21; → χάρις). The place which has been lost is described in Rom 5:2 as a condition determined by God's grace, but not unconditionally as a realm from which we could fall. It is comparable to faith. Rev 2:5 (v.l. for → πίπτω) refers to a fall from previous faithfulness.

d) In Rom 9:6 ἐκπίπτω has the meaning—not attested in the LXX—*lose validity, fail.* Paul states that God's promises to Israel as a whole *have* not *failed* on account of the present rejection of the gospel by some Israelites. Chs. 9–11 explain in what respect this is not the case. In 1 Cor 13:8 v.l. (Koine D G etc.) ἐκπίπτω has the meaning *cease.*

M. E. Glasswell

ἐκπλέω *ekpleō* set sail*

With εἰς, "toward" (Acts 15:39; 18:18); with ἀπό, "from" (20:6).

ἐκπληρόω *ekplēroō* fill up, fulfill*

In the NT only fig.: Acts 13:33: ὁ θεὸς ἐκπεπλήρωκεν τοῖς τέκνοις αὐτῶν ἡμῖν, God *"has fulfilled* [the promise] to us their children"; cf. also *Herm. Vis.* iii.7.6.

ἐκπλήρωσις, εως, ἡ *ekplērōsis* fulfillment, completion*

Acts 21:26: τὴν ἐκπλήρωσιν τῶν ἡμερῶν τοῦ ἁγνισμοῦ, the *completion* of the days of purification. Luke probably thinks here of the completion of the days of Paul's Nazirite vow. → ἁγνός 3.

ἐκπλήσσομαι *ekplēssomai* be beside oneself, be overwhelmed, be astonished*

In the NT this word is (as in the LXX) always pass., and is usually used of the reaction of bystanders to Jesus' teaching and deeds (exceptions are in Luke 2:48; Acts 13:12, but the latter is close: ἐκπλησσόμενος ἐπὶ τῇ διδαχῇ τοῦ κυρίου, *"astonished* at the teaching of the Lord"). In Matthew it always appears in association with Jesus' teaching: ἐξεπλήσσοντο . . . ἐπὶ τῇ διδαχῇ αὐτοῦ (Matt 7:28 par. Mark 1:22/Luke 4:32; Matt 22:33; Mark 11:18 [sg.]); ἐδίδασκεν αὐτοὺς . . . ὥστε ἐκπλήσσεσθαι αὐτοὺς καὶ λέγειν (Matt 13:54 par. Mark 6:2); ἀκούσαντες δὲ οἱ μαθηταὶ ἐξεπλήσσοντο σφόδρα (Matt 19:25 par. Mark 10:26: περισσῶς ἐξεπλήσσοντο, they were very *frightened*). In response to healings: . . . ἐπὶ τῇ μεγαλειότητι τοῦ θεοῦ, "all *were astonished* at the majesty of God"; absolute: ὑπερπερισσῶς ἐξεπλήσσοντο, "they *were astonished* beyond measure" (Mark 7:37).

ἐκπνέω *ekpneō* breathe out, breathe one's last, die*

Of the death of Jesus: ἐξέπνευσεν, *he expired* (literally "breathed out his life"; Mark 15:37 par. Luke 23:46; Mark 15:39).

ἐκπορεύομαι *ekporeuomai* go out, come out*

There are 33 occurrences of this vb. in the NT, which is esp. common in Mark (11 occurrences) and in Revelation (8 occurrences). It is frequently used in the Gospels in the literal sense: *come out* (from a place): With ἀπό (Matt 20:29; Mark 10:46); with ἐκεῖθεν (Mark 6:11); with ἔξω (11:19); with ἐκ (13:1; cf. ἐκ τοῦ θρόνου ἐκπορεύομαι, *burst forth, burst out* from the throne, Rev 4:5; 22:1). With the goal indicated by πρός (Mark 1:5 par. Matt 3:5); by εἰς (Mark 10:17; John 5:29); εἰσπορευόμενος καὶ ἐκπορευόμενος εἰς Ἰερουσαλήμ, "*he went* in and *out*... at Jerusalem" (Acts 9:28). With no indication of direction (Luke 3:7); ἐν τάχει ἐκπορεύεσθαι, "*go* there shortly" (Acts 25:4).

Used metaphorically and figuratively: frequently in the construction ἐκπορεύεσθαι ἐκ τοῦ στόματος, "*proceed* from the mouth" (Matt 15:11, 18; Luke 4:22; Eph 4:29; Rev 1:16; 9:17, 18 [pl.]; 11:5; 19:15; 19:21 v.l.); διὰ στόματος θεοῦ (Matt 4:4); ἐκ τοῦ ἀνθρώπου (Mark 7:15, 20); ἔσωθεν ... ἐκ τῆς καρδίας (v. 21); ἔσωθεν (v. 23); with εἰς (v. 19); ἐξεπορεύετο ἦχος περὶ αὐτοῦ εἰς πάντα τόπον, "reports of him *went out* into every place" (Luke 4:37; cf. Rev 16:14); τὸ πνεῦμα... παρὰ τοῦ πατρὸς ἐκπορεύεται, "the Spirit... *proceeds* from the Father" (John 15:26); with no indication of direction: ὥστε ... τά τε πνεύματα τά πονηρὰ ἐκπορεύεσθαι, "so that ... the evil spirits *came out*" (Acts 19:12; cf. Matt 17:21 C Koine D *pl* lat).

ἐκπορνεύω *ekporneuō* be very immoral*

Jude 7: ἐκπορνεύσασαι, of Sodom, Gomorrah, and the surrounding cities, which *had given themselves over to immorality.*

ἐκπτύω *ekptyō* spit out*

Gal 4:14 with a fig. meaning: τὸν πειρασμὸν ὑμῶν ἐν τῇ σαρκί μου οὐκ ἐξουθενήσατε οὐδὲ ἐξεπτύσατε, "you never showed the least sign of *being* revolted or *disgusted* by my disease that was such a trial for you" (JB; οὐδὲ ἐξεπτύσατε does not appear in 𝔭[46]!).

ἐκριζόω *ekrizoō* uproot, pull out by the roots*

Of weeds together with wheat (Matt 13:29); πᾶσα φυτεία ... ἐκριζωθήσεται, "*will be rooted up* [by God]" (15:13); ἐκριζώθητι, "*be rooted up,*" of a fig tree (Luke 17:6); δένδρα ... ἄκαρπα δὶς ἀποθανόντα ἐκριζωθέντα, "fruitless trees ..., twice dead, *uprooted,*" in Jude 12 as an image for ungodly people who have made their way into the Church (cf. also v. 5, τὸ δεύτερον).

ἔκστασις, εως, ἡ *ekstasis* a state of being outside oneself; "transport"

1. NT evidence and definition in the history of religions — 2. Ἔκστασις as a form-critical element indicating admiration in early Christian miracle stories — 3. Ἔκστασις as visionary "transport"

Lit.: H. R. Balz and G. Wanke, *TDNT* IX, 189-219. — G. Bertram, *TDNT* III, 4-7, 27-42. — H. Dörrie, *KP* II, 226. — G. van der Leeuw, *Phänomenologie der Religion* (1977). — A. Müller, *HWP* II, 434. — A. Oepke, *TDNT* II, 449-60; V, 220-38. — F. Pfister, *RAC* IV, 944-87. — E. Rohde, *Psyche* ([2]1898; reprint 1961). — A. Schimmel, *RGG* II, 410-12. — G. Theissen, *Urchristliche Wundergeschichten* (1974).

1. The noun ἔκστασις (Mark 5:42; 16:8; Luke 5:26; Acts 3:10; 10:10; 11:5; 22:17) occurs less frequently than the vb. → ἐξίστημι/ἐξιστάνω (not only) in the NT. Even the vb. appears only in the narrative sections of the NT (the Synoptics and Acts). The single exception, 2 Cor 5:13, is interesting because the contrast there of ἐκστῆναι to σωφρονεῖν (be in one's right mind) gives a negative meaning to the former. If a low estimate of ἔκστασις is more typical for Philo than for the NT, it is to be emphasized that ἔκστασις does not occur in the NT in theological and ethical reflections. One finds scarcely more than thin, uncertain traces of "ecstasy" in the full sense which it has in the history of religions (cf. Pfister; Schimmel; van der Leeuw, index s.v. *Ekstase*; Rohde II, index s.v. ἔκστασις). These traces are to be regarded as merely edifying and apologetic concessions to Hellenistic readers. Despite the enthusiastic experience of the Spirit, one should simply not render ἔκστασις in the NT with "ecstasy"; such an apparent nontranslation leads to overburdened associations.

Linguistically the LXX has certainly had an influence, at least in part. Philo is particularly to be observed, not so much because of his own position regarding the phenomenon, but because of the nuances of meaning for ἔκστασις in his time attested by him. Alongside *All.* ii.19, 31 (on Gen 2:21) and the quite extreme negative evaluations in *Cher.* 69, 116; *Plant.* 147; *Ebr.* 15; *Spec. Leg.* iii.99; *Vit. Cont.* 40, the section *Her.* 249-65 (on Gen 15:12) deserves special notice because of the four types described there (each with examples). Whereas the first of the four may be classified among the unfavorable statements, the second is important for the NT (→ 2): ἔκστασις as σφοδρὰ κατάπληξις (intense confusion, perhaps about something unusual; cf. also Περὶ ὕψους, 1:4; 38:5). For the visionary ἔκστασις in Acts both of the other meanings are to be considered: ἠρεμία διανοίας/νοῦ (rest for the spirit) and prophetic ἔνθεος κατοκωχή τε καὶ μανία (divinely inspired possession and delirium), which distinguishes the wise and the righteous and in which the divine pneuma takes the place of the human νοῦς.

2. In Mark 5:42 vb. and noun are connected in a *figura etymologica* (BDF §§153; 198), in a way reminiscent of LXX language (Gen 27:33; Ezek 26:26; 27:35; 32:10). The addition of μεγάλη (cf. Dan 10:7 Θ) with the dat. strengthens the expression. The full *being outside oneself* describes "the effect of captivation caused by the epiphany experienced in the miracle" (R. Pesch, *Markusevangelium* [HTKNT] I, ad loc.). Likewise as an aspect of the motif of admiration (Theissen 78-81), associated with the distinguishing mark of acclamation, ἔκστασις is decisive in the reaction to healing and the forgiveness of sins in Luke 5:26 (cf. the vb., 2:12). In Acts 3:10 ἔκστασις is connected with → θάμβος (astonishment), which indicates that the arrangement of the Synoptic healing miracles has influenced the narrative.

Ἔκστασις takes on a somewhat different color, i.e., that of fear, in connection with → τρόμος (trembling, otherwise connected with → φόβος) in the much-discussed end of

Mark (16:8). It is uncertain what is meant by the reference to the reaction of the women (an empty tomb? an appearance of angels?), whether historical experiences or only motifs from apocalyptic literature are reflected in their *amazement*.

3. Only with great reserve and with careful consideration of the conceptual nuances (→ 1) can one speak of visionary "ecstasy" (BAGD s.v.; "trance": Liddell/Scott 520) in the case of the experiences of Peter or Paul in Acts 10:10 (cf. the dependent 11:5) and 22:17. Ἔκστασις is schematically so connected with prayer and vision that little independent weight is given to describing the process as such. Along with the dream (→ ὄναρ), ἔκστασις is not the goal, but rather an apocalyptic means of presenting revelations.

M. Lattke

ἐκστρέφω *ekstrephō* pervert, confuse*

Titus 3:11: ἐξέστραπται ὁ τοιοῦτος, "such a [i.e., a heretic, v. 10] *is perverted.*"

ἐκσῴζω *eksǭzō* save

Acts 27:39B* C 88 cop[sa, bo] arm: ἐκσῶσαι in place of ἐξῶσαι (→ ἐξωθέω).

ἐκταράσσω *ektarassō* excite, stir up*

Acts 16:20: ἐκταράσσουσιν ἡμῶν τὴν πόλιν, "they *are disturbing* our city."

ἐκτείνω *ekteinō* reach out*

There are 16 occurrences in the NT, of which 6 are in Matthew. The vb. is particularly frequent in the construction ἐκτείνειν τὴν χεῖρα, "*stretch out* one's hand" (sg. in 13 of the occurrences: Matt 8:3; 12:13 bis, 49; 14:31; 26:51; Mark 1:41; 3:5 bis; Luke 5:13; 6:10; Acts 4:30; 26:1; also pl.: Luke 22:53; John 21:18). It is used in connection with the grasping of the hand of a person in healing the hand or the whole person. Extending the hands (pl.) can be a gesture of helplessness (ὅταν δὲ γηράσῃς, ἐκτείνεις τὰς χεῖράς σου, "when you are old, you will *stretch out* your hands, and another will gird you and carry you . . ." [John 21:18]) or of hostility (ἐπ' ἐμέ, against me [Luke 22:53]). In Acts 26:1 Paul, though a prisoner, takes the posture of the ancient orator: ἐκτείνας τὴν χεῖρα ἀπελογεῖτο, he "*stretched out* his hand and made his defense" (cf. Apuleius *Metamorphoses* ii.21). Acts 27:30 uses the vb. in a t.t. of seafaring: ἀγκύρας μελλόντων ἐκτείνειν, "under pretense of *laying out* anchors," i.e., of going a small distance out from the bow in the lifeboat to set the anchors (cf. E. Haenchen, *The Acts of the Apostles* [1971] ad loc.).

H. Balz

ἐκτελέω *ekteleō* complete, finish*

Used absolutely in Luke 14:29f. of someone who has laid a foundation for a tower and then "*is* not *able* to finish" it (μὴ ἰσχύοντος ἐκτελέσαι, v. 29; οὐκ ἴσχυσεν ἐκτελέσαι, v. 30).

ἐκτένεια, ας, ἡ *ekteneia* perseverance*

Acts 26:7: ἐν ἐκτενείᾳ, *"earnestly"*; 12:5 D.

ἐκτενής, 2 *ektenēs* persistent, continuous*

1 Pet 4:8: τὴν . . . ἀγάπην ἐκτενῆ ἔχοντες, cultivate love *continuously*; Acts 12:5 v.l.

ἐκτενῶς *ektenōs* constantly, fervently*

Acts 12:5: προσευχὴ δὲ ἦν ἐκτενῶς (v.l. ἐκτενής) γινομένη, prayer was *fervently* made; 1 Pet 1:22: ἀλλήλους ἀγαπήσατε ἐκτενῶς, "love one another *earnestly*"; comparative in Luke 22:44: ἐκτενέστερον προσηύχετο, "he prayed *more earnestly.*"

ἐκτίθημι *ektithēmi* explain; expose*

In the NT only in Acts: *explain:* 11:4 (ἐξετίθετο); 18:26 (ἐξέθεντο); 28:23 (ἐξετίθετο), regularly with the dat.; *be exposed:* 7:21: ἐκτεθέντος δὲ αὐτοῦ, "when he [the three-month-old Moses] *was exposed.*"

ἐκτινάσσω *ektinassō* shake off; shake out*

Mark 6:11: ἐκτινάξατε τὸν χοῦν, "*shake off* the dust"; par. Matt 10:14: ἐκτινάξατε τὸν κονιορτὸν τῶν ποδῶν ὑμῶν, "*shake off* the dust from your feet" (i.e., which is on your feet); cf. Acts 13:51; Acts 18:6: ἐκτιναξάμενος τὰ ἱμάτια, "he *shook out* his garments."

ἕκτος, 3 *hektos* sixth*

1. Ἕκτος occurs 14 times in the NT, most frequently in the Gospels (twice in Matthew, once in Mark, 3 times in Luke, twice in John), once in Acts, and 5 times in Revelation.

2. It is used 7 times for the time of the day; the *sixth* hour is *noon.* In the parable of the laborers in the vineyard workers are enlisted at equal intervals between the first and the last hours, including the middle of the workday (Matt 20:5), but the workers all receive the same pay. In Matt 27:45; Mark 15:33; and Luke 23:44 darkness falls at the *sixth* hour; according to Mark this took place from the midpoint of the time during which Jesus hung upon the cross until his death. According to John 19:14 Pilate undertook a last attempt to save Jesus at the *sixth* hour. Jesus thus died in the afternoon, while the Passover lambs

were being slaughtered, and was thus perhaps regarded as a Passover lamb as well as the true unleavened bread, which was probably eaten at that hour. John 4:6 can be brought into connection with this figuring of time, since Jesus' being thirsty, but not the coming of the woman, is understandable (cf. the word of judgment in v. 10). Acts 10:9 refers to prayer at noon (in accordance with Ps 55:17f.; cf. Dan 6:10; *Did.* 8:3), which of course is not rooted in Jewish law.

Luke 1:26, 36, by referring to the *sixth* month, connects Jesus' birth with that of his predecessor, John the Baptist.

3. In Revelation the word is used of a) the *sixth* seal (→ σφραγίς) opened by the lamb (6:12); b) the *sixth* angel (ἄγγελος) to blow his trumpet (→ σάλπιγξ; 9:13f.); c) the *sixth* angel to empty his bowl (φιάλη; 16:12); and d) the precious stone (σάρδιον) which portrays the *sixth* of the twelve foundations (→ θεμέλιος) of the heavenly Jerusalem (21:20). In the first three passages it is used for the sixth of seven—the perfect number; in the last it is used for the sixth of twelve—the symbol of the new Israel.

M. E. Glasswell

ἐκτός *ektos* outside, other than, except*

As improper prep. governing gen.: *with the exception of, apart from:* Acts 26:22: ἐκτὸς . . . ὧν, "nothing but"; 1 Cor 15:27 (cf. BDF §216.2); *outside:* ἐκτὸς τοῦ σώματος (1 Cor 6:18; 2 Cor 12:2; 12:3 v.l.; cf. BDF §184). As an adv.: Matt 23:26: τὸ ἐκτὸς αὐτοῦ (with μέρος understood), "the *outside* of the cup." Three times in the construction ἐκτὸς εἰ μή, *unless* (with ind., 1 Cor 15:2; with subjunc., 14:5; without the vb., 1 Tim 5:19: ἐκτὸς εἰ μὴ ἐπί, "*except for*"; cf. BDF §376).

ἐκτρέπομαι *ektrepomai* turn away; avoid; be out of joint*

In the NT always pass. with mid. meaning. Ἐξετράπησαν εἰς ματαιολογίαν, they "*have wandered away* into vain discussion" (1 Tim 1:6); ἐξετράπησαν ὀπίσω τοῦ σατανᾶ, they "have . . . *strayed* after Satan" (5:15); ἐκτρεπόμενος τὰς βεβήλους κενοφωνίας, "*avoid[ing]* the godless chatter" (6:20). Heb 12:13: ἵνα μὴ τὸ χωλὸν ἐκτραπῇ, ἰαθῇ δὲ μᾶλλον, a medical t.t., "so that what is lame may not continue to *be* [RSV "be put] *put out of joint* but rather be healed"; linguistically and according to the context also possible is "not *depart from the way*" (e.g., Xenophon *An.* iv.5.15; cf. BAGD s.v.; O. Michel, *Hebräer* [KEK] ad loc.).

ἐκτρέφω *ektrephō* nourish, bring up (children)*

Eph 5:29: ἐκτρέφει καὶ θάλπει, he "*nourishes* and cherishes"; 6:4: ἐκτρέφετε αὐτά, "*bring* them *up.*"

ἔκτρομος, 2 *ektromos* trembling

Heb 12:21 ℵ D* in place of ἔντρομος.

ἔκτρωμα, ατος, τό *ektrōma* miscarriage*

Lit.: J. Blank, *Paulus und Jesus* (1968) 185-97. — T. Boman, *Die Jesusüberlieferung im Lichte der neueren Volkskunde* (1967) 236-40. — E. Güttgemanns, *Der leidende Apostel und sein Herr* (1966) 88-93. — H. Müller and C. Brown, *DNTT* I, 182-84. — J. Munck, "Paulus tanquam abortivus, 1 Cor. 15:8," *NT Essays* (FS T. W. Manson; 1959) 180-93. — P. von der Osten-Sacken, "Die Apologie des paulinischen Apostolats in 1 Kor 15, 1-11," *ZNW* 64 (1973) 245-62 (250-57). — Bibliography up to 1939 in BAGD ad loc.; for further bibliography see *TWNT* X, 1072.

Ἔκτρωμα (related to vb. ἐκτιτρώσκω, "procure an abortion") occurs in the NT only in 1 Cor 15:8. In the LXX it appears three times (Num 12:12; Job 3:16; Eccl 6:3) with the otherwise attested meaning *miscarriage, stillbirth*; outside the canon the meaning "premature birth" is attested also (BAGD s.v.; Munck 184ff.).

In 1 Cor 15:8 the translation "premature birth" (Güttgemanns 90 with n. 196, etc.) is excluded because it would stand in contradiction to the preceding information, according to which Jesus appeared to Paul "last of all." The remaining translations *miscarriage* or *stillbirth* emphasize the nothingness of the one who is named. As the reason in v. 9 indicates, Paul uses this metaphor to interpret himself as persecutor of the community of Jesus before his conversion. The memory of this—introduced by the judgment "least of the apostles," which interprets the metaphor of v. 8—makes it possible for him to explain his call as a radical act of God's grace empowered by the success of the mission (v. 10; cf. Blank 192ff.). While he removes all doubt in this way about the reality of the appearance of Jesus Christ which served as the basis of his call, he defends the legitimacy of his late apostleship alongside the authorities previously named (vv. 3ff.).

The article before ἔκτρωμα thus does not demand the assumption that Paul has taken up a derogatory name from his opponents (agreeing with Munck 182, who gives a different reason; *contra* Boman, Güttgemanns, et al.). Rather "it gives to the figure a relationship to that which precedes and designates Paul as the one who is ἔκτρωμα in relation to the ones who have already been named" (P. Bachmann, *Der erste Brief des Paulus an die Korinther* [1921] 437). In this sense one may paraphrase: "(to me) as, so to speak, the *miscarriage* (among the apostles)" (so in detail Osten-Sacken 252f.).

The use of σκύβαλα in Phil 3:8 is comparable. Ign. *Rom.* 9:2 alludes to 1 Cor 15:8.

P. von der Osten-Sacken

ἐκφέρω *ekpherō* carry out, lead out, bring out*

Literally *carry out,* with acc. obj. (Luke 15:22; Acts

5:6, 9, 10, 15); ἐξήνεγκεν αὐτὸν ἔξω τῆς κώμης, he "*led him* out of the village" (Mark 8:23); ὅτι οὐδὲ ἐξενεγκεῖν τι δυνάμεθα, "we cannot *take* anything *out* of the world" (1 Tim 6:7); fig. of vegetation that the earth *brings forth:* ἐκφέρουσα in Heb 6:8.

ἐκφεύγω *ekpheugō* flee, escape*

Used absolutely: *escape:* Acts 16:27; absolute and fig.: *escape* (God's judgment): 1 Thess 5:3: οὐ μὴ ἐκφυγῶσιν; Heb 2:3: πῶς ἡμεῖς ἐκφευξόμεθα; 12:25: εἰ γὰρ ἐκεῖνοι οὐκ ἐξέφυγον; with acc. obj.: *escape:* Luke 21:36: ἐκφυγεῖν ταῦτα πάντα τὰ μέλλοντα; Rom 2:3: ὅτι σὺ ἐκφεύξῃ τὸ κρίμα τοῦ θεοῦ; 2 Cor 11:33: ἐξέφυγον τὰς χεῖρας αὐτοῦ; with ἐκ: Acts 19:16.

ἐκφοβέω *ekphobeō* terrify, intimidate*

2 Cor 10:9: ὡς ἂν ἐκφοβεῖν ὑμᾶς διὰ τῶν ἐπιστολῶν, as if I *wanted to intimidate* you with letters.

ἔκφοβος, 2 *ekphobos* terrified, afraid*

Mark 9:6: ἔκφοβοι γὰρ ἐγένοντο, "for they were *exceedingly afraid*"; Heb 12:21: ἔκφοβός εἰμι καὶ ἔντρομος (cf. Deut 9:19), I am *full of fear* and trembling.

ἐκφύω *ekphyō* put forth*

Mark 13:28 par. Matt 24:32: ὅταν . . . ὁ κλάδος . . . ἐκφύῃ τὰ φύλλα, "as soon as its branch . . . *puts forth* its leaves."

ἐκχέω, ἐκχύννω *ekcheō, ekchynnō* pour out*

1. Occurrences in the NT — 2. Basic meaning — 3. Phrases with special significance

Lit.: BAGD ad loc.; J. BEHM, *TDNT* II, 467-69. — BDF §§73; 74; 101 (s.v. χύν[ν]ειν). — B. KEDAR-KOPFSTEIN, *TDOT* III, 234-50. — R. PESCH, *Das Markusevangelium* (HTKNT) II (1977), 358-60.

1. Alongside the form ἐκχέω, used since Homer, which appears in the NT 16 times, both act. and pass. (Matt 9:17; John 2:15; Acts 2:17, 18, 33; Rom 3:15; Titus 3:6; Rev 16:1, 2, 3, 4, 6, 8, 10; 12:17), the pass. of the Hellenistic form ἐκχύννω appears 11 times (Matt 23:35; 26:28; Mark 14:24; Luke 5:37; 11:50; 22:20; Acts 1:18; 10:45; 22:20; Rom 5:5; Jude 11).

2. Ἐκχέω/ἐκχύννω appears with its basic meaning when it is said that wine (Matt 9:17 par. Luke 5:37), the coins of the money changers (John 2:15), or the contents of a bowl (God's wrath: Rev 16:1, 2, 3, 4, 8, 10, 12, 17) is *poured out* or *spilled out.* The phrase "all of his [Judas'] bowels *gushed out*" (Acts 1:18) is known from the OT (cf. 2 Kgs 20:10). Jude 11 associates with ἐκχέω/ἐκχύννω the idea of a person giving himself or herself to an object or a person: they "*abandon themselves* for the sake of gain to Balaam's error."

3. Ἐκχέω/ἐκχύννω is used formulaically with the obj. αἷμα, "blood," with the blood considered "the bearer of personally differentiated life, the vital element in the individual" (Kedar-Kopfstein 240). Αἷμα ἐκχεῖν/ἐκχύννειν means "destroy a life," "commit a murder," "kill," as in the OT (e.g., Gen 9:6; Ezek 18:10, etc.) so also in the NT. Rom 3:15 uses the language of Isa 59:7 (cf. Ps 13:3 LXX) to lament the murderous conduct of humanity. In the framework of a pronouncement of woe on the Pharisees, Q recalls the many murders, extending from the murder of Abel (Gen 4:8-10) to the last murder of a prophet mentioned in Scripture (2 Chr 24:20-22), and threatens that the blood *shed* innocently will be avenged on "this generation." According to Rev 16:6 mankind has *shed* the blood of both the saints and the prophets. Rev 16:1, 2, 3, 4, 8, 10, 12, 17 contrasts this *shedding* with the "pouring out" of God's wrath in the judgment.

Αἷμα ἐκχεῖν/ἐκχύννειν takes on theological significance in connection with ὑπέρ in the words of the Lord's Supper: Mark 14:24 par. Matt 26:28/Luke 22:20 (omission by D is secondary) proclaim that Jesus' "blood . . . *is poured out* for many" ("for you" in Luke 22:20 is redactional). In an allusion to Exod 24:8 ("the blood of the covenant") and with a "sovereign and free" (Pesch 359) use of Isa 53:12 (pertinent material!) the death of Jesus is interpreted in connection with the conception of "the atoning blood of the covenant" and "that of the vicarious offering of one's life with universal atoning results" (Pesch 359).

With ἐπί + acc. ἐκχέω/ἐκχύννω expresses metaphorically the *pouring out* of "divine gifts or powers" (Behm 468). According to Joel 3:1f. LXX God will *pour out* his Spirit like rain in the end time (cf. 2:23f.; Isa 32:15) "on all people." Acts 2:16ff. sees this OT prophecy fulfilled in the Pentecost miracle and emphasizes (v. 33) that Jesus "*has poured out* this [the Spirit] which you see and hear." This pouring out of the Spirit was present for the early Christian both repeatedly in the form of the Pentecost experience of glossolalia (10:45) and in baptism, in which God "*has poured out* [his Spirit] upon us richly through Jesus Christ our Savior" (Titus 3:6). Rom 5:5 refers to the mystery of the pouring out of the Spirit: "God's love *has been poured* into our hearts" (cf. Ps 44:3 LXX; Sir 18:11).

F. G. Untergassmair

ἐκχωρέω *ekchōreō* withdraw, escape*

Luke 21:21: ἐκχωρείτωσαν, they *should flee.*

ἐκψύχω *ekpsychō* breathe one's last, die*

Acts 5:5, 10; 12:23: ἐξέψυξεν, he/she *died.*

ἑκών, 3 *hekōn* voluntarily, of one's own accord*

Rom 8:20: οὐχ ἑκοῦσα, ἀλλὰ διὰ τὸν ὑποτάξαντα, "not *of its own will,* but for the sake of [RSV "by the will of"] him who subjected it"; 1 Cor 9:17: εἰ γὰρ ἑκὼν τοῦτο πράσσω, "for if I do this *of my own will.*"

ἐλαία, ας, ἡ *elaia* olive; olive tree*
ἐλαιών, ῶνος, ὁ *elaiōn* olive grove; the Mount of Olives*

Lit.: G. Dalman, *Jerusalem und sein Gelände* (1930) 21-56. — H. Frehen, *BL* 1258-62. — V. Hamp and H. Haag, *LTK* VII, 1138f. — E. Segelberg and G. Sauer, *BHH* II, 1337-40.

1. Of the 15 occurrences of ἐλαία in the NT, 9 are in the phrase τὸ ὄρος τῶν ἐλαιῶν (Mark 11:1; 13:3; 14:26; Matt 21:1; 24:3; 26:30; Luke 19:37; 22:39; John 8:1) for the *Mount of Olives,* which is a rise *ca.* 800 m. high to the north, northeast, and east of Jerusalem. It "had economic significance for old Jerusalem primarily because of its olives" (G. Dalman, *Orte und Wege Jesu* [1924] 278). According to the witness of the Gospels Jesus repeatedly stopped here. Luke 19:29 and 21:37 understand the absolute Ἐλαιῶν as the name of the mountain. Ἐλαιών is attested indisputably only in Acts 1:12. In Luke 19:29; 21:37 Ἐλαιῶν is the preferred reading (rather than ἐλαιών).

2. Rom 11:17, 24 is probably dependent on conceptions of Israel as the *olive tree* (cf. Jer 11:16). In Romans the Gentile Christians are wild seedlings which have been engrafted (cf. the related image in *b. Yebam.* 63a in Billerbeck III, 292). Branches of the wild olive are not grafted onto domestic olive trees, but rather the other way around; probably Paul contradicts actual practice not so much because of ignorance of the process as the transformation of the metaphor by the subject matter. His use of the metaphor is significant for determining the situation behind Romans (cf. H.-J. van der Minde, *Schrift und Tradition bei Paulus* [1976] 194-97).

Jas 3:12 uses the figure of an olive-bearing fig tree and a grape vine which bears figs to support his statement about misuse of the tongue in v. 10 (cf. Matt 7:16). In Stoicism the fig tree and the grape vine have a similar function (see M. Dibelius and H. Greeven, *James* [Hermeneia] 204f.).

In Rev 11:4 the two prophetic witnesses are called ἐλαῖαι, *olive trees.* The author probably did not understand this expression merely as an adoption of Zech 4:3; he probably also connected the olive tree with a positive allusion to anointing and thereby the charisma of these prophets (cf. H. Kraft, *Offenbarung* [HNT] 157). While the two witnesses have frequently been identified with Moses and Elijah, Kraft argues that identification of the two witnesses is impossible.

I. Broer

ἔλαιον, ου, τό *elaion* olive oil; oil; liquified fat*

1. Oil as a means of healing — 2. Anointing — 3. Oil as merchandise — 4. The use of oil in lamps

Lit.: R. J. Forbes, *Studies in Ancient Technology* III/1. *Cosmetics and Perfumes in Antiquity* (1965). — O. Haas, "Das Öl und die ersten Indoeuropäer Griechenlands," *Lingua Posnaniensis* 7 (1959) 54-76. — E. Kutsch, *Salbung als Rechtsakt im AT und im Alten Orient* (1963). — H. Schlier, *TDNT* II, 470-73.

Of the numerous associations in which ἔλαιον is used in ancient literature (cf. O. Böcher, *Dämonenfurcht und Dämonenabwehr* [1970] 216f. and Forbes 2ff.), only four appear in the NT.

1. The surprising report of the healing of the sick by the disciples' anointing them with oil (Mark 6:7, 13) presupposes the use of oil as a means of healing by the Jews; wine and vinegar were also used (so Luke 10:34; cf. Josephus *Ant.* xvii.172; *B.J.* i.657; Billerbeck I, 426ff.; II, 11f.). The report probably refers to more than an ordinary natural means of healing, since the exorcisms mentioned in the parallel clause go back to the authority granted by Jesus (certainly to speak with W. Grundmann, *Markus* [THKNT] 125 of a sacramental meaning is to go too far).

In Jas 5:14(f.) the healing effect is traced back more to the prayer than to the anointing; likewise here the oil can in no way be seen as a natural means of healing, for the anointing takes place with the appeal to the name of the exalted Jesus. Certainly one cannot speak here of an "instruction" from James (so F. Mussner, *Jakobus* [HTKNT] 220); instead the practice of anointing the sick with an appeal to the name of Jesus is assumed by the author as already in existence.

2. That anointing with oil was not done by Jesus' host (Luke 7:46) cannot be considered a violation of the rules of propriety, since the texts necessary to establish such a conclusion are scarcely sufficient. Thus it is agreed that the anointing of Jesus by the woman should be considered a service of love beyond the normal measure.

The use in Heb 1:9 of the passage from Ps 45:7f., which is difficult to explain, is probably to be interpreted in accordance with the evidence in Heb 1:13 as pointing to the act of exaltation as appointment to sonship. With this citation the "proof" is furnished for the sonship which is affirmed in the exordium in vv. 1-4 (cf. E. Grässer, EKKNT (V) 3 [1971] 71). "Oil of gladness" refers here to the oil at the happy occasion of the anointing of the king, which the psalm recalls on the occasion of the wedding of the king. Likewise the anointing is generally an expression of joy (cf. Amos 6:6; Ps 23:5; Prov 27:9; Eccl 9:8), as the omission of it on the occasion of mourning and fasting indicates.

3. With regard to oil as merchandise or part of one's property: The amount of oil owed in Luke 16:6 reflects

Palestinian relationships, for according to the OT and Josephus Palestine had a rich oil production; in Rev 18:13 oil is likewise mentioned in the catalog of merchandise offered by the merchants of Babylon. Rev 6:6 (cf. Schlier) is disputed; most likely it refers to the prediction of a partial crisis (see esp. H. Kraft, *Offenbarung* [HNT] 117, etc.).

4. Oil as fuel for lamps (or torches; → λαμπάς 3) is mentioned in Matt 25:3, 4, 8. This use of oil is attested throughout antiquity.

I. Broer

ἐλαιών, ῶνος, ὁ *elaiōn* olive grove; the Mount of Olives
→ ἐλαία.

Ἐλαμίτης, ου, ὁ *Elamitēs* (the) Elamite*

An inhabitant of Elymas, an area east of the lower Tigris. The "biblical" form of the name (as in Isa 21:2 LXX) appears in Acts 2:9 at the beginning of a list of peoples or lands (vv. 9-11): "Parthians and Medes and *Elamites*" (see H. Conzelmann, *Acts* [Hermeneia] 14).

ἐλάσσων, 2 / ἐλάττων, 2 *elassōn/elattōn* younger, smaller*

With the meaning *inferior:* John 2:10 (opposed to καλός); Heb 7:7: τὸ ἔλαττον (opposed to κρεῖττον). With the meaning *younger* (= less important in age): Rom 9:12 (opposed to μείζων); 1 Tim 5:9: μὴ ἔλαττον ἐτῶν ἑξήκοντα γεγονυῖα, "not *less* than sixty years of age."

ἐλαττονέω *elattoneō* suffer from want*

2 Cor 8:18: ὁ τὸ ὀλίγον οὐκ ἠλαττόνησεν (citing Exod 16:18), "he who gathered little *had* no *lack.*"

ἐλαττόω *elattoō* make inferior; pass.: diminish*

Heb 2:7, with παρά: "thou *didst make* him for a little while *lower* than the angels" (citing Ps 8:6 LXX); in reference to Jesus: v. 9; pass. John 3:30: ἐμὲ δὲ ἐλαττοῦσθαι, but I *decrease.*

ἐλάττων, 2 *elattōn* younger, smaller
→ ἐλάσσων.

ἐλαύνω *elaunō* drive, row, advance toward*

Absolute and intrans.: *make progress* (Mark 6:48: ἐν τῷ ἐλαύνειν); trans.: *travel, row* (John 6:19); pass.: ἠλαύνετο ὑπὸ τοῦ δαιμονίου εἰς τὰς ἐρήμους, he "*was driven* by the demon into the desert" (Luke 8:29); τὰ πλοῖα . . . ὑπὸ ἀνέμων σκληρῶν ἐλαυνόμενα, ships "*are driven* by strong winds" (Jas 3:4); ὁμίχλαι ὑπὸ λαίλαπος ἐλαυνόμεναι, "mists *driven* by a storm" (2 Pet 2:17).

ἐλαφρία, ας, ἡ *elaphria* irresponsibility*

2 Cor 1:17: μήτι ἄρα τῇ ἐλαφρίᾳ ἐχρησάμην; "did I act irresponsibly?" (NEB mg.).

ἐλαφρός, 3 *elaphros* light, easy to bear*

Matt 11:30: φορτίον ἐλαφρόν, a *light* burden; 2 Cor 4:17: τὸ γὰρ παραυτίκα ἐλαφρὸν τῆς θλίψεως ἡμῶν, "for this [our] momentary *slight* affliction. . . ," literally "the momentary *lightness* of our affliction."

ἐλάχιστος, 3 *elachistos* least*

Lit.: BAGD ad loc. — BDF §§60.2; 61.2. — W. Brandt, "Die geringsten Brüder," *JTSB* 8 (1937) 1-28. — Dalman, *Words* 113-15. — F. Dibelius, "Zwei Worte Jesu," *ZNW* 11 (1910) 188-92.

1. Ἐλάχιστος occurs 14 times in the NT in 11 contexts. It is formed from ἐλαχύς and used as the superlative of μικρός. It is additionally strengthened—apparently in a well-worn usage—by the comparative ἐλαχιστότερος (Eph 3:8).

2. Five usages of ἐλάχιστος can be distinguished: a) In Matt 5:19 the *least* place in the kingdom of heaven is threatened (cf. rabbinic material in Dalman 113) to be the fate of the one who declares one of the *least,* i.e., *most insignificant,* commandments invalid (*contra* Dibelius 188-90: "one of these shortest commandments," i.e., the Decalogue). The totality of Jesus' fulfillment of the Torah and the prophets (v. 17) encompasses the *smallest* commandment, just as it encompasses every iota and apostrophe (vv. 18f.). These words directed against antinomian enthusiasts instruct the leaders of the Church not in the direction of abolition of the Torah, but rather toward interpretation of the sayings of the Torah, i.e., its commandments (cf. vv. 21ff.). Principles of the Torah of Jesus (love of enemies, concern for the poor) are brought to bear implicitly when at the judgment of the world the decisive matter determining one's membership in the kingdom of heaven is what was done to the *least* of the brothers of Jesus (25:40, 45; i.e., to any suffering person [Brandt 26]). Both Matthew 5 and Matthew 25 thus determine as the confirmation of one's position or participation in the kingdom of God one's treatment of the *least.*

b) As with the occurrences of the word in Matthew, the Lukan passages are especially determined by the structure *a minore ad maius.* It is learned from experience that it is impossible for anyone to bring about *"so small a thing"* as adding a cubit to one's span of life. This knowledge should move a person to general lack of worry about the whole of life (Luke 12:26). In 16:10 Luke adds a rule of wisdom that states that the person who is faithful or unfaithful *in that which is relatively insignificant* will also be so in that which is important. This rule is given narrative elaboration in 19:11-27 (v. 17).

c) In Matt 2:6 the Scripture (Mic 5:1) is corrected; the statement about Bethlehem as the "least" among the princes of Judah is read qualitatively as *"least important"* and this position is negated with the coming of the Messiah from Bethlehem (οὐδαμῶς ἐλαχίστη). Similarly Paul characterizes himself in 1 Cor 15:9 interpretatively as a "miscarriage" and as the *least* of the apostles as a result of his activity of persecuting the Church. This he does in order to throw into bold relief the work of God's grace against this background and thus to transcend this position. The rhetorical purpose of this argumentation comes to light in Eph 3:8 through the self-designation as the very least of all the saints (not only of the apostles). In all of these passages the concern is with the denial or the transformation—in the light of a new event—of the judgment that something is insignificant.

d) The church's evaluation of the apostle amounts for Paul to *practically nothing* (1 Cor 4:3), because the legitimate court of judgment comes with the coming of the Kyrios (v. 4). Likewise, on the basis of expectation of the saints' future participation in the judgment of the cosmos, he is able to classify the legal actions of the Corinthians as κριτήρια ἐλάχιστα, *petty lawsuits* (BAGD; 6:3). In both instances the greater thing to come leads to a lower estimation of the significance of present matters.

e) The power of what is small to guide the greater whole of which it is a part is illustrated in Jas 3:4: just as the *smallest* or *tiny* rudder rules an entire ship as it is blown about by the wind and waves, so the one who bridles his tongue is able to rule his entire body (v. 2).

P. von der Osten-Sacken

Ἐλεάζαρ *Eleazar* Eleazar*

A personal name in Matt 1:15 (bis).

ἐλεάω *eleaō* have pity, exercise mercy
→ ἔλεος.

ἐλεγμός, ου, ὁ *elegmos* correction, reproof; conviction; punishment*

The word has a variety of meanings in the LXX: conviction (of a sinner), blame, correction, chastisement, punishment. In 2 Tim 3:16 it appears between διδασκαλία and ἐπανόρθωσις, indicating the meaning *correction.* F. Büchsel, *TDNT* II, 473-76; H.-G. Link, *DNTT* II, 140-42. → ἐλέγχω 1, 4.

ἔλεγξις, εως, ἡ *elenxis* correction, reproof, censure*

2 Pet 2:16: he received *correction* for his lawlessness. F. Büchsel, *TDNT* II, 473-76. H.-G. Link, *DNTT* II, 140-42. → ἐλέγχω 1, 4.

ἔλεγχος, ου, ὁ *elenchos* proof, evidence; rebuke, censure, correction; conviction
→ ἐλέγχω 1, 4.

ἐλέγχω *elenchō* blame, correct, punish
ἐλεγμός, ου, ὁ *elegmos* correction, reproof; conviction; punishment
ἔλεγξις, εως, ἡ *elenchis* correction, reproof, censure
ἔλεγχος, ου, ὁ *elenchos* proof, evidence; rebuke, censure, correction; conviction*

1. Occurrences in the NT — 2. Meanings — 3. The vb. in the NT — a) The Synoptics — b) The letters — c) John — 4. The nouns

Lit.: BAGD ad loc. — F. Büchsel, *TDNT* II, 473-76. — G. Dautzenberg, "Der Glaube im Hebräerbrief," *BZ* 17 (1973) 161-77. — *idem, Urchristliche Prophetie* (1975) 246-52 (on 1 Cor 14). — H. Dörrie, "Zu Hebr 11:1," *ZNW* 46 (1956) 196-202. — H. Frankemölle, *Jahwebund und Kirche Christi* (NTAbh new series 106, 1974) 180ff., 226-47. — J. Gnilka, *Der Epheserbrief* (HTKNT, 1971). — *idem,* "Die Kirche des Matthäus und die Gemeinde von Qumran," *BZ* 7 (1963) 43-63. — E. Grässer, *Der Glaube im Hebräerbrief* (MTSt 2, 1965). — H.-G. Link, *DNTT* II, 140-42. — O. Michel, *Der Brief an die Hebräer* (KEK, 1975) 372-79. — W. Pesch, *Matthäus der Seelsorger* (SBS 2, 1966) 36ff. — F. Porsch, *Pneuma und Wort* (FTS 16, 1974) 279-89. — R. Schnackenburg, *The Gospel according to St John* III (1982) 128-54. — W. Trilling, *Das wahre Israel* (SANT 10, [3]1964) 113-23.

1. While the three nouns appear in the NT only once each, the vb. appears 17 times, predominantly in the (later) epistles (11 times).

2. NT usage of ἐλέγχω involves almost its entire range of meaning. In the majority of passages, the influence of the wisdom literature is present, in which the vb.—together with παιδεύω—designates fatherly or divine correction and punishment for the purpose of improvement (cf. Sir 18:13; Prov 9:7f.; 3:11, cited in Heb 12:5 and Rev 3:19; also: 1 Tim 5:20; 2 Tim 4:2; Titus 1:13; 2:15; Jude 15). The intellectual aspect of refutation appears in Titus 1:9; cf. διακατελέγχομαι in Acts 18:28. (On philosophical usage in Greek literature cf. Büchsel 472f.). On the other hand, the convicting activity of the paraclete in John 16:8ff. (cf. Hos 5:9; Jer 2:19) is reminiscent of the prophetic proclamation of judgment.

3. a) Other than Luke 3:19 (Herod *is censured* by John the Baptist), the vb. is used in the Synoptics only in Matt 18:15, in "the passage on the practical behavior of the sons of the kingdom" (Frankemölle 226f.). The measures involving the correction of a brother are regulated according to a three-step procedure (cf. Luke 17:3).

The practice in Qumran was materially related but different in intention (cf. 1QS 5:26–6:1; CD 9:2-4). The OT foundation for both is found in Lev 19:17 (cf. Gnilka, *Kirche* 54ff.).

b) Paul uses ἐλέγχω only in 1 Cor 14:24, where it—together with ἀνακρίνω—characterizes the convicting and edifying activity of prophets endowed with the Spirit (cf. v. 5c; Dautzenberg, *Prophetie* 248f.). Eph 5:11 encourages Christians to *expose* "the unfruitful works of darkness," so that their true (dark) character might come to light (cf. v. 13). Jas 2:9 ascribes a convicting function also to the law.

c) In John 8:46 objective evidence is referred to, while 3:20 mentions the consequence of refusing to believe: Abiding in darkness or in a hardened condition prevents evil from "coming to light" (to the conscience of the evildoer). John 16:8ff. describes the work of the Paraclete as that of the defending attorney and the prosecutor in a trial. After the death of Jesus the Paraclete gives proof (to the believer's conscience) that Jesus is in the right as the Paraclete uncovers the nature of sin, righteousness, and judgment. Through this revelation the Paraclete *convicts* the world (cf. Porsch 279ff.).

4. The meaning of the three nouns cannot be differentiated (cf. 2 Tim 3:16: ἐλεγμός with v.l. ἔλεγχος). Ἔλεγξις in 2 Pet 2:16 refers to divine *correction.* Ἐλεγμός in 2 Tim 3:16 can be understood as *conviction, refutation,* or *revelation* (of the truth), for which God's inspired Scripture is useful.

Interpretation of ἔλεγχος in the *definition of faith* in Heb 11:1 varies from a purely subjective understanding *(lack of doubting)* and an objective understanding (*proof;* cf. Grässer 46ff.). Because the concern here is with the maintenance of persevering faithfulness in a time of trial and is probably intended to support the maintenance of belief described in 10:38 (which is then in the following materials illustrated by OT models), ἔλεγχος (with ὑπόστασις) must be seen as the opposite of the posture of shrinking back and languishing. A place to stand and stability can be found only in the invisible world that is the object of hope, which for faith is the only reality. In this context the author can "define" faith as "the basis of reality for the object of one's hopes and the *proof* of things which one cannot see" (cf. the German translation by U. Wilckens). In this—certainly not complete—definition both Greek philosophical thinking and the biblical understanding of faith are connected.

F. Porsch

ἐλεεινός, 3 *eleeinos* pitiable*

1 Cor 15:19: we are *more pitiable* than all (other) people"; Rev 3:17 in the letter to Laodicea: "not knowing that you are miserable (ταλαίπωρος), *pitiable. . . .*"

ἐλεέω *eleeō* have pity, help (someone) out of mercy, have mercy
→ ἔλεος.

ἐλεημοσύνη, ης, ἡ *eleēmosynē* pity, kindness; alms*

1. Occurrences in the NT; meaning — 2. NT usage — 3. Ἐλεήμων

Lit.: V. Balogh, *"Selig die Barmherzigen." Die christliche Barmherzigkeit bei Matthäus im allgemeinen und in der fünften Seligpreisung im besonderen im Lichte des AT* (1959). — H. D. Betz, "The Beatitudes of the Sermon on the Mount," *idem, Essays on the Sermon on the Mount* (1985) 17-36. — Billerbeck IV, 536-58. — H. Bolkestein and W. Schwer, *RAC* I, 301-7. — A. van den Born, *BL* 49f. — R. Bultmann, *TDNT* II, 477-87. — Dalman, *Words* 62f. — A. Descamps, *DBSup* IV, 1443f. — G. Eichholz, *Auslegung der Bergpredigt* (1965) 45f., 107-9. — H. H. Esser, *DNTT* II, 594-98. — J. Gamberoni, *SacVb* 16-19. — V. Hamp and A. Vögtle, *LTK* I, 359f. — J. Jeremias, *Jerusalem in the Time of Jesus* (1969) 111-19, 126-34. — M. Mees, "Die Hohepriestertheologie des Hebr im Vergleich mit 1 Clem," *BZ* 22 (1978) 115-24. — E. Neuhäusler, *Anspruch und Antwort Gottes* (1962) 141-85. — W. Pesch, "Zur Exegese von Mt 6, 19-21 und Lk 12, 33-44," *Bib* 41 (1960) 356-78. — H. Peucker, *BHH* I, 61f. — Schnackenburg, *Botschaft* 83-86, 102-7. — G. Schneider, *Botschaft der Bergpredigt* (1973) 45f., 93-96. — Schulz, *Q* 94-114, 142-45. — G. Strecker, "Ziele und Ergebnisse einer neutestamentlichen Ethik," *NTS* 25 (1978/79) 1-15. — H.-D. Wendland, *Ethik des NT* (1970) 16-22. — H.-T. Wrege, *Die Überlieferungsgeschichte der Bergpredigt* (1968) 25, 94-97. — H. Zimmermann, *Die Hohepriester-Christologie des Hebräerbriefs* (1964).

1. Of 13 NT occurrences, 3 are in Matthew, 2 in Luke, and 8 in Acts. In Matt 6:1 the TR, under OT influence, has ἐλεημοσύνη in place of δικαιοσύνη.

The word is unknown in classical Greek. The Greeks and Romans coined no term for "gift to the poor," although the giving of alms did occur; however, it was not considered meritorious. In secular literature ἐλεημοσύνη is first attested in Diogenes Laertius v.17. In Callimachus *Hymn.* iv.152 ἐλεημοσύνη is found for the first time with the meaning "pity." The restriction of the meaning of ἔλεος/ἐλεημοσύνη = pity to "mercy toward the poor," "gift to the poor," "alms" occurs first in the LXX (Prov 21:26; Dan 4:27; cf. *Sib. Or.* ii.79-82). In the LXX ἐλεημοσύνη is normally a translation of *ṣ*ᵉ*ḏāqâ* ("righteousness"), especially where the OT speaks of the gracious God in relation to his people or the pious (Isa 1:27; 59:16; 28:17; Pss 32:5; 23:5; 102:6, etc.). Ἐλεημοσύνη does not appear in Josephus or Philo.

In the NT ἐλεημοσύνη has the restricted meaning: *love for the poor* as a virtue and *giving to the poor* as a deed. In ἐλεημοσύνην ποιεῖν, "to give *alms* (Matt 6:2, 3; Acts 9:36; 10:2; 24:17; cf. Tob 1:3; 16:4, 7f.; Sir 7:10), and ἐλεημοσύνη διδόναι (Luke 11:41; 12:33) the wider original meaning echoes. Only Acts in the NT knows the pl. of ἐλεημοσύνη (9:36; 10:2, 4, 31; 24:17). *Did.* 1:6; 15:4; *2 Clem.* 16:4 use ἐλεημοσύνη in dependence on the NT.

2. In all NT occurrences ἐλεημοσύνη is scarcely or not

at all used for the emotional state of pity, but for a *charitable deed.* According to the introductory axiom in Matt 6:1 Jesus speaks in vv. 2-4 of almsgiving in order to characterize the disciple's true piety. What is decisive is sincerity of intention expressing itself in the spontaneity of the good deed not done for the sake of theatrical effect (cf. 25:37-39).

Almsgiving was considered meritorious in the OT and Jewish theology; it was thought to result in the forgiveness of sins (Prov 11:4; Dan 4:24, etc.), was regarded as a condition of salvation (Isa 58:6-12), and was equated with sacrifice (Tob 11:4; Sir 32:5). In contrast to *b. Sanh.* 92a, it is said in *b. Šabb.* 151b: "One who shows mercy to his fellow person is shown mercy from heaven."

In the speech against the Pharisees and scribes (Luke 11:37-54), which is shaped redactionally by Luke, God's concern is said to be not only with ritual washings (vv. 38-41); rather he demands of each person the sincere heart which gives alms (v. 41, from Q). Luke 12:33 (also from Q) develops the preceding v. 21 ("rich toward God"). The image, unlike that in Matt 6:19ff., refers to a careful and responsible relationship to money (heavenly capital) and, in connection with v. 34, has in mind the death of the individual (Pesch 374).

In the early Church what Jesus demanded took place in an exemplary way: The lame beggar at the "Beautiful Gate" receives not only alms (Acts 3:2, 3, 10); Easter salvation is also provided through Peter "in the name of Jesus Christ" (v. 6). Almsgiving, along with prayer, belongs to the special acts of piety done by the disciple Tabitha in Jaffa (9:36) and by Cornelius in Caesarea (10:2, 4, 31), of which God is mindful. Paul defends himself before Felix by referring to his collection for Jerusalem (24:17).

3. **Ἐλεήμων** *merciful, compassionate** appears in the NT only in Matt 5:7 and Heb 2:17. In the fifth beatitude (without parallel in Luke; cf., however, Luke 6:36) the concern is with the correct conduct of the disciple. Divine mercy is given to the *merciful* (cf. *2 Clem.* 4:3; *Did.* 3:8; Pol. *Phil.* 6:1). Matt 9:13 and 12:7 take up Hos 6:6; the parable in Matt 18:23-35 expands the theme of mercy.

The concluding and transitional statement in Heb 2:17f. (in the section on the redeeming solidarity of Christ with mankind, vv. 10-18) designates Jesus for the first time in this "word of exhortation" (13:22) as high priest (cf. 3:1; 4:14–5:10; 6:20; 7:1–10:18). In 2:17 an interpretation of what precedes is given: The meaning of Jesus' salvific deed and its connection with the preceding history of salvation outline Jesus' priesthood as a deed of mercy (ἐλεήμων) toward mankind and as a deed of faithfulness (πιστός) in fulfillment of the office commissioned by the Father. His office is intended especially to take away the deadly effect of sin.

F. Staudinger

ἐλεήμων, 2 *eleēmōn* merciful, compassionate

→ ἐλεημοσύνη 3.

Ἐλεισάβετ *Eleisabet* Elizabeth

Alternative form of the personal name → Ἐλισάβετ used in the Westcott-Hort edition (1881).

ἔλεος, ους, τό *eleos* pity, compassion, mercy*
ἐλεάω *eleaō* have pity, exercise mercy*
ἐλεέω *eleeō* have pity, help (someone) out of mercy, have mercy*

1. Occurrences in the NT — 2. Meaning — 3. Usage — a) Mercy of human to human — b) Jesus' mercy in the miracle stories — c) God's mercy in Luke 1 — d) The Pauline corpus — e) Hebrews — f) 1 Peter and Jude

Lit.: → ἐλεημοσύνη. Also: BAGD ad loc. — G. BORNKAMM, G. BARTH, and H. J. HELD, *Tradition and Interpretation in Matthew* (1963) 165-299. — R. BULTMANN, *TDNT* II, 477-87. — *idem, Theology* I, 285-91. — H. FRANKEMÖLLE, *In Gleichnissen Gott erfahren* (1977) 103-7. — FRISK, *Wörterbuch* I, 489f. — C. MÜLLER, *Gottes Gerechtigkeit und Gottes Volk. Eine Untersuchung zu Röm 9–11* (FRLANT 86, 1964). — PAPE, *Wörterbuch* I, 795. — C. PLAG, *Israels Wege zum Heil. Eine Untersuchung zu Römer 9 bis 11* (1969). — T. SCHLATTER, *CBL*[5] 126f. — H. SCHLIER, *Grundzüge einer paulinischen Theologie* (1978), esp. 48-54, 77-97, 158-73. — R. SCHNACKENBURG, "Mitmenschlichkeit im Horizont des NT," FS Schlier 70-92. — W. THÜSING, "Die Botschaft des NT—Hemmnis oder Triebkraft der gesellschaftlichen Entwicklung?" *GuL* 43 (1970) 136-48. — W. VOGELS, "Le Magnificat, Marie et Israel," *ÉeT* 6 (1975) 279-96. — H.-J. ZOBEL, *TDOT* V, 44-64. — For further bibliography see *TWNT* X, 1072f.

1. The noun ἔλεος appears in 27 passages in the NT (Titus 1:4 is to be excluded because the v.l. χάρις, ἔλεος [καὶ] εἰρήνη is attested only in A C^2 K minuscules and the fathers). In accordance with the usage in secular Greek ὁ ἔλεος appears in the TR of Matt 9:13; 12:7; 23:23; Titus 3:5 and Heb 4:16 (cf. Diodorus Siculus xii.18.4; Josephus *B.J.* i.560; *Ant.* iv.239); *UBSGNT* regularly has τὸ ἔλεος in these passages. Mark, John, and Acts do not have ἔλεος. In the Hatch/Redpath concordance of the LXX ἔλεος takes up more than four columns, most often as the translation of *ḥesed* (e.g., Ps 6:4).

The vb. ἐλεάω appears 3 times in the NT: Rom 9:16 (cf. Prov 21:26; 4 Macc 9:3; *1 Clem.* 13:2; Pol. *Phil.* 2:3; *Barn.* 20:2); Jude 22, 23. (Jude 22 has the v.l. ἐλέγχετε in A C* 33 and other minuscules in place of ἐλεᾶτε; 1505 has the more common vb.: ἐλεεῖτε διακρινομένῳ. In v. 23 ἐλεᾶτε does not appear in the TR; the minuscules 436, 629, and 1241 have ἐλεεῖτε; in place of ἐλεᾶτε the minuscules 88, 104, 945, and other witnesses have ἐλέγχετε.) Hatch/Redpath lists 10 passages with ἐλεᾶν, of which 4 are in Ecclesiastes.

The NT has 29 passages with the vb. ἐλεέω, none of them in John or Acts. Hatch/Redpath gives four columns to ἐλεέω, which often translates the qal of *ḥānan* in the LXX.

2. The noun and vb., attested since Homer, speak of the emotion experienced in the presence of an affliction that has come upon another and the action resulting from this emotion (Esser 594). The LXX, the Qumran texts (*KQT* has two columns of references to *ḥesed*), and the NT assume esp. Hebrew religious usage (cf. Zobel 54-64; Bultmann, *TDNT* II, 479-82). One may assume that ἔλεος and ἐλεεῖν entered into the religious language of the Bible from the secular realm.

The vb. ἐλεεῖν (ἐλεᾶν) in the sense of *have pity, be sorry for, help (out of pity), be merciful* is found in the Synoptics in narrative, where it signifies the coming of the divine mercy into the world of human misery (Mark 5:19), esp. in the imv. ἐλέησον (Mark 10:47, 48 par. Matt 20:30f./ Luke 18:38f.; Matt 9:27 [Matthean doublet to Mark 10:47]; Matt 15:22 [not in par. Mark 7:25]; Matt 17:15 [not in par. Mark 9:17]); elsewhere pass. (Matt 5:7; Rom 11:30, 31; 2 Cor 4:1; 1 Tim 1:13, 16; 1 Pet 2:10 bis). The pf. pass. partc. ἠλεημένος (1 Cor 7:25; 1 Pet 2:20) refers to the duration of the mercy that is discovered: Paul's appointment (1 Cor 7:25) is based on the mercy of the Kyrios; on that basis he gives his counsel in the question of remaining unmarried. The community addressed in 1 Pet 2:10 is and remains the "people of God" only on the basis of the divine mercy (cf. 1:6, 9).

The noun ἔλεος remains limited in the Synoptic tradition to discourse material (hymns), except for its use in narrative in Luke 1:58. Ἔλεος is connected with ποιεῖν in Luke 1:72; 10:37; Jas 2:13, while in 2 Tim 1:16 it is connected with δίδοναι to mean have *mercy,* do *good.* The epistolary introductions in 1 Tim 1:2; 2 Tim 1:2; 2 John 3 wish upon the readers ἔλεος alongside χάρις. In Matt 23:23 and Jas 2:13 ἔλεος stands in connection with κρίσις.

Ἔλεος and ἐλεεῖν find a rich diversity of usage in Paul's and the other NT epistles.

3. a) Ἔλεος and ἐλεέω designate, in accordance with the original OT meaning of *ḥesed* ("kindness") conduct demanded by God from person to person. With Hos 6:6 Jesus interprets God's will at the call of Levi and at the sabbath conflict (Matt 9:9-13; 12:1-8): "I desire *mercy* and not sacrifice" (9:13; 12:7). In the discourse against the Pharisees Matt 23:23 (ἔλεος is not in par. Luke 11:42) states the obligation of tithing (cf. Num 18:12; Deut 14:23) more precisely: One is to do justly in relationships with others, exercise mercy toward others, and practice faith. The illustrative narrative in Luke 10:25-37 characterizes the merciful deed of the Samaritan (v. 37) as a concrete demonstration of love.

In the discourse material of Matthew, the vb. ἐλεέω appears in 5:7; 18:33 for the mercy of human to human, as in the petition of the condemned rich man to the forefather Abraham, who lives in fellowship with God (Luke 16:24). In the parable of the unmerciful debtor (Matt 18:23-35), which elaborates on the problem of forgiveness that had been raised (vv. 21f.), v. 33 draws the compelling conclusion (ἔδει) from the mercy (of God) which has already been experienced: "Should not you *have had mercy* (ἐλεῆσαι) . . . , as I *had mercy* (ἠλέησα) on you?" A person's good fortune rests on his or her acceptance of another (Frankemölle 107). In Judaism as well the demand for mercy was motivated by the reminder of God's mercy (*b. Šabb.* 151b; *T. Zeb.* 5:3).

Jas 2:13 impresses on the inactive community that mercy (goodness) maintains its validity at the final judgment. According to 3:17 (in a catalog of virtues) knowledge of God's mercy in Christ establishes the new element in Christian argumentation with customary motifs. In a passage similar to Jas 3:17, Rom 12:8 encourages the readers with regard to the more general sense of "goodness": ὁ ἐλεῶν ἐν ἱλαρότητι (cf. *Did.* 5:2; *Barn.* 20:2). The texts mentioned speak of practical sympathy and mercy, which take active part in earthly need. The uncertainly transmitted verses Jude 22f. speak similarly, as does Justin *Apol.* 25:3; 57:1, of concern for the eternal salvation of the other (K. H. Schelkle, *Judasbrief* [HTKNT] 170-72).

b) In the Synoptic miracle stories the imv. ἐλέησον appears in the mouth of those who beseech Jesus for deliverance using a messianic appellative. The request has, esp. in Matthew, the form of a prayer. In Mark 10:47f. a blind man calls out to Jesus as Jesus departs from Jericho (in par. Luke 18:38f. Jesus is entering the city; cf. 19:1; Matt 20:30f. [redactional] speaks of two blind men): "Jesus, Son of David, *have mercy* on me!" The descendant of David gives him his eyesight and makes him a witness of the Passion in Jerusalem (cf. the Lukan accent). In Matt 9:27 also (cf. the structure of the miracle cycle in 8:1–9:34) two blind men request mercy from Jesus, the Son of David. In Matt 15:22 (par. Mark 7:25 lacks ἐλέησον) a Canaanite woman calls to Jesus: "*Have mercy* on me, O Lord, Son of David!" The expected descendant of David demonstrates that he is Kyrios when he acquiesces to the faith of the Gentile woman and banishes the demon from her daughter. The father of the epileptic boy (Matt 17:15; cf. Mark 9:17/Luke 9:28) implores: "Lord, *have mercy* on my son!" "The Lord" reveals himself, according to Matthew, with the wonder-working word, which his followers were unable to speak. The lepers of Samaria call for the mercy of the "master" in Jesus (Luke 17:13), in order to be accepted again into the cultic and village community. According to Mark 5:19 the Gerasene demoniac is sent by Jesus as a messenger of God's mercy to the family with whom he had previously lived, in order then to proclaim Jesus' deeds in the Decapolis.

c) Luke takes up the OT concept of *ḥesed* in its original sense of the gracious and creative faithfulness of God, esp. in OT citations and hymns which allude to the OT (Luke 1:50 [cf. Ps 102:17]; 1:54 [cf. Ps 97:3]; 1:72 [cf. Pss 105:8;

106:45]; 1:78 [cf. Isa 60:1f.]). There is joy, according to 1:58 (a Hebraism), over the *mercy* (grace) by which God favors Elizabeth. This mercy is a sign of God's creative omnipotence. The leitmotif of Luke is sounded in the infancy narrative: The promised mercy *(ḥesed)* of God, which in the OT is experienced in Israel's salvation history, reaches its fullness in the gracious self-revelation of God among the insignificant and the poor in the incarnation of his Son.

d) Paul interprets God's ἔλεος/ἐλεεῖν in Romans 9, 11, and 15 as the salvation-historical/eschatological deed in Jesus Christ. In 9:14-18 he refutes the objection that God is unjust, using Exod 33:19 (Rom 9:15) and Exod 9:16 (Rom 9:17), fitting the Exodus text freely to his train of thought. He interprets it as the direct expression of Yahweh and then follows: The God who is merciful (v. 16) claims the right to be merciful. God hardened Pharaoh "in order to complete his eternal purpose of self-glorification" (F. W. Maier, cited by O. Kuss, *Der Römerbrief* II [1959] 725). The point of departure of the Pauline train of thought is the fact that God is absolutely not at the disposal of humankind. In the prophetic image (of pots) in v. 23 "vessels of *mercy*" are contrasted to "vessels of wrath" (v. 22) in order to explain God's universal (inclusive of both Jews and Gentiles) appointment to glory.

In Rom 11:25-32 Paul offers his solution to the difficult problem ("mystery," v. 25) of how, despite Scripture, covenants, and revealed divine plans for salvation, things could come to the rejection of the message of faith in Jesus Christ by the overwhelming majority of the Jewish people (9:1–11:36). What Paul sets forth as a reality in 11:28f. (enemies of God, God's faithfulness in election, irrevocability of call and grace) and in v. 25 (partial hardening, the call of the full number of the Gentiles), he supports (ὥσπερ–γάρ, v. 30; οὕτως–ἵνα, v. 31; γάρ–ἵνα, v. 32) in his own fashion: "As you were once disobedient to God but now *have received mercy* (ἠλεήθητε) because of their disobedience, so they have now been disobedient *to the mercy* (ἐλέει) given to you, so that they also *have* now *received mercy* (ἐλεηθῶσιν) [RSV differently: "in order that *by* the mercy shown to you they also may receive mercy"]. For God has consigned all men to disobedience, that he *may have mercy* upon all (ἐλεήσῃ)" (vv. 30-32). Paul knows and recognizes God's salvific *mercy* as the only possible means by which all receive a share in salvation (Kuss 818f.). This is realized alone in Christ Jesus (Rom 3:21-31; Gal 2:16, etc.), now for the Gentiles (Rom 9:23; 11:30; 15:9), then also for the Jews (11:31). God's free mercy is not in conflict with his covenant faithfulness. The Gentiles may praise God for the mercy which he has shown to them in Christ (Rom 15:9).

At the conclusion of Galatians (6:16) Paul wishes "peace and *mercy*" on all who are "a new creation" (v. 15). This good wish is granted only where Christians make their new existence the basic principle of their life and conduct (cf. *Barn.* 15:2; *Herm. Vis.* iii.9.8; *1 Clem.* 22:8). God's *mercy* heals Epaphroditus from illness for Paul's sake (Phil 2:27). He and his fellow Christians are convinced that they must pass on God's mercy which they have experienced (2 Cor 4:1; cf. Rom 12:1: οἰκτιρμῶν) in zealous service and joy (Rom 12:8). It is not one's own works of righteousness, but God's mercy which is the basis of the salvation of the one who is raised to faith and renewed through the Spirit (Eph 2:4). God saves persons on the basis of his mercy (Titus 3:5, in a parenthesis).

Along with χάρις or εἰρήνη this mercy of God and of Jesus Christ is requested for the addressees in the Christianized epistolary prescripts in 1 Tim 1:2; 2 Tim 1:2; 2 John 3; Jude 2 (cf. Ign. *Phld.* superscription; *Mart. Pol.* superscription). 2 Tim 1:16 implores for the mercy of the resurrected Lord as a present salvific gift, while in v. 18 it is sought as a final, future gift. The anamnesis of Paul in 1 Tim 1:12-17 sees in the apostle and his conversion the forbearance of Christ at work; thus as a persecutor he has found mercy (vv. 13, 16).

e) Heb 4:16 unfolds what is first announced in 2:17. The high priest christology of Hebrews (5:1-10; 8:1–9:18) is oriented typologically to the OT high priesthood and its function on the Day of Atonement (Lev 16). That Christ the high priest is in total solidarity with humankind but essentially superior because of his divine sonship guarantees his merciful and unlimited understanding of the human situation (Heb 2:17; 4:15). He gives to the community which has become weak the confidence to approach the throne of grace to find mercy (4:16).

f) 1 Peter and Jude have already been mentioned. 1 Pet 1:3 begins with a song of praise to God's mercy. Rebirth to a living hope is given to Christians through the resurrection of Jesus Christ from the dead (cf. Eph 2:4; 1 Cor 15:19). 1 Pet 2:10 attests to the converted Gentiles (the non-people), with an appeal to Hos 2:25, that they have found mercy and are "God's people" since their conversion and baptism. Their new existence is for them both calling and sending.

In the introduction to the letter Jude 2 wishes the addressees mercy, peace, and love in their fullness. In a familiar phrase, v. 21 encourages the community threatened by false teaching: "keep yourselves in the love of God; wait for the *mercy* of our Lord Jesus Christ, who gives you [RSV "unto"] eternal life." From this flows the mercy of Church members toward one another (vv. 22f.).

F. Staudinger

ἐλευθερία, ας, ἡ *eleutheria* freedom

→ ἐλεύθερος.

ἐλεύθερος, 3 *eleutheros* free; subst.: free person
ἐλευθερόω *eleutheroō* liberate*
ἐλευθερία, ας, ἡ *eleutheria* freedom*
ἀπελεύθερος, ου, ὁ *apeleutheros* freedman*

1. Occurrences in the NT — 2. Meaning — 3. Paul — 4. Matthew — 5. John — 6. James — 7. 1–2 Peter

Lit.: H. R. BALZ, *Heilsvertrauen und Welterfahrung. Strukturen der paulinischen Eschatologie nach Röm 8, 18-39* (1971). — S. S. BARTCHY, *Μᾶλλον χρῆσαι. First Century Slavery and the Interpretation of 1 Cor. 7:21* (1973). — G. BORNKAMM, "Die christliche Freiheit," *idem, Aufsätze* I, 133-38. — G. BORNKAMM, G. BARTH, and H. J. HELD, *Tradition and Interpretation in Matthew* (1963) *passim* (on Matt 17:24ff.). — W. BRANDT, *Freiheit im NT* (1932). — R. BULTMANN, "Gnade und Freiheit," *idem, Glauben* II, 149-61. — *idem*, "Die Bedeutung des Gedankens der Freiheit für die abendländische Kultur," *ibid.*, II, 274-93. — *idem*, "Der Gedanke der Freiheit nach antikem und christlichem Verständnis," *ibid.*, IV, 42-51. — *idem, Theology* I, 330-40. — J. CAMBIER, "La liberté chrétienne selon Saint Paul," *SE* II (1964) 315-53. — K. DEISSNER, *Autorität und Freiheit im ältesten Christentum* (1931). — G. DELLING, *TDNT* VIII, 49-87. — M. DIBELIUS and H. GREEVEN, *James* (Hermeneia, 1976) 116-17. — C. H. DODD, *Das Gesetz der Freiheit. Glaube und Gehorsam nach dem Zeugnis des NT* (1960). — E. ESKING, *Fri och Frigjord* (1956). — H. FRANKEMÖLLE, *Jahwebund und Kirche Christi* (1974) 174ff. — G. FRIEDRICH, "Freiheit und Liebe im ersten Korintherbrief," *TZ* 26 (1970) 81-98. — E. FUCHS, *RGG* II, 1101-4. — E. GRÄSSER, "Freiheit und apostolisches Wirken bei Paulus," *EvT* 15 (1955) 333-42. — E. G. GULIN, "Die Freiheit in der Verkündigung des Paulus," *ZST* 18 (1941) 458-81. —B. HÄRING, "Paulinische Freiheitslehre, Gesetzesethik und Situationsethik," *Studiorum Paulinorum Congressus Internationalis Catholicus 1961* (1963) I, 165-73. — R. HUMMEL, *Die Auseinandersetzung zwischen Kirche und Judentum im Matthäusevangelium* (1966) 103ff. (on Matt 17:24ff.). — W. JOEST, "Paulus und das Lutherische *Simul Iustus et Peccator*," *KD* 1 (1955) 269-320. — H. JONAS, *Augustin und das paulinische Freiheitsproblem* (1965). — E. KÄSEMANN, *Jesus Means Freedom* (1969). — R. N. LONGENECKER, *Paul, Apostle of Liberty* (1964). — C. MAURER, "Grund und Grenze apostolischer Freiheit. Exegetisch-theologische Studie zu 1. Kor. 9," *Antwort* (FS K. Barth, 1956) 630-41. — M. MÜLLER, "Freiheit. Über Autonomie und Gnade von Paulus bis Clemens von Alexandrien," *ZNW* 25 (1926) 177-236. — F. MUSSNER, *Der Jakobusbrief* (HTKNT, 1975) 107ff., 126. — idem, Theologie der Freiheit nach Paulus (1976). — W. NAUCK, "Lex insculpta (*ḥwq ḥrwṯ*) in der Sektenschrift," *ZNW* 46 (1955) 138-40. — D. NESTLE, *Eleutheria. I: Die Griechen* (1967). —*idem, RAC* VIII, 269-306. — K. NIEDERWIMMER, *Der Begriff der Freiheit im NT* (1966). — F. NÖTSCHER, " 'Gesetz der Freiheit' im NT und in der Mönchsgemeinde am Toten Meer," *Bib* 34 (1953) 193-94. — F. PASTOR RAMOS, *La libertad en la carta a los Gálatas. Estudio exegético-teológico* (1977). — M. POHLENZ, *Griechische Freiheit. Wesen und Werden eines Lebensideals* (1955). — A. SAND, "Gesetz und Freiheit," *TGl* 61 (1971) 1-14. — H. SCHLIER, *TDNT* II, 487-504. — *idem*, "Über das vollkommene Gesetz der Freiheit," Schlier I, 193-265. — *idem*, "Zur Freiheit gerufen. Das paulinische Freiheitsverständnis," *ibid.*, III, 216-33. — O. SCHMITZ, *Der Freiheitsgedanke bei Epiktet und das Freiheitszeugnis des Paulus* (1923). — R. SCHNACKENBURG, "Christian Freedom according to Paul," Schnackenburg II, 31-53. — H. SCHÜRMANN, "Die Freiheitsbotschaft des Paulus—Mitte des Evangeliums?" *Orientierungen am NT. Exegetische Aufsätze* III (1978) 13-49. — G. STRECKER, *Der Weg der Gerechtigkeit. Untersuchung zur Theologie des Matthäus* (1971) 200f. and *passim* (on Matt 17:24ff.). — P. STUHLMACHER, *Der Brief an Philemon* (1975). — W. TRILLING, *Das wahre Israel. Studien zur Theologie des Matthäus-Evangeliums* (1964). — For further bibliography see esp. Schürmann and *TWNT* X, 1073-76; *DNTT* I, 720f.

1. Of the 23 NT occurrences of ἐλεύθερος, 14 appear in Paul's letters, 2 among Paul's "students" (in Ephesians and Colossians), 1 in Matthew, 2 in John, 1 in 1 Peter, and 3 in Revelation. Ἐλευθερόω occurs 7 times, 5 in Paul's letters, 2 in John. Ἐλευθερία occurs 11 times, of which 7 are in Paul's letters, 2 in James, and 1 each in 1–2 Peter. Ἀπελεύθερος occurs only in 1 Cor 7:22. The word group appears esp. frequently in the Pauline *Hauptbriefe* (Romans, 1–2 Corinthians, Galatians), where the question of Christian freedom is considered thematically. But only part of the history of liberation is seen in NT texts which have these words; that history begins already in the work of the earthly Jesus, esp. in the Easter experience and the experience of the Spirit.

2. Ἐλεύθερος originally characterizes one who belongs to a given group with the full rights of a member and fellow citizen (in contrast to aliens, non-citizens, conquered populations, and slaves). The word group has a long and complex developmental history, in the course of which new elements are added, including the freedom of the polis, the freedom of Greece (in regard to the Persian War), and finally freedom as a concept and problem of philosophy (the individual's inner freedom, the Cynic's freedom with respect to conventions, the freedom of the Stoic wise man who attains his self-sufficiency in submitting himself to the world-logos, etc.). On this see further Niederwimmer 1ff.; Nestle *passim.*

The word appears with its traditional legal and social meaning (the free man in contrast to the slave) several times in the NT (1 Cor 7:21; 12:13; Gal 3:28; 4:22 [παιδίσκη–ἐλευθέρα]; Eph 6:8; Col 3:11; Rev 6:15; 13:16; 19:18). In 1 Cor 7:22 there is a play on the words: the slave, who was called to Christ, is (in the eschatological sense) a *freedman* of Christ. The *free man* (in the legal-social sense) becomes again a slave of Christ (in the eschatological sense) through calling into Christian status.

According to Jewish law the wife becomes *free* from being bound to her husband at his death and acquires the right to remarriage (only in Rom 7:3; 1 Cor 7:39). Paul uses this legal statement in Rom 7:1ff. to portray "freedom from the law" (→ 3).

The dominant usage in the NT gives an *eschatological* sense to the word group: It represents the unsurpassed freedom that Christ gives to the believer, the citizen of the eschatological world.

3. This is most true of Paul. *Freedom* is the gift of Christ (Gal 5:1); the Christian has it ἐν Χριστῷ Ἰησοῦ (2:4). "Where the Spirit of the Lord is, there *freedom* rules" (2 Cor 3:17; RSV is different). "The law of the Spirit of life" *has liberated* the Christian (Rom 8:2). Christians have been called (Gal 5:13) to this *freedom* that has been opened up by Christ. As those who believe and have been baptized they belong to the multitude of the free, to the citizens of the coming world. They are God's children (Rom 8:21; cf. Gal 4:30f.; → τέκνον, υἱός). Freedom is the gift of the future (Rom 8:18ff.), but in the Spirit it is at the same time the preliminary gift of the present. Freedom has been given to the Christian already; this person can say "my *liberty*" (1 Cor 10:29), "our *freedom*" (Gal 2:4), "Am I not *free*?" (1 Cor 9:1). As the eschatological gift of salvation freedom is universal and unsurpassable (ἐλεύθερος . . . ὢν ἐκ πάντων, 1 Cor 9:19; cf. 3:21ff.; 6:12; 10:23)—but also remains misunderstood and endangered (see below).

How does freedom become concrete? It becomes concrete esp. as freedom *from sin,* i.e., from sin as a power which leads human existence into moral self-alienation (→ ἁμαρτία). Christ, to whom the believer now belongs, has effected liberation from sin's power. Freedom is granted to the Christian through baptismal death, in which the old person, the body of sin, dies and loses its power (cf. Rom 6:6, 11). Therefore the Christian no longer seeks his or her identity by affirming eschatological freedom to himself or herself, but rather by yielding to God's unconditioned love. The result is that the believer is liberated from the tyranny of sin's power (cf. Rom 6:12ff.; 8:2), as well as from the concealed fallenness and self-alienation under which all achievement-oriented piety stands.

Thus according to the Pauline view *the law* was not capable of removing human self-alienation, for it foundered on the → σάρξ (cf. Rom 8:3). Sin misused the law with the result that the law—against its intention—led not to life, but rather to the manifestation of self-alienation (cf. 3:20b; 5:20a; 7:7ff., 13ff.; → ἁμαρτία, θάνατος). The law reveals that the individual *extra Christum* stands in his or her conduct alienated from himself or herself. If Christ has liberated us from the power of sin, he has also liberated us from the way of the piety of achievement (7:5f.). Genuine righteousness is no longer sought by way of "the law [RSV "principle"] of works" (3:27), but rather is accepted in faith. Those who believe—and those alone—are those who are liberated (Gal 4:21-31, esp. vv. 23, 26).

Of course liberation from the piety of achievement does not mean that a person is released into empty free choice. It is true that the ritual commandments of the OT and Jewish tradition (circumcision, food laws, etc.) are abrogated for Paul; but obligation to the ethical commands of the Torah remains, insofar as they are harmonious with the demand which God addresses to mankind; i.e., the demand that is radicalized by the love command and protected from all "legalism." The one who loves does in freedom what the law demands and fulfills the law as it actually is meant to be fulfilled (Rom 13:8-10; Gal 5:14); ἐν πνεύματι such a person fulfills the will of God freely, from the center of his or her own person. Tfhe law is not against one who bears the fruit of the Spirit (Gal 5:22f.). Thus Paul can speak of "the law of the Spirit" (Rom 8:2), "the law [RSV "principle"] of faith" (3:27), and "the law of Christ" (Gal 6:2; cf. 1 Cor 9:21), i.e.—as one can perhaps paraphrase—of law without legalism.

In accordance with this the freedom which is attained must be protected against the danger of relapse into legalism (Gal 2:4; 5:1) and against the danger of antinomianism (5:13). Paul can say in reference to the latter: Those who are *freed* from sin "have become slaves of righteousness" (Rom 6:18; the reverse is stated in v. 20) or slaves of God (v. 22). Genuine freedom is demonstrated by the capacity for service to the neighbor (1 Cor 9:19; Gal 5:13) and by readiness to renounce the exercise of one's freedom for the sake of the neighbor (→ εἴδωλον 4.b, γινώσκω 3.f).

Cf. also the Pauline corrective to the sayings in 1 Cor 6:12; 10:23. On 1 Cor 7:21 → δουλεύω 5, χράομαι. On 1 Cor 10:29, → συνείδησις.

As eschatological freedom, freedom is a *universal* gift of salvation. It includes not only liberation from moral fallenness in itself, but also redemption and liberation from all *powers,* including death. (These ideas are of course only occasionally indicated by use of the word group under discussion.) Liberation from sin and death, which has already taken place, is proclaimed in Rom 8:2. The final liberation which is yet to come (i.e., the revealing of the hidden glory of the children) is proclaimed in vv. 19, 21. Paul reveals in this section (vv. 19ff.) that in the freeing of the children creation (→ κτίζω), which is now subjected to perishability and absurdity, is also included. The day on which the glory of the elect is revealed brings with it the redemption and liberation of the whole creation.

4. In the Synoptic tradition the word group appears only in Matt 17:26. The pericope beginning with v. 24 (a pre-Matthean nucleus revised by Matthew) answers the question whether the Jewish Christian followers of Jesus are obligated to pay the Jewish temple tax (δίδραχμον). The question indicates the early, Jewish Christian origin of the tradition (pre-70, possibly Syrian). The answer argues from the eschatological status of the "sons." "The sons" are fundamentally free. Just as earthly kings exact no tolls and taxes from their sons (their own children or their own countrymen), but only from foreigners, so the King of heaven demands no taxes from his sons, the Christians. But in order to avoid any offense, the temple tax should be paid. For the group which speaks here the temple cult and the temple tax have already become an adiaphoron. Thus eschatological freedom can be demonstrated by the relinquishing of its immediate accomplishment. (The interpretation which the Evangelist wants to give to the pericope cannot be recognized with certainty.)

5. Johannine use of the word group (only in 8:32-36) is connected with the contrast between divine truth (→ ἀλήθεια 4.b) and the deception "of this world," which is characteristic of John. The revealer promises to those who remain in his word the knowledge of the truth which *makes free*. The Jews—as representatives of the "world"—misunderstand the revelatory word. They understand themselves as Abraham's descendants to be *free* already (v. 33). However, the revealer indicates the fraudulent character of their presumed freedom; they are not free sons, but rather slaves—slaves of sin (v. 34). Only the Son himself is able to make free sons of servants. Only he, only his word, truly *frees* (v. 36).

6. Jas 1:25 (νόμος τέλειος ὁ τῆς ἐλευθερίας) and 2:12 (νόμος ἐλευθερίας) are difficult. Both phrases appear abruptly, suggesting that they were already fixed formulations. The formulations perhaps betray a knowledge of Stoic or popular philosophical motifs ("the wise man who is subject to the universal law is a king and is free"); but these motifs are present in James as they were mediated and reinterpreted in Jewish or Jewish Christian circles. What is referred to is the divine law as the standard for conduct (1:25) or for the future judgment (2:12), and indeed (naturally not the Stoic λόγος τῆς φύσεως, but rather) the divine law, as it is known and lived in the Christian Church. It is called (1:25) the "perfect" law in contrast to other laws; or (perhaps better) the "full, entire" law (cf. Delling 74), because it demands the undivided submission of the individual: It requires not partial obedience to partial instructions, but rather the "heart" in subjection to God's will. As such this law is not opposed to freedom, but rather creates freedom, i.e., it makes a person free to do deeds of love (cf. the νόμος βασιλικός, 2:8).

7. 1 Pet 2:16 is, on the other hand, reminiscent of Pauline associations (cf. Gal 5:13; Rom 6:18, 22). 2 Pet 2:19 opposes false teachers who ascribe to themselves possession of freedom in a special way. Probably it is concerned specifically with "Gnostic" antinomians, whom the author (taking up the old paradox) shows to be slaves of destruction.

K. Niederwimmer

ἐλευθερόω *eleutheroō* liberate
→ ἐλεύθερος.

ἔλευσις, εως, ἡ *eleusis* arrival*

Acts 7:52: "the *coming* of the Righteous One," in reference to the (first) coming of Christ (so also Pol. *Phil.* 6:3; *1 Clem.* 17:1). The word is used for the parousia (the second *coming*) in ms. D in Luke 21:7; 23:42 (so also *Acts Thom.* 28). J. Schneider, *TDNT* II, 675; G. D. Kilpatrick, "Acts VII.52 ΕΛΕΥΣΙΣ," *JTS* 46 (old series, 1945) 136-45.

ἐλεφάντινος, 3 *elephantinos* made of ivory*

Rev 18:12: "vessel [RSV "articles"] *of ivory,*" in the enumeration of the wealth of Babylon. *BRL* 67-72.

ἐλήλυθα *elēlytha* have come

Pf. of → ἔρχομαι.

'Ελιακίμ *Eliakim* Eliakim*

Personal name in Matt 1:13 (bis); Luke 3:30. Cf. 4 Kgdms 18:18; 23:24.

ἔλιγμα, ατος, τό *heligma* roll (noun)

John 19:39 B ℵ* W: "a *roll* of myrrh and aloes," v.l. (scribal error) in place of "a mixture (μίγμα) of. . . ."

'Ελιέζερ *Eliezer* Eliezer*

Personal name in Luke 3:29; cf. Gen 15:2; Exod 18:4 LXX.

'Ελιούδ *Elioud* Eliud*

Personal name in Matt 1:14f.

'Ελισάβετ *Elisabet* Elizabeth*

1. 'Ελισάβετ is the Grecized form of *'ᵉlîšeḇaʿ* (Exod 6:23), which can be explained etymologically both as "God has sworn" (*šāḇaʿ* I) or "God is fullness, perfection" (*šāḇaʿ* II; cf. KBL^2 942, 944). The LXX has 'Ελισάβε (A*) or 'Ελισάβετ (A^1 F). On the final τ, cf. the analogous name *Yehôšeḇaʿ* in 2 Kgs 11:2, which, already in Hebrew, is *Yᵉhôšaḇʿaṯ* in 2 Chr 22:11.

2. In the NT the name Elizabeth appears only in Luke 1 and in every instance refers to the same person, the wife of Zechariah. Nothing of her is known in extrabiblical literature. If one were to suppose that the name was chosen on theological grounds, one could assume a relationship to Luke 1:73 (on the basis of the etymology "God has sworn"). Such an assumption is not probable. More probable is an association with the wife of Aaron (Exod 6:23), who bore the same name and was related to his sister Miriam (= Mary; cf. esp. Luke 1:36).

Through Elizabeth's lineage from priestly circles (Luke 1:5), the honorable descent of John is underlined. Despite Elizabeth's barrenness and the advanced age of both her and her husband Zechariah (v. 7), he receives the promise of a son (v. 13). The twofold reason for the childlessness serves the purpose of increasing the miracle of God in this time of salvation (cf. the age of Abraham and Sarah in Gen 17:17; Sarah in 11:30; for the eschatological time, cf. Isa 54:1). Elizabeth "conceived" and remained in seclusion for five months (Luke 1:24). Consequently the assumption is made that the pregnancy can serve as a "sign" for Mary (v. 36).

In Luke 1:36 Elizabeth is called a relative of Mary. Because συγγενίς must mean membership in the same tribe (Levi), this is the only passage in the NT and early Christian literature that knows of Jesus' being from the tribe of Levi (not Judah, as is the case elsewhere). Early Christianity has this idea elsewhere only in the Christian revision of the *Testaments of the Twelve Patriarchs* (*T. Jos.* 19; *T. Sim.* 7). When Mary visited Elizabeth (Luke 1:40), the child leaped in Elizabeth's womb (v. 41). The witness of John to Jesus is thus traced back already to the mother's womb. Elizabeth, filled with the Holy Spirit, is able to interpret the sign (vv. 42-45). The birth of the Baptist is mentioned finally in v. 57, bringing the angel's promise to its fulfillment.

H. Weder

Ἐλισαῖος, ου *Elisaios* Elisha*

Luke 4:27 mentions the Israelite prophet Elisha and recalls the healing of Naaman the Syrian (2 Kings 5:1-14). The LXX gives the form of the name as Ἐλισαιέ; Josephus (*Ant.* viii.352-54; ix.28) and *Ep. Arist.* (47f., 50, 184) have the form Ἐλισσαῖος.

ἑλίσσω *helissō* roll, roll up*

This vb. appears twice in the NT, both times in metaphorical references to the end of the world. Heb 1:12: "like a mantle thou wilt *roll* them [(earth and) the heavens] *up*" (cf. Ps 101:27 LXX v.l.); Rev 6:14: "the sky vanished like a scroll that is *rolled up*" (cf. Isa 34:4 LXX [ἑλιγήσεται]).

ἕλκος, ους, τό *helkos* sore, wound*

Luke 16:21, of the *sores* of Lazarus; Rev 16:2: "evil *sore[s]* came upon the men"; v. 11: they "cursed the God of heaven for . . . their *sores*" (cf. the Egyptian plague, Exod 9:10f.; see also Deut 28:35).

ἑλκόω *helkoō* cause sores*

Luke 16:20, pf. pass. partc.: εἱλκωμένος, Lazarus was *covered with sores.* → ἕλκος.

ἕλκω *helkō* draw, drag*

Only trans. in the NT. Literal: John 18:10: Simon *drew* the sword; 21:6, 11, of dragging fishing nets; Acts 16:19: Paul and Silas are *dragged* before the archons; 21:30: Paul is *dragged* out of the temple; Jas 2:6: the rich *drag* you into court. Fig.: John 6:44: "unless the Father . . . *draws* him"; 12:32: "I, when I am lifted up from the earth, *will draw* all men to myself." A. Oepke, *TDNT* II, 503f.; R. Schnackenburg, *The Gospel according to John* II (1979) 50, 393f.

Ἑλλάς, άδος, ἡ *Hellas* Greece*

Lit.: LSJ s.v. — C. Schneider, *Kulturgeschichte des Hellenismus* (1967, 1969), esp. I, 158-977 (on Hellenistic culture, kingdoms, lands, cities; bibliography). — H. Koester, *History, Culture, and Religion of the Hellenistic Age* (1982).

Ἑλλάς, which in Homer (*Il.* ii.684) is still the name of an area in Phthiotis in southern Thessaly, gradually becomes after the 6th cent. the name of all Greece, including Thessaly, Epirus, the Peloponnesus, and the southwest coast of Asia Minor (Ionia) with the Aegean islands. According to 1 Macc 1:1 Ἑλλάς is identical with Alexander's empire. In 1:10 (and elsewhere) 1 Maccabees designates the Seleucids as rulers of the "Hellenes." In 8:9, however, Ἑλλάς is used in the narrower sense of the Achaean league (146 B.C., when Corinth was destroyed).

In the NT Ἑλλάς appears only in Acts 20:2. Here the name is used in the vernacular sense as a substitute for the normal provincial name Achaia (→ Ἀχαΐα; similarly Pausanias vii.16), which is the term used elsewhere in the NT (10 times). Achaia comprised central and southern Greece. In 146 B.C. the Romans conclusively defeated Achaia and placed it for a time under the control of the governor of Macedonia. In 27 B.C. it was made an independent (senatorial) province with the residence of the proconsul in Corinth (→ Γαλλίων).

J. Wanke

Ἕλλην, ηνος, ὁ *Hellēn* Greek man
Ἑλληνίς, ίδος, ἡ *Hellēnis* Greek woman

Lit.: C. H. Dodd, *The Bible and the Greeks* (1935). — J. Jüthner, *Hellenen und Barbaren* (1923). — M. Hengel, *Jews, Greeks and Barbarians* (1980). — *idem, Judaism and Hellenism* (1974). — C. Schneider, *Kulturgeschichte des Hellenismus* (two volumes, 1967, 1969). — P. Wendland, *Die hellenistisch-römische Kultur in ihren Beziehungen zum Judentum und Christentum* (HNT I/2, [2, 3]1912). — U. von Wilamowitz-Moelendorff, *Der Glaube der Hellenen* (two volumes, 1926, 1932; [2]1955). — U. Wilcken, "Hellenen und Barbaren," *NJKA* 17 (1906) 457-71. — H. Windisch, *TDNT* II, 504-16. — For further bibliography see Schneider; *TWNT* X, 1076.

1. Since *ca.* 700 B.C. the designation "Hellene" united the Greek tribes and city-states through language, culture, and religion. In the Hellenistic age there was a tendency to characterize non-Greeks who possessed Greek language and education as "Hellenes" (for texts see Windisch 505, n. 6). The LXX has Ἕλλην for Heb. *yāwān* and *y*[e]*wānîm* ("Ionian," Zech 9:13; Dan 8:21; 10:20; 11:2). In 1 Macc 1:10, etc. the Seleucids are called "Hellenes." The distinction between Greeks and "barbarians" was social and political (cf. Hengel, *Jews* 55-66); as the dominating upper class, the Greeks avoided any intermingling with the despised "barbarians" (to which the Jews belonged, according to the Greek view), whenever possible. Particular "barbarian" peoples sought to attain a higher cultural estimation by claiming an early relationship with the Greeks (cf. 1 Macc 7:21; Hengel, *Jews* 57). On the stresses involved in the encounter between Judaism and Hellenistic culture in pre-Christian Palestine, which are significant in the background of the gospel, see Hengel, *Judaism.*

2. In the NT the basic meaning *Greek* is dominant for Ἕλλην. In many passages the meaning "Gentile" resonates (unambiguously appearing first after the NT; cf. Jüthner 146), especially where "Jews and Hellenes" represents the totality of mankind divided according to a salvation-historically relevant distinction (Acts 19:10; 20:21; Rom 1:16; 2:9f.; 3:9; 10:12; 1 Cor 1:24, etc.). The "Hellene" functions (especially for Luke and Paul) as a significant representative of paganism (cf. Rom 3:9 with 3:29; 9:24 with 10:12). Nevertheless a distinction can be made between Greeks and "barbarians" (cf. Rom 1:14; Col 3:11).

Luke has Paul speak to "Jews and *Greeks,*" referring thus to all the inhabitants of particular Hellenistic cities (even in Syria and Asia Minor; Acts 11:19, 20 v.l. [→ Ἑλληνιστής]; 14:1; 18:4; 19:17). In Mark 7:26 the woman seeking help is called a "Greek"; the addition of "Syrophoenician by birth" affirms her pagan origin (cf. Acts 17:12). According to John 12:20f. there were "Greeks" "among those who went up [to Jerusalem] to worship at the feast" and these Greeks sought to see Jesus. The passage concerns "God-fearers" (cf. Acts 17:4), i.e., Gentiles who are closely associated with Judaism without converting (cf. K. G. Kuhn, *TDNT* VI, 727-44). John 7:35 ("Does he intend to go to the Dispersion among the *Greeks* and teach the *Greeks?*") has the Greek-speaking Gentile world in view. The genitive phrase "Diaspora of the Hellenes" refers to geographic area (A. Schlatter, *Der Evangelist Johannes* [1948] 198). Thus the reference is not to Diaspora Jews. The Evangelist has the confused Jews express the later reality without realizing it: The gospel will be preached to the Gentiles.

Paul, as "apostle to the Gentiles" (cf. Gal 1:16), one who is "under obligation both to *Greeks* and to barbarians" (Rom 1:14), maintains the precedence of the elect people in salvation history (cf. Rom 1:16; 2:9; *contra* Col 3:11!). He takes into consideration that "*Greeks* seek wisdom" (1 Cor 1:22; cf. Rom 1:14) and knowledge of God (cf. Rom 1:21). Yet as "the people of fallen wisdom" (Windisch 514) they stand, like the Jews, under the judgment (cf. Rom 3:9). In Christ the old characterizations of Jews and Greeks are abolished in the new genus of the Church (cf. 1 Cor 12:13; Gal 3:28). Paul can write to the Corinthians: "Give no offense to Jews or to Greeks or to the church of God" (1 Cor 10:32). Here the way is opened for the common threefold division into Greeks (= Gentiles), Jews, and Christians (cf. Harnack, *Mission* I, 302ff.).

J. Wanke

Ἑλληνικός, 3 *Hellēnikos* Greek*

Rev 9:11, of "the angel of the bottomless pit," who is named ἐν τῇ Ἑλληνικῇ (γλώσσῃ understood)—in *Greek*—Ἀπολλύων (destroyer). The adj. appears also in Luke 23:38 v.l. in a secondary insertion about the three languages of the inscription over Jesus' cross (cf. John 19:20).

Ἑλληνίς, ίδος, ἡ *Hellēnis* Greek woman
→ Ἕλλην.

Ἑλληνιστής, οῦ, ὁ *Hellēnistēs* Hellenist*

Lit.: E. C. Blackman, "The Hellenists of Acts VI, 1," *ExpTim* 48 (1936/37) 524f. — H. J. Cadbury, "The Hellenists," *Beginnings* V 59-74. — O. Cullmann, *The Johannine Circle* (1976), esp. 39ff. — E. Grässer, "Acta-Forschung seit 1960 (3. Teil)," *TRu* 42 (1977) 1-68. — F. Hahn, *Mission in the NT* (1965). — M. Hengel, *Between Jesus and Paul* (1983) 1-29 (+ 133-62), 48-64 (+ 166-79). — H. Kasting, *Die Anfänge der urchristlichen Mission* (1969), esp. 100-105. — C. F. D. Moule, "Once More, Who are the Hellenists?" *ExpTim* 70 (1958/59) 100-102. — G. Schneider, "Stephanus, die Hellenisten und Samaria," *Les Actes des Apotres* (ed. J. Kremer; 1979) 215-40. — M. Simon, *St. Stephen and the Hellenists in the Primitive Church* (1958). — H. Windisch, *TDNT* II, 504-16, esp. 508f. — For further bibliography see *TWNT* X, 1076.

1. Ἑλληνιστής, which is not attested in secular usage of the time, is found in the NT only in Acts 6:1; 9:29. In Acts 11:20 the reading Ἕλληνας ($\mathfrak{p}^{74}$ A D $\aleph^c$) is to be preferred over Ἑλληνιστάς (B D^b E Koine), because only so is the intended contrast to Ἰουδαῖοι (likewise Greek-speaking, v. 19) in effect. The v.l. is to be explained from the later assimilation of the meaning of Ἑλληνιστής to → Ἕλλην (= Gentile; for texts see Hengel 8, 139, n. 51). According to Acts 6:1 the *Hellenists* murmured against the "Hebrews" (→ Ἑβραῖος) because the Hellenists' widows were neglected in the daily distribution. In 9:29 it is said of Paul in Jerusalem: "He spoke and disputed against the *Hellenists;* but they were seeking to kill him."

Luke understands the "Hellenists" in Acts 9:29 probably as Jews of Jerusalem who spoke (only) Greek and who were distinguished from the Jews of the city who spoke Aramaic as their native tongue. According to 6:9 (cf. 24:12) they were organized by native country into various synagogues. The murmuring "Hellenists" of Acts 6:1 are thus the Christians of the early Jerusalem church who came from these Jewish circles. The form of Ἑλληνιστής is probably derived from ἑλληνίζειν, "to speak Greek." Only later did the vb. receive a negative connotation: "to adopt a Greek (i.e., pagan) lifestyle" (Cf. Hengel 9.)

The interpretation according to linguistic differences, although represented already by Chrysostom *Homily* 21 to Acts 9:29 (*PG* LX, 164), has frequently been thought too simple. One thus assumed that among the "Hellenists" there were Gentile Christians (e.g., Cadbury), Hellenistic proselytes (e.g., Blackman), or Hellenistic or Palestinian Jews of heterodox (perhaps Essene or Samaritan) origin who were open to syncretistic influences (Cullmann, who saw a connection with the "Johannine circle"; Simon 13: "paganizing"). On the history of interpretation see Hengel 4-11; Grässer 17-23.

2. In Jerusalem lived former Diaspora Jews, who had returned to the "holy" city for religious reasons (cf. the Greek Theodotus inscription from Ophel, *CIJ* II, no. 1404; Hengel 17f.). These people retained their native Greek tongue. The followers of Jesus who came from them joined together in the manner of a synagogue community (with their own Greek-speaking worship service). The group of seven in Acts 6:1-6 led by Stephen is probably to be regarded as the circle of leadership for the Hellenist Christians. The accusation against Stephen (cf. Acts 6:11, 13f.) indicates that the "Hellenists" had fallen into conflict with their former brothers in the faith because of their critical stance toward the Torah of Moses and the temple. Apparently in their preaching they recalled tendencies of Jesus' preaching and enthusiastically carried them further.

The persecution attested in 8:1, 4; 11:19 was directed principally against the Christian "Hellenists," not the "Hebrews" of Jerusalem (who retained more of observance of the law and temple piety). The obscure circle of "Hellenists" is "the most important historical connecting link between the proclamation of Jesus, on the one hand, and Paul before he was a Christian, on the other hand" (J. Blank, *Paulus und Jesus* [SANT 18, 1968] 247). From the same group the first impulse toward mission among the Samaritans (8:5ff.) and Gentiles (11:19) originated. In addition the transmission of the Aramaic Jesus tradition into Greek is probably to be ascribed largely to them.

J. Wanke

Ἑλληνιστί *Hellēnisti* in Greek*

The adv. refers to the Greek language in two NT passages: John 19:20, of the inscription at Jesus' cross (τίτλος), which "was written in Hebrew, in Latin, and *in Greek*"; Acts 21:37, the tribune's astonished question to Paul: "Do you know (γινώσκεις) *Greek?*"

ἐλλογέω, (ἐλλογάω) *ellogeō (ellogaō)* charge to someone's account*

This vb. is a contraction from ἐν λόγῳ (τίθημι), "charge to the account," and is a t.t. of mercantile language. The form -άω came into existence in the koine language through the mixing of the inflections -εῖν and -ᾶν (BDF §90). Rom 5:13: ἁμαρτία οὐκ ἐλλογεῖται, "sin *is* not *counted* where there is no law" (see G. Friedrich, "Ἁμαρτία οὐκ ἐλλογεῖται, Röm 5.13," *TLZ* 77 [1952] 523-28; H. Schlier, *Römerbrief* [HTKNT] ad loc., the latter on the background in the Jewish concept of "registration" of merit or transgression by "posting in heavenly books"); Phlm 18: Philemon should *charge* any damages by the runaway Onesimus *to the account* of Paul (ἐλλόγα). H. Preisker, *TDNT* II, 516f.

Ἐλμαδάμ *Elmadam* Elmadam*

Personal name in Luke 3:28.

ἐλπίζω *elpizō* hope (vb.)
→ ἐλπίς.

ἐλπίς, ίδος, ἡ *elpis* hope (noun), object of hope*
ἀπελπίζω *apelpizō* despair; hope for, expect*
ἐλπίζω *elpizō* hope (vb.)*
προελπίζω *proelpizō* hope in anticipation*

1. Occurrences in the NT — 2. Meaning and usage — 3. Usage in the individual writings of the NT — a) Acts — b) Paul — c) Colossians and Ephesians — d) The Pastorals — e) Hebrews — f) 1 Peter and 1 John — 4. Ἀπελπίζω and προελπίζω

Lit.: H. R. BALZ, *Heilsvertrauen und Welterfahrung. Strukturen der paulinischen Eschatologie nach Röm 8, 18-39* (1971). — G. BORNKAMM, "Die Hoffnung im Kolosserbrief," *idem, Aufsätze* IV, 206-13. — R. BULTMANN, "Die christliche Hoffnung und das Problem der Entmythologisierung," *idem, Glauben* III, 81-90. — *idem, TDNT* II, 517-23. — *idem, Theology* I, 324ff. — F. DE LA CALLE FLORES, "La esperanza de la creación, según el apóstol Pablo (Rom 8, 18-22)," *La Esperanza en la Biblia. XXX Semana Biblica Española* (1972) 169-86. — H. CONZELMANN, "Hoffnung," *RGG* III, 415-18. — *idem, Theology,* 184-91. — W. J. DALTON, " 'So that your Faith May Also Be your Hope in God' (1 Peter 1:21)," *Reconciliation and Hope* (FS L. L. Morris, ed. R. Banks; 1974) 262-74. — E. GAUGLER, *Der Epheserbrief* (Auslegung neutestamentlicher Schriften 6, 1966) 65-71. — E. GRÄSSER, *Der Glaube im Hebräerbrief* (1965). — F. KERSTIENS, *SM* III, 61-65. — B. KLAPPERT, *Die Eschatologie des Hebräerbriefs* (TEH 156, 1969). — O. KUSS, *Der Römerbrief* first fascicle ([2]1963) 195-98. — A. LINDEMANN, *Die Aufhebung der Zeit. Geschichtsverständnis und Eschatologie im Epheserbrief* (1975). — J. L. MORALES, "La Esperanza como objeto y virtud en las dos cartas más antiguas de San Pablo (1.2. Tesalonicenses)," *La Esperanza en la Biblia. XXX Semana Biblica Española* (1972) 131-67. — G. NEBE, *"Hoffnung" bei Paulus* (1983) — E. NEUHÄUSLER, *LTK* V, 416-18. — M. NICOLAU, "La esperanza en la Carta a los Hebreos," in *La Esperanza en la Biblia. XXX Semana Biblica Española* (1972) 187-202. — K. H. RENGSTORF, *TDNT* II, 523-29. — H. SCHLIER, "Über die Hoffnung," Schlier II, 135-45. — *idem, Nun aber bleiben diese Drei* (1971). — G. SEGALLA, "Gli Orizzonti della Speranza in S. Paolo," *Studia Patavia* 21 (1974) 5-27. — F. J. STEINMETZ, *Protologische Heils-Zuversicht. Die Strukturen des soteriologischen und christologischen Denkens im Kolosser- und Epheserbriefe* (FTS 2, 1969). — A. VÖGTLE, *Das Neue Testament und die Zukunft des Kosmos* (1970). — H. ZIMMERMANN, *Das Bekenntnis der Hoffnung* (BBB 47, 1977). — For further bibliography see *TWNT* X, 1076-78; *DNTT* II, 246.

1. The noun ἐλπίς does not appear in the Gospels. See CWSD
Outside the Pauline letters it appears most frequently in Acts (8 times). It appears 5 times in Hebrews; 3 times each in Ephesians, Colossians, Titus, and 1 Peter, and once each in 2 Thessalonians, 1 Timothy, and 1 John. In the Pauline

epistles (25 total occurrences), Romans has the most occurrences (13), followed by 1 Thessalonians (4); 1 Corinthians, 2 Corinthians (3 each); Galatians, Philippians (once each). The verb ἐλπίζω appears sporadically in the Gospels and in Acts: once each in Matthew and John, 3 times in Luke, and twice in Acts. It appears most frequently in Paul's letters (15 times), limited there to Romans (4), 1 Corinthians (3), 2 Corinthians (5), Philippians (2), and Philemon (1). Beyond that, it appears in 1 Timothy (4), Hebrews (1), 1 Peter (2), and 2–3 John (once each). The distribution of occurrences does not reflect the significance of the concept in the respective books. The compounds ἀπελπίζω (Luke 6:35) and προελπίζω (Eph 1:12) are hapax legomena. In Mark, 2 Timothy, James, 2 Peter, Jude, and Revelation the word group has no representatives.

2. The meaning of the four words is sufficiently grasped with the rendering *hope* (noun), *object of hope,* and *to hope.*

In Ephesians, Colossians, Hebrews, and 1 Peter ἐλπίς is used primarily for the *object of hope* (Paul only in Gal 5:5 and possibly also in Rom 8:24b). Those who hope are primarily the Christian Church, individual Christians, or Paul in his missionary activity; other than those they include: Christ (Acts 2:26), the twelve tribes of Israel (26:7), the Jews (John 5:45; Acts 24:15), the Gentiles (Matt 12:21; Rom 15:12), Abraham (Rom 4:18), the disciples on the road to Emmaus (Luke 24:21), "the holy women" (1 Pet 3:5), and the whole creation (Rom 8:20). While the hope of all those subjects is directed to objects relevant to salvation, the goals of the hearers of the "sermon on the plain" (Luke 6:34f.), the owners of the slave girl (Acts 16:19), the company on the ship (Acts 27:20), Herod (Luke 23:8), Felix (Acts 24:26), and those who plow and harvest (1 Cor 9:10) are of a varied nature: hope is aimed at compensation for what is loaned (Luke 6:34f.), profit (Acts 16:19; 24:26), rescue from distress at sea (Acts 27:20), a sign from Jesus (Luke 23:8), and the yield from plowing and harvesting (1 Cor 9:10). In addition the hope for an imminent meeting is also to be mentioned (1 Tim 3:14; 2 John 12; 3 John 14). In two passages the Gentiles are said to be excluded from the hope of salvation (Eph 2:12; 1 Thess 4:13). In only one passage (1 Cor 13:7) is an abstraction (love) the subject of hoping.

In the great majority of passages, therefore, hope is connected with salvation. Even within this relationship hope is viewed under a variety of perspectives. There are statements defining the nature of hope (Rom 8:24f.; cf. Heb 11:1). The content of eschatological hope is portrayed in a variety of ways. Likewise there are frequent statements about the basis of the hope of salvation, its outstanding characteristics, what reactions are seen in those who have such hope, and how one must exert oneself for it. In the Pauline letters hope determines also the relationship of the apostle to the Church.

3. a) Acts employs ἐλπίς and ἐλπίζω in a theologically significant way, and indeed only in speeches with an apologetic touch. Hope is directed toward the resurrection of the dead and the promise to Israel regarding the Messiah. Already David speaks in Psalm 15 LXX of the repose of the flesh "on the basis of *hope*" (RSV "in hope") and witnesses to the fact that Jesus cannot be held by death (Acts 2:26). Paul's affirmation that he stands before the court because of the hope for the resurrection of the dead leads to the division of the Pharisees from the Sadducees (23:6f.). In Paul's defense before Felix (24:15f.) hope for the resurrection of the righteous and the unrighteous is said to be an important motive for his reputable life. The hope directed toward the promise given to the fathers, i.e., the messianic expectation, is the reason why Paul stands before the court. On the other hand, faith in the resurrection must lead his opponents to Jesus the resurrected one, as the Messiah (26:6-8). Paul declares to the leaders of the Jews in Rome that he is imprisoned (28:20) "because of the *hope* of Israel." The author of Acts emphasizes in all these passages that this hope is not specifically Christian, but rather belongs to part of Israel (23:8) or to all of Israel (24:15; 26:7; 28:20).

b) According to Paul Abraham provides an example of true hope. Hope is based on the divine promise and leaves behind it any uncertainty, venturing against all hope (Rom 4:18). Hope, by its very nature, is associated with not seeing. "*Hope* that sees [or "is seen," as in RSV] is not *hope*" (Rom 8:24; βλεπομένη can be taken as act. or pass.). Thus existence in hope demands patient expectation (Rom 8:25; 1 Thess 1:3) of that which does not belong to the visible world. According to 1 Thess 1:3; 5:8 hope is, together with faith and love, the characteristic of being a Christian and is enumerated as part of the Christian armor. When Paul says in 1 Cor 13:13 that the triad faith–hope–love abides, this does not mean that hope lives on in the eschatological consummation, for that would hardly be possible for faith and hope. What is said applies to the present; the triad determines Christian existence in the present.

Hope is characteristic of the one who has been justified. The person who stands in grace possesses hope for the glory of God (Rom 5:1f.; cf. also 2 Thess 2:16). This hope is not disappointed because of God's love, which has already been demonstrated (Rom 5:5), i.e., because of the justification and reconciliation through Christ already effected by God (vv. 9f.). Finally this hope is supported by the divine predestination of the believer to salvation and thus receives the greatest possible basis for security (1 Thess 5:9). Anyone who is not included has no hope (4:13). Such hope for the coming salvation (5:9) is fulfilled in varied ways: Its object is the parousia of Jesus Christ the Lord (1:3, 10), Christ as the guarantee of the future of Christians (1 Cor 15:19), protection or rescue from the eschatological wrath (1 Thess 5:9; Rom 5:9f.), sonship, and "the redemption of our bodies" (Rom 8:23). Christians also await "righteousness" (→ δικαιοσύνη 3) as the object of hope (Gal 5:5)—a surprising affirmation, as Paul otherwise describes righteousness as a gift of salvation in the present (cf. Rom 5:1, 9; 8:30; Gal 2:16-21). One must understand righteousness as an object of hope as definitive and completed righteousness or simply as final salvation. The salvation hoped for consists of life shared with Christ (1 Thess 5:10).

In this understanding of Christian existence the Christian can boast even in the tribulations which befall him or her because they produce patience in persons defined by hope. Patience in turn produces character, which results in new hope (Rom 5:3f.). Just as one boasts on the basis of hope, so also can one rejoice in it (12:12). Indeed, Paul asks God, who is a "God of *hope,*" to fill the Church with all joy and all peace in believing (15:13). Here Paul is asking that God's promise might produce fullness of joy and peace through faith, and that joy and peace might in turn bring again abundance of hope by the Spirit's power (*contra* E. Käsemann, *Commentary on Romans* [1980] 387, according to whom ἐλπίς in 15:12 serves as a reminder of "the cosmic goal of redemption"). The example of Christ and the encouragement of Scripture are given to believers to maintain hope in the time of temptation (v. 4; *contra* Käsemann 383, according to whom hope in this verse "points forward to vv. 7-13, namely, the eschatological uniting of the church of Jews and Gentiles"). On the other hand, Paul emphasizes the delay of the parousia, perhaps over against pneumatic self-security and in awareness of the pressures of the present time (8:23ff.). Nevertheless in the presence of the future he does not lose his focus on the present salvation: "For *in* this *hope* (τῇ γὰρ ἐλπίδι) we were saved" (8:24a).

What is true for Christians as they live in hope is true also for creation. If it is subjected to decay, nevertheless it is "in hope" (Rom 8:20). It awaits "the revealing of the sons of God" (v. 19), but also its own liberation "from its bondage to decay" to "obtain the glorious liberty of the children of God" (v. 21). Of course the significance of what is said here about the future of the whole creation is rejected in various ways; e.g., what is said about the groaning of the creation is supposed to serve only to assure the elect that the eschatological woes have broken in and *their* (understood exclusively) consummation has come near. In 15:12 Christ is "an object of hope for all creation" (Käsemann 387; more circumscribed is Michel, *Römerbrief* [KEK] 360: hope of the Gentiles; H. Schlier, *Römerbrief* [HTKNT] 425 takes it as present: "Christ has filled all people with hope").

Paul uses ἐλπίς and ἐλπίζω in a variety of ways beyond the usual soteriological alignment of the terminology for hope. He especially has hope for the churches. Hope is the determining stance of Paul when his concern is to be accepted in the Corinthian church as apostle and to be able to stand the test before the church. He hopes that the Corinthians will understand him fully (2 Cor 1:13), that he will stand openly before their conscience just as he is known openly to God (5:11), and that they will recognize that he has not failed (13:6). He hopes to be able to stand even greater before them and to be able to preach beyond Corinth (10:15f.). He hopes also that the Corinthians understand their suffering as Christ's suffering and that they will consequently receive consolation just as he has himself (1:7). His hope is surprised by the readiness of the churches in Macedonia (8:5). The church of Thessalonica will be his hope, alongside others, at the return of Christ (1 Thess 2:19).

Hope in God fills the apostle in connection with his apostolic service. He hopes that God, who delivered him from death, will also deliver him again (2 Cor 1:10). He hopes finally that his ministry of the Spirit (3:8) and of righteousness (v. 9) will produce doxa in abundance (vv. 11f.). According to Phil 1:20 the apostle hopes that he will be ashamed in nothing. That he be ashamed is impossible, since Christ is glorified in the bodily fate of Paul, whether through his life or his death.

Hope extends finally to the realization of travel plans (1 Cor 16:7; Phil 2:19, 23; Phlm 22), so that Paul's planning is not only a human activity; it occurs also "in consciousness of a living relationship to the Lord Jesus" (J. Gnilka, *Philipperbrief* [HTKNT] 157).

c) In contrast to the authentic Pauline letters Colossians speaks only of the *spes quae speratur,* of the object of hope. It is kept in heaven, appears as content of the gospel, and shapes the Church toward faith and active love (Col 1:4f.). A condition for salvation is that the Church not allow itself to be diverted from the hope of the gospel (1:23). Colossians understands the preached Christ concretely as the hope of glory (1:27), he who, according to 3:1-4, sits above at the right hand of God. At his revelation those who believe will also appear with him in glory. "This shifts the concept of 'hope' from a temporal-eschatological orientation to one which has spatial characteristics" (E. Lohse, *Colossians and Philemon* [Hermeneia] 18).

Ephesians also speaks of hope as the object of hoping (Eph 1:18), where it treats hope in depth. When hope is characterized as ἐλπὶς τῆς κλήσεως (1:18; 4:4), this signifies that hope is closely associated with acceptance of the gospel and entrance into the Church. Only in the realm of the Church is hope possible. This hope is defined more precisely in a twofold way. In terms of content it is "the riches of his glorious inheritance among [RSV "in"] the saints" (1:18): completed doxa in community with the

ἐλπίς

angels, which is still expected (or "does Ephesians refer here to membership in the concrete Christian community"? Then the Church is "absolutely certain of the completion, so that it can speak in such confident words"; so J. Ernst, *Epheserbrief* [RNT] 288f.). This hope has its basis in the extraordinary greatness of God's power, which is made known to the believers (v. 19), as it has already been made known in Christ (vv. 20-23). For the author of Ephesians, this situation of being called in this one hope of their calling is an appropriate motif in calling for the preservation of unity in the Church (4:4).

d) According to the Pastorals Christ Jesus is the content of the hope of Christians (1 Tim 1:1). Their hope is aimed toward his parousia; they await "the appearing of the glory of the great God and our Savior Jesus Christ" (Titus 2:13 [RSV reads differently]; cf. 2 Tim 4:8). Their present conduct is determined by that fact. They await the inheritance of eternal life in the future, for, having been justified by grace on the basis of the washing of rebirth and renewal through the Spirit, which God has poured out generously, they are "heirs in accordance with the *hope* [RSV "in hope"] of eternal life" (Titus 3:5-7). The work of the apostle himself is determined by this hope for eternal life which God has promised (1:2). In some instances the hope is directed toward God himself. Thus the Christian's effort and striving is based on hope in the living God, whose will to save is universal and so pertains esp. to those who believe (1 Tim 4:10). A genuine widow is recognized by the fact that she sets her hope on God (1 Tim 5:5). And finally Timothy must warn the rich of a hope in the uncertain riches; the rich should instead direct their hope to God, who richly provides everything for our enjoyment (6:17).

e) Hebrews gives considerable emphasis to ἐλπίς. The prerequisite for the Church to be the house of Christ (or of God) is its holding fast to the confidence and pride of hope (Heb 3:6). When one compares this with the old order of the law, the law is seen to be weak and useless, while the new arrangement provides the better hope because it brings access to God (7:18f.). Thus in addition to active ministry on behalf of the other person, one must be concerned in the same way about the completion of hope until the end (6:11); this means either that one should hold on to the entire conviction of hope until the end (A. Strobel, *Hebräerbrief* [NTD] 140) or that one should make the effort until the fullness is attained of that which is hope's content and goal (O. Kuss, *Hebräerbrief* [RNT] 83).

On the basis of God's promise and the oath which confirms it—two unchangeable things—Christians have firm confidence to hold on to the hope which is made available to them (Heb 6:18). As the sure and firm anchor of the soul it gives them stability. When the anchor enters beyond the curtain (v. 19), what is meant is that it extends into the very place of God's presence and is established in the world of eternity. Because Jesus has already gone ahead as pioneer and high priest of the order of Melchizedek, the Church will reach this goal (v. 20). In 10:23 the hope is explicitly determined by the installation of Jesus as high priest. Confession of Jesus, the high priest, is "at the same time the confession of our hope" (Zimmermann 208). It "is called 'confession of hope' because confession of Jesus the high priest, which takes in the promise guaranteed by God, involves being able to go with Jesus on his high-priestly way" (*ibid.* 216).

f) In 1 Peter also hope stands at the center of Christian existence. When Christians are expected to be ready always "to make a defense to any one who calls you to account for the *hope* that you bear among you," i.e., "that is among [RSV "in"] you" (1 Pet 3:15), ἐλπίς is thereby made the decisive factor in Christian life. Furthermore, "the holy women" (3:5) are characterized more precisely as those "who *hoped* in God."

In the blessing in 1 Peter 1 there is an extended description of the object of hope which awaits Christians (1:3-9). They are reborn to a living hope, which is guaranteed and does not deceive because it is based on the resurrection of Jesus Christ from the dead (v. 3). This hope is defined as an imperishable, unspoiled, and unfading inheritance preserved in heaven (v. 4). God himself protects Christians by his power—nevertheless through faith—for salvation—another definition of hope—which lies ready to be revealed at the end (v. 5). In the face of such hope Christians will break out in eschatological jubilation, even though they now experience many temptations (v. 6). If they confess in faith that God raised Christ from the dead and glorified him, then this faith becomes hope that the same will be granted to them (v. 21). But they are encouraged to gird the loins (of their minds) and to be sober, awaiting with full hope the salvation that is described (v. 13) as "grace" to be given to them at the revelation of Jesus Christ.

In 1 John 3:3 *hope* is directed to Jesus, the one who returns. Because he appears then as the glorified one, Christians will also share in his glory. The basis for this conviction is given already in the fact that they are children of God.

4. The compounds **ἀπελπίζω** and **προελπίζω** only slightly alter the meaning of the simple verb, the prepositional prefixes ἀπό and πρό being used to give more precise distinctions. The decision to *give up hope* of receiving back what has been loaned (ἀπελπίζω, Luke 6:35) contains within it the promise that one will be a child of God. The definition of προελπίζω (Eph 1:12) depends on whether "we" is understood as Jewish Christians only or Christians in general. If it is Jewish Christians, then "before the Gentiles" or even "already before the Christ's appearance" is implied by προ- (see BAGD ad loc.); if it

is Christians in general, "the προ- refers to the present in relation to the eschatological consummation" (Bultmann, *TDNT* II, 535).

B. Mayer

Ἐλύμας, α *Elymas* Elymas*

A Jewish magician on Cyprus mentioned in Acts 13:8. According to v. 6 he was also called Bar-Jesus. Acts gives the impression in v. 8b that the two names were synonymous (BAGD ad loc.), but it is not to be ruled out that Luke understands ὁ μάγος as the interpretation of the name Elymas (E. Haenchen, *The Acts of the Apostles* [1971] 398). The latter view might receive support from the argument by L. Yaure ("Elymas, Nehelamite, Pethor," *JBL* 79 [1960] 297-314) that Elymas is derived from Aram. *ḥlm'*, "interpreter of dreams, magician." On the form of the name in D (Ἑτοιμᾶς) see *TCGNT* 402f. The similar name Αἰλύμας is attested in Diodorus Siculus xx.17.1, 18.3 as the name of a Libyan king.

ελωι *elōi* my God!*
λεμα *lema* why?*
σαβαχθανι *sabachthani* you have forsaken me*

1. Occurrences and variants — 2. Original form and the question of authenticity — 3. Theological significance

Lit.: J. Blinzler, *Der Prozeß Jesu* ([4]1969). — T. Boman, "Das letzte Wort Jesu," *ST* 17 (1963) 103-19. — H. Gese, "Psalm 22 und das NT," *ZTK* 65 (1968) 1-22. — J. Gnilka, " 'Mein Gott, mein Gott, warum hast du mich verlassen?' (Mk 15, 34 Par.)," *BZ* 3 (1959) 294-97. — A. Guillaume, "Mt 27:46 in Light of the Dead Sea Scrolls," *PEQ* 83 (1951) 78-81. — R. H. Gundry, *The Use of the OT in St. Matthew's Gospel* (NovTSup 18, 1967) 63-66. — Jeremias, *Theology* 5. — R. Pesch, *Das Markusevangelium* (HTKNT) II (1977) 494-96. — M. Rehm, "Eli, Eli, lamma sabacthani," *BZ* 2 (1958) 275-78. — H. Schützeichel, "Der Todesschrei Jesu. Bemerkungen zu einer Theologie des Kreuzes," *TTZ* 83 (1974) 1-16. — D. P. Senior, *The Passion Narrative According to Matthew. A Redactional Study* (BETL 39, 1975) 295-97.

1. Ελωι, ελωι, λεμα σαβαχθανι ("My God, my God, why have you forsaken me?") appears in Mark 15:34 as the cry of Jesus immediately before his death. It is a transliteration of the Aram. translation of Ps 22:2a. The parallel in Matt 27:46, which is dependent on Mark 15:34, offers a mixture of Hebrew and Aramaic: Ηλι, ηλι, λεμα σαβαχθανι. The text witness D exhibits in Mark 15:34 par. Matt 27:46 has Ηλι, ηλι, λαμα ζαφθανι, which conforms to Hebrew (on this scribal corrective see Dalman, *Words* 53). Both Gospels have Greek translations immediately after the Psalm citation, both of which deviate somewhat from the LXX form. In extracanonical literature the variant ἡ δύναμίς μου, ἡ δύναμίς (μου), κατέλειψάς με, "my power, my power, you have left me," is noteworthy (*Gos. Pet.* 19).

2. On the question of the original form of the prayer opinions vary (cf. Gnilka 295f.). An answer depends on how independent Mark 15:35f. (the Elijah misunderstanding) is. Unlike Mark 15:34, the Matthean version underlines the misunderstanding of the cry by having ηλι, which sounds similar to the name Elijah, in place of ελωι. The Matthean version and the D v.l. are to be understood as an interpretation, i.e., as an assimilation to the MT. The fundamental question is thus not whether the D v.l. is original in Matthew or Mark or both. It is, rather, whether the apparently primary Markan tradition in the present text tradition renders the Aram. translation of Jesus' cry from the cross, and even whether the cry is authentic (i.e., spoken by Jesus) at all. As it is a quotation of Scripture, the Hebrew form is conceivable in the mouth of Jesus. This would best explain the confusion of the name of God with the name of the prophet by the bystanders (Pesch 495 considers it "wanton distortion"). The Aram. form is, however, at least pre-Markan. Final certainty concerning the original form and the question of authenticity is not possible.

3. The cry of Jesus can be understood as answering to the preceding calumnies. It appears to confirm what the nearby scoffers think: his God has abandoned him. We cannot deny to the saying the character of deepest human abandonment and pain. But when Jesus in his abandonment "flees to the one by whom he feels abandoned" (Schützeichel 8), he reveals God (the one who is the answer that Jesus aims at) as the partner whom one may always address. What the centurion is to confess, "Truly, this man was the Son of God" (Mark 15:39), arises from and corresponds to this "my God" spoken in the darkest hour.

F. G. Untergassmair

ἐμαυτοῦ, ῆς *emautou* my, mine*

1. Occurrences and frequency in the NT — 2. As dir. obj. — 3. With a prep. — 4. As possessive gen. with a noun — 5. Referring to the subj. of the main clause

Lit.: BDF §64.1; 283; 284.2. — Kühner, *Grammatik* I/1, §168. — Mayser, *Grammatik* II/1, 65-72 (§15). — Moulton, *Grammar* III, 41-43

1. The first person reflexive pron. (the dat. and acc. forms are discussed here with the gen.) appears in the NT a total of 37 times, remarkably almost exclusively in John's Gospel (16 times) and Paul's letters (14 times in the undisputed authentic letters). Elsewhere it appears only in Luke-Acts (6 times) and Matt 8:9 (par. Luke 7:8). When one considers the frequency of pronouns in Hellenistic Greek, the small use of reflexive pronouns is remarkable. The reflexive pron. is used almost exclusively as dir. obj. of the vb. (→ 2), but other than that—except in prep. phrases (→ 3)—is almost totally neglected.

2. As dir. obj. ἐμαυτόν can come after the vb. (John 8:54; 14:21; 17:19; Acts 20:24; 26:2, 9; Rom 11:4; 2 Cor 2:1; 11:7) or before it (Luke 7:7; 1 Cor 4:3, 4; 9:19; 2 Cor 11:9; Gal 2:18; Phil 3:13).

3. Only in the Fourth Gospel do these prep. phrases appear: ἀπ' ἐμαυτοῦ, *of myself* (John 5:30; 7:17, 28; 8:28, 42; 10:18 *[of my own accord, voluntarily]*; 14:10) and ἐξ ἐμαυτοῦ, "on my own authority" (12:49). Here the "Johannine" Jesus speaks of himself, primarily in negative statements (5:30; 7:28; 8:28, 42; 12:49; 14:10): "The οὐκ ἀπ' ἐμαυτοῦ designates . . . the nature and character of Jesus in a comprehensive sense. . . . God speaks and acts through and in Jesus" (J. Blank, *Krisis. Untersuchungen zur johanneischen Christologie und Eschatologie* [1964] 112-14 [quoting 113]).

Other prep. phrases are: εἰς ἐμαυτόν (1 Cor 4:6; for εἰς ἐμέ, *to myself*), περὶ ἐμαυτοῦ, *about myself* (John 5:31; 8:14, 18; Acts 24:10 [τὰ περὶ ἐμαυτοῦ], πρὸς ἐμαυτόν, *to me* (John 12:32; 14:3; Phlm 13 ["with me"]), ὑπ' ἐμαυτόν, *under my authority* (Matt 8:9 par. Luke 7:8), ὑπὲρ ἐμαυτοῦ (2 Cor 12:5 for περὶ ἐμαυτοῦ; BDF §231.1).

4. 'Εμαυτοῦ appears as a possessive gen. with a noun in 1 Cor 10:33: μὴ ζητῶν τὸ ἐμαυτοῦ σύμφορον, "not seeking *my own* advantage," in contrast to τὸ τῶν πολλῶν, "that of many" (BDF §283.3).

5. In 1 Cor 7:7 Paul wishes that all men were ὡς καὶ ἐμαυτόν, "as *I myself* am," i.e., living in an unmarried state (ἄγαμος, v. 8). The reflexive pron. appears here because what is referred to is the subj. of the main clause (θέλω). It is acc. by attraction to πάντας (H. Conzelmann, *1 Corinthians* [Hermeneia] ad loc.).

G. Schneider

ἐμβαίνω *embainō* step (into)*

This vb. appears only in the Gospels (5 times in Matthew, 5 in Mark, 3 in Luke, 3 in John). It is used with εἰς of stepping into a boat (πλοῖον: Mark 4:1; 5:18; 6:45; 8:10, 13; Matt 8:23; 9:1; 13:2; 14:22; 15:39; Luke 5:3; 8:22, 37; John 6:17; 21:3) or boats (πλοιάρια: John 6:24). 'Εμβαίνω also appears in textual variants (Matt 14:32 [C Koine, etc.; πλοῖον]; John 5:4 [A C[3] K, etc.; of stepping into water]; 6:22 [ℵ* K Θ, etc.; πλοιάριον]; Acts 21:6 [B E *pc*; πλοῖον]).

ἐμβάλλω *emballō* throw (into)*

Luke 12:5: the one who "has power to *cast* into hell" (ἐμβαλεῖν εἰς τὴν γέενναν; cf. Schulz, *Q* 158, who considers Matt 10:28 ["destroy both soul and body in hell"] original).

ἐμβάπτω *embaptō* dip (into)*

Mark 14:20 par. Matt 26:23 (par. John 13:26 in 𝔭[66] Koine A D W, etc.), of dipping (the hand, in Matthew) into a dish (τρύβλιον). Mark 14:20 has the mid. form ὁ ἐμβαπτόμενος μετ' ἐμοῦ, "one who *is dipping [what he holds in his hand]* . . . with me." Within the framework of the betrayal sayings of Jesus, Mark 14:20c varies the allusion to Ps 40:10 (in the preceding v. 18) "in view of what actually happens in the Passover meal, the eating of the preliminary course, in which the participants in the meal dip the bitter herbs into the ground fruits" (R. Pesch, *Markus* [HTKNT] II, 350; cf. Billerbeck IV, 63-67).

ἐμβατεύω *embateuō* enter*

Col 2:18: ἃ ἑόρακεν ἐμβατεύων, to be translated *what he has seen at his entrance* (cf. E. Schweizer, *The Letter to the Colossians* [1982] 160). Here the word probably does not refer to an initiation into the mysteries (cf. BAGD ad loc.), but rather to a visionary experience in which the Colossians experienced the entrance into the heavenly sanctuary. *TWNT* X, 1078 (bibliography).

ἐμβιβάζω *embibazō* bring in, put on board (a ship)*

Acts 27:6: ἐνεβίβασεν ἡμᾶς, he (the centurion) *"put us on board,"* literally, "he let us enter (the ship)" (first aorist).

ἐμβλέπω *emblepō* look (at), view*

This vb. appears 12 times in the NT, all in the Gospels and Acts and all in the literal sense, not in the fig. sense (as in *1 Clem.* 19:3). Only in Matt 6:26 ("*Look* at the birds of the air") can the fig. meaning be considered (cf. Luke 12:24). There and in Acts 1:11 (A C Koine D; see *TCGNT*) ἐμβλέπω is used with εἰς; in Matt 19:26 par. Mark 10:27; Acts 22:11 the vb. is used absolutely. Mark demonstrates a relative preference for the vb. (Mark 8:25; 10:21, 27; 14:67). Further occurrences are in Luke 20:17 (not in par. Mark 12:10); 22:61 (not in Mark); John 1:36, 42; Acts 22:11.

ἐμβριμάομαι (ἐμβριμόομαι) *embrimaomai (embrimoomai)* snort; scold*

The vb. is attested in the meaning *snort* as an expression of rage (BAGD ad loc.; on the two forms see BDF §90). With dat. of the person, *scold* (Mark 1:43; 14:5); John 11:38f.: ἐμβριμώμενος ἐν ἑαυτῷ, *become indignant, be furious*; 11:33: ἐνεβριμήσατο τῷ πνεύματι, in the same sense (of an "inner" excitement of Jesus); cf. J. Beutler, "Psalm 42/43 im Johannesevangelium," *NTS* 25 (1978/79) 40-44 (33-57).

ἐμέω *emeō* spit (out)*

Rev 3:16, fig.: "I will *spit* [RSV "spew"] you out of my mouth." Cf. *T. Ash.* 7:3 (despised like bad water).

ἐμμαίνομαι *emmainomai* be enraged*

In Acts 26:11 (with dat., as in Josephus, *Ant.* xvii.174) Paul says about his past as a persecutor of Christians that he was fiercely *enraged* against them.

Ἐμμανουήλ *Emmanouēl* Emmanuel*

Lit.: R. E. BROWN, *The Birth of the Messiah* (1977) 143-53. — J. LANGE, *Das Erscheinen des Auferstandenen im Evangelium nach Matthäus* (Forschungen zur Bibel 11, 1973), esp. 329f., 344f., 348, 492-95. — W. ROTHFUCHS, *Die Erfüllungszitate des Matthäus-Evangeliums* (BWANT 88, 1969) esp. 33f., 57-60.

1. Ἐμμανουήλ is the transliteration of Heb. *ʿimmānû ʾēl*, "God (is/be) with us," appearing in Isa 7:14 LXX. It represents esp. a declaration of trust (cf. Ps 46:8, 12), which may have been at home in the temple liturgy of Jerusalem (H. Wildberger, *Jesaja 1-12* [BKAT] 293, 332f.; cf. also H. D. Preuss, *TDOT* I, 450-58; D. Vetter, *Jahwes Mit-Sein. Ein Ausdruck des Segens* [1971]). The prophet Isaiah cites this declaration in 8:10; and in a definite historical situation (the Syro-Ephraimitic war of 734/33?) he employs it as a "name with a meaning" in a message directed to Ahaz (7:14): in a short time a young woman (the wife of the king himself? so Wildberger 290f., where other identifications are discussed) will give birth to a son and call him "God with us": a sign of judgment on faithless Ahaz and at the same time a sign of God's constant faithfulness toward the "house of David" (Wildberger 288-300; somewhat different is Preuss 458-63). There is no indication that Isa 7:14 was understood in a messianic sense in Judaism (Billerbeck I, 75; Braun, *Qumran* I, 8).

2. Matthew has inserted at 1:23 the "fulfillment citation" (Rothfuchs) from Isa 7:14 into the narrative which he has received of the divine begetting of God's Son (Matt 1:18-21, 24-25; → παρθένος). Matthew is not in this way trying to convince Jews that the one so born is the Messiah (the Isaiah passage was scarcely able to do that; → 1); rather he wants to make clear to his church that the Jesus story is anchored in God's plan for salvation and announced previously by the prophets of the OT; thus the OT is understood as a "Christian" book of the story of Jesus.

Instead of "she (the mother of the child) will call him . . ." (Isa 7:14 MT; LXX has: "you will call him . . .") Matthew writes: "they will call him . . . ," i.e., as in RSV, "his name shall be called." Thus God is not described in a veiled way as the one who gives the name (so many exegetes). Rather Matthew takes into account that the Son does not receive the name Emmanuel at all, but is—in accordance with the instruction of the angel (Matt 1:21)—named Jesus.

Emmanuel remains a "name with meaning" in Matthew as the translation in Matt 1:23 explicitly shows: Jesus the "Savior" (v. 21b) will be understood, i.e., by the Christian community, as the one in whom God has shown himself as "God with us." This the reader should recall at the conclusion of the book (Matt 28:20b) where the resurrected Son says to the Church: "I am with you. . . ." Thus the confession "he is God-with-us" and the promise "I am with you" form an inclusio (Lange) around the whole of the story and work of Jesus according to Matthew.

N. Walter

Ἐμμαοῦς *Emmaous* Emmaus*

Lit.: ABEL, *Geographie* II ([3]1967) 314-16. — H. D. BETZ, "Ursprung und Wesen christlichen Glaubens nach der Emmauslegende (Lk 24, 13-32)," *ZTK* 66 (1969) 7-21. — BILLERBECK II, 269-71. — J. DUPONT, "Les pélerins d'Emmaüs," *Miscellanea Biblica b. Ubach* (1953) 349-74. — H. HAAG, *LTK* III, 848f. — KOPP, *Stätten*, 445-50. — L. PIROT, *DBSup* II (1934) 1049-63. — J. WANKE, *Die Emmauserzählung* (1973) (bibliography).

1. Ἐμμαοῦς, which is mentioned in Luke 24:13 and described there as a village (κώμη), is identified in early Church tradition (first attested by Eusebius, *Onomasticon* [ed. E. Klostermann, 90]) with the Emmaus of 1 Macc 3:40; 4:3.

This Emmaus lay *ca.* 28 km. (about 160-170 stadia) northwest of Jerusalem where the Judean mountainous terrain meets the coastal plain. In the NT era it was the administrative headquarters of a Judean toparchy (cf. Josephus, *B.J.* iii.55). At the instigation of the prefect Julius Africanus, an acquaintance of Origen, the city adopted the name Nicopolis around A.D. 223 (texts in Kopp 446, n. 120). In Arabian times it bore the name *ʿAmwâs.* The Dominicans of the École Biblique in Jerusalem excavated a basilica with three naves in *ʿAmwâs* in 1924-30. The basilica was built on the foundation of a late Roman villa (cf. L.-H. Vincent and F.-M. Abel, *Emmaüs, sa basilique et son histoire* [1932]). Vincent dates the basilica to the 3rd cent. However, this early date most probably can be given only to the older parts of the mosaics found in the Roman villa (cf. C. Watzinger, *Denkmäler Palästinas* [1935] 126, 149). The archeological evidence can confirm only the early existence of a Christian church in Nicopolis.

Because of its greater proximity to Jerusalem, the site named *el-Qubeibeh* (11 km. west of Jerusalem, about 60 stadia) has been regarded as the Emmaus of Luke 24:13 since the late Middle Ages (cf. Kopp 449f.). Also an Ἀμμαοῦς mentioned in Josephus, *B.J.* vii.217 (at the approximate location of the village *Qalôniyeh, ca.* 6 km. west of Jerusalem) is occasionally identified with Emmaus (so Billerbeck), but there is no support in tradition for this location.

2. The information about Emmaus given in Luke 24:13 contributes considerably to the confusion. The majority of the mss. read "60 stadia," while only a few (among them א) insert ἑκατόν (hundred) and read "160 stadia." Possibly the addition occurred because of the influence of the local tradition of Emmaus = Nicopolis. It is less probable, on the other hand, that an original number 160 was reduced to 60 without the support of a concrete tradition.

The tension between the better reading "60 stadia" and the tradition connecting it to the more distant Nicopolis can be solved by means of redaction criticism. Luke has little pertinent information about the location of Emmaus (cf. H. Conzelmann, *The Theology of St. Luke* [1961] 94).

He connects an appearance tradition (Jesus appears as one unknown but is recognized at the meal) that came to him with his resurrection chapter, which is concentrated in Jerusalem. Jerusalem has theological meaning for Luke; for him it is the place where the way of Jesus is completed and where the mission begins. The motif of the departure and the return of the "Emmaus disciples" subordinates the ancient Easter story to the intention of the Evangelist, who wants to bind the Easter kerygma (cf. 24:34) to Jerusalem (cf. Wanke 116-22).

J. Wanke

ἐμμένω *emmenō* remain (in), persevere (in)*

Paul *remained* for two years ἐν ἰδίῳ μισθώματι (Acts 28:30). All other NT uses of this word are to be rendered *continue, remain*: Acts 14:22: ἐμμένειν τῇ πίστει; Gal 3:10: ἐμμένει πᾶσιν τοῖς γεγραμμένοις (cf. Deut 27:26 LXX; on the alteration of the biblical wording by Paul, see BAGD s.v.); Heb 8:9: ἐνέμειναν ἐν τῇ διαθήκῃ μου. F. Hauck, *TDNT* IV, 576f.

Ἑμμώρ *Hemmōr* Hamor*

Personal name in Acts 7:16. According to *T. Levi* 5:4; 6:3 Hamor is progenitor of the υἱοὶ Ἑμμώρ. The sons of Hamor lived in the area of Shechem. Abraham purchased a burial place from them (Gen 33:19; 34:2; Josh 24:32).

ἐμός, 3 *emos* my, mine

1. Linguistic history — 2. Occurrences in the NT — 3. Usage — 4. Ἐμός in John

Lit.: BAGD s.v. — BDF §285. — G. D. KILPATRICK, "The Possessive Pronouns in the NT," *JTS* 42 (1941) 184-86. — LSJ s.v. — MAYSER, *Grammatik* II/2, 64-74. — MOULTON, *Grammar* III, 189-92. — MOULTON/MILLIGAN 206f. — PREISIGKE, *Wörterbuch* I, 474; IV, 777. — F. ROSTALSKI, *Sprachliches zu den apokryphen Apostelgeschichten* I (1909-10) 5-10. — SCHWYZER, *Grammatik* II, 200-205. — G. B. WINER and P. W. SCHMIEDEL, *Grammatik des neutestamentlichen Sprachidioms* ([8]1894/1903) 207-9.

1. The possessive adj. of the first person sg. belongs, along with the possessives σός, ἡμέτερος, ὑμέτερος, σφέτερος, to the most ancient elements of the Greek language. Until the beginning of the Hellenistic age it serves with these possessives as "the ordinary pronominal expression of the possessive relationship" (Schwyzer 200). In the course of time, however, the gen. of the personal pron. (μου, σου, etc.) was used increasingly; in addition circumlocutions with προσήκων, ὑπάρχων, etc., appear. In koine Greek and thus in the NT—as already in the LXX—the gen. of the personal pron. has become the ordinary usage, but without entirely supplanting the possessive adj.

2. In contrast to the other possessive adjectives ἐμός appears in the NT rather frequently; of a total of 76 occurrences 41 appear in John alone and 9 in 1 Corinthians.

3. In agreement with its usage in koine (see BAGD, Mayser, Preisigke) ἐμός is used in the NT both as an adj. and as a subst. With regard to adjectival usage one must distinguish between attributive and predicate usage. Used attributively, ἐμός sometimes has the function of an objective gen. (Luke 22:19; 1 Cor 11:24f.: εἰς τὴν ἐμὴν ἀνάμνησιν, "in remembrance *of me*"), but more often has the sense of a possessive gen. (e.g., John 12:26: ὁ διάκονος ὁ ἐμός; 1 Cor 9:3: ἡ ἐμὴ ἀπολογία [in both passages ἐμός, as often, in place of less emphatic μου]; Gal 6:11; Phlm 19, and other epistolary closings: τῇ ἐμῇ χειρί, "*my own* hand" [here the possessive is emphasized]). Predicate use of ἐμός is present in Matt 20:23 par. Mark 10:40: οὐκ ἔστιν ἐμὸν (τοῦτο) δοῦναι, it "is not *mine* to grant"; John 13:35: ὅτι ἐμοὶ μαθηταί ἐστε (in connection with a pred. nom.). Ἐμός occurs as a subst. in τὸ ἐμόν or τὰ ἐμά, *my property* (Matt 20:15; 25:27; Luke 15:31; John 16:14f.); οἱ ἐμοί, *those who are my own*, often in the papyri, but in the NT only in Rev 13:14 v.l.

4. The unusual frequency of ἐμός in John cannot be explained. If the use of the possessive adj. elsewhere demonstrates "a certain literary education and stylistic skill" (Mayser 67), this would scarcely be the case for the author of John's Gospel. Equally unlikely is the explanation of the form as an indication of the origin of John in Asia Minor, where the frequent usage of ἐμός would betray the characteristics of the dialect of the koine in the area of Pontus and Cappadocia (A. Thumb, *TLZ* 28 [1903] 421), inasmuch as other literature from Asia Minor from that period (Revelation, *Acts of Paul*) does not have the same usage (Moulton, *Grammar* I, 40; Rostalski).

E. Plümacher

ἐμπαιγμονή, ῆς, ἡ *empaigmonē* ridicule (noun)*

This hapax legomenon appears only in 2 Pet 3:3: In the last days "scoffers (ἐμπαῖκται) will come . . . with [their] *scoffing* (ἐν ἐμπαιγμονῇ)." G. Bertram, *TDNT* V, 635f.

ἐμπαιγμός, οῦ, ὁ *empaigmos* mocking, derision*

Used with μάστιγες to describe an experience of the martyrs, Heb 11:36: "Others suffered *mocking* and scourging." G. Bertram, *TDNT* V, 635f.

ἐμπαίζω *empaizō* mock, make fun of*

1. Occurrences in the NT — 2. Jesus as object of mockery

Lit.: BAGD s.v. — G. BERTRAM, *TDNT* V, 625-36. — J. BLINZLER, *Der Prozeß Jesu* ([4]1969). — R. DELBRUECK, "Antiquarisches zu den Verspottungen Jesu," *ZNW* 41 (1942) 124-45. — D. L. MILLER, "ΕΜΠΑΙΖΕΙΝ: Playing the Mock Game (Luke 22:63-64)," *JBL* 90 (1971) 309-13. — G. SCHNEIDER, *Verleugnung, Verspottung und Verhör Jesu nach Lukas 22, 54-71* (1969), esp. 96-104.

1. The vb. ἐμπαίζω is found only in the Synoptics (13 occurrences). It is used with the dat. (Mark 15:20a par. Matt 27:31a; Matt 27:29; Mark 10:34; Luke 14:29; 22:63; 23:36), with no obj. (Mark 15:31 par. Matt 27:41; Matt 20:19; Luke 23:11), and in the pass. (Matt 2:16; Luke 18:32). With the exception of Matt 2:16 ("trick") it is used with the basic meaning of *mock* (so often in the LXX). But other nuances are not excluded. In Luke 14:29 the ridicule of the people is directed at the builder who had acted without foresight. In all other passages Jesus is the object of the mockery.

2. In the "third" Passion prediction (Mark 10:34 par. Matt 20:19/Luke 18:32) Mark employs ἐμπαίζω for a single act within the framework of the mocking (to which also "spitting upon" is to be counted). Luke strengthens this impression. According to both Evangelists Jesus announces individual acts of his mocking. Matthew, on the other hand, employs ἐμπαίζω to describe the entire "event of the mocking," which is followed by the scourging and crucifixion.

In the Passion narrative itself Mark 15:20a par. Matt 27:31a uses ἐμπαίζω to emphasize the "mischievous game" of the soldiers with Jesus, which consisted in their furnishing Jesus with makeshift royal insignia, in their greeting him as a mock king, in their beating him, and finally in their spitting on him and kneeling before him in mock-homage. These individual acts are brought together under the one word "mockery."

Luke employs ἐμπαίζω in this comprehensive function when he reports concerning the mockery of Jesus at the trials before the Jews (22:63-65) and before Herod (23:11). The gorgeous apparel (cf. 15:17; on the subject of "clothing" cf. esp. Delbrueck) is meant to mock Jesus' "claim to kingship": "With the mock clothing he [Herod] indicated that he considered the man ridiculous rather than dangerous" (Blinzler 290).

In the pericope of the mocking of the crucified one (Mark 15:31 par. Matt 27:41/Luke 23:36) Mark and Matthew describe the scornful conduct of the high priest and the scribes with ἐμπαίζω. Luke substitutes another LXX word, ἐκμυκτηρίζω, which he takes from the Psalm passage which is similar to Luke 23:35 (Ps 21:8 LXX). Ἐκμυκτηρίζω appears to express more the "inward attitude of the mockers" (G. Bertram, *TDNT* IV, 799). In Luke 23:36 ἐμπαίζω describes the conduct of the soldiers as they play their mischievous game with Jesus. The "royal play" (cf. Miller) may illuminate the original background of the mocking of criminals by those around them. Jesus' experience has in common with it that open scorn strikes at the one who is apparently defenseless. This motif is developed in the Evangelists' increasingly deepening reflection on Jesus' suffering in the light of the OT "righteous one" (and of the Jewish martyrs).

F. G. Untergassmair

ἐμπαίκτης, ου, ὁ *empaiktēs* mocker*

According to 2 Pet 3:3 *mockers* are predicted in the "last days" (cf. Isa 3:4 LXX). According to v. 4 they are present and do their mocking in the face of the delay of the parousia. Jude 18 ascribes the prediction of the eschatological *mockers* to the apostles of Jesus Christ. G. Bertram, *TDNT* V, 636.

ἐμπεριπατέω *emperipateō* walk about*

2 Cor 6:16, in a (slightly altered) citation from Lev 26:12 LXX: I will live among them and *move.* H. Seesemann and G. Bertram, *TDNT* V, 940-45.

ἐμπίμπλημι (ἐμπιπλάω) *empimplēmi (empiplaō)* fill, satisfy*

Luke 1:53, of God, who *fills* the hungry with good things; 6:25, in the "woe" over those who are *full, satisfied*; John 6:12: "And when they *had eaten their fill*"; Acts 14:17 (with the alternate form ἐμπιπλάω) of God, who was "*satisfying* your hearts with food and gladness"; Rom 15:24: "once I have *satisfied myself* with [RSV "enjoyed"] your company for a little" (cf. 1:11f.). G. Delling, *TDNT* VI, 128-31.

ἐμπίμπρημι (ἐμπιπράω) *empimprēmi (empipraō)* ignite, burn*

Matt 22:7: the king "*burned* their city." In Acts 28:6 ℵ* *pc* (in place of πίμπρημι) the pass. appears, probably in the sense of *take a fever.*

ἐμπίπτω *empiptō* fall (into); fall (among)*

Matt 12:11; Luke 6:39: "it *falls* into a pit"; cf. Luke 14:5 v.l. The vb. is used metaphorically in Luke 10:36: "who *fell* among robbers"; 1 Tim 3:6: "*fall* into the condemnation of the devil"; v. 7: "*fall* into [the] reproach and the snare of the devil"; 6:9: they "*fall* into temptation, into a snare"; Heb 10:31: "It is a fearful thing to *fall* into the hands of the living God."

ἐμπλέκω *emplekō* oblige, ensnare*

This vb. appears in the NT only in the pass. and in a fig. sense. 2 Tim 2:4, of entanglement in civilian pursuits; 2 Pet 2:20: *ensnared* by "the defilements of the world."

ἐμπλοκή, ῆς, ἡ *emplokē* braiding*

1 Pet 3:3: ἐμπλοκῆς τριχῶν, *braiding* the hair.

ἐμπνέω *empneō* breathe, breathe heavily*

Acts 9:1: Paul *breathed* threats and murder against the disciples of the Lord. The threats are described in 26:11, the murder in 26:10. E. Haenchen, *The Acts of the Apostles* (1971) 319; E. Schweizer, *TDNT* VI, 452f.; P. W. van der Horst, "Drohung und Mord schnaubend (Acta IX 1)," *NovT* 12 (1970) 257-69.

ἐμπορεύομαι *emporeuomai* trade; purchase (vb.)*

Intrans. *trade,* Jas 4:13. Trans., 2 Pet 2:3: "in their greed they [the false teachers] *will exploit* you with false words."

ἐμπορία, ας, ἡ *emporia* business, commerce*

Matt 22:5: of those invited to the meal, "one [went] to his farm, another to his *business.*"

ἐμπόριον, ου, τό *emporion* public market*

John 2:16: "you shall not make my Father's house a house of trade (οἶκος ἐμπορίου)." The gen. is epexegetical.

ἔμπορος, ου, ὁ *emporos* merchant*

In general the wholesale dealer (in contrast to the retailer = κάπηλος) is intended: Matt 13:45 (pleonastic ἄνθρωπος ἔμπορος); Rev 18:3, 11, 15, 23. On "the merchants of the earth" in Revelation, see Ezekiel 27; H. Kraft, *Offenbarung* (HNT) 227f., 233, 239.

ἔμπροσθεν *emprosthen* before, in front (of), ahead (of), in the presence of, previously

1. Origin and usage — 2. In secular Greek, papyri, and the LXX — 3. NT occurrences and meanings

Lit.: BAGD s.v. — LSJ s.v. — MAYSER, *Grammatik* II/2, 539.

1. Ἔμπροσθεν is composed of the preps. ἐν and πρός (πρό), strengthened by the particle of direction -θεν. Thus in its origin it bears a local and a temporal element, supplemented by the designation of a relationship of precedence (not in the NT). Its meaning depends on the context in which it appears (e.g., local-static or temporal-dynamic) and on its grammatical function (i.e., as improper prep. with gen., as adj., or as adv.).

2. Secular Greek (e.g., Herodotus, Plato, Xenophon) uses ἔμπροσθεν as adj. or adv. as an indication of place (before, in front of), time (previously, for ages) and rank (more, higher than). Esp. noteworthy are the papyri from the Hellenistic period, which use ἔμπροσθεν in poetic and in prose texts, often in fixed phrases in place of πρό as an absolute adv. of time along with πρότερον. Prepositional usage is rare. The LXX adds nothing to this usage.

3. NT texts exhibit ἔμπροσθεν in various meanings and connections. Matthew has the most occurrences with 18, Luke has 10, and John 5. In the undisputed Pauline letters ἔμπροσθεν appears 7 times. It does not appear in the deutero-Pauline letters or the Pastoral Epistles.

Probably one of the earliest uses is found in the sayings source (Matt 10:32 par. Luke 12:8); here the local use is seen: confession (or denial) *before* humans corresponds to confession *before* God. The antithesis of the human realm and the divine forum, of positive and negative consequences with an emphasis on visibility, is significant: *before the face* (cf. Luke 12:9: ἐνώπιον as synonym). Another Q logion (Matt 11:26 par. Luke 10:21) underlines the dynamic perspective: being well-pleasing *before* the Father has earthly consequences. The local-demonstrative idea is present also in Mark 2:12; 9:2, once more with what is present thought of as "proof" for the reality of an event. The tangible function of a witness is found in the form of the Baptist in Matt 11:10 par. Luke 7:27 (probably from Q; Mark differs); here it is seen that ἔμπροσθεν can take on both a local *(in front of)* and a temporal *(previously)* aspect together.

Uses of ἔμπροσθεν in the Matthean special tradition emphasize the public character of the word (in a positive sense, Matt 5:16, 24; in a polemical context, 6:1f.; 23:13; in a forensic-eschatological context, 25:32 [judgment]; 26:70; 27:11, 29 [trial]). Despite the variety of sayings, the accent lies on the visibility and perceptibility of what is described. The Lukan tradition uses ἔμπροσθεν as an adv. in a distinct way in two passages: Luke 19:4 *(in front)* and 19:28 *(forward).* The special Lukan usage is seen in Acts 10:4 and 18:17 as an indication of direction and place.

In John the temporal aspect of the word is seen; ἔμπροσθεν is often used in antithesis to ὀπίσω ("after"; e.g., John 1:15, 27 v.l.). The demonstrative-visible meaning plays a role with respect to discipleship (10:4) and in connection with the signs of Jesus (12:37), here with a critical note.

Paul uses ἔμπροσθεν in the local and temporal senses to describe the direct imminence and presence of God in the expectation of the parousia (1 Thess 1:3; 2:19; 3:13), but also with respect to present relationships and events (e.g., Gal 2:14). Late NT uses of the word are local, as in Rev 4:6 (adv.); 19:10; 22:8. From the differing uses of ἔμπροσθεν local and temporal meanings crystallize with a demonstrative and witnessing element (the Synoptics), with a parenetic accent (John), and with an eschatological element (Paul).

A. Kretzer

ἐμπτύω *emptyō* spit (on)*

In the NT only in the Synoptics (Mark and passages dependent on Mark), in reference to the mistreatment of Jesus in the Passion: in the Passion predictions (Mark 10:34 par. Luke 18:32), in the Passion story itself (Mark 14:65 par. Matt 26:67 [in the Sanhedrin]; Mark 15:19 par. Matt 27:30 [by the Roman soldiers]). The vb. is always used with the dat. in Mark. Matt 27:30 has εἰς αὐτόν, while

26:67 has εἰς τὸ πρόσωπον αὐτοῦ. The pass. appears in Luke 18:32.

ἐμφανής, 2 *emphanēs* visible, manifest
→ ἐμφανίζω.

ἐμφανίζω *emphanizō* show, announce, reveal*
ἐμφανής, 2 *emphanēs* visible, manifest*

1. Occurrences and meaning — 2. The vb. in the NT — 3. Ἐμφανής

Lit.: R. BULTMANN and D. LÜHRMANN, *TDNT* IX, 7. — E. HAENCHEN, *The Acts of the Apostles* (1971) 645-47, 652. — O. MICHEL, *Der Brief an die Hebräer* (KEK, [6]1966) 324f. — A. SAND, "Die biblischen Aussagen über die Offenbarung," *Handbuch der Dogmengeschichte* I/1a (1971) 1-26 (significant bibliography).

1. The vb. occurs 10 times in the NT, the adj. twice. It is noteworthy that Acts uses the vb. 5 times, and the adj. one time. The remaining NT uses (vb.: once in Matthew, twice in John, twice in Hebrews; adj.: once in Romans) permit no inferences to be drawn about tradition-historical connections. In Greek the vb. has the sense of *prove,* then esp. of *declare, announce.* The LXX uses adj. and vb. in the same sense, but it knows also the religious sense *be visible, appear* with reference to the deity (cf. Wis 1:2; also as early as Exod 33:18 v.l. Moses asks God: Show yourself to me). Philo also uses the vb. of God's revelation of himself (*All.* iii.27, 101).

2. a) The vb. has the original sense of *report* in Acts 23:15, 22; 24:1; 25:2, 15. The Jews have conspired against Paul and have accused him before the Roman magistrates (23:12). In all of these passages the vb. means "make an official report" (BAGD s.v.).

b) The theological meaning *reveal* appears in John 14:21: One who loves Jesus will be loved in turn by Jesus, who will *manifest* himself to such a person (ἐμφανίσω), i.e., reveal himself to him or her. In Judas's question, which has been redactionally inserted after this statement (v. 22), the vb. is again taken up: Why does Jesus *manifest* himself only to the disciples and not to the world? Ἐμφανίζειν corresponds in both places to φανεροῦν, which is the word used by John elsewhere (9 times in the Gospel, 9 times in 1 John). The resurrected one makes himself known and reveals himself to the believers.

c) According to Matt 27:53 the dead who come out of the graves *manifest* themselves to the inhabitants of Jerusalem. This saying interprets Jesus' death soteriologically on the basis of his resurrection (cf. the parallel between the cosmic events of 27:51 and 28:2). While Heb 11:14 uses the vb. with reference to OT believers in the meaning *indicate* (but also with the secondary meaning *confess*), the pass. in 9:24 expresses the fact that Christ has not, like the high priest of the old covenant, entered into the most holy place, but *appears* instead directly before God's face, and indeed "on our behalf."

3. **Ἐμφανής** is used in Acts 10:40 with the meaning *visible,* in order to conclude the Christian kerygma: God raised Jesus on the third day and gave (ἔδωκεν) so that he might become *visible* (ἐμφανῆ γενέσθαι): The resurrected one is attested before the Christian witnesses (cf. 1:3f., 22). In Rom 10:20 Paul cites Isa 65:1 LXX; the meaning of the adj. is the same as in the passage cited: God has made himself *known* to those who did not seek him, who did not ask for him *(parallelismus membrorum).* God has hidden himself from Israel, but *revealed* himself to the Gentiles.

A. Sand

ἔμφοβος, 2 *emphobos* frightened, in fear*

In the NT only in the phrase ἔμφοβος γίνομαι and, except for Rev 11:13, only in Luke-Acts: Luke 24:5, 37, of the fear of the women in the presence of the angel and the disciples in the presence of the resurrected Jesus; Acts 10:4, of Cornelius, to whom an angel appeared; 24:25, of Felix, who heard Paul preach. In Acts 22:9 D E P Ψ and others insert "and fell in fear" (after "saw the light"); this reading may be original.

ἐμφυσάω *emphysaō* breathe on*

Jesus "*breathed on* them [the disciples in the evening of Easter day; ἐνεφύσησεν], and said to them, "Receive the Holy Spirit" (John 20:22). On the motif, cf. Gen 2:7 (ἐνεφύσησεν); Wis 15:11 (ἐμφυσήσαντα πνεῦμα ζωτικόν); Philo *Op.* 135 (ἐνεφύσησεν . . . πνεῦμα θεῖον). The context (John 20:23) indicates that the gift of forgiveness of sins is interpreted as a new creation of Easter. E. Stauffer, *TDNT* II, 536f.

ἔμφυτος, 2 *emphytos* implanted*

Jas 1:21: "receive . . . the *implanted* word [i.e., the word implanted in you], which is able to save your souls." The adj. refers in *Barn.* 1:2; 9:9 to "the grace of the gift of the Spirit" or "the gift of his teaching," which the addressees receive. It is associated with the typical forms of baptismal parenesis (F. Mussner, *Jakobusbrief* [HTKNT] s.v.).

ἐν *en* in, on, at

1. Occurrences in the NT; meaning — 2. Spatial — 3. Temporal — 4. Instrumental — 5. Modal — 6. In place of dat. or locative — 7. Semiticizing constructions

Lit.: On preps. in gereral → ἀνά. BAGD s.v. — BDF §§195; 218-20. — M. J. HARRIS, *DNTT* III, 1190-93. — KÜHNER, *Grammatik* II/2, 392-98. — MOULTON, *Grammar* III, 249-53, 260-65. — A. OEPKE, *TDNT* II, 537-43. — P. F. REGARD, *Contribution à*

l'étude des prépositions dans la langue du NT (1919) 227-376. — For further bibliography see *TWNT* X, 1078f.

1. 'Εν, with about 2700 occurrences, is by far the most frequent prep. in the NT. It occurs in all NT writings with no notable concentration in particular documents or groups of documents. The possibilities for usage, which already in classical Greek extended considerably beyond the original local meaning, have been greatly expanded in the NT, partially because of imitation of Hebrew constructions with b^e. Therefore meanings of ἐν cannot always be clearly distinguished from each other (e.g., Acts 17:28: ἐν αὐτῷ ζῶμεν, "*in* him we live" [local; so RSV], but also "*through* him we live" [causal]).

2. Spatial usage: a) 'Εν is used to designate the place *in, at,* or *on* which something is found (rarely in place of the expected εἰς: John 5:4; Rev 11:11): *in* the house, *in* the city, *in* the wilderness, *at* the well, "*at* the right hand" (ἐν δεξιᾷ), *on* the mountain, *at* the market. Esp. significant is ἐν (τοῖς) οὐρανοῖς (also sg.): "*in* heaven," predominantly in Matthew as the place of residence of God (Matt 10:32f.; 12:50, etc.; Mark 11:26) or of the angels (Matt 22:30), but also as the place of joy (Luke 15:7), of peace (19:38), of reward (Matt 5:12 par.), of the divine kingdom (Phil 3:20); however, in Mark 13:25; Acts 2:19: *in* the sky; note also the polar expression "*in* heaven and on earth" (Col 1:16, 20; Eph 1:10). 'Εν is also used to give location of scriptural passages (Acts 13:40, *in* the [books of the] prophets; Luke 24:44, *in the* law of Moses; Rom 11:2, *in* the account concerning Elijah).

b) 'Εν is used of things *in* which one finds oneself or *with* which one comes: *in* soft raiment (Matt 11:8; cf. Rev 3:5); *in* sheep's clothing (Matt 7:15); come *with* a rod (1 Cor 4:21; cf. Heb 9:25); of abstract concepts: coming *into (with)* his rule, the fullness of blessing, the gospel (Matt 16:28; Rom 15:29; 2 Cor 10:14).

c) 'Εν is used with respect to persons, *among* (1), *to* (2), or *in* (3) whom something occurs: 1) Matt 2:6: *among* the rulers; Gal 1:16: *among* the Gentiles; 1 Cor 2:6: *among* the mature; Luke 14:31: *with* ten thousand men; 2) do something *to* someone (Mark 14:6); happen *to* someone (1 Cor 9:15); 3) involving mental processes: to say, think, apprehend, be perplexed *to* oneself (Matt 3:9 par.; Mark 2:8; 5:30; Acts 10:17); "groan *inwardly*" (Rom 8:23); ἐν ταῖς καρδίαις, "*in* their hearts" (Mark 2:6, 8 par.); ἐν ταῖς συνειδήσεσιν, "*to* your conscience" (2 Cor 5:11).

d) In religious terminology ἐν is used: 1) In regard to a person being filled with something: Sin lives *in* a person (Rom 7:17, 20); likewise God's Spirit (8:9, 11; 1 Cor 3:16; cf. 1 Tim 4:14; 2 Tim 1:6); life, joy, faith, and the word (of Christ) are said to be *in* people (John 6:53; 15:11; 2 Tim 1:5; John 5:38, etc.). By contrast, all of the treasures of wisdom are *in* Christ (Col 2:3; cf. 1:19); the mystery and the life are hidden *in* God (Eph 3:9; Col 3:3).

2) For the inner relationship between God and a person: The frequent statement that God works *in* a person (1 Cor 12:6; Phil 1:6; 2:13; Col 1:29; cf. Mark 6:14 par.; Eph 2:2) is made most emphatically in the Pauline formula Χριστὸς ἐν ὑμῖν, "Christ *in* you" (Rom 8:10; 2 Cor 13:5; cf. Gal 2:20; 4:19). The reciprocity of this relationship is indicated in the Johannine formula of mutuality, "the Father *in* me and I *in* him" (John 10:38; similarly 14:10f., etc.; with μένειν, "remain": 6:56; 15:4-7; 1 John 4:13, 15, etc.; with the disciples included: John 14:20; 17:21, 23, 26). Paul emphasizes existence "*in* Christ" or "*in* the Lord" (ἐν Χριστῷ, ἐν κυρίῳ; 20 times each in Romans and 1 Corinthians, also Phil 1:1, 14; 4:7; 2 Cor 5:17, etc.), frequently in connection with vbs. (trust, speak, work), nouns (life, grace, freedom), and adjs. (wise, mature, beloved). 'Εν Χριστῷ thus refers not to mystical life in Christ; it serves rather, like the related formula ἐν πίστει, "*in* faith," as a characterization of one's realm of existence, which is often set in contrast to the worldly realm (ἐν σαρκί, "*in* the flesh," Phil 3:3; 1:21f.; Rom 8:8f.; 1 Tim 3:16; Phlm 16).

3. Temporal usage: 'Εν is used to refer to: a) A point in time: *in* that hour (Matt 8:13); *on* the sabbath (John 7:23); *on* the day of judgment (Matt 11:22; cf. John 6:44); *at* the sound of the trumpet (1 Cor 15:52).

b) Duration of time *during which* or *within which something occurs: within* three days (Matt 27:40); *in* the days (= at the time of) Herod (2:1); *during* the insurrection (Mark 15:7); *in* a short while (Luke 18:8; Rom 16:20); ἐν τῷ ἑξῆς, "afterward" (Luke 7:11); ἐν τῷ μεταξύ, "meanwhile" (John 4:31). Also with a substantival inf. (esp. in Luke): *at* the oars, i.e., while they were rowing (Mark 6:48); while sowing (Matt 13:4); ἐν τῷ εἶναι, "while they were there" (Luke 2:6); rarely with the aor. inf. to indicate punctiliar action: "as they entered the cloud" (Luke 9:34); *at* the sound of the voice (v. 36).

4. Instrumental usage: a) Use of ἐν to describe means is not unknown in classical Greek, but becomes common in the LXX, first under the influence of Hebrew b^e. The original spatial meaning is still apparent in βαπτίζειν ἐν ὕδατι, baptize "*(in) with* water" (Matt 3:11; John 1:33; cf. Rev 7:14); ἐν πυρί, burn "*in (with)* fire" (Rev 16:8; cf. Homer *Il.* vii.429); cf. simple ὕδατι (Mark 1:8; Luke 3:16) and πυρί (Matt 3:12); ἐν μαχαίρῃ, "with a sword" (Matt 26:52, etc.; without ἐν in Acts 12:2); ἐν (τῷ) αἵματι, "*by* the blood (of Christ)" (Rom 5:9; Heb 9:22; Rev 1:5, etc.); ἐν τῇ προσευχῇ, "*in* prayer" (Matt 21:22); διδάσκειν ἐν παραβολαῖς, teach "*in* parables" (Mark 4:2).

b) A person can also be named as the "instrument": cast out demons "*by* the ruler" (ἐν τῷ ἄρχοντι) of demons (Mark 3:22 par.); judge the world ἐν ἀνδρί, "*by* a man" (Acts 17:31; cf. 1 Cor 6:2); ἁγιάζεσθαι ἐν, be "consecrated *through*" (1 Cor 7:14).

c) Occasionally the instrumental usage comes close to being causal: ἐν τῇ πολυλογίᾳ, "*for* their many words" (Matt 6:7); ἐν τῷ λόγῳ τούτῳ, *because* of this word (Acts 7:29); ἐν τῇ ζωῇ αὐτοῦ, "*by* his life" (Rom 5:10); ἐν τούτῳ, "*by this,*" i.e., *therefore* (John 16:30); frequently with verbs of emotion: χαίρειν, "rejoice *over*"; εὐδοκεῖν, "delight *in*" (esp. in LXX); καυχᾶσθαι, "boast *of* a matter"; σκανδαλίζεσθαι, "take offense *at.*"

5. Modal usage (to designate circumstances or manner): *In* ecstasy (Acts 11:5); *in* torment (Luke 16:23); *in the face of* many battles (1 Thess 2:2); *in* corruptibility (1 Cor 15:42). Often in adverb-like phrases: ἐν δυνάμει, "*with* power" (Mark 9:1, etc.); ἐν δικαιοσύνῃ, "with righteousness" (Acts 17:31); ἐν χαρᾷ, "*with* joy" (Rom 15:32); ἐν κρυπτῷ, "*in* secret," ἐν παρρησίᾳ, "openly" (John 7:4); ἐν τάχει, "speedily" (Luke 18:8; Rom 16:20). With a substantival inf., *in the course of, while:* ἐν τῷ τὴν χεῖρα ἐκτείνειν σε, "*while* thou stretchest out thy hand" (Acts 4:30; cf. 8:6; Heb 8:13).

6. Occasionally a phrase with ἐν appears to stand in place of the simple dat.: Acts 4:12: no other name is given "to [RSV "among"] men" (ἐν ἀνθρώποις); Rom 1:19: it "is plain to them (ἐν αὐτοῖς)" (cf. 2 Cor 4:3); Luke 2:14: "peace to [RSV "among"] men" (ἐν ἀνθρώποις, parallel to θεῷ). However, in most such instances a local understanding is also possible. On 1 Cor 14:11 (ἐν ἐμοὶ βάρβαρος, "a foreigner to me") cf. Sophocles *Ant.* 925.

7. Constructions such as ὀμνύναι/ὁμολογεῖν ἐν, "swear *by* someone," "confess *to* someone," are based on Hebrew (or Aramaic).

W. Elliger

ἐναγκαλίζομαι *enankalizomai* embrace*

Mark 9:36; 10:16, of Jesus, who *embraced* a child or children (παιδίον, παιδία).

ἐνάλιος, 2 *enalios* belonging to the sea*

Jas 3:7: ἐνάλια, *sea creature* (in a list).

ἔναντι *enanti* opposite, before*

This adv. is used as an improper prep. with gen. It appears frequently in the LXX, in the NT only in Luke-Acts: Luke 1:8, of Zechariah's priestly service: "*before* God"; Acts 8:21, in Peter's criticism of Simon Magus, whose heart is not "right *before* God"; 7:10 $\mathfrak{p}^{74}$ א *al* (in place of ἐναντίον), of Joseph, to whom God granted "favor and wisdom *before* Pharaoh."

ἐναντίον *enantion* before, in the eyes of*

The neut. of ἐναντίος is used as an improper prep. with gen. It appears, except for Mark 2:12 C Koine A D, etc. (*before* all), only in Luke-Acts: Luke 1:6: "they were both righteous *before* God"; 20:26: "*in the presence of* the people"; 24:19: "mighty in deed and word *before* God and all the people"; Acts 7:10: "*before* Pharaoh"; 8:32: "a lamb *before* its shearer" (citing Isa 53:7 LXX). On adverbial usage (connected with the article) → τοὐναντίον.

ἐναντίος, 3 *enantios* opposite, hostile*

Mark 6:48 par. Matt 14:24, of a *contrary* wind; Acts 27:4, of winds; 1 Thess 2:15: *hostile, opposed* to all people; Acts 28:17: "I had done nothing *against* the people"; 26:9: ἐναντία πράσσω (as in Josephus *Ant.* xix.305); Mark 15:39: ἐξ ἐναντίας αὐτοῦ, "*facing him*"; with art., Titus 2:8: ὁ ἐξ ἐναντίας, the opponent.

ἐνάρχομαι *enarchomai* begin*

The compound appears in the NT only twice, both in Paul's letters and both times as an aor. partc. Gal 3:3 (with no obj.): once you *have made a beginning* in the Spirit; Phil 1:6 (with acc.): "who *began* a good work in you."

ἔνατος, 3 *enatos* (the) ninth*

Of the *ninth* hour (i.e., 3:00 p.m.) as the hour when Jesus spoke at his death (Mark 15:33, 34 par. Matt 27:46/ Luke 23:44). The *ninth* hour was considered a time of prayer (Acts 3:1; 10:3, 30; see Billerbeck II, 696-702). Matt 20:5 mentions the sixth and *ninth* hours, at which the householder goes out to find workers. Rev 21:20 (in the enumeration of the twelve foundations of the new Jerusalem): "the *ninth* [was] topaz."

ἐνγράφω *engraphō* write in, record

Alternative form of → ἐγγράφω.

ἐνδεής, 2 *endeēs* poor, needy*

Acts 4:34a, in the summary statement about the early Church: "There was not a *needy person* (ἐνδεής τις) among them"; cf. vv. 32, 34b, 35.

ἔνδειγμα, ατος, τό *endeigma* indication*

2 Thess 1:5: Steadfastness in persecutions and afflictions is "*evidence* of the righteous judgment of God, that you may be worthy of the kingdom of God, for which you are suffering."

ἐνδείκνυμαι *endeiknymai* show, prove, demonstrate*

In the NT only the mid. appears; all 11 NT occurrences are in the Epistles, and all have an acc. obj.: Rom 2:15: they *demonstrate* that the work of the law (i.e., the deeds demanded by the law) is written (double acc.: ἔργον . . .

γραπτόν); 9:17: my power; v. 22: the wrath (of God); Eph 2:7: the wealth of his grace; 1 Tim 1:16: his complete patience; 2 Tim 4:14: Alexander "*demonstrated* [RSV "did"] to me great harm"; Titus 2:10: good fidelity; 3:2: gentleness toward all persons; Heb 6:11: the same zeal; 2 Cor 8:24: τὴν οὖν ἔνδειξιν τῆς ἀγάπης ὑμῶν... εἰς αὐτοὺς ἐνδεικνύμενοι, while you *bring forth* "proof . . . of your love . . . to these men"; Heb 6:10: "the love, which [ἧς rather than ἥν, by attraction to ἀγάπης] you *showed* for his name [RSV "sake"]."

ἔνδειξις, εως, ἡ *endeixis* demonstration*

Lit.: E. Käsemann, "Zum Verständnis von Röm 3, 24-26," *idem, Versuche* I, 96-100. — W. G. Kümmel, "Πάρεσις und ἔνδειξις. Ein Beitrag zum Verständnis der paulinischen Rechtfertigungslehre," *idem, Heilsgeschehen und Geschichte* (MTSt 3, 1965) 260-70. — P. Stuhlmacher, "Recent Exegesis on Romans 3:24-26," *idem, Reconciliation, Law, and Righteousness* (1986) 94-109. — D. Zeller, "Sühne und Langmut. Zur Traditionsgeschichte von Röm 3, 24-26," *TP* 43 (1968) 51-80.

1. All four NT occurrences of ἔνδειξις are in the Pauline letter corpus.

2. Ἔνδειξις means, as the connection with → ἐνδείκνυμαι and → ἔνδειγμα indicates, *(distinct) sign, demonstration, proof.*

In Rom 3:25 Paul underlines with the use of traditional material (to which ἔνδειξις perhaps already belonged) the character of God's revealed righteousness. The double and emphatic use of ἔνδειξις in vv. 25f. accents the manifestation of God's righteousness both with respect to the forgiveness of past sins and with respect to the present.

In an abbreviated clause in 2 Cor 8:24 Paul asks the Corinthian church to show agape to Titus and the two (unnamed) delegates and thus to give evidence (ἔνδειξιν ἐνδείκνυσθαι) for Paul's boasting about the Corinthians' conduct. Such proof would be directed to the totality of the churches and would thereby shift behavior into the horizon of Pauline ecclesiology.

Phil 1:28 indicates that the unanimity of the Church becomes a clear proof (ἥτις attracted to ἔνδειξις) to the Church's opponents (and as the incomplete parallelism indicates, *only* to the opponents) of their destruction and of the presence of salvation in the Church. (Ἔνδειγμα is used in an analogous way in 2 Thess 1:5.)

H. Paulsen

ἕνδεκα *hendeka* eleven*

Lit.: J. Plevnik, " 'The Eleven and Those with Them' according to Luke," *CBQ* 40 (1978) 205-11. — For further bibliography → δώδεκα.

Ἕνδεκα occurs 5 or 6 times in the NT: Matt 28:16; Luke 24:9, 33; Acts 1:26; 2:14; Mark 16:14 (the longer ending). In Acts 2:14 the completed circle of twelve other than Peter and after the replacement of Judas by Matthias is referred to. In the other passages the word refers to the group of twelve after the loss of Judas. In Matt 28:16; Acts 1:26 the number appears as an adj. (in Matthew with μαθηταί, in Acts with ἀπόστολοι, in accord with how the two books regard the → δώδεκα [4.d]), but elsewhere it is a subst.

The occurrences and meaning (esp. Acts 2:14) of the word exclude the view that "the *eleven*" is "a fixed and ancient expression like the 'twelve' " (so E. Lohmeyer, *Matthäus* [KEK] 414, n. 2); the number is rather "calculated" from the number twelve. From unqualified use of "twelve" the use of ἕνδεκα developed in an analogous way. Nevertheless the *eleven* are not raised to the level of an institution; the number is instead used in reference to a definite number that has been calculated by subtraction of the fixed number twelve and not by addition. Thus ἕνδεκα is not intelligible apart from οἱ δώδεκα.

The reading of the "Western" text of 1 Cor 15:5 is altered, replacing δώδεκα by ἕνδεκα. This is a correction, which places the (correct) number in the place of the (assumed to be already known) institution.

T. Holtz

ἑνδέκατος, 3 *hendekatos* eleventh*

Matt 20:6, 9, of the *eleventh* hour (i.e., 5:00 p.m.); Rev 21:20, in the enumeration of the foundation stones of the new Jerusalem: "*the eleventh* [was] jacinth."

ἐνδέχομαι *endechomai* accept*

In Luke 13:33 the verb is used impersonally: οὐκ ἐνδέχεται, *it is not possible* (with complementary inf. and acc.).

ἐνδημέω *endēmeō* be at home*

In the NT only in a fig. sense: 2 Cor 5:6: "while we *are at home* in the body (σῶμα) we are away (→ ἐκδημέω) from the Lord"; v. 8, on the other hand, of the desire to "be away (ἐκδημῆσαι) from the body and *[to be] at home* with the Lord"; v. 9: "whether we *are at home* or [are] away (ἐκδημοῦντες)." W. Grundmann, *TDNT* II, 63f.; P. Hoffmann, *Die Toten in Christus* (1969) 253-85; H. Lietzmann and W. G. Kümmel, *An die Korinther I/II* (HNT, [5]1969) ad loc.; H. Bietenhard, *DNTT* II, 789f.; for further bibliography see Lietzmann and Kümmel 223.

ἐνδιδύσκω *endidyskō* dress, put on*

With double acc. in Mark 15:17: "they *clothed* him in a purple cloak"; mid. *clothe oneself* in Luke 16:19: "who *dressed* in purple and the finest linen" (NEB); 8:27 Koine D Θ *pl:* he *wore* no garment.

ἔνδικος, 2 *endikos* just, legal

Rom 3:8: ὧν τὸ κρίμα ἔνδικόν ἐστιν, "their condemnation is *just*"; Heb 2:2: "*just* retribution."

ἐνδοξάζομαι *endoxazomai* be glorified*

2 Thess 1:10: "when he comes . . . *to be glorified*"; v. 12, "so that the name of our Lord Jesus *may be glorified* in you." G. Kittel, *TDNT* II, 254.

ἔνδοξος, 2 *endoxos* famous, splendid, glorious*

1 Cor 4:10, in contrast to ἄτιμος: "you are *held in honor [esteem]*, but we in disrepute"; Luke 7:25, of *glorious* apparel; Eph 5:27, of the Church, which Christ presents *in glorious form* (ἔνδοξον); in Luke 13:17 τὰ ἔνδοξα are the *glorious deeds* (cf. Exod 34:10; Job 5:9; 9:10; 34:24) of Jesus, in response to which the people rejoice. G. Kittel, *TDNT* II, 254.

ἔνδυμα, ατος, τό *endyma* garment, clothing*

The word preferred by Matthew for *garment* in the general sense (7 occurrences); elsewhere only in Luke 12:23 (par. Matt 6:25). Literally: Matt 3:4: "of camel's hair"; 6:25: "the body [is] more than *clothing*"; v. 28: anxiety περὶ ἐνδύματος; 22:11f.: ἔνδυμα γάμου, "wedding *garment*"; 28:3: the *garment* of the angel at the tomb, which was "white as snow" (cf. Mark 16:5; Matt 17:2 D lat). Fig.: 7:15: wolves "in sheep's *clothing* (ἐν ἐνδύμασιν προβάτων)."

ἐνδυναμόω *endynamoō* strengthen*

Lit.: E. Fascher, *RAC* IV, 415-58. — W. Grundmann, *TDNT* II, 284-317, esp. 286, 313.

1. Of the 7 NT occurrences of ἐνδυναμόω 6 are in the Pauline letter corpus. In the Apostolic Fathers Hermas in particular uses it (cf. also Ign. *Smyrn.* 4:2). Like the related vb. → δυναμόω, ἐνδυναμόω means *strengthen, support;* pass. ἐνδυναμοῦσθαι means *become strong.*

2. Ἐνδυναμόω is used most of all in relation to the theology of the apostolate. In Phil 4:13 a fragment in diatribe style stands under the thought of the autarkeia of the apostle (4:11) as a high point in the statement about the apostle's strength in all things, a strength founded on Christ's δύναμις. Contacts with Stoic ideas are apparent here (cf. Marcus Aurelius *In semet ipsum* i.16.11). However, the decisive element is the Pauline understanding of the apostolate: Christ as the δύναμις of God empowers the apostle and is at the same time present in the apostle's proclamation.

Such correlations between the apostle and his Lord are consolidated in the Pastorals. 1 Tim 1:12 proceeds from the call to the apostle (cf. 1:12ff.) and describes Christ as the one who gives strength. This statement emphasizes not only that Paul's conversion was overwhelming, but also that it was a gift from the Lord. 2 Tim 4:17 makes a similar connection: The description of the apostle's destitution (4:16; cf. Phil 4:13) has its focus in the contrasting emphasis on assistance and strengthening by the Lord. In 2 Tim 2:1 Timothy is told to be strengthened (pass.) in the grace of Jesus Christ; ἐνδυναμοῦ marks a key movement in the argument: Just as Timothy is to pass on what he has received from Paul, his ἐνδυναμοῦσθαι corresponds also to the apostle's conversion.

Ἐνδυναμοῦσθαι is also used in regard to other topics: Rom 4:20 has an antithetic formulation in which → ἐπαγγελία remains formally and materially the primary subject: doubt and strengh are one contrasting pair, faith and unbelief are another. Faith is thus not thought of as the cause of the strengthening, but as a more precise definition of it. Such a connection between πίστις and ἐνδυναμοῦσθαι is used especially by Hermas (e.g., *Vis.* iii.12) and may also be at the basis of Acts 9:22. A reference in the latter to bodily health is, despite 9:19 (and Heb 11:34), less probable. In Eph 6:10 the vb. introduces the letter's final parenesis emphatically, but, unlike 2 Tim 2:1, is directed toward the whole Church. Eph 6:10 corresponds with 3:16 and Col 1:11 (→ δυναμόω); the frequency of terms of strength is striking (κράτος—ἐνδυναμοῦσθαι—ἰσχύς).

H. Paulsen

ἐνδύνω *endynō* go (in), break (in)*

2 Tim 3:6: "*make their way* into households."

ἔνδυσις, εως, ἡ *endysis* dressing, putting on*

1 Pet 3:3, in the exhortation to women (vv. 1-6): "Let not yours be the outward adornment with . . . *wearing* of fine clothing (ἐνδύσεως ἱματίων κόσμος)."

ἐνδύω *endyō* put on, dress*

1. Occurrences and meaning — 2. Usage — 3. Ἐπενδύομαι

Lit.: M. Bouttier, "Complexio Oppositorum: sur les Formules de I Cor. XII.13; Gal III.26-8; Col. III.10, 11," *NTS* 23 (1976/77) 1-19. — E. Brandenburger, *Fleisch und Geist* (1968), esp. 175-77. — H. Kaiser, *Die Bedeutung des leiblichen Daseins in der paulinischen Eschatologie* I (Diss. Heidelberg, 1974) 58-61. — A. Oepke, *TDNT* II, 318-21. — U. Wilckens, *TDNT* VII, 687-91.

1. Ἐνδύω is found with the meaning *put on, dress* 28 times in the NT. In the NT only 2 Tim 3:6 has the related form ἐνδύνω.

2. Besides the literal use (so Matt 6:25; 22:11; 27:28,

31; Mark 1:6; 6:9; 15:20; Luke 8:27; 12:22; 15:22; Acts 12:21; Rev 1:13; 15:6; 19:14; cf. → ἔνδυμα) ἐνδύω appears in theologically significant texts in a fig. sense, especially in the Pauline and deutero-Pauline literature (cf. also the eschatological use in Luke 24:49: ἐνδύειν τὴν δύναμιν). Three figurative uses can be distinguished; ἐνδύω is associated with a) baptism and christology, b) parenesis, and c) eschatology. These are connected in that all emphasize the newness of the reality mediated by Christ.

Paul (and the deutero-Paulines) refers in his usage of ἐνδύω to traditional topics and motifs. The connection with baptism and baptismal parenesis is apparent. On the other hand, explanation in history-of-religions terms has proven to be difficult, especially because of the extensive use of the garment and outer garment motifs. However, contacts with the wisdom-apocalyptic traditions of post-OT Judaism (cf. Brandenburger), with Philonic thought (Wilckens 688), and with the thought forms of the mysteries (cf. M. Dibelius, "Die Isisweihe bei Apuleius und verwandte Initiations-Riten," *idem, Botschaft* II, 30-79) and Gnostics or Gnosticizing texts are not to be overlooked (W. Schmithals, *Gnosticism in Corinth* [1971] 259-75, 401-7). The point remains obscure (cf. the critical comments of P. von der Osten-Sacken, *Römer 8 als Beispiel paulinischer Soteriologie* [1975] 104-24). Perhaps the history-of-religions explanation should not be made the starting point for discussion of the different usage of ἐνδύω within the NT.

a) Gal 3:27 shows that for Paul ἐνδύω is connected with baptism and is used of being covered by the Kyrios. This involves, according to v. 28, both incorporation into the σῶμα Χριστοῦ and the presence of the new creation. Rom 13:14 gives this incorporation a parenetic significance and makes it the constant task of the Christian (within a recognition of the indicative–imperative antithesis). When Col 3:10 and Eph 4:24 speak of putting on the "new person" (RSV interprets: "new nature"), the connection with baptism is maintained. This putting on occurs according to the → εἰκών of the Creator, thus according to Christ himself. Despite a closer association Christ and this new person are not identified with each other; the difference is maintained (cf. Col 3:10). Parenetic interests are given renewed dominance. As in 2 Cor 4:16, the concern is with the realization of the new (Christ-)person created in baptism.

b) On this basis ἐνδύω is used in specific parenetic statements. This is the case in the exhortation to put on spiritual weapons (1 Thess 5:8; Eph 6:11, 14; here a traditional image is used) and in Rom 13:12; Col 3:12. Again the concern is with the realization of the event that occurs in baptism, which is interpreted according to the dialectic between indicative and imperative.

c) 'Ενδύω's explicit eschatological character can be seen in 1 Cor 15:53f. The image of the garment is still resonant: the new garment is put on over the old garment, and death is "swallowed up" by life. As the motif of the transformation indicates (v. 52), the believer's identity in such an eschatological existence remains fundamental. Paul explains this with the use of traditional material in 2 Cor 5:1-5 (→ 3).

3. **'Επενδύομαι** *put on**. The future covering with the σῶμα πνευματικόν (1 Cor 15:44) is described in 2 Cor 5:2 as ἐπενδύσασθαι. The use of the compound is no accident. It indicates that in baptism an ἐνδύσασθαι (5:4) has already taken place. Paul thus sees death not as a condition of nakedness (a desirable nakedness according to parallels in the history of religions; cf. ἐκδύσασθαι, v. 4). It is, like entry into the heavenly οἰκοδομή, an ἐπενδύσασθαι that does not abolish the beginning which has occurred in baptism (v. 5)

H. Paulsen

ἐνδώμησις, εως, ἡ *endōmēsis* interior structure; substructure*

Rev 21:18: the new Jerusalem ἡ ἐνδώμησις τοῦ τείχους αὐτῆς ἴασπις, the *(sub-)structure* of its wall [is made of] jasper.

ἐνέδρα, ας, ἡ *enedra* ambush, attack*

Acts 23:16; 25:3: a planned *attack* against Paul (cf. 23:21).

ἐνεδρεύω *enedreuō* lie in wait for, ambush*

Luke 11:54: the scribes and Pharisees "*lying in wait* for him (αὐτόν)"; Acts 23:21: forty men "*lie in ambush* for him [αὐτόν, Paul]" to kill him.

ἔνεδρον, ου, τό *enedron* ambush, attack

Acts 23:16 v.l. in place of classical → ἐνέδρα.

ἐνειλέω *eneileō* force in, wrap up tightly*

Mark 15:46: Joseph of Arimathea *wrapped* Jesus' body with a linen cloth before burial.

ἔνειμι *eneimi* be inside*

Luke 11:41: τὰ ἐνόντα, *the contents, "things which are within"* (Thucydides iv.57.3; Pap. Tebt II, 414, 20; Josephus, *B.J.* vi.183).

ἕνεκα (ἕνεκεν, εἵνεκεν) *heneka (heneken, heineken)* because of, for the sake of*

Ἕνεκα is an improper prep. with gen. (BDF §216.1) occurring only in the Synoptics, Acts, Romans, and 2 Corinthians. Ἕνεκα (Matt 19:5; Luke 6:22; Acts 19:32; 26:21) is the Attic form. From the 3rd cent. B.C. ἕνεκεν came to be more common (e.g., LXX, *Epistle of Aristeas*) and is dominant in the NT (Matt 5:10f.; 10:18, 39; 16:25; 19:29; Mark 8:35; 10:7, 29 bis; 13:9; Luke 9:24; 18:29; 21:12; Acts 28:20; Rom 8:36; 14:20; 2 Cor 7:12 ter). Εἵνεκεν (BDF §30.3) is also attested (Luke 4:18; 2 Cor

3:10). Which passages have which of the three forms is subject to uncertainty in the text tradition (esp. in Matt 19:5, 29; Luke 4:18 [Isa 61:1]); 18:29; Acts 19:32; 28:20; Rom 8:36; 2 Cor 3:10; 7:12 ter).

Ἕνεκεν τούτου, *therefore* (Mark 10:7 par. Matt 19:5); ἕνεκα τούτων (Acts 26:21); with the rel. pron.: οὗ εἵνεκεν (Luke 4:18); ἕνεκεν τοῦ φανερωθῆναι, "in order that . . . [it] might be revealed" (2 Cor 7:12); τίνος ἕνεκα; *why?* (Acts 19:32).

ἐνενήκοντα *enenēkonta* ninety*

Matt 18:12f. par. Luke 15:4, 7: ἐνενήκοντα ἐννέα, "*ninety*-nine," referring to ninety-nine sheep or ninety-nine righteous persons.

ἐνεός, 3 *eneos* speechless, mute*

Acts 9:7: "the men stood . . . *speechless.*"

ἐνέργεια, ας, ἡ *energeia* working, power, effective action
→ ἐνεργέω 3.

ἐνεργέω *energeō* work, operate*

1. Occurrences and meaning — 2. Usage — 3. Ἐνέργεια — 4. Ἐνέργημα — 5. Ἐνεργής

Lit.: G. Bertram, *TDNT* II, 635-55, esp. 652ff. — E. Fascher, *RAC* V, 4-51.

1. Trans. ἐνεργέω is found in the NT 12 times with the meaning *work, bring about.* Intrans. ἐνεργέομαι, *prove to be effective,* occurs 9 times.

2. While Mark 6:14 par. Matt 14:2 speaks in the framework of demonological conceptions of the *working* of the δυνάμεις of the executed Baptist in Jesus, ἐνεργέω normally takes on a fixed theological meaning, esp. in the Pauline and deutero-Pauline literature. This is the case even in Phil 2:13, where ἐνεργέω refers to human actions (but cf. the connection with the preceding statement), and in Eph 2:2, where the partc., as a modifier of the appositional πνεῦμα, refers to the activity of "the prince of the power of the air."

1 Cor 12:4-6 is esp. important for a prominent theological statement. In a triadic series that moves toward a climax, χαρίσματα—διακονίαι—ἐνεργήματα are correlated with πνεῦμα—κύριος—θεός. Ὁ θεός is emphasized as the third member and by the (probably traditional) divine predicate ἐνεργῶν (v. 6). This predicate speaks of omnipotence (note τὰ πάντα): ἐνεργέω designates God as the one who is active in everything. That the relationship of ἐνεργέω and God should not be too strictly conceived is shown by v. 11, where ἐνεργέω stands in relation to πνεῦμα. This connection with πνεῦμα results, on the one hand, from the dominant role which πνεῦμα takes on in vv. 7ff. and, on the other hand, from the fact that in the πνεῦμα not only the Lord, but also God himself is manifest.

In a way not unlike 1 Cor 12:6, God is again the subject of this all-embracing activity: in Gal 2:8 (bis) as the one who *acts* in the apostles (there may be here an authentic statement from the Jerusalem conference), in 3:5 as the one who works δυνάμεις in the Church, in Phil 2:13 (bis) as the one who initiates human willing and activity, and in Eph 1:11 in the typical connection with the τὰ πάντα. Eph 1:20-22 is esp. characteristic: the ἐνεργεῖν of God is spelled out christologically, being related in turn to Christ's resurrection, the subjection of the powers, and Christ's installment as the Church's head.

Use of intrans. ἐνεργέομαι is less focussed than use of ἐνεργέω; the subj. is never God and, in fact, varies. On the one hand, ἐνεργέομαι is associated with godless powers that enslave and work in mankind (Rom 7:5: the passions of the ἁμαρτία; 2 Cor 4:12: the power of death; 2 Thess 2:7: the mystery of ἀνομία). On the other hand, the subj. can be the λόγος θεοῦ (1 Thess 2:13; cf. 1 Cor 16:9; Heb 4:12), παράκλησις (2 Cor 1:6; on the text criticism, cf. R. Bultmann, *The Second Letter to the Corinthians* [1985] 25), πίστις active in love (Gal 5:6), God's ἐνέργεια (Col 1:29), or, in the non-Pauline literature (Jas 5:16), prayer.

3. **Ἐνέργεια** *working, power, effective action** occurs 8 times in the NT (see Fascher on the distinctive emphatic usage in Hellenistic literature). It is close in meaning to δύναμις, but considerably less frequently used, being found only in the Pauline and deutero-Pauline literature. Phil 3:21, in dependence on traditional material, gives a christological formulation: As the σωτήρ, Christ receives the *power* to subject all things. In Eph 1:19; 3:7; 4:16; Col 1:29; 2:12 use of ἐνέργεια is consistent and almost without differentiation: always with κατά (except in Col 2:12) and always in proximity to the other expressions for strength and power (esp. in Eph 1:19). Along with use with reference to God (Col 1:29) and in the context of the idea of the σῶμα Χριστοῦ (Eph 4:16), the word is used particularly with reference to the *power* of the resurrection from the dead (Eph 1:19; Col 2:12; probably also Eph 3:7). In 2 Thess 2:9, 11 (→ also 2) use of the word underlines the demonic *power* of Satan and the πλάνη caused by him.

4. **Ἐνέργημα** *activity, effective power** occurs in the NT only in 1 Cor 12:6, 10. In both verses the word is close to the χαρίσματα; in v. 6 they are almost made equal, while v. 10 accents more strongly a relationship to the δυνάμεις (cf. esp. 2 Cor 12:12).

5. **Ἐνεργής** *effective, active** in 1 Cor 16:9 serves to clarify the missionary situation. While it occurs in the course of the metaphor of the open door (cf. 2 Cor 2:12),

it is oriented above all to the actuality represented by the metaphor and therefore breaks the metaphor apart; what is emphasized is the possibility of open and plain proclamation (cf. 1 Thess 2:13). Phlm 6 is essentially reminiscent of Gal 5:6 (→ 2): The community of faith proves to be effective by its knowledge of all that is good (on the interpretation cf. also P. Stuhlmacher, *Philemon* [EKKNT] 33f.). In Heb 4:12 ἐνεργής is used alongside ζῶν in another traditional predicate to grasp in gnomic fashion the significance of the λόγος τοῦ θεοῦ.

H. Paulsen

ἐνέργημα, ατος, τό *energēma* activity, effective power
→ ἐνεργέω 4.

ἐνεργής, 2 *energēs* effective, active
→ ἐνεργέω 5.

ἐνευλογέω *eneulogeō* bless*

Acts 3:25: "in your posterity [i.e., "seed"] *shall* all the families of the earth be *blessed*" (Gen 22:18 LXX); Gal 3:8: "In you *shall* all the nations *be blessed*" (Gen 12:3; 22:18 LXX). The form ἐνευλογηθήσονται stands in both of the cited OT texts. For this reason the variant εὐλογηθήσονται in Acts 3:25 (B A*) is to be preferred as the more difficult reading; cf. T. Holtz, *Untersuchungen über die alttestamentlichen Zitate bei Lukas* (1968) 71-76; H. W. Beyer, *TDNT* II, 765.

ἐνέχω *enechō* have a grudge against; pass.: be overcome*

Mark 6:19: Herodias *had a grudge against* John the Baptist; Luke 11:53: δεινῶς ἐνέχειν, *be very hostile,* of the opponents of Jesus; Gal 5:1: "do not *submit* again to a yoke of slavery" (imv. pass. ἐνέχεσθε). H. Hanse, *TDNT* II, 828.

ἐνθάδε *enthade* here; to this place*

In the NT only in Luke-Acts (6 occurrences) and John (2 occurrences): meaning *to this place:* John 4:15f.; Acts 25:17; meaning *here:* Luke 24:41; Acts 10:18; 16:28; 17:6; 25:24.

ἔνθεν *enthen* from there, from here*

Matt 17:20: "you will say to this mountain, 'Move *from here* to there (ἐκεῖ)"; Luke 16:26: "who would pass *from here* to you."

ἐνθυμέομαι *enthymeomai* consider, ponder*

Matt 1:20; 9:4; Acts 10:19 v.l. (in place of διενθυμέομαι). F. Büchsel, *TDNT* III, 172.

ἐνθύμησις, εως, ἡ *enthymēsis* thought, idea*

In the NT ἐνθύμησις is characterized by godless evil and foolishness. Matt 9:4; 12:25: Jesus knows "their *thoughts*"; Acts 17:29: ἐνθύμησις ἀνθρώπου, *thought, reflection* of a person, a human *idea*; Heb 4:12: God's word judges "the *thoughts* and intentions (ἐννοιῶν) of the heart." F. Büchsel, *TDNT* III, 172.

ἔνι *eni* there is*

Ἔνι appears in place of ἔνεστιν (BDF §98). In the NT always negative: οὐκ ἔνι, *there is not* (1 Cor 6:5; Gal 3:28 ter; Col 3:11; Jas 1:17).

ἐνιαυτός, οῦ, ὁ *eniautos* year*

Lit.: BAGD s.v. — LSJ s.v. — Pape, *Wörterbuch* s.v.

1. In classical Greek ἐνιαυτός is generally used of any fixed cyclic period of time (according to Plato it is derived from ἐν ἑαυτῷ) in distinction from → ἔτος, "year." In the koine Greek of the NT this distinction has largely been lost.

2. As a rule ἐνιαυτός is used in the NT as a neutral term in referring to time. John 11:49 (51); 18:13 refers to a fixed period of a year: "Caiaphas, who was high priest that *year.*" A definite (perhaps longer) period of time for a residency in a city is designated by ἐνιαυτός (acc.) in Acts 11:26; 18:11; Jas 4:13, in Acts referring to a period of missionary activity, in James, to an indefinitely long period of time (in contrast to the following day).

3. Time references are used in Hebrews in regard to cultic ritual activities. Heb 10:1, 3 speaks of the annual sacrifice of an animal prescribed in the law. The inadequacy of the sacrifice is emphasized; furthermore, in view of the new sacrifice of Jesus, the annual sacrifice no longer has any meaning, since it does not provide perfection, but rather, at best, leads to resignation by giving an annual reminder of sin. Heb 9:7, 25 refers to the OT ordinance that the high priest alone could enter the holy of holies, and that only once each year (Exod 30:10; Lev 16:2-28: Aaron); this practice is also surpassed by Jesus, who has effected final redemption in his once-for-all appearance at the end of the ages through his complete and final sacrifice.

4. Ἐνιαυτός has salvation-historical significance in Luke 4:19: Jesus cites Isa 61:1f. in the synagogue at Nazareth, and applies the scriptural passage to himself: "Today this scripture has been fulfilled in your hearing" (v. 21). The "acceptable" (δεκτός) *year* of Yahweh's grace—the "jubilee year" of emancipation (Lev 25:10 LXX), the time of the establishment of God's kingdom—has broken in, i.e., in the sense of the Lukan periodization of salvation (time of the old covenant—middle of time—time of the Church). This is the time that is free of Satan,

the time of Jesus. Significantly the citation breaks off before the announcement of God's vengeance (Isa 61:2b): the Messiah is bringer of salvation, not the messenger of judgment.

Jas 5:17 is not salvation-historical. To support the teaching about the power of prayer, the Elijah miracle in 1 Kgs 17:1; 18:1 is referred to: At the word of the prophet a sign of punishment follows; for three and one-half years it does not rain (cf. also Luke 4:25; Rev 11:6). The period of three and one-half years named here is not from the OT but from early Judaism. Beginning with Dan 7:25 (cf. Rev 11:2; 12:14) three and one-half years is used of times of persecution or calamity.

In Rev 9:15, at the sixth trumpet, the four angels bound at the Euphrates (probably referring to the kingdom of the Parthians) are released. These angels "had been held ready for the hour, and the day, and the month, and the *year*," i.e., for the great day of wrath (6:17); here apocalyptic traditions of the "day of Yahweh" are brought together (cf. Joel 2:1-11; 3:1-4; 4:15-17; Amos 5:18-20).

5. In Gal 4:10 Paul warns the church of a relapse into slavery to empty "world powers" (v. 9, RSV "elemental spirits"). Concretely this refers to a "calendar piety." He denounces, on the one hand, a superstitious astrological cult that was attractive to Gentiles; on the other hand, he also denounces a legalistic Jewish observance of time. He thus places Judaism on the same level with paganism. Paul is ultimately concerned here with the purity of Christian piety.

R. Kratz

ἐνίστημι *enistēmi* be at hand; in past tenses: be present*

Pf. ind. in 2 Thess 2:2: "the day of the Lord *is here* [ἐνέστηκεν, RSV "has come"]." Pf. partc.: Heb 9:9: ὁ καιρὸς ὁ ἐνεστηκώς, the *present* time; Gal 1:4: ὁ αἰὼν ὁ ἐνεστώς, the *present* age; Rom 8:38 and 1 Cor 3:22: the *present* (ἐνεστῶτα) contrasted to the future (μέλλοντα); but in 1 Cor 7:26: "the *impending* distress" (RSV mg.). Fut. ind. in 2 Tim 3:1 (probably like 1 Cor 7:26): "in the last days *there will come* times of stress." A. Oepke, *TDNT* II, 543f.; A. M. G. Stephenson, *SE* IV (1968) 442-51.

ἐνισχύω *enischyō* gain strength; trans.: strengthen*

Luke 22:43: an angel from heaven "*strengthening* him"; Acts 9:19: "he took food and *was strengthened*."

ἐνκ-
→ ἐγκ-.

ἐννέα *ennea* nine*

Luke 17:17: "Where are the *nine*?"; Matt 18:12f. par. Luke 15:4, 7: → ἐνενήκοντα ἐννέα, *ninety-nine*.

ἐννεύω *enneuō* nod, wave*

Luke 1:62: "they *made signs* to his father."

ἔννοια, ας, ἡ *ennoia* thought, insight, conviction*

Heb 4:12: the word of God is judge of "the thoughts and *intentions* (ἐννοιῶν) of the heart"; 1 Pet 4:1: "arm yourselves with the same *thought* [as the suffering Christ]." J. Behm, *TDNT* IV, 968-71.

ἔννομος, 2 *ennomos* lawful, under the law*

Lit.: C. H. Dodd, "ΕΝΝΟΜΟΣ ΧΡΙΣΤΟΥ," FS de Zwaan 96-110. — G. Friedrich, "Das Gesetz des Glaubens Röm 3, 27," *idem, Auf das Wort kommt es an. Gesammelte Aufsätze* (1978) 107-22, esp. 112f. — W. Gutbrod, *TDNT* IV, 1087f.

1. This adj. appears in the NT only in Acts 19:39 and 1 Cor 9:21; the adv. ἐννόμως appears as a v.l. in Rom 2:12 in place of ἐν νόμῳ and in contrast to ἀνόμως (like the adj. in 1 Cor 9:21). The few LXX uses (Sir prologue; 14:36 [adv.]; Prov 31:25 [adv.]) refer to behavior in conformity with God's law. In extrabiblical usage ἔννομος means generally "regulated by laws" and thus "just, orderly" (also of persons: "faithful to the law"), e.g., Plato *Lg.* 921c; *R.* 424e. Ἔννομος appears with the gen. as in 1 Cor 9:21, e.g., also in Sophocles *Ant.* 369.

2. In Acts 19:39 the phrase ἐν τῇ ἐννόμῳ ἐκκλησίᾳ (cf. *SIG* II, 672, 37) appears in the proposal of the Ephesus town clerk to let the dispute between Demetrius and Paul "be settled at the *regular* [not tumultuous] assembly," since the dispute concerned compensation for damages (v. 38). The opposite of the lawful assembly is the spontaneous "unlawful assembly" (συστροφή, v. 40; RSV "commotion"). According to Chrysostom (*Homily* 42.2), a regular people's assembly took place three times a month.

3. In 1 Cor 9:19-23 Paul develops apologetically the freedom of his apostolate as it is determined by the cross. To the Jews he can behave "as one under the law" (ὡς ὑπὸ νόμον, v. 20) and "to those outside the law" "as one outside the law" (ὡς ἄνομος, v. 21)—μὴ ὢν ἄνομος θεοῦ ἀλλ' ἔννομος Χριστοῦ, although Paul is not "outside God's law, being *under the law* of Christ" (v. 21 NEB). Gen. θεοῦ and Χριστοῦ are determined by νόμος, which is included in both adjectives (cf. BDF §182.3). Faith in Christ frees the apostle from "existence under the (Jewish) law," but in no way sets him free from the claim of God's law in general. Rather, God's law encounters Paul as the claim of Christ in a conclusive way. Thus Paul is himself a Jew to the Jews and can be a Gentile to the Gentiles, so that Gentiles are not brought under the law nor must Jews be torn away from the law. Thus his freedom to obey the commission of Christ alone is confirmed. Νόμος in ἔννομος is thus

"used here in an improper sense" (H. Conzelmann, *First Corinthians* [Hermeneia] 161); Paul gives us a play on words, i.e., a parallel formulation to the frequently used ἄνομος (cf. Friedrich 113: "ingenious formulation"; see also νόμος πίστεως, Rom 3:27; νόμος τοῦ πνεύματος, 8:2; νόμος τοῦ Χριστοῦ, Gal 6:2). There is not a "law of Christ" standing in contrast to the Jewish law; the formulation indicates rather that the one who is bound to the commission of Christ, whether he is a Jew or a Gentile, lives neither under the law nor free from the law, but in truth satisfies the claim of God's law (*contra* Dodd).

H. Balz

ἔννυχα *ennycha* at night*

The neut. acc. pl. of ἔννυχος, -ον, "nocturnal," appears as an adv. with the meaning *at night:* Mark 1:35: πρωῒ ἔννυχα λίαν, in the early morning, *when it was still* fully *night.*

ἐνοικέω *enoikeō* dwell within, live in/among*

Lit.: O. MICHEL, *TDNT* V, 119-61.

1. Ἐνοικέω is used in the LXX of human dwelling or settling on earth, in the land, on mountains, or in cities and therefore also human possession of these places. Thus the participle οἱ ἐνοικοῦντες is a fixed term for "inhabitants." God is never the subj. NT usage is totally different, however. Here mankind is never the subj.; instead the subj. is sin (Rom 7:17), God's Spirit (Rom 8:11; 2 Tim 1:14), Christ's word (Col 3:16), God (2 Cor 6:16), or faith (2 Tim 1:5). A human being or the Church (2 Cor 6:16; Col 3:16) becomes the obj., i.e., the dwelling place.

2. In Rom 7:17 Paul takes up the old and widely held view that external powers choose an individual to dwell in and are able to dominate that individual. The person's body becomes a "house" or "temple" of demons (→ δαιμόνιον, οἰκέω, κατοικέω; cf. Matt 12:45 par.; Billerbeck III, 239; Michel 125, n. 28). According to *T. Naph.* 8:6, e.g., the devil inhabits the sinner "as his own instrument." Thus it is decisive that the particular power continuously takes possession of a person, dominates that person, and has him or her in its power. Thus sin, according to Rom 7:7, not only controls the actions of the person (so C. K. Barrett, *Romans* [HNTC] ad loc.) but also acts in place of the person (v. 18) against his or her express will (8:20). It forces the person to do what he or she does not want to do, and drives the person to destruction. Only the Spirit of God can totally redeem one from the death-bringing powers (7:2ff.). When God makes his dwelling in a person (8:11) he takes total possession of the person and directs his or her entire life in a new way. At the same time the Spirit establishes a close relationship with Christ (vv. 9ff.) and is the guarantee of the resurrection (v. 11). (The idea that God dwells in the individual is found first in Philo. He designates, e.g., the soul as the "house of God" [*Som.* i.149].)

Col 3:16 has as a parallel to the exhortation "let the peace of Christ rule in your hearts" (v. 15): ὁ λόγος τοῦ Χριστοῦ ἐνοικείτω ἐν ὑμῖν πλουσίως. By the latter exhortation the Church is called on to give to the Christian message the position that is appropriate to it and to allow it to have sway. Thus Christ's word will be able to develop its effect and power and will produce behavior that corresponds to that word in the Church. Likewise the faith which dwells within a person must be continually realized (2 Tim 1:5f.) and must determine the life of the believer. God gives to Timothy, the bearer of Church office, power through his Spirit to preserve the Pauline tradition against false teachers. This power, which was mediated by the laying on of hands at ordination, now *dwells* in him (2 Tim 1:14).

In a combined citation of Ezek 37:27 and Lev 26:12, 2 Cor 6:16 sets out to prove that the Church is the temple in which God *dwells* (κατασκηνόω in the LXX) and moves. Here the OT conception, according to which God can dwell in the earthly temple, is taken up and applied to the Church (cf. 1 Cor 3:16f.).

R. Dabelstein

ἐνορκίζω *enorkizō* adjure*

1 Thess 5:27: "I *adjure* you by the Lord (τὸν κύριον)" with complementary inf. J. Schneider, *TDNT* V, 464.

ἑνότης, ητος, ἡ *henotēs* unity*

Lit.: M. BARTH, *Ephesians* II (AB, 1974) 464-67, 487-89. — K. M. FISCHER, *Tendenz und Absicht des Epheserbriefes* (1973) 40-78. — S. HANSON, *The Unity of the Church in the NT* (1946) 148-55. — E. KÄSEMANN, "Epheser 4, 1-6," "Epheser 4, 11-16," *idem, Versuche* I, 284-87, 288-92. — E. STAUFFER, *TDNT* II, 434-42, esp. 438f. — A. VANHOYE, "L'épître aux Ephésiens et l'épître aux Hébreux," *Bib* 59 (1978) 198-230, esp. 207-8.

Ἑνότης appears only twice in the NT, in Eph 4:3, 13 (the v.l. in Col 3:14 is secondary). In Ignatius ἑνότης is a catchword used many times (e.g., *Eph.* 4:2; 5:1; 14:1; *Phld.* 2:2; 3:2; 5:2; 8:1; 9:1).

In the parenetic section Eph 4:1-16, ἑνότης emphasizes, together with εἷς, οἱ πάντες, and σῶμα, the necessary but threatened unity of the Church (vv. 1-6, 12-16), which does nonetheless include a variety of ministries (vv. 7-11). "In no passage of the NT are the unity formulas so frequent as at the beginning of the parenetic part of our letter" (J. Gnilka, *Epheserbrief* [HTKNT] 145).

V. 3 ("[Be] eager to maintain the *unity* of the Spirit in the bond of peace") concludes a long παρακαλῶ sentence (vv. 1-3) and forms its high point. It is the Holy Spirit who produces this unity (τοῦ πνεύματος is subjective gen., but another translation might be "spiritual unity"). Unity is already present, but it must be preserved; it can be lost. The bond of peace, i.e., the bond which consists of peace, produces the unity. In vv. 4-6 seven εἷς phrases describe the content of this unity.

In v. 13 "until we all attain the *unity* of the faith and of the knowledge of the Son of God" is introduced by μέχρι, which points to both temporal aspect and goal. Together with the two other phrases in v. 13, which also speak about the goal (do all three stand on the same level?), this first part of the verse points to the final goal to which the various ministries must lead. Unity is described here as an ideal to be pursued. It consists of or grows out of faith and knowledge of the Son of God. With this qualification it is clear that the author again speaks of that which those who believe already possess. They should nevertheless deepen it; they can grow in it and increase it through their own effort.

J. Lambrecht

ἐνοχλέω *enochleō* plague, trouble*

Luke 6:18: "those who were *troubled* with unclean spirits (οἱ ἐνοχλούμενοι ἀπό . . .)"; absolute in Heb 12:15: *"cause trouble."*

ἔνοχος, 2 *enochos* guilty; subject to*

Lit.: H. Hanse, *TDNT* II, 828. — R. Pesch, *Das Markusevangelium* (HTKNT, 1976, 1977) I, 209-21, II, 439-41. — E. Schweizer, *The Good News according to Matthew* (1976) 114-17. — F. Thiele, *DNTT* II, 142f.

1. With its etymological derivation from ἐνέχομαι, ἔνοχος has the basic meaning *held in* something, in the fig. sense *subjected, exposed, subject to.* It is most often used forensically: *guilty, liable.* The adj. is used with gen. and dat. substantives, gen. for that which the subj. is guilty of (Mark 3:29), the object against which the subj. has erred (Jas 2:10; 1 Cor 11:27), or the appropriate punishment (Mark 14:64 par. Matt 26:66), dat. for the appropriate court of judgment (Matt 5:22).

2. The only passage in the NT in which ἔνοχος appears with neither connotations of judicial language nor a fig. meaning is Heb 2:15; there ἔνοχος is, to be sure, in a context in which it has a negative meaning ("*held* in slavery"); the slavery springs from the fear of death. Jesus has broken the power of death, whose lord is the devil, for he was like mankind and went through suffering and death. Through the sacrificial death of Jesus the high priest, the power of Satan and of death is conclusively defeated and mankind is redeemed.

3. Ἔνοχος is most often used forensically. In Mark 14:64 par. Matt 26:66, in his trial before the high court, Jesus is accused of blasphemy (the gesture of tearing the garment fits with this). The death penalty is given in cases of blasphemy according to Lev 24:10-16; Num 15:30f. The members of the court can legally determine that Jesus is worthy of death, but the decision of the Sanhedrin is to be understood only as a determination of guilt, not as a sentence of execution (cf. 15:1). The latter is reserved for Pilate, as apparently the sentencing authority in criminal proceedings has been taken from the Jews. As the story moved from Mark's narrative world into the world described by Matthew, it gained the stronger stylization in the Matthean version in comparison to the Markan version. Mark provides a narrative report which probably rests on an historical foundation.

4. Ἔνοχος followed by the dat. appears only in Matt 5:21f., where the dat. indicates the appropriate court of judgment. In the antithesis, which is certainly authentic (5:21a[-b?], 22a), Jesus presents a radically sharpened ethic of unlimited neighbor love. God's judgment becomes the final court of judgment for every act of unkindness. Because of the redactional addition of v. 22b-c (which is probably intended to caricature a Pharisaic-casuistic teaching of the law), κρίσις in v. 22a can mean only the local court, by which a progression in the levels of the court (local court—Sanhedrin—hell of fire) is established. The inconsistent climax in the statement of the offense and the court proceedings becomes intelligible when one understands "fool" as a disrespectful designation of the godless (cf. Pss 14:1; 94:8, etc.). What is indicated is that one who harms human relationships is subject to human judgment, while one who disturbs a relationship with God is subject to divine judgment.

5. It is against the background of Mark 14:64 that the indisputable word of Jesus in Mark 3:29 is seen in the right perspective. All lapses (against humans) and even blasphemies (against God) will be forgiven; only blasphemy against the Holy Spirit will not be forgiven. This means that anyone who rejects God's grace (which is given concrete form in God's unconditional readiness to forgive presented in Jesus) in the work of his Spirit is deserving of eternal damnation. This agrees with Jesus' proclamation, which is first of all the message of salvation; judgment is certainly not disregarded, for the freedom of human decision with respect to God's offer of grace remains unquestioned.

6. Jas 2:10 corresponds in its content to Matt 5:17-19. In 1 Cor 11:27 the forensic terminology is raised to the level of theological symbolic conceptuality (cf. also vv. 28ff.).

R. Kratz

ἐνπ-
→ ἐμπ-.

ἔνταλμα, ατος, τό *entalma* commandment*

Ἐντάλματα ἀνθρώπων (Isa 29:13), human *commandments* (Mark 7:7 par. Matt 15:9; Col 2:22).

ἐνταφιάζω *entaphiazō* bury*

Matt 26:12: πρὸς τὸ ἐνταφιάσαι με, for my *burial;* John 19:40: "as is the burial custom of the Jews."

ἐνταφιασμός, οῦ, ὁ *entaphiasmos* burial*

Mark 14:8: "she has anointed my body beforehand for *burying*"; John 12:7: "for the day of my *burial.*"

ἐντέλλομαι *entellomai* authorize, order, command*

Lit.: BAGD s.v. — H. H. ESSER, *DNTT* I, 331-39. — G. SCHRENK, *TDNT* II, 544-56. — For further bibliography → ἐντολή.

1. Ἐντέλλομαι is employed in classical as well as in later Greek normally in a purely secular sense of a commission, regulation, or commandment. Very early a transference takes place so that the vb. comes to refer to divine instructions and commandments; so in the LXX (cf. only Gen 2:16). In the OT the commands of kings (Gen 12:20: Pharaoh; 2 Kgs 18:5: David) and of Moses are referred to with the same word. A similar usage is seen in the NT.

2. In two NT passages ἐντέλλομαι refers to secular commandments (Mark 13:34; Heb 11:22).

3. In NT citations of the LXX one may find ἐντέλλομαι used with the force of a divine command in view (Matt 4:6 par. Luke 4:10 in the temptation story [Q]; Heb 9:20, citing Exod 24:8; cf. also Mark 14:24 par.); but the LXX has διέθετο. God's commands are in view in Matt 15:4 v.l. (א* C Koine L W 0106); here the moral obligation of the fifth commandment, which the Pharisees circumvent through the corban vow, is contrasted to the traditions of the ancients (παράδοσις). As pure law observance, this can work out as an appeal to God against God's will (e.g., purity regulations; cf. also Mark 2:27; 7:1-23). In Acts 13:47 the Gentile mission is justified with the divine authorization in Isa 49:6.

4. As in Jewish tradition, so in the NT the statutes and instructions of the Torah prescribed by Moses can be disregarded as commands (Mark 10:3 par. Matt 19:7 [the certificate of divorce: Deut 24:1]; John 8:5 [the stoning of an adulteress: Deut 22:23f.]).

5. In the Jesus tradition ἐντέλλομαι is used only in connection with the self-revelation speeches of Jesus.

Though the love commandment does not appear in the Synoptic sayings material, in John it is the sum of the commandments; nothing can be played off against love (cf. Matt 15:4, → 3). In John "love" is qualified in a christological and trinitarian manner, as well as soteriologically. The love between the Father and the Son effects eternal life in the sacrifice of the Son by the Father and by the Son's self-sacrifice for the sake of the disciples, and thus for the community of salvation. In the Son's love for the Father there is no contradiction between fulfillment of the Father's mandate (καθὼς ἐνετείλατό μοι ὁ πατήρ) and the obedience and freedom of the Son (14:31). Just as the Son keeps the Father's commandment and abides in his love, so the disciples will remain in the Son's love when they keep his commandments (15:9ff.: vv. 14, 17: ἐντέλλομαι ὑμῖν). That the Son loves to the point of sacrificing himself is the standard for the disciples' love for each other. Thus Jesus speaks the commission to his disciples: "love one another" (15:17). After the Son's departure the Holy Spirit, as the Paraclete, will call to mind the Son's instructions and see to their fulfillment.

Similarly, in the Lukan literature Jesus, before his ascension (Luke 24:44-53; Acts 1:1-8), admonishes the disciples to fulfill the law and promises them the Spirit, through whom he *gives commandment* (Acts 1:2) and who carries out their mission. Matt 28:20 is concerned with the keeping of all that Jesus *commanded,* i.e., with bringing together that which constitutes Jesus' proclamation and deeds (cf. chs. 5–7, 8–9 with the opening and concluding verses 4:23 and 9:35); keeping of the commandments also appears here in connection with the giving of the Spirit, mission, and eschatological consequences. In Matt 17:9 ἐντέλλομαι has an independent usage in the introduction to the demand for silence within the framework of the idea of the messianic secret.

R. Kratz

ἐντεῦθεν *enteuthen* from here*

As adv. of place: Luke 4:9; 13:31; John 2:16; 7:3; 14:31; 18:36. Ἐντεῦθεν καὶ ἐντεῦθεν (John 19:18) or ἐντεῦθεν καὶ ἐκεῖθεν (Rev 22:2): *on both sides.* To indicate grounds or source, Jas 4:1: *on the basis of* your lusts.

ἔντευξις, εως, ἡ *enteuxis* intercession, request*

1 Tim 2:1, in the summons to make δεήσεις, προσευχάς, ἐντεύξεις, εὐχαριστίας "for all men"; 4:5: Everything created is good, not to be rejected, being "consecrated by the word of God and *prayer,*" i.e., by thanksgiving for the receiving of things (vv. 3f.). O. Bauernfeind, *TDNT* VIII, 244f.

ἔντιμος, 2 *entimos* honored, esteemed, precious*

Luke 14:8: ἐντιμότερός σου, *more esteemed* than you; Phil 2:29: ἔντιμον ἔχω, hold *in honor;* Luke 7:2: *precious, valuable* (the centurion's servant); 1 Pet 2:4, 6, of a stone (used alongside ἐκλεκτός; see Goppelt, *Der erste Petrusbrief* [KEK] 141-44).

ἐντολή, ης, ἡ *entolē* command, order*

1. Occurrences in the NT — 2. Meaning — 3. Hellenistic Jewish understanding of ἐντολή — 4. The Synoptics — 5. The Pauline literature — 6. The Johannine literature — 7. The late apostolic literature

Lit.: K. BERGER, *Die Gesetzesauslegung Jesu* (WMANT 40, 1972). — G. BORNKAMM, "Sin, Law, and Death (Romans 7)," *idem, Early Christian Experience* (1969) 87-104. — C. BURCHARD, "Das doppelte Liebesgebot," FS Jeremias (1970) 39-62. — H. FRANKEMÖLLE, *Jahwebund und Kirche Christi* (1974) 95-98, 296-302 (on Matthew). — H. HÜBNER, *Law in Paul's Thought* (1984) 70-78. — R. HUMMEL, *Die Auseinandersetzung zwischen Kirche und Judentum im Matthäusevangelium* (1966). — E. KÄSEMANN, "Das Formular einer neutestamentlichen Ordinationsparänese," *idem, Versuche* I, 101-8. — W. G. KÜMMEL, *Römer 7 und die Bekehrung des Paulus* (1929), reprinted in *idem, Römer 7 und das Bild des Menschen im NT* (1974) ix-160, esp. 55f. — S. LYONNET, " 'Tu ne convoiteras pas' (Rom VII 7)," FS Cullmann (1962) 157-65. — *idem,* "L'histoire du salut selon le ch. 7 de l'épître aux Romains," *Bib* 43 (1962) 117-51. — A. NISSEN, *Gott und der Nächste im antiken Judentum* (WUNT 15, 1974). — S. PANCARO, *The Law in the Fourth Gospel* (NovTSup 42, 1975) 431-51. — B. RENAUD, "La loi et les lois dans les Livres des Maccabées," *RB* 68 (1961) 39-67. — A. SAND, *Das Gesetz und die Propheten* (1974) 33-36 (on Matthew). — G. SCHRENK, *TDNT* II, 544-56. — For further bibliography see *TWNT* X, 1079; *DNTT* I, 342f.

1. Ἐντολή occurs 67 times in the NT, of which 42 occurrences are sg. and 25 are pl. It is found in every NT writing except 2 Corinthians, Galatians, Philippians, 1–2 Thessalonians, 2 Timothy, Philemon, James, 1 Peter, 3 John, and Jude.

2. Ἐντολή means *command, order, charge.* In almost every instance in the NT where ἐντολή appears, it refers to a command ordained by God or Christ. However, it can also be used of a human *order* (Luke 15:29; John 11:57; Acts 17:15; Col 4:10; Titus 1:14).

3. The NT understanding of ἐντολή is connected with the usage of Hellenistic Judaism, which is determined by the LXX. In the LXX also ἐντολή can refer to a human decree (3 Kgdms 2:43; 4 Kgdms 18:36; 1 Macc 2:31; *T. Levi* 14:4; *T. Jud.* 13:7; Josephus *B.J.* i.209, 261, etc.). In most instances ἐντολή refers to the divine *miṣwâ,* "command, instruction," in the Torah (Gen 26:5; Exod 15:26; Lev 22:31; *T. Levi* 14:6f.; *T. Jud.* 16:3f.; Philo *All.* i.93; *Spec. Leg.* i.300; Josephus *Ant.* i.43, 47; v.76, 94; vi.60, 101, etc.), since the Torah (→ νόμος) encounters the individual as ἐντολή (cf. Prov 6:23 LXX; Deut 17:19 LXX; 4 Kgdms 21:8; *T. Dan* 5:1).

This interpretation of the Torah as *miṣwâ* is found already in Deut 6:1, 25; 7:11; 8:1; 11:8, 22 LXX, etc. The ἐντολή of the Torah is seen in ἐντολαί, individual *commandments* (cf. the traditional reference to *kol-hammiṣwâ,* translated as πᾶσαι αἱ ἐντολαί, Deut 8:1; 11:8, 22; 15:5; 26:13 LXX, etc.). It is incorrect to conclude that "Judaism is thus confronted by a plethora of commands which make it difficult to apprehend the unity of the divine will" (so Schrenk 547; cf. Sand 42). The unity of the divine will is given in the Torah (Nissen 330-416); consequently it is impossible in Judaism itself—not first in Matthew—to distinguish "between the law (νόμος as the sum of the νόμοι) and the individual commandments of the Torah (ἐντολαί)" (*contra* Frankemölle 296). LXX usage indicates already how little the νόμος was understood in Judaism as the sum of the νόμοι: With the exception of Neh 9:13, references to the νόμοι of the Torah come only in reference to the "Gentile milieu" (Jdt 11:12; Esth 1:15, 19; 3:8, 13; 8:11, 13; 1 Macc 10:37; on the particular usage in 2 Maccabees see Renaud).

4. Ἐντολή is used unproblematically in Luke for both human commandments (15:29; cf. Acts 17:15) and commandments of the Torah, whose validity and order is never questioned (Luke 1:6; 18:20; 23:56). Mark and Matthew use ἐντολή exclusively for the commandments of the Torah. They are God's word (Mark 7:13; Matt 15:4) and as such point the way to eternal life (Mark 10:17-19; Matt 19:16f.).

Despite this fundamental agreement, Mark and Matthew have considerable differences in their understanding of ἐντολή. Characteristic of this difference are the two renderings of the question of the greatest commandment (Mark 12:28-34; Matt 22:34-40): According to Mark 12:31 the commandments to love God and neighbor are the greatest in the law and cannot be surpassed by any other. An appraisal of this kind—which was also known in Diaspora Judaism (Burchard 55-57; Berger 137-40)—understands the Torah no longer as a unity of equal value throughout, but presupposes a distinction in significance among the commandments, making it possible to offer a critique of the (cultic) commandments (12:32f.).

For Matthew, however—as for rabbinic Judaism (Nissen 337-42)—such a differentiation is impossible: The first and second commandments are equivalent (22:38f.—only so in Matthew). The law hangs on both, as love is the object of both (→ ἀνομία 4, νόμος). Thus according to 5:19 it is forbidden to remove "the least of these *commandments*" or to teach anyone to do so.

Matt 5:19 is unclear because of the use of the demonstrative pron. τούτων: Does it refer to ἰῶται καὶ κεραίαι (v. 18)? Or to commandments disputed within the Church? Or is a semitism present here (corresponding to rabbinic usage) so that the demonstrative pron. has a general sense? Or does v. 19 already have in view the antitheses or commandments which follow? A definite answer is impossible. The meaning of v. 19 is nevertheless clear: "In the present context the iota and dot on the one hand and the least of the commandments on the other hand are an expression for the fact that the Torah is absolutely valid, without any diminution" (Hummel 67).

5. Connections with the Hellenistic Jewish under-

standing of ἐντολή can be observed in the use of the word in the Pauline literature: here also, with the exception of 1 Cor 14:37 (the command of the Lord) and Col 4:10 (human instructions), ἐντολή is used of (the) commands of the Torah (Rom 7:8-13; 13:9; 1 Cor 7:19; Eph 2:15; 6:2). The designation of "You shall love your neighbor as yourself" as the summary of all possible commandments of the law (Rom 13:9) is also to be found in Hellenistic Judaism.

Indeed, where Paul speaks both of Adam's reception of the Torah in Paradise and of Adam's temptation (→ ἐξαπατάω) and designates the commandment against coveting as the basic command of the Torah (7:7-13), he follows Jewish tradition (Lyonnet, *L'histoire* 135-45). This connection to tradition makes it improbable that Paul refers to covetousness as that which is contained in every sin (so H. Schlier, *Römerbrief* [HTKNT] 223; E. Käsemann, *Commentary on Romans* [1980] 194; Bornkamm 90, etc.). The ἐντολή evokes instead the will to possess, which cannot be satisfied.

Paul goes beyond Jewish tradition first when he not only sees the commandment (given to Adam) being used by sin as the occasion of all covetousness (7:8, 11) but also interprets the commandment, in which God's Torah encounters the individual (→ 3), as the means by which sin is shown to be sin and turns out to be excessively sinful (v. 13). Thus Paul agrees with Judaism that the commandment was given for life and that the law is holy and the commandment holy, righteous, and good (vv. 10, 12). Nevertheless the commandment possesses for Paul—in contrast to Judaism—no salvific meaning, since according to his understanding the commandment serves fundamentally as sin's "operational base" (Hübner 71) and thus produces death for the individual.

6. In contrast to the other NT writings, ἐντολή is never used in the Johannine literature of the Mosaic Torah. Instead ἐντολή stands for the commission of the Father given to the Son (John 10:18; 12:49, 50; 15:10) and for Christ's commandment to his disciples (13:34; 14:15, 21; 15:10, 12). In 1–2 John also ἐντολή refers to commandments which are valid for Christians, commandments whose singularity is associated with the coming of God's Son into this world (1 John 2:3f., 7f.; 3:22-24; 4:21; 5:2f.; 2 John 4-6). In both John and 1–2 John the ἐντολαί remain undefined, for ἐντολή is defined in numerous ways: According to John 10:18, for the Son it consists of the *charge* authorizing him to lay down his own life and to take it up again; according to 12:49; 14:31 what the Son says and does corresponds to the Father's ἐντολή, which is eternal life (12:50). For the disciples the ἐντολή of the Son consists of the commandment to "love one another as I have loved you" (13:34; 15:12; cf. 1 John 4:21; 2 John 6). According to 1 John 3:23 God's ἐντολή has a twofold meaning: faith in the Son, Jesus Christ, and mutual love.

7. In the late apostolic writings use of ἐντολή varies. In Heb 7:5, 16, 18; 9:19 ἐντολή is used for the commandments of the Torah. In 1 Tim 6:14 it is "the official charge" of the (Christian) leader of the church (Käsemann 106f.). In 2 Pet 2:21; 3:2 it is the Christian moral life or instruction in the faith which must be kept, while ἐντολή in Titus 1:14 stands finally for human instructions.

M. Limbeck

ἐντόπιος, 3 *entopios* local*

Acts 21:12: pl. subst. οἱ ἐντόπιοι, *the people there,* in contrast to Paul's companions (ἡμεῖς).

ἐντός *entos* inside, within*

Lit.: Mayser, *Grammatik* II/2, 530 (§134.6).

On Luke 17:20f.: Dalman, *Words* 145f. — R. Geiger, *Die lukanischen Endzeitreden* (1973) 29-53. — H. Hartl, "Die Aktualität des Gottesreiches nach Lk 17, 20f," *Biblische Randbemerkungen* (FS R. Schnackenburg, 1974) 25-30. — W. G. Kümmel, *Promise and Fulfillment* (1957) 33-36. — F. Mussner, "'Wann kommt das Reich Gottes?'" *BZ* 6 (1962) 107-11. — B. Noack, *Das Gottesreich bei Lukas* (1948). — N. Perrin, *Rediscovering the Teaching of Jesus* (1967) 68-74. — A. Rüstow, "ΕΝΤΟΣ ΥΜΩΝ ΕΣΤΙΝ. Zur Deutung von Lukas 17, 20-21," *ZNW* 51 (1960) 197-224. — R. Schnackenburg, "Der eschatologische Abschnitt Lk 17, 20-37," FS Rigaux 213-34. — A. Strobel, "Die Passa-Erwartung als urchristliches Problem in Lc 17, 20f," *ZNW* 49 (1958) 157-96. — *idem,* "A. Merx über Lc 17, 20f.," *ZNW* 51 (1960) 133f. — J. Zmijewski, *Die Eschatologiereden des Lukas-Evangelium* (BBB 40, 1972) 361-97.

'Εντός appears in the NT only as an improper prep. with the gen. and has the (spatial) meaning *within, in the realm of* (cf. Lucian *DMort.* 14.5; Josephus *B.J.* iii.175; Ign. *Eph.* 5:2; *Trall.* 7:2; Pol. *Phil.* 3:3).

1. In a metaphor in Matt 23:26 Jesus speaks of the *inside* of the cup (τὸ ἐντὸς τοῦ ποτηρίου), meaning what it contains (cf. 1 Macc 4:48: τὰ ἐντὸς τοῦ οἴκου; Isa 16:11: τὰ ἐντός absolute: the *inner part*). To make the *inward part* pure is more important than to purify the outer part (τὸ ἐκτός). The metaphor refers (according to the context) to elimination of "extortion and rapacity" (v. 25).

2. In Luke 17:21b Jesus says (to the Pharisees!): "Behold, the kingdom of God is ἐντός ὑμῶν." Here ἐντός is to be interpreted neither spiritualistically-individualistically nor collectively with reference to those present (i.e., the Pharisees: "in the midst of you" [RSV], "among you"). Rather, as Rüstow 214-17 has shown (referring to Xenophon *An.* i.10.3; *Cyr.* i.4.23; Pap. Oxy. no. 2342, ll. 1, 7f., etc.), ἐντός is to be understood as referring to the sphere of the kingdom's influence, authority, or effectiveness. The oldest interpretation of Luke 17:21b (Tertullian *Marc.* iv.35) agrees with this (similarly Athanasius *Contra Gen-*

tes 30; *Vita Antonii* 20; Cyril of Alexandria *Expl. in Lucam* [*PG* LXXII, 840f.]). Jesus is answering the Pharisees' question of when the kingdom will come (v. 20a). The negative part of his answer (vv. 20b, 21a) characterizes the question as wrongly put. The positive concluding part (v. 21b) seeks to turn the conduct of the (passively waiting) questioners toward active personal effort (Schnackenburg 218). Since vv. 20f. has been revised by Luke (v. 20a derives from him), one may ask if v. 21b also comes from him. In any case one may mention other examples in Luke in which the Evangelist aims at this kind of inversion of a question or redirection of expectation (13:23f.; 18:8a, b).

G. Schneider

ἐντρέπω *entrepō* make ashamed; mid.: have regard for*

1 Cor 4:14: "I do not write this to *make* you *ashamed*"; pass.: *be ashamed* (2 Thess 3:14; Titus 2:8); mid. with acc.: *have respect for* someone, *have regard for* (Mark 12:6 par. Matt 21:37/Luke 20:13; Luke 18:2, 4; Heb 12:9 [αὐτούς supplied on the basis of the context]).

ἐντρέφω *entrephō* nourish, bring up*

1 Tim 4:6, mid.: "*nourished* on the words of the faith."

ἔντρομος, 2 *entromos* trembling*

Acts 7:32; 16:29: ἔντρομος γενόμενος; Heb 12:21: ἔντρομος with ἔκφοβος (as in 1 Macc 13:2).

ἐντροπή, ῆς, ἡ *entropē* shame*

1 Cor 6:5; 15:34: "I say this to your *shame*."

ἐντρυφάω *entryphaō* revel*

2 Pet 2:13: ἐντρυφῶντες ἐν ταῖς ἀπάταις, "*reveling* in their dissipation."

ἐντυγχάνω *entynchanō* meet (someone), turn (to someone), appeal (for or against someone)*

Lit.: H. Balz, *Heilsvertrauen und Welterfahrung* (BEvT 59, 1971) 69-92 (bibliography). — O. Bauernfeind, *TDNT* VIII, 242f. — C. Brown, *DNTT* II, 882-85. — P. von der Osten-Sacken, *Röm 8 als Beispiel paulinischer Soteriologie* (FRLANT 112, 1975) 20-43, 271-77. — H. Paulsen, *Überlieferung und Auslegung in Röm 8* (WMANT 43, 1975) 141-47, 168-72.

1. Ἐντυγχάνω appears 5 times in the NT; 2 are in Acts 25:24: περὶ οὗ ἅπαν τὸ πλῆθος τῶν Ἰουδαίων ἐνέτεχόν μοι, "about whom [i.e., Paul] the whole Jewish people *petitioned* me" (cf. Dan 6:12 LXX; Josephus *Ant.* xii.18) and Rom 11:2: ὡς ἐντυγχάνει τῷ θεῷ κατὰ τοῦ Ἰσραήλ, Elijah "*pleads* with God against Israel" (cf. 1 Macc 8:32; 10:61-64; 11:25).

In the other 3 NT instances the vb. is used in a specific theological connection, always with ὑπέρ. In Rom 8:27 it is used of intercession by "the Spirit himself" (v. 26) "for the saints according to the will of God" (ὅτι κατὰ θεὸν ἐντυγχάνει ὑπὲρ ἁγίων; cf. ὑπερεντυγχάνει [v. 26], "intercedes vicariously [RSV "for us"]," not attested before Paul). It is also used of the exalted Christ's intercession "for us" (ὑπὲρ ἡμῶν, Rom 8:34) and "for them" (ὑπὲρ αὐτῶν), i.e., for those who come before God on the basis of Christ's priestly service (Heb 7:25; see Balz 75f.).

Outside the NT are found the special meanings "read" (= "take a book in hand," 2 Macc 2:25; 6:12; 15:39) and "request" ("approach [God] with requests," with the dat., Wis 8:21; 16:28; with πρός, *Herm. Sim.* 2:8; with περὶ, "make intercession," Pol. *Phil.* 4:3).

Ἐντυγχάνω is thus a many-sided word; it belongs primarily to the conceptual world of the ruler's court (cf. the occurrences in 1–2 Maccabees; further texts in BAGD s.v. 1), where accusations against another and where requests on behalf of another are made with the hope of receiving a hearing (see also Bauernfeind 243). The narrower theological usage of the verbs in Romans 8 and Hebrews 7 take on their meaning from this background.

2. In Rom 8:27 the Spirit appears as intercessor (here only in the NT) for the saints before God; the Spirit intercedes with "sighs too deep for words" (v. 26). Paul formulates his eschatological interpretation of the pneuma consciousness, which was widespread in the Hellenistic churches, against the background of Jewish ideas of the heavenly intercessor and mediator (see Balz 87-91) and the Jewish tradition of the work of the Spirit. In the (glossolalic) cries of the pneumatics in worship, what is heard is not the cry of liberation by the already-redeemed. It is rather the groaning of the faithful who are still bound to this world and still looking impatiently for the freedom to come. The Spirit brings about this groaning in them and at the same time brings it before God as their intercessor. The experience of salvation is at the same time the demand for final salvation and only as such is it really salvation (Balz 91f.; E. Käsemann, *Commentary on Romans* [1980] ad loc.).

In Rom 8:34 ὃς καὶ ἐντυγχάνει ὑπὲρ ἡμῶν is taken from pre-Pauline tradition (von der Osten-Sacken; Paulsen; Balz 119f.). Christ is the intercessor who appears for the believer at the heavenly court. In Heb 7:25 Christ is the one who is high priest for eternity (cf. vv. 21, 24). Early Christian tradition thus brings together the motif of Christ's exaltation (according to Ps 110:1) with that of the intercessory or priestly approach of the exalted one to God's right hand for the believer (see O. Michel, *Hebräerbrief* [KEK] ad loc.; → παράκλητος). Here Christ does not—as in Jewish texts—declare the merits of the faithful (cf. Billerbeck II, 560-62), but as the one who has always stood on their side interceding, he gives assistance.

H. Balz

ἐντυλίσσω *entylissō* wrap; fold up*

Matt 27:59 par. Luke 23:53: *covering* the body in the linen cloth; John 20:7: the burial cloth lay there *folded up.*

ἐντυπόω *entypoō* engrave*

2 Cor 3:7: "*carved* in letters on stone."

ἐνυβρίζω *enybrizō* abuse, revile*

Heb 10:29: one "who *has . . . despised* [RSV "outraged"] the Spirit of grace." G. Bertram, *TDNT* VIII, 306.

ἐνυπνιάζομαι *enypniazomai* dream, have visions*

Acts 2:17: "Your old men *will have visions* in dreams" (RSV "dream dreams"; cf. Joel 3:1 LXX); Jude 8: the false prophets "*in their dreamings* defile the flesh." H. Balz, *TDNT* VIII, 553.

ἐνύπνιον, ου, τό *enypnion* dream*

Acts 2:17: ἐνυπνίοις → ἐνυπνιάζομαι, "have visions *in dreams*" (acc. ἐνύπνια in Joel 3:1 LXX). H. Balz, *TDNT* VIII, 553.

ἐνώπιον *enōpion* (in the presence of) before*

Lit.: On preps. in general → ἀνά; BAGD s.v. (bibliography). — JOHANNESSOHN, *Präpositionen* 194-97, 359-61.

1. Ἐνώπιον (derived from ἐν + the root ὀπ-, "see/eye") is the neut. acc. sg. of the adj. ἐνώπιος used adverbially: *being in sight/before the face, present,* etc., and is used in Hellenistic Greek with the gen. as an improper prep. In the LXX (*ca.* 540 occurrences) it corresponds to various Hebrew prep. expressions with the general meaning "before" (cf. Johannesohn), most frequently *lipnê.* Yet it alternates, without any apparent reason (e.g., Num 17:19, 22, 25), with ἔναντι/κατέναντι for *lipnê,* and in Exod 34:23f. (Deut 16:16; 31:11), in a t.t. for pilgrimage, with ἐναντίον for *eṯ-pᵉnê* (suggestion by H.-P. Stähli, Bethel). Thus when ἐνώπιον is a v.l. in NT mss. (e.g., in Luke 1:6 for ἐναντίον, in Acts 8:21 for ἔναντι, in Acts 10:4 for ἔμπροσθεν), or is used in Luke 5:25 in place of the par. Mark 2:12 ἔμπροσθεν/ἐναντίον, and in Luke 12:8f. (in contrast to par. Matt 10:32f.) replaces ἔμπροσθεν in the second verse, one may ask how much the ὀπ- element in ἐνώπιον is still perceived. (The parallelism with τοῖς ὀφθαλμοῖς in Heb 4:13 can be understood in either way.)

Classifying the use of ἐνώπιον in the NT, including the OT formula ἐνώπιον τοῦ θεοῦ or κυρίου, "*before* God" or "the Lord," is at any rate a matter of strongly subjective judgment. The distribution of NT occurrences is noteworthy: Lukan writings and Revelation, each 35; Paul, 9; Pastorals, 8; Johannine literature, 3; Hebrews, 2; James and 1 Peter, 1 each; none, e.g., in Mark or Matthew. The compound κατενώπιον ("before") is found 3 times (all, probably coincidentally, with ἄμωμος, "blameless") for relation to God.

2. a) In *ca.* 30% of the occurrences ἐνώπιον has a purely local meaning (Luke 5:18; Rev 3:8; 12:4, etc.). John goes forth as herald and forerunner *before* the κύριος (Luke 1:17, 76); the angels stand *before* God (Luke 1:19; Rev 8:2). In Revelation the term is used most frequently of an occurrence *before* God's throne (1:4; 4:5f.; 7:9, 11, 15, etc.) or *before* the (enthroned) lamb (5:8; 7:9).

b) Ὀπ- appears to be still perceived in ἐνώπιον where "before" can be understood as *before the eyes,* i.e., *in the presence of:* to do something or say something *before* a group of people (Luke 5:25; 8:47; John 20:30; Acts 19:9, 19; 1 Tim 5:20, etc.) or a heavenly being (Rev 14:3, 10); "to eat *before the eyes of*" refers to table fellowship (Luke 13:26; 24:43, also Acts 27:35); in the fig. sense esp. ἐνώπιον τοῦ θεοῦ, "*before the eyes* of God," means *in accountability to* God, as in swearing before the guarantor or judge (Gal 1:20; 1 Tim 5:21; 6:13; 2 Tim 2:14; 4:1), keeping the faith (Rom 14:22), recommending oneself (2 Cor 4:2), not boasting (1 Cor 1:29). Through ἐνώπιον τοῦ θεοῦ, "*in the eyes* [i.e., *according to the judgment*] of God," the possible meaning of individual terms (esp. adj. and subst.) becomes limited (e.g., Luke 1:15; 16:15b; Acts 4:19; 1 Tim 2:3; 5:4; Heb 13:21; 1 Pet 3:4; 1 John 3:22; so also the compound κατενώπιον in Eph 1:4). In Rev 13:12, 14; 19:20 ἐνώπιον τοῦ θηρίου ποιεῖν τι, do something "*in the presence* of the beast," is to be understood as "*at the commissioning* of the beast."

c) In a few passages ἐνώπιον appears to have merely a connecting function in a verbal process, so that a pertinent translation must be chosen, e.g., remembered *by* God (Acts 10:31; Rev 16:19b), not forgotten *by* (Luke 12:6), find grace *with/from* (Acts 7:46), sin *against* (Luke 15:18, 21), what is considered good *before* (Rom 12:17); thus ἐνώπιον can also be just a circumlocution for the simple dat. (Luke 24:11; Acts 6:5, etc.).

H. Krämer

Ἐνώς *Enōs* Enosh*

Personal name in Luke 3:38: the son of Seth (Gen 4:26).

ἐνωτίζομαι *enōtizomai* give ear*

Acts 2:14: ἐνωτίσασθε τὰ ῥήματά μου (Job 32:11 LXX), "*give ear* to my [following] words." Ἐνωτίζομαι frequently occurs in the LXX in a request for attention, esp. in the prophets (e.g., Hos 5:1; Joel 1:2; Isa 1:2; 28:23; Jer 8:6; 13:15). J. Horst, *TDNT* V, 559.

Ἑνώχ *Henōch* Enoch*

Lit.: D. LÜHRMANN, "Henoch und die Metanoia," *ZNW* 66 (1975) 103-16. — H. ODEBERG, *TDNT* II, 556-60. — C. D. OSBURN, "The Christological Use of I Enoch I.9 in Jude 14, 15," *NTS* 23 (1976/77) 334-41. — For further bibliography see *TWNT* X, 1079.

Of the four persons with this name in the OT, only Enoch the son of Jared (Gen 5:18) has become important in Jewish and Hellenistic Jewish literature. Enoch is the collective name for an entire complex of conceptions (on this cf. Odeberg), which are already mentioned in Gen 5:21-24 and are alluded to in the NT.

In Luke 3:37 Enoch appears as the seventh in the first series of the genealogy of Jesus, which begins with God and follows in the traditional order from Adam. Enoch's position here can scarcely be interpreted theologically, because for Luke the division of the genealogy into eleven sets of seven (though perhaps decisive for the Lukan source) is no longer significant—as is seen in his disregard of that principle of organization at several points in the genealogy.

Heb 11:5 explicitly takes up the idea of the translation of Enoch (cf. the allusion to Gen 5:24), which also plays a great role in extrabiblical tradition (e.g., Sir 44:16; 49:16; *1 Enoch* 70:1-4; Wis 4:10ff.; cf. Philo *Mut.* 34; *Abr.* 17). Enoch is, after Abel, the second in the cloud of witnesses to *faith* (Heb 11:4; cf. 12:1). His translation is a sign of his being well-pleasing (as in Gen 5:21-24). Jewish tradition understands Enoch's translation as a sign of his righteousness (e.g., Sir 49:14ff.; *Jub.* 10:17; *1 Enoch* 1:2), his repentance (→ μετάνοια; Sir 44:16 LXX; Philo *Abr.* 17; see Lührmann 106), or his knowledge of God (Sir 44:16 in the Hebrew original). But in Hebrews it is attributed only to his faith (11:6!). Because it is possible to be pleasing to God only on the basis of faith, it is said of Enoch: πίστει . . . μετετέθη (v. 5).

Jude 14 designates Enoch explicitly as the seventh after Adam. Thereby (in dependence on traditional sayings; cf. *1 Enoch* 60:8; 93:3; *Jub.* 7:39; Billerbeck III, 787) the dignity and reliability of his prophecy are expressed. Vv. 14b-15 cite *1 Enoch* 1:9 (not exactly, to be sure). Accordingly Enoch appears here as one who knows apocalyptic mysteries (this idea was already traditional; cf. *1 Enoch* 1:2; *Jub.* 4:19). 2 Peter, which is dependent on Jude, expunges this citation and thus no longer counts *1 Enoch* among the writings worthy of being cited (extracanonical since Jamnia).

H. Weder